The Routledge Handbook of Language and Politics

The Routledge Handbook of Language and Politics provides a comprehensive overview of this important and dynamic area of study and research. Language is indispensable to initiating, justifying, legitimatising and co-ordinating action, as well as negotiating conflict and, as such, is intrinsically linked to the area of politics. With 45 chapters written by leading scholars from around the world, this Handbook covers the following key areas:

- Overviews of the most influential theoretical approaches, including Bourdieu, Foucault, Habermas and Marx;
- Methodological approaches to language and politics, covering – among others – content analysis, conversation analysis, multimodal analysis and narrative analysis;
- Genres of political action from speech-making and policy to national anthems and billboards;
- Cutting-edge case studies about hot-topic socio-political phenomena, such as ageing, social class, gendered politics and populism.

The Routledge Handbook of Language and Politics is a vibrant survey of this key field and is essential reading for advanced students and researchers studying language and politics.

Ruth Wodak is Emerita Distinguished Professor of Discourse Studies at Lancaster University, UK; she remains affiliated to the University of Vienna, Austria.

Bernhard Forchtner is a Lecturer at the School of Media, Communication and Sociology, University of Leicester, UK.

Advisory Board

Adam Jaworski, Hong Kong University
Barbara Johnstone, Carnegie Mellon University, USA
Deborah Stone, Brandeis University, USA
Teun van Dijk, Pompeu Fabra University, Spain

Routledge Handbooks in Linguistics

Routledge Handbooks in Linguistics provide overviews of a whole subject area or sub-discipline in linguistics, and survey the state of the discipline including emerging and cutting edge areas. Edited by leading scholars, these volumes include contributions from key academics from around the world and are essential reading for both advanced undergraduate and postgraduate students.

The Routledge Handbook of Semantics
Edited by Nick Riemer

The Routledge Handbook of Linguistic Anthropology
Edited by Nancy Bonvillain

The Routledge Handbook of the English Writing System
Edited by Vivian Cook and Des Ryan

The Routledge Handbook of Metaphor and Language
Edited by Elena Semino and Zsófia Demjén

The Routledge Handbook of Systemic Functional Linguistics
Edited by Tom Bartlett and Gerard O'Grady

The Routledge Handbook of Heritage Language Education
From Innovation to Program Building
Edited by Olga E. Kagan, Maria M. Carreira and Claire Hitchins Chik

The Routledge Handbook of Language and Humor
Edited by Salvatore Attardo

The Routledge Handbook of Language and Dialogue
Edited by Edda Weigand

The Routledge Handbook of Language and Politics
Edited by Ruth Wodak and Bernhard Forchtner

The Routledge Handbook of Language and Media
Edited by Daniel Perrin and Colleen Cotter

The Routledge Handbook of Ecolinguistics
Edited by Alwin F. Fill and Hermine Penz

Further titles in this series can be found online at www.routledge.com/series/RHIL

The Routledge Handbook of Language and Politics

Edited by
Ruth Wodak and Bernhard Forchtner

LONDON AND NEW YORK

First published 2018
by Routledge
2 Park Square, Milton Park, Abingdon, Oxon OX14 4RN

and by Routledge
711 Third Avenue, New York, NY 10017

Routledge is an imprint of the Taylor & Francis Group, an informa business

© 2018 selection and editorial matter, Ruth Wodak and
Bernhard Forchtner; individual chapters, the contributors

The right of the editors to be identified as the authors of the editorial
material, and of the authors for their individual chapters, has been asserted
in accordance with sections 77 and 78 of the Copyright, Designs and
Patents Act 1988.

All rights reserved. No part of this book may be reprinted or reproduced or
utilised in any form or by any electronic, mechanical, or other means, now
known or hereafter invented, including photocopying and recording, or in
any information storage or retrieval system, without permission in writing
from the publishers.

Trademark notice: Product or corporate names may be trademarks or
registered trademarks, and are used only for identification and explanation
without intent to infringe.

British Library Cataloguing-in-Publication Data
A catalogue record for this book is available from the British Library

Library of Congress Cataloging-in-Publication Data
Names: Wodak, Ruth, 1950–editor. | Forchtner, Bernhard.
Title: The Routledge handbook of language and politics/edited by Ruth
Wodak and Bernhard Forchtner.
Description: Milton Park, Oxon; New York, NY: Routledge,
[2017] |
Series: Routledge Handbooks in Linguistics | Includes bibliographical
references and index.
Identifiers: LCCN 2016056494| ISBN 9781138779167 (hardback) | ISBN
9781315183718 (ebook)
Subjects: LCSH: Language and languages–Political aspects.
Classification: LCC P119.3 .R68 2017 | DDC 306.44–dc23
LC record available at https://lccn.loc.gov/2016056494

ISBN: 978-1-138-77916-7 (hbk)
ISBN: 978-1-315-18371-8 (ebk)

Typeset in Times
by Saxon Graphics Ltd, Derby

Printed and bound in Great Britain by
TJ International Ltd, Padstow, Cornwall

Contents

List of figures	x
List of tables	xii
List of contributors	xiii
Introducing the language–politics nexus *Ruth Wodak and Bernhard Forchtner*	1

PART I
Theoretical approaches to language and politics   15

1. Rhetoric as a civic art from antiquity to the beginning of modernity   17
   Sara Rubinelli

2. From Karl Marx to Antonio Gramsci and Louis Althusser   30
   Bob Jessop

3. Jürgen Habermas: between democratic deliberation and deliberative democracy   43
   Simon Susen

4. Michel Foucault: discourse, power/knowledge and the modern subject   67
   Reiner Keller

5. Jacques Lacan: negotiating the psychosocial in and beyond language   82
   Yannis Stavrakakis

6. The discourse theory of Ernesto Laclau   96
   Christoffer Kølvraa

7. Pierre Bourdieu: ally or foe of discourse analysis?   109
   Andrew Sayer

Contents

8 Conceptual history: the history of basic concepts 122
   Jan Ifversen

9 Critical Discourse Studies: a critical approach to the study of
   language and communication 135
   Bernhard Forchtner and Ruth Wodak

PART II
Methodological approaches to language and politics **151**

10 Content analysis 153
    Roberto Franzosi

11 Corpus analysis 169
    Amelie Kutter

12 Cognitive Linguistic Critical Discourse Studies: connecting
    language and image 187
    Christopher Hart

13 Competition metaphors and ideology: life as a race 202
    Jonathan Charteris-Black

14 Legitimation and multimodality 218
    Theo van Leeuwen

15 Narrative analysis 233
    Anna De Fina

16 Rhetorical analysis 247
    Claudia Posch

17 Understanding political issues through argumentation analysis 262
    Ruth Amossy

18 Conversation analysis and the study of language and politics 276
    Steven E. Clayman and Laura Loeb

19 Politics beyond words: ethnography of political institutions 291
    Endre Dányi

PART III
Genres of political action   307

20 Parliamentary debates   309
    Cornelia Ilie

21 Government communication   326
    Sten Hansson

22 Press conferences   342
    Mats Ekström and Göran Eriksson

23 Policy-making: documents and laws   355
    Kristof Savski

24 The semiotics of political commemoration   368
    Martin Reisigl

25 Mediatisation and political language   383
    Michael Higgins

26 Performing politics: from the town hall to the inauguration   398
    Jennifer Sclafani

27 Genres of political communication in Web 2.0   412
    Helmut Gruber

28 Music and sound as discourse and ideology: the case of the
    national anthem   426
    David Machin

29 The language of party programmes and billboards: the example of
    the 2014 parliamentary election campaign in Ukraine   440
    Lina Klymenko

30 Caricature and comics   454
    Randy Duncan

31 Meetings   468
    Jo Angouri and Lorenza Mondada

Contents

PART IV
Applications and cases I: language, politics and contemporary socio-cultural challenges — 485

32 Climate change and the socio-ecological crisis — 487
    Anabela Carvalho

33 Old and dependent: the construction of a subject position for politics and care — 500
    Bernhard Weicht

34 Language and gendered politics: the 'double bind' in action — 514
    Tanya Romaniuk and Susan Ehrlich

35 Queering multilingualism and politics: regimes of mobility, citizenship and (in)visibility — 528
    Tommaso M. Milani and Erez Levon

36 Language and globalisation — 541
    Melissa L. Curtin

37 A cultural political economy of Corporate Social Responsibility: the language of 'stakeholders' and the politics of new ethicalism — 557
    Ngai-Ling Sum

38 The fictionalisation of politics — 572
    Ruth Wodak and Bernhard Forchtner

39 Religion and the secular — 587
    Teemu Taira

PART V
Applications and cases II: language, politics and (de)mobilisation — 601

40 Discursive depoliticisation and political disengagement — 603
    Matthew Flinders and Matt Wood

41 Identity politics, populism and the far right — 618
    Anton Pelinka

42 Race, racism, discourse — 630
    Dávid Káposi and John E. Richardson

43 The materiality and *semiosis* of inequality and class struggle and warfare: the case of home-evictions in Spain 646
David Block

44 Language under totalitarian regimes: the example of political discourse in Nazi Germany 660
Andreas Musolff

45 Discursive underpinnings of war and terrorism 673
Adam Hodges

Index *687*

Figures

5.1	Saussurean and Lacanian algorithms	85
5.2	Saussure and Lacan on trees	86
5.3	Saussure's and Lacan's trees – simplified version	86
5.4	Signification – real, symbolic and imaginary aspects	87
8.1	Ogden and Richard's linguistic triangle	124
9.1	FPÖ poster 2010 'We protect free women'	142
10.1	*Wordle* cloud of lynching words (PC-ACE, Georgia lynching project, 1875–1930)	159
10.2	Gephi network graph of actors involved in lynching violence (Georgia lynching project, 1875–1930)	159
10.3	Google Earth Pro map of lynching events in Georgia (1875–1930)	160
10.4	Google *n-gram* of selected words	165
11.1	Keywords of Period 2 when compared to Period 1	178
11.2	Number of keywords per period when compared to the previous period	182
11.3	Range of keyness per period when compared to the previous period	183
12.1	Action schemas	190
12.2	Potential points of view on the Anchorage Plane	192
12.3	Point of view in reciprocal constructions	193
12.4	Point of view in active versus passive voice	194
12.5	Point of view in pictures of protests	196
13.1	Frequency of 'rat race' in *Hansard* 1950–2005	211
14.1	Impersonal authority as a legitimation for jihad	223
14.2	'Freedom' according to Getty Images	229
20.1	Addressees and audiences targeted by parliamentary speakers	315
24.1	(Failing) commemorative speech as a linguistic action pattern	375
25.1	'I hope that in some […] small way'	388
25.2	Yes Scotland, *Why Independence Will Be the Best Thing for Generations*	392
25.3	Alex Salmond steps out from behind the podium	394
28.1	'Star Spangled Banner'	432
28.2	'O Canada'	432
29.1	Billboard of the Petro Poroshenko Bloc	446
29.2	Billboard of the Fatherland party	449
29.3	Billboard of the Radical Party of Oleh Liashko	450
30.1	Visually blending and associating concepts. 'The Carlyle Group' by Seth Tobacman from *The Bush Junta* (2004)	464

30.2 Caricature and cartooning create visual rhetoric. 'The Carlyle Group' by
     Seth Tobacman from *The Bush Junta* (2004)   465
37.1 An example of UNESCAP's way of identifying and prioritising
     stakeholders   566
38.1 *The West Wing* advisers rushing through the corridors of the White House   575

Tables

11.1	Collocates of *Staat* according to *T Score* and *MI Score*	176
13.1	'Racing and Competition' metaphor keywords	209
13.2	'Global race' metaphors in the Thatcher-period and New Labour	213
13.3	'Euro-sclerosis' metaphor in parliamentary debates on the European Union	215
20.1	Parliamentary participant roles and institutional identities	316
23.1	Levels of context and their relevance to policy	358
23.2	Comparison of RLP-14, first and second draft (deletions crossed out, additions underlined)	361
28.1	US and Canada national anthem lyrics	430
28.2	Meaning potentials of pitch	432
28.3	Meaning potentials of direction of pitch movement	433
28.4	Meaning potentials of pitch range	433
28.5	Meaning potentials of note articulation	434
29.1	Political parties that entered the Ukrainian parliament in the 2014 parliamentary election	444
34.1	Distribution of overall occurrences of laughter, Clinton and 'other politicians'	519
34.2	Distribution of overall occurrences in relation to interviewer's (IR's) talk	519
37.1	Knowledge produced through Wal-Mart supplier scorecards	561
40.1	'Supply-side' causes of public disengagement with politics	605
40.2	Typology of different logics of discursive depoliticisation	611
43.1	Typology of assets related to inequality	649

Contributors

Ruth Amossy is Professor Emeritus at Tel-Aviv University (Israel), and the coordinator (with R. Koren) of the research group ADARR (*Analyse du discours, argumentation, rhétorique*). She is the chief editor of the French online journal *Argumentation et Analyse du Discours*. She is the author of numerous publications on the subject of stereotypes and clichés, argumentation, ethos and public controversies. Among her recent publications are *La presentation de soi. Ethos et identité verbale* (2010) and *Apologie de la polémique* (2012).

Jo Angouri is an Associate Professor at The University of Warwick, UK. Her research expertise is in sociolinguistics, pragmatics and discourse analysis. She has carried out projects in a range of corporate and institutional contexts, and her work concerns both online and face-to-face interaction. She has published widely on language and identity, as well as teamwork and leadership in professional settings. Her current research includes a project on teamwork in medical emergencies and multidisciplinary work on migration and the labour market. She has recently edited a volume on *Boundaries at Work* (with M. Marra and J. Holmes, EUP, 2016) and is currently working on a monograph on *Intercultural Communication at Work* for Routledge. Jo is co-editing *DAPSAC* for Benjamins and *Language at Work* for Multilingual Matters.

David Block is ICREA (*Institució Catalana de Recerca i Estudis Avançats*) Research Professor in Sociolinguistics at the University of Lleida (Spain). He is interested in the impact of political economic, sociological, anthropological and geographical phenomena on multimodal practices of all kinds (including social movements, multiculturalism, bi/multilingualism and the acquisition and use of languages). In recent years, he has focused specifically on neoliberalism as the dominant ideology in contemporary societies and social class as a key dimension of identity. He is author of *Social Class and Applied Linguistics* (Routledge, 2014) and co-author (with John Gray and Marnie Holborow) of *Neoliberalism and Applied Linguistics* (Routledge, 2012). He is Editor of the Routledge book series *Language, Society and Political Economy* and Associate Editor of the journal *Applied Linguistics Review*.

Anabela Carvalho (PhD, University College London) is Associate Professor at the Department of Communication Sciences of the University of Minho, Portugal. Her research focuses on various forms of environment, science and political communication, with a particular emphasis on climate change. She is editor of *Communicating Climate Change: Discourses, Mediations and Perceptions* (2008), *As Alterações Climáticas, os Media e os Cidadãos (Climate Change, Media and Citizens)* (2011), *Citizen Voices: Enacting Public*

Participation in Science and Environment Communication (with L. Phillips and J. Doyle, 2012), *Climate Change Politics: Communication and Public Engagement* (with T.R. Peterson, 2012), *Academics Responding to Discourses of Crisis in Higher Education and Research* (with Z. Pinto-Coelho, 2013) and of two journal special issues. Anabela Carvalho is on the Board of Directors of the International Environmental Communication Association, and is co-founder, former Chair and currently Vice-Chair of the Science and Environment Communication Section of ECREA.

Jonathan Charteris-Black is Professor of Linguistics at the University of the West of England, UK. His research interests are metaphor, rhetoric and political discourse. He is the author of *Fire Metaphors: Discourses of Awe and Authority* (Bloomsbury, 2017); *Analysing Political Speeches: Rhetoric, Discourse and Metaphor* (Palgrave Macmillan, 2014); *Politicians and Rhetoric: The Persuasive Power of Metaphor* (Palgrave Macmillan, 1st edition 2005, 2nd edition, 2011); *Gender and the Language of Illness* (Palgrave Macmillan, 2010); *The Communication of Leadership: The Design of Leadership Style* (Routledge, 2007); *Corpus Approaches to Critical Metaphor Analysis* (Palgrave Macmillan, 2004) as well as numerous other articles and book chapters.

Steven E. Clayman is Professor of Sociology at UCLA. His research addresses the interface between language, interaction, and media/politics. He is the co-author (with John Heritage) of *The News Interview: Journalists and Public Figures on the Air* (Cambridge, 2002), and *Talk in Action: Interactions, Identities, and Institutions* (Wiley-Blackwell, 2010).

Melissa L. Curtin, University of California, Santa Barbara (USA), is a Researcher in Language, Culture and Communication and Adjunct Assistant Professor in the Departments of Education, Global Studies, and Linguistics. Focusing on identity politics and belonging, she investigates ways that language/semiotic practices are used in processes of identification, the social construction of place, and the production of frames of 'differential belonging'. She is on the editorial board of the *Journal of International and Intercultural Communication*, and her critical ethnographic research is published in several edited volumes (*Handbook of Critical Intercultural Communication*; *Globalizing Intercultural Communication*; *Seeking Identity: Language in Society*; *Linguistic Landscape: Expanding the Scenery*; and *Conflict, Exclusion and Dissent in the Linguistic Landscape*) and journals (*International Journal of Sociology of Language*; *Social Semiotics*).

Endre Dányi is postdoctoral research fellow at the Department of Sociology at the Goethe University in Frankfurt am Main, Germany. Influenced by Science and Technology Studies (STS) and historical sociology, he wrote his PhD thesis at the Department of Sociology at Lancaster University about the Hungarian Parliament, more precisely about the ways in which material practices associated with democratic politics are being coordinated and distributed by the parliament building in the centre of Budapest. In his postdoctoral research, he traces the limits of such material practices by examining the ways in which the state, groups of policy experts and civil organisations constitute the 'outside' of parliamentary politics.

Anna De Fina is Professor of Italian Language and Linguistics in the Italian Department and Affiliated Faculty with the Linguistics Department at Georgetown University, USA. Her interests and publications focus on identity, narrative, migration and diversity. Her books include *Identity in Narrative: A Study of Immigrant Discourse* (John Benjamins, 2003),

Analyzing Narratives (co-authored with Alexandra Georgakopoulou, Cambridge University Press, 2012) and the *Handbook of Narrative Analysis* (co-edited with Alexandra Georgakopoulou, Wiley, 2015).

Randy Duncan is Professor of Communication at Henderson State University, USA. He is co-author, with Matthew J. Smith, of *The Power of Comics: History, Form and Culture* (Continuum, 2009) and co-editor, with Smith, of the Eisner-nominated *Critical Approaches to Comics: Theories and Methods* (Routledge, 2011) and the *Icons of the American Comic Book* (Greenwood Press, 2013). He is co-author, with Michael Ray Taylor and David Stoddard, of *Creating Comics as Journalism, Memoir and Nonfiction* (Routledge, 2015). Dr. Duncan is co-founder, with Peter Coogan, of the Comics Arts Conference. In 2009, Duncan received the Inge Award for Outstanding Comics Scholarship. In 2012, he received the Inkpot Award for Achievement in Comics Arts.

Susan Ehrlich is Professor of Linguistics in the Department of Languages, Literatures and Linguistics at York University, Toronto, Canada. She has published in the areas of discourse analysis, language, gender and sexuality, and language and the law. Her books include *The Handbook of Language, Gender and Sexuality*, 2nd edition (edited with M. Meyerhoff and J. Holmes, Wiley-Blackwell, 2014), *'Why do you ask?': The Function of Questions in Institutional Discourse* (edited with A. Freed, Oxford, 2010) and *Representing Rape* (Routledge, 2001).

Mats Ekström is Professor in the Department of Journalism, Media and Communication at the University of Gothenburg, Sweden. His research focuses on media discourse, conversation in institutional settings, political communication and young people's political engagement.

Göran Eriksson is Professor of Media and Communication Studies at Örebro University, Sweden. He has written extensively in the areas of politics and media, mainly studying televised political interviews and representations of politics and journalism. His most recent papers deal with reality television and multimodal representations of working-class participants.

Matthew Flinders is Professor of Politics and Founding Director of the Sir Bernard Crick Centre for the Public Understanding of Politics at the University of Sheffield, UK. He is also Chair of the Political Studies Association of the United Kingdom.

Bernhard Forchtner is a Lecturer at the School of Media, Communication and Sociology, University of Leicester (UK) and has previously worked as a Marie Curie Fellow at the Institute of Social Sciences, Humboldt-University of Berlin where he conducted a project on far-right discourses on the environment (project number 327595). He has published in the field of memory studies, at the interface of sociological theory and Critical Discourse Analysis, and on prejudice and discrimination.

Roberto Franzosi (BA in Literature, University of Genoa; PhD in Sociology, Johns Hopkins University) is Professor of Sociology and Linguistics at Emory University, USA. His main substantive interest has been in social protest, with projects on Italian strikes (*The Puzzle of Strikes*, Cambridge University Press, 1994) and two current projects on the rise of Italian fascism (1919–22) and on lynchings in Georgia (1875–1930) that have led to the publication of several journal articles. Franzosi has had a long-standing methodological interest in issues of language and measurement of meaning in texts, with several journal articles and four books published: *From Words to Number* (Cambridge University Press, 2005), *Content Analysis* (Sage, 2008), *Quantitative Narrative Analysis* (Sage, 2010), *Landmark Essays: Tropes and Figures* (Routledge, 2016).

Helmut Gruber is an Associate Professor at the Department of Linguistics at Vienna University, Austria. His research interests include discourse analysis and pragmatics, conflict communication, communication in the new media, academic writing research and discourse and politics. He has published in all these areas. He is co-editor of *Pragmatics*, member of the International Pragmatics Association (IPrA) consultational board, member of the editorial board of the *Journal of Language and Politics*, and president of the Austrian association of academic writing (GEWISSS).

Sten Hansson is exploring new ways of analysing public communication by executive governments, with a particular focus on blame, scandal and crisis. Sten has recently published his research in the *Journal of Pragmatics*, *Discourse & Society* and the *Journal of Language and Politics*. He is currently teaching political discourse analysis at the University of Tartu.

Christopher Hart is a senior lecturer in linguistics at Lancaster University, UK. He is author of *Critical Discourse Analysis and Cognitive Science: New Perspectives on Immigration Discourse* (Palgrave Macmillan, 2010) and *Discourse, Grammar and Ideology: Functional and Cognitive Perspectives* (Bloomsbury, 2014).

Michael Higgins is Senior Lecturer in the School of Humanities at the University of Strathclyde in Glasgow, UK. He has published widely in the areas of political communication and media discourse, including the books *Media and Their Publics* (Open University Press, 2008) and as lead-editor of *The Cambridge Companion to Modern British Culture* (Cambridge University Press, 2010). His latest book, written with Angela Smith, is *Belligerent Broadcasting: Synthetic Argument in Broadcast Talk* (Routledge, 2017).

Adam Hodges is a Visiting Assistant Professor of English at Carnegie Mellon University in Qatar. He is author of *The 'War on Terror' Narrative: Discourse and Intertextuality in the Construction and Contestation of Sociopolitical Reality* (Oxford University Press, 2011), editor of *Discourses of War and Peace* (Oxford University Press, 2013), and co-editor of *Discourse, War and Terrorism* (2007, John Benjamins). His research draws from sociolinguistics, linguistic anthropology and discourse analysis to examine the social, cultural and political dimensions of language use.

Jan Ifversen is currently Vice-Dean for the Faculty of Arts at Aarhus University (Denmark) and Professor of European studies. He has been writing on conceptual history for many years. In 1998, he founded an international group on the *History of Concepts*, together with colleagues. He is a member of the editorial committee of *Contributions to the History of Concepts*.

Cornelia Ilie is currently Full Professor of Business Communication at Zayed University, United Arab Emirates. Prior to that, she was Full Professor of English Linguistics at the

University of Malmö, Sweden. She held visiting professorships at several universities in Austria, Finland, Italy, Spain and Romania. She is the founder of EPARDIS (Europe and Parliamentary Discourses), founder and president of ESTIDIA (European Society for Transcultural and Interdisciplinary Dialogue), a board member of IPrA and a member of the Reference Group of Experts (Higher Education and Education For All) of the IAU (International Association of Universities). Her research interests are mainly interdisciplinary, and she has published extensively on institutional pragmatics and discourse practices (particularly political, media and academic discourses), intercultural rhetoric, and dialogic argumentation. In addition to numerous book chapters, refereed journal and encyclopaedia articles, her publications include the following authored or edited books: *Language and Ideology, Vol. 2: Descriptive Cognitive Approaches* (John Benjamins, 2001); *European Parliaments Under Scrutiny: Discourse Strategies and Interaction Practices* (John Benjamins, 2010); *Evolving Genres in Web-mediated Communication* (Peter Lang, 2012); *International Encyclopedia of Language and Social Interaction* (Wiley-Blackwell, 2015); *Parliaments and Parliamentarism: A Comparative History of Disputes about a European Concept* (Berghahn Books, 2016).

Bob Jessop is Distinguished Professor of Sociology and Co-Director of the Cultural Political Economy Research Centre at Lancaster University, UK. He is best known for his contributions to state theory, critical political economy and social theory and, more recently, has developed, together with Ngai-Ling Sum, a trans-disciplinary approach in the social sciences known as cultural political economy. This takes semiosis (sense- and meaning-making) seriously within the framework of political economy. Recent publications include: *The Future of the Capitalist State* (Wiley, 2002), *Beyond the Regulation Approach* (co-authored with Ngai-Ling Sum, Edward Elgar, 2006), *State Power* (Wiley, 2007), *Towards Cultural Political Economy* (co-authored with Ngai-Ling Sum, Edward Elgar, 2013), and *The State: Past, Present, Future* (Wiley, 2015).

Dávid Kaposi received his PhD at Loughborough University and is currently working at the Open University (UK) as Lecturer in Social Psychology. His publications include work on Imre Kertész's novels, the correspondence between Hannah Arendt and Gershom Scholem, as well as theoretical issues about truth, memory and identity. His latest project involved publication of the monograph *Violence and Understanding in Gaza: The British Broadsheets' Coverage of the War* (Palgrave Macmillan, 2014), where he was looking for instances of discourse where dialogue amid violent conflict was, and where it was not, possible. He plans to devote his future projects to the ensuing question: *why* was it (not)?

Reiner Keller is Professor of Sociology at Augsburg University, Germany. He is founder and Co-Editor of the *Journal for Discourse Research/Zeitschrift für Diskursforschung*. His research centres on knowledge and culture, discourse studies, sociological theory, pragmatist sociology, risk and environment, and French sociology. He has published widely in these areas, including the books *Wissenssoziologische Diskursanalyse* (*The Sociology of Knowledge Approach to Discourse*; VS-Verlag, Wiesbaden; Engl. Translation in preparation for Springer, 2017), *Michel Foucault* (Universitätsverlag Konstanz, 2008), *Doing Discourse Research* (Sage, 2013) as well as several co-edited volumes on discourse research, including *The Sociology of Knowledge Approach to Discourse: Conceptual and Methodological Applications for Research* (Routledge, 2017, in prep.). For updated information see http://kellersskad.blogspot.de.

Contributors

Lina Klymenko is a Researcher at the Karelian Institute and an Adjunct Professor at the Department of Social Sciences of the University of Eastern Finland, Finland. She holds a PhD in Political Science from the University of Vienna, Austria. Her research interests include politics of memory and national identity, political culture and democratisation in post-Soviet countries, and teaching and learning politics.

Christoffer Kølvraa is Associate Professor in the Section for European Studies, Department of Culture and Society, Aarhus University, Denmark. His research interests are oriented towards the construction of European identity, nationalism and extreme-right movements, theories of ideology and issues of political affect and mobilisation. His recent publications include: 'European Fantasies: On the EU's political myths and the affective potential of utopian imaginaries for European identity' (in *Journal of Common Market Studies*, 2016); 'The nature of nationalism: "Populist radical right parties" on countryside and climate' (in *Nature and Culture*, 2015).

Amelie Kutter is Researcher and Lecturer in European Politics and Discourse Studies at the European University Viadrina in Frankfurt (Germany). She holds a PhD (from Viadrina) and an MA (from Freie Universität Berlin) in political science and a BA in political and Slavic studies (Technische Universität Dresden). She is currently directing a project on the reconfiguration of centre and periphery in the European Union within the framework of a Marie Curie grant funded by the European Commission. Amelie Kutter has worked on the financial crisis, European integration, post-socialist transformation and transnational political communication at Lancaster University, FU Berlin, European University Viadrina, TU Dresden and CERI/Sciences Po. She specialises in discursive political studies and methods of textual analysis.

Erez Levon is Reader in Sociolinguistics at Queen Mary University of London, UK. His work focuses on language, gender and sexuality, and in particular, how gender and sexuality intersect with other categories of lived experience (including race, nation and social class).

Laura Loeb is a PhD candidate at University of California, Los Angeles, USA. Her research explores political interviews and interaction practices outside the traditional news programme, focusing specifically on talk shows. Her dissertation research on political talk-show interviews looks at the 2012 election season, combining conversation analysis with a quantitative comparison.

David Machin is Professor of Media and Communication at Örebrö University, Sweden. His books include *Introduction to Multimodal Analysis* (Bloomsbury, 2007), *Analysing Popular Music* (Sage, 2010), *The Language of Crime and Deviance* (Bloomsbury, 2012) and *The Language of War Monuments* (Bloomsbury, 2013).

Tommaso M. Milani is Professor of Multilingualism at the University of Gothenburg (Sweden). His broader areas of research encompass language–politics, media discourse, multimodality, and language gender and sexuality. His recent publications include the book *Language Ideologies and Media Discourse* (co-edited with Sally Johnson, Continuum, 2010), as well as articles in several international journals. He is the editor of the book series *Advances in Sociolinguistics* (Bloomsbury) and of the journals *African Studies* and *Gender & Language*.

Contributors

Lorenza Mondada is Professor for Linguistics at the University of Basel and Distinguished Professor at the University of Helsinki, Finland. Her research deals with social interaction in ordinary, professional and institutional settings, within an ethnomethodological and conversation analytic perspective. She has extensively published in *Journal of Pragmatics, Discourse Studies, Language in Society, ROLSI* and has co-edited several collective books (for Cambridge University Press, De Gruyter, Benjamins and Routledge) on multimodality, mobility, multiactivity and knowledge in interaction.

Andreas Musolff graduated from Düsseldorf University and is Professor of Intercultural Communication at the University of East Anglia, Norwich, UK. His research interests focus on Intercultural and Multicultural Communication, Cultural Metaphor Studies and Critical Discourse Analysis. His publications include the monographs *Political Metaphor Analysis: Discourse and Scenarios* (Bloomsbury, 2016), *Metaphor, Nation and the Holocaust: The Concept of the Body Politic* (Routledge, 2010), *Metaphor and Political Discourse: Analogical Reasoning in Debates about Europe* (Palgrave Macmillan, 2004), and the co-edited volumes *Metaphor and Intercultural Communication* (Bloomsbury, 2014), *Contesting Europe's Eastern Rim: Cultural Identities in Public Discourse* (Multilingual Matters, 2010) and *Metaphor and Discourse* (Palgrave Macmillan, 2009).

Anton Pelinka is Professor of Political Science at the University of Innsbruck, Austria (from 1975 to 2006), Professor of Nationalism Studies and Political Science, Central European University, Budapest, Hungary (since 2006). Publications on Democratic Theory (e.g. *The Politics of the Lesser Evil*, Transaction, 1999) and Comparative Politics (e.g. *Democracy Indian Style*, Transaction, 2003).

Claudia Posch is Assistant Professor for Feminist Linguistics and Political Rhetoric, University of Innsbruck, Austria and Visiting Researcher at University of Zurich, Switzerland. Research interests include: rhetoric and argumentation, feminist discourse analysis, language and gender, and corpus linguistics.

Martin Reisigl holds a PhD in Applied Linguistics and is teaching at the Department of Linguistics at the University of Vienna. Between 2011 and 2017, he has been an Assistant Professor for Sociolinguistics at the Institute for German Studies and the Center for the Study of Language and Society (CSLS), University of Bern. He was a Substitute Professor for German Linguistics at the Technical University Dortmund (2016–2017) and the University of Hamburg (2009–2010). Furthermore, he was a visiting professor at the Central European University (CEU) in Budapest (2009 and 2011). For many years, he worked as a Lecturer for Applied Linguistics at the University of Vienna. His research interests include (Critical) Discourse Analysis and discourse theory, text linguistics, sociolinguistics, pragmatics, politolinguistics, rhetoric, language and history, linguistics and literature, argumentation analysis and semiotics.

John E. Richardson is a Reader in Critical Discourse Studies, Department of Social Sciences, Loughborough University, UK. His research interests include structured social inequalities, British fascism, racism, Critical Discourse Studies and argumentation. His publications include the books *(Mis)Representing Islam: The Racism and Rhetoric of British Broadsheet Newspapers* (John Benjamins, 2004), *Analysing Journalism: An Approach from Critical Discourse Analysis* (Palgrave Macmillan, 2007), *Analysing Fascist Discourse: European*

Fascism in Talk and Text (Routledge, 2013, co-edited with Ruth Wodak) and *Cultures of Post-War British Fascism* (Routledge, 2015, co-edited with Nigel Copsey); and academic articles on Critical Discourse Studies, newspaper representations of Muslims, balance and impartiality in BBC reporting of Israel/Palestine, argumentation in readers' letters, political communications and party political leaflets. He is currently writing a book offering a Discourse Historical Analysis of British fascist discourse (2017, ibidem-Verlag) and researching the commemoration of Holocaust Memorial Day in Britain. He is Editor of the international peer-reviewed journal *Critical Discourse Studies* and is on the editorial boards of various journals.

Tanya Romaniuk is Assistant Professor in the Department of Communication at Portland State University, Portland, USA. She has published in the areas of discourse analysis, language and gender, and political discourse in mass media. Her recent publications include 'Text trajectories and media discourse: Tracking gendered representations in presidential politics' in *Gender and Language* (2014), 'Pursuing answers to questions in broadcast journalism' in *Research on Language Social Interaction* (2013), and 'Questioning candidates' (with S. Clayman) in *Talking Politics in the Broadcast Media* (John Benjamins, 2011).

Sara Rubinelli holds a degree in Classics and Philosophy from the Catholic University of Milan, Italy and a PhD from the University of Leeds, UK in the areas of logic, argumentation theory and rhetoric. From 2003 to 2009, she was the Scientific Coordinator of the Institute of Communication and Health of the University of Lugano, Switzerland. Since September 2009, she has been Scientific Coordinator of the Human Functioning Unit at Swiss Paraplegic Research, Switzerland and leads the Person-Centred Healthcare Group there. Since September 2012, she has been Assistant Professor in Health Sciences, with a focus on communication sciences, at the Department of Health Sciences and Health Policy of the University of Lucerne (CH). Sara Rubinelli's topics of research and teaching include theories and models of communication rhetoric, argumentation theory, argument effects and persuasion, health communication, knowledge translation, advertising, semiotics, critical thinking and communication skills in academic and professional curricula.

Kristof Savski is a Lecturer at Prince of Songkla University, Hat Yai, Thailand. His main research interests include historical and critical sociolinguistics, with a particular focus on the role of linguists in the development of the Slovene language in the 19th and 20th centuries, and on contemporary Thai language-in-education policies.

Andrew Sayer is Professor of Social Theory and Political Economy at Lancaster University, UK. His publications have been in the areas of philosophy of social science (e.g. *Realism and Social Science*, Routledge, 2000), ethics and social science (*Why Things Matter to People*, Cambridge University Press, 2011), class (*The Moral Significance of Class*, Cambridge University Press, 2005) and political economy (e.g. *Why We Can't Afford the Rich*, Policy Press, 2014).

Jennifer Sclafani is an Assistant Professor of Applied Linguistics at Hellenic American University in Athens, Greece and Visiting Assistant Professor of Linguistics at Georgetown University, USA. She researches the discursive construction of political identity in US presidential campaigns and teaches courses in sociolinguistics, cross-cultural communication, and language and gender.

Yannis Stavrakakis studied political science at Panteion University, Athens (Greece) and received his MA from the Ideology and Discourse Analysis Programme at the University of Essex, UK, where he also completed his PhD under the supervision of Ernesto Laclau. He has worked at the Universities of Essex and Nottingham, UK, before taking up a position at the Aristotle University of Thessaloniki, Greece, in 2006. He is the author of *Lacan and the Political* (Routledge, 1999) and *The Lacanian Left* (Edinburgh University Press/ SUNY Press, 2007) and Co-Editor of *Discourse Theory and Political Analysis* (Manchester University Press, 2000) and *Lacan & Science* (Karnac, 2002). He is Principal Investigator of the research project 'POPULISMUS: Populist Discourse & Democracy': www.populismus.gr

Ngai-Ling Sum is Senior Lecturer in the Politics, Philosophy and Religion Department and Co-Director (with Bob Jessop) of the Cultural Political Economy Research Centre at Lancaster University, UK. She has research and teaching interests in regulation approach, (international) political economy, Gramsci and Foucault, globalisation and competitiveness, Corporate Social Responsibility, etc. She was awarded (with Bob Jessop) the Gunnar Myrdal Prize by the European Association of Evolutionary Political Economics (EAEPE) for their co-authored book, *Beyond the Regulation Approach* (Wiley, 2006). In 2013, she co-authored with Bob Jessop a companion volume titled *Towards a Cultural Political Economy* (Edward Elgar). She publishes in journals such as *Economy and Society, Critical Policy Studies, Development Dialogue, New Political Economy, Critical Asian Studies, Competition & Change, Capital & Class, Urban Studies*, and *Language and Politics* as well as contributing book chapters to many edited collections.

Simon Susen is a Reader in Sociology at City University of London, UK. He is the author of *The Foundations of the Social: Between Critical Theory and Reflexive Sociology* (Bardwell Press, 2007), *The 'Postmodern Turn' in the Social Sciences* (Palgrave Macmillan, 2015), *Pierre Bourdieu et la distinction sociale. Un essai philosophique* (Peter Lang, 2016), and *The Sociology of Intellectuals: After 'The Existentialist Moment'* (with Patrick Baert, Palgrave Macmillan, 2017). Along with Celia Basconzuelo and Teresita Morel, he edited *Ciudadanía territorial y movimientos sociales. Historia y nuevas problemáticas en el escenario latinoamericano y mundial* (Ediciones del ICALA, 2010). Together with Bryan S. Turner, he edited *The Legacy of Pierre Bourdieu: Critical Essays* (Anthem Press, 2011), *The Spirit of Luc Boltanski: Essays on the 'Pragmatic Sociology of Critique'* (Anthem Press, 2014), as well as a Special Issue on the work of *Shmuel Noah Eisenstadt*, which appeared in the *Journal of Classical Sociology* (2011). In addition, he edited a Special Issue on *Bourdieu and Language*, which was published in *Social Epistemology* (2013). He is an Associate Member of the Bauman Institute and, together with Bryan S. Turner, editor of the *Journal of Classical Sociology*.

Teemu Taira is Senior Lecturer in the Department of Study of Religions, University of Helsinki, Finland. He is a co-author of *Media Portrayals of Religion and the Secular Sacred* (Ashgate 2013, with Kim Knott and Elizabeth Poole), Co-Editor of *The New Visibility of Atheism in Europe* (with Ruth Illman, special issue in *Approaching Religion*, 2012) and author of three monographs in Finnish. His articles have been published in journals such as *Religion, Culture and Religion* and *Journal of Contemporary Religion*. http://teemutaira.wordpress.com/

Theo van Leeuwen is Emeritus Professor at the University of Technology, Sydney (Australia), and Professor of Language and Communication at the University of Southern

Denmark. He has published widely on Critical Discourse Analysis, multimodality, social semiotics and visual semiotics. His books include *Reading Images: The Grammar of Visual Design* (with Gunther Kress, Routledge, 2006); *Introducing Social Semiotics* (Routledge, 2004); *Speech, Music, Sound: The Language of Colour* and *Discourse and Practice* (Palgrave Macmillan, 2010). He is a founding editor of the journal *Visual Communication*.

Bernhard Weicht has studied (Social) Economics in Vienna, Austria and Social Policy in Nottingham, UK. He received his PhD in Sociology from the University of Nottingham researching the social and moral construction of care for elderly people (2010). He is currently based at the University of Innsbruck, Austria. Bernhard has published on the construction of care, ideas of dependency, migrant care workers, the intersection of migration and care regimes and the construction of ageing and older people. He is Vice-Chair of the European Sociological Association Research Network, Ageing in Europe, and a member of the editorial board of the *Journal of International and Comparative Social Policy*.

Ruth Wodak is Emerita Distinguished Professor of Discourse Studies at Lancaster University, UK, and affiliated to the University of Vienna. Besides various other prizes, she was awarded the Wittgenstein Prize for Elite Researchers in 1996 and an Honorary Doctorate from the University of Örebrö in Sweden in 2010. She is a member of the British Academy of Social Sciences and a member of the *Academia Europaea*. In 2008, she was awarded the Kerstin Hesselgren Chair of the Swedish Parliament (at the University of Örebrö). She is co-editor of the journals *Discourse and Society*, *Critical Discourse Studies*, and *Language and Politics*. Her research interests focus on (Critical) Discourse Studies, gender studies and language, politics, prejudice and discrimination, and on ethnographic methods of linguistic field work. Recent book publications include *The Politics of Fear. What Right-wing Populist Discourses Mean* (Sage, 2015; translated into German *Politik mit der Angst. Zur Wirkung rechtspopulistischer Diskurse.* Konturen, 2016); *The Discourse of Politics in Action: 'Politics as Usual'* (Palgrave Macmillan, 2nd revised edition 2011); *Migration, Identity and Belonging* (with G. Delanty, P. Jones, Liverpool University Press, 2011); *The Discursive Construction of History. Remembering the German Wehrmacht's War of Annihilation* (with H. Heer, W. Manoschek, A. Pollak, EUP, 2008); *The Politics of Exclusion. Debating Migration in Austria* (with M. Krzyżanowski, Transaction, 2009); *The SAGE Handbook of Sociolinguistics* (with Barbara Johnstone and Paul Kerswill, Sage, 2010); *Analyzing Fascist Discourse. Fascism in Talk and Text* (with John Richardson, Routledge, 2013), and *Rightwing Populism in Europe: Politics and Discourse* (with Majid KhosraviNik and Brigitte Mral, Bloomsbury, 2013).

Matt Wood is a Lecturer in the University of Sheffield Department of Politics, UK. He is also Deputy Director of the Sir Bernard Crick Centre for the Public Understanding of Politics. Dr Wood's work focuses on the phenomenon of anti-politics and how it affects the legitimacy and authority of public figures and institutions. His work has appeared in diverse journals including *Deviant Behavior*, *Government and Opposition*, *British Journal of Politics and International Relations*, *New Political Science*, and *Critical Policy Studies*.

Introducing the language–politics nexus

Ruth Wodak and Bernhard Forchtner

Sketching out a long history

Given the significance of actual language use, and meaning-making more generally, in politics since at least the rise of rhetoric in Ancient Greece, and the ever more discursive nature of late modern politics in the twentieth and twenty-first centuries, *The Routledge Handbook of Language and Politics* contributes a single-volume reference work to this field. More specifically, this handbook adds to existing scholarship by providing a comprehensive overview of influential theoretical approaches, as well as common methodologies, classic genres and contributions on salient, socio-cultural challenges.[1]

In this introduction, we situate the 45 contributions to this volume both historically, that is, in a wider context of how language use has been viewed in relation to politics, and theoretically, that is, pointing to perspectives when approaching the language–politics nexus. We close with an overview of the various contributions to this volume.

Research in the field of language and politics has expanded enormously in recent years (for example, Cap & Okulska 2013; Fairclough & Fairclough 2012; Wodak 2011; Wodak & de Cillia 2006; Chilton 2004). From a Western point of view, the significance of skilful, persuasive language use is, of course, connected to rhetoric in Ancient Greece. Starting with councils as advisory bodies and, ultimately, the emergence of democracy in Athens, the art of persuasion (rhetoric) became an increasingly necessary prerequisite for successful participation in public life (Murphy et al. 2013; Fuhrmann 2011). This significance of actual language use for politics is visible, for example, in Aristotle's *Politics* (for an overview of thoughts on the co-evolution of language and politics, see Chilton 2004, pp. 16–19; for the following, see also Chilton, 2004, p. 5). The treatise is concerned with the polis, the political community and its best constitution; in a well-known passage, Aristotle addresses man as a 'political animal', stating that it is clear why:

> man is a political animal in a greater measure than any bee or any gregarious animal [...]. For nature, as we declare, does nothing without purpose; and man alone of the animals possesses speech. The mere voice, it is true, can indicate pain and pleasure,

and therefore is possessed by the other animals as well [...], but speech is designed to indicate the advantageous and the harmful, and therefore also the right and the wrong [...]

(Aristotle 1944, 1253a)

This quote captures our attention due to its emphasis on 'speech' in the process of sharing viewpoints. And even though today's understanding of politics is not limited to Aristotle's concern for households and city states, the importance of speech, and here, we include other modes of meaning-making, such as writing, visuals, music etc., in politics has hardly diminished. Indeed, rhetoric has evolved in manifold ways throughout subsequent centuries until today.

With the development of mass communication in the nineteenth and early twentieth centuries, interest in language use, in communication and its effects, entered a new stage. Seminal texts were stimulated by the (perceived) effectiveness of mass media and propaganda at the beginning of the twentieth century in 'the manufacture of consent' (Lippmann 1998 [1922], p. 248) and include, besides Walter Lippmann's and John Dewey's (1927) work, for example, Harold Lasswell's *Propaganda techniques in the World War* (1927). Important research was, furthermore, conducted by Jewish refugees in the United States, such as Paul Lazarsfeld in the context of the *Office of Radio Research* and later the *Bureau of Applied Social Research*. After the Second World War, Lasswell and Nathan Leites (1949) published one of the most important studies on quantitative semantics in the field of language and politics, developing approaches from communication and mass media research. Another tradition characterised by a more qualitative orientation is that proposed by members of the Frankfurt School, such as Theodor W. Adorno (Adorno et al. 1950) and Leo Löwenthal (Löwenthal & Guterman 1949).

Influenced by the use of propagandistic language during the Second World War and in the emerging Cold War era, research on the intricate links between language and politics (re-)emerged throughout Europe. Here, the dystopian novel *1984* by George Orwell (2008 [1949]) was a significant point of departure for the development of an entire new field. In Germany, critical linguistic research into the interdependence of language and politics during National Socialism was primarily conducted by Victor Klemperer (1947) and by Rolf Sternberger, Gerhard Storz and Wilhelm Emanuel Süskind (1957). Klemperer as well as Sternberger, Storz and Süskind sampled, categorised and described the words used during the Nazi regime: many words had acquired new meanings, other words were forbidden (words borrowed from other languages, such as *cigarette*), and neologisms (new words) were created; similar language policies were adopted by former communist totalitarian regimes (Wodak & Kirsch 1995). Controlling language in this way implies an attempt to control (the thinking and practices of) people.

A similar focus characterised the development of French discourse analysis in the 1960s and 1970s, that is, the work carried out by Michel Pêcheux on automated discourse analysis (for example, Pêcheux 1995). Here, language use was analysed in order to uncover deeper, ideological meanings. This interest in language was part of a wider shift towards recognising its significance in the 1960s (albeit with its roots in the nineteenth and early twentieth centuries). Among others, language plays an important role in Peter L. Berger and Thomas Luckmann's *The social construction of reality* (1991 [1966]), as well as, although in a different manner, by focusing on discourse in post-structural approaches most prominently represented by Michel Foucault.

From 1990 onwards, research on *political discourse* expanded further (for example, Wilson 1990). Studies were conducted on communication within political organisations (for example, European Union committees and decision-making processes, Krzyżanowski & Oberhuber 2007; Muntigl, Weiss & Wodak 2000; the United Nations, Holzscheiter 2010; the European Parliament, Wodak 2011), as well as on the unique (charismatic) style of politicians (for example, Tony Blair, Fairclough 2000; Jörg Haider, Wodak & Pelinka 2002; US senators, Duranti 2006), on political speeches and the politics of the past (for example, Austermuhl 2014; Heer et al. 2008; Charteris-Black 2004; Ensink & Sauer 2003; Martin & Wodak 2003), on right-wing political and fascist rhetoric (Richardson 2017; Wodak 2016, 2015; Wodak et al. 2013), on legitimation and persuasion (for example, Cap 2010; Chouliaraki 2006; van Dijk 2006; van Leeuwen 1996), and on interviews with politicians in the media (for example, Tolson & Ekström 2013).

Against the background of this diverse research, Armin Burkhardt, among others, proposed a typology by emphasising the use of:

> "political communication" as a generic term comprising all types of public, institutional and private talks on political issues, that is, all types of texts and genres typical of politics and political action, as well as the use of lexical and stylistic linguistic instruments characterizing text and talk about political contexts.
> (Burkhardt 1996, p. 5)

While attempting to transcend purely hermeneutic or philological approaches to text and talk, he lists four different procedures as particularly promising methods and techniques to be used for 'ideological reconstruction': *lexical-semantic techniques* (analysis of catchwords and value words, of euphemisms, and of ideological polysemy); *sentence and text-semantic procedures* (analysis of tropes, of semantic isotopes, and of inclusion and exclusion strategies); *pragmatic text-linguistic techniques* (analysis of forms of address, speech acts, allusions, presuppositions, argumentation, rhetoric, quotations, genres and intertextuality); and finally, *semiotic techniques* (icon, symbol and semiotic analysis). These distinctions have recently been taken up and further elaborated by German-speaking scholars (for example, Reisigl 2008, 2007) – but however these categories are defined, language use is intrinsically linked to them, and to what we label 'doing politics' (Wodak 2011).

Understanding politics

Mentioning Burkhardt furthermore raises the question of what constitutes 'political issues'? For Burkhardt, political communication is concerned with all types of public, institutional and private talk about political issues; thus, the topics are clearly marked as dealing with official political agendas. But as feminists have long argued, the boundaries between the private and the public, what is traditionally viewed as the sphere of the political, are shifting. Subsequently, and in light of both the plurality of theories in general and the wide range of perspectives held by contributors to this volume in particular, this handbook abstains from offering one stable, single definition or understanding of 'politics' and 'political issues'.

One such understanding could refer to individuals coming together in order to take decisions, and this is famously illustrated by Hannah Arendt's work in which political power is perceived as the result of acting in concert, that is, of actors coming together in order to achieve a certain purpose. Political power is thus based on consent and rational exchange, and not on coercion. As Arendt (1972, p. 151) notes, '[p]ower springs up whenever people get together and act in concert' – and it is in such a realisation of potential, coming together and deliberating, that power (that is, political power) can be considered to be legitimate; it is reproduced as such through constant deliberation.

Although within a different framework, Jürgen Habermas' (1979, p. 9) model of communicative action and discourse ethics radicalises this approach to the extent that understanding and co-operation are rooted in *'the intuitive knowledge of competent subjects'*. Consequently, procedures should warrant a deliberative exchange of arguments and the ability to discuss one's interests in light of norms that are acceptable to all those involved and affected (Habermas 2002, 1997). The deliberative model is thus one in which legitimate power is exercised collectively – and decisions that affect a group must be based on more or less free and equal exchange between individuals.

Such a conception does not deny conflict and disagreement – indeed, it is based on the very fact that disagreements exist, although framed by an orientation towards understanding and agreement. A sharp foregrounding of the conflictual dimension of politics (and beyond) is highlighted in Marxist-inspired approaches that stress class antagonism as the driving force of political developments. Here, politics is not – at least not in a classic understanding – viewed as an autonomous field, but ultimately tied to economic relations. Expanding and going beyond this view, Pierre Bourdieu argues that:

> [...] politics is a struggle to impose the legitimate principle of vision and division, in other words, the one that is dominated and recognized as deserving to dominate, that is to say, charged with symbolic violence.
>
> (Bourdieu 2005, p. 39)

Such a focus on conflict and struggle, on attaining hegemony, is most strongly associated with post-foundational approaches such as those from Ernesto Laclau and Chantal Mouffe (Mouffe 1999; Laclau 1994; Laclau & Mouffe 1985), who view politics as a matter of exclusion and decision, as that type of action which aims, ultimately, to implement one single perspective as hegemonic. Here, politics concerns the fixing of meaning, of social relations, in a context of radical contingency. Mouffe (1999) links such an understanding to the distinction between *politics* and *the political*. The latter refers to the ontological level, where antagonism is viewed as a principle characterising human relations. *Politics*, in contrast, concerns actual party programmes, institutions, and so on – the ontic level – and 'indicates the ensemble of practices, discourses and institutions which seek to establish a certain order' (ibid., p. 754). In Mouffe's (ibid.) agonistic model of democracy, politics 'consists in domesticating hostility and [...] trying to defuse the potential antagonism that exists in human relations' by turning enemies into adversaries on the basis of shared principles of liberal democracy, liberty and equality, in turn, on the basis of a basic consensus.

Vis-à-vis the aforementioned, we have not adopted an understanding of politics being either restricted to the sphere of government and policy, elections and so forth, or a specific theoretical tradition. As such, politics here is broadly viewed as being ubiquitous, as being about the ordering of social relations in both public and private life. Making something 'political' (or aiming to do so) thus concerns changing social relations, that is, negotiation and struggle over the distribution and use of power and resources. Indeed, where there is power, there is politics, as Colin Hay (2002, p. 3) maintains.

David Held and Andrew Leftwich offer a similarly broad working definition of politics, defining the latter as:

a phenomenon found in and between all groups, institutions (formal and informal) and societies, cutting across public and private life. It is involved in all the relations, institutions and structures which are implicated in the activities of production and reproduction in the life of societies. It is expressed in all the activities of co-operation, negotiation and struggle over the use, production and distribution of resources which this entails. [...] Thus politics is about power; about the forces which influence and reflect its distribution and use; and about the effect of this on resource use and distribution; it is about the 'transformative capacity' of social agents, agencies and institutions: it is not about Government or government alone.

(Held & Leftwich 1988, p. 144)

By thus going beyond a focus on government, orienting instead towards scarcity and diversity, towards the negotiation of interests, we view politics as being concerned with conflict and co-operation, as being the kind of human activity that revolves around dealing with diverging interests (differences in opinion, over scarce resources, etc.). This can result in either *imposing* a particular perspective, which is subsequently recognised as 'legitimate' by others, or reaching a collectively binding understanding of what to do through means of *deliberation*. Both perspectives, however, concern formal and informal practices that address a demarcation between the public and the private, a debate about the definition of what is (or might be) a legitimate (public) topic, the use and distribution of resources, and an attempt to affect the balance of forces within political institutions, such as the state, but also beyond them, and within different groups involved in these activities.

Language and politics – an interdisciplinary endeavour

Currently, language and politics are being studied from the perspectives of a number of disciplines, including political science, journalism and communication studies, sociology, law, economics and management studies, linguistics, psychology, philosophy and education. Each of these fields and approaches tends to presuppose certain sets of theoretical and methodological points of departure, which may not always be compatible with or easily comparable to others. However, there seems to be a consensus among most scholars that research on political communication generally requires some kind of inter- or transdisciplinary approach.

Clearly, this follows from the aforementioned: if every social process is potentially political – one concerned with the distribution of power, with power relations – then economic and social processes, for example, are part of this scope of understanding, to the extent that they affect these relations (Hay 2002, p. 4). A perspective that is thus able to capture the economic, the bodily, natural life, and so on, is therefore needed – be it called inter-, post- or transdisciplinary.

When analysing political communication and, more specifically, political 'spin', Brian McNair (2004) points to *source-centred approaches* to political communication (if they focus on politicians' strategic actions as information sources). Moreover, we can also distinguish *message/ discourse-centred* approaches (if the focus is on the linguistic analysis of language use in the manifold genres of political text, talk and images), the mediatisation of politics (if mainly interested in the practices of media professionals as transmitters of political information), or *reception-centred* approaches (focusing on how citizens participate in political communication).

Scholars who adopt a source-centred approach focus on the communicative behaviour of powerful groups and individuals in society: rulers, political elites. For example, McNair (2003, p. xv) emphasises how the actions of politicians and journalists influence media content and focuses 'on the nature of the interface between politicians and the media, the extent of their interaction, and the dialectic of their relationship'. Many studies, moreover, illustrate how politicians use numerous strategies and techniques to *attract public attention*, present themselves in a positive light and their adversaries in a negative one, convince audiences to support certain policy programmes, and so forth. These activities are labelled in manifold ways, such as political public relations, strategic communication, political propaganda, political media management, political marketing (Henneberg et al. 2009), political (or party) branding, 'spin' or 'spin-doctoring' (Hood 2011), image-making and mass self-communication (Castells 2009), and so forth.

Furthermore, we can observe an increase in the *'mediatisation of politics'* – a process by which politics (and society in general) becomes more and more dependent on the media (Strömbäck 2008); this contributes to the increasing professionalisation of political communication. Importantly, public office-holders' communication seems to be influenced by their preoccupation with individual blame avoidance (Hansson 2015), a perceived risk of mediated scandal (Allern & Pollak 2012) and constant concern with their organisational reputation (Carpenter & Krause 2012). More specifically, scholars working within *Discourse Studies* (Angermuller et al. 2014) and *Critical Discourse Studies* (Flowerdew & Richardson 2017; Hart & Cap 2014; Wodak & Meyer 2015) have developed innovative tools for systematic and detailed analyses of political text and talk. This *discourse-centred* research includes, among other topics:

- Studies of political metaphor and discursive framing in persuasive political text and talk.
- Cognitive and evolutionary linguistic analyses of political discourse, with a focus on expressions of spatial, temporal and modal dimensions.
- Corpus-assisted and qualitative research on political parties and/or politicians.
- Studies of rhetoric and argumentation in parliamentary debates, speeches, committees, and government reports.

In sum, we would like to emphasise that understanding politics, the procedures of decision-making, conflict and conflict resolution are not only of theoretical interest as an interdisciplinary endeavour; analysing, understanding and explaining the dynamics of everyday politics on the frontstage and backstage are also of eminent relevance in practice. As politics is increasingly perceived as an elitist endeavour, with participation by citizens often seen as lacking, this volume also hopes to contribute to making politics more transparent.

Outline of *The Routledge Handbook of Language and Politics*

This volume is divided into five sections: *Theoretical approaches to language and politics*, *Methodological approaches to language and politics*, *Genres of political action* and two final sections containing studies on salient debates that utilise various theories and methods, thus offering a series of analyses of 'language in/and politics'.

The first section on *Theoretical approaches to language and politics* outlines perspectives on how, on a fundamental, conceptual level, this nexus has been understood. This is not to suggest that approaches and theorists not presented in this section are not relevant, but developments sometimes beyond the editors' remit have prevented the inclusion of further chapters. In the first chapter, Sara Rubinelli reconstructs the development of rhetoric, the classic area in which language and politics have first met, by examining relevant authors from classical Greece to the beginning of modernity. This is followed by Bob Jessop's chapter on Karl Marx, Antonio Gramsci and Louis Althusser, in which he introduces and compares their thoughts on language, ideology and politics, emphasising continuities as well as discontinuities, and assessing their contemporary relevance.

The third chapter by Simon Susen deals with Jürgen Habermas' attempt to locate the normative grounds of deliberative democracy in the rational foundations of language. Indeed, Susen maintains that Habermas's conception of democracy is inseparably linked to his conception of language. Although sceptical of the extent to which aspects of this deliberative model of democracy can be applied to large-scale societies, the chapter concludes by addressing a number of issues that arise when confronted with the task of assessing both the validity and the usefulness of Habermas's communication-theoretic account of democracy.

Reiner Keller's discussion of Michel Foucault's work introduces the latter's focus on the modern subject as being established through 'games of truth' and power/knowledge regimes, including discussions of key concepts, such as archaeology, genealogy, discursive formations, *dispositif*, bio-politics, governmentality, and analytics of power. In his chapter on Jacques Lacan, Yannis Stavrakakis reflects on the role of language in psychoanalytic theory, especially Lacan's original reworking of Saussurean linguistics, and thus Lacan's psychosocial conceptualisation of the *symbolic,* before examining how Lacan shifted his attention from language to *jouissance*. Christoffer Kølvraa discusses Ernesto Laclau's discourse theory and the emergence and dynamics of political hegemonies therein. After elaborating on a post-structuralist understanding of discourses and their dislocation, Kølvraa points to how affect and emotion function as core elements in political discourses struggling for hegemony.

Andrew Sayer introduces Pierre Bourdieu's tension-laden relationship with actual language use and discourse by discussing the main concepts through which Bourdieu interprets social practices (such as habitus, field, capital and symbolic power), and reconstructs the relevance of Bourdieu's work for understanding the interdependence of language and politics.

In Chapter 8, Jan Ifversen turns to conceptual history and its analysis of basic social concepts in their range of semantic relations. The history of concepts, he maintains, is interested in the emergence, stability and changes to concepts in different historical contexts. Indeed, concepts are viewed as indicators of specific historical changes. The final chapter in this section, by Bernhard Forchtner and Ruth Wodak, introduces Critical Discourse Studies (CDS), a heterogeneous framework that facilitates the analysis of meaning-making in relation to wider societal (power) structures. As CDS recontextualises various concepts from a range of social theories, which subsequently influence empirical analysis, this chapter is characterised by a certain overlap of theoretical and methodological foci and thus serves as a transition towards Section 2.

Methodological approaches to language and politics introduces a range of methods for analysing 'language and politics'. Instead of attempting to offer an overview of the greatest possible number of methods of data analysis, we have attempted to provide a useful overview of tools for the analysis of *semiosis*. The opening chapter of this second section is provided by Roberto Franzosi, who discusses content analysis. He traces the development of this quantitative method of text analysis and illustrates a novel approach – Quantitative Narrative Analysis – by investigating newspaper articles reporting lynchings in Georgia (1875–1930).

Chapter 11, by Amelie Kutter, reviews corpus analysis, that is, computer-aided statistical analysis of large samples of digitised texts. Kutter provides an overview of the tool-kit of corpus linguistics and illustrates this method by drawing on an analysis of crisis discourse in financial commentary.

Christopher Hart subsequently turns to cognitive linguistics and the significance of conceptual structures that are invoked by language, and the ideological potential of those conceptual structures, in communication contexts. He argues for a connection between cognitive linguistics and multimodal approaches, and illustrates his claims by analysing discourses on political protests. Chapter 13, by Jonathan Charteris-Black, is also concerned with cognition and introduces the reader to conceptual metaphor, looking at the use of the 'competitive race' metaphor in debates of the British parliament.

The next chapter, by Theo van Leeuwen, offers an overview of ways to analyse multimodal legitimation in discourse and highlights three types of legitimation – legitimation through authority, moral evaluation legitimation and rationalisation legitimation – which are exemplified by a plethora of examples. Anna De Fina introduces narrative analysis in much detail and emphasises its significance for the study of politics in Chapter 15. Among other things, De Fina discusses 'master narratives' and the narratives as an everyday, context-sensitive practice. She concludes her chapter with a brief discussion of video narratives posted by members of the 'Dreamers' as part of their campaign to push for migration reforms in the United States.

The subsequent chapter by Claudia Posch discusses rhetorical analysis by first looking at the interdependence of rhetoric and politics. She then presents a number of rhetorical devices and their functions for the interpretation of persuasive strategies in political language. Ruth Amossy subsequently elaborates the meaning of political argumentation in Chapter 17 before approaching argumentation in relation to discourse analysis. Amossy illustrates the 'argumentation in discourse' approach to political discourse via an analysis of a speech delivered by Israeli Prime Minister Benjamin Netanyahu at the United Nations. Steven E. Clayman and Laura Loeb introduce the method of conversation analysis as an adequate approach to the detailed study of interaction in language and politics, including the characteristic forms of data that are employed and methods of analysis. This is illustrated by reference to exemplary work in the analysis of radio phone-in shows, political speeches and interviews.

In Chapter 19, Endre Dányi considers ethnography as an entry point to understand the connection between meaning-making and politics. The author illustrates a way of analysing a 'politics beyond words' by using the Hungarian parliament as a case in point and demonstrates how ethnography sheds light on the complex relationship between bodies, texts, symbolic objects, communication technologies and many other entities.

Section 3, *Genres of political action,* moves on to the description of a range of ways in which politics is performed. Cornelia Ilie's opening chapter reconstructs the particular ratified practices underlying parliamentary debates, drawing on a series of examples. Here, Ilie illustrates the mechanisms of deliberation, adversariality and polarisation that underpin political negotiation and power struggles. Focusing on government communication, Sten Hansson provides suggestions as to how communication practices of executive government institutions can be conceptualised. Hansson supports his analysis with examples taken from an extract from a UK Cabinet Office news release, a controversial campaign by the UK Home Office and public policy consultation papers on education. Next, Mats Ekström and Göran Eriksson examine another relevant genre in and through which politics are publicly performed and negotiated: press conferences. More specifically, they introduce a range of relevant aspects, from the history of the genre to press conferences as resources in news production and related practices of quoting and recontextualising political actions. Chapter 23, by Kristof Savski, describes the particularities of policy documents and laws. His analysis focuses on: first, the language of politics and laws; second, the analysis of policy genres in institutional contexts; third, the genesis of policy texts; and, fourth, the trajectory of policy meanings.

This is followed by Martin Reisigl's account of the genre of political commemoration. He argues that commemoration needs to be viewed as a multimodal process and event which serve the (trans)formation of political identities. Chapter 25, by Michael Higgins, examines the relationship between media and political language by deploying the concept of 'mediatisation', that is, of political discourse being ever more entwined with the logics and imperatives of the media. Higgins claims that the political use of language continues to evolve in parallel with ongoing developments in media technology and practice, and provides a range of examples.

Jennifer Sclafani, in Chapter 26, focuses on genres of political speeches, from town hall to inauguration, as *identity performances*. Drawing on interactional sociolinguistics, she illustrates how United States Senator Joni Ernst and Hillary Clinton use particular discourse strategies in various roles (as first lady, senator, secretary of state and presidential candidate) and in different contexts (town hall meetings, debates, campaign advertisements and speeches).

Helmut Gruber introduces genres of political communication in Web 2.0, presenting an activity-oriented genre conception that is adequate for describing and analysing dynamic multimodal interactions on social-media platforms. More specifically, he reviews the vast literature on: first, politician to citizen communication and, second, on citizen to citizen communication. David Machin investigates the particularities of the use of music in politics by looking at national anthems as a genre. He points to the affordances of sound and music in general, and how anthems in particular play an important part in legitimising and naturalising political ideologies.

Chapter 29, by Lina Klymenko, summarises research on the characteristics of billboards and party programmes as genres of political communication. She illustrates how these genres enabled political parties in the 2014 parliamentary election campaign in the Ukraine to approach voters concerning solutions to security and national unity issues. In Chapter 30, Randy Duncan similarly focuses on the visual by introducing caricatures and comics. He points to modes of simplification, techniques of exaggeration and sequencing in order to engage in political rhetoric, facilitating, for example, the undermining of authority. Jo Angouri and Lorenza Mondada close this section by approaching the genre of meetings in terms of social gatherings of small – as well as larger – groups of people for institutional and professional purposes. They discuss examples from political, business and multilingual meetings, while highlighting similarities and differences. The authors argue that this form of institutional talk promotes several important issues, the politics of meetings, such as the right to speak and to be listened to, of choices which lead to varying degrees of participation.

The final two sections illustrate applications of the aforementioned theories, methodologies and genres, pointing to particular links between language and politics. The first of these sections, entitled *Applications and cases I: language, politics and contemporary socio-cultural challenges*, includes eight chapters. Chapter 32, by Anabela Carvalho, addresses the perhaps most urgent challenge of our time: climate change. Here, Carvalho argues that responses to the issue have been increasingly privatised as techno-managerial approaches have gained currency – though alternative voices do exist. Chapter 33, by Bernhard Weicht, deals with another topic often presented in apocalyptic terms: the construction of 'the old and dependent'. His analysis stresses that becoming old is not to be understood as a continuous process; associations and symbols create a dichotomy of the young on one side, and an ageing population on the other. While drawing on an analysis of newspapers and focus groups from the UK and Austria, Weicht illustrates how the elderly are represented and how, consequently, the discursive constructions of 'being old' define and shape the possibilities of political action and struggle.

The next chapter, by Tanya Romaniuk and Susan Ehrlich, addresses language and gendered politics, that is, the distinctively masculine culture that continues to characterise politics. Following a review of the literature dealing with women in politics – and their representation – the authors analyse the different reception of laughter during the presidential primaries by Hillary Clinton in 2007, and close by arguing that women's performances as politicians are still evaluated according to a dominant, cultural script steeped in masculine hegemony.

In Chapter 35, Tommaso M. Milani and Erez Levon argue for the queering of multilingualism and politics by focusing on the relationships between mobility, sexuality and citizenship, and the role played by multilingualism and multi-semioticity in mediating such relationships. They illustrate their approach via a detailed analysis of multilingual practices in Israel/Palestine.

The next chapter in this section is provided by Melissa L. Curtin who emphasises refined conceptualisations of globalisation, language and linguistic practices by discussing: first, the 'language of globalisation'; second, 'the globalisation of language'; and third, particular linguistic practices and ideologies situated in specific contexts. She concludes with an appeal for a 'language and globalisation social-justice movement', which should support positions of alter-globalisation. Chapter 37, by Ngai-Ling Sum, investigates the discourses and practices of Corporate Social Responsibility (CSR) in the context of global, neo-liberal capitalism. She first introduces cultural political economy as an approach to understand the interdependencies of language and politics, and then focuses on the rise of global production-retail chains, such as Wal-Mart and, third, on criticism of the latter's practices. Sum, finally, argues that CSR operates in terms of a 'new ethicalism' which seeks to stabilize and enhance neo-liberalism.

Chapter 38, by Ruth Wodak and Bernhard Forchtner, investigates increasingly popular television programmes about backstage politics, such as the UK's *Yes Minister*, Denmark's *Borgen* and the US' *The West Wing*. Here, information about politics is provided in an accessible, often simplified way, which appeals to viewers dissatisfied with conventional media-reporting. The authors discuss this development by focusing on two episodes of *Borgen* and *The West Wing* – pointing to differences and similarities between the two.

The final chapter in this section, by Teemu Taira, explores how the modern distinction between religion and the secular has become a contested discursive tool in modern societies. Taira presents two approaches to the study of religion and the secular, one which views the two as analytical concepts, the other one being interested in their actual use.

The final section on *Applications and cases II: language, politics and (de)mobilisation* also deals with challenges. Here, however, we focus on mobilisation and demobilisation – even though the boundaries between the contributions in this and the previous section remain blurred. The first chapter in this section, Chapter 40 by Matthew Flinders and Matt Wood, is arguably the most general in its concern for discursive depoliticisation and political disengagement. The authors propose a typology of three 'logics of denial' –

denial in relation to the past, present and future – and illustrate these logics by drawing on speeches from then leading Conservative politicians in the UK.

The next chapter, by Anton Pelinka, deals with identity politics, populism and the far right. The article offers a historical overview of far-right parties and their development since the nineteenth century, followed by a discussion of populism as a concept and its particular understanding of democracy. Pelinka, then, turns to inclusion and exclusion in far-right politics before reflecting, finally, on recent developments. The focus on mobilisation through exclusion is further specified in Chapter 42. Here, Dávid Kaposi and John E. Richardson examine race and racism, and the relations between social ideas, social stratification based on these ideas, and discourse. The chapter analyses, first, a rather clear-cut case of racism, before moving on to less conspicuous and more ambivalent examples, thereby also illustrating the value of close analysis when examining discourse on this topic.

David Block examines the materiality and *semiosis* of inequality, class struggle and warfare by discussing the case of home evictions in contemporary Spain. Exploring this case in closer detail, Block focuses on the struggle between two crucial actors, the conservative *Partido Popular* and the *Plataforma de Afectados por la Hipoteca* (the latter being a grass-roots organisation which works on behalf of individuals and families who are threatened with eviction).

Chapter 44, by Andreas Musolff, discusses language use in totalitarian regimes and, in particular, the example of political discourse in Nazi Germany. Musolff arrives at a general characterisation of totalitarian language use as the construction of a strict demarcation between *us* and *them* in the context of latent state-terrorism, with the consequence of stigmatizing, isolating and possibly destroying the latter.

The final chapter in this section, and the Handbook, returns to the present and considers contemporary, discursive underpinnings of war and terrorism. Adam Hodges elaborates how forms of organised group violence are made acceptable or unacceptable, legitimate or illegitimate. More specifically, he analyses terrorism as a form of political communication and focuses the narrative construction of war and the properties of characters which populate these stories, while drawing, *inter alia*, on President George W. Bush's 'war on terror' narrative.

We hope that the focus of all these contributions on the role of language use – and meaning-making more generally – in political activities, offers innovative perspectives to readers who take the power of actual language use seriously for negotiation of the common good.

Note

1 For related volumes, see, for example, Semetko & Scammell 2012; Wodak & Koller 2008; Hellinger & Pauwels 2007; Gee & Handford 2012; Kaid 2004; Schiffrin et al. 2003; Shapiro 1984; O'Barr & O'Barr 1976.

References

Adorno, T W, Frenkel-Brunswik, E, Levinson, D J & Sanford, R N, 1950, *The authoritarian personality*, Harper & Brothers, New York.
Allern, S & Pollack, E, eds., 2012, *Scandalous! The mediated construction of political scandals in four Nordic countries*, Nordicom, Göteborg.
Angermuller, J, Maingueneau, D & Wodak, R, eds., 2014, *The discourse studies reader. Main currents in theory and analysis*, John Benjamins, Amsterdam.
Arendt, H, 1972, *Crises of the republic*, Harcourt Brace Jovanovich, New York.
Aristotle, 1944, *Politics. Aristotle in 23 volumes, vol. 21*, William Heinemann, London.
Austermuhl, F, 2014, *The great American scaffold. Intertextuality and identity in American presidential discourse*, John Benjamins, Amsterdam.
Berger, P L & Luckmann, T, 1991 [1966], *The social construction of reality: A treatise in the sociology of knowledge*, Penguin, London.
Bourdieu, P, 2005, 'The political field, the social science field, and the journalistic field', in *Bourdieu and the journalistic field*, eds. R Benson & E Neveu, Polity Press, Cambridge, pp. 29–47.
Burkhardt, A, 1996, 'Politolinguistik. Versuch einer Ortsbestimmung', in *Sprachstrategien und Dialogblockaden. Linguistische und politikwissenschaftliche Studien zur politischen Kommunikation*, eds. J Klein & H Diekmannshenke, de Gruyter, Berlin, pp. 75–100.
Cap, P, 2010, *Legitimization in political discourse: A cross-disciplinary perspective on the modern US war rhetoric*, Cambridge Scholars Publishing, Cambridge.
Cap, P & Okulska, U, 2013, *Analyzing genres in political communication: Theory and practice*, John Benjamins, Amsterdam.
Carpenter, D P & Krause, G A, 2012, 'Reputation and public administration', *Public administration review*, vol. 72, no. 1, pp. 26–32.
Castells, M, 2009, *Communication power*, Oxford University Press, Oxford.
Charteris-Black, J, 2004, *Corpus approaches to Critical Metaphor Analysis*, Palgrave Macmillan, Basingstoke.
Chilton, P, 2004, *Analysing political discourse. Theory and practice*, Routledge, London.
Chouliaraki, L, 2006, *The spectatorship of suffering*, Sage, London.
Dewey, J, 1927, *The public and its problems*, Alan Swallow, Denver.
Duranti, A, 2006, 'The struggle for coherence: rhetorical strategies and existential dilemmas in a campaign for the U.S. Congress', *Language in Society*, vol. 35, no. 4, pp. 467–497.
Ensink, T & Sauer, C, eds., 2003, *Framing and perspectivising in discourse*, John Benjamins, Amsterdam.
Fairclough, I & Fairclough, N, 2012, *Political discourse analysis*. Routledge, London.
Fairclough, N, 2000, *New Labour, new language*, Routledge, London.
Flowerdew, J & Richardson, J, 2017, *The Routledge handbook of Critical Discourse Studies*, Routledge, London.
Fuhrmann, M, 2011, *Die antike Rhetorik*, Artemis & Winkler, Mannheim.
Gee, J P & Handford, M, 2012, *The Routledge handbook of discourse analysis*, Routledge, London.
Habermas, J, 1979, 'What is universal pragmatics?', in *Communication and the evolution of society*, ed. J Habermas, Heinemann, London, pp. 1–68.
Habermas, J, 1997, *Between facts and norms: Contributions to a discourse theory of law and democracy*, Polity Press, Cambridge.
Habermas, J, 2002, *Inclusion of the other: Studies in political theory*, Polity Press, Cambridge.
Hansson, S, 2015, 'Discursive strategies of blame avoidance in government: A framework for analysis', *Discourse & Society*, vol. 26, no. 3, pp. 297–322.
Hart, C & Cap, P, eds., 2014, *Contemporary Critical Discourse Studies*, Bloomsbury, London.
Hay, C, 2002, *Political analysis*, Palgrave Macmillan, Basingstoke.
Heer, H, Manoschek, W, Pollak, A & Wodak, R, 2008, *The discursive construction of history: Remembering the Wehrmacht's war of annihilation*, Palgrave Macmillan, Basingstoke.

Held, D & Leftwich, A, 1988, 'A discipline of politics?', in *What is politics? The activity and its study*, ed. A Leftwich, Blackwell, Oxford, pp. 139–159.

Hellinger, M & Pauwels, A, 2007, *Handbook of language and communication: Diversity and change*, Mouton de Gruyter, Berlin.

Henneberg, S C, Scammell, M, & O'Shaughnessy, N J, 2009, 'Political marketing management and theories of democracy', *Marketing Theory*, vol. 9, no. 2, pp. 165–188.

Holzscheiter, A, 2010, *Children's rights in international politics: The transformative power of discourse*, Palgrave Macmillan, Basingstoke.

Hood, C, 2011, *The blame game: Spin, bureaucracy and self-preservation in government*, Princeton University Press, Princeton.

Kaid, L L, ed., 2004, *Handbook of political communication research*, Lawrence Erlbaum Associates, Mahwah.

Klemperer, V, 1947, *LTI. Notizbuch eines Philologen*, Aufbau Verlag, Berlin.

Laclau, E, 1994, 'Why do empty signifiers matter to politics?', in *Emancipation(s)*, ed. E Laclau, Verso, London, pp. 36–46.

Laclau, E & Mouffe, C, 1985, *Hegemony and socialist strategy: Towards a radical democratic politics*, Verso, London.

Lasswell, H D, 1927, *Propaganda technique in the World War*, Kegan Paul & Company, London.

Lasswell, H D & Leites, N, 1949, *Language of politics: studies in quantitative semantics*, G W Stewart, New York.

Lippmann, W, 1998 [1922], *Public opinion*, Transaction Publishers, New Brunswick.

Löwenthal L & Guterman N, 1949, *Prophets of deceit. A study of the techniques of the American agitator*, Harper and Brothers, New York.

Martin, J R & Wodak, R, eds., 2003, *Re/reading the past: Critical and functional perspectives on time and value*, Amsterdam, John Benjamins.

McNair, B, 2003, *An introduction to political communication*, Routledge, London.

McNair, B, 2004, 'PR must die: Spin, anti-spin and political public relations in the UK, 1997–2004', *Journalism Studies*, vol. 5, no. 3, pp. 325–338.

Mouffe, C, 1999, 'Deliberative democracy or agonistic pluralism', *Social Research*, vol. 66, no. 3, pp. 745–758.

Muntigl, P, Weiss, G, & Wodak, R, eds., 2000, *European Union discourses on un/employment. An interdisciplinary approach to employment policy-making and organizational change*, John Benjamins, Amsterdam.

Murphy, J, Katula, R & Hoppmann, M, 2013, *A synoptic history of classical rhetoric*. 4th ed., Routledge, London.

O'Barr, W M & O'Barr, J F, eds., 1976, *Language and politics*, Mouton de Gruyter, The Hague.

Oberhuber, F & Krzyżanowski, M, 2007, *(Un)doing Europe: Discourses and practices of negotiating the EU constitution*, Peter Lang, Bruxelles.

Orwell, G, 2008 [1949], *1984*, Penguin, London.

Pêcheux, M, 1995 [1969], *Automated discourse analysis*, Rodopi, Amsterdam.

Reisigl, M, 2007, *Nationale Rhetorik in Fest- und Gedenkreden: Eine diskursanalytische Studie zum "österreichischen Millennium" in den Jahren 1946 und 1996*, Stauffenburg Verlag, Tübingen.

Reisigl, M, 2008, 'Rhetoric of political speeches' in *Handbook of communication in the public sphere*, eds. R Wodak & V Koller, de Gruyter, Berlin, pp. 271–289.

Richardson, J E, 2017, *British fascism. A discourse-historical analysis*, ibidem, Stuttgart.

Schiffrin, D, Tannen, D & Hamilton, H E, eds., 2003, *The handbook of discourse analysis*. Blackwell, Oxford.

Semetko, H A & Scammell, M, eds., 2012, *The Sage handbook of political communication*, Sage, London.

Shapiro, M J, ed., 1984, *Language and politics*, Basil Blackwell, Oxford.

Sternberger, D, Storz, G & Süskind, W E, 1957, *Aus dem Wörterbuch des Unmenschen*, Clausen, Hamburg.

Strömbäck, J, 2008, 'Four phases of mediatization: An analysis of the mediatization of politics', *International Journal of Press/Politics*, vol. 13, no. 3, pp. 228–246.

Tolson, A & Ekstroem, M, 2013, *Media talk and political elections in Europe and America*, Palgrave Macmillan, Basingstoke.

van Dijk, T A, 2006, 'Discourse and manipulation', *Discourse & Society*, vol. 17, no. 3, pp. 359–383.

van Leeuwen, T, 1996, 'The representation of social actors', in *Texts and practices: Readings in Critical Discourse Analysis*, eds. C R Caldas-Coulthard & M Coulthard, Routledge, London, pp. 32–70.

Wilson, J, 1990, *Politically speaking: The pragmatic analysis of political language*, Blackwell, Oxford.

Wodak, R, 2000, 'From conflict to consensus? The co-construction of a policy paper', in *European Union discourses on un/employment. An interdisciplinary approach to employment policy-making and organizational change*, eds. P Muntigl, G Weiss & R Wodak, John Benjamins, Amsterdam, pp. 73–114.

Wodak, R, 2011, *The discourse of politics in action: Politics as usual*, Palgrave Macmillan, Basingstoke.

Wodak, R, 2015, *The politics of fear. What right-wing populist discourses mean*, Sage, London.

Wodak, R, 2016, *Politik mit der Angst. Zur Wirkung rechtspopulistischer Diskurse*, Konturen, Wien.

Wodak, R & de Cillia, R, 2006, 'Politics and language: Overview' in *Encyclopedia of language & linguistics*. 2nd ed., ed. K Brown, Elsevier, Oxford, pp. 707–719.

Wodak, R & Kirsch, F P, eds., 1995, *Totalitäre Sprache – Langue de bois – Language of dictatorship*, Passagen, Vienna.

Wodak, R & Koller, V, eds., 2008, *Communication in the public sphere. Handbook of applied linguistics*, vol. 4, De Gruyter, Berlin.

Wodak, R & Meyer, M, eds., 2015, *Methods of Critical Discourse Studies*. 3rd ed., Sage, London.

Wodak, R & Pelinka, A, eds., 2002, *The Haider phenomenon*, Transaction Publishers, New York.

Wodak, R, KhosraviNik, M, Mral, B, eds., 2013, *Right-wing populism in Europe: Politics and discourse*, Bloomsbury, London.

Part I
Theoretical approaches to language and politics

1

Rhetoric as a civic art from antiquity to the beginning of modernity

Sara Rubinelli

Introduction

Language is essential to politics as politics exercises its power of making decisions and influencing citizens through language. The ancient Greeks started a tradition of the study of language focused on this power of influencing civic life under the field of 'rhetoric'.

When thinking about 'rhetoric' currently, we are often confronted with negative connotations. As the 'intellectual art or study of persuasion', intimately connected with oratory as 'verbal communication with the intent to persuade' (Worthington 1994, p. viii), rhetoric is often perceived as a field of study leading to the acquisition of skills to unethically deceive people. Within this connotation, rhetoric is also considered to be the study of how to support both sides of an argument and, thus, how to give credit to whatever is in the best interests of the speaker, regardless of its truth (Parker 1972).

If mastering the art of rhetoric can lead to the power to greatly harm people by unjustly using the strategies of language, Aristotle was keen to underline that, without knowledge of persuasion, it is not easy to convince an audience of good, constructive, or true ideas. Audiences will not be able to evaluate claims and standpoints in the correct way if such points are not presented and supported persuasively (Aristotle's *Rhetoric* A 1, 1355a, pp. 20–23, Bodéüs 1992). This is why, despite the 'dark side' of rhetoric, the study of persuasion is a key source of empowerment for those citizens who have vital interests and core values to defend (Vickers 1989, preface and pp. 1–80). Rhetoric is a discipline of study that leads to personal growth and, in politics, it is a laboratory for developing democratic processes (Ober 1994; Lunsford et al. 2009, p. 290). Thus, since Greek antiquity, rhetoric has focused on what counts as an argument of quality, on how to recognise fallacious arguments and, overall, on how to use language in order to persuade people to act upon beneficial ideas (see, for instance, Aristotle's *Rhetoric* B 23). To use concepts from the modern theory of argumentation, there was a tradition beginning in classical Greece concerned with the study of the relationship between reasonableness and effectiveness in argumentation (i.e. on the use of appropriate reasons to support a point of view while, at the same time, aiming for effectiveness) (van Eemeren 2010). Rhetoric developed as a discipline that deals with the requirements and characteristics of persuasive discourse and, as such, flourished as a key discipline in the education system (Milanese 1989).

The objective of this chapter is to examine the development of rhetoric as the study of language in the context of politics from antiquity to the beginning of modernity. More specifically, it examines the way in which the principal classical authors dealt with rhetoric in light of its power 'to cultivate citizens' (Glenn & Carcasson 2010) in both thinking and speaking and, from there, to impact civic life.

Rhetoric in Ancient Greece

The Sophists and Isocrates

The rise of rhetoric as a discipline of study in Ancient Greece can be seen as a recognition of the importance of language in political society. Historically, the origin of the art of speaking is said to be found in the second quarter of the fifth century BC in the newly established democracy of Syracuse. Citizens' effective participation in political debate required that there be an exchange of opinions to enable them to make good and wise decisions on issues of social interest (Kennedy 1963; Cole 1991). Skillful oratory played an instrumental role for power in Athenian society (Ober 1994); it was a precondition for political success as well as a form of self-defence.

With this in mind, it is not surprising that, in the second half of the fifth century BC, the teaching of persuasion became a key business, especially for the itinerant professional teachers known as the Sophists. The most famous of these teachers were Protagoras (490–420 BC), Gorgias (485–380 BC) and Prodicus (465–395 BC). The Sophists made rhetoric the core of their education programme as, in their view, the acquisition of rhetorical skills and of competence in using rhetorical devices was the best equipment for fulfilling any political ambition (Guthrie 1971; Kerferd 1981).

Protagoras stressed that every argument has two contradictory sides, both of which could well be argued. In his teaching, Gorgias specifically focused on how to lead souls (*psychagogia*) by using figures of speech and working on stylistic elements. He also focused on the so-called art of the propitious moment (*kairos*) as the ability to say the right thing at the right time. For this purpose, students were taught to memorise specific speeches that they could use at any time so they were always ready with an appropriate response (Rubinelli 2009, pp. 43–72).

The Sophists elevated rhetoric to an autonomous discipline, the study of which was essential for personal empowerment. However, rhetoric was taught as being detached from personal qualities such as justice, respect and honesty, and this evident limitation did not go unnoticed from an ethical point of view.

In the treatise *Against the Sophists*, Isocrates (436–338 BC) condemned the main principles behind the educational programme of the Sophists. He portrayed rhetoric as 'that endowment of our human nature which raises us above mere animality and enables us to live the civilised life' (Norlin 1928, p. ix). There is no absolute truth on which human beings can base their judgement; nevertheless, human beings can be reliable judges and so not entirely susceptible to manipulation through speech (Balla 2004). Through pioneering ideas that were most successful in the Roman rhetorical tradition, Isocrates conceived the ideal orator as a person not only skilful in the art of speaking, but also gifted in history, culture, science and, ultimately, morality. It was this notion that led to Isocrates being known today as the father of 'liberal education' (Corbett 1989; Benoit 1991).

Plato

Isocrates looked at rhetoric as a practical skill to be coupled with education. But, in the same period as Isocrates, this constructive idea of rhetoric was strongly rejected by Plato (436–338 BC) who, at an early stage in his career, condemned rhetoric as simply being the expression of a decline of values in society (Wardy 1996; Ryan 1979; Cole 1991). For Plato, a competence in rhetoric was all about appearing to know things and flattering the audience through skilful usage of the language. In *Gorgias* (464b–465d), Plato presented a remarkable analogy when comparing rhetoric and justice with cookery and medicine: medicine and justice aim towards the good, cookery and rhetoric aim towards pleasure. Thus, within the educational model presented in the *Republic*, rhetoric does not hold a position. For Plato, what is important to those individuals who will guide the city are disciplines including music, gymnastics, mathematics and dialectic (*Republic* 521d–541b).

Yet, Plato could not avoid admitting that oratory is an important component of human communication. Thus, later in his career, he reflected on whether there could be a way to think about rhetoric more constructively. In the second half of the *Phaedrus*, Plato re-evaluated the possibility that rhetoric could be a real art by pointing out that it is not speaking or writing that are shameful *per se*, but that what is bad is when people engage in them shamefully (*Phaedrus* 258d, pp. 4–5). Indeed, Plato recognises that rhetoric is the primary way 'of leading the soul by means of speech' (*Phaedrus* 261a, 8). As such, it can to be used to enhance society for the good, provided that it is assisted by a rigorous study of nature, of psychology and of argumentation techniques (*Phaedrus*, pp. 269e–272b).

Overall, it is clear that for Plato, rhetoric should be subordinated to philosophy, as it is philosophy that offers the knowledge and moral virtues necessary to use rhetoric for the benefit of the city.

Aristotle

Plato never wrote a handbook of rhetoric. It was only his pupil Aristotle (384–322 BC) who, in the *Rhetoric*, pioneered that which Plato had left unexamined.

For Aristotle, rhetoric, as the counterpart of dialectic, can enable speakers to strengthen their ability to construct sound arguments (*Rhetoric* A 1, 1355a, pp. 20–33) (Rubinelli 2009, pp. 50–58).

In the *Rhetoric*, Aristotle gave clear indications of what students had to learn. They had to be trained in the discovery of 'artistic' arguments (*Rhetoric* A 2, 1355b, pp. 35–39) that result from a reflection on the speaker, the audience and the topic. Orators can design their arguments by playing on the character of the speaker (the *ethos*), by disposing the listener in some way (with attention to *pathos*) and by playing on the rational appeal (the *logos*) with induction and deduction (*Rhetoric* A 2, 1356a, pp. 1–4).

Aristotle considered the rational appeal to be particularly important in shaping persuasive speeches. To teach students this task, he introduced in the *Rhetoric* the method of argumentation presented in his *Topics*, which instructs students how to build arguments by reflecting on the formal aspects of argumentation (Rubinelli 2009, pp. 59–90).

To increase students' knowledge of emotions is one target of rhetorical education, and that is why, in the *Rhetoric*, Aristotle presented the first systematic discussion of human psychology. In Book 2 of the *Rhetoric* he analysed 15 emotions, including anger/mildness, love/friendship, pity and envy (Wisse 1989). As for the other role of the speaker, Aristotle emphasised the value of ethical appeal. When speakers gain trust and admiration, they increase their credibility (*Rhetoric* 2, pp. 12–17).

In Book 3 of the *Rhetoric*, Aristotle addressed the issue of style as another topic in which students must be trained and enquired what a good prose style comprises. Aristotle recognised the importance of the actual delivery of a speech in terms of its linguistic format. (*Rhetoric* 3, pp. 1–19).

Overall, Aristotle is recognised as having made the greatest contribution to rhetorical theory in the sense that he offered a theory of persuasive speech communication that could train and reinforce the skills of students. He developed this theory by reflecting on the fact that rhetoric was indeed used to influence events in the city and also on the evidence that there was a lack of theoretical insight in the current teaching of rhetoric (*Rhetoric* 1–3) (Grimaldi 1972, pp. 60–66). He was aware that rhetoric is morally free and that, as such, it can be used or abused. Nevertheless, he was optimistic enough to believe that empowering citizens in terms of their persuasion skills would have offered a valuable tool with which to transmit the best ideas for human progress.

Rhetoric in Ancient Rome

The ability to design and deliver persuasive speeches was perceived as a precondition for success in the popular assemblies and the Roman senate (Kennedy 1972, pp. 23–37; Bonner 1998). Rome was, at the time, based on a form of democratic oligarchy where several hundred men in the senate would each need the skill to present their points of view to gain the approval of the audience, as well as to influence the passing or vetoing of various laws and legislation (Crook 1967). One priority in rhetorical training in the Roman context focused on teaching students how to successfully plead a case.

The two Roman thinkers who most influenced the development of rhetoric as an educational discipline, namely Cicero (106–43 BC) and Quintilian (35–96 AD), were themselves highly competent lawyers.

Cicero

Thanks to the status of his father, an equestrian knight, Cicero received the best education in philosophy, history and rhetoric through classes with famous Greek teachers. At the age of 15, he wrote *De inventione*, which, together with the contemporary anonymous work known as *Rhetorica ad Herennium*, represent the first extant treatises of Roman rhetoric. Cicero's early interest in rhetoric was influenced by the idea that eloquence is one of the most important traits for a man who contends on behalf of his country (Powell & Paterson 2004). Indeed, as he explained at the beginning of *De inventione*, the ability to deliver persuasive speeches facilitated the use of wisdom in settling many important issues for cities. Rhetoric was, thus, for the young Cicero, an element of political science.

As the title *De inventione* underlines, the rhetorical training to empower citizens focused on the elaboration of a speech known as *inventio*, concerned with the 'discovery of valid or seemingly valid arguments to render one's cause plausible' (*De inventio* I, 9). Within the context of *inventio*, Cicero, by following ideas already discussed in the Greek tradition, proposed an extended version of the distinction of the parts of a speech, namely: the introduction [*exordium*], the beginning of the discourse; the narration [*narratio*] of the events that occurred, or that might have occurred; the division [*divisio* or *partitio*], about what is agreed upon and what is a matter of controversy; the proof [*confirmatio*], as the presentation of arguments; the refutation [*refutatio*] of the adversaries' arguments; and the conclusion [*conclusio*] of the discourse (*De inventione* I, 9). According to the above categories, speakers were taught how to create a successful oration by reflecting on the construction of a speech according to certain specific tasks.

In his later work, Cicero himself further refined his conceptualisation of the art of rhetoric. During his studies, he reflected upon what the ideal role and education of an orator should have been. In 55 BC, he composed a dialogue entitled *De Oratore* where he presented the idea that rhetoric has to be joined by philosophy (I, 3, 9) and by an overall knowledge of humanity, culture and society (Narducci 1994, pp. 5–82).

Orators must possess the acumen of dialecticians, the mind of philosophers, an almost poetical expression, the memory of lawyers, the voice of tragic actors and the gestures of the most advanced actor (*De Oratore* I, 28, 128). All of these characteristics must be mastered to the highest degree (*De Oratore* III, 20, 76). These principles were further explained and supported in the *Brutus*, Cicero's treatise on the history of Roman oratory, and in the *Orator*, his last work on rhetoric.

On a more operational level, in *De Oratore*, Cicero echoed the Aristotelian motto of *ethos*, *logos* and *pathos* as representing in practice the main qualities of a skilful orator. As he expressed through the character of the orator Antonius, there are three main functions of the orator: to gain the sympathy of the audience, to demonstrate what is true and to stir emotions (*De Oratore* II, pp. 114–115). These functions of the orator's mission have been transmitted through the ages as the *officia oratoris*.

Overall, Cicero attempted to rebase the discipline of rhetoric in its more fundamental theoretical foundation in response to a practical orientation codified in the post-Aristotelian schools of rhetoric. In so doing, he attempted to develop a model of the perfect orator in the format of an almost ideal one.

Quintilian

The battle of Actium (31 BC) signalled the end of the Roman republic and the beginning of the Empire under Octavian. In this period, the teaching of a special form of exercise called *declamation* became the real passion of rhetorical schools. In the basic form of declamation, the student was given a set of hypothetical circumstances and had to support one of these hypotheses as in a genuine judicial or deliberative context (Heath 1995; Kennedy 1994).

The practice of declamation spread widely among the private schools of rhetoric. Yet, this spread gave rise to a rather arid and artificial declamatory style, resulting in the increasing use of short sentences, forced metaphors and ready-made arguments. These changes, seen as a corruption of the Ciceronian standards, provoked the reaction of rhetoricians, among whom Quintilian was considered to be the greatest teacher of rhetoric in Rome (Gwynn 1926). Asked by his friends to write a treatise to re-evaluate rhetoric as a discipline, in 93 AD Quintilian began writing the first of the 12 books of *Institutio oratoria*, which is usually translated as *The Education of the Orator*.

The title reflects Quintilian's desire to explain the ideal course of study through which to became a perfect orator 'who will be not only an eloquent speaker but a political leader and moral spokesman for Roman society' (Kennedy 1972, p. 509). For Quintilian, the orator should be *vir bonus dicendi peritus* (a good man skilled in speaking) (*Institutio oratoria*, XII, 1).

The first book of the *Institutio oratoria* is devoted to those things that take place prior to the work of rhetoricians, namely the earliest training at home and study in a grammar school.

The core of the *Institutio* is a discussion of rhetoric. Quintilian explained all the traditional phases of elaboration and parts of a speech by adding some elements not found in other Latin treatises. For example, he included a book devoted to how an orator can obtain ideas and expressions by reading and writing. For this purpose, he explained what a student should read in Greek and Latin. In another section, the focus is on the theory of 'imitation' (*mimesis* in Greek). As defined by the historian and rhetorician Dionysius of Halicarnassus (first century AD), imitation is 'an activity of the soul moved toward admiration of what seems fine' (Kennedy 1994, p. 78). In Quintilian's book, speakers are invited to imitate the techniques of a classical writer in order to understand the special qualities of writers and learn how to acquire their skills.

Within his educational programme, all forms of knowledge were important, although speaking, writing and reading were the best skills to obtain. Quintilian perceived education as the tool to create an upstanding citizen; within the field of education, oratory was considered majestic as it was the best gift from the gods to man (Book XII), and it is precisely because of their reasoning and speaking skills that human beings achieve superiority over animals (Book II).

The Roman Empire

The influence of Quintilian's enterprise was significant at an educational level. Because of it, rhetoric became a key component in the general curricula in all public professions. Under the Roman Empire, however, despite Quintilian's enterprise, the general understanding of rhetoric changed significantly. The Empire started to impose constraints of freedom of thought and expression. Juridical rhetoric started to lose its power because of the professionalisation of the procedures in the law courts. Knowledge of the law became more important as judges became less tolerant of rhetorical style (Kennedy 1972, pp. 100–150).

Rhetoric as a whole became increasingly identified with what classical rhetoricians, such as Aristotle and Cicero, had regarded as but one of its parts (indeed, one of its less important parts), namely *elocutio* (or stylistic expression).

Historical changes also affected the social considerations of rhetoric. Beginning in the last third of the second century, the East and West of the Roman Empire started to have distinct governments with the consequence that, by the fourth century, there were two empires with different languages (Greek and Latin). The Eastern schools of rhetoric were still active until the reign of Justinian (527–65 AD). The basic rhetorical textbook was the *Hermogenic corpus*, a series of handbooks of exercises under the name of the Greek rhetorician Hermogenes (late second century AD) (Heath 1995). But teachers of rhetoric were no longer paid for public services. Some schools of rhetoric continued to exist, but even they were eventually replaced by the study of rhetoric in some monasteries. In the West, schools of rhetoric continued their activity through the fourth century. Then, Rome was sacked and devastated by the Visigoths in 410, and the year 476 marked the political end of the Western Empire.

Rhetoric in the Middle Ages

The medieval take on classical rhetoric began in the fourth century BC. There, amid a climate of historical turbulence, there were some remarkable attempts to revive an interest in the art of rhetoric. Yet, rhetoric was not directly linked to the politics of cities, it did not have a civic function, and so its status somehow declined. Rhetoric no longer played a central role in education and was instead in competition with grammar (the study of style and language composition) and dialectic (the study of argumentation) (McKeon 1941).

Augustine of Hippo

It is with Augustine of Hippo, also known as St Augustine (354–430 BC), that the art of persuasion nevertheless receives some importance as a powerful tool to support the spread of Christianity (Murphy 1981, pp. 43–89).

At the time of Augustine, the Church was challenged by heresies, such as those of the Manichaeans and Pelagians. Although the sophistic abuses of rhetoric were condemned, the discipline was valued for its prominent role in empowering future apologists. Thus, in *De doctrina Christiana* (I, 1.1) Augustine claimed that the two things necessary for appropriately dealing with the Scriptures are 'a way of discovering' (*modus inveniendi*) what people should understand, and 'a way of expressing to others' (*modus proferendi*).

Later in the treatise, he echoed ideas from the classical tradition when claiming that an empty flow of eloquence is dangerous, as fluency can give the impression that someone 'speaks with truth' (*De doctrina Christiana* IV, 5.8). Thus, defenders of authentic truth cannot stay unarmed if they want to have an effect (*De doctrina Christiana* IV, 2.3). The man who possesses the truth is not necessarily able to communicate it; rhetorical knowledge and knowledge of the Scriptures have to go together, and a training in rhetoric is thus important to strengthen the individual's own expression and counteract potential negative influences.

Martianus Capella

About the same time that Augustine was completing *De doctrina Christiana*, Martianus Capella framed the role of rhetoric in his masterpiece, *On the wedding of philology and Mercury and of the seven liberal arts*, considered as fundamental in the history of education. Martianus Capella proposed to write an encyclopaedia of the liberal culture of the time. There, rhetoric was mentioned in the theory of education called *trivium* (the three roads) after logic and grammar. These disciplines were considered preparatory for the *quadrivium*, comprising arithmetic, geometry, music and astronomy. The quadrivium was the educational entry point for the serious study of philosophy and theology (Stahl 1965).

The definition and order of the disciplines of the *trivium* testify to the different approach to rhetoric, compared to the breadth assigned to it in the classical Greek and Roman ages. In a context where logic was presented as the art of thinking, and grammar as the art of combining symbols to express thoughts, rhetoric was related to the application of language to persuade an audience. Within such a framework, the discipline was progressively reduced to a body of rules mainly derived from those found in Cicero's *De inventione*, as the other main classical works on the subject were unknown in this period of the Middle Ages (Murphy 1981).

Boethius

It was Boethius (480–524 AD), the leading statesman-orator at the Ostrogothic Court, who further reinforced the idea of rhetoric having a different status from the classical discipline and its educational canons.

Boethius was among the major characters responsible for the transmission of Aristotle's logical works to the medieval West (Stump 1988).

Although Boethius was not particularly interested in rhetoric, in his treatise on logic known as *De Differentiis Topicis* he framed a conceptualisation of rhetoric where he subordinated it to dialectic. Rhetoric was no longer perceived as a civil science; it cannot generate knowledge and it is not interrelated with philosophy. Aristotle saw the educational value of rhetoric in the fact that he conceived it as being parallel to dialectic. Cicero theorised that dialectic is even subordinate to rhetoric. In *De Differentiis Topics* Book IV, Boethius made rhetoric an appendage of dialectic: dialectic has a philosophical breadth as it deals with theses, that is, general discussion about universal issues (for instance, should man marry?); rhetoric deals with hypothesis, that is, questions that involve individual circumstances (for instance, should Cato marry?) (Stump 1989).

Thomas Aquinas

This treatment of rhetoric as being separate from dialectics and, moreover, from a civil output was further supported by Thomas Aquinas, also known as St Thomas (1225–1274), who made a clear statement that rhetoric essentially deals with conjectural probability; it has nothing to do with demonstrative proof. It has an inferior epistemological status to dialectic and so might only be of value for dealing with the business affairs of human beings through its persuasive power (Smith 2012, pp. 172–175; Barilli 1989, pp. 46–48).

Towards modernity

Sixteenth century

Renaissance rhetoric was characterised by the discovery of important manuscripts of classical rhetoric, such as Aristotle's *Rhetoric*, the entire Ciceronian corpus and the work of Quintilian. The availability of texts from the classical traditions favoured a revival and reorientation of rhetoric that, after an epistemological decline in the Middle Ages, regained popularity as a field of study. Indeed, in the early Renaissance, rhetoric was again perceived in light of Cicero's ideal that the discipline was the force of human society. From this, rhetoric again held a privileged position in education (Mack 2011a).

Desiderius Erasmus (1467–1536) was a prominent protagonist in the rediscovery of the power of rhetoric in education. In his work, *De ratione studii*, he expressed his innovative views on students' education by claiming that the knowledge of words (learned as grammar, rhetoric and logic) is a precondition for the knowledge of things. This is because, ultimately, ideas are intelligible only by means of the words that describe them. The educational role of rhetoric in Erasmus' framework was further reinforced by the epistemological status he accredited to the discipline. Informed by Aristotle's ideas as found in the *Rhetoric*, for Erasmus, rhetoric had a value as an instrument for probable argumentation. While the medieval authors attributed key importance to dialectic as the science for the discovery of truth, for Erasmus and other Renaissance authors, rhetoric was the best approach to determine the probabilities of outcomes for certain issues under discussion (Nauert 2006, pp. 102–172).

Erasmus was himself the author of rhetorical tracts that aimed to disseminate his ideas. In the *Colloquies*, he used the technique of dialogical investigation where the protagonists engage in discussion to reach an agreement over the most probable solution to a certain issue (Mack 2011a, pp. 76–103).

With Petrus Ramus (1515–1572), the separation between rhetoric and dialectic became even sharper, with rhetoric favoured as a fully autonomous discipline, but rather far away from the breadth of the classical tradition (Jasinski 2001, pp. xvii–xviii). By accusing Aristotle and Cicero of having brought confusion to the fields of dialectic and rhetoric, Ramus subdivided the two domains. He shifted to the domain of dialectic what were – in the classical tradition –the parts of rhetoric dealing with the discovery of arguments (the *inventio*) and argumentation itself (the *confirmatio* and *refutatio* in Cicero's *De inventione*). As a consequence, he conceptualised rhetoric as the domain of style (*elocutio*) and its delivery, including the effective use of language and pronunciation (Mack 2011b). Within this framework, rhetoric became a discipline to empower students in the art of speaking well, ornately and correctly. From there, rhetoric entered into the field of literature and its stylistic parameters (Vickers 1989, p. 206).

Seventeenth century

Ramus' approach to rhetoric was questioned at an early stage by Francis Bacon (1561–1626) who, although he was not a rhetorician, developed a rhetorical theory as a means of communicating scientific knowledge. Bacon perceived empowerment in rhetoric as being central to active civic life. For him, the focus of the art of rhetoric went back to the discovery and use of arguments, and he explicitly praised Aristotle for placing rhetoric between logic and moral knowledge. Bacon attributed considerable importance to argumentation, but not to dialectic *per se*, as the preferred method for the discovery of things (Vickers 1996). For Bacon, there had to be a strong connection between the knowledge derived from empirical investigation and its transfer through words. This is why he merged together what – in previous years – was distinguished under dialectic and rhetoric; he wrote about the four 'arts intellectuall', referring to the discovery of argument, argumentation, memory and style. Style alone is not condemnable *per se*, although Bacon recognised its value in disseminating knowledge convincingly. Yet, human knowledge may be hindered by the 'aesthetic satisfaction' produced by style, as it can prevent people from deepening their knowledge (Smith 2012, pp. 239–241).

However, a more sceptical account of the value of rhetoric was given by Thomas Hobbes (1588–1679) who was educated in the humanistic tradition (Skinner 1996). Hobbes wrote *A briefe of the art of rhetorique: Containing in substance all that Aristotle hath written in his three bookes of that subject*, and he knew the classical tradition remarkably well. Nevertheless, he was Platonic in his conviction that eloquence can destroy civil life. For Hobbes, while logic is connected to thought and wisdom, rhetoric favours a competition to win (*De cive*, pp. 154–155). When politicians are empowered with eloquence, they somewhat prevent the reaching of truth through reason, as personal interests are supported by playing on passions and emotions (*Leviathan*, p. 119, II. xvii).

In some ways, Hobbes was acutely hostile to persuasion, but in others, especially in the *Leviathan*, he showed his mastery of eloquence. Indeed, from his perspective, if science were to be promoted by people equipped with morality, and were to be based on certain and not probabilistic reasoning, eloquence could be an aid for science. In an overt disagreement with the rhetorical style praised by the Renaissance humanists, Hobbes made use of the rhetorical precepts to argue with irony against philosophical claims that he did not support.

Eighteenth century

While the seventeenth-century tradition had focused more on the epistemological characteristics of rhetoric, in the eighteenth century, rhetoric received significant attention in European formal education, from elementary to university levels. Here, the study of rhetoric was pursued with the aim of equipping students for the rhetorical analysis of literary texts and in what is nowadays known as public speaking. Students were trained in composition, in writing through the principles of imitation and of the comparison of classical authors, as well as in refining texts with elegant prose (Kennedy 1997, pp. 330–346).

In France, the masterpiece of Charles Rollin (1661–1741), *Traité des etudes de la manière d'enseigner et d'étudier les Belles-Lettres*, proposed an innovative system of education with entire sections on the teaching of rhetoric and the practice of eloquence. For Rollin, education was mainly aimed at forming the tastes of students; this aim was achieved by emulating those considered to be models in the field of eloquence (Warnick 1993, pp. 1–14). A study of the best examples of eloquence would, in fact, allow students to reflect on the principles of composition behind these examples.

The Rollin book was also among those works that emphasised the importance of an approach to rhetoric known as the belletristic (from the French Belles-Lettres) movement. In the eighteenth century, neoclassical trends in the study of rhetoric, such as those promoted by John Lawson (1709–1759) and John Ward (1679–1758), were still anchored by the Greek-Roman approach to the art of persuasion. Yet, the belletristic scholars promoted an idea of rhetoric joined to related fields, including art, poetry and history. This trend of thought was introduced into the study of rhetoric elements found in a tradition starting with Aristotle's *Poetic* and those treatises that centred on the quality of style in prose, writing and artistic products generally (Kennedy 1999, pp. 259–289).

The other most successful contributions to the content of rhetoric as an educational discipline in the eighteenth century were made by Hugh Blair (1718–1800) and George Campbell (1719–1796). They were both Protestant ministers and theologians who saw in rhetoric an instrument to preach the Christian mission and to help human beings be redeemed from degeneration. In the *Lectures on Rhetoric and Belles-Lettres*, Blair explained how knowledge of rhetoric and literature is an asset for social success as it can promote virtue and moral ideals.

Campbell's main development of rhetoric derived from overcoming what he saw as the main limitations of the classical tradition. In Book 1 of the *Philosophy of Rhetoric*, he introduced a psychological and behavioural flavour into the domain of rhetoric. To be skilful in persuasion, orators must adapt their discourses to the needs of the audience. These needs are four in number: understanding, imagination, passions and will. The orator has to help the audience to understand and, through imagination and passion, to convince them. In Campbell's view, rhetoric is not only related to civic affairs, but has to be conceived as a universal theory of human communication.

The breadth of Campbell's reflection on rhetoric was somehow narrowed down and reshaped by Richard Whately (1787–1863). In his treatise, *Elements of Rhetoric*, which also falls under the genre of ecclesiastical rhetoric, Whately did not intend to make a theoretical inquiry into the nature of communication. By recalling the Aristotelian design of rhetoric as an 'off-shoot from Logic', he renewed the understanding of rhetoric as the art of reasoned discourse, and focused on argumentation as the essence of the discipline (Whately 1828).

Conclusion

This chapter, far from being an exhaustive history of rhetoric, highlights the main arguments on the link between rhetoric, as the study and use of language, and its value as an educational discipline for political life, from the classical world to the beginning of modernity.

It is apparent from observing the conceptual developments of rhetoric through the centuries that they are rather circular; similar claims about the high or low status of the discipline, according to its relation to the rigorousness of dialectic and morality, have been discussed by different authors in different contexts. Rhetoric was hardly to be relegated to being a question of language and style, even if a captivating style was considered to be important in attracting the audience. Rhetoric advanced as a discipline by reflecting on the educational equipment of the orator, where vast knowledge, moral values and communication skills must come together to the point where the ethically good orator is almost an ideal one. When it was clear that rhetoric could be powerfully used without the capacity and the wish to think philosophically for the good of the city, then it was criticised for the nature of the empowerment it endowed upon people.

Civic life was never, and will never be, without rhetoric because the language of politics is essentially rhetorical. Thus, the issue is whether to banish rhetoric from a conceptual point of view, knowing, however, that people will still use it, or to elevate it to the rank of a key educational discipline to empower those who have constructive ideas to successfully dismantle and contrast manipulation. Overall, the authors discussed in this chapter decided to take the second route and, in one way or another, operationalised the philosophical discussions on rhetoric into usable precepts that are nowadays vital to any training in persuasion for – and beyond – politics.

References

Augustine, 1995, *De doctrina Christiana*, tr. RPH Green, Clarendon Press, Oxford.
Balla, C, 2004, 'Isocrates, Plato, and Aristotle on rhetoric', *Rhizai*, vol. 1, pp. 45–71.
Barilli, R, 1989, *Rhetoric*, University of Minnesota Press, Minneapolis.
Benoit, WL, 1991, 'Isocrates and Plato on rhetoric and rhetorical education', *Rhetoric Society Quarterly*, vol. 21, no. 1, pp. 60–71.
Blair, H, 1993 [1793], *Lectures on rhetoric and belles lettres*, Scholars' facsimiles and reprints, Delmar, NY.
Bodéüs, R, 1992, 'Des raisons d'être d'une argumentation rhéthorique selon Aristotle', *Argumentation*, vol. 6, no. 3, pp. 297–305.
Boethius, 1988, *De topiciis differentiis*, tr. E Stump, Cornell University Press, Ithaca, NY.
Bonner, S, 1998, *Education in Ancient Rome*, University of California Press, Berkeley, CA.
Campbell, G, 1992 [1776], *The philosophy of rhetoric*, Scholar's facsimiles and reprints, Delmar, NY.
Cicero, 1939, *Brutus. Orator*, tr. G L Hendrickson & HB Hubbell, Harvard University Press, Cambridge, MA.
Cicero, 1976, *De invention*, tr. H M Hubbell. Harvard University Press, Cambridge, MA.
Cicero, 2001, *On the ideal orator*, trs. J M May & J Wisse, Oxford University Press, Oxford.
Cole, T, 1991, *The origins of rhetoric in ancient Greece*, John Hopkins University Press, Baltimore and London.
Corbett, EPJ, 1989, 'Isocrates' legacy. The humanistic stand in classical rhetoric', in *Selected essays of Edward P. J. Corbett*, ed. R J Connors, Southern Methodist University Press, Dallas, TX, pp. 267–277.
Crook, JA, 1967, *Law and life of Rome*, Cornell University Press, Ithaca, NY.
Erasmus, D, 1901 [1511], *De ratione studii*, tr. W H Woodward, Longmans, Green and Co., London.
Glenn, C & Carcasson, G, 2009, 'Rhetoric as pedagogy' in *The SAGE handbook of rhetorical studies*, eds. AA Lunsford, KH Wilson & RA Eberly, SAGE Publications, Thousand Oaks, CA, pp. 285–292.
Gorgias, 1990, 'Encomium of Helen' in *The rhetorical tradition: Readings from classical times to the present*, eds. P Bizzell & B Herzberg, Bedford Books, Boston, MA.

Grimaldi, WMA, 1972, *Studies in Aristotle's rhetoric*, Hermes Einzelschriften, vol. 25, pp. 1–151.
Guthrie, WKC, 1971, *The Sophists*, Cambridge University Press, Cambridge.
Gwynn, ASJ, 1926, *Roman education from Cicero to Quintilian*, Teachers College Press, New York.
Heath, M, 1995, *Hermogenes on issues: strategies of argument in later Greek rhetoric*, The Clarendon Press, Oxford.
Hobbes, T, 1983, *De cive*, ed. H Werrender, Oxford University Press, Oxford.
Hobbes, T, 2012, *Leviathan*, ed. N Malcolm, Oxford University Press, Oxford.
Isocrates, 1929, *Against the Sophists*, tr., G Norlin, Harvard University Press, Cambridge.
Jasinski, J, 2001, *Sourcebook on rhetoric*, Sage Publications, Thousand Oaks, CA.
Kennedy, GA, 1963, *The art of persuasion in Greece*, Princeton University Press, Princeton, NJ.
Kennedy, GA, 1972, *The art of rhetoric in the Roman world*, Princeton University Press, Princeton, NJ.
Kennedy, GA, 1991, *Aristotle on rhetoric. A theory of civic discourse*, Oxford University Press, New York and Oxford.
Kennedy, GA, 1994, *A new history of classical rhetoric*, Princeton University Press, Princeton, NJ.
Kennedy, GA, 1997, *The Cambridge history of literary criticism, vol. 4: The eighteenth century*, Cambridge University Press, Cambridge.
Kennedy, GA, 1999, *Classical rhetoric and its Christian and secular tradition from ancient to modern times*, The University of North Carolina Press, Chapel Hill, NC.
Kerferd, GB, 1981, *The sophistic movement*, Cambridge University Press, Cambridge.
Lunsford, AA, Wilson, KH & Eberly, R, 2009, *The SAGE handbook of rhetorical studies, part III: Rhetoric and pedagogy*, SAGE Publications, Thousand Oaks, CA.
Mack, P, 2011a, *A history of Renaissance rhetoric*, Oxford University Press, Oxford.
Mack, P, 2011b, 'Rhetoric and dialectic', in S J Reid & EA Wilson, *Ramus, pedagogy and the liberal arts*, Ashgate, Burlington, VT.
Martianus Capella and the seven liberal arts: The marriage of Philosophy and Mercuri, 1971, tr. W H Stahl, Columbia University Press, New York.
McKeon, R, 1941, 'Rhetoric in the Middle Ages', *Speculum*, vol. 17, pp. 1–32.
Milanese, G, 1989, *Lucida carmina. Comunicazione e scrittura da Epicuro a Lucrezio*, Vita e Pensiero, Milano, pp. 31–33.
Murphy, JJ, 1981, *Rhetoric in the Middle Ages. A history of rhetorical theory from St. Augustine to the Renaissance*, University of California Press, Berkeley and London.
Narducci, E, 1994, *Cicerone: dell'oratore*, BUR, Milano.
Nauert, CG, 2006, *Humanism and the culture of Renaissance Europe*, 2nd ed, Cambridge University Press, Cambridge.
Norlin, G, 1928, *Isocrates*, Harvard University Press, Cambridge, vol. 1, ix–xiviii.
Ober, J, 1994, 'Power and oratory in democratic Athens: Demosthenes 21, against Meidias', in *Greek rhetoric in action*, ed. I Worthington, Routledge, London and New York, pp. 85–108.
Parker, AD, 1972, 'Rhetoric, ethics and manipulation', *Philosophy & rhetoric*, vol. 5, no. 2, pp. 69–87.
Plato, 1994, *Gorgias*, tr. R. Waterfield, Oxford University Press, Oxford.
Plato, 2000, *Republic*, ed. GRF Ferrari, tr. T Griffith, Cambridge University Press, Cambridge.
Plato, 2002, *Phaedrus*, tr. R. Waterfield, Oxford University Press, Oxford.
Powell, JGF & Paterson, J, eds., 2004, *Cicero the advocate*, Oxford University Press, Oxford.
Quintilianus, Marcus, Fabius, 1920, *Institutio oratoria*, tr. HE Butler, Cambridge University Press, Cambridge.
Rhetorica ad Herennium, 1954, tr. H Caplan, Cambridge University Press, Cambridge.
Rollin, C, 1819, *De la manière d'enseigner et d'étudies les Belles Lettres*, Russand, Lyon.
Rubinelli, S, 2009, *Ars topica. The classical techniques of constructing arguments from Aristotle to Cicero*, Springer, New York.
Ryan, EE, 1979, 'Plato's Gorgias and Phaedrus and Aristotle's theory of rhetoric: a speculative account', *Athenaeum*, vol. 57, pp. 452–461.

Skinner, G, 1996, *Reason and rhetoric in the philosophy of Hobbes*, Cambridge University Press, Cambridge.
Smith, CR, 2012, *Rhetoric and human consciousness*, Waveland Press, Long Grove, IL.
Stahl, WH, 1965, 'To a better understanding of Martianus Capella', *Speculum* vol. 40, no. 1, pp. 102–115.
Stump, E, 1988, *Boethius's in Ciceronis Topica*, Cornell University Press, Ithaca, New York.
Stump, E, 1989, *Dialectic and its place in the development of medieval logic*, Cornell University Press, Ithaca, New York.
van Eemeren, FH, 2010, *Strategic maneuvering in argumentative discourse. Extending the pragma-dialectical theory of argumentation*, John Benjamins, Amsterdam and Philadelphia.
Vickers, B, 1989, *In defense of rhetoric*, Oxford University Press, Oxford.
Vickers, B, 1996, 'Bacon and rhetoric' in *The Cambridge companion to Bacon*, ed. M Peltonen, Cambridge University Press, Cambridge, pp. 200–208.
Wardy, R, 1996, *The birth of rhetoric: Gorgias, Plato and their successors*, Routledge, London.
Warnick, B, 1993, *The sixth canon: Belletristic rhetorical theory and its French antecedents*, University of South Carolina, Columbia, SC.
Whately, R, 1828, *Elements of rhetoric*, John Murray, London.
Wisse, J, 1989, *Ethos and pathos from Aristotle to Cicero*, Adolf M Hakkert, Amsterdam.
Worthington, I, ed. 1994, *Greek rhetoric in action*, Routledge, London and New York.

2
From Karl Marx to Antonio Gramsci and Louis Althusser

Bob Jessop

Introduction

This chapter explores the work on language, ideology, and politics of Karl Marx (1818–1883), Antonio Gramsci (1891–1937), and Louis Althusser (1918–1990). While only the first two explicitly considered language, all three adopted a totalising approach, forcefully critiqued ideologies and domination, and stressed the unity of social theory and political practice. I first address Marx's ideas on language and consciousness, ideology and its critique, and political struggle and domination. Friedrich Engels (1820–1895) is included both for his work with Marx and his own contributions. Second, I review Gramsci's pre-prison writings and prison notes on language, economic base-superstructure relations, the state and intellectuals and link them to his university studies in philology. Third, I examine Althusser's views on ideology, the state and politics. In all cases, I relate these topics to their broader theoretical and strategic views.

Karl Marx

Five remarks will help to situate Marx's analyses of language and politics. First, a critical understanding of philology was central to university education in Marx's youth – thanks in part to Hegel's effort to get 'philosophy to speak German', not Latin, to help build a German nation; second, Marx and Engels aimed to demystify not only religion, as did other Young Hegelians, but also, unlike them, the secular language of the ruling class, including bourgeois morality, bourgeois 'theory', and the ideas of leading German intellectuals (Cook 1982; Williams 1977, pp. 21–26); third, Marx wanted to help the masses to develop their own language, their own 'poetry' or political imaginary to better express their own needs and demands; consequently, fourth, he engaged in 'translational' work to turn mystifying speculation into more prosaic language suited for articulating a scientific socialist programme; and, fifth, Marx himself used language skilfully for political as well as scientific effect (Marx 1979, pp. 14–16).

I begin with a disparate set of manuscripts drafted by Marx and Engels in 1845–1846. Although consigned to 'the gnawing criticism of the mice' (Marx 1987b, p. 264), these drafts were later compiled into one text, *Die deutsche Ideologie* (*The German ideology*), first published in Russian in 1924 and then in various versions in other languages (on this history, see Carver 2010). Part one introduces, *inter alia*, the authors' views on language, political economy, and ideology. Later parts illustrate how they critique specific intellectuals and ideological currents. Marx and Engels argue that a materialist conception of history must begin with living human individuals, not abstract man, analysing how they organise material life to satisfy their changing needs and to propagate the species. These activities form humankind's material mode of production and underpin a definite mode of life. The need to co-ordinate interaction with nature and/or other people gives rise to language, which, in its plain, ordinary or everyday form, they write, can be understood as practical consciousness. This consciousness exists for other people as well as the speaker. The unity of hand, larynx and brain as the biological foundation of language is matched on the social level by the unity of labour/production, language and consciousness (Höppe 1982, p. 28; Marx & Engels 1976, pp. 36, 44; cf. Engels 1987). Thus, Marx and Engels treat language both as an *intellectual* force of production that arises from and enables social co-operation and as a necessary, constitutive part of any mode of life (Marx & Engels 1976, pp. 51–60; cf. Marx 1975, pp. 298–299, 304; Marx 1987a, pp. 538–540, 548–549; Höppe 1982, p. 55).

The pair add that social development involves a growing division between mental and manual labour. Moreover, the more autonomous mental labour becomes, the more do people tend to treat ideas as lacking foundations in material life, almost as if ideas descend from heaven. This generates the 'pure', even esoteric, language of ideologists in fields such as theology, metaphysics and ethics, which are far removed from material production, and, they note, it also inclines intellectuals to explain events and practices in terms of free-floating ideas, cut loose from reality (Marx & Engels 1976, pp. 44–45, 55–56, 92; Engels 1990, pp. 392–394; on intellectuals, see also pp. 35–37). This view also appears implicitly in Marx's critiques of Hegel on the state and of Feuerbach on religion. An analogous division of manual–mental labour occurs within the ruling class itself – it contains not only practical 'men of affairs', but also specialists in ideas (*ibidem*, p. 60).

Building on such arguments, Marx and Engels suggest that the state is an independent social form standing above and outside society and acting in the name of its (necessarily illusory!) collective interests (*ibidem*, p. 90). They also interpret political struggles as the illusory forms in which the real struggles of different classes are fought out. They posit that every class struggling for domination must first gain political power in order to represent its interest as the general interest (*ibidem*, p. 90). Language is the medium in and through which interests are articulated and, hence, a crucial medium of political struggle too (see below). Furthermore, 'the ideas of the ruling class are in every epoch the ruling ideas, i.e. the class that is the ruling *material* force of society, is at the same time its ruling *intellectual* force' (*ibidem*, p. 59, italics in original). This is grounded, in part, on the ruling class' control over the means of mental as well as material production. This invites, one might add, reflection on changing modes of mental production, such as writing, print media, radio, television and social media. These comments were intended for self-clarification rather than publication (Marx 1987b, p. 262) and, in more elaborate forms, can be discerned in the later work of both Marx and Engels.

Part I of *The German ideology*, together with the 1859 preface to the *Contribution to the critique of political economy* (Marx 1987b) are often invoked to justify the claim that Marx had a reductionist model in which an economic base generates a matching juridico-political superstructure, forms of life, and social consciousness. In early work, this base-superstructure model had a diacritical role. In some ways, it shifted attention from an *idealist critique of religion and theology to a materialist critique of law and politics,* and, in others, in treating language as practical consciousness, *its materialism excluded any claim that the social world can exist prior to thought.* Viewed substantively, however, this metaphor does injustice to the richness of Marx's critique of political economy as well as his and Engels' historical analyses.

Further remarks on Marx's work on language and ideology are hindered by its disparate, unfinished nature. But it is possible to contrast his approach positively with the usual linguistics approach to the social character of language. For, as Norman Fairclough and Phil Graham note, the usual approach involves a double movement:

> [...] *first* abstracting language from its material interconnectedness with the rest of social life, treating language as an 'ideal' and non-material entity, and *then* construing the sociality of language as relations 'between' language [...] and society, as if these were two separately constituted realities which subsequently, or even accidentally, come into contact with each other.
>
> (Fairclough & Graham 2002, p. 187, italics added)

In contrast, Fairclough and Graham continue, Marx emphasised:

> the dialectical interconnectivity of language and other elements of the social and can therefore do full justice to [the] social power of language in [...] capitalism without reducing social life to language, removing language from material existence, or reifying language.
>
> (Fairclough & Graham 2002, p. 187)

To support this claim, they give many examples of Marx's anticipation of what would now count as Critical Discourse Analysis and/or argumentation analysis, ranging from the early 1840s to the late 1870s (see below on *The Eighteenth Brumaire of Louis Bonaparte*).

Although Marx's later work was less directly concerned with language, he still explored its nature as practical consciousness and examined the semantics and pragmatics of political language. Marx and Engels also considered how ideologies differ from other sets of ideas insofar as they serve the interests of power and domination, and, relatedly, how ideological effects emerge – consciously or not – from language use in diverse contexts. So, their later, more or less systematic efforts at *Ideologiekritik* were directed against *specific* ideologies – technological paradigms, economic doctrines, legal systems, political imaginaries, party programmes, religious-belief systems, philosophies and general systems of ideas – in terms of how they obscured, mystified and legitimated social relations of exploitation and/or domination (cf. McCarney 1980, pp. 10–11). An example is the degeneration of classical political economy, with its real scientific achievements, into mere bourgeois apologetics as the working-class movement grows stronger and challenges the logic of capital (Marx 1967, pp. 23–26). Marx and Engels also recognised that the most powerful ideological effects may be sedimented in language, language use, practical consciousness and other forms of signification. In this regard, they both noted: the class character of language; its implicit value judgements; its role in generalising bourgeois mentality through turns of phrase, figures of speech and commercial language; the status of economic categories as objective forms of thought (*Gedankenformen*); and the mystifying effects of commodity fetishism and the juridical world-view (Engels 1976; Marx 1967, pp. 29, 49; Marx 1987a, pp. 538–541, 547–550; Marx & Engels 1976, pp. 102–103, 231; for many further examples, see Höppe 1982, pp. 97–105, 199–203, 222–247).

Finally, although Marx starts from the social relations of production, he argues that social transformation is mediated through the political sphere. Indeed, he emphasises the primacy of the political over the economic. For example, in *The Eighteenth Brumaire of Louis Bonaparte*, written in 1851, Marx noted that, while 'men make their own history; they do not make it under circumstances chosen by themselves' (1979, p. 103). He then remarked that it was hard for revolutionaries to develop new political practices because the available political lexicon limits their ability to represent their own class interests and voice new demands. Thus, he refers to limits rooted in 'the tradition of all the dead generations', 'superstition about the past', and 'an entire superstructure of different and distinctly formed sentiments, illusions, modes of thought and views of life' (1979, pp. 103, 106, 128). This suggests, as James Martin noted, that Marx recognised 'the "performative" character of politics, that is, the manner in which the symbolic is not simply some secondary "level" perched upon the hard rock of property relations but is itself integral to the materialisation of class power' (Martin 2002, pp. 132–3).

Throughout *The Eighteenth Brumaire*, Marx explores the *language and other symbols* in and through which the class content of politics gets represented or, more commonly, misrepresented. He dissects the semiotic forms, genres, and tropes through which political forces articulate their identities, interests and beliefs. He reveals the articulation between: (1) the phrases and tropes of language and custom borrowed from the past or recontextualised through intertextual weaving in the present; and (2) current political and social realities, such that old phrases sometimes lead to spirited revolutionary action but, more often, prove to be empty signifiers open to manipulation for political or economic advantage (Marx 1979, pp. 103–112, 126–131, 142–146, 148–150, 190–193 and *passim*). Here and elsewhere, Marx also reflects on the type of political language in which the proletariat might formulate its demands, arguing that it must develop its own novel, political language rather than draw, as did earlier revolutions, on the 'poetry of the past' (Marx 1979, p. 106). In short, this and other texts can be read as contributions to the critique of *semiotic* economy, that is, to an account of how language and symbolism are involved in the imaginary (mis)recognition and (mis)representation of class interests.

Antonio Gramsci

In terms of the all-too-familiar base-superstructure metaphor, Gramsci is often regarded as a *theorist of the superstructures* (especially politics, civil society and culture) rather than of the material base (the forces and social relations of production) (for an important, more nuanced dispute along these lines between Norberto Bobbio and Jacques Texier, respectively, see the texts reprinted in Mouffe 1979, pp. 21–79). Another misleading interpretation sees Gramsci as pioneering a Marxist approach to cultural criticism, or cultural studies, as if he saw culture as separate from the economy, politics, law, or other fields. Yet, Gramsci explicitly rejected the validity of an *ontological* distinction between base and superstructure (while conceding its *analytical* or methodological value) and sought to transcend it by exploring the interpenetration and co-evolution of these allegedly separate social spheres. This is especially clear in his discussion of Americanism and Fordism (see below). Among other reasons for his rejection of the metaphor, one might be the difficulties of locating language within this schema. Thus, to cite Peter Ives, Gramsci regarded language as 'material, albeit historically material. [...] Language is rooted in the materiality of the production of words' (Ives 2004, p. 34). Although this recalls arguments in *The German ideology*, Gramsci was unaware of this text, given its publication history (see above). His arguments were, in this regard, his own.

As Italian commentators have noted for many decades (see especially Lo Piparo 1979 and Carlucci 2013; and, for illustrative Italian work, contributions to Ives & Lacorte 2011) and anglophone scholars have begun to argue more recently (e.g. Ives 2004), Gramsci's whole approach was inspired by his university studies in philology under the direction of Matteo Bartoli, who initiated an approach called neo-linguistics (in opposition to the German neogrammarian school, which had affinities with Saussure's semiology) and later known, more substantively, as *linguistica spaziale* (spatial linguistics). This approach was rooted in the idealism of the Italian philosopher and organic intellectual, Benedetto Croce, modified by broadly contemporaneous work in linguistic geography and historical linguistics. Neo-linguistics emphasised that language is an evolving human creation and that linguistic innovation is normal.

Significantly, Bartoli argued that language diffuses geographically and socially in regular ways mediated through relations of prestige and power (Bartoli 1925; also Ives 2004b, pp. 44–55). He explored 'how a dominant speech community exerted prestige over contiguous, subordinate communities: the city over the surrounding countryside, the "standard" language over the dialect, the dominant socio-cultural group over the subordinate one' (Forgacs & Smith 1985, p. 164). He also charted how innovations flowed from the prestigious *langue* to the receiving one, such that 'earlier linguistic forms would be found in a peripheral rather than central area, an isolated rather than an accessible area, a larger rather than a smaller area' (Brandist 1996, pp. 94–95). This is reflected in Gramsci's comments on the stratification of language use (e.g. how countryfolk copy urban manners, how subaltern groups imitate the upper classes, how peasants speak when they move to the cities, etc.) (Gramsci 1985, pp. 180–181; in Gramsci 1975, the Italian critical edition of the prison notebooks, this corresponds to *Quaderno*, or notebook, Q29, §2, pp. 2342–2343). This comparative historical and spatial linguistics strongly influenced Gramsci's ideas on hegemony before he met the term in Lenin's analysis of party and class alliances. In contrast to its conventional meaning in international relations and Marxist-Leninist alliance theory, Gramsci redefined hegemony to denote the formation and organisation of consent (see below).

Gramsci applied historical and spatial linguistics in much of his work, even describing his overall method as *philological*. He argued that: 'the whole of language is a continuous process of metaphor, and the history of semantics is an aspect of the history of culture; language is at the same time a living thing and a museum of fossils of life and civilisations' (1971, p. 450; Q11, §24, p. 1427). Like Marx and Engels, Gramsci emphasised that language permeates all social relations and secretes a particular view of the world into everyday life and special social fields. He also argued that:

> All men are philosophers. Their philosophy is contained in: 1. *language itself*, which is a totality of determined notions and concepts and not just words grammatically devoid of content; 2. 'common sense' and 'good sense'; 3. popular religion and, therefore, also in the entire system of belief, superstitions, opinions, ways of seeing things and of acting which are collectively bundled together under the name of 'folklore'.
> (Gramsci 1971, p. 323; Q11, §12, p. 1375)

Thus social relations can only be fully understood and explained through the 'determined notions and concepts' (Marx's term for these was 'categories') in and through which determinate social practices develop and get institutionalised.

Peter Ives even describes Gramsci's approach as 'vernacular materialism'. This applies 'the tenets of a historical materialist approach to language and [develops] a linguistically concerned theory of politics and society' (Ives 2004a, p. 3). A deliberate play on words, this term serves to: (1) oppose vernacular to vulgar materialism; (2) establish the dialectical nature of Gramsci's work, with its focus on the organic relationship between language and social structures; (3) identify Gramsci's concern to develop a political programme that would 'popularise' culture rather than impose the culture of the dominant class from above, or force the development of a national – or international – culture through the imposition of an official, normative grammar, or resort to an artificial language, such as Esperanto; and (4) promote the historical materialist analysis of society (Ives 2004a, p. 4). It is worth noting the continuities between point two and Marx's historical materialist analysis of language as practical consciousness and, for point three, the similarities to Hegel's efforts to make philosophy speak German and Marx's commitment to developing a plain language with which workers could develop the poetry of the future. Indeed, as Gramsci wrote, Italian unification occurred without a popular revolution or radical social transformation such as that in France. This was reflected in the well-known aphorism from the 1870s: *Italia fatta, bisogna fare gli Italiani* (loosely translated, 'now we've made Italy, we must make the Italians'). For Gramsci, this required the development of a national-popular collective will grounded in a shared language, shared world-view, and shared hegemonic project that would encompass a new economic and political order.

These claims can be illustrated from Gramsci's analyses of the articulation of base and superstructure, the relations between political and civil society, and intellectuals' major and vital role in creating and reproducing these mediations in capitalist societies.

First, to replace the base-superstructure distinction, Gramsci redefined the meaning of base via the concept of *mercato determinato* (determinate market), which he misattributed to David Ricardo (Potier 1991, p. 87). For Gramsci, this is 'equivalent to [a] determined relation of social forces in a determined structure of the productive apparatus, this relationship being guaranteed (that is, rendered permanent) by a determined political, moral and juridical superstructure' (Gramsci 1971, p. 410; Q11, §52, p. 1477). This highlighted the need for an integral (totalising) analysis of historically specific economic regimes, their modes of social regulation, and their contingent, tendential laws of motion. For example, in his famous notes on Americanism and Fordism, Gramsci showed the importance of new economic imaginaries and organic intellectuals in promoting 'Americanism' as a mode of growth in response to the crisis of liberal capitalism and also identified how new social and cultural practices helped to consolidate Fordism as a new mode of regulation and societal organisation (1971, pp. 310–313; Q22, §13, pp. 2171–2175). He also noted, in remarks reminiscent of *The Eighteenth Brumaire*, that it would be hard to implant Fordism in Europe. This is because of the dead-weight of tradition, the incrustations of the past that must be swept away, and the presence of parasitic classes and strata (1971, pp. 281, 285, 317; Q22, §2, pp. 214–247, §15, p. 2179). These arguments put the struggle for political, intellectual and moral leadership at the heart of efforts to build and embed new economic regimes in capitalist societies.

Second, another, broader, concept is that of 'historical bloc': rather than redefining the base, this covers base-superstructure relations. Gramsci asked how and why 'the complex, contradictory and discordant ensemble of the superstructures is the reflection of the ensemble of the social relations of production'. He answered that it reflects 'the necessary reciprocity between structure and superstructure' (1971, p. 366; Q8, §182, pp. 1051–1052). This is realised through specific intellectual, moral and political practices. These translate narrow sectoral, professional, or local (in his terms, 'economic-corporate') interests into wider 'ethico-political' ones. Agreement on the latter not only helps to co-constitute economic structures (by providing a shared orientation), but also gives them their rationale and legitimacy. Analysing the historical bloc also shows how 'material forces are the content and ideologies are the form, though this distinction between form and content has purely didactic value' (1971, p. 377; Q7, §21, p. 869).

Third, in his best-known concept, Gramsci related hegemony (*egemonia*) to the capacity of dominant groups to establish and maintain political, intellectual and moral leadership and secure the 'broad-based consent' of allied and subordinate groups to the prevailing relations of economic and political domination. Just as he studied the economy in its integral sense as a determined market, Gramsci studied the state in its integral sense. He defined it as 'political society + civil society' and examined state power, in liberal democracies based on mass politics, as 'hegemony protected by the armour of coercion' (1971, p. 263; Q6, §88, pp. 763–765). His analysis of hegemony–consent–persuasion is not restricted to civil society, but extends into what are conventionally regarded as economic and political spheres. Paraphrasing, effective hegemony depends on the capacity of dominant groups to suture the identities, interests, emotions and values of key sectors of subordinate classes and other subaltern groups into a hegemonic vision and embed this in institutions and policies – leading in turn to their translation into 'good' common sense. At the same time, reflecting the 'material' as well as the discursive moment of social practice, hegemony depends on material concessions to subaltern groups, and this means that it must rest on 'a decisive function exercised by the leading group in the decisive nucleus of economic activity' (Gramsci 1971, p. 161; Q 13, §18, p. 1591).

For Gramsci, just as the moment of force is institutionalised in a system of coercive apparatuses (that may not always coincide with the state's formal juridico-political boundaries), hegemony is crystallised and mediated through a complex system of ideological (or hegemonic) apparatuses located throughout the social formation. While present in the juridico-political apparatuses, hegemonic practices are largely concentrated in normal circumstances in civil society (i.e. the 'ensemble of organisms commonly called "private"') (Gramsci 1971, p. 12; Q8, §182, p. 1518). Relevant 'hegemonic apparatuses' include the Church, trade unions, schools, the mass media, or political parties (Gramsci 1971, pp. 10–14, 155, 210, 243, 261, 267; Q12, §1, pp. 1518–1524; Q13, §23, pp. 1602–1603; Q13, §27, pp. 1619–1620; Q26, §6; pp. 2302–2303; Q17, §51, pp. 1947–1948).

Fourth, Gramsci's interest in the determined market, historical blocs, and state power was closely related to his studies of intellectuals (also broadly defined). He observed that, while everyone is an intellectual, not everyone in society has the function of an intellectual (Gramsci 1971, p. 9; Q12, §1, p. 1516). This claim has a dual significance. It rejects an elitist or vanguard role for intellectuals, stressing the need for hegemony to be rooted in everyday practices and interests. At the same time, those with the function of intellectuals are regarded as the creators and mediators of hegemony, as crucial bridges between economic, political and ideological domination, and as active agents in linking culture (especially common sense, or everyday knowledge, passions, feelings and customs) and subjectivity in the production of hegemony. Specifically, Gramsci saw hegemony as being anchored in the activities of traditional and/or organic intellectuals whose specialised function in the division of labour is to elaborate ideologies, educate the people, organise and unify social forces, and secure the hegemony of the dominant group (Gramsci 1971, pp. 5–23; Q12, §1–3, pp. 1511–1552; for an excellent review of intellectuals' role in this regard, especially in forming a historical bloc, see Portelli 1972). Thus, the task of organic intellectuals is to promote and consolidate a conception of the world that gives homogeneity and awareness to a fundamental class in the economic, political and social fields; this, in turn, becomes the basis for efforts to create hegemony within the wider society (Gramsci 1971, p. 5; Q12, §1, p. 1513; cf. Althusser 1990, p. 258). Whereas organic intellectuals identify with the dominant classes, or at least, have roles coeval with the specific forms of their economic, political and ideological domination, traditional intellectuals have roles dating from earlier modes of production, or ways of life (e.g. priests) and have weaker ties to the currently dominant classes.

Louis Althusser

Louis Althusser was a Marxist philosopher and member of the French Communist Party who criticised Stalinist doctrines and party practices. He researched political theory, wrote some major essays on Marx's philosophical and theoretical development and, with four students, presented an influential structuralist reading of Marx's *Capital* (Althusser et al., 1968; cf. Althusser & Balibar 1970). Here I focus on his views on language, ideology and politics. In contrast to Marx and Gramsci, Althusser did not study language, as such. Instead, he focused on ideology, which he regarded as 'a "representation" of the imaginary relationship of individuals [members of social classes in class societies] to their real conditions of existence' (1971b, p. 162; cf. 1971a, p. 241; 1990, p. 25). This definition draws on Claude Lévi-Strauss' notion of *culture*, that is, the languages, the unconscious categories, through which people give meaning to experience (Althusser 1971a, p. 241). Another direct influence was Jacques Lacan (whose work he would later reject), who, inspired by de Saussure, wanted to reorientate psychoanalysis on the assumption that the unconscious is structured *like* a language (e.g. Lacan 1993, 166–67). Nonetheless, while there are cultural and linguistic influences in Althusser's work, language is not, for him, a crucial topic.

Let me explore Lacan's influence. He distinguished three registers of analysis. The *imaginary* is the restricted, superficial, non-psychoanalytic level of everyday lived experience. It denotes, he wrote, my imagined relation to myself, to my feelings, to others, to others' perceptions of me, and to the real world. For Althusser, ideology is so pervasive in individuals' thoughts and deeds that it is '*indistinguishable* from their lived experience' (1990, p. 25, italics in original). These imaginary relations, which have real effects, are structured and overdetermined by the *symbolic* order. This register comprises sociolinguistic structures, rules and dynamics, and the wider moral and institutional order (cf. Althusser 1990, p. 26). The third register is the Real, which is less relevant here, because Althusser does not discuss reality in Lacanian terms (see Johnson 2013; on Freud and Lacan, Althusser 1971a; for the wider Althusser–Lacan connection, Resch 1992, pp. 208–213).

Althusser argued that, because individuals' lived experience of real conditions is always mediated through language and/or practice, it is not possible to equate ideology with false consciousness of the real world, for our reliance on language to construe the world traps us permanently inside *ideology in general*. However, we can compare *particular ideologies*, that is, different imaginary representations of our relationship to that world. Indeed, one task of science is to test the practical adequacy of different ideologies, to separate good and bad ideological thinking – Gramsci writes here of organic versus arbitrary, rationalistic and willed ideologies (1971, pp. 376–377; Q7, §19, p. 868). Another task of science is to identify what is possible in specific conjunctures – although, for Althusser (1990), even scientific practices are also shaped by ideological concepts, metaphors, and so on, as regards their presentation, reception and effects.

Furthermore, against a purely ideational account of ideology as comprising only ideas or representations, Althusser claims that ideology has a material existence (1971b, pp. 165, 169–170). It 'always exists in an apparatus, and its practice, or practices' (1971b, p. 166).

Thus, ideology has real effects. One of these is *interpellation*. Specifically, Althusser suggests that 'all ideology hails or interpellates concrete individuals as concrete subjects' (1971b, p. 115). Language has a key role here: indeed, Althusser's example is the hailing of a pedestrian by a police officer with the phrase, 'hey, you!' This also illustrates how, in acting towards others as subjects, we also reproduce institutions, here the police apparatus (Althusser 1971b, pp. 167–168, 170–171, 173). Furthermore, 'individuals are always-already subjects' (1971b, pp. 175–176) because they are interpellated even in the womb thanks to naming and other practices that occur in 'the specific familial ideological configuration' (1971b, p. 176). This *assujetissement* (or process of subjectivation) is the crucial ideological mechanism because it forms our reality and makes it appear natural, true, or self-evident. Indeed, a key ideological effect 'is the practical denegation of the ideological character of ideology by ideology' (1971b, p. 175).

In contrast to his direct references to Lévi-Strauss and Lacan, Althusser does not mention Marx or Gramsci in his remarks on ideology *as lived experience*, or how it is structured *like* a language. While generally supportive of Marx's later, scientific work (in contrast to his youthful humanism), Althusser was hostile to Gramsci's allegedly unscientific philosophy of praxis (for reasons noted in my conclusions). But he did recognise the latter's major contributions to political analysis and ranked him next to Marx and Lenin in this regard. In particular, he praised Gramsci's innovative notion of hegemony, broad concept of intellectuals and recognition of how civil society helped to reproduce class domination (see 1969, pp. 114, 114n, 105n, respectively). That said, Althusser did not engage seriously with these insights because he read them through the Marxism-Leninist optic that Gramsci aimed to overturn (Thomas 2009, pp. 26–35). So, profound differences remained in their respective studies of ideology and politics.

Althusser emphasised the importance of *assujetissement* to economic reproduction, which depends on the 'superstructural ensemble'. Yet, he tried to go beyond the purely *descriptive* value of the base-superstructure metaphor (1971b, p. 136) to ground it *scientifically* in the causal power of the superstructure, especially its juridico-political institutions and the ideological field (Althusser 1969, pp. 113–14; cf. 1971b, pp. 134–137). This opens space for a half-hearted rehabilitation of Gramsci, which Althusser attempted in his famous note on ideology and ideological state apparatuses:

> Gramsci is the only one who went any distance in the road I am taking. He had the 'remarkable' idea that the state could not be reduced to the (Repressive) State Apparatus, but included [...] institutions from '*civil society*': the Church, the Schools, the trade unions, etc. Unfortunately, Gramsci did not systematise his institutions.
> (Althusser 1971b, p, 142n; cf. 1990, p. 257; 2006, pp. 138–139)

In addressing this defect, Althusser even claimed to have completed the Marxist state theory that Marx, Lenin and Gramsci had only sketched in a series of pre-theoretical intuitions. He formulated this account in five theses: (1) the core of the state is its repressive (state) apparatus, or RSA; (2) the state also includes various ideological state apparatuses, or ISAs; (3) each ISA has its own particular ideology and apparatus logic; (4) the state plays a vital role in reproducing the relations of production and intervenes in all areas that bear on their reproduction; and (5) while economic exploitation is foundational, changes in the state form must precede reorganising the economic base. These theses were first published in an extract (Althusser 1971b) from a longer, but incomplete, work, *On reproduction*, published posthumously (see Althusser 2014).

For Althusser, whereas the RSA functions mainly via repression (including physical violence), the ISAs function primarily through ideology (1971b, pp. 144–146, 149). The latter are so diverse, relatively autonomous, and wide-ranging that the entire society becomes saturated by class relations and submitted to a class power that acquires coherence through 'a certain *political* configuration [...] imposed and maintained by means of material force (that of the State) and of moral power (that of the ideologies)' (Althusser 1968). What unifies the ISAs is: (1) their common subordination to the ideology of the ruling class (1971b, pp. 146, 149, 154–157); and (2) the RSA's role in securing the political conditions for the functioning of the ISAs, 'which largely secure the reproduction specifically of the relations of production, behind a "shield" provided by the repressive State apparatus' (1971b, p. 150). This last phrase, which recalls Gramsci on 'hegemony protected by the armour of coercion', is explained in terms of a 'logic of the supplement', whereby something apparently secondary is actually crucial to the existence of what appears original or primary (Derrida 1976, p. 315). As applied here, the relations of production/exploitation determine, *in the last instance*, the character of the state (RSA + ISAs) that underwrites the political and ideological relations of domination that, *in their turn*, ensure the reproduction of the social relations of production/exploitation that would otherwise fail or collapse.

Denying that Gramsci's work on hegemony anticipated his analysis of ISAs, Althusser protested that Gramsci's 'answer to the question of the *material* infrastructure of the ideologies' was rather mechanistic and economistic, that he never talked about ISAs, but only 'hegemonic apparatuses', and that he failed to explain the 'hegemony-effect'.

> Gramsci, in sum, defines his apparatuses in terms of their effect or result, *hegemony*, which is also poorly conceived. I, for my part, was attempting to define the ISAs in terms of their 'motor cause': ideology. Furthermore, Gramsci affirms that the hegemonic apparatuses are part of 'civil society' [...] on the pretext that they are 'private'.
> (Althusser 2006, pp. 138–139, italics in original)

Althusser claims superiority, quite unfairly, because he can explain the hegemony-effect through the ideological mechanism of interpellation and does not erroneously take the 'public–private distinction' as real when it is just one result of bourgeois juridico-political ideology. More generally, in a class society, ideology helps individuals to 'bear' their condition, whether this be one of exploitation, or exorbitant privilege (Althusser 1990, p. 25). Moreover, subaltern individuals who reject their condition are disciplined by the RSA as 'bad' subjects who reject the dominant ideology (1971b, pp. 137, 149–150, 181). In sum, while hegemony depends on ISAs, the RSA is also needed (cf. Gramsci above). Finally, while ideology is located in the superstructure and has its own logic and effects there vis-à-vis law and the state, it also penetrates the entire social edifice (not the continued use of the base-superstructure metaphor) and provides the *cement* [sic] that assures the cohesion of subjects in their roles, functions and social relations (1990, p. 25).

Althusser develops his theses in various pseudo-dialectical and formalistic ways. For example, he mentions the secondary ideological functions of the RSA, the secondary repressive functions of ISAs, and the possibilities that specific institutions may switch between primarily ideological and primarily repressive functions. But he provides no substantial historical analyses and few clues about how different political and ideological fields are articulated, let alone unified ('cemented'), apart from the equally formal claim that this occurs when one ISA is dominant. For Althusser, this was currently the school system (1971b, pp. 152–155), although followers, such as Régis Debray (1981) and Nicos

Poulantzas (1978), later claimed that the mass media held this place. Overall, this argument seems quite functionalist. There is no sense that the ISAs may be riven by contradictions and class struggle, that there is a specific role for intellectuals, political forces, and so on, in class struggle, or, indeed, that ideology may also be secreted in the organisation of production (cf. the critiques by Buci-Glucksmann, 1980, pp. 64–67; Poulantzas 1973, pp. 300–305). Later, in a post-script to his famous ISAs essay, Althusser tried to correct its functionalist tenor by insisting on the primacy of class struggle over institutions (2006, p. 112). In contrast to Gramsci, however, he made no effort to produce appropriate concepts to explore the forms, modalities and potential disjunctions of class struggle in and across different fields.

Such reflections prompted a return to another classical political theorist. In *Machiavel et nous* (1972–1986), Althusser attempted to theorise the state and politics without resort to the deterministic and economically reductionist base-superstructure schema. His proposed replacement is an *aleatory materialism* that focuses on historical becoming based on the primacy of events or contingent encounters, rather than on the operation of 'iron laws', or an inevitable social progress. Althusser (1999) claims that Machiavelli raises the crucial question of how a durable political state emerges *ex nihilo*. Machiavelli's answer, he argues, was that, while the prince founds the modern state, it can only be stabilised through a shift from a despotic principality to a modern republic based on the rule of law. Moreover, while Althusser once regarded people as passive subjects to be interpellated and mobilised by the ISAs, and disciplined by the RSA if they resisted, his reading of Machiavelli leads him to see 'the people' as the prime source of refusal and struggle against political repression and ideological subjectivation. In these respects, Althusser's interpretation marks a radical epistemological break with the functionalism of his ISA texts. It grounds social order in the contingent, aleatory historical development and succession of state forms (cf. Vatter 2004). It also marks another shift towards Gramsci's views insofar as the latter had already updated Machiavelli's call for 'a new prince in a new [Italian] principality' by positing the need for a 'modern prince' to create a unified Italian republic. This would not be a dictatorial vanguard party, but a communist party operating as a hegemonic social force, one that is in continuing dialogue with the popular masses and, on this basis, can develop a political, intellectual and moral hegemony that advances the national-popular will.

Conclusions

Marx interpreted language as an expression of practical consciousness and critiqued the effects of the manual–mental division of labour, which inclined intellectuals to believe that ideas were the motor force of history. He engaged in systematic, even symptomatic, critiques of the basic categories that organised capitalist relations of production and corresponding juridico-political, intellectual and philosophical social forms and consciousness. Given that politics, not the development of the productive forces, was the key moment of social development, Marx also paid much attention to the role of language in politics and to the specificities of political struggle, especially to develop and secure support for an illusory account of the general interest.

Gramsci elaborated many of these ideas (on the basis of limited access in prison to key Marxian texts, ignorance of some and over-familiarity with others, notably the 1859 *Preface*), based on his prior training in historical and spatial linguistics. He also emphasised the need to develop hegemony (political, intellectual and moral leadership) that would articulate a national-popular will as the basis for a revolutionary transformation of society. He was also interested in how intellectuals secured the unity of the power bloc and the hegemony of the power bloc over the popular classes. Developing a common language grounded in common sense and orientated to good sense was a crucial dimension of the struggle for hegemony (cf. Carlucci 2013).

Althusser cannot be read as the natural successor of Marx and Gramsci. On the contrary, he criticised Marx's views on ideology and the state as, at best, descriptive and pre-theoretical, and he falsely accused Gramsci's 'philosophy of praxis' of trying to explain historical development through the evolution of consciousness. Yet, Gramsci stressed that concepts, institutions and practices only gain meaning and significance in particular circumstances and that one task of the philosophy of praxis is to explain this historical contingency. While Althusser tended to conflate language with 'ideology in general' and his approach also inclined to functionalism, he also noted the role of language in *assujetissement* via interpellation and emphasised the materiality of ideology as expressed in specific apparatuses. Others have done this better. Thus, of the three figures considered above, those interested in Marxist approaches to language and politics would be well advised to start with Marx and Gramsci.

References

Althusser, L, 1969, *For Marx*, Allen Lane, London.
Althusser, L, 1971a [1964/1969], 'Freud and Lacan', in *Lenin and philosophy and other essays*, New Left Books, London, 195–219.
Althusser, L, 1971b [1969], 'Ideology and ideological state apparatuses (notes towards an investigation', in *Lenin and philosophy and other essays*, New Left Books, London, pp. 127–86.
Althusser, L, 1990, *Philosophy and the spontaneous philosophy of the scientists, and other essays*, New Left Books, London.
Althusser, L, 1999 [1972–1986], *Machiavelli and us*, Verso, London.
Althusser, L, 2006 [1978], 'Marx in his limits', in idem, *The philosophy of the encounter*, Verso, London, pp. 7–162.
Althusser, L, 2014 [1995], *On the reproduction of capital: Ideology and ideological apparatuses*, Verso, London.
Althusser, L & Balibar, E, 1970 [1968], *Reading capital*, New Left Books, London.
Althusser, L, Balibar, E, Establet, R, Macherey, P & Rancière, J, 1968, *Lire le capital*, 4 volumes, Maspero, Paris.
Bartoli, M, 1925, *Introduzione alla neolinguistica: principi, scopi, metodi*, Olschki, Florence.
Brandist, C, 1996, 'Gramsci, Bakhtin, and the semiotics of hegemony', *New Left Review*, no. 216, pp. 94–110.
Buci-Glucksmann, C, 1980, *Gramsci and the state*, Lawrence & Wishart, London.
Carlucci, A, 2013, *Gramsci and languages: Unification, diversity, hegemony*, Brill, Leiden.
Carver, T, 2010, 'The German Ideology never took place', *History of Political Thought*, vol. 31, no. 1, pp. 107–127.
Cook, D J, 1982, 'Marx's critique of philosophical language', *Philosophy and Phenomenological Research*, vol. 42, no. 4, pp. 530–554.
Debray, R, 1981 [1979], *Teachers, writers, celebrities: The intellectuals of modern France*, New Left Books, London.
Derrida, J, 1976, *Of grammatology*, Johns Hopkins University Press, Baltimore, MD.
Engels, F, 1967 [1845], 'The condition of the working class in England', in *MECW*, vol. 4, Lawrence & Wishart, London, pp. 295–583.
Engels, F, 1987 [1876], 'The part played by labour in the transition from ape to man', in *MECW*, vol. 25, Lawrence & Wishart, London, pp. 452–64.

Engels, F, 1990 [1886], 'Ludwig Feuerbach and the end of classical German philosophy', in *MECW*, vol. 26, Lawrence & Wishart, London, pp. 353–398.

Fairclough, N, & Graham, P, 2002, 'Marx as a critical discourse analyst: The genesis of a critical method and its relevance to the critique of global capital', *Estudios de sociolingüística*, vol. 3, no. 1, pp. 185–229.

Forgacs, D & Smith, G N, 1985, 'Introduction', in A Gramsci, *Selections from cultural writings*, Lawrence & Wishart, London, pp. 1–15.

Gramsci, A, 1971, *Selections from the prison notebooks*, Lawrence & Wishart, London.

Gramsci, A, 1975, *Quaderni del carcere, edizione critica del'Istituto Antonio Gramsci*, ed. V Gerratano, Einaudi, Rome.

Gramsci, A, 1985, *Selections from cultural writings*, Lawrence & Wishart, London.

Höppe, W, 1982, *Karl Marx–Friedrich Engels: Sprache und gesellschaftlicher Gesamtkomplex. Das Verhältnis von Sprache zu Basis und Überbau nach den Sprachtheoremen in den Werken von Marx und Engels*, Bouvier Verlag, Bonn.

Ives, P, 2004a, *Gramsci's politics of language. Engaging the Bakhtin Circle and the Frankfurt School*, University of Toronto Press, Toronto.

Ives, P, 2004b, *Hegemony and language in Gramsci*, Pluto Press, London.

Ives, P & Lacorte, R, eds., 2010, *Gramsci, language, and translation*, Lexington Books, Oxford.

Johnson, A, 2013, 'Jacques Lacan', *Stanford encyclopedia of philosophy*, 2 April 2013. Online. Available from: http://plato.stanford.edu/entries/lacan/ [accessed 15 March 2017].

Lacan, J, 1993, *The seminar of Jacques Lacan, book III. The psychoses 1955–1956*, Routledge, London.

Lo Piparo, F, 1979, *Lingua, intellettuali, egemonia in Gramsci*, Laterza, Rome and Bari.

Martin, J, 2002, 'Performing politics: class, ideology and discourse in Marx's *Eighteenth Brumaire*', *Marx's 'Eighteenth Brumaire': (Post-)modern interpretations*, eds. M Cowling & J Martin, Pluto, London, pp. 129–142.

Marx, K, 1967 [1890], *Capital, volume 1*, 3rd edn, Lawrence & Wishart, London.

Marx, K, 1975 [1844], 'Economic and philosophical manuscripts', in *MECW*, vol. 3, Lawrence & Wishart, London, pp. 229–346.

Marx, K, 1979 [1851–1852], 'The eighteenth Brumaire of Louis Bonaparte', in *MECW*, vol. 11, Lawrence & Wishart, London, pp. 99–197.

Marx, K, 1987a [1879], 'Marginal notes on Adolph Wagner's "Lehrbuch der politischen Ökonomie"', in *MECW*, vol. 26, Lawrence & Wishart, London, pp. 531–559.

Marx, K, 1987b [1859], 'Preface' (to *Contribution to the critique of political economy*), in *MECW*, vol. 29, Lawrence & Wishart, London, pp. 261–265.

Marx, K & Engels, F, 1976 [1845–46], 'The German ideology', in *MECW*, vol. 5, Lawrence & Wishart, London, pp. 19–581.

McCarney, J, 1980, *The real world of ideology*, Harvester, Brighton.

Mouffe, C, ed., 1979, *Gramsci and Marxist theory*, Routledge, London.

Portelli, H, 1972, *Gramsci et le bloque historique*, Maspero, Paris.

Potier, J P, 1991, *Piero Sraffa, unorthodox economist (1898–1983): A biographical essay*, Routledge, London.

Poulantzas, N, 1973 [1968], *Political power and social classes*, Sheed & Ward and New Left Books, London.

Poulantzas, N, 1978, *State, power, socialism*, New Left Books, London.

Resch, R P, 1992, *Althusser and the renewal of Marxist social theory*, University of California Press, Berkeley CA.

Vatter, M, 2004, 'Machiavelli after Marx: the self-overcoming of Marxism in the late Althusser', *Theory and event*. Available from: https://muse.jhu.edu/journals/theory_and_event/v007/7.4vatter.html [Accessed 15 March 2017].

Williams, R, 1977, *Marxism and literature*, Oxford University Press, Oxford.

3

Jürgen Habermas
Between democratic deliberation and deliberative democracy

Simon Susen

Introduction

It is widely acknowledged that Jürgen Habermas is an advocate of a deliberative model of democracy.[1] In essence, Habermas's discourse ethics constitutes a systematic attempt to locate the normative grounds of deliberative democracy in the rational foundations of language. From a Habermasian point of view, every time we engage in the co-existential exercise of seeking mutual understanding (*Verständigung*), we anticipate that we are capable of reaching agreements (*Einverständnisse*). Put differently, our communicative ability to understand one another equips us with the deliberative capacity to reach agreements with one another. Thus, the emancipatory potential of communicative action manifests itself not only in our 'weak' orientation towards intelligibility (*Verständlichkeit*) but also in our 'strong' orientation towards consensus-formation (*Konsensbildung*). Language use, irrespective of its quasi-transcendental features, is embedded in the pragmatics of interaction. Symbolic forms emerge in relation to spatio-temporally contingent modes of existence, whose political constitution is reflected in the socio-ontological significance of discursively motivated practices, which are vital to the construction of democracy. This chapter aims to demonstrate that Habermas's concern with democracy is inseparably linked to his interest in language. More specifically, it seeks to illustrate that the following ten elements are central to Habermas's multifaceted account of democracy: (1) deliberation, (2) reciprocity, (3) self-determination, (4) citizenship, (5) the state, (6) sovereignty, (7) communicative rationality, (8) regulation, (9) will-formation and (10) constitutional law. The chapter concludes by addressing a number of issues that arise when confronted with the task of assessing both the validity and the usefulness of Habermas's communication-theoretic account of democracy.

1. Democracy and deliberation

One of the most fundamental features of democracy is that it allows human beings to engage in processes of *deliberation*. Acts of collective deliberation are processes of intersubjective contemplation aimed at the construction of symbolically mediated and materially relevant arrangements shaped by potentially empowering dynamics of action co-ordination. To deliberate, then, means to reflect, to ponder and to contemplate. More specifically, to deliberate with others obliges us to navigate our way through situations of purposeful interaction that require context-sensitive frameworks of communication. If, following Habermas, we 'shift the burden of justifying the effectiveness of practical reason from the mentality of citizens to the *deliberative forms of politics*' (Habermas, 1998b, p. 386, italics added), we move the weight of substantiating the anthropological distinctiveness of communicative reason from the cognitive capacity of the subject to the recognitive potential built into experiences of intersubjectivity. Democratic decision-making processes can never be based solely on the self-referential motivations of isolated individuals; rather, they are founded on the mutually dependent wills of interconnected actors. One of the main objectives of deliberative forms of democracy is to give a rationally grounded voice to members of a particular community, whose capacity to develop a sense of solidarity constitutes a precondition for guaranteeing the relative stability of symbolically mediated and relationally constructed realities.

Democratic modes of social organisation cannot dispense with rationally determined processes of collective deliberation. Only insofar as we deliberate collectively over the purposive organisation and normative habitualisation of society can we ensure that the course of history is guided by the transperspectival force of shared responsibility. In this sense, *the 'linguistic turn'*[2] *in the social sciences*, which is motivated by the rejection of the atomistic presuppositions underlying traditional philosophies of consciousness and the defence of the intersubjectivist assumptions underpinning post-metaphysical sociologies of language,[3] is homological to *the 'deliberative turn' in social reality*, which is characterised by a shift from an arbitrarily ruled collective entity to a discursively constituted order, whose key institutions enjoy a considerable degree of legitimacy in terms of their capacity to regulate behavioural and ideological reference points shared by members of a given community (cf. Susen, 2010c, pp. 110–111, 116–117; cf. also Susen, 2014b). If, following Habermas, 'a *discursive or deliberative model* replaces the contract model' (Habermas, 1994, p. 137, italics added) and if, as a result, 'the legal community constitutes itself not by way of a social contract but on the basis of a *discursively achieved agreement*' (Habermas, 1994, p. 137, italics added), then the normative cornerstone of a democratically organised society is not simply its formal commitment to producing and protecting judicially confined social relations but, rather, its *substantive* capacity to enhance its members' active participation in collective processes of consensus-oriented deliberation.[4]

2. Democracy and reciprocity

A further central feature of democracy is that it permits human beings to build social relations based on *reciprocity*. Indeed, systems of democracy depend on relations of reciprocity; that is, we can shape the development of society democratically only insofar as we co-ordinate our actions reciprocally. The whole point of democracy is to do justice to the fact that human existence is a condition of *discursive reciprocity*: not only do we need to reciprocate each other's socially embedded actions, but we also need to reciprocate each other's linguistically articulated reflections, in order to provide society with the solidity of a collectively sustained, communicatively structured and rationally justified background of normativity for the daily construction of reality. The overall stability of society is contingent upon its capacity to incorporate, and to respond to, the demands of its members' intersubjectively negotiated search for context-specific forms of validity.

Our quotidian quest for symbolically mediated modes of validity is indicative of the meaning-laden nature of society. Our constant exchange of linguistically uttered claims to validity illustrates that even large-scale systems of political representation hinge upon small-scale spheres of communicative deliberation. Thus, 'the *reciprocity* of raising and responding to validity claims' (Habermas, 2005, p. 384, italics added) is maintained by an intersubjectively constituted process derived from the co-existential necessity of articulating and exchanging legitimacy claims: the validity of collectively co-ordinated actions depends on the normative power they obtain through *mutually* established codes of legitimacy.[5] Democracy, then, is inconceivable without reciprocity because of the interdependence of individual and collective freedom: 'the individual liberties of the subjects of private law and the public autonomy of enfranchised citizens *reciprocally* make each other possible' (Habermas, 1994, p. 141, italics added; cf. Susen, 2009b, pp. 104–105). Just as the discursively motivated reciprocity between subjects is crucial to the functioning of democratic processes of collective deliberation, the confluence of autonomy and solidarity is central to successful bonding processes generating empowering dynamics of social integration.[6]

3. Democracy and self-determination

Another significant feature of democracy is that, due to its capacity to foster social relations based on mutual understanding and agreement, it allows for the emergence of both individual and collective forms of *self-determination*. Individual self-determination and collective self-determination are two complementary moments in the human striving for autonomy: the self-determination of individuals is pointless if not granted by collectives, just as the self-determination of collectives is worthless if not supported by individuals.[7]

Following Habermas, there are four conditions for subjects' free association within a democratic framework:

a. the consolidation of an effective political *apparatus*,
b. the formation of a more or less clearly defined *'self'*,
c. the construction of a *citizenry*, and
d. the creation of an economic and social *milieu*.

(see Habermas, 2003, pp. 88–89)

In other words, genuine forms of democracy need to draw on various *political, cultural, institutional* and *economic* resources of a given society to claim that they have the legitimate power to affirm their bonding function within the domain of a territorially circumscribed reality.

To the extent that '[t]he identity requirement for the determination of a collective subject capable of *self-determination* and *self-direction* is fulfilled by the *sovereign territorial state* of classical international law' (*ibidem*, p. 89),[8] the right to both individual and collective autonomy is inscribed in the agenda of democratically organised societies. In essence, the right to self-determination and self-direction designates the legitimate capacity to define what one does and where one goes – individually or collectively. If subjects are granted the right to self-determine their actions, they are entitled to fill the space of historical indeterminacy with the self-empowering force of autonomy.[9]

According to Habermas's account of autonomy, however, the right to both individual and collective self-determination obtains not only *force* but also *legitimacy* insofar as its carriers are *actively* and *directly* involved in discursive processes of opinion- and will-formation. For assertions of self-determination are embedded in processes of communication. In this sense, self-government rests upon both communicative power and political power. '*Communicative power* is the power that emerges from the exercise of political autonomy, and hence cannot be separated from the discursive processes of will-formation, i.e., from *democracy*' (Preuss, 1998, p. 331, italics added). And *political power* is the power that emerges from the exercise of communicative freedom, and thus cannot be divorced from the linguistic processes of social integration, that is, from *everyday intersubjectivity*. Democracy and self-determination, then, are intimately intertwined because our ability to shape the course of history through communicative processes of critical intersubjectivity is indivisible from our capacity to develop a sense of individual and social responsibility by mobilising our species-constitutive resources[10] through which we, as human beings, acquire a sense of both personal and collective sovereignty.[11]

4. Democracy and citizenship

A further key component of democracy in modern society is its dependence on different forms of *citizenship*. According to *universalist* conceptions of citizenship, *civil, political and social rights* constitute integral elements of modern democracies.[12] According to *differentialist* conceptions of citizenship, *numerous* rights – that is, not only *civil, political and social rights*, but also several other rights, such as *cultural, sexual and human rights* – represent vital ingredients of late modern democracies.[13]

The historical significance of civil, political and social rights manifests itself in the existence of three institutions that are central to the functioning of modern society: the law courts, the parliament and the welfare system (see Turner, 1994 [1990], p. 202; see also Turner, 2009, p. 68). The present-day relevance of the struggle over further – for instance, cultural, sexual and human – rights is illustrated in the commitment of an increasing number of modern democracies to protecting their citizens from both hidden and overt mechanisms of social discrimination. In the modern world, the pursuit of democracy cannot be disconnected from 'the struggle for, and attainment of, citizenship'[14] – the ideal of democratic freedom cannot be realised without a commitment to the construction of democratic citizenry (cf. Habermas, 2003, p. 88).

It is far from uncontroversial, however, what the main elements of a democratic citizenry are and to what extent complex forms of society require complex forms of citizenship (see Susen, 2010b). Notwithstanding the issue of addressing the multiple challenges posed by high levels of societal complexity, it is hard to deny that the genealogy of large-scale systems of democracy is inconceivable without the establishment of differentiated models of citizenry.

When reflecting upon the relationship between democracy and citizenship in the contemporary context, we need to face up to three historical processes, which – from a sociological perspective – are of paramount importance: (a) the consolidation of the *neoliberal* project, (b) the emergence of a *post-communist* world and (c) the rise of *multicultural* politics (see *ibidem*, pp. 260–262).

a. If, under the *neoliberal* model, citizenship has been converted into a privatised affair of an increasingly *commodified* society, the question remains to what extent modern democratic systems have the capacity to undermine, rather than to reinforce, the detrimental effects of economic reification processes.[15]

b. If, in the *post-communist* context, citizenship has been transformed into a universalised affair of an ever more *globalised* society, the question remains to what extent modern democratic systems have the capacity to cope with both the intra-national demands 'from below' and the supra-national pressures 'from above' in a world characterised by an intensified degree of interdependence of local and global developments.[16]
c. If, following *multicultural* agendas, citizenship has been turned into a hybridised affair of a culturally *fragmented* society, the question remains to what extent modern democratic systems have the capacity to translate the presence of advanced levels of cultural complexity into an empowering resource, rather than a disempowering obstacle, in the pursuit of social stability, economic prosperity and developmental elasticity.[17]

In short, the increasing differentiation of society has led to the complexification of the dynamic relationship between democracy and citizenship.[18]

5. Democracy and the state

One of the most controversial issues in contemporary social and political theory is the question of the extent to which democracy and *the state* constitute two irreducible components of modern society. More precisely, the question in this regard concerns the degree to which *democracy* and *the state* can be considered two *interdependent* foundations of highly advanced civilisational formations. From a historical point of view, it appears that the creation of modern democracies is inextricably linked to the consolidation of legitimate states. If there is a predominant – and, indeed, appropriate – consensus according to which, the ideal of democracy in the modern world can be realised only through the construction of a legitimate political state, then another controversial question arises, namely the following: What should such a state look like, in terms of both its ideological outlook and its institutional set-up?

From a Weberian perspective, 'the *sovereign territorial state*' constitutes a cornerstone of modern societies (Habermas, 2003, p. 89, italics in original). From a Habermasian standpoint, the 'sovereign *Rechtsstaat*' represents an indispensable source of political legitimacy in modern democracies (see, for example, Habermas, 1996 [1992]-a). Both interpretations illustrate that, in a world characterised by the ubiquity of large-scale bureaucratic organisations, it is difficult – or, perhaps, implausible – to examine the concepts of 'democracy' and 'the state' in isolation from one another. To the degree that the question of 'democracy' and the question of 'the polity' are intimately intertwined, it is impossible to dissociate the possibility of collective deliberation from the necessity of political organisation. Just as we need to accept that a 'distinctive feature of the modern state is the possession of the monopoly of the means of *violence* within a given territory' (Hirst & Thompson, 1995, p. 410, italics added), we need to recognise that a predominant feature of modern democracy is the possession of the monopoly of the means of political *discourse* within a given society (cf. Susen, 2010c, pp. 110–111, 116–117). The territorial integrity of the modern polity is a precondition for the legitimate affirmation of the state's institutionally established sovereignty, and the pluralistic elasticity of modern democracy is a prerequisite for the legitimate consolidation of the state's discursively negotiated autonomy.[19]

6. Democracy and sovereignty

Another key issue arising from debates around the constitution of democracy is its relation to the idea of both individual and collective *sovereignty*.

a. The legitimacy of democracy depends on its capacity to protect and to promote the *individual sovereignty* of the members of a given society. At this level, democracy is aimed at converting the philosophical ideal of personal autonomy into a social reality based on individual responsibility and accountability (*Mündigkeit*) (see Habermas, 1987 [1965/1968], p. 311; see also Susen, 2007, pp. 37, 40, 69, 72, 82, 251).

According to the early Habermas, we – as a species capable of cognition and action – possess *knowledge-constitutive interests*, which manifest themselves in our ability to control, to comprehend and to critique particular aspects of reality by generating, and making use of, technological, hermeneutic and critical forms of knowledge (see esp. Habermas, 1987 [1965/1968]). According to the late Habermas, we – as a species capable of speech and action – possess *language-constitutive interests*, which permeate our ability to represent, to regulate and to relate to particular aspects of reality by raising assertive, normative and expressive validity claims.[20] Owing to the socio-ontological significance of our *species-constitutive interests*, we are obliged to recognise that the pursuit of individual and collective forms of sovereignty (*Eigenständigkeit*) is built into the nature of human linguisticality (*Sprachlichkeit*).

Our '*emancipatory* cognitive interest' (Habermas, 1987 [1965/1968], pp. 310, 314, italics added) in personal and social liberation from 'dependence on hypostatized powers' (*ibidem*, pp. 310, 313) enables us to pursue our 'human interest in autonomy and responsibility (*Mündigkeit*)' (*ibidem*, p. 311). Our linguistic capacity to question the unquestioned and to discuss the undiscussed permits us to follow our human interest in acquiring an empowering degree of individual sovereignty by immersing ourselves in discursively mediated forms of critical intersubjectivity. In other words, the *emancipatory* value of democracy – in the Habermasian sense – depends on its capacity to defend both *the right* and *the will* to individual sovereignty, which is indispensable to both the construction of personal autonomy and the development of a sense of responsibility (cf. Susen, 2009a, 2015b). Put differently, democracy – understood in Habermasian terms – is inconceivable without the emergence of linguistically anchored and discursively cultivated modes of sovereignty.

b. The legitimacy of democracy depends on its capacity to protect and to promote the *collective sovereignty* enjoyed by the members of a given society. In the modern world, *collective* sovereignty is typically associated with *national* sovereignty, that is, the sovereignty of nation-states. In essence, two key levels underlying collective sovereignty can be distinguished: *internal sovereignty and external sovereignty*.

Whereas *internal* sovereignty stems from a political body's capacity to claim legitimacy in relation to a particular society, *external* sovereignty is reflected in a political body's capacity to claim legitimacy in relation to other political bodies. The former enables a given government to assume the supreme command over civil society by virtue of both *de jure* – that is, legal – and *de facto* – that is, coercive – institutionalised means. The latter, by contrast, is derived from nation-states' *mutual recognition* of their respective territorial integrity and political legitimacy. Put differently, collective sovereignty is consolidated and sustained on the basis of both internal *and* external sovereignty. Hence, rather than presuming that the capacity for sovereignty simply emanates 'from within', we need to acknowledge the fact that 'to a significant degree the capacity for sovereignty came from *without*' (Hirst & Thompson, 1995, p. 410, italics in original; on this point, see also Susen, 2015a, pp. 126, 127, 133, 134, 216, 225, 229).

If, therefore, we accept that the seemingly endogenous power of sovereignty is inextricably linked to its exogenous conditioning, we are compelled to concede that democracy is never simply a *local* or *national* affair, but always, at least in principle, also a *global* and *transnational* matter. Internally, democracy can work only insofar as the members of a given society are willing to engage in discursive forms of communicative intersubjectivity oriented towards collective deliberation. Externally, democracy can work only insofar as different polities are prepared to commit to transnational co-operation and transcultural dialogue, both of which are central to generating fruitful communication processes between different societies.

In brief, democracy and sovereignty are two elements necessary for the construction of a society that is shaped by discursively constituted and morally valuable modes of agency.[21]

7. Democracy and communicative rationality

Democracy, in the Habermasian sense, has another crucial ingredient: *communicative rationality*. Indeed, Habermas's plea for an *ethics founded on communicative rationality* can be conceived of as a proposition for a set of principles oriented towards deliberative democracy. The paradigmatic primacy ascribed to the construction of a discursively configured reality is motivated by the conviction that, as linguistic beings able to raise rationally justifiable validity claims, we can mobilise the empowering resource of communicative rationality to determine both the constitution and the evolution of society.

In order to make sense of the discursive nature of democracy, we need to reflect upon five – interrelated – dimensions of *communicative rationality*.[22]

a. Communicative rationality is based on *Verstand* (reason): as such, it is derived from our rational capacity to attribute meaning to the world by virtue of linguistically articulated claims to validity.
b. Communicative rationality enables us to engage in processes of *Verständigung* (communication): as such, it permits us not only to co-ordinate our actions, but also to attribute meaning to them by virtue of intersubjective practices oriented towards mutual understanding.
c. Communicative rationality is the main driving force guiding our species-constitutive search for *Verstehen* (understanding): as such, it allows us to imbue the givenness of reality with the meaning-ladenness of language and thereby to permeate the facticity of worldly objectivity with the normativity of lifeworldly intersubjectivity.
d. Communicative rationality is both a means and an end of our orientation towards *Verständlichkeit* (intelligibility): as such, its existence is symptomatic of the fact that, as subjects capable of speech and action, we make sense of the world by making sense of each other.
e. Communicative rationality is the principal socio-ontological force behind our ability to reach an *Einverständnis* (agreement): as such, its presence demonstrates that we – as a communicative species – are capable of mutual understanding and that we – as a discursive species – are capable of reaching agreements.

This is the point at which *democracy* comes into play. Democracy rests upon the empowering potential of communicative rationality, because the symbolically mediated and intelligibly structured co-ordination of our actions within the sphere of reality lies at the heart of every discursively organised society.

a. Democracy is inconceivable without *Verstand*: in democratic societies, the ultimate resource of justification is not faith but *reason*.
b. Democracy is unthinkable without *Verständigung*: in democratic societies, the ultimate resource of argumentation is not monologue but *dialogue*.
c. Democracy is impossible without *Verstehen*: in democratic societies, the ultimate resource of signification is not the acceptance of facticity but the struggle over *normativity*.
d. Democracy is unimaginable without *Verständlichkeit*: in democratic societies, the ultimate resource of action co-ordination is not egotistic self-referentiality but mutual *intelligibility*.
e. Democracy is unimaginable without *Einverständnis*: in democratic societies, the ultimate resource of both small-scale and large-scale organisation is not violence but the search for *agreements*, including – if necessary – the agreement to disagree.

In short, deliberative democracy and communicative rationality are two mutually inclusive conditions for the understanding-oriented co-existence of interdependent subjects.[23]

8. Democracy and regulation

It would be overly optimistic to suggest that the running of democracy is driven by exclusively empowering – notably, deliberative, communicative and discursive – forces. In fact, one of the less obvious dimensions of democracy is its *regulative* function (see Habermas, 1994, p. 138), which may be perceived as ambivalent in that it contains both positive and negative aspects:

- On the *positive* side, the regulative function of democracy is illustrated in the fact that its existence allows for the establishment of relatively *predictable* – and, thus, fairly stable – forms of both small-scale and large-scale social interaction.
- On the *negative* side, the regulative function of democracy is reflected in the fact that its existence can trigger inconveniently *rigid* – and, hence, excessively synchronised – forms of both small-scale and large-scale social interaction.

If 'morality and law both serve to regulate interpersonal conflicts' (*ibidem*, p. 138) and if 'both are supposed to protect the autonomy of all participants and affected persons equally' (*ibidem*, p. 138), a key function of democracy consists in organising human life forms in terms of both micro-sociological concerns, arising from people's tangible experiences of *Gemeinschaft*, and macro-sociological issues, emerging from people's intangible experiences of *Gesellschaft*. The validity claims of moral commands raised in the lifeworld (see *ibidem*, p. 139) and the legitimacy claims of legal norms imposed upon ordinary actors by the system (see *ibidem*, p. 139) form a dual regulative totality that permeates the praxeological horizon of every modern democracy.

Democracy, then, is not only a 'legislative practice of justification' (*ibidem*, p. 139), but also a regulative process of normalisation. Just as 'different types of reason' (*ibidem*, p. 139) can be brought forward to make a case for a particular kind of legislation, different collective strategies can be employed to shape the development of a given society by specific patterns of regulation. Indeed, what manifests itself in the functional interdependence of legislative practices of justification and regulative practices of normalisation is the intertwinement of validity and normativity: rationally justified claims to validity that are aimed at equipping a collective entity with a framework of legislative regularity express a demand for normativity, without which there would be no meaningful organisation of society.

In this sense, 'law has a more complex structure than morality' (*ibidem*, p. 139): whereas the latter serves to regulate people's interactions in the concrete realm of *Gemeinschaft*, the former operates as a legislative umbrella that stipulates people's interactions in the abstract realm of *Gesellschaft*. The distinctive power of democracy, in this context, is its capacity to make both ordinary claims to moral validity and institutional claims to judicial legitimacy subject to critical scrutiny by virtue of communicative rationality. In a democratic society, understood in the Habermasian sense, it is not the *forceful force of symbolic or physical violence* but, on the contrary, the *forceless force of the better argument* which gives *validity* to moral patterns of justification as well as *legitimacy* to legislative patterns of normalisation.[24] In short, an important function of democracy is to guarantee the *regulation* of society – not by relying upon arbitrary forms of authority, but by drawing upon communicative rationality. Hermeneutically equipped entities capable of speech and action can determine the course of history by mobilising the discursive resources inherent in linguistically mediated practices of intersubjectivity.[25]

9. Democracy and will-formation

The construction of democracy is inextricably linked to the formation of both individual and collective *wills*. Put differently, democratic power is expressed in *will power*. Yet, democratic and non-democratic modes of will-formation are fundamentally different in the following sense:

- In the former, every member of society has the right to express their opinion and, consequently, to participate in both private and public debates.
- In the latter, some members or groups of society may be excluded from collective decision-making processes on relatively arbitrary – for example, economic, ideological, religious, cultural, ethnic, 'racial' or gender-specific – grounds.

The universal right to be directly and actively involved in collective processes of will-formation, then, is a *sine qua non* of genuine articulations of democracy – notwithstanding the question of whether they are supposed to operate as models of deliberative or representative participation. Collective processes of democratic will-formation, however, are far from straightforward and can be successful only to the extent that people are able to question – that is, both to recognise and to relativise – the perspectival determinacy of their claims to discursive validity.

> Thus the opinion- and will-formation of the democratic legislature depends upon *a complicated network of discourses and bargaining* – and not simply on moral discourses. And unlike the clearly focused normative validity claim of moral commands, the legitimacy claim of legal norms – like the legislative practice of justification itself – is supported by *different types of reason*.
>
> (Habermas, 1994, p. 139, italics added)

In other words, what we, as critical theorists of democracy, need to examine are the sociological implications of the fact that collective will-formation – as a process based on discursive negotiation and consensus-oriented communication – constitutes a normative challenge that requires actors who participate in practices of argumentation to *transcend* the perspectival determinacy of their claims to validity by engaging in the dialogical exercise of communicative intersubjectivity. *Different people* with *different backgrounds, standards, principles and convictions* will mobilise *different types of reason* to describe, to analyse, to interpret, to explain and to assess *different kinds of situation*. The world of reason cannot be dissociated from the realm of experience. The manifold ways in which communicative actors make rational judgements are inevitably shaped by the normative standards to which they are exposed, and by the socio-culturally specific horizons in which they are embedded, when experiencing both the material and the symbolic dimensions of their lifeworlds. Collective will-formation is always a matter of social life-formation: what we want and how we decide is contingent upon what we have learned to want and how we have learned to decide. Our discursive problematisation of the world cannot be separated from our assimilative, adaptive and purposive immersion in the lifeworld.

To accept that in democratic systems 'all government is by the people' (Habermas, 2001b, p. 768; cf. Ferrara, 2001) means to do justice to the fact that 'all society is by the people'. From a democratic point of view, those who make up society should also be those who decide over the context-laden roles of both the individual and the collective aspects of their everyday reality. Will-formation, in the democratic sense, is not a privilege of those who govern society 'from above', through the systemic force of the state, but, rather, a right of those who build society 'from below', through the communicative force of the lifeworld. Hence, 'the discourse-theoretic interpretation of the democratic self-constitution of the constitutional state *[Verfassungsstaat]*' (Habermas, 2001b, p. 776) concerns not only the systemic sphere of administrative structures put in place to determine the development of society 'from above', through processes of 'functional integration' (see Susen, 2007, pp. 67–68, 237), but also the ordinary sphere of communicative interactions whose linguistic resources are mobilised to shape the development of society 'from below', through processes of 'social integration' (see *ibidem*, pp. 67, 68, 69, 70, 71, 237, 258). In brief, collective will-formation cannot dispense with the communicative practices accomplished by human actors, whose quotidian performances are mediated by linguistically organised processes.[26]

10. Democracy and constitutional law

As elucidated above, democracy has a regulative function: democratic institutions and democratic practices allow for the regulation – and, thus, for the normalisation – of the interactions taking place between members of a given society. In the context of modern society, the institutional inscription of practical prescriptions into consolidated democracies reflects the systemic necessity to solidify interactional regularity through the consolidation of normative frameworks founded on *constitutional legality*. From a Habermasian point of view, the complementary connection between morality and law (see, for example, Habermas, 1994, pp. 139–141) is entrenched in the tension-laden relationship between lifeworld and system,[27] for the institutionalisation of legislative arrangements cannot be divorced from the socialisation processes of communicatively sustained engagements. If we regard 'positive law as a functional complement to morality' (Habermas, 1994, p. 140), then we locate the abstract superstructure of legislative imperatives in the concrete infrastructure of communicative practices.

Yet, not only is there an intimate link between the rule of law and everyday intelligibility, but, in addition, there is an 'internal relation between the rule of law and democracy' (*ibidem*, p. 141). Just as regulative processes of formal legislation are anchored in communicative processes of informal co-operation, the long-term acceptability of the rule of law depends on its capacity to gain legitimacy through democratic procedures based on transparency, accountability and reasonability. As Habermas reminds us, '[l]ike morality, so also legitimate law protects the equal autonomy of each person: no individual is free so long as all persons do not enjoy an equal freedom' (Habermas, 2001b, p. 779). Put differently, private and civic autonomy are complementary and mutually dependent elements of constitutionally legitimated democracies and democratically legitimated constitutions: '[t]he interdependence of constitutionalism and democracy comes to light in this complementary relationship between private and civic autonomy: each side is fed by resources it has from the other' (*ibidem*, p. 780).

If the *Dasein* (being-there) of every member of humanity cannot be detached from the *Miteinandersein* (being-with-one-another) experienced by all members of society, then the affirmation of personal autonomy is contingent upon the assertion of civic autonomy. It is the function of constitutional law to ensure that individual self-government and collective self-government co-exist as two complementary preconditions for the attainment of political legitimacy within democratically organised societies.[28]

Conclusion

As illustrated in the previous analysis, Habermas's concern with democracy is inseparably linked to his interest in language. This chapter has aimed to demonstrate that ten elements are particularly important to Habermas's multifaceted account of democracy: (1) deliberation, (2) reciprocity, (3) self-determination, (4) citizenship, (5) the state, (6) sovereignty, (7) communicative rationality, (8) regulation, (9) will-formation and (10) constitutional law. From a Habermasian point of view, the construction of an emancipatory society is inconceivable without the sustained attempt to bring about a solid form of democracy based on the deliberative power that is embedded in people's communicative capacity. Subjects capable of speech and action are equipped with the competence to take both individual and collective decisions that are derived from intersubjective processes of reflection, justification and deliberation. The preceding enquiry has sought to identify the principal components underlying Habermas's conception of democracy. This concluding section endeavours to address a number of issues that arise when confronted with the task of assessing both the validity and the usefulness of Habermas's communication-theoretic account of democracy. Following the structure of the foregoing study, these issues can be summarised as follows:

1. There is no democracy without processes of *deliberation*. It is far from clear, however, to what extent *direct and deliberative* models of democracy are viable in large-scale societies, which – owing to their demographic and systemic complexity – tend to rely on *indirect and representative* forms of political participation.
2. There is no democracy without both dynamics and structures of *reciprocity*. It is not obvious, however, to what extent asymmetrical and power-laden modes of reciprocity can be challenged in order to build a society in which fundamental sociological variables – such as class, ethnicity, gender, age and ability – cease to have both a determining and a detrimental impact upon the political agendas set under the banner of democracy.
3. There is no democracy without the possibility of *self-determination*. It remains open to scrutiny, however, to what extent it is achievable to grant every individual or collective actor not only the *formal right* to, but also the *substantive resources* for, autonomy, self-government and self-realisation – especially in light of the fact that behavioural, ideological and institutional patterns are shot through with power relations.

4. There is no democracy without *citizenship*. It is a matter of debate, however, to what extent it is feasible to strike a healthy balance between, on the one hand, *rights and entitlements* and, on the other hand, *duties and obligations* – notably in societies that are characterised by high levels of internal cultural diversity and, hence, by advanced degrees of behavioural, ideological and institutional heterogeneity.
5. There is no democracy without a *state* – at least not in large-scale societies. One of the key issues that remain crucial in this respect, however, is the question of the extent to which it may be both viable and desirable to create a society whose members are capable of co-ordinating their actions and managing their affairs *without* relying on an institutional entity equivalent to a state or a polity. The question, then, is not simply to what degree and in which specific areas of social life the state should, or should not, have the right to intervene; more fundamentally, the question is whether or not, in the course of human history, the consolidation of a highly differentiated society *without* a polity can be considered a realistic possibility.
6. There is no democracy without *sovereignty*. Irrespective of whether we reflect on individual or collective, internal or external, real or imagined forms of sovereignty, it is far from evident, however, to what extent, in a global network society, actors have the potential, let alone the factual, power to make decisions as genuinely autonomous entities. In an age of increasing interconnectedness, the pivotal sources of agency appear to have shifted from a hitherto self-empowered humanity to an assemblage of constantly changing parameters of performativity, with no sense of direction, let alone an underlying teleology.
7. There is no democracy without *communicative rationality*. To be exact, the socio-ontological forces of *Verstand* (reason), *Verständigung* (communication), *Verstehen* (understanding), *Verständlichkeit* (intelligibility) and *Einverständnis* (agreement) play a foundational role in the construction of democracy. No less central, however, is the function of seemingly uncomfortable – yet, vastly influential – elements of democracy, such as the following: (a) not only belief and faith, but also madness and fanaticism; (b) not only miscommunication, but also silence and disengagement; (c) not only misunderstanding, misinterpretation and misconception, but also confusion, perplexity and bewilderment; (d) not only unintelligibility, incomprehensibility and obscurity, but also misrepresentation, distortion and manipulation; (e) not only disagreement, discrepancy and controversy, but also rupture, friction and hostility.
8. There is no democracy without *regulation*. The question that poses itself in this context, however, is to what extent democratically controlled processes of regulation can be converted into oppressive mechanisms of normalisation, habitualisation and disciplination capable of undermining human empowerment, autonomy and self-realisation.
9. There is no democracy without *will-formation*. The mere fact that, in democratic societies, subjects capable of speech and action are engaged in processes of opinion- and will-formation, however, does not reveal anything about the extent to which their views, beliefs, judgements and decisions are universally defensible, rather than applicable only to the limited horizon of context-specific modes of individual or collective agency. The construction of *value-laden, meaning-laden, perspective-laden, interest-laden, power-laden* and *tension-laden* realities manifests itself in the emergence of normativities, reflecting the contestability that inhabits symbolically mediated life forms as they evolve throughout history.
10. There is no democracy without *constitutional law* – at least not in highly differentiated societies. The fact that something is legal, however, does not make it legitimate. Constitutional legality is by no means a guarantee of social, political or moral legitimacy.

What is more, grass-roots democracy can dispense with the formalised rules, criteria and standards that are imposed 'from above' by constitutionally founded systems of legality. Genuine democracy is not simply a matter of imposing the lawfulness of procedural politics upon the relative arbitrariness of everyday occurrences; rather, it involves the challenge of ensuring that those whose lives are shaped – if not governed – by customs, conventions and principles are not only *entitled* but also *empowered* to negotiate – and, if necessary, to define – the normative parameters underlying their existence *themselves*.

Notes

1 See, for instance: Brookfield (2005); Conover & Searing (2005); Cooke (2000); Eriksen & Weigård (2003); Festenstein (2004); Günther (1998); Habermas (1996 [1992]-b); Habermas (1998b); Habermas (2005); Janssen & Kies (2005); Johnson (1993); Pellizzoni (2001); Power (1998); Sintomer (1999); Susen (2009a); Susen (2010c: 110–111, 116–117); Young (1997b).
2 On *the 'linguistic turn'*, see, for example: Apel (1976); Bohman (1996); Bourdieu (1982); Bourdieu (1992); Bourdieu (1993 [1984]); Fairclough (1995); Fillmore (1985); Gebauer (2005); Goldhammer (2001); Habermas (1988 [1967/1970]); Habermas (1976); Hacking (1975); Hacking (1982); Jäger (2002); Kirk (1997 [1994]); Krämer (2002); Krämer & König (2002); Lafont (1993); Lafont (1997); Lafont (1999 [1993]); Lee (1992); May (1996); Rigotti (1979); Rorty (1967a); Rorty (1967b); Rossi-Landi (1974 [1972]); Schöttler (1997); Susen (2007: chapters 1–4); Susen (2009a); Susen (2010c); Susen (2013a); Susen (2013c); Susen (2013d); Susen (2013e); Susen (2015a: 34, 244, 288 n. 159); Taylor (1991 [1986]); Wellmer (1977 [1976]).
3 On *Habermas's conception of 'postmetaphysical thinking'*, see, for instance: Habermas (1987 [1985]); Habermas (1992 [1988]); Habermas (2004). Cf. Rorty (1967b).
4 On *the relationship between democracy and deliberation*, see, for example: Brookfield (2005); Conover & Searing (2005); Cooke (2000); Eriksen & Weigård (2003); Festenstein (2004); Günther (1998); Habermas (1996 [1992]-b); Habermas (1994: 137); Habermas (1998b); Habermas (2005); Janssen & Kies (2005); Johnson (1993); Pellizzoni (2001); Power (1998); Sintomer (1999); Susen (2009a); Susen (2010c: 110–111, 116–117); Young (1997b).
5 On *the link between 'validity claims' and 'legitimacy claims'*, see, for instance: Susen (2007: 248, 253, 257, 263, 286); Susen (2009b: 99, 100, 102, 103, 105, 113, 114, 115, 117, 119); Susen (2010c: 104, 106, 108, 109, 110, 111, 112, 114, 115, 116); Susen (2011b: 46, 55, 57, 58); Susen (2011c: 49, 53, 57, 60, 63, 64, 69, 70, 71, 75, 77, 80, 82); Susen (2013d: 200, 213, 218, 235 n. 87); Susen (2013e: 330, 331); Susen (2014b: 91, 92, 94, 95, 96, 97, 99, 100).
6 On *the relationship between democracy and reciprocity*, see, for example: Habermas (1994: 141); Habermas (2005: 384); Susen (2007: 23, 41, 51, 52, 72, 81, 84, 90, 91, 118, 124, 193, 194, 198, 201 n. 84, 311); Young (1997a).
7 On this point, see, for instance, Susen (2010a: 151–158, 198–208). See also, for instance: Browne & Susen (2014); Holloway & Susen (2013); Susen (2008a); Susen (2008b); Susen (2009a); Susen (2010d); Susen (2011b); Susen (2012a); Susen (2013d); Susen (2013e); Susen (2014a).
8 Italics added to '*self-determination*' and '*self-direction*'; '*sovereign territorial state*' is italicised in the original version.
9 On *the concepts of 'indeterminacy' and 'autonomy'*, see Susen (2015a: esp. Chapter 4 and Chapter 5, respectively).
10 See Susen (2007: esp. Chapter 10). See also, for example: Boltanski, Honneth & Celikates (2014 [2009]); Boltanski, Rennes & Susen (2010); Boltanski, Rennes & Susen (2014 [2010]); Holloway & Susen (2013); Susen (2009a); Susen (2010c); Susen (2011a); Susen (2012b); Susen (2013d); Susen (2013e); Susen (2014 [2012]); Susen (2015b); Susen (2017).
11 On *the relationship between democracy and self-determination*, see, for example: Browne & Susen (2014); Habermas (2003: 88–89); Holloway & Susen (2013); Preuss (1998: 331); Susen (2008a); Susen (2008b); Susen (2009a); Susen (2010a: 151–158, 198–208); Susen (2010d); Susen (2011b); Susen (2012a); Susen (2013d); Susen (2013e); Susen (2014a); Young (1997b).
12 On this point, see Susen (2010b: 262–265) and Susen (2015a: Chapter 5). See also Marshall (1964 [1963]), Marshall (1981) and Turner (2009).

13 On this point, see Susen (2010b: 265–268, 271–274) and Susen (2015a: Chapter 5). See also, for instance, Young (1994 [1989]), Young (1997a) and Young (1997b).
14 Mann (1994 [1987]: 63). On this point, see also, for example: Basconzuelo, Morel & Susen (2010a); Basconzuelo, Morel & Susen (2010b); Susen (2010a); Susen (2015a: 127, 173, 174, 175, 177, 190, 207, 212, 216, 221, 222, 226, 274, 276).
15 On *the concept of neoliberalism*, see, for example: Berberoglu (2010); Browne & Susen (2014); Davies (2014); Harvey (2006); Marcos (1997); Outhwaite (2006: esp. Part I); Soederberg, Menz & Cerny (2005); Susen (2010b: 260–262); Susen (2012a); Susen (2015a: esp. Chapter 3 and Chapter 5).
16 On *the concept of globalisation*, see, for example: Amin-Khan (2012); Axford (2013); Bauman (1998); Bhambra (2007); Centeno & Cohen (2010); Chirico (2013); Dicken (2011 [1986]); Drake (2010); Featherstone, Lash & Robertson (1995); Franklin, Lury & Stacey (2000); Fraser (2007b); Hirst & Thompson (1995); Hirst & Thompson (1996); Hoogvelt (1997); Lash & Lury (2007); Martell (2010); Mayo (2005); Mittelman (1996); Mouzelis (2008: 159–161); Nederveen Pieterse (1995); Outhwaite & Ray (2005); Paulus (2001: 745); Petrella (1996); Piketty (2013); Redner (2013); Ritzer (2013 [1993]); Robertson (1995); Sassen (2004); Sklair (1995 [1991]); Sloterdijk (2013 [2005]); Susen (2010a: 182–197); Susen (2010b: 260–262); Susen (2015a: esp. Chapter 3); Tomlinson (1999); Williams, Bradley, Devadson & Erickson (2013).
17 On *the concept of multiculturalism*, see, for example: Barry (2001); Chevallier (2008 [2003]); Crowder (2013); Jullien (2014 [2008]); Kelly (2002); Khory (2012); Kymlicka (2005); Kymlicka (2007); Kymlicka & He (2005); Lutz, Herrera Vivar & Supik (2011); Modood (2013 [2007]); Nemoianu (2010); Parekh (2008); Phillips (2007); Schweppenhäuser (1997); Susen (2010a: 204–208); Susen (2010b: 260–262, 271–274); Susen (2013b: 93, 97, 100 n. 35); Susen (2015a: Chapter 5); Taylor & Gutmann (1992); Yar (2001).
18 On *the relationship between democracy and citizenship*, see, for example: Archibugi (2008); Bridges (1994); Crouch, Eder & Tambini (2001); Delanty (2000); Fraser (2007a); Habermas (2003: 88); Hutchings & Dannreuther (1999 [1998]); Isin (2000); Janoski (1998); Mann (1994 [1987]); Marshall (1964 [1963]); Marshall (1981); Mayo (2005); Miller (1993); Mouffe (1993); Smith (2007); Susen (2010b: 260–262, 262–265, 265–268, 271–274); Taylor (1989); Turner (1994 [1990]: 202); Turner (2009: 68); Vandenberg (2000); Young (1994 [1989]).
19 On *the relationship between democracy and the state*, see, for example: Anderson (1986); Armaline, Glasberg & Purkayastha (2014); Baraith & Gupta (2010); Boyer & Drache (1996); Chernilo (2007); Chernilo (2008); Crouch, Eder & Tambini (2001); Cudworth, Hall & McGovern (2007); Dunn (2000); Evans, Rueschemeyer & Skocpol (1985); Gill (2003); Habermas (1996 [1992]-a); Habermas (1999); Habermas (2001 [1998]); Habermas (2003: 89); Hall (1986); Hall (1994); Hall & Ikenberry (1989); Hay, Lister & Marsh (2006); Held (1991); Held (1995); Held (1985 [1983]); Hirst & Thompson (1995: 410); Jessop (2007); Keane (1988); King & Kendall (2004); Lachmann (2010); Pierson (2004 [1996]); Poggi (1978); Poggi (1990); Reid, Gill & Sears (2010); Skinner (1989); Skinner & Stråth (2003); Sørensen (2003); Thornhill (2013); van Creveld (1999); Wertheim (1992).
20 On this point, see, for instance: Habermas (1984 [1976]); Habermas (2001 [1984]-b); Habermas (2001 [1984]-c); Habermas (2001 [1984]-d). See also, for instance: Heath (1998); Ilting (1990 [1982]); Niemi (2005); Susen (2007: 75-95); Thompson (1982); Whitton (1992).
21 On *the relationship between democracy and sovereignty*, see, for example: Brittan (1998); Habermas (1987 [1965/1968]: 314); Hinsley (1986 [1966]); Hirst (1997); Hirst & Thompson (1995: 410); Khory (2012); King & Kendall (2004); Krasner (1988); Sassen (1996); Spruyt (1994); Susen (2007: 37, 40, 69, 72, 82, 251).
22 Cf. Susen (2013d) and Susen (2013e: 326). Cf. also, for instance, Susen (2007: 20, 49, 51, 52, 53, 54, 67, 69, 70, 72, 86–87, 97 n. 54, 107, 108, 110, 112, 116, 118, 119, 125, 161, 253, 255, 256, 260, 276, 304, 305, 307, 308, 314).
23 On *the relationship between democracy and communicative rationality*, see, for example: Abbas & McLean (2003); Apel (1990 [1985]); Benhabib & Dallmayr (1990); Bjola (2005); Breen (2004); Callinicos (1989); Eriksen & Weigård (2003); Gamwell (1997); Grant (2003); Günther (1998); Habermas (1970); Habermas (1985 [1984]); Habermas (1987 [1981]-b); Habermas (1987 [1981]-a); Habermas (1990 [1983]); Habermas (2001 [1984]-a); Habermas (2001a); Heath (2001); James (2003); Johnson (1991); McCarthy (1973); Outhwaite (2009 [1994]); Preuss (1998); Steinhoff

(2001); Stryker (2000); Susen (2007: 97 n. 54); Susen (2009a); Susen (2010c); Susen (2013d); Susen (2013e: 326); Thompson (2000); Thompson (1983); Warnke (1995).
24 On this point, see, for example: Habermas (2001: 13, 45, 79). See also, for example: Apel (1990 [1985]: 35, 41–42, 50); Ray (2004: 317–318); Susen (2007: 114, 244, 251, 286); Susen (2009: 102–103, 114); Susen (2010: 109, 116); Whitton (1992: 307).
25 On *the relationship between democracy and regulation*, see, for example: Black (2000); Black (2001); Deflem (1994a); Deflem (1994b); Habermas (1994: 138–139); Palast, Oppenheim & MacGregor (2002); Starkey (2007); Williams & Matheny (1995).
26 On *the relationship between democracy and will-formation*, see, for example: Crouch, Eder & Tambini (2001); Ferrara (2001); Habermas (1994: 139); Habermas (1996 [1992]-a); Habermas (2001b: 768, 776); Mayo (2005); Mouffe (1993); Susen (2007: 116); Williams & Matheny (1995); Vandenberg (2000); Young (1994 [1989]).
27 On *Habermas's account of the relationship between 'lifeworld' and 'system'*, see, for example, Susen (2007: 61, 70, 71-73, 239, 245, 246, 305).
28 On *the relationship between democracy and constitutional law*, see, for example: Alexy (1998); Black (2000); Black (2001); Deflem (1994a); Deflem (1994b); Ferrara (2001); Guibentif (1994); Günther (1998); Habermas (1996 [1992]-a); Habermas (1998a); Habermas (1998b); Habermas (2001b); Hall (1986); Poggi (1978); Power (1998); Preuss (1998); Rasmussen (1994); Rosenfeld & Arato (1998); Thornhill (2013).

References

Abbas, A & McLean, M, 2003, 'Communicative competence and the improvement of university teaching: Insights from the field', *British Journal of Sociology of Education* 24(1), pp. 69–81.
Alexy, R, 1998, 'Jürgen Habermas's theory of legal discourse' in *Habermas on law and democracy: Critical exchanges*, eds. M Rosenfeld & A Arato, University of California Press, Berkeley, CA, pp. 226–233.
Amin-Khan, T, 2012, *The post-colonial state in the era of capitalist globalization: Historical, political and theoretical approaches to state formation*, Routledge, New York.
Anderson, J, ed., 1986, *The rise of the modern state*, Wheatsheaf, Brighton.
Apel, K-O, ed., 1976, *Sprachpragmatik und Philosophie*, Suhrkamp, Frankfurt am Main.
Apel, K-O, 1990 [1985], 'Is the ethics of the ideal communication community a utopia? On the relationship between ethics, utopia, and the critique of utopia' in *The Communicative Ethics Controversy*, eds. S Benhabib & F R Dallmayr, MIT Press, Cambridge, MA, pp. 23–59.
Archibugi, D, 2008, *The global commonwealth of citizens: Toward cosmopolitan democracy*, Princeton University Press, Princeton, NJ.
Armaline, W T, Glasberg, D S & Purkayastha, B, 2014, *The human rights enterprise: Political sociology, state power, and social movements*, Polity, Cambridge.
Axford, B, 2013, *Theories of globalization*, Polity, Cambridge.
Baraith, R S & Gupta, D, eds., 2010, *State and globalization*, Rawat Publications, Jaipur.
Barry, B, 2001, *Culture and equality: An egalitarian critique of multiculturalism*, Polity, Cambridge.
Basconzuelo, C, Morel, T & Susen, S, eds., 2010a, *Ciudadanía territorial y movimientos sociales. Historia y nuevas problemáticas en el escenario latinoamericano y mundial*, Ediciones del ICALA, Río Cuarto.
Basconzuelo, C, Morel, T & Susen, S, 2010b, 'Prólogo' in *Ciudadanía territorial y movimientos sociales. Historia y nuevas problemáticas en el escenario latinoamericano y mundial*, eds. C Basconzuelo, T Morel & S Susen, Ediciones del ICALA, Río Cuarto, pp. 7–10.
Bauman, Z, 1998, *Globalization: The human consequences*, Polity, Cambridge.
Benhabib, S & Dallmayr, F R, eds., 1990, *The communicative ethics controversy*, MIT Press, Cambridge, MA.
Berberoglu, B, ed., 2010 *Globalization in the 21st century: Labor, capital, and the state on a world scale*, Palgrave Macmillan, Basingstoke.

Bhambra, G K, 2007, *Rethinking modernity: Postcolonialism and the sociological imagination*, Palgrave Macmillan, Basingstoke.

Bjola, C, 2005, 'Legitimating the use of force in international politics: A communicative action perspective', *European Journal of International Relations* 11(2), pp. 266–303.

Black, J, 2000, 'Proceduralizing regulation: Part I', *Oxford Journal of Legal Studies* 20(4), pp. 597–614.

Black, J, 2001, 'Proceduralizing regulation: Part II', *Oxford Journal of Legal Studies* 21(1), pp. 33–58.

Bohman, J, 1996, 'Two versions of the linguistic turn: Habermas and poststructuralism' in *Habermas and the unfinished project of modernity*, eds. M P d'Entrèves & S Benhabib, Polity, Cambridge, pp. 197–220.

Boltanski, L, Honneth, A & Celikates, R, 2014 [2009], 'Sociology of critique or critical theory? Luc Boltanski and Axel Honneth in conversation with Robin Celikates' in *The spirit of Luc Boltanski: Essays on the 'pragmatic sociology of critique'*, eds. S Susen & B S Turner, tr. S Susen, Anthem Press, London, pp. 561–589.

Boltanski, L, Rennes, J & Susen, S, 2010, 'La fragilité de la réalité. Entretien avec Luc Boltanski. Propos recueillis par Juliette Rennes et Simon Susen', *Mouvements* 64, pp. 151–166.

Boltanski, L, Rennes, R & Susen, S, 2014 [2010], 'The fragility of reality: Luc Boltanski in conversation with Juliette Rennes and Simon Susen' in *The spirit of Luc Boltanski: Essays on the 'pragmatic sociology of critique'*, eds. S Susen & B S Turner, tr. S Susen, Anthem Press, London, pp. 591–610.

Bourdieu, P, 1982, *Ce que parler veut dire. L'économie des échanges linguistiques*, Fayard, Paris.

Bourdieu, P, 1992, *Language and symbolic power*, ed. J B Thompson, trs. G Raymond & M Adamson, Polity, Cambridge.

Bourdieu, P, 1993 [1984], 'The linguistic market' in *Sociology in question*, P Bourdieu, tr. R Nice, Sage, London, pp. 78–89.

Boyer, R & Drache, D, eds., 1996, *States against markets: The limits of globalization*, Routledge, London.

Breen, K, 2004, '*Understanding Habermas: Communicative action and deliberative democracy*. By Erik Oddvar Eriksen and Jarle Weigård', *German Politics* 13(1), pp. 152–153.

Bridges, T, 1994, *The culture of citizenship: Inventing postmodern civic culture*, State University of New York Press, Albany.

Brittan, L, 1998, *Globalisation vs. sovereignty? The European response: The 1997 Rede lecture and related speeches*, Cambridge University Press, Cambridge.

Brookfield, S, 2005, 'Learning democratic reason: The adult education project of Jürgen Habermas', *Teachers College Record* 107(6), pp. 1127–1168.

Browne, C & Susen, S, 2014, 'Austerity and its antitheses: Practical negations of capitalist legitimacy', *South Atlantic Quarterly* 113(2), pp. 217–230.

Callinicos, A, 1989, 'The limits of communicative reason' in *Against postmodernism: A Marxist critique*, A Callinicos, Polity, Cambridge, pp. 92–120.

Centeno, M A & Cohen, N J, 2010, *Global capitalism: A sociological perspective*, Polity, Cambridge.

Chernilo, D, 2007, *A social theory of the nation-state: The political forms of modernity beyond methodological nationalism*, Routledge, London.

Chernilo, D, 2008, 'Classical sociology and the nation-state: A re-interpretation', *Journal of Classical Sociology* 8(1), pp. 27–43.

Chevallier, J, 2008 [2003], *L'État post-moderne*, 3e édition, LGDJ, Collection Droit et Société, Paris.

Chirico, J A, 2013, *Globalization: prospects and problems*, Sage, London.

Conover, P J & Searing, D D, 2005, 'Studying "everyday political talk" in the deliberative system', *Acta Politica* 40(3), pp. 269–283.

Cooke, M, 2000, 'Five arguments for deliberative democracy', *Political Studies* 48(5), pp. 947–969.

Crouch, C, Eder, K & Tambini, D, eds., 2001, *Citizenship, markets, and the state*, Oxford University Press, Oxford.

Crowder, G, 2013, *Theories of multiculturalism: An introduction*, Polity, Cambridge.

Cudworth, E, Hall, T & McGovern, J, 2007, *The modern state: Theories and ideologies*, Edinburgh University Press, Edinburgh.
Davies, W, 2014, *The limits of neoliberalism: Authority, sovereignty and the logic of competition*, Sage, London.
Deflem, M, 1994a, 'Social control and the theory of communicative action', *International Journal of the Sociology of Law* 22(4), pp. 355–373.
Deflem, M, 1994b, 'Introduction: Law in Habermas's theory of communicative action', *Philosophy & Social Criticism* 20(4), pp. 1–20.
Delanty, G, 2000, *Citizenship in a global age: Society, culture, politics*, Open University Press, Buckingham.
Dicken, P, 2011 [1986], *Global shift: Mapping the changing contours of the world economy*, 6th ed., Sage, London.
Drake, M S, 2010, *Political sociology for a globalizing world*, Polity, Cambridge.
Dunn, J, 2000, 'The state' in *The cunning of unreason: Making sense of politics*, J Dunn, HarperCollins, London, pp. 48–92.
Eriksen, E O & Weigård, J, 2003, *Understanding Habermas: Communicative action and deliberative democracy*, Continuum, London and New York.
Evans, P B, Rueschemeyer, D & Skocpol, T, eds., 1985, *Bringing the state back in*, Cambridge University Press, Cambridge.
Fairclough, N, 1995, *Critical discourse analysis: The critical study of language*, Longman, London.
Featherstone, M, Lash, S & Robertson, R, eds., 1995, *Global modernities*, Sage, London.
Ferrara, A, 2001, 'Of boats and principles: Reflections on Habermas's "constitutional democracy"', *Political Theory* 29(6), pp. 782–791.
Festenstein, M, 2004, 'Deliberative democracy and two models of pragmatism', *European Journal of Social Theory* 7(3), pp. 291–306.
Fillmore, C J, 1985, 'Linguistics as a tool for discourse analysis' in *Handbook of discourse analysis. Volume 1: Disciplines of discourse*, ed. T A van Dijk, Academic Press, London, pp. 11–39.
Franklin, S, Lury, C & Stacey, J, 2000, *Global nature, global culture*, Sage, London.
Fraser, N, 2007a, 'Transnationalizing the public sphere: On the legitimacy and efficacy of public opinion in a post-Westphalian world' in *Identities, affiliations, and allegiances*, eds. S Benhabib, I Shapiro & D Petranovi, Cambridge University Press, Cambridge, pp. 45–66.
Fraser, N, 2007b 'Re-framing justice in a globalizing world' in *(Mis)recognition, social inequality and social justice: Nancy Fraser and Pierre Bourdieu*, ed. T Lovell, Routledge, London, pp. 17–35.
Gamwell, F I, 1997, 'Habermas and Apel on communicative ethics: Their difference and the difference it makes', *Philosophy & Social Criticism* 23(2), pp. 21–45.
Gebauer, G, 2005, 'Praktischer Sinn und Sprache' in *Pierre Bourdieu: Deutsch-französische Perspektiven*, eds. C Colliot-Thélène, E François & G Gebauer, Suhrkamp, Frankfurt am Main, pp. 137–164.
Gill, G J, 2003, *The nature and development of the modern state*, Palgrave Macmillan, Basingstoke.
Goldhammer, A, 2001, 'Man in the mirror: Language, the enlightenment, and the postmodern' in *Postmodernism and the enlightenment: New perspectives in eighteenth-century French intellectual history*, ed. D Gordon, Routledge, New York, pp. 31–44.
Grant, C B, ed., 2003, *Rethinking communicative interaction: New interdisciplinary horizons*, John Benjamins, Amsterdam.
Guibentif, P, 1994, 'Approaching the production of law through Habermas's concept of communicative action', *Philosophy & Social Criticism* 20(4), pp. 45–70.
Günther, K, 1998, 'Communicative freedom, communicative power, and jurisgenesis' in *Habermas on law and democracy: Critical exchanges*, eds. M Rosenfeld & A Arato, University of California Press, Berkeley, CA, pp. 234–254.
Habermas, J, 1970, 'Towards a theory of communicative competence' *Inquiry* 13(4), pp. 360–375.
Habermas, J, 1976, 'Was heißt Universalpragmatik?' in *Sprachpragmatik und Philosophie*, ed. K O Apel, Suhrkamp, Frankfurt am Main, pp. 174–272.

Habermas, J, 1984 [1976], 'What is universal pragmatics?' in *Communication and the evolution of society*, J Habermas, tr. T McCarthy, Polity, Cambridge, pp. 1–68.

Habermas, J, 1985 [1984], 'Remarks on the concept of communicative action' in *Social Action*, eds. G Seebaß & R Tuomela, trs. Ruth Stanley & D. Reidel, Kluwer Academic Publishers, Dordrecht and Boston, pp. 151–178.

Habermas, J, 1987 [1965/1968], 'Knowledge and human interests: A general perspective' in *Knowledge and human interests*, J Habermas, tr. J J Shapiro, Polity, Cambridge, pp. 301–317.

Habermas, J, 1987 [1981]-a, *The theory of communicative action. Volume 2: Lifeworld and system: A critique of functionalist reason*, tr. T McCarthy, Polity, Cambridge.

Habermas, J, 1987 [1981]-b, *The theory of communicative action. Volume 1: Reason and the rationalization of society*, tr. T McCarthy, Polity, Cambridge.

Habermas, J, 1987 [1985], 'The undermining of Western rationalism through the critique of metaphysics: Martin Heidegger' in *The philosophical discourse of modernity*, J Habermas, tr. F Lawrence, Polity, Cambridge, pp. 131–160.

Habermas, J, 1988 [1967/1970], 'The linguistic approach' in *On the logic of the social sciences*, J Habermas, trs. S Weber Nicholsen & J A Stark, MIT Press, Cambridge, MA. pp. 117–143.

Habermas, J, 1990 [1983], *Moral consciousness and communicative action*, trs. C Lenhardt & S Weber Nicholsen, MIT Press, Cambridge, MA.

Habermas, J, 1992 [1988], *Postmetaphysical thinking: Philosophical essays*, tr. W M Hohengarten, MIT Press, Cambridge, MA.

Habermas, J, 1994, 'Postscript to *Faktizität und Geltung*', *Philosophy & Social Criticism* 20(4), pp. 135–150.

Habermas, J, 1996 [1992]-a, *Between facts and norms: Contributions to a discourse theory of law and democracy*, tr. W Rehg, Polity, Cambridge.

Habermas, J, 1996 [1992]-b, 'The sociological translation of the concept of deliberative politics' in *Between facts and norms: Contributions to a discourse theory of law and democracy*, J Habermas, tr. W Rehg, Polity, Cambridge, pp. 315–328.

Habermas, J, 1998a, 'Paradigms of law' in *Habermas on law and democracy: Critical exchanges*, eds. M Rosenfeld & A Arato, University of California Press, Berkeley, CA, pp. 13–25.

Habermas, J, 1998b, 'Reply to the symposium participants' in *Habermas on law and democracy: Critical exchanges*, eds. M Rosenfeld & A Arato, University of California Press, Berkeley, CA, pp. 381–452.

Habermas, J, 1999, 'The European nation-state and the pressures of globalization', *New Left Review* 235, pp. 46–59.

Habermas, J, 2001 [1984]-a, *On the pragmatics of social interaction: Preliminary studies in the theory of communicative action*, tr. B Fultner, Polity, Cambridge.

Habermas, J, 2001 [1984]-b, 'The phenomenological constitutive theory of society: The fundamental role of claims to validity and the monadological foundations of intersubjectivity' in *On the pragmatics of social interaction: Preliminary studies in the theory of communicative action*, J Habermas, tr. B Fultner, Polity, Cambridge, pp. 23–44.

Habermas, J, 2001 [1984]-c, 'Universal pragmatics: Reflections on a theory of communicative competence' in *On the pragmatics of social interaction: Preliminary studies in the theory of communicative action*, J Habermas, tr. B Fultner, Polity, Cambridge, pp. 67–84.

Habermas, J, 2001 [1984]-d, 'Truth and society: The discursive redemption of factual claims to validity' in *On the pragmatics of social interaction: Preliminary studies in the theory of communicative action*, J Habermas, tr. B Fultner, Polity, Cambridge, pp. 85–103.

Habermas, J, 2001 [1998], *The postnational constellation: political essays*, etc., tr. M Pensky, Polity, Cambridge.

Habermas, J, 2001a, *Kommunikatives Handeln und detranszendentalisierte Vernunft*, Reclam, Ditzingen, Stuttgart.

Habermas, J, 2001b, 'Constitutional democracy: A paradoxical union of contradictory principles?', *Political Theory* 29(6), pp. 766–781.

Habermas, J, 2003, 'Toward a cosmopolitan Europe', *Journal of Democracy* 14(4), pp. 86–100.
Habermas, J, 2004, 'Die Grenze zwischen Glauben und Wissen. Zur Wirkungsgeschichte and aktuellen Bedeutung von Kants Religionsphilosophie', *Revue de métaphysique et de morale* 4, pp. 460–484.
Habermas, J, 2005, 'Concluding comments on empirical approaches to deliberative politics', *Acta Politica* 40(3), pp. 384–392.
Hacking, I, 1975, *Why does language matter to philosophy?*, Cambridge University Press, Cambridge.
Hacking, I, 1982, 'Language, truth and reason' in *Rationality and Relativism*, eds. M Hollis & S Lukes, Blackwell, Oxford, pp. 48–66.
Hall, J A, 1986, *States in history*, Basil Blackwell, Oxford.
Hall, J A, 1994, *Coercion and consent: Studies on the modern state*, Polity Cambridge.
Hall, J & Ikenberry, G J, 1989, *The state*, Open University Press, Milton Keynes.
Harvey, D, 2006, *Spaces of global capitalism: Towards a theory of uneven geographical development*, Verso, London.
Hay, C, Lister, M & Marsh, D, eds., 2006, *The state: Theories and issues*, Palgrave Macmillan, Basingstoke.
Heath, J, 1998, 'What is a validity claim?', *Philosophy & Social Criticism* 24(4), pp. 23–41.
Heath, J, 2001, *Communicative action and rational choice*, MIT Press, Cambridge, MA.
Held, D, ed., 1985 [1983], *States and societies*, 2nd ed., Basil Blackwell in association with the Open University, Oxford.
Held, D, 1991, 'Democracy, the nation-state and the global system', *Economy and Society* 20(2), pp., 138–172.
Held, D, 1995, *Democracy and the global order: From the modern state to cosmopolitan governance*, Polity, Cambridge.
Hinsley, F H, 1986 [1966], *Sovereignty*, 2nd ed., Cambridge University Press, Cambridge.
Hirst, P, 1997, 'The international origins of national sovereignty' in *Politics and the ends of identity*, ed. Kathryn Dean, Aldershot: Ashgate, pp. 265–287.
Hirst, P & Thompson, G, 1995, 'Globalization and the future of the nation state', *Economy and Society* 24(3), pp. 408–442.
Hirst, P Q & Thompson, G, 1996, *Globalization in question: The international economy and the possibilities of governance*, Polity, Cambridge.
Holloway, J & Susen, S, 2013, 'Change the world by cracking capitalism? A critical encounter between John Holloway and Simon Susen', *Sociological Analysis* 7(1), pp. 23–42.
Hoogvelt, AMM, 1997, *Globalization and the postcolonial world: The new political economy of development*, Macmillan, Basingstoke.
Hutchings, K & Dannreuther, R, eds., 1999 [1998], *Cosmopolitan citizenship*, Macmillan Press, Basingstoke.
Ilting, K-H, 1990 [1982], 'The basis of the validity of moral norms' in *The communicative ethics controversy*, eds. S Benhabib & F R Dallmayr, MIT Press, Cambridge, MA, pp. 220–255.
Isin, E F, ed., 2000, *Democracy, citizenship and the global city*, Routledge, London.
Jäger, L, 2002, 'Medialität und Mentalität. Die Sprache als Medium des Geistes' in *Gibt es eine Sprache hinter dem Sprechen?*, eds. S Krämer & E König, Suhrkamp, Frankfurt am Main, pp. 45–75.
James, M R, 2003, 'Communicative action, strategic action, and inter-group dialogue', *European Journal of Political Theory* 2(2), pp. 157–182.
Janoski, T, 1998, *Citizenship and civil society: A framework of rights and obligations in liberal, traditional, and social democratic regimes*, Cambridge University Press, Cambridge.
Janssen, D & Raphaël K, 2005, 'Online forums and deliberative democracy', *Acta Politica* 40(3), pp. 317–335.
Jessop, B, 2007, *State power*, Polity, Cambridge.
Johnson, J, 1991, 'Habermas on strategic and communicative action', *Political Theory* 19(2), pp. 181–201.

Johnson, J, 1993, 'Is talk really cheap? Prompting conversation between critical theory and rational choice', *American Political Science Review* 87(1), pp. 74–86.

Jullien, F, 2014 [2008], *On the universal: The uniform, the common and dialogue between cultures*, trs. M Richardson & K Fijalkowski, Polity, Cambridge.

Keane, J, ed., 1988, *Civil society and the state: New European perspectives*, Verso, London.

Kelly, P J, ed., 2002, *Multiculturalism reconsidered: Culture and equality and its critics*, Polity, Cambridge.

Khory, K R, ed., 2012, *Global migration: Challenges in the twenty-first century*, Palgrave Macmillan, Basingstoke.

King, R & Kendall, G, 2004, *The state, democracy and globalization*, Palgrave Macmillan, Basingstoke.

Kirk, N, 1997 [1994], 'History, language, ideas and postmodernism: A materialist view' in *The postmodern history reader*, ed. K Jenkins, Routledge, London, pp. 315–340.

Krämer, S, 2002, 'Sprache und Sprechen oder: Wie sinnvoll ist die Unterscheidung zwischen einem Schema und seinem Gebrauch? Ein Überblick' in *Gibt es eine Sprache hinter dem Sprechen?*, eds. S Krämer & E König, Suhrkamp, Frankfurt am Main, pp. 97–125.

Krämer, S & König, E, eds., 2002, *Gibt es eine Sprache hinter dem Sprechen?*, Suhrkamp, Frankfurt am Main.

Krasner, S D, 1988, 'Sovereignty: An institutional perspective', *Comparative political studies* 21(1), pp. 66–94.

Kymlicka, W, 2005, 'Liberal multiculturalism: Western models, global trends and Asian debates' in *Multiculturalism in Asia*, eds. W Kymlicka & B He, Oxford University Press, Oxford, pp. 22–55.

Kymlicka, W, 2007, *Multicultural odysseys: Navigating the new international politics of diversity*, Oxford University Press, Oxford.

Kymlicka, W & He, B, eds., 2005, *Multiculturalism in Asia*, Oxford University Press, Oxford.

Lachmann, R, 2010, *States and power*, Polity, Cambridge.

Lafont, C, 1993, *La razón como lenguaje. Una revisión del 'giro lingüístico' en la filosofía del lenguaje alemana*, Visor, Madrid.

Lafont, C, 1997, *Lenguaje y apertura del mundo. El giro lingüístico de la hermenéutica de Heidegger*, Alianza Universidad, Madrid.

Lafont, C, 1999 [1993], *The linguistic turn in hermeneutic philosophy*, tr. J Medina, MIT Press, Cambridge, MA.

Lash, S & Lury, C, 2007, *Global culture industry: The mediation of things*, Polity, Cambridge.

Lee, D, 1992, *Competing discourses: Perspective and ideology in language*, Longman, London.

Lutz, H, Herrera Vivar, M T & Supik, L, eds., 2011, *Framing intersectionality: Debates on a multi-faceted concept in gender studies*, Ashgate, Farnham.

Mann, M, 1994 [1987], 'Ruling class strategies and citizenship' in *Citizenship: critical concepts*, eds. B S Turner & P Hamilton, vol. 1, Routledge, London, pp. 63–79.

Marcos, Sous-Commandant, 1997, 'Sept pièces du puzzle néolibéral : la quatrième guerre mondiale a commencé', *Le Monde Diplomatique*, août, pp. 4–5.

Marshall, T H, 1964 [1963], *Class, citizenship, and social development*, intro. S M Lipset, Doubleday, Garden City, NY.

Marshall, T H, 1981, *The right to welfare and other essays*, intro. R Pinker, Heinemann Educational, London.

Martell, L, 2010, *The sociology of globalization*, Polity, Cambridge.

May, T, 1996, 'The linguistic turn in critical theory' in *Situating social theory*, T May, Open University Press, Buckingham, pp. 139–157.

Mayo, M, 2005, *Global citizens: Social movements and the challenge of globalization*, Zed,. London.

McCarthy, T, 1973, 'A theory of communicative competence', *Philosophy of the Social Sciences* 3(2), pp. 135–156.

Miller, T, 1993, *The well-tempered self: Citizenship, culture, and the postmodern subject*, Johns Hopkins University Press, Baltimore.

Mittelman, J H, ed., 1996, *Globalization: critical reflections*, Lynne Rienner Publishers, Boulder, CO.
Modood, T, 2013 [2007], *Multiculturalism: A civic idea*, 2nd ed., Polity, Cambridge.
Mouffe, C, 1993, *The return of the political*, Verso, London.
Mouzelis, N P, 2008, *Modern and postmodern social theorizing: Bridging the divide*, Cambridge University Press, Cambridge.
Nederveen Pieterse, J, 1995, 'Globalization as hybridization' in *Global modernities*, eds. M Featherstone, S Lash & R Robertson, Sage, London, pp. 45–68.
Nemoianu, V, 2010, *Postmodernism & cultural identities: Conflicts and coexistence*, Catholic University of America Press, Washington, DC.
Niemi, J I, 2005, 'Habermas and validity claims', *International Journal of Philosophical Studies* 13(2), pp. 227–244.
Outhwaite, W, 2006, *The future of society*, Blackwell, Oxford.
Outhwaite, W, 2009 [1994], *Habermas: A critical introduction*, 2nd ed., Polity, Cambridge.
Outhwaite, W & Ray, L J, 2005 *Social theory and postcommunism*, Blackwell, Oxford.
Palast, G, Oppenheim, J & MacGregor, T, 2002, *Democracy and regulation: How the public can govern essential services*, Pluto, London.
Parekh, B C, 2008, *A new politics of identity: Political principles for an interdependent world*, Palgrave Macmillan, Basingstoke.
Paulus, A L, 2001, 'International law after postmodernism: Towards renewal or decline of international law?', *Leiden Journal of International Law* 14(4), pp. 727–755.
Pellizzoni, L, 2001, 'The myth of the best argument: Power, deliberation and reason', *The British Journal of Sociology* 52(1), pp. 59–86.
Petrella, R, 1996, 'Globalization and internationalization: The dynamics of the emerging world order' in *States against markets: The limits of globalization*, eds. R Boyer & D Drache, Routledge, London, pp. 62–83.
Phillips, A, 2007, *Multiculturalism without culture*, Princeton University Press, Princeton, NJ.
Pierson, C, 2004 [1996], *The modern state*, 2nd ed., Routledge, London.
Piketty, T, 2013, *Le capital au XXIe siècle*, Éditions du Seuil, Paris.
Poggi, G, 1978, *The development of the modern state: A sociological introduction*, Hutchinson, London.
Poggi, G, 1990, *The state: Its nature, development and prospects*, Stanford University Press, Stanford, CA.
Power, M K., 1998, 'Habermas and the counterfactual imagination' in *Habermas on law and democracy: critical exchanges*, eds. M Rosenfeld & A Arato, University of California Press, Berkeley, CA, pp. 207–225.
Preuss, U K, 1998, 'Communicative power and the concept of law' in *Habermas on law and democracy: Critical exchanges*, eds. M Rosenfeld & A Arato, University of California Press, Berkeley, CA, pp. 323–335.
Rasmussen, D M, 1994, 'How is valid law possible? A review of *Faktizität und Geltung* by Jürgen Habermas', *Philosophy & Social Criticism* 20(4), pp. 21–44.
Redner, H, 2013, *Beyond civilization: Society, culture, and the individual in the age of gobalization*, Transaction Publishers, New Brunswick.
Reid, A, Gill, J & Sears, A M, eds., 2010, *Globalization, the nation-state and the citizen: Dilemmas and directions for civics and citizenship education*, Routledge, London.
Rigotti, E, 1979, *Principi di teoria linguistica*, La Scuola, Brescia.
Ritzer, G, 2013 [1993], *The McDonaldization of society, 20th Anniversary Edition*, 7th ed., Sage, London.
Robertson, R, 1995, 'Glocalization: Time–space and homogeneity–heterogeneity' in *Global modernities*, eds. M Featherstone, S Lash & R Robertson, Sage, London, pp. 25–44.
Rorty, R, ed., 1967a, *The linguistic turn: Essays in philosophical method*, University of Chicago Press, Chicago.

Rorty, R, 1967b, 'Metaphilosophical difficulties of linguistic philosophy' in *The linguistic turn: Essays in philosophical method*, ed. R Rorty, University of Chicago Press, Chicago, pp. 1–39.

Rosenfeld, M & Arato, A, eds., 1998, *Habermas on law and democracy: Critical exchanges*, University of California Press, Berkeley, CA.

Rossi-Landi, F, 1974 [1972], *Ideologías de la relatividad lingüística*, tr. Juan Antonio Vasco, Ediciones Nueva Visión, Buenos Aires.

Sassen, S, 1996, *Losing control? Sovereignty in an age of globalization*, Columbia University Press, New York.

Sassen, S, 2004, 'Local actors in global politics', *Current Sociology* 52(4), pp. 649–670.

Schöttler, P, 1997, 'Wer hat Angst vor dem "linguistic turn"?', *Geschichte und Gesellschaft*, Vandenhoeck & Ruprecht, Göttingen. Jahrgang, Heft 1, pp. 134–151.

Schweppenhäuser, G, 1997, 'Paradoxien des Multikulturalismus' in *Postmoderne Kultur? Soziologische und philosophische Perspektiven*, eds. C Rademacher & G Schweppenhäuser, Westdeutscher Verlag, Opladen, pp. 181–195.

Sintomer, Y, 1999, 'Bourdieu et Habermas' in *La démocratie impossible ? Politique et modernité chez Weber et Habermas*, Y Sintomer, La Découverte & Syros, Paris, pp. 158–162.

Skinner, Q, 1989, 'The state' in *Political innovation and conceptual change*, eds. T Ball, J Farr & R L Hanson, Cambridge University Press, Cambridge, pp. 90–131.

Skinner, Q & Stråth, B, eds., 2003, *States and citizens: History, theory, prospects*, Cambridge University Press, Cambridge.

Sklair, L, 1995 [1991], *Sociology of the global system*, 2nd ed., Prentice Hall/Harvester Wheatsheaf, London.

Sloterdijk, P, 2013 [2005], *In the world interior of capital: For a philosophical theory of globalization*, tr. W Hoban, Polity, Cambridge.

Smith, W, 2007, 'Cosmopolitan citizenship: Virtue, irony and worldliness', *European Journal of Social Theory* 10(1), pp. 37–52.

Soederberg, S, Menz, G & Cerny, P G, eds., 2005, *Internalizing globalization: The rise of neoliberalism and the decline of national varieties of capitalism*, Palgrave Macmillan, Basingstoke.

Sørensen, G, 2003, *The transformation of state: Beyond the myth of retreat*, Palgrave Macmillan, Basingstoke.

Spruyt, H, 1994, *The sovereign state and its competitors: An analysis of systems change*, Princeton University Press, Princeton, NJ.

Starkey, G, 2007, *Balance and bias in journalism: Representation, regulation and democracy*, Palgrave Macmillan, Basingstoke.

Steinhoff, U, 2001, *Kritik der kommunikativen Rationalität. Eine Gesamtdarstellung und Analyse der kommunikationstheoretischen jüngeren Kritischen Theorie*, Die Deutsche Bibliothek, Marsberg.

Stryker, S D, 2000, 'Communicative action in history', *European Journal of Social Theory* 3(2), pp. 215–234.

Susen, S, 2007, *The foundations of the social: Between critical theory and reflexive sociology*, Bardwell Press, Oxford.

Susen, S, 2008a, 'Poder y anti-poder (I–III)', *Erasmus: Revista para el diálogo intercultural* 10(1), pp. 49–90.

Susen, S, 2008b, 'Poder y anti-poder (IV–V)', *Erasmus: Revista para el diálogo intercultural* 10(2), pp. 133–180.

Susen, S, 2009a, 'Between emancipation and domination: Habermasian reflections on the empowerment and disempowerment of the human subject', *Pli: The Warwick Journal of Philosophy* 20, pp. 80–110.

Susen, S, 2009b, 'The philosophical significance of binary categories in Habermas's discourse ethics', *Sociological Analysis* 3(2), pp. 97–125.

Susen, S, 2010a, 'Los movimientos sociales en las sociedades complejas' in *Ciudadanía territorial y movimientos sociales. Historia y nuevas problemáticas en el escenario latinoamericano y mundial*, eds. C Basconzuelo, T Morel & S Susen, Ediciones del ICALA, Río Cuarto, pp. 149–226.

Susen, S, 2010b, 'The transformation of citizenship in complex societies', *Journal of Classical Sociology* 10(3), pp. 259–285.
Susen, S, 2010c, 'Remarks on the concept of critique in Habermasian thought', *Journal of Global Ethics* 6(2), pp. 103–126.
Susen, S, 2010d, 'Meadian reflections on the existential ambivalence of human selfhood', *Studies in Social and Political Thought*, 17, pp. 62–81.
Susen, S, 2011a, '*Kritische Gesellschaftstheorie* or *kritische Gesellschaftspraxis*? Robin Celikates, *Kritik als soziale Praxis. Gesellschaftliche Selbstverständigung und kritische Theorie* (Frankfurt am Main, Campus Verlag, 2009)', *Archives Européennes de Sociologie/European Journal of Sociology* 52(3), pp. 447–463.
Susen, S, 2011b, 'Critical notes on Habermas's theory of the public sphere', *Sociological Analysis* 5(1), pp. 37–62.
Susen, S, 2011c, 'Epistemological tensions in Bourdieu's conception of social science', *Theory of Science* 33(1), pp. 43–82.
Susen, S, 2012a, '"Open Marxism" against and beyond the "Great Enclosure"? Reflections on how (not) to crack capitalism', *Journal of Classical Sociology* 12(2), pp. 281–331.
Susen, S, 2012b, 'Une sociologie pragmatique de la critique est-elle possible? Quelques réflexions sur *De la critique* de Luc Boltanski', *Revue Philosophique de Louvain* 110(4), pp. 685–728.
Susen, S, ed., 2013a, *Special issue: 'Bourdieu and language'*, *Social Epistemology*, 27(3–4), pp. 195–393.
Susen, S, 2013b, 'Comments on Patrick Baert & Filipe Carreira da Silva's *Social Theory in the Twentieth Century and Beyond* – Towards a "Hermeneutics-Inspired Pragmatism"?', *Distinktion: Scandinavian Journal of Social Theory* 14(1), pp. 80–101.
Susen, S, 2013c, 'Introduction: Bourdieu and language', *Social Epistemology* 27(3–4), pp. 195–198.
Susen, S, 2013d, 'Bourdieusian reflections on language: Unavoidable conditions of the real speech situation', *Social Epistemology* 27(3–4), pp. 199–246.
Susen, S, 2013e, 'A reply to my critics: The critical spirit of Bourdieusian language', *Social Epistemology* 27(3–4), pp. 323–393.
Susen, S, 2014 [2012], 'Is there such a thing as a "pragmatic sociology of critique"? Reflections on Luc Boltanski's *On Critique*' in *The spirit of Luc Boltanski: Essays on the 'pragmatic sociology of critique'*, eds. S Susen & B S Turner, tr. S Susen, Anthem Press, London, pp. 173–210.
Susen, S, 2014a, '15 theses on power', *Philosophy and Society* 25(3), pp. 7–28.
Susen, S, 2014b, 'Reflections on ideology: Lessons from Pierre Bourdieu and Luc Boltanski', *Thesis Eleven* 124(1), pp. 90–113.
Susen, S, 2015a, *The 'postmodern turn' in the social sciences*, Palgrave Macmillan, Basingstoke.
Susen, S, 2015b, 'Emancipation' in *The encyclopedia of political thought*, vol. 3, eds. M T Gibbons, D Coole, E Ellis & K Ferguson, Wiley-Blackwell, Oxford, pp. 1024–1038.
Susen, S, 2017, 'Remarks on the nature of justification: A socio-pragmatic perspective', in *Justification, evaluation and critique in the study of organizations: Contributions from French pragmatist sociology*, eds. C Cloutier, J-P Gond & B Leca, Research in the sociology of organizations 52, Emerald, Bingley, pp. 349–381.
Taylor, C, 1991 [1986], 'Language and society' in *Communicative action: Essays on Jürgen Habermas's 'The theory of communicative action'*, eds. A Honneth & H Joas, trs. J Gaines & D L Jones, Polity, Cambridge, pp. 23–35.
Taylor, C & Gutmann, A, 1992, *Multiculturalism and 'the politics of recognition': An essay*, with commentary by A Gutmann, Princeton University Press, Princeton, NJ.
Taylor, D, 1989, 'Citizenship and social power', *Critical Social Policy* 9(26), pp. 19–31.
Thompson, J, 2000, 'A defence of communicative ethics', *The Journal of Political Philosophy* 2(3), pp. 240–255.
Thompson, J B, 1982, 'Universal pragmatics' in *Habermas: critical debates*, eds. J B Thompson & D Held, Macmillan, London, pp. 116–133.
Thompson, J B, 1983, 'Rationality and social rationalization: An assessment of Habermas's theory of communicative action', *Sociology* 17(2), pp. 278–294.

Thornhill, C, 2013, 'Natural law, state formation and the foundations of social theory', *Journal of Classical Sociology* 13(2), pp. 197–221.
Tomlinson, J, 1999, *Globalization and culture*, Polity, Cambridge.
Turner, B S, 1994 [1990], 'Outline of a theory of citizenship' in *Citizenship: Critical Concepts*, vol. 1, eds. B S Turner & P Hamilton, Routledge, London, pp. 199–226.
Turner, B S, 2009, 'T.H. Marshall, social rights and English national identity', *Citizenship Studies* 13(1), pp. 65–73.
van Creveld, M, 1999, *The rise and decline of the state*, Cambridge University Press, Cambridge.
Vandenberg, A, ed., 2000, *Citizenship and democracy in a global era*, Macmillan Press, Basingstoke.
Warnke, G, 1995, 'Communicative rationality and cultural values' in *The Cambridge companion to Habermas*, ed. S K White, Cambridge University Press, Cambridge, pp. 120–142.
Wellmer, A, 1977 [1976], 'Communications and emancipation: Reflections on the "linguistic turn" in critical theory' in *On Critical Theory*, ed. J O'Neill, Heinemann Educational, London, pp. 231–263.
Wertheim, W F, 1992, 'The state and the dialectics of emancipation' in *Emancipations, modern and postmodern*, ed. Jan Nederveen Pieterse, Sage, London, pp. 257–281.
Whitton, B J, 1992, 'Universal pragmatics and the formation of Western civilization: A critique of Habermas's theory of human moral evolution', *History & Theory* 31(3), pp. 299–313.
Williams, B A & Matheny, A R, 1995, *Democracy, dialogue, and environmental disputes: The contested languages of social regulation*, Yale University Press, New Haven, CT.
Williams, S, Bradley, H, Devadson, R & Erickson, M, 2013, *Globalization and work*, Polity, Cambridge.
Yar, M, 2001, 'Recognition and the politics of human(e) desire', *Theory, Culture & Society* 18(2–3), pp. 57–76.
Young, I M, 1994 [1989], 'Polity and group difference: A critique of the ideal of universal citizenship' in *Citizenship: Critical concepts*, vol. 2, eds. B S Turner & P Hamilton, Routledge, London, pp. 386–408.
Young, I M, 1997a, 'Asymmetrical reciprocity: On moral respect, wonder and enlarged thought' in *Intersecting voices: Dilemmas of gender, political philosophy, and policy*, I M Young, Princeton University Press, Princeton, NJ, pp. 38–59.
Young, I M, 1997b, 'Communication and the other: Beyond deliberative democracy' in *Intersecting voices: Dilemmas of gender, political philosophy, and policy*, I M Young, Princeton University Press, Princeton, NJ, pp. 60–74.

4
Michel Foucault
Discourse, power/knowledge and the modern subject

Reiner Keller

Introduction

French philosopher Michel Foucault (1926–1984) is among the most influential thinkers of the twentieth century. His ideas exhibit an extraordinary reach across the social sciences and the humanities, even gaining considerable popularity outside academia.[1] Foucault has been considered a structuralist, a historian, a philosopher, a sociologist, a left radical, an anarchist, a threat to youth, a neoconservative, a nihilist and a positivist, among many other labels. In a revealing interview, he conceived of himself as an 'experimenter', not as a theoretical thinker (Foucault 2000b). Experimenting implied, according to Foucault, not seeking to confirm a priori established theory via empirical proof, but to enter fields of inquiry with curiosity and to emerge from them as a different person, with new ideas and concepts. The focus of his work was on the historical and empirical genealogy of the modern subject (Foucault 1983, 2000c).

From the late 1940s, Foucault studied philosophy and psychology in Paris at the prestigious *École Normale Supérieure* and at the *Sorbonne* University. His habilitation thesis, written in the late 1950s, became his first widely known book, *History of madness* (Foucault 2009a [1961]). His 1966 book, *The order of things* (Foucault 2001a), was a veritable public event throughout France and sold several hundreds of thousands of copies. After professorships in Clermont-Ferrand (France), Tunis (Tunisia), and Paris-Vincennes (France), Foucault in 1970 was awarded a professorship in the *History of Systems of Thought* at the most prestigious academic institution in France, the *Collège de France* in Paris. His annual series of public lectures were 'must-go' events. Through his academic work and political engagements, Foucault became an iconic figure of fresh and emancipatory thinking all over the world.

The reception of Foucault's writings has varied widely. His outstanding and innovative originality results from his turning philosophy from theoretical and speculative thinking into an empirical and historical discipline. This is to be understood against the background of the most influential and hegemonic French intellectual movements of his time. First, there was the *philosophy of the subject*, as represented, among others, by leading French philosopher, writer, and public intellectual Jean-Paul Sartre (1905–1980) and his work on *existentialism*.[2]

Philosophies of the subject seek to grasp the very substance of what the universal or transcendental subject is, regardless of historical, social and cultural contexts. Sartre's existentialism claimed the absolute ethical responsibility of the free human subject, thrown into the world, where it has to act and make moral choices according to its own will. Second, and in complete contrast, there were *Hegelian and Marxist philosophies of history* and the intellectual movement of *structuralism*, led by French ethnologist and anthropologist Claude Lévi-Strauss (1908–2009). Structuralism was based on the theory of language as a system of differences as established by Swiss linguist Ferdinand de Saussure (1857–1913), inspired by the sociology of Émile Durkheim (1858–1917). With branches in Marxism (Louis Althusser, 1918–1990), psychoanalysis (Jacques Lacan, 1901–1981), linguistics, semiotics and cultural theory (Roland Barthes, 1915–1980), structuralism asserted the function of pre-established systems of differences as hidden forces that organise human life and practices.

Foucault, although flirting with structuralism in the early 1960s, essentially opposed philosophies of history and structuralism as well as philosophies of the subject. Instead, he argued for, and established, a third space of historical inquiry and analysis, which accounted for the empirical becoming and continuous transformation of modes of existence of human subjects and orders of practice.[3] He transformed theoretical philosophy of the subject into empirical research on historical subject formation and situated subjectivity, and the philosophy of history and structuralist thinking into historical research on contingent constellations of heterogeneous elements and practices. In so doing, he established a huge range of now-famous analytic and diagnostic concepts, including *discourse, dispositive, power/knowledge, archaeology, genealogy, discipline, biopower, governmentality* and many others. These were not arbitrary creations *ex nihilo*. They emerged out of concrete research interests and outcomes that relied upon several intellectually close thinkers. Foucault was influenced by philosophers Immanuel Kant (1724–1804) and Friedrich Nietzsche (1844–1900), his mentor, philosopher of science Georges Canguilhem (1904–1995), the historian and cultural anthropologist Georges Dumézil (1898–1986), as well as by the French *Annales School in History*, the *philosophy of language* and *American pragmatism*.[4] The following text discusses first the *general concern and intent* of Foucault's work. Second, it considers his methodology and, third, his concept of discourse. A fourth section explains his *analytics of power*. In the guise of a conclusion, a fifth and final section points to his *legacy* and *current developments*.

Concern and intent

Foucault owes the extraordinary impact of his work to his impressive material analyses and conceptual innovations. His research examined the history of accounting for the reasonable subject through the separation of sanity from insanity (Foucault 2008, 2009a), of the healthy human body (Foucault 1994), of the emerging importance of the modern subject in the humanities (Foucault 2001a), of illegal action, discipline and punishment (Foucault 1995), and of 'normal vs. abnormal' sexuality (Foucault 1998). As he was primarily interested in the historical constitution of modern subjectivity, he collected data mostly from the seventeenth century to the nineteenth century in France, the period generally recognised as the establishment of the modern subject and society. Foucault (1983; 2000b; 2000c) explained that each of his historical inquiries followed a different rationale, shaped by the specific questions and objects he was interested in. He therefore compiled all kinds of data according to his research interests – and not in order to build up 'representative samples'. Furthermore, he noted the focal point of his work: across such different fields of institutional, organisational, scientific, juridical and administrative practices, his analyses were guided by his core interest in the historically shifting formations of 'modern subjects'. How did the actors in science, law, politics and so on define and identify the insane, the sick body, the criminal subject, the sexually perverse? And how did they treat the 'abnormal'? The so-called modern subject is revealed as a bundle of empirical and historical formations that take place in and between institutions, discourses and practices. In his late works, Foucault (1990a, 1990b) adds an interest in ethically responsible behaviour via technologies of the self (Foucault 2000a; Martin, Hutton & Gutman 1988), analysing advice books for ethically sound male behaviour in ancient Greek and Roman culture.

Such a project was not conceived of as a purely academic or intellectual endeavour. Referring to Immanuel Kant's concept of 'critique' and discussion of 'enlightenment', Foucault (1984, 2007) claims to establish a *history of the present*, of the historical becoming of our current moment, especially focusing on a *critical ontology of ourselves*, the modern subjects. This 'critical ontology' reveals the contingent historical constellations and transformations that brought about modern subjectivities – demonstrating that there is neither determining nature and essence nor ontological necessity involved. Nor does the idea of *critique* here point to Marxist versions of ideological critique, or to the Frankfurt School of Critical Theory. Rather, Foucault refers to the analyses of conditions of possibility of some phenomenon. The difference to Kant in this is Foucault's turn towards empirical and historical inquiry instead of philosophical introspection. Foucault's critical intent aims to make visible the historical contingency of the present and 'to show people that they are much freer than they feel' (Foucault 1988, p. 10). Such an *ethos* of research is grounded in a Foucauldian constructivist project of enlightenment, understood as a never-ending inquiry into the given conditions of power/knowledge and their historical contingency. Because history is not a conditioned movement towards better life and progress, but a discontinuous series of contingent historical transformations of power/knowledge regimes, the work of critical ontology can never come to an end.

Methodology

Given his focus on historical processes of subject formation and his critical intent, what then is Foucault's general 'methodology of experimenting'?[5] Subsequent work in history or the social sciences has drawn upon several core concepts and upon his general 'mode of thinking', often in a rather loose way, while discourse research has concentrated mostly upon his 1969 methodological book *The archaeology of knowledge* (Foucault 2010a) as an account of his general methods. That book had a somewhat programmatic tone. Foucault tried to give a systematic account of what he did in his earlier work. But he seldom returned to this work, disputed its rationale and preferred the perspective of *genealogy* (see p. 71) in his later writings. In their comprehensive interpretation of Foucault's work, Hubert Dreyfus and Paul Rabinow (1983, pp. 104–125) account for the Foucauldian methodology as 'interpretive analytics'. This is an appropriate description of his strategy of research and analysis. *Interpretation* here does not refer to some strategy of text analysis, but to a more general approach involving the creation of far-reaching diagnostic concepts (like 'governmentality') for larger historical constellations and patterns of practices. Analytics points towards the way Foucault approaches his research themes. Here, it is important to note that Foucault avoids theory or pre-established theorising when carrying out empirical research and analysing data. This is quite the opposite of, for example, a Marxist perspective. Analytics refers to a procedure of splitting up apparently coherent unities, looking for complex constellations and empirical relations between heterogeneous elements.

What is his concrete way of doing research? As philosophers and historians attacked him for being too close to empirical reality for solid analytical distance, yet not close enough for sound research, he tried to explain why he argued a problem-driven approach on a middle-ground level (Foucault 1980b). Foucault generally assumes the relevance and performance of institutions, discourses and practices. He then starts with a particular research interest inspired by contemporary social phenomena, such as psychiatric treatment of 'insane' people, the prisoner movement, or prosecution of 'illegal (homo)sexuality'. The next step is collecting all kinds of available and relevant data from the historical period considered most important for the present condition – such as documents, reports, paintings, novels, laws, institutional orders, academic writing, proceedings of juristic disputes – which purport to deal with these questions in a given period of time. In order to account for the points of interest that would lead into inquiry, Foucault proposed the idea of *problematisation* and the related term *eventualisation* (see Foucault 1991, p. 76). Why and how did insanity become, at a specific moment in recent historical time, a problem in need of institutional work and solutions that then led to our modern dispositives for dealing with the insane? Through which particular social or institutional practices and epistemic procedures did it appear on society's agenda as an 'event to act upon'? Why and how did the relation between criminal acts and practices of punishment become a problem at the end of the eighteenth century? How do transformations in historical periods occur, if we do not assume a natural mode of progression? How can we compare them? And how can our research contribute to make something an event on today's agenda? The experimental part of Foucault's thinking could be resumed as follows:

- Consider your case in a pragmatic way as an opportunity for new experience.
- Return from your analysis with new diagnostic concepts which make you (and others) see the phenomenon at the heart of your inquiry in a different way.
- Do not dip into *hermeneutics of suspicion* (Ricœur 1970), as in Marxist, Freudian, Heideggerian, or structuralist thinking, in which a piece of given data is accounted for in terms of a pre-established theoretical model, for example, the relationships of production, or the ego, id and super-ego structure.
- Avoid mono-causality or cause-effect thinking as an explanation and look for historical ruptures or *discontinuities* (rather than continuities) as well as for *causal multiplication*, which implies accounting for the multiple, heterogeneous and perhaps conflicting – but always singular – elements that constitute a given historical constellation.

There are two main conceptual tools Foucault uses in his empirical work, *discourse* and *dispositive*. Both are heuristic devices intended to somehow name and fix the elements of his inquiries. *Discourse* refers to institutional and language-based modes of meaning-making and ordering of people, objects and practices. It will be explained in detail in the next section. *Dispositive*, since the 1970s, has referred to a network of heterogeneous, but related, elements such as texts, laws, buildings, practices, legal and procedural measures, organised processes, objects – in short: sayings, doings and materialities – assembled to solve or treat an 'urgency', a problem, identified via occurring processes of problematisation. The term 'dispositif' is common in French; it refers to an ensemble of measures that is made available for a specific purpose, such as for a political, economic, or technical undertaking. For example, in *The will to knowledge*, Foucault (1998, p. 106) talks about the *dispositif d'alliance* as a particular institution to organise 'relations of sex', which included strategic marriage in order to maintain property (kingdoms, industries, farms). A dispositive is a complex of heterogeneous, but related, elements (actors, discourses, practices, objects), drawn together as strategies, without strategic masterplan, to intervene into some 'problem to be solved'. This, for example, might include laws, architectural manifestations – such as the prison design concept in Jeremy Bentham's *Panopticon* – practices of surveillance, discipline and punishment, sacramental confession (Foucault 1990a), as well as other *practices*. As a methodological device, *dispositive* allows for an analytical perspective on the different elements appearing in descriptions of historical events, or constituting contemporary interventions into society and nature.

In the 1960s, Foucault, working at the cross-roads of philosophy, history and historical sociology (of knowledge), called his perspective *archaeology* in order to distinguish it from the established history of ideas, people, institutions and big events. From the 1970s, he preferred the notion of *genealogy*, without completely abandoning the former (Foucault 1984, 2000c, 2007). *Archaeology* referred to the usages of this term in the works of Immanuel Kant, Georges Canguilhem and Georges Dumézil. It is conceived as a methodological device or research perspective that implies inquiring into a particular historical constellation and its elements considered as 'monuments' (a term used by Georges Canguilhem).[6] This implies, much as in the academic discipline of archaeology, accounting for the socio-cultural patterns of a given historical moment through an analysis of its immanent historical situatedness. A case in point is his book *The order of things*, which analyses patterns of scientific knowledge-making in three distinct historical periods. However, influenced by the social protest movements of the late 1960s and early 1970s, Foucault shifted his attention to the analytic strategy of *genealogy*. This perspective, taken from Friedrich Nietzsche, traces the discontinuities and transformations of historical constellations – which can be identified as *regimes of power-knowledge* (see below) – through time. As with Nietzsche, it avoids both the idea of a single point of origin far back in history and the related (Hegelian or Marxist) ideas of ongoing development and progress, starting from that original point. *Genealogy* instead is about *games of power* and *games of truth*, about conflict, struggle, domination and historical transformation, without implying a trajectory towards brighter futures.

A final point to discuss here is the question of data. Reference to data is important in Foucault and his move from theoretical philosophy to empirical research. In a famous statement, he considered himself to be a 'happy positivist' (Foucault 2010a, p. 125). This ironic confession implicitly addressed a harsh critique of his previous work as 'having a positivist style', voiced by a long-standing intellectual enemy, French feminist philosopher and writer Simone de Beauvoir (1908–1986). In so doing, Foucault pointed to his strong commitment to concrete work on empirical data. Such data were available basically as texts (books, documents, leaflets, proceedings, etc.), and sometimes as paintings or photographs. He worked through textual data much like historians do, via close reading, guided by analytical questions.[7] His detailed pre-iconographic account of the figural elements of the painting *Las Meninas* by *Velasquez* (1599–1660) is a good illustration (Foucault 2001a). He then developed concepts in order to name what was done and accounted for in the (mostly written) documents: patterns of practices, elements of processes, ordering of perspectives. In fact, the chapter subtitles of much of his work indicate such classification procedures and category building out of data, which seem close to some versions of today's grounded theory methodology in the social sciences. Two examples will illustrate this. In *Discipline and punish*, Foucault (1995, pp. 141–149) discusses 'the art of distributions'. This subtitle can be considered as a category that emerged out of empirical analysis (close reading, sorting and category building). He explains what he means by such 'arts of distribution' in accounting for and quoting different excerpts from historical texts. Here is one example presented under the quoted heading:

> Jean-Baptiste de La Salle dreamt of a classroom in which the spatial distribution might provide a whole series of distinctions at once: according to the pupils' progress, worth, character, application, cleanliness and parents' fortune. [...] Each of the pupils will have his place assigned to him and none of them will leave it or change it except on the order or with the consent of the school inspector.
> (Foucault 1995, p. 147)

A second example comes from *The order of things*, which deals exclusively with academic texts. Therein, Foucault explains, for example, the core organising pattern of scientific knowledge-making, the *episteme* established by the end of the sixteenth century, as 'resemblance'. Such resemblance appears in texts as discussions of 'similitudes'. Here is the quote:

> As Crollius says: 'The stars are the matrix of all the plants and every star in the sky is only the spiritual prefiguration of a plant, such that it represents the plant, and just as each herb or plant is a terrestrial star looking up at the sky, so also each star is a celestial plant in spiritual form' [...].
> (Foucault 2001a, p. 20)

Foucault was well aware that 'not all texts are equal'. The documents he used had a different status and symbolic-performative power according to their functional context (see Prior 2003). He combined such textual analysis with data on institutions, law procedures, experiments, public events, material devices – core textual data are only one (important) element in a relational constellation of heterogeneous parts. But as he worked on historical phenomena, somehow all of his data were textual (or, to a lesser degree, painted, photographed) – there was no other way to get access.

Analytics of discourse(s)

Foucault is probably the most influential thinker ever in discourse research and discourse analysis in linguistics, the humanities, cultural studies and the social sciences. It is important to note that he did not establish a *theory* of discourse, but a heuristic toolbox, an analytics of discourse, which clarifies the object of inquiry (discourse) and some strategies to approach it. Although his conception of 'discourse' shifts somewhat in his writings, the main reference is *The archaeology of knowledge* (Foucault 2010a). In fact, he considered this book a failure and never returned to it – he never realised an empirical analysis according to the conceptual framework he proposed. Despite this, the book can be considered a milestone in the inquiry into language, knowledge and meaning-making. This is due to at least three core elements. First, he succeeds in establishing a rationale for the empirical analysis of historical and current knowledge-making by introducing given textual and institutional data as solid grounds for analysis. Second, while being informed by contemporary philosophy of language, he argued that analysis has to move beyond linguistic interests in languages and their functions (*ibidem*, pp. 79–134) in order to address serious speech acts as ways of constituting reality in institutional settings. Third, he accordingly introduced, beyond representationalism, the term *discourse* for the ordered practices of knowledge-making, which themselves are the object of such inquiry. The analytic task 'consists of not – of no longer – treating discourses as groups of signs (signifying elements referring to contents or representations) but as practices that systematically form the objects of which they speak.' (Foucault 2010a, p. 49)

In French, the common term '*discours*' refers to all kind of 'important' speeches or longer statements (e.g. during a wedding ceremony, a fiftieth birthday, a lecture at an academic conference) and written academic treatises (such as René Descartes' *Discourse on method*). Such speech events have in common the fact that language use here is embedded in a particular institutional context, which shapes its 'worth'. From Foucault's perspective, discourse as a conceptual framework refers to a series of discursive events and practices that are ordered by some regularity or 'rules of formation'. Single discursive events and statements obtain their meaning from the network of statements and formation patterns to which they 'belong'. A statement may have a different function in different networks and thus be a different statement. The regularity in each case shapes what can be said, by whom and to what effects. It has to be reconstructed by the analyst from empirical data. Foucault identified four dimensions of 'rules of formation':

1. The *formation of objects* of concern to a discourse can be understood by reconstructing the rules according to which the objects – of which discourses speak – are created: Which scientific disciplines play a role, and in which way? Which patterns of classification are used?
2. The *formation of enunciative modalities* refers to questions such as: Who is a legitimate speaker, or what are the institutional locations and subject positions from which objects of discourse are spoken about? How do different forms of enunciation – statistics, narratives, experiments, and so on – relate to each other?
3. The *formation of concepts* refers to rules that form the basis of the respective statement: How are textual elements connected to each other? Which rhetorical schemas are used? How is the statement positioned regarding other texts, for example, through the respective mode of citation? How are quantitative statements translated into qualitative statements?
4. The *formation of strategies* refers to the external relationships of a discourse: What are the topics and theories of a discourse? How do they interact with other discourses? To what extent do they purport to be better solutions to problems than those others?

Foucault insisted in opposition to structuralism that he is interested in historically situated practices and their regularities. Religious discourses can be distinguished from legal, economic, political, or scientific discourses by their different formative principles of statement production. The interest of analysis lies in examining the rules that conditioned what was (and only could be) 'actually' said in 'serious speech acts' (Dreyfus & Rabinow 1983, p. 48) at a given historical and institutional moment. The intent is to reconstruct the institutionalised regulations of discursive practices in observable games of truth, their elements, functions and effects. Discourse, therefore, is his way of apprehending the institutional patterns that make seemingly disparate empirical occurrences, as products of enunciations, belong to a common frame of reference or institutional structuring. Such occurrences are serial and regulated sequences of historically situated practices of producing statements. To Foucault, the use of language in institutional discourse is a social act of constituting reality that cannot be equated with the intentional actions of single speakers, nor to the syntactical rules of language use, but instead is shaped by the institutionally stabilised rules and orders of discourses. This allows for the analysis of regular patterns, their historical and institutional emergence, stabilisation and transformation. And this furthermore is the solid basis for discursive meaning-making and construction of knowledgeable objects via sign use and the performative references to a 'signified', or *interpretans*. Discourse is not about signifying given things 'out there', but about the very production of such 'things'.

Soon after *The archaeology of knowledge*, Foucault's perspective on discourse shifted. During the wave of student revolts in the late 1960s, he became more explicitly interested in power (see p. 75). Again, he followed his own original approach. In contrast to social movements and (for example, Marxist) academics who opposed truth or knowledge to power – take, for instance, the case of 'unmasking the hidden reality of power relations in society' – Foucault insisted that power and knowledge are closely intertwined. For him, it was important to do away with a tradition of thinking which claimed that knowledge can be established only when there is no more power, or that knowledge is somewhere outside of power. Instead, arguing once again in line with Nietzsche, he stated that power and knowledge imply each other: there is no power relation without a particular field of knowledge, and no knowledge that does not presuppose and constitute power relations. This claim has important implications for the position of the researcher or 'knowing subject', which cannot assume an external position free of influence by a given system of power. Instead, the knowing subject, the object of inquiry, and the epistemological practices are all together effects of historical power/knowledge regimes and their transformations (Foucault 1995, pp. 27–28).

In Foucault's short inaugural speech at the *Collège de France* in Paris in December 1970 (Foucault 2010a, pp. 215–238) this interest in power became clear in his discussion of internal and external elements that structure the unfolding of discourses. At this point, he was less concerned with general rules that account for the identity of a discourse than with dimensions that refer to the concrete processing of institutional discourse. These include situational contexts and taboos and the field of appliance of true/false statements, which all allow for some ideas to be voiced, but not others. Academic degrees and titles, commentaries and the principle of authorship permit some categories of people to speak while silencing others. Discourses are structured by mechanisms of exclusion and empowerment that produce 'scarcity' in the fields of serious speech acts.

Close to this, Foucault returned to various ideas of speech-act theory and Wittgensteinian philosophy of language (Wittgenstein 2009), but again, to mark a difference. His concept of *games of truth* adopts the latter's notions of 'language-games' and 'family resemblances'. Games of truth focus on the procedures that separate truth from error, or false knowledge. This might occur in the (human) sciences, but also, for example, in legal realms. Furthermore, Foucault now refers to discourses as strategic-tactical confrontations and conflicts. The interest is no longer in the analysis of individualised discursive formations *per se*, but in the role of conflicting, clashing, or collaborating discourses in given historical and local constellations of problematisation. In a series of lectures, he explained his new interest in investigating the role of discourse:

> The first inquiry is historical: How have domains of knowledge been formed on the basis of social practices? [...] The second line of research is a methodological one, which might be called discourse analysis. [...] to consider these facts of discourse [...] as games, strategic games of action and reaction, question and answer, domination and

evasion, as well as struggle. [...] This analysis of discourse as a strategic and polemical game is, in my judgment, a second line of research to pursue. Last of all, the third line of research [...] what we should do is show the historical construction of a subject through a discourse understood as consisting of a set of strategies which are part of social practices.

(Foucault 2000d, pp. 6–7)

The *Pierre Rivière* case (Foucault 1982) can be considered a nice illustration. Rivière, a young man in early nineteenth-century French Normandy, had murdered his mother, sister and brother in order to re-establish, as he affirmed, the honour of his father. He gave a long, written account of his motives and wanted to be punished with death. But then the different actors involved in the trial – the judge, police, medical doctors and psychiatrists representing different schools of psychiatry – entered into a conflict in order to clarify his mental state when committing the killings. Foucault accounted for this event as manifesting a battle between competing discourses, which all claim to account for the legitimate 'definition of the situation' (Thomas & Thomas 1928, pp. 571–572): 'Indeed it is in discourse that power and knowledge are joined together. [We must imagine the world] as a multiplicity of discursive elements that can come into play in various strategies. It is this distribution, that we must reconstruct [...].' (Foucault 1998, p. 100) This is quite a comprehensive research programme for subsequent discourse research in the social sciences and the humanities.

To sum up, it is safe to say that theorising and defining discourse or discourse analysis was not a primary concern for Foucault. There are elements of a never-completed and employed methodology. And there are several conceptual devices to analyse the role of conflicting discourses and other elements in situations of problematisation. The different accentuations of 'discourse' in Foucault, taken together, constitute a rich toolbox, despite the fact that Foucault, as we have seen, did not say much about ways of analysing discourse as data.

Analytics of power

Power plays a major role in Foucault's work. Political institutions, devices and actions are elements of the historical processes of problematisation he was interested in (Kelly 2014). But to Foucault, power implies much more than simply state action or class dominance.[8] Power is not a singular instance 'up there', but a basic dimension of human action and human relations. It is a core part of power/knowledge regimes: '[T]he smallest glimmer of truth is conditioned by politics' (Foucault 1998, p. 5; 1980a). Power relations can be found at every level of social action and society; they 'are not in a position of exteriority with respect to other types of relationships (economic processes, knowledge relationships, sexual relations), but are immanent in the latter.' (Foucault 1998, p. 94) Power is a play of distribution, rather than a quality of a position: 'the multiplicity of force relations immanent in the sphere in which they operate' (Foucault 1998, pp. 92). It is the central mechanism of producing subjects and objects. Playing with the connotations of the French (or Latin) word 'subjection/subjectification', which implies 'becoming a subject' as well as 'being subjected', Foucault addresses power as a productive, enabling and constraining force at the same time.

So, what is his conception of power? Foucault (1983, pp. 217–219) distinguishes between operations on things, which he calls 'capacity', relationships of communication (the circulation of meaning) and relationships of power. Exercising power happens between individual or collective actors and means, according to Foucault, *acting upon the actions of others*, that is, via different modalities, shaping their actions. This therefore implies degrees of freedom of action on the side of the others concerned and possibilities of resistance; otherwise, there would be no need to shape their actions. Power as subjection historically tends to fail; it always produces resistance. Foucault then adds another category: 'Relations of strategy' (*ibidem*, pp. 224–226) emerge in confrontations between actors if the goal is to win over the adversary. If they succeed, they create an asymmetric constellation for action and re-action. When such a constellation is locked together in a stable way with relations of power, then an enduring situation of 'domination' occurs.

Here again, Foucault refused a general theory of power and replaced it by an 'analytics'. Such a perspective implies historical diagnostics of the multiple forms, exercises and historical transformations of power, including its most productive realm – bringing particular kinds of subjects and objects into being. The core question, then, is: How, by which means, is power exercised? And what happens then? Foucault (1983, pp. 223–224; 1998, pp. 92–102) has given some general advice on how to explore power: Analysis should look for the systems of societal 'differentiation' (by law, statues, privilege, etc.) which, as a condition and a result of power relations, allow some people to act upon the actions of others. A second dimension is the type of objectives pursued by such actors (e.g. profit making). Third, the means of establishing power relations should be addressed. Finally, the forms of institutionalisation (e.g. the state form), as well as the degrees of effectiveness or rationalisation of power are of interest. His insistence on the omnipresence of power relations does not imply that the way they are right here and now is the best way or the only way. As history tells us, struggles abound within the transformation of powers and power/knowledge regimes.

The analytics of power imply that every single historical phenomenon of interest needs its own empirical inquiry. Foucault therefore came out of his research with different diagnostic concepts of power – each one accounting for a specific historical modality of 'acting upon the action of others'. In *Discipline and punish*, Foucault (1995) introduces several concepts to identify historical transformations of power relations since the classical age. *Sovereign power* refers to the former concentration of the locus of power in the position and person of the king, who had to decide – and was allowed to decide – on giving life or death to individuals (Foucault 1998, p. 135). *Microphysics of power* accounts for the new emerging modes of intervening into the body parts and movements of persons, for example in military or prison contexts, by making them stand, walk, look here and there, or follow this or that rationale for movement. *Disciplinary power* is the most comprehensive term for the new technologies and templates of disciplining bodies and persons, including, for example, carrying out examinations and giving grades in schools.

The will to knowledge presents the concepts of *biopower* and *biopolitics*. These are set against a view that identified power with established law and 'the' state, named *juridical power* or *power of the law* – a position, which, according to Foucault, was widely and wrongly used in debates in the 1960s/1970s (Foucault 1980c, pp. 139–143). *Biopolitics* is complementary to disciplinary power and refers to state interventions and measures to produce 'normal' populations, for example, by acting on birth rates, health practices and conditions. *Biopower* is the more general term Foucault suggests for the combination of disciplinary power and biopolitics. It 'brought life and its mechanisms into the realm of explicit calculations and made knowledge-power an agent of transformation of human life' (Foucault 1998, p. 143; see Foucault 2003, 2009b, 2010b).

Governmentality, one of the most prominent terms created by Foucault (2009b, 2011, 2012), refers to the elements and properties of individual or collective state-based 'governing' of conduct, to the 'conduct of (one's own or others') conduct'. Governing refers to practices of guiding the way a person – or people in general – acts, for example by making people behave in a certain way (e.g. not drinking in order to be fit for work). It occurs in very different situations and constellations. There is governing of others in families, in schools, in monasteries, in all kind of institutions and in states: 'To govern, in this sense, is to structure the possible field of action of others' (Foucault 1983, p. 221). In two influential lectures Foucault (2009b) dealt with transformations of liberal state government from the eighteenth to the early twentieth century. He was interested in political economy's ideas on the market, its functioning and its structuring effects on the conduct of citizens, as well as its beneficial role in nation building during the nineteenth and early twentieth centuries. 'Governmentality', according to Foucault, indicates a new 'economy' of power. It implies:

> the ensemble formed by institutions, procedures, analyses and reflections, calculations, and tactics that allow the exercise of this very specific, albeit very complex, power that has the population as its target, political economy as its major form of knowledge, and apparatuses of security as its essential technical instrument.
> (Foucault 2009b, p. 144)

Moreover, it refers to the process by which (state) 'government' and its dispositives became the dominant mode of exercising power, with the state itself becoming governmentalised. Foucault further distinguishes between governance through external *technologies of discipline*, which refer to the individual as object, through close *technologies of dominance* (ways of leading and subjugating others) and through *technologies of the self*, which refer to the individual as a moral, confessing, reflecting subject of self-conduct.

Conclusion

Foucault's work and concepts have travelled across the world. He has stimulated most contemporary social sciences and linguistic research on discourses and power relations, as well as academic disciplines, such as cultural studies, feminist studies, social studies of science and technology, and post-colonial studies. A full account of his influence and the critiques of his work are far beyond the scope of this conclusion.[9] Subsequent *discourse research*, even when claiming to be 'Foucauldian', has used his toolbox in rather loose ways, added other concepts to it and concentrated on the ways discourses establish ordered realities in political conflicts, public debate and scientific knowledge-making.[10] His *analytics of power*, especially the concepts of biopower and governmentality, have provoked a huge amount of in-depth discussion and empirical work, for example, on the logics of neo-liberal government and government of risk populations.[11] Perhaps not all such usage is 'true' to the Foucauldian concepts, but nevertheless, the subsequent debates have been stimulating.[12] Interestingly, despite the huge amount of research into power relations inspired by Foucault, only a few newer conceptual propositions have been made. French sociologist Pierre Lascoumes (1995) introduced the notion of *ecopower* ('éco-pouvoir') for a constellation that emerged in the 1970s in the realm of environmental concern. Michael Power (1999) accounted for the 'audit society' and its 'rituals of verification'. Keller (2011b) proposed the concept of *positioning power* to name the current constellations of ranking, audit and evaluation as structuring devices for the distribution of resources, chances and risk, ranging from clients' comments on web pages to large financial audit infrastructures.

Leading cultural studies author Stuart Hall (1932–2014) argued for the integration of Foucauldian, Marxist and Weberian sociological approaches. Edward Saïd and other prominent authors in post-colonial studies use(d) Foucauldian concepts in order to account for the post-colonial condition. Anthropologist Paul Rabinow develops his Anthropology of the Contemporary by building on Foucault. Prominent science and technology studies writers Bruno Latour and John Law, feminist thinkers such as Karen Barad, as well as philosophers Antonio Negri and Gorgio Agamben, draw on Foucault's influential work to 'move beyond'. Empirical studies in history, sociology and political science have been profoundly shaped by him and today show a mix of Foucauldian and 'post-Foucauldian' approaches. Most prominently, philosopher Judith Butler (1990, 1997) built largely on Foucault's analysis of discourse, body and power, adding psychoanalytical and deconstructivist elements in order to account for the bases of power. It is certain that his legacy will inform future inquiry into discourse, language, power and politics, even in research 'beyond Foucault'. If inquiry tries to stay close to a 'Foucauldian state of mind', it would have to use his methodology and concepts, not as a sacred, enshrined system of analysis, but as a toolset at hand – which implies that it should be worked on, modified, or expanded according to the research questions of interest.

Notes

1 I would like to thank the editors for their helpful suggestions. For comprehensive presentations of Foucault's work and life, please refer to Dreyfus & Rabinow (1983), Deleuze (1988), Downing (2008), Keller (2008), O'Farrell (2005); on Foucault's biography see Macey (1995) and Eribon (1991); for current work see *Foucault Studies*, http://rauli.cbs.dk/index.php/foucault-studies/index [accessed 30 January, 2016]. See Foucault (1999, 2000a, 2001b) for compilations of shorter key texts and interviews.
2 Other then-prominent positions in France include phenomenologist Maurice Merleau-Ponty (1908–1961), Edmund Husserl (1859–1938), and Martin Heidegger (1889–1976).
3 The term 'practices' refers to conventionalised or institutionalised patterns of behaviour and action.
4 See the special issue of *Foucault Studies* (2011).
5 Foucault only slightly touched upon his methodology (Foucault 1991, 1980b; Kendall & Wickham 1999, Keller 2008). Conceptual tools are very important in this and will be discussed below.
6 The book established an influential rationale for empirical discourse research, which will be discussed on pp. 72–73. But it differs largely from Foucault's own practice of, and interest in, analysis as explained above.
7 In his public lectures at the Collège de France, as well as in his two last books (Foucault 1990a, 1990b), Foucault commented on a narrow selection of (e.g. antique) texts, reporting what they say and discussing implicit assumptions, historical connotations and ethical aspects – thereby exposing his way of 'doing textual work'.
8 The state indeed is an effect of particular power relations rather than their site of origin.
9 For an early feminist critique of a 'male-centred view' in Foucault's last books see, e.g., Foxhall (1994). Marxist critique addressed a lack of explanatory theory on power relations. Critical theory authors and positivists attacked his historical relativism. Post-Foucauldian approaches today argue the need to go 'beyond discourse' to the heterogeneous materialities or material-semiotic dimensions of the world.
10 See, e.g., Said (1978), Hajer (1995), Darier (1998), Bührmann et. al (2007), Keller (2011a, 2013), Clarke (2005).
11 See Dean (2009; 2014); Lemke (2012), Burchell, Gordon & Miller (1991), Rose (2007), Walthers & Haahr (2005), Rose & Miller (2008), Bröckling, Krasmann & Lemke (2010).
12 See Rabinow & Rose (2006) for a critique of the use of *biopower* in the works of Antonio Negri & Michael Hardt or Gorgio Agamben.

References

Bröckling, U, Krasmann, S & Lemke, T, eds., 2010, *Governmentality. Current issues and future challenges*, Routledge, London.

Bührmann, A D, Diaz-Bone, R, Gutiérrez Rodriguez, E, Kendall, G, Schneider, W & Tirado, F J, eds., 2007, 'From Michel Foucault's theory of discourse to empirical discourse research', *Forum Qualitative Social Research*, vol. 8, no. 2, available from: http://www.qualitative-research.net/index.php/fqs/issue/view/7 [accessed January 31 2016].

Burchell, G, Gordon, C & Miller, P, eds., 1991, *The Foucault effect. Studies in governmentality*, The University of Chicago Press, Chicago, IL.

Butler, J, 1990, *Gender trouble. Feminism and the subversion of identity*, Routledge, New York and London.

Butler, J, 1997, *The psychic life of power. Theories in subjection*, Stanford University Press, Stanford, CA.

Clarke, A, 2005, *Situational analysis. Grounded theory after the postmodern turn*, Sage, London.

Darier, F, ed., 1998, *Discourses of the environment*, Wiley-Blackwell, London.

Dean, M M, 2009, *Governmentality: Power and rule in modern society*, 2nd ed., Sage, London.

Dean, M M, 2014, *The signature of power: Sovereignty, governmentality and biopolitics*, Sage, London.

Deleuze, G, 1988, *Foucault*, The University of Minnesota Press, Minneapolis.

Downing, L, 2008 *The Cambridge introduction to Michel Foucault*, Cambridge University Press, Cambridge.

Dreyfus, H L & Rabinow, P, 1983, *Michel Foucault. Beyond structuralism and hermeneutics*, 2nd ed., The University of Chicago Press, Chicago, IL.

Eribon, D, 1991, *Michel Foucault*, Harvard University Press, Boston, MA.

Foucault, M, 1980a, *Power/knowledge: Selected interviews and other writings, 1972–1977*, ed. C Gordon, Vintage Books, New York.

Foucault, M, 1980b, 'La poussière et le nuage' in *L'impossible prison. Recherches sur le système pénitentiaire au XIXe siècle*, ed. M Perrot, Éditions du Seuil, Paris, pp. 29–39.

Foucault, M, 1980c, 'The confession of the flesh' in Foucault, M., *Power/knowledge*, ed. C Gordon, Vintage Books, New York, pp. 194–228.

Foucault, M, 1982, *I, Pierre Rivière, having slaughtered my mother, my sister, and my brother: A case of parricide in the 19th Century*, University of Nebraska Press, Lincoln, NE.

Foucault, M, 1983, 'The subject and power' in H L Dreyfus & P Rabinow, *Michel Foucault. Beyond structuralism and hermeneutics*, 2nd ed., The University of Chicago Press, Chicago, IL, pp. 208–228.

Foucault, M, 1984, 'What is Enlightenment?', in *The Foucault reader*, ed. P Rabinow, Pantheon Books, New York, pp. 32–50.

Foucault, M, 1988, 'Truth, power, self: An interview with Michel Foucault October 25 1982', in *Technologies of the self: A seminar with Michel Foucault*, eds. L H Martin, H Guttman & P H Hutton, University of Massachusetts Press, Massachusetts, pp. 9–15.

Foucault, M, 1990a [1984], *The history of sexuality vol. 2: The use of pleasure*. Vintage Books, New York.

Foucault, M, 1990b [1984], *The history of sexuality vol. 3: The care of the self*, Vintage Books, New York.

Foucault, M, 1991, 'Questions of method', in *The Foucault effect. Studies in governmentality*, eds. G Burchell, C Gordon & P Miller, The University of Chicago Press, Chicago, IL, pp. 73–86.

Foucault, M, 1994 [1963], *The birth of the clinic*, Vintage Books, New York.

Foucault, M, 1995 [1975], *Discipline and punish*, Vintage Books, New York.

Foucault, M, 1998 [1976], *The will to knowledge. The history of sexuality vol. 1*, Penguin Books, London.

Foucault, M, 1999, *Aesthetics, method, and epistemology: Essential works of Foucault, 1954–1984 vol. 2,* ed. J D Faubion, The New Press, New York.
Foucault, M, 2000a, *Ethics: subjectivity and truth. The essential works of Michel Foucault 1954–1984, vol. 1,* ed. J D Faubion, The New Press, New York.
Foucault, M, 2000b [1980], 'Interview with Michel Foucault', in *Power. The essential works of Michel Foucault 1954–1984,* ed. J D Faubion, The New Press, New York, pp. 240–299.
Foucault, M [as M Florence], 2000c [1984], 'Foucault', in *Aesthetics, method, and epistemology: Essential works of Foucault 1954–1984 vol. 2,* ed. J D Faubion, The New Press, New York, pp. 459–464.
Foucault, M, 2000d [1973/1974], 'Truth and juridical forms', in M Foucault, *Power,* ed. J D Faubion, The New Press, New York, pp. 6–89.
Foucault, M, 2001a [1966], *The order of things: An archaeology of the human sciences.* 2nd ed. Routledge, London.
Foucault, M, 2001b, *Power: Essential works of Foucault, 1954–1984 vol. 3,* ed. J D Faubion, The New Press, New York.
Foucault, M, 2003, *'Society Must Be Defended': Lectures at the Collège de France, 1975–1976,* Palgrave Macmillan/Picador, New York.
Foucault, M, 2007 [1978], 'What is critique?', in M Foucault, *The politics of truth,* ed. S Lothringer, Semiotext(e), Los Angeles, pp. 41–77.
Foucault, M, 2008, *Psychiatric power: Lectures at the Collège de France, 1973–1974,* Palgrave Macmillan/Picador, New York.
Foucault, M, 2009a [1961], *History of madness,* Routledge, London.
Foucault, M, 2009b, *Security, territory, population: Lectures at the Collège de France 1977–1978,* Palgrave Macmillan/Picador, New York.
Foucault, M, 2010a [1969], *The archaeology of knowledge & the discourse on language,* Vintage Books, New York.
Foucault, M, 2010b, *The birth of biopolitics: Lectures at the Collège de France, 1978–1979,* Palgrave Macmillan/Picador, New York.
Foucault, M, 2011, *The government of self and others: Lectures at the Collège de France, 1982–1983,* Palgrave Macmillan/Picador, New York.
Foucault, M, 2012, *The courage of truth: The government of self and others II; Lectures at the Collège de France, 1983–1984,* Palgrave Macmillan/Picador, New York.
Foucault Studies, 2011, *Special Issue: Foucault and Pragmatism,* no. 11, available from http://rauli.cbs.dk/index.php/foucault-studies/issue/view/408/showToc [accessed 31 January, 2016].
Foxhall, L, 1994, Pandora unbound. A feminist critique of Foucault's *History of sexuality,* in *Dislocating masculinity. Comparative ethnographies,* eds A Cornwall & N Lindisfarne, Routledge, London, pp. 133–145.
Hajer, M, 1995, *The politics of environmental discourse,* Polity Press, Cambridge.
Keller, R, 2008, *Michel Foucault,* Universitätsverlag Konstanz, Konstanz, Germany.
Keller, R, 2011a, 'The sociology of knowledge approach to discourse (SKAD)', *Human Studies,* vol. 34, no. 1, pp. 43–65.
Keller, R, 2011b, 'Drama, baby, drama. Über Macht, Herrschaft und Gouvernementalität in der zweiten Moderne', in *Macht und Herrschaft im Wandel,* eds. W Bonß, & C Lau, Velbrück, Weilerswist, Germany, pp. 76–98.
Keller, R, 2013, *Doing discourse research,* Sage, London.
Kelly, GMK, 2014, *Foucault and politics. A critical introduction,* Edinburgh University Press, Edinburgh.
Kendall, G & Wickham, H, 1999, *Using Foucault's methods,* Sage, London.
Lascoumes, P, 1995, *L'éco-pouvoir. Environnements et politiques,* Éditions de la Découverte, Paris.
Lemke, T, 2012, *Foucault, governmentality, and critique,* Routledge, London.
Macey, D, 1995, *The lives of Michel Foucault,* Vintage Books, New York.

Martin, L H, Hutton, P H & Gutman H, eds., 1988, *Technologies of the self: A seminar with Michel Foucault*, The University of Massachusetts Press, Massachusetts.

O'Farrell, C, 2005, *Michel Foucault*, Sage, London.

Power, M, 1999, *Audit society. Rituals of verification*, Oxford University Press, Oxford.

Prior, L, 2003, *Using documents in social research*, Sage, London.

Rabinow, P & Rose, N, 2006, 'Biopower today' *BioSocieties* vol. 1, no. 2, pp. 195–217.

Ricœur, P, 1970, *Freud and philosophy: An essay on interpretation*, Yale University Press, New Haven, CT.

Rose, N, 2007, *The politics of life itself: Biomedicine, power, and subjectivity in the twenty-first century*, Princeton University Press, Princeton, NJ.

Rose, N & Miller, P, 2008, *Governing the present: Administering economic, social and personal life*, Polity Press, Cambridge

Saïd, E W, 1978, *Orientalism*, Vintage Books, New York.

Thomas, W I & Thomas, D S, 1928, *The child in America*, Knopf, New York.

Walters, W & Haahr, J H, eds., 2006, *Governing Europe: Discourse, governmentality and European integration*, Routledge, London

Wittgenstein, L, 2009, *Philosophical investigations*, 4th ed., Wiley-Blackwell, Oxford.

5

Jacques Lacan

Negotiating the psychosocial in and beyond language

Yannis Stavrakakis

Introduction: symbolic, imaginary and real

It is generally accepted that Lacanian theory has advanced a distinct and challenging take on 'pure' as well as 'applied' psychoanalysis by focusing on the nodal status of language in human experience. Lacan himself quite often presented his teaching as consisting of 'simply language, and absolutely nothing else' (Lacan 2008, p. 26). Indeed, from a Lacanian point of view, psychoanalysis as a process remains overdetermined by the social institution of language. It can function as the 'talking cure' and constitute itself as a science of the unconscious only to the extent that the latter is understood as structured like a language. And yet, this focus on language does not involve a reduction of psychoanalysis to linguistics: 'The fact that I say that the unconscious is structured like a language is not part and parcel of the field of linguistics' (Lacan 1998, p. 15). In its unfolding, Lacan's take on psychoanalytic theory will itself push 'language' and 'discourse' to their extremes.

Now, registering the importance of language presupposes at least one extremely important theoretical and clinical precondition: to move beyond a common misunderstanding concerning the nature of psychoanalysis. Namely, that it focuses on individuality: on individual symptoms, lives and persons. According to Lacan, however, the subject of psychoanalysis emerges beyond any naïve individualism. It is not the self-sufficient, 'autonomous' subject of knowledge as it is constructed in the tradition of philosophy, that is to say, as corresponding to the conscious *cogito*, but an eccentric, split subject, one structured around a central division, a radical lack.

The implications of such a conceptualisation are indeed paramount. It moves beyond psychological reductionism towards a thorough grasping of the socio-symbolic dependence of subjectivity: against this lack, the constitution of every identity has to rely on processes of identification with socially available objects of identification such as political ideologies, patterns of consumption and social roles.[1] Language thus emerges as a crucial resource available to the lacking subject in order to attempt the constitution of her/his identity within civilisation. This orientation becomes central in Lacan's teaching following an initial stage in which the *imaginary* figures as dominant. Furthermore, through his continuous interaction with the structuralist and post-structuralist field, it will overdetermine his complex theoretical and clinical contributions at least from the 1950s onwards. This is precisely the period in which his so-called 'Return to Freud', the cornerstone of his multifaceted work, will be articulated. No wonder that the 'symbolic', together with the aforementioned 'imaginary' and the 'real' – to which we shall return – constitute the core conceptual triad of Lacanian theory.

At any rate, it is clear that the symbolic has a far more important structuring role than the imaginary in Lacan's theorisation of how human reality is constructed (Lacan 1993, p. 9). By submitting to the laws of language, every human becomes a subject in language – it inhabits and is inhabited by language at the most ontological level: 'Not only is man born into language in precisely the way he is born into the world; he is born through language' (Lacan 2008, p. 27). The subject truly comes to being as long as 'it agrees' to be represented by the signifier: 'the subject is the subject of the signifier – determined by it' (Lacan 1979, p. 67). Hence Lacan's insistence on the subject as *l'etre parlant*, which, as he points out in a rare filmed lecture at Louvain University (1972), obviously designates a *pleonasm*: it is the reliance on language that makes her/him a (social) being.

This, however, should not lead to the conclusion that entering the symbolic overcomes the constitutive alienation marking the split Freudian/Lacanian subject by providing it with a solid identity. On the contrary, the symbolic dependence of the subject is bound to fail on this front because, apart from conditioning our (symbolic) identifications, it is also, paradoxically, what limits their scope. In fact, it may very well be – in itself, yet not entirely on its own – what causes lack in the first place. The reliance of human sociality on language is thus revealed as both a blessing and a curse, a source of both *jubilation* and *alienation*.[2] On the one hand, due to the 'universality' of language, to the linguistic constitution of human reality, the signifier offers the subject an ostensibly stable and guaranteed representation; only this representation is incapable of capturing and communicating the real 'singularity' of the subject, a *real* that is sacrificed – *castrated* – upon our entering the symbolic.

The emergence of the subject in the socio-symbolic terrain thus presupposes a division between reality (which denotes social construction and representation) and the real (a concept designating whatever escapes such representation). Reality is dynamic and meaningful, but ultimately, limited and alienating; the real, however, denotes what insists beyond – but also within – this reality by lacking nothing. Reality, the psychosocially overdetermined materiality of the signifier always attempts to symbolise the real of human and physical nature: to introduce meaning to the banality/stupidity of animal life, to the meaningless materiality of (biological) need. And yet, relying on the fundamental loss of the real – the word, the symbol, is the murder of the thing, Hegel tells us (Lacan 2006, p. 104) – it can only produce *retroactive, partial* and ultimately *illusory* simulations (imaginarisations) of this real in fantasy.[3] For better or worse, these are always – and simultaneously – more *and* less than the real itself. Retroactivity is the keyword here, and Lacan is correct to highlight his role in asserting its force: 'No one before me had ever noticed the importance of this *nachträglich*, even though it is there on every page of Freud' (Lacan 2008, p. 47).

Uniting the *necessary* with the *impossible* in a retroactive loop, the real is clearly foundational in an always escaping and mystifying way: impossible to avoid and yet impossible to meaningfully master, to accurately represent, to adequately symbolise. The resulting failure marks all encounters between the symbolic and the real, splitting subjective and objective reality: *if the subject is a lacking subject the Other is also a lacking Other*. Indeed, moving towards the concluding phase of Lacan's teaching, Lacanian theory will increasingly account for this lack in the Other, the lack that splits subjective and objective reality, as a lack of *jouissance*, of an enjoyment that, although castrated upon our entry into symbolic reality, never stops influencing our lives, interacting with language in a plurality of often paradoxical ways. And yet, to the extent that speaking beings can only access it from within a limited and alienating symbolic, all the retroactive attributes of real *jouissance* and the ensuing choreography between the real, the symbolic and the imaginary, will never manage to lift the ambiguity and ambivalence marking our linguistically mediated relationship towards the real.

Lacan has orchestrated his semiotic 'Return to Freud' through a thorough reconceptualisation of Saussurean linguistics. The following sections provide an overview of this project, highlighting Lacan's contribution to a novel take on psychosocial semiosis that insists on the pivotal role of language and discourse in the constitution of human reality, registering, at the same time, the complex encounter between symbolic and real, as well as the importance of retroactivity in trying to grasp it. We subsequently follow Lacan's shift of focus from language to affect and *jouissance*, placing emphasis on the articulations between the two fields. Both Lacan's conceptualisation of the symbolic, especially the importance he assigns to the role particular signifiers play in structuring whole fields of signification, as well as his highlighting of the role of *jouissance*, have influenced enormously the study of political discourse and ideology (Laclau & Mouffe 1985; Žižek 1989, 1993, 1994; Laclau 2005; Stavrakakis 1999, 2007). Thus, this chapter will conclude by briefly alluding to some of the political implications of Lacanian semiotics, discussing empirical examples.

The symbolic: Lacanian semiotics

If the main aim of Lacan's 'Return to Freud' was to reinvigorate analytic theory by taking into account developments in the vanguard of the scientific thought of his age, it is clear that he initially considered modern linguistics, as shaped by Saussure (Lacan 2006, p. 344), as the guide in such an enterprise. Linguistics is credited with such a crucial role in facilitating the adequate formalisation of analytic theory precisely because analysis functions through language (Lacan 2006, p. 235). Lacan's advice 'Read Saussure' (Lacan 2006, p. 344) is furthermore legitimised by the fact that Freud himself seems to have placed linguistic phenomena at the forefront of his discovery of the unconscious: 'What is Freud […] dealing with? No matter whether it is the text of the dream, the text of the joke or the form of the slip, he is manipulating articulations of language, of discourse' (Lacan 2008, p. 81). In doing that, he is seen as anticipating some of Saussure's insights: 'You will see that Freud talks about them in such a way that the structural laws Mr de Saussure disseminated all over the world are written out there in full' (Lacan 2008, pp. 27–8).

Undoubtedly, it is possible to recognise here a mark of Lacan's general argumentative strategy vis-à-vis Freud: by crediting Freud for a certain linguistic *prefiguration*, Lacan reconstructs Freud in a way influenced by modern linguistics. The stratagem implicit in Lacan's move is that while interpreting Freud according to his own view of modern linguistic theory, he can also claim to recover the lost meaning of Freud. And yet, this is not to say that, for Lacan, psychoanalysis is reducible to linguistics. When using structural linguistics to clarify Freudian doctrine, we must also recognise that Freud introduces insights that go well beyond Saussure; it is not as if Freud simply refers us to the structuralist theory of language, since psychoanalysis takes us to the limits of formalisation, towards the element of the real that escapes symbolic closure (Shepherdson 2008, p. 11). As we shall see then, it is a particular reading of linguistics that is deemed relevant for analytic theory. This is again a two-way movement marked by retroactivity. Lacan's innovative gaze is revealed here as the vanishing mediator between the proper names 'Freud' and 'Saussure', as offering the keys that overdetermine the specific terms of the relation between the two domains these proper names represent, namely psychoanalysis and linguistics.

In mediating between Freud and Saussure, Lacan has managed to avoid certain contradictions haunting the Saussurean schema he is creatively re-appropriating. For example, despite his efforts to avoid such a development, Saussure appears to be reintroducing a *representationalist* conception of signification. Despite his insistence on arbitrariness (Saussure 1959, p. 67), in Saussure, the distinction between signifier and signified can be described as 'a relic, within a theory allergic to it, of a representationalist problematic of the sign' (Borch-Jacobsen 1991, p. 175). As Derrida has put it, in such a schema, not only do signifier and signified seem to unite, 'but in this confusion, the signifier seems to be erased or to become transparent so as to let the concept [a concept linked to external reality] present itself, just as if it were referring to nothing but its own presence' (Derrida 1981, p. 32–3).[4] It is clear that, given his take on the relationship between symbolic and real, Lacan's reformulation of Saussurean linguistics was bound to move beyond any such kind of representationalism. How does Lacan deal with this metaphysical trap? In order to answer this question, we need to engage seriously with Lacanian semiotics.

For Lacan, a theory of meaning founded on a recourse to some kind of referent, to a supposedly accessible order of objective reality, is clearly insufficient. Lacanian theory offers a tentative solution to this insufficiency by *subverting* the relation between the signifier and the signified. Instead of the unity between the signifier and the signified about which Saussure speaks, Lacan stresses their division; if unity prioritises the signified, division gives priority to the signifier over the production of the signified, a production which only now becomes fully elucidated. Thus, although starting from a Saussurean angle, Lacan draws a very different distinction between signifier and signified from that of Saussure: it is the structure of the first that governs the direction of the second (Lacan 2006). Thus, in 'Agency of the Letter' (1957) Lacan makes a crucial move with reference to the Saussurean algorithm, which he presents as S/s, where capital S designates the signifier and small s the signified (see Figure 5.1; Saussure 1959, p. 66; Lacan 2006, p. 415).

Both algorithms illustrate the relation between signifier (sound image) and signified (concept). And yet the second is not far from being the inversion or subversion of the first. A similar conclusion is reached if comparing Saussure's and Lacan's respective diagrams on signification vis-à-vis the example of the 'tree' (see Figure 5.2; Saussure 1959, p. 67; Lacan 2006, p. 416). To the extent that the use by Saussure of the Latin signifier '*arbor*' slightly complicates things, a simplified version of the comparison may be useful (see Figure 5.3; Fink 2004, p. 81).

This radical inversion does not, however, discourage Lacan from attributing this primordial position of the signifier to Saussure himself, a move allowing him to adapt the Saussurean concept to the analytic framework, and, at the same time, to lay his claim on

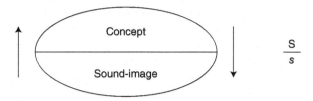

Figure 5.1 Saussurean and Lacanian algorithms

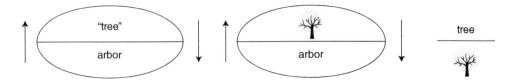

Figure 5.2 Saussure and Lacan on trees

Figure 5.3 Saussure's and Lacan's trees – simplified version

Saussure's legacy (a strategy that, as we have seen, he used with much success in his reading of Freud). Here, the signifier (S) is located over the signified (s), this 'over' corresponding to the bar separating them, a barrier resisting signification. This barrier is exactly what makes possible 'an exact study of the connections characteristic of the signifier, and of the magnitude of their function in generating the signified' (Lacan 2006, p. 415).[5] If the dominant factor here is the bar that disrupts the unity of the Saussurean sign, then the unity of signification, the linguistic sign as the 'union' posited by Saussure, can only be an illusion, a retroactive fantasmatic construction. And yet it is a functional illusion with a multiplicity of stabilising – as well as stagnating – effects both for subjective and collective life.

What creates this illusion (the effect of the signified) is the play of the signifiers. In Lacan's schema then, the signifier is not something that functions as a representation of the signified. Simply put, meaning is produced by signifiers; it springs from the signifier to the signified and not vice versa.[6] The signifier manifests the presence of difference and nothing else, making impossible any direct connection between signs and things. In other words, reference to signs implies a reference to things as guarantees of signification, a correspondence theory of truth along the lines of the Aristotelian tradition of 'truth and metaphor as homoiosis' (Chaitin 1989, p. 999), something that Saussure himself was ultimately unable to avoid. On the contrary, the notion of the primacy of the signifier breaks with such representationalist connotations. Signification is now articulated around an illusion – that of attaining the signified as real; most importantly, this illusion of a stable meaning itself is revealed as a result of the signifying play. What Lacan seems to mean by this is that if there is a signified it can only be a signifier to which we retroactively attribute a transferential signified function. The conceptual content of an utterance, as Jameson points out, has to be seen as a meaning effect; it is the relationship between signifiers that produces the objective *mirage* of signification (Jameson 1991, p. 26).

However, a certain confusion seems to contaminate the argument at this point. What is the exact status of the signified? Is the signified real or imaginary? It is possible to argue that the signified can only be an effect of transferential illusion – an imaginary entity. Conversely, Lacan also treats the signified as pertaining to the real order, an order beyond signification, the locus of an absence. Lacan seems to be accepting two opposite definitions of the

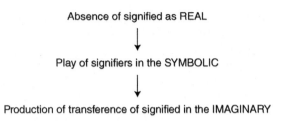

Figure 5.4 Signification: real, symbolic and imaginary aspects

signified. A more careful examination reveals, however, that this is not the result of some kind of conceptual confusion but Lacan's ingenious solution to the problem of meaning. A rigorous Lacanian approach to the terrain of meaning and signification, a true Lacanian semiotics, has to take into account all the three dimensions involved; the real, the imaginary and the symbolic register. It also has to capture their *retroactive* choreography. According to Lacan, the signified, what is supposed to be, through its links to external reality, the source and guarantor of signification, indeed belongs to the real. But this is a real that, as we have seen, resists symbolisation. Surely, if this real is always absent from the level of signification – within which socialisation entraps us – it cannot be in itself and by itself the source of this same signification. Its absence, however, the constitutive lack of the signified as real, can. Lack thus constitutes something absolutely crucial for signification. This absence has to be compensated for if signification is to acquire any coherence. It is the absence of the signified in its real dimension, then, which triggers the emergence of the transference of the signified. What emerges, thus, is the signified in its imaginary dimension: fantasy. There is, however, one more dimension to this signifying play. This transference of the signified, the emergence of the imaginary signified, can only be the result of a play between signifiers. This is how the third dimension, the dimension of the symbolic, overdetermines signification. It is the predominance of the signifier that produces the imaginary signified in order to cover over the absence of the real signified, or rather, of the signified as real (Stavrakakis 1999, p. 28).

Semiological affinities and socio-political implications of Lacan's 'Return to Freud'

Notwithstanding all the important differences, it is possible to discern here certain similarities with the function of *myth* in Barthes; something that will give us the opportunity to start encompassing some of the implications for the socio-political field. In both cases, we have a dialectic between emptiness/absence and imaginary fullness: 'The signifier of myth presents itself in an ambiguous way: it is at the same time meaning and form, full on one side and empty on the other' (Barthes 1973, p. 126). Furthermore, myth emerges retroactively through signification: 'When it becomes form, the meaning leaves its contingency behind; it empties itself, it becomes impoverished, history evaporates, only the letter remains' (Barthes 1973, p. 127). This produces a certain ideological illusion by camouflaging a contingent symbolic construction as an objective and eternal truth supposedly anchored on the real of nature. Indeed, for Barthes, such a naturalisation constitutes 'the very principle of myth: it transforms history into nature', 'making contingency appear eternal' and thus depoliticising what is at stake (Barthes 1973, pp. 140, 155). This is, then, why myth is experienced as 'innocent speech': 'what allows the reader to consume myth innocently is that [...] the signifier and the signified have, in his eyes, a natural relationship. [...] myth is read as a factual system, whereas it is but a semiological system' (Barthes 1973, p. 142).

We know today that such a naturalistic fantasy can indeed persist in a perverse 'as if' form, even when naturalism itself is delegitimised – what often dominates is a cynical 'enlightened false consciousness' (Žižek 1989, p. 29) that is fully aware of the artificial mask of naturalisation, but nevertheless clings to the natural guarantee, or refers it to a number of other guarantees. This is why an efficient argumentative deconstruction of political identifications that seem to rely on such naturalisations (for example, racism) often fails to displace them to the extent that innocence is not the only way to consume myth; the deconstruction of innocence can leave intact the force and affective intensity of a commonly invested transferential signified now reproduced through shared *guilt* and/or shared *disavowal,* even through *cynicism*. When Lacan talks about a 'transference of the signified', he alludes to the fact that what is at stake here is no longer merely a symbolic matter, but a sort of 'affective tie', that marks the limit of symbolisation while functioning as its formal support (Shepherdson 2008, p. 14).

The name Lacan will eventually give to this signified effect, in order to highlight its excessive implications that escape the scope of the symbolic, is first *phallus* and then *objet petit a*: object little-a. Through symbolisation, the play of signifiers produces 'a kind of excess, a remainder or surplus-effect, that is not at all equivalent to reality, but is, rather, an effect of the symbolic order, though not reducible to it' (Shepherdson 2008, p. 37). What accounts for the ideological efficacy of this entity, of this weird symbolically produced object compensating for real absence with a deferred imaginary fullness, is the fact that it is by constitution 'lost': 'The idea that this object was once possessed is strictly a retroactive fantasy – but an illusion that is inseparable from the symbolic order itself and does not cease to have effects, even when its non-existence has been demonstrated' (Shepherdson 2008, p. 49).[7]

We can provide many concrete examples of these processes demonstrating their important socio-political implications. Shepherdson, for instance, has utilised the Derridean account of the Gold Standard in the economy.[8] Given the homology or equivalence between linguistic and monetary systems, substantiated in detail by Goux (partly with reference to the gold standard as well), this seems to be a fitting example (Goux 1990; Goux 1996, p. 36). When we speak of money today, we usually treat it in symbolic terms, that is to say as:

> a conventional system of representation governed by certain internal laws, [...] we are concerned [...] with relations between signifiers, and not with what the signifier represents outside the system. Accordingly, 'ten dollars' is not defined by what it will buy, or by its relation to external reality. That is a purely contingent and constantly changing relation – today it will buy three loaves of bread, but next year it only serves as change to ride the bus.
>
> (Shepherdson 2008, p. 21)

And yet, this is not the end of the story: 'there is a point at which the structure is, paradoxically, attached to the very reality it is supposed to exclude' (*ibidem*). It is here that the operation of the gold standard acquires its paradoxical relevance. What is the paradox with gold? 'On the one hand, it is a pure convention: unlike bread (which we *need*), gold has no value in itself, but is entirely symbolic (a pure signifier without any use value)' (*ibidem*). On the other hand, it functions as a ground 'that stands outside the system of exchange, giving value to the symbolic elements – whose purely formal relations are supposed to operate precisely by excluding any such outside' (*ibidem*). No wonder that More's Utopians were rather astonished with this paradox and its implications: 'They [Utopians] are surprised that gold, a useless commodity in itself, is everywhere valued so highly that man himself, who for his own purposes conferred this value on it, is considered far less valuable than the gold' (More 2002, p. 63).

This scandalous and paradoxical character of gold should not be merely discarded 'as a confusion that might be removed (e.g., when we finally come to our senses and realize that gold is merely symbolic), but as its positive content: it is to be understood (in Derrida's words) precisely as "something which no longer tolerates the nature/culture opposition"' (Shepherdson 2008, p. 22). In this sense, gold thus seems to function, in the first instance, as a kind of what Lacan called a *point de capiton*, an anchoring or quilting point, an element that is neither inside nor outside the structure:

> The enigma of gold as a 'quilting point' is that it has no value in itself, but acquires its status as a 'natural value' from the system itself […] in the sense that it is a 'surplus-effect', a 'product' of the system that expels it from the chain of representations, and buries it in the earth, where it can be 'found again'.
> (Shepherdson 2008, p. 21)

Hence, beyond the deconstruction of the illusion of the 'natural and foundational character of gold' and the reassertion of the 'purely symbolic', socially constructed character of 'value', the crucial task here is rather to register the paradoxical fact that a system founded on convention nevertheless comes to rely on the apparent 'exteriority' and 'naturalness' of a chosen and retroactively invested object, of gold as an *objet petit a*.[9]

From the symbolic to the real: language and *jouissance*

From the intersection of psychoanalysis with linguistics we have slowly started moving into social and political theory, enlisting examples from the domain of socio-political reality. This choreography will be further enhanced as we shift our emphasis from the symbolic to the real, something consistent with the trajectory of Lacan's teaching itself. Although he himself provided numerous instances of legitimising such a view, 'the dominant reading of Lacan, as a thinker of the symbolic order, mistakenly reduces his work to a thought of nothing but the symbolic order, which is obviously a very different thing'. Indeed, precisely as 'a thinker of the symbolic order, Lacan brought to light many aspects of human existence that are irreducible to language' (Shepherdson 2008, p. xv). And yet, throughout his radical embrace of the real towards the end of his teaching – when *jouissance* acquired a certain conceptual and causal priority over the signifier (Miller 2002, p. 47) – language and discourse remained the background against which this real could be grasped in ways that hugely influenced socio-political reflection. How is this possible?[10]

Although the real is *ex definitione* irreducible to the field of construction and symbolic representation, it nevertheless shows itself in the first instance – and indirectly – through the disruption of the symbolic, through the kinks and inconsistencies of the latter's functioning: 'In all those failed acts in which Freud saw the operation of the unconscious – slips, dreams, symptoms, jokes, free associations – there is a truth striving to appear. But this truth can only manifest itself as an interruption of discourse, in the form of a mistake, precisely because […] the word is always lacking' (Chaitin 1996, p. 133). This psychoanalytic idea of distortion or disruption as a (negative) index of the real has been cogently captured by

Ernesto Laclau in his political theorisation of discourse through his category of 'dislocation', a concept introduced to encircle the limits of signification. Laclau even goes on to explicitly link his treatment of the issue with the Lacanian problematic of the real: 'we are trying to signify the limits of signification – the real, if you want, in the Lacanian sense – and there is no direct way of doing so except through the subversion of the process of signification itself' (Laclau 1996, p. 39).

One must not forget, however, that in Lacanian theory, the real is not only associated with moments of disruption, with traumatic, or dislocatory experiences. First of all, *the real in itself cannot be disruption or lack.* Disruption is certainly one way of *showing* the constitutive inability of the symbolic to represent the real, of demonstrating the symbolic order's lack of resources. But that can only mean that the real should rather be thought of as a 'lack of lack'. Moreover, for Lacan, this lack in the symbolic is not simply a lack of symbolic resources. Rather, it also has to be acknowledged as a lack of the real *jouissance*, castrated through socialization. In this sense, the lack in the Other is a lack of a pre-symbolic real enjoyment or satisfaction which – at least in its fullness, as the lack of lack – retroactively presents itself as lost, as the part of ourselves that is sacrificed when we enter the socio-symbolic system – a system that, as we have seen, regulates the discursive articulation of human reality. Last, but not least, in order for the social world to retain any consistency and appeal, this lack of the real, the negative mark of symbolic castration, needs to be *positivised* (imaginarised). To stimulate the desire for identification, for social and political life, to imaginarise lack, is the function of *fantasy*. Fantasy attempts that by offering us what Lacan calls the *objet petit a*, the object-cause of desire, embodying, in a double movement, the lack in the Other, together with the promise of its filling, the promise of a miraculous encounter with castrated *jouissance*. At the imaginary level then – or rather at the level of an imaginarised real – the limits of the symbolic are positivised in the form of an *objets petits a*: '*Objet [petit] a* is a kind of "positivisation", filling out, of the void…' (Žižek 1993, p. 122). It incarnates 'simultaneously the pure lack, the void around which the desire turns and which, as such, causes the desire, *and* the imaginary element which conceals this void, renders it invisible by filling it out' (Žižek 1994, pp. 178–9).[11]

Likewise, Laclau's dislocation, any encounter with the real that disrupts a given discursive field, is not only something traumatic – an experience of *negativity* – but also the condition of possibility for social and political *creation* and re-articulation (Laclau 1990, p. 39). Dislocation *qua* encounter with the impossible real functions as both the limit and the ontological condition of identity formation. In particular, for Laclau, this dual nature of dislocation is *positivised* in what he calls 'empty signifiers', referring to a dialectic between emptiness and fullness not unrelated to the one employed by Barthes in formulating 'myth'. If our continuous experiences of dislocation reveal that the full closure of the Other is impossible, that the real is ultimately unrepresentable, that lack is an irreducible characteristic of socio-political reality, this does not mean that positivisation in terms of closure, fullness or full representation disappears from political discourse. Politics comprise all our (partial) attempts to fill in this lack in the Other: 'although the fullness and universality of society is unachievable, its need does not disappear: it will always show itself through the presence of its absence' (Laclau 1996, p. 53). And this is precisely where Laclau's category of the empty signifier becomes relevant:

> In a situation of radical disorder 'order' is present as that which is absent; it becomes an empty signifier, as the signifier of this absence. In this sense, various political forces can compete in their efforts to present their particular objectives as those which carry out

the filling of that lack [...] Politics is possible because the constitutive impossibility of society can only represent itself through the production of empty signifiers.
(Laclau 1996, p. 44)

Laclau suggests, moreover, that signifiers other than 'order' – signifiers such as 'unity', 'revolution', 'justice', 'change', 'happiness', and so on. – can function in a similar way. Clearly, therefore, there is an immediate theoretical affinity holding between Lacan's positivisations of the real through the fantasmatic *objet petit a* and Laclau's positivisation of the limits of signification in terms of 'empty signifiers.' What both gestures have in common is the acknowledgement of the need to positively index these limits in the psychic economy and the discursive identity of the social subject.

Last but not least, through the intervention of empty signifiers qua *objets petits a*, linguistic articulation acquires an extra dimension, which is necessary for its sedimentation and hegemonic appeal through its affective investment. This is how *jouissance* enters the picture to interact with language. Together, they produce discourse. No wonder that, in Vanier's words, for Lacan '"discourse" is a collective organization for managing jouissance' (Vanier 2001, p. 41), something that will eventually resurface in Laclau's theorisation:

That is why I have extracted some categories – such as discourse – from any regional connotation and I have attempted to give to them a more primary ontological role. The complexes that I call 'discursive' include both affective and linguistic dimensions.
(Laclau 2003, pp. 283–4)

Hence, hegemony and ideological attachment cannot be fully explained at a formal level, the level of discursive articulation and signification. The *force* of a discourse, its hegemonic appeal, cannot be reduced to its *form*. Form and force need to be conceptually distinguished, in their mutual constitution, and this is something Ernesto Laclau forcefully registered in his recent work:

For what rhetoric can explain is the *form* that an overdetermining investment takes, but not the *force* that explains the investment as such and its perdurability. [...] something belonging to the order of *affect* has a primary role in discursively constructing the social. Freud already knew it: the social link is a libidinal link. And affect [...] is not something *added* to signification, but something consubstantial with it.
(Laclau 2004, p. 283; also see Laclau 2005, p. 110)

Conclusion

Let us recapitulate our argument so far. The symbolic, in Lacan, is not the order of the sign, as in Saussurean linguistics, but the order of the signifier. Meaning is produced by the signifier. As for the signified, this is understood by Lacan as an effect of *transference*. If we speak about the signified, it is only because we need to believe in its existence. It is a belief crucial for our construction of reality as a coherent, 'objective' whole; a belief in something that guarantees the validity of our knowledge, sustaining the fantasy of an *adaequatio* between language and the world. But for Lacan, as he argues in his seminar on *The psychoses* (1955–1956), even 'the transference of the signified, so essential to human life, is possible only by virtue of the structure of the signifier' (Lacan 1993, p. 226). Lacan, then, is radicalising the semiological idea, implicit in Saussure and expressed by Barthes, that 'it appears increasingly more difficult to conceive a system of images and objects whose signifieds can exist independently of language [...] The world of signifieds is none other than that of language' (Barthes 1973, p. 10). And yet, language does not exhaust the real; it is obliged to interact – negatively as well as positively, through the dual nature of dislocation and its retroactive positivisation in the production of empty signifiers – with an (internal) beyond – with the 'intimate alterity of the real' (Shepherdson 2008) – in order to allow the articulation and affective investment of discourses constructing our socio-political reality.

Needless to say, this process is also crucial for the formation of collective identity. For Lacan, it is clear that 'what constitutes a collectivity – what I called men, women, and children – means nothing qua pre-discursive reality' (Lacan 1998, p. 33). We can thus assume that constructing a sense of collective identity is also subject to the retroactive operations of signification implicit in Lacanian semiotics as well to the same discursive choreography between language, affect and *jouissance*. An example from socio-political analysis may serve to elucidate this point. Notice how Pierre Bourdieu conceives of the constitution of an organised social or political movement out of the mass of a dominated group, through, for example, the act of symbolisation by which the spokesperson of the movement is chosen:

> the sign creates the thing signified, the signifier is identified with the thing signified which would not exist without it, and which can be reduced to it. The signifier is not only that which expresses and represents the signified group: it is that which signifies to it that it exists, that which has the power to call into visible existence, by mobilizing it, the group that it signifies.
>
> (Bourdieu 1991, p. 207)

This radical retroactive ontology constitutes the cornerstone of Ernesto Laclau's theory of populism as formulated in his book *On populist reason*: 'the construction of the "people" is a radical one – one which constitutes social agents as such, and does not express a previously given unity of the group' (Laclau 2005, p. 118). The 'people' – what is supposed to be the foundation of modern democracy – is always something retroactively constructed, an empty signifier that needs to be invoked, a call incarnated in a proper name that (partially) creates what it is supposed to be expressing (a sovereign collective identity). And yet, no real politics and no real popular-democratic advances are possible without such a retroactive mobilising construction, as well as without taking the risk of its distortion (for example, its corruption from an inclusionary towards an exclusionary populist orientation).

Given that, under a strong Lacanian influence, Laclau has re-conceptualised discourse with *jouissance* and affect as its crucial internal moments, the Lacanian theorisation of *jouissance* emerges here as an integral aspect of a discursive theory of hegemony and populism: apart from such a process of retroactive construction, a hegemonic populism presupposes a radical affective investment. Interestingly enough, on top of being phrased in straightforward psychoanalytic jargon, this argument also concludes by highlighting no less than the 'identity' between the hegemonic logic and the psychoanalytic logic of the *objet petit a*:

> No social fullness is achievable except through hegemony; and hegemony is nothing more than the investment, in a partial object, of a fullness which will always evade us because it is purely mythical [...] The logic of the *objet petit a* and the hegemonic logic are not just similar: they are simply identical.
>
> (Laclau 2005, p. 116)

The registering of affectivity and enjoyment allows, thus, a more comprehensive account of the psychosocial dynamics at play adding to discourse theory an important new angle.

In a bid to demonstrate the importance of a Freud- and Lacan-inspired retroactivity in critical political theorisation, we can perhaps bring this chapter to a close by interpreting the recent resurgence of populism globally, in both its inclusionary and exclusionary forms (incarnated in certain Latin-American governments, as well as in European parties, such as Podemos and Syriza, and in European right-wing populist forces, such as the *Front National,* respectively), as an indication of a deepening discontent and dissatisfaction with the functioning of global democracy under conditions of a crisis-ridden neo-liberal globalisation:

> If a society managed to achieve an institutional order of such a nature that all demands were satisfied within its own immanent mechanisms, there would be no populism but, for obvious reasons, there would be no politics either. The need to constitute a 'people' (a plebs claiming to be a populus) arises only when that fullness is not achieved, and partial objects within society (aims, figures, symbols) are so cathected that they become the name of its absence.
>
> (Laclau 2005, pp. 116–7)

For example, in countries of the European South, such as Greece, social and political dislocations were positively indexed through the articulation and investment of new such partial objects; newcomers, such as Podemos, or previously marginal political forces, such as Syriza, were de facto entrusted with the task of representing the absence/dislocation, voicing the despair and indignation associated with it, as well as with restoring the dignity and well-being of the citizenry (fullness).

A psychoanalytic framework focusing on the role of language can also account for the turn of events culminating in the second victory of Syriza in September 2015, following a six-month long, tortuous negotiation with international and European institutions and its eventual capitulation to the austerity diktats. Indeed, how can Syriza's second victory in the face of such a failure be explained? Going back to our introduction (also see note 3), we could risk offering an explanation based on the Lacanian distinction between need, demand and desire. As we have seen, in humans, every need has to be articulated in language, in a demand to the Other (initially, the mother), who is invested with the power to satisfy or frustrate them. In that sense, on top of expressing biological *need*, *demand* also functions as the vehicle of *desire*, with the subject thus implicated in a relation of dependence to the Other, whose recognition, approval and love acquires a supreme value: 'Desire begins to take shape in the margin in which demand rips away from need' (Lacan 2006, p. 689). Thus, if a baby is hungry and cries, but the mother cuddles it, without offering any food, the chances are that the baby will stop crying (albeit temporarily), because part of the demand has been satisfied, even if need has remained unsatisfied. In many cases, in social life, an effective structuration of desire can sustain itself for long periods. Perhaps the second victory of Syriza should be interpreted along similar lines: What if the first Syriza government has been rewarded for satisfying desire, for offering recognition and approval, for voicing the demands of the Greek people to the European institutions and the world media (Stavrakakis 2015), even though needs remain frustrated? Only time will, of course, tell whether this choreography of desire will manage to sustain itself in the longer term, for how long and under which particular conditions.

Notes

1 Availability here indicates a multitude of ways through which the social world actively and/or passively, in a rigorous or a banal way, *interpellates* the lacking subject, instituting thus a two-way movement.
2 A constitutive ambivalence also characteristic of the imaginary, of what Lacan calls the 'mirror stage'.
3 This is also what conditions *desire*: 'In "murdering" the real world of objects and thereby constituting a reality inherently structured by the system of language, the human subject undergoes a transformation from a biological organism with needs that can be simply satisfied to a human being with unavoidable and fundamentally frustrating desires' (Lee 1990, p. 94). From now on, things get quite complicated; in Lacan's own words, 'It is when the Word is incarnated that things really start going badly. Man is no longer at all happy, he no longer resembles at all a little dog who wags his tail or a nice monkey who masturbates. He no longer resembles anything. He is ravaged by the Word' (Lacan 2013, p. 74).
4 Also see, for more details, Stavrakakis (1999, p. 24).
5 This is why, as Bruce Fink has highlighted, 'Lacan unceremoniously abolishes the enclosure, eliminating the apparent harmony of the image and the seeming totality it forms' (Fink 2004, p. 80). For a detailed analysis, see Stavrakakis (1999, p. 24).
6 See, for a lengthier exposition, Stavrakakis (1999, p. 25).
7 On another level, it could also be argued that, even when it is revealed, this nonexistence of the mythical guarantee of symbolic reality can always be *ad hoc* administered through the continuous deferral of signification, through the passage from signified effect to signified effect: 'Of course, such an idea is mythical, but it does nevertheless play an important role in our lived experience of language. But this fixed meaning is in fact always just another signifier, evoking others, generating yet another signified effect' (Pluth 2007, p. 33).
8 For another relevant example, see the discussion of the Longitude problem in Stavrakakis (1999, pp. 60–62).
9 This 'natural' illusion can, of course, be replaced by any other type of supposedly extra-discursive *guarantee* (God, mathematics, etc.), something extending the scope of this mechanism beyond this particular type of mythical transference.
10 Part of this section creatively rearticulates and expands arguments initially developed in Stavrakakis (2007, ch. 2).
11 A paradoxical status that, as we have seen, was also visible in the function of the Gold Standard.

References

Barthes, R, 1973, *Mythologies*, Paladin, London.
Borch-Jacobsen, M, 1991, *Lacan, the absolute master*, Stanford University Press, Stanford, CA.
Bourdieu, P, 1991, *Language and symbolic power*, Polity, Cambridge.
Chaitin, G, 1989, 'Lacan's Letter', *MLN*, vol. 103, no. 5, *Comparative Literature*, pp. 995–1011.
Chaitin, G, 1996, *Rhetoric and culture in Lacan*, Cambridge University Press, Cambridge.
Derrida, J, 1981, *Positions*, University of Chicago Press, Chicago, IL.
Fink, B, 2004, *Lacan to the letter*, University of Minnesota Press, Minneapolis, MN.
Goux, J-J, 1990, *Symbolic economies*, Cornell University Press, Ithaca, NY.
Goux, J-J, 1996, *The coiners of language*, University of Oklahoma Press, Norman, OK.
Jameson, F, 1991, *Postmodernism or the cultural logic of late capitalism*, Verso, London.
Lacan, J, 1979, *The four fundamental concepts of psychoanalysis*, Penguin, London.
Lacan, J, 1993, *The seminar of Jacques Lacan. Book III: The psychoses, 1955–56*, Routledge, London.
Lacan, J, 1998, *The seminar of Jacques Lacan. Book XX: Encore, on feminine sexuality, the limits of love and knowledge, 1972–3*, Norton, New York.
Lacan, J, 2006, *Ecrits*, Norton, New York.
Lacan, J, 2008, *My teaching*, Verso, London.
Lacan, J, 2013, *The triumph of religion*, Polity, Cambridge.
Laclau, E, 1990, *New reflections on the revolution of our time*, Verso, London.

Laclau, E, 1996, *Emancipation(s)*, Verso, London.
Laclau, E, 2003, 'Discourse and jouissance: A reply to Glynos and Stavrakakis', *Journal for Lacanian Studies*, 1(2), pp. 278–85.
Laclau, E, 2004, 'Glimpsing the future: A reply', in *Laclau: A critical reader*, eds. Simon Critchley & Oliver Marchart, Routledge, London, pp. 279–328.
Laclau, E, 2005, *On populist reason*, Verso, London.
Laclau, E & Mouffe, C, 1985, *Hegemony and socialist strategy*, Verso, London.
Miller, J-A, 2002, 'Enjoyment as axis of Lacan's teaching', *Psychanalysi*, vol. 5, pp. 43–51 (in Greek).
More, T, 2002, *Utopia*, Cambridge University Press, Cambridge.
Pluth, E, 2007, *Signifiers and acts*, SUNY Press, Albany, NY.
Shepherdson, C, 2008, *Lacan and the limits of language*, Fordham Press, New York.
Stavrakakis, Y, 1999, *Lacan and the political*, Routledge, London.
Stavrakakis, Y, 2007, *The Lacanian left*, SUNY Press, Albany, NY.
Stavrakakis, Y, 2015, 'Populism in power: Syriza's Challenge to Europe', *Juncture*, vol. 21, no. 4, pp. 273–280.
Žižek, S, 1989, *The sublime object of ideology*, Verso, London.
Žižek, S, 1993, *Tarrying with the negative*, Duke University Press, Durham, NC.
Žižek, S, 1994, *The metastases of enjoyment*, Verso, London.

6

The discourse theory of Ernesto Laclau

Christoffer Kølvraa

Introduction

A core concern in the study of the interface between language and politics is the issue of how ideological power is attained and maintained through certain types of language use, resulting in a distinct kind of symbolic structuring of the socio-political space. This issue is at the heart of Ernesto Laclau's work on discourse and hegemony. Here, for a start, hegemony can be taken to signify the kind of political power constituted not through brute repression or domination, nor through the inertia of tradition or convention, but by way of formulating a political or ideological programme for society with which people can actively identify and invest in emotionally.

What has become known as 'discourse theory' was first formulated in the book *Hegemony and socialist strategy* (1985 [2001]) by Ernesto Laclau and Chantal Mouffe. In it, they attempted to formulate a 'post-Marxist' theory of the formation of hegemonic struggles by drawing on post-structuralism. In describing their approach as post-Marxist, they wished to convey that, while their notion of hegemony rested on a rejection of central tenets in classical Marxist thought, it was, nonetheless, still inspired by, and formulated in and through, the conceptual universe of Marxist theory (Laclau & Mouffe 1985 [2001], p. 4). In particular, Antonio Gramsci and his theory of hegemony is a source of inspiration, because Gramsci's idea of hegemony as the 'organization of consent' seeks to escape the economic determinism of 'vulgar Marxism' and to afford the ideological superstructure relative autonomy. But according to Laclau and Mouffe, Gramsci still considers the central role of the working class to be determined by economic location, and thus, ultimately, he does not escape the economic essentialism inherent in Marxism (Barrett 1994). Hence the notion of hegemony in *Hegemony and socialist strategy* is developed through a detailed discussion of Marxist theorising, while clearly superseding this in a fuller engagement with an insistence on contingency and the anti-foundationalism present in various strands of post-structuralist thought.

Since the publication of *Hegemony and socialist strategy*, however, the theory has been substantially broadened and, in some cases, altered by Ernesto Laclau, primarily in such works as *New reflections on the revolution of our time* (1990), *Emancipation(s)* (1996) and, more recently, *On populist reason* (2005). Although his 1985 work with Chantal Mouffe remains the best-known and most widely cited of these, it does, nonetheless, not do justice to either Laclau or discourse theory if considering an introduction such as this without taking later developments on board. But what follows will not take the form of a 'history' of discourse theory, focusing closely on the various reformulations and the context and reasons for their introduction. Rather, the aim here is to relay to the reader, not necessarily already familiar with discourse theory, its fundamental arguments, assumptions and potential applications. Although Chantal Mouffe has also developed her own strand of discourse theory, here, I will focus primarily on Laclau's work.

Despite various developments and changes, Laclau's discourse theory does, nevertheless, remain constant in its concern to explain and understand the deeper dynamics of political dominance and conflict in society. It differs therefore from a more Foucauldian ambition to explore extensive knowledge systems (cf. Foucault 1972) and from the preoccupation central to Critical Discourse Analysis to understand the finer rhetorical strategies and manoeuvres embedded in media and political texts (cf. Reisigl & Wodak 2001; Wodak, de Cillia, Reisigl & Liebhart 1999). Furthermore, discourse theory differs from these approaches in that it rejects the former's reliance on the 'extra-discursive' and is fundamentally at odds with the often Habermasian foundations of the latter (Forchtner 2011).

As has been pointed out by David Howarth (2000, p. 117; 2004, p. 266), Laclau's interests are primarily of an ontological nature, seeking to question the very foundations on which any construction and investigation of society, politics and power must ultimately rest, and thus to challenge and criticise other ontologies, primarily of an essentialist or objectivist bent. The ontic level of exploring 'the nature of specific types of object, practice, institutions or even concrete discourses' (Howarth 2004, p. 266) receives much less attention in Laclau's work (see also Mouffe 2005, pp. 8–9). This means that, as regards the application of discourse theory to a concrete empirical material or case – not to mention the development of suitable 'methods' – this is something that Laclau tends to leave to others. Indeed, as Jacob Torfing points out, the critical reflection on the choice of suitable methods in concrete analysis is thus made the responsibility of anyone employing discourse theory, even if its founder shows very little interest in such issues (Torfing 2005, p. 25).

Thus, even if I include some explanatory analytical examples in what follows, I will nevertheless primarily seek to explain the major theoretical building blocks of Laclau's theory, starting with his understanding of 'Discourse' as being equally constituted by the dynamics of articulation and dislocation, and from there, moving on to the more overtly political concepts of hegemony, empty signifiers and their relationship to the development of ideological affect or political passion.

Discourse, articulation and dislocation

The starting point for Laclau and Mouffe is Ferdinand de Saussure's idea of language as a system of signs whose meaning is determined solely by their relation to each other (Howarth 2000, pp. 18–23). On the basis of this understanding of meaning as a strictly relational phenomenon, Laclau and Mouffe first define the concept of articulation as 'any practice establishing a relation among elements such that their identity is modified as a result of the articulatory practice' (Laclau & Mouffe 1985 [2001], p. 105), and from this a first notion of discourse as simply 'the structured totality resulting from the articulatory practice' (Laclau & Mouffe 1985 [2001], p. 105). Discourse should, at its most basic, be perceived as 'any complex of elements in which relations play the constitutive role' (Laclau 2005, p. 68, see also Laclau & Mouffe 1985 [2001], pp. 106–110). As this might indicate, Laclau furthermore emphasises that his notion of discourse is one of 'a meaningful totality which transcends the distinction between the linguistic and the extra-linguistic' (Laclau 1993, p. 435). Discourse is not simply 'text and talk', but also entails anything meaningful, including individuals, objects, actions and practices. Discourse in this sense is very much material, or rather it includes the material alongside the linguistic insofar as it is meaningful (Laclau & Mouffe 1987, pp. 82–84).

This means that Laclau and Mouffe manifestly reject the legitimacy of a distinction between discursive and non-discursive practices – a distinction that is still present in the work of Foucault (Laclau & Mouffe 1985 [2001], pp. 107–108). Discourses are not determined or secured by some non-discursive context or ground, because, insofar as this ground or context is meaningful, it too is discursively structured. This means that Laclau and Mouffe reject any Marxist notion of determination in the last instance by the economy, and also any idea of a subject external to, and able to, autonomously master discourse. Rather, they accept Foucault's notion of subject positions in order to emphasise that the position of the speaking individual too is constructed in and through discourse. This in no way entails a denial of a world external to thought, only an insistence that the world ('reality'), insofar as it is meaningful, is discursively structured. In a classical example, they argue that:

> An earthquake or the falling of a brick is an event that certainly exists, in the sense that it occurs here and now, independent of my will. But whether their specificity as objects is constructed in terms of 'natural phenomena' or 'expressions of the wrath of God', *depends on the structuring of a discursive field.*
> (Laclau & Mouffe 1985 [2001], p. 108)

Laclau and Mouffe therefore speak of *elements* which, when incorporated in a discursive structure and thus given meaning, become *moments* (Laclau & Mouffe 1985 [2001], p. 106).

But it is not just that there is nothing extra-discursive which can ground or stabilise the discursive order, it is also that such a differential system would be unable to stabilise itself. Crucial to Laclau's thinking is the (post-structuralist) notion that no differential discursive structure can ever attain full closure. It cannot constitute itself as a full and stable totality in the sense that Saussure imagined the language-system to be. Laclau argues that, for such a differential system to constitute itself as a 'finished' totality, it would need to be able to constitute its clearly defined limits, and this would mean that the system as such would itself need to be constituted against an 'outside' beyond these limits. But the consequence of this would be that, in relation to the system's limits and beyond, the internal differences (of which it consists) would be subverted; they would become equated qua their common differentiation from the 'constitutive' outside. What emerges then is the paradox that such systemic limits are both the condition of possibility for a differential system and its conditions of impossibility. The limits and the outside make the system possible, but they simultaneously subvert the internal relations of difference that define it. A fundamental split and ambivalence thus enters every moment of the system as they become undecidably suspended between their (internal) differential identities, and their identity as similar moments qua their being part of the same system vis-à-vis its outside (Laclau & Mouffe 1985 [2001], pp. 110–112, Laclau 1996a, pp. 37–38).

In a more direct sense, this means that whatever a discursive order excludes returns to haunt it. The excluded elements remain as a destabilising factor always preventing 'full closure'. This destabilising 'outside' of excluded or alternative meanings, undermining a given discursive order, is what Laclau and Mouffe call the 'field of discursivity', a potential 'surplus of meaning' consisting of elements that cannot be fixed as moments in the discursive structure. Therefore, any discursive order remains, fundamentally, only one contingent configuration or construction and never becomes able to domesticate the entirety of the field of discursivity, or shut down what, as such, remains a fundamental 'openness' of the social (Laclau & Mouffe 1985 [2001], pp. 110–114). An example might be the notion of an essential link between the people, territory and culture found in nationalism. Then, the point that Laclau and Mouffe are making would be that, no matter how dominant such a nationalist discourse becomes, it is still confronted by what it cannot integrate, by the elements in the social space that do not fit its harmonious image of an ideal national reality. Historically, these excluded – and (for nationalists) haunting – elements have often taken the form of transnational or migrant minorities which, as such, can be said to challenge (or 'dislocate') the dominant discourse, not simply because they do not 'fit', but because this very 'misfitting' reveals that the version of reality portrayed in 'nationalist' discourse is a construction; it is only one possible image of reality among others.

This does not of course amount to an argument that meaning, as such, is impossible. As Laclau and Mouffe note, a world without *any* fixation of meaning would be a world of the psychotic (Laclau and Mouffe 1985 [2001], p. 112). But fundamental to their thinking is an insistence that discourses are only ever a partial fixation of meaning. Indeed, without such insistence, the very concept of articulation would be redundant; social life would take the form of an endless re-enactment of structurally prescribed practices and statements, and we would simply have moved determinism from the extra-discursive to the discursive realm (cf. Laclau 1997, p. 299).

The partial fixity nevertheless achieved relies on what Laclau and Mouffe call *nodal points*. These are (socially) privileged signifiers around which other meanings can stabilise. Indeed, the idea of nodal points borrows heavily from the Lacanian idea of a discursive *point de caption*, a notion that trades on the metaphor of a 'quilting button' (Laclau and Mouffe 1985 [2001], p. 112). The basic idea is that, even if the discursive structure never attains its own full stability and 'closure', its relative coherence is still secured by it being 'tied down' around certain such nodal points. In concrete terms, a nodal point might be a central concept, in relation to which, other ideas in the same discourse or ideology are defined or restricted, as for example might be said to be the case for 'Volk' in National Socialism, which heavily influenced the meaning of signifiers from 'Art' to 'foreign policy'. However, it is crucial to note that nodal points can also take other linguistic forms; they may take the form of an especially evocative metaphor, a name, or even an image. Thus, in a fuller definition of articulation, Laclau and Mouffe can state that:

> The practice of articulation, therefore, consists in the construction of nodal points which partially fix meaning; and the particular character of this fixation proceeds from the openness of the social, a result in its turn, of the constant overflowing of every discourse by the infinitude of the field of discursivity.
>
> (Laclau and Mouffe 1985 [2001]:113)

Although the inherent contingency and partial instability of any discursive order is, as such, fundamental to the theory, Laclau and Mouffe are of course aware that the social sphere is, most of the time, experienced as a relatively stable conglomerate of 'taken for granted' practices, relationships and identities. They thus introduce the notion of sedimentation in order to capture the point that even if, in the last instance, contingency is ineliminable, certain meanings can settle over time and come to appear as 'natural and unalterable' (Laclau 1990, pp. 34–35). Indeed, what they term 'the social' designates those social practices that have become sedimented, whereas 'the political' is the realm of conflict and contestation, of breaking and making new and old meanings. The insistence on a fundamental contingency would then mean that, even if it is, at times, experienced as though society is characterised by great stability, moments of the social could always, in the right circumstances, become re-politicised and thus again enter the realm of the political (Laclau 1990, pp. 34–36). Such circumstances are what Laclau later comes to designate as 'dislocation' (Laclau 1990, pp. 39-43). Dislocation refers to 'the process by which the contingency of discursive structures is made visible' (Howarth & Stavrakakis 2000, p. 3), meaning the impact of developments or events that destabilises the discursive structure, which literally throws it 'out of joint'. Prominent examples of such processes are revolutions, natural disasters or wars, but more extensive phenomena, such as the impact of globalisation on the nation-state, or the emergence of mass migration, may also be thought of as dislocatory processes. Even a political scandal or a spectacular election defeat, while on a smaller scale, might be thought of as carrying dislocating potential. The concept of dislocation is associated with developments or events that bring about a feeling of insecurity, change and possibility, and thus with situations where hitherto-accepted structural conditions, or limitations, are experienced as loosening or falling away. This is central to discourse theory because its core arguments and ideas aim precisely at understanding the political processes released in such turbulent times of change.

It is at times of dislocation that the (increasingly destabilised) discursive structures leave most room for subjects to formulate new political projects, new power relationships and ultimately, new forms of societal discursive order. In order to capture this, Laclau argues that beyond the structural dimension of the subject – its subject-position – we must also consider a more manifest and autonomous form of political subjectivity (Laclau & Zac 1994; Laclau 1996a, pp. 47–65; Laclau 1990, pp. 60–67). This notion of political subjectivity would then capture the dimension of radical agency in the subject, its ability (in times of dislocation) to do more than merely reproduce the structural conditions of its subject-position. Indeed, as 'dislocation is the source of freedom' (Laclau 1990, p. 60), Laclau describes the subject as 'nothing but this distance between the undecidable structure and the decision' (Laclau 1990, p. 30). The subject is never a transcendental one in total command of its discourses, but neither is it simply a structural product – a mere position in the structure. This is precisely because the structure is constitutively 'damaged' or incomplete. There is, in other words, true political subjectivity only because the structure does not manage to (fully) produce the subject, and thus cannot ultimately fully determine its decisions (cf. Laclau 1996b). At times of dislocation, when the world seems literally to be 'thrown out of joint' a space opens up in which political subjects can remake the structural conditions of their world, sometimes to a radical extent.

It is, however, crucial that this is not misunderstood as meaning that the subject thrives on the kind of insecurity and instability characterising periods of radical dislocation. Rather, Laclau continually emphasizes that, even if a fully stable discursive order of society is never achieved, it is, nonetheless, what is continually being attempted and sought after. The paradox here is then that, even if such totalising closure is impossible, it is nonetheless necessary, because without the endeavours to establish a fully coherent order there would be no meaning or identity at all (Laclau 2005, p. 70). Put somewhat more substantially, the fundamental idea is that what Laclau calls the 'fullness of society' (i.e. a society in which everything makes sense and total harmony rules) is constitutively unachievable, but it does nonetheless remain necessary to maintain such an idea of full closure as something akin to a communal ideal or common utopian horizon. Otherwise, the entire fabric of society would dissolve into its contingent elements; the illusion of a socially cohesive community guided by certain rules of behaviour, hierarchies of power and practices of exchange, would be revealed as a mere construction and would cease to exercise any regulatory influence.

As such, dislocation might be a moment of freedom, but it is a freedom that the subject employs to fight dislocation, to articulate new discursive structures, to establish new societal orders that, themselves, will never be complete and therefore require their own utopian horizons to achieve a partial stability. Dislocation is, as such and at once, a moment of emancipation and of trauma; it opens a space for the subject to act beyond the confines of established subject positions, but in so doing, it literally puts the subject in an 'identity crisis', in dire need of identifying in new ways, and with new political projects (Laclau 1990, p. 39; Howarth & Stavrakakis 2000, pp. 12–14).

An example that might serve to pull these various theoretical strands together is to consider the dislocatory impact of globalisation on the national welfare state and the rise of the so-called populist radical-right parties. Whereas the existence of the European welfare states and their relatively culturally homogenous societies did, in the post-war decades, increasingly come to be taken for granted – that is, they did to some extent become a de-politicised socially sedimented expectation of citizens – the impact of a globalising economy and other trans-border flows have served to re-politicise the cultural form and political futures of European states and societies. As such, the weakening of the welfare state has, in some ways, opened up the political field to new kinds of political projects, for example, the reformulated ethno-nationalism of the European populist radical right. The dislocation from globalisation has, as it were, introduced increased freedom for subjects in relation to more traditional (political) subject positions, such as 'socialist', 'liberal', and so on, and allowed for a fuller 'political subjectivity', through which such genuinely new political formations, ideas and projects can be formulated. In other ways, however, the attractive promise of these new ethno-nationalist political projects is precisely to reduce or even eliminate the felt dislocation from which they sprang, to reconstitute national sovereignty, bring the economy under domestic control, secure the borders and reinvigorate national culture. It is the process through which different groups or identities are, in times of dislocation, joined together in such new and forceful common political projects, that Laclau seeks to understand through his concept of hegemony.

Hegemony, empty signifiers and affect

In order to understand the theory of hegemony offered by Laclau (and Mouffe) it is necessary to move from their general understanding of the discursive construction of meaning to a more specific one of the constitution and dynamics of a political space and of the groups and forces operating therein. Already, in *Hegemony and socialist strategy*, Laclau and Mouffe offer the idea that political spaces are at the most abstract level constituted by two, in fact opposite, articulatory logics. What this means is that the relations forged by articulation can in general be viewed as expressions or combinations of a logic of difference and/or a logic of equivalence. The logic of difference is that fundamental rule of the Saussurean idea of language that operates as a differential system; it is a logic that secures the identity of a specific element (which can be a demand, a group, a voter, etc.) by differentiating it from other elements; it is a logic that produces particularity by way of distinction. The logic of equivalence, in contrast, forges relations between elements by emphasising their similarity, by grouping, categorising or linking them together on the basis of something held in common. As such, it is a logic that tends towards the universal, in that it actually weakens distinctions between elements, which thereby enter into what Laclau and Mouffe call a 'chain of equivalences' (Laclau & Mouffe 1985 [2001], pp. 127–134; Butler, Laclau & Žižek 2000, pp. 302–304; Laclau 2005, pp. 77–78). Laclau considers these two kinds of dynamics to be fundamental and argues that even if he uses the terms logic of difference/ equivalence specifically about the form these dynamics take in a political space, the same duality is present in linguistics as the distinction between the syntagmatic (combination/ difference) and the paradigmatic (similarity/substitution) poles of language, and in rhetoric as the difference between metonymy and metaphor (Laclau 1988, p. 256). As should be clear from such parallels, these two logics are not simply to be understood as embodying a dichotomy between one that produces (political) meaning and one that undermines it. Rather, the meaning of a political space (its nodal points) is constituted by the tenuous compromise between the two dynamics, and the total domination of either is equally untenable. If the logic of difference ruled supreme, then no wider groups, political programmes or alliances between different interests could emerge; the political space would be completely fragmented and atomistic. But if the logic of equivalence were to rise to total dominance, there would only be sameness and no possibility of differentiation. In such a case, meaning – the foundation of which is still difference – would itself evaporate (Butler, Laclau & Žižek 2000, pp. 304–307, Torfing 1999, pp. 96–99).

The fundamental dynamics of a political space is as such conceived as a game of both differences and equivalences that proceed from the various attempts at linking and contrasting different groups, ideas and interests in wider alliances and conflicts. And this dynamic is played out as different political forces, actors or groups seek to link various so-called 'floating signifiers' into certain 'chains of equivalences', or at least to loosen them from the chains of opponents. A floating signifier is an element that has not (yet) received a definite meaning, either because a process of dislocation has detached it from its traditional sedimented position, or because various political forces seek to ascribe it meaning in radically different ways (Laclau & Mouffe 1985 [2001], p. 113; Andersen 2003, pp. 53–54). In essence, the cut and thrust of politics can be understood as 'a double operation of breaking and extending chains of equivalence' (Butler, Laclau & Laddaga 1997, p. 8), by way of rearticulating the floating signifiers of a given situation or period.

As such, the partial fixing of political meaning requires and retains both these logics. If we take the example of the nodal point of communism quilting the elements of democracy, freedom, the state, and so on, then, as Jacob Torfing puts it, what actually happens is that 'a variety of signifiers are floating within the field of discursivity as their traditional meaning has been lost; suddenly some master signifier [the nodal point] intervenes and retroactively constitutes their identity by fixing the floating signifiers within a paradigmatic chain of equivalence' (Torfing 1999, p. 99). The signifiers 'quilted' by the nodal point are clearly not simply synonymous, they retain some of their individual meaning. Equivalence is not identity and the individual links never become completely equivalent to the extent that all distinction between them is subverted. But in being collectively linked to communism, a certain equivalence *is* constructed between the linked concepts (democracy, freedom, the state) qua their (new) status as various elements of communism. A crucial point here is, however, that the construction of equivalence must rely on common external differentiation. Given that there is nothing essentially communist in these signifiers, their linking in the equivalential chain of communism proceeds from the positing of a 'common outside', that is, of something that they are collectively differentiated from (e.g. the false democracy, exploitation and bourgeois state of capitalism). Here we are of course simply returning to the same dilemma, one which was formulated around the undecidability of a differential system and its limits. The unstable compromise between the two logics thus invades even the nodal point and ensures that these can only ever be points of *partial* fixity.

However, the hegemonic process that emerges at times of dislocation involves the rising to dominance of a logic of equivalence in political life and from this the production of empty signifiers and antagonism. As argued, the starting point (both theoretically and analytically) is a situation of dislocation, for example, a society where an uprooting force or process has thrown traditional identities, hierarchies and social relations into doubt. In a broader sense, it could be said that this is a situation where there is a proliferation of floating signifiers, where old ideas and institutions are suddenly open to reinterpretation or rejection. In such a situation of insecurity, demands will be made by a broad range of societal groups, which are – qua the logic of difference – initially differentiated by the particularity of each of their specific demands or identities. However, if the dislocation of the societal order proceeds, a situation gradually emerges where an increasing number of various demands cannot be accommodated, or in more general terms where an increasing number of groups do not feel that their identities are being recognised, their privileges respected or their interests protected. Laclau argues that an equivalential logic will potentially begin to emerge between these groups, not necessarily because of any deep or substantial overlap between their particular demands, but simply because these demands are equally frustrated in a given situation (Laclau 1996a, pp. 40–45; Laclau 2005, pp. 72–78). However, if the chain is gradually extended by adding more disappointed or oppressed groups to this emerging political front, then the political space will gradually shift from being characterised by the presence of multiple different demands and interests (that is from a situation where the logic of difference is dominant), to a more dichotomous form in which society appears increasingly split between the 'chain' of groups thus made equivalent in and by their frustration, and the regime, power or outside group against which their protests and demands are aimed (i.e. to a situation where a logic of equivalence is dominant). As the chain extends and ever more demands are added to it, so increasingly less substantial content will be shared by all the demands. Finally, the equivalential chain will express little more than a gesture of opposition to the current order with which its individual links have been disappointed in multiple different ways. The chain thereby eventually tends towards representing nothing other than the absence of a societal order able to honour all the various demands (Laclau 1997, pp. 304–311). As Laclau writes, 'the community created by this equivalential expansion will be, thus, the pure idea of communitarian fullness which is absent – as a result of the presence of the repressive power' (Laclau 1996a, p. 42). However, this 'pure idea' of a better society will still need to be represented somehow, to attain some kind of political signification. Yet any signifier assigned to represent the totality of the chain (i.e. to formulate the content of its overarching common demand) will, Laclau argues, tend towards a certain emptiness, given that it must denote, not an individual link in the chain (and its concrete demand), but must, as such, become a unifying signifier for the chain. This 'empty signifier' must, so to speak, mean everything to everybody (ideally embodying all the various demands in the chain in one grand demand), and can in reality, therefore, only be a signifier that means very little, or more precisely, one that has very little precise and concrete content. Thus, an empty signifier does not of course simply mean a signifier without any signified (which would simply be noise (Laclau 2005, p. 105)); rather, Laclau gives the example of slogans such as 'Justice' or 'Respect', arguing that the extremely malleable meaning of such terms allows them to function as empty signifiers denoting little more than the absent societal fullness represented in extensive equivalential chains (Laclau 1997, pp. 308–309; Laclau 1996a, pp. 36–46). These signifiers are thus empty, simply because they are made to signify something, which in essence, cannot be signified, namely, the totality of grievances and demands in society, or rather the very fullness that would harmoniously resolve these. The empty signifier therefore has a utopian dimension, it designates, so to speak, the necessarily vague hope for a new and better order in society.

Once again, however, it is crucial for Laclau to emphasize that this equivalential forging of a common utopian hope for a better society can only proceed with the construction of a common enemy. The equivalential chain of demands is initially unified against the 'repressive' power, which cannot or will not, honour these demands. But as the unity of the chain tends towards a more empty utopian form, so too does the construction of the common enemy become less concrete (Laclau 2006, p. 655). If the empty signifier ultimately signifies only a common hope for a better society, then the enemy against which it is united comes to signify everything that is wrong with the present one. It is this kind of enmity towards a common enemy, constructed in contrast to an equivalential chain unified around an empty signifier, which Laclau designates as antagonism. For Laclau, antagonism designates the kind of difference that distinguishes different players from the cheat (Laclau 1990, p. 11). The antagonist does not simply represent 'another way of playing the game' – that is, an alternative yet legitimate view (of society) – but an opponent who undermines and wrecks the game. As such, antagonistic difference is certainly not the kind that is internal to a discursive order that produces and secures particular identities through differentiation, but a kind of difference that is experienced to prevent, block or undermine identity. In the presence of the antagonist, I cannot be fully myself; the antagonist represents an outside that is experienced as threatening the 'inside' (Laclau & Mouffe 1985 [2001], pp. 122–127, Laclau 2005, pp. 83–87).

There are thus strong similarities between the idea of antagonism and the foundational argument about the differential system and its constitutive limits and beyond (cf. Laclau 2004, pp. 318–319). Indeed, in *Hegemony and socialist strategy,* Laclau and Mouffe conceive of the presence of an antagonist as the source of contingency and dislocation. But in his later works, Laclau instead argues that '"dislocation" is an experience more primary than "antagonism", that the latter is already a discursive inscription of dislocation and that, as such, it is purely contingent and needs discursive conditions of possibility' (Laclau 1999, p. 96). Thus, antagonism is not the source of contingency and dislocation in discursive structures, but rather its symptom. It might be said that there is a certain projection going on; in times of dislocation where the coherence of discursive order is indeed destabilised and threatened, an antagonist is constructed as a tangible explanation for this, as an enemy that can embody and bear responsibility for everything that is wrong with society. If we take the example of current nation-state societies affected in various ways by globalisation, the growing support of far-right parties is, of course, accompanied by a growing enmity towards immigrant populations. What Laclau's understanding of dislocation and antagonism is able to grasp is the potential disconnect between the forces actually challenging various traditional forms of life and the concrete actors who end up being blamed and ostracised. Again, framing such a situation in Laclau's terms, it might be said that the partial fixity of a national discursive order – secured around the nodal point of the sovereign nation-state – is challenged by various dislocating forces, often grouped under the common heading of globalisation, and this results in an experience of weakened national sovereignty and security in relation to global finance, transnational threats, 'foreign' cultural influences, migrant flows or technological developments. In this situation, a variety of demands will be left unfulfilled, for example, demands for job security, for welfare, for public order/security, or for the preservation of traditional cultural forms. Although these demands are initially logically addressed to state authorities, far-right parties can be said to have successfully equivalated any of these under the empty signifier of national identity, and thus installed immigrant communities as the antagonist thereby experienced as blocking or preventing the utopian unfolding of the harmonious national community with jobs for all, extensive welfare services, safe streets and a familiar cultural homogeneity. The far right has, as such, been able to relaunch the image of a traditional, culturally uniform, national community as an empty signifier around which a wide range of contemporary fears and worries can be equivalated. The hegemony of such parties is, then, a consequence of them being able to offer and embody the empty signifier, and to style themselves as the primary guarantors of its utopian promise and staunch defenders against the antagonistic forces supposedly preventing its realisation.

If, then, the context for hegemony is a dichotomised situation between, from one perspective, an equivalential chain unified around empty signifiers, and on the other, an antagonist constructed to embody everything evil and threatening, then what Laclau calls the hegemonic relationship is exactly what happens when a specific group is able to offer itself as the body or incarnation of the common empty signifier, when, for example, a certain party or leader is able to become the incarnation of 'justice' or 'respect' (Laclau 1996a, p. 43). It is this dynamic, through which a certain particularity (a distinct group with its own demands and interests) comes to represent the universality of multiple demands and grievances, which Laclau understands as the secret to hegemony. The point, in other words, is that if the equivalential chain has, in the end, little that is concrete and in common, other than a vague utopian notion of 'justice' to be attained, then there is immense power available to the group or leader that successfully presents itself, or him- or herself, as the very embodiment of the communal hope for 'justice'.

In order to explain how something empty of concrete meaning can nevertheless become the lynchpin of a political project, Laclau in his latest work stresses that the empty signifier – although emptied of what we might call strict semantic meaning (i.e. something like a concrete content or definition) – must nevertheless be understood as filled by affect (Laclau 2005, p. 110). The empty signifier is 'meaningful' or 'makes sense' in an affective mode; it is the object of a radical emotional investment, and can be so only because it is no longer tied to a restrictive semantic meaning. Slavoj Žižek has given the example that the heart of communities is most often made up by exactly such seemingly empty signifiers, claiming that what:

> guarantees the community's consistency is a signifier whose signified is an enigma for the members themselves – nobody really knows what it means, but each of them somehow presupposes that others know it, that it has to mean "the real thing", and so they use it all the time.
>
> (Žižek 2005, p. 305)

Thus, although the heart of a community is intensely emotionally invested in by its members, the attempt to precisely and concretely signify the essence of a community (i.e. what it really means to be English, Danish, Austrian, etc.) is rarely successful and often ends up recycling a set of stereotypically conventional expressions or metaphors. This mysterious core of community is never adequately captured – no matter how many concepts are loaded onto it, there is always something more that could be said – or rather 'it' (e.g. Englishness, Danishness, etc.) is always somehow more than can be articulated.

In Laclau's latest book, *On populist reason,* he increasingly draws on Lacanian psychoanalysis. He can thus point out that the hegemonic process through which a particular element or actor comes to embody the empty signifier, unifying a vast equivalential chain, can be understood as a political version of the logic of sublimation defined by Lacan as 'the elevation of an ordinary object to the dignity of the Thing [das Ding]' (Laclau 2005, p. 113). In Lacan's thinking, the Thing is the original site of *jouissance* (a state of affective intensity, of bliss or joy, sometimes given as the experience in the mother–child dyad), which is forever lost as the subject enters the world of language in the Symbolic realm. And yet, the desire for this *jouissance* remains and leads the subject to affectively invest in, or more precisely sublimate, various partial objects (which Lacan calls *objet petit a)* imagined to embody the *jouissance* of the Thing. In comparing this kind of dynamic with the one he himself has described as core to the hegemonic relationship, Laclau goes so far as to conclude that '[t]he logic of the *objet petit a* and the hegemonic logic are not just similar: they are simply identical' (Laclau 2005, p. 116). In Lacanian psychoanalysis, Laclau has found an explanation, or at least corroboration, for the fact that empty signifiers seem to command a radical emotional or affective investment. The crucial insight that Laclau embeds in his theory of hegemony is then that semantic vacuity is no obstacle to affective investment – quite the opposite, in fact. And as such, the process of hegemony – of assembling a political front across concrete interests and demands – unfolds in the realm of affect, rather than through semantic stringency or precision.

An apt example that can sum up many of the points made so far might be former US President Obama's first campaign for office in 2008. The presidential campaign in 2008 certainly proceeded, in a US context seemingly dislocated in various ways. Not only did the financial crisis burst into the public's awareness amid the election campaign, with the collapse of Lehman Brothers in September 2008, but also, in a wider sense, it could be suggested that the kind of purpose and zeal that had succeeded 9/11, and galvanised American society behind President Bush in the War on Terror, were waning and fragmenting as it became clear that such a war would tend to drag on, and, as critique of the US mounted in the wake of, for example, the Abu Ghraib scandal and the disregard the Bush administration had shown to the UN and to the traditional European allies of the US. There was, in other words, a wide range of grievances and demands that addressed the supposed shortcomings of the Bush administration, varying from its foreign policy and its 'pampering' of big business and Wall Street to its lack of initiative on issues of welfare and healthcare, and so on. Obama's actual political programme did of course concretely address some of these, but it quickly became apparent that his appeal was somehow more than the sum of his concrete answers. Increasingly, the Obama Campaign zoomed in on a few successful empty signifiers, namely 'Hope' and 'Change'. Indeed, it must be admitted that little could have been found as a campaign slogan that would have been less concrete than these two concepts. It seemed now that the promise of, or indeed the hope for, a different societal order – for a changed society – was able to unify a long list of different groups, minorities and interests in an equivalential chain, and that whatever each was more concretely hoping for and believed the concrete necessary change to be, it was, for everyone, Obama who came to embody the utopian emptiness of 'Change' and 'Hope' themselves. Clearly then, the rush of support that was later termed 'Obamamania' was precisely not constituted by the 'semantic precision' or argumentative rigour of Obama's political discourse, but rather by the affective investment through which various groups seemed to sublimate him into something almost akin to a national saviour.

Conclusion

In the end, it is worth re-emphasising that Laclau himself is first and foremost a political philosopher who is primarily interested in the ontological preconditions for the political. What he offers is a field of concepts that allows us to think about what political hegemony entails outside or across any specific political contexts, and thus an idea of what kinds of questions might be posed and what kind of dynamics might be tracked in a concrete instance of political struggle. But Laclau's theory does not entail anything resembling a hands-on method of investigation. When David Howarth (2004, p. 267) at one point raised the need for a so-called 'middle-range' theorisation that would better connect the ontological arguments in Laclau's work with concrete 'ontic' cases and analyses, Laclau wholly agreed, but did not then see the need for it to be him that developed such a middle-range tier of arguments (Laclau 2004, p. 321). To work with Laclau's theory in concrete cases will always involve looking for means to cover this middle-range ground, and it will analytically involve asking how elements recognised through the theory (e.g. an antagonistic conflict, a chain of equivalence, a hegemonic relationship, or an empty signifier) appear and are constructed in specific political, historical and cultural circumstances.

The original formulation of Laclau's (and Mouffe's) discourse theory in *Hegemony and socialist strategy* is now some 30 years old. However, due to its constant development and re-articulation, both by Laclau himself and by others, it has not been allowed to become dated. Concepts and ideas, such as chains of equivalence, nodal points, empty signifiers, dislocation and antagonism have spread and found many uses in constructivist or post-structuralist social and political analyses. And with Laclau's final turn to psychoanalysis, he was again changing the agenda for the study of political hegemonies. While *Hegemony and socialist strategy* left behind Marxist ideas of a material basis for society, in favour of an uncompromising insistence on its discursive constitution, Laclau's Lacanian engagements in *On populist reason* suggest – in his own terms – an expansion of the theoretical focus from one concerned most with the (discursive) 'form' of political hegemonies, to one which seeks to understand the sources of their (affective) 'force' (Laclau 2005, p. 110). This certainly is still a central and crucial ambition in any attempt to analyse contemporary political phenomena.

References

Barrett, M, 1994, 'Ideology, politics, hegemony: From Gramsci to Laclau and Mouffe' in *Mapping Ideology*, ed. S Žižek, Verso, London, pp. 235–264.
Butler, J, Laclau, E & Laddaga, R, 1997, 'The uses of equality', *Diacritics*, vol. 27, no.1 (Spring), pp. 2–12.
Butler, J, Laclau, E & Žižek, S, 2000, *Contingency, hegemony, universality*, Verso, London
Forchtner, B, 2011,'Critique, the discourse-historical approach and the Frankfurt School', *Critical Discourse Studies*, vol. 8, no.1, pp. 1–14.
Foucault, M, 1972, *The archaeology of knowledge & the discourse of language*, Pantheon Books, New York.
Howarth, D, 2000, *Discourse*, Open University Press, Buckingham.
Howarth, D, 2004, 'Hegemony, political subjectivity, and radical democracy', in *Laclau – a critical reader,* eds. S Critchley & O Marchart, Routledge, London, pp. 256–276.
Howarth, D & Stavrakakis, Y, 2000, 'Introducing discourse theory and political analysis', in *Discourse theory and political analysis*, eds. D Howarth, A Norval & Y Stavrakakis, Manchester University Press, Manchester.

Laclau, E, 1988, 'Metaphor and social antagonism', in *Marxism and the interpretation of culture*, eds. C Nelson & L Grossberg, University of Illinois Press, Illinois, pp. 249–257.
Laclau, E, 1990, *New reflections on the revolution of our time*, Verso, London.
Laclau, E, 1993, 'Discourse' in *A Companion to contemporary political philosophy*, eds., RE Goodin & P Pettit, Blackwell, Oxford, pp. 541–548.
Laclau, E, 1996a, *Emancipations(s)*, Verso, London.
Laclau, E, 1996b, 'Deconstruction, pragmatism, hegemony', in *Deconstruction and pragmatism*, ed. C Mouffe, Routledge, London, pp. 47–67.
Laclau, E, 1997, 'The death and resurrection of the theory of ideology', *MLN*, vol. 112, no.3, pp. 297–321.
Laclau, E, 2004, 'Glimpsing the future', in *Laclau – a critical reader,* eds. S Critchley & O Marchart, Routledge, London, pp. 279–328.
Laclau, E, 2005, *On populist reason*, Verso, London.
Laclau, E, 2006, 'Why constructing a people is the main task of radical politics', *Critical Inquiry*, vol. 32 (summer), pp. 646–680.
Laclau, E & Bowman, P, 1999, 'Politics, polemics and academics: An interview by Paul Bowman', *Parallax*, vol. 5, no.2, pp.93–107.
Laclau, E & Mouffe, C, 1987, 'Post-Marxism without apologies', *New Left Review*, vol. 166, pp. 79–106.
Laclau, E & Mouffe, C, 2001 [1985], *Hegemony and socialist strategy – towards a radical democratic politics*, Verso, London.
Laclau, E & Zac, L, 1994, 'Minding the gap: The subject of politics', in *The making of political identities*, ed. E Laclau, Verso, London, pp. 11–39.
Mouffe, C, 2005, *On the political,* Routledge, London.
Reisigl, M & Wodak, R, 2001, *Discourse and discrimination*, Routledge, London.
Torfing, J, 1999, *New theories of discourse*, Blackwell, Oxford.
Wodak, R, de Cillia, R, Reisigl, M & Liebhart, K, 1999, *The discursive construction of national identity*, Edinburgh University Press, Edinburgh.
Žižek, S, 2005, *Interrogating the real*, Continuum, London.

7
Pierre Bourdieu
Ally or foe of discourse analysis?

Andrew Sayer

Introduction

More than anything, Pierre Bourdieu's work was concerned with power. He was particularly interested in the 'soft forms of domination' that operate largely unnoticed and without coercion, and through which, in his view, many inequalities are reproduced. Discourse is a medium of such power, and his interest in language was primarily concerned with this aspect, for he considered it rare for language in everyday life to operate purely as a means of communication. His social theory of action emphasised embodied dispositions and semi-conscious practical skills and tendencies rather than discourse and conscious reasoning, know-how rather than knowing-that, and he continually attacked the academic or 'scholastic' tendency to reconstruct action in terms of reason, and indeed to reduce action to understanding, or discourse. For Bourdieu, much of what influences us does so below our reflexive radar, and is all the more powerful for that. Not surprisingly, his analyses are marked by a hermeneutics of suspicion rather than a hermeneutics of sympathy that affirms peoples' self-understanding. The result is a series of powerful, stinging critiques of domination, including that exercised unknowingly in the educational field by academics.

Although Bourdieu's writing contains examples of analyses of discourse – most formally in his studies of teacher–student interactions in schools and universities, and more informally in his discussions of political discourse, he was a fierce critic of 'discourse analysis', and of what he saw as excessive and misplaced emphasis on discourse in some parts of social science (Bourdieu 1991, p. 28). His own use of language has received much comment, particularly regarding his use of unusually long sentences with multiple subordinate clauses – a practice he defended, in a somewhat paranoid manner, as necessary for pre-empting any possible misreadings, especially where critics quote his work. Linguists might be tempted to dismiss Bourdieu for all these reasons. But it would be a grave mistake, for his work is immensely useful for anyone interested in discourse, particularly Critical Discourse Analysis and sociolinguistics, and indeed for anyone interested in language and power. He was a formidable and remarkably perceptive writer. It would be hard to read his most famous work, *Distinction*, one of the most important books in twentieth-century social science, without being struck by his command of the language of critical description in his analyses of everyday actions and ideas, and his ability to name normally hidden forms of domination (Bourdieu 1986).

To understand Bourdieu, it is necessary to grasp his key concepts – particularly habitus, field and capital – and how they complement each other in the study of social life. Yet, he always emphasised that they could only be assessed when put to use in studying the social world. Bourdieu's researches were always much more than a 'naming-of-parts' through the deployment of these terms; by engaging with the content of the practices and discourse in their social context, he produces interpretations of striking critical power. I recommend, for example, his brilliant analyses in *Language and symbolic power* of condescension, euphemism, working-class masculinity and the silencing power that legitimate language and its users can have over others, and of political discourse (Bourdieu 1991).

So, I shall first outline his primary concepts of habitus, field and capital, and his critique of what he called 'the scholastic fallacy' in interpreting the role of discourse in social life. I shall then show, via examples relating to language, how he combined these to analyse symbolic domination and the struggles or competitions of the social field, and then conclude with a brief evaluation.

Habitus

Habitus, Bourdieu's most famous concept, refers to the set of durable dispositions that individuals acquire through socialisation, particularly in early life, and which orient them towards the social and physical world around them. Given that these dispositions are acquired and embodied through repeated involvement in social relations and practices of the kinds peculiar to their situation, Bourdieu argues that there is a rough fit between the habitus and the individual's habitat, between their dispositions and their social positions. These dispositions in turn give rise to behaviours that tend to reproduce the very conditions in which those dispositions were formed. The dispositions are semi-conscious, involving a kind of 'feel for the game' that can neither be reduced to discursive knowledge, nor adequately explained by it. The expert tennis player can return the ball skilfully without thinking about it or being able to offer a good explanation of how it was done. The dispositions are acquired *semi-consciously*, partly with awareness, partly without, and they involve comportment and ways of using the body, including in speech. We know so much more than we can tell, and are affected by so much more than words and other influences that we are aware of. We have a feel for the game of talking in familiar situations, but feel awkward and 'don't know what to say' in a situation to which our habitus is not adjusted.

The different habitus of working-, middle- and upper-class speakers involves not only different vocabularies and ways of speaking, but different relations *to* language. In France, among the educated classes, articulacy and command of language are highly valued, whereas it is less so among the equivalent class in the United States, as research by Michèle Lamont – inspired by Bourdieu – shows (Lamont 1992). In the UK, there is often a certain disdain among working-class people for such articulacy, indicating a mistrust of those whose command of language indicates not only a different social class, but a removal from the world of work and necessity, and possibly lack of appreciation of it (Charlesworth 2000). Being a man or woman 'of few words', and 'just getting on with it' implies strength and solidity, down-to-earthness, and has greater value for them. Those in the middle, the petty-bourgeois, tend to develop a habitus characterised by social anxiety in relation to the dominant classes – through fear of being 'found out', and fear of slipping down into the working class or being mistaken for them. Linguistically, this comes out in self-consciousness, hyper-correctness and affectation ('commencing' work, instead of starting it). (These are, of course, general observations made by Bourdieu from his researches, and there are many exceptions – for a host of possible reasons, mostly to do with particularities of socialisation.)

Linguistic capacities are *embodied*, most obviously, in the way the mouth is used when speaking. Compare the loose, free speech of many working-class people with the precise, measured, drawn-in, 'tight-lipped' talk of some members of the dominant classes, suggesting mastery, carrying the threat of a precisely aimed put-down, but also inviting suspicions of coldness, misanthropy and lack of generosity ('tight-arsed'). Since the habitus is classed and gendered, so too are ways of talking and writing, but always in relation to, and in distinction from, others. Addressing this relation requires the next key concept.

Fields

Individuals, organisations, practices (including uses of language) and objects are located within *fields* of relationships to other individuals, organisations, practices and objects, and their behaviour can only be understood by reference to those fields. Within the general social field, there are local fields specific to major activities, such as the fields of politics or education. The concept of field involves a triple metaphor: a space in which action takes place and actors act, a magnetic field of forces and a battlefield – an arena of competition and struggle for power. The behaviour and fortunes of a particular university, for example, can only be understood by reference to its position in the national or international university field, itself part of the educational field and social field. What my own university does and does not do, for example, depends on how it relates comparatively and competitively both to Oxbridge and a small number of other universities traditionally favoured by the British elite, and to new, less prestigious universities recently created from former colleges and polytechnics. What a person can say, and with what effect, depends on their position within the social field relative to others. The ability of the army officer to order the private to clean the latrines, and the consequences of any attempt by the private to tell the officer to clean them, are a product of the inequalities and power relations of the social field. The tendency of the same speech behaviour to be regarded as 'assertive' in men and 'strident' or 'bossy' in women is also a field effect.

Bourdieu repeatedly criticises 'interactionist' approaches that abstract discourses and interlocutors from the fields in which they exist, and thereby ignore the power relations within which speakers, writers, listeners and readers are located; they reduce relations of power to relations of communication (Bourdieu 1977; 1991). What words mean depends on location within the field – what is valued by some may be an object of scorn for others – not just because of different 'values', but because of the objective differences in their position within the social field, which give rise to different dispositions or habitus.

At times, Bourdieu uses the metaphors of 'games' or 'markets' to characterise fields. Each game/field has its own rules and goals: the rules of the art game, of producing, selling, acquiring and displaying art, are different from those of the science game, or the political game. Referring to fields as markets, hence, 'the linguistic market', allows Bourdieu to emphasise their competitive character and the differences in power of the players, and the stakes over which they compete. Particular speech acts have 'prices' determined not only by their linguistic content, but by the speaker's position in the social field relative to interlocuters and observers.[1] Thus, as Johann Unger shows, Scots language speakers are aware that their language has different 'prices' in different markets, being valued positively in some, and negatively in others (Unger 2013). And, of course, there are linguistic sub-markets or fields such as those of education, politics, socialising, sports or entertainment. Bourdieu's use of this and other economic metaphors – 'capital', 'symbolic profit' – leads him to develop accounts that give a predominantly instrumental character to action, albeit one that is less a matter of actors' intentions or reasons than unconscious or semi-conscious strategies that are already inscribed in the habitus.

Thus, one chapter of his *Language and symbolic power* is entitled 'Price formation and the anticipation of profits' (Bourdieu 1991). The latter refers to the way in which speakers have to anticipate the reception of their words in order to communicate as they intend; this involves an awareness (or feel for the game) of the field in which their words are produced and received, and what is safe or risky. Again, as Unger's study of Scots shows, as a language that is widely spoken, but only rarely written, it cannot generally be used in formal situations. For those in a subordinate position, communicating with those above them often requires accepting and attempting to reproduce styles of speaking and writing approved by the dominant groups. This generally fails because, although they can *recognise* 'legitimate language', their position in the social field means they are unlikely to have acquired the appropriate habitus and hence the ability to use it. Bourdieu et al.'s *Academic discourse* shows how this applies to students with different class backgrounds (Bourdieu et al. 1994). The field thus exerts a kind of censorship on discourse via agents' dispositions and their grasp and expectations of the form in which it will be acceptable.

> Any kind of discourse, whatever it may be, is the product of an encounter between a *linguistic habitus*, i.e. a competence that is inextricably both technical and social (both the ability to speak and the ability to speak in a certain socially marked fashion), and a *market*, i.e. a system of price formation that contributes to give linguistic production an orientation in advance.
>
> (Bourdieu 2008, p. 133)

In the case of strongly unequal fields, the inability of those in subordinate positions to speak in the form that is deemed legitimate by the dominant can condemn them 'to either silence or shocking outspokenness.' (Bourdieu 1991, p. 139)

This combination of an instrumental view of action with downplaying of conscious reasoning makes Bourdieu extremely sceptical about assumptions that some kinds of reason or action are 'disinterested'; for example, the art collector's professed belief to be interested only in the art itself, not its economic or symbolic value, is likely to increase its value (Bourdieu 1993b).

Capital

Bourdieu's analysis of inequality and domination is distinctive in that it goes beyond differences in economic capital to differences in social and cultural capital (Bourdieu 1986b). Social capital refers to connections and networks that give agents advantages vis-à-vis others, while cultural capital derives from possession of, and involvement in, the practice and enjoyment of cultural goods that are highly valued within the social field through association with dominant classes. Cultural capital is partly embodied – involving a certain disposition towards the goods in question, so that, for example, the relation of the bourgeois to opera might be one of entitled ease, and of the petit-bourgeois one of anxiety to be accepted as knowledgeable about, and comfortably familiar with, opera. As such, the latter risks being found out by trying too hard, appearing pretentious, lacking an effortless ownership of the art form that characterises the dominant classes' relation to the most prestigious goods. Cultural capital is not just a matter of knowing about or liking particular valued cultural goods, but of the whole relation to them. Educational capital (qualifications) and linguistic capital, are varieties of cultural capital, and they exhibit the same general features in that they are *relational* insofar as their 'price' depends on the valuation of the whole field and the position of the agent within the field relative to others – superior, equal or inferior – and, like the habitus, *embodied*. Although each field is different, there are often homologies between them. So, those that are in a dominant position in one field, say the arts, are likely to share a similar mix and volume of capital and tastes and dispositions to those in a dominant position in another field, such as education.

Bourdieu argues and demonstrates that the relation between different tastes and ways of acting and speaking of agents and their location within the relevant fields are not arbitrary, but betray their relation to the world and to the field. Underlying oppositions between refined or distinguished versus vulgar or common, is a distinction between the *distance from necessity* that marks the lives of the dominant classes and the closeness to necessity of the subordinate classes. Thus, as regards taste, the dominant have time and leisure and can enjoy superfluity in such forms as abstract art, poetry, classics and history, while the subordinate expect art to be representational and education to be functional for making a living. This is evident in language, too, where superfluity (or less charitably, verbosity), carefully measured words, slow delivery and freedom from the fear of interruption suggest superiority and a confident command of the listener's attention. At a largely pre-reflexive level, this not only expresses dominance, but confirms it to both speaker and listener.

Having introduced these concepts, we can now proceed to show how they are applied, though we must first apply them to the position of academics themselves in order to combat a common fallacy.

The scholastic fallacy

Bourdieu did not exempt the academic world from his critiques of social practices (Bourdieu 1988, 1994, 1996). While he devastatingly analysed the class co-ordinates and traits of academia, his most fundamental critique of academia concerned its methodology – its susceptibility to 'the scholastic fallacy'. This involves the tendency of academics to project (unknowingly) the perspective and dispositions of their peculiarly contemplative relation to the social world onto those whose relation to the world is primarily practical. Habermas' treatment of 'communicative reason' is taken to task for this as an extreme example, but the fallacy is much more pervasive (Bourdieu 2000). It allows actions to be treated, not merely as meaningful, but as always consciously intended, and in so doing, it misunderstands the nature and 'logic' of the practice and the position of those who do not share the contemplative stance of academics. It is closely associated with 'the interactionist fallacy', in which conversations or discourses are examined in abstraction from the position of the interlocutors in the social field, their capital and relative power, thereby ignoring their profound shaping of the communications, and their production and reception (Bourdieu 1977; 1991).

Of all the academic disciplines, philosophy and linguistics are most likely to be guilty of this fallacy. Along with it goes an implicitly classed hierarchy of mind (the professions, management) over body (manual work). It need not take a rational choice form; ethnographic accounts that seek to render practices as texts, are also susceptible to the fallacy. The fallacy unknowingly reflects academics' distance from necessity, and the ease and time for reflection available to them.

The disposition towards reflection and scholastic reason are embodied capacities of the academic habitus, which, in its distance from practical necessity, gives it affinities with the habitus of the dominant classes, and this helps to explain the easy assimilation of students with high cultural capital into the academic field, relative to that of working-class students. It is not only the latter's lack of familiarity with books and high culture, but their habitus, characterised by the dominance of practical necessity, and the need to take orders from their superiors rather than reason why, that impede them. Furthermore, where social classifications and the contingent social divisions in which people live correspond, they are likely to become 'doxa' – taken for granted, self-evident, undiscussed; as Bourdieu puts it, it 'goes without saying because it comes without saying' (1977, p. 167).

Symbolic power and fields of struggle

Symbolic power is the target of much of Bourdieu's work, but again, despite the emphasis on discourse and imagery, knowledge and recognition, he argues that it operates substantially without 'intentional acts of consciousness.' It is generally not even recognised by the dominated as a form of domination, indeed dominant discourses and framings of issues may be accepted and affirmed by those who are its victims.

For Bourdieu, this acquiescence is less a product of ideology (a term he avoids), 'false consciousness' or even dominant discourses, than the facticity of the social world in which people act. It is primarily a product of habituation to subordinate positions and lack of experience of alternatives, which produces a bodily attunement to them (2000, p. 181); '[...] of all the forms of "hidden persuasion", the most implacable is the one exerted, quite simply, by the *order of things*' (Bourdieu & Wacquant 1992, p. 168, emphasis in original). Recognition is less a matter of conscious assessment and deliberation than a product of:

> the set of fundamental, pre-reflexive assumptions that social agents engage by the mere fact of taking the world for granted, of accepting the world as it is, and of finding it natural because their mind is constructed according to cognitive structures that are issued out of the very structures of the world.
>
> (Bourdieu & Wacquant 1992, p. 168)

Likewise, hegemony is less imposed from above discursively than acquired semi-consciously from engaging in everyday life within unequal societies. The dominated may dream of coming into money and luxury, yet such dreams do not subvert the social field, but merely involve imagining occupying a different place within it, thereby confirming its legitimacy. Envisaging radical alternatives is easier for those whose position affords some distance from necessity.

This emphasis on practice rather than ideology is a powerful counter to those who imagine that only the artful and energetic production of 'ideological discourse' by the dominant stops an imagined latent protest bursting out at any moment. Nevertheless, one has only to look at newspapers, TV and social media to see that there is a huge effort given to producing discourses that mostly affirm the dominant interpretations of the world.

For Bourdieu, the nature and effects of discourse and other practices cannot be understood just at the semantic level, but always require consideration of the field as a material as well as a semantic space. Symbolic power is always field-dependent: it depends not only on the powerful, but the susceptibilities of others to their actions, intended or unintended. It is not a tautology to say that intimidating or stigmatising speech only works on those who are susceptible to them. In everyday life, language is rarely analysed as a linguist or philosopher might, for it operates partly below the level of consciousness, because the dominated accept and misrecognise the terms in which it is expressed. And the 'acceptance' comes not just from the words, but from the dispositions of deference, and felt sense of inferiority that have come to constitute their habitus, just as the complementary felt sense of entitlement, superiority and condescension are part of the upper-class habitus.

> Symbolic violence is a violence practised in and through ignorance, and all the more readily in that those who practise it are unaware they are doing so, and those experiencing it unaware they are experiencing it.
>
> (Bourdieu 2008, p. 322)

So, the submission of a woman to an order from a man does not come just from the words he uses, or from what she understands them to mean, but from the respective habitus they have acquired through their gendered upbringings that already predispose one to defer, acquiesce, serve and appease and the other to command, lead and expect compliance. Of course, the ways of exerting this power vary with context, including not just the kind of situation, but the positioning of the two within the social field. However, again, they derive more from habituation and a feel for the game acquired through practice than calculation or analytic understanding; and even to the extent that the words and actions are calculated, they must take into account the relations and inequalities of the social field, so as to assess how direct or euphemised the requests or commands need to be. It might therefore be expected that a woman who had encountered and accepted feminist discourses might nevertheless still find it difficult to override the tendencies of her habitus when faced with instances of masculine domination. Resistance has to be practised repeatedly to change the habitus and become second nature.

Symbolic violence is always most effective when the dominated share with the dominant the schemes of perception and appreciation through which they are perceived by the dominant (as inferior) and through which the dominant perceive themselves (as superior). This 'knowledge and recognition have to be rooted in practical dispositions of acceptance and submission, which, because they do not pass through deliberation and decision, escape the dilemma of consent or constraint' (Bourdieu 2000, p. 198). The critic who challenges the common sense shared by the dominant and dominated can easily be dismissed by pointing to the acquiescence of the dominated as evidence of their being 'out of touch' with those whom they claim to represent. Tabloid newspapers make money from selling stories of welfare 'benefit cheats' to people, many of whom are likely to receive welfare benefits. Whereas mechanisms producing economic inequalities and physical coercion operate without consent, the use of elements of the dominant discourse by the dominated gives at least the appearance of consent and agreement, simply because communication requires the shared capacity to communicate in both parties. And each party has, at a basic level, to accept the other as an interlocutor. But what is shared ('accepted') may be a product of misrecognition. Symbolic violence therefore is a more hidden 'soft' form of power. Bourdieu argues that 'all power owes part of its efficacy – and not the least important part – to misrecognition of the mechanisms on which it is based' (Bourdieu 1993a, p. 14).

This misrecognition is compounded by those social scientists and philosophers who succumb to the scholastic fallacy. According to Bourdieu, their misrecognition of their own social position in relation to that of students of different classes is revealed in the nuances of condescension, scorn and praise to be found in their comments on students' work and the correspondences between these and students' class position (Bourdieu 1996). *Academic discourse* argues that tutors typically fail to appreciate the nature of the power relations of the educational field that press students into writing what they do not understand – a kind of misrecognition of misrecognition (Bourdieu et al, 1994).

Fields (or markets) are arenas of struggle and competition in which, among other things, symbolic power is reproduced and contested. The struggles of the social field are not to be reduced simply to randomly located competing views and interests, but always relate to the competing positions and practices of those involved. The fields are always unequal, but the dominant tend to represent the competitive struggles as taking place on a level playing field and without any shortages, so everyone can win, even though the prizes are few and monopolised by the dominant (Bourdieu 2000, p. 225). This, for example, allows modern incarnations of the traditional distinction between the deserving and the undeserving poor to emerge and to be mobilised against the losers.

The struggles have a three-fold character, involving:

1. competition *for* valued goods, practices and positions, for capital;
2. struggle over *what* is worthy of value, worthwhile, prestigious, and how things are to be named, particularly insofar as names secrete evaluations;
3. struggle over *who* has the authority to determine what is of value.

Language itself can be an object of struggle. There can be competition to acquire and use ways of speaking that are accepted as authoritative, 'posh' or 'cool' (1, above); struggles over *what* is legitimate language – often partly taking place through ridicule, for example, over which accents and kinds of speech or writing allow their producers to be taken seriously (2); and struggles (3) over *who* defines it – in the UK, this usually involves references to 'the Queen's English', 'received pronunciation' and people who are 'well-spoken' (as opposed to 'rough spoken'), in which the class locations are unmistakeable, if not explicit.

Bourdieu analyses the struggles of the social field as 'strategies', though he applies this to cases where people are acting 'on automatic', spontaneously according to their habitus, rather than consciously. If we ignore the awkwardness of this use of a term normally implying conscious reasoning and planning for behaviour, which does not (necessarily) involve them, certain typical patterns can be identified.

Those who are in dominated positions in the field often use 'strategies' of deference and compliance, accepting their place and seeking confirmation of respectability from those above. As Bourdieu repeatedly notes, they tend to choose what is chosen for them, refusing what they are refused, as 'not for the likes of us' (e.g. Bourdieu 1986a, p. 374). This refusal is then open to being taken by those in more advantageous positions as confirmation of their inferiority, or a 'poverty of aspiration' as UK Prime Minister David Cameron put it. The dominant in politics can also reward this acceptance by the dominated of their inferior position and keep them in their place through reciprocal gestures of condescension, as when they refer to them as 'hard-working people'.

Frequently, these dominant ways of seeing are internalised by the dominated or used to condemn others: the American working-class men studied by Lamont who blamed themselves for their lack of 'success' (Lamont 2000); the British people on welfare benefits who suspect their neighbours of being 'benefit cheats' and thereby seek to exempt themselves from the charge (Shildrick & MacDonald 2013); the young women who look down on others who do not achieve the required feminine appearance, and mobilise a 'nice girl/slag' distinction; the poor working-class people in France, studied by Bourdieu and co-researchers, who direct their anger at their immigrant neighbours (Bourdieu et al. 1999). Often, those who police these distinctions most avidly are themselves at risk of falling foul of them; where dignity and respect are in question, small differences may seem to matter. These are horizontal deflections of symbolic violence.

In many cases, the most dominated are *unable* to comply with norms of what is acceptable – because, for example, there are not enough jobs to go around, so they cannot be 'hard-working families' – and they often lack the economic, political, educational and linguistic resources to resist. Where they do resist, for example, by refusing to comply and by demanding *respect* on their own terms, rather than seeking *respectability* on the terms of the dominant (Sayer 2005), they open themselves to counter-attacks. Those who do not, or cannot, comply with ways of life misrecognised as available and desirable are fully exposed to a more open kind of symbolic violence – what Bourdieu terms 'class racism' (Bourdieu 1986a, p. 179) as 'chavs', 'trailer trash', 'scroungers', 'skivers', and as exemplified in the US and UK by TV programmes recently dubbed 'poverty porn', such as *The Jerry Springer Show*, and *Benefits Street*, respectively.

Whether resistance or compliance is involved, it is necessary to appreciate the nature of the particular habitus of participants in discourse to understand what they say and how they interpret others. Thus, in the UK, the common male working-class disregard for, and ridicule of, correctness according to dominant, legitimate language is a form of opposition to class position constructed via gender that defends a notion of masculinity based on toughness, and it refuses refinement and a desire to please others as 'effeminate' (1991, p. 100). What is going on here cannot be understood without reference to their habitus and the field or market in which they interact.

Political discourse

Bourdieu's treatment of the discourse of politics is in keeping with this emphasis on the field and habitus, and his insistence on going beyond the meaning of the discourse itself. For him, political discourse attempts to defend (or challenge) the correspondence between the ways in which people classify and categorise their world ('wealth creators', 'working people', 'scroungers', 'investors') and the objective divisions and practices that sustain, and are sustained by, current common-sense thought and that are reflected in the habitus. Oppositional political discourses attempt to break this pre-reflexive acceptance of the prevailing structures of the world ('doxa') and create a new common sense. The power of naming[2] is central to this ('criminal immigrants', 'skivers', 'chattering classes', 'idle rich', etc.), and considerable political effort is devoted to manipulating such terms in the hope that they will resonate with, or 'touch raw nerves', in others.

As always, the likelihood of such discourse being produced and the particular way in which it is received or ignored, depends on the structure of the field; in the case of oppositional discourse, Bourdieu argues that it will have an effect only if there is also some (extra-discursive) objective crisis to which it draws attention. (We can of course add that it also depends on understandings of such words and the contexts in which they have been used before, but Bourdieu wants to counteract the temptation to reduce reception simply to the level of discourse.) Political discourse involves a struggle to conserve or transform the social world by conserving or transforming the vision of this world and its systems of classifications and the objective 'di-visions' of the social world which these classifications sustain and reflect (Bourdieu 1991, p. 181). What he terms 'strong discourses' are backed by dominant social and economic forces; a contemporary example might be the discourse of austerity.

The discourse of politicians has to be seen in terms of the special relation of representation to supporters and the electorate, and the interests politicians have in the persistence of the institution and the specific profits it brings them. In some ways, being invested with political powers by those they represent, this represents a concentration of the means of production of discourse and political acts. Delegates consecrate themselves as representatives of the group, usurping power by presenting themselves as their servants, while treating their own values as universal, whether knowingly or unknowingly. As Bourdieu said, 'when it comes to the state, one never doubts enough' (1998, p. 36).

Evaluation and conclusions

The occupational hazard of all academic disciplines is reductionism – the temptation to try to make the discipline's defining objects and approaches do more explanatory work than they can. Linguistics' occupational hazard is overextending the scope and influence of language in explaining social phenomena. The prevalence of the scholastic fallacy in social science increases this problem. It assumes that minds are independent of bodies and their social development. Developments in neuroscience are increasingly showing that the left-brain scholastic emphasis on analytical reason and language underestimates the importance of right brain pre-linguistic understanding and responses to the world, which have a gestalt, big-picture, and often emotional character, much of which does not get consciously registered, interpreted and articulated (McGilchrist 2009). Neuroscience and psychology provide evidence for something like the habitus, and for the lasting importance of social influences on dispositions and behaviour. Much goes on below the radar of linguistically constructed understanding, including where communication is involved, and this hidden surplus is inherently difficult to describe in words, thereby eluding formulation in given categories and analysis by breaking down wholes into parts, which is the method the scholastic standpoint values.

The critical reception of Bourdieu's work has been dominated by debates about whether his work is excessively deterministic and pessimistic. The dominated classes seem doomed to accept their inferior position as a result of having developed a habitus adapted to it, and having been subject to symbolic power operating pre-reflexively, so they make a virtue of what is actually necessity, and thereby reproduce their position. What anyone thinks, says or does is seen overwhelmingly as a reflection of their social position and habitus (an internalisation of the social field). In effect, the explanation is 'they would say that given their location and history', which leaves little or no room for individual reflexivity and responses that might not be read off from their position in the social field. Luc Boltanski and Jacques Rancière, among others, have attacked the real or apparent fatalism in Bourdieu's characterisation of the dominated, and his belittling of their ability to see their situation more consciously and critically (Boltanski 2011; Rancière 2004). At worst, it involves sociological reductionism and inverts the problems of interactionist approaches so that the content and meaning of discourse is treated as unimportant relative to its positioning with the social field and its 'pre-reflexive' reception. At the least, this underestimates the endless possibilities for novel meanings to develop in discourse. Margaret Archer has countered Bourdieu's fatalism both theoretically and through empirical research on reflexivity in everyday life, through attending to people's 'internal conversations', and how they monitor and reflect upon the constraints and influences they encounter, and hence mediate their impact (Archer 2007). Although she rejects the concept of habitus, others argue we can acknowledge this lay reflexivity without abandoning it, as if nothing that influenced us escaped our awareness (Archer 2010).

Yet, the concept of habitus is not wholly deterministic anyway, for it involves semi-conscious awareness and monitoring, indeed there would seem to be a continuum from the unconscious reception through this awareness to careful, self-conscious deliberation. At times, Bourdieu defends his argument by saying he is 'bending the stick' as a way of correcting the opposite error of assuming all action to be based on universal, conscious deliberation.

Tendencies towards determinism and fatalism also beg the question of where resistance comes from. Bourdieu's main answer is that it is most likely to come from those who find themselves participating in a social field or location that differs from that to which their habitus has accommodated, or which changes more rapidly than they can adapt. Given its opposition to individualistic explanations, this is always the answer that sociological reductionism has to give to the question of sources of resistance. Yet, it is simply false not only in ignoring individuals' reflexivity and capacity for critical thought, but also in implying that there are no habitats to which people cannot adjust through the acquisition of a habitus, and no difference between adjustments that are comfortable and others that are painful. Moreover, it ignores the extent to which discourse and practice are characterised by dilemmas and conflicting ideas and actions (Billig 1996).

Bourdieu is further limited by his disregard of emotions, both in terms of their cognitive content and their motivating power, for it ignores the emotional force of particular kinds of discourse.

> When people speak of class struggle, they never think of the class struggles in everyday life, the contempt, the arrogance and crushing ostentation (about children and their successes, holidays and cars), the wounding indifference and injury, and so on. Social misery and resentment – the saddest of social passions – arise from these everyday struggles, in which the issue at stake is dignity, self-esteem.
>
> (Bourdieu 2008, p. 73)

This statement – about everyday conversations – is full of terms that refer to moral emotions and dispositions and which presuppose reflexivity – yet, they are not acknowledged as such theoretically by Bourdieu.

However, in his later, more political work, for example, *The weight of the world* (Bourdieu et al. 1999), he does pay more attention to what lay people say, though retaining his primary emphasis on the hermeneutics of suspicion. And he also discusses the scope for politicisation, arguing that it depends on making connections that enable people to see that their problems are not merely individual misfortunes, but consequent upon contingent social processes. His own energetic involvement in the struggle to politicise the public and foment resistance suggests a softening of his reductionism.

A less-noted problematic feature of Bourdieu's work is his reluctance to acknowledge that communicative intentions and receptions can be non-instrumental, open and involving judgements of the good that are not reducible to reflections of self-interest or the habitus. He therefore tends to portray all practices and struggles of the social field as a Hobbesian war of all against all, and to deflate any claims to disinterested goals, or divergence between commitments and self-serving beliefs. In so doing, he generally fails to acknowledge that which acceptance of his own analysis presupposes, namely, that sometimes communication (including self-talk) is disinterested. (If we accept his approach, do we do so merely because our habitus disposes us to do so and because doing so serves as a strategy of distinction in the academic world?; or do we accept it because we think it is right, useful, revealing?) He would probably have said that it is necessary to find out how far any communicative act is interested, how far it is conditioned by speakers' and listeners' position in the social field and the 'profits' available to them, in order to know how far it is *not* influenced in those ways. But the opposite also applies.

In bending the stick to correct for the interactionist error and the scholastic fallacy, in acknowledging the unconscious or semi-conscious part of communication, and the effects of the habitus and the social field on communication, it is important not to neglect the analysis of the meanings of the discourse. For example, how else can we understand why countries with similar inequalities and social fields produce different political responses? Why is anti-immigrant feeling strong in the UK, but limited in Spain, despite the latter's much higher unemployment; why are French workers more politicised than US workers? Here, it is necessary to look at the cultural and political histories of the countries and their *different* dominant discourses. To explain this would mean having to take the *content* of discourses, and not only their situation in fields of power, into account.[3]

While Bourdieu's approach might seem to involve a sociologically reductionist treatment of language, his intent is clearly to find out what is communicated and with what effect. Academics unaware of their habitus and position within the social field and the scholastic fallacy, are likely to reproduce, rather than avoid, distorted communication. Bourdieu's scathing remarks about the scholastic fallacy and discourse analysis seem to assume that the latter must always abstract from social context and actions in which it is always embedded, and treat practical action as primarily communicative. Neither need be true, though these are dangers to keep in mind. His view of linguistics is partly unfair, particularly in representing it as looking for the meanings of words only in words, 'where it is not to be found', (Bourdieu 1993a, p. 107), but insofar as it has some truth, his critique and his approach to language need to be taken seriously. Discourse is indeed a crucial form and mediator of power, so anyone wanting to understand it needs to consider his work.

Notes

1 For a critique of Bourdieu's use of economic metaphors with regard to language, see Grin (1994).
2 Bourdieu's own concept of 'cultural capital' is a striking example of this power.
3 Bourdieu does allude to this problem occasionally and acknowledge the remedy (e.g. 2000, p. 173). However, given that he mainly wrote either in general terms about symbolic dominance, or through French examples, rather than comparative studies, like those of Lamont (1992; 2000), as far as I am aware, he did not provide the historical analyses of culture and politics that are so important for identifying the meaning and affective load of the particular terms used in political language, as analysed for example in Ruth Wodak's studies of right-wing political discourses (Wodak 2015).

References

Archer, M, 2007, *Making our way through the world*, Cambridge University Press, Cambridge.
Archer, M, ed., 2010, *Conversations about reflexivity*, Routledge, London.
Billig, M, 1996, *Arguing and thinking: a rhetorical approach to social psychology*, Cambridge University Press, Cambridge.

Boltanski, L, 2011, *On critique: A sociology of emancipation*, Polity Press, Cambridge.
Bourdieu, P, 1977, *Outline of a theory of practice*, Cambridge University Press, Cambridge.
Bourdieu, P, 1986a, *Distinction*, Routledge, London.
Bourdieu, P, 1986b, 'The forms of capital', in *Handbook of theory and research for the sociology of education,* ed. J Richardson, Greenwood, New York, pp. 241–258.
Bourdieu, P, 1988, *Homo academicus*, Polity Press, Cambridge.
Bourdieu, P, 1991, *Language and symbolic power*, Polity Press, Cambridge.
Bourdieu, P, 1993a, *Sociology in question*, Sage, London.
Bourdieu, P, 1993b, *The field of cultural production*, Polity, Cambridge.
Bourdieu, P, 1996, *The state nobility: Elite schools in the field of power*, Polity Press, Cambridge.
Bourdieu, P, 1998, *Practical reason*, Polity Press, Cambridge.
Bourdieu, P, 2000, *Pascalian meditations*, Polity Press, Cambridge.
Bourdieu, P, 2008, *Political interventions*, Verso, London.
Bourdieu, P & Wacquant, L, 1992, *An introduction to reflexive sociology,* Sage, London.
Bourdieu, P, Passeron, J-C & de Saint Martin, M, 1994, *Academic discourse*, Polity Press, Cambridge.
Bourdieu, P et al., 1999, *The weight of the world*, Polity Press, Cambridge.
Charlesworth, S, 2000, *The phenomenology of working class life*, Cambridge University Press, Cambridge.
Grin, F, 1994, 'The economics of language: match or mismatch', *International Political Science Review*, 15.1, pp. 25–42.
Lamont, M, 1992, *Money, morals and manners: The culture of the French and American upper-middle class*, Chicago University Press, Chicago, IL.
Lamont, M, 2000, *The dignity of working men: Morality and the boundaries of race, class and imagination*, Russell Sage Foundation and Harvard University Press, New York.
McGilchrist, I, 2009, *The master and his emissary: the divided brain and the making of the western world,* Yale University Press, Yale, CT.
Rancière, J, 2004, *The philosopher and his poor,* Duke University, Durham, NC.
Sayer, A, 2005, *The moral significance of class*, Cambridge University Press, Cambridge.
Shildrick, T & MacDonald, R, 2013, 'Poverty talk: how people experiencing poverty deny their poverty and why they blame "the poor"', *The Sociological Review*, 61.2, pp. 285–303.
Unger, J W, 2013, *The discursive construction of the Scots language*, John Benjamins, Amsterdam.
Wodak, R, 2015, *The politics of fear*, Sage, London.

8
Conceptual history
The history of basic concepts

Jan Ifversen

Introduction

Historians have an issue with language. Most of the accessible information on what happened in the past is derived from written sources. Source criticism was developed to deal with the language of the past. Despite the importance that language has in forming what we might know of the past, historians have in general been quite reluctant to see this as a specific challenge. Until the so-called linguistic turn left its imprint on the discipline in the 1980s, only a few historians had engaged directly with the challenge presented by language. In 1930, Lucien Febvre and Marc Bloch introduced a permanent section in their famous journal, *Annales d'histoire économique et sociale*, on words and things because of the need to direct the attention of historians to 'the delicate problem of the history and evolution of the semantics of words' (Febvre 1930, p. 234). Decades later, the German-Israeli historian Richard Kroebner wrote an insightful article on semantics and historiography, which highlighted the role of words for the study of historical consciousness (Kroebner 1953). But it was only in the 1960s and 1970s that the role of language was forcefully recognised in historical studies and particularly in studies focusing on intellectual history.[1] In 1969, Michel Foucault published his *Archaeology of knowledge*, which presented discourse as a linguistically anchored approach to the study of epistemic changes. The same year, a young Quentin Skinner introduced a new programme for the history of ideas based on how meaning and understanding were formed in constant exchanges of speech acts (Skinner 1988). Foucault and Skinner both dug deep into linguistics in order to privilege the role of language in historical changes.

In 1967, the German historian Reinhart Koselleck introduced conceptual history (*Begriffsgeschichte*) as an approach developed to write a lexicon of political and social concepts in modern times (Koselleck 1967). Although *Begriffsgeschichte* had been coined by Hegel in his *Lectures on the philosophy of history* and adopted by the philosophers who, in 1955, established the journal *Archiv für Begriffsgeschichte* in order to develop building blocks for a future historical dictionary of philosophy (published in thirteen volumes between 1971 and 2007), Koselleck was the first to call for a study of concepts within the discipline of history. While he drew from his engagement with hermeneutics, and was influenced by Carl Schmitt's work on legal and political theory, he was also strongly inspired by linguistics.[2] This chapter focuses on his encounter with linguistics. First, I will discuss how conceptual history in its linguistic orientation develops in three steps. In the first section, I look at the representational dimension where concepts are anchored in a historical semantics. The second section deals with the question of referentiality and extra-linguistic reality. The third section discusses the contextual aspects of concepts in action. In the third section, I give an example of how key concepts can be studied.

Language

Koselleck's interest in language is founded on the basic premise of historical science – that the interpretation of past events mainly rests on sources in the form of texts. The historian is always confronted with the challenge that whatever the sources refer to in the past is rendered by the art of language. The interest in language was further nourished by the influence of Hans Georg Gadamer's philosophy of hermeneutics. Gadamer succinctly condensed his theory in this statement: 'All understanding is interpretation, and all interpretation takes place in the medium of language' (Gadamer 1975, p. 350). Interpreting past experiences therefore relies on the language of the past. For Gadamer, as well as for Koselleck, this language is constituted by concepts. As Koselleck expressed it, conceptual history is an approach that 'interprets history through its prevailing concepts' (Koselleck 1985a, p. 85). But unlike Gadamer, who never went beyond a general acceptance of the necessary representational character of language, Koselleck took an interest from the beginning in the way language operated in order to represent objects.

The assumption that historians can only understand the past through the medium of the language expressed in the sources is just a first condition. Koselleck also endorsed the claim that language forms the reality of the historical actors. 'Without common concepts there is no society' (Koselleck 1985a, p. 74), as he pointedly remarked. His statement that '[a] concept is not simply indicative of the relations which it covers; it is also a factor within them' (Koselleck, 1985a, p. 84) has become something of a trademark for conceptual history. Before we place Koselleck too solidly in the company of social constructivism (itself a broad umbrella for different approaches as to how language is a 'factor'), it is worth noting that he still upholds the idea that concepts are also determined by what they refer to. But he repeatedly highlighted the formative role of concepts in language. Drawing on inspiration from the first generation of structural semantics, he stressed the link between concepts and words within the language system. He relied on Ogden and Richard's classic linguistic triangle, in which the left leg illustrated the signifying or symbolising mechanism within the language system based on the link between thought and symbol, or, in his own terminology, concepts and world (Ogden & Richard 1923). The right leg indicated the capacity of language to denote or refer to objects or matters of fact (*Sache* in German) through the relation between the concept and the referent.

Here, I will take a closer look at how Koselleck developed his theory of conceptual history based on the two legs in the linguistic triangle. To guide this journey into the language theories that undergird conceptual history, I rely on Ekkehard Felder's elaboration of the triangle (Felder 2006, p. 15). According to Felder, the legs indicate the two ways of understanding the sign. The first way, which he terms the representational understanding of the sign, corresponds to what, since Saussure, has been called signification. Here signs (or words) relate to a cognitive world of concepts. The second understanding of the sign is referential because signs refer to, or denote, things or matters in the world. To these two

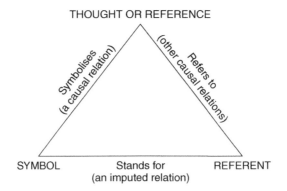

Figure 8.1 Ogden and Richard's linguistic triangle (Ogden & Richard 1923, p. 11)

understandings, he adds a third, which points to the effect of speech actions on the sign. Representation and reference are also dependent on the use of the sign in actual speech and on the conventions underlying communication in specific contexts. In the following section, I will consider the linguistic reflections that Koselleck presented in support of his conceptual history, based on these three forms of understanding: representation, reference and action.

Representation

In his programmatic outline for a theory of conceptual history (Koselleck 2011), Koselleck underlines the importance of investigating the relations between concepts and words. In traditional semantics, and even more so in lexicography, representation concerns the meaning of particular words in the lexicon (de Saussure 1969). This semasiological approach was soon joined by an onomasiology that 'takes its starting-point in a concept, and investigates by which different expressions the concept can be designated or named' (Geeraerts 2006, p. 37). Koselleck emphasised that conceptual history was anchored in an onomasiological approach, which looked at the way actors had conceptualised their experiences in the past. As he noted, conceptual history 'must register the variety of names for (identical?) materialities in order to be able to show how concepts are formed' (Koselleck 1985a, p. 86). He used the word *state* as an example of the difference between word and concept. As a concept, STATE can include other words such as territory, sovereignty, legislation and administration.[3] The onomasiological approach will open up for a study of the semantic range of the concept state, or – to use Andreas Blank's elegant formulation – the lexical pathway that concepts take (Blank 2001, p. 7). Koselleck was certainly aware of the complex relations between word and concept. Unlike his predecessors within the historical discipline, who rather directly connected words to things, he emphasised that not only were concepts bound to words, but that a concept was more than a word (Koselleck 1985a, p. 84). Although he did not clearly distinguish between when he was studying the lexical pathways of a concept, and when he was interested in the emergence of a basic concept in a particular historical situation, he was conscious of the mechanism for lexical change. His primary focus was 'the semantic field' in which a concept moved. The term 'field' was directly borrowed from Jost Trier, who shifted the focus of structural semantics from the paradigmatic relations introduced by Saussure to a larger understanding of how words related to each other characterised 'a conceptual field' (Trier 1931). Koselleck used the example of FEDERATION to demonstrate how a semantic field around words such as *Bund, Liga, Union* and *Einigung* formed the concept. Koselleck has been criticised for not being terribly precise in his definition of concept. Linguists will certainly accept that concepts are not necessarily tied to a single lexeme. But some clarity of the semantic boundaries between concepts is needed if onomasiological studies are to be conducted.

The fact that Koselleck might have conflated the representational link between words and concepts with a referential understanding of how specific concepts became basic within communication in historical situations does not invalidate his claim that concepts are tied to words and therefore have to be studied in semantics. As a historian, he is mainly interested in studying how concepts partake in historical change. At one level, he is well aware that concepts can have their own rhythm of change, which is not directly aligned to changes occurring in broader social and cultural contexts. Sometimes, he speaks of semantics as having a slower rate of change than the events themselves (Koselleck 1989, p. 657). This observation opens up the possibility for a more systematic study of semantic change.

Within structuralist semantics, there is a long tradition for the study of semantic change. Koselleck mentioned Eugenio Coseriu's seminal study of structural diachrony of signification (Coseriu 1964). Although Koselleck did not subscribe completely to Coseriu's structuralist approach to change, he borrowed his view of privileging the concepts and not the signs, and he included semantic fields in his study of how concepts were formed or changed. The acceptance that semantic structures had their own rhythm of change did not lead him to study the mechanism of lexical change in more detail. The conceptual changes he observed were explained by changes of a socio-cultural nature. As Andreas Blank has succinctly pointed out, 'new concepts emerge when we change the world around us or our way of conceiving it' (Blank 2013, p. 71). Semantic change, narrowly understood, concerns the particular verbalisation of these new concepts. If we stay within semantics proper, we look at the mechanisms that make changes possible. Among the most effective mechanisms is the broadening or the narrowing of a word, the change from positive to negative, or vice versa, borrowing from foreign languages, and not least, the use of metaphor and metonymy. In the view of many linguists, metaphorisation – 'using words for the look-alikes of what you mean' – or metonymisation – 'using words for the near neighbours of the things you mean' (Nerlich & Clarke 1992, p. 137) are the most effective operators of semantic change. Of the different semantic mechanisms that lead to concepts, Koselleck only really considered metaphorisation.[4] Koselleck's interest in the transfer of concepts from one field to another is a step in this direction. So is his sensitivity towards the polysemic or blurry nature of conceptual meaning. He clearly understood that polysemy is at the core of semantic change. When concepts enter new fields and emerge in the shape of new verbalisations, earlier meanings tend to live on. As Traugott states, 'all semantic change arises by polysemy' (Traugott 2006, p. 126).

Koselleck studied the emergence and change of an array of concepts. Many studies were undertaken in the monumental work on basic historical concepts in Germany, *Geschichtliche Grundbegriffe: Historisches Lexicon zur politisch-sozialen Sprache in Deutschland*, which appeared in seven volumes with him as the main editor between 1972 and 1997. He had a particular interest in following the emergence of temporal concepts such as CRISIS, PROGRESS, REVOLUTION, HISTORY and their role in the formation of modern German society. The lexicon covered a broad range of concepts, but tended to focus on those concepts that dominated the political imaginary in the crucial period of transformation towards modernity. As Koselleck pointed out in the introduction to the lexicon, the main assumption behind studying the history of these basic concepts was that the period from around 1750 to 1850 was marked by the dramatic emergence of the concepts that formed our society. 'What is posited', he said, 'is the emergence of a threshold period (*Sattelzeit*) in which the past was gradually transformed into the present' (Koselleck 2011, p. 9).

In his many studies of concepts, he was certainly aware of tracing out the different semantic paths that a concept would take on its way to becoming an important modern concept. By following the verbalisations in different national languages, and the borrowings that took place, he was able to observe important conceptual transfers. When studying the concept of CRISIS, he noticed that it transferred from religion and medicine into first the psychological and then the political and economic sphere (Koselleck 2006a, p. 362). In his study of REVOLUTION, he underlined the role of metaphorisation as the concept moved from a naturalistic universe and to denote political events (Koselleck 1985b,). He might not have examined these transfers in all their semantic complexity, but they are precisely at the core of conceptual history. His typology of concepts entails quite a number of ordering principles in the form of 'totalising concepts', 'distributional concepts', 'supraconcepts' and 'counterconcepts', but they are not related to the traditional semantic taxonomy with their synonyms, antonyms, hyponyms, hyperonyms, and so on. Koselleck did not conduct any systematic studies of the paradigmatic relation, and he hardly gave any thought to the syntagmatic relations through which language operates.

The challenge of developing a more systematic approach to semantic relations in conceptual history was taken up by the historian Rolf Reichardt, who, together with Hans-Jürgen Lüsebrink, edited a *Handbuch politisch-sozialer Grundbegriffe in Frankreich 1680–1820*. Reichardt worked out a method to describe what he called semantic nets in small text corpora.[5] He was particularly interested in locating the central concepts in these nets. To do this, he examined the collocations as they appeared in syntagmatic relations and also looked at the paradigmatic link between the search word and other words to determine those words that could function as a 'switch' between different semantic fields. He also included frequency to determine the centrality of a concept. Although he did not draw on corpus linguistics, he came close to using what has later been termed KWIC (key words in context).[6] The lack of digitalised corpora did, however, severely limit the scope of the analysis.

Reference

Within semantics, the referential or denotational dimension of language has typically been treated as independent from the internal language system. It is generally accepted that denotation is not simply the answer to a philosophical question of how to deal with reality, but also a formal question of understanding the relationship between representation and what is represented. Here, I will rely on Felder's view that referentiality concerns the ways in which non-linguistic objects and matters are expressed linguistically in specific situations of utterance.[7] Koselleck repeatedly insisted on the importance of the non-linguistic or the world in conceptual history. He sometimes referred to the relation between the world and language as ambiguous:

> Language is and remains ambiguous: on one hand, it registers [...] what happens outside itself; it states what pushes itself onto [...] the world, that is, as the latter presents itself pre- and extralinguistically. On the other hand, language actively transforms all extralinguistic objects and facts.
>
> (Koselleck 2006b, p. 6, my translation)

Language is thus not only a factor, it is also 'indicative'. Gadamer had insisted that there is no point of view outside the experience of the world in language (Gadamer 1975, p. 410). Koselleck critically replied that 'experience goes much beyond its linguistic interpretation' (Sebastián & Fuentes 2006, p. 125). He even saw the ambiguity of language as a tension between representation and world: 'There exists between concept and materiality a tension which now is transcended, now breaks out afresh, now appears insoluble' (Koselleck 1985a, p. 85) The analysis of this tension is at the core of conceptual history.

Koselleck moves rather hastily from pointing to the referential function of language (where language 'registers') to granting the world its own being, omitting any mentioning of the formal features of referentiality within language. He furthermore opens a Pandora's box of complex ontological questions by granting the world a being-in-itself independent of language. Critics have claimed that by overstressing the indicative role of language, he risks facing 'the danger of a realistic ontology' (Bödeker 1998, p. 60). As I see it, whether this claim is dangerous or not depends on how the world in itself is understood. Through the influence of existential phenomenology, he posits human experience as the basic point of orientation. Experiences are formed by concepts, but they are also structured by universal or metahistorical categories that make social life possible. Temporality or being-in-time is one of these categories. As long as language is seen as referring to object or matters, and not simply mirroring the world, there is no risk of any strong realism.

Koselleck always insisted that conceptual history had to be paired with a social history. He opened his most programmatic text on conceptual history by first stating that politics and even social life as such would be unimaginable without common concepts, but then added that 'concepts are founded in socio-political systems that are far more complex than would be indicated by treating them simply as linguistic communities organized around specific key concepts' (Koselleck 1985a, p. 76). These systems were to be studied by a social history, which would unveil the social structures of the common space of experience. Although a social history would need a conceptual history to 'unlock' the language of the past in order to access the structures, it also contained its own method oriented towards the study of 'extra-linguistic series of events' (Koselleck 1998, p. 33). At first glance, this division of labour between conceptual history and social history seems reasonable. But it begs the question of how the latter can circumvent the linguistic nature of the historical sources. While social facts can be used to demonstrate social structures, they have to be interpreted mostly from written sources.

Koselleck uses the division between concept and world as the basis for understanding historical change. From a theoretical point of view, both language and society have their own systems or structures. Structures are not simply abstract ordering principles: they also express themselves in the constant repetition of human activity. Koselleck makes use of the well-known distinction between structure and event to emphasise that every expression is a unique event, which, when repeated, manifests a structure. Language has its own semantic system, which is expressed through utterances. Society is permeated by a multitude of daily actions whose constant repetition reveals the social structures. Since historians see structures in a temporal perspective, they prefer to talk about duration and change. Koselleck focused on durations and temporal layers. Within language, these layers were represented by the duration of the various concepts. Some concepts had entered the language a long time ago and were deeply layered in the vocabulary; others were of more recent provenance. But the main point is that conceptual history as a method allows us to study the ways linguistic events are 'semantically preprogrammed' (Koselleck 1989, p. 685).

The nature of historical analysis is also, however, to explain historical change. Linguistic events cannot be reduced to individual speech acts. Conceptual history has to explain semantic changes. The first step in explaining semantic change is to bring forward the asymmetry between changes in language and changes in the world. Koselleck expresses this asymmetry in a remarkable way: 'The transformation of words and the transformation of things, the change of situation and the urge to rename, correspond diversely to each other' (Koselleck 1985a, p. 85). The asymmetry lays out a matrix of change. The world might be changing rapidly without the concepts following. But the existence of semantic structures will certainly also determine what might occur in the future. Our horizons of expectations – to take a term Koselleck used to understand the future-orientated behaviour of all human existence – are grounded in existing concepts. Our plans for the future are formed by concepts of the past. Logically, as pointed out by Heiner Schulz, the asymmetries could be reduced to four modes (Schultz 1978, pp. 65–67). The first mode would characterise all situations where the reference of a concept would stay unaltered. A good number of trivial examples could be mentioned. The referent of HORSE has probably not changed much over the centuries. It does not make much sense, however, to claim that abstract concepts referring to political life have stayed unchanged. The second mode describes situations where the world changes without concepts following. Life is full of situations in which human beings encounter objects or matters they unsuccessfully try to understand using existing concepts. Sometimes, they have to recognise that there are things they cannot conceptualise. Koselleck gives the example of how the Soviet communists used the concept of fascism after 1945 to fit Western capitalism into their ideology of progress in an effort to deny that the world had changed. In the third mode, we find situations where a new concept is introduced without any worldly changes 'calling' for it. The concept somehow belongs to an imaginary, which is unfounded in the context. Koselleck mentions REVOLUTION, which became a concept for constitutive but peaceful political change in the latter half of the eighteenth century. But in the French Revolution, the concept was used to describe the kind of violent events that had previously been described as CIVIL WAR. The fourth mode points to situations where a concept follows its own path independently of what happens in the world. This mode is the most difficult to grasp in Koselleck's matrix of change. He takes the example of STATE, which – in German – changes the concept of STAND (estate) into a unifying and totalising entity. It becomes what he calls 'a collective singular', which is introduced to capture the direction of the future (just like HISTORY, CIVILISATION, or PROGRESS). STATE is therefore a concept for something that does not exist yet. Because it is out of sync with the world, it is contested. However, the problem with this mode is that the conceptual changes mentioned (from STAND to STATE) are not completely independent of how the political system develops. It would probably be more correct to say that STATE as a new concept only affects the world slowly and therefore does not have a clear reference, or that there is a difference between how the concept evolves and how it intersects with political life.

With his matrix of change, Koselleck demonstrates that the relations between concepts and the world are complex. Even if concepts are to be understood as factors in social life, they do not control the world. The dynamics of historical change are produced by a constant tension between what is semantically manageable and what is not. The latter depends on what happens in the world. What is missing in Koselleck's matrix is, however, the innovative force of language itself, as well as of the language users, who in their dialogue with the world, invent new concepts. There is an evident risk that if the two legs of the linguistic triangle (representation and reference) are separated, his theory breaks apart. Conceptual history is first and foremost a history of how conceptual changes take shape through semantic changes that were produced in a dialogue with the world.

Action and context

Referentiality is the dimension through which language is orientated towards the world. Although it is a formal element within the language system, it is also an element in language use. Our words are used to communicate messages about objects or matters. Communication has a purpose. Precisely what the purpose might be depends on our intentions, as well as on the situation in which we speak. The latter I will call the context. This term is purely analytical and must not be conflated with world. Context is what orientates language users when they communicate. Language users address their communication to an audience and have knowledge of the context in which communication takes place. But the context is also what sets the rule of communication. These might be the various media or genres; they can be existing conventions or institutions. Communication is thus dependent on a particular context. To understand how concepts have changed in history, we therefore need to reconstruct the processes of communication in which concepts were used and transmitted. This involves reconstructing the contexts that informed and restrained communication. Koselleck is certainly aware of this. As he states: 'Intellectual or material meanings are indeed bound to the word, but they feed off the intended content, the written or spoken context, and the historical situation' (Koselleck 1985a, p. 85). 'The intended content' is what the speaker or writer wants to achieve when communicating. The intention is dependent on contexts. Obviously, there may be many reasons for communicating, one of which could be to invent new concepts and words. The example of the American engineer who constructed the torpedo and invented the word is well known. As a historian, Koselleck is careful when reconstructing contexts. They might be linguistic contexts, that, is, the semantics and the discourses available, or they could be an institutional framework. The only problem, as I see it, is that due to his alignment with social history, he tends to turn contexts into a world of their own. His contextualism is thus hampered by a realist approach that actually tends to disclose the contextualist features, which inform the text.

Koselleck underlined the importance of studying the use of concepts in communication. He emphasised the need to examine who used concepts, who the addressees were, and how concepts were used by the communicating subject. He stressed the fundamental role of studying language use: 'The record of how their uses were subsequently maintained, altered or transformed may properly be called the history of concepts' (Koselleck 1998, p. 62–63). To underline the importance of language use, he distinguished between semantics and pragmatics within conceptual history.[8] Semantics concerned the structures of meaning, whereas pragmatics was about 'what, where, why somebody says something' (Koselleck 2003, p. 14). He used the distinction to differentiate between the semantic reservoir available for the actors and the particular choices made by specific actors in political or intellectual controversies. In his reference to pragmatics, he sometimes refers to the approach developed by the so-called Cambridge School, and in particular, Quentin Skinner. But he does not include speech act theory in his theoretical reflections – as Skinner did – and nor does he agree with Skinner's main theoretical argument that conceptual changes can only be observed in language use.

Koselleck never grounded his use of pragmatics in any strong, theoretical reflections. Within linguistics, there has been a long discussion on how to draw the borders between semantics and pragmatics. A narrow definition restricts pragmatics to those relations between language and context that are encoded in the structure of language (Levinson 1983, p. 9). These would typically be features such as deixis, presuppositions and speech acts. But a broader definition would also include conversational implicatures and capture the differences between the literal meaning of an utterance and what the speaker means to say. In speaking of pragmatics, Koselleck avoids the use of linguistic terminology. But he is aware of the formal linguistic features through which communication operates. At one point he speaks of how 'reified units of actions' such as states, churches, classes or parties act through linguistic patterns of identification (Koselleck 1998). In a study on how counterconcepts are used to exclude others from a concept with universalising potentials, he examines how the pronoun *we* plays a strategic role. The most remarkable influence from pragmatics within conceptual history is, however, to be found in the understanding of how concepts formed part of political and social struggles. Koselleck speaks of concepts 'consciously developed as weapons' (*Kampfbegriffe*) in political struggles (Koselleck 1985a, p. 78). Not only are concepts introduced by political actors to change a political situation, they can also become objects that actors will struggle for. Let us take the concept of human rights as an example. In one way, the concept is introduced in a struggle against a hierarchically organised society. In another, it is controversial and will be fought over. It is thus formative as well as being itself formed by action. As Hans-Erich Bödeker, a leading conceptual historian, has constantly reminded us, concepts do not act by themselves, they are invoked by actors in particular situations (Bödeker 2011, p. 34). The history of concepts is therefore also a history of what actors do with concepts.

Due to his intuitive understanding of the pragmatic dimension, Koselleck could point out different functions that concepts could have in historical change. He persistently lists these functions. Among the more general, we find concepts of movement, concepts of time, concepts of expectation, concepts of the future, concepts of action, intentional concepts and not least basic concepts (to which we shall return in a moment). He kept refining this list, albeit without developing a clear system. But more importantly, the functions that the different concepts were set to perform were related to a grand social change that began around 1750. What took shape was modernity (*die Neuzeit*), which marked a radical break with the existing space of experience and the introduction of our modern political and social concepts. According to Koselleck, four major processes incorporated the new experiences and laid out the patterns for the use of political and social concepts. The first was a process of democratisation, which dramatically broadened the use of political language; the second process indicated a temporalisation of concepts in order to capture the growing expectations about the future. The third process was characterised by the insertion of concepts into ideologies, where they acquired strong universalising potentials in the form of collective singulars. The fourth process, finally, was an increasing politicisation of concepts, during which, they became attuned to political conflict. By outlining these processes, Koselleck was able to place the different uses of concepts in a larger sociological perspective, which could be said to underline major patterns of speech action.

Conceptual history can no doubt be developed further in the direction of pragmatics. There are certainly advantages to be gained by taking a more formal look at speech actions as done by Quentin Skinner, at the manifestation of subject positions in line with discourse analysis, at speaker positions as they manifest themselves in the semantic designators, or in the strategic use of deictic references,[9] and at the conventions and rules embedding political communication as practised by Willibald Steinmetz and his colleagues.[10]

Basic concepts and politics

The goal of conceptual history is to study the changes of basic concepts in the political and social lexicon. Koselleck limited his study of historical semantics to what he termed basic concepts. In order to properly understand his theory and method, we need to take a closer look at his use of the term. Basic concepts do not only belong to the domain of representation. To grasp the full range of the term, we have to include the two other dimensions of language we have scrutinised. If basic concepts are simply seen as concepts within the representational understanding of meaning, they hardly make sense (as many linguists have critically remarked). As all concepts, basic concepts too are linked to words, but this link does not make them basic. Koselleck makes a careful distinction between word and concept: 'In terms of our method, a word becomes a concept when a single word is needed that contains – and is indispensable for articulating – the full range of meanings derived from a given sociopolitical context' (Koselleck 2001, p. 19). Obviously, the formulation only makes sense if the term 'concept' as used here is understood as 'basic concept'. Consequently, a word can become the label for a basic concept, which includes a range of meaning in a particular context. Basic concepts are not only the result of activities in a particular context, they also 'condense' an entirety of experience in the context, to use another formulation by Koselleck (1985a, p. 85). This 'condensation' is a way of saying that basic concepts are made into headers in order to influence or even control a situation. If we take basic concepts in politics (itself a basic concept), they appear and are used to influence and frame events. Condensation works through the ability of a word to label a concept of a rather general or abstract nature. The word *state* labels the concept STATE, which contains a range of meaning. This polysemy is thus an inherent part of a basic concept. But basic concepts are precisely also basic in the sense that they 'become indispensable to any formulation of the most urgent issues of a given time' (Koselleck 1996, p. 64). It is up to the conceptual historian to demonstrate how concepts become basic by being 'an inescapable, irreplaceable part of the political and social vocabulary' (*ibidem*). To do this, we need the long-term perspective of the historian. In the Lexicon, Koselleck and his co-editors chose those political and social concepts that they saw as irreplaceable in our modern society. The basic concepts studied in the Lexicon, in their view, made up the conceptual architecture of modern politics and modern social life. The general nature of basic concepts also made them controversial and contested. By their nature, they contained a political dimension in the sense that they would always generate debate or conflict. In a larger perspective, they might become conventionalised, or part of a dominant discourse, but they would still be subject to different interpretations and play the role of empty or floating signifiers, to borrow a terminology from Ernesto Laclau.

The pivotal role of basic concepts can be seen as central to efforts for ordering and managing society. Basic concepts are carriers of discourses framing social and political expectations. Koselleck's understanding of basic concepts bears resemblances to Raymond Williams' famous work on keywords. Williams studied the changing experiences following modernisation through the changing meaning of a number of keywords that were able to 'bind' meanings together and 'indicate' important thoughts (Williams 1976, p. 15). He had a particular eye to those situations in which keywords were at the centre of conflicts of values. While drawing less on semantic theory in his studies of keywords, Williams still placed his work within historical semantics. In the lexicon project, Koselleck and his colleagues precisely undertook a study of key concepts in the sense that they were factors in the emergence of our modern society. They followed the semantic forms in which concepts were verbalised and pointed out the context in which they became central or even inescapable.

Conclusion

Although linguists working within the field of historical semantics have shown some interest in conceptual history, the relations between linguistics and conceptual history are weak. Conceptual history is not mentioned in standard encyclopedia of linguistics. There have been closer ties to discourse analysis. Koselleck mentions the role of the discursive context in which concepts move. Foucault points to the role of the conceptual architecture in the formation of discourses. In France, in particular through the works of Jacques Guilhaumou, conceptual history has thrived in an encounter with discourse analysis (Ifversen 2009). Guilhaumou combined the analysis of relations and position within discourses with the semantics at use in designations of symbolic positions such as people, aristocracy, nation and revolutionaries. Scholars working within Critical Discourse Analysis have made use of conceptual analysis to demonstrate how policy discourses are being framed through the semantic relations of key concepts (Krzyżanowski & Wodak 2011). In a similar vein, studies of political ideology have focused on the role of conceptual morphologies in forming and changing ideology (Freeden 1996). Scholars drawing on the Cambridge School have been engaged in discussions with conceptual historians on how to include language use, and more specifically rhetoric in the analysis of conceptual change (Palonen 2014). In more recent years, conceptual history has been strongly inspired by methods from corpus linguistics, not least in dealing with digitalised corpora. It is expected that this new encounter with linguistics – hosted within the umbrella of digital humanities – will increase the interest for studying conceptual changes.

Conceptual history is to be understood as a historical investigation of those semantic, referential and contextual conditions in which basic concepts were formed. The approach follows the long diachronic lines that concepts will take on their way to becoming basic concepts. Concepts develop through semantic changes. The meaning of words is changed, new words appear and words go out of use. Through the investigation of conceptual changes, the focus is on the durations and rhythms of concepts. When looked at synchronically, the different rhythms are perceived by the historian as different time layers forming the experiences of past actors. The study of semantic changes is only the first dimension in conceptual history. The work on historical semantics is followed by a study of the dynamic relation between concept and world. The second dimension of conceptual history examines this relation as it is played out linguistically in what the concepts refer to. Sometimes, concepts directly form the world. At other times, things happen that need conceptualisation. But in order to identify basic concepts, conceptual history draws in a third dimension, which allows it to follow what actors do with concepts when they communicate with each other in particular situations. Only the study of how concepts are formed in language use and influenced by specific contexts will fulfil the requirements for a history of basic concepts.

Notes

1 In line with the programmatic statement of Lucien Febvre, some French historians also called for a closer engagement with semantics or lexicography, notably Louis Girard (1963) and Alphonse Dupront (1969).
2 For an overview of the different intellectual inspirations that formed Koselleck's conceptual history, see Richter (1995) and Olsen (2012).
3 I have followed the conventions within the study of semantics and write the lexemes in italics and the concepts in capital letters.
4 Schäfer (2012).

5 Reichardt developed his method in a number of articles (see Reichardt 1985).
6 According to the corpus linguist Paul Baker, keyness is simply defined through relative frequency: 'any word is potentially to be key if it occurs frequently enough when compared to a reference corpus' (Baker 2004, p. 347).
7 John Lyons prefers to distinguish between denotation, which is utterance-independent and thus part of the systemic meaning, and reference, which is utterance-dependent and therefore part of a speech act (Lyons 1995, p. 79).
8 The distinction was used as the subtitle for one of his books, published after his death, *Begriffsgeschichten: Studien zur Semantik und Pragmatik der politischen und sozialen Sprache*.
9 The role of designators has been studied extensively by what I have called the French school of conceptual history, and in particular by the linguist and historian Jacques Guilhaumou (see Ifversen 2009).
10 Steinmetz 2012, p. 89.

References

Baker, P, 2004, 'Querying keywords: Questions of difference, frequency, and sense in keywords analysis', *Journal of English Linguistics*, vol. 32, no. 4, pp. 346–59.

Blank, A, 2001, 'Words and concepts in time: Towards diachronic cognitive onomasiology', available from: www.metaphorik.de/de/journal/01/words-and-concepts-time-towards-diachronic-cognitive-onomasiology.html [accessed 1 March 2015].

Blank, A, 2013, 'Why do new meanings occur? A cognitive typology of the motivations for lexical semantic change', in *Cognitive linguistic research: historical semantics and cognition*, eds. A Blank & P Koch, Walter de Gruyter, Tübingen, pp. 61–90.

Bödeker, H E, 1998, 'Concept – meaning – discourse: Begriffsgeschichte reconsidered' in *History of concepts: Comparative perspectives*, eds. I Hampsher-Monk, K Tilmans & F K de Vrees, Amsterdam University Press, Amsterdam, pp. 51–64.

Bödeker, H E, 2011, 'Begriffsgeschichte as the history of theory. The history of theory as Begriffsgeschichte: An essay', in: *Political concepts and time*, ed. J F Sebastián, University of Cantabria Press, Santander, pp. 19–44.

Coseriu, E, 1964, *Pour une sémantique structural diachronique*, Klincksieck, Strasbourg.

de Saussure, F, 1969, *Cours de linguistique générale*, Payot, Paris.

Dupront, A, 1969, 'Sémantique historique et histoire', *Cahiers de Lexicologie*, no. 14. pp. 15–25.

Febvre, L, 1930, 'Les mots et les choses en histoire économique', *Annales d'histoire économique et sociale*, vol. 2, no. 6, pp. 231–234.

Felder, E, 2006, *Semantische Kämpfe: Macht und Sprache in den Wissenschaften*, Walter de Gruyter, Berlin.

Freeden, M, 1996, *Ideologies and political theory*, Oxford University Press, Oxford.

Gadamer, H-G, 1975, *Truth and method*, The Seabury Press, New York.

Geeraerts, D, 2006, 'Onomasiology and lexical variation' in *Encyclopedia of language and linguistics*. 2nd ed., ed. K Brown, Elsevier, Amsterdam, pp. 37–40.

Girard, L, 1963, 'Histoire et lexicographie', *Annales. Économies, Sociétés, Civilisations*, vol. 18, no. 6, pp. 1128–1132.

Ifversen, J, 2009, 'Jacques Guilhaumou and the French School', *Redescriptions. Yearbook of political thought, conceptual history and feminist theory*, no. 12, pp. 244–261.

Koselleck, R, 1967, 'Richtlinien für das Lexicon politisch-sozialer Begriffe der Neuzeit', in *Archiv für Begriffsgeschichte* no. 11, pp. 81–99.

Koselleck, R, 1985a, 'Begriffsgeschichte and social history', in *Futures past: On the semantics of historical times*, R Koselleck, MIT Press, Cambridge, MA, pp. 75–92.

Koselleck, R, 1985b, 'Historical criteria of the modern concept of revolution', in *Futures past: On the semantics of historical times*, R Koselleck, MIT Press, Cambridge, MA, pp. 43–57.

Koselleck, R, 1989, 'Linguistic change and the history of events', *The Journal of Modern History*, vol. 61, no. 4, pp. 649–666.

Koselleck, R, 1996, 'A response to comments on the *Geschichtliche Grundbegriffe*' in *The meaning of historical terms and concepts*, eds. H Lehmann & M Richter, German Historical Institute, Washington, pp. 59–70.

Koselleck, R, 1998, 'Social history and Begriffsgeschichte', in *History of concepts: Comparative perspectives*, eds. I Hampsher-Monk, K Tilmans & F K de Vrees, Amsterdam University Press, Amsterdam, pp. 23–36.

Koselleck, R, 2003, 'Zeit, Zeitlichkeit und Geschichte – sperrige Reflexionen: Reinhart Koselleck im Gespräch mit Wolf-Dieter Narr und Kari Palonen', in *Zeit, Geschichte und Politik: Zum achtzigsten Geburtstag von Reinhart Koselleck,* eds. J Kurunmäki & K Palonen, University of Jyväskylä, Jyväskylä, pp. 9–34.

Koselleck, R, 2006a, 'Crisis', *Journal of the History of Ideas*, vol. 67, no. 2, pp. 357–400.

Koselleck, R, 2006b, 'Die Geschichte der Begriffe und Begriffe der Geschichte', in Koselleck R *Begriffsgeschichten: Studien zur Semantik und Pragmatik der politischen und sozialen Sprache,* Suhrkamp Verlag, Frankfurt am Main, pp. 56–76.

Koselleck, R, 2011, 'Introduction and prefaces to the *Geschichtliche Grundbegriffe*' [1972], *Contributions to the History of Concepts*, vol. 6, no. 1, pp. 1–37.

Kroebner, R, 1953, 'Semantics and historiography', *Cambridge Journal*, no. 7, pp. 131–144.

Krzyżanowski, M & Wodak, R, 2011, 'Political strategies and language policies: the European Union Lisbon strategy and its implications for the EU's language and multilingualism policy', *Language Policy*, vol. 10, no. 2, pp. 115–136.

Levinson, S C, 1983, *Pragmatics*, Cambridge University Press, Cambridge.

Lyons, J, 1995, *Linguistic semantics: An introduction*, Cambridge University Press, Cambridge.

Nerlich, B & Clarke D D, 1999, 'Elements for an integral theory of semantic change and semantic development', in *Meaning change – meaning variation. I*, eds. R Eckardt & K Heusinger K, Arbeitspapier 106, Universität Konstanz, pp. 123–134.

Ogden, C K & Richards, I A, 1923, *The meaning of meaning: A study of the influence of language upon thought and of the science of symbolism,* Routledge & Kegan Paul, London.

Olsen, N, 2012, *History in the plural. An introduction to the work of Reinhart Koselleck*, Berghahn, New York.

Palonen, K, 2014, *Politics and conceptual Histories. Rhetorical and temporal perspectives,* Bloomsbury, London.

Reichardt, R, 1985, 'Einleitung', in *Handbuch politisch-sozialer Grundbegriffe in Frankreich 1680–1820,* vol. 1, eds. R Reichardt R & E Schmitt, R Oldenbourg Verlag, Munich, pp. 39–85.

Richter, M, 1995, *The history of political and social concepts. A critical introduction*, Oxford University Press, Oxford.

Schäfer, R, 2012, 'Historicizing strong metaphors. A challenge for conceptual history', *Contributions to the History of Concepts*, vol. 7, no. 2, pp. 28–51.

Schultz, H, 1978, 'Begriffsgeschichte und Argumentationsgeschichte', in *Historische Semantik und Begriffsgeschichte,* ed. R Koselleck, Klett-Cotta, Stuttgart, pp. 43–74.

Sebastián, J F & Fuentes, J F, 2006, 'Conceptual history, memory, and identity: An interview with Reinhart Koselleck', *Contributions to the History of Concepts*, vol. 2, no. 1, pp. 99–127.

Skinner, Q, 1988, 'Meaning and understanding in the history of ideas', in *Meaning and context: Quentin Skinner and his critics,* ed. J Tully, Polity Press, Cambridge, pp. 29–67.

Steinmetz, W, 2012, 'Some thoughts on a history of twentieth-century German basic concepts', *Contributions to the History of Concepts,* vol. 7, no. 1, pp. 87–100.

Traugott, E C, 2006, 'Semantic change: bleaching, strengthening, narrowing, extension', in *Encyclopedia of language and linguistics,* 2nd ed., ed. K Brown, Elsevier Science, Amsterdam, pp. 124–136.

Trier, J, 1973, *Der deutsche Wortschatz im Sinnbezirk des Verstandes* [1931], Winter, Heidelberg.

Williams, R, 1976, *Keywords. A vocabulary of culture and society*, Oxford University Press, New York.

9
Critical Discourse Studies
A critical approach to the study of language and communication

Bernhard Forchtner and Ruth Wodak

Introduction

The theoretical frameworks reviewed in this first section have all pointed to the relevance of language and semiosis in the way politics is not only performed, but also conceptualised. Here, we add to this endeavour by introducing another, more recent way of approaching the *nexus of language, discourse* and *politics* and discussing the burgeoning field of Critical Discourse Studies (CDS, also known as Critical Discourse Analysis, CDA; see Flowerdew & Richardson 2017; Wodak & Meyer 2015 for a comprehensive overview). More specifically, we reflect on how CDS has drawn on a variety of theoretical approaches and utilised them in empirical research. In this chapter, we thus present research conducted within the framework of CDS, which deals with political issues of various kinds, exploring how it draws on a range of theories in its multi-, inter-, trans- or post-disciplinary empirical work.[1]

The range of different approaches within CDS cannot be viewed as theories on their own; none of these approaches has put forward, for example, a notion of 'discourse' comparable in its level of abstraction with that of Michel Foucault, Jürgen Habermas or Ernesto Laclau (for more details, see Chapters 3, 4 and 6). At the same time, it would be wrong to understand approaches associated with CDS purely in terms of methodology (Angermuller et al. 2014; Hart & Cap 2014; Wodak 2013; van Dijk 2007). Indeed, while all these approaches focus on the detailed analysis of text in context and thus draw on concepts taken from argumentation theory, linguistic pragmatics, rhetoric, semantics and syntax, the underlying goal is to understand the complex workings of language within society, a concern for how socio-cultural structures influence and, at the same time, are influenced by, language use (Fairclough & Wodak 1997, p. 258). There is thus an attempt to situate 'textually oriented discourse analysis' (Fairclough 1992, p. 55) within (socio-)theoretical frameworks and, thereby, also to shift the boundaries of these grand theories. Accordingly, Lilie Chouliaraki and Norman Fairclough (1999, pp. 113ff.) view CDS as a principle that draws together, that is, recontextualises, different theoretical traditions while integrating them with an empirical orientation. Similarly, Gilbert Weiss and Ruth Wodak (2003, p. 9) view CDS as addressing the 'problem of mediation', of integrating insights from linguistic and other disciplines, the mediation between communication and structure, discourse and society. However, before turning to a discussion of how approaches within CDS have, to varying extents, recontextualised theoretical frameworks, we consider the basic notions of 'discourse', 'critique' and 'power'.

Discourse is a concept used in a plethora of ways – ranging from notions oriented towards Foucault (that is, describing a system of rules of formation and, later, discourse as a specific, historical power/knowledge regime) to a concept inspired by Habermas focusing on challenging, criticizing and justifying validity claims (based on idealizing presuppositions of equal rights to speak, freedom of repression and manipulation, inclusiveness and sincerity). The latter, for example, partly informs in the Discourse-Historical Approach's (DHA) conceptualisation of discourse as centred on topic-related semiotic practices, which are socially constituted as well as socially constitutive, and which consist of truth and rightness claims involving several actors with different perspectives (Reisigl & Wodak 2009, p. 89). The former appears to inspire, for example, Theo van Leeuwen's approach (2008, p. vii), while Fairclough's approach in CDS has most extensively – though also critically – drawn on Foucault's work.

Critique is supposed to make visible existing interconnections (between structure and language use, or between structures) – something that might be based on (neo-)Marxist views, or derive from a Foucault-inspired attempt to problematise (Foucault 1981a). As Paul Chilton, Hailong Tian and Ruth Wodak state:

> the term 'critical' is associated with currents of thought whose recent sources are in the eighteenth-century European Enlightenment but whose roots are in ancient Greek philosophy. Etymologically, the verb 'criticize' derives from a Greek word *krinein* 'to separate, decide', in the sense of making a judgement or a distinction.
> (Chilton, Tian & Wodak 2010, p. 490)

Moreover, Gunther Kress (1996, p. 15), in line with other authors, is concerned with unequal 'distributions of economic, cultural and political goods in contemporary societies', and thus summarises the project of CDS as follows: 'The intention has been to bring a system of excessive inequalities of power into crisis by uncovering its workings and its effects through the analysis of potent cultural objects – texts – and thereby to help in achieving a more equitable social order.'

Martin Reisigl and Wodak (2001, pp. 32ff.) make useful, conceptual distinctions between *text-immanent critique, socio-diagnostic critique* and *prospective (retrospective) critique*. Their view of text-immanent critique is based on hermeneutics and pursues one of the early ideas of Critical Theory, namely, the unearthing of inherent contradictions via linguistic means. While text-immanent critique is inherently text-oriented, socio-diagnostic critique is based on theoretical assumptions, which go hand in hand with the analyst's social and political commitments. At this level, the aim is also to reveal multiple interests and contradictions of text producers, on the basis of evidence in the text and its broad and narrow contexts. Prospective critique builds on these two levels to identify areas of social concern that could be addressed by direct social and political engagement in many Western polities (Reisigl & Wodak 2001, p. 34; see also Chilton, Tian & Wodak 2010, p. 495).

All approaches share a view that CDS 'highlights the substantively linguistic and discursive nature of social relations of *power* in contemporary societies. This is partly the matter of how power relations are exercised and negotiated in discourse' (Wodak 1996, p. 18). While some approaches and/or studies favour a more traditional, Weberian definition of power, others subscribe to a productive notion of power in the post-structural tradition.

Yet, approaches generally view power as being present 'in discourse' (some positions will hold greater potential to influence others), 'over discourse' (for example, the question of access and agenda setting), 'and of discourse' (an understanding of power which points to latent conflicts; see Lukes 2005, p. 29).

Such an agenda cannot be built on one disciplinary foundation, but requires varying degrees of co-operation spanning disciplinary boundaries (Weiss & Wodak 2003, p. 18; van Leeuwen 2007). The extent of such co-operation might vary; for example, *multidisciplinarity* is linked to disciplines that offer different perspectives on the issue in question, usually under the lead of one discipline. In contrast, *interdisciplinarity* implies two or more disciplines that explore a problem in an equal way. *Transdisciplinarity* describes the interpenetration of methods and common theory/ies across different disciplines, which cluster around particular problems. Finally, *postdisciplinarity* (or *predisciplinarity*) postulates neglecting disciplinary boundaries in favour of pure problem orientation. Andrew Sayer (1999, p. 6), for example, has pointed to Adam Smith, who was concerned with moral philosophy and, as such, also with the social order (sociology). However, he also acknowledged psychological factors and is, today, famous for his contribution to the field of economics. As Sayer maintains, this did not result in a reductionism of any kind.

Independent of whichever perspective is subscribed to, CDS, as an overarching framework, necessarily spans disciplinary boundaries in its problem-oriented focus. Hence, middle-range theories usually provide the necessary conceptual apparatus to approach a particular problem. This does not, however, reduce the influence of more abstract frameworks through which complex issues become identified.

While focusing on how research in CDS has drawn on a range of theoretical frameworks and disciplinary fields (including sociology, history, and so forth), we first look at the most explicit references to Marx and the neo-Marxism of Gramsci before moving, second, to Foucault and the discourse theory of Laclau. We then return, third, to neo-Marxism and discuss the Critical Theory of the first generation of the Frankfurt School and Habermas. Fourth, we move on to Pierre Bourdieu's influence on CDS before providing a brief summary of the impact of *Begriffsgeschichte* (conceptual history) on CDS. The chapter closes with a brief summary.

CDS and the influence of Marx and Gramsci

Marx's understanding of society in terms of modes of (currently capitalist) production and struggle underpins many CDS approaches. This is especially the case in Fairclough's approach, and explicitly discussed in *Marx as Critical Discourse Analyst* (Fairclough & Graham 2002). Here, Fairclough and Phil Graham that language has become ever more central in late modernity and claim (*ibidem*, p. 201) that, with respect to language as being produced by as well as reproducing material circumstances, practices, social consciousness and human experience, 'Marx's method and the methods of CDA are identical'. In one way, the authors base this claim on their reading of Marx as being well aware of the link between language use and other dimensions of the social, thus stressing the dialectics between the discursive and the material dimensions of social life. In another, the authors illustrate that even Marx engaged in empirical Critical Discourse Analysis when, for example, discussing Hegel's concept of 'state'. Due to reasons of space, we cannot go into more details of Fairclough and Graham's complex analysis. Suffice to say that they illustrate how Marx, also at the level of actual language use, rejected Hegel's claim that 'the idea' takes the position of the subject, that is, how Hegel endowed 'the idea' erroneously with agency.

Fairclough has also drawn on Antonio Gramsci's approach (Fairclough 2010; 1992, pp. 91–96; see also Chouliaraki & Fairclough 1999; Chapter 2 in this volume). By utilising the concept of 'hegemony', Fairclough attempts to explain the fact that various domains of today's society are shaped by naturalised practices and relations without being directly forced to do so. Such naturalised conventions are made transparent by means of discourse analysis.

For example, Fairclough (*ibidem*, p. 129) turns to doctor–patient consultations, linking such everyday experiences to conventional hegemonic relationships between doctor and patient. The cultural hegemony of this mode of interaction can, of course, be challenged – leading to struggles over hegemony (for example in and through the rise of alternative medicine). Turning to the micro-level, Fairclough analyses a conversation between a patient (an alcoholic) and a doctor, and emphasises that the doctor's questions ('are you back, are you back on it'), the doctor's assessment of advice given ('I think that's wise') and his directive ('I'd like to keep you know seeing you') seem to reproduce traditional patterns of interaction. However, vague formulations ('are you back on it'), the use of modality markers ('I think') and the hedged directive 'you know' contradict such traditional modes of interaction characterised by domination. Embedding this interpretation in a wider socio-cultural context, Fairclough presents the analysed conversation as an example of a doctor open to alternative, non-hegemonic practices, as a case of 'conversationalisation'. This type of discourse, which emerged in the private sphere, has since colonised public institutions and bears the potential for both democratic renewal and the regression of the active subject into a consumer.

Another analysis inspired by Gramsci's understanding of hegemony is proposed by Can Küçükali (2015), who applies the DHA, specifically its framework of discursive strategies (nomination, predication, argumentation, perspectivisation and intensification/ mitigation; see below), to the ruling Turkish Justice and Development Party's (AKP) attempts to establish and maintain its political hegemony. Indeed, the party has managed to construct a hegemonic bloc in order to secure the (neo-liberal and religious-conservative) transformation of Turkish society. While drawing on a post-foundational understanding of politics, on conflict and contingency, Küçükali favours a critical realist reading of Gramsci. Accordingly, language use is understood as 'a sphere of political struggle which is based on social structures and which has material effects on society' (*ibidem*, p. 51). The focus on discursive aspects of hegemonic projects implies a detailed analysis of *topoi* and rhetorical figures in argumentation. The following example is taken from a parliamentary reply by the-then Foreign Minister, Ahmet Davutoğlu, in 2012 in response to criticism of Turkey's Syrian policy (*ibidem*, pp. 133–134).

> Yesterday, I listened to a highly credible official from Syria. Filled with tears, he said: 'My honourable minister, because a father who lost his child in an air bombardment could not go out and bury him, he put the child in the fridge to avoid a stink. I personally saw it.' What kind of torture is this? In the past, we gave friendly advice to Syria but we didn't impose anything. But whenever folk are overrun, then it changes at that time. […] We cannot do it [not being interested] as humans. […] Like the Bosnian government of the time, which struggled with snipers, I am memorizing it with appreciation; we too, should adopt a certain attitude.
>
> (Küçükali 2015, pp. 133–134)

In the following, we briefly summarise Küçükali's analysis of this quote: the first four lines start with an *argumentum ad exemplum,* in which a tragic example is used to operationalise a threat to the Syrian government, further supported with an *argumentum ad misericordiam* (appeal to pity), a rhetorical question, the *topos of authority* ('highly credible official') and the *topos of personal experience* (the pronoun 'I'). The latter points to an interesting shift as, subsequently, the pronoun 'we' emphasises the power of the state and, ultimately, results in a threat (from 'friendly advice' to 'not to impose anything' to 'a certain attitude'). This attitude is legitimised through a *topos of humanity* and an analogy with the Bosnian war, an analogy further legitimised by cutting off the flow of the argument (*parenthesis*) so as to indicate the speaker's personal stance in support of the Bosnian government's attitude. Here, Küçükali's critical realist perspective on hegemony becomes manifest as he evaluates this analogy not simply in terms of meaning-making but as fallacious. While arguing that, in the first example, the indicated actor is defending his own country, Turkey, vis-à-vis Syria, is in fact an external actor intervening in another, sovereign state. In so doing, the author traces in detail how a hegemonic project is discursively realised.

CDS and the influence of post-structuralist approaches: Foucault and beyond

Given that the notion of discourse – and the wider shift towards an interest in language – has been closely linked to (post-)structuralist concerns for meaning-making, it is not surprising that Foucault has influenced the approaches of CDS. It has been primarily in the work of Fairclough and the Duisburg School (see below) that a strong Foucauldian influence on text-oriented discourse analysis is noticeable. Generally speaking, Fairclough (1992, pp. 55ff.), and other proponents of CDS, embrace Foucault's view of discourse as constitutive of subjects, social relationships, objects and conceptual frameworks; the insistence that discourse practices are interdependent (thus intertextually related); the discursive nature of power, the political nature of discourse and the discursive nature of social change. This does not imply, however, that Fairclough (1992, pp. 56–61) and others have accepted every aspect of Foucault's programme; for example, the former is critical of a too-abstract notion of discourse (without analysing actual language use), an exaggerated understanding of power and a relativist outlook. Yet, Fairclough and Siegfried Jäger, in particular, have repeatedly drawn on Foucault in a productive way, some of which we introduce briefly in the following.

First, Fairclough draws on Foucault's notion of 'order of discourse' (2015, pp. 88–89; Fairclough 1992; Foucault 1981b), which he defines as particular combinations of genres (ways of acting), discourses (ways of representing) and styles (ways of being). The way these orders, modes of legitimate meaning-making, are structured is continuously contested and subject to constant struggle. Here, we refer again to doctor–patient communication (see above) – a relation, which is characterised by a particular order, which might well change over time as new styles and representations of the human body gain legitimacy.

Second, and also explicitly linked to Foucault, is the notion of the 'technologisation of discourse' (*ibidem*). Drawing on Foucault's idea of technologies as constitutive of power in modern society and, more particularly, on Rose and Miller's work on the Foucauldian idea of bio-power and 'technologies of government', Fairclough (*ibidem*, pp. 137ff.) views the 'technologisation of discourse' as a conscious effort to understand, reshape and reproduce discursive practices that benefit certain hegemonic projects and ideological effects. Examples can easily be envisaged, such as the constant demand for further training in the area of communication, which leads to particular knowledge being circulated in institutions, such as universities. Through technologisation, actors attempt to influence these orders and change them in a certain way. This requires experts, the policing of these interventions, their design and simulation, as well as subsequent normalisation – illustrated by the analysis of an extract from a British university prospectus. Fairclough then identified a trend, which has become ever more pervasive since the early 1990s (see Rheindorf & Wodak 2015; Jessop et al. 2008).

This genre has developed from densely written texts on basic requirements to ever more colourful publications, consisting of short paragraphs and promises of opportunities. Fairclough (2010, p. 142) points out that instead of formulations such as *'we require'*, the investigated prospectus speaks of *'you will need'*; and instead of stating what is required, assurances (*'students will gain valuable experience'*, the lure of employability as it is known nowadays) and descriptions (*'students pursue'*) are supposed to create a positive impression. These micro-observations are then linked back to the macro level: Fairclough points to the educational system at large and the increasing significance attached to spoken language and face-to-face interaction.

Siegfried and Margaret Jäger, key proponents of the Duisburg School of CDS (see Jäger & Maier 2015), draw on Foucault's notion of discourse, Alexej N. Leont'ev's (1978) speech activity theory and Jürgen Link's (1982) focus on collective symbols. As institutionalised and conventionalised speech modes, discourses express legitimate knowledge and thus societal power relations (which in turn are impacted upon by discourses). Knowledge, its effects, function, evolution and transmission, have to be reconstructed in order to analyse and problematise power relations and the 'truths' they legitimise. By focusing on *dispositives* – 'heterogeneous ensemble[s] of discourses, institutions, architectural forms, regulatory decisions, laws, administrative measures, scientific statements, philosophical, moral and philanthropic propositions – in short, the said as much as the unsaid' (Foucault 1977, p. 194) – the Duisburg School furthermore emphasises the intertwining of discursive and non-discursive practices as well as their materialisations.

Discourse becomes manifest in different 'discourse strands' (composed of discourse fragments, texts on the same topic that are launched from different 'discourse positions', that is, the position of the participant) on different discourse planes (science, politics, media, etc.). Every discourse is historically embedded and has repercussions for current and future discourse. The discourse of the so-called 'new right' in Germany was analysed by Jäger and Jäger (2008), who based their research on different right-wing print media. They identified important common characteristics, such as the use of specific symbols, 'ethno-pluralism' [*apartheid*], aggressiveness and anti-democratic attitudes, as well as significant linguistic and stylistic differences due to the different target audiences of the newspapers. Concerning '*apartheid*', for example, Jäger (2008, p. 340) reveals the many linguistic devices employed when media and politicians make clear-cut distinctions between 'our white people' and 'others' (migrants, such as Turks or Bosnians), which subsequently enhances nativist nationalism.

Post-Foucauldian approaches, in particular Laclau's discourse theory (DT), have been greeted with enthusiasm – as well as scepticism and attempts at reformulation. In particular, Chouliaraki and Fairclough (1999, pp. 121–126) discuss DT as a possibility to integrate Marxism with post-structuralist theories of discourse. Here, the concept of '*articulation*' is viewed as valuable in order to understand the openness and continuous reconstitution of the social, although strong arguments are made in favour of recognising the significance of social structures, of the non-discursive, which, the authors claim, should be taken more seriously than in Laclau's DT.

While both approaches more or less agree that meaning depends on discourse, Chouliaraki and Fairclough insist that the social arises out of dialectical relations between *semiosis* (discourse) and non-discursive aspects. One case in point is Nicolina Montesano Montessori's (2011) work on the Zapatistas and their struggle in Mexico. While attempting to design a framework that brings together CDS and DT, Montesano Montessori, among other things, draws on Fairclough's notion of 'orders of discourse', his critique of what she (*ibidem*, p. 172) describes as Laclau's 'idealist social ontology', and the DHA's methodology in analysing discourse at (a) the level of topic(s), (b) discursive strategies and (c) relevant linguistic realisation(s). For example, Montesano Montessori's (*ibidem*, p. 178) analysis of texts produced by the *Ejército Zapatista de Liberación* (EZLN) and the-then Mexican President Salinas results in the claim that 'modernisation' (a keyword in Salinas' texts) is characterised as an urgent project that has ultimately reformed the country and is grammatically supported by a verbal system that indicates material achievement and progress (Montesano Montessori supports her claims by drawing on computer-assisted collocation analysis). In contrast, 'democracy', a keyword in texts floated by the Zapatistas, is linked to terms indicating transition and movement. There is thus a level of insecurity attached to 'democracy' (understood as an *empty signifier*), an openness that leaves space for various parties to join this *chain of equivalence*.

Another scholar who draws on DT is Felicitas Macgilchrist (2011), who analysed the role of journalism in the discursive construction of Russia. She draws on DT's constructivist premises and its interest in hegemonic projects as means to fix contingent social relations, but also on CDS in order to identify how the construction of such hegemonic projects (and their possible failure) operate in detail through language.

In her research on the Russian–Chechen conflict, Macgilchrist analyses the use of metaphors in order to trace how international news coverage construes *us* and *them*. More specifically, she focuses on the articulation of metaphors and its consequences. Macgilchrist analyses what Lakoff (2002) described as two kinds of the 'nation-as-a-family' metaphor, that is, either the *strict father* or the *nurturing parent* model. The former envisages authority, strength, independence and the need to advise and regulate 'the children' – which in cases of transgression need to be punished 'for their own good'. In contrast, the nurturing parent model endorses empathy, discussion and compromise; negotiations are favoured over displays of strength and the use of force. Among many cases, and drawing on these two models, Macgilchrist (*ibidem*, pp. 91ff.) investigates the representation of the-then Prime Minister Putin's military response to Islamic militants entering Dagestan in August 1999 – and whether or not this representation follows a '*weak father* story-line' or that of the '*neglectful parent*'. While a strict father would, at least, achieve a quick victory, Russia fails this test, as manifested in a German newspaper article: 'Russia missed its opportunity, following the disaster in Chechnya, to prepare its army better to fight in the mountains. The armed forces are already underpaid, poorly equipped and have little motivation.' Different, but yet similar in constructing the Russian 'other', stories about Russia as a neglectful parent focus on the worsening of the situation through military action, as in *The Guardian*'s appeal to avoid 'excessive and badly-aimed firepower'. In sum, both projects *other* Russia, either by articulating it as incompetent and weak (and, subsequently, too brutal) or not civilised enough, not 'in the know' about how to solve conflicts properly.

CDS and the influence of Critical Theory and Jürgen Habermas

Returning to neo-Marxist influences, references to Critical Theory in CDS are prominently placed (e.g. Reisigl & Wodak 2001, p. 32; Fairclough & Wodak 1997, pp. 260ff.) – though operationalisation of these approaches in empirical research remains rare. To a certain extent, this is surprising given that interdisciplinarity is a frequent self-description of CDS practitioners. As such, Max Horkheimer's (1993, p. 11) call for theoretically informed, empirical investigations of the link between economy, psychology and culture (including areas such as fashion, law, public opinion, etc.) suggests the first generation of Critical Theory as a useful framework. Indeed, these scholars elaborated a rich, empirical programme, a mixture of detailed discussions of empirical data related to theoretical arguments.

In *The salaried masses*, originally published in 1930, Siegfried Kracauer (1998, p. 29), for example, provides an ethnographic study of the 'exoticism of a commonplace existence' of white-collar workers. Leo Löwenthal and Norbert Guterman's (1949) book *Prophets of deceit*, a study of American agitators, resembles language-sensitive work on the contemporary far right in CDS in many ways. A study based on analyses of focus groups dealt with the legacies of National Socialism in post-war Germany (see, for example, Adorno 2010) while *The authoritarian personality* (Adorno et al. 1950), combines statistical analysis with discussions of extracts from interviews. The latter is mentioned in Reisigl and Wodak (2001, pp. 13ff.) and has been taken up in Wodak's *Politics of fear* (2015, pp. 154ff.), in which *The authoritarian personality* informs Wodak's analysis of right-wing populist gender politics. Drawing on Adorno, Wodak's description of the link between authoritarian patterns and '*pseudo-masculinity*'/'*pseudo-femininity*', that is, a fantasy of masculine virility and feminine qualities, helps to explain the attraction of strong men for many (right-wing populist) voters. Pointing to a poster from the local Viennese elections in 2010 by the Austrian Freedom Party (FPÖ), Wodak (*ibidem*, p. 163) analyses the, at first glance, paradox appeal to liberate Muslim women from being coerced into wearing a headscarf.

While the in-group ('We') articulated by the leader of the FPÖ, H C Strache, on the right comprises the FPÖ and 'proper' Viennese who 'protect[s] free women', it is (fallaciously) juxtaposed with 'The SPÖ [the Social-Democratic Party, until then holding an absolute majority in the local government] [protects] the compulsory wearing of head-scarves.' The verb, 'to protect', is missing in this elliptic sentence, but easily inserted via implicature from the first sentence. By arguing for the prohibition of religiously connoted – more precisely, Muslim – head-scarves, the campaign suggests purging public space of 'foreign' presence and enforcing conformity on an idea of 'modern' (Christian) femininity. The brand-like slogan at the bottom of the poster, 'WE [capitalised and thus emphasising contrast] are here for the Viennese' signifies the in-group. The latter, the 'proper Viennese', consist of free women, but not of Muslims and those apparently complicit in constraining women's freedoms and rights (the Social-Democratic Party and multicultural policies).

Compared with the influence of the first generation, Habermas' work has had a more direct influence. The key concepts are: *public sphere* and '*deliberative democracy*', in which the free and equal raising of validity claims in debate, critique and decision-making

Figure 9.1   FPÖ poster 2010 'We protect free women' (http://www.ceiberweiber.at/index.php?p=news&area=1&newsid=541 [12.08.2014])

is enabled (Chilton et al. 2010, p. 496; Reisigl & Wodak 2001, p. 34). In line with this focus on the exchange of validity claims (Reisigl & Wodak 2009, p. 89), 'truth and normative validity' are a constitutive part of their definition of 'discourse'. As part of their analysis of an intervention in debates about climate change by the-then Czech President Václav Klaus, Reisigl and Wodak analyse the following passage in Klaus' statement.

> [...] the biggest threat to freedom, democracy, the market economy and prosperity at the beginning of the 21st century is not communism or its various softer variants. Communism was replaced by the threat of ambitious environmentalism. This ideology preaches earth and nature and under the slogans of their protection – similarly to the old Marxists – wants to replace the free and spontaneous evolution of mankind by a sort of central (now global) planning of the whole world.
> (Reisigl & Wodak 2009, pp. 100–118)

This entails both a *claim to truth* ('ambitious environmentalism' as dangerous) and a *claim to rightness* (a free society has to be protected against global planning). These claims are realised via particular lexical choices in order to label (discursive strategy of nomination) actors, objects and processes, including ideological (derogatory) anthroponyms such as 'old Marxists' and 'ideology', as well as negatively representing (discursive strategy of predication) environmentalists as a 'threat'. In addition, these claims rest on specific argumentation schemes (formal and content-related *topoi*) and *fallacies*, such as the *topos* of comparison of communism and environmentalism (reconstructed as: since communism threatened freedom, democracy and the market economy, its contemporary equivalent 'ambitious environmentalism' will do the same). In this way the analysis of positive self and negative other representation is inherently substantiated by deconstructing validity claims and related argumentation schemes.

Bernhard Forchtner (2011; see also Forchtner and Tominc 2012) further elaborates the link between Habermas' approach and the DHA by identifying weak, but unavoidable, pragmatic presuppositions of communication oriented towards understanding, as reconstructed in Habermas' work. These presuppositions are viewed by Habermas (2008, p. 28) in terms of 'a world of independently existing objects, the reciprocal presupposition of rationality or "accountability," the unconditionality of context-transcending validity claims such as truth and moral rightness, and the demanding presuppositions of argumentation'. The latter, including inclusiveness, equal communicative rights, sincerity and freedom from repression and manipulation, are counter-factually presupposed in particular as soon as validity claims in communication oriented towards understanding are not any longer 'naively' accepted, but challenged and justified.

Forchtner and Christian Schneickert (2016) have further elaborated this line of thinking: while focusing on the aforementioned presuppositions and the subsequent possibility for collective learning processes (that is, processes through which intersubjective relations become more open and egalitarian) and their blocking, they integrate aspects of Bourdieu's and Habermas' approaches with the DHA. The authors draw on work inspired by Habermas in which the idea of learning processes and their blocking is conceptualised. For example, Max Miller (2006) offers a four-dimensional conceptualisation of blocked learning. Such blockage of interaction could be caused by, first, an existing consensus or a disagreement that, second, cannot be challenged due to references to an authority, be it an individual/ corporate actor or an idea/institution. *Dogmatic learning* leads to consensus, which is not challenged because of legitimising references to an individual or corporate actor. *Defensive learning* views collectively shared knowledge and practices by a group as protected from criticism through reference to a particular idea or institution. *Regressive learning* excludes the *other per se* (for example through an *argumentum ad hominem*) from those who decide what is collectively shared. *Ideological learning* claims the existence of a fundamental antagonism/disagreement, which cannot be challenged by a certain idea.

For instance, ideological learning is detected in a document entitled *Doctrine on research and teaching regarding Marxist-Leninist theory and the organisation of sciences in the GDR* (quoted in Forchtner & Schneickert 2016, p. 303), in which certain ideas ('e.g. of bourgeoisie sociology of knowledge') are excluded *per se* on the basis of antagonism: 'Neutralistic positions or even the uncritical adoption of principles (e.g. of bourgeoisie sociology of knowledge) and its results are incompatible with a Marxist theory of knowledge.'

This proposal is still very much linked to traditional assumptions about rational and transparent argumentation. Against this background, Forchtner (2016) combines a Habermasian perspective with a narrative approach, arguing that *modes of emplotting stories* (that is, the selective arrangement of events as romantic/melodramatic, tragic, comic, or ironic; see White 1973; Frye 1957) provide a more 'realistic' approach to assess intersubjective relations. Here, the focus is on the ways actors, events, objects and processes feature in a narrative, and the expectations, emotional states and levels of certainty and self-righteousness, of more-or-less self-critical subjects, which emerge from these stories.

Stories, which are melodramatically emplotted, depict the world as being divided into 'black and white', and the main protagonist of the story (with whom the audience is asked to identify) stands on the right side. Comedies too, though less clear-cut, offer reassurance to the subject (indeed, they offer a happy ending) and, thus, there is little reason for self-critique. The closure of subjectivity through these two modes does not facilitate the use of Habermasian presuppositions, or the rise of open and egalitarian exchange. In contrast, tragic stories thematise past failures, the possibility of their repetition, and difficult choices to be made by *us* as well as inner tensions, while ironic ones deal even more explicitly with 'the shifting ambiguities and complexities of an unidealized existence' (Frye 1957, p. 223), with puzzling defeats and the demise of the heroic. As such, these modes might serve as a mechanism for enabling or blocking collective learning processes. One of the examples analysed by Forchtner, while drawing on the DHA, concerns a text critical of the then looming US-led war against Iraq in 2003 by a German writer. Forchtner claims, that this contribution to the debate is characterised by comic elements, such as (European) reconciliation, rebirth and, thus, a happy ending (Forchtner 2016, pp. 171–182). Narrating past and present in such a way enables the construction of others, in this example: the United States, as lacking knowledge and having not learnt, thus facilitating self-righteousness and closure. By integrating Habermasian Critical Theory with narrative theory, this recent attempt points to both the importance of recontextualising social theories in CDS and a stronger awareness of the significance of the narrative form for CDS.

CDS and the influence of Bourdieu's social theory

Chouliaraki and Fairclough (1999) engage in a detailed discussion of Bourdieu's toolkit (field, habitus, symbolic capital and power) and stress his assumption of differentiated fields with their own logics. They furthermore point to his notion of '*linguistic capital*' and the '*linguistic market*' (see Chapter 7, this volume), while criticising a lack of theory of contemporary forms of mediation as fields (for example, the journalistic field), his view of language use as a by-product of sociological categories that does not acknowledge the 'generative force' of discourse, and a lack of detailed analysis of actual interaction.

The DHA has attempted to operationalise some Bourdieusian categories; for example, the concept of *habitus* features in *The discursive construction of national identity* (Wodak et al. 2009 [1999]) as well as in Wodak's (2011) study of frontstage and backstage politics and the manifold ways MEPs are socialised into the 'political profession'. The habitus concept denotes Bourdieu's attempt to overcome the objectivism:subjectivism dichotomy referring to incorporated experiences from the past (acquired through socialisation), in particular '*beliefs or opinion*', '*emotional attitudes*' and '*behavioural dispositions*'. Another key concept utilised in this study (and beyond) is Bourdieu's notion of *strategy,* which describes subconscious moves in fields 'based on the dialectic between habitus and fields' (Bourdieu 1988, pp. 147ff.). This rejection of conscious choices has subsequently become key for understanding the notion of *discursive strategies* (Wodak et al. 2009, pp. 31ff.), one of the three levels of analysis in the DHA (see above). Moreover, the DHA distinguishes between five macro-strategies of *positive self and negative other representation* (nomination, predication, argumentation, perspectivisation and mitigation/ intensification) (Reisigl & Wodak 2001, pp. 44ff.), The authors (*ibidem*, p. 96) note, for example, that public discourse in Austria in 1986, during heated debates over the country's involvement in the Second World War and the Holocaust during the so-called 'Waldheim Affair', was increasingly characterised by a shift in nomination, realised through, among others, the metonymic-synecdochic *totum pro parte* ('Austria') and the *pars pro toto* 'Waldheim' (for all 'respectable' Austrians). Hence, anyone who dared to criticise the-then Austrian candidate for presidency, Kurt Waldheim, was immediately implied as having criticised the entire nation-state of Austria (Wodak et al. 1990).

Finally, Forchtner and Schneickert (2016) have recently attempted to integrate the concepts of *field, habitus* and *strategy* systematically in, and with, Habermasian elements characterising the DHA (see above), thereby strengthening the explanatory power of the DHA with respect to theoretical assumptions about actions, structures and power relations. This includes, first, the reconstruction of objective *positions* from which actors in fields operate by means of principal component analysis, multidimensional scaling and correspondence analysis.

Second, in order to identify and reconstruct individual and/or collective *dispositions*, that is, habitus, several methods of data collection, which belong to the DHA's traditional repertoire (such as [biographic] interviews, ethnographic observation or argumentation-oriented analysis), could be used. Third, the more-or-less skillful positioning of actors in a specific field is linked to strategies (for example, actions by European Union politicians on the frontstage, see Wodak 2011) and can be analysed by drawing on the DHA's traditional, text-analytical toolkit. For example, an analysis of the position of (male) professors in Germany in the 1960s reveals the hegemony of this type of actor in the academic field (see an interview with a German professor about female scholars in the 1960s discussed by Forchtner & Schneickert 2016, p. 302). This power imbalance involved utterances such as 'logical thinking is not a quality of the woman. The work of the university professor is hard work, which requires robust strengths, a strong personality, and having a strong voice. That goes beyond the powers of a woman.' The socialisation of university staff at German universities, which especially in the past shared a male, bourgeois disposition, puts the speaker in a dominant position in the academic field. Finally, positioning is enabled through the strategy of argumentation, the latter being realised through the *topos of male strength* (to be reconstructed as: 'Since males are robust and strong, have a strong personality and a strong voice, certain jobs should only be implemented by them').

CDS and *Begriffsgeschichte*

Ideas rooted in conceptual history (more particularly the Koselleck-inspired *Begriffsgeschichte*, see Chapter 8, this volume) are also influential in CDS. An interest, not in events but in the development of concepts, such as 'democracy' or 'state', characterises this academic field. Such an endeavour is necessarily concerned with lexical items. Bo Stråth and Wodak (2009) as well as Michał Krzyżanowski (2010) have pointed to the fact that both approaches share the idea that discourses and concepts are recontextualised across fields and genres. Krzyżanowski and Wodak (2011) and Krzyżanowski (2016) have analysed conceptual changes concerning the European Union's (EU) Language and Multilingualism Policy (EULMP) between 1997 and 2015 in 35 relevant documents. This field has become a key site of the EU Lisbon Strategy 2000, an attempt at 'modernising' the association of states in a neo-liberal spirit (focusing on competitiveness, a knowledge-based economy, skills and life-long learning etc.). They argue that the concept of 'multilingualism' was increasingly endowed with neo-liberal meaning – and that this was also the case in respect to its sister concepts, such as a 'multilingual society' (e.g. Krzyżanowski 2016, pp. 316ff.).

In a recent study about Austrian media debates on the so-called 'refugee crisis', Markus Rheindorf and Wodak (2017) analyse how prominent political actors in government are forced to publicly negotiate key terminology regarding the 'management' of migration and refugees. Competing terms for apparently identical entities and differing meanings ascribed to a single term represent distinct ideological positions. The study traces this mediatised struggle over meanings in the autumn and spring of 2015/16 by considering spatial metaphors in *border politics*, a strong interdiscursivity with debates on terrorism and concordances all of which manifest the appropriation of semantic fields. For example, the authors point to heated ideological debates over the supposedly adequate labelling of the number of refugees to be allowed to cross the border and apply for asylum – as either a 'maximum limit' (*Obergrenze*) or a 'reference point' (*Richtwert*).

Conclusion

This chapter has introduced CDS, an empirically oriented framework for discourse and text analysis, a framework that is, however, also characterised by an intimate relationship with a range of broader, (socio-)theoretical approaches. Such analyses of language in use in different political activities are thus not to be reduced to a method – even though this framework is certainly not claiming the status of a grand theory. Rather, this problem-oriented framework draws eclectically on a range of theoretical traditions and recontextualises these within distinct research programmes. *Discourse*, as the main concept, thus implies actual analysis, but also remains, depending on the specific approach of the respective researcher, entangled in a net of relations with sociological and philosophical concepts. In particular, we have focused on how studies conducted within the framework of CDS have utilised concepts recontextualised from authors such as Marx and Gramsci, Foucault and Laclau/Mouffe, as well as the Critical Theory of the Frankfurt School (including Habermas), Bourdieu and the tradition of *Begriffsgeschichte*.

As recent years have witnessed a tendency towards more and more differentiation of CDS, so too have ever more theoretical perspectives inspired CDS-studies. For example, this includes attempts to queer CDS (Thurlow 2016; Milani 2015). The wide range of theoretical approaches utilised in classic and more recent studies implies the risk of an unproductive eclecticism, a mixture of concepts and theoretical approaches which, due to contradictory assumptions, might raise more questions than they solve. However, a careful and reflective adoption of different theoretical perspectives will certainly enrich the further study of language in use in ever more complex contexts and strengthen the explanatory power of problem-oriented critical research.

Note

1 For a more extensive discussion of how many of these approaches have influenced CDS, see Forchtner 2017.

References

Adorno, T W, Frenkel-Brunswik, E, Levinson, D J & Sanford, R N, (1950), *The authoritarian personality*, Harper & Brothers, New York.
Adorno, T W, 2010, *Guilt and defense: on the legacies of National Socialism in postwar Germany*, Harvard University Press, Cambridge, MA.
Angermuller, J, Maingueneau, D & Wodak, R, 2014, *The Discourse Studies reader: main currents in theory and analysis*, Benjamins, Amsterdam.
Bourdieu, P, 1988, *Homo academicus*, Polity, Cambridge.
Chilton, P, Tian, H & Wodak, R, 2010, 'Reflections on discourse and critique in China and the West', *Journal of Language and Politics*, vol. 9, no. 4, pp. 489–507.
Chouliaraki, L & Fairclough, N, 1999, *Discourse in late modernity: rethinking Critical Discourse Analysis*, Edinburgh University Press, Edinburgh.
Fairclough, N, 1992, *Discourse and social change*, Polity, Cambridge.
Fairclough, N, 2010, 'Discourse, change and hegemony' in *Critical Discourse Analysis. The critical study of language*, N Fairclough, Longman, London, pp. 125–145.
Fairclough, N, 2015, 'A dialectical-relational approach to Critical Discourse Analysis in social research' in *Methods of Critical Discourse Studies*. 3rd ed., eds. R Wodak & M Meyer, Sage, London, pp. 86–108.
Fairclough, N & Graham, P, 2002, 'Marx as critical discourse analyst: the genesis of a critical method and its relevance to the critique of global capital', *Estudios de Sociolinguistica*, vol. 3, no. 1, pp. 185–229.
Fairclough, N & Wodak, R, 1997, 'Critical Discourse Analysis', in *Introduction to Discourse Studies. Discourse and interaction. Volume 2*, ed TA van Dijk, Sage, London, pp. 258–284.
Flowerdew, J & Richardson J E, 2017, *The Routledge handbook of Critical Discourse Studies*, Routledge, Oxon.
Forchtner, B, 2011, 'Critique, the discourse-historical approach and the Frankfurt School', *Critical Discourse Studies*, vol. 8, no. 1, pp. 1–14.
Forchtner, B, 2016, *Lessons from the past? Memory, narrativity and subjectivity*, Palgrave Macmillan, Basingstoke.
Forchtner, B, 2017, 'Critical Discourse Studies and social theory', in *The Routledge Handbook of Critical Discourse Studies*, eds. J Flowerdew & J E Richardson, Routledge, Oxon, pp. 259–271.
Forchtner, B & Schneickert, C, 2016, 'Collective learning in social fields: Bourdieu, Habermas and Critical Discourse Analysis', *Discourse and Society*, vol. 27, no. 3, pp. 293–307.
Foucault, B & Tominc A, 2012, 'Critique and argumentation: on the relation between the discourse-historical approach and Pragma-dialectics', *Journal of Language and Politics*, vol. 11, no. 1, pp. 31–50.
Foucault, M, 1977, 'The confession of the flesh' in *Power/knowledge. Selected interviews and other writings*, ed. C Gordon, 1980, Pantheon Books, New York, pp. 194–228.
Foucault, M, 1981a, 'So it is important to think?' in *Essential works of Foucault 1954–1984. Vol. III*, Penguin, London, pp. 454–464.

Foucault, M, 1981b, 'The order of discourse' in *Untying the text: a post-structuralist reader*, ed. R Young, Routledge, London, pp., 48–78.
Frye, N, 1957, *Anatomy of criticism: four essays*, Princeton University Press, Princeton.
Habermas, J, 2008, 'Communicative action and the detranscendentalized "use of reason"', in *Between naturalism and religion: philosophical essays*, J Habermas, Polity, Cambridge, pp. 24–76.
Hart, C & Cap, P, eds., 2014, *Contemporary Critical Discourse Studies*, Bloomsbury, London.
Horkheimer, M, 1993, 'The present situation of social psychology and the tasks of an Institute for Social Research' in *Between philosophy and social science: selected early writings*, MIT Press, Cambridge, MA, pp. 1–14.
Jäger, S, 2008, 'Zwischen den Kulturen: Diskursanalytische Grenzgänge', in *Kultur – Medien – Macht: Cultural Studies und Medienanalyse*, eds. A Hepp & R Winter, Verlag für Sozialwissenschaften, Wiesbaden, pp. 327–352.
Jäger, S & Maier, F, 2015, 'Analysing discourses and dispositives: a Foucauldian approach to theory and method' in *Methods of Critical Discourse Studies. Third edition*, eds. R Wodak & M Meyer, Sage, London, pp. 109–136.
Jessop B, Fairclough, N & Wodak, R, 2009, *Education and the knowledge-based economy in Europe*, Rotterdam, Sense Publishers.
Kracauer, S, 1998, *The salaried masses: Disorientation and distraction in Weimar Germany*, Verso, London.
Kress, G, 1996, 'Representational resources and the production of subjectivity: questions for the theoretical development of Critical Discourse Analysis in a multicultural society' in *Texts and practices. Readings in Critical Discourse Analysis*, eds. C R Caldas-Coulthard & M Coulthard, Routledge, London, pp. 15–31.
Krzyżanowski, M, 2010, 'Discourses and concepts: interfaces and synergies between Begriffsgeschichte and the discourse-historical approach in CDA' in *Diskurs-Politik-Identität/Discourse-Politics-Identity*, eds. R de Cillia, F Menz, H Gruber & M Krzyżanowski, Stauffenburg Verlag, Tübingen, pp. 125–137.
Krzyżanowski, M, 2016, 'Recontextualisation of neoliberalism and the increasingly conceptual nature of discourse: challenges for Critical Discourse Studies', *Discourse and Society*, vol. 27, no. 3, pp. 308–321.
Krzyżanowski, M & Wodak, R, 2011, 'Political strategies and language policies: the European Union Lisbon strategy and its implications for the EU's language and multilingualism policy', *Language Policy*, vol. 10, no. 2, pp. 115–136.
Küçükali, C, 2015, *Discursive strategies and political hegemony. The Turkish case*, Benjamins, Amsterdam.
Lakoff, G, 2002, *Moral politics. How liberals and conservatives think*. University of Chicago Press, Chicago, IL.
Lakoff, G & Johnson, M, 2003, *Metaphors we live by*, University of Chicago Press, Chicago, IL.
Leont'ev, A N, 1978, *Activity, consciousness, and personality*, Prentice Hall, Englewood Cliffs, NJ.
Link, J, 1982, 'Kollektivsymbolik und Mediendiskurse', *kulturRRevolution*, vol. 1, pp. 6–21.
Löwenthal, L & Guterman, N, 1949, *Prophets of deceit. A study of the techniques of the American agitator*, Harper and Brothers, New York.
Lukes, S, 2005, *Power: a radical view*, Palgrave Macmillan, Basingstoke.
Macgilchrist, F, 2011, *Journalism and the political. Discursive tensions in news coverage of Russia*, Benjamins, Amsterdam.
Milani, T M, 2015, 'Sexual citizenship. Discourses, spaces and bodies at Joburg Pride', *Journal of Language and Politics*, vol. 14, no. 3, pp. 431–454.
Miller, M, 2006, *Dissens*, Transcript, Bielefeld.
Montesano Montessori, N, 2011, 'The design of a theoretical, methodological, analytical framework to analyse hegemony in discourse', *Critical Discourse Studies*, vol. 8, no. 3, pp. 169–181.
Reisigl, M & Wodak, R, 2001, *Discourse and discrimination: rhetorics of racism and antisemitism*, Routledge, London.

Reisigl, M & Wodak, R, 2009, 'The discourse-historical approach (DHA)' in *Methods of Critical Discourse Analysis. Second edition*, eds. R Wodak & M Meyer, Sage, London, pp. 87–121.

Rheindorf, M & Wodak, R, 2015, 'Der Wandel des österreichischen Deutsch: Eine textsortenbezogene Pilotstudie (1970–2010)', *Zeitschrift für Deutsche Sprache*, vol. 42, pp. 139–167.

Rheindorf, M & Wodak, R, 2017, 'Borders, fences and limits – protecting Austria from refugees. Metadiscursive negotiation of meaning in the current refugee crisis', *Journal of Immigrant and Refugee Studies*. doi: 10.1080/15562948.2017.1302032.

Sayer, A, 1999, 'Long live postdisciplinary studies! Sociology and the curse of disciplinary parochialism/imperialism', Department of Sociology, Lancaster University, available from: http://www.comp.lancs.ac.uk/sociology/papers/Sayer-Long-Live-Postdisciplinary-Studies.pdf [accessed 25 August 2015].

Stråth, B & Wodak, R 2009, 'Europe–discourse–politics–media–history: constructing crises' in *The European public sphere and the media: Europe in crisis*, eds. A Triandafyllidou, R Wodak & M Krzyżanowski, Palgrave Macmillan, Basingstoke, pp. 15–33.

Thurlow, C, 2016, 'Queering Critical Discourse Studies or/ and performing "post-class" ideologies', *Critical Discourse Studies*, vol. 13, no. 5, pp. 485–514.

van Dijk, T, 2007, 'The study of discourse: an introduction' in *Discourse studies*, ed. T van Dijk, Sage, London, pp. xix–xlii.

van Leeuwen, T, 2007, 'Three models of interdisciplinarity' in *A new agenda for (critical) discourse analysis*, eds. P Chilton & R Wodak, Benjamins, Amsterdam, pp. 3–18.

van Leeuwen, T, 2008, *Discourse and practice: new tools for Critical Discourse Analysis*, Oxford University Press, Oxford.

Weiss, G & Wodak, R, 2003, 'Introduction: theory, interdisciplinarity and Critical Discourse Analysis' in *Critical Discourse Analysis: theory and interdisciplinarity*, eds. G Weiss & R Wodak, Palgrave Macmillan, Basingstoke, pp. 1–32.

White, H, 1973, *Metahistory. The historical imagination in nineteenth-century Europe*, John Hopkins University Press, Baltimore, MD.

Wodak, R, 1996, *Disorders of discourse*, Longman, London.

Wodak, R, 2011, *The discourse of politics in action. Politics as usual. Second revised edition.* Palgrave Macmillan, Basingstoke

Wodak, R, 2013, 'Critical Discourse Analysis – challenges and perspectives' in *Critical Discourse Analysis*, eds. R Wodak, Sage, London, pp. xix–xxxxiii.

Wodak, R, 2015, *The politics of fear. What right-wing populist discourses mean*, Sage, London.

Wodak, R & Meyer, M, eds., 2015, *Methods of Critical Discourse Studies. Third edition*, Sage, London.

Wodak, R, de Cillia, R, Reisigl, M & Liebhart, K, 2009, *The discursive construction of national identity. Second edition*, Edinburgh University Press, Edinburgh.

Wodak, R, Nowak, P, Pelikan, J, Gruber, H, de Cilla, R & Mitten, R, 1990, *"Wir sind alle unschuldige Täter". Diskurshistorische Studien zu Nachkriegsantisemitismus*, Suhrkamp, Frankfurt.

Part II

Methodological approaches to language and politics

10
Content analysis

Roberto Franzosi

Content analysis

What makes Bunin's *Gentle breath* 'one of the best short stories ever written … a true model of its genre'? Vygotsky entertains that question in *The psychology of art*.[1] It is a question about beauty and art in writing. It is a question of little concern to content analysis in its approach to writing. Harold D Lasswell, the 'father' founder of content analysis, made that clear: 'Content analysis will not tell us whether a given work is good literature', whether it is "beautiful writing"' (Lasswell et al. 1952, pp. 45, 22) Rather, Lasswell looked at writing for what it would tell him about propaganda[2] and communication – propaganda as 'the control of opinion by significant symbols… [and by] forms of social communication'; and communication as answers to the questions 'Who, says what, how, to whom, with what effect?', the 'what' question being the primary concern of content analysis (Lasswell 1926, p. 11, see also 1927, p. 627; Lasswell et al. 1952, p. 12).

The study of propaganda and communication had been Lasswell's interest as early as his PhD dissertation in Political Science at the University of Chicago (1926), a study of the propaganda symbols and themes used by the various belligerent countries during the First World War.[3] By 1938, when he published the short article 'A provisional classification of symbol data', Lasswell was pursuing new substantive and methodological avenues. After reading Freud and visiting European universities, Lasswell's study of symbols had shifted from propaganda to psychoanalytic interviews; to his earlier theoretical and historical approach, he had added a concern with classifying, counting and quantifying:

> We may classify references[4] into categories according to the understanding which prevails among those who are accustomed to the symbols. References used in interviews may be quantified by counting the number of references which fall into each category.
> (Lasswell 1938, p. 198)

No doubt, Lasswell's foray in the novel field of Freudian psychiatry based on 'prolonged (psychoanalytic) interviews' was pushing him in novel directions: 'Lacking precedents in this matter, it was necessary to invent somewhat novel categories and methods' (1935,

p. 15). And while measuring a patient's physiological reactions (e.g. pulse rate, electrical conductivity of the skin, blood pressure, 1935, 1936b), he was also measuring the rate of words uttered per minute, was noting the association of these words, and was classifying them into 'numerous categories of verbal reference' (1936b, p. 242). As an undergraduate at the University of Chicago, Lasswell had already shown an interest in measurement and hypothesis testing, in methodology. In a letter from Europe to his parents – he would write weekly long letters – the twenty-one-year-old Lasswell muses about ideas he is mulling over in his head; the word *methodology* appears several times in the letter. Young Harold has the sense of humour to acknowledge to his parents that the letter could only be of interest to 'a technically trained psychologist and social scientist; and even he might yawn and give it up in disgust' (cited in Muth 1990, p. 6).

In *World revolutionary propaganda* (1939), Lasswell returned to his earlier interest in propaganda symbols and themes (e.g. 1927), but with a new methodological approach based on frequency counts of those themes and words.[5] The book's focus was communist propaganda in Chicago as found in documents (namely, American Communist Party leaflets, shop papers and speeches, Lasswell 1939, pp. 101–164). The drive to quantify permeates the entire book. In the 'Preface', Lasswell and Blumenstock (1939, p. vii) write: 'Events ... are described as quantitative changes of variables.' We find here the embryo of Lasswell's later famous manifesto 'Why be quantitative?' (1949), an apology for theme counts in texts.

The technique of content analysis[6] really came of age during the years 1941 and 1943, when Lasswell became Director of The War Communications Research Unit,[7] a new special project, funded by the Rockefeller Foundation.[8] Some of the key methodological developments of the technique came out of the Unit.[9] And building upon Lasswell's earlier attempts to quantify through counts, the technique was born quantitative. 'There is clearly no reason for content analysis unless the question one wants answered is quantitative' (Lasswell et al. 1952, p. 45). Lasswell proposed to quantify by counting words, themes, symbols ('a technical term for words', Lasswell et al. 1952, p. 29), symbol clusters, but also concepts and ideas (Lasswell et al. 1952, pp. 29, 27, 34, 54, 69). He would apologetically write:

> content analysis is not a cheap technique. But the advance of science has always been expensive. Our advantage over Plato and Ibn Kaldun is certainly not that we have more insight. We cannot expect to go far beyond their results without introducing tools which they did not have.
>
> (Lasswell et al. 1952, pp. 46, 45)

He was hopeful that '*Someday there may be a handbook* which will specify standardized types of investigations that may be undertaken with confidence by moderately skilled personnel' (Lasswell et al. 1952, pp. 46, 45, emphasis added). That day came sooner than anticipated. In that same year of 1952, the first such handbook was published (Berelson 1952) and others followed in rapid succession (Budd et al. 1967; Holsti 1969). And they have continued to be published, a testimony to the popularity of the technique (Krippendorff 1980, Weber 1990, Neuendorf 2002, Krippendorff 2004).

How content analysis deals with a text

The press was certainly Lasswell's favourite source for the study of symbols (Lasswell et al. 1952, pp. 17, 40). Let us follow Lasswell in his preferences and focus on newspaper articles on race relations in the American South, Georgia in particular, during the period 1875–1930. Let us start with an article that appeared in *The Atlanta Constitution* (8 December 1897, p. 1) about the yearly meeting at Tybee Island, Georgia, of the Georgia Agricultural Society. Mrs W H Felton was one of several speakers. Mrs W H Felton (after her husband's first and last name, Dr William H Felton, member of the US House of Representatives and of the Georgia House of Representatives), would later be remembered as Rebecca Latimer Felton, the first woman representative to the US Senate, albeit for one day only: 21 November, 1922. But on the day of 11 August, 1897, she was undoubtedly the star of the day at Tybee Island, as we read in *The Atlanta Journal*:

> It was reserved for Mrs. W.H. Felton... to make the speech of the day... she declared it to be the duty of the white man to protect the women of his home, no matter how much rope it required, or how much some people might howl against lynching, the convention arose in tumultuous applause.
>
> (1897, p. 1)

Mrs. Felton's speech may well have gone unnoticed beyond the enthusiastic audience of the Society had it not been picked up by a scathing, 'hot editorial' of the *Boston Transcript* (*The Atlanta Constitution*, 18 August, 1897, p. 1). Mrs. Felton replied to the *Boston Transcript* with an open letter in *The Atlanta Constitution*:

> I took the position that the churches seemed to be incapable of handling the subject of lynching... and our young women were violently destroyed in their homes and on the public highways by black fiends and rapists. I also said that the courts seemed to be incapable of protecting the innocent from the guilty; that the 'law's delay' had apparently become the villain's bulwark. I also said that the manhood of the country seemed to be incapable of enforcing a regard for law... IF IT NEEDS LYNCHING to protect woman's dearest possession from the ravening human beasts, then I say lynch a thousand a week if necessary.
>
> (20 August 1897, p. 4; original emphasis)

Mrs. Felton repeated those arguments about the vulnerability of white women to black brutes in several speeches (Whites 1992). What would content analysis do with Felton's speeches? Let Lasswell answer: 'Conceive of a newspaper as a collection of responses to questions we wish to ask it. This is indeed a fruitful way of conceiving the research situation in which content analysis operates.' (Lasswell et al. 1952, p. 78) Again, following Lasswell's analogy, what questions do we want to pose? What themes do we want to record? Unfortunately, there is no single answer to these questions. Basically, 'the choice ... depends on what one wishes to find out'... 'The choice is entirely a function of the goals at hand.' (Lasswell et al. 1952, pp. 30, 54; also 35). While avoiding specifics, Lasswell makes two general recommendations for the design of a coding scheme and its categories, that is, for the questions to ask:

1. Avoid abstract coding categories (a recommendation often ignored in content analysis projects). Reliability increases with 'coding by explicit symbol rather than by more interpretive categories.' (Lasswell et al. 1952, p. 62)
2. Avoid 'attempting to reproduce all the possible complexities of language' (Lasswell et al. 1952, p. 52). Simplify, 'painful' as simplification may be. Or... You may end up with too

much (costly) data only a fraction of which you will ever use or data that will require 'a content analysis of one's collected content-analysis data' (Lasswell et al. 1952, p. 52).

With that in mind, what do we want to know about Mrs Felton's letter to *The Atlanta Constitution*? Southern attitudes about race (and gender) relations in Jim Crow South? About lynching? The role (failure) of religion in instilling morality into individuals? The role (failure) of the courts in upholding the law? The design of coding categories does indeed reflect the questions asked of texts.

Vygotsky, Bunin, and the question of artistic writing

'The sound of the coffin hitting earth/is a sound utterly serious', Machado writes in a gem of twentieth-century Spanish poetry, 'En el entierro de un amigo' (The burial of a friend). There is nothing of Machado's heaviness and the silence-breaking 'loud thump' of a coffin, in Bunin's opening scene of *Gentle breath* at a cemetery. Even the 'heavy' 'cross... made of oak' is 'a pleasure to look at' (Vygotsky 1971, p. 161). That, for Vygotsky, is Bunin's mastery as a writer: turn light what is heavy, bright what is dark, in a form of rhetorical redescription or paradiastole (on rhetorical figures, see Franzosi 2017). The troublesome image of what lies beneath that cross, 'buried in the frozen earth', does not hit the reader until the end of Bunin's short story when other images come to make light of it (Vygotsky 1971, p. 165). No doubt, through rhetorical redescription, Bunin masterfully turns into artistic beauty the ordinary 'material' of his story – material that 'differs in nothing', except perhaps in its tragic ending, 'from the usual life of pretty, well-to-do girls living in provincial Russian towns' (Vygotsky 1971, p. 150): the story of Olia Meshcherskaia, a beautiful Russian high-school girl – 'at fifteen everyone said she was a beauty' – who seduces her school mates, her father's best friend and a Cossack officer who ends up shooting her at the railroad station.

Of course, 'of great bearing on the artistic treatment' of the story are also:

> the manner in which the author narrates the events, the language he uses, the tone, the mood, his choice of words, his construction of sentences, whether he describes scenes or gives only a brief summary, whether he transcribes the dialogues of his characters or just tells us what they have said, and so forth.
>
> (Vygotsky 1971, p. 158)

But the main tool in Bunin's hands for artistic production is his savvy use of story and plot, between the chronological order of the events narrated (story or disposition) and the arrangement of these events in an order aimed at maximising the rhetorical grip on the reader (plot or composition). Vygotsky even provides a table (Vygotsky 1971, p. 151) where the events of Bunin's short story are placed side-by-side in their story and plot order to show that in *Gentle breath* 'the chronological sequence is completely disrupted' (Vygotsky 1971, p. 151). It is that disruption that gives Bunin's writing 'artistic form', that makes him a Nobel writer, the first Soviet Nobel laureate, in 1933 (Vygotsky 1971, p. 152).

(Quantitative) Narrative Analysis

We owe the distinction between story and plot (*fabula* versus *sjužet*) to Tomashevsky, Vygotsky's contemporary and a member of the school of 'Russian formalists'. For

Tomashevsky (1965, p. 70), 'A story may be thought of as a journey from one situation to another... Motifs which change the situation are dynamic motifs; those which do not are static.' Propp, another formalist, further argued that in Russian folktales the number of dynamic motifs is limited (31 in total) and their sequence invariant.[10] Half a century later, American socio-linguist Labov would similarly search for invariant macro-level structures of narrative. Such is his classification of parts of narrative in Abstract, Orientation, Complicating action, Evaluation, Result or resolution, Coda (Labov 1972, pp. 362–370), where each functional part answers the following set of questions: what was this about? (abstract) who, when, what, where? (orientation), then what happened? (complicating action), so what? (evaluation) what finally happened? (resolution) (Labov 1972, p. 370). Not all narratives contain all these functional parts; only 'the complicating action, is essential if we are to recognize a narrative' (Labov 1972, p. 370). For Labov, micro-level narrative clauses are based on the structure *who-what*, where the *what* is further characterised by time (*when*), location (*where*), mode (*how*) and instrument (this corresponds to the 5 Ws + H of American journalism: who, what, when, where, why and how) (Labov 1972, pp. 375–376).[11] French structuralist Todorov similarly argued that Tomashevsky's dynamic motifs or Labov's orientation are expressed in (narrative) clauses consisting of two basic elements: *who* and *what*, agent and predicate (Todorov 1969).

It is with a structure of this kind, the 5 Ws + H, a 'story grammar', that I started toying with in the early 1980s as a way to study historical processes using newspapers as sources of data (on newspapers as data sources, see Franzosi 1987). I used rewrite rules to formalise the relation of every object in the grammar to all other objects. I developed a computer-assisted program that would make the grammar practically usable in larger-scale historical projects (Franzosi 2010, 2014a; www.pc-ace.com).

How (Quantitative) Narrative Analysis deals with a text

Beautiful writing was hardly the goal of newspaper articles on lynching. A typical article, taken from my project on Georgia lynchings between 1875 and 1930, would look like the following string of 'factual' information, with no literary pretence:

> ANOTHER LYNCHING. *Special to the Journal.* HAWKINSVILLE. Owen Jones, colored, was hanged by a mob in this county day before yesterday for an outrage on Miss Howell, a daughter of Mr. Sanders Howell, who lives in the upper edge of Pulaski. The crime was committed while the young lady was alone at the home. The negro confessed. He was left swinging to the limb all night last night and nearly all day today.
> (*The Atlanta Constitution*, 1 November 1890, p. 9)

Coded output for part of this article within the objects of a complex story grammar would look something like this:

> (Participant-S: (Actor: (Individual: (Name of individual actor: *negro*) (Personal characteristics: (First name and last name: (First name: *Owen*) (Last name: *Jones*)) (Race: *negro*) (Type (adjective): *colored*)))))) (Process: (Simple process: (Verbal phrase: *outrages*))) (Participant-O: (Actor: (Individual: (Name of individual actor: *young lady*) (Personal characteristics: (First name and last name: (Last name: *Howell*)) (Gender: *female*) (Age: (Qualitative age: *young*)) (Race: *white*) (Family relationship: (Type of relationship: *daughter*) (Actor: (Individual: (Name of individual actor: *man*)

(Personal characteristics: (First name and last name: (First name: *Sanders*) (Last name: *Howell*)) (Residence: (Space: (Territory: (Spatial direction: *Upper part*) (Type of territory: (County: *Pulaski*)))))))))))))

This snippet of coded output clearly shows the main features (advantages) of QNA: 1. output preserves both the words and the narrative qualities of input; 2. each coded object is related to all other objects through formal relations set up in the grammar. What the output does not show is QNA disadvantage: coding based on a story grammar as coding scheme (the 5 Ws + H) works well when the input text is a story, a narrative (indeed, the example shown here); it breaks down for different types of texts (e.g. Mrs. Felton's letter to *The Atlanta Constitution*), or even for those macro-structures of narrative (e.g. evaluation) that do not display the 'basic narrative clause' of the 5 Ws + H. Content analysis, where the design of the coding scheme reflects the interests of the investigator, rather than underlying linguistic properties of the text, does have its advantages, as Lasswell noted: 'content analysis is, in principle, a method of unlimited applicability', with 'no limits, in principle, to the applicability of content-analysis technique' (Lasswell et al. 1952, pp. 36, 39).

'Words as Data'

Back in 1989, as I was working on ways of going 'from words to numbers,' (some) colleagues in the sociology department of the University of Wisconsin-Madison, where I was an assistant professor, asked: 'What's Franzosi gonna do with thousands of words in the computer?' Legitimate question (and one that would cost me dearly). The web, data mining, big data, digital scholarship were yet to come. Back then, data were numbers, not words. Yet, even further back, in 1952, Lasswell was already conceiving of 'words as data' (Lasswell et al. 1952, p. 29) and was asking himself: What's Lasswell gonna do with thousands of words (on paper coding sheets)? He approached that question in a section titled, 'How Content-Analysis data are analyzed' (Lasswell et al. 1952, p. 36). The answers (plural) were modest, within the limits of available technology (and methodology): indices, covariates, time plots.

The methods of analysis currently available for QNA-type data go far beyond what Lasswell could do with words in the dawn of quantification in the social sciences. From dynamic network graphs to dynamic GIS modelling, QNA allows the user to apply techniques of data analysis that are true to the fundamental properties of story grammars: relations between actors via their actions (network models), and actions that are set in time and space (GIS modelling) (on these issues and applications, see Franzosi 2010, 2014). There are answers (plural) to the question of what to do with thousands (now millions) of words in the computer!

To stay with Lasswell's counts of symbols, but 'introducing tools which ... [Lasswell] did not have', I can 'go far beyond ... [his] results', as he himself went further than Plato and Ibn Kaldun. I can use word-cloud software, such as Wordle, to visualise the actors and actions found in my database for the Georgia lynchings project (Figure 10.1, words coded verbatim from newspaper sources).[12] I can also use network software such as Gephi to visualise in a network graph the relations of violence between the social actors involved in lynching (Figure 10.2).[13]

I can also use GIS (Geographic Information System) software such as Google Earth Pro to visualise in a map the lynching events known to have occurred in Georgia between 1875 and 1930, with the ability to display information on each event by clicking on a selected pin (Figure 10.3).

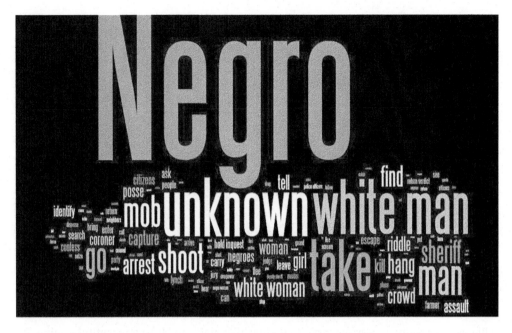

Figure 10.1 Wordle cloud of lynching words (PC-ACE, Georgia lynching project, 1875–1930)

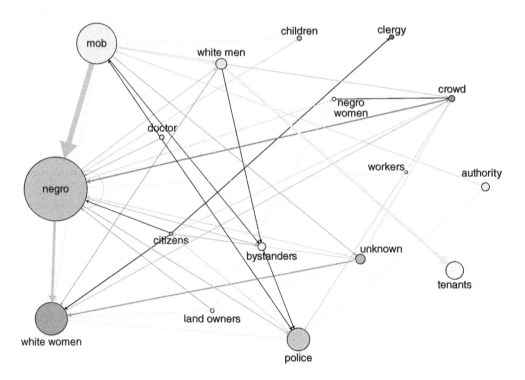

Figure 10.2 Gephi network graph of actors involved in lynching violence (Georgia lynching project, 1875–1930)

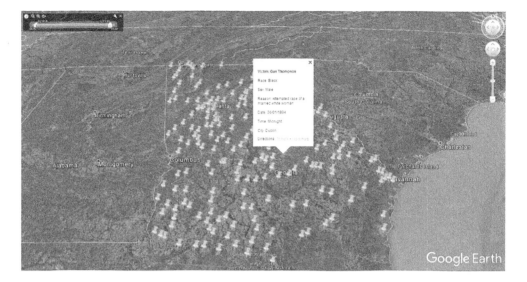

Figure 10.3 Google Earth Pro map of lynching events in Georgia (1875–1930)

Although, certainly, newspaper articles on lynching make no claim to beautiful writing, the visual representation of their words can still produce 'beautiful evidence', based on colour, shape and movement (unfortunately, neither colour nor movement can be reproduced in these pages; Tufte 2006; on the relationship between QNA and aesthetics, see also Franzosi 2014b). And for those detractors who would argue that there is nothing but description in the graphs of Figures 10.1 and 10.2, Lasswell already had an answer: 'research is important [even] when it goes no further than to describe trends and distributions' (Lasswell et al. 1952, p. 21).

Beyond CA & QNA: discourse analysis

A lynching provides the 'material' for another masterful short story by another Nobel Prize winner (in 1950), William Faulkner. Except that in *Dry September*, rhetorical redescription plays no part in making bright of dark, light of heavy. Both Bunin and Faulkner open and close their stories with descriptive lines. In between, ordinary tragedies of Bunin's and Faulkner's ordinary worlds are consumed. Bunin opens with a short description of Russian grey, cold, and wind-swept April days; Faulkner with 'the bloody September twilight, aftermath of sixty-two rainless days' of the American South. Bunin closes with Olia's gentle breath, a requirement for 'what a woman's beauty should be' – Olia tells her best friend – "I have it, don't I? Listen, how I sigh. It's there, isn't it?" And now this gentle breath is dissipated again in the world, in this cloud-covered sky, in this cold spring wind.' There is no redemption in Faulkner's closing lines. The last scene is not one of gentle breath, but one of violence of a lynch mob leader. After which, the reader is left with the words: 'There was no movement, no sound, not even an insect. The dark world seemed to lie stricken beneath the cold moon and the lidless stars.' If with Bunin 'we experience an almost pathological lightness', with Faulkner it is 'painful tension and suspense' (Vygotsky 1971, p. 160).

The unsigned journalist who penned *The Atlanta Constitution* article on the lynching of Peter Stamps (26 July 1885, p. 7), one of the few articles on lynching that goes beyond the factual, also uses the script of the natural world as background to the social world, a frame for tragic human events: the dark night, the heavy clouds hanging below the sky, the quiet town, with which the newspaper article opens:

> His body cut down. Peter Stamps laid out in an old stable. ... The negro admits his guilt... The town is quiet again. Peter Stamps has been hung and the body of the unfortunate girl has been laid to rest in the cold and silent grave. When Stamp's life was choked out of his body by the rope, the hands of the clock pointed to twelve minutes after one o' clock. The night was dark. Heavy clouds hung below the sky.
> (*Atlanta Constitution* article on the lynching of Peter Stamps, 1885, p. 7)

As in *Dry September*, there is no room for rhetorical redescription in this newspaper article. If anything, the description of nature underscores the heaviness of the events. But a close linguistic reading of the article has many surprises in store for us.

Overall, despite its brevity, the article does present the macro-level structural features outlined by Labov. The 'abstract' is given in the lead. Orientation and complicating actions are fused together to give us the who, what, when, where and why of the story. In keeping with Labov's comment (1972, p. 369) that the 'evaluation of the narrative ... may be found in various forms throughout the narrative', the entire article may serve that function. Lasswell himself had noted: 'We made the mistake of assuming that in editorials, unlike news stories, judgments would be numerous. Consequently, we defined judgments narrowly, requiring that they be quite explicit. In fact, however, explicit judgments proved to be fairly rare' (Lasswell et al. 1952, pp. 51–52). Indeed, evaluation is not always explicit in lynching articles (e.g. 'a justly merited death', even though outside the law), or taken up in separate, complete clauses. It is often confined to the choice of adjectives and nouns, such as the 'fiend,' 'the brute,' 'human beast,' 'animal in human disguise.' And if *The Atlanta Journal* of 1 November 1890, in reporting the lynching of Owen Jones provides no explicit evaluation of the event, *The Atlanta Constitution* of 1 November 1890, reporting the same lynching, starts right with evaluation: 'Owen Jones, a negro, met *a justly merited death* at the hands of a crowd of deeply incensed citizens...' (emphasis added).

Closer analysis of *The Atlanta Constitution* article on the lynching of Peter Stamps (26 July 1885, p. 7) reveals that nearly all opening sentences have passive constructs (except for 'the Negro admits his guilt', of course, right in the lead). Nominalisation creeps in ('the lynching'). Such linguistic features are of little interest to content analysis, but discourse analysis has shown that they play key functions.[14] They help to deny or hide agency: Who did it? Who is responsible? To probe further into the language of the article, the word 'hung' appears twice, once in the passive form ('Peter Stamps has been hung'), once in the active form ('Heavy clouds hung') – an uncomfortable association of the verb 'hang'. There are no words of sympathy or human compassion for Peter Stamps, while the unnamed girl is 'unfortunate' and the image of a girl resting 'in the cold and silent grave' makes us shudder. 'Peter Stamps has been hung... When Stamps' life was chocked out of his body by the rope'... Ah! Now it is clear. The rope did it, not the 'determined and quiet mob'. Remarkably, in the second part of this sentence about Stamps' choking, we learn that 'the *hands* of the clock pointed to twelve minutes after one o'clock' (in the active form). Yet another uncomfortable association of Stamps' choking and hands (of the clock, not of mob members). A few sentences down – 'When Stamps' heavy body stretched the rope' – makes it seem like Stamps' choking was his own doing, the result of a heavy body that stretched the rope that eventually would choke him. 'Unfortunate' Stamps. A lighter body may have saved him. The rope returns as a semantic agent a few sentences down when 'The mob knew that STAMP'S [sic] EARTHLY CAREER was over when they heard the dull, heavy thud made by the rope as it went taut.'

The uneasiness of language in the opening lines of the newspaper article on Peter Stamps' lynching betrays perhaps the journalist's uneasiness with the content of the story – of Peter Stamps, 'colored', and of a white girl, Ida Abercrombie, 'daughter of a well-to-do white farmer' – a story, to remind the reader, told from the perspective of a white Southern journalist, in the context of Jim Crow anti-miscegenation laws. Peter is 45, married. Ida is 13. When she confesses to her father that she is pregnant with Peter Stamps' child, Stamps is lynched and Ida is found dead the day after the lynching. Poisoned. Did she commit suicide? Did Stamps give her the poison? Did her father, her step-mother, her uncle, a physician, poison her? Whatever the answers to these questions, raised by the journalist and forever left unanswered, the post-mortem autopsy would find poison in Ida's body and a black foetus in her womb. The journalist remarks: 'The people here are more than satisfied that Stamps richly deserved his fate. They all believed the story of the girl's innocence...' Rhetorical redescription does play a role in this newspaper article after all, turning evil into good, guilt into innocence: Ida 'was pure and honest, and though she did a great sin she was sinless.' The myths of the purity of white Southern women and of black 'ravening human beasts' is safely reestablished, the order of things is linguistically restored. 'No other story will ever be believed by the people of Douglasville. On this point they are satisfied.'

'Reading between the lines': the linguistic construction of facts

The front flap of Lasswell's *World revolutionary propaganda: A Chicago study* in the Alfred Knopf's edition (Lasswell and Blumenstock 1939) tells us that 'The purpose [of the book] is to give the facts and to tell what they mean. For this book is first of all a fact book. ... And these facts are given by methods which are both precise and original. ... And the book analyzes facts.' Lasswell and Blumenstock (1939, p. v) themselves state in the 'Preface' to the book: 'We are interested in the facts. We have taken care to find them. But we are chiefly concerned with the meaning of the facts for the understanding of the future.' Facts. Methods. Precision. Originality. As Lasswell would put it in a later work: 'Through the use of statistical methods, content analysis aims at achieving objectivity, precision, and generality.' (Lasswell et al. 1952, pp. 31, also 32–33) These are the buzz words of social scientific language to which Lasswell was one of the early contributors. Yet, facts imply choices; 'what they mean' implies interpretation. For Vygotsky, 'the choice of facts' is one of the ingredients of artistic writing (1971, p. 158). But the silence on some facts and the emphasis on others is not just a matter of artistic writing. It is a general characteristic of all writing, including scientific writing.[15]

The subtleties of language are of little interest to content analysts. They go at language with a hatchet, rather than a razor. Only *manifest*, rather than *latent* content is of interest.[16] Anything else would lead to a 'coy approach' to words, to imprecision, vagueness, uncertainty, and '"impressionistic" analysis' (Lasswell et al. 1952, p. 32).

> This coy approach to the human vocabulary shows among scholars in such habits as 'reading *between* the lines' of verbal texts used as data. Such habits, when used by a skilled person, produce insights which are often brilliant but usually unverifiable. Content analysis is, in the first place, a method for 'reading *on* the lines' and for reporting the results which can be verified.
>
> (Lasswell et al. 1952, p. 32; original emphasis)

Coy, no doubt, would have been for Lasswell's later social science approaches to text, such as discourse analysis or frame analysis.[17] That Lasswell's own approach could be weird, rather than coy ... that criticism had yet to be formulated (Henrich et al. 2010): coding for content analysis projects being typically carried out by undergraduate college students, WEIRD, indeed (Western, Educated, Industrialised, Rich and Democratic). And since these weird people are hardly 'skilled' in language, intractable issues of interpretation are turned into more numbers as indices of inter-coder reliability. Much scholarly ingenuity has gone into the construction of these indices (Krippendorff 2004, pp. 221–56).

'Reading between the lines', *Dry September* would suggest other interpretations of lynching stories over outrages. Could Miss Howell have lied about her outrage at the hand of Owen Jones, colored? 'The negro confessed', we are told. In many other Georgia newspaper stories of lynchings, the 'negro' professes his innocence, even with a noose around his neck. Does it make a difference to the outcome of the event? '"Wont you take a white woman's word before a nigger's?" ... "you'd take a nigger's word before a white woman's? Why, you damn niggerloving—"' (*Dry September*). Could Miss Howell and Owen Jones have had a consensual relationship, consumed in Miss Howell's house when alone? Would she, might she, be forced to scream rape when caught? In the 200 or so lynching events over 'outrages' of white women that occurred in Georgia between 1875 and 1930, the 'facts' suggested by these questions are never part of the newspaper narratives. The story of Peter Stamps and Ida Abercrombie, the white girl for whom he was lynched, comes close to a publicly admitted consensual relationship between a black man and a white woman. Yet... it is a love story that leaves us uneasy, at least as told by a Southern newspaper in Jim Crow culture. There *is* more to 'the string of factual information' of newspaper articles on lynching.

Of terrible, horrible objects: language and politics

You will be hard pressed to find literary beauty in newspaper articles on lynching across the US South – even if you apply 'coy' approaches to texts, even if, Vygotsky at hand, you start looking for rhetorical figures (e.g. paradiastole), for style, for story and plot, for silence and emphasis in the selection of facts.

If not art, what then was the purpose of those newspaper articles? Why do they tell lynching stories? For Labov, the 'story point' is typically part of the 'evaluation' section of narrative, where the narrator indicates 'the point of the narrative, its raison d'être: why it was told, and what the narrator is getting at' (Labov 1972, p. 366). Lasswell offers clues for an answer to these questions, taking them from one of his most cited books: 'successful violence is relatively more dependent upon proper coordination with propaganda' (Lasswell 1936a, p. 63). 'An act of violence becomes "propaganda of the deed"' (1936, p. 65) a deed leading to a 'loss [that] will terrorize the enemy' (1936a, p. 66). 'Stamps, as he hung from that bridge, made a fearful picture, one which will live long in the minds of many of those who saw it' (*The Atlanta Constitution*, 26 July 1885, p. 7). And 'those who saw it' were 'men, women and children, both black and white,' a motley crowd that 'contained the lawyer, the physician, the merchant, the barroom keeper, the planter, the man servant, the maid servant, the wife, the maid, the child and the babe. No class, sex or color was wanting in the crowd, every member of which had his eyes riveted upon the same terrible, horrible object' (*The Atlanta Constitution*, 26 July 1885, p. 7).

And terrorised it was, the 'enemy' of this white Southern culture obsessed with the purity of white Southern women: members of a black community struck by a lynching would not claim the body for proper burial for fear of reprisal, would lock themselves up in their homes, take to the woods and swamps to hide, or leave the South for good, heading North (on the reactions of the black community to a lynching, see Franzosi et al. 2012). The body – 'this terrible, horrible object' – would often be left hanging for a couple of days, 'a fearful picture' for all, for those whites tempted to be 'damn niggerlovers' (*Dry September*) and for those blacks who could use a reminder for a lesson to be taught. As Mrs W H Felton put it in her letter to *The Atlanta Constitution* (20 August 1897, p. 4): 'when a human beast gets ready to thus destroy my child or my neighbor's child the beast should be taught to expect a quick bullet or a short rope.' No doubt, as Calabrese (2010) aptly puts it, Southern culture was 'sending a message' through lynching: violence as political communication.[18] And that message was often explicit. Pinned to the lynched bodies, in the case of outrages, you would sometimes find a sign 'We must protect our ladies' (on one side) and 'Beware all darkies. You will be treated the same way' (on the other side) (*Newnan Herald and Advertiser* 28 April 1899), 'This is the penalty for rape. Yours truly Brother Dooley' (*The Augusta Chronicle* 16 May 1904).

'Imagine ... some mysterious method'

Weird it may well have been this content analysis, this new social science approach to words. But prolific it turned out to be, across different fields, from political science to sociology and particularly mass communication. Hundreds of journal articles have been written with their 'data and methods' based on content analysis.

Writing in 1952, Lasswell had a vision, a vision for content analysis, a vision for a day when counting key symbols in countless documents 'may reveal truths not heretofore established': 'New lines of research may open new vistas: Perhaps *the new technique of counting key symbols* may reveal truths not heretofore established. That, at least, is a provisional hope of the social scientist' (Lasswell et al. 1952, p. 26, emphasis added).

We take these words from one of Lasswell's books available on the web, originally held at the library of the University of Michigan and digitised by Google. Using tools such as *Google ngrams* (books.google.com/ngrams) we can turn into reality a figment of Lasswell's imagination: 'Imagine that we are transported by some mysterious method to the year 1900, carrying back with us our present knowledge' (Lasswell et al. 1952, p. 6). The time plots of Figure 10.4 do bring us back to the year 1900, carrying back our current knowledge of the millions of books digitised by Google. And just as Lasswell imagined, but on a scale beyond even *his* imagination, through frequency measures we can get trends, comparisons, covariances (Lasswell et al. 1952, pp. 36–37).

Using the 'mysterious method' of Google ngram, we can track Lasswell's academic fortunes over the twentieth century in US published books, compared to his closest early competitors as writers of handbooks of content analysis (Berelson and Holsti). We can compare the popularity of content analysis to its 'coy' competitors of discourse analysis, frame analysis, or narrative analysis. And while *quantitative* content analysis still comes on top at a steady level since the late 1960s, *qualitative* discourse analysis is rapidly surging to threaten that position of dominance.

We learn all that through counting symbols taken from millions of documents. One of 'the weirdest people in the world' – Professor of Political Science at the University of Chicago, where he had started as an undergraduate student at the age of 16, Professor of Law at Yale, President of the American Political Science Association,[19] 'a bit of a freak: pedantic, verbose, and quite ill at ease', in the recollection of one of his first students in 1927

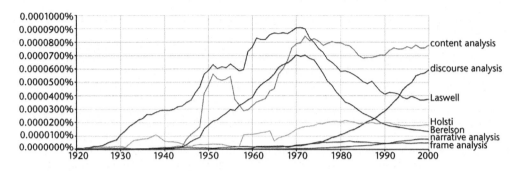

Figure 10.4 Google *ngram* of selected words

(Rosten 1969, p. 1) – could have predicted that: 'The sequence of movements in history can be conveniently read by scanning the dominant symbols of successive epochs'[20] (Lasswell et al. 1952, p. 15). Weird, then, as Janowitz noted (1969, p. 156), that in a book Lasswell published in 1963 on 'the future of political science from the viewpoints of scope, method, and impact', he would make only one passing reference to his own method of content analysis without dignifying it with an index entry (Lasswell 1963, p. 45). Weird, perhaps, that Gottschalk, who applied Lasswell's content analysis to Lasswell's psychoanalytic verbal data, would make no references to Lasswell's work (e.g. Gottschalk & Gleser 1969, Gottschalk et al. 1986).

As for the social science approaches to text… Weird or coy? Quantitative or qualitative? Which road should we follow? Let qualitative historian G R Elton give the answer (to us and to his sparring partner, quantitative historian Robert Fogel, 1993 Economics Nobel laureate, in their book *Which road to the past?*): 'I should like to think that each will go to heaven his own way, and to the other for answers to the questions properly investigated by either sort' (Fogel & Elton 1983, p. 83).

Acknowledgements

My thinking about the language of lynching has benefited from a fellowship at the Fox Center for Humanistic Inquiry of Emory University (2011–2012) and a sabbatical year (2013–2014) with fellowships at the Italian Academy of Columbia University, Nuffield College (University of Oxford), University of Trento, and Ca' Foscari (University of Venice). The project on lynching in Georgia (1875–1930) was made possible by funding from the University Research Committee at Emory University. Woody Beck kindly provided the cross-references between each lynching event and newspaper articles. The *Atlanta Constitution* article on Peter Stamps and Ida Abercrombie was discussed at a talk I gave at the Free University of Amsterdam (Critical Discourse Community ACDC) on 23 April 2014.

Notes

1 Vygotsky (1971:4). Vygotsky completed *The psychology of art* in 1925; the manuscript was published posthumously in 1965, some 30 years after Vygotsky's death.
2 On this point, see Lasswell et al. (1952, p. 40).
3 For a reflection on the propaganda themes discussed in his dissertation, see Lasswell (1927); Themes return briefly in his 1930 *Psychopathology and politics*.

4 In the same article, Lasswell defines references as 'a sentence or part of a sentence' (1938, p. 201; see also 1935, p. 16, 1936b).
5 There is no mention of content analysis, under any label, or quantification of symbols, themes, or words in two crucial publications prior to 1938, Rice (1931) and Lasswell et al. (1935).
6 For the story of the label 'Content Analysis', see Franzosi (2008). Lasswell himself wavered between different labels. Two different consecutive sections in Lasswell et al. (1952, pp. 29, 31) bear the two different headings of 'Why symbol analysis?' and 'Why content analysis?' As a way of explanation, Lasswell writes: 'The general method involved we have been calling symbol analysis, and the special technique used in the RADIR Project is known as content analysis (or quantitative semantics). The exposition of what content analysis is becomes somewhat easier if one deals first with its more technical name, quantitative semantics' (Lasswell et al., 1952, p. 31).
7 'Content Analysis, as practiced today, is a development of the past decade. Although some important thinking in this direction was done earlier, the elaboration of the technique was not accomplished until the Experimental Division for the Study of Wartime Communications was established at the Library of Congress during World War II.' (Lasswell et al., 1952, p. 40).
8 The Unit, known as the Experimental Division for the Study of Wartime Communications, was housed in the basement of the Library of Congress in Washington, DC. For a brief sketch of that period, see Muth (1990, p. 15).
9 For that story and for a reprint of some of those hitherto unpublished documents, see Franzosi (2008). See also Franzosi & Sevin (2014).
10 For a lengthier treatment of the characteristics of narrative briefly traced here, see Franzosi (2012).
11 That structure, in turn, has a very long history in rhetoric and the theory of circumstances (Franzosi 2012).
12 For visualization purposes, most verbs have been lemmatized (e.g. shoots, shot, will shoot – shooting lemmatized as shoot).
13 In network graphs, the thickness of the line ('edge') is roughly proportional to the number of events between a pair of actors ('nodes') and the arrow represents the direction of the action (e.g. violence).
14 Johnstone (2007), Billig (2008), van Dijk (2008); for a history of discourse analysis and its basic concerns, see Wodak & Meyer (2009).
15 Franzosi (2004a, pp.147–53, 175–77, 202–14, 219–22); see also the emphasis of early content analysis on issues of measurement (Franzosi 2008); on historical evidence and facts, see Franzosi (2006).
16 Laswell et al. discuss ways of assessing latent structures through manifest content (Lasswell et al. 1952, pp. 75–77).
17 On frame analysis and its foundations in rhetoric, see Franzosi and Vicari (2014).
18 On violence as a means of political communication, see also Arendt (1969) and Apter (1997).
19 On Lasswell's life and achievements, see Muth et al. (1990).
20 'When it is desired to survey politically significant communication for any historical period on a global scale, the most practicable method is that of counting the occurrence of key symbols and clichés. Only in this way can the overwhelming mass of material be reliably and briefly summarized.' (Lasswell et al. 1952, p. 16).

References

Apter, D E, 1997, 'Political violence in analytical perspective', in *The legitimization of violence*, ed. David Apter, New York University Press, New York, pp. 1–32.

Arendt, H, 1969, 'On violence', in *Crises of the republic*. Harcourt Brace Jovanovich, New York, pp. 103–184.

Berelson, B, 1952, *Content analysis in communication research*, The Free Press, Glencoe, IL.

Billig, M, 2008, 'The language of Critical Discourse Analysis: The case of nominalization', *Discourse and Society* 19, pp. 783–800.

Budd, R W, Thorp, R K & Donohew, L, 1967, *Content analysis of communications*, Macmillan, New York.

Calabrese, A, 2010, 'Sending a message: Violence as political communication', *International Journal of Media and Cultural Politics*, vol. 6, no. 1, pp. 109–114.
Fogel, R W & Elton, G R, 1983, *Which road to the past? Two views of history*, Yale University Press, New Haven, CN.
Franzosi, R, 1987, 'The press as a source of socio-historical data', *Historical Methods* 20, pp, 5–16.
Franzosi, R, 2004a. *From words to numbers: Narrative, data, and social science*, Cambridge University Press, Cambridge.
Franzosi, R, 2004b, 'Content analysis' in *Handbook of data analysis*, eds. A Bryman & M Hardy, Sage, Beverly Hills, CA, pp. 547–66.
Franzosi, R, 2006, 'Historical knowledge and evidence' in: *Oxford handbook of contextual political studies*, eds. R E Goodin & C Tilly, Oxford University Press, Oxford, pp. 438–53.
Franzosi, R, 2008, *Content analysis (benchmarks in social research methods series)*, 4 vols., Sage, Thousand Oaks, CA.
Franzosi, R, 2010, *Quantitative narrative analysis*, Sage Publications, Los Angeles.
Franzosi, R, 2012, 'On quantitative narrative analysis' in *Varieties of narrative analysis*, eds. J A Holstein & J F Gubrium (eds.), Thousand Oaks, CA, Sage, pp. 75–98.
Franzosi, R, 2014a, 'Analytical sociology and quantitative narrative analysis: Explaining lynchings in Georgia (1875–1930)' in *Analytical sociology: Actions and networks*, ed. G Manzo, Wiley, Hoboken, NJ, pp. 127–148.
Franzosi, R, 2014b, 'Of stories and beautiful things: Digital scholarship, method, and the nature of evidence', unpublished paper.
Franzosi, R, 2017, *Tropes and figures*, Routledge, New York.
Franzosi, R & Sevin, E, 2014, 'The dawn of a popular methodology: Content analysis. The Washington Years of Harold D. Lasswell (1941–1943)', unpublished paper.
Franzosi, R & Vicari, S, 2014, 'What's in a text? Answers from frame analysis and rhetoric for measuring meaning systems and argumentative structures,' unpublished paper.
Franzosi, R, De Fazio, G & Vicari, S, 2012, 'Ways of measuring agency: An application of quantitative narrative analysis to lynchings in Georgia (1875–1930)' in *Sociological Methodology Vol. 42* ed. T F Liao, Sage, Thousand Oaks, CA, pp. 1–41.
Gottschalk, L A & Gleser, G C, 1969, *The measurement of psychological states through the content analysis of verbal behavior*, University of California Press, Berkeley, CA.
Gottschalk, L A, Lolas, F & Viney, LL, 1986, *Content analysis of verbal behavior: Significance in clinical medicine and psychiatry*, Springer-Verlag, Berlin.
Henrich, J, Heine, S J & Norenzayan, A, 2010, 'The weirdest people in the world?' *Behavioral and Brain Sciences*, vol. 33, pp. 61–135.
Holsti, O, 1969, *Content analysis for the social sciences and humanities*, Addison Wesley, Reading, MA.
Janowitz, M, 1969, 'Content analysis and the study of the "symbolic environment"' in *Politics, personality, and social science in the twentieth century: Essays in honor of Harold D. Lasswell*, ed. A A Rogow, University of Chicago Press, Chicago, Il, pp. 155–170.
Johnstone, B, 2007, *Discourse analysis*, Blackwell Publishing, Malden, MA.
Krippendorff, K, 1980, *Content analysis. An introduction to its methodology*, Sage, Beverly Hills, CA.
Krippendorff, K, 2004, *Content analysis. An introduction to its methodology*, 2nd ed., Sage, Thousand Oaks, CA.
Labov, W, 1972, *Language in the inner city*, University of Pennsylvania Press, Philadelphia, PA.
Lasswell, H D, 1926, *Propaganda technique in the world war*, PhD Dissertation, University of Chicago.
Lasswell, H D, 1927, 'The theory of political propaganda', *The American Political Science Review*, vol. 21, no. 3, pp. 627–631.
Lasswell, H D, 1930, *Psychopathology and politics*, University of Chicago Press, Chicago, Il.
Lasswell, H D, 1935, 'Verbal references and physiological changes during the psychoanalytic interview: A preliminary communication,' *Psychoanalytic Review*, vol. 22, no. 1, pp. 10–24.

Lasswell, H D, 1936a, *Politics: Who gets what, when, how*, McGraw-Hill, New York.

Lasswell, H D, 1936b, 'Certain prognostic changes during trial (psychoanalytic) interviews', *Psychoanalytic Review*, vol. 23, no. 3, pp. 241–247.

Lasswell, H D, 1938, 'A provisional classification of symbol data', *Psychiatry*, no. 1 pp. 197–204.

Lasswell, H D, 1948, 'Structure and function of communication in society', in *The communication of ideas: A series of addresses*, ed. L Bryson, Institute for Religious and Social Studies, New York, pp. 37–51.

Lasswell, H D, 1949, 'Why be quantitative?' in *Language of politics: Studies in quantitative semantics*, eds. H D Lasswell, N Leites and associates, George W. Stewart, New York, pp. 40–52.

Lasswell, H D, 1963, *The future of political science*, Atherton Press, New York.

Lasswell, H D & Blumenstock, D, 1939, *World revolutionary propaganda: A Chicago study*, Alfred A Knopf, New York.

Lasswell, H D, Casey, RD & Lannes Smith, B, 1935, *Propaganda and promotional activities: An annotated bibliography*, University of Chicago Press, Chicago, IL.

Lasswell, H D, Lerner, D & de Sola Pool, I, 1952, *The comparative study of symbols: An introduction*, Stanford University Press, Stanford, CA.

Muth, R, 1990, 'Harold D. Lasswell: A Biographical Profile' in *Harold D. Lasswell: An annotated bibliography*, eds. R Muth, M M Finley & M F Muth, Kluwer, Dordrecht, pp. 1–480.

Muth, R, Finley, M M & Muth, M F, eds., 1990, *Harold D. Lasswell: An annotated bibliography*, Kluwer, Dordrecht.

Neuendorf, K A, 2002, *The content analysis guidebook*, Sage, Newbury Park, CA.

Rice, S A, ed., 1931, *Methods in social science: A case book*, University of Chicago Press, Chicago, IL.

Rosten, L, 1969, 'Harold Lasswell: A memoir' in *Politics, personality, and social science in the twentieth century: Essays in honor of Harold D. Lasswell*, ed. A A Rogow, University of Chicago Press, Chicago, IL, pp. 1–13,

Todorov, T, 1969. 'Structural analysis of narrative,' *NOVEL: A Forum on Fiction*, vol. 3, no. 1, pp. 70–76.

Tomashevsky, B, 1965 [1925], 'Thematics' in *Russian Formalist Criticism: Four Essays*, eds. L T Lemon & M J Reis, tr. L T Lemon & M J Reis, University of Nebraska Press, Lincoln, NE, pp. 61–95.

Tufte, E R, 2006, *Beautiful evidence*, Graphics Press, Cheshire, CT.

van Dijk, Teun, 2008, 'Critical discourse analysis and nominalization: Problem or pseudoproblem?' *Discourse and Society* 19, pp. 821–28.

Vygotsky, L S, 1971, *The psychology of art*, MIT Press, Cambridge, MA.

Weber, R P, 1990, *Basic content analysis*, Sage, Newbury Park, CA.

Whites, L A, 1992, 'The diversity of Southern gender and race: Women in Georgia and the South', *The Georgia Historical Quarterly*, vol. 76, no. 2, pp. 354–372.

Wodak, R & Meyer, M, 2009, 'Critical discourse analysis: History, agenda, theory, and methodology' in *Methods of Critical Discourse Analysis*, eds. R Wodak & M Meyer, Sage, Thousand Oaks, CA, pp. 1–33.

11
Corpus analysis

Amelie Kutter

Introduction

The past decade has seen a surge in digitisation. Web-based access to digital sources has widened, coupled with advances in general-purpose technologies for the automated processing of digital documents. Searches in web archives, networking in social media, marketing targeting web users, virtual financial transactions, or international cyber intelligence and policing: contemporary social practices rely on digital documents and their automated processing. This is also true for politics and the involvement of language in political struggles. Politics is more radically being subjected to the logics and technological trends of mass mediation. It comes as no surprise then that *corpus analysis*, with its potential to work with large numbers of digital texts, has become popular beyond the confines of computational and corpus linguistics. Notably, in linguistic discourse studies, using collections of digital texts and specialised analytical software has become something of a must. Pushed by new technologies, traditions of automated textual analysis, such as computer-aided content analysis and lexicometrics, have been revived in the social sciences, too. Corpus analysis, more precisely: the semi-automated analysis of numerical-linguistic patterns in a specified text collection, promises to link these traditions to current technological and social trends.[1]

The popularity of corpus-analytical techniques has revived controversies about the advantages and drawbacks of computer-aided textual analysis that have structured the field ever since digital documents were first processed by computers. Current debates centre on the opposition between 'corpus-driven' and 'corpus-based' approaches, or 'unsupervised' and 'supervised' approaches. Corpus-driven approaches entrust lexicometric or corpus linguistic software with the task of revealing patterns of language use that may be associated with social meaning, while corpus-based approaches insist that such investigations should be theory-driven, rather than technology- or data-driven (Gür-Şeker 2014). Unsupervised approaches expect recent advances in text mining to generate the artificial intelligence necessary for automated text comprehension, while supervised approaches doubt that any meaningful interpretation can be made based on text mining unless this is consistently controlled by human interpretive effort (Scharkow 2012 in Wiedemann 2013). These labels, apparently relating to the use of technology, involve tacit positioning alongside established divides in the philosophy of science (see the sub-section on 'Dilemmas of conducting corpus research' on p. 172). They show that corpus analysis has become subject to struggles for scholarly authority.

The objective of the present contribution is to give an overview of the field of corpus analysis so that entering the field and navigating field-specific controversies become easier. Readers will get to know the plurality of approaches to corpus analysis, familiarise themselves with the specificities of text-statistical methods and learn about possible applications, all illustrated by examples from a study on crisis discourse (Kutter 2013a). The contribution argues that corpus analysis is a valid addition to the tool-box of the discourse researcher, in particular, when used as an *explorative technique for heuristic and reflexive purposes*. Corpus analysis enables a specific macro-view of text material and supports the development of questions and hypotheses (heuristic potential). It also productively disturbs our intuitive and preconceived views of the subject studied and, thereby, contributes to a multi-layered interpretation of language and meaning (reflexive potential). In the following sections, the reader will learn how to exploit these potentials for political discourse studies. Information is provided on approaches and dilemmas of corpus research, specificities of lexicometrics and corpus linguistics, and the development of a discourse-analytical strategy involving corpus analysis.

Corpus analysis: a multi-disciplinary and difficult field or research

Corpus analysis has been emerging since the 1960s, in parallel with the digitisation of documents and computation. It is now an independent field of research that deals with the *semi-automated statistical analysis of patterns of language use* that reveal themselves in a specific *corpus*. In general terms, a corpus is a collection of semiotic artefacts, whether of linguistic, or other quality, that are the subject of interpretive enquiry. In the more specific terms of corpus analysis, a corpus is a collection of digital texts that has been compiled and annotated according to specific criteria with a view to statistically analysing linguistic, or other, characteristics of the whole collection.

Approaches to corpus analysis

Corpora are used in a growing number of sub-disciplines in linguistics, the humanities and the social sciences.[2] *Corpus linguists* construct corpora in order to investigate patterns of language use in a natural, specialised, or group-specific language. They build large corpora that serve as reference corpora of a specific natural language, design technologies for automatically compiling and annotating digital texts with linguistic information, and develop formulae and software for the statistical analysis of distributional patterns in corpora. The steps of analysis usually comprise semi-automated annotation, automated statistical analysis of distributional patterns and further manual analysis of the patterns revealed. Applications include the construction of digital dictionaries and thesauruses, or the study of linguistic varieties, translation and language acquisition (McEnery & Wilson 2001, Tognini-Bonelli 2001). *Computational linguists* and computer scientists use corpora as resources for Natural Language Processing (NPL), for developing and testing the automated classification and processing of digital data with regard to their linguistic characteristics, including morphological, syntactic, semantic or pragmatic aspects. They develop algorithms that are based on formal models of knowledge of language and recognise character strings or sound bites as graphemes and morphemes; parse the grammatical structure of a sentence, recognise parts of speech or named entities; and infer speech acts and semantic categories from this information. Increasingly, such processing of linguistic data is based on probabilities and machine learning. Algorithms learn from existing annotated corpora how to process and classify large samples of digital texts and employ statistical models to project such information onto un-annotated text samples (Clark, Fox & Lappin 2013; Jurafsky & Martin 2009).

While corpus and computational linguists seek to construct a corpus in a way that shows language use in (a representative segment of) a natural language, *discourse linguists* focus on (a segment of) the totality of texts that, through semantic, functional, intertextual and pragmatic relations, connect with the issue being investigated (Busse & Teubert 1994, p. 14f). Such *issue-specific corpora* have been used in two ways in discourse linguistics. On the one hand, they facilitate a description of language use in a specific socio-cultural domain that draws on traditions of semantics, stylistics and pragmatics in corpus linguistics (Baker 2006, Stubbs 1996, Stubbs 2001). On the other hand, issue-specific corpora assist in the analysis of culturally dense language use that borrows from historical semantics and cultural studies (Busse & Teubert 2013; Wengeler 2006) and focuses on the corpus linguistic exploration of categories such as *topoi* or semantic frames, which are rooted in traditions of philological-hermeneutic text critique (Bubenhofer 2009; Gür-Şeker 2012; Spitzmüller & Warnke 2011; Ziem, Scholz & Römer 2013).

Issue-specific corpora are also used in *Critical Discourse Analysis* (CDA), which highlights the discursive constitution of symbolic power and social exclusion, linking categories from socio-, text- or systemic-functional linguistics to social theory and theories of discourse (Fairclough & Wodak 1997; Forchtner & Wodak in this volume). Corpus analysis is here employed as an ancillary tool, to better contextualise small-scale studies of detailed discourse analysis. For instance, a query of words regularly co-occurring with the search word 'unemployed' in a newspaper corpus was used to obtain a rough idea of how that specific newspaper lexicalised unemployment – here relating to either structural disadvantage or individuals' failure (Mautner 2009). The distributional-semantic patterns revealed by corpus linguistic procedures also facilitate the systematic focusing and selection of individual texts for an otherwise unaltered CDA methodology (Baker et al. 2008; Kutter 2013b).

An ancillary approach towards issue-specific corpora is also applied by *content analysts in the social sciences*. They use computational and corpus linguistic tools to either automatically retrieve lexical-semantic information from large amounts of texts, or automatically assign content-related information to them that matters in relation to a specific social-science research question. The objective is thus to extend the analysis beyond the few texts that can be handled manually by hermeneutic methods. Following the example of *The General Inquirer*, the first influential content-analytical software, such analysis is usually based on an abductively generated dictionary (or 'code book') that defines how single terms, specific word clusters or passages of text shall be read in terms of the social-science categories investigated. The annotations are then queried with regard to salience, co-occurrence, relations to meta-information, and so on. Recent developments in NPL, in particular topic models, word-sense disambiguation, or named entity recognition, promise to replace dictionary-based annotation with machine-learning algorithms (Wiedemann 2013), or inform and prepare smaller-case hermeneutic content analysis (Kutter & Kantner 2012).

Lexicométrie (henceforth lexicometrics) is yet another approach to the analysis of issue-specific corpora. It is rooted in French lexical statistics and has, since the 1960s, been continuously developed as a method for tracing lexical shifts in political discourse over a longer period of time (Lebart, Salem & Berry 1998). Statistical procedures, implemented by specialised software, are geared towards comparing different time periods, speakers or text genres. The objective is to establish the overall structure and dynamic of an issue- or domain-related discourse in a systematic manner (Scholz & Mattisek 2014). Recently, lexicometrics has gained resonance beyond its pioneer hubs in French political history, in cultural geography and discourse semantics (Glasze 2013, Scholz & Ziem 2013).

Dilemmas of conducting corpus research

The surge in digitisation, automated text processing, Big Data, and funding for digital humanities has enhanced the aforementioned uses of corpus analysis. Scholars in the social sciences and discourse studies hoped to boost the basis and plausibility of their research, while computational and corpus linguistics expected their techniques to be straight-forwardly applicable in other disciplines. But pioneers soon discovered that the tools provided little more than an overview of the distribution of lexis in texts, while the time needed to develop an interpretive approach towards these revelations had gone on the establishment of data and technical infrastructure, the development of tools and interdisciplinary co-ordination. Conducting corpus analysis in sustainable ways requires taking decisions early on with regard to corpus size, tools, middle-range theories and the philosophy of science. The appropriate *size* of text collections depends on the research purpose: general statements about a natural language require extra-large reference corpora of several billion words; the study of distinct vocabularies of a specific debate or institution will draw on a smaller issue-specific corpus of a million words or so, and the systematic comparison of historical varieties on a few texts. However, given that corpus analysis relies on statistics, a critical mass of 'tokens', that is, of computable (linguistic) items, is necessary to ensure that distributional features can actually be calculated and regular patterns represented. The compilation, cleaning and pre-processing of larger corpora is labour-intensive, though, and sustainable only if corpora are (re-)used in long-term projects.

The choice of *tools* is a related problem: tools in NPL, corpus linguistics and lexicometrics require some form of prior or dynamic linguistic annotation, time-consuming pre-processing and, occasionally, support from computational linguists (see section on 'Focus and procedures'). NPL tools are particularly suited for data management and pre-classification. For example, a tailored web crawler can compile a corpus automatically from the web; duplicates and sampling errors can be discovered by text mining, and topic models or supervised vector machines can identify texts containing similar content (Kantner et al. 2011; Wiedemann 2013). Using corpus linguistic and lexicometric tools is advisable if there is interest and skill in linguistic and statistical interpretation. Scholars focusing on the distribution of content or interpretive categories such as 'frames' might be well advised to use content-analytical software, such as *MAXQDA* or *Atlas.ti*, instead. What is important to keep in mind is that corpus analysis operates on linguistic categories: it is telling with regard to lexical, semantic, syntactic, grammatical and pragmatic characteristics of texts, insofar as these reveal themselves in the distribution and clustering of words. Taken by themselves, these insights are not necessarily relevant to social and discourse researchers. The further research questions go beyond linguistics proper, the more urgent is, therefore, the adoption of *middle-range theories* that specify how the issue being investigated is likely to be constructed discursively and how this can be studied in terms of the distributional features of language use of a specific corpus (see section on 'Analytical strategy...' on p. 179).

Along with the question of how to approach linguistic information comes the question of how to conduct corpus analysis scientifically. Should we take sides with those discourse linguists who suggest that corpus-driven approaches, because they proceed inductively, are more scientific than corpus-based 'intuition-led' approaches (Bubenhofer 2009)? Should we align ourselves with discourse scholars who, mirroring this (mis)representation, reject corpus-driven approaches as a-theoretical (Fairclough 2014) or incompatible with a social-studies understanding of text collections (Angermüller 2014)? Or, should we focus on the operational level of method triangulation, instead (Baker & Levon 2015)? Rather than providing a fair portrayal of alternative routes into corpus analysis, these stances suggest an alignment with specific positions in the 'boot-camp debate' in corpus linguistics (Worlock Pope 2010) and the schism between the quantitative (nomothetic-deductive) and qualitative (interpretive) paradigms in the social sciences. A more productive way of resolving research-philosophical issues is to acknowledge that purist corpus-driven approaches, too, start from some conception of language (McEnery & Gabrielatos 2006), that the coupling of data-driven assessment with introspection and of automated-quantitative assessment with manual-interpretive analysis is an established practice in contemporary corpus analysis (Fillmore 1992), and that the critical appropriation of corpus analysis, rather than its rejection, is an appropriate way of dealing with the new dispositive of text processing in qualitative social research.

The crucial decision concerning what *philosophy of science* should guide one's corpus-analytical project, then, no longer relates to the choice between corpus-driven and corpus-based approaches. Instead, the question is whether corpus-driven *and* corpus-based research should be conducted from the perspective of a positivist or post-positivist philosophy of science. Adopting a positivist stance means accepting as scientific only those insights that are generated by applying quasi-experimental methods to data sets, which are representative of the subject studied. Corpus-analytical expertise, then, centres on constructing corpora in line with principles of representativeness and reliability, so that text-statistical analysis will yield patterns that can be regarded as evidence of a 'general truth' about language use (Gabrielatos 2007; Gür-Şeker 2014; Kantner, Kutter, Hildebrandt & Püttcher 2011). When adopting a post-positivist stance, one will accept as scientific only those insights that are produced by reflexive methods and facilitate a complex reading of the issue investigated, which extends, instead of confirms, conventional ways of interpretation (Andersen Åkerstrøm 2003). While corpora used for exploration have to be constructed in a way that plausibly supports the research objective, the main emphasis is on revealing the analytical strategy applied (see section on 'Analytical strategy...', p. 179).

In short, as with any other method, corpus analysis comes with a range of technical issues and disputed research-philosophical assumptions. They need careful consideration before proceeding to implementation. The following section will provide a basis on which to decide whether or not corpus analysis is the way to go, more particularly, it highlights the specificities and limitations of corpus analysis and descriptive-statistical applications in lexicometrics and corpus linguistics. The examples given below were produced with the help of the corpus linguistic tool *Wordsmith* and are taken from a German-language corpus of financial commentary that was part of a larger study on crisis discourse (Kutter 2013a).

Focus and procedures of corpus analysis

Corpus analysis starts from the *word as the basic unit of analysis*.[3] Words are taken as principal entities embodying content (in content analysis and lexicometrics) or lexical-syntactic and pragmatic meaning (in NPL, corpus and discourse linguistics and corpus-based CDA). Words function as the primary unit even when analysis extends to word clusters, phrases, texts or hypertexts: 'the word is the peg that everything else is hung on' (Mautner 2009, p. 124).

The focus on words and their distributional characteristics within a given corpus corresponds to a certain conception of language and meaning. With the exception of content-analytical applications in the social sciences, where a theory of language is missing, corpus analyses usually draw on linguistic structuralism and its pragmatic turn. They assume the meaning of the analysed words to be given by their relational positioning, which can be characterised in paradigmatic (logical-hierarchical) or syntagmatic (sequential) terms. These relations are seen as being given by the 'language in use' manifest in concrete artefacts of written and spoken speech, rather than by a universal linguistic structure. Lexicometrics, corpus linguistics and NPL further stress that these relations can be partially revealed by computing the distribution of words in a text collection. Specific to corpus linguistics is the Firthian assumption that relations recurring in the immediate neighbourhood of a word determine the meaning it tends to have in a specific text collection (McEnery & Gabrielatos 2006; Tognini-Bonelli 2001).

The conceptual focus of corpus analysis is reflected in the view of computer-aided 'word statistics'. Statistical analysis organises ungrouped numerical data that are characterised by either a quantitative measure, such as score or weight, or some quality, such as a common property. Performing such analysis on texts with the help of computers means transforming texts into numerical data. The basic unit, 'word', becomes a set of bytes or a string of characters that is more or less different from other character strings in numerical terms. These 'tokens' can be computed with regard to frequency, distribution and co-occurrence and subjected to descriptive or inferential statistics. Their recognition by corpus-analytical software as linguistic units does, however, presuppose pre-processing, in the course of which information modelled on linguistic theory is read from or assigned to character strings. The recognition of bytes as *graphemes* (as units of a writing system of a natural language) depends on standardised character encoding, such as UNICODE or UTF 8, whereas the recognition of various graphemes as forms of a *lexeme* (a lexical-morphological unit of a natural language) or as *parts of speech* presupposes lexical and syntactic parsing. In the course of such parsing, character strings are matched with and classified as matching given information on lemmas and parts of speech of a natural language.[4] In addition, texts may be annotated with (and subsequently queried with regard to) meta-information, such as information on text production or text reception.

What procedures of statistical analysis are then applied, and how the results of computation are represented, largely depends on the chosen school and tool of corpus analysis. Lexicometric and corpus linguistic tools operate on descriptive statistics; they focus on properties of distribution in a given static corpus. Occurrences of a word or word type are counted in terms of absolute or normalised frequencies and these numbers are subsequently subjected to automated statistical procedures. One standard procedure is to calculate the extent to which individual words, pairs of words or patterns of word distribution in one corpus or corpus partition deviate from those in another corpus or corpus partition and from a central tendency (contrasting). Another common procedure is to measure the probability according to which two or more words co-occur in a given corpus (concordancing).

Contrasting in lexicometrics

Lexicometric software, such as *Alceste*,[5] *Lexico3* or *Hyperbase*[6], is particularly strong in corpus-driven contrasting. It focuses on revealing lexical macro structures of a discourse or topic in a given corpus by comparing partitions of an issue- or actor-specific corpus with each other. These partitions are defined by the researcher beforehand, following criteria that are external to the texts, such as sequences of the period under investigation, authors, speakers or geographical origin. The objective of such contrasting is to reveal, in a systematic manner, whether and how lexical preferences converge or differ between the subdivisions of a corpus both across time (diachronically) and across segments and types of discourse (synchronically). Standard procedures include *specificity tests*, which establish what words are statistically significantly over-represented in a corpus division when compared to another corpus division, or the overall corpus, and *factor analyses* that compute latent interdependencies and joint variations in the total of tokens of a corpus before then calculating statistically significant degrees of convergence between these summarising factors. Lexicometric software also provides for a *co-occurrence analysis*, which establishes what words frequently co-occur in a text passage of specified length, either in terms of a simple co-occurrence (A~B), poly-occurrence (A~B~C~D), or reciprocal co-occurrence (A~B, B~A). Using specificity tests, it is possible, for instance, to calculate and then display in a bar graph how the salience of words such as 'junior professor', 'BA' or 'strikes' changes over time in texts on the Bologna reform of Higher Education in Germany. Employing factor analysis, it is possible to show, in a four-dimensional dispersion plot, which speaker aligns with what group in terms of wording and lexical preferences. Using co-occurrence analysis, it is possible to draw a semantic web or tree graph, from the same text material, which highlight the proximity of expressions such as 'area of Higher Education' with 'European', 'unified' or 'mobility' (Scholz & Mattisek 2014).

Concordancing in corpus linguistics

Corpus linguistic tools, such as *AntConc*[7] or *Wordsmith*[8], are particularly suited to a type of concordancing that focuses on selected search words and their co-text. Co-occurring words are shown in the concordance lines of a keyword-in-context (KWIC) display and listed according to absolute or normalised frequencies, or according to the number of texts in which they co-occur. The fact of co-occurrence can be further assessed by computing different types and measures of probable co-occurrence while considering the different degrees of closeness or distance that the search word and co-occurring words tend to have in a corpus. Depending on the formula chosen, different features of collocation are highlighted. For instance, a *T score* will foreground those collocates that frequently occur next to the search word, while a *Mutual Information (MI) score* will rank highest those collocates that may not be particularly frequent but, compared to other collocates, tend to co-occur only in close proximity to the search word, not further away (Hoffmann et al. 2008, pp. 139–158; McEnery & Wilson 2001, p. 86f). These measures may be combined with tests of statistical significance, such as *log-likelihood* (*LL*), which establishes the level of confidence that the revealed feature is not due to chance (Gabrielatos & Baker 2008). The *Collocates* thus calculated may be assessed with regard to the frequency with which they occur in specific positions to the left or right of the search word within a specified span of words, using the *Patterns* display, or as part of multiword units that are based on n-grams, using the *Clusters* display of the concordancing tool in *Wordsmith*.

Table 11.1 shows the co-occurrences of *Staat* ('state') highlighted by *T score* vs *MI score* as they occurred in the investigated German-language corpus of financial commentary. The *T score* foregrounds conjunctions (if, then, so that) and modal verbs (has to, ought, should, may), financial means (money, billions) and quantifiers (more, many, billions), or specific actors

Amelie Kutter

Table 11.1 Collocates of *Staat* according to *T Score* and *MI Score*

T Score Word 2	Joint	T Score	MI Score Word 2	Joint	MI
dass (so that, in order to)	167	12,13	*schlanker* (lean)	5	9,62
wenn (if)	103	9,63	*zurückzieht* (withdraws)	3	9,15
muss (has to)	85	8,99	*erpressen* (blackmail [verb])	4	8,71
vom (by, from)	74	8,47	*Vater* (father, nanny)	10	8,50
kann (can)	73	8,22	*mischt* (meddles)	3	8,47
mehr (more)	74	8,06	*subventioniert* (subsidises)	3	8,30
Geld (money)	61	7,56	*regelt* (regulates)	4	8,08
Banken (banks)	55	7,00	*heraushalten* (step back)	3	8,01
soll (ought)	43	6,46	*bürgt* (guarantees)	3	8,01
sollte (should)	38	5,93	*zurückziehen* (withdraw)	6	8,01
Milliarden (billions)	37	5,91	*einspringen* (jump in)	13	8,00
viel (much, many)	27	4,84	*übernimmt* (takes over)	9	7,56
helfen (help [verb])	23	4,73	*ruft* (calls [verb])	4	7,30
dann (then)	27	4,72	*Großaktionär* (main investor)	3	7,30
Wirtschaft (economy, business)	25	4,66	*starker* (strong [nominative])	6	7,22
Unternehmen (firms)	22	4,37	*eingreifen* (intervene)	8	7,10
darf (may)	20	4,37	*sichert* (secures)	3	6,88
müssen (have to)	22	4,32	*rufen* (call [verb])	7	6,86
starken (strong)	19	4,32	*behält* (retains)	3	6,82
Markt (market)	19	4,25	*starken* (strong [accusative])	19	6,77
Bürger (citizen/s)	19	4,24	*gerettet* (rescued)	12	6,73
damit (so that, in order to)	21	4,23	*Notfall* (emergency)	4	6,71
können (can)	21	4,17	*Anteile* (shares [noun])	3	6,71
ob (whether)	20	4,17	*Ruf* (call [noun])	9	6,70

Note: The table shows the frequency with which the investigated pair of words occurred within the entire span of words (Joint) and the density of relationship according to T score or MI score.

(business, firms, citizens) as collocates of *Staat*. In contrast, the *MI score* highlights as collocates of *Staat* words associating with state intervention (subsidies, regulate, intervene, rescue, guarantee, Nanny) and state retreat (withdraw, step back, retreat) and related adjectives (strong vs lean) (see Table 11.1). The two measures, when studied across the different displays of *Wordsmith's* concordancing tool, facilitate a syntagmatic analysis of the semantic field of *Staat* in the corpus investigated. The modal verbs revealed by the *T score* turn out to be predicates, and financial resources and actors turn out to be objects of clauses, in which *Staat* appears as the grammatical subject. The state thus seems to be regularly portrayed by financial journalists as an agent that is expected to act upon redistribution and dispose of capacities to do so vis-à-vis specific recipients. The collocates highlighted by the *MI score* suggest that financial journalists conceive of the state not only primarily as a regulatory-redistributive agent that is expected to act upon economic problems (rather than, for instance, a polity), but also relate that conception to catchwords of habitual debates on regulatory policy and idiomatic phrases related to liberal state critique. Such insights into patterns of word use at the macro level of the entire corpus may inform further explorations in a corpus-based content analysis (Kutter & Kantner 2012) or a corpus-based conceptual history (Kutter 2013b).

Contrasting in corpus linguistics

Along with concordance analyses of word co-occurrences, corpus linguistic software also provides procedures for contrasting corpora that are similar to specificity tests in lexicometrics: *keyword analysis* and *consistency analysis*. Keywords are those words in the corpus being investigated that are considered to be distinct or 'key' in that corpus because they are over-represented or under-represented when compared to the distribution of the same words in another corpus (the reference corpus). In order to identify keywords, corpus linguists generate *word lists*, which rank the words in a corpus according to frequency. Keywords are then calculated by cross-tabulating the frequency of a single item and the total of tokens in the wordlist of one corpus and the frequency of a single item and the total of tokens in the wordlist of the other corpus. These numbers are subjected to statistical tests, such as *chi-square* or *log-likelihood*, to estimate what difference in frequency is likely to be stronger than random and, hence, points to words that are 'key' (McEnery & Wilson 2001, p. 84). Keyword analyses are often used to establish the distinct lexical features of an issue- or realm-specific corpus in comparison to a general language corpus, such as the BNC. But they can also be applied in comparisons of partitions of a corpus where each comprises texts associated with a specific time span, genre or speaker. Figure 11.1 shows which words were key in German financial commentary during the period in which the financial crisis emerged and escalated (P_2: February 2007 to August 2008) when compared to the preceding period of relative calm (P_1: January 2006 to January 2007, reference corpus). The figure ranks the words according to positive and negative keyness, which is the score that measures the degree to which words are statistically significantly over- or under-represented when compared to words in the reference corpus (Figure 11.1; see also Figures 11.2 and 11.3). The method of consistency analysis compares the frequencies of individual words across text files, or across word lists and the keyword lists of different corpora. The procedure is usually applied in order to determine the lexical, stylistic, and so forth, variance of (historical) versions or types of texts. It may also, however, be used to establish consistent word use across different partitions of a corpus where each comprises texts associated with a specific time span, genre, or speaker (see section on 'Methods...', p. 181).

Implications of the corpus-analytical view

The given examples illustrate that corpus analysis yields a very specific view of the investigated texts. The complexity of texts is radically reduced: first, through quantitative abstraction that highlights distributional features of words; and second, by abstracting search words and their immediate co-text from the rest of the texts. This condensed representation of texts does not result from a process of interpretation, but from statistical procedures applied to linguistic units according to algorithms modelled on theories of natural language. It is conceptually selective as it highlights the unit 'word' as carrier of meaning, rather than, for instance, structures that ensure the consistency and coherence of texts, and conceives of meaning constitution in syntagmatic terms only insofar as syntagmatic relations can be revealed by statistical methods. Moreover, context is primarily conceived in terms of the statistically defined co-text of a specific word (the words regularly co-occurring in the neighbourhood of a search word). Of course, the larger co-text can be zoomed in on by additionally consulting the embedding text using a KWIC display, or by jumping to the full text. The historically specific context of text production and comprehension may be integrated, too, by relating information on word distribution to additionally collected

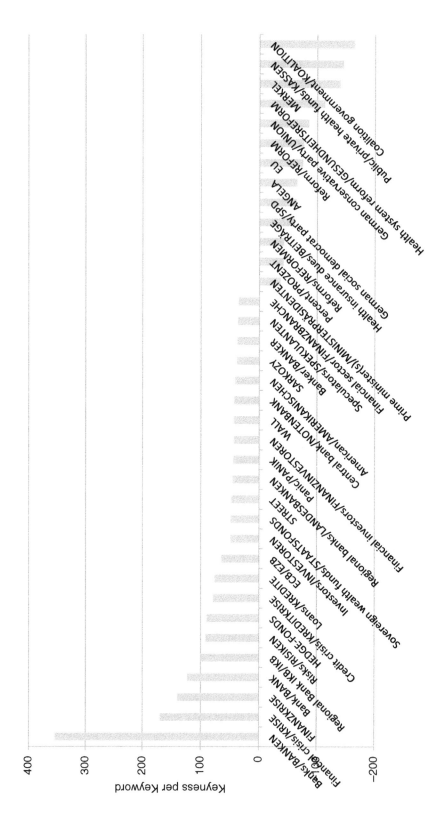

Figure 11.1 Keywords of Period 2 when compared to Period 1

Source: Kutter 2013a (log-likelihood; p-value: 0.000001; stop list applied)

meta-information. It may also be considered by designing an issue-specific corpus in a way that already reflects the specificity of the context of utterance, for example, by selecting a text genre, such as a column on financial pages that enacts the institutionalised practice of financial journalism, and so on. However, the very analytical procedures of corpus analysis are meant to abstract from an individual text and its specific conditions of emergence. Instead, they draw our attention to regular, statistically significant patterns of language use in an entire text collection. In what sense the results of a corpus analysis are meaningful to a particular discourse-analytical project, or question of political studies, depends on the analytical strategy that has been chosen to arrive at an informed interpretation.

Analytical strategy: the example of crisis discourse

An analytical strategy constructs the researcher's perspective on the subject of investigation in an explicit way; it specifies 'how the [researcher] will construct the observations of others to be the object of his or her own observations' (Andersen Åkerstrøm 2003, p. xiii). It determines from what research-philosophical viewpoint and macro-theoretical assumptions the study starts, and how these inform the conceptualisation of the research subject. Specific to a discourse-analytical strategy is to additionally point out what *theory of discourse* guides the study, which defines how reality is expected to be (co-)constituted through acts of uttering and signification. Based on these general decisions, it is necessary to adopt *middle-range theories* about the discursive construction of the subject of investigation that are concrete enough to inform *categories and methods of discourse analysis* and abstract enough to translate insights back into the macro-theoretical framework. A discourse study employing corpus analysis will further specify how insights generated by corpus-based or corpus-driven methods will be read in light of general assumptions and middle-range concepts.

The study on crisis discourse in financial commentary illustrates how such an analytical strategy involving corpus analysis can be formed. It was part of a larger project called 'Cultural political economy of crisis and crisis management', which aimed to include the perspective of culture (here understood as semiotic practice) into a political-economic examination of the conditions for the emergence and resolution of the North-Atlantic financial crisis (Jessop 2013).[9] A more specific objective of the discourse study was to explore how professional producers of economic discourse, such as financial journalists, represented and explained the crisis, and whether they adjusted conceptions of economic policy and theory. To this end, we employed the discourse-analytical repertoire of CDA, supported by corpus analysis. The corpus comprised commentaries on macroeconomic policy published by reputable financial columnists between 2006 and 2010. They were manually compiled by three people from papers ascribed priming authority in public debates on economic policy, including: *The Financial Times*, *The Economist* and *The Guardian* in the UK; *The Wall Street Journal*, *The New York Times* and *The Washington Post* in the US; and *Handelsblatt*, *Financial Times Deutschland* and *Süddeutsche Zeitung* in Germany. The German sample used for illustration here contained 2,025 commentaries and amounted to 1,172,111 tokens (Kutter 2013a).

The overall project was motivated by a critical-realist philosophy of knowledge and science, which posits that objective mechanisms exist outside subjective perceptions and can partially be disclosed by humans provided they adopt scientific methods that account for the mutual constitution of human agency and social structure (philosophy of knowledge and science).[10] This research-philosophical stance suggested using reflexive methods and open-ended empirical-theoretical exploration. It also implied a moderate constructionist ontology, presuming that economies are constituted through both collective imagination *and* structuration (ontology). Using theories from heterodox political economy and interpretive strands therein, this ontological perspective was substantiated in conceptions of economy and crisis (macro theory). Economies were seen to be historically specific constellations of economic structures, institutions and technologies of economic governance, actors' strategic coalitions and prevalent discourses that, together, temporarily contain inherent contradictions of capitalist accumulation (Jessop 2013). A crisis in such constellations, when mobilised as a decisive moment of political intervention in public debate, may challenge fortifying discourses. New conceptions of economy may emerge, depending on whether collective actors perceive a specific conjuncture of crisis as opening up horizons for action and whether structural-economic conditions lend plausibility to new complexity reduction (Kutter & Jessop 2014).

The framework implied focusing the discourse study on complexity reduction in financial commentary, while considering the conjunctural conditioning of this selective process. The theory of discourse developed in CDA, which posits that intersubjective meaning emerges from correspondence between linguistic interaction and the context of expression, helped to align these assumptions with a theoretically grounded discourse analysis (theory of discourse) (Kutter & Jessop 2014). The challenge consisted, however, of developing concepts that would grasp shifts in the discursive construction of crisis and inform the choice of categories and methods (middle-range theories). We drew inspiration from the concepts of 'periodisation' and 'crisis narratives'. Periodisation conceptualises social change in line with conjunctural analysis. In contrast to a chronology, which sorts events by putting them on a linear time axis in a simple narrative of succession and simultaneity, periodisation constructs a sequence of periods according to specific criteria, which are relevant to the practical and theoretical topic in question and account for the specific temporality of the phenomenon under investigation, such as economic cycles, discourse events, or *longue durée* (Jessop 2002). In line with this assumption and drawing on secondary analyses and economic data, we divided the period of investigation (2006–2010) into six phases, with each being characterised by new crisis developments and new sets of priorities in crisis management and, therefore, likely to mark crucial temporal horizons in financial commentary. This included: a period of relative calm and moderate growth or stagnation (P_1: January 2006 to February 2007); a period of emerging crisis (P_2: March 2007 to August 2008); a period of panic (P_3: September to November 2008); a period of normalisation in finances (P_4: December 2008 to March 2009); recession and crisis in real economy (P_5: April 2009 to February 2010); and the emerging Eurozone crisis (P_6: March to December 2010).

The concept of crisis narratives is based on the assumption, developed in narrative policy analysis, that humans structure experiences and define problems through narration. The construction of a crisis as a moment of specific decisive political intervention is seen to rely upon narration and its mobilisation in mediatised public debate. In the course of this debate, individual stories about the emergence and specific quality of the crisis are mapped into a more general template of interpretation (a meta-narrative) that recruits only specific events and only specific attributions of causation and responsibility to the public agenda (Hay 1999). The construction of crisis could, consequently, be text-analysed by establishing what events and topics were selected as newsworthy in financial commentary, what stories about causation and responsibility were developed, and which of them became most persuasive through moves of generalising abstraction (Kutter 2014).

Methods: the example of intra-corpus comparison

Corpus analysis, supported by the corpus linguistic tool *Wordsmith*, promised to capture efficiently the lexical-semantic dimensions of the categories that we had established with the help of middle-range theories. We expected keyword analysis to reveal the salient lexis of each crisis period, hinting at events and topics to us that were virulent during these periods. Via concordance analysis, we hoped to gain an overview of the connotations of fundamental concepts of macroeconomic policy, such as 'state'. As a result of corpus exploration, three methods could be consolidated, and these suggest themselves for use beyond the study of financial commentary: corpus-based conceptual history, corpus-based content analysis and intra-corpus comparison (Kutter 2013b; Kutter & Kantner 2012). Intra-corpus comparison draws on earlier work (Koller & Farrelly 2010) and will be presented here as an example of corpus-driven methods.

Periodised intra-corpus comparison

Intra-corpus comparison, when applied to the category of time, helps to establish how salient lexis changes over the period of investigation and how the use of words broadens or narrows down. It is corpus-driven because it trusts corpus-analytical software to produce relevant insights. Basic corpus linguistic procedures used in this method are keyword analysis and consistency analysis (see section on 'Focus and procedures...').[11] However, instead of comparing the language use in the corpus being investigated with the language use in a general corpus of a natural language, following the procedure that corpus linguists usually apply, one compares the periodized partitions of the corpus being investigated with each other. The partitions cover periods of time during which changes in discursive practice, which are relevant from the perspective of the research question, are likely to have occurred (periodisation, see the previous section). For the study on crisis discourse, we divided the period of investigation (2006–2010) into six phases, each being marked by different crisis developments, and divided the corpus in corresponding partitions (see the previous section). The steps of exploration included:

- a comparison of individual period-specific corpus partitions to the overall corpus, which reveals word use that distinguishes the respective crisis period from the rest of the period of investigation;
- a comparison of succeeding periods to preceding periods (P_2 to P_1; P_3 to P_2 and so on), which reveals in what way word use in the succeeding periods differs from that of respective previous periods;
- a consistency analysis that establishes what words are more or less consistently used over the period of investigation.

Applied to the periodised corpus of financial commentary, the first step of exploration suggested that journalists did indeed shift their attention corresponding to those events and issues that we had considered relevant during periodisation. For instance, while using words in P_1 that related to adjustments to German fiscal policy and health-system reform agreed upon by the new federal coalition government, journalists employed words in P_2, which are associated with the US housing and subprime crisis, the successive defaults of US and German financial institutions, and rescue actions (see Figure 11.1; section on 'Focus and procedures...'). The second step revealed, however, that despite these distinct features,

Amelie Kutter

overall word use differed considerably only between P_1 and P_2: here, both the number of keywords and their *keyness* proved very high. In contrast, word use during subsequent periods (P_3 to P_5) seemed to remain largely the same: only some words of little *keyness* were added and a few dropped out again, with the emerging Eurozone crisis (P_6) deviating again from that pattern (see Figures 11.2 and 11.3). Scrutiny of actual keywords revealed that the lexis, which was salient during P_1 and mainly related to welfare-state adjustment and fiscal reform, was largely replaced by a rich variety of financial-market lexis in P_2 (see Figure 11.1; section on 'Focus and procedures...'). During subsequent periods, words entered and dropped out again, which pointed to new sites of trouble and new crisis managers. The financial-market lexis, however, seemed to remain; it did not surface according to any threshold of significant deviation. This also held for the period of the emerging Eurozone crisis P_6, which had seemed different when looking at the numbers.

The exploration of crisis labels (compound nouns built from the German word *Krise*) in the third step further indicated that the consolidation of financial-market lexis corresponded to a narrowing of conceptions of crisis. During the period of emerging financial crisis, P_2, a variety of crisis labels was used, including housing crisis, mortgage crisis, subprime crisis, banking crisis, crisis of confidence, and so on. In the panic period, P_3, however, the term *Finanzkrise* (financial crisis) became the default label. It was hitherto consistently used, complemented only by *Wirtschafts- und Finanzkrise* (economic and financial crisis) during P_4 and P_5 and *Griechenlandkrise* (Greek crisis) and *Eurokrise* (Eurozone crisis) during P_6.

The revelations regarding the diachronic features of word distribution had great heuristic value for the study. Read in light of the interpretive scheme of crisis narratives, these revelations suggest that financial journalists developed a crisis narrative as early as 2007, which hitherto remained largely the same and which emphasised, above all, financial-sector issues. Commentators seemed to have consolidated their conception of the crisis as being a

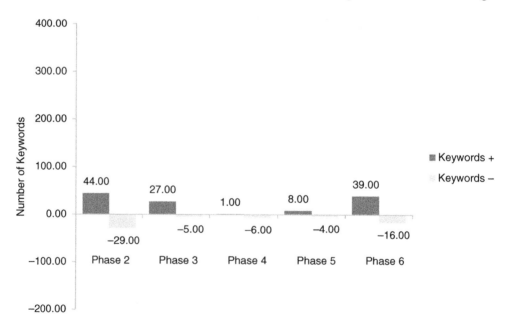

Figure 11.2 Number of keywords per period when compared to the previous period

Source: Kutter 2013a (log-likelihood; p-value: 0.000001; stop list applied)

Corpus analysis

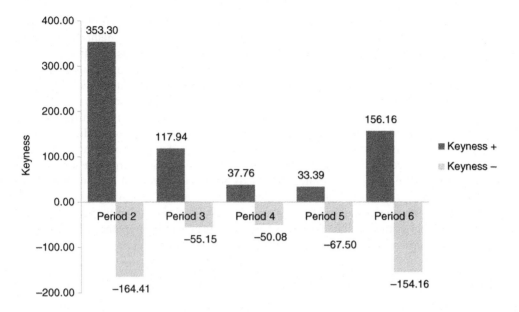

Figure 11.3 Range of keyness per period when compared to the previous period
Source: Kutter 2013a (log-likelihood; p-value: 0.000001; stop list applied)

financial-system crisis no later than 2008. They applied this reading to subsequent crisis displacements, too, regardless of whether these related to fiscal squeeze, social-humanitarian calamities and political turmoil. The insights obtained by intra-corpus comparison were also valuable because they induced reflexivity. They challenged conclusions drawn from the content and discourse analysis of causal stories, which had suggested that crisis conceptions and lessons drawn changed during the period of investigation (Kutter 2014). More generally, the insights obtained by this method suggested that, when studying crisis-induced shifts in debates on economic policy, one has to take prevalent conceptions of crisis into account to gain a fair understanding of perpetuation or change.

Conclusions: using corpus analysis in political discourse studies

In this chapter, discourse researchers, who are considering using computer-aided textual analysis, can familiarise themselves with the field and method of corpus analysis, more precisely: the semi-automated statistical analysis of large collections of digital texts called 'corpora'. The chapter has promoted the argument that the distinct view of corpus analysis, the sort of abstraction that it generates from large amounts of texts, is the particular value that corpus analysis adds to the discourse study of social and political issues. Corpus analysis does not present texts according to their linear or intertextual composition. Instead, it highlights patterns of regular use of single words or word clusters as they appear in a large collection of texts. Whether showing these words in situ, or in quantified abstraction, this reading provides us with a bird's eye view of the use of specific words *across* all the texts contained in a corpus. In addition, the display of word clusters reveals patterned semantic, syntactic, and so on, relationships between words. This provides us with an additional layer of interpretation, which cannot be gained otherwise. Corpus analysis may challenge not only our habitual way of linear reading, but also our preconceived views about the subject studied.

However, the results of such corpus exploration are often not meaningful in themselves. In order to relate to discourse studies of social and political issues, methods of corpus exploration have to be made part of an analytical strategy. In other words: big data and smart tools are nothing without theory. Neither should we expect procedures of corpus analysis to replace human-manual efforts to disentangle discourse (as many advocates of corpus-driven and unsupervised approaches do). Nor should we nourish the hope that corpus analysis will free us from the bias of small-scale studies and decisively help us in reconstructing the larger context of utterance (as corpus-based and supervised studies often do). Precisely because of its selective focus on the distributional properties of words, corpus analysis is not suited to reproduce the deep comprehension that hermeneutic-interpretive or detailed linguistic discourse analysis generates from texts and their contextual and interdiscursive conditioning. If discourse researchers take on the huge task of compiling, preparing and analysing corpora, they should rather use corpus analysis as an explorative technique. As such, it will yield distinct insights into texts and facilitate generating hypotheses and research questions for further investigation by other methods of textual analysis.

Notes

1 I wish to thank the two editors and Costas Gabrielatos for their helpful comments on an earlier version.
2 An exhaustive account of the growing field of corpus analysis is beyond the scope of this chapter; the review is meant to illustrate the plurality of the field, instead.
3 The following will elaborate on word-based languages only. For an equivalent approach to symbol-based languages, see Jurafsky and Martin (2009).
4 When using corpus linguistic or lexicometric software, this information has to be physically inscribed into texts using algorithmic processing tools, such as tree tagger or the tagging functionalities of analytical software. Text-mining tools, on the contrary, process texts dynamically. Note that standard character encoding, provided by standard corpus-analytical software, is usually enough for a rough analysis of lexis.
5 http://www.image-zafar.com/en/alceste-software
6 http://www.tal.univ-paris3.fr/lexico/
7 www.antlab.sci.waseda.ac.jp/software.html
8 www.lexically.net/wordsmith
9 The North-Atlantic financial crisis emerged as a consequence of the 2006 US housing crisis. It had global repercussions when mortgage-backed securities crashed in 2007, followed by a crash of banks and stocks in 2008, and recession and fiscal crisis in 2009. The label highlights the regional origin of the crisis.
10 This is the author's ex-post reading of the project in light of an analytical strategy. It is based on a series of discussions with the principal investigator, Bob Jessop, but might not be identical with his views.
11 In lexicometrics, the procedure of specificity tests and factor analyses may yield similar insights.

References

Andersen Åkerstrøm, N, 2003, *Discourse analytic strategies. Understanding Foucault, Koselleck, Laclau, Luhmann*, The Policy Press, Bristol.
Angermüller, J, 2014, '»Der« oder »das« Korpus? Perspektiven aus der Sozialforschung' in *Diskursforschung. Ein interdisziplinäres Handbuch*, eds. J Angermüller, M Nonhoff, E Herschinger, F Macgilchrist, M Reisigl, D Wrana, J Wedle & A Ziem, transcript, Bielefeld, pp. 604–613.
Baker, P, 2006, *Using corpora in discourse analysis*, Continuum, London and New York.
Baker, P & Levon, E, 2015, 'Picking the right cherries? A comparison of corpus-based and qualitative analyses of news articles about masculinity', *Discourse and Communication*, vol. 9, no. 2, pp. 1–16.

Baker, P, Gabrielatos, C, KhosraviNik, M, McEnery, T & Wodak, R, 2008, 'A useful methodological synergy? Combining Critical Discourse Analysis and corpus linguistics to examine discourses of refugees and asylum seekers in the UK press', *Discourse & Society*, vol. 19, no. 3, pp. 273–305.

Bubenhofer, N, 2009, *Sprachgebrauchmuster. Korpuslinguistik als Methode der Diskurs- und Kulturanalyse*, de Gruyter, Berlin.

Busse, D & Teubert, W, 1994, 'Ist Diskurs ein sprachwissenschaftliches Objekt?' in *Begriffsgeschichte und Diskursgeschichte. Methodenfragen und Forschungsergebnisse der historischen Semantik*, eds. D Busse, F Hermanns & W Teubert, Westdeutscher Verlag, Opladen, pp. 10–28.

Busse, D & Teubert, W, 2013, *Linguistische Diskursanalyse: neue Perspektiven*, VS Springer, Wiesbaden.

Clark, A, Fox, C & Lappin, S, 2013, *The handbook of computational linguistics and Natural Language Processing*, Wiley-Blackwell, Chichester.

Fairclough, N, 2014, *Language and power*, 2nd revised edition, Routledge, London.

Fairclough, N & Wodak, R, 1997, 'Critical Discourse Analysis' in *Discourse as social interaction*, ed. T A v Dijk, Sage, London, Thousand Oaks, New Delhi, pp. 258–284.

Fillmore, C J 1992, '"Corpus linguistics" or "Computer-aided armchair linguistics"' in *Directions in Corpus Linguistics. Proceedings of the Nobel Symposium 82 Stockholm, 4–8 August 1991*, ed. J Svartik, Mouton de Gruyter, Berlin, pp. 35–60.

Gabrielatos, C, 2007, 'Selecting query terms to build a specialised corpus from a restricted-access database', *ICAME Journal*, vol. 31, pp. 5–43.

Gabrielatos, C & Baker, P, 2008, 'Fleeing, sneaking, flooding: A corpus analysis of discursive constructions of refugees and asylum seekers in the UK press 1996–2005', *Journal of English Linguistics*, vol. 36, no. 1, pp. 5–38.

Glasze, G, 2013, *Politische Räume: Die diskursive Konstitution eines 'geokulturellen Raums' Frankophonie*, transcript, Bielefeld.

Gür-Şeker, D, 2012, *Transnationale Diskurslinguistik*, Hempen, Bremen.

Gür-Şeker, D, 2014, 'Zur Verwendung von Korpora in der Diskurslinguistik' in *Diskursfoschung. Ein interdisziplinäres Handbuch*, eds. J Angermüller, M Nonhoff, E Herschinger, F Macgilchrist, M Reisigl, D Wrana, J Wedle & A Ziem, transcript, Bielefeld, pp. 583–603.

Hay, C, 1999, 'Crisis and the structural transformation of the state: interrogating the process of change', *British Journal of Politics and International Relations*, vol. 1, no. 3, pp. 317–344.

Hoffmann, S, Evert, S, Smith, N, Lee, D & Berglund Prytz, Y, 2008, *Corpus linguistics with BNCweb – a practical guide*, Peter Lang, Frankfurt (Main).

Jessop, B, 2002, 'The political scene and politics of representation. Periodising class struggle and state in "The Eighteenth Brumaire"' in *Marx's Eighteenth Brumaire. (Post)modern interpretations*, eds. M Cowling & M James, London, Pluto Press, pp. 179–94.

Jessop, B, 2013, 'A Cultural Political Economy of Crisis Construal in the North Atlantic Financial Crisis' in *Sprachliche Konstruktionen von Krisen. Interdisziplinäre Perspektiven auf ein fortwährend aktuelles Phänomen*, eds. M Wengeler & A Ziem, Hempen, Bremen, pp. 31–52.

Jurafsky, D & Martin, J H, 2009, *Speech and language processing. An introduction to natural language processing, computational linguistics and speech recognition*, Prentice-Hall, New Jersey.

Kantner, C, Kutter, A, Hildebrandt, A & Püttcher, M, 2011, 'How to get rid of the noise in the corpus: Cleaning large samples of digital newspaper texts', *International Relations Online Working Paper Series*, no. 2011/2.

Koller, V & Farrelly, M, 2010, 'Darstellungen der Finanzkrise 2007/2008 in den britischen Printmedien', *Aptum*, vol. 6, no. 2, pp. 179–192.

Kutter, A, 2013a, 'Zur Analyse von Krisendiskursen. Korpusgestütze Explorationen der nordatlantischen Finanzkrise aus politisch-ökonomischer Perspektive' in *Sprachliche Konstruktionen von Krisen. Interdisziplinäre Perspektiven auf ein fortwährend aktuelles Phänomen*, eds. M Wengeler & A Ziem, Hempen, Bremen, pp. 241–266.

Kutter, A, 2013b, 'Totgesagte leben länger. Die Fortschreibung ökonomischer Ordnung in Krisenlektionen der deutschen Finanzpresse' in *Ökonomie, Diskurs, Regierung: Interdisziplinäre Perspektiven*, ed. J Maeße, VS Verlag, Wiesbaden, pp. 95–120.

Kutter, A, 2014, 'A catalytic moment: the Greek crisis in the German financial press', *Discourse & Society*, vol. 25, no. 4, pp. 445–465.

Kutter, A & Jessop, B, 2014, 'Culture as discursive practice: combining cultural political economy and discursive political studies in investigations of the financial crisis' in *Financial cultures and crisis dynamics*, eds. B Jessop, B Young & C Scherrer, Routledge, London, pp. 64–82.

Kutter, A & Kantner, C, 2012, 'Corpus-based content analysis: A method for investigating news coverage on war and intervention', *International Relations Online Working Paper Series*, no. 2012/01.

Lebart, L, Salem, A & Berry, L, 1998, *Exploring textual data*, Kluwer, Dordrecht.

Mautner, G, 2009, 'Checks and balances: How corpus linguistics can contribute to CDA' in *Methods of critical discourse analysis*, eds. R Wodak & M Meyer, Sage, London, pp. 122–143.

McEnery, T & Gabrielatos, C, 2006, 'English Corpus Linguistics' in *The handbook of English linguistics*, eds. B Aarts & A McMahon, Blackwell Publishing Ltd, pp. 33–70.

McEnery, T & Wilson, A, 2001, *Corpus linguistics*, Edinburgh University Press, Edinburgh.

Scholz, R & Mattisek, A 2014, 'Zwischen Exzellenz und Bildungsstreik. Lexikometrie als Methodik zur Ermittlung semantischer Makrostrukturen des Hochschulreformdiskurses' in *Diskursforschung. Ein interdisziplinäres Handbuch*, eds. J Angermüller, M Nonhoff, E Herschinger, F Macgilchrist, M Reisigl, J Wedle, D Wrana & A Ziem, transcript, Bielefeld, pp. 86–112.

Scholz, R & Ziem, A, 2013, 'Lexikometrie meets FrameNet: das Vokabular der "Arbeitsmarktkrise" und der "Agenda 2010" im Wandel' in *Sprachliche Konstruktion von Krisen. Interdisziplinäre Perspektiven auf ein fortwährend aktuelles Phänomen*, eds. M Wengeler & A Ziem, Hempen, Bremen, pp. 155–183.

Spitzmüller, J & Warnke, I H, 2011, 'Discourse as a "linguistic object": Methodical and methodological delimitations', *Critical Discourse Studies*, vol. 8, no. 2, pp. 75–94.

Stubbs, M, 1996, *Text and corpus analysis*, Blackwell, Oxford, Cambridge MA.

Stubbs, M, 2001, *Words and phrases. Corpus studies of lexical semantics*, Blackwell, Oxford.

Tognini-Bonelli, E, 2001, *Corpus linguistics at work*, John Benjamins, Amsterdam, Philadelphia.

Wengeler, M, 2006, 'Linguistik als Kulturwissenschaft. Eine Einführung in diesen Band' in *Linguistik als Kulturwissenschaft*, ed. M Wengeler, Olms, Hildesheim, pp. 1–23.

Wiedemann, G, 2013, 'Opening up to big data: Computer-assisted analysis of textual data in social sciences', *Forum Qualitative Sozialforschung/Forum: Qualitative Social Research*, May 2013. Available from: www.qualitative-research.net/index.php/fqs/article/view/1949 [Accessed 4 July 2017].

Worlock Pope, C, 2010, 'The bootcamp discourse and beyond', *Special Issue of International Journal of Corpus Linguistics,* 2010, vol. 15, no. 3.

Ziem, A, Scholz, R & Römer, D, 2013, 'Korpusgestützte Zugänge zum öffentlichen Sprachgebrauch: spezifisches Vokabular, semantische Konstruktionen, syntaktische Muster in Diskursen über "Krisen"' in *Faktizitätsherstellung in Diskursen. Die Macht des Deklarativen*, ed. E Felder, de Gruyter, Berlin/New York, pp. 329–358.

12

Cognitive Linguistic Critical Discourse Studies

Connecting language and image

Christopher Hart

Introduction

In this chapter, I introduce one cognitive school of Critical Discourse Studies (CDS) in the form of cognitive linguistic approaches. Cognitive Linguistic CDS (CL-CDS) is characterised by an emphasis on the conceptual dimensions of semiosis. Specifically, it addresses the conceptualisations invoked by language and the ideological or legitimating potentials that those conceptualisations might realise in political contexts of communication. I begin the chapter by providing an overview of the different frameworks in CL-CDS before focusing specifically on image schema analysis, illustrated with examples from discourse on political protests. I then go on to make a connection between cognitive linguistic and multimodal approaches to CDS. The claim made is that understanding language involves fully modal rather than *a*modal mental representations. I therefore argue that existing research on the social semiotics of multimodal representation is an important source in considering the meanings of language in use. I illustrate this claim by relating linguistic instances of discourse on political protests to visual instances.

Cognitive Linguistic CDS

It is now increasingly recognised in CDS that any connection between language and social action is mediated by cognition (Wodak 2006). A number of cognitive approaches to CDS may therefore be identified, including van Dijk's socio-cognitive approach (e.g. van Dijk 1998, 2008, 2014) and several approaches that draw on cognitive linguistics (e.g. Cap 2013; Charteris-Black 2004; Chilton 2004; Hart 2010, 2015; Koller 2004, 2014; Marín Arrese 2011; Musolff 2004, 2011). Although some researchers have sought to unify these perspectives (e.g. Koller 2005), a number of distinctions between them may be discerned (see Hart 2014b for discussion). For example, while van Dijk's socio-cognitive approach focuses more on the role of context models in text-production, cognitive linguistic approaches focus more on the mental processes involved in text interpretation. A further difference lies in their 'methodological attractors' (Hart & Cap 2014). While the socio-cognitive approach draws eclectically on various aspects of cognitive psychology, cognitive linguistic approaches draw more or less exclusively on specific theories in cognitive linguistics. A fundamental difference between them, which arises as a consequence of this, is in their characterisations of meaning. In the socio-cognitive approach, meaning is characterised in more or less propositional terms. In cognitive linguistic approaches, by contrast, meaning is treated as imagistic or conceptual in nature. This chapter aims to introduce readers to cognitive linguistic approaches to CDS specifically.

CL-CDS is concerned with analysing conceptualisation in discourse and specifically the ideological and legitimating qualities that alternative conceptualisations may carry in contexts of political communication (Chilton 2004; Hart 2013a, 2013b, 2014a, 2014b). Linguistic units (lexical, grammatical and textual) are seen, from this perspective, as prompts for the activation of various kinds of conceptual structures and processes, which are constitutive of meaning. The conceptual structures and processes involved are said to be imagistic in nature, grounded in prior visual and other forms of embodied experience (Lakoff & Johnson 1999; Langacker 2008). Crucially, from a critical standpoint, conceptualisation is subject to *construal* as alternative patterns in language use prompt for the same target situation to be conceptualised in different ways.[1] It is thus through the process of conceptualisation that language is able to enact ideology as alternate language usages conjure competing images of the same material situation. At least three CL approaches to CDS may be identified, focused on different features of conceptualisation.

The most developed of these is Critical Metaphor Analysis (e.g. Koller 2004; Musolff 2004; Charteris-Black 2004, 2006; see also Charteris-Black, this volume, p. 202). In Critical Metaphor Analysis, based in Lakoff and Johnson's (1980) Conceptual Metaphor Theory, metaphorical expressions in discourse are seen as linguistic reflexes of, or prompts for, conceptual structures and processes. Metaphors are not seen as mere tropes, then, but rather, the conceptual structures and processes involved in metaphor shape our thoughts and actions. Conceptual metaphors involve a mapping from a source domain onto a target domain in order to provide it with structure. Conceptual metaphors are ideological in so far as the source domain provides a refracting medium through which the target domain is construed and where the particular choice of source domain leads to particular patterns of inference within the target domain. Source domains are provided by concrete or salient domains of experience encoded in image schemas (see below), or frames (Fillmore 1982, 1985). Recurring source domains in social and political discourses include frames for JOURNEY, BUILDING, WAR, GAMES and GAMBLING, orientational schemas such as UP-DOWN and NEAR-FAR, and naturalised themes such as FIRE, WATER, ILLNESS or WEATHER. However, one particular schema, which has been found to function as a source domain across several social and political discourses, is the CONTAINER schema (e.g. Charteris-Black 2006; Chilton 1994, 1996; Hart 2010; Nuñez Perucha 2011). The CONTAINER schema is an especially powerful conceptual structure in political discourse where the inherent topology of the schema, defining an inside versus an outside, 'operates as a principle of division' (Chilton 1996, p. 147). It is thus an image schema through which one of the fundamental features of ideologies – polarisation between Us and Them (van Dijk 1998) – is enacted. In the context of the Cold War, for example, Chilton (1996) showed how a conceptual metaphor STATE AS CONTAINER, which underpinned public discourse at the time, 'provided a cognitive basis for variant policies of containment, and for imagining "two worlds"' (Chilton 1996, p. 415). A conceptual metaphor found to be salient in immigration discourse is IMMIGRATION IS FLOOD (Charteris-Black 2006; Hart 2010; Santa Ana 2002). The FLOOD frame in this metaphor serves to present immigrants as an inanimate substance and therefore discourages human empathy and ignores individual motives and life stories. It further presents immigration as excessive. The interaction between this metaphor and the COUNTRY IS CONTAINER metaphor, moreover, is likely to invoke emotional responses as it creates an image of the container being perforated, thereby allowing the inflow of liquid (Chilton 2004).

Critical Metaphor Analysis is not restricted to the linguistic modality, but has been usefully applied to the visual modality, too (e.g. Bounegru & Forceville 2011; El Rafaie 2003; Forceville & Urios-Aparisi 2009). Here, scholars have shown that many of the conceptual metaphors evidenced by patterns of linguistic discourse find expression in visual discourse, too. For example, El Refaie (2003) shows how the FLOOD frame is invoked in political cartoons depicting refugees. This cross-modal realisation is predicted by a Cognitive Linguistic perspective, where metaphors are seen as a feature of the conceptual system, rather than belonging to any particular communicative modality. It therefore makes sense that they should be reflected in, or articulated through, alternative semiotic modes.

A second strand of CL-CDS is found in applications of Discourse Space Theory (e.g. Chilton 2004; Cap 2006, 2013; Dunmire 2011; Filardo Llamas 2013; Filardo Llamas, Hart & Kaal 2015; Kaal 2012). This approach aims to account for meaning construction in discourse 'beyond the sentence'. According to this approach, meaning is created through the construction of 'discourse worlds' – conceptual structures that represent the *ontologies* defined in, or presupposed by, a text (Chilton 2004; Gavins 2007). These discourse worlds are constructed inside a deictically defined mental or 'discourse' space consisting of three dimensions: space, time and (epistemic and deontic) evaluation. The actors, actions and events explicitly or implicitly referenced in texts get positioned in the three-dimensional space at distances relative to a spatial, temporal and evaluative 'deictic centre' presumed to be shared between speaker and hearer. The co-ordinates of elements in the discourse world may be indexed by linguistic features of various types, including tense, prepositional phrases, pronouns, and modal expressions, or may be derived from frame-based knowledge accessed by the discourse (Chilton 2004, p. 61). Discourse worlds are important structures in the cognitive study of ideology since they represent a particular world-view, which, through discourse, hearers are invited to share in. Based in Discourse Space Theory, and further developing its central notion of (metaphorical) distance in conceptualisation, Cap (2006, 2008, 2011, 2013) outlines a model of legitimation by *proximisation*. Within this framework, proximisation is defined as a rhetorical strategy involving a contraction of the conceptual space between elements initially located at distal points in spatial, temporal or evaluative dimensions and the speaker and hearer's deictic co-ordinates in one or other of these dimensions (see Hart 2014a for a revised typology of proximisation strategies). Proximisation has been shown as particularly powerful in interventionist discourses because it construes evolving actions or situations as personally consequential. It has been shown to operate in a range of interventionist discourses, including American and British political discourse on action in Iraq (Cap 2006; Hart 2014a), media and political discourses on immigration (Hart 2010, 2014a), and the discourse of the Irish Republican Army (Filardo Llamas 2013).

One final strand of CL-CDS is found in the form of image schema analysis drawing on Langacker's (1991, 2008) Cognitive Grammar (e.g. Hart 2011, 2013a, 2013b, 2015). Image schema analysis addresses the basic structuring of situations and events through the imposition of image schemas. Image schemas are abstract holistic knowledge structures that emerge from repeated patterns of embodied experience (Johnson 1987; Mandler 2004). They arise in basic domains such as SPACE, ACTION, FORCE and MOTION to encode relational information pertaining, for example, to topology, sequence and causation. Image schemas form the foundations of the conceptual system and provide 'folk theories' of the way the world works. They later 'work their way up into our system of meaning' (Johnson 1987,

p. 42) to become paired with lexical and grammatical units inside the system of symbolic assemblies that makes up language. In discourse, they are invoked by their reflexes in text to constitute our most basic understanding of the referential event, defining its type and internal structure. Their selection in discourse thus serves an ideological function in categorising and organising reality, as well as in directing inference. Different schemas, furthermore, define different semantic roles within the event-structure, thus attributing particular qualities to the actors involved. There is also, then, an ideological dimension in assigning social actors to the different roles specified within the schema (Wolf & Polzenhagen 2003, p. 265). I illustrate this form of CL-CDS in more detail in the following section before drawing some connections between cognitive linguistic and multimodal approaches to CDS. Examples come from media discourse on political protests.

Example analysis: a partial grammar of political protest reporting

Consider the contrast between (1) and (2):

1. A number of police officers were injured after [they $_{PATIENT}$] [came under attack from $_{ACTION}$] [youths $_{AGENT}$], some wearing scarves to hide their faces. (*The Telegraph*, 10 November 2010).
2. [Activists who had masked their faces with scarves $_{AGENT}$] [traded punches with $_{ACTION}{}^R$] [police $_{AGENT}$]. (*The Guardian*, 10 November 2010)

At the level of lexico-grammar, the main difference between (1) and (2) lies in the alternative grammatical constructions used to describe the event. In (1), we find a regular transitive construction, while in (2) we find a reciprocal construction. Conceptually, the difference between (1) and (2) lies in the alternative image schemas that these grammatical choices invoke to construe the scene in question – a process referred to as *schematisation* (Croft & Cruse 2004; Hart 2014a). The alternative schemas are modelled in Figure 12.1.

The two schemas are grounded in embodied experience of observing interactions between elements in our physical environments. The one-sided schema in Figure 12.1(a) represents a unidirectional transfer of energy from the element 'upstream' in the energy flow to the element 'downstream', resulting in a change of state to the downstream element. The two-sided schema in Figure 12.1(b) represents events in which there is a bidirectional transfer of energy between two equally active elements.[2] These schemas come to form the meaningful

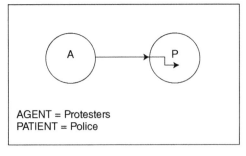

(a) One-sided action schema

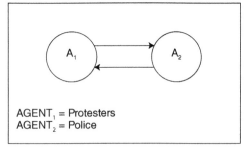

(b) Two-sided action schema

Figure 12.1 Action schemas

basis of regular transitive versus reciprocal constructions, respectively. In the regular transitive construction, an AGENT (A) acts upon a PATIENT (P). The vector in the corresponding image schema represents the force and direction of the action designated in the verb. In the reciprocal construction, one participant cannot be said to be active and the other passive, but, rather, both participants are equally agentive. The twin vectors in Figure 12.1(b) thus represent the bi-directionality of the force designated in the semantics of the verb. These alternate schemas, then, are invoked in discourse by the selection of their linguistic counterparts, whereupon they serve to configure the internal structure of the referential situation in different ways: (1), for example, construes the event in terms of the one-sided action schema modelled in Figure 12.1(a), while (2) construes the same material event in terms of the two-sided action schema modelled in Figure 12.1(b). The construal invoked by (1) serves to assign sole responsibility for the violence that occurred to the protesters, while the construal in (2) recognises the role of the police in the violence that occurred. The alternative conceptualisations may be reflective/constitutive of wider ideologised discourses on the relationship between state and citizen. The construal in (1) may be seen as instantiating a right-wing conservative discourse in which political protest is demonised and the actions of authorities are not debated, while the construal in (2) may be seen as instantiating a more left-wing liberal discourse, which at least calls into question the actions of the authorities. And indeed, in distributional analyses (Hart 2013a, 2013b), it has been found that regular transitive constructions, such as (1), with protesters as sole agents, occur more frequently in newspapers expected to espouse a more conservative discourse on political protests, while reciprocal constructions, such as (2), occur more frequently in newspapers expected to espouse a more liberal discourse.[3] These two examples illustrate the ideological and legitimating significance of schematisation. The schemas discussed, however, are just two, which, within the parameter of schematisation, contribute to the grammar of protest reporting (see Hart 2013b, 2014a, 2014b for others).

A second dimension of construal addressed in image schema analysis is 'point of view'. In Cognitive Grammar (Langacker 1987, 1991, 2002, 2008), it is argued that alternate grammatical constructions include within their semantic values a point-of-view specification. That is, grammatical constructions not only evoke a particular image schema, but also encode a point of view from which that image schema is experienced. This arises from the embodied basis of language where our experience as visual actors – who, at any moment experience a scene from a different point of view – is exploited to provide meaning to language. The point-of-view variables available to language cover the full range of this experience. Language, however, seems, in practice, to make use of only a restricted set of cardinal points of view.

In discourse, these conceptual processes – schematisation and point of view – take place in and across networks of mental spaces (Fauconnier 1994, 1997). Image schemas are defined inside an 'event-space' (Hart 2010, 2014a) while point of view is defined inside a 'base space' (Radden & Dirven 2007), which acts as a grounding space. Variation in point of view operates in at least three dimensions: horizontal, vertical and distal. Here, I illustrate variation in point of view on only the horizontal or 'anchorage' plane (see Hart 2014a, 2015 for a detailed discussion of point-of-view shifts in all three dimensions). On the anchorage plane, four cardinal points may be identified, which correspond to 90° rotations relative to the inherent or construed directionality of elements within the scene under conception. For example, actions and motions are conceived in terms of vectors that inherently possess directional properties. Points of view may be defined perpendicular to the vector, whose direction is then either left-to-right or right-to-left, relative to the point of view, or in line

Christopher Hart

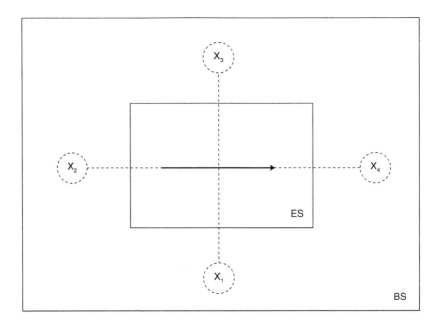

Figure 12.2 Potential points of view on the anchorage plane

with the vector, which then either points towards or away from the point of view. This is modelled in Figure 12.2 where the four potential points of view are represented as broken circles. We can assign the potential points of view arbitrary numerical values X 1–4.[4]

All four points of view are exploited in media discourse on political protests and thus make up part of the grammar of protest reporting. For example, reciprocal constructions encode a point of view from either cardinal point X_1 or X_3, while regular transitive constructions encode a point of view from either cardinal point X_2 or X_4 (see Hart 2014a, 2015). Which particular point of view is determined by further grammatical distinctions within the two types of construction, namely, information structure and voice choice, respectively. Consider the contrast between (3)–(4) and (5)–(6).

3. [Protesters $_{AGENT}{}^1$] [clashed with $_{ACTION}{}^R$] [police $_{AGENT}{}^2$] around the Bank of England. (*The Telegraph*, 1 April 2009).
4. [Riot police $_{AGENT}{}^2$] [clash with $_{ACTION}{}^R$] [demonstrators $_{AGENT}{}^1$]. (*The Guardian*, 1 April 2009).
5. A number of police officers were injured as [they $_{PATIENT}$] [came under attack from $_{ACTION}$] [the protesters $_{AGENT}$] (*The Times*, 10 November 2010).
6. [About 50 riot police $_{AGENT}$] [tried to drive $_{ACTION}$] [the crowd $_{PATIENT}$] back. (*The Independent*, 10 November 2010).

Both (3) and (4) are examples of reciprocal constructions, and thus, both invoke the two-sided action schema modelled in Figure 12.1(b) to construe the event. However, the point of view from which the conceptual content in the event space is construed is different in each case. Assuming a configuration as in Figure 12.1(b) (A_1 = protesters, A_2 = police), the point of view from which the reader is invited to construe the scene in (3) is X_1. The point of view that the reader is asked to assume in (4) is X_3. This is modelled in Figure 12.3(a) versus 12.3(b), respectively.

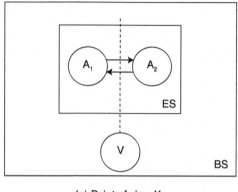 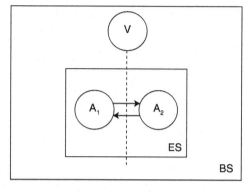

(a) Point of view X₁   (b) Point of view X₃

Figure 12.3 Point of view in reciprocal constructions (A₁ = protesters, A₂ = police)

The contrasting points of view are motivated by an iconic correspondence between the linear organisation of the clause and the left-right organisation of conceptual content (cf. Perniss et al. 2010). Based on this correspondence, the information sequence in (3) promotes a point of view that organises the event relative to this point of view, as in Figure 12.3(a), with the protesters on the left and the police on the right, while the information sequence in (4) promotes a point of view that results in the relative spatial organisation in Figure 12.3(b), with the police on the left and the protesters on the right.

In the case of regular transitive constructions, the point of view is determined by voice choice. Here, the active voice invites a construal from cardinal point X_2, while the passive voice invites a construal from cardinal point X_4. Thus, the regular transitive construction in (5) invites the reader to construe the scene from cardinal point X_4, at the head end of the vector and downstream of the energy flow. In the richer simulation, this point of view invites the reader to place themselves in the shoes of the PATIENT. This is achieved at the level of schematisation by means of a *role connector (R)* (Fauconnier 1994, 1997), which links participants across mental spaces. This is modelled in Figure 12.4(a). In contrast to (5), the transitive construction in (6) is in the active voice. The point of view promoted is thus from cardinal point X_2 at the tail end of the vector. From this point of view, the reader is asked to assume in the simulation the role of the AGENT, again achieved at the level of schematisation by means of a role connector. This is modelled in Figure 12.4(b).

The ideological significance of the point-of-view distinctions found in (3)–(6) can be examined through their distributions in a corpus of protest reports. Here, for example, Hart (2013a, 2013b) found that when reciprocal constructions are used, the construal modelled in Figure 12.3(a) is preferred by more conservative newspapers, for whom the police/protesters typically constitute the in/out-group, respectively, while more liberal newspapers tend to favour the construal modelled in Figure 12.3(b). Similarly, when regular transitive constructions are used, the passive voice – and thus the construal modelled in Figure 12.4(a) – tends to be favoured when police are patients in a violent action, but the active voice – and thus the construal modelled in Figure 12.4(b) – is preferred when the police are encoded as agents in legitimated actions, such as 'drive back', which construe the police as defenders of civil order, rather than perpetrators of state violence.

The ideological significance of both schematisation and point of view, however, as well as the other construal operations described in CL-CDS, can also be explored through more

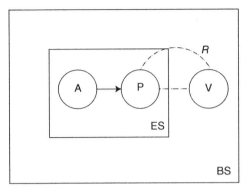 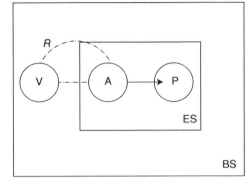

(a) Point of view X_4
transitive passive construction

(b) Point of view X_2
transitive active construction

Figure 12.4 Point of view in active versus passive voice

qualitative functional analyses. Here, CL-CDS can gain valuable insights from multimodal approaches to CDS. Indeed, the critical impetus of CL-CDS can be seen, at least in part, to emerge from the combination of cognitive linguistic and multimodal forms of analysis (Hart 2014a, 2015, 2016).

Connections with multimodality

At the level of schematisation described above, the abstract mental imagery invoked by language encodes information relating to basic structural properties of the scene, such as spatial topology and sequential organisation (Langacker 1991; Talmy 2000). Conceptualisation, however, involves at least two levels of mental representation. At a higher level, it involves much richer, more specified imagery, not designated in the lexical or grammatical units of the utterance, but derived from background knowledge and past experience, encoded in a mental *simulation* of the target scene (see Bergen 2012 for an overview). By simulation, it is meant an 'experience resembling perceptual or motor experience occurring in the absence of the relevant external stimuli, in the case of perceptual experience; or without actual execution of motor actions, in the case of motor imagery' (Bergen et al. 2007, p. 735). That is to say, in other words, that language use involves the activation of imagery and imagined scenarios based on past experience including, presumably, mediatised visuo-semiotic experience (see Hart 2016 for extensive discussion of this and its implications for CDS).

Information included in mental simulations pertains, *inter alia*, to the colour, shape, size, and orientation of objects (Stanfield & Zwaan 2001; Zwaan et al. 2002) as well as to the length, rate and direction of motion of described objects (Glenberg & Kaschak 2002; Kaschak et al. 2005; Matlock 2004). Simulations, moreover, are not run in a disconnected way, but with *simulated situatedness*, run from the perspective of an 'immersed experiencer' (Bergen 2012; Zwaan 2004). That is, the conceptualiser imagines the scene unfolding from the perspective of an actor (i.e. AGENT or PATIENT) in, or a witness to, the scene. The particular perspective corresponds with the point-of-view specification determined by the semantic values of alternative grammatical constructions (Bergen et al. 2004; Bergen & Chang 2005). Conceptualising a scene from the perspective of an immersed experiencer also means that affective systems that serve to guide judgement, reasoning and decision-making processes (Damasio 1994) are run concomitantly as part of the simulation.

Colour, shape, size, orientation, rate and direction of motion, and point of view are, of course, precisely the kind of semiotic variables whose functions have been extensively studied in multimodal (Critical) Discourse Analysis (e.g. Kress & van Leeuwen 2006; Machin 2007; Machin & Mayr 2012; O'Halloran 2004; van Leeuwen 2010; see also van Leeuwen, this volume). Multimodal studies can therefore provide important insights into linguistic meaning. If language prompts for the construction of fully modal mental representations, possessing properties whose meaning potentials have already been analysed in multimodal discourse analysis, then it follows that multimodal discourse analysis can shed light on the nuances of meaning communicated through language. A good starting point here, I suggest, is with Kress and van Leeuwen's (2006) 'grammar of visual design', or the systems of FORM (including COLOUR and SHAPE) and PERSPECTIVE (including DEEP SPACE and POINT OF VIEW) proposed by Lim (2004, p. 236).

Relatedly, since there is no principled reason to suppose that such semiotic variables should function differently in linguistic versus visual modes of communication, critical insights from multimodal studies into the ideological and/or legitimating potentials of values within these systems can be directly brought to bear in analysing the ideological and/or legitimating potentials of language. A second important corollary is that the processes involved in linguistic meaning can be characterised in the same terms as in multimodal studies. The point-of-view shifts described above, for example, can be characterised as *panning* (Hart 2014a, 2014b, 2015). This is more than just an analogy and reflects instead the principle that language is embodied, related in particular to visual experience. A third consequence for CDS is that the meanings of language usages in any given context are dependent on patterns in visual articulations of the same discourse. This works as follows: In the case of most social and political discourses, language users do not have first-hand experiences of the situations being described. Rather, such situations are experienced second-hand through images. The meaning of a linguistic expression in social and political discourse is thus, at least in part, a function of the images to which an individual has previously been exposed in contexts of similar language usages. To study the meaning of language in social and political discourses therefore entails studying patterns of visual representation within the same discourse. It may further suggest, specifically, investigating the extent to which configurations of linguistic and visual representation correspond with one another when they co-occur in multimodal texts (for example, in the case of photographs and their captions).

Let us now see how all this relates to examples of linguistic discourse on political protests. Figure 12.5 shows four photographs documenting political protests in London.[5] The photographs reflect the kind of conceptual content likely to be encoded in the simulations invoked by examples (1)–(6). Information relating to the participants, including their age, race, gender, facial expressions, body postures, clothing (type and colour) and effectors (shields, truncheons, sticks, bottles, etc.), present in the images, will all form part of the mental representations invoked by utterances such as (1)–(6). These features should all, therefore, enter into any linguistic analysis, too. My focus in this chapter, however, is on one particular contrasting feature presented by the images, namely, point of view. The images each present a different point of view on the anchorage plane relative to actors and/or vectors in the image.[6] The semiotic experience provided by these images is thus likely to be reflected in the simulated experiences evoked by language usages such as (1)–(6). Specifically, the images in Figure 12.5(a)–(d) share corresponding point-of-view specifications with the grammatical constructions exemplified in (3)–(6), respectively. The simulated experience, that is, the meaning, evoked by linguistic instantiations (3)–(6) will therefore reflect the semiotic experiences we have in encountering images such as those in Figure 12.5(a)–(d), respectively. Thus, the ideological/(de)delegitimating functions of linguistic examples such as (3)–(6) are best illuminated by critically analysing, in light of findings from multimodal discourse analysis, images such as those in Figure 12.5.

The images in Figure 12.5(a) and 12.5(b) both present a point of view in which the actors in the image are seen in profile orientation. The angle between the sight-line of the viewer and vectors in the image representing action is perpendicular. For Kress and van Leeuwen (2006, p. 136), this oblique angle creates a sense of detachment. The viewer is positioned outside the event depicted. The position, moreover, is one of relative neutrality as the point of view is not from one side or the other but, rather, the viewer is forced to occupy the middle ground between the police and protesters. As a consequence of the contrasting points of view they present, however, the two images differ in the spatial organisation of the actors involved. In 12.5(a) the protesters occupy the left region of the image and the police the right, while in 12.5(b), it is the police who occupy the left region of the image and the protesters the right. The two images are not completely neutral, therefore, since left versus right are found in multimodal studies to have different value associations. There is disagreement, though, in precisely what the value associations of left and right are. In Kress

(a) Point of View X_1
© EPA

(b) Point of View X_3
© Tim Ireland/PA

(c) Point of View X_4
© James Veysey/Camera Press

(d) Point of View X_2
© Dan Kitwood/Getty

Figure 12.5 Point of view in pictures of protests

and van Leeuwen (2006), for example, spatial left and spatial right are treated as signifying 'given' versus 'new' information. Elements in the left region of an image are thus attributed the status of 'established' or 'unquestioned' while elements in the right region are attributed the status of 'controversial' or 'contested'. Casasanto (2009), by contrast, has shown experimentally that left positioning is associated with negative valence, while right positioning is associated with more positive valence. Elements in the left region of an image, on this account, are therefore attributed the status of 'bad' while elements in the right region are attributed the status of 'good'.[7] The reality in practice is that the particular associations of left and right are likely to be culture-, context-, and/or individual-specific. Nevertheless, Casasanto's work at least demonstrates a default tendency which would suggest that, for many readers, the image in Figure 12.5(a) will invite a more negative appraisal of the protesters relative to the police, while the image in Figure 12.5(b) is likely to invite a more negative appraisal of the police relative to the protesters.[8] Based on the argument made above, then, that grammatical constructions encode spatialised mental representations, and that the point-of-view specifications encoded by reciprocal constructions, such as those in (3) and (4), invoke mental experiences resembling those invoked by the images in Figure 12.5(a) and 12.5(b), respectively, we may say that while (3) and (4) are more neutral in comparison to (5) and (6), (3) confers a more negative evaluation on the protesters relative to the police, while (4) confers a more negative evaluation on the police relative to the protesters.

In the simulations invoked by (3) and (4), the viewer is asked to adopt the situated perspective of an eye-witness. In parallel with the images in Figure 12.5(a) and Figure 12.5(b), we can characterise the points of view encoded in these constructions as an 'observer's' perspective. This is in contrast to the 'involved' perspective encoded in the regular transitive constructions exemplified in (5) and (6), whose meanings reflect the semiotic experience presented by the images in Figure 12.5(c) and 12.5(d), respectively. The point of view in Figure 12.5(c) and 12.5(d) is one in which the sight-line of the viewer, and the vectors in the image representing action, are not perpendicular to one another, but are more or less overlain. For Kress and van Leeuwen (2006), this straight angle positions the viewer, not as an eye-witness to the scene, but as a participant in it. Which participant depends on the particular point of view presented and the relationship this sets up with action vectors in the image. When the point of view is such that the vector is pointing away from the viewer, the viewer is invited into the role of AGENT. When the point of view is such that the vector is pointing towards the viewer, they are invited into the role of PATIENT. In Figure 12.5(c), where the process depicted is a violent action, the point of view is at the head of the vector. The viewer is therefore positioned on the side of the PATIENT, in this case the individualised police officer, and sees the scene unfolding from this perspective. In Figure 12.5(c), the viewer is thus asked to identify with the police rather than the protesters, with whom they are placed in confrontation.[9] From this point of view, not only is the viewer in a position of alignment and confrontation with the police and protesters, respectively, but the aggressive action depicted in the image is seen as directed towards the viewer themselves. The image is thus highly rhetorically charged. In Figure 12.5(d), the point of view is from the tail of the vector, with the viewer positioned on the side of the AGENT. In this image, the police are agentive, and so the viewer is similarly asked to identify with the police and imagine themselves as agents in the action depicted. From this perspective, however, the action the viewer is invited into is not one of 'attacking' but, rather, 'defending'.

The two images are highly ideologised. In both of these images, the viewer is asked to see the world from the point of view of the police, who are only agents in legitimated actions, but who have to face the violent actions of protesters. The argument being made here is that, in the case of regular transitive constructions such as (5) and (6), the passive versus the active voice invite simulations from the perspective of the PATIENT versus the AGENT, respectively. The meaning of (5) and (6) will thus resemble the visuo-semiotic experience presented by the images in Figure 12.5(c) and 12.5(d), along with all the ideological and rhetorical force that these experiences carry. In the simulation evoked by (5), the conceptualiser 'sees' the event from the perspective of the police as PATIENT. They therefore experience the event as if they were on the receiving end of the violent action. In the simulated experience, systems of affect are integrated to create a similar sense of threat as conjured by the image in Figure 12.5(c).[10] In the simulation evoked by (6), the conceptualiser 'sees' the event from the perspective of the police as AGENT. They therefore experience police action in the same way as evoked by the image in Figure 12.5(d). Examples such as (5) and (6) can thus, on the back of combined insights from cognitive linguistics and multimodal discourse analysis, and beyond what is revealed by a transitivity analysis alone, be said to instantiate a discourse of legitimation/delegitimation in relation to police and protesters, respectively. More than instantiating a particular world-view, however, examples such as (5) and (6) invite the hearer to at least temporarily inhabit the world of the police, as it is presented by the discourse.

Conclusion

In this chapter, I have introduced the cognitive linguistic school of Critical Discourse Studies. CL-CDS comes with a particular model of language in which both lexical and grammatical units are seen, when selected in discourse, as prompts for a variety of construal operations in the cognitive process of conceptualisation. Conceptualisation is held to be imagistic in nature, involving the activation of abstract schematic images, as well as richer imagery provided by embodied simulations. I have focused on two conceptual processes, schematisation and point of view, in the context of discourse on political protests. Since understanding language involves the activation of imagery, I have argued that the ideological import of linguistic constructions can be most clearly gleaned from analyses, based in multimodal discourse analysis, of images with corresponding content and structural properties. A number of questions remain to be addressed here. However, I hope to have at least demonstrated the merits of cognitive linguistics applied in CDS and of integrating cognitive linguistic and multimodal methods.

Notes

1 The notion of critique in CL-CDS corresponds most closely with that in Critical Linguistics (Fowler 1991; Hodge & Kress 1993) or what Reisigl and Wodak (2001) refer to as socio-diagnostic critique aimed as 'the demystifying exposure of the – manifest or latent – persuasive, propagandist, populist, "manipulative" character of discursive practices' (p. 32).
2 Imagine a moving object crashing into a stationary object compared to two moving objects colliding with one another.
3 Of course, the distribution of constructions may also be used diagnostically to determine the political positions of different institutions.
4 Note that the direction of the action and point of view are not fixed in an absolute sense relative to a geographical frame of reference (cf. Levinson 2003) but, rather, are defined relative to one another.
5 I am using these photographs only to illustrate the theory. I make no claim as to their representativeness, which would require semantic tagging and statistical analyses of a large corpus of images.

6 For Kress and van Leeuwen (2006), action and motion in images are represented by vectors created within the image.
7 For Casasanto, this is down to the positive embodied experience most people have, given their right-handedness, of controlling objects located to the right, compared to objects located to the left. This raises interesting questions as to the effect of handedness on interpreting image and language.
8 A corpus analysis comparing distributions across newspapers known to adopt competing ideological stances would add to the weight of evidence here.
9 That we make a link between spatial point of view and social value positions is evidenced in metaphorical expressions such as 'we see things the same way' or 'we share the same outlook on life'.
10 This raises questions concerning the orthodox view of the ideological functions of the passive voice (cf. Fowler at al. 1979; Hodge & Kress 1993).

References

Bergen, B, 2012, *Louder than words: The new of science of how the mind makes meaning*, Basic Books, New York.
Bergen, B & Chang, N, 2005, 'Embodied construction grammar in simulation-based language understanding' in *Construction grammars: Cognitive grounding and theoretical extensions,* eds, J O Östman & M Fried, John Benjamins, Amsterdam, pp. 147–190.
Bergen, B, Chang, N & Narayan, S, 2004, 'Simulated action in an embodied construction grammar', in *Proceedings of 26th annual conference of the Cognitive Science Society,* Erlbaum, Mahwah NJ, pp. 108–113.
Bergen, B, Lindsay, S, Matlock, T & Narayanan, S, 2007, 'Spatial and linguistic aspects of visual imagery in sentence comprehension', *Cognitive Science*, vol. 31, no.5, pp. 733–764.
Bounegru, L & Forceville, C, 2011, 'Metaphors in editorial cartoons representing the global financial crisis', *Visual Communication*, vol. 10, no. 2, pp. 209–229.
Cap, P, 2006, *Legitimization in Political Discourse*, Cambridge Scholars Publishing, Newcastle.
Cap, P, 2008, 'Towards a proximisation model of the analysis of legitimization in political discourse', *Journal of Pragmatics*, vol. 40, no. 1, pp. 17–41.
Cap, P, 2011, 'Axiological proximisation', in *Critical Discourse Studies in context and cognition*, ed. C Hart, John Benjamins, Amsterdam, pp. 81–96.
Cap, P, 2013, *Proximization: The pragmatics of symbolic distance crossing*, John Benjamins, Amsterdam.
Casasanto, D, 2009, 'Embodiment of abstract concepts: good and bad in right- and left-handers', *Journal of Experimental Psychology,* vol. 138, no. 3, pp. 351–367.
Chilton, P, 2004, *Analysing political discourse: Theory and practice*, Routledge, London.
Croft, W & Cruse, D A, 2004, *Cognitive linguistics*, Cambridge University Press, Cambridge.
Damasio, A R, 1994, *Descartes' error: Emotion, reason and the human brain*, Penguin, New York.
Dunmire, P, 2011, *Projecting the future through political discourse*, John Benjamins, Amsterdam.
El Refaie, E, 2003, 'Understanding visual metaphor: The example of newspaper cartoons', *Visual Communication*, vol. 2, no. 1, pp. 75–96.
Fauconnier, G, 1994, *Mental spaces: Aspects of meaning construction in natural language*, Cambridge University Press, Cambridge.
Fauconnier, G, 1997, *Mappings in thought and language*, Cambridge University Press, Cambridge.
Filardo Llamas, L, 2013, '"Committed to the ideals of 1916". The language of paramilitary groups: The case of the Irish Republican Army', *Critical Discourse Studies*, vol. 10, no. 1, pp. 1–17.
Filardo Llamas, L, Hart, C & Kaal, B, 2016, *Space, time and evaluation in ideological discourse*, Routledge, London.
Forceville, C & Urios-Aparisi, E, 2009, *Multimodal metaphor*, Walter de Gruyter, Berlin.
Fowler, R, 1991, *Language in the news: Discourse and ideology in the press,* Routledge, London.
Fowler, R, Hodge, R, Kress, G & Trew, T, 1979, *Language and control*, Routledge and Kegan Paul, London.

Gavins, J, 2007, *Text world theory: An introduction*, Edinburgh University Press, Edinburgh.

Glenberg, A & Kaschak, M, 2002, 'Grounding language in action', *Psychonomic Bulletin & Review*, vol. 9, pp. 558–565.

Hart, C, 2010, *Critical discourse analysis and cognitive science: New perspectives on immigration discourse*, Palgrave Macmillan, Basingstoke.

Hart, C, 2011a, 'Force-interactive patterns in immigration discourse: A Cognitive Linguistic approach to CDA', *Discourse & Society*, vol. 22, no. 3, pp. 269–286.

Hart, C, 2011b, 'Moving beyond metaphor in the Cognitive Linguistic Approach to CDA: Construal operations in immigration discourse' in *Critical Discourse Studies in context and cognition*, ed. C Hart, John Benjamins, Amsterdam, pp. 171–192.

Hart, C, 2013a, 'Event-construal in press reports of violence in political protests: A Cognitive Linguistic Approach to CDA' *Journal of Language and Politics*, vol. 12, no. 3, pp. 400–423.

Hart, C, 2013b, 'Constructing contexts through grammar: Cognitive models and conceptualisation in British newspaper reports of political protests' in *Discourse and contexts*, ed. J Flowerdew, Continuum, London, pp. 159–184.

Hart, C, 2014a, *Discourse, grammar and ideology: Functional and cognitive perspectives*, Bloomsbury, London.

Hart, C, 2014b, 'Construal operations in online press reports of political protests' in *Contemporary Critical Discourse Studies*, eds. C Hart & P Cap, Bloomsbury, London, pp. 167–188.

Hart, C, 2015, 'Viewpoint in linguistic discourse: Space and evaluation in news reports of political protests', *Critical Discourse Studies*, vol. 12, no. 3, pp. 238–260.

Hart, C, 2016, 'The visual basis of linguistic meaning and its implications for Critical Discourse Analysis: Integrating Cognitive Linguistic and multimodal methods', *Discourse & Communication*, vol. 27, no. 3, pp. 335–350.

Hodge, R & Kress, G, 1993, *Language as ideology*, 2nd ed., Routledge, London.

Johnson, M, 1987, *The body in the mind: The bodily basis of meaning, imagination, and reason*, University of Chicago Press, Chicago, IL.

Kaal, B, 2012, 'Worldviews: Spatial ground for political reasoning in Dutch election manifestos', *CADAAD*, vol. 6, no. 1, pp. 1–22.

Kaschak, M, Madden, C J, Therriault, D J, Yaxley, R H, Aveyard, M, Blanchard, A A & Zwaan, R A, 2005, 'Perception of motion affects language processing', *Cognition*, vol. 94, no. 3, B79–B89.

Koller, V, 2004, *Metaphor and gender in business media discourse: A critical cognitive study*, Palgrave Macmillan, Basingstoke.

Koller, V, 2005, 'Critical discourse analysis and social cognition: Evidence from business media discourse', *Discourse & Society*, vol. 16, no. 2, pp. 199–224.

Koller, V, 2014, 'Cognitive linguistics and ideology' in *The Bloomsbury companion to cognitive linguistics*, ed. J Littlemore & J Taylor, Bloomsbury, London, pp. 234–252.

Kress, G & van Leeuwen, T, 2006, *Reading images: The grammar of visual design*, 2nd ed., Routledge, London.

Langacker, R W, 1987, *Foundations of Cognitive Grammar, vol. I: Theoretical prerequisites*, Stanford University Press, Stanford, CA.

Langacker, R W, 1991, *Foundations of Cognitive Grammar, vol. II: Descriptive application*, Stanford University Press, Stanford.

Langacker, R W, 2002, *Concept, image, and symbol: The cognitive basis of grammar*, 2nd edn, Mouton de Gruyter, Berlin.

Langacker, R W, 2008, *Cognitive Grammar: A basic introduction*, Oxford University Press, Oxford.

Levinson, S, 2003, *Space in language and cognition: Explorations in cognitive diversity*, Cambridge University Press, Cambridge.

Lim, F V, 2004, 'Developing an integrative multisemiotic model' in *Multimodal discourse analysis*, ed. K L O'Halloran, Continuum, London, pp. 220–246.

Machin, D, 2007, *An introduction to multimodal analysis*, Bloomsbury, London.

Machin, D & Mayr, A, 2012, *How to do Critical Discourse Analysis: A multimodal approach*, Sage, London.
Mandler, J M, 2004, *The foundations of mind: Origins of conceptual thought*, Oxford University Press, Oxford.
Marín Arrese, J, 2011, 'Effective vs. epistemic stance and subjectivity in political discourse: Legitimising strategies and mystification of responsibility' in *Critical Discourse Studies in context and cognition*, John Benjamins, Amsterdam, pp. 193–224.
Matlock, T, 2004, 'Fictive motion as cognitive simulation', *Memory & Cognition*, vol. 32, pp. 1389–1400.
Musolff, A, 2004, *Metaphor and political discourse: Analogical reasoning in debates about Europe*, Palgrave Macmillan, Basingstoke.
Musolff, A, 2011, 'Migration, media and 'deliberate' metaphors', *Metaphrik.de*, vol 21, pp. 7–19.
Musolff, A, 2012, 'The study of metaphor as part of critical discourse analysis', *Critical Discourse Studies*, vol. 9, no. 3, pp. 301–310.
O'Halloran, K L, 2004, *Multimodal discourse analysis*, Continuum, London.
Perniss, P, Thompson, R, & Vigliocco, G, 2010, 'Iconicity as a general property of language: Evidence from spoken and signed languages', *Frontiers in Psychology*, vol. 1, pp. 227.
Radden, G & Dirven, R, 2007, *Cognitive English grammar*, John Benjamins, Amsterdam.
Stanfield, R A & Zwaan, R A, 2001, 'The effect of implied orientation derived from verbal context on picture recognition', *Psychological Science*, vol. 12, pp. 153–156.
Talmy, L, 2000, *Toward a cognitive semantics*, MIT Press, Cambridge, MA.
van Dijk, T A, 1998, *Ideology: A multidisciplinary approach*, Sage, London.
van Dijk, T A, 2008, *Discourse and context: A sociocognitive approach*, Cambridge University Press, Cambridge.
van Dijk, T A, 2014, *Discourse and knowledge: A sociocognitive approach*, Cambridge University Press, Cambridge.
van Leeuwen, T, 2010, *The language of colour: An introduction*, Routledge, London.
Wodak, R, 2006, 'Mediation between discourse and society: Assessing cognitive approaches in CDA', *Discourse Studies*, vol. 8, no. 1, pp. 179–90.
Wolf, H G & Polzenhagen, F, 2003, 'Conceptual metaphor as ideological stylistic means: An exemplary analysis, in *Cognitive models in language and thought: Ideology, metaphors and meanings*, eds. R Dirven, R Frank & M Putz, Mouton de Gruyter, Berlin, pp. 247–76.
Zwaan, R A, 2004, 'The immersed experiencer: Toward an embodied theory of language comprehension' in *The psychology of learning and motivation, volume 44*, ed. B H Ross, Academic Press, New York, pp, 35–62.
Zwaan, R A, Stanfield, R A & Yaxley, R H 2002, 'Do language comprehenders routinely represent the shapes of objects?', *Psychological Science*, vol. 13, pp. 68–171.

13
Competition metaphors and ideology
Life as a race

Jonathan Charteris-Black

Introduction: ideological metaphor

It is now well accepted that metaphors perform a range of rhetorical purposes in political genres that are broadly associated with persuasion.[1] The choice of metaphor is governed by the political context and the nature of the genre, since debates, conference speeches and social media platforms differ in their rhetorical needs. Such metaphors influence public events by reinforcing and legitimising the outlooks and beliefs of supporters and by attacking and delegitimising those of opponents. In either case, where there is evidence of the realisation of a predetermined strategy I have proposed the term 'purposeful metaphor' and argued that there is often corroborating linguistic and contextual evidence of this purpose (Charteris-Black 2012). Linguistic evidence of purpose is often provided by semantically related metaphor clusters. For example, words from the semantic fields of war, illness, journeys or the human body may refer to political struggle, opponents, political actions or the state of the nation, respectively. Reiteration of metaphors encourages ways of thinking about the entity referred to, and contributes to, conceptually based outlooks. The rhetorical context supplies the identity of a nation or social group, or the nature of a social problem. Clusters of cognitively related metaphors are typically represented using conceptual metaphors (Lakoff & Johnson 1980). Another form of contextual evidence of purpose is when metaphors contribute to a wider discourse in public debates, in which the metaphors of one group are contested by the alternative ones proposed by an opposing group. Metaphors are purposeful when they contribute to a speaker's efforts to convince others that he or she is right.

Purposeful metaphors become ideological when they express a set of beliefs and values that are shared by a particular social group and contribute to a world-view that unites and defines this group. I view ideology as pyscho-social in nature because it provides a means through which individuals are able to establish group identities that influence the social order (see Seliger 1976, p. 14; Charteris-Black 2011, p. 22). A world-view is a set of concepts that is required both to understand the world and to provide the justification for an individual's – or a group's – actions and behaviours in the world. In this chapter, I therefore use the term 'ideological metaphor' to refer to a metaphor that is both purposeful – because it has a distinct persuasive role – and ideological – because it legitimises the world-view[2] of a social group. The purposes of such ideological metaphors are most readily identifiable when they ostracise an Out-group by using a metaphor vehicle such as a disease (cancer, Ebola, etc.) or an animal (e.g. cockroach, or tiger) or dehumanise them altogether by metaphors based on dangerous climatic conditions (e.g. storms, floods) or environmental disasters (e.g. melt-downs, tsunamis). The idea shared by clusters of systematically related metaphors may be represented conceptually as IMMIGRANTS ARE ANIMALS/NATURAL DISASTERS, etc. Musolff (2015) argues that the metaphor of the German nation as a body needing to be rescued from a deadly poison should be viewed as the conceptual basis for the Nazi genocidal policies that culminated in the Holocaust; Wodak (2015) provides many fascinating illustrations of ideological metaphors in more recent right-wing populist rhetoric. By contrast, an In-group may be identified using family and home metaphors that may be conceptually represented as THE NATION IS A FAMILY/HOME. In some cases, the rhetorical motivation for such colourful uses of metaphor is fairly 'transparent', in the sense that the intention behind them is readily identifiable, however the deeper cognitive roots of an ideology may not be. Musolff (2015) demonstrates how metaphors deriving from the human body derive from deeply embedded ways of thinking that underlie much Western political thought. In such cases, ideological metaphors require considerable critical expertise to capture and elucidate because they *covertly* encapsulate a set of beliefs that permeates a way of thinking, a way of talking and a way of doing and acting in the world.

In this chapter, I analyse a metaphor that I suggest has sometimes gone unrecognised in the discussion of left- and right-wing perspectives on capitalism: a competitive sports metaphor in which social progress is framed as a race; I will refer to this as the 'Competitive Race metaphor'. My interest in competitive sports metaphors is partly because I love sports: whether or not this is because I attended a British public school and enjoyed playing in hockey and cricket 'first elevens', I do not know. However, it was also sparked by recent use in British politics when this rather invisible metaphor was brought to our attention as a way of formulating ideological differences between the political left and right. In the following extract from a speech by a former leader of the British Labour Party, Competitive Race metaphors are shown in italics:

> Let me explain why. You see he believes in *this thing called the global race,* but what he doesn't tell you is that he thinks for Britain *to win the global race* you have *to lose,* lower wages, worse terms and conditions, fewer rights at work. But Britain can't *win a race for the lowest wages* against countries where wages rates are pennies an hour and the more we try the worse things will get for you. Britain can't *win a race for the fewest rights at work* against the sweat shops of the world and the more we try the worse things will get for you. And Britain *can't win a race for the lowest skilled jobs* against countries where kids leave school at the age of 11. And the more we try the worse things will get for you. *It is a race to the bottom.* Britain cannot and *should not win that race.*
>
> (Miliband, 24 September 2013)

Miliband begins by introducing the counter-position of 'he' (his opponent, the-then Prime Minister, David Cameron) in which international relations are framed in terms of nations competing as individuals in a race, with the assumption that winning the race is desirable. As Underhill observes:

> From the nineteenth century onwards, attempts had been made to define the nature of 'the character of nations' and races, which were then compared and contrasted in order

to allow us to establish hierarchies which attributed a transcendental justice to transient reigns of power and spheres of influence...

(Underhill 2012, p. 138)

Without rejecting the Competitive Race metaphor, Miliband elaborates it by drawing attention to Cameron's assumption that the 'race' is one where international 'performance' is measured by GDP and introduces social criteria by which the performances of nations can be measured. The race is no longer one of economic competition in which 'coming first' means earning the most money. Cameron's Competitive Race metaphor is contested by drawing on another aspect of competitive events – the league table – in which a team can move 'upwards' or 'downwards' in relation to other teams. Miliband's use of metaphor draws attention to an ideology that is covert in Cameron's use of 'global race' by drawing attention to it as a 'competition' by repetition of 'race' and then reframing and elaborating the metaphor by drawing attention to the aspects of 'progress' that it ignores. In a typical race, the competitors run towards a finishing line; there is a single winner, many losers and no prizes for being runner-up. When used by the political right, 'global race' assumes that we all know what race we are in, that we all want to be participants in it and we want to win it. But as Underhill (2012, p. 154) reminds us: 'Competitors in sports became an expression of the "Will to Power", the will to destroy opposition ... The sportsman was reduced to a conqueror who imposed himself by crushing others'. The will to power of one nation over another was originally found in the concept of 'the arms race' that was prominent in the 1930s and 1980s when there was political confrontation between nation-states as they sought to crush each other. Miliband's 'race to the bottom' reframes the Competitive Race metaphor by redefining what is meant by 'winning' away from economic measures such as GDP, trade and profitability towards measures of social progress.

Once metaphors are viewed as characterising and influencing thought rather than just as stylistic preferences, it is necessary to consider the cognitive semantic approach initiated by Lakoff and Johnson (1980) and developed extensively elsewhere (e.g. Lakoff 1996; Charteris-Black 2004). From this view, the systematic correspondences between the primary and secondary senses of words – their original senses when used literally, and their extended senses when used metaphorically – imply a single underlying idea known as a conceptual metaphor that constitutes a way of thinking. The original, earlier, more basic or literal sense of a word is known as a 'source domain' and the extended, later and more abstract metaphorical sense is known as a 'target domain'. A conceptual metaphor is inferred from the systematic correspondences, or mappings, between source and target domains. So that, if words from the semantic field of 'racing' – such as 'rat race', 'overtake' or 'catch up' – are used systematically to describe life in general, then we can infer a conceptual metaphor LIFE IS A RACE. If such 'racing' metaphors regularly occur in the political discourse of particular politicians, then this is because they attach ideologically motivated positive values to competition. They may also value the attributes that make winning more likely: fitness, strength, organisation, training, teamwork, strategy, etc. Notice how the conceptual metaphor always commences with the target domain – the concept that the metaphors refer to – here LIFE, and then follows with the semantic field of the more basic sense of these words – here A RACE; they are then joined by the copula. The conceptual metaphor is intended to describe the relatedness of these metaphors through a single cognitive representation that is orthographically represented in upper case. They are not grammatically fixed; for example, the above nominal form could be re-phrased verbally as LIVING IS RACING. The conceptual metaphor can be thought of as the shadow of individual metaphors, like their reflections on the wall of the mind's cave.

Conceptual metaphors are motivated by ways of thinking, or frames, that place constraints on other ways of thinking and often exist in a relationship of complementary distribution with alternative frames. For example, Lakoff (1996) contrasts two alternative politically motivated frames: adherents of traditional social values who follow the Strict Father frame use language based on conceptual metaphors such as MORALITY IS STRENGTH, BEING GOOD IS BEING UPRIGHT and MORALITY IS PURE. By contrast, adherents of socially progressive outlooks use language that is conceptually based on opposing conceptual metaphors such as MORALITY IS EMPATHY, MORAL ACTION IS NURTURANCE and MORAL GROWTH IS PHYSICAL GROWTH. Conceptual metaphors therefore constitute arenas of contested ideological outlook that are manifest in language.

In this chapter, after discussing some related studies, I consider some methodological issues confronting those who seek to research ideological metaphor. I then illustrate how the Competitive Race metaphor can be analysed using the published online records of the British parliament: *Hansard*. Throughout, my purpose is to show the ideological motivation that underlies much choice of language and to demonstrate how the process of identifying metaphors, and the concepts that they assume, is a way of revealing their rhetorical role in the creation of power.

Related studies

Research into ideological metaphor has occurred across a wide range of settings and across diverse genres. Researchers move from identification of particular metaphors in a corpus of texts to claims regarding the cognitive processes involved in their production; these are represented by conceptual metaphors that connect the semantic fields of the metaphor. Researchers provide an explanation of why these metaphors occur, although they differ in the emphasis they place on rhetorical purpose. Their explanations imply that metaphors can be attributed to ideological motives to varying degrees – although it is not always clear how conscious their producers were of such motives because it is difficult for text-based studies to explore the processes behind the production of ideological metaphors.

The idea that analysis of metaphors could identify ideologies originated in Sontag (1989) who argued the use of 'war' metaphors in the treatment of cancer was insensitive to those experiencing the illness. In a political context, Dirven (1994) grouped together various metaphors to identify the differences between Afrikaans and Dutch metaphors in a South African newspaper corpus. As regards competition and sports metaphors, Straehle et al. (1999) found evidence of the notion of 'struggle metaphors' in EU discourse, and as they summarised:

> 'Survival of the fittest' is the general organising principle of human life; economism has adapted this idea and reframed it in terms of competition and rivalry. From the perspective of economism, society exists as a site for permanent competition and struggle, a place where individuals only 'survive' if they internalise the struggling. According to such a world-view, the forces guiding society are not co-operation and solidarity, but competition and rivalry, such that the individual ability to act becomes synonymous with competitiveness.
>
> (Straehle et al. 1999, p. 94)

Howe (1988) identified the use of sports and war metaphors in American political discourse, noting their appeal to men in particular. Semino and Masci (1996) identified the use of football metaphors by the Italian media tycoon Silvio Berlusconi, and Jansen and Sabo (1994) examined the role of sports metaphors in the first Gulf War.

A number of studies have identified a competition frame in business-related genres; for example, Boers (1997) examined a corpus of editorials from *The Economist*, suggesting that competition metaphors were indicative of a free-market ideology and that this was evident from clusters of metaphors relating to the notions of health, fitness and racing. These were classified as ECONOMICS IS HEALTH CARE and ECONOMIC COMPETITION IS RACING, concepts that imply a set of value judgements that impact on decision-making. He argues that most novel figurative language arises from taking established conceptual metaphors, rather than inventing new ones, or from including peripheral aspects of the source domain. Koller (2004) examined marketing texts and proposed that MARKETING IS A SPORTS COMPETITION. In a rigorous study of ideology and metaphor, Goatly (2007) analyses the ideological evidence for the metaphor theme SPEED IS SUCCESS. Downing et al. (2013) examined a corpus of multimodal advertisements to identify e-BUSINESS IS A RACE and HIGH PERFORMANCE e-BUSINESS IS A SPORTS COMPETITION. The authors propose that as e-business has become more familiar, ICT companies have moved away from conventional journey and race metaphors to represent technology companies as animals, drawing on attributes such as speed and agility to compete.

The above studies show how insights from critical linguistics could be applied to metaphor studies, and Critical Metaphor Analysis (Charteris-Black 2004) offered a methodology for this approach. It proposed that in order to understand many different types of metaphor in political and social contexts, it was necessary to examine the contexts in which metaphors occurred. It invited approaches that make inferences about *why* speakers had chosen a metaphor rather than a literal alternative for conveying the same propositional meaning. Examination of the contexts in which metaphors occur provided evidence of speakers' intentions. This approach towards meaning was governed by the tradition of British linguistics, such as Firth and Halliday, which emphasised the importance of context. Critical Metaphor Analysis sought to combine the methodology proposed by Fairclough (1995, p. 6) of identifying linguistic features, and then interpreting and explaining these choices with reference to how far they could be accounted for by differences in power relations.

The distinctive hallmark of the approach is the claim that speakers make linguistic choices in order to achieve rhetorical and ideological purposes. In more recent work (Charteris-Black 2012, 2014), I have emphasised the importance of purpose over intention since speakers – even when their purposes are clear from text-based methodologies – may not be fully conscious of how they achieve them, and because metaphors can simply pop out automatically, as the most persuasive way of framing a particular issue. In political contexts effect is more important than intention. Rhetoric, according to James Berlin (1988), is the study of language in the service of power. From this point of view, what is 'critical' about metaphor choice is that metaphors contribute to the formation of an ideology, and by interpreting and explaining metaphor choices, we can better understand this ideology. Ideology is 'the basis of the social representation shared by members of a group. This means that ideologies allow people, as group members, to organise the multitude of social beliefs about what is the case, good or bad, right or wrong, for them to act accordingly' (van Dijk (1998, p. 8). Ideology may therefore be described as 'meaning in the service of power' (Thompson 1984, quoted in Goatly 2007:1).

After discussing some of the different methodologies used by researchers in the next section, I will analyse the Competitive Race metaphor in British parliamentary debates by tracing its discourse history. Since racing is related to embodied experience of fast movement, I will also illustrate the frame of health and disease that is used to generate ideological metaphors for an anti-EU ideological position through the concept of 'Eurosclerosis'. Competitive running (racing), fitness and health are conceptually related because the body becomes fitter and healthier by running; by contrast, the body that avoids exercise becomes less fit and therefore less healthy. Historically, issues of fitness have become socially important in relation to the threat of international conflict and the fitness level of army recruits – rather than because of concerns for individual health. This was especially the case in the periods prior to the two World Wars when neo-Darwinist views predominated, and wars between nation-states have been viewed as struggles to the death. As Goatly (2007, p. 54) notes: '…constructing activity as a competitive race relates to the question of HUMAN IS ANIMAL metaphor, through neo-Darwinians' and socio-biologists' construction of human society as inexorably competitive'.

I will argue that cultural assumptions of the social value of 'health' has led to a resurgence of the 'fitness' frame and – less visibly – encouraged an orientation towards individualism that Cameron's use of the Competitive Race metaphor assumes. Miliband re-activates another aspect of racing, which is that sports is also a social activity and that 'health' can also be interpreted as having *social* value as well as being *individually* virtuous. By drawing attention to the fact that such metaphors are ideologically contested, I will be encouraging their critical re-evaluation and reframing.

Researching ideological metaphor

Researchers encountering metaphor in political contexts usually start with a hunch about their ideological motivation, either by analysing explicit metaphors (e.g. the use of 'disease' and 'fitness' frames that are activated by metaphoric uses of words such as 'sclerosis', 'cancer', 'overweight' or 'obese'), or by identifying phrases that we might not initially even think of as metaphors because they have become conventional ways of talking about a topic ('the race to the top'). We should immediately notice that this introduces two problems: first, there may be variation in what counts as a metaphor, depending on what cognitive frames are activated by a word for a particular individual; and second, that a single 'metaphor' may spread over several words. I suggest that 'race to the top' is a single metaphor, although it is apparently four words; this is because it contains a single idea. Both problems invite empirical responses: the first by drawing on expert informants; the second by examining a corpus. The identification of possible metaphors leads the researcher to explore hunches by developing research questions that explore issues such as the *topic* and the *genre* of language where such ideological metaphor may occur. Genres include political speeches, the press or broadcast media, or other types of text that has the purpose of influencing how people think – such as political banners/slogans, campaign posters or press releases. The ideological potential of metaphor may be enhanced by a semiotic analysis of images or visual-verbal representations, particularly where these seek to subvert power elites (e.g. satirical cartoons).

Taking into account the geographical and temporal specifications of the discourse topic (such as 'British parliamentary debates in the 1980s'), metaphor researchers may then assemble a dataset/(s) and corpus/corpora (verbal or visual) for the identification of candidate metaphors. This will entail identifying political actors and other agents of social cognition who use metaphor (e.g. politicians, demonstrators, journalists). Researchers will need to fix a time frame for compilation of a dataset that can be examined for metaphor. Taken together, these stages require attention to the issue of genre that overlaps closely with 'political discourse': language designed for a particular ideological effect or purpose. In some cases, researchers undertake empirical research whereby they record focus groups, or undertake psycholinguistic experiments. The design of an appropriate dataset is crucial if claims for ideological metaphor are to be upheld empirically.

Identifying metaphor(s) relating to a political issue(s) entails deciding who will undertake such a task, how they will do it, and perhaps counting metaphors. Typically, this requires an operational definition of metaphor, the use of reference works, corpora, reliability considerations and the use of several analysts' views on whether a particular word or phrase is a metaphor. A common method is to identify a candidate metaphor, say 'fitness' and then search for words in the same semantic field, say 'overweight', 'obese', 'sprint' and 'marathon', all of which could potentially be related to 'fitness'; I have described these as 'metaphor keywords' (Charteris-Black 2004, p. 35). It may also involve initial categorisation of metaphor as conventional, novel or dead. Visual metaphors can be identified by establishing underlying concepts that are evident from semiotic analysis of multimodal genres, such as satirical cartoons.

Once metaphors have been identified, the next stage of analysis requires classification. Initially this may be either by the semantic fields of the words classified as metaphors ('source domains') when they are used with their literal senses, or by the topics they refer to when used with metaphoric senses ('target domains'). Researchers then identify patterns of metaphors and identify their shared cognitive frames, as described above in the introduction (p. 202); this often requires an abstract category to represent a concept shared by a number of metaphors. Depending on the theoretical approach adopted, researchers may propose a conceptual metaphor such as THE NATION IS A BODY to represent this concept.

Once language and concepts have been analysed, and depending again on the theoretical approach, researchers usually make claims that metaphors contribute to the formation of ways of thinking, or 'frames' that influence the current social perceptions that govern future ways of thinking. Van Dijk refers to this process as 'social cognition'. For example, thinking about the nation as a 'body' may frame policies in terms of essential 'surgery'. It may require the leader to 'inject' into the 'patient' a 'medicine' that is necessary to 'cure' a political or economic 'disease'. The post-2008 financial collapse policies of reduced public expenditure are often described as 'austerity'; but whether this is necessary suffering, or a pain inflicted unnecessarily on a long-suffering 'patient' depends on ideological outlook. What is certain is that the metaphor of 'austerity' evokes an argument (with dubious evidence) that short-term sacrifice is a necessary precondition for long term 'health'.

There may, of course, be more than one metaphor frame, and frequently metaphors are contested areas of language use – as we have seen in the contrast between the 'global race' and the 'race to the bottom' metaphors in the discourses of Cameron and Miliband. This is when we move to an explanation of ideological metaphor; this may involve identifying how features occurring in conjunction with metaphor contribute to the identification of ideological metaphor. Analysis of additional discursive features contributes to the identification of underlying purpose and may facilitate triangulation of data by combining verbal and visual evidence of ideology.

The 'Competitive Race' metaphor

In this section, I illustrate how Critical Metaphor Analysis can be employed to identify an ideological metaphor. I do this by outlining the method I have used to identify evidence of the Competitive Race metaphor in the range of British parliamentary genres that are collectively known as *Hansard*. This includes all debates in the House of Lords and House of Commons and those in Westminster Hall; it also includes Written Answers, Written Statements, Lords reports and Grand Committee reports.[3]

'Race' as a noun has three separate entries in the Oxford English Dictionary (2nd edition, 2003): the first is 'A competition between runners, horses, vehicles, boats etc. to see which is the fastest in covering a set course' and I will refer to this as the 'competition sense'. This sense of 'race' originates in the Old Norse *rás* meaning 'current' and was originally a northern English word with the sense 'rapid forward movement'. The second sense is 'each of the major divisions of human kind, having distinct physical characteristics', and it originates from the Italian *razza* (via French) meaning 'a group with common features'. The two senses of the word 'race' are in complementary distribution: that is, the competition sense does not occur in those texts in which the ethnicity sense occurs, and vice versa. The ethnicity sense is relevant in discussions of ideology concerned with national identity, whereas this chapter focuses on the competition sense.

My procedure was first to map out the semantic field for racing, competition and fitness to identify metaphor keywords, and then search on the Hansard web site to establish whether the use of these keywords was metaphoric because a more basic or literal sense of the word or phrase was not relevant in this context. Table 13.1 shows which terms were searched:

One of the difficulties with a large database is the number of 'hits' generated; for example, 'race' alone produced 51,637 hits. The solution I adopted was to search for metaphoric phrases or compound forms containing the word 'race', such as 'rat race' (329 hits) and 'race against time' (105 hits). Once candidate phrases were identified I could produce a much more manageable dataset. For example, 'fast' produced 40,342 hits, whereas 'super-fast' produced only 9 hits. Clearly, a larger study could examine uses of all lemmas in a semantic field, but analysis of phrases, compound forms and less-frequent words allowed sufficient examination of a large data set to identify ideological metaphors.

The database also provided valuable contextual information, for example, the earliest use of 'global race' in parliamentary debates was as follows: 'Jobs have been lost in the textiles industry – because we cannot compete *in the global race to the bottom* with Morocco, Sri Lanka and the far east' (Judy Mallaber, 16 December 1997).

The contextual information shows the name of the speaker, the genre, the topic and date of the debate. A bar graph at the top of the page also shows the frequency of the search term by year and by decade, so it is easy to identify shifts in frequency over time. An advantage of a chronological database of this kind is that it facilitates identification of whether a metaphor was novel when first introduced and to trace its conventionalisation and eventual

Table 13.1 'Racing and Competition' metaphor keywords

Racing and competition general	Fast motion and fitness	Slow motion and unfitness
rat race	super-fast	slow
race against time	high speed	lag
race to the top	sprint	laggard
race to the bottom	pace	tortoise
fast-track	stride	slug
track record	overtake	sluggish
relay	accelerate	sclerosis
	catch up	sclerotic

entrenchment. A lack of awareness of a word being used as a metaphor implies a gradual normalisation process in which a concept becomes cognitively embedded, with clear ideological implications. Psycholinguistic processing of metaphor depends on the extent to which a comparison is cognitively active. For example, I would suggest that the phrase 'rat race' in the 1970s became so entrenched that there was no longer any comparison with the behaviour of rats, as the term came to evaluate negatively any aspect of an unpleasantly competitive life-style. Similarly, in the 1990s, the gradual shift to accepting competition as normal reflects how the competition frame became similarly ideologically entrenched; part of the contestation of metaphor relies on recognising that a use of language is, or once was, a metaphor.

I would like to focus on the ideological motivation of the competition frame that has emerged in the construal of global capitalism as a 'race' of nations seeking to outperform their 'competitors'. I propose that the shift away from the unpleasant evaluation of competition implied by 'rat race' is grounded in neo-Darwinist outlooks that view human progress as some sort of struggle for survival in which those nations with powerful 'genes' in the form of 'transferable skills' in technology and science, are better 'equipped' for survival. The neo-liberal concept of the 'global race' originated in the earlier political concept of nations being involved in an 'arms race'. A search of Hansard in the 1930s shows the rapid emergence of the expression 'arms race'; this was associated with the rise of Hitler and the attempts of Nazi Germany to circumvent the impositions on re-armament that had been imposed by the Treaty of Versailles after the First World War. The concept of an 'arms race' continued in the Cold-War period and enjoyed a considerable resurgence in relation to the foreign policy of Margaret Thatcher and Ronald Reagan. However, the point I would like to emphasise is that throughout the period 1930s–1980s, the notion of 'an arms race' was exclusively negative – irrespective of whether or not speakers supported or opposed military expenditure, and it was rhetorically deployed as an argument to *reject participation in such a race.* A more positive prosody for 'race' began to emerge in the metaphor of the 'space race' – whose original reference was to the competition to put a man on the moon; however, most of the references to 'space race' in *Hansard* are by speakers who criticise the cost of being involved in this 'race', as British political opinion was not favourable towards space exploration at that time.

The idea that social relations between nations can be viewed in terms of a 'race' as compared with other frames, such as co-operation, has become a metaphor of the political right and can be illustrated in the following use by David Cameron when describing the ideological context for policy:

> Because the truth is this. *We are in a global race today*. And that means an hour of reckoning for countries like ours. Sink or swim. Do or decline. To take office at such a moment is a duty and an honour ... and we will rise to the challenge. If we're going to be *a winner in this global race* we've got to beat off this suffocating bureaucracy once and for all.
>
> (Cameron, 15 October 2012)

As well as when announcing policy:

> Today we announce a *new fast-track system* for international patents to reduce the global backlog which stifles growth and enterprise and costs the global economy £7.6 billion for every year patents are delayed.
>
> (Cameron, 28 May 2010)

Competition metaphors and ideology

Enterprise is associated with speed and progress and to be slow is retrograde. I will now summarise findings for three 'competition' metaphors: two based on speed – 'the rat race' and 'the global race' – and one on slowness and illness – 'Euro-sclerosis'.

'The rat race'

In the 1970s, 'the rat race' implied that a 'race' was not something in which any right-minded person would wish to participate and contributed to an ideology of the time that questioned the value of sacrificing quality of life for the accumulation of wealth. Figure 13.1 shows this phrase peaked in the 1970s, and has since declined.

The decline in the negative use of 'arms race' and 'rat race' and their replacement by 'global race' in Tony Blair's and David Cameron's discourse was a purposeful attempt to reverse the negative semantic prosody of the 'race' metaphor. The 'rat race' and the 'arms race' were races to be avoided. By contrast, we are all supposed to want to participate in the 'global race': things are only worth doing if 'we' are going to win because there are no prizes for the also-rans. This indicates a shift in ideology that is indicative of globalisation, the spread of international capitalism and the normalisation of competition. This is a shift away from a society where quality of life was measured in terms of global peace, lower personal stress and where having enough time was more important to national welfare than material advantage and never-ending competition. This shift is illustrated in the following:

> She [Margaret Thatcher] believes that the smaller the size of the public sector in the economy and the larger the market economy, the better. However, that is taken one stage further by the Prime Minister and her Government. The market economy is not just to be let loose in Britain, but is to be seen on a world-wide basis. We are to play our part in that and we must produce, become more efficient and *pay our way in an international rat race*.
>
> (Spearing, 23 July 1981)

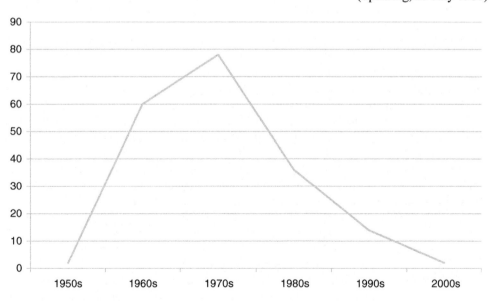

Figure 13.1 Frequency of 'rat race' in *Hansard* 1950–2005

Here the 'rat race' metaphor expresses an ideological opposition to the global market-orientated economy of the type that began to develop in the 1990s and has continued until the present.

'The global race'

The Competitive Race metaphor is evident in Cameron's understanding of the world and of the relationships between individuals and society:

> To get decent jobs for people, you've got to recognise some fundamental economic facts. *We are in a global race today.* No one owes us a living. Last week, our ambition *to compete in the global race* was airily dismissed as *a race to the bottom* ... that it means competing with China on sweatshops and India on low wages. No – those countries are becoming our customers ... and we've got to compete with California on innovation; Germany on high-end manufacturing; Asia on finance and technology.
>
> (Cameron, 2 October 2013)

The value placed on competition was surely instilled [and] nurtured by his education at Eton and Oxford – as well as by his family values (Elliott & Hanning 2012). Cameron assumes an unquestioning sense of legitimacy around the idea of competing. His construal of political policy has also been influenced by the 'speed' frame in literal language as shown in the value placed on projects related to speed:

> My Government will support investment in new *high-speed broadband* internet connections, enable the construction of a *high-speed railway network* and reform the economic regulation of airports to benefit passengers.
>
> (Cameron, 22 May 2010)

> The *super-fast broadband cables* are going to be laid. And *high-speed rail* is going to criss-cross this country.
>
> (Cameron, 28 January 2011)

Here, there is a curious conflation of the speed frame in reference to two otherwise apparently unrelated policy areas: cable networks and rail transport.

However, Competitive Race metaphors were equally prevalent in the discourse of New Labour who, in turn, inherited the racing frame from Margaret Thatcher. Table 13.2 illustrates how, over a relatively long period of time, speed-related metaphors were deployed by Margaret Thatcher and then continued in the discourse of Tony Blair.

There are many other such metaphors characterising the discourse of New Labour that reinforced an ideology based on unregulated market competition – such as being on the 'right track' and gauging policy with reference to a 'track record'. Goatly (2007, p. 53) proposes that they can be conceptually represented as SUCCESS IS SPEED, and reminds us that etymologically 'speed' meant 'success' or 'prosperity' before there were means available for the measurement of speed. However, here it is the competitive element that is salient, implying that LIFE IS A RACE and NATION-STATES ARE COMPETITORS. New Labour became well known for the introduction of 'targets' and 'league tables' in most areas of public life – in particular education and health. Clearly, there was a broad acceptance by both major

Competition metaphors and ideology

political parties of a cognitive construal of government and social relations as a competitive race. In

Table 13.2 'Global race' metaphors in the Thatcher-period and New Labour

Speaker	Metaphors (in italics)
Thatcher, 12 Oct. 1979	The world has never offered us an easy living. There is no reason why it should. We have always had to go out and earn our living – the hard way. In the past we did not hesitate. We had great technical skill, quality, reliability. We built well, sold well. We delivered on time. The world bought British and British was best. Not German. Not Japanese. British. It was more than that. We knew that *to keep ahead* we had to change. People looked to us *as the front runner for the future*.
Thatcher, 8 Oct. 1982	Far-away countries scarcely heard of ten years ago now *overtake us* in our traditional industries. Suddenly we are faced with the need to do everything at once – to wake up, catch up and then *overtake*, even though the future is as hard to predict as ever.
Thatcher, 14 Oct. 1983	Our competitors are improving all the time and some of them *started well ahead of us*. So we must improve *even faster* than they do *if we are to catch up*. It is no good just *beating our previous best*; we have to *beat our competitors*.
Thatcher, 14 Oct. 1988	At home, *the fast pace* of economic growth has put more money into people's pockets and more money into industry's profits.
Blair, 26 Sept. 2000	Don't tell me that a country with our history and heritage, that today boasts six of the top ten businesses in the whole of Europe, with London the top business city in Europe, that *is a world leader* in technology and communication and the businesses of the future, that under us *has overtaken* France and Italy to become the fourth largest economy in the world…
Blair, 1 Oct. 2007	And this underscores I think the profound characteristic of the modern world: *the speed of change*. In truth, globalisation is a fact. It's why resisting it is self-defeating and even absurd. But the inevitable consequence of it, is unquestionably challenging because *it makes change happen at break neck speed* and indeed if you decide to open up, and if you are on the open side of the argument, it happens *even faster*. That's why the natural inclination is to ward it off or seek to place limits on it … So I'm saying this – that globalisation, and the interdependence and *speed of change* that accompanies it, is a fact. However, what we do about it is a choice.
Blair, 1 Oct. 2007	And this is a different type of argument, but it awakens all the old primeval fears about the nature of capitalism. And recent events in the financial market show again the truth of the proposition that globalisation *presses the fast forward button* of world events.
Blair, 18 Mar. 2007	China's wind turbine technology *still lag* [sic] *a few years behind* the state of the art, but is priced at about 30% less than European products – If the level of technology keeps improving China could become *the world leader* in both construction and production of wind energy.

some cases, the competition frame allowed me to identify the theme of a whole speech. From the table above, we see that the speed element of the competition frame was active in a speech given by Blair on the topic of globalisation. This speech starts:

> What I want to talk to you about tonight is really how I see the debate about globalisation in politics today. And the real dividing line to think of in modern politics has less to do with traditional positions of *right* versus left, more to do today, with what I would call the modern choice, which is *open* versus closed. If you take any of the big motivating debates in politics today, in *Europe* or America, *international engagement* or isolation, immigration – is it *good* or bad, free trade – *a benefit* or a fear. Each essentially has, at its core, this question: '*Do we open up*? Albeit with rules and controls, or do we hunker down, do we close ourselves off and wait till the danger has passed? Is globalisation a threat or an *opportunity*?'
>
> (Blair, 1 October 2007)

Here, metaphors occur in combination with antithesis; political choices are presented as stark alternatives in which, in each case, the first item (italicised) is the option that is positively evaluated, while the second (underlined) is the negative option, that is until the *final* question where 'threat *precedes* opportunity' and hence gains added impact. It seems that there is no choice as to whether to engage in the race, because globalisation is represented as 'open', 'good' a 'benefit', and so on – so the answer to the rhetorical question is that globalisation is an opportunity and not a threat.

As Goatly (2007, p. 56ff.) argues, the association between speed and success originates in the treatment of time as a commodity that could be measured, bought and sold, so that time became equivalent to money. Urbanisation, mechanisation and digitalisation all seek to reduce the time involved in production and to make access to markets quicker through accelerating the ordering and transportation processes. However, there are costs entailed by an obsession with speed, such as reduced quality and increased stress: these are much more difficult to measure.

'The Euro-sclerosis metaphor'

Within the competitive frame, 'fast' metaphors convey the positive values of the 'we' group, while 'slow' metaphors convey the negative values of the opposition. A particularly good example of this is the metaphoric use of 'sclerosis' in debates on the European Union. The ubiquitously negative compound form 'Euro-sclerosis' has frequently been used to frame an ideological position on the European Union, as illustrated in Table 13.3.

Conceptually, for its opponents, THE EUROPEAN UNION IS AN ILLNESS, and measures that seek to protect workers are 'sclerotic' because they encourage government regulation and conflict with the Anglo-American business model with its competitively orientated values of being 'lean' and 'fit'. In a study of American political discourse, Howe (1988) argued that the most pervasive sports metaphor was based on the notion of a 'team'. It is employed during campaigns to create a bond between candidate and electorate, or to express a sense of common enterprise and loyalty, while the Competitive Race frame more typically activates individualism and argues against the values of team membership. In other cases, particular aspects of the competition frame are highlighted; for example, the 'relay' metaphor can be used to argue for collective rather than individual effort. The relay is the closest that competitive running gets to being a team sport – as team members have, like politicians, shared objectives. However, in practice 'relay' is more commonly used as a way of criticising those individuals who are *letting down* the team:

The Government should not just thank the commission, as we do, but should apologise to it. *It is as though the captain of the relay team had instructed the runners of the first legs to sprint around the track at high speed, but when the baton was handed over to the captain for the final lap, he relaxed into a leisurely stroll.*

(Young, 19 June 2000)

Table 13.3 'Euro-sclerosis' metaphor in parliamentary debates on the European Union

Speaker	'Euro-sclerosis' metaphors (in italics)
Hurd, 22 Apr. 1993	I find the attitude of the Liberal Democrats more puzzling, because their leader was clear at the outset. A few days before Maastricht, looking ahead as is his wont, he warned that the social chapter could lead to *a form of Euro-sclerosis.*
Lord Alexander of Weedon, 7 Jun. 1993	Europe as a whole has lost its competitiveness over recent years. It is in danger of what a decade ago used to be called '*Euro-sclerosis*'. It is going through a period of structural change.
Major, 15 Jul. 1993	I am glad that the right hon. Gentleman has not forgotten, but perhaps I can remind the House what he said: I believe what is now being put forward in the social chapter may *well lead to a form of Euro-sclerosis.*
Lord Alexander of Weedon 22 Jul. 1993	They are concerned about the high rate of non-wage labour costs. *The spectre of Euro-sclerosis is back* with us again.
Sir Peter Hordern 23 Jul. 1993	*It is an example of Euro-sclerosis.* European companies are increasingly investing overseas because the costs of employment in the Community are becoming prohibitive.
Lord Taverne 14 Mar. 2001	They (the Conservatives) contrast the low tax, low spending and dynamic economy across the Atlantic with its recent high rate of growth and low unemployment on the one hand, with the *so-called 'sclerotic' economies* across the Channel, weighed down with high taxes and high spending which have resulted in low growth and high unemployment…
Campbell, 9 Jul. 2003	It is of course true that there could be enlargement without these provisions being enacted, but it would be a curious European Union which emerged as a result, and one that would be all the more likely to be subject to *paralysis and sclerosis.*

So *after a brisk sprint round the first lap* by Lord Wakeham, *the baton was handed over to a jogger in rather poor shape*, and it has taken the Government nearly two years to produce their response, optimistically entitled 'Completing the Reform'.

(Young, 10 January 2002)

This implies that individualism pervades the Competitive Race frame: the onus is on the individual to stay in shape so as not to let the side down – as in a true public school sporting ethos. It is a doctrine of individual moral responsibility with implications for an individualist society in which 'Let the devil take the hindmost'.

Conclusion

This investigation of metaphors from the semantic field of racing and competition has identified an ideological orientation that has coloured British – and to some extent 'world' – politics during this period. Until recently, there has been an uncritical advocacy of global capitalism within a competitive framework in which countries are equated with runners in a ruthless race in which there are only winners and losers, a race in which the rewards for the winners are high, while there are none for the losers – although a 'safety net' may be provided to prevent social collapse. This has been summarised as NATION-STATES ARE COMPETITORS and LIFE IS A RACE. This implies an acceptance of evolutionary psychological views of an inherent and biologically determined aggression and what Goatly summarises as the 'naturalistic fallacy' that nature is inherently competitive and that humans are driven to self-perpetuate their genes: 'Most theories that accept HUMAN IS ANIMAL as the best explanatory model take as the ground for the model/metaphor the aggression and competitiveness on which Darwinian theories of evolution are based…' (Goatly 2007, p. 159). Not only may models based on aggression be damaging to individual mental health and well-being, but global political stability requires co-operation between nation-states to overcome problems, such as environmental disasters that threaten all states equally. The Competitive Race metaphor is therefore one that is ideologically contested between supporters and opponents of unregulated capitalism and the 'free' market.

More generally, I have tried to demonstrate how clusters of metaphors can be shown to reveal the cumulative cognitive, or cultural, models that constitute the collective beliefs of a community as represented in the minds of its individual members. These models have been summarised using conceptual metaphors. If I have succeeded in raising awareness of how a capitalist ideology underlies many Competitive Race metaphors, then Critical Metaphor Analysis can be said to have done its job of revealing metaphor in the service of power.

Notes

1   See, Charteris-Black (2014) and Perrez & Reuchamps (2015) *Metaphor and the Social World* vol. 5 no. 2 – a special issue on the political impact of metaphors.
2   See Underhill (2012) for a discussion of the term 'world-view'.
3   Available from: http://hansard.millbanksystems.com/. There is also a new online version of Hansard at http://www.hansard-corpus.org.

References

Berlin, J, 1988, 'Rhetoric and ideology in the writing class', *College English* vol. 50, pp. 477–493.
Boers, F, 1997, '"No pain, no gain" in a free market rhetoric: A test for cognitive semantics?' *Metaphor and Symbol*, vol. 12, no. 4, pp. 231–241.
Charteris-Black, J, 2004, *Corpus approaches to Critical Metaphor Analysis*, Palgrave Macmillan, Basingstoke.
Charteris-Black, J, 2011, *Politicians and rhetoric: The persuasive power of metaphor*, 2nd ed., Palgrave Macmillan, Basingstoke & New York.
Charteris-Black, J, 2012, 'Forensic deliberations on "purposeful metaphor"'. *Metaphor and the social world* vol. 2, no. 1, pp. 1–21.
Charteris-Black, J, 2014, *Analysing political speeches: Rhetoric, discourse and metaphor.* Palgrave Macmillan, Basingstoke & New York.
Dirven, R, 1994, *Metaphor and nation: Metaphors Afrikaners live by*, Peter Lang, Frankfurt.

Downing, H, Kraljevic, B, Mujic, B & Núnez-Perucha, B, 2013, 'Metaphorical creativity and recontextualization in multimodal advertisements on e-business across time', *Metaphor & the social world*, vol. 3, no. 2, pp. 199–219.
Elliott, F & Hanning, J, 2012, *Cameron: Practically a Conservative*, Fourth Estate, London.
Fairclough, N, 1995, *Critical Discourse Analysis: The critical study of language*, Longman, London.
Goatly, A, 2007, *Washing the brain: Metaphor & hidden ideology*, John Benjamins, Amsterdam & Philadelphia.
Hansard 1803–2005, ND, Digitised editions of Commons and Lords *Hansard*, available from: http://hansard.millbanksystems.com.
Howe, N, 1988, 'Metaphor in contemporary American political discourse', *Metaphor and Symbolic Activity*, vol. 3, no. 2, pp. 87–104.
Jansen, S C & Sabo, D, 1994, 'The sport/war metaphor: Hegemonic masculinity, the Persian Gulf War, and the new world order', *Sociology of Sport Journal*, vol. 11, pp. 1–17.
Koller, V, 2004, *Metaphor and gender in business media discourse: A critical cognitive study*, Palgrave Macmillan, Basingstoke.
Lakoff, G, 1996, *Moral politics*, University of Chicago Press, Chicago IL.
Lakoff, G & Johnson, M, 1980, *Metaphors we live by*, Chicago University Press, Chicago, IL.
Musolff, A, 2015, *Metaphor, nation and the Holocaust: The concept of the body politic*, Routledge, London.
Perrez, J & Reuchamps, M, eds., 2015, *Metaphor and the social world*, vol. 5 no. 2.
Seliger, M, 1976, *Ideology and politics*, Allen & Unwin, London.
Semino, E & Masci, M, 1996, 'Politics is football: Metaphor in the discourse of Silvio Berlusconi in Italy', *Discourse and Society* vol. 7, no. 2 pp. 243–269.
Sontag, S, 1989, *AIDS and its metaphors*, Allen Lane, London.
Straehle, C, Weiss, G, Wodak, R, Muntigl, P & Sedlak, M, 1999, 'Struggle as metaphor in European Union discourse on unemployment', *Discourse & Society*, vol. 10 no. 1, pp. 67–99.
Thompson, J B, 1984, *Studies in the theory of ideology*, Polity Press, London.
Underhill, J, 2012, *Creating worldviews: Metaphor, ideology & language*, Edinburgh University Press, Edinburgh.
van Dijk, T A, 1998, *Ideology: A multidisciplinary approach*, Sage, Newbury Park, CA.
Wodak, R, 2015, *The politics of fear*, Sage, London.

14
Legitimation and multimodality

Theo van Leeuwen

Legitimation, language and multimodality

The legitimations by means of which individuals or groups 'seek to secure consent to their power from at least the most important among their subordinates' (Beetham 1991, p. 3), has for some time been an important area in the study of language and politics (e.g. Rojo & van Dijk 1997; van Leeuwen & Wodak 1999) and more recently, also in organisation and management studies (e.g. Vaara & Tienar 2008). Such studies consider how language is used to legitimate the power of individuals or groups, and also, more broadly, how social practices are legitimated in all their aspects; not only the individuals and groups that have agentive power in them, but also the actions that constitute them, the ways in which these actions are undertaken, the places where – and the times when – they are undertaken, and the resources that are used to do so (van Leeuwen 2008, pp. 8–12). The legitimacy of the law, for instance, is not only realised linguistically, through the written and spoken language of the law, but also through the layout of courtrooms, the dress (and in some countries, wigs) of lawyers, and so on. The same applies to the legitimacy of the practices that constitute politics. In studying legitimation, attention must therefore be paid, not only to language, but also to the other forms of expression that combine with language in many forms of contemporary political discourse, in short, to multimodality.

The change from power as invested in individuals and groups to power as invested in social practices was strongly influenced by the work of Michel Foucault (e.g. 1977) for whom power is enacted in the practices of institutions such as schools and prisons. Habermas (1976, pp. 71–2) also points out the importance of everyday practices, but with a greater emphasis on agency, viewing practices as planned and implemented through administrative interventions in schooling, city planning, health planning, family and marriage planning, and so on, and stressing that they are not always legitimated through formal legislation, but may also be legitimated through the personalisation of substantive issues, symbolic hearings, expert judgements, expert discourses, advertising techniques and the 'strategic employment of cultural traditions' (*ibidem*, p. 70).

In short, all aspects of practices need legitimation, especially when practices are in the process of being established or changed. This can take many different forms, and is closely connected to the different kinds of normative discourses that regulate practices. Above all, legitimations seek to give meaning to social practices, linking practices to the 'human craving for meaning that appears to have the force of instinct' and the human 'compulsion to impose a meaningful order upon reality' (Habermas 1976, p. 118). Finally, the inclusion of all the various elements of social practices – actions, participants and their roles, manner, times, places and resources – points to the need for a multimodal approach to the analysis of legitimation (or of de-legitimation, critique), which includes the behavioural style and dress and grooming of powerful (and less powerful) actors, the way power is expressed by spatial arrangements, the multimodal technological resources involved, and so on.

An account of the meanings people attach to the practices they engage in is, by nature, descriptive – such meanings vary historically and contextually. In a fragmented and heterogeneous society, the same practices may be legitimated differently in different social contexts, or by different groups of people. Kress (1985) described how Helen Caldicott, in a speech at an anti-nuclear rally in Sydney, legitimated the action of taking part in the protest in many different, sometimes even contradictory ways: 'medical, Christian, populist, (Jungian) psychiatric, patriotic, sentimental/parental, romantic, patriarchal, technological, prophetic, feminist' (Kress 1985, p. 17). In other words, Caldicott showed she was aware that the participants in the rally were united in what they did, participating in a protest, but divided in the meanings they attached to it. But if meaning is fragmented, if it is *doing* rather than meaning that provides social cohesion, what replaces legitimation? Is meaning, as Habermas said, 'a scarce resource becoming scarcer' (1976, p. 73), reduced to clichés and superseded by function (Zijderveld 1979)? Has the separation of instrumental functions from expressive symbols released an 'unspecific readiness to follow' (Habermas 1976, p. 70), stimulated by advertising techniques that appeal to unconscious and emotive – rather than rational and moral – motives, and underpinned by anti-humanist theories that seek to explain human behaviour by analogy to animal behaviour? If so, attention to multimodality is crucial for a critical analysis of these phenomena, given the role of visual and musical communication in many important domains of communication, and their ability to link aesthetics and affect to functional purposes. And attention to advertising, which has pioneered this kind of multimodality and which, in the age of the 'marketization of discourse' (Fairclough 1993), has deeply influenced many other forms of discourse, including politics, is equally crucial.

A few further points need to be made. First, legitimation will take different forms, depending on whether it is persuasive or confirmatory. The persuasive role of legitimation comes to the fore when new or changed practices are proposed. This involves the de-legitimation of existing practices, as well as the legitimation of the proposed changes – or, when changes are being opposed, the de-legitimation of the proposed changes and the re-legitimation of the established practices. All this must be done with the kind of strategies that will be discussed below. Once a practice is established, however, critique is likely to be disempowered or isolated from the mainstream, institutionalised in ways that remove its power to mount effective challenges. The values that underlie the persuasive arguments are now objectivated, given 'cognitive validity' (Berger & Luckmann 1966, p. 111). Here, language plays a crucial role, described by Berger and Luckmann as 'incipient legitimation' (*ibidem*, p. 112):

> Incipient legitimation is present as soon as a system of linguistic objectifications of human experience is transmitted. For example, the transmission of a kinship vocabulary

ipso facto legitimates the kinship structure. The fundamental legitimating 'explanations' are, so to speak, built into the vocabulary.

(Berger & Luckmann 1966, p. 111)

However, incipient legitimation can also be realised visually or musically. Visual stereotypes, though usually originating in explicit scientific and other discourses, can communicate social relations of class, gender, race and ethnicity (van Leeuwen 2008), and stereotypes also exist in music: the 'representative style' of Western music, for instance, originally developed in seventeenth-century Italian opera, created musical motifs to signify gender stereotypes, which have continued into contemporary film music and are recognised and understood by audiences who may not consciously be aware of what it is they respond to (McClary 1991). Discourse analysts should therefore not only focus on the analysis of texts, but also on the analysis of vocabularies of this kind, especially now they have become readily available through digital image banks and music libraries for use, not just by specialists, but also by ordinary people creating multimodal messages on social media, such as Instagram. This should include tracing such stereotypes back to the more explicit discourses that originated them. Nederveen Pieterse (1992) has, for instance, described how racist stereotypes of black people were developed (and linked to negative character traits) by late eighteenth and early nineteenth century scientists, thus legitimating slavery and colonisation – but while these explicit discourses have been forgotten, the visual stereotypes they gave rise to continue, especially in comic strips, advertisements, computer games and other entertainment media.

In sum, the critical analysis of meaning-making should attend to multimodality for a number of reasons:

- Legitimation is not just realised linguistically, but also visually and musically. Just as in the Middle Ages, visual art and church music expressed the theological ideas that legitimated the power of the Church, so today visual art and music express many of the neo-liberal values that underlie contemporary society, especially in advertising and entertainment media.
- At the same time, de-legitimation plays a crucial role in critiquing oppositional values (and of course also in oppositional discourses themselves). De-legitimation, too, can be multimodally realised. Terms like 'flood' and 'influx' have their visual equivalents in the current 'refugee crisis', in the images of large groups of dishevelled refugees that can legitimate the closing of borders and the erection of walls, while shots of a single refugee looking dismally at the tents of the Calais camp and the sea beyond, can legitimate helping refugees – through the kind of personalisation and emotivisation that Habermas noted.
- Finally, discourse analysts should also analyse the digital 'vocabularies' of images and music that provide the resources for expressing the dominant legitimation discourses.

This chapter will therefore attempt to show in some detail how legitimation may be realised multimodally and outline an approach to analysing it. It is based on an earlier framework for analysing linguistic realisations of legitimation (van Leeuwen & Wodak 1999; van Leeuwen 2008), and will discuss three types of legitimation, which can of course occur in various combinations: (1) authority legitimation based on the authority of people who can exercise power, or of documents that bestow that power (p. 221); (2) moral evaluation legitimation, legitimation based on moral values (p. 226); (3) rationalisation legitimation, legitimation based on theories of reality (p. 229).

Authority legitimation

I will distinguish three kinds of authority legitimation. The first is *authority* properly speaking. In this case, a practice, or some element or part of it, is legitimate because someone in whom authority is vested says so (personal authority), or because it says so in a document or other artefact with normative power, for instance a legal document or a set of rules. The second I will refer to as *commendation* legitimation. In this case, a practice, or some element or part of it, is legitimate because it is recommended by an acknowledged expert or engaged in by a role model, whether a peer leader, or a distant celebrity, hero or saint. The third is legitimation by *custom*, which may either be a matter of *conformity*, in which case a practice is legitimate 'because everyone does it', or a matter of *tradition*, in which case it is legitimate because 'it has always been done this way'. In what follows, I will discuss how each of these may be realised linguistically, visually and musically, and hence multimodally, when such realisations are combined in a single text or communicative event.

Personal authority

In the case of *personal authority*, legitimate authority is vested in a person because their status or role in a particular institution affords them agentive power in the relevant social practice, for example, parents and teachers in the case of children. Such authorities then do not need to justify what they do to others – or require others to do – other than by a mere 'because I say so' – although in practice, they may provide reasons and arguments, and although their authority may ultimately be based on impersonal grounds, for example, on religious ideas about the role of the father in a family, or the king in a monarchy, or on the job description of a manager. Bernstein (1971, p. 154) saw personal authority as one of the hallmarks of the 'positional family' in which 'judgements are a function of the status of the member' and 'disputes are settled by the relative power inhering in the respective statuses'. It is therefore not surprising that many examples of personal authority can be found in children's books, usually taking the form of a verbal process clause in which the authority's utterance contains some form of obligation modality, linking the mandatory nature of the action to its legitimacy, as in these quotes from children's books:

> Magnus sat down. Because the teacher said they had to.
> (van Leeuwen 1981, author translation)

> 'It's time to go home', she said [i.e. the Mother].
> (Leete-Hodge ND)

But personal authority may also be expressed in other ways, as in the opening sentence of former US President George W. Bush's declaration of war:

> On my orders, coalition forces have begun striking selected targets of military importance.
> (Bush 2003)

Or as in this quote from the CEO of Rank Xerox, London, taken from an in-house staff magazine:

> I want to see leadership deeper in the organization. I want to extend the management of our company beyond the first line. I want all 143 senior managers to take ownership of the business.
>
> (Rank Xerox 1996a)

Visual personal authority legitimation can be realised by visual signifiers of rank and status. On the famous First World War recruitment poster ('Your Country Needs You') Lord Kitchener is not only shown in military uniform, but also sports an intimidating Prussian moustache as he imperiously points his finger at the viewer. As Bush declared war on Iraq, the camera showed the US flag and the presidential seal, to lend authority to his words. Judges, ministers of religion and police officers wear uniforms to signify their powers. In short, the visual realisation of personal authority rests on dress, grooming and accessories of authority.

Impersonal authority

Impersonal authority legitimation rests on the authority of laws, rules and regulations. It, too, often takes the form of verbal process clauses, with the carrier of the impersonal authority ('policy', 'regulation', 'law', etc) as the 'sayer' of statements ('The rules state…', 'The law says…', *The Bible* says…'), or the doer of actions for which power is required, as in the following quotes, again from the Rank Xerox staff magazine, relating to an obligatory training programme (despite the term 'encourage'), and a *Guardian* newspaper column on the refugee crisis:

> The 3D Programme – Define, Decide and Develop – encourages every individual to take control of his/her own career.
>
> (Rank Xerox 1996b)

> The international law of refugees (including the 1951 convention) bars the forced return of refugees
>
> (Sachs 2015)

Visually, impersonal authority legitimation may be realised by visual elements of documents – seals, coats of arms, signatures, certain forms of typography, and so on, and 'Jihad' is often legitimated by showing a copy of *The Quran* (Figure 14.1).

Authority can also be realised through musical signifiers associated with authoritative institutions such as the Church or the nation-state, and the emotive power of music plays a key role in creating and sustaining emotive allegiance to such institutions. After the French Revolution, a National Institute of Music was created to 'support and bestir by its accents, the energy of the defenders of equality, and to prohibit the music which softens the soul of the French with effeminate sounds' (quoted in Attali 1985, p. 55), and music played an equally important role in legitimating and supporting power in Nazi Germany and Stalinist Russia (van Leeuwen 1999).

A key function of authority music is the *heraldic* function of music, its function of announcing authoritative statements and actions, for instance, the arrival of an authority at an official event, or the national news bulletin. Heraldic music of this kind tends to use energetic ascending melodies in major key, martial tempos, dotted rhythms, and brass instruments in musical motifs, which musicologists have also called 'masculine' and 'heroic'

Legitimation and multimodality

Figure 14.1 Impersonal authority as a legitimation for jihad[1]

(van Leeuwen 1999). Such music is to be listened to with the same deference also accorded to powerful people – standing up, and listening silently and solemnly. The audio-visual logos of many major corporations use similar heraldic motifs, but with different timbres. IT companies, such as Microsoft, Intel and others, for instance, combine the electronic sounds that signify technological excellence with warmer instrumental sounds that add a human touch.

Expert authority

Expert authority legitimation rests on expertise rather than status. Such expertise is often stated explicitly, by mentioning the expert's credentials, but if the expert is well known, this can be omitted. Expert authority is not as binding as personal or impersonal authority, but expertise is nevertheless a powerful force in society, frequently used in the media, which play a key role in translating science (especially psychology) into legitimate practices, especially in areas that are not formally regulated and yet play a significant role in social life – health, beauty, relationships, and so on. Typically, it takes the form of verbal process clauses with the well-credentialed expert as subject, as in these quotes from *Cosmopolitan* magazine and from a *Guardian* report criticising the UK Government's foreign policy

> 'We know that the combination of a healthy diet, regular exercise and positive visualization yields optimal results', says Robert Wolff, PhD, author of *Home Body Building* and creator of greatbodygreatlife.com
>
> (*Cosmopolitan*)

> Authors of the report prepared by a commission convened by the London School of Economics include the former head of intelligence Sir Richard Dearlove, the prime minister's former adviser in international affairs Jonathan Luff and HSBC's chief economist Stephen King. The report claims that 'successive prime ministers and foreign secretaries have shied away from significant foreign policy engagements'
>
> (Wintour & Sparrow 2015)

In the age of professionalism, expertise gradually acquired authority in many domains of practice including child rearing, nutrition, and eventually even sexuality. 'In any area where a human need can be imagined', wrote Ivan Illich (1977, p. 19) 'the new professions, dominant, authoritative, monopolistic, legalised – and at the same time debilitating and effectively disabling the individual – have become the exclusive experts of the public good'. Today, however, experts increasingly have to surrender their professional autonomy to management structures, while the public is increasingly made aware that most problems have more than one expert solution, as instantiated, for instance, by the replacement of expert columns in magazines with the 'hot tips' genre (cf. Machin & van Leeuwen 2008b), which positions readers as consumers of advice, rather than, for instance, as 'patients' or 'counsellees'.

Visually, expertise will be signified by laboratory paraphernalia, books, stethoscopes or other professional attributes – in other words, by the superficial badges of expertise, rather than by a visualisation of their expert judgements. Advertisements freely make use of such signifiers to support claims for products no actual expert would endorse.

Role model authority

Role models legitimate practices by engaging in them or endorsing them. Role model authority plays a particularly important role in advertising and lifestyle media. Home decoration magazines, for instance, legitimate ways of decorating private homes by presenting stories of the way media personalities renovate and decorate their homes, and magazine celebrity profiles often describe their diets, health and exercise routines, and so on in enough detail for readers to adopt them. But it can play a role in politics too, as when stars of stage and screen endorse US presidential candidates. After the Second World War, American popular culture spread the idea of the role model, encouraging young people across the world to take their cues from their peers and from popular culture, rather than from their elders and from tradition. This in turn facilitated the rapid turnover of consumer preferences that has become so vital to the contemporary economy and to the 'lifestyle identities' it has fostered. The linguistic examples below are from a teacher-training textbook and a *Cosmopolitan* magazine feature, illustrating role modelling by exemplary peers and distant celebrities:

> Experienced teachers involve the whole class in supporting the newcomer
> (Cleave, Jowett & Bate 1982)

> Halle Berry is wearing Revlon LipGlide Colour Gloss in Cherry Ice
> (*Cosmopolitan*)

Visually, celebrities are often instantly recognisable, so that role model authority can be conveyed simply by showing celebrities engaged in the to-be-legitimated actions or with to-be-legitimated actors. In a video of Obama's second election campaign, Robert de Niro is instantly recognised, standing to the right of Obama, and strategically positioned behind a lectern that carries the slogan 'Change we can believe in'.

In a study of advertisements for contraception (van Leeuwen et al., forthcoming), many of the ads show women or couples talking together and exchanging experiences, for instance, about contraceptive implants, complete with lines of dialogue ('No scars and a fast recovery made our decision easy'). Even though these ads are directed at general practitioners, because most countries do not allow direct advertising of pharmaceuticals products to consumers, they show no discussions between women and their doctors, as if peers are a more reliable source of information than experts.

Insofar as singers are role models, and they often are, music can play a significant role in legitimating practices. Songs provide, for instance, scenarios for dating and relationships of different kinds, and although these are formulated linguistically in the lyrics, the music can add value to this, using principles, which will be discussed under the heading of 'moral evaluation' (p. 226). Another musical realisation is the 'call and response' song structure in which a leader sings a line or a whole verse and is then responded to by a choir. In television commercials aimed at children, for instance, the leader tends to be either another child, the 'opinion leader' of the peer group, as it were, or an adult who sings in a funny 'clown' voice, that is, an adult who is definitely not a parent or a teacher and acts out a kind of funny-uncle-who-always-brings-a-present role. These, so advertisers apparently think, are the types of 'leaders' who children will follow (van Leeuwen 1999).

The authority of tradition

Although the authority of tradition has been declining in many domains, tradition legitimation is still common, linguistically realised through key words such as 'tradition', 'practice', 'custom', 'habit', as for instance, in this example:

> Tony Abbott defended the canvassing of political donations from big business as a time-honoured practice which prevents taxpayers from being forced to subsidise election campaigns.
>
> (Owens 2014)

The term 'time-honoured' is the key in this example, suggesting the practice 'has always been done this way'. In fact, many traditions are much more recent than is often assumed (Hobsbawn & Ranger 1983). A mythical origin, further back in time, may then be invoked. Recently, for instance, politicians everywhere have celebrated the Magna Carta (which dates from 1215) as the origin of practices such as habeas corpus, jury trial, equality before the law, the independence of the judiciary, and representative government – all of which did not in fact emerge until much later (Krygier 2015). Thus, David Cameron could say:

> The great charter shapes the world for the best part of a millennium to promote arguments for justice and freedom.
>
> (Cameron cited in Krygier 2015, p. 1)

Tradition lends itself well to visual and musical realisations, simply by relating past practices and products and past forms of music to contemporary practices and products. Advertisements for certain products often stress tradition, for instance, by showing traditional craft workers in commercials for mass-produced products, or using classical music to accompany commercials for cars. The past still holds considerable value, especially in contexts where past glory is revered.

The authority of conformity

The implied message of conformity legitimation is that if everyone else does it, so should you. It is used to legitimate practices for which no formal regulation exists, but it can nevertheless have mandatory force because of the social pressure it invokes. Linguistically, it often manifests itself in statements that include high-frequency modality, whether through words like 'many' or 'most' or through fine-grained statistics, as in this example from the *Guardian*, which repeats the large number of protestors to de-legitimate bull-fighting:

> Hundreds of thousands of Spaniards have lodged their opposition to plans by the conservative government to introduce a two-year bull-fighting course in state schools. More than 430,000 people have signed a petition against the idea.
>
> (*The Guardian*)

Even in practices such as city planning, practices may be legitimated by 'what the others do', as in this example, quoted from the *Sydney Morning Herald*:

> Madrid is now following the example of other European cities by building a new light rail system.
>
> (*Sydney Morning Herald*)

Conformity can also be realised visually. Advertisements often show a range of users of the advertised product or service to indicate that it has something to offer to all: 'Something is provided for all, so that none may escape' (Horkheimer & Adorno 1982, p. 123). There may then be subtle differences between the users to signify that using the same products as everyone else can combine with unique individuality.

Musically, conformity can be realised by unison singing, which is a feature of many practices – from church services to soccer matches. Here, too, a measure of individuality can be retained through differences in 'vocal blend', the degree to which individual timbres blend or can still be discerned. The male choirs in beer commercials are often rough, with individual voices standing out clearly, while the female choirs in many other commercials tend to be well blended. This constructs men as being more individuated than women – and less orientated towards values of solidarity (cf. van Leeuwen 1999)

Moral evaluation

Moral evaluation legitimation is based on moral values rather than on authority. In some cases it is simply asserted by troublesome words such as 'good' and 'bad', which freely travel between moral, aesthetic and hedonistic territories, and this may of course be combined with authority legitimation, as when George W. Bush legitimised the War on Terror by calling his enemies an 'axis of evil'. But in most cases, moral evaluation is linked to specific discourses of moral value. However, these values are not explicitly asserted, and hence not opened up to debate. They are only hinted at, by means of adjectives such as 'healthy', 'normal', 'natural', 'useful', and so on. These then form the top of a submerged iceberg of moral values, which is never explicated. They trigger a moral concept, but are detached from the system of interpretation they derive from. In other words, they transmute moral discourses into the kind of 'generalized motives', which Habermas said 'are now widely used to ensure mass loyalty' (1976, p. 36).

As a result, moral evaluations, whether linguistically or multimodally expressed, cannot be identified on the basis of explicit signifiers. We can only recognise them – without fully knowing what it is we recognise. John Berger described this well in relation to advertising:

> Vague historical or poetic or moral references are always present. The fact that they are imprecise and ultimately meaningless is an advantage: they should not be understandable, they should merely be reminiscent of cultural lessons half-learnt.
> (Berger 1972, p. 140)

Only the discourse *historian* can explain the moral status of these expressions, by tracing them back to the moral discourses that underlie them and making explicit what was lost over time.

Three types of moral evaluation can be discerned: 'evaluation', 'analogy' and 'abstraction'.

Evaluation

Evaluative adjectives play a key role in moral evaluation. Here are some linguistic examples from my study of the legitimation of schooling:

> It is perfectly normal to be anxious about starting school.
>
> Showing signs of stress about starting school is a natural and healthy response.
> (van Leeuwen 2008)

'Naturalisation' ('it is only natural') is a specific form of moral evaluation that legitimates social practices, in principle on the basis of (socio-)biological arguments, but here, no detailed arguments are given. 'Normalisation' suggests norms, but what these norms are and where they come from, we do not learn. And few would stop to ask themselves in which ways stress might be healthy. Here are some further examples, from a recent *Guardian* commentary on the refugee crisis:

> Asserting that Europe's door is open to migrants and refugees without limit is reckless, not compassionate.
>
> Wide-open doors are unfeasible and unmanageable.
> (Sachs 2015)

Here, a commentator rejects compassion and asserts 'good management' as acceptable legitimations for a European refugee policy and, indirectly, recommends adopting 'risk aversion' instead – as well as, throughout the column, refusing to distinguish between migrants and refugees.

Analogy

Another way of expressing moral evaluations is by analogy – comparisons in discourse almost always have a legitimating or critical function. In other words, they say 'this is legitimate because it is *like* something else which we all agree is legitimate', or 'this is not legitimate because it is like something which we all agree is not legitimate'. Sometimes, the comparison is implicit. An activity that belongs to one social practice is described in terms which, literally speaking, belong to another social practice.

Visual analogy is quite common, for instance in political cartoons. In a Gulf War cartoon by the Australian cartoonist Moir, a nurse shouting 'Emergency!' rushes a patient on a stretcher labelled 'Arab goodwill' into an operating theatre, towards a surgeon labelled 'The West'. Here, the operation of emergency diplomacy is compared to surgery – a comparison that is often used to legitimate practices, for instance, military operations, as being effective and precise (Moir 1991).

Abstraction

In the case of abstraction, the terms that are used to refer to social practices, or to their component actions, are abstract in the sense that they represent not the actions themselves, but some quality of them that can be linked to discourses of moral value. To again, give some examples from my study of the legitimation of schooling, instead of 'the child goes to school for the first time', we say 'the child takes up independence', so that the practice of schooling is legitimised in terms of a discourse of 'independence'. Instead of 'playing in the playground', we get 'co-operate', which legitimises playing in terms of a discourse of sociability, in other words, as an activity from which something is to be learnt. Instead of attending parents' nights, we say 'build up a relationship with the school' or 'be involved with the school', abstractions which foreground desired and legitimate qualities of co-operation, engagement and commitment. In the following example, practices supported by international aid are legitimated on economic grounds, as 'building stable economic futures', without any indication of what they would actually consist of:

> Europe's aid budgets are being swallowed in caring for refugees on European soil, when that money should be used to build stable economic futures in the source countries.
> (Sachs 2015)

The visual and musical representation of moral values is becoming increasingly important and dominant. Just as there was, in Medieval and Renaissance art, a vocabulary of emblems to visualise virtues and vices, so, today, vocabularies are developing for the visualisation of contemporary neo-liberal values. Machin (2004) has researched one of these, the Getty Image Bank. It allows images to be searched with keywords that are every bit as vague as 'building stable economic futures', but also every bit as indicative of neo-liberal values, for instance 'exploration', 'curiosity', 'innovation', 'growth', 'spirituality', 'balance', 'satisfaction', 'freedom', 'fun', 'creativity', 'learning', 'expertise', and so on. When 'freedom' is searched, tens of thousands of images of freedom can be inspected – for the most part women jumping, on the beach, or in a wide-open field where there are no other people in sight (Figure 14.2). The only political images in this category are a few images of US jet fighters and of the Statue of Liberty, with or without war planes overhead. As Machin comments, freedom here 'is not ideological, not something that needs to be protected or fought for, it is a mood, a passing feeling, and drawing on individualistic new age concepts such as serenity and spirituality' (*ibidem*, p. 332). These images are well produced, and Getty provides them cheaply, with all rights pre-paid. As a result, they are ubiquitous across the globe – in advertisements, in magazines, in health brochures, and even in news magazines.

Music, too, can express moral values. Anyone who is at all exposed to contemporary media can recognise the musical signifiers of love, nature, technology, innocence and many

Legitimation and multimodality

Figure 14.2 'Freedom' according to Getty Images

other highly valued notions – without necessarily knowing what it is they recognise. And here, too, music libraries classify music in terms that include such values (cf Tagg 1983). Different kinds of music can also be associated with periods, countries, social classes, age groups, and so on, and hence with the values, or 'myths', in Barthes' terms (1973) which, in the given cultural context, are associated with these periods, countries, classes and age groups.

Rationalisation

In the case of moral evaluation, rationality has gone underground. In the case of rationalisation, morality remains oblique and submerged, even though no rationalisation can function without it. The following, for instance, is, on the surface, a carefully worded rational argument, but it cannot serve to de-legitimate 'opening Europe's doors' without value-laden terms like 'unviable', 'catastrophe' and 'crisis', as in this sentence from a *Guardian* commentary:

> If conditions abroad are unviable, the wars, migrations and environmental catastrophes driving today's crisis will continue to be replicated and expanded.
>
> (Sachs 2015)

I have distinguished two main types of rationalisation. Instrumental rationality legitimates practices by reference to their goals, uses and effects. Theoretical rationality legitimates practices by reference to a theory of 'how things are'.

Instrumental rationalisation

Like legitimations, purposes are constructed in discourse in order to explain why social practices exist, and why they take the form they do. In order to serve as legitimations, purpose constructions must contain an element of moralisation, in the sense in which I have described it in the previous section. Only this can turn purposes and purposiveness into what Habermas has called (1976, p. 22) a strategic-utilitarian morality. Here is the purpose of 'honest reflection' (by means of which the *Guardian* commentator both reflects back to the argument against 'opening Europe's doors' and legitimates that argument), complete with moral evaluations ('clear thinking' and 'least bad options'):

> Such honest reflection could, by itself, help our societies think more clearly about the least bad options
>
> (Sachs 2015)

Theoretical rationalisation

In the case of theoretical rationalisation, legitimation is grounded, not in whether the action is morally justified or not, nor in whether it is purposeful or effective, but in whether it is founded in some kind of truth, some account of 'the way things are', for instance through definitions, in which one activity is defined in terms of another, moralised activity; for example, school signals that the child is growing up.

In the case of explanations, it is not the practice that is defined or characterised, but one of the actors involved. The action is legitimate because it is considered appropriate to the nature of the actors, their general attributes or habitual activities.

Berger and Luckmann distinguished between 'experiential' and 'scientific' rationalisations. Experiential rationalisations they described as 'various explanatory schemes relating sets of objective meanings', and they added that 'these schemes are highly pragmatic, directly related to concrete actions', typically taking the form of 'proverbs, moral maxims and wise sayings' (Berger & Luckmann 1966, p. 112). Scientific rationalisations are 'differentiated bodies of knowledge' that are developed to legitimate specific institutions, as we have seen. Psychology, for instance, produces discourses that can be used to legitimise social practices, through the way they inform 'the changing popular syntheses of isolated items of scientific information' (Habermas 1976, p. 80). In this example, a psychological study legitimises sex between older people (read 're-legitimise' instead of 'rediscover'):

> A study in the journal *Psychology and Aging* surveyed 5,500 people aged 20–95 and found that desire was just as important as companionship for those aged 60 and over. What's interesting is that this has to be rediscovered again and again, as though it so contradicts the dominant narratives around ageing and sex that we can't believe it.
>
> (Karpf 2015)

Images and music, and even typography, can of course express the characteristics of social actors. Erving Goffman (1976) brilliantly analysed the gendered poses that express gender characteristics in advertisements. Again, certain kinds of irregular and multi-coloured fonts immediately suggest children's books, or invitations to children's parties, but also express a view of what children are like – unruly, not yet able to produce neat, ordered writing, but also joyful and exuberant. Such traits also rest on theories. But these are not made explicit in the way that definitions are. They are moral evaluations rather than rationalisations. Images can also display the trappings of rational discourses – graphs, tables, and so on. But as in the case of visual expert authority legitimation, these only connote rationality, and do not provide actual rationalisations.

Conclusion

In this chapter I have attempted to show that most forms of legitimation can be expressed visually and musically, and I have tried to indicate how this can be done.

I have argued that visual and musical legitimation, as they are currently used, and in contradistinction to written texts, can legitimate only with reference to the outward manifestations of authority, rather than to any arguments that actually ground such authority, and that moral evaluations, whether linguistically or multimodally expressed, are detached from the discourses that underlie them and make them explicit.

Finally, I have argued that these forms of legitimation originated in the practices of advertising, and have now permeated many other domains, including digital technologies such as image banks and music libraries that now play such an important role in communication.

For discourse analysts, it is therefore important to mount a critique of these forms of legitimation and to recognise that, as a result, meaningful legitimation, legitimation that can be seen as valid across fragmented and heterogeneous societies, is indeed becoming scarcer, so that legitimation can indeed be said to be in crisis. Just as the discourse historian needs to rediscover where today's moral buzzwords come from, the critical analyst needs to rediscover sources of legitimation that can be meaningful in complex and diverse societies. And finally, in all this, it should be remembered that the visual and music are not restricted to the legitimating uses to which today's strategic-functional communication puts them. A rescue operation may be in order.

Note

1 From: http://republic.buzz.com/Obama-islam-prohibits-terrorist-for-the-quran-says-whoever-kills-an-innocent-it-is-as-if-he-has-killed-all-mankind.

References

Attali, J, 1985, *Noise – The political economy of music*, Manchester University Press, Manchester.
Barthes, R, 1973, *Mythologies*, Paladin, London.
Beetham, D, 1991, *The legitimation of power*, Macmillan, Basingstoke.
Berger, J, 1972, *Ways of seeing*, Penguin, Harmondsworth.
Berger, P & Luckmann, T, 1966, *The social construction of reality*, Penguin, Harmondsworth.
Bernstein, B, 1971, *Class, codes and control* 1, RKP, London.
Bush, G W, 2003, 'War declaration', available from: http://edition.cnn.com/2003/US/03/19/sprj.irq.int.bush.transcript/.
Cleave, S, Jowett, S & Bate, M, 1982, *And so to school*, NFER-Nelson, Windsor, p. 41.
Fairclough, N, 1993, 'Critical Discourse Analysis and the marketization of public discourse: the universities', *Discourse & Society* 4(2), pp. 133–169.
Foucault, M, 1977, *Discipline and punish – the birth of the prison*, Allen Lane, London.
Goffman, E, 1976, *Gender advertisements*, Macmillan, London.
Habermas, J, 1976, *Legitimation crisis*, Heinemann, London.

Hobsbawn, E & Ranger, T, 1983, *The invention of tradition*, Cambridge University Press, Cambridge.

Horkheimer, M & Adorno, T, 1986, *Dialectic of enlightenment*, Continuum, New York.

Illich, I, 1977, *Disabling professions*, Marion Boyars, London.

Leete-Hodge, L, ND, *Mark and Mandy*, Peter Haddock, London.

Karpf, A, 2015, 'Sex isn't the preserve of the young', *The Guardian*, 6 November 2015, available from: www.theguardian.com/commentisfree/2015/nov/06/sex-young-over-60s.

Kress, G, 1985, *Linguistic processes in sociocultural practice*, Deakin University Press, Geelong, VIC.

Krygier, M, 2015, 'Magna Carta and the rule of law tradition', presentation at the Magna Carta 800 Symposium, Parliament House, 30 October 2015.

Machin, D, 2004, 'Building the world's visual language: The increasing global importance of image banks in corporate media', *Visual Communication* 3(3), pp. 316–336.

Machin, D & van Leeuwen, T, 2008, *Global media discourse – a critical introduction*, Routledge, London.

McClary, S, 1991, *Feminine endings: Music, gender and sexuality*, University of Minnesota Press, Minneapolis, MN.

Moir, A, 1991, *Moir's Gulf*, Wild and Woolley, Sydney.

Nederveen Pieterse, J, 1992, *White on black: Images of Africans and Blacks in Western popular culture*, Yale University Press, New Haven, CT.

Owens, J, 2014, 'Joe Hockey seeks legal advice over corporate donor accusations', *The Australian*, 5 May 2014, available from: www.theaustralian.com.au/national-affairs/joe-hockey-seeks-legal-advice-over-corporate-donor-accusations/news-story/b0f205fce7bc9f0829f7e297158bd4f4.

Rank Xerox, 1996a, *XL The Document*, iss. 5.

Rank Xerox, 1996b, *Document Matters*.

Rojo, L M & van Dijk, T A, 1997, 'There was a problem and it was solved: Legitimating the expulsion of illegal migrants in Spanish parliamentary discourse', *Discourse & Society* 8(4), pp. 523–566.

Sachs, J, 2015, 'There's no perfect answer to the migrant crisis and we must face it', *The Guardian*, 2 November 2015, available from: www.theguardian.com/opinion/migration.

Tagg, P, 1983, 'Nature as a musical mood category', Göteborg, *IASPM Internal Publications* P 8206.

Vaara, E & Tienar, J, 2008, 'A discursive perspective on legitimation strategies in multinational corporations', *Academy of Management Review* 33(4), pp. 985–993.

Van Leeuwen, J, 1981, *De Metro van Magnus*, Omniboek, Den Haag.

van Leeuwen, T, 1999, *Speech, music, sound*, Macmillan, London.

van Leeuwen, T, 2008, *Discourse and practice: New tools for Critical Discourse Analysis*, Oxford University Press, New York.

van Leeuwen, T & Wodak, R, 1999, 'Legitimizing immigration control: A discourse-historical analysis', *Discourse Studies* 1(1), pp. 83–118.

van Leeuwen, T, Bateson, D J, Inoyue, K, Le Hunt, B, Barratt, A, Black, K, Kelly, M, Rutherford, R, Stewart, M, Richters, J (forthcoming) 'Swallowing the pill: A multimodal discourse analysis of contraceptive advertising to doctors'.

Weber, M, 1947, *The theory of social and economic organization*, Oxford University Press, New York.

Weber, M, 1976, *The protestant ethic and the spirit of capitalism*, Allen and Unwin, London.

Wintour, P & Sparrow, A, 2015, 'British foreign policy is in crisis, warn senior diplomatic figures', *The Guardian*, 9 November 2015, available from: www.theguardian.com/politics/2015/nov/08/british-foreign-policy-report-senior-diplomatic-figures.

Zijderveld, A C, 1979, *On clichés: The supersedure of meaning by function in modernity*, Routledge, London.

15
Narrative analysis

Anna De Fina

The narrative mode has a special significance for the study of politics in that it has been long regarded as basic to the ideological construction of events and to the manipulation of public opinion. From Hayden White's theorisations about the relations between narrative, politics and ideology to modern-day investigations about the way stories are embedded into different forms of political communication, narrative has always been at the centre of reflections about political discourse.

In this chapter, I approach the topic of the relations between storytelling and politics from the point of view of discourse analysis. As I will show below, narrative analysis in the area of political discourse studies is not a unified field. Indeed, researchers employ a variety of theoretical methodological instruments and focus on very different kinds of texts and contexts. These differences reflect not only diverging conceptions of narrative and politics, but also alternative ways of approaching discourse itself. Nonetheless, two general trends can be devised in the field of narrative analysis. In the first trend, the focus is on 'master-narratives,' intended as overarching structures that underlie and organize discourse and interpretation. Applications of this approach have mostly concentrated on public discourse and on discourse directly intended as politically motivated. A second approach treats narratives as a set of everyday discourse practices and genres that acquire specific characteristics in specific contexts. Applications of narrative analysis from this perspective have been much more varied since a view of narrative as a tool for making sense of and constructing experience also allows for an understanding of politics as an aspect of everyday life. The distinction between these two conceptions of narrative will guide the organisation of this chapter.

In the first part, I will introduce some theoretical methodological issues and definitions. I will then concentrate on studies that conceive of political narratives as grand narratives that are either controlled by, or reflect the influence of, politically powerful agents such as governments, international organisms or mainstream media. Here, the emphasis will be on master-narratives. I will also discuss work on the conflicts between expected narrative contents and forms and actual storytelling needs and practices in institutional settings (e.g. the Truth and Reconciliation Commission (TRC) in South Africa, or asylum-seeking procedures). The following section will discuss how narrative analysis has contributed to the study of political discourse by looking, for example, at studies about the use of stories and anecdotes as instruments of persuasion in the discourse of politicians and in media aligned with political parties. I will then review work that has illuminated the way narratives are used to make sense of political issues in different domains. I will focus on studies that come from different theoretical methodological approaches showing how they have contributed to understanding ways in which narratives turn the personal into the political. In this section, I will also devote attention to recent developments that show a growing interest in digital media.

Theoretical methodological issues

Definitions of narrative

Before discussing narrative analysis and its application to the field of politics, it is important to briefly review some general issues, such as definitions of narrative and ways of conceiving politics, and to introduce narrative analysis as a field within discourse studies, together with some of the main concerns and debates in the area that are relevant to research in politics.

The definition of narrative is perhaps the most controversial issue in the field. Indeed, there is little agreement among linguists on the criteria that distinguish narratives from other discourse genres. It is to be noted here that the terms 'narrative' and 'story' are often used interchangeably in the literature, but in reality, a distinction should be made between the notion of 'story' as a prototypical narrative and the notion of 'narrative' as a genre that comprises different types of stories. Narratologists, that is, scholars who study narrative from a literary perspective, have focused on finding the constitutive elements of the prototypical story. They describe it as comprising a sequence of related events, with chronological ordering as the main criterion (Chatman 1990), but have added causal links as an important organising principle (Prince 2003). As narratology developed over time, the list of defining characteristics of stories increased and scholars started including elements such as the presence of human agency and the communication of human experience (Fludernik 1996). Even so, most narratologists would agree on the idea that a story could be defined as representing temporally and causally related events, dealing with some sort of complication, presenting goal-directed actions and having animate protagonists (for a discussion, see De Fina & Georgakopoulou 2012, ch. 1). These basic ideas have been retained in linguistic models of narrative.

The most popular among them has been, and still is, the one proposed by the sociolinguist William Labov who focused on narratives of personal experience, which he defined as 'one verbal technique for recapitulating past experience' (Labov & Waletzky 1967, p. 13). In his model, prototypical stories consist of an abstract (a kind of story summary), orientation (clauses or sections offering guidance to the listener in terms of time, space and story characters), complicating action (the main events reported), evaluation (clauses or sections expressing the point of view of the narrator on the events and characters) and a coda (a closing statement that connects the story to the present interaction). Not all these components were deemed necessary for a text to be regarded as a story, since the story may also simply focus on a series of actions in the past, but Labov showed that well-performed stories included all components and had developed evaluation sections. Most narrative analysts would agree on a basic definition of stories as concerning past events, chronologically and or causally connected by a narrator whose point of view they encode. However, many would also question the excessive focus on the prototypical story, the neglect of different narrative models and formats, the scarce consideration of alternative storytelling formats (for example, of the presence of multiple narrators and differentiated audiences), practices (including the selection of specific addressees among possible audiences, the effect of audience reactions and feedback on storytelling, and so forth) and contexts (for example, mediated ones), which are typical of Labov's model (see contributions in Bamberg 1997 for a discussion of some of these issues).

For the study of narratives in relation to political issues, we will see, for example, that many different genres besides the narrative of personal experience are relevant, such as the anecdote, the chronicle, the life story, the testimonial, the small story, and so forth, and that the contexts and media in which such narratives are embedded are also very important to understanding the way they are used.

Narrative as methodology or as epistemology

Another important issue that concerns narrative analysts is the ambiguity and overlaps between a conception of it as a methodological instrument (i.e. a tool for eliciting first-hand experience) and as a specific epistemological mode (i.e. a way of understanding reality). Indeed, many discourse analysts, particularly after the narrative turn's stress on the legitimacy of qualitative research paradigms (Bruner 1986) take the view that eliciting stories or analysing existing narrative testimonials about particular experiences (e.g. political ones) is the best way to get to participant understandings of particular events or social experiences. Such preference for narrative is based on the idea that narrative is one of the most widespread and preferred modes of encoding and understanding human experience.

We will review debates around the epistemological status of narrative more in detail below, but here it is important to note how the conflation between narrative as a tool and narrative as a mode presents many possible complications and has therefore led to polemics and debates in the field. Indeed, while using narrative as a tool for eliciting experiential accounts and subjective perceptions is an accepted and largely uncontroversial practice, embracing the view of narrative as an epistemic mode has led many analysts to interpret narratives (elicited or spontaneous) as unmediated and transparent reports about experience, without paying sufficient attention to the conditions of production of such stories and therefore treating them simply as vehicles for the communication of content. Scholars who approach storytelling as practice (De Fina & Georgakopoulou 2008) have focused on the importance of this issue, for example, highlighting the role of the interviewer in the context of elicited stories (De Fina 2009, De Fina & Perrino 2011) and the influence of different kinds of contextual factors on the shape and function of narratives.

Narratives and politics

The special relationship between narratives and politics has been noted over and over again in the literature on both topics. Bottici argues, for example, that:

> Narratives are ways to connect events in a nonrandom way, and therefore they are powerful means to provide meaning to the political world we live in. [...] They tell us both what is the sense of our political world in general and also of our place within it.
> (Bottici 2010, p. 920)

Scholars note that since stories are the most ubiquitous of discourse genres, they are necessarily connected with politics, both in the sense that personal and private narratives, such as autobiographical stories and anecdotes, are used by politicians and political movements, and in the sense that narratives, such as news stories, stories on social media and a variety of historical narratives, circulate and are widely shared, thereby shaping public perception about politically relevant events, relations and people.

However, the way in which narrative practices may be related to the political realm crucially depends on the conception and definition of what politics is. Hoare (2010) takes up and discusses a useful distinction originally proposed by Freeden between 'thinking politically' and 'thinking about politics'. In his words: 'thinking politically refers to a range of particular thought practices of, and concerning, collectivities', while thinking about politics refers to 'the patterns and ranges of views that people hold when their thoughts concern the central issues and challenges their societies encounter: the core domain of politics' (Freeden 2008, pp. 197–198, quoted p. 6). Taking inspiration from this distinction, it could be said that politics can be conceived both as the realm of action and thought about how issues and problems concerning individuals intersect with issues and problems concerning society as a collective entity, and also as the realm of direct engagement with issues of power. If politics and the political include, as I believe, both the realm of public struggles and discourses about social issues, and the domain of private (or less public) discourses and practices that pertain to the individual as a member of society at large, then our definition of what kinds of narratives are political also needs to be expanded. At the same time, if the notion of politics is not reduced to the negative connotations that are attached to it when regarded as not simply an arena for the imposition of power, but also as terrain for the proposal of solutions and new ways of tackling social questions, then again, the range of narratives that can be seen as political expands. In her work on political narratives, Molly Andrews espouses the latter view when she declares:

> I am then interested in what kinds of stories people tell about how the world works, how they explain the engines of political change, and the roles they see themselves, and those whom they regard as being part of their groups, as playing in this ongoing struggle.
>
> (Andrews 2007, p. 8)

As we will see, narrative analysts have focused on one or the other of these two meanings depending on their theoretical background and object of study (see also the introduction to this volume for a discussion on this point).

Grand narratives

A great deal of work on narratives and politics focuses on what many call 'master' narratives, that is public dominant discourses about particular social issues. Such discourses are seen as frames through which other discourses (including political discourses and stories) are interpreted. For example, examining narratives told by Korean women who were sex slaves to the Japanese military, Murph argues that:

> The relentless accusations and framing of the survivors' experiences as prostitution and the survivors as prostitutes – who volunteered to work in lucrative war zones and who were not coerced to do so by the Japanese government – continually evoke the master narrative of prostitution.
>
> (Murph 2008, p. 50)

Such narrative positions these subjects in a way that corners them into delicate identity work to propose alternative interpretations of their past.

Much of the literature on master-narratives comes from a Critical Discourse Analysis (CDA) framework and examines politics as the imposition of frames of understanding by the powerful. Therefore, it focuses mostly on reports of events in the press and on political discourses.

The examination of ideological bias in press articles has a long tradition. Authors have of course dealt with the coverage of political events, but also with the political motivatedness of event construals and the possible impact of such narratives on audiences. Studies look at how events are connected to each other and, in turn, at how such connections represent and convey particular ideological viewpoints. Scholars have shown that events of political significance in the press are emplotted in certain ways through processes of selection, temporal and causal ordering, attributions of agency to different protagonists, focus on particular occurrences, and choices at the lexical or syntactic level (see Fowler 1991, Hall et al. 1978, Matheson 2005; Jacobs 2000). They have also pointed to the role of these press reports in fitting into dominant models and value-systems that are reproduced and circulated. In a recent article on reports of political protests by the British press, Hart (2013) shows, for example, that these kinds of events are always construed as episodes of violence through the use of many different strategies: from the fact itself of treating them as violent episodes and therefore undermining their motivations, to constructing asymmetrical schemas about agents and patients of actions and to applying a selective focus on certain kinds of semantic relations within event clauses.

Another strand of CDA looks at the role of master or 'hegemonic' narratives in public political discourse. Particularly significant here is work on national identities and on how states, politicians and organisations construct a story about the identities of nations. Such collective representations then become frames within which individual stories can be understood. For these studies, narratives are interpretations of the past and therefore they are based on discourses and counter-discourses about history. For example, Wodak et al. (2009) examine how national identities are constructed within official commemorations. In particular, they analyse the discourses produced by politicians in 2005 on the occasion of the sixtieth anniversary of the end of the Second World War and the liberation in Austria. They argue that stories about traumatic events in the past can be seen as 'attempts to create consensual images of history which unify a whole nation' (p. 206) and to find a common core of images and explanations. Their analysis centers on linguistic/rhetorical strategies, temporal and spatial deixis, the naming of actors, syntactic constructions, such as active or passive, modality, metaphors and *topoi*, and their use in the building up of success or catastrophe.

Public narratives about the nation are seen by others as windows into the motivations and future objectives of political regimes. In a study about public discourse in the Putin-Medvedev era, Bacon (2012) defines public political narratives as 'a sequential account given by political actors connecting selected, specific developments so as to impose a desired order on them' (p. 768). In his view, being selective, such narratives construct a political point of view, but they are also predictive in that they indicate possible developments and future actions. Bacon stresses that for this reason, narrative analysis can illuminate actors' views, motifs, priorities, instead of focusing exclusively on effects of power processes. These grand narratives are dominant because they are circulated through the media and repeated through a process of 'accrual', that is, they become part of people's habitus.

Similar views of narrative as a kind of meta-discourse about recent or past history are found also in Hodges' (2011) work on the 'War on terror' narrative propagated by George W. Bush about the 9/11 events in the US and in Kubiak's (2014) analysis of the 'War narrative' as legitimation of American politics.

Most of the works reviewed above rely on a variety of data (such as different political speeches, interviews, articles in the press, books and interviews) and stress the importance of intertextuality, that is of connections between different texts and how such connections and metaphors are reflected in more private discourses.

In the work discussed above, narratives are seen from a macro perspective as cohesively constructed interpretations or all-encompassing metaphors about the past. I will come back to the issues related to the definition of what exactly is a meta or ideological narrative below but now I will briefly turn to work that examines the role of narratives in institutional processes.

Nowhere is the political effect of narratives clearer than in institutional settings that directly depend upon and affect policy making. Examples of these kinds of settings are truth commissions and asylum-seeking settings. In the case of truth commissions, scholars have underlined how the process of storytelling is deeply embedded within government policies of reconciliation. In a study about TRC narratives in South Africa during the post-apartheid period, Andrews (2007) shows, for example, that the TRC had the role to restore a narrative fashioned by the state as part of a project to recreate and maintain national identity. Narratives were supposed to demonstrate a process of healing for the nation and the Truth Commission carefully controlled which stories could be told by setting criteria that excluded many of the testimonies. Andrews makes the important point that the individual stories fitted into larger meta-narratives: one was about the Truth Commission itself, the second was the assumed relationship between telling and healing, and the third was the idea that individual stories of suffering put together would allow the construction of a collective identity for the country. Similar arguments about the 'hearability' of narratives that did not conform to TRC expectations, are made by Blommaert, Bock and McCormick (2006).

Work on asylum seekers' narratives also points to how political processes constrain the criteria for tellability and create clashes between asylum seekers and reviewing officials' expectations about what can and should be narrated, and how. Maryns and Blommaert (2001) and Maryns (2005) analysed asylum seekers' storytelling processes in Belgium and pointed to differences in perspectives on the events taken by the two sides and on the inequality determined by the fact that narrators did not tell their story in their own language, but had to use a lingua franca. Differences in event perspectives arise given the different roles that officials and narrators play in the interaction and their, often conflicting, objectives in terms of what they want to achieve in the communicative event. While asylum seekers are protagonists of the events they tell, and regard them as highly charged lived experiences, officials may define them as collections of facts that have to eventually fit into bureaucratic categories. Having no first-hand knowledge of these experiences, officials do not necessarily empathise with the narrators; however, their interpretations of, and judgement about, asylum seekers' stories will affect the result of their pleas.

Jacquemet (2005) studied interviews that took place at the United Nations High Commission on Refugees in Tirana, Albania, for the granting of refugee status to Kosovars seeking UN protection during the 2000 conflicts in former Yugoslavia. He noted the disrupting effect that the prejudice against stories had on asylum seekers who were trying to convey dramatic experiences and who wanted to relate them in detail to officials who had been instructed to reject personal stories in favour of detailed responses to questions. In these environments, although stories are not directly concerned with political issues, they are embedded in important political processes.

Before I turn to narratives told by politicians, let me summarise some of the criticism and objections that have been addressed to accounts of narrative that use the construct of the meta- or the master-narrative. Even though it is important to recognise the significance of the link between individual narratives and more macro constructs, such as ideologies and discourses, the use of the term 'narrative' to refer to such macro-level phenomena may have the effect of effacing the textual and interactional nature of storytelling and of stories as such. There is a danger of substituting the term 'narrative' for any kind of macro-level discourse, thus leading to a misunderstanding of what narratives actually are in context. Such a tendency can be corroborated in the ambiguity and lack of precision with which the terms master-, meta- or hegemonic-narrative are used in the literature. Scholars (particularly in the CDA camp) tend to employ such terms to refer to ideologies, discourses, scenarios, historical reconstructions, and so forth, often without exactly clarifying what they mean by them. As we will see below, in more recent studies, there has been a shift towards a view of narratives as practices and therefore a much greater attention on the embedding of narratives in particular interactional and semiotic contexts, and on the use of specific resources and affordances by narrators.

Narratives in the discourse of politicians

Many scholars have noted that narrative plays an important part in discourses produced by politicians. Narratives are often used as a more immediate way of connecting with audiences and readers because they are seen as representing a non-argumentative, more common-sense and therefore more grass-roots inspired mode of conveying political views. In a review and critical assessment of CDA use of narrative, Souto Manning (2014) illustrates how politicians use everyday narratives to their advantage. She presents the case of a political speech by Bush in which he used an anecdote about a Texan painter whose work was showcased at the Oval office to come across as compassionate and optimistic. She also uses the case of a government campaign in Brazil to analyse how narratives are used in political advertisements on TV in order to garner support from audiences for public policies. Because stories have a more immediate quality than arguments, and are presented as conveying the experience of common people, their message is more easily internalised by audiences.

The tendency to tell stories as a way to connect with the public is recognised by some as a phenomenon that is closely related to the informalisation of public life. Paul Goetsch noted, for example, that the spread of television not only added a visual component to the experience of listening to political speeches, but also 'encouraged Presidents to break with the conventions of formal oratory and to adopt an informal, sometimes conversational and narrative style' (1994, p. 26, quoted in Schubert 2010, p. 144). In a study of former Italian Prime Minister Berlusconi's and politician Grillo's rhetoric styles, Ruggiero (2012) argued, for example, that both tend to communicate in the most direct way through the use of slogans and narratives that tap into common sense and subvert traditional categories of the symbolic use of language (Edelman 1988), achieving thereby, the 'primacy of the narrative in political discourse' (p. 307, see also Paternostro and Sottile 2014, on the same topic). Studying a collection of political speeches by UK and US leaders and politicians, Schubert proposes a taxonomy of narrative functions of political speeches. He distinguishes between 'personalizing', 'integrating', 'exemplifying' and 'polarizing'. When politicians personalise, they use stories to present themselves as particular kinds of individuals. An integrating function 'can be discerned in narrative passages that emphasise common achievements or values of a nation or a political party, while the speaker is a representative of the group' (2010, p. 11). Narratives can also exemplify particular argumentative points a politician is making, and finally, a polarising narrative uses historical reconstruction or anecdotes to construct enemies.

Studies have also addressed particular kinds of narratives or narrative functions. This is the case with Shenav's (2005) analysis of what he calls 'concise' narratives in the speech of Israeli politicians, that is, narratives that summarise entire historical periods to the advantage of a particular argument. Fetzer (2010) talked about 'small stories' as allowing the intersection of public and private spheres in political discourse. Archakis and Tsakona provide yet another example of specific narrative types in their investigation of the role of humorous narratives in Greek parliamentary debates (also see Perrino 2015 on the use of humorous stories by politicians). They argue that:

> such informal conversational resources and themes originating in local social networks and entering political discourse and oratory are strategically employed by politicians in their attempt to create a more personalised view of political affairs, hide the unequal distribution of discursive resources along different social groups, and avoid political argumentation.
> (Archakis & Tsakona 2011, p. 62)

Narratives as political sense making

In this section, we turn to the use of narratives by individuals to deal with their particular experiences as integral to social experiences, as instances of social problems and as windows into their understanding of socio-political processes. In that sense, this kind of understanding of narratives also conveys a conception of politics as a domain in which the private and the public are closely interwoven. In a series of studies about how individuals construe social processes (from political changes in East and West Germany to war fought by the US), Andrews states that she is:

> interested in what kinds of stories people tell about how the world works, how they explain the engines of political change, and the roles they see themselves, and those whom they regard as being part of their groups, as playing in this ongoing struggle.
> (Andrews 2007, p. 8)

Narrative inquiry that takes this approach uses as a point of reference the idea, dear to 'narrative turn' scholars in the social sciences (see Bruner 1986), that getting people to narrate experiences, is a good way of understanding social problems from the point of view of their protagonists, or their victims. Thus, many of these studies take as their data, narratives told in interviews or in focus groups, and examine ways in which narrators portray their experiences and their role in a wide variety of contexts that can be seen as 'political' in the sense sketched above. For example, narrative analysts have looked at the wide issue of migration, studying how migrants construct experiences connected with ethnic and racial discrimination (see Baynahm 2003; De Fina 2003; van de Mieroop 2012) or linguistic discrimination (De Fina & King 2011; Relaño Pastor 2014). Other studies have focused on different groups' construction of social problems, such as homelessness (Trimingham 2015), gender oppression (Murph 2008; Latvala 2015), survival from wars and mass killings, such as the Holocaust (Schiffrin 2002; Piazza & Rubino 2015; Wodak & Rheindorf 2017).

Most of these works use qualitative methodologies with a variety of instruments taken from discourse analysis and sociolinguistics, work on small data corpora, that is narratives told by a limited number of subjects and offer close textual analyses of the fragments under investigation. In these studies, the connections between the individual and the social is seen as residing in the way narrators and interviewers interactionally position themselves with respect to social issues. Stress is placed on the centrality of the interactional context, that is on the relationships established between interlocutors through the storytelling (not only on the content of the stories) and on the dynamic construction of context, which includes incorporation into the present discourse of 'enregistered' identities (that is, identities that are more generally associated with social roles, see De Fina 2014) and ideologies or capital D discourses. But such wider constructs are evoked and made relevant by the narrators and listeners, not presupposed by the analyst. Common analytic instruments include the notions of positioning, agency, stance and participation frameworks. *Positioning* (as defined by Bamberg 1997b, but also as reinterpreted later, see De Fina 2013 on this point) refers to positions taken by narrators with respect to:

a. the story world, that is, characters in the story;
b. the storytelling world, that is, present interlocutors;
c. the social world, that is, common ideologies and stereotypes.

Agency is seen as the degree of initiative implicitly taken in story worlds and/or assigned in storytelling worlds to themselves by narrators. *Stance-taking* refers to 'the expression of an attitude, evaluation, or judgement as the speaker's own point of view' (Lampropoulou & Myers 2012). All these tools involve the analysis of linguistic strategies, such as pronoun choice and switches, passive and active constructions, modality, reported speech, time and place reference, linguistic devices conveying presuppositions, lexicon and syntactic expressions conveying emotions, and so on.

The concept of *participation frameworks* (Goffman 1981) proposes the idea that both the notion of speaker and hearer can be deconstructed in order to include different roles. For example, the speaker can take the role of author, animator (someone who just utters the words), or principal (someone who speaks on behalf of someone else). The audience in turn can include ratified addressees, but also non-ratified addressees and overhearers. The ways narrators and audiences play, impersonate or reject all or some of these roles determines the way stories convey meanings as much as the referential worlds that they evoke.

The studies mentioned above have centered on storytelling, particularly in interviews and research-generated environments. They have also focused on verbal devices and on self-representation. However, as is the case with discourse analysis in general, in the last decade, narrative analysis has widened its scope to include new ways of creating and communicating stories. Within this still-young field, the stress is on narrative as practices (see De Fina & Georgakopoulou 2008). From this perspective, narratives should be seen as embedded within other semiotic practices and as inscribed within the affordances and frames created and established in them. Narrative genres, therefore, are not seen as fixed, but as emerging within particular kinds of interactions, and the inventory of narrative resources necessarily widens to open up to non-verbal and multimodal tools. If storytelling is seen as practice, then participation frameworks also become more important and significant as co-narration or co-authorship and multiple listenership or readership also acquire greater relevance.

Studies of narratives as practices within the scope of discourse and politics have concentrated on computer-mediated communication as it is within digital media, such as social media, that new forms of political participation are taking shape. Analysts have underscored, for example, the power of social-media participants in shaping, reshaping and circulating stories about politicians and politics, but also in terms of how new media are exploited by political powers to tell certain stories. In the study of political speeches that was quoted earlier, Schubert (2010) analyzes, for example, how speeches embedded within government-controlled sites are surrounded by electronic hypertexts that create new potential frames. He shows that hyperlinks allow users to access further narrative genres, such as photo contexts, biographies and historical surveys, which constitute kinds of meta-narratives that guide interpretation. At the same time, users are free to create their own 'narrative paths' as they navigate the websites.

As mentioned above, recent investigations are interrogating the participatory power of new media narratives. In a study of Chilean students, participation in demonstrations against educational policies, García Agustín and Aguirre Díaz (2014) show how the students combined the appropriation of public spaces through 'flash mob' events, that is, mobilisations organised through social media, performed and then circulated again through the same media, and within the frame of reference of popular narratives and characters taken from Japanese comics. Students perform roles that are taken from those characters and use the comics' storylines to reinterpret present conflicts. These new forms of participation have completely transformed storytelling by giving users of social media power over encoding and circulation (see also Georgakopoulou 2014 on media transposition of stories about the Greek crisis).

There are yet other ways in which new media have broken established storytelling formats. Recent research on the construction of identities in public space has also demonstrated how stories and media are tightly intertwined. Analyses of narratives told, for example, by members of LGBTQ communities, have illustrated how coming-out narratives acquire power through the construction of collective frames and through the availability of testimonials on the internet, but also how these new spaces have allowed for the creation of hybrid genres (see Gray 2009; Jones 2015). The appropriation of the internet by oppressed and minority groups has also allowed these groups to get their messages across to a wide audience and to position themselves strategically. Storytelling has played an important role in such processes; therefore, to conclude this chapter, I will briefly discuss the example of video narratives posted by members of the 'Dreamers' movement as part of their campaign to push for migration reforms.

The Dreamers movement started in 2010 when four undocumented students occupied the office of an Arizona Senator in the US to pressure him to support a reform of legislation that would allow undocumented students to enrol in university. Such legislation came to be known as the DREAM act, hence their name. The Dreamers have since grown into a national organisation, with organisations in 26 states and with more than 100,000 members. They have organised countless events and protests and successfully pushed for approval, in 2012, of DACA ('Deferred Action for Childhood Arrivals'), a piece of legislation that allows a certain number of young migrants to stay legally in the US. The 15 narratives that I use as data for this exemplification were part of a set of stories posted online in 2014 as part of a campaign to support an extension of DACA to a greater number of immigrants and to stop deportation of their parents. The narratives demonstrate the role that new media can have in the creation of a strategic collective identity that may serve the political objectives of the movement. The initiative called for stories to be posted on the United We Dream Movement site;[1] these stories would focus on the authors sharing their own dreams, or their parents' dreams, in order to prod migration reform. The resulting stories were actually posted mostly by movement activists rather than by audience members. Through them, young Dreamers present themselves and explain, through accounts of their own and their parents' experiences, to the public and the-then President Obama in particular, why DACA extension and migration reform are so important to them. Stories are organised around thematic components that appear in all or most of the narratives. Among such components are: personal information, narratives about what the author was doing at the time of first hearing the announcement of DACA, a hypothetical story about what the author would do if DACA were extended, the telling of a crucial moment in which the author realised how being undocumented would affect everyday life, but also the telling of dreams. The organising principles behind the way these pieces were put together are strategic: one is a shared self-presentation (and presentation of in-group members) as loyal, family-orientated, altruistic, and hard-working; the second is an argumentative move in which the qualities attributed to self and family are used to support the plight for new legislation. Verbal strategies are complemented with multimodal strategies, such as the use of music and photos.

Due to limited space, I can only briefly discuss verbal strategies and reproduce some fragments from one of these narratives:

> you know I: I love my dad to death he is like my best friend↑
> because uh anything ((photo of dad)) anything that happens to me like I confide in him,
> and his his ((ends photo) ultimate dream is to see me and my sister succeed which is why we came to the United States in the first place
> um he wanted me to get a better education→
> he wanted me to have a better future
> uhm you wanted me to have the things that that he didn't
> uhm and so I I want him to be happy
> I want my family to be happy
> ((some lines deleted))
> I would look President Obama straight in the eyes and tell him that I am
> I wouldn't be the man who I am today I'm if it weren't for my father
> I would not have uhm any of my traits,
> uhm I would not be as hard working, I would not be as honest or
> just want a better future for everyone
> if it weren't for him I'm
> he taught me everything I know↑
> uhm and I'm that my father and my mother are human beings and that
> I am a by product of that
> and that they deserve a better future and that they deserve to not fear whether or not they would be able to come home
>
> (Jose 2014)

As we see in this fragment, Ray is presenting himself and his family as desirable citizens in terms that appeal to typical US values of honesty, hard work and care for others. This allows him to articulate the plea to President Obama that concludes his narrative. This way, self-presentation positions the listener towards a moral stance in which rejection of the plea of immigrants would be felt as unjust. As we see, there is very little in terms of a radical request here. Youth migrants adopt a conciliatory discourse in these narratives that is strategically useful to them, while still presenting much more aggressive profiles on other occasions, such as in videos taken during their marches.

This succinct example shows how narratives may be used as a vehicle to build and circulate collective identities that are strategically important to win political battles.

Conclusion

In this chapter, I have reviewed the many links that connect narratives to politics. We have seen that narratives can convey and reflect meta-discourses about society and identity, that through stories, both politicians and members of society at large position themselves with respect to socio-political issues and that narratives can provide strategic sites for the construction and negotiation of politically expedient identities. In all these ways, storytelling can be seen as political practice.

Note

1   http://unitedwedream.org/twoyears/

References

Andrews, M, 2007, *Shaping history: Narratives of political change*, Cambridge University Press, Cambridge.
Archakis, A & Tsakona, V, 2011, 'Informal talk in formal settings: Humorous narratives in Greek parliamentary debates', in *Studies in political humour: In between political critique and public entertainment*, eds. D Popa & V Tsakona, John Benjamins, Amsterdam, pp. 61–82.
Bamberg, M, 1997a, ed, 'Oral versions of personal experience: three decades of narrative analysis', Special Issue of *Journal of Narrative and Life History*, 7(1–4).
Bamberg, M, 1997b, 'Positioning between structure and performance', *Journal of Narrative and Life History* 7(1–4), pp. 335–342.
Blommaert, J, Bock, M & McCormick, K, 2006, 'Narrative inequality in the TRC hearings. On the hearability of hidden transcripts', *Journal of Language and Politics* 5(1), pp. 37–70.
Bottici, C, 2010, 'Narrative', in *Encyclopedia of Political Theory*, ed. M Bevir, pp. 919–920. Sage, Thousand Oaks, CA, pp. 919–920.
Bruner, J, 1986, 'Two modes of thought', in *Actual minds possible worlds*, J Bruner, Harvard University Press, Cambridge, MA, pp. 11–43.
Chatman, S, 1990, *Coming to terms: the rhetoric of narrative in fiction and film*, Cornell University Press, Ithaca, NY.
De Fina, A, 2003, *Identity in narrative: A study of immigrant discourse*, John Benjamins, Amsterdam.
De Fina, A, 2009, 'Narratives in interview – the case of accounts. For an interactional approach to narrative genres', *Narrative Inquiry* 19(2), pp. 233–258.
De Fina, A, 2013, 'Positioning level 3: Connecting local identity displays to macro social processes', *Narrative Inquiry* 23(1), pp. 40–61.
De Fina, A, 2014, 'Enregistered and emergent identities in narrative', in *Researching identity and interculturality*, eds. F Dervin & K Risager, Routledge, London, pp. 46–66.
De Fina, A & Georgakopoulou, A, 2008, 'Analysing narratives as practices', *Qualitative Research*, 8(3), pp. 379–387.

De Fina, A & King, K, 2011, 'Language problem or language conflict? Narratives of immigrant women's experiences in the US', *Discourse Studies*, 13(2), pp. 163–188.

De Fina, A & Perrino, S, eds, 2011, 'Narratives in interviews, interviews in narrative studies', Special Issue *Language in Society*, 40(1), pp. 1–11.

Fetzer, A, 2010, 'Small stories in political discourse', in *Narrative revisited in the age of social media*, ed. C R Hoffmann, John Benjamins, Amsterdam, pp. 163–184.

Fludernik, M, 1996, *Towards a 'natural' narratology*, Routledge, London.

Fowler, R, 1991, *Language in the news: discourse and ideology in the press*, Routledge, London.

Freeden, M, 2008, 'Thinking politically and thinking about politics: Language, interpretation, and ideology', in *Political theory: Methods and approaches*, eds., D Leopold & M Stears, Oxford University Press, Oxford, pp. 196–215.

García Agustín, O & Aguirre Díaz, F, 2014, 'Spatial practices and narratives. The GenkiDama for education by Chilean students', *Journal of Language and Politics*, 13(4), pp. 732–754.

Georgakopoulou, A, 2014, 'Small stories transposition and social media: A micro-perspective on the "Greek crisis"', *Discourse & Society*, 25(2), pp. 519–539.

Goetsch, P, 1991, 'Presidential rhetoric: An introduction', in *Important Speeches by American Presidents after 1945*, eds. P Goetsch & G Hurm, Winter, Heidelberg, pp. 7–31.

Goffman, E, 1981, *Forms of talk*, University of Pennsylvania Press, Philadelphia, PA.

Gray, M, 2009, 'Negotiating identities/queering desires: Coming out online and the remediation of the coming-out story', *Journal of Computer-Mediated Communication*, 14(4), pp. 1162–1189.

Hall, S, Critcher, C, Jefferson, T, Clarke, J & Roberts, B, 1978, *Policing the crisis: Mugging, the state, and law and order*, Palgrave Macmillan, Basingstoke.

Hart, C, 2013, Event-construal in press reports of violence in two recent political protests: A cognitive linguistic approach to CDA. *Journal of Language and Politics*, 12(3), pp. 400–424.

Hoare, G, 2010, 'Telling stories about politics: The concept of political narrative and "Left Versus Right": Politics in Strange Places: Breaking the Boundaries of the Definition of the Political', available from: https://podcasts.ox.ac.uk/telling-stories-about-politics-concept-political-narrative-and-case-left-versus-right [accessed 1 July 2015].

Hodges, A, 2011, *The 'War on Terror' narrative: Discourse and intertextuality in the construction and contestation of sociopolitical reality*, Oxford University Press, New York.

Jacobs, R, 2000, 'Narrative, civil society and public culture', in *Lines of narrative: Psychosocial perspectives*, ed. M Andrews, Routledge, London, pp. 18–35.

Jacquemet, M, 2005, 'The registration interview: Restricting refugees' narrative performances', in *Dislocations/relocations: Narratives of displacement*, eds. M Baynham & A de Fina, St. Jerome Publishing, Manchester, pp. 194–216.

Jones, R, 2015, 'Generic intertextuality in online social activism: The case of the It Gets Better project', *Language in Society*, 44(3), pp. 317–339.

Jose, R, 2014, *United we dream*, available from: https://unitedwedream.org/twoyears/.

Kubiak, J, 2014, *War narratives and the American will in war*, Palgrave Macmillan, New York.

Lampropoulou, S & Myers, G, 2012, 'Stance-taking in Interviews from the Qualidata Archive', *Forum Qualitative Sozialforschung/Forum: Qualitative Social Research*, 14(1), art. 12, available from: http://nbn-resolving.de/urn:nbn:de:0114-fqs1301123 [accessed 22 August 2015].

Maryns, K, 2005, 'Displacement and asylum seekers' narratives' in *Dislocations/relocations: Narratives of displacement*, eds. M Baynham and A de Fina, St. Jerome Publishing, Manchester, pp. 174–193.

Maryns, K & Blommaert, J, 2001, 'Stylistic and thematic shifting as a narrative resource', *Multilingual: Journal of Cross-cultural and Interlanguage Communication* 20(1), pp. 61–84.

Matheson, D M, 2005, *Media discourses*, McGraw-Hill Education, Berkshire.

Murph, K, 2008, 'Negotiating the master narratives of prostitution, slavery, and rape in the testimonies by and representations of Korean sex slaves of the Japanese military (1932–1945)', unpublished PhD Dissertation, Department of Linguistics, Georgetown University, Washington, DC.

Paternostro, G & Sottile, R, 2014, 'In alto i cuori/L'Italia cambia verso', *Discorso politico e interazione nei social network.* Paper presented at AISLI Convention, Naples, 21 November 2014.

Perrino, S, 2015, 'Performing extracomunitari: Mocking migrants in Veneto barzellette', *Language in Society*, 44(2), pp. 141–160.

Piazza, R & Rubino, A, 2015, '"Racial laws turned our lives positively": Agentivity and chorality in the identity of a group of Italian Jewish witnesses' in *Marked identities. Narrating lives between social identities and individual biographies*, eds. A Fasulo & R Piazza, Palgrave Macmillan, Basingstoke, pp. 98–122.

Prince, G, 2003 [1987], *A dictionary of narratology*, University of Nebraska Press, Lincoln, NE.

Ruggiero, C, 2012, 'Forecasting in the politics of spectacle: From Berlusconi to Grillo: The narrative of impolite politics', *Bulletin of Italian Politics* 4(2), pp. 305–322.

Schiffrin, D, 2002, 'Mother and friends in a Holocaust survivor oral history', *Language in Society*, 31(3), pp. 309–354.

Schubert, C, 2010, 'Narrative sequences in political discourse. Forms and functions in speech and hypertext frameworks', in *Narrative revisited telling a story in the age of new media*, John Benjamins, Amsterdam, pp. 143–162.

Shenav, S, 2005, 'Concise narratives: A structural analysis of political discourse', *Discourse Studies*, 7(3), pp. 315–335.

Souto-Manning, M, 2014, 'Critical narrative analysis: the interplay of critical discourse and narrative analyses', *International Journal of Qualitative Studies in Education*, 27(2), pp. 159–180.

Trimingham, P, 2015, 'They paint everyone with the same brush but it just simply isn't the case' in *Marked identities. Narrating lives between social identities and individual biographies* eds. A Fasulo & R Piazza, Palgrave Macmillan, Basingstoke, pp. 58–78.

van de Mieroop, D, 2012, 'Maneuvering between the individual and the social dimensions of narratives in a poor man's discursive negotiation of stigma', *Narrative Inquiry*, 22(1), pp. 122–145.

Wodak, R & Rheindorf, M, 2017, '"Whose story?" – Narratives of persecution, flight and survival told by the children of Austrian Holocaust survivors', in *Diversity and superdiversity: Sociocultural linguistic perspectives*, eds. A De Fina, D Ikizoglu & J Wegner, Georgetown University Press, Washington, DC, pp. 17–35.

Wodak, R, de Cillia, R, Reisigl, M & Liebhart, K, 2009, *The discursive construction of national identity*, Edinburgh University Press, Edinburgh.

16
Rhetorical analysis

Claudia Posch

Introduction

Rhetorical analysis is concerned with ways of finding and interpreting persuasive strategies in language. The language of politics particularly is in the focus of rhetorical analysts as it 'is both the result of rhetorical creativity and the object of rhetorical analysis' (Lunsford, Wilson & Eberly 2009, p. 433). Rhetoric and rhetorical analysis have always been an important skill or even art (*artis rhetoriquae*). In ancient Greece, rhetoric was viewed as a crucial discipline, the 'queen of all subjects' (Kienpointner 1995a). In his famous treatise,[1] Aristotle identified rhetoric as an essential part of the ethical discipline *politics* (Sloane 2001, p. 612). The art of rhetoric was practised in political settings and assemblies, as well as in public discussions in order to persuade audiences of certain political acts. Thus, there has always been a close relationship between rhetoric and politics: 'All the major classical rhetorical scholars [...] focused on politics as the "principal locus" for rhetoric and their rhetorical theory and practice were aimed at citizens as political agents' (Rutten, van Belle & Gillaerts 2014, p. 4). The contrast between the philosophical paradigm and linguistic practice has also been an area of conflict. Over time, rhetoric gained a negative connotation in the form of 'mere rhetoric' meaning 'empty words', or even manipulative speech and propaganda (Kienpointner 2005). In the twentieth century, however, the occupation with rhetoric became increasingly scientific and new research traditions with multiple approaches developed.

Kienpointner (1995a) identifies two general theoretical perspectives on which rhetorical analysis typically draws:

- traditional or classical rhetoric approaches;
- approaches based on the *New rhetoric* or contemporary rhetoric.

These perspectives are often integrated with other analytic frameworks from different fields, such as philosophy, social sciences and especially linguistics (for example, Critical Discourse Studies [CDS], the Discourse Historical Approach [DHA] and politolinguistics).

In the following paragraphs, first, the traditional approaches to rhetorical analysis will be discussed with a focus on Aristotelian concepts, which were a basis for all later frameworks.

Then, contemporary approaches to rhetorical analysis are introduced and a more detailed overview of linguistic and discourse approaches is given. Thereafter, methods of analysing rhetorical devices are explored, such as logical structure analysis of argumentation, the semantics of arguments and fallacious argumentation. Finally, some figures of speech, especially metaphors, are sketched out in more detail.

Traditional approaches to rhetorical analysis

Traditional theoretical perspectives on rhetorical analysis are based on pre-modern concepts and 'have conditioned more recent thinking about the nature of rhetoric' (Zachry 2009, p. 68). In particular, they rely on Aristotelian notions, many of which remain valid and important today. Aristotle offered the first systematic theory aiming at exploring how persuasion works 'by identifying and defining its constituent parts' (Zachry 2009, p. 71). Working from a traditional perspective, many present-day rhetorical analysts especially in the North American tradition, draw on Aristotle's rhetoric (Zachry 2009, p. 71).

According to Aristotle's theory, there are three means (called proofs, '*písteis*') by which a communicator persuades an audience: the character of the speaker or the source of communication ('*éthos*'), the emotion of the person or people being persuaded ('*páthos*'), or the arguments presented in a speech ('*lógos*') (Kienpointner 1995a). Following these basic categories, rhetorical analysis of political language is conducted to this day (Zachry 2009, p. 71).

Aristotle further developed a rhetorical theory of speech genres, which is based on the goals and subjects of speeches. Three types of oratory are distinguished: *forensic* (judicial), *political* (deliberative) and *epideictic* (demonstrative) speech (Reisigl 2008, p. 244; Zachry 2009, p. 68). Forensic rhetorical performances are concerned with the justness or unjustness of past actions, with the question of whether a past event is justifiable from a present point of view. Political or deliberative rhetorical acts deal with the question of whether 'future political actions are useful or disadvantageous for the state' (Kienpointner 1995a). The third type is about the question of whether the distinctive actions and behaviours of a person in the present should be praised or reprimanded. In rhetorical analysis, this typology of speech genres is useful 'for making sense of communicative events' in context (Zachry 2009, p. 71).

Aristotle and his followers also developed a framework along the lines of which communicative acts may be analysed. According to Kienpointner (1995a) this framework represents a set of five rules or 'tasks' of a speaker as well as stages of speech:

- finding arguments or invention ('inventio');
- structuring or arranging ('dispositio');
- formulation and style ('elocutio');
- memory ('memoria'); and
- delivery ('actio').

The first category *invention* is about discovering the most important instrument of the art of rhetoric, the argument, in communications. Aristotle's *invention* aims at providing a systematic way to discover arguments in certain 'places', which he calls '*tópoi*',[2] and he distinguishes 28 'common arguments' (Forchtner 2014, p. 30; Lauer 2004, p. 19)[3]. Researchers differently interpreted what exactly Aristotle meant by '*tópos*' and it has been described as both a 'device to find arguments' (Kienpointner 1995a) and a 'warrant' connecting arguments with conclusions (Kienpointner 1995a; Lauer 2004, p. 20). A more detailed description of *topoi* as understood today will be given in the section Semantics of arguments (p. 252). *Disposition* is the structuring and arranging of a communicative act. Traditional rhetoric entails a fine-grained structuring quite similar to that known from composition: introduction, presentation of facts, argumentation and epilogue. The third element in the framework is about formulation and style ('*elocutio*') and includes the 'virtues of style' (Kienpointner 1995a) of linguistic expression: grammatical correctness, clarity, adequacy, brevity and 'embellishment' or ornaments of speech. *Memory* ('*memoria*') refers to the practice of communication, to reflection on the form of presentation and remembering of ideas for presentation. *Delivery* means the act of carrying out a communication and is thus concerned with the performance of a rhetor. With these so-called *canons*, Aristotle and his followers provided a stable and robust rhetorical genre theory, which is still considered to be important for rhetorical analysis.

Until the twentieth century, little changed about the general theory of rhetoric, even if extensive catalogues of concepts and categories were developed or adapted throughout the Middle Ages and Renaissance. Rhetoric went out of fashion as a discipline and was 'gradually reduced to a theory of style' (Kienpointner 1995a). As mentioned earlier, in the twentieth century, with the linguistic turn in the humanities, interest in rhetoric as an important element of public discourse increased again.

Contemporary rhetorical analysis

Zarefsky speaks of the chief responsibility of rhetoric today as being the 'display of public reason' and the justification of 'contingent claims in the public forum' (Zarefsky 2014, p. 49). Rhetoric constitutes a public or community by construing and negotiating 'common bonds, [...], interests, experiences, and aspirations as consubstantial' (Zarefsky 2014, p. 53). Contemporary approaches to rhetoric are strongly influenced by the work of Chaïm Perelman and Lucie Olbrechts-Tyteca. Their *Traité de l'argumentation: La nouvelle rhétorique* (Perelman & Olbrechts-Tyteca 2004 [1969]) brought rhetoric as a heuristic tool back into academic discussion. They viewed rhetoric as a 'theory of plausible argumentation', as a valid alternative to strictly mathematical and logical approaches in the fields of ethical and political argumentation (Kienpointner 1995a). Rhetoric was re-established as 'a sophisticated framework for analysing and thus making sense of how human beliefs and behaviours are shaped by patterns of communicative practices as well as by discrete communication events' (Zachry 2009, p. 68). Perelman and Olbrechts-Tyteca presented a comprehensive typology of argumentative schemes, which has been taken up and used in numerous fields of study and research (Kienpointner 2011, p. 512). Starting with Perelman and Olbrechts-Tyteca's work, new developments in rhetoric were triggered and contributions were made by researchers such as Kenneth Burke (2004–2014), Michel Meyer (1994), Stephen Toulmin (2003) and Karlyn Kohrs Campbell (Campbell & Huxman 2009). Its aims are defined differently by these scholars, either as 'a tool for *identification*' or 'a tool to enable our understanding of *contextualized* reasoning or argumentation' and also 'a tool to avoid violence and build community through a *listening rhetoric*' (Rutten, van Belle & Gillaerts 2014, p. 4–5). The *Toulmin schema*,[4] for example, tries to include all essential components of argumentation. Current approaches in the US and Canada are much influenced by Toulmin, especially the research programme known as *informal logic*. Informal logic looks at argumentation in everyday language. Argument schemes for reconstructing, assessing, criticising and construing arguments are developed within this framework (van Eemeren 2008, p. 4217; Hansen 2008). Approaches vary from those closer to formal logic (Johnson 2000) to those that take a more dialectical stance (Tindale

1999; Walton 2008). One of the most influential schools of argumentation research today is *Pragma-dialectics*, established by Frans van Eemeren and Rob Grootendorst (1992). The aim of this approach is to create a link between formal dialectics and rhetoric, or more specifically 'to provide a sound integration of both dialectics – the study of critical exchanges – and pragmatics – the study of language use in actual communication' (van Eemeren & Houtlosser 2006, p. 1). What is pragmatic about this approach is that it is also influenced by 'speech act theory, Grice's logic of conversation, and discourse analysis' (van Eemeren 2008, p. 4218). In this way, the pragma-dialectical method 'enables the analyst of argumentative discourse to make a theoretically motivated reconstruction of the discourse' and detect those elements applicable to critical assessment (van Eemeren & Houtlosser 2009, p. 1).

Linguistic rhetorical analysis

Meynet describes rhetorical analysis as an activity or field that belongs to linguistics 'by reason of its object, even if it also works beyond the limits of the sentence; it also belongs to it by reasons of its method and its procedures' (Meynet 2012, p. 23). It shares many characteristics with different textual analysis approaches within linguistics. Thus, rhetorical and linguistic analysis often go hand in hand. Even if there is no such thing as a 'linguistic rhetoric', there are various approaches within linguistic communication and argumentation research that investigate persuasive strategies used by communication participants. These research activities could be viewed as 'linguistic rhetoric' (Kindt 2008, p. 147). In the context of political language it is possible to speak of politolinguistics as proposed by Reisigl: 'Politolinguistics theoretically relies on actual concepts in political science, as well as on rhetorical and discourse-analytical categories […]' (Reisigl 2008, p. 244). A thorough analysis of political language may benefit significantly from approaches connecting rhetoric, political science and linguistic discourse analysis (Wodak 2014a, p. 525). Rhetoric in politics today is much characterised by persuasiveness, because a democracy depends on agreements for decision-making processes. Thus, political discourse shaped by rhetoric has become an important field for rhetorical analysis. Because political decision-making processes are largely reliant on the willingness of people to agree, there is a strong preference for persuasive language. Most political interactions, as well as texts, are influenced by this preference and their lexis – as well as the structure of their speech acts – are formed by persuasive language (Klein 2009, p. 2113).

Discursive approaches to rhetorical analysis

Researchers, referring to their own work as 'rhetorical criticism or rhetorical theory', unfortunately often are not familiar with the multidisciplinary field Critical Discourse Studies (Eisenhart & Johnstone 2008, p. 14). Discourse-centred approaches – with their major exponents, Ruth Wodak (Wodak & Chilton 2005; Wodak & Meyer 2001; Wodak 2012), Paul Chilton and Christina Schäffner (2002), Teun van Dijk (2008), and Isabella and Norman Fairclough (2012) – combine the traditional modes of rhetorical criticism with the tools of linguistic analysis.[5] The Discourse-Historical Approach (DHA), for instance, is a three-dimensional model connecting 'formal, functional and content-related aspects of argumentation in an integrative framework' (Reisigl 2014, p. 69). The DHA specifically stresses the importance of the historical dimension in the analysis of political discourse. In this way, a multi-perspective interpretation of text is possible and intertextual, interdiscursive, diachronic as well as synchronic links can be drawn. Texts are never isolated, but are parts of greater temporal and spatial nexuses. Discourses overlap, and texts and genres thus are of a hybrid nature. Therefore, the DHA 'facilitates looking at latent power dynamics and the range of potential in agents' (Forchtner, Krzyżanowski & Wodak 2013, p. 211). The DHA aims at bringing to mind the relationship between power and language and at producing 'enlightenment and support emancipation' (Wodak & Köhler 2010, 36–37; Forchtner 2011, p. 2). The DHA criticises political language, and there is a special focus on right-wing and populist rhetoric (Wodak & de Cillia 2007; Wodak & Köhler 2010; Wodak 2014b). *Topics* of specific discourses, discursive strategies and the linguistic means by which they are constructed are analysed within the following five heuristic categories (Wodak 2001, p. 93). A focus on *nomination*, for instance, reveals how social actors or events (anthroponyms, tropes, etc.) are linguistically constructed. *Predication* refers to strategies, which attribute negative or positive characteristics to the social actors identified in a text, for example, via certain figures of speech, such as euphemisms or dysphemisms. In a further step, *argumentative strategies*, which are used to justify, for example, predications, are identified. In this step, *topoi* and argumentation patterns/fallacies are evaluated. By looking for *mitigation/intensification*, ways of modifying utterances are detected. Furthermore, *strategies of perspectivation* are assessed – here, the point of view of a rhetor in the production of the communicative piece is of importance (Forchtner, Krzyżanowski & Wodak 2013, p. 211). The DHA is 'particularly interested in the analysis of contents of argumentation schemes' and 'stresses the importance of mapping out sound or fallacious argumentation' (Reisigl 2014, p. 69). The approaches described above have in common that they analyse specific devices of rhetoric, some of which will be described in more detail in the next sections.

Analysing rhetorical devices

Fairclough and Fairclough (2012, p. 17) define public discourse, especially political discourse, as 'primarily argumentative discourse'. Hence, it makes sense that many rhetorical analyses focus on evaluating and critically assessing arguments. Argumentation schemes and typologies form a basis for carrying out argumentation analysis. They have been criticised (Öhlschläger 1979) and modified by more recent researchers (Manfred Kienpointner; Douglas Walton) and modern typologies also 'try to improve standards of explicitness and demarcation and sometimes also incorporate normative aspects by asking critical questions on argumentative schemes' (Kienpointner 1995a). Two main areas of argumentation analysis are generally conducted and briefly discussed in the following sections.

Logical structure analysis of argumentation

Formal structures underlying argumentation are omnipresent in everyday language and even more so in political arguments. To reconstruct the logical structure of arguments found in a discourse, so-called argumentation schemes are useful. The most basic structure of an argumentative utterance consists of a major premise and a conclusion that follows it and may look like this:

Major Premise: A
thus
Conclusion: B

(Posch 2014, p. 39)

In complex discourse, argument structures are often much less transparent, thus argument schemes were proposed to help identify and reconstruct structure to enable argument evaluation. For example, Walton and Hansen (2013, p. 79) propose the following argument scheme for the logical structure analysis of an *argument from fairness*:

> Major Premise: If A treats B and C equally then A is fair (just).
> Minor Premise: Action (policy) A treats B and C equally.
> Conclusion: A should be carried out.
> (A is an action, or in some instances a general policy for action. B and C are agents or groups of agents)
>
> (Walton & Hansen 2013, p. 79)

Walton and Hansen demonstrate how this scheme works via the example of a text concerning a programme suggested for criminals in Ontario. This programme requires criminals to do community work. In a press conference, the politician Tim Hudak said: 'We're just asking the prisoners to do what every other hard-working Ontarian does – an honest day's work instead of spending the day working out to become better criminals' (Mackrael 2011). According to Walton and Hansen, this is an *argument from fairness*, because it suggests that criminals and citizens should be treated in the same way with respect to having to work (Walton & Hansen 2013, p. 79). With the argumentation scheme above, the argument can be broken down into the following structure:

> Major Premise: If the work programme treats criminals and citizens equally, then the work programme is fair (just).
> Minor Premise: The work programme treats criminals and citizens equally.
> Conclusion: The work programme should be carried out.[6]

The argument scheme as such does not automatically make a claim about how justified an argument is, or whether it is good or bad. It only identifies the structure underlying the argument. In order to assess an argument more profoundly theoreticians suggest asking critical questions about it.[7]

In traditional logic, arguments that are not formally valid are generally viewed as fallacies. For everyday language, however, this strict distinction is not useful and therefore recent approaches evaluate fallacies differently by bearing in mind linguistic and communicative aspects. One basic assumption here is that even emotional appeals can be acceptable in certain circumstances and some traditional fallacies can be 're-evaluated as forms of presumptive reasoning' (Kienpointner 1995a; Walton 1995). The important question in recent structure analysis is whether or not emotive language in arguments is acceptable and when. Macagno and Walton (2013, p. 5) consider emotive words 'extremely effective instruments to direct and encourage certain attitudes and choices' which makes 'words' key in rhetorical analysis: they describe and hide reality at the same time. What we name is equally important as what we omit. Thus, the focus of rhetorical analysis cannot be on the structure of arguments alone, as this is not sufficient to evaluate arguments as plausible or fallacious.

Semantics of arguments. Topics

Textual aspects of argumentation have to be examined closely, which can only be done if the meaning of 'extra logical vocabulary' is also considered (Kienpointner 2008, p. 711). An analyst has to assess the actual meaning of the words used in the context of an argumentation, the 'argumentative *topoi*' (Kienpointner 2008, p. 710). *Topoi* (singular *topos*) are a concept frequently used in rhetorical analysis: 'They are the content-related warrants or 'conclusion rules' connecting the argument or arguments with the conclusion, the claim. As such, 'they justify the transition from the argument or arguments to the conclusion' (Kienpointner 1992, p. 192).[8] *Topoi* could be described as thought markers that lie behind the argument and indicate the route to a certain conclusion. *Topoi* are always connected to the context of an argumentation and they are likely to 'proliferate according to the range of specific rhetorical situations for which arguments are necessary' (Klein 2014, p. 133). Lists of frequent *topoi* are a background for analysing typical content-related argumentation schemes, even if they are 'incomplete and not always disjunctive' (Wodak 2001, p. 74). In a case study of a petition issued by the Austrian right-wing party FPÖ in 1992–1993, Wodak (2001, p. 75) distinguishes 15 *topoi* as typical for discriminatory discourses. One is exemplified here: the *topos of danger and threat*. In its simplest form, this *topos* can be paraphrased as 'if there are specific dangers and threats, one should do something against them' (Wodak 2001, p. 75). This *topos* appears frequently in discriminatory discourses on immigration, which argue that something should be done against too many immigrants. In these discourses, immigrants are viewed as threats to a country or society,[9] often with a demand for political action. Forchtner, Krzyżanowski & Wodak (2013, pp. 211–217) identify this *topos* in a series of election campaign posters advertising Austria's Freedom Party *inter alia* arguing for 'More courage for our "Viennese Blood"' and 'too much otherness is not good for anybody'.

In an extensive study of the Austrian 'rhetoric of the national' Reisigl (2007) analyses politicians' speeches on the 'Austrian nation' and 'Austrian national identity', which were held at especially staged commemorative events with the slogan '950 years Austria' and '1000 years Austria'. Reisigl identifies 34 notable *topoi* in the Austrian discourse on 'nation' and 'national identity', for example the so-called *singularity topos*.[10] The *singularity topos* in Reisigl's study refers to the explicit and implicit idea of Austria's uniqueness or singularity within Europe, which is generally assumed and sometimes argumentatively highlighted in the speeches analysed. Former Federal President Thomas Klestil argues that he 'does not know any other country' which has been so closely connected to the idea of Europe from its very beginning (Reisigl 2007, pp. 171–72). 'Any other country' is also phonetically emphasised to strengthen the argument. *Topoi* in discourse serve as a connection or thread providing the content-logic of an argument.

Fallacious arguments

Since the beginning of the occupation with rhetoric, deficient arguments have been called fallacies, and typologies of fallacies have been created. Aristotle already provided catalogues of fallacies, which were not changed much or criticised until recently (Kienpointner 2008, p. 715). Today, research defines fallacies as rule violations in reasonable argumentation, corresponding to a pragmatic theory of fallacies (van Eemeren & Grootendorst 1992). The related pragma-dialectical perspective on fallacy (Reisigl 2014; Walton 1987; Walton 1995) defines it as:

> an argument, a pattern of argumentation, or something that purports to be an argument, that falls short of some standard of correctness as used in a conversational context but that, for various reasons, has a semblance of correctness about it in context, and poses a serious obstacle to the realization of the goal of the dialog.
>
> (Walton 2011, p. 380)

Reisigl (2014, p. 82) emphasises that a fallacy need not necessarily be restricted to single speech acts and also that 'sequences of related speech acts' can become fallacious. Thus, if one is to analyse argumentation, some normative model that provides guidelines for distinguishing sound from fallacious argumentation, is needed. Even so, it is difficult to make this distinction, because it also 'heavily depends on the previous topic-related knowledge of the analysts and on the respective "field" in which the argumentation is embedded' (Reisigl 2014, p. 79). Pragma-dialectics provides such a set of ten normative rules (van Eemeren & Grootendorst 1992), which are supplemented by eight more rules in the Discourse-Historical Approach (Reisigl 2014, p. 83). Forchtner (2011, p. 10) argues that for an analysis of fallacies Habermas' language-philosophy which 'gives an account of *why* fallacious arguments are fallacious at all' should also be given more weight in the future.

Names of fallacies are often composed of *argumentum ad* and another Latin component describing its meaning. Some terms for fallacies also have numerous, descriptive English equivalents. Argument schemes, as well as rule sets, can be used to analyse fallacies such as *argumentum ad misericordiam* (appeal to pity), *argumentum ad populum* (appeal to popularity, consensus fallacy), *argumentum ad hominem* (personal attack), *argumentum ad baculum* (appeal to force), the *Straw Man Fallacy*, and many more. Lists of informal and formal fallacies are abundant on the internet, even though sites of course greatly vary in quality. Many fallacies may be acceptable in distinctive circumstances and in particular dialogue types, even if they form weak or presumptive arguments to support a certain standpoint. To evaluate at which point a fallacy becomes unacceptable in a certain discourse, analysts ask critical questions. For example, *argumentum ad misericordiam* (appeal to pity) is an argument in which the arguer tries to evoke feelings of pity in order to persuade. Walton (1997) suggests that an *appeal to pity* is fallacious if it is either formulated in such a way that it blocks further questions, or if its dramatic impact is severely exaggerated. A fallacious *appeal to pity* mentioned by Kienpointner (2009) is often used by so-called Pro-Life activists. In one example, US abortion laws are compared to the Nuremberg laws and to slavery, drastically accompanied by explicit pictures on a website. Such arguments prevent rational discussions of the topic by 'using excessively drastic verbal and visual means of argumentation for their standpoint in order to seal off the discussion and to silence the opponent' (Kienpointner 2009, p. 71). This makes them highly problematic strategic moves in a discussion.

A major problem arising when classifying arguments as fallacies is that 'we have to explain how each of them is used as an effective deceptive tactic that does work to fool people' (Walton 2011, p. 381). To solve this problem, the concept of *strategic manoeuvring* was introduced by van Eemeren (2008) to account for actions arguers take to achieve both their rhetorical and dialectical goals. Here, rhetorical strategies are registered and evaluated to determine at which point emotional argumentation becomes unacceptable or fallacious (Kienpointner 2011, p. 513).

Figures of speech

Figures of speech (FSP) are another important instrument in rhetoric, especially political rhetoric, and they have been studied as one of the main branches of rhetoric from antiquity onwards. They are small rhetorical units and, from a classical perspective, they were viewed as linguistic ornaments or stylistic means. Recent approaches influenced by modern linguistics, however, also concentrate on the mechanisms and structures of FSP (Gévaudan 2009) and rather view them as semiotic categories. Extensive typologies specifying and describing the five traditional categories of FSP – simile, metaphor, hyperbole, personification and synecdoche – were developed. Tzvetan Todorov (1966) and Geoffrey Leech (1979 [1966]) undertook modern attempts at the classification of FSP.[11]

However, what exactly are FSP? A broad definition is given by Kienpointner (1995b), who states that they: 'are the output of discourse strategies which we use to select units from linguistic paradigms of different levels (phonetics/phonology, morphology, syntax, semantics) to create texts (in the sense of both written and spoken genres of discourse) which are adequate as far as their communicative purpose in some context is concerned'. FSP can be distinguished by a) the linguistic levels on which they are operating, and b) the operations that occur when figures of speech are realised (Kienpointner 1995b).

A brief explanation of these distinctions will be given in the following short sections. On the linguistic level of sound (phonology) FSP such as alliteration, assonance, consonance or onomatopoeia are situated. Put simply, FSP on this level achieve attention because they do something with sound, for example, repeating the initial consonant sound of a word (alliteration). The following example from George W. Bush's State of the Union Address in 2002 demonstrates this effect (alliteration highlighted): 'The American people have responded magnificently, with courage and compassion, strength and resolve' (Posch 2006, p. 94). FSP may also be at work on a meaning-level of language (semantics) as is the case with euphemisms, metaphors, metonymies, personifications, and many more. In political discourses especially, euphemisms are frequently used as stylistic elements. Their ability of blurring or disguising a meaning in an utterance is in parts responsible for the sometimes negative conception of the term rhetoric. One example of this is a regional political campaign in Austria titled '*sauberes Graz*' (clean Graz). This campaign focused on the terms 'clean' or 'to clean' which alludes to the terrible euphemisms Nazi propaganda frequently used. 'To clean' was used to camouflage genocide (Wodak & Köhler 2010, p. 41). Many more types of FSP are also located on other linguistic levels such as morphology (*anaphora, anadiplosis, archaism, epiphora*) and syntax (*ellipsis, parallelism, chiasmus, asyndeton, polysyndeton*).[12]

FSP can also be categorised along the lines of how they operate. For example, the aforementioned figure 'alliteration' is defined as a figure of repetition, because it achieves an effect by repeating sounds. Other operational modes are subtraction, permutation and substitution. Again, these types of operation can appear on all levels of language. An FSP that operates by substitution, the re-arranging of an element, is metonymy. Metonymy refers to a type of relation between two linguistic entities. On a word level, for instance, this would be achieved by using one name to stand in for the name of an entity that is closely related to it (Wodak & de Cillia 2007, p. 43). This can be observed when the name of a country is used to refer to the people living in it, such as 'Austria is World Champion' (Wodak & de Cillia 2007, p. 43) or 'America has a window of opportunity to extend and secure our present peace […]' (Posch 2006, p. 86).

Parallelisms are, for example, pairs of utterances in which syntax and lexis are coordinated in such a way that they are short and easy to remember. According to Charteris-Black (2005, p. 5) such short 'sound bites' are often selected because they suggest certainty and simplicity with the aim to persuade the audience of a certain argument. Parallelisms are figures of repetition – one element (for example sound or word), or even a broader structure (phrase, sentence) is repeated. The following short excerpt from a speech delivered by George W. Bush to the US troops in Qatar on 5 June, 2003 demonstrates this (Posch 2006, p. 107): 'We believe that liberty is God's gift to every individual on the face of the earth. We believe people have the right to think and speak and worship in freedom.' This FSP operates by parallelism and is called *anaphora*. The phrase 'we believe' is repeated at the beginning of each sentence, thus the linguistic level on which it operates is syntax and the operation that occurs is repetition.

The use of FSP does not automatically turn rhetoric into something negative, or make it fallacious. Rather, FSP are more or less present in any utterance. Particularly in political rhetoric, the overall aim is to convince audiences of a standpoint and FSP are a tool that may or may not help to achieve this goal. A rhetorical analyst may categorise FSP used in a discourse and take a close look at the effects that are achieved with their use.

Reconstructing metaphors

In a traditional sense, metaphors are often viewed as purely ornamental, as subsets of FSP. In modern discourse-centred approaches, however, metaphors are no longer viewed as artificially crafted linguistic tools, but rather as instruments that structure thinking and are deeply anchored in the human mind. Charteris-Black (2005, p. 13) views metaphors as important in any persuasive discourse, because they mediate between 'conscious and unconscious means of persuasion – between cognition and emotion' and they are therefore 'a central strategy for legitimization in political speeches'. Charteris-Black also assumes that metaphors are the most important rhetorical and stylistic device in political discourses. It is a linguistic characteristic of metaphors that they produce semantic tension. Pragmatically, the aim of metaphor use, as everyday their use may be, is to persuade (Charteris-Black 2005, p. 13). Most approaches dealing with metaphor in language today are based on the definition of metaphor as cognitive structures by Lakoff and Johnson (2011) from their famous book *Metaphors we live by*. Metaphors are understood in such a way that they do not only appear on the linguistic surface, but rather that the linguistic metaphor is cognitively preceded by a so-called 'conceptual metaphor'. Conceptual metaphors are, simply put, 'pathways' of thinking we are used to taking, they hint at our thinking habitus (Leech 1979 [1966], p. 331). Conceptual metaphors in metaphor analysis are usually indicated by capital letters. Frequent metaphors, especially in political discourses, are war metaphors. Posch, Stopfner, and Kienpointner (2013, p. 113) identified the POLITICS IS WAR metaphor as a metaphor that is frequently used by right-wing populists.

In a study on media reports of the worldwide financial crisis, Posch (2010) found that conceptual metaphors that frame the international financial crisis as a phenomenon occurring without any external influences are frequent; for example, the CRISIS AS SICKNESS or AS NATURAL CATASTROPHE metaphors. They linguistically manifest in phrases such as 'there is no recovery' or the 'crisis has become virulent', and in sentences such as 'There is a storm brewing: It is about low paid salespeople and business groups heading towards crisis' (Posch 2010, 133). The CRISIS AS SICKNESS metaphor entails that the financial crisis is, rather, a danger that comes from outside and not anything produced by humans. This danger is spreading autonomously, the crisis itself becomes the acting subject of the discourse. In this way, the discourse obscures those responsible for the crisis. The same is true for the CRISIS AS NATURAL CATASTROPHE metaphor. People as well as business are cognitively construed as actors in nature who are endangered by the catastrophe, rather than as responsible agents.

Prospect

Research into speech communication continues the tradition of classical rhetoric with a focus on critical rhetorical analysis (Campbell & Jamieson 1990; Gévaudan 2009) as well as composition (Raskin & Weiser 1987). Furthermore, especially in linguistics, the focus now is on the use of computerised methods for applied and critical research into rhetoric and discourse analysis. Corpus linguistics aims to develop new methods for finding arguments and rhetorical devices in huge numbers of texts, which may contribute empirical support to the findings of discourse analysis. The research programme of sentiment analysis, for example, aims to develop machine algorithms to detect subjective emotions in a text (Généreux, Poibeau & Koppel 2011). Other corpus linguistic approaches seek to combine ideas and concepts from discourse analysis and rhetoric with the analysis of large corpora (Baker 2006; Bubenhofer 2013; Bubenhofer & Scharloth 2013; Felder 2012; Mautner 2001; Volk et al. 2010). Rhetorical analysis is now key in all of these disciplines and presumably will continue to blossom as a field of interest in the years to come.

Notes

1 For a translated version of Aristotle's work, see Roberts 1984.
2 Singular: '*tópos*'.
3 In his *Topics*, Aristotle lists more than 300 tópoi, see Kienpointner 1995a.
4 For a short overview, see Kienpointner 2011, p. 512.
5 For a general introduction on CDA, see Forchtner 2012; for a view on the relation of rhetoric and CDA, see for instance, Forchtner & Tominc 2012.
6 In Walton and Hansen's (2013, p. 79) analysis, the scheme is more detailed and there are different versions of it.
7 For an example of critical questions concerning the above argument on fairness, see Walton and Hansen 2013, p. 82.
8 On *topoi*, see also: Klein 2014, p. 133; Forchtner 2014; Wodak 2001, p. 110; for a critique of the concept of *topoi* as it is applied by rhetorical analysts, see Žagar 2010; for a reply to Žagar's critique, see Reisigl 2014, p. 85.
9 For example, as 'economic threat' see Baker, McEnery & Gabrielatos 2007.
10 The *singularity topos* can also be found in nomination strategies referring to the 'real Austrian' and 'Viennese Blood', see Wodak 2014b, p. 111; Forchtner et al. 2013, p. 217.
11 For a more detailed overview, see Dubois 1981 [1970].
12 Abundant catalogues and glossaries with examples of types of FSP can be found on the internet (e.g. http://rhetoric.byu.edu or http://americanrhetoric.com).

References

Baker, P, 2006, *Using corpora in discourse analysis*, Continuum, London.
Baker, P, McEnery, T & Gabrielatos C, 2007, *Using collocation analysis to reveal the construction of minority groups: The case of refugees, asylum seekers and immigrants in the UK press*, Workshop paper, available from: http://eprints.lancs.ac.uk/id/eprint/602 [accessed 31 January 2016].
Bubenhofer, N, 2013, 'Quantitativ informierte qualitative Diskursanalyse: Korpuslinguistische Zugänge zu Einzeltexten und Serien' in *Angewandte Diskurslinguistik: Felder, Probleme, Perspektiven*, eds. K S Roth & C Spiegel, Akademie-Verlag, Berlin, pp. 109–134.
Bubenhofer, N & Scharloth, J, 2013, 'Korpuslinguistische Diskursanalyse: Der Nutzen empirisch-quantitativer Verfahren' in *Diskurslinguistik im Spannungsfeld von Deskription und Kritik*, eds. I H Warnke, U Meinhof & M Reisigl, Akademie-Verlag, Berlin, pp. 147–168.
Burke, K, 2004–2014, 'Works by Kenneth Burke (full list)', *The Journal of the Kenneth Burke Society*, available from: http://kbjournal.org/node/58, [accessed 31 January 2016].
Campbell, K K & Huxman, S S, 2009, *The rhetorical act: Thinking, speaking and writing critically*, 4th ed., Wadsworth, Belmont, CA.
Campbell, K K & Jamieson, K H, 1990, *Deeds done in words: Presidential rhetoric and the genres of governance*, University of Chicago Press, Chicago, IL.

Charteris-Black, J 2005, *Politicians and rhetoric: The persuasive power of metaphor*, Palgrave Macmillan, New York.

Chilton, P A & Schäffner, C, 2002, *Politics as text and talk: Analytic approaches to political discourse*, Benjamins, Amsterdam.

Dubois, J 1981 [1970], *A general rhetoric*, Johns Hopkins University Press, Baltimore, MD.

Eisenhart, C & Johnstone, B, 2008, 'Discourse analysis and rhetorical studies' in *Rhetoric in detail: Discourse analyses of rhetorical talk and text*, eds. B Johnstone & C Eisenhart, Benjamins, Amsterdam, pp. 3–21.

Fairclough, I & Fairclough, N, 2012, *Political discourse analysis: A method for advanced students*, Routledge, London.

Felder, E, ed., 2012, *Korpuspragmatik: Thematische Korpora als Basis diskurslinguistischer Analysen*, de Gruyter, Berlin.

Forchtner, B, 2011, 'Critique, the discourse-historical approach, and the Frankfurt School', *Critical Discourse Studies*, vol. 8, no. 1, pp. 1–14.

Forchtner, B, 2012, 'Critical Discourse Analysis', in *The encyclopedia of applied linguistics*, ed. CA Chapelle, Blackwell, Oxford, pp. 1–7.

Forchtner, B, 2014, '*Historia magistra vitae*: The *topos* of history as a teacher in public struggles over self- and other-representation', in *Contemporary Critical Discourse Studies*, eds. C Hart & P Cap, Bloomsbury, London, pp. 19–43.

Forchtner, B & Tominc, A, 2012, 'Critique and argumentation: On the relation between the discourse-historical approach and Pragma-dialectics', *Journal of Language and Politics*, vol. 11, no. 1, pp. 31–50.

Forchtner, B, Krzyżanowski, M & Wodak, R, 2013, 'Mediatization, right-wing populism and political campaigning: The case of the Austrian Freedom Party' in *Media talk and political elections in Europe and America*, eds. M Ekström & A Tolson, Palgrave Macmillan, Basingstoke, pp. 205–228.

Généreux, M, Poibeau, T & Koppel, M, 2011, 'Sentiment analysis using automatically labelled financial news items', in *Affective computing and sentiment analysis*, ed. A Khurshid, Springer, Dordrecht, pp. 101–114.

Gévaudan, P, 2009, 'Tropen und Figuren', in *Rhetorik und Stilistik: Ein Handbuch historischer und systematischer Forschung*, ed. U Fix, de Gruyter, Berlin, pp. 728–742.

Hansen, H V, 2008, 'Rhetoric and logic', in *The international encyclopedia of communication*, ed. W Donsbach, Blackwell, Malden, MA, pp. 4268–4271.

Johnson, R H, 2000, *Manifest rationality: A pragmatic theory of argument*, Lawrence Erlbaum Associates, Mahwah, NJ.

Kienpointner, M, 1992, *Alltagslogik: Struktur und Funktion von Argumentationsmustern*, Frommann-Holzboog, Stuttgart-Bad Cannstatt.

Kienpointner, M, 1995a, 'Rhetoric', in *Handbook of pragmatics*, eds. J Verschueren, J O Östman & J Blommaert, Benjamins, Amsterdam, Available from: https://benjamins.com/online/hop/link/articles/rhe1.hop.m.html, [accessed 31 January 2016].

Kienpointner, M, 1995b, 'Figures of speech', in *Handbook of pragmatics*, eds. J Verschueren, J O Östman & J Blommaert, Benjamins, Amsterdam, available from: https://benjamins.com/online/hop/link/articles/fig1.hop.5.html [accessed 31 January 2016].

Kienpointner, M, 2005, 'Rhetorik im 21. Jahrhundert. Probleme, Positionen und Perspektiven', *RhetOn - Online-Zeitschrift für Rhetorik & Wissenstransfer*, available from: http://www.rheton.sbg.ac.at/rheton/2007/04/manfred-kienpointner-rhetorik-im-21-jahrhundert-probleme-positionen-und-perspektiven/ [accessed 31 January 2016].

Kienpointner, M, 2008, 'Argumentationstheorie', in *Rhetorik und Stilistik: Ein Internationales Handbuch historischer und systematischer Forschung*, eds. U Fix, A Gardt & J Knape, de Gruyter, Berlin, pp. 702–717.

Kienpointner, M, 2009, 'Plausible and fallacious strategies to silence one's opponent', in *Examining argumentation in context: Fifteen studies on strategic maneuvering*, ed. F van Eemeren, Benjamins, Amsterdam, pp. 61–75.

Kienpointner, M, 2011, 'Rhetorik', in *Aristoteles-Handbuch: Leben, Werk, Wirkung*, eds. C Rapp & K Corcilius, Metzler, Stuttgart, pp. 510–515.

Kindt, W, 2008, 'Die Rolle sprachlicher Indikatoren für Argumentationsanalysen. Ein Ergebnisbericht aus der Linguistischen Rhetorik', in *Rhetorische Wissenschaft: Rede und Argumentation in Theorie und Praxis*, ed. G Kreuzbauer, Lit, Wien, pp. 147–162.

Klein, J, 2009, 'Rhetorisch-stilistische Eigenschaften der Sprache der Politik', in *Rhetorik und Stilistik: Ein Handbuch historischer und systematischer Forschung*, ed. U Fix, de Gruyter, Berlin, pp. 2112–2131.

Klein, J, 2014, *Grundlagen der Politolinguistik: Ausgewählte Aufsätze*, Frank et Timme, Berlin.

Lakoff, G & Johnson, M, 2011, *Metaphors we live by*, 6th ed., University of Chicago Press, Chicago, IL.

Lauer, J M, 2004, *Invention in rhetoric and composition*, Parlor Press, West Lafayette, IN.

Leech, G N [1966] 1979, 'Linguistics and the figures of rhetoric', in *Essays on style and language: Linguistic and critical approaches to literary style*, ed. R Fowler, Routledge and Kegan, London, pp. 135–156.

Lunsford, A A, Wilson, K H & Eberly, R A, eds., 2009, *The SAGE handbook of rhetorical studies*, SAGE, Thousand Oaks, CA.

Macagno, F & Walton, D, 2013, *Emotive language in argumentation*, Cambridge University Press, New York.

Mackrael, K, 2011, 'Prison guard union not endorsing Ontario PC chain-gang plan', *The Globe and Mail*, 29 September. Available from: http://www.theglobeandmail.com/news/politics/prison-guard-union-not-endorsing-ontario-pc-chain-gang-plan/article596143/ [accessed 31 January 2016].

Mautner, G, 2001, 'Checks and Balances: How corpus linguistics can contribute to CDA', in *Methods of critical discourse analysis*, eds. R Wodak & M Meyer, Sage, London, pp. 155–179.

Meyer, M, 1994, *Rhetoric, language, and reason*, Pennsylvania State University Press, Pennsylvania, PA.

Meynet, R, 2012, *Treatise on biblical rhetoric*, Brill, Leiden, Boston, MA.

Öhlschläger, G, 1979, *Linguistische Überlegungen zu einer Theorie der Argumentation*, Niemeyer, Tübingen.

Perelman, C, Olbrechts-Tyteca L, Kopperschmidt, J, Varwig, F & Ehni, H, 2004 [1969], *Die neue Rhetorik: Eine Abhandlung über das Argumentieren*, Frommann-Holzboog, Stuttgart-Bad Cannstatt.

Posch, C, 2006, *'This world he created is of moral design': The reinforcement of American values in the rhetoric of George W. Bush*, Praesens, Wien.

Posch, C, 2010, '"Ich halte es für den falschen Weg, sich täglich weiter in die Krise hineinreden zu lassen" Das (nicht) Sprechen über die globale Wirtschafts- und Finanzkrise in den österreichischen Medien', *aptum: Zeitschrift für Sprachkritik und Sprachkultur*, no. 2, pp. 121–137.

Posch, C, 2014, *Argumentieren, aber richtig: Praxisbuch für Studierende*, Tectum, Marburg.

Posch, C, Stopfner, M & Kienpointner, M, 2013, 'German postwar discourse of the extreme and populist right', in *Analysing fascist discourse: European fascism in talk and text*, eds. R Wodak & J E Richardson, Routledge, New York, pp. 97–121.

Raskin, V & Weiser, I, 1987, *Language and writing: Applications of linguistics to rhetoric and composition*, ABLEX, Norwood, N.J.

Reisigl, M, 2007, *Nationale Rhetorik in Fest- und Gedenkreden*, Stauffenburg, Tübingen, Wien.

Reisigl, M, 2008, 'Rhetoric of political speeches', in *Handbook of communication in the public sphere*, eds. R Wodak & V Koller, de Gruyter, Berlin, pp. 243–269.

Reisigl, M, 2014, 'Argumentation analysis and the discourse-historical approach: A methodological framework', in *Contemporary Critical Discourse Studies*, eds. C Hart & P Cap, Bloomsbury, London, pp. 67–95.

Roberts, W W, 1984, 'Rhetoric', in *The complete works of Aristotle*, Princeton University Press, Princeton, NJ, pp. 4618–4866.

Rutten, K, van Belle, H & Gillaerts, P, 2014, 'Let's talk politics: Introduction', in *Let's talk politics: New essays on deliberative rhetoric*, ed. H van Belle, Benjamins, Amsterdam, pp. 3–9.

Sloane, T O, 2001, *Encyclopedia of rhetoric*, Oxford University Press, Oxford.

Tindale, C W, 1999, *Acts of arguing: A rhetorical model of argument*, State University of New York Press, Albany, NY.

Todorov, T, 1966, 'Les anomalies sémantiques', *Languages*, vol. 1, no. 1, pp. 100–123.

Toulmin, S 2003, *The uses of argument*, Cambridge University Press, Cambridge.

van Dijk, T A, 2008, *Discourse and context: A socio-cognitive approach*, Cambridge University Press, Cambridge, MA.

van Eemeren, F H, 2008, 'Rhetoric, argument, and persuasion', in *The international encyclopedia of communication*, ed. W Donsbach, Blackwell, Malden, MA, pp. 4215–4219.

van Eemeren, FH & Grootendorst, R, 1992, *Argumentation, communication, and fallacies: A pragma-dialectical perspective*, Erlbaum, Hillsdale, NJ.

van Eemeren, FH & Houtlosser, P, 2006, 'The case of Pragma-dialectics', in *Argumentation in multi-agent systems: Second International Workshop*, ed. S Parsons, Springer, Berlin, pp. 1–28.

van Eemeren, F H & Houtlosser P, 2009, 'Strategic maneuvering: Examining argumentation in context', in *Examining argumentation in context: Fifteen studies on strategic maneuvering*, ed. F H van Eemeren, Benjamins, Amsterdam, pp. 1–24.

Volk, M, Bubenhofer, M, Althaus, A, Bangerter, M, Furrer, L & Ruef, B, 2010, 'Challenges in building a multilingual alpine heritage corpus', in *Seventh international conference on Language Resources and Evaluation* (LREC), Malta, 19-21 May 2010, pp. 1653–1659. Available from: http://www.zora.uzh.ch/34264/2/volk_et_al_text_n_berg_for_LREC_2010V.pdf [accessed 31 January 2016].

Walton, D, 1987, *Informal fallacies*, Benjamins, Amsterdam.

Walton, D, 1995, *A pragmatic theory of fallacy*, University of Alabama Press, Tuscaloosa, AL.

Walton, D, 1997, *Appeal to pity: Argumentum ad misericordiam*, State University of New York Press, Albany, NY.

Walton, D, 2008, *Informal logic: A pragmatic approach* 2nd ed., Cambridge University Press, New York.

Walton, D, 2011, 'Defeasible reasoning and informal fallacies', *Synthese*, vol. 179, no. 3, pp. 377–407.

Walton, D & Hansen, H V, 2013, 'Arguments from fairness and misplaced priorities in political argumentation' *Journal of Politics and Law*, vol. 6, no. 3, pp. 78–94.

Wodak, R, 2001, 'The discourse-historical approach', in *Methods for Critical Discourse Analysis*, eds. R Wodak & M Meyer, Sage, London, pp. 63–94.

Wodak, R, ed., 2012, *SAGE major works in Critical Discourse Analysis*, 4 volumes, Sage, Los Angeles, CA.

Wodak, R, 2014a, 'Political discourse analysis – Distinguishing frontstage and backstage contexts. A discourse-historical approach', in *Discourse in context*, ed. J Flowerdew, Bloomsbury, London, pp. 522–549.

Wodak, R, 2014b, 'The strategy of discursive provocation: A discourse-historical analysis of the FPÖ's discriminatory rhetoric', in *Doublespeak: The rhetoric of the far right since 1945*, eds. M Feldman & P Jackson, Ibidem, Stuttgart, pp. 101–119.

Wodak, R & Chilton, P A, 2005, *A new agenda in (critical) discourse analysis: Theory, methodology, and interdisciplinary*, Benjamins, Amsterdam.

Wodak, R & de Cillia, R, 2007, 'Commemorating the past: the discursive construction of official narratives about the "Rebirth of the Second Austrian Republic"', *Discourse & Communication*, vol. 1, no. 3, pp. 337–363.

Wodak, R & Köhler, K, 2010, 'Wer oder was ist »fremd«? Diskurshistorische Analyse fremdenfeindlicher Rhetorik in Österreich', *SWS-Rundschau*, vol. 50, no. 1, pp. 33–55.
Wodak, R & Meyer, M, 2009, *Methods of Critical Discourse Analysis*, Sage, London.
Zachry, M, 2009, 'Rhetorical analysis', in *The handbook of business discourse*, ed. F Bargiela-Chiappini, Edinburgh University Press, Edinburgh, pp. 68–79.
Žagar, I, 2010, '*Topoi* in Critical Discourse Analysis', *Lodz Papers in Pragmatics* vol. 6, no. 1, pp. 3–27.
Zarefsky, D, 2014, *Rhetorical perspectives on argumentation: Selected essays*, Springer, Heidelberg.

17
Understanding political issues through argumentation analysis

Ruth Amossy

Introduction

Is political discourse intrinsically linked to argumentation? Today, public opinion is often inclined to doubt it, partly due to the popular notion that politicians resort to rhetorical strategies in order to better manipulate their audience, with little consideration for valid reasoning and genuine debate. If we follow Aristotle's *Rhetoric*, however, the answer to this question can be considered as a matter of fact: political discourse corresponds to the 'deliberative' mode, one of the three genres upon which rhetorical argumentation is traditionally built (together with the forensic and the epideictic). Deliberation is mainly 'concerned with determining whether a course of action or a policy [is] useful or harmful (expedient or inexpedient)' (Jasinski 2001, p. 160). It can be defined as a verbal attempt to reach an agreement on the most suitable choice for the common good in situations where different, if not contradictory, opinions are possible. The practice of *logos* as both discourse and reason is supposed to pave the way for conflict resolution, thus allowing for a peaceful management of the various problems facing the *polis*. This view is at the basis of quite divergent approaches to argumentation such as that of Perelman's and Olbrecht Tyteca's *New rhetoric* (1969 [1958]) and van Eemeren's Amsterdam School of Pragma-dialectics (1996).

Argumentation in political discourse is not, however, limited to an activity of reason weighing the *pros* and *contra* of a line of action, or of looking for a negotiated solution on controversial issues. Although practical reasoning does rely on logical processes linking premises to a conclusion, rhetorical argumentation in the Aristotelian tradition includes *pathos*, or appeals to emotions that act upon the audience, and *ethos*, or the presentation of self that confers credibility upon the orator (Amossy 2001, 2010b). The relevance of these elements for contemporary political discourse is obvious. Notably, *ethos* is understood more and more in light of the necessity for speakers to build a favourable image of themselves, so that it can enhance their public reputations and add weight to their propositions or programmes – or simply bring about their election, or maintain them in power.

Two more dimensions of rhetorical argumentation in its relation to political discourse should be emphasised: the epideictic and the polemical. Political discourse is meant not only to persuade by rationally justifying a choice, but also to reinforce existing values and shared opinions, so that citizens can be mobilised, in times of crisis, to defend these values. This is why the epideictic mode (although, in its traditional form – speeches of praise and blame, eulogies, and so on – it is often defined as merely ceremonial), actually plays a crucial socio-political role (Perelman & Olbrechts Tyteca 1969 [1958], pp. 47–55). Last but not least, political discourse displays fierce controversies in which two or more parties, overtly hostile to each other, do not necessarily reach an agreement. This polemical dimension, often blamed for its excess of passion and verbal violence, tends to be excluded from the realm of argumentation by those who promote a purely rational definition of public debate. However, in a pluralistic democracy where divergences of opinions are permanent and conflicts constitute the very heart of political life (Mouffe 2000), polemical exchanges constitute a fully argumentative modality defined by the confrontation of dichotomised stances in a dynamic of polarisation (dividing the public into antagonistic groups) (Amossy 2010a, 2014). In short, political argumentation includes not only deliberation as rational debate, but also a value-based discourse looking for communion, and an adversarial discourse that highlights sharp confrontations.

This extension of the limits and goals of political discourse has to be understood against the background of contemporary practice with its various institutional sub-genres, going from formal debate at the Chamber to TV addresses or informal discussions on the Web. If we view political discourse as the oral and written discourse of the politicians, but also as any discourse dealing with the problems of the *polis* (public affairs), we can see that the aforementioned aspects of argumentation are differently integrated in each political genre. Thus, a debate in Parliament is by definition deliberative, although it presents a varying degree of *ethos* building and of polemical confrontation. Electoral discourse heavily relies on *ethos* construction as a means of persuasion, while also playing on direct or indirect verbal confrontation. Each generic framework has its own constraints, allowing speakers to use its rules for their own purposes on the condition that they do not transgress the borderlines of what is allowed and tolerable in a given institutional or social space.

In the subsequent section, I will clarify the meaning of argumentation, before looking in the next section (p. 264) at argumentative analysis in relation to discourse analysis and giving an overview (p. 266) of a few contemporary approaches, some normative (such as Critical Discourse Analysis), and some non-committed and analytical. There will then follow an argumentative and discursive approach to political discourse –mainly borrowed from Amossy's 'argumentation in discourse', exemplified on a UN speech delivered by Israeli Prime Minister (PM) Benjamin Netanyahu (2014).

What is argumentative analysis? A communicational and discursive perspective

The main objective of argumentation analysis is to disclose the mechanisms and internal logic of political discourse through the way it constructs patterns of reasoning and puts them into words in a given generic and institutional framework. Practically, it unveils the way underlying arguments and argument schemes are embedded into words in order to act upon an audience, orient collective decisions and action, oppose conflicting stances, or simply reinforce pre-existing choices and points of view. Examining how political discourse works does not mean confining the exploration to formal features. Argumentation analysis sheds light on the intrinsic link between discursive elements, logical patterns of reasoning, and political issues in their specific socio-historical and cultural environment. In this perspective, it aspires to a better understanding of how discourse frames reality, defines collective problems, manages disagreement, reinforces power or allows for empowerment.

Such an approach to argumentation is communicational and discursive, defining argumentation as a verbal exchange (be it actual or virtual) between speakers who use *logos* – language and reason – in order to act on the outside world by acting upon each other. This is the perspective of the *New rhetoric* (Perelman & Olbrechts Tyteca 1969 [1958]), anchored in the great Aristotelian tradition. Defining rhetorical argumentation as the verbal attempt to bring about the adherence of an audience to a thesis, Perelman and Olbrechts Tyteca place addressees and their premises at the heart of the persuasion enterprise. Speakers have to adapt to their audiences; moreover, an audience can be defined as a construction of the orator who builds attempts at persuasion on the beliefs and ways of thinking attributed to the addressee (1969 [1958], p. 18). Common deliberation and mutual persuasion feed not on absolute truth – which does not exist in human affairs – but on *doxa* defined as common knowledge and common opinion: the series of values and recognised truths or facts that are widely circulated in a given community (Amossy & Sternberg 2002). The main task of the orator is to transfer to the conclusion the adherence that the audience grants to the shared premises.

The communicational bias entails a discursive one. When viewed not as reasoning *per se*, but as a social practice in which the participants share and discuss ways of defining and interpreting reality, argumentative patterns are necessarily rooted in natural language. Refusing to isolate logical propositions from the discourse that conveys them, argumentation analysis does not view natural language as an obstacle (as is the case in frameworks privileging abstract reasoning and logically valid arguments). On the contrary, natural language, with its polysemy and unavoidable ambiguity, is 'the necessary condition for argumentation' (Plantin 1995, p. 259). In short, argumentative speech does not take place within the space of pure logic, but within a communication situation and a socio-cultural context in which speakers interact by using a whole array of verbal means. All these discursive elements contribute to the argumentative enterprise in its social and cultural dimensions, and have to be closely analysed.

Argumentation analysis and discourse analysis

Viewing argumentation analysis as the attempt at understanding how political discourse, in its communicational and discursive dimensions, works in the field raises the question of its similarity and difference with discourse analysis (DA) and Critical Discourse Analysis (CDA). Although the latter promotes social critique, whereas DA offers a non-committed analytical approach, both are trends subsuming a variety of approaches, which deal not only with language in use and in context, but more broadly with discourse as a social practice. For Maingueneau, a main representative of the French trend, the object of DA is 'to apprehend discourse as articulating texts and social places. Consequently, its object is not textual organisation, nor communicative situation (as it can be described by traditional sociology), but what knots them together is a certain genre of discourse practice' (2007, p. 7).[1] In CDA terms, the analyst explores 'the dialectical relationship between a particular discursive event and all the diverse elements of the situation(s), institution(s) and social structures which frame it' (Fairclough, Mulderrig & Wodak 2013, p. 79). In the same perspective, the American branch of DA emphasises that 'Discourse is shaped by the world, and discourse shapes the world' (Johnstone 2008, p.10). Claiming that 'functionally, discourse is used (simultaneously) to represent, evaluate, argue for and against, and ultimately to legitimate or delegitimate social actions' (Hart & Cap 2014, p.1), and focusing on 'how decisions are made, resources allocated, and social adaptation or conflict accomplished in public and private life' (Johnstone 2008, p. 7), such an analytical framework is quite close to argumentation analysis in the study of the verbal management of social problems and collective choices. Some theories even consider that argumentativity constitutes an inherent feature of any discourse (Amossy 2009, p. 254; Reisigl 2014, p. 69).

Thus, argumentation analysis calls for laying bare the various patterns of reasoning underlying the verbal surface, thus exposing the logical foundation of political communication and its attempts at mutual influence. Patterns of reasoning include various argument structures such as *syllogisms* and *enthymemes*, examples and analogies, manifold types of arguments (arguments by the cause, from consequences, by the definition, etc.). They feed on *topoi* pertaining to *invention* and understood as logical underlying structures – such as the *topos* of quantity: what is good for a greater number is better than what is good for a smaller number; or the *topos* of quality: what is considered good by superior beings is better than what is considered good by the crowd. The analyst can use the tools provided by various argumentation treatises going from Aristotle to Perelman, Toulmin (2003 [1958]) or informal logicians (Johnson & Blair 2000). However, in order to explore discourse as a social practice, argumentation analysis needs linguistic insights and tools that neither ancient rhetoric nor contemporary theories of argumentation based on philosophical grounds can provide. Having uncovered the underlying abstract schemes, the analyst has to examine how they are put into words. In so doing, the analyst can feed on the notions and analytic tools of today's language studies, including major linguistic trends such as Benveniste's theory of enunciation (1974, 2014), Bakhtin's explorations of dialogism[2] (1986), pragmatics – with its emphasis on performatives, Ducrot's study of connectives and polyphony (1972, 1996, Anscombre & Ducrot 1988), and many others. The analyst can thus explore political discourse with the help of notions such as speaker and addressee, intersubjectivity and interaction, axiological and affective markers (Kerbrat Orecchioni 1980), presuppositions and implicatures (Amossy 2012 [2000], pp. 190–196; Wodak 2013a), nominalisation, connectives and hedges, phraseology, repetition and rhythm, and so on.[3]

This is why argumentation analysis calls for a merging of disciplines that, although very close, have historically developed as autonomous fields often ignoring each other, and are to this day institutionally kept apart. To develop a comprehensive approach of argumentation in discourse, analytical tools have to be borrowed from both fields of studies, while trying to work out a coherent framework where rhetorical argumentation and DA (or CDA) can harmoniously complement and enrich each other.

Last, but not least, let us emphasise that argumentation analysis in its connection to DA and CDA closely links verbal patterns of reasoning and figural constructions to their social and cultural context and promotes the notion of interdiscourse. '"Interdiscursivity" signifies that discourses are linked to each other in various ways' (Reisigl & Wodak 2015, p. 28). A central notion in all DA and CDA approaches, it reframes the rhetorical tradition of *doxa*, now conceived in a socio-historical perspective as the totality of the discourses circulating in the public space at a particular moment, with their stereotypes and frozen formulas, collective images, symbols and myths, basic beliefs and dominant ideas expressed through recurrent verbal means. Interdiscourse includes *topoi* understood, not as formal structures leading to a conclusion, but rather as content-related arguments, in the vein of Cicero's or Quintilianus' rhetoric (the so called commonplaces): 'they tell about [...] subjects' positions, controversial claims, justification strategies, ideologies, etc.' (Reisigl 2014, p. 77). Interdiscourse also includes fixed sets of arguments that have taken the form of reservoirs – a 'repertoire of arguments' in the formulation of Rennes

(2007), or 'rhetorical arsenal' as coined by Angenot (1997, 2004) (the French conveniently use the term '*argumentaire*'). The discursive and argumentative analysis has to show how interdiscourse is interwoven in the fabric of the new discourse that integrates, modifies and sometimes subverts it.

This leads us to a question partly accounting for the divide that often separates rhetorical argumentation from DA and CDA. The latter, with their strong emphasis on interdiscursivity, as well as on institutional and generic frameworks, emphasise the constraints put on speakers, and the extent to which they are determined and 'spoken' by the discourse of the time. As a consequence, the autonomy of the speaking subject as a unique individual endowed with reason will appear as illusory. Rhetorical argumentation, on the contrary, traditionally emphasises agency – free choice and the capacity to act by verbal means. This apparent incompatibility can, however, be resolved by a balanced approach, taking into account both the constraints determining discourse and, in this very framework, the possibility for individual or collective initiative and choice at the heart of the rhetorical enterprise.

DA or CDA

Before going back to argumentation analysis of political discourse, a short comment on the way the connection between (rhetorical) argumentation and DA has been viewed in different theoretical frameworks is needed. We have first to distinguish normative approaches based on CDA and mainly drawing on Pragma-dialectics, from non-normative DA approaches aiming at analytical understanding rather than assessment, based on the tradition of rhetorical argumentation and Perelman's and Olbrechts Tyteca's *New rhetoric*. The vocation of CDA is social critique: it 'studies the way ideology, identity and inequality are (re)enacted through texts produced in social and political contexts' (van Dijk 2001, p. 352); it is '*characterized by the common interests in demystifying ideologies and power through the systematic and retroductible investigation of semiotic data (written, spoken, or visual*' (Wodak 2013b, p. xxiii,). No wonder, thus, that Fairclough or Wodak turned to a normative theory of argumentation distinguishing between sound and fallacious argumentation. Pragma-dialectics provides ten rules for rational dispute, such as: parties must not prevent each other from advancing or casting doubts on standpoints, or whoever advances a standpoint has the obligation to defend it, and so on (van Eemeren et al. 1996). The violation of these rules points to fallacies – arguments that look valid on the surface but are not. Thus, arguments can be both described and assessed, denouncing manipulation and unethical discussions.

Other approaches are analytical rather than overtly critical: they do not seek to pass judgement on the texts they explore, nor do they confront them with a pre-established model (implying a preliminary ideological or political choice, and thus a declared commitment, on the part of the analyst). In this perspective, Amossy's Argumentation in discourse (2012 [2000]) borrows from the *New rhetoric* rather than from Pragma-dialectics, or Informal logic, that focuses on the detection of fallacies. In other words, argumentation analysis does not deal with the validity of arguments, nor does it confront the analysed address or debate to pre-established norms of political communication in order to assess its capacity of solving conflicts, or its adequacy as regards genuine democracy (in opposition, for instance, to Habermas' approach). Drawing on the French trend of DA (as represented by Charaudeau & Maingueneau 2002) that does not focus on social critique, Argumentation in discourse, unlike CDA, does not demand any overt commitment on the part of the analyst. According to Maingueneau, however, this mission has by itself a critical force: it 'destroys any illusion of transparency and self-evidence by linking discourses to the institutional settings that produce them, to the social practices of which they are part, and to situated power relationships' (Maingueneau 2012, p. 206). Johnstone (2008, p. 29) also claims that beyond the difference between critical and non-critical approaches, 'discourse analysis is, at root, a highly systematic, thorough approach to critical reading […], and critical reading almost inevitably leads to questioning the status quo' – even when social critique is not the objective.

Let us start with CDA's efforts at integrating argumentation. A theoretical framework was worked out in 2008 by Fairclough and Fairclough on the basis of Norman Fairclough's version of Critical Discourse Analysis (CDA). The latter is understood as a branch of critical social analysis, throwing light on its crucial linguistic dimension, and defined as a normative enterprise (criticising political reality on normative grounds). *Political Discourse Analysis* adds to this theory an argumentative approach called for by the deliberative nature of political discourse: according to the authors, practical reasoning has to be thoroughly explored because it determines choices leading to action. Thus, the necessity to find out formal models of practical reasoning in order to see how they are constructed in political discourse – which is done here in terms of claims and counter-claims in their relation to goals anchored in values, to circumstances, to means of achieving the goal, with a view on possible negative consequences (see Fairclough & Fairclough 2012, pp. 45, 51, 126, 148). The uncovering of underlying schemes – namely, argument reconstruction – is accompanied by a critical evaluation of the argument partly based on the normative approach of Pragma-dialectics, and called for by CDA's objective to disclose power relations, to denounce forces associated with capitalism, and so on, an approach justified by the idea that CDA is part of a social critique meant to change reality. Thus, this CDA approach to argumentation analysis is both explanatory, and evaluative.

Another interesting attempt at integrating discursive and argumentative analysis can be found in the Discourse-Historical Approach (DHA), another version of CDA 'with a strong and organized focus on argumentation' (Reisigl 2014, p. 67). Borrowing from Kopperschmidt (2000), its promoters understand argumentation as a persuasion enterprise focusing on the 'systematic challenging or justification of validity claims, such as truth and normative rightness', the first relating to knowledge and degrees of certainty, the second to practical norms or ethical and moral standards (Reisigl & Wodak 2016, p. 27). Thus, validity in argumentation is both logical, and ethical. Argumentation analysis is functional (it looks at claim, argument/premise, conclusion rule; here, Toulmin provides a good model); formal (it lays bare the formal *topoi* and arguments underlying discourse); macro structural (it investigates stages and complexity of argumentation as well as the interdependency of arguments); and content-related (it analyses *topoi* as recurrent elements of content) (*ibidem*). For DHA, content-related *topoi* are of the utmost importance, as they unveil world-views and ways of reasoning typical of a given period and place: they allow for ideological analysis and disclose subject positions as well as justification strategies. An example of a content-related *topos* would be the anger of the person in the street as expressed in Austrian populist discourse (according to Reisigl 2014, p. 78): it claims that if the ordinary citizen is angry, political action has to be taken (or not) in order to resolve that anger. Moreover, the DHA proposes a context-dependent approach, trying to integrate in its analysis 'all available background information', and examining each utterance in context: its analytical practice is by definition socio-historical. It also combines argumentative and discursive analysis as it explores the linguistic means mobilised by the discourse in contexts – for example, antisemitic language behaviour is studied by Wodak (2013a, p. 360), who also closely links CDA with pragmatics as the study of insinuations and allusions, presuppositions and implicatures, and so on. Finally, it is important to bear in mind that the DHA is normative insofar as its mission is to assess the cognitive and ethical validity of the respective discourse. In other words, it highlights the detection of fallacies – here again, on the basis of the Pragma-dialectic rules, to which Reisigl would, however, like to add some insights from Hannah Arendt or Jürgen Habermas, and include 'democratic norms and ethical principles of justice and equality' (2014, p. 22).

Among the non-normative approaches, let us first mention Barbara Johnstone's interesting attempt at linking linguistic investigation with rhetoric. Though mainly working in sociolinguistics, the American scholar has published a book on *Discourse analysis* (2008 [2007]), followed by a collective work edited by herself and Christopher Eisenhart, entitled *Rhetoric in detail* (2008). Their premises are that 'linguistic discourse analysis can provide a grounded, rigorous set of analytical methods for answering rhetorical questions' (2008, p. 13). The book presents a series of detailed analyses showing how stylistic moves and variations, rhetorical micro-strategies, use of transitivity and naming, representation of the others' voices, and so on, allow for an understanding of political issues such as the construction of political legitimacy, government control, agency of disabled or disadvantaged groups, and so on. In its focus on specific linguistic and stylistic devices and on their social functions, *Rhetoric in detail* is a valuable contribution to an argumentation analysis of political discourse – formulated by the editors as the filling of a gap in rhetorical studies (2008, p. 18), a statement to be understood against the background of the institutional importance conferred upon rhetoric in American academic studies.

Another non-normative approach is Argumentation in discourse (AD) as elaborated by Amossy from 2000 onwards. It aims at integrating the study of arguments, argumentative structures and figures as described by traditional and contemporary rhetorical argumentation in discourse analysis, understood as a non-normative and non-ideological enterprise in the wake of both the *New rhetoric* of Perelman, and the French contemporary trend of DA. In *L'argumentation dans le discours* (2012 [2000]), argumentation is defined in a broad sense as the totality of verbal means trying to elicit adherence to a thesis (when discourse has an argumentative goal), or to orient ways of thinking, perceiving the surrounding world, and feeling (when discourse has an argumentative dimension with no declared persuasive aim). Unlike some other trends (for instance, Pragma-dialectics and Fairclough's work borrowing from it), this approach does not make a clear-cut distinction between argumentation and rhetoric, nor does it confine it to the art of persuading by reasoning: *logos* is closely connected to *ethos* and *pathos*. Moreover, persuasion, as well as *ethos* construction, value-based agreement or polemics are achieved, not only through rational arguments, but also through the multiple and complex discursive means in which schemes of reasoning are embedded. Thus, the reconstruction of arguments and the exploration of discursive features mingle in a single analytical enterprise. The argumentative patterns underlying discourse are brought to the surface, while minute attention is paid to micro-discursive phenomena in order to see how the respective argument is embodied in natural language. At the same time, discourse is analysed in context, and in its generic and institutional frameworks. A central place is given to its dialogical (or interdiscursive) dimension, thus actual or virtual reactions (of confirmation, re-elaboration or opposition) to pre-existing discourses. In this perspective, the study of political discourse explores the way interpretations of the surrounding reality are constructed, and how social problems are framed and managed.

Analysis of an example: Israeli PM Netanyahu's address at the UN (2014)

In order to show how argumentation theory and DA can be used in an integrated approach, I will analyse a short fragment of Israeli PM Netanyahu's speech at the UN 69th General Assembly (September 2014). The address participates in political deliberation insofar as it deals with the UN assessment of the military operation (Protective Edge) launched in July 2014 by Israel against Gaza, governed by the Islamic Hamas (labelled as a terrorist organisation),[4] and put under Israeli blockade. Systematic launching of rockets from Gaza on Israeli cities resulted in retaliation, taking the form of a massive bombing of the Gaza strip. Two contradictory stances confronted each other at the UN, expressed in the speech of Mahmud Abbas, President of the Palestinian Authority, speaking in the name of all Palestinians, despite his tense relations with Hamas (26 September 2014), and in Netanyahu's address on 29 September 2014. Even if the session of the General Assembly is not meant to take an immediate practical decision, the judgement passed by its members on Protective Edge was bound to have an impact, both on the international image of Israel (which was quite damaged by multiple UN condemnations), and on the future resolutions concerning the management of the Middle East conflict. However, the address also dealt with *ethos* construction – trying to reinforce the authority of the speaker in a period of crisis, and displayed a polemical confrontation – it fiercely attacked the Palestinian discourse, intending to undermine its credibility and that Mahmud Abbas cannot, consequently, be a valid partner for the peace process.

The audience (a crucial element of rhetorical argumentation) is by definition heterogeneous: in the Assembly as well as in the international public watching the speech on TV or the internet, or reading it in its totality, or in fragments, through the press, we can find unconditional pro-Palestinian and pro-Israeli members, but also relatively neutral ones. Moreover, the performance is also meant for the Israelis; it contributes to the construction of the PM's *ethos* at home. In this perspective, the speech has to impress a variety of addressees who hold divergent, if not contradictory, views. Let us first explore the following passage of Netanyahu's address, while shortly elaborating on the means and procedures of the analysis:

> Antisemitism [...] is now spreading in polite society, where it masquerades as legitimate criticism of Israel. For centuries the Jewish people have been demonised with blood libels and charges of deicide. Today, the Jewish state is demonised with the apartheid libel and charges of genocide.
>
> (*Haaretz* 2014)

Our first stage will be to look for the underlying argumentative structures of the PM's speech. Obviously, the central one is analogy, one of the two main modes of reasoning (together with syllogism) according to Aristotle. Perelman describes it as 'A is to B as C is to D'. The first one (A is to B) is the theme dealt with, which has to be clarified and better understood (here: today's accusations against Israel); the second is called the *phoros*, and consists of familiar elements (here the traditional accusations against the Jews), which can throw light on the theme being discussed (Perelman 1982 [1977], pp. 114–120). Thus, apartheid libels and charges of genocide (A) are to Israel (B) what blood libels and charges of deicide (C) were to the Jewish people (D). Accusations against Israel are presented as analogous with antisemitic defamation and thus factually and morally wrong. As the charges of having killed Christ and of using the blood of innocent children for Passover have long

269

been held against the Jews, the *phoros* is here grounded in history: the analogy takes the form of a historical example, or of what Reisigl and Wodak (2001, p. 80) call the *topos* of history: 'because history teaches that specific actions have specific consequences, one should perform or omit a specific action in a specific situation (allegedly) comparable with the historical example referred to'. Forchtner (2014, p. 34) offers a category into which Netanyahu's example perfectly fits: 'the rhetoric of judging', where 'the *topos* links the data (a past wrongdoing committed by an out-group) and the conclusion (that similar actions proposed today by *others* should be avoided)'.

The conclusion of the argument is given at the beginning of the paragraph to make it more salient: being equivalent to antisemitism, sharp political criticism against Israel should not only be avoided, but condemned and silenced. The metaphor of the 'masquerade' is meant to denounce false appearances. But above all, the affirmative utterance, examined separately from the arguments by analogy that sustain it, has its own force insofar as it reproduces a recurrent and already-familiar argument. The notion that the new antisemitism acquires its legitimacy today by usurping the form of a political criticism of Israel is a commonplace (a content-related argument) elaborated both in the academic[5] and in lay debates; it has become part of an argumentative arsenal on which defenders of Israel regularly draw, so that the reader can easily recognise it (for the best if adhering to the stereotypical judgement, for the worst if disagreeing).

On the stylistic level, a well-wrought syntactic, semantic and even phonetic parallelism emphasises the similitude between political critique of Israel and antisemitism, suggesting that the one cannot be distinguished from the other. The *Jewish* people are equated with the *Jewish* State (the very Zionist definition of Israel that the Palestinians refused to recognise), blood libels with apartheid (where the common denominator is the axiological term 'libel'), charges of deicide with charges of genocide (where repetition is reinforced by the play upon dei- and genocide, both built on the suffix, *cidius*, killing). Although contents change from one period of time and one domain to the other, what remains the same over the ages is the process, the perpetual and unjustified act of accusation against the Jews.

On the lexical level, the choice of 'demonisation', borrowed from an interdiscourse familiar to all, is particularly poignant. The Jew is depicted as Satan, the incarnation of evil on earth, with the only difference being that religious accusations have been translated into political ones. The selection and repetition of 'demonised', with its strong religious and symbolic connotations, connects the speech to a widely circulated discourse in the pro-Israeli spheres, with its long memory of antisemitic violence. The lexical choice of terms referring to the history of antisemitism (Poliakov 1980) is quite loaded from the axiological and affective vantage: human beings should not be presented as targets of fear, hatred and rejection, if not of murder. Let us also emphasise that in the context of antisemitism, the genocide attributed to Israel is brought back to its supposed etymological source – it was coined by the legal scholar Raphael Lemkin in 1944 in reference to the extermination of the Jews by the Nazis, and discloses the rhetorical process of '*retorsion*' (turning the argument against the arguer) through which the Jews are accused of the very crime committed against them by those who negated their humanity.

These argumentative and discursive features allow for a plea that refutes the accusations by proposing an alternative script. It tacitly inverts the dominant distribution of roles where Israel is the oppressor, and the colonised and massacred Palestinians, the victim. This script, meant to reframe the situation, is tuned to a global context of 'competition between victims', as well as to the Israeli imaginary, obsessed by a history of hatred and persecution culminating in the Holocaust. It addresses both the feelings of the Jews, and the democratic (mostly

Western) countries that acknowledge their guilt and vehemently condemn antisemitism. *Pathos* appears here as a powerful adjuvant to *logos*, meaning that emotions and reasoning are closely interconnected and not, as some would have it, that the presence of emotions is synonymous with lack of reasoning.[6] On the stage of the international community, the address endeavours to construct an alternative image of Israel, better suited to elicit understanding and compassion, if not indignation against an unremitting injustice.

In the following utterances of the same paragraph, the claim made by Netanyahu about the illegitimacy of a political critique feeding on antisemitism is supported by a development on the already-mentioned notion of genocide. The passage is overtly polemical as it endeavours to refute and discredit the discourse of Mahmud Abbas, who launched the following accusation in the opening sentence of his UN speech (September 26, 2014): 'In this year, proclaimed by the United Nations General Assembly as the International Year of Solidarity with the Palestinian People, Israel has chosen to make it a year of a new war of genocide perpetrated against the Palestinian people.'

To this, Netanyahu replies with a vehement counter-discourse:

> Genocide? In what moral universe does genocide include warning the enemy's civilian population to get out of harm's way? Or ensuring that they receive tons, tons of humanitarian aid each day, even as thousands of rockets are being fired at us? Or setting up a field hospital to aid their wounded?
>
> (Netanyahu, United Nations 2014)

The focus on 'genocide' rather than on the current accusations of 'massacres' or 'disproportionate use of force', allows for a reframing of the problem, if not a shift from the ongoing debate. The question is no longer whether Israel reacted in the right manner and proportion to Palestinian attacks, but whether it is acting with the intention to annihilate the Palestinian people. Moreover, the deliberation as an attempt to weigh the pros and the cons of Defensive Edge is replaced by a polemical exchange with its dichotomisation (radicalisation of two options presented as incompatible), its polarisation (reinforcing antagonism between groups) and its attempt at discrediting the Other (Amossy 2014). This does not mean that formal arguments are not mobilised. In his polemical attack, Netanyahu refutes the charge against Israel on the basis of an argument by definition: genocide being the deliberate extermination of an ethnic group or a people, helping the civil population to survive not only does not fit the definition, but even appears as the antonym of genocide.

The argumentative strategy is completed by a discursive one. The utterances heavily rely on the use of implicit elements to be filled in by the addressee, so that the latter is called upon to co-operate by co-constructing the meaning of the discourse. The definition of genocide at the basis of the argument is not formulated and the audience has to supply it from common knowledge; the denial of the accusation is not achieved in negative form, but through rhetorical questions that include their own (negative) answer, so that the conclusion has to be drawn by the audience. Moreover, by uncovering the incompatibility between the nature of genocide and what he presents as the reality on the ground, Netanyahu taints his comment with irony, calling for the audience's complicity.

To this, we have to add the functions of the presuppositions. 'In what moral universe does genocide include warning the enemy's civilian population to get out of harm's way?' does not raise the question of whether or not this warning actually existed, it takes it for granted, presupposing that the Israelis did ask the population to leave the premises before bombing. Presuppositions present the alleged facts as already known and escaping discussion (Ducrot

1972). But they do not necessarily rely on common knowledge: thus Abbott (2000, pp. 1422–1423), following Grice, emphasises that they can bring in a new information, which the addressee activates as if he already knew it. Thus, information about the way Israel dealt with civilians can be brought indirectly to the knowledge of the audience. Netanyahu also uses a technique of indirection to link the military actions of Israel to ethics by using the term 'moral universe', implying that the fighting was a matter, not only of military efficiency, but also of moral values (this is an allusion to the topic of 'purity of arms' related to Tsahal, presented in Israel as a 'moral army').

Denying the Palestinian claim of genocide and replacing it by a moral representation of Israel amounts to a process of image reparation (Benoit 1995). A crescendo is reached with the *chiasmus* of 'tons, tons of humanitarian aid' (for the Gaza civilians) and 'thousands of rockets fired at us'. The hyperbolic tone emphasises the importance of humanitarian considerations for Israel, and its capacity to transcend a war situation in favour of an act of decency and generosity. This picture encapsulates the image of Protective Edge as the majority of Israeli citizens – as well as large parts of the Jewish populations in the world – see it, thus fulfilling an epideictic role: the community can gather around the same beliefs. It also aspires to enlightening those who ignore the facts presented by the PM – thus playing a persuasive role. Here again, *pathos* in the guise of questions ('Genocide?'), repetitions and oppositions, reinforces the argumentative structure by colouring the speech with indignation at an accusation considered as distorted and abusive.

Through his UN speech, Netanyahu constructs an *ethos* targeting both the international audience, and his home audience. His speech aims to present him in the face of the world as a leader fiercely defending his country, and a principled orator moved by moral feelings. At the same time, the Israeli PM seizes the opportunity to improve an image of self severely impaired during a war during which (Israel being for weeks under rocket attacks) he was severely criticised in his own country. He was attacked by his right wing who claimed that he was not reacting powerfully enough against Hamas and failed to defeat it. He was blamed by the left who claimed that such a bloody military operation was unnecessary and, moreover, that the disastrous situation as a whole was a result of Netanyahu government's failure to engage in a real peace process. A large part of the population, especially in the south of the country – where the bombing was the most intense and where murderous tunnels leading to civil habitations were discovered – simply felt that the government was not able to protect the population. This explains the necessity to refurbish a tarnished image and to project, on a prestigious international stage, an image of a leader able to confront the world and make a vibrant plea for his people, representing them on all the topics where a wide national consensus was achieved. Caring for his own power position, as well as for Israel's international reputation, Netanyahu thus engages in a double process of image repair intended to maintain his own power and prestige as well as to influence the UN's future deliberations.

Conclusion

I have chosen to engage in a brief analysis of a situated discursive fragment in order to exemplify the procedures and notions of argumentation analysis, and show how they interact on different levels, shifting from deliberation to polemical exchange and exploiting *ethos* construction and image reparation. In the limits of a short presentation where an extensive survey of argumentative and discursive means is not possible, my main purpose has been to show how we can use various analytical tools borrowed from different trends of language studies, as well as argumentation theories, while linking the text to its targeted audience as well as to its context, and examining the particular management of verbal argumentation in its generic framework. Argumentation in discourse unveils the mechanisms of the discourse without engaging in explicit critique – it analyses without assessing.

Although I have chosen to exemplify a non-normative approach, drawing on DA rather than on CDA, and despite the differences in approaches (notably, in what concerns critique and commitment), we can see that the various trends of argumentation analysis share some features: focus on arguments, argumentative schemes and formal *topoi* (with occasional preference for content-related *topoi*); emphasis on the socio-historical and institutional situation in which the argumentation is embedded; close linguistic analysis of the way arguments are put into words, and of the discursive means (syntactic, lexical, pragmatic, etc.) mobilised by the overall persuasion enterprise; and use of discursive and argumentative analysis to shed light on political issues and the management of public affairs.

Notes

1. 'Its object is neither the textual organization, nor the communication situation, but what links them together through an enunciation system. Such a system falls both within the verbal and the institutional provinces' (Maingueneau in Charaudeau & Maingueneau 2002, p. 43).
2. For an interesting integration of Bakhtin's dialogism into argumentation theory, see Tindale 2004, ch. 4.
3. It goes without saying that these few bibliographical items are purely indicative.
4. Hamas – its military wing, together with several charities it runs – has been designated as a terrorist organisation by Israel (1989), the United States (1996), Canada (2002), the European Union (2001/2003), Japan (2006) and Egypt (2015), and it was outlawed in Jordan (1999). It is not regarded as a terrorist organisation by Iran, Russia, Norway, Switzerland, Turkey, China and Brazil. An EU court found the EU's earlier designation flawed, but its decision has been appealed by the European Council. It is a point of debate in political and academic circles over whether or not to classify Hamas as a terrorist group (Wikipedia ND).
5. It is fully elaborated in the writing of Taguieff – among others (Taguieff 2002).
6. On this much-debated topic, see Walton 1992; Micheli 2010.

References

Abbott, B, 2000, 'Presuppositions as nonassertion', *Journal of Pragmatics*, vol. 32, pp. 1419–1437.
Amossy, R, 2001, 'Ethos at the crossroad of disciplines: Rhetoric, pragmatics, sociology', *Poetics Today*, vol. 22, no 1, pp. 1–23.
Amossy, R, 2009, 'The new rhetoric's inheritance: Argumentation and discourse analysis', *Argumentation*, vol. 23, no 2, pp. 313–324.
Amossy, R, 2010a, 'The functions of polemical discourse in the public sphere', in *The responsibilities of rhetoric*, eds. M Smith & B Warnick, Waveland Press, Long Grove, pp. 52–61.
Amossy, R, 2010b, *La présentation de soi. Ethos et identité verbale*, PUF, Paris.
Amossy, R, 2012 [2000], *L'argumentation dans le discours*, Dunod, Paris.
Amossy, R, 2014, *Apologie de la polémique*, PUF, Paris.
Amossy, R & Sternberg, M, eds., 2002, *Doxa and discourse; How common knowledge works*, Poetics Today, vol. 23, no 3.
Angenot, M, 1997, *La propagande socialiste. Six essais d'analyse du discours*, Les éditions Balzac, Montréal.
Angenot, M, 2004, *Rhétorique de l'anti socialisme. Essai d'histoire discursive. 1830–1917*, Les Presses de l'Université Laval, Laval.
Anscombre, J C & Ducrot, O, 1988, *L'argumentation dans la langue*, Mardaga, Liège.

Aristotle, *Rhetoric*, translation W Rhys Roberts, a hypertextual resource compiled by Lee Honeycutt, available from: http://rhetorigc.eserver.org/aristotle/index.html [accessed 27 February 2016].

Bakhtin, M, 1986, *Speech genres and other late essays*, tr. V W McGee, University of Texas Press, Austin, TX.

Benoit, W L, 1995, *Accounts, excuses, and apologies. A Theory of Image Restoration*, State University of NY Press, Albany, NY.

Benveniste, E, 1974, *Problèmes de linguistique générale 2*, Gallimard, Paris.

Benveniste, E, 2014 [1970], 'The formal apparatus of enunciation', in *The Discourse Studies reader. Main currents in theory and analysis*, eds. J Angermuller, D Maingueneau, & R Wodak, John Benjamins, Amsterdam/Philadelphia, pp. 140–145.

Charaudeau, P & Maingueneau, D, eds., 2002., *Dictionnaire d'analyse du discours*, Seuil, Paris.

Ducrot, O, 1972, *Dire et ne pas dire. Principes de sémantique linguistique*, Hermann, Paris.

Ducrot, O, 1996, *Slovenian lecture*, ed. I Zagar, ISH, Lubjubljana.

Eemeren, F H, van Grootendorst, R, Snoek Hoekemans, F, 1996, *Fundamentals of Argumentation Theory*, Lawrence Erlbaum, New Jersey and London.

Fairclough, I & Fairclough, N, 2012, *Political discourse analysis*, Routledge, London and New York.

Fairclough, N, Mulderrig, J & Wodak, R, 2013, 'Critical Discourse Analysis', *Critical Discourse Analysis, vol. I. concepts, history, theory*, ed. R Wodak, Sage, Los Angeles and London, pp. 79–102.

Forchtner, B, 2014, '*Historia magistra vitae*: The *topos* of history as a teacher in public struggles over self and other representation', in *Contemporary Critical Discourse Studies*, eds. C Hart & P Cap, Bloomsbury, London, pp. 19–44.

Haaretz, 2014, 'Transcript of Benjamin Netanyahu's Address to the 2014 UN General Assembly', *Haaretz*, 29 September 2014, available from: www.haaretz.com/news/diplomacy-defense/1.618308 [accessed 27 February 2016].

Hart, C & Piotr C, 2014, 'Introduction', *Contemporary Critical Discourse Studies*, eds. C Hart & P Cap, Bloomsbury, London, pp. 1–16.

Jasinski, J, 2001, *Sourcebook on rhetoric. Key concepts in contemporary rhetorical studies*, Sage, Thousand Oaks, CA.

Johnson, R H & Blair, J A, 2000, 'Informal logic: An overview', *Informal Logic*, vol. 20, no. 2, pp. 93–99.

Johnstone, B. 2008 [2002], *Discourse analysis*, Blackwell Publishing, Malden, Oxford and Victoria.

Johnstone, B & Eisenhart, C, eds., 2008. *Rhetoric in detail*, John Benjamins, Amsterdam/Philadelphia.

Kerbrat Orecchioni, C, 1980, *L'énonciation de la subjectivité dans le langage*, Colin, Paris.

Maingueneau, D, 2006, 'Is Discourse Analysis Critical?', *Critical Discourse Studies*, vol. 3, no 2, pp. 229–230.

Maingueneau, D, 2007, 'Discourse analysis in France: A Conversation', Entretien avec J. Angermüller. *Forum Qualitative Social Research*, vol. 8, no. 2, art. 21, available from: www.qualitative research.net/fqs texte/2 07/07 2 21 e.htm [accessed 27 February 2016].

Maingueneau, D, 2012, 'Que cherchent les analystes du discours', Argumentation et analyse du discours [En ligne], 9 | 2012, mis en ligne le 26 Septembre 2012, consulté le 13 Décembre 2014. Available from: http://aad.revues.org/1354

Micheli, R, 2010, 'Emotions as objects of argumentative constructions', *Argumentation. An International Journal on Reasoning*, vol. 24, no 1, pp. 1–17.

Mouffe, C, 2000, *The democratic paradox*, Verso, London, New York.

Perelman, C, 1982 [1977], *The realm of rhetoric*, University of Notre Dame Press, Notre Dame and London.

Perelman, C & Olbrechts Tyteca, L, 1969 [1958], *The new rhetoric. A treatise on argumentation*, University of Notre Dame Press, Notre Dame and London.

Plantin, C, 1995, 'L'argument du paralogisme', Hermès 15, *Argumentation et rhétorique I*, pp. 245–262.

Poliakov, L, 1980, *La causalité diabolique. Essai sur l'origine des persécutions*, Calmann Lévy, Paris.

Reisigl, M, 2014, 'Argumentation analysis and the Discourse Historical Approach. A methodological framework', in *Contemporary Critical Discourse Studies*, eds. C Hart & P Cap, Bloomsbury, London, pp. 67–96.

Reisigl, M & Wodak, R, 2001, *Discourse and discrimination: Rhetorics of racism and anti semitism*, Routledge, London.

Reisigl, M & Wodak, R, 2009, 'The Discourse-Historical Approach', in *Methods of Critical Discourse Analysis* (2nd revised ed.), eds. R Wodak & M Meyer, Sage, London, pp. 87–121.

Reisigl, M & Wodak, R, 2016, 'The discourse historical approach (DHA)', in *Methods of Critical Discourse Studies* (3rd revised ed.) eds. R Wodak & M Meyer, Sage, London, pp. 23–61.

Rennes, J, 2007, *Le mérite et la nature. Une controverse républicaine: l'accès des femmes aux professions de prestige*, Fayard, Paris.

Taguieff, P A, 2002, *La nouvelle judéophobie*, Fayard, Paris.

Tindale, C W, 2004, *Rhetorical argumentation. Principles of theory and practice*, Sage, Thousand Oaks, CA.

Toulmin, S, 2003 [1958], *The uses of argument*, Cambridge University Press, Cambridge.

van Dijk, T A, 2001, 'Multidisciplinary Critical Discourse Analysis: a plea for diversity', in *Methods of Critical Discourse Analysis*, eds. R Wodak & M Meyer, Sage, London, pp. 95–120.

Walton, D, 1992, *The place of emotion in argument*, Pennsylvania State University Press, Pennsylvania, PA.

Wikipedia, ND, 'Hamas', available from: https://en.wikipedia.org/wiki/Hamas [accessed 20 March 2017].

Wodak, R, 2013a, 'Pragmatics and Critical Discourse Analysis: A cross disciplinary inquiry', in *Critical Discourse Analysis', vol. I, concepts, history, theory*, ed. R Wodak, Sage, Los Angeles, London, pp. 372–413.

Wodak, R, 2013b, 'Editor's introduction: Critical Discourse Analysis – challenges and perspectives', in *Critical Discourse Analysis, vol. I, concepts, history, theory*, ed. R Wodak, Sage, Los Angeles, London, pp. xx–xliv.

# 18

Conversation analysis and the study of language and politics

Steven E. Clayman and Laura Loeb

Introduction

Conversation analysis (henceforth CA) has long served as an approach to the study of language and politics. Although CA research initially focused on generic interactional practices largely within the domain of ordinary conversation, a shift toward task-oriented forms of institutional talk emerged by the 1980s, with political speeches and broadcast news interviews figuring prominently in this line of work. Other politically relevant forms of talk soon became the focus of study, including radio call-in shows, presidential news conferences, campaign debates, and participatory democracy meetings. As should be apparent from this list, CA studies have illuminated the production of talk *about* political matters as well as talk that is central to the *doing* of politics itself. Scholarly attention to these areas has not been evenly distributed, but there are now few politically relevant interactional forms that have not been subject to scrutiny from a conversation analytic perspective. And while CA studies have not always explicitly addressed the political dimensions of such talk, nor even language *per se* as opposed to multimodal forms of vocal and non-vocal behaviour, many such studies nonetheless yield insight into the nexus of language, interaction and politics.

CA exploits the concreteness and specificity of language practices to illuminate political meanings, tasks, norms, relationships and institutions. In this respect, it has much in common with other approaches to language and politics. What is most distinctive about the CA approach is a persistent empirical focus on language practices in the context of *direct interactional encounters* between some combination of political figures, media professionals and ordinary people. As a corollary of this interactional focus, language practices are understood to be: (1) housed within turns at talk, (2) produced in the service of specifiable actions, and (3) both responsive to prior actions and consequential for the actions that follow.

The focus on interactional materials necessarily excludes written contexts of political language use, but it is otherwise wide-ranging and has a variety of substantive and methodological affordances. The sequencing of interaction is a primary locus for the production of action, for displays of understanding of action, and for the exercise of agency and social influence (Heritage 1984a, Schegloff 2007). These dimensions of action, understanding, and influence are thoroughly intertwined in the move-by-move unfolding of interaction, as each contribution simultaneously displays understanding of what came before, acts on that understanding and shapes what happens next. Accordingly, by examining how language is put to use within interaction, it is possible to gain a lively sense of the utility of specific practices, how they operate on prior actions produced by other interactional participants and are consequential for what happens next. At the same time, it is also possible to gain a sense of the social meaning of such practices for the interactants themselves, with the speaker's understanding evident in the specifics of how they deploy each practice, and the recipient's understanding evident in how they respond. Examining the sequencing of language practices in interaction thus provides a means of justifying and validating analytic claims.

Moreover, this research has yielded interlocking and cumulative findings about the inner workings and norms of conduct in a wide range of interactional arenas, which together comprise an important part of the contemporary mediated public sphere.

This chapter provides a brief introduction to the conversation analytic approach to language and politics. We begin with a discussion of some of the methodological principles characteristic of this approach, and we then review some exemplary research studies relevant to language and politics. It bears emphasis that the discussion of both methods and findings are far from exhaustive, and readers interested in delving deeper into the approach are urged to consult other relevant literature.[1]

CA methodology

Getting started

Conversation analysis is concerned with the detailed study of interaction as it naturally occurs. Experimental manipulations and role-playing are avoided on the grounds that such circumstances almost always impose motivations or simplifying constraints on the participants, resulting in interactional conduct that bears on uncertain relationship to ordinary talk. Within the parameters of naturally occurring interaction, primacy is placed on data that have been audio- or video-recorded to enable repeated scrutiny, and systematically transcribed so as to capture the details of what was actually said and done (for transcription conventions in general as well as those utilised when analysing examples below, see Hepburn & Bolden 2012).

Interactional activities can be investigated at varying levels of granularity. At a broad level are overarching *tasks* and *norms*, such as the politician's impetus to appeal to both partisan and centrist voters, and the journalist's obligation to be non-partisan and objective. Such tasks and norms typically serve as a vernacularly familiar starting point for analysis, which then focuses on the less-familiar practices through which they are enacted. In some settings, there may also be specialised *turn-taking systems* that specify how opportunities to speak are distributed between the participants, imposing constraints on participation and the production of action. Specialised turn-taking systems tend to be operative in settings that are 'formal' (e.g. news interviews, campaign debates) or involve multiple participants (e.g. news conferences, participatory democracy and town meetings, political speeches).

At a finer level of granularity are discrete *sequences of action*, which may be analysed for their relatively generic sequential properties (e.g. as paired actions), or for type-specific characteristics (e.g. as question–answer sequences, disagreement sequences, sequences of political rhetoric and audience applause, etc.). Next come the *actions* that comprise sequences and are often accomplished through a single turn at talk, such as questioning, praising or criticising, responding to these various actions, and so on. Finally, there are *practices mobilised within turns*, such as lexical choices, prosodic features and non-vocal behaviours, which may be relevant to the action in progress, or more overarching tasks and norms.

As should be apparent from the preceding list, virtually everything that happens in interaction is fair game for analysis. Contrary to the assumption that much interactional conduct can be dismissed as random noise, conversation analysts proceed from the premise that all elements of interaction are *potentially* orderly and meaningful for the participants (Sacks 1984). This attitude opens up a wealth of possibilities for analysis. Specific lines of inquiry may be motivated by the goal of building on previous research findings, exploring new forms of interactional data, or explicating new practices.

Since the latter type of inquiry – research stimulated by previously unnoticed and unexamined interactional practices – is a hallmark of CA, but relatively marginal to social science more generally, we dwell on this at greater length. Purely unmotivated observation is, of course, an unattainable ideal, as analysts necessarily approach data with a conceptual foundation grounded in previous research, which affects what they are inclined to observe. Nevertheless, it is possible to notice and be intrigued by practices that are not directly related to a pre-existing research agenda. Such 'noticings' can prompt the analyst to explicate what, if anything, the practice might be 'doing' or accomplishing. This typically involves examining where and how it contributes to the stream of interaction, and with what consequence.

To illustrate, Heritage (2002) noticed that journalists would sometimes depart from the more commonplace grammatical format for polar questions by incorporating a negative into the copula (e.g. *Isn't it...*, *Aren't you...*, etc.). Since this practice, termed a negative interrogative, is an optional grammatical choice in the design of polar questions, what is the import of this choice? A clue may be gleaned from the responses that negative interrogatives tend to attract, in which the recipient claims to 'agree' or 'disagree' with the proposition framed by the negative interrogative. For instance, President Bill Clinton responds to a negative interrogative about campaign funding irregularities in just this way ('I disagree with that...').

```
1  IR:      W'l Mister President in your zea:l (.)  for funds during
2      →    the last campaign .hh didn't you put the Vice President   (.)
3           an' Maggie and all the others in your (0.4) administration
4           top side .hh in a very vulnerable position, hh
5           (0.5)
6  BC:  →   I disagree with that .hh u– How are we vulnerable because ...
                                        (1, Clinton News Conference, 7 March 1997)
```

The negative interrogative recurrently receives this type of response in news interviews and news conferences, and it is the only grammatical form to do so (Heritage 2002). The pattern suggests that the form is relatively assertive, with questions formatted in this way treated as opinionated and as straddling the boundary between seeking and expressing information. Correspondingly, the frequency with which negative interrogatives are used in the design of yes/no questions later served as an index of the propensity for journalists to depart from strict neutrality and express a point of view under the guise of 'asking questions' (Clayman & Heritage 2002a; Clayman et al. 2006; Heritage & Clayman 2013).

Grounding analytic claims

In the broad tradition of interpretive social science, CA seeks analyses that are 'emic' and hence grounded in the understandings and orientations of the participants themselves. Within interaction, the understandings that matter most are those that participants display, act on, and thus render consequential for the interaction's subsequent development (Schegloff & Sacks 1973).

A central resource for tapping into such understandings, already glimpsed in excerpt 1 above, is embodied in how recipients respond to the practice in question. Since contributions to interaction are, to some extent, directed to or conditioned by the previous contribution, each contribution will normally display that speaker's understanding of what was just said and done by the prior speaker (Sacks, Schegloff & Jefferson 1974). Interactants themselves rely on such retrospective displays of understanding to ascertain whether and how they were understood, and this 'architecture for intersubjectivity' (Heritage 1984b) is also a resource for grounding and validating analytic claims.

For instance, Clayman (1992a) advanced the claim that when journalist-interviewers shift footings – by attributing their remarks to a third party either overtly (i.e. *Critics say that...*), or by implication (i.e. *It is said that...*) – this serves to maintain a formally neutral or 'neutralistic' posture. The most straightforward evidence for this claim is that recipients, in responding to attributed talk, often treat such talk as belonging to the same third party. For instance, in a discussion of nuclear waste, the interviewer expresses the view that waste disposal is a readily soluble problem (lines 5–11), directly contradicting the pessimistic view expressed just previously by a critic of the nuclear industry (lines 1–4). As he introduces this oppositional viewpoint, he makes a special point of indicating that it belongs to another interviewee from earlier in the programme ('Doctor Yalow said... her own opinions... she seems to feel...'), and he also refrains from endorsing, rejecting, or otherwise commenting on that view.[2]

```
1    JS:       And if you look et– simply the record in the
2              low level waste field over the last fifteen to
3              twenty years... the record is not very good (0.3)
4              an' it doesn't give one a cause for optimism.=
5    IR:  →    =You heard what Doctor Yalow said earlier in
6         →    this broadcast she'll have an opportunity to
7         →    express her own opinions again, but she seems to
8              feel that it is an EMinently soluble problem,
9              and that ultimately that radioactive material
10             can be reduced, to manageable quantities, 'n' put
11             in the bottom of a salt mine.
12   JS:  →    The p– the point that she was making earlier
13             about (.) reprocessing of: the fuel rods goes
14             right to the heart (.) of the way a lotta
15             people look at this particular issue...
                            (2, US ABC Nightline, 6 June, 1985, Nuclear Waste)
```

This neutralistic posture may, of course, be a façade, but it is subsequently validated and reinforced by the response ('The point she was making earlier' in line 12).

Just as responses yield insight into recipient's understanding of the practice in question, the specifics of the practice's deployment are often revealing of the speaker's own grasp of the practice. With regard to the footing-shift practice, its neutralistic import is further apparent in the selectivity with which this practice is used by interviewers. Consider this question to Senator Bob Dole, the Reagan-era majority leader for the Republican Party, which begins with an extended preface comprised of three declarative assertions.

```
1    IR:   1→   Senator, (0.5) uh: President Reagan's elected
2                thirteen months ago: an enormous landslide.
3                (0.8)
4          2→   It is s::aid that his programs are in trouble,
5                though he seems to be terribly popular with the
6                American people.
7                (0.6)
8          3→   It is said by some people at the White House
9                we could get those programs through if only we
10               ha:d perhaps more: .hh effective leadership
11               on on the Hill and I [suppose] indirectly=
12   BD:                              [hhhheh ]
13   IR:         =that might (0.5) relate t'you as well:. (0.6)
14               Uh what do you think the problem is really.
15               Is=it (0.2) the leadership as it might be
16               claimed up on the Hill, or is it the
17               programs themselves.
              (3, US NBC Meet the Press, 8 December, 1985: Troubled Programs)
```

The first assertion (beginning at arrow 1) – that Reagan was elected 'thirteen months ago' in 'an enormous landslide' – reports a concrete historical fact and a matter of public record, and this fact is asserted straightforwardly. In contrast, the subsequent claim that Reagan's programmes are 'in trouble' (beginning at arrow 2) and the suggestion that Dole is to blame for this (beginning at arrow 3) are, by comparison, matters of judgement and interpretation. Correspondingly, the interviewer distances himself from these latter assertions, first by means of the passive voice with agent deletion ('it is said'), and second by attribution to 'some people at the White House'.

Footing shifts are also deployed selectively over the course of a single sentence, such that a contentious word or phrase is singled out for attribution. In the next example, from an interview with an anti-apartheid activist in South Africa, the IR begins (lines 1–2) by attributing an upcoming viewpoint in its entirety to a third party ('the Ambassador'), and this footing is later renewed just prior to a specific term ('collaborator', arrowed) which is re-attributed to that party.

```
1    IR:     Reverend Boesak lemme a– pick up a point uh the
2             ambassador made. What– what assurances can you
3             give u:s .hh that (.) talks between moderates
4             in that see:ms that any black leader who is
5             willing to talk to the government is branded
6       →    as the Ambassador said a collaborator and is
7             then punished.=
8    AB:     =Eh theh– the– the ambassador has it wrong.
```

9	It's not the people who want to talk with
10	the government that are branded collaborators...

(4, US ABC Nightline, 22 July, 1985, Unrest in South Africa)

The term *collaborator* has strong negative and accusatory overtones here, in effect characterising moderate black activists as agents of the apartheid regime. It is precisely this contentious term that the IR disavows, in addition to the overall viewpoint of which it is a part. Here again, the resulting neutralistic stance is subsequently validated by the IE ('The ambassador has it wrong' in line 8).

Working through collections

The objective of CA is to elucidate socially shared methods used to build interaction. Although the close study of single specimens or cases is fundamental to this process, a full analysis transcends any particular case and sheds light on practices that operate across a range of participants and social contexts. As Sacks has observed:

> Thus it is not any particular conversation, as an object, that we are primarily interested in. Our aim is to get into a position to transform... our view of 'what happened,' from a matter of a particular interaction done by particular people, to a matter of interactions as products of a machinery. We are trying to find the machinery. In order to do so we have to get access to its products.
>
> (Sacks 1984, pp. 26–27)

This requires working case by case through collections of candidate instances of a given practice. This process enriches an analysis initially arrived at through a single case, in the first instance confirming (or disconfirming) that the practice has a recurrent and consequential import. It also illuminates such matters as the practice's various forms, the boundaries that separate it from related practices, and its scope and normativity.

When building collections of a given practice, it is advisable to cast a wide net. This means including what appear to be clear cases of the practice in question, as well as cases in which the practice is present in an atypical or partial form, and also what appear to be negative or 'deviant' cases. Analyzing such cases, rather than dismissing them as random noise, almost always yields a richer and more encompassing analysis.

Once a collection is assembled, analysis proceeds on a case-by-case basis, with the aim of developing a comprehensive account that encompasses all relevant instances in the collection. The process is roughly analogous to analytic induction (Katz & Emerson 1983), although in CA the objective is not causal explanation, but an analysis that will encompass a practice's varying occurrences across a range of interactional contexts and exigencies.

Central to this process is the analysis of problematic or deviant cases. Some such cases are shown, upon analysis, to result from interactants' orientation to the same considerations that produce the 'regular' cases; they are 'exceptions that prove the rule'. In other instances, deviant cases can prompt the researcher to replace the initial analysis with a more general formulation that encompasses both the regular cases and the anomalous departure. Finally, some deviant cases may, upon analysis, turn out to fall beyond the parameters of the phenomenon being investigated. Such cases are not genuinely 'deviant' at all, and they serve to clarify the boundaries of the phenomenon in question.

Quantitative extensions

CA has, in recent years, begun to supplement case-by-case analysis with formally quantitative methods. This development brings various trade-offs. With the aggregation of cases required of such methods, analysis is necessarily removed from the specifics of the participants' orientations in any particular case. Such aggregation is, however, integrated with and built upon a foundation provided by prior case-by-case research, with coding systems derived explicitly from previous 'emic' or participant-centred investigations. Moreover, the quantitative extension of CA has enabled researchers to work with larger datasets and investigate distributional and causal associations between interactional practices, more diffuse dimensions of context and outcomes. In the field of language and politics, quantification has been most prominent in studies of the journalistic questioning of public figures, illuminating such matters as long-term historical trends in vigorous or adversarial questioning (Clayman et al. 2010; Clayman et al. 2006), the impact of socio-economic conditions on adversarialism (Clayman et al. 2007), partisan bias (Ekström et al. 2013; Gnisci et al. 2013; Huls & Varwijk 2011), and the comparison of journalistic versus 'infotainment' interviews (Loeb 2015).

Exemplary CA studies

Conversation analysis has been applied to a range of empirical domains relevant to the study of politics. Although language and politics shape one another out of the public eye (Clayman & Reisner 1998; Ekström & Kroon Lundell 2011), here, we focus on public interactions: participatory democracy meetings, political speeches and various forms of broadcast talk, including radio phone-in programmes, journalistic and 'infotainment' interviews, and news conferences. These studies are all conversation analytic in character, although some include multimodal and quantitative elaborations of CA work. Taken together, these studies illustrate the capacity of the CA approach to illuminate diverse public interactional environments and the complex relations between language and politics.

Participatory democracy meetings

One context for the application of CA involves direct public input into governmental processes, namely participatory democracy meetings (Mondada 2011; Mondada 2013). At these meetings, examined in Lyons, France, community members come together to discuss and debate the prospect of a public park in the area, and what form that new park should take. As these meetings involve large numbers of community residents, one area of interest is how participation is managed through the regulation of turn taking (Mondada 2013). The research traces how participants gain access to the floor and are ratified to speak, noting that in this large group setting, taking a turn at talk requires multimodal resources beyond those needed in smaller groups (Sacks, Schegloff & Jefferson 1974). Speakers are ratified by the meeting chairperson in a process that requires close attention, not only to the verbal cues of the turn-taking system, but also to embodied cues. These embodied signals allow the chairperson to co-ordinate the next speaker, or even a series of next speakers (Mondada 2013). Mondada notes that this turn-taking system, like all such systems, shapes the capacity of the assembled participants to exert agency within the proceedings and thereby influence its political outcomes.

Radio phone-in shows

Another domain of public participation is the radio phone-in programme. These types of programmes have been researched by a number of scholars (Hutchby 2006; Scannell 1996; Thornborrow 2001a; Thornborrow 2001b). Thornborrow has examined various phone-in radio interviews from Britain in 1987, prior to a general election. Using CA, she highlights how the institutional structure of the radio phone-in programme shapes the actions available to the citizen callers, as well as the politicians.

On these programmes, callers are pre-screened, so that only those with questions approved by the show's production team are granted air time to ask questions. The host takes on the role of first speaker, introducing the caller, which sparks a round of greetings between host, caller and political guest (Thornborrow 2001a). Only then is the caller able to introduce their question. For the caller, this is their main opportunity to engage the politician directly.

Even when granted the turn space in which to query the politician, callers often work to justify their question as in the excerpt below.

```
1    PM:      [--]'n we now take our first call (.) it's Jim
2             In Finchampstead who wants to talk about the teachers
3             good morning Jim
4    Caller:  good morning
5    MT:      .hh good morning (.) [sir
6    Caller:                       [good morning prime minister=
7    MT:      =good morning
8    Caller:  uh my question is– follows on from (.) the uh subject
9             you've been talking about [--] I'm the parent of two boys
10            (.) my question how are you going to get the teachers
11            back to work and get politics out of the classroom
```
(5, IRP/MT, Thornborrow 2001a, p. 464)

Here the host indicates what the topic will be (at line 2), but the guest still does work to ground their question in their experience and identity (lines 10–12). In doing this, the guest draws on resources outside the immediate interview context to justify their role as questioner (Thornborrow 2001b). These practices shape how questions are asked and suggests that only some questions might be viewed as justifiable in this context.

Once the guest's question is asked, a host may, or may not, ask a follow-up question on the topic, or ask the caller to do so, but the caller cannot direct the path they take (Thornborrow 2001a). Finally, the host decides when to move to close the call, with the caller not participating in this sequence in most interviews (Thornborrow 2001a). Thornborrow's research shows the power of interactional structures to shape political moments. Here, although the phone-in is a place where members of the voting public can interact with the major political figures of the day, their participation is substantially constrained by the interactional structure of the phone-in programme.

Hutchby's research focuses on radio programmes where callers discuss issues of civic importance with the host. Although these interviews differ from those studied by Thornborrow in terms of participants, some of the practices used by both guests and hosts are similar. One such practice is callers using their personal experience to justify the stances they are taking, in a process he calls 'witnessing' (Hutchby 2006). Like Thornborrow, Hutchby is interested in the power dynamics between callers and hosts on radio phone-in programmes. He uses CA to explore the common perception that hosts have significantly more authority and power in these situations, allowing them to control the call. His work shows how the structure of the call allows hosts a measure of power in determining the direction the call will take. In these interactions, callers are expected to state their opinion first, which places the host in the responsive or second position. From this second position, hosts are more able to critique or problematise the caller's turn, potentially undermining their observations (Hutchby 2006).

In the following example, a caller has made a point about the difficulty of securing childcare (lines 1–6). The host responds with an interrogative that calls into question the relevance of the caller's point (line 7), and obliges the caller to defend what they have said (lines 8–9).

```
1 Caller:   When you look at e:r the childcare facilities in
2           this country, .hh we're very very low, (.) i-on
3           the league table in Europe of (.) you know if
4           you try to get a child into a nursery it's very
5           difficult in this country. .hh An' in fa:ct it's
6           getting wor::se.
7 Host:     What's that got to do with it.
8 Caller:   .phh Well I think whu– what's 'at's gotta d– do
9           with it is . . . ((Continues))
```

(6, H:21.11.88:11:1; Hutchby 2006, p. 92)

This is just one example of how a host can use the responsive or second position to challenge a caller's perspective. Hosts can also summarise the gist of a caller's remarks, allowing them to subtly shade what the caller has said (Hutchby 2006). Additionally, hosts can use this second-position slot to undermine the use of personal experience, problematising a caller's use of witnessing (Hutchby 2006). However, Hutchby also notes that while the typical structure of a radio phone-in call favours the host, the caller can take steps to turn the tables. This demonstrates that power relations are not exogenous to interaction, but are enacted through the practices of talk and are in the same way transformable.

Political speeches

Political speeches constitute yet another domain of direct public involvement in the discourse of politics, although here, public participation typically takes the form of simultaneous collective behaviour, responses such as applause, booing, and laughter (Atkinson 1984; Clayman 1993; Heritage & Greatbatch 1986). Most research in this area has focused on the organisation of applause and how it may be 'invited' by political speakers. This pioneering research has been undertaken in Britain and the US, democratic societies where applause plays a key role in shaping perceptions of the popularity of both politicians and their views and policies.

That applause behaviour is socially organised is apparent in the fact that bursts of applause typically begin within 0.2 seconds following the completion of the message to which they are responsive and rise to maximum amplitude in less than 1 second (Atkinson 1984). The timing and placement of applause indicates that many audience members decide to clap independently of one another, while also suggesting that certain points within a political speech not only provoke applause, but also provide for its co-ordinated onset. Researchers have found that specific rhetorical formats stand out from the background of a speech and provide clearly projectable completion points, and are thus associated with the majority of applause responses (Atkinson 1984; Heritage & Greatbatch 1986). With these devices, the orator and the audience are able to work together to create a prompt and favourable response.

One of the most common and effective rhetorical devices a speech-maker can use to project an impending applause point is a contrast (Heritage & Greatbatch 1986). In a contrast, a political point is delivered in two parts, the second of which is designed to contrast with the first. Contrasts in speeches often use closely parallel language, which allows the audience to predict its point of completion (Atkinson 1984). In the following excerpt from a 1992 Democratic Party convention speech, the speaker uses a contrast (arrowed) to attack a political opponent (independent presidential candidate, Ross Perot).

```
1    Pol:        He says he's an outsi::der who will shake up the
2                system in Washington. (0.4) But as far back as 1974
3                he was lobbying Congress for tax breaks, (0.4) He tri:ed
4                to turn fifty five thou:sand dollars in contributions
5                into a special (.) fifteen mill::ion dollar tax
6                loopho:le that was pa– tailor ma:de. (.) for him.
7                (1.8) ((light cheering))
8                Sounds to me like (1.0)
9         A→    instead o'shakin' the system (0.2) u:p
10               (0.9)
11        B→    Mister Perot's been shakin' it dow:n.
12   Aud:       xxxXXXXXXXXXXXXXXXXXXXXXXXXX...
```
                (7, Georgia Governor Zell Miller, 1992 Democratic Convention;
                                         Heritage & Clayman 2010, pp. 267–268)

In lines 1–8, the speaker presents evidence of hypocrisy in Perot's actions. This receives some light cheering (line 7), but the audience withholds clapping as he had not yet reached a significant applause point. He then launches a contrast, asserting that Perot is not 'shaking the system up' (i.e., instituting government reforms, lines 8–9), but rather 'shaking it down' (i.e., engineering self-interested tax breaks, line 11). This formatted contrast both emphasises the substantive message while also providing a clearly projectable completion point, and applause follows promptly thereafter (line 12).

Researchers have outlined a number of effective rhetorical formats beyond contrasts, such as three-part lists, puzzle-solutions, and headline-punchlines (Atkinson 1984). These various formats can also be combined, generating complex and highly effective applause points. Furthermore, quantitative research by Heritage and Greatbatch (1986) demonstrates that these formats have a statistically significant impact on the occurrence of applause. Messages formatted in these ways were two-to-eight times more likely to receive applause than messages that were not rhetorically formatted (Heritage & Greatbatch 1986). A prerequisite for these devices to work is for the audience to be in agreement with the speaker, but the rhetorical format makes it easier for audience members to collectively express their agreement in the form of applause.

These moments of applause indicate affiliation between speaker and audience, but other research has examined the organisation of responses that disaffiliate from the speech and its speaker (Clayman 1993; Clayman 1992b). Clayman finds that unlike applause, booing tends to be delayed and builds more gradually as audience members successively join in the response. Moreover, because booing tends to be delayed, other response behaviours tend to serve as the proximate 'trigger' for the response (e.g. a murmur or 'buzz' of disapproval, or clapping by other audience members). Booing is used by audiences to disaffiliate from either the speaker *per se*, or from the speaker in conjunction with other audience members who are applauding (Clayman 1993). These two forms of response show that while speeches are not always thought to be particularly interactive, audiences can express their reactions and make their approval or disapproval heard.

Journalistic and 'infotainment' interviews

Broadcast news interviews are an arena of direct encounters between political figures and media professionals, and as such, have been the site of much scholarly interest. Within conversation analysis, a good deal of work has been done on the distinctive turn-taking system that characterises news interview talk and guides participation, as well as the professional norms that inform practices of question design (Clayman 1988; Clayman 1991; Clayman & Heritage 2002b; Greatbatch 1988). Clayman and Heritage have analysed two norms of news interview questioning. The norm of neutralism, which is rooted in the broader ideal of journalistic objectivity, restricts interviewers to the activity of questioning and prohibits declarative assertions, except as prefaces to a question, or as attributed to a third party (Clayman & Heritage 2002b). The norm of adversarialism, rooted in the ideals of independence, balance and the watchdog role, favours questions that critically scrutinise politicians' positions and remarks. While these two norms are not a universal feature of journalistic questioning (Montgomery 2007, 2011), they are broadly relevant in news interviews with politicians and shape many aspects of question design (Clayman 1992a; Clayman 1988; Clayman and Heritage 2002b; Romaniuk 2013). For instance, the footing shifts discussed earlier in this chapter (excerpts 2, 3, 4 on pp. 279–281) enable the journalist to adversarially challenge the politician, while maintaining a neutralistic posture.

One variant of news interview research concerns interviews with campaigning politicians. This research has shown that campaign interviews entail much the same norms and practices as other news interviews, but they are mobilised in the service of specialised tasks relevant to the questioning of political candidates (Clayman & Romaniuk 2011). One type of question designed for political candidates is the 'pop quiz question' (Roth 2005), which tests the candidate's knowledge of current affairs. With this type of question, the newsworthiness of the answer lies not in its informational content, but in what it reveals about the politician's ability or inability to answer. By asking pop quiz questions, interviewers suggest that politicians should have the targeted knowledge, while also implying that they might not. The following exchange with presidential candidate George W Bush, which quizzes him on his knowledge of contemporary world leaders, illustrates this practice:

1 Hiller: Can you name the president of Chechnya?
2 Bush: No, can you?
3 Hiller: Can you name the president of Taiwan?
4 Bush: Yeah, Lee.
5 Hiller: Can you name the general who is in charge
6 of Pakistan?
7 Bush: Wait, wait. Is this 50 Questions?

(8, Roth 2005, p. 33)

Notice that Bush is resistant to the line of questioning, which he correctly identifies as unlike typical interview questions. Exchanges like this can be extremely newsworthy, but also controversial (Roth 2005). Accordingly, journalist-interviewers have more subtle ways of testing candidates' knowledge, as well as performing other tasks relevant to screening candidates for elective office (Clayman & Romaniuk 2011).

Other interview genres relevant to politics and political campaigns have also been investigated. The celebrity talk-show interview (e.g. *The Tonight Show, The Late Show, The View*), which is generally seen as an exercise in 'infotainment', rather than straight journalism, is becoming an increasingly important arena for politicians on the campaign trail (Baum 2005; Baum & Jamison 2006; Farnsworth & Lichter 2007; Jones 2010) and a focus of conversation analytic investigation (Loeb 2014; Loeb 2015). Such interviews are characterised by a distinctive matrix of norms and practices, with the host's interviewing practices normally embodying qualities of personalisation rather than neutralism, and congeniality rather than adversarialness. However, when politicians appear on such programmes, the resulting interviews become a hybrid of the political and celebrity interview forms, with statistical analysis documenting a blend of interviewing norms and practices (Loeb in press). This results in a unique form of campaign interview, and a distinctive arena in which politicians appear before the public.

News conferences

News conferences have also been examined from a CA perspective. Here, the focus has been on formal quantitative analysis of aggressive or adversarial questioning, with initial work focusing on the US context and tracing historical trends in the aggressiveness of questions directed toward the president (Clayman et al. 2010; Clayman et al. 2006; Clayman et al. 2007; Clayman et al. 2012; Heritage & Clayman 2013). Five dimensions of aggressive questioning have been examined: initiative, directness, assertiveness, adversarialness and accountability. All dimensions have exhibited a rising trend in aggressiveness from 1953 to 2000 (Clayman et al. 2006), with directness rising relatively gradually, while other dimensions have been more volatile over time (Clayman et al. 2006). Further research looking at the specific question form of the negative interrogative supported and strengthened this finding (Heritage & Clayman 2013). These findings, in turn, provide ample evidence of growing press independence in the US and an increasingly adversarial relationship between the press and the presidency.

Subsequent research has suggested that this shift was driven in part by a normative shift that took place following the era coinciding with the Nixon administration, which reframed how journalists relate to the president (Clayman et al. 2010). Other research has identified a range of other circumstantial factors associated with more aggressive questioning. At the level of journalistic attributes (Clayman et al. 2012), female journalists were more aggressive than male journalists from 1953–1968, although the gender difference has attenuated since that time. A contrast that has persisted is between journalists who are regulars at press conferences and those who appear less frequently, with the former being significantly more aggressive (Clayman et al. 2012). Beyond the level of the individual journalist, question content is also demonstrably consequential, with domestic policy questions more aggressive than questions dealing with foreign affairs or national security (Clayman et al. 2007). The economic context is also significant, with questions more aggressive when unemployment rates and interest rates are on the rise (Clayman et al. 2007). This research shows how conversation analysis can provide the foundation for formal quantification of language practices, which, when applied to news conference data can shed light on the dynamic and evolving relationship between press and state.

Conclusion

The research studies reviewed here demonstrate how a focus on language practices *within interaction* can inform the study of politics from the vantage point of direct encounters between political figures, media personnel and ordinary people.

While a variety of politically relevant interactional forms have been investigated, progress has not been evenly distributed. Among interactions between political figures and media professionals, journalistic interviews and presidential news conferences have until recently overshadowed the study of 'infotainment' talk shows – even though the latter are becoming an increasingly important venue for public appearances by elected officials and political candidates. Among interactions between political figures and ordinary people, political speeches involving collective audience behaviour have, until recently, overshadowed contexts in which members of the public participate as individuals in governmental and political processes. By the same token, new research initiatives in the study of celebrity talk shows, direct democracy meetings and other environments of public participation (Thornborrow 2014) have begun to rectify this. Furthermore, the addition of statistical techniques, with coding systems built upon, and validated by, prior qualitative research, has begun to add range and depth to this work, enabling the study of distributional patterns and causal associations between language practices and socio-political contexts. All this work has yielded expanding insight into the diverse interactional arenas in which such language is deployed, and the political processes and institutions to which it contributes.

Notes

1 For more thorough discussions of CA methods, see ten Have (1999), Heritage (1997), and Clayman & Gill (2012). For more comprehensive reviews of politically relevant research studies, see Clayman (2012) and Hutchby (2006).
2 This excerpt, and the next two to follow, are from network television news interview programmes in the US.

References

Atkinson, M, 1984, *Our masters' voices: The language and body language of politics*, Methuen, London.

Baum, M A, 2005, 'Talking the vote: Why presidential candidates hit the talk show circuit', *American Journal of Political Science* 49(2), pp. 213–234.

Baum, M A & Jamison, A S, 2006, 'The *Oprah* effect: How soft news helps inattentive citizens vote consistently', *The Journal of Politics* 68(4), pp. 946–959.

Clayman, S E, 1988, 'Displaying neutrality in television news interviews', *Social Problems*, 35(4), pp. 474–492.

Clayman, S E, 1991, 'News interview openings: Aspects of sequential organization', in *Broadcast Talk*, ed. P Scannel, Sage, London, pp. 48–75.

Clayman, S E, 1992a, 'Footing in the achievement of neutrality: The case of news interview discourse', in *Talk at work: Interaction in institutional settings*, ed. P Drew & J Heritage, Cambridge University Press, Cambridge, pp. 163–198.

Clayman, S E, 1992b, 'Cavet orator: Audience disaffiliation in the 1988 presidential debates', *Quarterly Journal of Speech*, 78, pp. 33–60.

Clayman, S E, 1993, 'Booing: The anatomy of a disaffiliative response', *American Sociological Review*, 58(1), pp. 110–130.

Clayman, S E & Heritage, J, 2002a, 'Questioning presidents: Journalistic deference and adversarialness in the press conferences of US Presidents Eisenhower and Reagan', *Journal of Communication*, 52(4), pp. 749–775.

Clayman, S E & Heritage, J, 2002b, *The news interview: Journalists and public figures on the air*, Cambridge University Press, Cambridge.

Clayman, S E & Reisner, A, 1998, 'Gatekeeping in action: Editorial conferences and assessments of newsworthiness', *American Sociological Review*, 63(2), pp. 178–199.

Clayman, S E & Romaniuk, T, 2011, 'Questioning candidates', in *Talking politics in broadcast media: Cross-cultural perspectives on political interviewing, journalism and accountability*, eds. M Ekström & M Patrona, John Benjamins, Amsterdam, pp. 15–32.

Clayman, S E, Elliott, M N, Heritage, J & Beckett, M K, 2010, 'A watershed in White House journalism: Explaining the post-1968 rise of aggressive presidential news', *Political Communication*, 27(3), pp. 229–247.

Clayman, S E, Elliott, M N, Heritage, J & McDonald, L L, 2006, 'Historical trends in questioning presidents, 1953–2000', *Presidential Studies Quarterly*, 36(4), pp. 561–583.

Clayman, S E, Heritage, J, Elliott, M N & McDonald, L L, 2007, 'When does the watchdog bark? Conditions of aggressive questioning in presidential news conferences', *American Sociological Review* 72(1), pp. 23–41.

Clayman, S E, Elliott, M N, Heritage, J & Beckett, M K, 2012, 'The president's questioners consequential attributes of the White House press corps', *The International Journal of Press/Politics*, 17(1), pp. 100–121.

Ekström, M & Lundell, A K, 2011, 'Beyond the broadcast interview: Specialized forms of interviewing in the making of television news', *Journalism Studies*, 12(2), pp. 172–187.

Ekström, M, Eriksson, G, Johansson, B & Wikström, P, 2013, 'Biased interrogations?: A multi-methodological approach on bias in election campaign interviews', *Journalism Studies*, 14(3), pp. 423–439.

Farnsworth, S J & Lichter, S R, 2007, *The nightly news nightmare: Television's coverage of U.S. presidential elections, 1988–2004*, Rowman & Littlefield Publishers, Lanham, MD.

Gnisci, A, Zollo, P, Perugini, M & Di Conza, A, 2013, 'A comparative study of toughness and neutrality in Italian and English political interviews', *Journal of Pragmatics*, 50(1), pp. 152–167.

Greatbatch, D, 1988, 'A turn-taking system for British news interviews', *Language in Society* 17(3), pp. 401–430.

Hepburn, A & Bolden, G, 2012, 'The conversation analytic approach to transcription,' in *The handbook of conversation analysis*, eds. J Sidnell & T Stivers, Wiley-Blackwell, Oxford, pp. 57–76.

Heritage, J, 1984a, 'A change-of-state token and aspects of its sequential placement,' pp. 299–345 in *Structures of social action: Studies in conversation analysis*, eds. J M Atkinson & J Heritage, Cambridge University Press, Cambridge, pp. 299–345.

Heritage, J, 1984b, *Garfinkel and ethnomethodology*, Polity Press, Cambridge.

Heritage, J, 2002, 'The limits of questioning: Negative interrogatives and hostile question content', *Journal of Pragmatics* 34(10), pp. 1427–1446.

Heritage, J & Clayman, S E, 2010, *Talk in action: Interactions, identities and institutions*, Wiley Blackwell, Boston, MA.

Heritage, J & Clayman, S E, 2013, 'The changing tenor or questioning over time: Tracking a question form across US presidential news conferences, 1953–2000', *Journalism Practice* 7(4), pp. 481–501.

Heritage, J & Greatbatch, D, 1986, 'Generating applause: A study of rhetoric and response at party political conferences', *American Journal of Sociology* 92(1), pp. 110–157.

Huls, E & Varwijk, J, 2011, 'Political bias in TV interviews', *Discourse & Society*, 22(1), pp. 48–65.

Hutchby, I, 2006, *Media talk: Conversation analysis and the study of broadcasting*, Open University Press, New York.

Jones, J P, 2010, *Entertaining politics: Satiric television and political engagement*, Rowman & Littlefield Publishers, Lanham, MD.

Katz, J & Emerson, R M, 1983, 'Analytic induction: A theory of qualitative methodology', in *Contemporary field research*, Waveland, Prospect Heights, IL, pp. 127–187.

Loeb, L, 2014, 'Presidential candidates and the celebrity talk show'. Paper presented at the National Communications Association, Chicago, IL.

Loeb, L, 2015, 'The celebrity talk show: Norms and practices', *Discourse, Context & Media*, 10, pp. 27–35.

Loeb, L, in press, 'Politicians on celebrity talk shows', *Discourse, Context, and Media*.

Mondada, L, 2011, 'The interactional production of multiple spatialities within a participatory democracy meeting', *Social semiotics* 21(2), pp. 289–316.

Mondada, L, 2013, 'Embodied and spatial resources for turn-taking in institutional multi-party interactions: Participatory democracy debates', *Journal of Pragmatics*, 46(1), pp. 39–68.

Montgomery, M, 2007, *The discourse of broadcast news: A linguistic approach*, Routledge, London.

Montgomery, M, 2011, 'The accountability interview, politics and change in UK public service broadcasting', in *Talking Politics in Broadcast Media*, eds. M Ekström & M Patrona, John Benjamins, Amsterdam, pp. 33–55.

Romaniuk, T, 2013, 'Pursuing answers to questions in broadcast journalism', *Research on Language & Social Interaction*, 46(2), pp. 144–164.

Roth, A L, 2005, '"Pop quizzes" on the campaign trail: Journalists, candidates, and the limits of questioning', *The Harvard International Journal of Press/Politics*, 10, pp. 28–46.

Sacks, H, 1984, 'Notes on methodology', in *Structures of social action*, eds. J M Atkinson & J Heritage, Cambridge University Press, Cambridge, pp. 21–27.

Sacks, H, Schegloff, E A & Jefferson, G, 1974, 'A simplest systematics for the organization of turn-taking for conversation', *Language* 50(4), pp. 696–735.

Scannell, P, 1996, *Radio, television, and modern life*, Blackwell, Oxford.

Schegloff, E A, 2007, *Sequence organization in interaction: A primer in conversation analysis I*, Cambridge University Press, Cambridge.

Schegloff, E A & Sacks, H, 1973, 'Opening up closings', *Semiotica* 8(4), pp. 289–327.

ten Have, P, 1999, *Doing conversation analysis: A practical guide*, Sage, London.

Thornborrow, J, 2001a, 'Questions, control and the organization of talk in calls to a radio phone-in', *Discourse Studies* 3(1), pp. 119–143.

Thornborrow, J, 2001b, 'Authenticating talk: Building public identities in audience participation broadcasting', *Discourse Studies* 3(4), pp. 459–79.

Thornborrow, J, 2014, *The discourse of public participation media: From talk show to Twitter*, Routledge, Abingdon and New York.

19
Politics beyond words
Ethnography of political institutions

Endre Dányi

The politics of words

Democratic politics is envisioned primarily as a politics of words. Nothing illustrates this better than the etymology of the term 'parliament', which comes from the Old French '*parlement*' and refers to speaking or talk. Yet, as the imposing parliament buildings all over the world show, the politics of words is highly dependent upon a complex, well-aligned infrastructure that involves bodies, texts, symbolic objects and many other entities. Using the Hungarian parliament as a specific case, this chapter shows how ethnography might help in tracing and describing such alignments in practice, pointing at what could be called a 'politics beyond words'. Before doing that, however, a short historical detour is necessary.

Ethnography as a research method comes from anthropology, and its development in the late nineteenth and early twentieth centuries was strongly intertwined with the internal and external colonisation projects of Europe and North America. Knowing indigenous people, their languages, rituals and relations was a way of managing difference between 'their' culture and 'ours' – using the latter as a constant point of reference. Words played an important role in this undertaking in at least two ways: they were used to record cultural differences (see Malinowski 1922 on participant-observation), and they helped to make sense of cultures as if they were texts waiting to be read, compared and analysed by a competent reader (see Geertz 1977 on the interpretation of cultures).

After the Second World War, with many colonial territories becoming independent states, the artificial distinction between 'us' and 'them' was becoming untenable. While many indigenous groups were eager to develop understandings of their own cultures, a number of social and cultural anthropologists in Europe and North America – strongly influenced by poststructuralist theories concerned with the complex relationship between knowledge and power – began to argue for a radical reconceptualisation of *ethnography as a mode of carrying out research*. Possibly the most important attempt to do so was the Writing Culture workshop, held in Santa Fe in 1984. In his introduction to the edited volume that grew out of the workshop, James Clifford argued that the reconceptualisation of ethnography needed to begin 'not with participant-observation or with cultural texts (suitable for interpretation), but with writing, the making of texts' (Clifford & Marcus 1986, p. 2). This required the problematisation of such taken-for-granted notions as 'the object of research', 'the fieldsite', 'the natives', 'the fieldworker', and 'the author'.

It is difficult to overestimate the significance of Writing Culture within cultural anthropology and its impact on several neighbouring disciplines and interdisciplinary fields (Rabinow et al. 2008; Starn 2012). Over recent decades, ethnography has become a popular mode of carrying out research, from medicine through organisation studies and human geography to cultural history. When it comes to the empirical study of politics, ethnographic works have made significant contributions in at least three ways. First, treating politics as a distinct domain of modern life, several scholars have focused on the ethnographic analysis of various political institutions. From a sociological and political scientific point of view, this approach is based on the recognition that certain aspects of the workings of those institutions cannot be fully captured by formal descriptions of political systems – aspects that could collectively be referred to as a political culture (Almond & Verba 1989; see also Auyero et al. 2007; Schatz 2009). The importance of political culture has been elegantly demonstrated, for example, in detailed analyses of the architecture and infrastructure of local councils and national parliaments (Abélès 1991; Crewe 2005, 2015; Gardey 2015), the complex ways in which bureaucracies organise themselves and the world around them (Farrelly 2015; Hull 2012; Riles 2006; Scheffer 2010), the embodied practices of 'doing politics' as activists (Graeber 2009) and elected politicians (Muntigl et al. 2000; Wodak 2000, 2011), the often invisible work that goes into making policies meaningful across different places (Clarke et al. 2015; Freeman 2014; Shore & Wright 2003; Yanow 1996), and the discursive and material tinkering that goes into the constitution of such supranational entities as the European Union (Abélès 1992; Barry 2001; Krzyżanowski & Oberhuber 2007; Wodak 2011; Wodak et al. 2012). What these and other ethnographic analyses of politics as a domain show is that political culture is not simply an 'add-on' to political systems. Quite the contrary: our ways of thinking about systems and system-ness should be seen as the result of historically and culturally specific developments.

The second way in which ethnographic works have contributed to ongoing debates in political science and political sociology is concerned less with politics as a domain than with political processes – or, to put it differently, processes through which things become political. The main sources of inspiration in this regard are Science and Technology Studies (STS) and Foucauldian governmentality studies, which have both been concerned with the political effects of such seemingly apolitical practices as technological innovation (Suchman 2006), scientific knowledge production (Knorr-Cetina 1981, 1999; Latour 1987; Latour & Woolgar 1986; Law 1994; Lynch 1997), the performance of market economies (Callon et al. 2007; Mackenzie et al. 2007), the running of evaluations and audits (Power 1997; Strathern 2000), the organisation of healthcare (Mol 2002; Mol et al. 2010) and education (Sørensen 2011; Verran 2001), and the conduct of social and personal life (Rose 2007; Rose & Miller 2008). These and similar practices participate in politics precisely by denying their being political. Studying them ethnographically does not only show how sciences, technologies, economies, and so on work, but also provides new possibilities to articulate how they could work differently.

This points at the third way in which ethnographic works have engaged with politics, which – following the German philosopher and literary critic Walter Benjamin (1969) – could be called the politics of storytelling. As several ethnographers working with Benjamin's concepts and style of thought have convincingly argued, ethnographic accounts are difficult to locate on a single plane, being defined by both facts and fictions (Raffles 2010; Shelton 2007, 2013; Stewart 2007; Stone 2012; Taussig 2006). As stories, their main aim is not necessarily to offer explanations of various phenomena (which would contribute to the disenchantment of the world), but to highlight the cracks on the apparently smooth glass and steel surfaces of modern life (and thereby engage in an act of re-enchantment). Benjamin himself tried to put this understanding of storytelling to use in the realm of consumer capitalism (see Benjamin 1999). What would such an approach look like in the realm of democratic politics?

Taking inspiration from the three above-mentioned sets of sources, the main aim of this chapter is to make ethnography more visible and accessible for social scientists interested in politics – not by offering a how-to manual, but by indicating in what ways an ethnographic approach can transform our understanding of what politics *is*. Drawing on fieldwork conducted in Budapest between 2008 and 2010, I will use the Hungarian parliament building as a methodological device to analyse what could be called 'politics beyond words'. The fieldwork itself consisted of several research visits, which could also be seen as distinct stages of my ethnography (see Krzyżanowski 2011, p. 287). The first visit involved a recontextualisation of my research object, which I had known well as a Hungarian citizen, but which I had to learn to see anew in light of my research interest and the available literature. The second, third and fourth visits were dedicated to the collection of a wide range of empirical materials, a selection of which will appear in this chapter, either as fieldnotes (indented) or as vignettes. These will be used, not as illustrations of politics in general, but as empirical arguments that reflect the situated and inherently material character of political practices. The fifth and final visit was an attempt to relate my findings to a constantly changing scientific and political discourse about the crisis of democracy in Hungary – I return to this problem in the last section of this chapter.

The text is structured as follows. After a brief introduction of the parliament building as the main stage of Hungarian democracy, I will first discuss the role of politicians (and their bodies) in ever-changing staging processes. I will then switch focus to the roles different kinds of texts and text-producing devices play in the delineation of political activities from other, largely technical procedures. While this delineation is supposed to secure the ongoing operation of the parliament as a legislative machine, in the subsequent section, I will use the example of the Holy Crown of Hungary to show how the parliament as a place and an institution is caught up in politics that works as much on the level of symbols as on the level of laws. Finally, I will reflect on the politics of ethnographic stories, that is, their potential to perform critique within a democratic setting.

Staging politics

The Hungarian parliament building is a large neo-Gothic palace in the centre of Budapest, on the east bank of the Danube, just below Margaret Island. Its construction began in the early 1880s and when completed in 1902, it was the largest – and arguably the most impressive – parliament building in the world. Back then, Hungary was still part of the Austro-Hungarian Monarchy, which means that by today's standards, the legislature played a rather restricted role in the political system. Still, between the signing of the Austro-Hungarian Compromise in 1867 and the outbreak of the First World War in 1914, the focus of politics had gradually shifted from the Royal Palace to the parliament, turning the latter into the iconic site of Hungarian politics (Dányi 2015; Gábor & Verő 2000).

In the last two decades of the nineteenth century, the main task of the architect of the new parliament building, Imre Steindl, was nothing less than to design a structure that would convey a sense of political stability for many centuries to come. Steindl took the task seriously, but the political system fell apart sooner than anyone could imagine, and throughout the twentieth century, there were hardly any periods when the grandiose parliament building in Budapest could function as the true centre of Hungarian politics. As cultural historian András Gerő (2010) has pointed out, in the inter-war period, everyone knew that most decisions were made by Admiral Miklós Horthy, Governor of Hungary, who lived and worked in the Royal Palace, while in the communist period, everyone knew that most decisions were made in the headquarters of the Hungarian Socialist Workers' Party, a few hundred metres north of the parliament.

It is difficult to tell when exactly the bad spell of the twentieth century broke in Hungary. One possible answer is that it happened on 23 October 1989, when – commemorating the outbreak of the 1956 revolution – interim President Mátyás Szűrös used one of the balconies above the main entrance of the parliament building to declare the Third Republic. By then, the communist National Assembly had already modified the Constitution, which clearly stated that in the new republic, all power belonged to the people, who exercised their sovereign rights primarily through elected representatives. Subsequently, the first free general election was held in the spring of 1990, and by the time the first post-communist National Assembly was set up, the parliament building was refigured as the grand theatre of democratic politics.

The theatre metaphor, introduced to sociological analysis by Erving Goffman (1959), is neither accidental nor surprising. As political theorist Yaron Ezrahi (2012) argues, democratic politics has often been described in theatrical terms – as a spectacle where the public is allowed to see and hear all the debates, but it is not supposed to directly participate in them. In fact, one of the hardest challenges for the architects of modern parliament buildings – including Steindl – was to find a good way of accommodating 'the public' in the legislature. The visual and acoustic logic dictated that plenary halls – with the exception of the Palace of Westminster in London – take the shape of a semi-circle or a horseshoe, creating a theatrical setting in which political speeches could come across as individual performances on the frontstage of democratic politics (Friedland 2002; Manow 2010).

While the conceptualisation of the parliament as the Goffmanian frontstage of democratic politics, where official performances are put on public display, is certainly not wrong, it suggests that speeches in the legislature are 'mere performances' while real politics happens elsewhere, behind the scenes, somewhere in the proverbial smoke-filled rooms that collectively constitute the backstage of democracy. Although it is tempting to portray ethnography as a method that could be used to explain how politics *really* works, its main contribution to empirical analyses of democracy lies more in its capacity to shift the attention from an ongoing oscillation between front- and backstages to various staging processes (Disch 2008; Latour 1999). Let me illustrate what this might mean by sharing excerpts from my fieldnotes about a series of events I observed in Budapest in April 2008. Incidentally, this was the time that the Alliance of Free Democrats (AFD) decided to quit the governing coalition with the Hungarian Socialist Party (HSP) once they found out the socialist Prime Minister had decided to sack the liberal Minister of Health for her failed attempt to reform the healthcare system.

Monday, 7 April 2008
It is nine o'clock in the morning, and the AFD faction is holding its weekly meeting in the faction office in the Parliament. Members of the faction are preparing for the upcoming plenary sitting. Péter Gusztos, deputy faction leader and party whip, has a

double role to play. On the one hand, he has to make sure everyone understands and follows the party line; on the other hand, he needs to pursue his own agenda. At some point he asks the faction whether they should make anything of the attack against a ticket office, which happened in Hollán Street in Budapest a few days earlier. According to a conservative newspaper, the employees of the ticket office refused to sell tickets to a concert of a 'patriotic rock band'. In turn, someone threw a Molotov cocktail at the shop. Péter thinks it would be important to publicly condemn the event, but others in the faction argue the party should focus on the coalition crisis instead. As a compromise, they decide to connect the attack to a larger issue, namely the regulation of hate speech, which has for a very long time been a source of controversy between socialist and liberal politicians. Péter volunteers to give a short speech in the parliament.

Tuesday, 8 April 2008
At nine o'clock in the morning, the debating chamber of the House of Representatives is almost completely empty. Only a handful of MPs are present when the Deputy Speaker opens the sitting, and even they look like they would prefer to be somewhere else. Before the National Assembly begins the general debate of a bill that aims to modify an existing law on financial service provision, each faction has a chance to present an early day motion in five minutes. Péter is the third in line – the title of his speech is 'On the responsibility of public figures'. In the beginning of his speech, Péter briefly presents two cases, which in his opinion relate to a debate Hungarian politicians have been having for almost two decades about hate speech and political extremism. One of the cases is an implicitly antisemitic opinion piece published in a conservative newspaper, while the other is the arson attack against the ticket office in Hollán Street. Péter was happy to see that, irrespective of party affiliation, several politicians condemned the two events, but strongly disagrees with those who think the solution to the growing problem of political extremism lies in the stricter regulation of hate speech. He shares the view of those who argue that further regulation could only be introduced at the expense of the freedom of speech, which would be unacceptable. He continues:

> we, liberals, have said it countless times in this debate that we find it imperative that politicians discuss not only what can and cannot be done in terms of legislation, but also what the responsibility of public figures is in such situations; what room there is for social action for politicians, journalists, intellectuals when they encounter such phenomena.[1]

Péter finishes his speech by claiming that taking a common stance against the extreme-right in public would be much more productive than any debate in the legislature. The speech ends with weak applause, and a member of the Government stands up to give a short response. He speaks on behalf the Ministry of Education and Culture, but his position is exactly the same as that of the Hungarian Socialist Party: it is the moral duty of the state to protect all victims of hate speech, and he believes the best way to do it is through strict legal regulation. Of course, he adds, no regulation can be successful without the support of civil society, so in that sense, he says he shares Péter's concern. Once again, there is weak applause in the chamber, and the Deputy Speaker calls on the next MP on the list.

Friday, 11 April 2008
Péter's speech on Tuesday morning went largely unnoticed, and he would have certainly forgotten about it, had a journalist not called him this morning to ask if he's planning to attend an anti-fascist demonstration in Hollán Street. Allegedly, it is organised by a civil organisation, and the Prime Minister has already announced that he is going to be there, along with former German Chancellor Gerhard Schröder, who happens to be in Budapest. Péter has not yet heard about the demonstration, but after his speech in the parliament it is clear that he, too, has to be there.

Hollán Street is just ten minutes' walk from the parliament. Early in the afternoon, the otherwise quiet area is getting visibly tense. Several far-right groups, including Jobbik (Movement for a Better Hungary), had announced they would hold a counter-demonstration just a few blocks down the road, and given the heated political situation, I would not be surprised if there were clashes between them and the heavily armed police. In the narrow streets around the ticket office, there are a couple of vans belonging to large television channels.

By the time we arrive, there are already two or three thousand people gathered together in the street. Some of them are holding 'Say no to neo-Nazis' signs; others are distributing small Hungarian flags. The event is organised by a civil group, so there are no political speeches in the programme, but quite a few socialist and liberal politicians can be spotted in the crowd, along with Gerhard Schröder. Showing up is already a political act, Péter tells me. All of a sudden, a group of counter-demonstrators appears at the far end of the street, but the police successfully block their way to the ticket office. The far-right groups are clearly outnumbered, but this does not prevent them from making a lot of noise to disturb the programme. Apart from this incident, however, everything goes as planned, and around 6pm, the demonstration comes to an end. In the evening, the event is leading news on all television channels.

Monday, 14 April 2008
In the afternoon, the corridors leading to the debating chamber in the House of Representatives are full of people. The lounge near the Secretariat of the Office of the National Assembly is surrounded by television cameras, spotlights and microphone stands. In accordance with the faction's decision, today, Péter is going to make another speech in the parliament related to hate-speech regulation. He enters the debating chamber, occupies his seat in the middle of the horseshoe and waits for his turn. When the Speaker announces the title of his speech – 'Hungarians against neo-Nazis' – Péter stands up and begins to address the plenum. In the introduction, he briefly summarises what had happened at the ticket office in Hollán Street, and calls last week's demonstration the victory of freedom and democracy. He then says:

> we, liberals, have argued countless times that no hate speech regulation can be as effective as what we saw on last Friday. […]

> Extremist groups exist everywhere, neo-Nazis appear in almost all European countries, and let me tell you, antisemitic articles are published outside the borders of Hungary, too – this is not the question. The question is how a country responds to such phenomena. […]

Last week Hungary, this tolerant, inclusive, freedom-loving and freedom-protecting country, knew what needed to be done. What needed to be done and how it needed to be done. [...]

In the future, in similar situations – and let us not have any illusions, unfortunately, there will be many similar situations – we have to demonstrate ourselves in a similar way (The Speaker indicates that time is up.), we have to demonstrate the strength of a courageous and inclusive Hungary.[2]

Parts of Péter's speech sound very similar to the one he gave in parliament on last Tuesday, except then, the debating chamber was practically empty. Once again, he connects the arson attack to the larger issue of hate-speech regulation and emphasises the importance of social action in the face of political extremism. However, there is a subtle, but all-the-more-important difference between the two speeches: whereas last week by 'liberals' Péter meant a small group of invisible politicians who had some disagreement with their socialist partners, now he uses the term to denote those freedom-loving and freedom-protecting Hungarians who had the courage to attend the Hollán Street demonstration. To be sure, they might not have all been liberal voters, but Péter implies they were liberal people, whose interests in the National Assembly are best represented by the Alliance of Free Democrats.

(Dányi fieldnotes 2008)

There is nothing particular about this series of events, recorded in my fieldnotes – Péter Gusztos's speeches in parliament had no important implications in the midst of the coalition crisis, and the demonstration after the arson attack certainly did not stop the far right from gaining more ground in Hungary. My purpose for recounting this series of events, however, was neither to evaluate politicians' frontstage performances, nor to provide glimpses into the backstage of parliamentary politics. Rather, my aim was to show how politicians are constantly involved in staging processes that connect party meetings, plenary sessions, street demonstrations, media studios and other locations in inventive ways. What such a multi-sited ethnography (Marcus 1995) allows us to see is how diverse locations collectively constitute a political market of parties and their programmes, the value of which are determined at regularly held elections.

The political and the technical in the legislative process

Regularly held elections indicate that, in some sense, parliamentary democracy is an inherently unstable system: governments change, politicians come and go, parties appear and disappear all the time. What grants this political system its stability? In this section, drawing on the insights of institutional ethnography (Holmes 2013; Hull 2012; Latour 2010; Riles 2006; Scheffer 2010; Suchman 2006), I argue that texts play a crucial stabilising role in at least three distinct ways.

First, it is possible to think of the legislation process as a complex collective work *on texts*. Proposals for creating new laws or for modifying existing ones – so-called bills – are typically documents that need to be formatted in a particular way to be recognised by parliament's bureaucratic machinery (see the chapter by Ilie in this book, p. 309). In Hungary, bills can only come from four specific entities: the President, the government, standing committees and individual MPs. They need to be addressed to the Speaker, and have to contain the title and the text of the proposed law, a justification for its submission, and a brief description of its anticipated economic effects and social implications. The Department of File Registry checks whether the nearly two-hundred bills that are submitted each year meet the formal criteria. All proposals begin their parliamentary life in this department, where – if everything goes well – they get a sticker with a bar code, and within half an hour, their scanned version appears on the legislature's intranet. A copy of the paper version is then forwarded to the Speaker, whose responsibility is to decide whether bills are, indeed, suitable for debate. If they are, the Speaker adds them to the National Assembly's tentative schedule, which is in effect a detailed timetable that determines when each bill should be debated by the National Assembly, for how long and in what order.

The debates typically take place in the debating chamber of the parliament, and are organised into two rounds. The first round is about the general principles of a bill and the text of the proposed law. The core of the debate consists of speeches by principal speakers from each party faction. It is then the individual MPs' turn to comment on the bill, alternating between the government and the opposition. All participants have a second chance to speak, and in the end, the sponsor is allowed to respond to the debate as a whole. Once the first round is over, the National Assembly decides whether the bill is ready for the second round, which focuses exclusively on various amendments submitted by the MPs and the relevant standing committees. This often appears to be an endless process, but at some point, even the longest disputes come to an end, and then the speaker convenes the National Assembly to decide the fate of the proposed law.

Most decisions need a simple majority, but the modification of some laws, for example, the amendment of the Constitution, requires a qualified majority. Similar to the debate, the vote on a bill happens in two rounds, but in a reverse order: first the National Assembly decides upon all amendments, and then upon the proposed law as a whole. Once the National Assembly passes a law, the final version of the text is sent to the Speaker, who signs to certify that everything during the legislative process went according to the rules and procedures established in the Standing Orders, and forwards it to the President, who in turn examines the content of the new law and decides whether it is in harmony with the general principles of the Constitution. If it is, the new law is promulgated in the *Official Gazette of the Republic of Hungary*.

The Speaker's and President's signatures on all laws passed by the National Assembly indicate a second way in which texts play a stabilising role in a parliamentary democracy. The two signatures point at two meta-documents – the Standing Orders and the Constitution – that together determine the rules of parliament's operation, down to such minute details as the length of speeches, and by doing so perform an important distinction between *the political* and *the technical*. The former is figured as a series of debates about well-defined objects between the government and the opposition, which end with clear decisions made by the National Assembly, while the latter denotes all the bureaucratic work that is required to ensure that all bills that enter parliament are treated equally, efficiently and transparently.

Transparency indicates a third way in which texts play a central role in the legislative process. In the previous section (p. 294) I could quote excerpts by Péter Gusztos only because his speeches, along with all the other speeches made by all the other MPs in the Hungarian legislature, are publicly accessible.[3] The transcripts of parliamentary speeches are prepared by the National Assembly's stenographers, who – as specified by Imre Steindl back in the early 1880s – sit right in the centre of the debating chamber, between the rostrum and the desks of the members of the government. Working in ten-minute shifts, their task is to produce faithful records of parliamentary debates. To be able to do so, they need to take minutes, not only of the speeches (which is difficult enough, since their hands have to move as fast as the politicians' mouths – see also Gardey 2015), but also every declaration and interruption, as well as any loud expression of approval or disapproval. Once their shift is over, stenographers leave the debating chamber through a door under the rostrum and rush into their office in the mezzanine to turn their notes into typewritten text. After several rounds of corrections and revisions, their texts are certified by the notaries and within three days, the official transcript is uploaded to the parliament's website. Within a week, the formatted transcript appears in print in the *Official Journal of the House of Representatives*. This, however, is not the end of the texts' journey: on the internet, in the archives, and in the parliament's library, the traces of previous debates constitute the parliament's institutional memory (Bowker 2008) that reaches back to the mid nineteenth century, forming and informing future debates and inquiries.

The problem of dis/continuity

The composition of the parliament might constantly change, but thanks to an artificial distinction between *the technical* and *the political* the legislature can operate in an eternal present, in which all issues concerning the political community can be dealt with through a standardised legislative procedure. But what about issues that concern the composition of a political community itself? Drawing on the works of Hannah Arendt and Jacques Derrida, in political theory, this question is usually referred to as 'the problem of founding a republic' (Honig 1991). In a constitutional sense, the Third Republic of Hungary was born on 23 October 1989, but it was the last communist parliament that had modified the Constitution so that a new, democratically elected parliament could be set up in 1990. In what sense is the Third Republic the continuation of the People's Republic of Hungary? How do both regimes relate to earlier ones, such as the Austro-Hungarian Monarchy and the Kingdom of Hungary? And what role does the parliament play in managing such dis/continuities? In order to address these questions, it is important to switch attention from politicians and texts to symbolic objects.

Consider, for example, the Holy Crown of Hungary (see also Dányi 2013). On 1 January 2000, the royal jewels of Hungary – the crown, the orb, the sceptre and the royal sword – were carried from the National Museum to parliament in an armoured vehicle, accompanied by a police motorcade. It took about quarter of an hour for the bullet-proof car to reach the parliament building, where it was received by a joyous crowd and the Corporation of the Holy Crown – a special committee that consisted of the President of the Republic, the Prime Minister, the Speaker of the National Assembly, the President of the Constitutional Court and the President of the Hungarian Academy of Sciences. After saluting the national flag and listening to the national anthem, four members of the Republican Guard carried the special earthquake-proof glass cabinet containing the regalia up the main stairs, and put it on permanent display in the centre of the Cupola Hall.

The idea of the royal jewels' transfer came up in 1999, when the Hungarian government proposed a bill to commemorate the thousandth anniversary of the coronation of St Stephen, Hungary's first Christian king. The preamble of the draft law acknowledged St Stephen's role in integrating the Hungarian people into Europe and recounted the development of his realm in the Carpathian Basin. It emphasised the importance of the Christian faith during times of occupation and dictatorship, and, without any further explanation, declared the Holy Crown of Hungary the relic that, in the consciousness of the nation, 'live[d] as the embodiment of the continuity and independence of the Hungarian state.' Finally, it proposed that:

Endre Dányi

> [o]n the occasion of the thousandth anniversary of the foundation of the state, Hungary elevates the Holy Crown to its appropriate place, and from the museum of the nation lays it under the protection of the representative of the nation, the National Assembly.
>
> (Hungarian Government draft bill 1999)

The text of the draft law did not clarify how St Stephen and the Holy Crown related to each other, but the preamble reiterated a well-known myth, popularised by Bishop Hartvic in the twelfth century, according to which, the crown currently on display in the Cupola Hall of the parliament is the same object used to crown St Stephen on 1 January 1000. It was supposedly given by Pope Sylvester II as a formal acknowledgement of Hungary becoming a Christian country, and as a guarantee of her independence from the Holy Roman Empire and the Byzantine Empire. In the period of growing tension between Rome and Constantinople, this account was clearly an important reference point and strengthened the cult of St Stephen, whom Bishop Hartvic portrayed, not only as the founder of the Hungarian state, but also as a strong defender of the Christian faith.

Despite the fact that most statues and paintings of St Stephen show him with the Holy Crown on his head, archaeologists currently think that the crown is younger than Bishop Hartvic had claimed. The first written document that refers to the crown as St Stephen's Crown dates back to the end of the thirteenth century, by which time, it was considered to be more than a royal jewel. As Ernst Kantorowicz observes, it was 'at once the visible holy relic of St. Stephen, Hungary's first Christian king, and the invisible symbol and lord paramount of the Hungarian monarchy' (Kantorowicz 1997, p. 339). As Kantorowicz's classical work on political theology argues, the conceptual separation of the king as a human being from kingship in general was common in medieval Europe. What made Hungary different was that the physical object came to be seen as the sole sovereign of the country. This meant that anyone who wanted to be recognised as a legitimate King of Hungary had to be crowned with the very same object.

Who exactly was the first king crowned with the Holy Crown of Hungary is difficult to tell. What is certain, is that the last king who was crowned with it was Charles IV, Francis Joseph's grand-nephew, in 1916. A contemporary photo shows that the crown was too big for his head – it almost fell off during the coronation ceremony. Not a good omen; no wonder, then, when, two years later, the Austro-Hungarian Monarchy lost the First World War and consequently five states announced their secession from the Empire. In the course of less than twelve months, Hungary witnessed a Bolshevik revolution and a Christian-nationalist counter-revolution, led by Admiral Miklós Horthy. His authoritarian regime was defined in opposition to the peace treaty that ended the First World War, as a result of which, Hungary had lost two-thirds of its pre-war territory and more than half of its population. The Horthy regime claimed the state lived on in the Holy Crown, and when, between 1938 and 1940, parts of Czechoslovakia and Romania were reattached to Hungary, it announced that those territories 'had returned to the body of the Holy Crown.'

Needless to say, the reattachment of parts of the lost territories to Hungary would not have been possible without the external support of Nazi Germany. In the first years of the Second World War, Hitler regarded Horthy as a strategic ally, but when he learned that the Hungarian government had begun to negotiate armistice with the Western Allies, he ordered the invasion of the country. In October 1944, Ferenc Szálasi, leader of the national-socialist Arrow-Cross Party, was appointed to form a government. Szálasi took his oath on the Holy Crown in the Buda Castle.

As the German forces were losing ground, the regalia were taken to Austria, where they were captured by the US Army. After the war, the Holy Crown was taken to Fort Knox, to the United States Gold Reserve in Kentucky, where it was held as a 'property of special status' for more than three decades. It was only in 1977 that President Jimmy Carter announced that the US would return it to Hungary. On 5 January 1978, the regalia once again arrived at Budapest, and after a brief stopover in the parliament's Cupola Hall, they were put on display in the National Museum as objects devoid of any political significance.

Many Hungarians, especially those who were born after the Second World War, might have thought the National Museum was the natural place for the royal jewels, so when, in 1999, the conservative government announced that for the thousandth anniversary of St Stephen's coronation it wanted to transfer them to the parliament, the socialist and liberal opposition was outraged. In the parliamentary debate of the bill, members of the opposition objected that the transfer would reinstitute the Holy Crown as a political object, which would go against the logic of parliamentary democracy (see, for example, Péter 2003). In the Third Republic of Hungary, they claimed, it is the President who symbolises the unity of the state, not the crown, or any other object. Unlike kings, the President is elected by the parliament, which in turn is elected by the people – this logic of sovereignty is based on the rejection of the logic the Holy Crown stands for.

On these grounds, the opposition considered the draft law unconstitutional, and asked the Constitutional Court to determine, whether the Holy Crown had any political function in the Third Republic of Hungary. After some deliberation, the Constitutional Court declared that the Holy Crown had no political function and *therefore* the government could place it wherever it wanted – even in the Cupola Hall of the parliament. This is where it was transferred to on 1 January 2000, and it has been on public display there ever since, configuring parliament into a profane shrine of Hungarian stateness.

The politics of storytelling

It would be possible to tell different stories about democratic politics through the Hungarian parliament building, and it would be equally possible to tell the same stories differently. The possibilities, however, are not endless. The parliament building, and various entities associated with it, make some stories more tell-able than others. One of the purposes of this chapter has precisely been to make such entities and their involvement in storytelling more visible. Drawing on the insights of cultural anthropology after the Writing Culture debate, I wanted to shift attention from a politics of words (e.g. debates, speeches, pamphlets, op-ed pieces in daily newspapers) to what I have called a 'politics beyond words', that is, the politics of settings responsible for making words meaningful in a political way.

After briefly introducing the Hungarian parliament building as a culturally and historically specific setting, I have focused on the roles politicians' bodies, different kinds of texts, and symbolic objects play in the constitution of a political reality called parliamentary democracy. While the material practices associated with regularly held elections, the legislative process and the making of historical dis/continuities might be seen as different aspects or layers of this political reality, what I have tried to show through my ethnographic story fragments is that they do not necessarily add up. Staging processes might be crucial for individual politicians, but from the legislature's perspective, they are feeble events that hardly ever become visible during the legislative procedure. The trajectory of a bill in the legislative machine might be measured in weeks, but it is shaped by the trajectories of thousands of other bills that had passed through the same machine since the mid nineteenth century. The past does therefore matter, but the *ways in which* it matters are constantly being negotiated by a succession of governments and politicians.

These slippages between material practices associated with parliamentary democracy often come across as moments of frustration, as they make politics rather 'unpindownable'. At the same time, however, they offer possibilities of political engagement that do not necessarily correspond to established forms of political participation. In 2010, the socialists lost the general election and the conservatives got a two-thirds majority in the National Assembly. Not long after the start of the new term, the government unilaterally drafted a new Constitution, the preamble of which named the Holy Crown as the single most important symbol of the Hungarian state. At the same time, practising full control of the legislative machine, the governing party undertook a comprehensive reconfiguration of the political system, as a result of which, a whole series of formerly independent institutions – from the Constitutional Court through the Central Bank to Public Service Broadcasting and other media outlets – were either marginalised or made subordinate to the logic of party politics. Many of these moves triggered fierce criticism from a number of scholars and international NGOs, claiming that, a little more than two decades after the collapse of communism, parliamentary democracy in Hungary was once again in danger of falling apart. Although such criticisms have more than a grain of truth in them, they operate along a democracy/non-democracy dichotomy, which tends to reinforce a sense of political apathy. What I have tried to demonstrate in this chapter is that the politics of ethnographic storytelling lies exactly in its capacity to change the frame of critique by opening up new spaces for specific articulations of good and bad democracy.

This, of course, is easier said than done. Like every research strategy, ethnography has its limitations. When it comes to 'studying up' (Nader 1972), that is, studying institutions of high political importance, for example, the success of ethnographic research greatly depends on the level of access researchers manage to negotiate, as well as the level of confidentiality they are asked to adhere to. Another limitation is what Marcus and Rabinow refer to as 'untimeliness' (Rabinow et al. 2008). While in their ways of collecting data, ethnographers are often indistinguishable from journalists, they also greatly differ in what they consider worthy of writing down. Journalists tend to focus on actual, pressing, newsworthy events, whereas ethnographers often engage with seemingly boring, uninteresting, mundane practices, many of which – as in the case of the Hungarian parliament – may already be out-dated by the time the findings of the research are published. The most complex limitation of ethnography, however, has less to do with restricted access or untimeliness than with the act of writing as such. As Stefan Hirschauer (2007) argues, ethnography is primarily about putting things into words that did not exist in language before. This requires not only constant translation work between linguistic and non-linguistic practices, but also a continuous formation of theoretical concepts, which cannot be detached from the empirical practices that had given birth to them.

Such limitations may come across as weaknesses or shortcomings of *ethnography as a method*, but they may just as well be seen as the strengths – or at least the potentially transformative capacities – of *ethnography as a mode of doing research*, insofar as they highlight the contingent and situated character of all forms of knowledge, and thereby help us rethink their implications for democratic politics and its institutions.

Acknowledgements

This chapter is based upon ethnographic research I conducted in Budapest between 2008 and 2010. I am grateful to The Leverhulme Trust for their financial support (award reference

F/00185/U), to my supervisors and examiners in Lancaster and London – John Law, Lucy Suchman, Andrew Barry and Yoke-Sum Wong – for their careful engagement with my work at various stages, and Thomas Scheffer and the Political Ethnography Working Group in Berlin and Frankfurt for sustained discussions about the limits of democracy.

Notes

1 Official Journal of the House of Representatives, 2006–2010 (9.38 am, 8 April 2008) – my translation.
2 Official Journal of the House of Representatives, 2006–2010 (1.40 pm, 14 April 2008) – my translation.
3 Available from: www.parlament.hu/orszaggyulesi-naplo-elozo-ciklusbeli-adatai.

References

Abélès, M, 1991, *Quiet days in Burgundy*, Cambridge University Press, Cambridge.
Abélès, M, 1992, *La vie quotidienne au Parlement européen*, Hachette, Paris.
Almond, G A & Verba, S, 1989, *The civic culture*, Sage, London.
Auyero, J, Joseph, L & Mahler, M, 2007, *New perspectives in political ethnography*, Springer Verlag, New York.
Barry, A 2001, *Political machines*, Continuum, London.
Benjamin, W, 1969, 'The storyteller' in *Illuminations: Essays and reflections*, Schocken, New York, pp. 83–110.
Benjamin, W, 1999, *The arcades project*, Harvard University Press, Cambridge, MA.
Bowker, G C, 2008, *Memory practices in the sciences*, The MIT Press, Cambridge, MA.
Callon, M, Millo Y & Muniesa, F, 2007, *Market devices*, Wiley Blackwell, Chichester.
Clarke, J, Bainton, D, Lendvai & Stubbs, P, 2015, *Making policy move*, Policy Press, Bristol.
Clifford, J & Marcus, G E, 1986, *Writing culture*, University of California Press, Berkeley, CA.
Crewe, E, 2005, *Lords of Parliament*, Manchester University Press, Manchester.
Crewe, E, 2015, *The House of Commons*, Bloomsbury Publishing, London.
Dányi, E, 2013, 'Democracy in ruins', in *The Inhabited Ruins of Central Europe*, eds. D Gafijczuk & D Sayer, Palgrave Macmillan, London, pp. 55–78.
Disch, L J, 2008, 'Representation as "spokespersonship": Bruno Latour's political theory', *Parallax*, vol. 14, no. 3, pp. 88–100.
Ezrahi, Y, 2012, *Imagined democracies*, Cambridge University Press, Cambridge.
Farelly, M, 2015, *Discourse and democracy*, Routledge, London.
Freeman, R & Sturdy, S, 2014, *Knowledge in policy*, Policy Press, Bristol.
Friedland, P, 2002, *Political actors: Representative bodies and theatricality in the age of the French Revolution*, Cornell University Press, Ithaca, NY.
Gábor, E & Verő, M, 2000, *The house of the nation: Parliament plans for Buda-Pest, 1784–1884*, Szépművészeti Múzeum, Budapest.
Gardey, D, 2015, *Le linge du Palais-Bourbon*, Le Bord de l'Eau, Lormont.
Geertz, C, 1977, *The interpretation of cultures*, Basic Books, New York.
Gerő, A, 2010, *Public space in Budapest: The history of Kossuth Square*, East European Monographs, Columbia University Press, New York.
Goffman, E, 1959, *The presentation of self in everyday life*, Doubleday, Garden City, NY.
Graeber, D, 2009, *Direct action*, AK Press, Oakland, CA and Edinburgh.
Hirschauer, S, 2007, 'Putting things into words. Ethnographic description and the silence of the social', *Human Studies*, vol. 29, no. 4, pp. 413–441.
Holmes, D, 2013, *Economy of words*, University of Chicago Press, Chicago IL.

Honig, B, 1991, 'Declarations of independence: Arendt and Derrida on the problem of founding a republic', *The American Political Science Review*, vol. 85, no. 1, pp. 97–113.

Hull, M S, 2012, *Government of paper*, University of California Press, Berkeley, CA.

Kantorowicz, E H, 1997, *The king's two bodies*, Princeton University Press, Princeton, NJ.

Knorr-Cetina, K, 1981, *The manufacture of knowledge*, Pergamon Press, Oxford.

Knorr-Cetina, K, 1999, *Epistemic cultures*, Harvard University Press, Cambridge, MA.

Krzyżanowski, M, 2011, 'Political communication, institutional cultures and linearities of organisational practice: A discourse-ethnographic approach to institutional change in the European Union', *Critical Discourse Studies*, vol. 8, no. 4, pp. 281–296.

Krzyżanowski, M & Oberhuber, F, 2007, *(Un)Doing Europe: Discourses and practices of negotiating the EU constitution*, Peter Lang, Brussels and New York.

Latour, B, 1987, *Science in action*, Harvard University Press, Cambridge, MA.

Latour, B, 1999, *Pandora's hope: Essays on the reality of science studies*, Harvard University Press, Cambridge, MA.

Latour, B, 2010, *The making of law*, Polity, Cambridge.

Latour, B & Woolgar, S, 1986, *Laboratory life: The construction of scientific facts*, Princeton University Press, Princeton, NJ.

Law, J, 1994, *Organizing modernity*, Wiley Blackwell, Chichester.

Lynch, M, 1997, *Scientific practice and ordinary action*, Cambridge University Press, Cambridge.

MacKenzie, D, Muniesa, F & Siu, L, 2007, *Do economists make markets? On the performativity of economics*, Princeton University Press, Princeton, NJ.

Malinowski, B, 1922, *Argonauts of the Western Pacific*, Routledge, London.

Manow, P, 2010, *In the king's shadow*, Polity, Cambridge.

Marcus, G E, 1995, 'Ethnography in/of the world system: The emergence of multi-sited ethnography', *Annual Review of Anthropology*, vol. 24, pp. 95–117.

Mol, A, 2002, *The body multiple*, Duke University Press, Durham, NC.

Mol, A, Moser, I & Pols, J, 2010, *Care in practice*, Transcript Verlag, Bielefeld.

Muntigl, P, Weiss, G & Wodak, R, 2000 *European Union discourses on unemployment*, John Benjamins, Amsterdam.

Nader, L, 1972, 'Up the anthropologist: Perspectives gained from studying up', in *Reinventing anthropology*, ed. D Hymes, Vintage Books, New York, pp. 284–311.

Péter, L, 2003, 'The holy crown of Hungary, visible and invisible', *Slavonic and East European Review*, vol. 81, no. 3, pp. 421–510.

Power, M, 1997, *The audit society*, Oxford University Press, Oxford.

Rabinow, P, Marcus, G E, Faubion, J D & Rees, T, 2008, *Designs for an anthropology of the contemporary*, Duke University Press, Durham, NC.

Raffles, H, 2010, *Insectopedia*, Vintage, New York.

Riles, A, 2006, *Documents*, University of Michigan Press, Ann Arbor, MI.

Rose, N, 2007, *The politics of life itself*, Princeton University Press, Princeton, NJ.

Rose, N & Miller, P, 2008, *Governing the present. Polity Press*, Cambridge.

Schatz, E, 2009, *Political ethnography*, University of Chicago Press, Chicago, IL.

Scheffer, T, 2010, *Adversarial case-making*, Brill Academic Publisher, Leiden.

Shelton, A C, 2007, *Dreamworlds of Alabama*, University of Minnesota Press, Minneapolis, MN.

Shelton, A C, 2013, *Where the North Sea touches Alabama*, University of Chicago Press, Chicago, IL.

Shore, C & Wright, S, 2003, *Anthropology of policy*, Routledge, London.

Sørensen, E, 2011, *The materiality of learning*, Cambridge University Press, Cambridge.

Starn, O, 2012, 'Writing culture at 25: Special editor's introduction', *Cultural Anthropology*, vol. 27, no. 3, pp. 411–416.

Stewart, K, 2007, *Ordinary affects*, Duke University Press, Durham, NC.

Stone, D, 2012, *Policy paradox*, W W Norton & Co, New York.

Strathern, M, 2000, *Audit cultures*, Routledge, London and New York.

Suchman, L, 2006, *Human-machine reconfigurations: Plans and situated actions*, 2nd ed., Cambridge University Press, Cambridge.
Taussig, M, 2006, *Walter Benjamin's grave,* University of Chicago Press, Chicago, IL.
Verran, H, 2001, *Science and an African logic,* University of Chicago Press, Chicago, IL.
Wodak, R, 2000, 'From conflict to consensus? The co-constitution of a policy paper', in *European Union discourses on unemployment*, eds. P Muntigl, G Weiss & R Wodak, John Benjamins, Amsterdam, pp. 73–114.
Wodak, R, 2011, *The discourse of politics in action: Politics as usual*, Palgrave Macmillan, London.
Wodak, R, Krzyżanowski, M & Forchtner, B, 2012, 'The interplay of language ideologies and contextual cues in multilingual interactions: Language choice and code-switching in European Union institutions', *Language in Society*, vol. 41, no. 2, pp. 157–186.
Yanow, D, 1996, *How does a policy mean?* Georgetown University Press, Washington, DC.

Part III
Genres of political action

20
Parliamentary debates

Cornelia Ilie

Parliamentary institutions: systems and functions

Parliament is a democratically elected, representative political assembly that ensures responsiveness and accountability of government to citizens by performing two vital political functions: first, by conducting free and open political debate regarding government legislation, financial records, and implementation of policies; second, by representing and championing the interests of citizens and groups in their dealings with government. The organisation, powers and effectiveness of parliaments vary widely, depending on the surrounding governance context, the relations between the state, the market and civil society, the extent of political space and support for active citizenship, and last but not least, the parliamentary culture, including motivating and constraining beliefs and practices. Members of parliament (henceforth MPs) and parliamentary staff carry out their tasks in four main lines of activity: the parliamentary chamber, committees, party caucuses and constituencies (Müller & Saalfeld 1997). In Westminster-system parliaments (the UK parliament and the parliaments of Commonwealth countries), government accountability concerns the relationship between government and opposition parties in parliament, with MPs and parliamentary committees controlled by party discipline. Whereas in Westminster-system parliaments, debates in the plenary chamber (displaying frontstage parliamentary performance) tend to assume a more prominent role than debates in parliamentary committees (carrying out current backstage parliamentary activities), the opposite situation prevails in European-model parliaments. In terms of the scope and focus of parliamentary procedures, two categories of parliaments are distinguished, namely *debate parliaments* and *working parliaments* (Gallagher, Laver & Mair 2011). To the first category, belong Westminster-type parliaments, such as the UK House of Commons, which are known to favour the parliament's close political connection with the government, and to function largely as an arena for lively adversarial debate and display of rhetorical skills. By contrast, most European parliaments can be regarded as working parliaments, with less spectacular and less confrontational interactions or statements, placing the emphasis on legislative proceedings and committees, rather than on the political struggle with the government.

An important power of parliament, which is less visible to the general public, is exercised through its oversight of the executive by parliamentary committees whose task it is to track the work of individual government departments and ministries, and to conduct specific investigations into salient aspects of their policy and administration. Crucial to the effectiveness of committee investigations is the power to require ministers and civil servants to provide information, to answer questions and to produce relevant documents. The outcome of a committee's investigations typically takes the form of a published report, addressed to the government with recommendations, which is laid before parliament as a whole. It is then up to parliament to decide its priority for debate, and how the government response is to be followed up. Another important mechanism of parliamentary oversight consists in questioning ministers in the plenum on a regular basis, both orally and in writing. Parliamentary questioning practices (see p. 313) represent an important contribution to accountability in that they impose on ministers the obligation to explain and justify their policies to parliament on a regular basis, and to answer publicly for any shortcomings (Inter-Parliamentary Union, 2006).

In parliamentary government systems, the struggle for political power is extensively deployed in intra-party and inter-party politics. Parliamentary debates constitute institutionally ratified practices of multi-party-political deliberation through pro and con dialogue between democratically elected representatives of the citizens (Ilie 2016). The discourse and rhetorical patterns of parliamentary debates display ideological visions, party affiliations, institutional position-takings and political agendas of the members of parliament as representatives of citizens in terms of their social, professional, gender and ethnic backgrounds. Essentially, parliamentary debates are prototypical instantiations of parliamentary government, which was aptly described by Thomas Babington Macaulay as 'government by speaking' (2005/1860, p. 353). In a parliamentary government, the power of speaking is the power of acting, and consequently the social and political outcomes of parliamentary debates show that 'what can be done (*das Machbare*) is to a large extent dependent on what can be said (*das Sagbare*)' (Steinmetz 2002, p. 87).

The European Parliament (henceforth EP) is a special parliament in several respects, one of which is its multilingualism: it consists of members of the European Parliament (MEP) from 28 EU member states speaking 24 official languages, which involves a large number of translators and interpreters. Moreover, the EP is a parliament in development: it has developed and increased its legislative powers with each treaty reform, and the 2007 Treaty of Lisbon represents a significant step in this evolution (Kreppel 2002). The EP is a working parliament and the only directly elected EU institution. It functions like parliaments in semi-presidential systems, since it interacts with a dual executive: the European Commission and the Council of Europe. As the EP's focus on legislative matters has moved to the parliamentary committees, it is through these committees and the key functions of committee chairpersons and rapporteurs that political groups exert power (Mamadouh & Raunio 2003). Despite ongoing formation of EU-level political parties, MEPs are in general more independent of national parties than their national counterparts. At the same time, the Treaty of Lisbon strengthened the role of national parliaments within the EU, especially by participating in the EU legislative process. National parliaments can, for instance, scrutinise draft EU laws to see if they respect the principle of subsidiarity, participate in the revision of EU treaties, or take part in the evaluation of EU policies on freedom, security and justice. An important forum for enhanced participative and open forms of deliberation, including national parliaments and the EP, was offered by the 2002 Convention on the Future of Europe. This Convention emerged, through a consensual process, as intergovernmental and democratic, and as a parliamentary assembly in that it does not follow the process of bargaining behind closed doors, but the process of deliberation.

This chapter outlines, illustrates and discusses the following major issues related to parliamentary debates: parliamentary deliberation practices (p. 311), parliamentary discourse genre and its subgenres (p. 312), parliamentary addressees and parliamentary audiences (p. 315), parliamentary participant roles (p. 315), key research topics on parliamentary debates (p. 317), and final remarks (p. 321).

Deliberation in parliament

The primary goals of parliamentary debates are to negotiate political solutions, to reach agreements and to make decisions, the results of which affect people's everyday lives. The deliberative dialogue between MPs exhibits both histrionic features, that is, elements of a theatre scenario, and agonistic features, that is, elements of a competition scenario (Ilie 2003a). Building on and fostering democratic processes of political deliberation, opinion-building, and decision-making in the public sphere, parliaments are 'open forums where elected representatives engage in arguments over policy', and parliamentary debate is 'a fundamental part of democratic lawmaking'. (Proksch & Slapin 2015, p. 1). Parliamentary debates are audience-orientated in that they are enacted by fellow parliamentarians before a wide (present and virtual) audience that is comprised, not only of parliamentarians, but also of members of the electorate, the general public and the media. If we envisage the debate as a rhetorical enterprise, parliamentary debates should be regarded as institutionalised rhetorical modes of action for collective decision-making. As has been argued in Ilie (2010b, p. 61), the discourse of MPs 'is meant to call into question the opponents' *ethos*, i.e. political credibility and moral profile, while enhancing their own *ethos* in an attempt to strike a balance between *logos*, i.e. logical reasoning, and *pathos*, i.e. emotion eliciting force'.

Parliamentary debates display interaction patterns characterised by two apparently contrary, yet complementary, principles: in some ways, a spirit of adversariality, which is manifested in position-claiming, opponent-challenging acts, and polarising argumentation, and in others, a spirit of co-operativeness, which is manifested in joint decision-making and cross-party problem-solving processes in order to reach commonly acceptable goals regarding suitable lines of action at a national level. It is precisely these dimensions of parliamentary practice that prompted theoreticians of deliberative politics, such as Habermas (1996), to argue that parliaments are an important sphere of deliberation since they fulfil essential legitimising and social integrative functions. His two tracks of political deliberation can be identified in parliamentary debates, as a 'problem-solving process' and a 'power-generating process'. Both combine to uphold the presumption of rationality for the outcomes, and, at the same time, to maintain the legitimacy of MPs' political decisions.

Using the Habermasian interpretation of deliberation, Bächtiger (2014) has analysed the extent of deliberative action in three legislatures: the US Congress and two parliaments with different legislative systems: the Swiss and the German. The Swiss parliament is regarded as a 'non-parliamentary' consensus system, the German parliament is regarded as a competitive parliamentary system, whereas the US Congress is regarded as an example of a competitive presidential system. The findings confirm that the Swiss grand coalition setting enhances the respectful behaviour of MPs. In contrast, government-opposition settings, such as the German parliament and the US Congress are conducive to zero-sum games, undermining respectful behaviour and constructive problem-solving activities.

Parliamentary discourse genre and its subgenres

From a pragma-linguistic perspective, the parliamentary discourse genre belongs to the wider field of political discourse, displaying particular institutional discursive features and complying with a number of specific rules and conventions. Parliamentary debates are meant to achieve a number of institutionally specific purposes, namely position-claiming, persuading, negotiating, agenda-setting and opinion-building, usually along ideological or party lines. The discursive interaction of parliamentarians is constantly marked by their institutional role-based commitments, by the ongoing dialogically shaped institutional confrontation, and by the awareness of acting in front of, and for the benefit of, a multi-layered audience. When debating, 'parliamentary identities are co-constructed by MPs complying with institutionally established communication constraints, while they resort to particular linguistic choices, discourse strategies and emotional/rational appeals to circumvent the institutional constraints' (Ilie 2010b).

From a rhetorical perspective, parliamentary discourse essentially belongs to the deliberative genre of political rhetoric, targeting an audience that is asked to make a decision by evaluating the advantages and disadvantages of a future course of action. At the same time, it also displays, even if rather occasionally and to a lesser extent, elements of the forensic and epideictic genres, which confirms the Bakhtinian view that genres are heterogeneous. One of the major responsibilities of MPs is to contribute to problem-solving tasks regarding legal and political deliberation, as well as decision-making processes. A major incentive for parliamentarians' active participation in debates is the constant need to promote their own image in a competitive and performance-oriented institutional interaction.

The parliamentary discourse genre displays several subgenres, that is, procedure-based communicative interactive tools that are subordinated to specific parliamentary goals. They include goal-orientated forms of demands or requests for action, reaction and/or information, as well as confrontational exchanges across party-political lines. Some of the most representative subgenres of parliamentary discourse are *ministerial statements, interpellations, parliamentary speeches, parliamentary debates, Parliamentary Questions (oral and written)* and *Question Time*.

In Westminster-type parliaments, government ministers can address written, as well as oral, statements to parliament. *Oral ministerial statements* often regard major incidents, policies and actions. *Written ministerial statements* are normally used to put the day-to-day business of government on the official record and in the public domain. *Oral ministerial statements* are made in the House of Commons after questions and urgent questions, before the public business of the day. Their purpose is to announce new policies or to provide specific information about current or urgent political matters.

A common feature of many parliaments is the *interpellation*, a formal (often written) request for information on, or clarification of, the government's policies. It is used as an instrument for the scrutiny of government, whereby a group of MPs can call for a debate on a topical issue or a matter of public concern. Interpellations are normally distinguished from ordinary questions by their more critical and extensive content in that they tend to address matters of national importance. The procedure of interpellation differs across parliaments. In several parliaments, interpellations can only be issued by a group of MPs or by recognised parliamentary political groups.

Parliamentary speeches are traditionally established forms of MPs' discourse. In most parliaments, speeches are addressed to the presiding officer, who is most commonly called the speaker in unicameral parliaments, or in the lower house of bicameral parliaments, and president in the upper house or second chamber. The Opening Speech is the first speech introducing the annual parliamentary session, and in many parliaments, it is given by the head of state. In some parliaments, the speech is given by the head of the executive and is usually followed by debates.

A *parliamentary debate* can be described as a formal discussion involving (often heated) exchanges of opinion and is intended to facilitate the chamber's informed collective decision-making on specific issues. A debate serves to hold the government to account by enabling focused discussion and eliciting clarifications about government policies. Votes are often held to conclude a debate. Parliamentary debates are particularly effective when the sittings are broadcast and/or the minutes are made public. A special case is the British style of debate, which exhibits a notorious rough-and-tumble debate style, accompanied by loud shouting, cheering and heckling.

Parliamentary questions are used by MPs to hold the government to account by criticising government policies, exposing abuses and seeking redress. According to Rogers and Walters, parliamentary questions serve as 'the best-known inquisitorial functions of Parliament' (2006, p. 311). MPs can address oral or written questions requesting information about various government policies or recent events to ministers of any government department every day during Oral Questions. As was pointed out by Franklin and Norton (1993), in the UK parliament *oral questions* are most frequently asked when MPs want to score points and attract publicity, whereas *written questions* are normally asked when the primary goal is indeed to obtain information. Asking an oral question is usually a pretext to attack, if asked by opposition MPs, or to praise the government, if asked by government MPs; it involves much information that is already known, as illustrated in excerpt (1) from the sitting on oral answers to questions on migration:

(1) Joanna Cherry (SNP, Edinburgh South West): (regarding the influx of refugees in Europe) [...] In her statement, the Home Secretary [Theresa May] said: 'The response of the British public has been one of overwhelming generosity'. Why are her Government unable to match that overwhelming generosity?
(Hansard Debates, 16 September 2015, c. 1056)

One of the prototypical forms of parliamentary questioning discourse is *Question Time* (henceforth QT), a regular session in a parliament's agenda that is set aside for questions to the government and answers from its ministers (Franklin & Norton 1993). QT has different names in different parliaments: *Question Period* in the Canadian Parliament, *Frågestund* in the Swedish Riksdag, *Questions au Gouvernement* in the French parliament, *Heure des Questions* in the Belgian parliament, to name but a few. This questioning procedure was also introduced in the EP in 1973. In many parliaments, this is the media highlight of the parliamentary agenda. In the UK parliament and other Westminster-type parliaments, there is also a session called *Prime Minister's Questions* (henceforth PMQs), which gives MPs the chance to address questions to the Prime Minister. During QT and PMQs, complaints and criticisms are raised by MPs, and information is sought about the government's plans and policies; QTs and PMQs are notorious for their adversarial and often aggressive language, and the use of hostile questions serving as face-threatening acts (Bull & Wells 2012). The nature and intensity of the debates during QT may be a good indicator of the political climate and of the power balance between the representatives of the major political parties at that very moment. The results of Bates et al.'s (2012) comparative analysis of the opening sessions of PMQs from Thatcher to Cameron indicate that PMQs has become increasingly a focal point for shallow political point scoring and increasingly dominated by the main party leaders. Their findings also suggest that, at the beginning of their premierships at least, Thatcher and Brown appear the most accomplished in terms of the fullness of their answers, and Blair and Cameron the least accomplished.

Unlike the questioning strategies in courtroom interaction, which are meant to elicit specific answers and to exclude unsuitable ones, parliamentary questioning strategies, especially during QTs and PMQs, are not intended to elicit particular answers, but rather to embarrass and/or challenge the respondent to make uncomfortable, damaging or self-revealing declarations. In their turn, responding government MPs, including the prime minister, resort to counter-attacks by refuting, challenging and/or dismissing the questioners' accusations and face-threatening acts (Ilie 2015). Excerpt (2) illustrates a typical instance of ritual confrontational exchange during PMQs.

> (2) Yvonne Fovargue (Makerfield) (Labour): Wigan council has had a cut of over 40% in its funding over the past five years and lost a third of its staff. Does the Prime Minister advise that I should write to the leader of the council regarding the consequent reductions in services, or should I place the blame firmly where it belongs: in the hands of his Government?
> The Prime Minister (David Cameron, Conservative): If the hon. Lady is looking for someone to blame, she might want to blame the Labour party, which left this country with the biggest budget deficit anywhere in the western world. [...]
> (Hansard Debates, 18 November 2015, cc. 675–676)

It is significant that in addition to questions from opposition MPs, the prime minister and government ministers also receive a significant number of friendly and co-operative questions – called *partisan* or *planted questions* – from MPs belonging to the government party (Ilie 2001; 2015). Asking partisan questions is a recurrent practice promoted by party whips to advance the party-political agenda by encouraging backbench MPs to 'plant' questions that help increase the chance of government-favourable subjects dominating QT and PMQs. Very often, planted questions are asked by government MPs to defend and reinforce the power of the government, but also to attack the opposition, as illustrated in excerpt (3):

> (3) Caroline Dinenage (Gosport) (Conservative): Does the Prime Minister agree with the comment of Lord Glasman, special adviser to the Leader of the Opposition, that the last Government lied to the British people about the extent of immigration?
> The Prime Minister (David Cameron, Conservative): My hon. Friend raises an important point, which is that the last Government did not tell it straight to people about what was happening on immigration and that it has fallen to this Government to take the steps to get the numbers under control.
> (Hansard Debates, 4 May 2011, c. 668)

The rules controlling parliamentary forms of interaction are subject to a complex interplay of institutional and socio-cultural constraints: the overall goal and impact of the institutional activity in which the MPs are engaged, the nature of the institutionalised relationships (social distance and dominance) between MPs, the extent to which MPs share common sets of assumptions and expectations with respect to the parliamentary activity and speech events that they are involved in (Ilie 2000; 2003a).

Parliamentary addressees and parliamentary audiences

In all parliaments, MPs engage in parliamentary interaction both as speakers and as interlocutors or audience members. MPs are involved in an institutional *co-performance* whereby they both address and involve (sometimes even *co-act* with) an audience of fellow MPs as active participants, expected to contribute explicit forms of *audience-feedback*, such as questions, responses, comments, or disruptive interventions. The various categories of directly or indirectly targeted addressees in parliamentary speakers' interventions are represented schematically in Figure 20.1 (Ilie 2010, p. 66).

When taking the floor, speaking MPs target their interlocutors (primary addressees), while at the same time, they address a multiple parliamentary audience (fellow MPs, members of the press, members of the public at large) and TV-audiences. However, according to parliamentary conventions, MPs can only address their fellow MPs through a moderator, that is, the speaker or president of the parliament. As a rule, only the speaker or president is addressed directly by MPs. But parliaments differ with respect to the ways in which the current interlocutor is addressed, that is, indirectly (in the third person) and/or directly (in the second person). The MPs in several parliaments, such as the French and the Italian parliaments, are normally addressed in the second person. In some parliaments, such as the Swedish Riksdag, both strategies of parliamentary address are used, although the MPs' officially recommended form of address is the third person (Ilie 2010). In others, such as the UK and Canadian parliaments, for example, MPs consistently follow the rule of addressing fellow MPs in the third person.

Parliamentary participant roles

As a result of the increasing mediatisation of parliamentary proceedings, MPs perform a major part of their work in the public eye, namely in front of several kinds of audiences made up of MPs, journalists, politicians and laypersons (Müller & Saalfeld 1997). On examining the nature of multi-party dialogues in comparison with two-party dialogues, it is essential to consider factors such as: common ground, group homogeneity/heterogeneity,

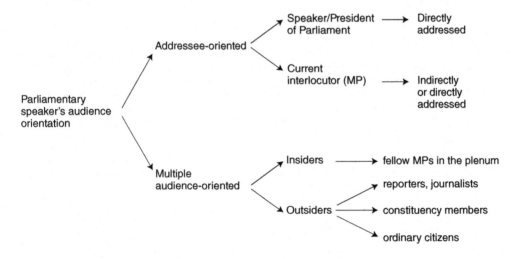

Figure 20.1 Addressees and audiences targeted by parliamentary speakers (Ilie 2010, p. 66)

dialogue conventions, as well as participant roles and identities. In a two-party dialogue, there is always a speaker (addresser) and a hearer (addressee), both of whom are regarded as ratified participants. In a multi-party dialogue, several participant roles can be identified. Goffman (1981) introduced a useful distinction between *direct participants* (speakers and addressees directly involved in the dialogue), *side-participants* (present, but not directly involved in the dialogue) and *overhearers* (passive observers, onlookers). This classification was further developed by Clark (1996), who proposed to add the distinction between *participants* and *non-participants*. The participants include the speaker and the currently addressed hearer, as well as other co-locutors taking part in the conversation, but not currently being addressed, that is, *side-participants*. In principle, side-participants have a choice: they may or may not actively contribute to the dialogue. Overhearers, who are regarded as non-participants, fall into two main categories: *bystanders* and *eavesdroppers*. Bystanders are those who are openly present, but not part of the verbal interaction. Eavesdroppers are those who listen in without the speakers' awareness. Overhearers generally have more limited access to relevant information and thus to the main interlocutors' mutual understanding because they have no opportunity to intervene and negotiate an understanding or clarification of the issues under consideration. These role distinctions apply to multi-party dialogue in general and can be used for mapping parliamentary participant roles and political identities. Table 20.1 maps the main categories of parliamentary participant roles and institutional identities.

An investigation of parliamentary interaction between debating MPs reveals role shifts between their institutional roles as elected representatives of part of the electorate and their non-institutional roles as members of the same electorate they represent. MPs who are current speakers, as well as their fellow MPs acting as targeted addressees, can be regarded as *direct participants*. The audience of listening and onlooking fellow MPs are acting as side-participants. Unlike certain kinds of non-institutional multi-party dialogue, parliamentary interaction exhibits a supplementary institutional role, namely the role of dialogue *moderator* or chairperson, assigned to the speaker or president. As far as the category of overhearers is concerned, it is rather difficult to designate a prototypical category in parliament. However, the category of parliamentary bystanders can be seen to consist both of *insiders* (parliamentary reporters and political journalists) and *outsiders* (members

Table 20.1 Parliamentary participant roles and institutional identities (Ilie 2010, p. 69)

Multi-party dialogue roles	Parliamentary roles	Institutional identities
Direct participants	MP = Current speaker (questioner, respondent)	Government or opposition member
Moderator	Speaker/president of the parliament	Parliamentary chair/referee
Side-participants	Fellow MPs	Government or opposition members
Overhearers Bystanders	Parliamentary reporters and political journalists	Insiders (semi-institutional identity)
	Occasional visitors	Outsiders = ordinary citizens (non-institutional identity)
Eavesdroppers	TV-viewers, parliamentary channel viewers	Insiders/Outsiders = non-institutional, institutional or semi-institutional identity

of the electorate, ordinary citizens, visitors). We can also distinguish the category of parliamentary eavesdroppers as represented by the more remote audience of TV-viewers, who may be either political insiders, or political outsiders, and may consequently display non-institutional, institutional or semi-institutional identities in relation to parliamentary interaction.

In all parliaments, MPs are involved in a co-performance that is meant to both address and engage (sometimes even co-act with) an audience of MPs as active participants. What is important for MPs is to consistently promote a political line that meets the general wishes of the voters (as expressed at general elections), to put certain issues on the political agenda, as well as to take desirable initiatives and effective measures.

Key research topics on parliamentary debates

Ever since the latter half of the twentieth century, parliamentary discourse and parliamentary rhetoric have gradually become a topical object of scholarly research in the fields of political sciences and sociology, several of which showed an increasing interest for the usages, functions and effects of parliamentary language. Significant scholarly contributions were made by political scientists, philosophers and media scholars, who specialised in parliamentary studies (Chester & Browning 1962; Franklin & Norton 1993), who pointed out institutional and language-related aspects of parliamentary debating strategies, emphasising the interplay between parliamentary procedures, socio-historical traditions and political speaking styles. However, it was only recently, in the past few decades, that the study of parliamentary discourse has acquired truly interdisciplinary scope, as a result of contributions made by scholars from the fields of rhetoric and linguistics (particularly pragmatics, rhetoric, discourse analysis, critical discourse analysis and cognitive linguistics), several of whom have developed and used integrative analytical tools in multi-disciplinary and cross-cultural approaches (Bayley 2004; Ilie 2010c; Ihalainen, Ilie & Palonen 2016). The discourse-focused research into parliamentary practices and interaction strategies has benefited from cross-fertilisation of linguistic studies with social and political sciences for in-depth exploration of shifting and multi-level institutional uses of language, interpersonal behaviour patterns, interplay between institutional and non-institutional language use, as well as interdependence between language-shaped facts and reality-prompted language ritualisation and change.

Since it is during debates that most of the parliamentary confrontation takes place, it is hardly surprising that several studies on parliamentary discourse have focused their analysis on topical issues discussed in parliaments. For example, one of the recurrent themes has been the dispute on immigration (Wodak & van Dijk 2000), and more specifically, legitimating the expulsion of illegal immigrants in the Spanish parliament (Martín Rojo 2000), the argumentation and counter-argumentation strategies in Italian parliamentary debates on immigration (ter Wal 2000) and the debates on immigration and nationality in the French parliament (van der Valk 2000).

The discursive and argumentative strategies displayed in parliamentary discourse make frequent use of *metadiscourse*, which accounts for (re)shaping institutional relationships and for producing shifts in the balance of power from the micro- to the macro-level (Ilie 2003a). Parliamentary metadiscourse is also intended to enable its multiple audiences (specifically addressed MPs, listening MPs, journalists, parliamentary reporters, general public, TV-viewers) to identify significant shifts and overlaps between institutional and interpersonal levels of discourse. Several metadiscursive strategies have been identified in

British parliamentary debates, for example, metadiscursive argumentation through the use and misuse of clichés (Ilie 2000), metadiscursive attribution, reporting, and quoting strategies (Ilie 2003a). An important category of frequently used metadiscursive strategies was identified in Ilie (2003b) as *parliamentary parentheticals*, an example of which is provided in excerpt (4).

(4) Mr. Bercow (Conservative): I am grateful to the Foreign Secretary [Mr. Cook, Labour] for giving way. No sensible person – from which category one should probably exclude the right hon. Gentleman – would favour European Union enlargement at any price.
(Hansard Debates, 22 November 1999, c. 367)

Through the insertion of the (underlined) parliamentary parenthetical, Bercow is deliberately operating a shift from his discursive role of MP to the metadiscursive role of observer and commentator, which enables him to practically dismiss his interlocutor (and political opponent) in derogatory terms.

Adopting interdisciplinary perspectives, several scholars have examined, defined and analysed some of the distinctive elements of parliamentary questioning practices. Sánchez de Dios and Wiberg (2012) carried out a comparison of questioning procedures in several European parliaments in terms of particular parameters, such as form and content of questions, timing of questioning, maximum number of questioners and allocation of the duty to answer. Two of the most widely explored parliamentary subgenres in the UK parliament are QT and PMQs and they were found to be particularly 'face-threatening' (Harris 2001; Pérez de Ayala 2001; Ilie 2003c; Bull & Wells 2012) and prone to (un)parliamentary practices, such as insults (Ilie 2001, 2004) and interruptions (Carbó 1992; Ilie 2005).

In the UK parliament, two main types of interruptions have been identified by Ilie (2005): 'authorised', that is, performed by the speaker, as illustrated in excerpts (5) and (6), and 'unauthorised', that is, tokens of approval or disapproval performed by MPs, as illustrated in (6):

(5)
   Mr Speaker: Order. The Minister for Children is under no obligation to behave like a child. It is not required.
(Hansard Debates, 4 May 2011, c. 668)

(6)
   Hon. Members: Oh, no.
   Mr Speaker: Order. It is very discourteous of the House to issue a collective groan— notably on the Opposition Benches.
(Hansard Debates, 13 February 2013, c. 857)

In the case of debates in the Austrian parliament, interruptions were found to have teasing and ridiculing functions, resulting in interlocutors' utterances being twisted (Zima, Brône & Feyaerts, 2010), whereas in the Italian parliament, interruptions were found to be less personalised and therefore more likely to be used as a signal of shifting from a two-party towards a multi-party discourse (Bevitori 2004).

In a systematic discourse-analytical study of interruptions in Mexican parliamentary discourse, Carbó (1992) showed that, although interruptions are forbidden by the rules of procedure, they occur frequently as a practice tacitly accepted by all participants. Her text-based analysis provides evidence for the fact that interruptions perform a double function: to legitimate the pluralistic ideology of the Mexican regime in a strongly presidential system where one party has monopolised the power, and also to allow the manifestation of genuine disaffection, sometimes in an ironical way.

Regarding parliamentary questioning-answering strategies, in an investigation of QT in the Australian Parliament, Rasiah (2010) found recurrent cases of evasion, whereby MPs 'resist' answering questions. Responses that were considered to be evasions were further analysed to determine the levels of evasion, whether they were covert or overt in nature, and the types of 'agenda shifts' that occurred in the question-response sequences.

Harris (2001) identified a mixture of negative politeness and positive impoliteness, as well as swift transitions from positive politeness to positive impoliteness, in British parliamentary discourse. Her findings were confirmed by subsequent researchers, such as Lovenduski (2012), who pointed out that systematic impoliteness is not only sanctioned, but rewarded in accordance with the expectations of British MPs who are socialised into an extremely adversarial and confrontational parliamentary culture. The use of face-threatening acts is counterbalanced by a wide range of politeness strategies, including strategic uses of parliamentary forms of address (Ilie 2010a). The study of covert and overt impoliteness strategies in parliamentary debates has also focused on the use of *unparliamentary language*. As has been shown in Ilie (2001, 2004) and Pérez de Ayala (2001), parliamentary debates exhibit systematic face-threatening acts articulated through unparliamentary language and behaviour. These acts cover a continuum that ranges from milder/mitigated acts, such as reproaches, accusations and criticisms, to strong ones, such as insults.

The various instantiations of unparliamentary language provide important clues about moral and social standards, prejudices and taboos, as well as value judgements of different social-political groups, as well as individuals. A multi-level cross-cultural analysis of several cognitive and rhetorical aspects of unparliamentary language in the UK parliament and in the Swedish Riksdag carried out by Ilie (2004) provided evidence for the fact that the preference for certain types of rhetorical appeals is rooted in political traditions, such as higher or lower levels of competition and conflict tolerance, higher or lower political control of societal developments, tendency towards open or closed confrontation, and process- or result-orientated consensus. The results of her contrastive analysis indicate that British unparliamentary language is marked particularly by pathos-orientated logos, whereas Swedish unparliamentary language is marked particularly by *ethos*-orientated *logos*.

In a study on the construction of the addresser in the Portuguese parliament, Marques (2010) examined the use of markers of personal deixis in the construction of discursive voices and of the relationships between addressers and addressees in the Portuguese parliament. Her findings show a convergence of the uses of first-person singular pronouns and first-person plural pronouns, which contribute to emphasising the various manifestations of collective and individual voices and to indicating relationships of group proximity anchored in the delegation of political power.

Recurrent instances of humour and irony appear to be the hallmark of parliamentary debates, particularly in political cultures where the display of wit and verbal eloquence is expected and praised as a sort of histrionic co-performance in a rather conventional and strictly regulated institutional setting. Exchanges of parliamentary joking and sarcastic statements, often based on recycled stereotypes, are meant to reinforce in-group solidarity and inter-group dissent, for example, through a combination of unparliamentary language and insults in the UK parliament (Ilie 2001, 2004), of lightly playful or moralising irony in the Swedish Riksdag (Ilie 2004), and of punning and ironical interruptions/challenges in the Greek parliament (Tsakona 2011, 2013).

Throughout their (longer or shorter) history, most parliaments have undergone several stages, with more-or-less-dramatic metamorphoses regarding parliamentary norm reinforcement, gender-representation balance and degree of tolerance to MP rule violations. While each individual parliament exhibits its own oratorical preferences and specific debating styles, a closer look at their overall evolution reveals comparable dialectics of interconnectedness between patterns of parliamentary continuity and change, and sometimes even of continuity *in* change (e.g. Ilie 2010d on managing dissent in Romanian parliamentary discourse; Ornatowski 2010 on changes in discursive practices and behaviour in the Polish Sejm). After 1989, in the post-communist period, the fledgling democracies of Central and Eastern European countries have undergone similar or comparable processes of reinvention and reactivation of their respective parliaments, by removing communist 'pseudo-parliamentary' constraints, by reactivating historical parliamentary practices, rituals and traditions, and by reinventing new (post-communist) parliamentary norms and conventions (e.g. Ornatowski 2010 on the Polish parliament; Bruteig 2010 on the Czech parliament). Although these countries experienced a relatively similar political system during the communist era, they nevertheless display significant differences due to their distinctive historically rooted political cultures, which are still reflected in their specific parliamentary practices. For example, both the Romanian and the Polish parliaments shared the experience of communist censorship that did not allow actual debates, but only well-rehearsed speeches followed by applause on command. At the same time, as Ilie and Ornatowski (2016) convincingly show, while the Romanian parliament (The Great National Assembly) served mainly as a political platform for the Romanian Communist Party, especially during the time of Ceaușescu's personality cult, the Polish parliament (Sejm) was actually more than a mere rubber stamp, especially throughout the 1980s. Another telling example is provided by the debates in the German parliament (Bundestag), which underwent a significant transition from discussion parliament via working parliament to today's media-oriented display-window parliamentarism (Burkhardt 2004).

A fast-growing body of research on parliamentary discourse has been devoted to the ways in which gender roles are instantiated in parliament (Wodak 2003; Lovenduski & Karam 2005; Ilie 2010a). For example, undertaking a comparative approach (of Australian, Canadian and UK Westminster-style bureaucracies), Chappell (2002) found that the reliance on masculine gender norms in institutions such as parliament, made them hostile to the presence of women and led to the production of gender-insensitive laws. Walsh (2013) pointed out that 'the overall culture of the Commons resembles a gentleman's club' (p. 70), whereas Ross (1995) and Puwar (1997) carried out surveys that identified instances of verbal sexual harassment of women MPs. In a comparative study of the linguistic behaviour of male and female politicians in the House of Commons and the Scottish parliament, Shaw (2002) found that in both parliaments, male MPs make more interventions than women MPs overall, and this practice constructs male MPs as more powerful participants as they assume the entitlement to break the rules. At the same time, while in the House of Commons, humour, sexist jokes and filibustering were identified as gendered linguistic practices, in the Scottish parliament, humour was frequently produced by female as well as male MPs and no sexist jokes were made.

Based on research exploring language use and gender in the Italian parliament, Formato (2014) found that both female and male MPs still tend to stereotypically use masculine unmarked terms (in singular and plural forms) when addressing female politicians. At the same time, on a more promising note, her results indicate that the use of (semi-)marked forms of address by both genders is gradually emerging in Italian parliamentary debates.

Analysing gendered discourses in the Cameroonian parliament within a 'masculine' society, with patriarchal ideologies, Atanga (2009) looked at the way men's and women's identities are constructed using traditional discourses of gender differentiation and how some of these discourses get challenged, appropriated or subverted using progressive gendered discourses that advocate equal opportunities and gender equality. She identified linguistic practices that reflect asymmetrical power relations in the way female and male MPs are addressed differently by government ministers, the speaker and other MPs.

Ilie (2013) compared the ways in which female and male MPs (mis)use addressing strategies in the UK parliament and the Swedish Riksdag, by examining how gender identities are negotiated, reinforced and/or challenged by observing or violating institutional norms of interaction. Berit Ås's theory of master suppression techniques was used to account for interpersonal discursive behaviours whereby debaters are being acknowledged and appreciated, or are being ignored, ridiculed and under-rated (Ås 1978). The findings show that subversive uses of addressing strategies can both reinforce and challenge the power balance between MPs, both within same-gender and mixed-gender interactions. While the two parliaments display certain similarities, there are also differences with regard to particular institutional and culture-specific features. Thus, in the analysed British QT sessions, the cross-gender adversarial confrontation is largely ritualistic (Rai 2010) and consists in consistently and openly challenging the power balance between female and male interlocutors. In the Swedish Interpellation sessions, the cross-gender adversarial confrontation appeared to be more subtle and apparently more subdued, although it also involves challenging the power balance.

Apart from a number of similarities, European parliaments display great variation, both with respect to institutional norms/procedures and to discourse practices. The growing interest in the structures, functions, discourses and roles of national parliaments in Europe has stimulated the research into the rising role and the discourse practices of the EP. One of the targets of these complementary strands of research is the ongoing debate about changing discourse practices and the diversified roles of national parliaments, including their role as European institutions involved in European decision-making (Morgan & Tame 1996; Katz & Wessels 1999; Hix, Noury & Roland 2007). Examining the functioning of the EP, Raunio (1996) found that parliamentary questions can serve as a two-way informational channel – MEPs use questions not only to obtain information, but also to highlight problems to the Council and Commission. In a more recent critical ethnography of the EP, Wodak (2011) explored the discursive and social practices of MEPs and showed how politicians construct and are constructed discursively by backstage and frontstage identities. She identified typical 'orders and disorders of discourse' that illustrate the discursive mechanisms by which politics is organised in this transnational and multinational arena. Roald and Sangolt (2011) carried out a multi-level analysis of debates on climate change in the EP, using a Habermasian perspective and a rhetorical approach. A major part of their analysis regarded topical issues related to the relationship between emotion and deliberation in political discourse, questioning the possibility of systematically measuring the role of emotions in political debate.

Final remarks

Many of the recent and current research studies on parliamentary debates point to a number of partly common and partly specific challenges that are facing parliaments in the post-modern world. We are witnessing changing discourse practices and institutional relations that parliament maintains with the public, the media, the executive branch and the international organisations. However, there is a growing representation in parliament of diverse parts of society, men and women, minorities and marginalised groups. As parliamentary debates are assuming an increasingly decisive role in (re)shaping political confrontation practices and in articulating the most topical social, economic and political issues on national and international agendas, further empirical research is necessary. Furthermore, in order to identify and better understand the common, as well as the distinctive features of parliamentary practices in national parliaments, more cross-cultural studies need to be carried out.

References

Ås, B, 1978, *Hersketeknikker* [*Master suppression techniques*], Kjerringråd, Bern.
Atanga, L L, 2009, *Gender, discourse and power in the Cameroonian Parliament*, RPCIG, Langaa.
Bächtiger, A, 2014, 'Debate and deliberation in legislatures', in *The Oxford Handbook of Legislative Studies*, eds., S Martin, T Saalfeld, & K W Strøm, Oxford University Press, Oxford, pp. 145–166.
Bates, Stephen R., Kerr, Peter, Byrne, Christopher & Stanley, Liam, 2012. 'Questions to the Prime Minister: A comparative study of PMQs from Thatcher to Cameron', *Parliamentary Affairs* 67(2), pp. 1–28.
Bayley, P, ed., 2004, *Cross-cultural perspectives on parliamentary discourse*, John Benjamins, Amsterdam.
Bevitori C, 2004, 'Negotiating conflict: Interruptions in British and Italian parliamentary debates', in *Cross-cultural perspectives on parliamentary discourse*, ed. P Bayley, John Benjamins, Amsterdam, pp. 87–109.
Bruteig, Y M, 2010, 'Czech parliamentary discourse: Parliamentary interactions and the construction of the addressee', in *European Parliaments under scrutiny: Discourse strategies and interaction practices*, ed. C. Ilie, John Benjamins, Amsterdam, pp. 265–302.
Bull, P & Wells, P, 2012, 'Adversarial discourse in Prime Minister's Questions', *Journal of Language and Social Psychology*, 31(1), pp. 30–48.
Burkhardt, A, 2004, *Zwischen Monolog und Dialog. Zur Theorie, Typologie und Geschichte des Zwischenrufs im Deutschen Parlamentarismus*, Niemeyer, Tübingen.
Carbó, T, 1992, Towards an interpretation of interruptions in Mexican parliamentary discourse, *Discourse & Society*, 3(1), pp. 25–45.
Chappell, L, 2002. *Gendering government: Feminist engagement with the state in Australia and Canada*, University of British Columbia Press, Vancouver.
Chester, D N & Bowring, N, 1962, *Questions in parliament*. Clarendon Press, Oxford.
Formato, F, 2014, Language use and gender in the Italian Parliament, unpubl. PhD thesis, Lancaster University.
Franklin, M & Norton, P, eds., 1993, *Parliamentary questions*, Oxford University Press, Oxford.
Gallagher, M, Laver, M & Mair, P, 2011, *Representative government in modern Europe*, McGraw-Hill, London.
Goffman, E, 1981, *Forms of talk*, University of Pennsylvania Press, Philadelphia.
Habermas, J, 1995, *Between facts and norms*, MIT press, Cambridge, MA.
Harris, S, 2001, 'Being politically impolite: Extending politeness theory to adversarial political discourse', *Discourse & Society* 12(4), pp. 451–472.
Hix, S, Noury, A & Roland, G, 2007, *Democratic politics in the European Parliament*, Cambridge University Press, Cambridge.
Ihalainen, P, Ilie, C & Palonen, K, 2016, *Parliament and parliamentarism: A comparative history of disputes about a European concept*, Berghahn Books, New York.

Ilie, C, 2000, 'Cliché-based metadiscursive argumentation in the Houses of Parliament', *International Journal of Applied Linguistics*, 10(1), pp .65–84.

Ilie, C, 2001, 'Unparliamentary language: Insults as cognitive forms of confrontation', in *Language and ideology*, Vol. II: *Descriptive cognitive approaches*, eds. R. Dirven, R. Frank & C. Ilie, John Benjamins, Amsterdam, pp. 235–263.

Ilie, C, 2003a, 'Discourse and metadiscourse in parliamentary debates', *Journal of Language and Politics*, 1(2), pp. 269–291.

Ilie, C, 2003b, Parenthetically speaking: Parliamentary parentheticals as rhetorical strategies, in *Dialogue Analysis 2000: Selected papers from the 10th IADA Anniversary Conference, Bologna 2000*, eds. M Bondi & S Stati, Niemeyer, Tübingen, pp. 253–264.

Ilie, C, 2003c, 'Histrionic and agonistic features of parliamentary discourse', *Studies in Communication Sciences*, 3(1), pp. 25–53.

Ilie, C, 2004, 'Insulting as (un)parliamentary practice in the British and Swedish Parliaments: A rhetorical approach', in *Cross-cultural perspectives on parliamentary discourse*, ed. P Bayley, John Benjamins, Amsterdam, pp. 45–86.

Ilie, C, 2005, 'Interruption patterns in British parliamentary debates and drama dialogue', in *Dialogue Analysis IX: Dialogue in Literature and the Media. Selected Papers from the 9th IADA Conference, Salzburg 2003*, eds. A Betten & M Dannerer, Niemeyer, Tübingen, pp. 415–430.

Ilie, C, 2010a, 'Strategic uses of parliamentary forms of address: The case of the U.K. Parliament and the Swedish Riksdag', *Journal of Pragmatics* 42(4), pp. 885–911.

Ilie, C, 2010b, 'Identity co-construction in parliamentary discourse practices', in *European parliaments under scrutiny: Discourse strategies and interaction practices*, ed. C. Ilie, Benjamins, Amsterdam, pp. 57–78.

Ilie, C, ed., 2010c, *European parliaments under scrutiny: Discourse strategies and interaction practices*, Benjamins, Amsterdam.

Ilie, C, 2010d, 'Managing dissent and maximising interpersonal relations in parliamentary discourse' in *European parliaments under scrutiny: Discourse strategies and interaction practices*, ed. C Ilie, John Benjamins, Amsterdam, pp. 193–221.

Ilie, C, 2013, 'Gendering confrontational rhetoric: Discursive disorder in the British and Swedish parliaments', *Democratization*, vol. 20(3), pp. 501–521.

Ilie, C, 2015, 'Follow-ups as multifunctional questioning and answering strategies in Prime Minister's Questions', in *The dynamics of political discourse: Forms and functions of follow-ups*, eds. A Fetzer, E Weizman & L Berlin, John Benjamins, Amsterdam, pp. 195–218.

Ilie, C, 2016, 'Parliamentary discourse and deliberative rhetoric', in *Parliaments and parliamentarism: A comparative history of disputes about a European concept*, eds. P Ihalainen, C Ilie & K Palonen. Berghahn Books, New York, pp. 133–145.

Ilie, C & Ornatowski, C, 2016, 'Central and Eastern European parliamentary rhetoric since the nineteenth century: The case of Romania and Poland' in *Parliaments and parliamentarism: A comparative history of disputes about a European concept*, P Ihalainen, C Ilie & K Palonen, Berghahn Books, New York, pp. 192–215.

Inter-Parliamentary Union, 2006, *Parliament and democracy in the twenty-first century: A guide to good practice*, Geneva, Le Grand Saconnex.

Katz, R A & Wessels, B, 1999, *European Parliament, the national parliaments and European integration*, Oxford University Press, Oxford.

Kreppel, A, 2002, *The European Parliament and the supranational power system: A study of institutional development*, Cambridge University Press, Cambridge.

Lovenduski, J, 2012, 'Prime Minister's Questions as political ritual', *British Politics* 7(4), pp. 314–340.

Lovenduski, J & Azza K, 2005, 'Women in parliament: Making a difference', in *Women in parliament: Beyond numbers*, eds. J Ballington & A Karam, IDEA, Stockholm, pp. 187–212.

Macaulay, T B, 2005 (1860), *Miscellaneous essays and lays of ancient Rome*, Cosimo Inc, New York.

Mamadouh, V & Raunio, T, 2003, The committee system: Powers, appointments and report allocation, *Journal of Common Market Studies* 41(2), p. 333–351.

Marques, M A, 2010, 'The public and private sphere in parliamentary debate: The construction of the addresser in the Portuguese parliament', in *European parliaments under scrutiny: Discourse strategies and interaction practices*, ed. C Ilie, John Benjamins, Amsterdam, pp. 265–302.

Martín Rojo, L, 2000, 'Spain, outer wall of the European fortress: analysis of parliamentary debates on immigration policy in Spain', in *Racism at the top: parliamentary discourses on ethnic issues in six European states*, eds. R Wodak & T van Dijk, Drava Verlag, Klagenfurt, ch. 6.

Morgan, R & Tame, C, eds., 1996, *Parliaments and parties: The European Parliament in the political life of Europe*, Macmillan, London.

Müller, W C & Saalfeld, T, eds., 1997, *Members of parliament in Western Europe: Roles and behaviour*, Frank Cass, London.

Ornatowski, C, 2010, 'Parliamentary discourse and political transition: Polish parliament after 1989' in *European Parliaments under scrutiny: Discourse strategies and interaction practices*, ed. C Ilie, John Benjamins, Amsterdam, pp. 223–264.

Pérez de Ayala, S, 2001, 'FTAs and Erskine May: Conflicting needs? – Politeness in Question Time', *Journal of Pragmatics* 33(2), pp. 143–169.

Proksch, S-O & Slapin, J B, 2015, *The politics of parliamentary debate: Parties, rebels and representation*, Cambridge University Press, Cambridge.

Puwar, N, 1997, 'Reflections on interviewing women MPs', *Sociological Research Online* 2(1). Available at http://www.socresonline.org.uk/2/1/4.html.

Rasiah, P, 2010, 'A framework for the systematic analysis of evasion in parliamentary discourse', *Journal of Pragmatics* 42(3), pp. 664–680.

Raunio, T, 1996, 'Parliamentary questions in the European Parliament: Representation, information and control', *Journal of Legislative Studies* 2(4), pp. 356–382.

Roald, V & Sangolt, L, 2011, *Deliberation, rhetoric and emotion in the discourse of climate change in the European Parliament*, Eburon Academic Publishers, Delft.

Rogers, R & Walters, R, 2006, *How Parliament works*, 6th ed., Routledge, Oxford.

Ross, K, 1995, 'Gender and party politics – how the press reported the Labour leadership campaign, 1994', *Media, Culture & Society* 17(3), pp. 499–509.

Sánchez de Dios, M & Wiberg, M, 2012, 'Questioning in European parliaments', in *The roles and function of parliamentary questions*, eds. S Martin & O Rozenberg, Routledge, Oxford, pp. 96–109.

Shaw, S, 2002, *Language and gender in political debates in the House of Commons*, unpubl. PhD thesis, The Institute of Education, University of London.

Shirin, R, 2010, 'Ceremony and ritual in parliament', *The Journal of Legislative Studies* 16(3), pp. 281–297.

Steinmetz, W, 2002, 'A code of its own: Rhetoric and logic of parliamentary debate in modern Britain', *Finnish Yearbook of Political Thought* 6, LIT Verlag, Münster, pp. 84–104.

ter Wal, J, 2000, 'Comparing argumentation and counter-argumentation in Italian parliamentary debate on immigration', in *The semiotics of racism*, eds. M Reisigl & R Wodak, Passagen Verlag, Vienna, pp. 129–154.

Tsakona, V, 2011, 'Irony beyond criticism: Evidence from Greek parliamentary discourse', *Pragmatics and Society* 2(1), pp. 57–86.

Tsakona, V, 2013, 'Parliamentary punning: Is the opposition more humorous than the ruling party?' *European Journal of Humour Research* 1(2), pp. 101–111.

van der Valk, I, 2000, 'Parliamentary discourse on immigration and nationality in France', in *Racism at the top: parliamentary discourses on ethnic issues in six European states*, eds. R Wodak & T van Dijk, Drava Verlag, Klagenfurt, ch. 7.

Walsh, C, 2013, *Gender and discourse: Language and power in politics, the church and organisations*, Routledge, London.

Wiberg, M, 1995, 'Parliamentary questioning. Control by communication?, in *Parliaments and Majority Rule in Western Europe*, ed. H Döring, Campus Verlag, Frankfurt, pp. 179–222.

Wodak, R, 2003, 'Multiple identities: The roles of female parliamentarians in the EU parliament', *The handbook of language and gender*, eds. in J Holmes & M Meyerhoff, Blackwell, Oxford, pp. 671–698.

Wodak, R, 2011, *The discourse of politics in action: Politics as usual*, 2nd ed., Palgrave Macmillan, Basingstoke.

Wodak, R & van Dijk, T A, eds., 2000, *Racism at the top. Parliamentary discourses on ethnic issues in six European states*, Drava Verlag, Klagenfurt.

Zima, E, Brône, G & Feyaerts, K, 2010, 'Patterns of interaction in Austrian parliamentary debates. The pragmasemantics of interruptive comments', in *European Parliaments under scrutiny: Discourse strategies and interaction practices*, ed. C Ilie, John Benjamins, Amsterdam, pp. 135–164.

21
Government communication

Sten Hansson

In modern democracies, governments produce vast amounts of text, talk and images that are made available to the public: news releases, social media postings, policy documents, televised speeches, broadcast interviews, advertisements, and so forth. In this chapter, I provide suggestions as to how communication practices of executive government institutions could be conceptualised and operationalised for a discourse-analytic study. I delineate several competing ways in which scholars have written about government communication, flesh out three example analyses of government officeholders' strategic language use, and point at some conflictual aspects of government communication that would merit further linguistic study.

Introduction: government, communication and communicators

From a linguistic perspective, 'government communication' can be conceived of as oral, written and visual language used by, and on behalf of, government officeholders, directed at the general public or particular groups in society. Hence, government communication belongs to the arena of political action. The word 'political' has several meanings and dimensions (see, for instance, Palonen 2003), but in broad terms, it integrates two contradictory senses:

> On the one hand, politics is viewed as a struggle for power, between those who seek to assert and maintain their power and those who seek to resist it. [...] On the other hand, politics is viewed as cooperation, as the practices and institutions that a society has for resolving clashes of interest over money, influence, liberty, and the like.
>
> (Chilton 2004, p. 3)

In government communication, as in politics in general, language is used strategically, that is, text, talk and images are employed with a goal to manage the interests of the speaker/writer.[1] Discourse analyst Paul Chilton (2004, pp. 45–46) posits that language use in politics can serve three broad and often intertwined strategic functions: coercion, (de)legitimisation, and (mis)representation. This three-fold distinction can be usefully applied to guide our thinking about the functions of language in government communication.

1   Language use of the executive government can be backed by legal and physical sanctions. A government can issue commands and use its non-linguistic resources (e.g. the police, courts and prisons) to punish those who do not comply. Governments and government officeholders are therefore often perceived as powerful, high-status actors. Their requests, choices of conversational topics, and assumptions of shared knowledge and beliefs are frequently accepted by government outsiders even without the actual threat of coercion. Coercive power is also exercised by government officeholders when they censor others' language use, limit the public dissemination of certain kinds of information, and regulate the arenas of communication (e.g. by introducing policies that affect the work of journalists or social media platforms).
2   Governments use language to establish and maintain their right to be obeyed by citizens. Such legitimising may involve arguing in favour of certain courses of action chosen by the officeholders and engaging in positive self-presentation (e.g. boasting about achievements of the government). However, governments also use language to delegitimise various opponents by presenting them in a more negative light, sometimes blaming, insulting, or marginalising them, and presenting as undesirable any alternative courses of action proposed by opponents.
3   Governments try to control the amount and the quality of information that they dispense. When government officeholders produce linguistic representations of events, actors, or objects, they often omit or substitute some elements. They may also add new elements, or rearrange the sequence of events in their stories. Misrepresentation can involve manipulative moves such as lying, verbal evasion and the use of euphemisms with the goal of 'blurring' the audience's understanding of some aspect of reality.

The actions of the government officeholders – including their public use of language – potentially affect the lives of thousands or millions of people. Therefore, unsurprisingly, a large proportion of the daily news served by the mainstream media is about governments or somehow related to the members and activities of governments, ranging from topics such as road safety, education reform and international diplomacy, to social inequality, government debt, and the occasional resignation of a cabinet minister. Governments have become increasingly 'mediatised' (Couldry & Hepp 2013; Strömbäck & Esser 2014) by adopting communication techniques, selecting employees and devising policies on the basis of how well they seem to fit into a society where media plays a central role. This means that government officeholders themselves produce a lot of text, talk and images for public consumption: they draw up policy documents, deliver televised speeches, distribute news releases via email, respond to reporters' questions at press briefings, create websites, and post comments, photos and videos on social media, give broadcast interviews, launch advertising campaigns, and so forth. However, government officeholders may also be tempted to monitor and control the flows of information, including restricting access to some knowledge, or making attempts to distract certain audiences from paying attention to certain problems in society, including the (possible) failures and misdeeds of policy-makers and public administrators.

A number of terms are used to denote these activities, including 'government communication', 'administrative communication' (Garnett & Kouzmin 1997), 'government information' (Graber 2003), 'government public relations' (Lee, Neeley & Stewart 2012), 'government publicity' and 'government media management'. Some of these activities are carried out, at least in part, by the top executive politicians themselves (e.g. the president's weekly video address in the US), while the bulk of the daily planning, preparation and presentation of a government's messages and interacting with the press and the public is the full-time job of (in some cases, fairly large) teams of communication experts, special advisers, press officers and spokespersons who have been specially hired by government departments for these tasks. Importantly, their action is both enabled and constrained by various regulations and institutions that determine what they can or cannot do and say (Yeung 2006). For example, freedom of information laws may establish what kind of government-held data should be made public, and civil service legislation may stipulate that civil servant communicators should always remain 'impartial' and avoid taking sides in party-political struggles. Hence, professional government communicators may try to cast themselves as 'neutral transmitters' of administrative information (te Molder 1999).

The tasks of professional government communicators typically include producing and publicising texts about policies, public services and institutional arrangement of the incumbent government, and giving advice and orders to people, for example, on how to submit annual tax returns, and how to behave in case of crises such as floods and pandemics (see, for instance, Government Communication Service, 2015). The 'government communication' sub-domain of political communication usually does *not* cover distributing information about, and on behalf of, political parties (including election campaigns and party-political advertising), communication activities of legislatures such as parliaments and congresses, and communication of the heads of state who are not heads of executive government and serve in mainly ceremonial roles (e.g. presidents in parliamentary democracies). Notably, in comparison to party-political communication and election campaigns where the 'struggle for power' is perhaps more central and explicit, government communication in its many guises has received somewhat less scholarly attention (Canel & Sanders 2013).

Ways of conceptualising government communication

Scholars who study government communication position themselves in relation to the subject matter of their research in different ways. This involves more-or-less-explicit perspective-taking: looking at communication either from the point of view of government (the ruler, officeholder, institution, political leader, campaign manager), or a government outsider (the ruled, citizen, individual, oppressed group). The former perspective is adopted by authors who write instructional literature on how to govern or how to run public services. The latter perspective is typical of authors who are more interested in how *not* to be governed or how to be governed otherwise. Along these lines, in communication studies, a basic distinction has been made between 'administrative' and 'critical' research (Lazarsfeld 1941). A more detailed review of literature within both of these distinctive streams of research reveals that government communication in modern democracies has been conceptualised by scholars in four competing ways: as a policy instrument, as a commodity, as manipulation, and as a factor in (un)doing democracy (Hansson, forthcoming). Each of these ways of talking about government communication may be seen as reflecting distinctive historically sedimented sets of normative ideas about political life that its proponents subscribe to.

Government communication as a policy instrument

Many authors adopt the perspective of a government or a top officeholder, and conceptualise communication as a necessary 'tool' that the government uses to exert authority and maintain control. Governments use three general types of policy instruments: they issue orders that people are obliged to follow (regulation backed up by coercion), they give or remove material resources (e.g. subsidies and taxes), and they use text and talk (issuing voluntary appeals). Such policy instruments may be defined as 'the set of techniques by which governmental authorities wield their power in attempting to ensure support and effect or prevent social change' (Vedung 2003, p. 21). In searching answers to the central question of 'what works' in government, the authors of instructional texts on government communication deal with the practicalities of exerting influence on 'governees'. Some of the typical recurrent concepts that are used with a predominantly positive connotation in such literature are reminiscent of military language: 'strategic', 'tactical', 'operation', 'target', 'officer'. Works in this tradition generally adhere to a functionalist presumption that the society should be characterised by social order, stability, and productivity. They more or less explicitly idealise the state of play in which the government as a system 'runs like clockwork' without facing any serious internal or external obstacles, or disturbances such as resistance, scandals, or crises. A well-known historical example of such an instrumental conceptualisation of government communication is found in *The Prince* by Niccolò Machiavelli (2006 [1513]), a Renaissance-era statesman who provided detailed advice to a monarch on how to hold on to power.

Government communication as a commodity

Communication can be understood as a set of services provided by the government to specific groups of customers. The authors who take this view place an emphasis on governing and communicating according to the logic and values of the market. They write of people as 'customers' (rather than 'citizens' or 'governees'), who are generally presumed to be self-interested and rational utility-maximisers. From this perspective, the goal of the government and its communication activities is to guarantee 'customer satisfaction'. Some of the key words that signal this approach include 'efficiency', 'competence', 'management skills', 'training' and 'innovation'. Public communication is primarily regarded as a means for selling more goods or services produced by the organisation ('marketing', 'promotion', 'publicity', 'advertising') and guaranteeing the survival and smooth functioning of the organisation via 'building goodwill' among people external to the organisation ('public relations', 'branding', 'reputation management', 'public affairs', 'corporate social responsibility'). This conceptualisation of government communication shares its historical roots with the instructional literature on scientific management (e.g. Taylor 1911) and public relations (e.g. Bernays 1928).

Government communication as manipulation

Some authors side with individuals and groups who feel oppressed by the government and see government communication mainly as top-down manipulation of public perceptions and behaviour by the self-serving ruling elite. Many government outsiders share a distrust of government and its communication activities. From this perspective, government is depicted as posing an inevitable threat to its 'governees' due to its permanent disposition to abuse its power and isolate outsiders by mystifying its action. A concern about people being oppressed by malicious discursive manipulation, government-perpetrated propaganda and 'spin-doctoring' can be traced back to the premises laid out in Marxist conflict theory in the nineteenth century. Major influences include the Marxist notion of 'false consciousness',

Gramscian conceptualisation of 'hegemony', and the critical tradition of the Frankfurt School that focuses on the often subtle cultural and psychological factors that limit the capacity for critical thought among 'the masses'.

Government communication as a factor in doing or undoing democracy

Some authors recognise that public communication on the part of the government is an integral component of policy-making and the provision of public services, but they also express critical awareness of its manipulative tendencies (e.g. image-making and spin). Government communication, therefore, could be seen as one of the factors in larger societal processes that either advance or limit public participation in political debates. 'Democratic deficit' or 'political disenchantment' in contemporary societies is a standard theme of many critical studies (see, e.g. Hay 2007; Norris 2011). Much of the discussion in this camp has been revolving around the Habermasian conception of the emergence of the 'public sphere' and the normative theories of democracy, where communication is central. From this perspective, governments should ideally observe high standards of integrity and commit themselves to certain criteria for ethical communication. Major influences include Max Weber's early twentieth-century sociology that provided an effective blueprint for analysing contradictions in modern societies (e.g. acknowledging that while bureaucracy is a prevalent and efficient form of governing, it poses a threat to people's individuality and social meaning-making), and the interpretive, linguistic and cultural turns in social sciences in the second half of the twentieth century.

Much of the literature under the rubrics of critical linguistics and critical discourse studies is in line with the latter two conceptualisations of government communication. The first two – the administrative conceptualisations – are more or less explicitly adopted by applied linguists who write instructional works on how to use language more 'effectively' or 'efficiently' in law, management, service provision, marketing and advertising.

Some critical discourse analysts (e.g. Fairclough 2000) point out how government officeholders increasingly use managerial and promotional language to present certain processes in society as inevitable, and normalise a particular business-centric understanding of the social world that may ultimately increase inequality and suffering. By actively promoting certain managerial actions as 'solutions', governments discourage public debate. Managerial discourse in government is characterised, not only by the use of lexis that is typical of those who run for-profit businesses (e.g. 'customers', 'marketing', 'benchmarking'), but also by some more subtle persuasive linguistic constructions. For example, Mulderrig (2011a) shows how officeholders represent some actions in ways that seem to reduce government agency and increase agency for others: they portray government as an overseer, a leader, or a facilitator, thereby masking its coercive power (see Example 3 p. 335). Linguistically informed critical studies of government communication have also involved contrasting language use and actual behaviour of the government of the day. For example, Farrelly (2015) highlights the ways in which government officeholders in the UK make frequent references to 'democracy' in their text and talk, while some of their deeds are rather non-democratic.

Critical discourse analysts have made substantial contributions to our understanding of expressions of social and political exclusion and discriminatory prejudices in government discourses. They have pointed out the ways in which government officeholders try to consolidate public support by exploiting xenophobia, ethnocentrism, racism and prejudices in their language, thereby normalising the omission of certain groups of people from political life (Krzyżanowski & Wodak 2009; Wodak, KhosraviNik & Mral 2013; Wodak 2015). They have also provided detailed analyses of the discursive construction of history and national identity (Martin & Wodak 2003; Heer, Manoschek, Pollak & Wodak 2008; Wodak, de Cillia, Reisigl & Liebhart 2009), dissected the language use of totalitarian governments (Wodak & Kirsch 1995), and carried out ethnographic studies of how language is used in the backstage of political institutions (Wodak 2011).

Analysing government communication: examples

The language-orientated researchers of government communication often focus their studies on a particular genre or medium used by officeholders. For example, some scholars have specifically addressed the rhetoric of presidential or (prime) ministerial speeches (Reisigl 2008; Kienpointner 2011, 2013), the discourses used in public policy documents (Scollon 2008; Wodak 2000), the pragmatics of presidential, (prime) ministerial, or departmental press conferences (Bhatia 2006; Ekström 2009; Eriksson 2011; Jacobs 2011) and press releases (Jacobs 1999). Depending on the research question and data at hand, scholars may adopt various approaches, methods and tools, such as discourse-historical analysis (Reisigl & Wodak 2015), socio-cognitive analysis (van Dijk 2015), ethnographic fieldwork (Gobo 2008), argumentation analysis (Reisigl 2014; van Eemeren 2010; Walton 2008), corpus-assisted discourse analysis (Mulderrig 2011a, 2011b), conversation analysis (Tolson & Ekström 2013), and so forth.

As should be clear from reading the previous sections, strategic use of language is a constitutive part of governing, administering and other aspects of 'doing politics'. Accordingly, a basic orientating question for an empirical linguistic study of government communication could be: *How are various linguistic resources, strategies, techniques, or devices employed by executive officeholders to achieve certain (political) goals?*

Depending on the apparent goals of the participants in a particular episode of communication at hand, it might also be worth asking: (1) *How do executive officeholders use language to claim and maintain their right to be obeyed?* (2) *How do executive officeholders use language to exercise their right to be obeyed?* I will expand on these questions in turn and provide some examples of data analysis.

Using language to hold on to power

Seeking an answer to the first of these two questions involves analysing the language of self-presentation and self-legitimation of government actors. How do governments and individual government officeholders present themselves linguistically? How do executive officeholders use language to construct and defend certain socially shared representations of the government, its members, goals and actions? How do officeholders build rapport with various government outsiders by casting them linguistically as an 'in-group', as members of a collective with shared values and interests (e.g. a nation, an ethnic community, citizenry)?

A practical methodological scaffolding, as well as a useful set of analytic tools for tackling these kinds of questions, has been developed by linguists working within the discourse-historical tradition of discourse studies (see, e.g. Reisigl & Wodak 2015; Wodak 2011, 2015). Following this approach, self-presentation of a government can be operationalised for a linguistic study by focusing on the following set of discursive strategies:

- *Naming* and *attributing* can be used by officeholders strategically to induce compliance by establishing in-groups and out-groups, and labelling actors, actions, and outcomes of the government as more positive (e.g. 'our long-term economic plan') and those of the opponents as negative (e.g. 'their reckless and appalling behaviour'). This often involves the use of linguistic membership categorisation devices and references to stereotypes.
- Officeholders may use *argumentation* schemes and warrants that lead to the conclusion that the government should be obeyed (e.g. appeals to force and authority).
- *Perspective-taking* involves using a variety of linguistic devices (e.g. deictics, reported speech) to indicate the speaker's or writer's point of view and involvement. For example, officeholders may try to portray themselves positively by using direct quotations of non-government actors who praise the government.
- *Intensifying* and *mitigating* devices (e.g. hyperboles, vague expressions) can be used to modify the epistemic status and illocutionary force of what is being said or written, to emphasise the positive and de-emphasise the negative utterances about the government.

In the face of being criticised for possible mistakes or transgressions, officeholders may try to use a variety of linguistic strategies defensively to ward off blame. Such strategies of blame-avoidance may be realised in a variety of ways (Hansson 2015a, 2017):

- *argumentation*: using argument schemes to support the standpoint that the negative event or outcome has been brought about either unintentionally, unknowingly, involuntarily, or by someone else; such defensive argumentation is often characterised by the use of certain topic-specific conclusion rules or *topoi* (see Reisigl & Wodak 2001, pp. 74–80; Reisigl 2014);
- *framing*: representing the self metaphorically/narratively as a Hero, a Helper of a Hero, or a Victim, and/or representing someone else as a Villain, to escape being assigned the role of the Villain by a blame-maker; such formulaic narrative frames have been described and discussed by Propp (1968 [1928]) and Lakoff (2008), among others;
- *denying*: rejecting agency (via act-denial, control-denial, intention-denial) and loss (via mitigations, downtoning) in response to accusations (see van Dijk 1992);
- *social actor and action representation*: exclusion, suppression, and backgrounding (e.g. by impersonalisation or nominalisation) of harmful actions, victims, and/or those actors who could possibly attract blame (see van Leeuwen 2008); and
- *legitimation*: providing explanations and justifications of possibly blameworthy actions by using references to authority, moral evaluation, rationalisation, and mythopoesis (see van Leeuwen 2007).

Example 1: 'eradicating waste in Whitehall'[2]

To illustrate how government may use language defensively, I analyse an extract from the UK Cabinet Office's news release in response to an investigative story on government overspending published in *The Times* on 9 January 2012. The story, entitled 'Whitehall waste: the £31 billion cost of failure', constituted a well-grounded (based on the National Audit Office's data) blame attack by a major newspaper on the government on an issue that was at the time at the core of its programme and thus also its collective identity. The story provoked the government to make an unusual move and issue a carefully crafted official response in the form of a Cabinet Office news release, entitled 'Eradicating waste in Whitehall saves £3.75 billion', on 11 January 2012. The news release contained a statement by Francis Maude, Minister for the Cabinet Office. Here are the first three sentences from his statement:

```
1  When we arrived in government we pledged to be ruthless in hunting down and
2  eradicating waste in Whitehall and that is precisely what we have done.
3  Just in the first ten months to last March we saved £3.75 billion – equivalent to
4  twice the budget of the Foreign Office, or to funding 200,000 nurses.
5  This has not been easy; spending hours renegotiating contracts, tackling vested
6  interests and large suppliers and cutting back on spend on consultants and
7  advertising does not make for glamorous or headline grabbing work.
```
(Cabinet Office, 11 January 2012)

In lines 1–2, Minister for the Cabinet Office uses the argumentative strategy of parading the government's own qualities (*argumentum ad verecundiam*) by claiming that it has fulfilled its pledge. Importantly, this sentence also implies a total act-denial: the Minister states that the government has 'eradicated waste', that is, he and his colleagues have done the opposite of 'wasting'. The Minister represents wasting, not as an action carried out by his fellow officeholders, but as a nominalised entity: 'waste in Whitehall'. Moreover, he diffuses blame by portraying the government metaphorically as a 'container' ('when we arrived in government...'), rather than a specific group of human actors who could be held responsible. He frames 'waste' as a Villain (or perhaps as some kind of a dangerous wild animal) and the government as a Hero (perhaps a gunman) who 'hunts it down' and 'eradicates' it.

In lines 3–4, the Minister backs up his claim by using a particular conclusion rule, *topos of numbers*, by suggesting that a given statistical figure (£3.75 billion allegedly saved in ten months) serves as proof that the government has not wasted money and should not be blamed. However, the Minister does not directly counter the central accusatory claim put forward by *The Times* that 'more than £31 billion of taxpayers' money has been wasted across government departments in the past two years'. Thus, he may be seen as committing a 'straw man' fallacy and violating a pragma-dialectical rule of reasonable discussion that requires the debater to use correct reference to previous discourse by the antagonist.

In lines 5–7, the Minister represents government's activities at a high level of abstractness ('renegotiating contracts', 'tackling vested interests', 'cutting back on spend'), thereby making it more difficult to understand the exact nature of the activities. This, in turn, may evoke a sense of mystery and awe among his audiences and therefore function as a kind of appeal to authority. In addition, he casts the government as a selfless Hero by claiming that the work of the government has been neither easy nor glamorous.

To illustrate how blame avoidance may involve negative other-presentation, I examine another extract from that news release. In his statement, Minister for the Cabinet Office says:

```
1  And I am not alone in highlighting all the good work we have done so far;
2  the Public Accounts Committee recently recognised and welcomed
3  our transparent approach to savings.
4  Meanwhile other countries, especially in troubled Europe,
5  are now looking to us for how this is done.
```
(Cabinet Office, 11 January 2012)

In lines 1–3, the Minister uses *ad populum* argumentation and authority legitimation in service of positive self-presentation of the government. He supports the position that the government should be praised (or at least not blamed) for its financial conduct by claiming that a collective actor who apparently holds high status in society – a parliamentary committee – has given the government a positive evaluation. In terms of representation, Maude nominalises the government's action: 'our transparent approach to savings' (line 3). This nominalised construction is remarkable for its ambivalence. It presupposes that the government is acting transparently and is saving money – both of which are supposedly regarded as worthy of public praise rather than blame. However, it is sufficiently vague to permit an opposite interpretation: that it might be possible to 'have a transparent approach to savings', but actually not save any money.

In lines 4–5, the Minister juxtaposes the actions of the UK government with those of other countries, evoking an 'Us vs Them' opposition. The suggestion that other governments regard the UK as a positive example (or perhaps a mentor or a role model) is not supported by any data – it ultimately relies on a presumption that his audience is likely to agree with the statements that reaffirm positive in-group feelings. The perceived opposition is intensified by negative other-presentation: 'troubled Europe' (line 4) is a salient linguistic construction that is based upon a presumption that the audience regards 'Europe' as an out-group (i.e. that the UK citizens do not belong to 'Europe') and also implies that the UK is not financially 'troubled' (problem denial). This kind of discursive triggering of group polarisation may be regarded as manipulative, if it is carried out systematically with the purpose of deflecting blame for possible financial misconduct of the government.

Using language to exert power

A linguistic study of how executive officeholders exercise their right to be obeyed involves analysing communication in relation to particular policies, that is, certain courses of action taken by a government organisation. Public policy-making involves inevitable trade-offs between goals and criteria such as equity, efficiency, security and liberty (Stone 2012). Governments' decisions as to 'who gets what, when, and how' seem to provide a constant source of discontent for groups and individuals who see themselves as 'losers' or 'bearers of a burden' under a particular distribution regime. Governments' attempts to maintain order and safety in society necessarily involve setting restrictions to human behaviour and limiting individual liberty.

Using language as a policy tool, that is, as an instrument for either encouraging or discouraging certain behaviour among diverse actors, may take various forms. Government officeholders may issue direct commands and requests that are backed up by coercion, or use some more subtle persuasive linguistic strategies that are designed to bring about a behaviour change, but mask the underlying threat of punishment. Here are two example analyses of such instrumental applications of language by the UK government.

Example 2: 'go home or face arrest'

In July 2013, the UK Home Office launched a communications pilot campaign, in which a van carrying a large billboard drove around six boroughs of London with sizeable migrant populations. The billboard displayed a photo of handcuffs, the logo of the Home Office and the following text:

1 In the UK illegally?
2 106 arrests last week in your area
3 GO HOME OR FACE ARREST
4 Text HOME to 78070
5 for free advice, and help with travel documents
6 We can help you to return home voluntarily without fear of arrest or detention

(Home Office 2013)

In line 1, a question is used to elicit self-identification by (potential) individual violators of immigration rules as addressees of the advertisement. In line 3, a contingent threat is constructed, specifying that the addressee must comply with a demand of the source ('go home') or else suffer a cost inflicted by the threatener ('face arrest'). Numerical data about previous arrests is presented in line 2 to increase the addressees' perceived risk of suffering a cost in case of non-compliance. In line 4, a concrete order is given: the addressee must send a particular text message to a certain number. Lines 5 and 6 include lexis that seems to indicate that complying with the given order has positive consequences for the addressee: 'free advice', 'help' and 'without fear'.

In this case, language use is explicitly backed up by coercion: an order is followed by a promise to punish those who do not obey. Indeed, it is an official task of the Home Office to ensure that the immigration rules are complied with and that immigration offenders are removed from the UK. According to the report published by the Home Office (2013), their pilot campaign with 'ad-vans' resulted in a total of 18 cases of voluntary departure, and helped to save money, because the campaign cost less than enforced removal.

However, in her critical discussion of this campaign, discourse analyst Ruth Wodak (2015, pp. 84–87) argues convincingly that the mobile ad campaign should be seen as 'fear-mongering', the discursive construction of 'the stranger' and 'fear of the stranger', and thus as an attempt by the UK government to win favour with certain kinds of voters who share xenophobic and anti-immigration sentiments. This observation helpfully reminds us that when we analyse a particular instance of instrumental-language use by a government, we should also study its broader socio-political context: only then can we understand how the text or utterance in question could be interpreted by various readers/hearers, and how it may have been designed to simultaneously serve multiple political goals.

Example 3: managing actions

Discourse analyst Jane Mulderrig (2011a) describes with much insight some of the subtle ways in which modern governments use language to attract rather than coerce people into behaving in certain ways. She shows that officeholders try to accomplish this by textual mechanisms that she calls 'Managing Actions': by using managing verbs (such as *let*, *allow*, *help*, *enable*, *require* and *expect*), presenting certain actions or outcomes as desirable, presupposing their necessity, and assuming volition of the 'managed actors' (i.e. governees or manipulees) rather than giving them direct orders. The following three short textual examples are taken from her corpus of public policy consultation papers on education issues between 1972 and 2005 in England and Wales (Mulderrig 2011a). Note that in these sentences, the personal pronoun 'we' is used to refer to the government.

(1) We will ensure that young people [...] achieve National Curriculum level 5

(Mulderrig 2011a, p. 60)

In this example, the government ('we') is construed as an 'overseer' who is in control of the behaviour of the managed actors ('we will ensure that [managed actors] do X'), completion of the activity is assumed semantically, the outcome seems inevitable, and the independence of the managed actors is comparatively limited.

> (2) We encourage [...] schools to work together in local 'families' to help share [best practice]
> (Mulderrig 2011a, p. 60)

In this second example, the government ('we') is construed as a 'leader' who has authority to instigate others' actions ('we encourage [managed actor] to do X'), the action is represented as desirable (or important, attractive), but there is no assumption of its completion. Other linguistic constructions that have a similar effect include, for instance, 'require [managed actor] to' and 'expect [managed actor] to'.

> (3) The government is concerned to enable the ethnic minority communities to play their full part in contributing to the education of ethnic minority pupils
> (Mulderrig 2011a, p. 57)

Here, the government is construed as a 'facilitator' whose authority over others' actions is assumed, but completion of the action is not necessarily assumed. Most importantly, the volition of the managed actors ('ethnic minority communities') is assumed here: they are represented as if they wanted to do X ('play their full part'), but needed help or support from the government to 'enable' that. Other linguistic constructions that have a similar effect include, for example, 'support [managed actor] to', 'allow [managed actor] to', 'free [managed actor] to', 'make it easier for [managed actor] to', 'provide the opportunities for [managed actor] to'.

Suggestions for future research: conflictual aspects of government communication

Governing is marked by both external (more visible) and internal (often less visible) conflict tendencies. Traces of various struggles and dilemmas can be illuminated by analysing government officeholders' strategic uses of spoken and written language. Next, I list some themes and questions that may provide a particularly fertile ground for future (critical) discourse studies.

Intra-governmental strifes

It would be a mistake to regard government as a homogeneous 'in-group'. Within all kinds of government organisations, including the ones at the very top of institutional hierarchy, interpersonal clashes and tensions often rise for various reasons and interdepartmental rivalry may easily emerge over allocation of power and resources. In coalition governments, where top executive power is shared between ministers from two or more political parties, governing is furthermore affected by inter-party competition, divergence in policy preferences within the cabinet, and struggles to make compromises with coalition partners, while maintaining integrity in the eyes of the party's supporters (Strøm, Müller & Bergman 2008). There are only a few linguistically informed empirical studies that focus on analysing backstage activity in political organisation (e.g. Wodak 2000, 2011). The question of how officeholders use language to mitigate or aggravate various conflicts in the workplace, construct in-groups and out-groups, make decisions, and address and persuade several audiences at once, would certainly merit further research.

Compromised impartiality of non-elected administrators

In many Western countries, there is an immanent tension between the widely observed trend of personalisation of politics (e.g. Castells 2009; Stanyer 2012) and the traditional public expectations and norms that demand formal impersonality and impartiality of public administration (Weber 1978). For example, the non-partisan civil servant communicators working in UK government departments are faced with a difficult task. They have to provide advice and support to their ministers, who are routinely engaged in personalised politics and a struggle for electoral support. However, as civil servants, professional communicators have to retain impartiality, that is, to avoid 'political bias' in their behaviour, as postulated by the UK Civil Service Code. While professional government communicators tend to claim neutral or impartial status by casting themselves as mere disseminators of messages about policies, they are, in practice, often engaged in formulating or reformulating government policies (te Molder 1999). Therefore, it seems necessary to investigate in more detail how civil servants use language and other symbolic resources in an attempt to construct and sustain an impression of impartiality.

Mediated scandals and blame avoidance

Political opponents make attempts to overthrow the incumbent by representing the policy-makers publicly in a negative light, blaming them for behaving in norm-violating ways, and causing bad outcomes. Strategic 'character assassinations' (Castells 2009) of individual officeholders help to fuel mediated scandals that undermine the overall trust in government (Thompson 2000; Adut 2008). Journalists are usually interested in seeking out and running 'scandalous' stories and are often (but not always, see Entman 2012) eager to publicise blistering criticism of political elites and powerful officeholders (Allern & Pollack 2012). While those in power usually try to avoid getting in the middle of a scandal, opposition politicians may deliberately use controversial discursive strategies (e.g. making a racist comment) to provoke and sustain scandals around themselves in order to dominate the media agenda – a dynamic that Wodak (2015, p. 19) has termed the 'populist perpetuum mobile'. Executive politicians may respond to public blame attacks by providing an apology (Harris, Grainger & Mullany 2006; Kampf 2008, 2009), or by employing other defensive discursive strategies, such as denying, counter-attacking the blame-maker, or distracting the critical audience (Hansson 2015a, 2015b). Future studies could provide further insights into the ways in which government-related political scandals are linguistically constructed in media, as well as the ways in which government officeholders use linguistic resources to respond to public verbal attacks and mediated scandals.

Concluding remarks

While there is a wealth of literature on the election campaigns of political parties and the rhetoric of certain celebrity politicians, relatively little has been written about contemporary day-to-day language use of government communicators. Admittedly, dealing with 'banal' data such as news releases, posters and policy documents produced by government agencies may perhaps seem less exciting compared to dissecting more 'noble' presidential speeches or party election manifestos. However, the seemingly dull everyday flows of text and talk coming from public policy-makers and their spokespersons can have profound societal implications, as these often construct and sustain particular unequal relations of power between certain 'in-groups' and 'out-groups'. Hence, I hope that the handful of basic conceptual distinctions, examples of analytical approaches and research themes that I have sketched out in this chapter will inspire new linguistically informed critical research projects in this understudied field.

Notes

1. It should be noted, however, that acting strategically does *not* always mean following well-thought-through, meticulous, rational and logical plans: it may involve acting in particular goal-orientated ways that are conventional or have become routine or 'automatic' in certain contexts for a certain community (Wodak, de Cillia, Reisigl & Liebhart 2009; Culpeper 2015).
2. The name 'Whitehall' is frequently used as a metonym for British central government.

References

Adut, A, 2008, *On scandal: Moral disturbances in society, politics and art*, Cambridge University Press, Cambridge.

Allern, S & Pollack, E, 2012, 'Mediated scandals', in *Scandalous!: the mediated construction of political scandals in four Nordic countries*, eds. S Allern & E Pollack, Nordicom, Göteborg, pp. 9–28.

Bernays, E, 1928, *Propaganda*, Horace Liveright, New York.

Bhatia, A, 2006, 'Critical Discourse Analysis of political press conferences', *Discourse & Society*, 17(2), pp. 173–203.

Cabinet Office, 2012, 'Eradicating waste in Whitehall saves £3.75 billion', available from: www.gov.uk/government/news/eradicating-waste-in-whitehall-saves-3-75-billion [accessed 10 March 2014].

Canel, M J & Sanders, K, 2013, 'Introduction: Mapping the field of government communication', in *Government communication: Cases and challenges*, eds. K Sanders & M J Canel, Bloomsbury, London, pp. 1–26.

Castells, M, 2009, *Communication power*, Oxford University Press, Oxford.

Chilton, P, 2004, *Analysing political discourse: Theory and practice*, Routledge, London.

Couldry, N & Hepp, A, 2013, 'Conceptualizing mediatization: Contexts, traditions, arguments', *Communication Theory*, 23(3), pp. 191–202.

Culpeper, J, 2015, 'Impoliteness strategies', in *Interdisciplinary studies in pragmatics, culture and society*, eds. A Capone & J L Mey, Springer, London.

Ekström, M, 2009, 'Power and affiliation in presidential press conferences: A study on interruptions, jokes and laughter', *Journal of Language and Politics*, 8(3), pp. 386–415.

Entman, R M, 2012, *Scandal and silence: Media responses to presidential misconduct*, Polity Press, Cambridge.

Eriksson, G, 2011, 'Follow-up questions in political press conferences', *Journal of Pragmatics*, 43(14), pp. 3331–3344.

Fairclough, N, 2000, *New Labour, new language?* Routledge, London.

Farrelly, M, 2015, *Discourse and democracy: Critical analysis of the language of government*, Routledge, London.

Garnett, J L & Kouzmin, A, eds., 1997, *Handbook of administrative communication*, Marcel Dekker, New York.

Gobo, G, 2008, *Doing ethnography*, Sage, London.

Government Communication Service, 2015, *Government Communication Service (GCS) Handbook*, available from: https://gcs.civilservice.gov.uk/wp-content/uploads/2015/09/GCSHandbook.pdf [accessed 10 October 2015].

Graber, D, 2003, *The power of communication: Managing information in public organizations*, CQ Press, Washington, DC.

Hansson, S, 2015a, 'Discursive strategies of blame avoidance in government: A framework for analysis', *Discourse & Society*, 26(3), pp. 297–322.

Hansson, S, 2015b, 'Calculated overcommunication: Strategic uses of prolixity, irrelevance, and repetition in administrative language', *Journal of Pragmatics*, 84, pp. 172–188.

Hansson, S, 2017, 'Anticipative strategies of blame avoidance in government: The case of communication guidelines', *Journal of Language and Politics*, 16(2), pp. 219–241.

Hansson, S, forthcoming, 'Four conceptualisations of government communication'.

Harris, S, Grainger, K & Mullany, L, 2006, 'The pragmatics of political apologies', *Discourse & Society*, 17(6), pp. 715–737.

Hay, C, 2007, *Why we hate politics*, Polity Press, Malden, MA.

Heer, H, Manoschek, W, Pollak, A & Wodak, R, 2008, *The discursive construction of history: Remembering the Wehrmacht's war of annihilation*, Palgrave Macmillan, Basingstoke.

Home Office, 2013, 'Operation Vaken evaluation report – October 2013', available from: www.gov.uk/government/uploads/system/uploads/attachment_data/file/254411/Operation_Vaken_Evaluation_Report.pdf [accessed 3 May 2014].

Jacobs, G, 1999, *Preformulating the news: An analysis of the metapragmatics of press releases*, John Benjamins, Amsterdam.

Jacobs, G, 2011, 'Press conferences on the internet: Technology, mediation and access in the news', *Journal of Pragmatics*, 43(7), pp. 1900–1911.

Kampf, Z, 2008, 'The pragmatics of forgiveness: Judgments of apologies in the Israeli political arena', *Discourse & Society*, 19(5), pp. 577–598.

Kampf, Z, 2009, 'Public (non-) apologies: The discourse of minimizing responsibility', *Journal of Pragmatics*, 41, pp. 2257–2270.

Kienpointner, M, 2011, 'Rhetoric', in Pragmatics in Practice, eds. J Östman & J Verschueren, John Benjamins, Amsterdam, pp. 264–277.

Kienpointner, M, 2013, 'Strategic maneuvering in the political rhetoric of Barack Obama', *Journal of Language and Politics*, 12(3), pp. 357–377.

Krzyżanowski, M & Wodak, R, 2009, *The politics of exclusion: Debating migration in Austria*, Transaction Publishers, New Brunswick, NJ.

Lakoff, G, 2008, *The political mind: Why you can't understand 21st-century American politics with an 18th-century brain*, Penguin Group, New York.

Lazarsfeld, P F, 1941, 'Remarks on administrative and critical communications research', *Studies in Philosophy and Science*, 9, pp. 2–16.

Lee, M, Neeley, G & Stewart, K, eds., 2012, *The practice of government public relations*, CRC Press, Boca Raton.

Machiavelli, N, 2006 [1513], *The Prince*, available from: www.gutenberg.org/files/1232/1232-h/1232-h.htm [accessed 10 October 2015].

Martin, J R & Wodak, R, eds., 2003, *Re/reading the past: Critical and functional perspectives on time and value*, John Benjamins, Amsterdam.

Mulderrig, J, 2011a, 'The grammar of governance', *Critical Discourse Studies*, 8(1), pp. 45–68.

Mulderrig, J, 2011b, 'Manufacturing consent: A corpus-based critical discourse analysis of New Labour's educational governance', *Journal of Educational Philosophy and Theory*, 43(6), pp. 562–578.

Norris, P, 2011, *Democratic deficit: Critical citizens revisited*, Cambridge University Press, Cambridge.

Palonen, K, 2003, 'Four times of politics: Policy, polity, politicking, and politicization', *Alternatives*, 28(2), pp. 171–186.

Propp, V, 1968 [1928], *Morphology of the folktale* (2nd ed.), tr. L Scott, University of Texas Press, Austin, TX.

Reisigl, M, 2008, 'Rhetoric of political speeches', in *Handbook of communication in the public sphere*, eds. R Wodak & V Koller, de Gruyter, Berlin, pp. 271–289.

Reisigl, M, 2014, 'Argumentation analysis and the discourse-historical approach: A methodological framework', in *Contemporary critical discourse studies*, eds., C Hart & P Cap, Bloomsbury, London, pp. 67–96.

Reisigl, M & Wodak, R, 2001, *Discourse and discrimination*, Routledge, London.

Reisigl, M & Wodak, R, 2015, 'The discourse-historical approach' in *Methods of Critical Discourse Studies*, 3rd ed., eds. R Wodak & M Meyer, Sage, London, pp. 23–61.

Scollon, R, 2008, *Analyzing public discourse: Discourse analysis in the making of public policy*. Routledge, London.

Stanyer, J, 2012, *Intimate politics: Publicity, privacy and the personal lives of politicians in media saturated democracies*, Polity, Cambridge.

Stone, D, 2012, *Policy paradox: The art of political decision making*, 3rd ed., W W Norton, New York.

Strøm, K, Müller, W C & Bergman, T, 2008, *Cabinets and coalition bargaining: The democratic life cycle in Western Europe*, Oxford University Press, Oxford.

Strömbäck, J & Esser, F, 2014, 'Introduction: Making sense of the mediatization of politics', *Journalism Practice, 8*(3), pp. 245–257.

Taylor, F W, 1911, *The principles of scientific management*, Harper, New York.

te Molder, H F M, 1999, 'Discourse of dilemmas: An analysis of communication planners' accounts', *British Journal of Social Psychology, 38*(3), pp. 245–263.

The Times, 2012, 'Whitehall waste: The £31bn cost of failure', available from: www.thetimes.co.uk/article/whitehall-waste-the-pound31bn-cost-of-failure-c2k87swn39d [accessed 10 March 2014].

Thompson, J B, 2000, *Political scandal: Power and visibility in a media age*, Polity Press, Cambridge.

Tolson, A & Ekström, M, eds., 2013, *Media talk and political elections in Europe and America*, Palgrave Macmillan, Basingstoke.

van Dijk, T A, 1992, 'Discourse and the denial of racism', *Discourse & Society, 3*(1), pp. 87–118.

van Dijk, T A, 2015, 'Critical discourse studies: A sociocognitive approach', in *Methods of Critical Discourse Studies* (3rd ed.), eds. R Wodak & M Meyer, Sage, London, pp. 62–85.

van Eemeren, F H, 2010, *Strategic maneuvering in argumentative discourse: Extending the pragma-dialectical theory of argumentation*, John Benjamins, Amsterdam.

van Leeuwen, T, 2007, 'Legitimation in discourse and communication', *Discourse & Communication, 1*(1), pp. 91–112.

van Leeuwen, T, 2008, *Discourse and practice: New tools for critical discourse analysis*, Oxford University Press, New York.

Vedung, E, 2003, 'Policy instruments: Typologies and theories', in *Carrots, sticks, and sermons: Policy instruments and their evaluation*, eds. M L Bemelmans-Videc, R Rist & E Vedung, Transaction Publishers, London, pp. 21–57.

Walton, D N, 2008, *Informal logic: A pragmatic approach*, 2nd ed., Cambridge University Press, Cambridge.

Weber, M, 1978, *Economy and society*, University of California Press, Berkeley, CA.

Wodak, R, 2000, 'From conflict to consensus? The co-construction of a policy paper', in *European Union discourses on un/employment. An interdisciplinary approach to employment policy-making and organizational change*, eds. P Muntigl, G Weiss & R Wodak, John Benjamins, Amsterdam, pp. 73–114.

Wodak, R, 2011, *The discourse of politics in action: Politics as usual*, Palgrave Macmillan, Basingstoke.

Wodak, R, 2015, *The politics of fear: What right-wing populist discourses mean*, Sage, London.

Wodak, R & Kirsch, F P, eds., 1995, *Totalitäre Sprache – Langue de bois – Language of Dictatorship*, Passagen Verlag, Vienna.

Wodak, R, de Cillia, R, Reisigl, M & Liebhart, K, 2009, *The discursive construction of national identity*, 2nd ed., Edinburgh University Press, Edinburgh.

Wodak, R, KhosraviNik, M & Mral, B, eds., 2013, *Right-wing populism in Europe: Politics and discourse*, Bloomsbury, London.

Yeung, K, 2006, Regulating government communications, *The Cambridge Law Journal*, 65(1), pp. 53–91.

22
Press conferences

Mats Ekström and Göran Eriksson

Introduction

In many political systems, the press conference is an institutional arrangement of public political communication, and has, as Kumar (2007, p. 255) puts it, 'come to be regarded as part of the foundation of democratic government'. It gradually progressed during the twentieth century from controlled and confidential, off-the-record meetings between leading politicians and journalists into an arena for public accountability with great significance for the news production cycle (Eriksson & Östman 2013). A press conference takes place on the political institution's initiative to announce policies, decisions, and so on, but occasionally also for handling challenging events, such as accidents, catastrophes, or even political scandals. There are differences between national contexts, but as a communicative genre, press conferences are characterised by certain standards (see Bhatia 2006; Eriksson, Larsson & Moberg 2013; Kumar 2007). The events are typically embedded in political processes and normally announced through press releases. The two main parts of the events involve the pre-planned speech by one politician (or sometimes two or more) and a question-and-answer session in which journalists pose questions. Through the subsequent news-construction phase, journalists process these different instances of talk and other information into news items that provide the public with a chance to know about politicians' actions.

The following chapter focuses on how politics and political actions are publicly performed, negotiated, and transformed (recontextualised) in the context of press conferences. It will show how power is exercised and negotiated in different phases of the communication processes, and how it relates to language and discourse on different levels. The chapter is based on research from disciplines such as conversation analysis, Critical Discourse Analysis, media discourse analysis and historical approaches to political communication and governmental PR. This research ranges from detailed studies of press-conference interaction (see e.g. Clayman et al. 2006, 2007; Clayman & Heritage 2002; Ekström 2009; Eriksson 2011) to broader approaches focusing on the origin and the development of press conferences as a forum for PR activities (Kumar 2007; Larsson 2012). Although there is now a growing body of research on political press conferences, two national contexts and forms of press conferences, in particular, have been explored most thoroughly: press conferences with the Swedish government (see e.g. Eriksson 2011; Eriksson & Eriksson 2012; Eriksson, Larsson & Moberg 2013; Larsson 2012) and those with the President of the United States of America (see, e.g. Clayman et al. 2006; Clayman & Heritage 2002; Clayman et al. 2007; Kumar 2005, 2007). This chapter relies extensively on these studies and it is organised as follows. In the next section, we describe the historical development of the political press conference. Thereafter, we discuss it as a genre, comprising a mix of sub-genres. This is followed by a section describing the different activities of talk that are crucial for press conferences. The chapter ends with a discussion on how the press conference is integrated into the news-production cycle and explores the recontextualising power of news journalism.

Historical developments: the organisation of public political performances

In many countries, press conferences are a routinised and frequent form for meetings between journalists and politicians. They are public events in the sense that they are often broadcast live (via traditional television or the web) and they generally receive extensive news media attention. In contrast to other public events, such as news interviews, a political press conference takes place on the initiative of a political institution and is an arrangement where the politician meets many journalists at one time. The form for press conferences has altered over the years – they started as informal off-the-record meetings to which chosen reporters were invited – but they nevertheless emanate from a need to communicate with the public and to handle the pressure of intensified media attention (Kumar 2007; Larsson 2012). Historical developments reflect changes in the strategic organisation of mediatised political performances.

Kumar (2005) describes the development of US presidential press conferences in four different steps. Although Theodore Roosevelt was the first president of the United States (1901–1909) to arrange regular off-the-record meetings with a handful of chosen reporters, the first period (1913–1933), started with the Woodrow Wilson administration (1913–1921). President Wilson saw such an arrangement as a way to reduce the total number of meetings he had to attend. These conferences were off-the-record sessions for the president to respond to questions, but reporters were not allowed to reproduce these responses without permission from the White House. Kumar (2005) depicts these meetings as 'reactive'; the president mainly answered questions that were posed beforehand and used a limited extent of the time to make statements. In the succeeding Warren Harding (1921–1923) administration, White House staff constructed a box in which the reporters put their queries when entering the conference room. As the number of reporters was rather large – between 50 and 200 – only a few questions could be responded to and the president could choose which ones gave him opportunities to decide what should be stressed during the meeting.

During the next period (1933–1953), the conditions for press meetings altered slightly. Off-the-record exchanges were still held, but the requirement for reporters to submit questions in advance ceased during Franklin D Roosevelt's administration (1933–1945), which affected meeting dynamics. The president would talk according to his own agenda and more thoroughly express his opinions and explanations. Another crucial change was the introduction of joint press conferences with foreign political leaders and with members of the president's administration, arrangements that are frequently used today (see Bhatia 2006; Kumar 2007).

The most dramatic changes in the press-conference format took place during the third period (1953–1981) when press conferences were put on record and televised. An obvious consequence of that change was that presidents could no longer control what was reported or how they were cited. According to Kumar (2005, p. 183), these changes 'transformed the forum from a low-risk to a high-risk performance', but they also provided presidents with the possibility to talk directly to the public. It nevertheless led to increased concern about communicative strategies. Certain organisations aimed at planning and working with such strategies were established. One aspect of this was to keep press conferences to times when it seemed most appropriate, from a strategic point of view, for instance, in the evening on prime time, which gave the president a chance to reach a wide audience. Kumar characterizes this format also as part of the extended fourth period, dated 1981 to 2004, but this era involved an augmented awareness of strategic communication intended to manage the president's exposure to an increasingly aggressive journalistic style (Clayman & Heritage 2002). As a result, the president often appeared in joint press conferences with foreign leaders or other public figures, which have become a form of press conference considered more advantageous for the president's image (Bhatia 2006).

According to Larsson (2012; see also Eriksson, Larsson & Moberg 2013), the outbreak of the Second World War led to the Swedish government's increased interest in having regular meetings with the press. Such meetings had, until then, been infrequent and random occurrences. The press conferences that took place four to six times a year were both a way for the government to provide information about its reaction to the ongoing war, and also an opportunity to control press reporting about the aggressors, that is, to show cautious opinions, especially about German and Soviet rulers. Normally, the information provided by the government was confidential, which meant the press was well-informed about governmental actions, but prevented from writing about them.

The arrangement of regular and confidential governmental press conferences (normally one each month with a limited number of journalists) continued after the war (Larsson 2012, pp. 266–267). It should be noted that the prime minister's office during the 1950s comprised a minimal staff consisting of a secretary and a typist. Journalists had no problem contacting the prime minister or the secretary. In 1963, the first press officer was appointed and was so influenced by President Kennedy's televised conferences that he launched a new form of press conference that was open to accredited journalists. The agenda was open and journalists were now free to report from them. However, these conferences never worked well; neither politicians nor journalists found them fruitful.

At the end of the 1960s and in the early 1970s, the Swedish government's press relations changed drastically (Eriksson, Larsson & Moberg 2013). After a less successful election in 1967, the social democratic government identified a need to strengthen press relations and recruited press secretaries to the different ministries. Olof Palme, who was appointed prime minister in 1969, was clearly a 'press-minded' person (Larsson 2012). During his first period in office (1969–1976), he had almost daily contact with several journalists, but on some occasions, he also arranged press conferences that became the institutional form of press conferences. Contact with individual journalists had become too time-consuming and the press conference was a way to handle increased demands from the media to obtain information about governmental actions. With all the technological landmarks arising in the last decade, press conferences seem old-fashioned for today's political communication, but they are still a crucial arrangement for political meetings with journalists. In Sweden, the number of press conferences has risen steadily during the last twenty years (Larsson 2012).

The history of press conferences in US and Sweden shows national specificities as well as general trends most likely found also in other countries. It is reasonable to see the development of more frequent and institutional forms for meetings between journalists and politicians against a background of a general 'mediatisation' of politics (e.g. Asp & Esaiasson 1996; Mazzoleni & Schulz 1999; Strömbäck 2008); a process of growing mutual dependency between political institutions and journalism, and increased adaptation of political strategies, performances and language to the media. Historical research on press conferences suggests that, during the twentieth century, political institutions recognised the need to communicate their policies and ideas with the public, and the press conference was one crucial means to achieve that. It was a way to handle growing media attention. Accordingly, journalism progressed during this era to become an institution fulfilling a 'watchdog role', legitimised as essential for democracy. For today's political institutions, the actual organisation of press conferences involves management of public performances. Important strategic decisions concern the timing of the event and its relation to other activities, location, formats, and so on (cf. Kumar 2005).

Press conferences as genre and sub-genre

The press conference can be classified as a broad genre of public political talk. It is organised by political institutions with the overall purpose of releasing public statements and making officials available for questions from the public (or, more specifically, from journalists who are assumed to act on behalf of the public). Among the various genres of political talk, the press conference thus stands out as being a distinctly formalised frontstage activity. The politicians literally come forward on a stage arranged for a particular public activity. It involves the dramaturgical components that Goffman (1959) identified as central to audience-oriented performances in social interaction; the setting that provides the scenery and appropriate location for performances; the expressive resources related to the performer (speech, bodily posture, gestures, etc.); and the collaborative work of team performances (cf. Wodak 2011, pp. 8–9). In press conferences, the boundaries between the front and the politics behind the scene are also constantly negotiated. Politicians prepare speeches to announce certain messages. Journalists push the boundaries and indicate concealments in questions that go beyond what politicians are prepared to talk about. The performances may indicate an event of strategic PR activities as well as transparency and public accountability.

The rationale for this communicative genre is manifest in the generic structure comprising a number of instances for talk and interaction (Bhatia 2006). These include: an opening and welcoming, the pre-planned speech, the interactional question-answer session, the closing, and, in many cases, a session of post-interviews. The roles and resources of the participants (as chair, speaker, interviewer, interviewee and audience) are partly pre-allocated in relation to these activities. They will be described in more detail on pp. 347–349.

The research, however, also shows that there are substantial differences between types of press conferences in terms of their rationale, conventional practices and communicative styles. They can be conceptualised in sub-genres. The following are three examples: first, government press relations officials invite journalists to press conferences to announce policies, reforms and other political initiatives. These events are typically part of proactive public relations and designed to demonstrate the capacity of the government to address problems and deliver good policy. The timing and packaging of messages are often the result of strategic planning where PR managers have a central role. The frequency of such conferences varies partly in relation to the cycles in mediatised politics. They are, for example, frequently organised to announce policy agreements between the political parties in new government coalitions and to intensify efforts to influence the media agenda during election campaigns.

The official diplomacy press conference is another sub-genre. A primary objective of these events is to display mutual relationships between governments, states, and international organisations. They are organised as joint sessions in connection to, for example, official state visits. The performances have ceremonial character, comprising a mix of official joint statements, friendly conversation and handshakes. As noted by Bhatia (2006, p. 176) the conferences represent a 'mediatization of political actions' in which the success and important outcomes of the meetings are often emphasised and conflicts are concealed. (The rhetorical features are further described in the next section on p. 347.) The diplomatic character of the conferences is reflected also in the interview session. In some cases, the time allotted for questions is restricted and researchers have observed a tendency for journalists to avoid aggressive questioning (Banning & Billingsley 2007). For prime ministers and presidents, diplomatic press conferences thus involve delicate performances of politeness, agreement and disguising problems, and at the same time create a lower risk of critical questions posed by journalists (Kumar 2003, p. 8).

A third and considerably different type of political press conference is that organised to manage criticism and political crises in the context of media scandals. It can be about norm transgressions of individual politicians, or serious deficiencies in governmental management of crisis situations (Ekström & Johansson 2008). Those press conferences often involve processes of blaming, articulated in acts of accusations and managed in blame avoidance strategies (Angouri & Wodak 2014; Hansson 2015). In these contexts, journalists claim to act on behalf of an accusatory public. The blaming is carefully managed in the design of questions, and its consequences for the politicians are negotiated in the interactions. Partly depending on the phase of the media scandal, the individual speech of the politician and their answers to critical and accusatory questions could, for instance, be designed as justifications, denials of the problem (that it never happened, or is not true), or public apologies (that to some extent, or fully, admit the problem). It could also involve a resignation announcement. Accountability questions are common in such interview sessions and can easily progress into a rather aggressive discourse. Emotional intensity is a common feature of these events.

It is a task for PR managers to help politicians handle media scandals. There is no simple answer to the question of what is the most successful strategy, although PR managers have reasons to generally recommend politicians to be open and apologise in order to terminate the narrative of the media scandal as quickly as possible. It also happens that politicians' conduct in press conferences develops into new media scandals. Ekström and Johansson (2008) provide an example when a Swedish government minister invited journalists to a press conference in order to handle a criticism (and what was about to develop into a typical power scandal) regarding the appointment of the director of the State Audit Institution. The press conference, which was broadcast in the news, began with the minister reading a scripted message. This message was then repeated, almost verbatim, regardless of what questions the journalists asked. This staying-on-message strategy, however, brought extensive criticism in the media. It developed into a 'talk scandal' (Ekström & Johansson 2008) in which the minister's reputation was seriously threatened. The minister transgressed the interactional norms and expectations by not responding properly to journalists' questions. He failed in at least giving the impression of being open to answering questions asked on behalf of the public. In the media, the minister was described as totally incompetent; he was ridiculed and asked to resign. The politician's performance in the press conference was thus planned as a way to handle the boundaries between the front- and backstage of politics, but rather, it appeared as an act of concealment and political ignorance.

Three activities of talk

The communicative activities in press conferences constitute significantly different contexts for political performances and journalism. This is manifest in the participant roles and relationships, expected contributions and the discursive orientation to particular tasks. In this section, we describe results from studies that have analysed language and discourse within three main activities of press conferences.

The political speech

Appearances in political press conferences are characterised by discursive and rhetorical strategies aimed at achieving certain goals. The first phase is the introductory speech in which politicians have opportunities to thoroughly announce policies, justify ideas and actions, or counter critiques directed at them (often without being interrupted). Normally, such statements are carefully prepared and can, to varying extents, set the agenda for the entire event. A good example of such rhetorical strategies is given by Bhatia (2006), who studies the performance of joint diplomacy talk by political leaders from different ideological backgrounds. Based on Critical Discourse Analysis, she investigated the discursive strategies used to dispel the differences and conceal potential conflicts in a joint press conference with Chinese President Jiang Zemin and US President George W Bush. The study shows how the two presidents make use of a variety of strategies (evasions of controversial issues, inclusive 'we' statements, and humour and informality) to accomplish a diplomatic performance. The discourse is, however, anything but unambiguous, and Bhatia shows that the statements can be interpreted as 'having one value on the surface and quite the opposite implied' (*ibidem*, p. 200). Language, she states, 'is used to choreograph a game of cat and mouse between the two diametrically opposed speakers' (*ibidem*, p. 194).

Moberg and Eriksson (2013) explore a similar rhetorical situation when studying press conferences with the leaders of the four parties forming the Swedish government. The particular events they study are press conferences in which politicians present major policy issues. Although the four parties' ideologies differ significantly in some important matters, it is crucial for them to appear united – to present a joint front – and this is handled through certain uses of the personal and plural pronoun, 'we'. For instance, the prime minister, who starts the speech phase, addresses subsequent utterances from the other politicians, which is a way to demonstrate their co-ordinated opinions. He does so by repeatedly using 'we' to refer to the actions of the four parties as a unit. Another key strategy is the use of a block of plural pronouns, as in the following example, in which one of the politicians (the leader of the Centre Party, Maud Olofsson) underlines the four parties being united as if one:

Example 1

    Politician: we are saying half of our energy shall be renewable
                  we are saying that ten percent of our energy in transport shall be renewable

we are saying that we must increase the energy efficiency by twenty percent and we are saying that we shall reduce emissions by forty percent...
(Moberg and Eriksson 2013)

Here the politician starts in the same way in four clauses in a row ('we are saying'), and she thereby demonstrates the government is talking with one voice. Although 'we' can be used in such a way that its reference is vague and signals ambiguousness in political matter, it can also, as Moberg and Eriksson (2013) show, be used to demonstrate a united front and tone down ideological differences.

The question-and-answer session

The political speech is typically followed by a session in which journalists pose questions and the politician provides answers. This is a moment when journalists can perform their role as a public watchdog institution and hold politicians accountable for their words and actions, a phase considered as absolutely crucial for the press conference as an arrangement for political communication (Clayman et al. 2006, 2007; Ekström 2009; Eriksson & Östman 2013). The interaction involves power in at least two related aspects: the actors' access to the floor (territorial power), and the power over the topic agenda and actions performed, negotiated through the exchange of questions and answers.

The journalists' access to the floor is regulated through pre-planned arrangements and negotiations in the interaction. Modern press conferences are public events that are often open to all accredited journalists. The time given for questions from journalists, however, varies. Press conferences are more or less strictly scheduled, and there are sometimes reasons for the organisers to limit the interrogation session. This can almost reduce the event to the individual voice of the politician.

The journalists' access to the floor also depends on the intensity of competition during the question-answer sessions. There are prestigious, high-intensity, live-broadcast events involving struggles for the floor between politicians and journalists and within the group of journalists. By asking questions in competitive contexts, the journalists not only influence the topical and action agendas that politicians have to deal with, but at the same time, they perform in positions of power and status. As part of their public-relations activities, government officials, however, also issue invitations to press conferences that receive such low interest from journalists that they are closed before the deadline.

The allocation of journalists' questions can be pre-scheduled in different ways. There are press conferences in which the journalists are expected to announce their questions in advance. Often, there is a formal or informal division within the group of journalists, based on the medium they represent and their status, which manifests itself according to where they are seated in the room and in the order in which they are invited to ask a question. Research based on conversation analysis has shown how the allocation of question turns is negotiated during the interaction (Ekström 2009). The politicians have potential power in their roles as both interviewee and as chairperson who selects the next speaker. The journalists are often selected by the politician as a second pair part response to a hand gesture, or they self-select and start talking without being invited. In some situations, the politicians make use of their role as a chair to avoid risky reporters or non-preferable follow-up questions (cf. Eriksson 2011; Eshbaugh-Soha 2003). In a study of George W Bush's press conferences, Ekström (2009) shows how the president uses his position to interrupt initiatives for self-selections and follow-ups and also to prevent self-selections by latching the selection of the next speaker onto his answering turns. Compared to individual interviews, the question-and-answer session in a press conference can be challenging for politicians if they encounter a number of journalists who have planned their best and toughest questions. However, a group of competing journalists can also be a resource for politicians who, in their role as a chair, can control the allocation of turns and, for example, interrupt follow-ups on the (normative) grounds that other people also have to ask their questions (Ekström 2009).

What has been discussed as *politically controlled* versus *journalist-controlled* press conferences are, to a large extent, the result of the various regulations of territorial power already discussed. This distinction is best understood, not as a dichotomy, but rather as a matter of degree. It can be used to explore differences between press conferences in various institutional settings, political events and political cultures. Yan and Tsan-Kuo (2012), for example, show how the regulation of question turns in the Chinese premier's press conferences make these events highly politically controlled. The question-answer session that followed the political speech included a few questions from selected media organisations, which were mainly decided by the political administration.

The design of questions is the key resource available for journalists to not only search for information, but also to influence the interactions and the context for political performances. Based on conversation analysis, Clayman and Heritage (2002; see also Clayman et al. 2006, 2007, 2010) show how questions alternatively set the topical and action agenda that politicians have to handle in their role as interviewees. The politicians can use strategies to – either overtly or covertly – evade questions, shift the agenda and perform actions not asked for. The questions, however, create conditions and expectations in relation to the answers, which can be recognised as particular actions. Clayman and Heritage explore the variety of resources in question designs used by journalists to put pressure on politicians, to criticize and create potential communicative conflicts, without having to take a clear stance while staying within the role of a formal neutral interrogator. An often-occurring technique is to refer statements to a third party, a move that is conceived of (with reference to Goffman) as a 'footing shift' (Clayman & Heritage 2002). In the following example, which comes from a press conference with the Swedish government the journalist makes such a shift by referring a statement to political opponents.

Example 2

> Interviewer: the opposition says that of these ten billions that you are assigning to labor market policies the main part goes to unemployment benefits is that correct?
>
> (Eriksson, Larsson & Moberg 2013, p. 116)

In this case, the opponents are identified as the alliance of political opponents, but footing shifts can also be achieved with reference to unspecified parties in constructions such as 'many people claim that' or 'critics say that'.

This research on question design has deepened our knowledge about how journalists enact the 'watchdog role' and critically scrutinise politicians' words and actions in the interactional phase. A key work is Clayman and colleagues' historical investigations of journalistic interrogations, focusing on the levels and changes of aggressiveness (Clayman et al. 2006, 2007, 2010). Based on detailed analyses of question design, they have developed a conceptualisation of five overall dimensions: initiative, directness, assertiveness, adversarialness and accountability. The conceptualisation is applied in empirical studies of president–journalist relationships from the 1950s to the 2000s. They found that from the Nixon era (1969–1974) journalists' questions became increasingly more characterised by directness and adversarialness, and journalists paid more attention to accountability. Generally, the study provides evidence for a normative shift in journalism in the 1960s and 1970s towards a more critical style of political interviewing. The level of aggressiveness is, however, dependent on contextual factors. The journalists, for example, tend to be significantly less critical when interviewing a president on foreign affairs.

The post-interviews

The post-interviews are, in many cases, an important part of a press conference, in particular from the perspective of journalism. In relation to the more public events, the post-interviews represent an exclusive context for questioning. The situations can be competitive for the journalists. The exclusivity not only concerns the particular questions that individual journalists would like to ask and the information and answers they hope to obtain, but in the production of broadcast news, the exclusiveness also relates to the production format as such and the fact that sound bites from individual interviews are often preferred to sound bites from the question-and-answer session. The individual interview displays journalists at work undertaking interviews. It is considered an important format to produce voices possible to use in segments of news stories. As in non-live interviews in general, these communicative activities involve particular asymmetries of relevance when it comes to power. Experienced politicians design their answers with respect to the potential to include all single utterances in a news report. However, the journalists not only set the topic and action agenda through their questions, but also decide what utterances are in the end treated as quote-worthy and how they are edited and recontextualised into the news reports (Ekström & Kroon Lundell 2010).

Press conferences and news production: the recontextualisation of political voices and actions

Press conferences are a crucial part of the news production process and the routine report on political institutions' activities, at least for high-status media (Eriksson & Östman 2013). Previous research on news journalism shows that news production relies on detailed organisation, routinised working procedures, established networks of sources, and that following political institutions is essential (see, e.g. Tuchman 1978; Gans 1979; Golding & Elliot 1979). After all, politics is, as McNair (2000, p. 43) states, 'the staple food of journalistic work', and press conferences typically provide pre-scheduled events. In reporting on governmental activities, journalism at the same time demonstrates an authoritative role in democracy. It is also central to how journalists perceive themselves. They see one of the most important journalistic enterprises as monitoring politicians and political institutions (Wiik 2009).

In relationship to press conferences, journalistic work can be described as a process consisting of several different moments or phases (Eriksson & Östman 2013). As press conferences take place on the initiative of political institutions, journalists normally receive a press release announcing time, place and theme for the event. How they are scheduled and what agenda is announced partly influence editorial decisions to prioritise events and also how journalists plan and prepare for possible news stories. The activities during the press conference – the speech, the question-and-answer session and the post-interviews – are opportunities for journalists to obtain (and produce) statements or comments that can be used to quote or cite in other ways in the news report, something that is crucial for news production (Kroon Lundell & Ekström 2010; Kroon Lundell & Eriksson 2010).

Even if the question-and-answer sessions of press conferences can be considered an 'adversarial moment' where the watchdog function can be performed, they are clearly characterised by co-operation between journalists and politicians. Studies of Swedish press conferences demonstrate that many of them are characterised by an *exchange model* (see Blumler & Gurevitch 1995) and shaped by a mutual dependency (Eriksson & Östman 2013; Eriksson, Larsson & Moberg 2013). For journalists, there are often good reasons for this. To produce news items, journalists need valid information and the collaborative approach can be a fruitful way to obtain such information.

The news-construction phase, following the interactional phase, is the moment when diverse material and data are assembled, edited and made ready for publication (Eriksson & Östman 2013; cf. Cook 1998; Reich 2006). Depending on whether the news product is published in a newspaper, aired on the radio, or broadcast on TV, the character of this moment of production will vary, but the end product – the particular news item – will be a heavily edited text. This phase thus involves discursive practices through which political voices are transformed into news and represented as particular actions.

A particular question explored in a few empirical studies is how political talk influences the news media. Based on a comparison of transcripts from a selection of US presidential press conferences from 1990 to 2010 and transcripts from the *CBS Evening News*, Eshbaugh-Soha (2013, p. 549) concluded that the news reports 'rely heavily on the president's own words'. The study measured the extent to which such words appeared in the news. The empirical result suggests that press conferences are effective ways for the president to influence the news agenda. As indicated by the author in the conclusion, the study, however, does not reveal how the words were used in the news, that is, how political voices (and actions) are recontextualised in the news discourse.

This is investigated by Eriksson and Östman (2013) who explore how statements from press conferences are compared and played out against other sources, often in ways that imply criticism of the initial political source. Criticism could, for instance, be ascribed by directly or indirectly quoting oppositional politicians, or, as in Example 3, be ascribed by journalism itself.

Example 3

> One day he makes an agreement on budget policy with two EU-hostile parties, at least one of which, the Green Party, does not consider economic growth to be a central issue. The next day he puts forward a government declaration that reshuffles the cabinet with an orientation toward the EU and economic growth.
>
> (*Dagens Nyheter* 7 October 1998)

In this case the text points out discrepancies between the politician's different actions.

Eriksson's and Östman's study show that journalists often add a high level of criticism when press-conference utterances and actions are reported in news stories, and they suggest that an adversary model is the most valid way to grasp what takes place in this phase of news production. After attending a press conference, journalists work independently of the initial source, that is, the politician, and they also include other actors. They contact other sources who represent alternative perspectives and can take a critical stance of the initial source. But, by using certain discursive techniques, it is also possible for journalists to criticize the initial source without using the voices of other actors. In the Swedish context, this latter form of criticism was the most common form in the news-construction phase (Eriksson & Östman 2013). This confirms previous studies showing that the various methods and devices used when voices (from interviews and press conferences) are quoted, referred to, and recontextualised in, news discourse, constitute key resources when news journalists adopt the expected critical stance in relation to the political elite (Ekström 2001).

Summary

The press conference, in its various forms, represents an institutionalised arena for political actions and journalistic interrogations. They have a ceremonial character, and they can serve as symbolic representations of public political accountability, but they are also a context in which political discourses are articulated, (re)enacted and negotiated. In this chapter, we have shown how press conferences have evolved over time as part of a growing mutual dependency between political institutions and journalists. We have suggested that press conferences are analysed as both platforms for strategic political communication, genres, contexts for audience-orientated talk and interaction, and resources in news production.

Press conferences are frontstage activities that take place on the initiative of political institutions and are characterised by discursive and rhetorical strategies aimed at achieving particular political goals, to convincingly present policies or reforms, to show a shared front (e.g. between states or within governments), or to manage criticism and crises. The introducing political speech is, as demonstrated by previous research (Bhatia 2006; Moberg & Eriksson 2013), crucial for these strategies. The following question-and-answer session is the part of the conference when journalists can perform the watchdog role by posing challenging questions to politicians. Politicians can, to some extent, regulate the talk by choosing the next speaker and preventing follow-up questions, but journalists can nevertheless scrutinise the politicians' words and deeds and pursue evasive or vague answers when they get the floor. It is more or less routine for high-status news media to report from press conferences, and this is the phase when political statements are recontextualised and integrated in news stories. Views from other sources can be added and played out against press-conference statements. Other information can be included in ways that imply criticism of these statements. Research on Swedish press conferences has shown that while the interactional phase is best characterised by a co-operative model, the news-construction phase is best characterised by an adversarial model as news stories generally involve criticism aimed at the initial political source.

References

Angouri, J & Wodak, R, 2014, '"They became big in the shadow of the crisis": The Greek success story and the rise of the far right', *Discourse & Society*, vol. 25, no. 4, pp. 540–565.

Asp, K & Esaiasson, P, 1996, 'The modernization of Swedish campaigns: Individualization, professionalization, and medialization', in *Politics, media and modern democracy: An international study of innovations in electoral campaigning and their consequences*, eds. D L Swanson & P Mancini, Praeger, Westport, CT, pp. 73–90.

Banning, S A & Billingsley, S, 2007, 'Journalist aggressiveness in joint versus solo presidential press conferences', *Mass Communication & Society*, vol. 10, no. 2, pp. 461–78.

Bhatia, A, 2006, 'Critical Discourse Analysis of political press conferences', *Discourse & Society*, vol. 17, no. 2, pp. 173–203.
Blumler, J G & Gurevitch, M, 1995, *The crisis of public communication*, Routledge, London.
Clayman, S E, 2006, 'Arenas of interaction in the new media era', in *News from the interview society*, eds. M Ekström, Å Kroon & M Nylund, Nordicom, Göteborg, pp. 239–64.
Clayman, S E & Heritage, J, 2002, 'Questioning presidents: journalistic deference and adversarialness in the press conferences of U.S. Presidents Eisenhower and Reagan', *Journal of Communication*, vol. 52, no. 4, pp. 749–75.
Clayman, S E, Elliott, M N, Heritage, J & Beckett, M K, 2010, 'A watershed in White House journalism: Explaining the post-1968 rise of aggressive presidential news', *Political Communication*, vol. 27, no. 3, pp. 229–47.
Clayman, S E, Elliott, M N, Heritage, J & McDonald, L, 2006, 'Historical trends in questioning presidents, 1953–2000', *Presidential Studies Quarterly*, vol. 36, no. 4, pp. 561–83.
Clayman, S E, Heritage, J, Elliott, M N & McDonald, L, 2007, 'When does the watchdog bark? Conditions of aggressive questioning in presidential news conferences', *American Sociological Review*, vol. 72, no. 1, pp. 23–41.
Cook, T, 1998, *Governing with the news: The news media as a political institution*, University of Chicago Press, Chicago, IL.
Ekström, M, 2001, 'Politicians interviewed on television news', *Discourse & Society*, vol. 12, no. 5, pp. 563–584.
Ekström, M, 2009, 'Power and affiliation in presidential press conferences: A study on interruptions, jokes and laughter', *Journal of Language and Politics*, vol. 8, no. 3, pp. 386–415.
Ekström, M & Johansson, B, 2008, 'Talk Scandals', *Media, Culture & Society*, vol. 30, no. 1, pp. 61–79.
Eriksson, G, 2011, 'Follow-up questions in political press conferences', *Journal of Pragmatics*, vol. 43, no 14, pp. 3331–3344.
Eriksson, G & Eriksson, M, 2012, 'Managing political crisis: An interactional approach to "image repair" in political press conferences', *Journal of Communication Management*, vol. 16, no. 3, pp. 264–277.
Eriksson, G & Östman, J, 2013, 'Cooperative or adversarial? Journalists' enactment of the watchdog function in political news production', *International Journal of Press/Politics*, vol. 18, no. 3, pp. 304–324.
Eriksson, G, Larsson, L & Moberg, U, 2013, *Politikernas arena: En studie av presskonferenser på regeringsnivå* [*The politicians' arena: A study of press conferences with the government*]. Studentlitteratur, Lund, Sweden.
Eshbaugh-Soha, M, 2013, 'Presidential influence of the news media: The case of the press conference', *Political Communication*, vol. 30, no. 4, pp. 548–564.
Gans, H 1979, *Deciding what's news*, Pantheon Books, New York.
Goffman, E, 1959, *The presentation of self in everyday life*, Doubleday & Company Inc, New York.
Golding, P & Elliot, P, 1979, *Making the news*, Longman, London.
Hansson, S, 2015, 'Discursive strategies of blame avoidance in government: A framework for analysis', *Discourse & Society*, vol. 26, no. 3, pp. 297–322.
Kroon Lundell, Å & Ekström, M, 2010, 'Beyond the broadcast news interview: Specialized forms of interviewing in the making of television news', *Journalism Studies*, vol. 12, no. 2, pp. 172–187.
Kroon Lundell, Å & Eriksson, G, 2010, 'Interviews as communicative resource in news and current affairs broadcast', *Journalism Studies*, vol. 11, no. 1, pp. 20–35.
Kumar, M J, 2005, 'Source material: Presidential press conferences: The importance and evolution of an enduring forum', *Presidential Studies Quarterly*, vol. 35, no. 1, pp. 166–192.
Kumar, M J, 2007, *Managing the president's message: The White House communications operation*, Johns Hopkins University Press, Baltimore.
Larsson, L, 2012, 'From yearly to daily press meetings: The development of the government press relations in Sweden', *Public Relations Inquiry*, vol. 1, no. 3, pp. 257–283.

Mazzoleni, G & Schulz, W, 1999, 'Mediatization of politics: A challenge for democracy?' *Political Communication*, vol. 16, no. 3, pp. 247–261.
McNair, B, 2000, *Journalism and democracy: An evaluation of the political public sphere*, Routledge, London.
Moberg, U & Eriksson, G, 2013, 'Managing ideological differences in joint political press conferences: A study of the strategic use of the personal pronoun "we"', *Journal of Language and Politics*, vol. 12, no. 3, pp. 315–334.
Reich, Z, 2006, 'The process model of news initiative: Sources lead first, reporters thereafter', *Journalism Studies*, vol. 7, no 4, pp. 497–514.
Strömbäck, J, 2008, 'Four phases of mediatization: An analysis of the mediatization of politics', *The International Journal of Press/Politics*, vol. 13, no. 3, pp. 228–246.
Tuchman, G, 1978, *Making news: A study in the construction of reality*, The Free Press, New York.
Wiik, J, 2009, 'Identities under construction: Professional journalism in a phase of destabilization', *International Review of Sociology*, vol. 19, no. 2, pp. 351–365.
Wodak, R, 2011, *The discourse of politics in action: Politics as usual*, Palgrave Macmillan, Basingstoke.
Yan, Y & Chang, T-K, 2012, 'Institutionalizing public relations in China: A sociological analysis of the Chinese premier's press conference', *Public Relation review*, vol. 38, no. 5, pp. 711–722.

23
Policy-making
Documents and laws

Kristof Savski

Introduction

In this chapter, I see policies and laws as located at the intersection of two major fields, whose social practices, discourse and unique organisation (Bourdieu 1984) define the textual genres that constitute them (cf. Bhatia 2004). Many of these practices, actors and communities are linked to *politics*, a fluid field oriented towards shaping the exercise of state power, but whose boundaries are routinely redrawn in public discourse (Jessop 2014). It is this close relation to politics that differentiates policy from *law*, which is ultimately a much more strictly bounded field with an established historical narrative, settings, actors and linguistic practices (e.g. Tiersma 1999). In the following, I discuss how the social roles of policy and law impact linguistic approaches to the texts or genres that constitute both those fields.

Fairclough understands a genre as 'a relatively stable set of conventions that is associated with, and partly enacts, a socially ratified type of activity' (Fairclough 1992, p. 126). Investigating genres can therefore be carried out from two perspectives: from the text itself, with a close linguistic analysis of the language choices made in it, or from the practices in which it is embedded (cf. Bhatia 2004). This chapter attempts to take both perspectives into account, and most importantly, to create links between them by showing the ways in which policies and legal texts reflect the practices of which they are products. The core of the chapter is therefore devoted to three interlocking key areas of investigation outlined in the following.

In the case of policies and laws, the activities or social practices that the texts reflect and enact are geared towards the exercise of power within a certain community: in order to achieve a certain set objective, policies and laws mandate or ban certain types of activities. Policies and laws are therefore intrinsically linked to organisational structure and hierarchy, and can be seen as an exercise of institutional power that is dependent on the trust of the members of the community where it is to be applied (see, e.g. Jenkins 2007). In the case of state policy, this, for example, refers to the pre-supposed universal acceptance of the state as acting in common interest and following general will (Jessop 1990, p. 341). One section of this chapter therefore focuses on how analysing the genres that constitute policy and law also involve analysing the organisation they are embedded in.

However, policies and laws are not only about 'making rules': from a discursive perspective, every policy or law codifies a particular construction of social reality, and the transformative goal as well as the projected means required to achieve that goal are part and parcel of this construction (Levinson, Sutton & Winstead 2009, p. 770). From this perspective, the making of policies and laws is also a site of constant tension between different world-views or ideologies, and has evolved as a set of practices to allow for this tension to be overcome in the search for consensus. The law or policy text, itself most often the work of several different authors, is located at the meeting point of these commonly opposed views (e.g. Savski 2016a; Wodak 2000). The second focus of this chapter is therefore on analysing the genesis of such texts and, by extension, the different interests that collide within them.

However, while policy- and law-making go hand in hand with social power and hierarchy, this does not mean that it should be seen as a simple and linear top-down imposition of will. Just as 'the state' (or any organisation for that matter) is not an actor in itself, but an array of spaces that offer various actors unequal opportunities to exercise power (Jessop 2007, p. 37), policy- and law-making can be seen as a diverse spectrum of possible constraints of structure and openings for agency. Another set of major questions to be addressed is therefore when such opportunities for agency come about, who is able to take advantage of them, and what they are able to achieve through policy (cf. Levinson, Sutton & Winstead 2009). The final section in this chapter therefore focusses on analysing what happens to policies and laws once they become durable and officially adopted texts, and different audiences begin to engage with their contents.

Each of these three sections overviews the concepts that are key to understanding their respective area, and also overview existing studies as well as proposing different analytical frameworks that can help prospective analysts collect and understand their data at these different levels. Each section also includes a short illustrative case study that is intended to show how relevant concepts can be applied to a specific example policy. As these three areas, when seen from a linguistic perspective, build on an existing tradition of analysing legal language, the following section is intended to bridge the gap between them by providing a brief overview of this established field of inquiry.

The language of policies and laws

In recent history, a number of researchers have examined the language associated with the fields of law and policy. In the broadest sense, this includes, not only analyses of the language of policies and laws or statutes, but also language use in the courtroom (e.g. Cotterill 2003), in mediation sessions (e.g. Conley & O'Barr 1998), all of which are seen as sub-fields in the larger field of 'legal language' (e.g. Melinkoff 1963). Though the scope of this chapter is somewhat different, as it focuses mostly on policy-making from the governmental perspective, the characteristics of legal language described by these authors are also highly relevant as they remain central text-internal criteria for what is considered a law or policy – though text-external criteria play an equally key part, as discussed below.

As the social role of policies and laws is to establish norms (though they are not necessarily binding, as discussed below), it is understandable that linguistic resources commonly used to express obligation and/or volition are common in legal texts. In English-language legal texts, the deontic modal 'shall' was traditionally used to express legal obligation and 'may' to confer power to an actor or institution (Charnock 2009; Maley 1994). However, as Williams (2009) indicates, the growing demands for clearer modes of expression in the late twentieth century has meant that many legislative texts now avoid 'shall' in favour of other modes of expressing obligation, such as the present simple tense.

Legal texts make great use of terminology, often drawing on several different codes (e.g. an English text may include expressions in Latin and French). As such texts aim to avoid any possible ambiguity or lack of clarity, their lexis is also characterised by frequent repetitions, and conversely, infrequent use of pro-forms or synonyms (Maley 1994; Williams 2004). Similarly, legal texts will often include a section where key terms are defined to avoid any possible uncertainty resulting from cases where a single term has been used with different meanings across different texts. However, to enable flexible application of legislation, such texts are also typically written in a highly generic manner, creating a constant tension between the two extremes of unambiguity and flexibility (Engberg & Heller 2008; Maley 1994).

Another key characteristic of legal texts is the fact that, while they were written by a set of actors (often in a complex genesis, see below), they are ultimately not associated with those writers. Rather, they become associated with the institution or polity that they govern. In Goffman's terms, while the *authors* of the text, that is, those who provided the words it contains, are backgrounded, the text becomes associated almost exclusively with a *principal*, that is, the actor or institution who is committed to the words and whose beliefs or authority they represent (Goffman 1981, pp. 144–145). For example, EU legislation typically begins with a statement setting out the principal, such as 'The Council of the European Union […] has adopted this regulation'.

Analysing policy genres in institutional context

For contemporary analyses of policies and laws, the tradition of analysing legal language continues to be of importance, as it provides a key means of distinguishing what is typical in such texts from what is atypical and therefore of potential interest. However, legal texts are not defined only by their language use, but also, and perhaps more dramatically so, by their shared discursive characteristics. As already mentioned, a key feature of such texts is that they attempt to oblige or forbid certain actions or practices: they do so by constructing a particular picture of the state of affairs in society, and the norms they aim to impose on society reflect a particular social set of social values, that is, a particular view of what society should be like (Levinson, Sutton & Winstead 2009). Laws and policies are therefore expressions of the particular moralities and/or ideologies that exist in their context, and their analysis should take this into account.

However, as the language used in legal texts and policies is often highly economised and condensed, creating a link between a particular feature of such a text and any ideologies in its context can be a major challenge if the text is analysed simply *in and of itself*. Instead, analysing policy texts is an exercise of constant recursion, that is, of constant interaction between the macro-, meso- and micro-levels of analysis. In practice this means, for example, examining a sentence in a policy text in light of its linguistic structure, its immediate co-text, the entire text, the policy-making practices that produced the sentence, the political agenda in which it is embedded, and finally how that sentence is understood by the different readers of the policy text.

One key consideration is therefore the question of what makes a particular text a policy: if not merely its form, is it its author, the institutional power it is associated with, or the way it was written and/or distributed within that particular polity? For instance, while a 'policy' in the contemporary state can take the form of a law, a strategy, a programme, or a white paper, with each of these having a particular status in the polity (see below for an example). In a different type of context, such as a small business, a policy can be an email sent out by the CEO to every employee. As they are both legitimated by the hierarchical structure of the polity, both will be accepted as 'policies' by its members (citizens or employees), though their linguistic form may ultimately be different.

Analysing this complexity requires a multi-levelled view of context, such as that proposed by Wodak (2008, pp. 10–14), and a recursive approach, where the different levels are explored flexibly, with the scope of contextualisation being constantly adjusted depending on what facets are highlighted as relevant by the data. Table 23.1 offers several policy-relevant potential research questions for each level.

To answer such research questions, recent linguistic analyses of policy have drawn on different types of data sets. Grue's (2009) analysis of discourses about disability in the policies of a Norwegian non-governmental organisation (NGO) covered the documents written in response to various legislative initiatives, as well as the programme statements of the NGO itself. In her historical investigation of UK educational policy, Mulderrig (2011) created a corpus of policy documents adopted by the UK government between 1972 and 2005. Other analyses have preferred to broaden their scope, and have included not only traditional 'policy documents', but also secondary sources of policy discourse. While approaching the same broad topic as Mulderrig – trends in educational policy in light of broader discourses – Holm and Londen's (2010) study of Finnish multicultural education policy relies on a data set adapted to the field of inquiry, including not only government strategies, but also national and local curricula, an important secondary genre in that field. To show the various considerations guiding data collection when conducting such research, I overview how various studies of policy in the European Union have responded to its complexity by gathering broader data sets.

Example: policy genres in the European Union

The way EU policy texts are related to each other is governed by the EU's complex institutional and multilingual structure. The EU has 24 official languages as of 2015, and it

Table 23.1 Levels of context and their relevance to policy

Level of context	Research questions for policy analysis
Co-text and co-discourse	What is the relationship between the different parts of a policy text? Has the text changed during drafting? Does this reflect the existence of multiple voices in the surrounding discourse?
Intertextuality and interdiscursivity	How does the text relate to other current or past policies in the same area, or in other areas? How does the policy text relate to those from other polities (e.g. EU-level vs. member state)?
Social and institutional properties of the context	What are the policy-making practices in the polity and what is their relevance to the policy text? What key actors became involved with the policy during its development?
Socio-political and historical context	How is the policy embedded in broader social and political processes? What is its relation to dominant historical narratives?

has its own set of language policies to deal with the complexity that this can cause, with one key principle being that policy texts are equivalent irrespective of which official language they are in. However, the situation is more complex: even though these 24 languages are *de jure* equal in EU institutions, there are *de facto* conventions that govern language choice, particularly in smaller, informal settings. Here, the more dominant working languages have a privileged status, and knowledge of them is a key strategic advantage for political actors (Wodak, Krzyżanowski & Forchtner 2012). In terms of the way policy texts are produced, and the status they have, this therefore indicates that the relationship between different language variants of the same policy text is not necessarily equal.

As a polity, the EU is a complex multi-level organisation whose 'politics and policy-making must be seen as inherently bound by the constant mediation between different (i.e. European, national and regional) levels of governance and between different level-specific institutions' (Krzyżanowski 2013, p. 109). There are three major institutions, the European Parliament (representing party interests), the European Council (representing state governments) and the European Commission (the 'European government') – all three share policy-making duties and must thus find agreement on key points. Due to the potentially overwhelming complexity that this entails, policy-making practices in the EU have developed to ensure that consensus is reached at an early stage (Huber & Shackleton 2013). While this has improved efficiency, it also means that policy-making has been effectively shifted out of public sight, and that a compromise has been made on democracy (Krzyżanowski 2013).

Another key property that defines EU policies is their complex relation to policies in the member states. In principle, EU policy is intended to take precedence over various national policies, and is considered to be binding to various extents, depending on the genre to which a particular policy is assigned (see below). To facilitate this, policy texts are written with a view towards enabling flexible application across the various different national contexts, although the extent to which they are implemented, or the pace of their enactment, varies greatly across these member states (Falkner et al. 2005), and the dynamics of recontextualisation of EU policy therefore differ from state to state (e.g. Wodak & Fairclough 2010).

This complexity means that several different genres are available to EU policy-makers. The exact status of these is set by another text, the Treaty on the Functioning of the European Union (2007):

> To exercise the Union's competences, the institutions shall adopt regulations, directives, decisions, recommendations and opinions.
> A regulation shall have general application. It shall be binding in its entirety and directly applicable in all Member States.
> A directive shall be binding, as to the result to be achieved, upon each Member State to which it is addressed, but shall leave to the national authorities the choice of form and methods.
> A decision shall be binding in its entirety. A decision which specifies those to whom it is addressed shall be binding only on them.
> Recommendations and opinions shall have no binding force.
> (Article 288, ex-Article 289 in the Treaty of the European Union)

To a certain extent, this text also codifies the policy-making practices through which others are produced. This is, however, not exclusive, as various other practices and genres are not prescribed in this way. Genres such as *Green papers* and *White papers* serve to highlight a particular area for future policy intervention at EU level, and potentially also an early vision of what the scope of such a policy would be. Additionally, a number of genres co-exist in the related field of policy communication, such as leaflets, fact-sheets, and so on. Rather than establishing policy directly, these are directed specifically at mediating policy objectives, priorities and decisions to various interested publics (Krzyżanowski 2013).

Analyses of EU policy have integrated many of these different genres into their data collection, aiming both to create a better account of policy discourse in a particular area, as well as to show its development through time, from early agenda-setting documents to binding legislation. Krzyżanowski (2013), for instance, shows how a major discursive shift occurred in EU environmental policy between 2007 and 2011, and how this was first announced by changes in green papers, intended to stimulate a broad public debate, before being integrated into other genres, which began to specify future policy action in more concrete terms. Krzyżanowski and Wodak (2011) take an even broader approach in their historical analysis of EU language policy, examining not only policy texts, but also speeches and surveys to show how EU discourse about multilingualism was embedded into a larger-scale political agenda.

Analysing the genesis of policy texts

As I discuss above, policy is an area where different world-views come into contact, and often, into conflict. With any policy, the engagement of actors or communities with different backgrounds means that potentially competing policy meanings are generated (see below). These reflect the different situated understandings of social reality, different concerns and proposals for solutions that such actors will have. From the earliest stages of planning and drafting, policy texts constantly come into contact with such communities as various public consultations are conducted (Scollon 2008).

This ultimately contributes to the creation of a polyphonic policy text containing the voices of different actors (Savski 2016b), which, while being interwoven and dialogically linked (see Bakhtin 1981), remain distinct and separate, reflecting the power relations between the actors contributing to the policy (Wodak 2000). All these voices are artificially merged with the finalisation of the policy text (Wodak 2000) and become associated with the authority of the polity in which they apply (Tiersma 2010).

Reconstructing these voices is therefore one possible approach to policy-text analysis. Ideally, this can be done directly if the researcher is granted access to the drafting process: Wodak (2000), for example, combines observation with textual analysis to show how the language of an EU document on unemployment developed as different stakeholders made contributions to it. In many cases, however, access to such backstage settings is not possible, and in such cases, the researcher has to employ alternative methods of data collection. Often, while meetings cannot be accessed, early drafts and feasibility studies can be found and can yield useful information about key issues, particularly if combined with research interviews. Examining different policy genres (see p. 357) can also be a useful tool in identifying the key trends in the genesis of a policy document.

Example: the genesis of a Slovene language policy document

Studying policy in the contemporary state presents a new challenge, as the researcher has to take into account the dynamic character of mediatised late-modern politics – where constructing a distinctive and likeable identity is as important as providing reasoned arguments (see, e.g. Wodak 2011, 2015). An example that typifies this is the Resolution for a National Language Policy Programme for 2014–2018 (RLP-14), a strategic document intended to establish a common frame of reference for all state institutions involved in language policy. The text was drafted over an extended period of time, from 2010 to 2013, during which time, a number of political shifts occurred in Slovenia.

In 2010, under the left-centre government led by social democrat Prime Minister Borut Pahor, several preparatory studies were conducted to set the format of the future strategy, and a drafting team began to write the text in mid 2011. However, by the time the first draft of RLP-14 was finished at the end of 2011, Pahor's government had collapsed, a snap election had taken place and a right-centre government under Janez Janša took power. This signalled a change of agenda, and following a public consultation regarding RLP-14, a new team was named and began a major rewrite of the existing text. By January 2013, this rewrite had been completed, and a new version of the text was published, creating a hybrid document that already contained several different voices, which can be uncovered by analysing the additions, deletions and rephrasings made during the redrafting (Wodak 2000).

As the examples in Table 23.2 demonstrate, the rewrite of RLP-14 enabled a major change in the Slovene language policy agenda and signalled a broader ideological shift in the text itself. While the original version had prioritised the area of multilingualism and minority rights as one where major improvement was needed, the rewritten version saw various hedging devices being used to reduce the force of such statements (Example 1). More generally, the new version moved away from the earlier text's equal treatment of different minorities, and established clear boundaries between the indigenous minorities protected by the Slovene constitution, and the non-indigenous minorities, or immigrants (see Example 2). Elsewhere, the focus of the text was shifted from the promotion of a development-minded and tolerant society to the protection of a monolingual Slovene-speaking community (see Example 3).

These changes indicate that the change of government sparked a major ideological shift in RLP-14: instead of a late-modern language ideology, to which values such as mobility and diversity are central, the text was now predominantly based on a more traditional nationalist ideology centred on a rigid levelling of nation, language and state (Savski 2016b). However, in many cases, only small changes had been made to the existing wordings to achieve this, creating a hybrid text, one which contained elements pertaining to both language ideologies, and written by two different drafting teams. This is the case with most,

Table 23.2 Comparison of RLP-14, first and second draft (deletions crossed out, additions underlined)

1	Alongside this, [the minority members'] rights to use their own language and culture must be guaranteed within legal and budgetary means.
2	At the same time, the Republic of Slovenia cares for the strengthening and full enactment of the language rights of the constitutionally defined minorities, and enables the maintenance and revitalisation of the use of languages of other language communities and immigrants.
3	A language policy oriented towards development is based on the belief that the Slovene state, Slovene language, and Slovene language community are vital and dynamic entities, which should be developed and strengthened ~~in a way that will enable all inhabitants to live in freedom, welfare, as well as tolerance and responsibility~~. In those areas which require special care in order to maintain the scale, vitality and dynamicity of the Slovene language, measures must be ensured to improve the situation when required.

if not all, policy texts: despite their 'fixed' appearance, the many language choices made within them have been made by different actors with different belief systems and intentions. The importance of studying this genesis process becomes clear when examining the stage of policy implementation, when such individual pieces of language become crucial to how texts such as RLP-14 are put into action.

Analysing the trajectories of policy meanings

As texts, policies are intended for varied audiences: some have to allow for broad application, while others are written for a small audience, and only play an administrative role (Tiersma 2010, pp. 165–167). However, the ways in which such audiences 'read' policy are varied. Various scholars in the field of policy analysis have stressed that the interpretation of policy texts is a complex process where, depending on what epistemic community it encounters, such a text will be received differently (Yanow 2000; see also Stone 2012). This presents a move from traditional conceptualisations of policy implementation as a linear process with no space for agency, part of a 'linguistic turn' in policy analysis (Fischer & Forrester 1993).

Policy meanings are discursively constructed as actors engage with policy in various texts and contexts (Savski 2016a), such as the genres of policy communication (see p. 357), political speeches (Koller & Davidson 2008, p. 316) and local administrative settings tasked with the implementation of a policy (p. 363). In these contexts, both hegemonic as well as subversive policy meanings are constructed in the discourse that surrounds a policy text (Savski 2016a). Which policy meanings dominate this discourse, therefore, becomes a central issue when considering how policies are put into action by grass-roots actors (p. 362). This brings about a significant implication for the study of policy texts, as a clear-cut assumption of equivalence between sign and meaning is no longer possible (Hutton 2009).

To overcome the potential insecurity that this would bring to the legal system, different legal traditions have suggested a number of theories of statutory interpretation, which are intended to guide the decisions of actors interpreting laws and policies. In the British context, an early example of such a theory was the *plain meaning rule*, which broadly placed the focus on the 'ordinary' meanings of the language used by law-makers, rather than on the context (Tiersma 2010, p. 156). In the US, a number of competing theories also exist, such as *intentionalism*, which involves investigation of context to reconstruct the intentions of law-makers (*ibidem*, pp. 159–163). In European legal theory, a similar approach is *systematic interpretation*, which involves making comparisons between different legislative texts in order to arrive at a valid meaning (Schütze 2012, p. 137).

For policies to be successfully enacted in real-world situations, the language used in them has to be flexible enough to enable application in changed contexts, while also being precise enough to avoid unwanted ambiguity (Tiersma 1999, pp. 79–85). Two principle perspectives have developed in the study of policy implementation: a *top-down* view that studies implementation from the perspective of policy-makers, in terms of the generalizability of policy problems and solutions, and a *bottom-up* view, which looks at implementation from the standpoint of the local actors. The latter perspective sees local policy actors as key decision-makers who are afforded a large amount of agency in order to enact the different provisions of a policy (Lipsky 2010).

This focus on the role of individual actors in policy has led Levinson, Sutton and Winstead to propose the concept of *appropriation* instead of implementation, to indicate 'the ways that creative agents interpret and take in elements of policy, thereby incorporating these discursive resources into their own schemes of interest, motivation, and action' (Levinson, Sutton &

Winstead 2009, p. 779). The role of policy texts in appropriation is to open (or close) *ideological spaces*, potential policy meanings that enable these agents to pursue a particular policy agenda in the local *implementational spaces* available to them (Hornberger 2005).

Example: policy appropriation in a US school district

In 2002, US President George W. Bush signed into law the bipartisan No Child Left Behind Act (NCLB), an educational policy that aimed to improve student achievements across states and school districts, with a particular focus on improving the academic proficiency of socially and/or economically disadvantaged students. Its various provisions were distributed into several sub-sections (titles). Title III, entitled 'Language Instruction for Limited English Proficient and Immigrant Students', represented a particular shift from previous policy, as it foregrounded English proficiency, and saw bilingual education as a means to that goal, rather than a value in itself.

The initial version of that text was, in fact, almost exclusively focused on English-language education, and it was only after extensive negotiation in the two houses of the US Congress that a compromise version was finalised (Johnson 2009, pp. 147–149). The final Act was dominated by two voices, one advocating knowledge of English as a focus of bilingual education, supported particularly by members of the House of Representatives, and one that supported bilingual education and was mainly introduced through amendments made by members of the Senate (*ibidem*). As Johnson comments, this ultimately made the bill acceptable to both sides, as either could interpret the text according to its own interests (*ibidem*).

Johnson (2009, 2013a, 2013b) conducted a detailed ethnographic study of how Title III was appropriated by local actors in the Philadelphia school district. One of his particular interests was the role of local decision-makers, or *language policy arbiters*, particular individuals whose institutional role granted them the ability to dictate policy interpretation (Johnson 2013b). He interviewed two such arbiters, two administrators who held positions of power in the office that co-ordinated bilingual education in the district, and uncovered how different their interpretations of NCLB were:

> Dixon-Marquez and Sánchez [*the two school district administrators*] interpreted Title III in very different ways, which led to different forms of implementation of the policy. In a discussion about NCLB in 2003, which was then a new policy, Dixon-Marquez said, 'There's an emphasis on English language acquisition [in NCLB] but it doesn't mean that's all they're going to fund – we haven't changed our programs dramatically – we're pretty much going to do what we've been doing' (11 April 2003). What they 'had been doing' was further developing the additive bilingual programs in the district. Dixon-Marquez made this quite clear in her proposal to the Federal Department of Education, and, she got the money. So, it appears that her interpretation of Title III was not rejected by the Department of Education even though her intention was to use Title III money to support additive bilingual education programs.
>
> During the 2003–2004 school year, there was a shake-up of the administrative personnel in the ESOL/bilingual office and Lucia Sánchez stepped in as the head of the office. Her ideas about language education, in general, and her interpretation of Title III and the goals of NCLB, in particular, were very different than her predecessors. In a discussion about Title III, she said: 'Title III was created to improve English language acquisition programs by increasing the services or creating situations where the students

would be getting supplemental services to move them into English language acquisition situations' (13 June 2005). Sánchez' interpretation of Title III is much different than Dixon-Marquez' and this interpretation helped guide the implementation of Title III and radically changed the direction of language education in the school district. [...]
(Johnson 2013a, pp. 211–212; my addition in italics)

This demonstrates not only that a plurality of policy meanings can co-exist, but also that such meanings matter, or rather, that who is in a position to establish a preferred policy meaning is crucial to how policy is appropriated. In this case, one key finding of Johnson's study is that while NCLB narrowed the ideological space for bilingual education, a potential remained for local actors to find implementational spaces (Johnson 2013a, pp. 212–213). It was, however, down to the individual initiative and beliefs of the local actors to take advantage of such spaces. The fact that both administrators from the example successfully applied and won funding awarded on the basis of NCLB shows that decision-makers can be equally permissive of different policy interpretations (Johnson 2013a, p. 211).

Concluding remarks and future challenges

I have overviewed three perspectives of contemporary discourse-orientated policy analysis. Ideally, the three should be joined together to form a comprehensive analytical framework suitable to the research questions that guide a particular policy study. In practical terms, this is not always possible, for instance, if the policy being analysed was drafted entirely behind closed doors and only limited information regarding its genesis can be recovered. In such cases, the use of research interviews with key actors, coupled with a detailed review of the discourses surrounding a policy, can still enable the dominant voices within a policy text to be identified. Alternatively, following implementation processes can give policy analysts vital clues as to how the text is 'read', once again indicating the key discourses with which it interacts.

For many, if not most, discourse-orientated approaches to politics and policy-making, the *text* remains the primary object of analysis. However, as discussed, policy texts are characterised by their complex genesis, where the voices of multiple contributors become entangled before a final version is adopted. During this complex process, because different contributors can independently write and rewrite (or give advice on) various sections, the text can also be seen as a series of developing fragments rather than a homogeneous whole. In addition to this, the fact is that even when these texts are finalised and officially adopted, their meaning and function continue to be a matter of debate.

Hutton (2009) argues that all this is a major theoretical – as well as practical – challenge for the structuralist systemic view of language that still represents the intellectual foundation of much of contemporary linguistics. For a discipline that continues to largely assume that the meaning of a piece of language in a text can be isolated and generalised as part of a broader system, the very notion that textual meanings are context-bound and can be contested or changed is highly problematic (Hutton 2009, pp. 44ff). While his interpretation can be seen as an overgeneralisation, given the diverse nature of contemporary linguistics – Hutton himself acknowledges that there are currents in sociolinguistics that can and do take flexibility of meaning into account – it does serve as a reminder of the theoretical and methodological flexibility needed to approach such texts.

When considering policy interpretation, the relationship between *structure* and *agency* also requires some reconsideration. As I have highlighted above, policy texts have the potential to empower grass-roots actors, but it is often left to the initiative and creativity of such local 'policy-makers' to take advantage of such potential. However, as tools of top-down state power, policy texts can also disempower by limiting space for interpretation, and thus for agency. The key question to be answered here is whether these two explanations are ultimately two sides of the same coin, or whether one should ultimately be seen as more crucial to understanding contemporary politics.

Another challenge that requires a similarly flexible approach is the question of how to integrate the study of power and polyphony: if policies and legal texts are seen as fragments produced by different actors, how do we account for and describe the power relations between the different voices in the resulting text? Do we assume that the 'loudest' voice (i.e. the one that we find is most commonly 'heard' in the text) is hegemonic? Or do we examine how the text is read, and thus see whether the way it is interpreted is actually governed by the 'loudest' voice, or whether the reading in fact reflects the polyphonic nature of the text in a more inclusive manner?

References

Bakhtin, M M, 1981, *The dialogic imagination: four essays*, University of Texas Press, Austin, TX.
Bhatia, V K, 2004, *Worlds of written discourse: A genre-based view*, Continuum, London.
Bourdieu, P, 1984, *Distinction: a social critique of the judgement of taste*, Routledge, London.
Charnock, R, 2009, 'When may means must: Deontic modality in English statute construction' in *Modality in English: Theory and description*, eds. R Salkie, P Busuttil & J van der Auwera, Mouton De Gruyter, Berlin, pp. 177–198.
Conley, J M & O'Barr, W M, 1998, *Just words: law, language, and power*, The University of Chicago Press, Chicago, IL.
Cotterill, J, 2003, *Language and power in court: a linguistic analysis of the O. J. Simpson trial*, Palgrave Macmillan, Basingstoke.
Engberg, J & Heller, D, 2008, 'Vagueness and Indeterminacy in Law' in *Legal discourse across cultures and systems*, eds. V K Bhatia, C Candlin & J Engberg, Hong Kong University Press, Hong Kong, pp. 145–168.
Fairclough, N, 1992, *Discourse and social change*, Polity, Cambridge.
Falkner, G, Treib, O, Hartlapp, M & Leiber, S, 2005, *Complying with Europe: EU harmonisation and soft law in the member states*, Cambridge University Press, Cambridge.
Fischer, F & Forester, J, 1993, *The argumentative turn in policy analysis and planning*, Duke University Press, Durham, NC.
Goffman, E, 1981, *Forms of talk*, Blackwell, Oxford.
Grue, J, 2009, 'Critical discourse analysis, topoi and mystification: disability policy documents from a Norwegian NGO', *Discourse Studies*, vol. 11, no. 3, pp. 305–328.
Holm, G & Londen, M, 2010, 'The discourse on multicultural education in Finland: education for whom?', *Intercultural Education*, vol. 21, no. 2, pp. 107–120.
Hornberger, N H, 2005, 'Opening and filling up implementational and ideological spaces in heritage language education', *Modern Language Journal*, vol. 89, no. 4, pp. 605–609.
Huber, K & Shackleton, M 2013, 'Codecision: A practitioner's view from inside the Parliament', *Journal of European Public Policy*, vol. 20, no. 7, pp. 1040–1055.
Hutton, C, 2009, *Language, meaning and the law*, Edinburgh University Press, Edinburgh.
Jenkins, R, 2007, 'The meaning of policy/policy as meaning' in *Policy reconsidered: Meanings, politics and practices*, eds. S Hodgson & Z Irving, The Policy Press, Bristol, pp. 21–36.
Jessop, B, 1990, *State theory: Putting the capitalist state in its place*, Pennsylvania University Press, Pennsylvania.
Jessop, B, 2007, *State power: a strategic-relational approach*, Polity, Cambridge.

Jessop, B, 2014, 'Repoliticising depoliticisation: theoretical preliminaries on some responses to the American fiscal and Eurozone debt crises', *Policy and Politics*, vol. 42, no. 2, pp. 207–223.

Johnson, D C, 2009, 'Ethnography of language policy', *Language Policy*, vol. 8, no. 2, pp. 139–159.

Johnson, D C, 2013a, *Language Policy*, Palgrave Macmillan, Basingstoke.

Johnson, D C, 2013b, 'Positioning the language policy arbiter: Governmentality and footing in the School District of Philadelphia', in *Language policies in education: Critical issues*, 2nd ed., ed. J W Tollefson, Routledge, London, pp. 116–136.

Koller, V & Davidson, P, 2008, 'Social exclusion as conceptual and grammatical metaphor: A cross-genre study of British policy-making', *Discourse & Society*, vol. 19, no. 3, pp. 307–331.

Krzyżanowski, M, 2013, 'Policy, policy communication and discursive shifts: Analyzing EU policy discourses on climate change', in *Analysing genres in political communication: Theory and practice*, eds P Cap & U Okulska, John Benjamins, Amsterdam, pp. 101–134.

Krzyżanowski, M & Wodak, R, 2011, 'Political strategies and language policies: the European Union Lisbon strategy and its implications for the EU's language and multilingualism policy', *Language Policy*, vol. 10, no. 2, pp. 115–136.

Levinson, B, Sutton, M & Winstead, T, 2009, 'Educational policy as a practice of power: Theoretical tool, ethnographic methods, democratic options', *Educational Policy*, vol. 23, no. 6, pp. 767–795.

Lipsky, M, 2010, *Street-level bureaucracy: dilemmas of the individual in public services* (30th anniversary expanded ed.), Russell Sage Foundation, New York.

Maley, Y, 1994, 'The language of the law', in *Language and the law*, ed. J Gibbons, Longman, Harlow, pp. 11–50.

Melinkoff, D, 1963, *The language of the law*, Little, Brown & Co., Boston, MA.

Mulderrig, J, 2011, 'Manufacturing consent: a corpus-based critical discourse analysis of New Labour's educational governance', *Journal of Educational Philosophy and Theory*, vol. 43, no. 6, pp. 562–578.

Savski, K, 2016a, 'Language policy in time and space', in *Discursive approaches to language policy*, eds. E Barakos & J W Unger, Routledge, London, pp. 51–70.

Savski, K, 2016b, 'Analysing voice in language policy: Plurality and conflict in Slovene government documents', *Language Policy*, vol. 15, no. 4, pp 505–524.

Schütze, R, 2012, *European Constitutional Law*, Cambridge University Press, Cambridge.

Scollon, R, 2008, *Analyzing public discourse: Discourse analysis in the making of public policy*, Routledge, London.

Stone, D A, 2012, *Policy paradox: The art of political decision making*, 3rd ed., W W Norton & Co., New York.

Tiersma, P M, 1999, *Legal language*, University of Chicago Press, Chicago, IL.

Tiersma, P M, 2010, *Parchment, paper, pixels: Law and the technologies of communication*, The University of Chicago Press, Chicago, IL.

Williams, C, 2004, 'Legal English and plain language: An introduction', *ESP Across Cultures*, vol. 1, pp. 111–124.

Williams, C, 2009, 'Legal English and the "modal revolution"', in *Modality in English: Theory and description*, eds. R Salkie, P Busuttil & J. van der Auwera, Mouton de Gruyter, Berlin, pp. 199–210.

Wodak, R, 2000, 'From conflict to consensus? The co-construction of a policy paper', in *European Union discourses on un/employment: An interdisciplinary approach to employment, policy-making and organizational change*, eds. P Muntigl, G Weiss & R Wodak, Benjamins, Amsterdam, pp. 73–114.

Wodak, R, 2008, 'Introduction: Discourse Studies – important concepts and terms', in *Qualitative discourse analysis in the social sciences*, eds. R Wodak & M Krzyżanowski, Palgrave Macmillan, Basingstoke, pp. 1–29.

Wodak, R, 2011, *The discourse of politics in action: Politics as usual*, Palgrave Macmillan, New York.

Wodak, R, 2015, *The politics of fear*, Sage, London.

Wodak, R & Fairclough, N, 2010, 'Recontextualizing European higher education policies: The cases of Austria and Romania', *Critical Discourse Studies*, vol. 7, no. 1, pp. 19–40.

Wodak, R, Krzyżanowski, M & Forchtner, B, 2012, 'The interplay of language ideologies and contextual cues in multilingual interactions: Language choice and code-switching in European Union institutions', *Language in Society*, vol. 41, no. 2, pp. 157–186.

Yanow, D, 2000, *Conducting interpretive policy analysis*, Sage Publications, Thousand Oaks, CA.

24
The semiotics of political commemoration

Martin Reisigl

Introduction

Commemoration is a multimodal semiotic (including verbal) practice and – with respect to its purpose – an important political activity that serves the formation, reproduction and transformation of political identities. Typically, it is organised around the cyclical return of an occasion that relates to a meaningful moment in the past of a political community and its 'lessons' for the present and future. Commemoration involves the political dimension of polity, that is, the general framework for political action, including political culture, rules and values. With respect to this political dimension, commemoration primarily has an integrative function. However, it can also play a disintegrative role if negative experiences are recollected in order to stir up collective aversions towards an enemy.

The topic of political commemoration is dealt with in many disciplines, for example, in historical research (Koselleck & Jeismann 1994), sociology (Durkheim 1995, p. 487; Halbwachs 2002, 2004; Zerubavel 1995; Olick 2003; Zifonun 2004; Levy & Sznaider 2005), cultural studies (e.g. A Assmann 2006, 2007; J Assmann 2007), political science (Meyer 2003, 2009), geography (McDowell & Braniff 2014), and philosophy (Ricœur 2004). The present chapter cannot do justice to this wide-ranging field of research. It will primarily focus on salient semiotic dimensions of political commemoration.

This chapter is divided into five parts. It begins with an explanation and discussion of the fundamental characteristics of political commemoration. This followed by a description of the commemorative speech as a basic format of communication that allows for 'bringing to remembrance' a particular reading of the past in the context of a ritualised public event. The next section briefly focuses on important semiotic aspects of commemoration beyond the verbal dimension. It is followed by a look at the salient discursive features of political commemoration from the perspective of the Discourse-Historical Approach (DHA), taking Austrian commemoration as an example. The selective focus will concentrate on the representation of social actors and events, on argumentation referring to commemorated events, on tropes (metaphors, metonymies and synecdoches) relating to the commemorated past and the representation of historical changes as well as continuities. The chapter will be rounded up with a short conclusion.

Fundamental characteristics of political commemoration

Commemoration comes from the Latin noun *commemoratio*, which derives from the Latin verb *commemorare*. The verb is composed of the prefix *con* – which in our case becomes *com* due to the phonological contact assimilation, meaning 'altogether', and *memorare*, meaning 'relate', 'to mention from memory'. Literally, the etymology tells us that *commemoration* means 'remembering together', that some individuals come together and bring some things (people and and/or events) into remembrance. This means that commemoration is a social activity involving various people and various remembered things, and it means that commemoration does not just involve mental processes, but also verbal and other forms of semiotic externalisation. Commemoration is a joint multimodal performance, event and experience that includes speeches, images, music, material places with monuments and buildings, front- and backstage, platforms, stands, requisites, parades or processions.

Commemoration is a significant social, religious and political practice that serves the formation, reproduction and transformation of social, religious or political identities. During ancient times and the Middle Ages, commemoration only took place in ritualised religious, cult-related and magic-related contexts. From the period of Reformation and Enlightenment onwards, the state was gradually separated from religion and the political sphere gradually became secularised. Thus, commemoration also developed into a secular political practice. Historical events became an object of public ceremonies of remembrance, in which fights for liberation and independence, battles, victories, fallen 'heroes', national poets, and monarchs' birthdays and coronations were remembered. During this process of secularisation, many semiotic elements of formerly religious commemorations were adapted for political practice in order to institutionalise a 'national liturgy'. The commemorating religious community was transformed into a commemorating political community, the commemorative speech replaced the sermon, patriotic hymns and songs were substituted for religious chants (the introit, Kyrie and Gloria), the national anthem received the function of a chanted prayer, processions changed into (military) parades, and the patriot profession of faith replaced the Christian creed (Mosse 1993, pp. 28, 93, 97, etc.). The new secularised commemoration served the function of political integration and mobilisation of the bourgeoisie, which became a new collective political actor.

In order to promote national identification of the new 'collective political subject', commemorative references to matters of alleged national importance are instrumentalised, for instance, the reference to the birth, life or death of figures considered to be important for the political community (e.g. 'heroes' and 'founding fathers'), the reference to victims of political suppression, victories, defeats, catastrophes and fortunes, the reference to agreements, treaties or other political documents (e.g. a document that mentions the name of a political unit for the first time; see Reisigl 2007), the reference to the foundation of a state, political system or form of government, and the reference to the community itself or the formation of a new policy.

The nature of this 'collective' memory is of a special kind. It is not a 'common memory', but a 'shared memory'. This conceptual distinction has been introduced by Avishai Margalit (2000, pp. 34ff.). Whereas 'common memory' refers to the recollection of an episode (e.g. a war episode) that has been experienced personally by various individuals and is remembered by these individuals, 'shared memory' refers to the recollection of past episodes that, for the most part or entirely, have not been experienced personally by those who recollect these experiences by communicating about them within a community of practice. As Margalit

(2000, p. 37) sets out for modern societies, memory shared by communication is the object of a mnemotechnical labour division. Shared memory is 'carried' by institutionalised professions and institutions, by special semiotic materialisations, such as street names, monuments and memorials, archives, museums, and so on. In other words: shared memory, is, for the most part, remembrance of remembrance (Margalit 2000, p. 41). This holds true for the most part of political commemoration, except for cases in which witnesses of the times participate in the commemoration as survivors, or provide testimonies and recall their personal experiences. A great deal of political commemoration is not rooted in individual and bodily engraved knowledge about an individual's own past, but in knowledge about narrated, described and explained past events, in a communicatively mediated past. This fact is often covered or confused by rhetorical devices, such as the historically expanded 'we' or the historical 'we'. These synecdochic or metonymic forms of 'we' encompass a trans-generational political (often national) community that includes persons from several centuries, or that suggests living members of an alleged national collective have participated in events that took place centuries ago (Wodak, de Cillia, Reisigl & Liebhart 2009, pp. 46ff.).

The integrative function of political commemoration can go hand in hand with a socially disintegrative function, for instance, with the function of social exclusion and separation from other national collectives. This close relationship between integration and disintegration is based on the Janus-faced process of identity formation: identity always relies both on sameness or similarity, and difference, distinction or diversification against others. The latter is most salient in secessionist nationalism that strives to break apart multiethnic political units (for the disintegrative function of political commemoration in Austria, see also Reisigl 2008, p. 251).

A tripartite question runs through political commemoration like a thread: where do we come from, who are we, where are we going? This triadic question relates to the three basic dimensions of time. The question is sometimes asked explicitly in commemorative speeches of presidents. The answer to it is organised around the cyclical – annual, fifth, tenth, twentieth, fiftieth, centenary, millenary – return of a specific occasion. This occasion appears to be an important moment in the past of a political community that both influences and 'instructs' the present and future.

The central political dimension of political commemoration is the polity. Commemoration supports a common framework for political action. This is not only due to the facts that commemoration is usually a consent-orientated political practice aiming to strengthen political cohesion and that the orators are often politicians with an integrative role, such as presidents and chancellors. Commemoration represents and sustains a political culture; in our times and European latitudes, a democratic culture, in former times, a monarchic culture, or sometimes a dictatorship (e.g. in Nazi Germany, or in the German Democratic Republic). Commemoration follows specific rules of communication, and it affirms specific political rules (e.g. democratic rules) and political values (e.g. political autonomy, independence, sovereignty, unity, singularity, solidarity, co-operation, community, peacefulness, etc.).

Commemorative speeches

The commemorative speech forms the basic type of communication that allows for 'bringing to remembrance' a particular reading of the past in the context of a ritualised public event. It forms a consent-orientated sub-genre of political speech and is located in the field of the formation of public attitudes, opinions and will.

The genre structure of commemorative speeches is often connected with patterns of the epideictic genre. According to ancient rhetoric, the epideictic genre relates to the speaker's demonstration (the Greek word *epideiktikós* means 'demonstrating', 'showing') of praiseworthy or blameworthy social and political – but also rhetorical – values (Dominicy & Fréderic 2001), as well as the demonstration of the speaker's rhetorical ability and ethos. In contrast, the function of the judicial genre is to prepare a jurisdictional decision by focusing on the past of the defendant and questions of (in)justice. The purpose of the deliberative genre consists in the preparation of a political decision by advising (exhorting or dissuading). When analysing particular commemorative speeches, it becomes clear that the genre of commemorative speech shows many features classically attributed to the epideictic speech, but that it rests across the three ideal-typical genres. In fact, a commemorative speech often deals with the problematic past of a political community. Thus, it also adopts elements of the judicial genre. Its parts on the political present and future include deliberative elements. Thus, commemorative speeches are best described as a generic mix of epideictic, judicial and deliberative elements.

When it comes to the macro-structure of the commemorative speech, we can describe it with the help of the classical distinction of functional speech sections:

The introduction (*exordium*) establishes the contact between the speaker and her or his audience by an initial vocative and salutation (*salutatio*). This phatic start is followed by attempts to attract the listeners' interest. In addition, the introduction of a commemorative speech familiarises the addressees with the topic and occasion of commemoration. This functional part is sometimes treated as a separate speech section (*propositio*) and sometimes as a part of the narration (Ueding & Steinbrink 2005, p. 263).

The main part of the speech conventionally consists of a narrative or explanation and an amplification of the issue in question (*narratio*), which is typically followed by a section containing arguments that are designated to persuade the listeners to adopt the speaker's opinion (*argumentatio*). The argumentation is considered to be the most important sub-section of the main part. It is classically divided into a sub-section aiming to argue for something (*probatio*) and a sub-section arguing against something (*refutatio*). Often, the narrative section also serves argumentative purposes. The argumentation section of commemorative speeches includes passages dedicated to the political present and future. This sub-section also includes prescriptive and directive elements that should help to obtain the listeners' consent, solidarity, identification and disposition to act in accordance with the values of the political community.

The final part of a speech (*peroratio*) has the double function of summarising the most important claims of the speaker and of re-intensifying the contact between the speaker and the listeners in order to make them emotionally and cognitively inclined to adopt the speaker's perspective. The summary often takes the form of an emphatic enumeration that fulfils a mnemonic function. Furthermore, the last part contains directive speech acts, such as requests and pleas, exhortations and warnings, as well as expressive speech acts, such as optative wishes, and – sometimes – compliments, congratulations and thanks. The illocutionary quality of these speech parts is to mobilise the listeners and to move them emotionally.

Spelling out the political functions of commemorative speeches in more detail, a series of sub-functions can be identified. Among them are the establishment of in-group consent, solidarity, identification and the disposition to act in accordance with what the speaker proposes. The complex action pattern of the commemorative speech can be sub-specified with respect to various tasks, and here again it becomes clear that the commemorative speech has a part in all three genres distinguished in rhetoric. Among the epideictic purposes of commemorative speeches are the laudatory, vituperative, retrospective or anamnestic, admonitory, consolatory, thanking, congratulatory, optative, promising and teaching functions. Among the deliberative purposes of commemorative speeches are the conciliatory, admonitory, promising and teaching functions (as we see, some deliberative and epideictic functions overlap). Lastly, the three typical judicial purposes of commemorative speeches are the accusing, exculpatory and justificatory functions.

In the twentieth and twenty-first centuries, commemorative speeches played an important role as an established form of public political speech when it comes to the retrospective historical self-presentation of a political community. Historical occasions for national days of remembrance include Independence Day (4 July) and Thanksgiving (fourth Thursday in November) in the US, the anniversary of the October Revolution in the former Union of Soviet Socialist Republics (7 November), the 'Oath on Rütli' and the signing of the Federal Pact in Switzerland (1 August), the anniversary of the storming of the Bastille as the beginning of the French Revolution (14 July), the Norwegian Constitution Day (17 May), the Liberation Day in Italy (25 April) commemorating the capitulation of the armed National Socialist forces on Italian territory, the anniversary of the military capitulation of the National Socialists celebrated as 'Day of Liberation' in the former German Democratic Republic (8 May), the German Unity Day commemorating the anniversary of the German reunification in 1990 (3 October), the National Holiday in Austria as the anniversary of the day on which Austria declared and enacted its 'permanent neutrality' (26 October), the 'Koninginnedag' as the anniversary of the coronation day of Queen Beatrix and the birthday of her mother, Princess Juliana, in the Netherlands (30 April; the name has now been changed to 'Koningsdag', because King Willem-Alexander is the successor to the throne), the anniversary of the beginning of the liberation fight against Turkey in Greece (25 March) and – in former colonies – the anniversary of the beginning of independence from the colonial power (6 March in Ghana, 21 March in Namibia, 24 May in Eritrea, 5 July in Algeria, 15 August in India).

Depending on the political system of a state and the political orientation of a political orator, the specific commemorative speech will aim to construct and reproduce a democratic political identity, or to pursue ideological indoctrination legitimising an undemocratic, for example, autocratic or dictatorial political identity (Haspel 1996, p. 642).

The purpose of commemorative speeches given in the first half of the twentieth century in many European states was primarily political propaganda and agitation of the masses. Until the First World War, they were employed to suggest historical continuities. The alleged continuities were referred to in order to support nationalist claims, and expansionist as well as imperialist aspirations. From the 1920s onwards, Italian fascists and National Socialists utilised commemorative speeches to glorify their own political movement by monumentalist, mythical and apotheotic self-presentations. The glorification relied on the invocation of a splendid history. Aesthetical scenery with imposing architecture, masses marching, huge choruses, fanfares and ideological creeds charged with a triumphalist and para-religious fervour produced an atmosphere of mass hysteria and a reverential shiver, in which participants fanatically identified with the 'leader, people and fatherland' and adopted the attitude of being ready to sacrifice themselves (see Mosse 1993, p. 238).

The rhetoric of commemoration typical for fascist and National Socialist states in Europe has implications for the development of post-war commemoration after 1945. Formerly fascist and National Socialist nation-states have to confront themselves with their problematic political past. This negative history becomes a central topic of the speeches (Haspel 1996,

p. 643). Several remarkable commemorative speeches given in West Germany have focused on the period of National Socialism. Richard von Weizsäcker gave a speech on 8 May 1985 on the occasion of the fortieth anniversary of the liberation from National Socialism that assumed the character of an admonitory speech in empathetic solidarity with the victims of the National Socialist dictatorship and critical of the German perpetrators and the German post-war society that tried to evade political responsibility (Haspel 1996, p. 643). This speech has become a rhetorical and ethical benchmark against which every other speech on the topic is measured and evaluated up until today. Furthermore, the disastrous speech given on 10 November, 1988 by the former president of the German parliament, Phillip Jenninger, on the occasion of the fiftieth anniversary of the anti-Jewish pogrom (the night from 9 November to 10 November, 1938), differed considerably from Weizsäcker's speech (see Kopperschmidt 1989; von Polenz 1989; Linn 1991; Wodak, Menz, Mitten & Stern 1994). Jenninger's commemorative retrospection lacked the respectful empathy with the victims of National Socialism and their immense suffering. It included formulations and stylistic meanings of discourse representation (i.e. free indirect speech) suggesting that Jenninger was adopting and partly justifying the perspective of National Socialist perpetrators. The failed speech seemed to relativise the Nazi crimes and to insinuate the unavoidability of the historical development. The 'Jenninger case' shows at least two things: first, Jenninger's subsequent resignation made clear that commemorative speeches are of vital importance for the public sphere of a modern democracy (see Haspel 1996, p. 643) and do not just assume the status of grandiloquent 'Sunday speeches'. Second, the reactions of other parliamentary representatives showed that a commemorative speech is not just a monological piece of communication, but an interactive genre (see Figure 24.1). More than 40 representatives left the room during the speech, and various representatives started to shout spontaneous hecklings of disapproval at Jenninger. This interactive character of a commemorative speech is often not noticed. It becomes conspicuous if the speech fails and the expected consent of the hearers does not follow, or if non-verbal acclamations presupposed as applauding 'minimal responses' are missing or replaced by reactions of dissent.

The political commemoration of the National Socialist dictatorship is also an issue in post-war Austria. Until the end of the 1980s, however, the commemoration was conspicuous by the absence of condolences and sincere sympathy with the Nazi victims. Up until then, politicians primarily produced half-hearted confessions of an Austrian responsibility for National Socialist crimes. They hardly ever publicly expressed their regret and hardly ever asked the surviving victims and their relatives for forgiveness. Most of the commemorative speeches reproduced the claim that Austria and the Austrians had been the first victims of Nazi Germany. Only after the-then Chancellor Franz Vranitzky made a declaration on 8 July 1991 in the Austrian parliament and confessed the guilt of the Austrian Nazis (see Wodak, de Cillia, Reisigl, Liebhart, Hofstätter & Kargl 1998, pp. 213ff.; Wodak, de Cillia, Reisigl & Liebhart 1999, pp. 89ff.), did the public dealing with the Austrian National Socialist past start to change (see also Ziegler & Kannonier-Finster 1997; Uhl 2011). Since then, victims of National Socialist persecution and extermination are commemorated with more compassion and regretful apologies based on the recognition of past wrongdoings, and the perpetrators are named and condemned more clearly.

The difficulties of 'saying sorry' in political commemoration (see Brooks 1999; Harris, Grainger & Mullany 2006) are also an issue in other countries with a highly problematic past. Efe and Forchtner (2015), for instance, focus on the example of Turkey and how the Turkish Prime Minister, Recep Tayyip Erdoğan, publicly addresses and admits the Massacre of thousands of Kurds in Dersim during the 1930s. From the example of Turkey, but also other countries, we can learn that strong nationalism is one of the principal obstacles to performing a clear and unmitigated (e.g. non-conditional) political apology based on the recognition of wrongdoing and the assumption of political responsibility.

As observed, the commemorative speech is not a monological event. As a genre, it is a communicative action pattern with an interactive structure. This becomes most clear if a commemorative speech fails, as in the case of Jenninger's speech in 1988. Figure 24.1 is designed to visualise both what the schematic interaction structure of a commemorative speech looks like and how the conventionalised interaction may be disrupted. The figure represents three kinds of speech-relevant processes, videlicet: (a) mental processes of the orator on the left, (b), semiotically externalised elements produced by the orator and the hearers in the middle, and (c) the mental processes of the hearers on the right. The rectangular double-lines mark the borders of the communicative action pattern. The rhombus symbolises a decisional nodal point with various alternatives, the small rectangles stand for specific mental, actional and interactional processes. The arrow represents the direction of the consecutive processes, and the broken and dotted lines denote the boundaries between the functional interactional meso-units (speech parts). Finally, on the right side, we perceive the (partial) breaking up of the communicative action.

Commemoration as a multimodal semiotic process and event

As already touched upon, commemoration involves various semiotic (e.g. symbolic, indexical and iconic) dimensions beyond the purely verbal dimension. Often, political commemoration is a complex multimodal ceremony and event that includes visuals, music, place arrangements, architecture and processes of collective action or interaction. It follows from this that the research on the semiotics of political commemoration has to take into account a series of interrelated elements. These elements are:

a. the selection of a specific place and architectural scenery with buildings, monuments, etc.;
b. the announcement of the speech event by strategic media activities of political mobilisation via fliers, press advertisements, appeals and organisational instructions, etc., and the often very selective invitation to participate in the commemorative event on the spot;
c. the preparation of the speech by a team consisting of the orator, advertisers and ghostwriters;
d. the preparation of the multimodal scenery and place by arranging the frontstage with the platform for the speaker(s) and the stands for the audience, by decorating the scenery with requisites, by choreographing the performance and eventually the parade or procession (for the distinction between *frontstage* and *backstage*, see Goffman 1959; Wodak 2011);
e. the musical framing of the commemorative event by hymns, anthems, (military) marches, etc.;
f. the dress rehearsal of the speech performance and the greater communicative event;
g. the delivery of the speech as a multimodal event that involves verbal and non-verbal aspects and that often shows discrepancies between the written and the oral speech;
h. the 'after story' of the speech performance, due to which the speech may become a *media spectacle* (Kellner 2003, pp. 160–178), i.e. the distribution of the registered speech or event by mass media, the reception of these recorded pieces of commemorative communication, and the reactions to the distributed semiotic pieces in the media.

Each of these elements or stages is significant for the process of political commemoration (see also Alexander 2006, pp. 66ff., who refers to the productive, distributive and

The semiotics of political commemoration

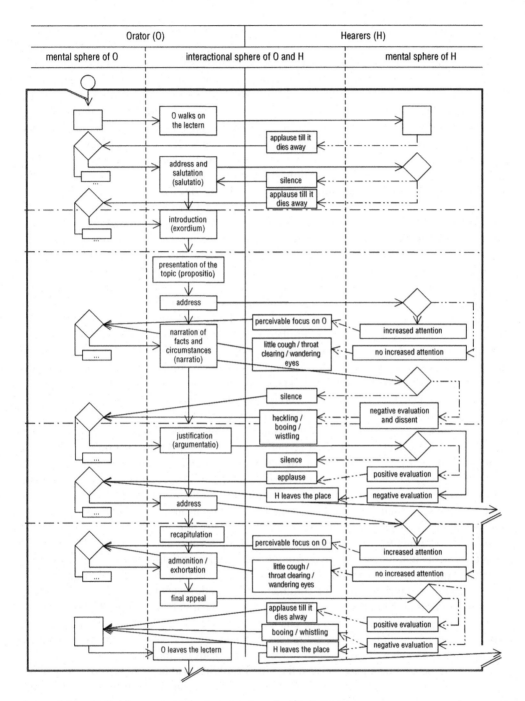

Figure 24.1 (Failing) commemorative speech as linguistic action pattern

hermeneutical powers interfacing with the *mise-en-scène* of social performances), though the commemorative speech is usually of crucial importance. Particular semiotic elements, such as pictures, can become as influential or even more influential than the commemorative speech itself. Here, we may think of the 'Warsaw Genuflection' of the former chancellor of the Federal Republic of Germany, Willy Brandt, who had actively resisted the Nazi regime (see also Rauer 2006). The picture or series of pictures show the chancellor kneeling in Warsaw on 7 December 1970 in front of a monument dedicated to the uprising against the Nazis in the Warsaw Ghetto. Willy Brandt performed this gesture of penance and admittance of responsibility supposedly spontaneously during his visit to the monument and the related wreath-laying ceremony. Brandt's visit took place in a specific historical context. He had come to Poland to sign the Treaty of Warsaw. In this treaty, the Oder-Neisse line was acknowledged as the final German border with Poland. The genuflection was, and is, perceived as an image of commemoration with a strong symbolic meaning. The picture of the emblematic gesture went around the world. While it was discussed controversially in West Germany, internationally, it was perceived as an important step towards a reconciliation and rapprochement between Germany and Eastern Europe. The respective images show a serious-looking man kneeling down, folding his hands and remaining silent for about 30 seconds. The shot is taken from above, that is, from a higher angle, and shows the politician on the right side, in social semiotic terms, as the new and most important information in the image. This non-verbal act of empathic commemoration was so impressive and influential that it has become, in turn, an important political event that has been regularly commemorated since. Thus, we observe here the commemoration of commemoration, since the commemorative genuflection itself is commemorated. Furthermore, Willy Brandt was dedicated a place name and monument in Warsaw for his gesture and policy. This means that the semiotic act of commemoration is collectively memorised in the form of a memory place, by the symphysical fixation of Brandt's name to a street sign and a monument at a specific place.

Other examples of a visual policy of commemoration through gestural symbols could be mentioned, such as the handshake of the former German Chancellor Helmut Kohl and the former French President François Mitterrand on 22 September 1984 at the war cemetery Douaumont in Verdun. During the playing of the Marseillaise, the two politicians shook hands unexpectedly and remained in this position of bodily closeness for some time – in front of two wreaths and a coffin adorned with the flags of France and Germany. The music of the two anthems seemed to have emotionally touched the two men. Mitterand started to reach out for Kohl's hand during the pause after the German anthem and immediately before the beginning of the French anthem in order to overcome his solitude of grief (as he explained). The pictures of this gesture of friendship went round the world. The example also documents that music can have strong effects on the participants of a commemorative event and move them to perform an unexpected gesture of high symbolic importance.

In contrast, a controversial joint commemoration took place a year later, when Ronald Reagan and Helmut Kohl participated in a ceremonial visit in Bitburg in 1985. The pictures show the president of the US and the chancellor of the Federal Republic of Germany at a military cemetery with two-thousand graves of fallen soldiers, 49 of whom were members of the *Waffen-SS*. They show Reagan in front of a wreath for the German soldiers. Within this context, the president had declared that the SS soldiers had been victims of fascism like the prisoners killed in the Nazi concentration camps. Understandably, this equation and the reverential act of commemoration at that very specific place became an object of international public critique.

All in all, the semiotics of political commemoration is becoming more and more important as an interdisciplinary research object. Various semiotic facets of commemoration are studied from different angles and with respect to different historical times, places, speakers and materialisations such as monuments (e.g. war monuments), museums and visitor books.

Among the many studies focusing on states such as Argentina, Austria, Egypt, Germany, Great Britain, South Africa and Uruguay are Aboelezz 2014; Abousnnouga & Machin 2013; Achugar 2009; Anthonissen 2006; Bietti 2014; Duncan 2014; Ensink 2009; Ensink & Sauer eds., 2003; Kopperschmidt 1999; Kohn & Rosenberg 2013; Matuschek 1994; Noy 2011; Sauer 1997; Staudinger 1994; Weedon & Jordan 2012; Zinsmaier 1999. Due to restricted space, they cannot be discussed in this chapter.

The discourse-historical focus on salient discursive features of political commemoration

During the last few decades, proponents of the DHA have carried out various discourse-analytical case studies on political commemoration with respect to public commemoration in Austria and partly also in Germany and elsewhere (Wodak et al. 1994; Wodak et al. 1998; Reisigl 1998; Wodak et al. 2009; Reisigl 1999, 2007, 2008, 2009; Wodak 2006; de Cillia & Wodak, 2009; Wodak & Richardson 2009, 2013; Tominc 2014, Forchtner 2014a, 2014b). From this specific theoretical and methodical perspective (see Reisigl & Wodak 2016), salient occasions have been looked at, among other things, the foundation of the First Austrian Republic in 1918 and the Second Austrian Republic in 1945, the signing of the so called 'State Treaty' in 1955, the liberation of the Nazi victims imprisoned in the Austrian concentration camp Mauthausen on 5 May 1945, the military capitulation of the National Socialists on 8 May 1945, the first documentation of the toponym 'ostarrîchi' in the year 996 (from which the name 'Austria' is derived), the enactment of the 'permanent Austrian neutrality' in 1955, and Austria's joining of the European Union in 1995.

Among the general discourse topics analysed in the respective commemorative speeches are: (1) the representation of Austrians and non-Austrians, (2) the narration of a national political history, (3) the reference to a common (national) culture, (4) the reference to a national present and future, and (5) the discursive construction of a 'national body' or 'national territory'.

In addition to the general characteristics and genre-related features mentioned on pp. 371f. and 374f., significant discursive features relating to commemoration and focused on in the respective DHA studies are: (a) the discursive representation (by nomination and predication) of social actors and crucial events as well as actions relating to commemorated events, (b) argumentation patterns referring to causes and consequences concerning the commemorated events, (c) tropological patterns employed in order to discursively deal with the commemorated past and to construct or represent historical changes and continuities.

The analysis of the commemorative representation of social actors and events brings to the fore a series of nomination and predication strategies employed for the depiction of single, nationally important individuals (e.g. 'founding fathers' or national 'heroes' and shining examples) by proper names, honorifics and positive national attributes. The national in-group and various out-groups are further represented by collective nouns, toponyms, relational anthroponyms as well as deictics such 'we' and 'you' and anaphoric pronouns such as 'they'. A crucial point of commemoration is the question of how certain historical events, actions and processes are named, for instance, whether a historical turning point is named as 'liberation', 'occupation' or 'defeat', or whether another turning point is named as voluntary 'Anschluss' or 'unification', or as compulsory 'annexation'. Predications used in commemorative semiosis are analysed with respect to national auto- and hetero-stereotypes.

Many argumentation patterns (*topoi*) have been identified in the above-mentioned Austrian case studies. They are employed in order to justify specific claims regarding the national past, present and future. Among these argumentation patterns are the *topos* of autonomy, the *topos* of heteronomy, the *topos* of singularity, the *topos* of will, the *topos* of difference, the *topos* of sameness and justice, the *topos* of the victim, the *topos* of culture, the *topos* of danger, the *topos* of responsibility, and the *topos* of history. In various Austrian commemorative speeches given by conservative politicians, this last *topos* is realised as a *topos* of the history as a teacher of lessons (*historia magistra vitae*). It refers to a positive change of the past and serves the positive national self-presentation by praising the we-group for having learned from its own past and by distracting the commemorative attention from the victims who deserve to be the main focus of attention.

Furthermore, tropes, that is, content-related rhetorical figures such as metaphors, metonymies and synecdoches, play a crucial role in the political commemoration in Austria and elsewhere. They help to construct historical continuities and historical change. They are not simply rhetorical decorations, but function as fundamental cognitive principles which – often unconsciously – shape and structure human perception and thinking. First, they are used to promote identification with political actors (e.g. the collective actor of the state or nation) and their aims, for instance via the metaphor of the 'core' with respect to Austria in relation to other nation-states of the European Union. Second, they are employed to promote in-group solidarity, for instance with the help of the family or kinship metaphor referring to the imagined community of the nation, or with the help of the bridge metaphor. Third, they support out-group segregation and discrimination, for instance via spatial metaphors implying strict frontiers between inside and outside. Fourth, tropes are used to generate a feeling of security, stability and order, for instance via construction and building metaphors referring to a state. Fifth, tropes fulfil justificatory or delegitimising functions with respect to specific political actions or their omission in the past, present or future, for instance via metaphors of gain or price relating to the consequences of a specific action or omission of action. Sixth, they may assume a relativising function, for instance via the metaphor of natural disasters and catastrophes for war, military actions and other cruelties willingly authored and committed by human beings, or via the metaphor of the rebirth of an 'innocent' national being without any problematic prehistory, or via the metaphor of the bridge that covers contradictions and antagonistic social structures that ought to be named explicitly and cleared by an adequate policy, or via expansive temporal synecdoches that disguise historical discontinuities and breaks (for details, see Reisigl 2009). Seventh, tropes are instrumental if it comes to mobilise political supporters to perform particular actions, for instance via inciting moving metaphors, journey metaphors or – in some cases – even militarising metaphors relating to political collaboration.

Conclusions

Within this chapter, I could only give some basic hints to important aspects of the topic. A comprehensive theory of the semiotics of political commemoration still awaits its elaboration. Such a theory is best constructed within the framework of an interdisciplinary co-operation that brings together historical research, political science, linguistics and semiotics in order to shape the contours of a historical politolinguistics that is connected with the DHA and Social Semiotics. Such a historical politolinguistics has to take into consideration the historical variability of the phenomenon. It has, for instance, to be aware of the fact that the political commemoration of periods such as National Socialism will change as soon as eyewitnesses from that time are no longer alive. The social demographic change has the effect that 'common memory' will successively disappear and be replaced by 'shared memory'. Historical politolinguistics also has to deal with new challenges following increased international migration, because the multitude of ethnic und cultural backgrounds has to be addressed adequately, that is, in an integrative way, in the practice of political commemoration. Furthermore, historical politolinguistics specialised for the analysis of political commemoration has to take into account that supranational commemoration is becoming more and more important.

With respect to the different semiotic modes, we have seen that, in the multimodal practice of political commemoration, non-verbal communication can have as much impact as verbal communication, and that music may sometimes trigger an unexpected non-verbal gesture of central political actors that assumes a strong symbolic meaning. All these dimensions are worthy of being accurately analysed, in addition to genre-specific elements of commemorative speeches and their interaction patterns, discourse topics, nominations, predications, argumentation schemes and tropes.

Finally, critical politolinguistics carrying out research on the semiotics of political commemoration may engage in speech criticism and political language advising (see Reisigl 2008, pp. 261ff.; Reisigl 2009, pp. 236ff.). Here, the practical critique has to rely on an accurate description and identification of *bad practices* as well as *good practices* of political commemoration. The respective evaluation should be based on a solid historical knowledge and on transparent semiotic (e.g. iconic, indexical, symbolic), cognitive (e.g. rational) as well as political (e.g. democratic) and ethical principles (e.g. of empathy and solidarity with the victims). In this sense, we analysts are ourselves part of an ongoing democratic project.

References

Aboelezz, M, 2014, 'The geosemiotics of Tahrir Square: A study of the relationship between discourse and space', *Journal of Language and Politics*, 13(4), pp. 599–622.
Abousnnouga, G & Machin, D, 2013, *The language of war monuments*, Bloomsbury, London.
Achugar, M, 2009, 'Constructing the past and constructing themselves: the Uruguayan military's memory of the dictatorship', *Critical Discourse Studies*, 6(4), pp. 283-295.
Alexander, J C, 2006, 'Cultural pragmatics: Social performance between ritual and strategy', in *Social performance. Symbolic action, cultural pragmatics, and ritual*, eds. J C Alexander, B Giesen & J L Mast, Cambridge University Press, Cambridge, pp. 29–90.
Anthonissen, C, 2006, 'The language of remembering and forgetting', *Journal of Language and Politics*, 5(1), pp. 1–13.
Assmann, A, 2006, *Der lange Schatten der Vergangenheit. Erinnerungskultur und Geschichtspolitik*, Beck, Munich.
Assmann, A, 2007, *Geschichte im Gedächtnis. Von der individuellen Erfahrung zur öffentlichen Inszenierung*, Beck, Munich.
Assmann, J, 2007, *Das kulturelle Gedächtnis: Schrift, Erinnerung und politische Identität in frühen Hochkulturen*, 6th ed., Beck, Munich.
Bietti, L M, 2014, *Discursive commemoration. Individual and collective remembering as a discursive, cognitive and historical process*, de Gruyter, Berlin and New York.
Brooks, R, ed., 1999, *When saying sorry isn't enough: The controversy over apologies and reparations for human injustice*, NYUP, New York.
de Cillia, R & Wodak, R, eds., 2009, *Gedenken im 'Gedankenjahr'. Zur diskursiven Konstruktion österreichischer Identitäten im Jubiläumsjahr 2005*, StudienVerlag, Innsbruck, Vienna, Bolzano.
Dominicy, M & Frédéric, M. eds., 2001, *La Mise en scène des valeurs. La Rhétorique de l'éloge et du blame*, Delachaux & Niestlé, Lausanne and Paris.
Duncan, P T, 2014, 'Remembering the future. Temporal tensions in the discursive construction and commemoration of Israel', *Critical Discourse Studies*, 11(4), pp. 416–440.

Durkheim, É, 1995, *The elementary forms of religious life*, Free Press, New York.
Efe, I & Forchtner, B, 2015, '"Saying sorry" in Turkey: The Dersim massacre of the 1930s in 2011', *Journal of Language and Politics*, 14(2), pp. 233–257.
Ensink, T, 2009, 'Resolving antagonistic tensions. Some discourse analytic reflections on verbal commemorative processes', in *Justice and memory. Confronting traumatic pasts. An international comparison*, eds. R Wodak & G Auer Borea, Passagen, Vienna, pp. 169–193.
Ensink, T & Sauer, C, eds., 2003, *The art of commemoration. Fifty years after the Warsaw Uprising*, Benjamins, Amsterdam and Philadelphia.
Forchtner, B, 2014a, '*Historia magistra vitae*: The *topos* of history as a teacher in public struggles over self- and other representation', in *Contemporary studies in Critical Discourse Analysis*, eds. C Hart & P Cap, Bloomsbury, London, pp. 19–43.
Forchtner, B, 2014b, 'Rhetorics of judge-penitence: Claiming moral superiority through admissions of past wrongdoing', *Memory Studies*, 7(4), pp. 409–424.
Goffman, E, 1959, *The presentation of self in everyday life*, Anchor Books, New York.
Halbwachs, M, 2002, La mémoire collective, Albin Michel, Paris.
Halbwachs, M, 2004, *Les cadres sociaux de la mémoir*, Albin Michel, Paris.
Harris, S, Grainger, K & Mullany, L, 2006, 'The pragmatics of political apologies', *Discourse & Society*, 17(6), pp. 715–737.
Haspel, M, 1996, 'Gedenkrede', in *Historisches Wörterbuch der Rhetorik (HWRh). Band 3. Unter Mitwirkung von zahlreichen Fachgelehrten herausgegeben von Gert Ueding*, Niemeyer, Tübingen, pp. 639–644.
Kellner, D, 2003, *Media spectacle*, Routledge, London and New York.
Kohn, A & Rosenberg, H, 2013, 'Collapsing walls and the question of commemoration: graffiti in the Israeli withdrawal, August 2005', *Social Semiotics*, 23(5), pp. 606–631.
Kopperschmidt, J, 1989, 'Öffentliche Rede in Deutschland. Überlegungen zur politischen Rhetorik mit Blick auf zwei Gedenkreden im Deutschen Bundestag', *Muttersprache*, 99(3), pp. 213–230.
Kopperschmidt, J, 1999, 'Über die Unfähigkeit zu feiern. Allgemeine und spezifische deutsche Schwierigkeiten mit der Gedenkrhetorik', in *Fest und Festrhetorik. Zu Theorie, Geschichte und Praxis der Epideiktik*, eds. J Kopperschmidt & H Schanze, Fink, München, pp. 149–172.
Koselleck, R & Jeismann, M, 1994, *Der politische Totenkult: Kriegerdenkmäler in der Moderne*, Fink, Munich.
Levy, D & Sznaider, N, 2005, *Holocaust and memory in the global age*, Temple University Press, Philadelphia.
Linn, A, 1991, *"... noch heute ein Faszinosum ..." Phillip Jenninger zum 9. November 1938 und die Folgen*, Lit, Münster.
Margalit, A, 2000, *Ethik der Erinnerung. Max Horkheimer Vorlesungen*, Fischer, Frankfurt am Main.
Matuschek, S, 1994, *Epideiktische Beredsamkeit. In: Historisches Wörterbuch der Rhetorik (HWRh). Band 2. Unter Mitwirkung von zahlreichen Fachgelehrten herausgegeben von Gert Ueding*. Niemeyer, Tübingen, pp. 1258–1267.
McDowell, S & Braniff, M, 2014, *Commemoration as conflict. Space, memory and identity in peace processes*, Palgrave Macmillan, London.
Meyer, E, 2003, 'Erinnerungskultur als Politikfeld. Geschichtspolitische Deliberation und Dezision in der Berliner Republik', in *Die NS-Diktatur im deutschen Erinnerungsdiskurs*, ed. W Bergem, VS für Sozialwissenschaften, Opladen, pp. 121–136.
Meyer, E, 2009, *Erinnerungskultur 2.0: Kommemorative Kommunikation in digitalen Medien*, Campus, Frankfurt am Main and New York.
Mosse, G L, 1993, *Die Nationalisierung der Massen. Von den Befreiungskriegen bis zum Dritten Reich*, Campus, Frankfurt am Main and New York.
Noy, C, 2011, 'Articulating spaces: inscribing spaces and (im)mobilities in an Israeli commemorative visitor book', *Social Semiotics*, 21(2), pp. 155–173.
Olick, J K, ed., 2003, *States of memory: Continuities, conflicts, and transformation in national retrospection*, Duke University Press, Durham, NC.

Rauer, V, 2006, 'Symbols in action: Willy Brand's kneefall at the Warsaw Memorial', in *Social performance. Symbolic action, cultural pragmatics, and ritual*, eds. J C Alexander, B Giesen & JL Mast, Cambridge University Press, Cambridge, pp. 257–282.

Reisigl, M, 1998, '"50 Jahre Zweite Republik" – Zur diskursiven Konstruktion der österreichischen Identität in politischen Gedenkreden', in *Fahnenwörter in der Politik – Kontinuitäten und Brüche*, ed. O Panagl, Böhlau, Vienna, pp. 217–251.

Reisigl, M, 1999, '"1000 Jahre Österreich" – Ein nationaler Mythos im öffentlichen Gedenken der Zweiten Österreichischen Republik', in *Fest und Festrhetorik. Zu Theorie, Geschichte und Praxis der Epideiktik*, eds. J Kopperschmidt & H Schanze, Fink, München, pp. 281–311.

Reisigl, M, 2007, *Nationale Rhetorik in Fest- und Gedenkreden. Eine diskursanalytische Studie zum 'österreichischen Millennium' in den Jahren 1946 und 1996*, Stauffenburg, Tübingen.

Reisigl, M, 2008, 'Rhetoric of political speeches', in *Handbook of communication in the public sphere (HAL 4: Handbooks of Applied Linguistics. Volume 4)*, eds. R Wodak & V Koller, Mouton de Gruyter, Berlin and New York, pp. 243–269.

Reisigl, M, 2009, 'Spoken silence – bridging breaks. The discursive construction of historical continuities and turning points in Austrian commemorative speeches by employing rhetorical tropes', in *Justice and memory. Confronting traumatic pasts. An international comparison*, eds. R Wodak & G Auer Borea, Vienna, Passagen, pp. 213–240.

Reisigl, M & Wodak, R, 2016, 'The discourse-historical approach', in *Methods of Critical Discourse Analysis*. 2nd revised edition, eds. R Wodak & M Meyer, Sage, London & Thousand Oaks, New Delhi, pp. 23–61.

Ricœur. P, 2004, *Memory, history, forgetting*, University of Chicago Press, Chicago, IL.

Sauer, C, 1997, 'Echoes from abroad – speeches for the domestic audience: Queen Beatrix's address to the Israeli parliament', in *Analysing political speeches*, ed. C Schäffner, Multilingual Matters Ltd, Clevedon, pp. 33–67.

Staudinger, A, 1994, '"Durch Gedenkfeiern gelegentlich zur Vergessenheit emporgehoben ..." Anmerkungen zur Funktion von Gedenktagen und zur grassierenden Jubiläumshistorie', in *Der literarische Umgang der Österreicher mit Jahres- und Gedenktagen*, ed. W Schmidt-Dengler, ÖBV Pädagogischer Verlag, Vienna, pp. 17–24.

Tominc, A, 2014, 'Transforming national holidays: identity discourse in the West and South Slavic countries, 1985–2010', in *Critical Discourse Studies*, 11(3), pp. 373–376.

Ueding, G & B, Steinbrink, 2005, *Grundriß der Rhetorik. Geschichte – Technik – Methode*, 4th ed. Metzler, Stuttgart and Weimar.

Uhl, H, 2011, 'Vom "ersten Opfer" zum Land der unbewältigten Vergangenheit: Österreich im Kontext der Transformationen des europäischen Gedächtnisses', in *Arbeit am europäischen Gedächtnis*, eds. V Knigge, H-J Veen, U Mählert, F-J Schlichting, *Diktaturerfahrungen und Demokratieentwicklung*, Böhlau, Köln, Weimar and Vienna, pp. 27–46.

von Polenz, P, 1989, 'Verdünnte Sprachkultur. Das Jenninger-Syndrom in sprach-kritischer Sicht', *Deutsche Sprache*, 4, pp. 289–316.

Weedon, C & Jordan, G, 2012, 'Collective memory: theory and politics', *Social Semiotics*, 22(2), pp. 143–153.

Wodak, R, 2006, 'History in the making/The making of history: The "German Wehrmacht" in collective and individual memories in Austria', *Journal of Language and Politics*, 5(1), eds. C Anthonissen, & J Blommaert, 'Critical linguistic perspectives on coping with traumatic pasts', pp. 125–154.

Wodak, R, 2011, *The discourse of politics in action: Politics as usual*, 2nd ed., Palgrave Macmillan, Basingstoke.

Wodak, R & Richardson, J E, 2009, 'On the politics of remembering (or not)', *Critical Discourse Studies*, 6(4), pp. 231–235.

Wodak, R & Richardson, J E, 2013, 'On the politics of remembering (or not)', in *Advances in Critical Discourse Studies*, eds. J Richardson, M Krzyżanowski, D Machin & R Wodak, Routledge, London. pp. 1–5.

Wodak, R, de Cillia, R, Reisigl, M, Liebhart, K, Kargl, M & Hofstätter, K, 1998, *Zur diskursiven Konstruktion nationaler Identität*, Suhrkamp, Frankfurt am Main.

Wodak, R, de Cillia, R, Reisigl, M & Liebhart, K, 2009, *The discursive construction of national identity*, 2nd ed., Edinburgh University Press, Edinburgh.

Wodak, R, Menz, F, Mitten, R & Stern, F, 1994, *Die Sprachen der Vergangenheiten: Öffentliches Gedenken in österreichischen und deutschen Medien*, Suhrkamp, Frankfurt am Main.

Zerubavel, Y, 1995, *Recovered roots. Collective memory and the making of Israeli national tradition*, Chicago University Press, Chicago, IL.

Ziegler, M & Kannonier-Finster, W, 1997, *Österreichisches Gedächtnis. Über Erinnern und Vergessen der NS-Vergangenheit*, 2nd ed. Böhlau, Vienna, Cologne and Weimar.

Zifonun, D, 2004, *Gedenken und Identität. Der deutsche Erinnerungsdiskurs*, Campus, Frankfurt am Main, New York.

Zinsmaier, T, 1999, 'Epideiktik zwischen Affirmation und Artistik. Die antike Theorie der feiernden Rede im historischen Aufriß', in *Fest und Festrhetorik. Zu Theorie, Geschichte und Praxis der Epideiktik*, eds. J Kopperschmidt & H Schanze, Fink, Munich, pp. 375–398.

25
Mediatisation and political language

Michael Higgins

Introduction

Concerns over the relationship between media and politics have echoed over much of the last century. Remarking that 'if Stalin smiles at a visitor, the news is flashed to the world before the smile has left his face', Gorman (1945, p. v) alludes to a quickening effect of mass media on the fortunes of politicians and to its supposed preference for demeanour over matters of substance. Jamieson (1996) and Franklin (2004) describe an emerging dynamic between the politicians, their communications advisers, industry lobbyists and media organisations, all vying to influence the 'packaging' of politics for public consumption. These efforts to reshape politics are a partial response to broader social and cultural changes, including the development of media platforms, as well as changing public attitudes. Corner and Pels (2003) describe the increasing roles of 'consumerism, celebrity and cynicism' in the mediation of politics, where voter disengagement and disillusionment is countered using the techniques of political marketing (Savigny 2008) and the political realm is left beholden to popular culture (Street 2004). In surveying this mediated politics, Corner (2003) points to the foregrounding of the politician as a 'mediated persona', schooled in performances that align with dominant political values and trained to pander to expectations around popular appeal (Langer 2012; Street 2011).

Various forms of language and discourse analysis have looked at the public discourse of contemporary politics. These range from the everyday pragmatics of political speech (Wilson 1990) to the continuing influence of classical rhetoric (Martin 2013). Also, various scholars associated with Critical Discourse Analysis (CDA) have sought to keep pace with the tactical dynamics of political language, from its articulation with various national identities (Higgins 2004; Wodak et al. 2009) to its strategic alignment with populism (Forchtner, Krzyżanowski & Wodak 2013). As an ever-greater proportion of exposure to politicians occurs through various media platforms, CDA has also sought to examine how political language and practice has reshaped to accommodate the imperatives of mediation, often in ways that have altered and diminished the value of political discourse (Fairclough 1995; Wodak 2009).

The chapter will proceed as follows. The first section discusses the role of 'media visibility' in the political realm, and its relationship with the personalisation of politics. This is followed by a discussion of the usefulness of 'mediatisation' in understanding the dynamic influence between political discourse and 'media logic'. After this, we outline the media imperative of 'sociability', and its relationship with 'conversationalisation' in media discourse. We then look at how this is manifest in language and representation across a number of political contexts, starting with an example of the televised performance of sincerity set against a more conventional political address. This is followed by a discussion of the production and contestation of the populist media persona of UK politician Boris Johnson: constructed in personalised and anti-political terms, but, as we will see, remaining vulnerable to the purposeful redirection of those same discourses. Then, we look at the institutional discourse of the party leaflet, again finding strategies of conversationalisation directed towards the playful destabilisation of the political lexicon, allied with intertextual references to popular culture. In the last section, on political debates, we examine the performance of 'affective empathy', and see a tactical combination of political and popular language co-ordinated with an embodied dis-alignment from political conventionality in favour of association with the audience.

Mediated visibility and political personality

Thompson (1995, 2000) deploys the term 'mediated visibility' to help us understand how these struggles of representation take place. As a key part of the experience of modernity (Thompson 1995), mediated visibility refers to a configuration of 'public exposure', around which mediation takes prominence over co-presence. Public space is constituted and populated through the technologies of media, leaving political figures to live by their success in 'fabricating a self-image of appeal' (Thompson 2000, p. 38). Our apocryphal example of Stalin's smile, doubly articulated towards its recipient and the wider media audience, hints at the skills of 'non-reciprocal intimacy at a distance' (Thompson 2000, p. 41) that have become essential across an increasing range of media platforms.

As Corner (2003) has pointed out, in an environment dominated by media visibility, the focus is on the expressive capabilities of politicians and political institutions and the adequacy of their media performance. Over the past few decades in particular, Street (2011, p. 244) identifies a fusion between personalisation and popular culture, associating politicians with the performative practices of celebrity culture. As we will see, such performances are animated in a number of ways, 'kinetic and gestural; visual as well as oral and aural' (Drake & Higgins 2012, p. 386), and extend through modes of 'conversationalisation' to the written word (Fairclough 1995). This amounts to a repertoire of situation-appropriate activities, producing facades ranging from resolve to candour, and offering various degrees of emotional empathy (Corner 2003, p. 94).

Mediatisation and politics

'Mediatisation' provides a useful way of conceptualising this relationship between politics and media. Its basis is that 'media logic' exercises growing authority over the organising principles of our everyday lives (Esser & Strömbäck 2014; Hjarvard 2013). According to Mazzoleni and Schulz (1999, p. 250), the political consequences of mediatisation emerge when policies and innovations proceed to the stage of 'publicity', and ideas, themes and candidates are presented to the political polity. Whatever the ideological, economic or social basis for backstage political decisions, the proposal is that their shape and delivery will be determined by the organising principles of media rather than those of politics, and this will be reflected in the associated language and other communicative activities.

As we note above, this places new demands on the aspiring political actor, whose success hinges upon the maintenance of media appeal and the cultivation of media skills (Mazzoleni & Schulz 1999, p. 251). This is a relationship in which politicians have at least partially internalised the expectations of media, and laud the demands of news value as professional goals. As Forchtner, Krzyżanowski and Wodak (2013, p. 207) suggest, what is produced is a 'performance of politics' informed by, and geared towards, the production priorities and presentational styles of the medium involved.

There is, of course, an intricate network of influence in play. Political actors retain some measure of commitment to party histories and core beliefs, as well as a formal obligation to democratic arrangements and procedures. And even as media institutions exercise influence in setting and pursuing agendas, any power is curtailed by sets of technical, conventional and regulatory limitations. In the example of the televised debates we will look at later, for example, the formalised practices of turn-taking and audience participation are negotiated between producers and political representatives, with close attention to the rules governing impartiality (Coleman 2000).

Media sociability and the conversationalisation of political discourse

As many of the concept's critics have pointed out, the explanatory purchase of mediatisation rests upon a clear idea of those qualities that characterise 'media logic'. In a discussion of broadcast media, Scannell (1996, p. 23) suggests the currency of 'sociability': the art of sustaining the company of an audience 'who have no particular reason, purpose or intention for turning on the radio or television set'. The imperative to be 'sociable' has a complex relation with media practice. For example, in parallel with their obligation to be engaging, broadcasts are motivated by 'strategic purposive intentions', such as the provision of information, or the sale of a product. Also, audience members congregate with incentives and demands of their own, ranging from enlightenment to idle distraction. Furthermore, as digital and social media come to prominence, there emerges an increasing variety of media platforms through which political and other types of information may be drawn, each offering their own appeals to their audiences and publics (Couldry, Livingstone & Markham 2007; Higgins 2008). Indeed, as participation and conversation become a more prominent part of the everyday experience of technology, the obligation for mediated discourse to be successfully 'engaging' becomes all the more pronounced.

If political communication is to be successful in a media context, it is therefore important that it adapts to the developing expectations of media form. While figuring as just one of these expectations, the imperatives of sociability are aided by a shift in style towards what Fairclough (1995) calls 'conversationalisation'. For Fairclough (1995, p. 142), the political consequences of this are rooted in its association with 'common sense' and its foregrounding intuitive forms of knowledge associated with the life-world: 'the voice of ordinary experience' (Fairclough 1995, p. 144). Later in the chapter, we will find this manifest as the 'populist ventriloquism' of the plain-speaking journalist, with an expressive commitment to 'how things seem' (Brundson & Morley 1978, p. 83). But for these efforts in conversationalisation to be apparent to those listening or watching, they often need sustained emphasis using a conspicuously colloquial lexicon, along with such indicators of conversational speech as the use of first person and hesitancy markers (Fairclough 1995).

Developing this association between conversationalisation and the predominance of the 'informal', Pearce (2005) charts the rise of conversational tokens in party-election broadcasts from the 1960s. Consistent with Scannell (1996), Pearce finds that discourse proceeds less on the basis of communicating policy intentions and bureaucratic ordinances than on the production of markers of a mutually supportive exchange. Accordingly, Pearce argues (2005, pp. 73–75) that features associated with formality such as elaborated noun-phrases have declined over time, to be replaced by tokens of informality, such as personal pronouns directed towards the listener, as well as those 'discourse markers' – contextual 'fillers' such as 'I mean' (Schiffrin 1987) – associated with spontaneous speech.

Yet, news and political coverage depend upon a constant negotiation of this informality with a necessary attitude of authority. Mediated strategies of conversationalisation therefore emerge in parallel with a display of political lexicon sufficient to associate the presenter with political access and competence. In line with our earlier remarks on political celebrity, Fairclough (1995, p. 147) and Higgins (2010) note that these negotiations may involve the 'personality' of the presenter as broadcaster, combining professional renown and performance with the institutional imperatives of the programme and format. In trying to identify the language patterns that underpin this personalisation, Pearce (2005, p. 75) points to an increased expression of 'stance', animating 'attitudes, value judgements or assessments'. While a number of these take the 'epistemic' form that may be expected of information-laden political discourse, many are also 'attitudinal' in 'reporting personal attitudes or feelings'. To some extent, personalisation has imported performative styles alien to early broadcasting into political journalism – aggression dominating over sociability, for example – which have subsequently developed as legitimated forms of media discourse (Clayman 2002; Higgins 2010).

Mediated political sincerity

So how do the qualities associated with conversationalisation aide political discourse? The figures that follow exemplify a conventional political ritual: statements issued by political leaders on a tragedy of national consequence. Such rituals are creatures of mediation in their very essence, and Boorstin (1963) sees these public statements as 'pseudo-events' initiated solely to be broadcast. However, they also amount to a communicative act of 'tribute'; of placing on record the personal torment of those in political power on occasions of collective mourning. In both cases, they draw upon the various traditions of political speaking described by Ilie and Sclafani in this volume (pp. 309 & 398, respectively) and include the communicative intentions of those press conferences discussed by Ekström and Eriksson also in this collection.

The statements we look at date from 1996 and are by then Prime Minister John Major and Leader of the Opposition Tony Blair, talking in response to the murder of a number of primary school children and their teacher in the town of Dunblane. Bracketed ellipses are used to mark pauses, a colon indicates the stretching of a sound or word, and underlining marks the speaker's emphasis:

1 JM We met a number of th:e (.) patients (.) some of whom had been (..) very severely
2 injured and (.) they are in (..) re<u>mark</u>ably good shape and there'd no doubt that they
3 had the most tremendous treat<u>ment</u> (..) and I was delighted to be here this morning
4 with Tony (.) to express (.) <u>our</u> thanks to th<u>em</u> for the work that they've done

Mediatisation and political language

```
 5  TB  I share all those (..) sentiments entirely (...) I think we were both struck by (.) the
 6      quite extraordinary dedication of the hospital staff here the way they have worked as
 7      a team in partnership together (..) and the dedication of the police and of course all
 8      those people at the school (...) it's been a quite (..) remarkable coming together and
 9      (...) I hope that in some (...) small way (..) I think we both found this rather distressing
10      and certainly very moving (..) our coming (.) today in uniting together can symbolise
11      (..) the unity of the country (.) and of people all around the world (.) in sympathy and
12      respect (.) for the people here in Dunblane [thank you]
13      [change of setting to street outside primary school]
14  JM  I don't think it is (.) possible (...) to put into words (.) precisely what they have had (.)
15      to deal with (..) and I think the way in which they have coped with all this (.) has been
16      quite (.) remarkable in every respect (....) the community and the school (..) will need
17      to put itself together over th:e months ahead (...) but I think that the strength (.) and
18      the resolution (...) that Tony and I found here in that school today suggests to us that
19      (..) hugely difficult task can be done
20  TB  I would (.) I would echo entirely what the (..) Prime Minister has just said (...) we
21      have seen for ourselves both th:e (..) enormity of the evil act that was (.) perpetrated at
22      the school (..) but also the quite (.) extraordinary (.) courage and resilience (...) of the
23      staff (..) of everyone connected with the school (.) and the local community (..) and I
24      know that we are both (...) absolutely proud to have been here (.) and to have paid
25      our respect to them (...) this community has suffered so much (..) and yet there is
26      such strength in it
```

(BBC 15 March 1996)

This extract produces what Montgomery (1999) has identified as a 'televisual' mode of public speaking by politicians that foregrounds sincerity and emotion over the conventional decorum of the political statement. As Smith and Higgins (2012) argue, the emotional trauma around Dunblane was manifest not only in the manner of its mediation, but in public and industry reception to the coverage and its tone. Fairclough (2000, p. 101) has already identified the prominence of 'ordinary' language and emotional empathy in Tony Blair's media performance, and the fraught emotions of the setting are reflected most vividly in Blair's lexical choice, such that references both to his own emotional state and to those of the local community figure strongly in his contributions ('rather distressing and certainly very moving' from lines 9 and 10 in the first address, and 'this community has suffered so much' from line 25 in the second).

We can also see evidence of what Montgomery (1999, p. 7) refers to as the rhetorical tactic of 'amplification', designed to emphasise the speakers' commitment, as well as the use of 'tact' in lending appropriateness to this expression of emotion. Instances of amplification come, first, in the use of adverbial phrases designed to stress the exceptionalness of the circumstances ('the quite extraordinary dedication' from Blair in line 6 and 'quite (..) remarkable coming together' from Blair and 'hugely difficult' from Major in line 19). In another example, this amplification is what Montgomery refers to as 'graduated'; thereby exercising tact in developing from a weaker to stronger formulation by situating sentiments first in the two political leaders themselves and then on behalf of the nation, before attributing them to the world as a whole ('our coming (.) today in uniting together can symbolise (..) the unity of the country (.) and of people all around the world (.) in sympathy and respect' on lines 10 and 11). In terms of emphasising measure and appropriateness, perhaps the most notable example of tact is Major's hedge on the expressive limits of his claim to empathy with the victims and community ('I don't think it is (.) possible (...) to put into words (.) precisely what they have had (.) to deal with' on line 14 and 15).

Another quality to characterise these extracts is the predominance of pauses and the stretching of words. One such pause is emphasised by Blair's switch in gaze to the side of the camera (Figure 25.1). These are not evenly spread across the extracts or speakers, such that Tony Blair produces many more pauses than John Major, and the second statement by Major makes more use of pauses than his first. (One way of interpreting this might be that Blair sets a performative tone in his initial contribution to which Major is then obliged to respond.) There are a number of purposes that pauses might serve in these extracts: one being the separation of passages of speech, and other being rhetorical effect, such that the measured use of pause in speech is essential to conventional political rhetoric, usually deployed in the service of devices such as contrast or accumulation (cf. Martin 2014). In Blair's second speech, the extract 'they have worked as a team in partnership together (..) and the dedication of the police and of course all those people at the school (...) it's been a quite (..) remarkable coming together' (lines 6 and 7) sees the first two pauses set between clauses, while the third separates 'remarkable' from its modifying advert 'quite'. This produces a performance of unscriptedness or sincerity, where Blair seems to be either searching for an appropriate word or struggling to contain his emotions. Likewise, in Major's second speech, 'and the resolution (...) that Tony and I found here in that school today suggests to us that (..) hugely difficult task can be done' the pauses are in keeping with the portrayal of an endeavor of such magnitude that it demands reflection; occasioning a hesitant and considered delivery. While there are embodied components to such a performance that we will turn to later, we can see here how Blair, especially, begins to dominate in using a combination of language choice and tactical use of pace to secure a mood of emotional commitment and authenticity.

Figure 25.1 'I hope that in some [...] small way'

Authentic personalities and the language of the popular

It is therefore clear that particular media performances foreground sincerity and emotional commitment, but there are related forms of media language dedicated towards expressing 'the popular' for party political purposes. The assumption of an institutionally-authored line is characteristic of much political talk, where party policies are enunciated and defended. Such institutional expression contrasts with what Wodak (2015, p. 131) describes as the populist drive to appear 'authentic', and of 'the people' in terms of taste, daily life and language. In echoes of Blair's speech from earlier (in the extract on p. 386), 'authentic' non-political discourse downplays education and refinement in favour of hesitancy and colloquialism (Wodak 2015, p. 132). In betokening the 'authenticity' of the speaker, colloquial language foregrounds the expression and commitment of the individual in political discourse. That is, while it is possible to be consistent and truthful in expressing a mutually agreed policy line and intentions, doing so while projecting an authentic performance is a statement of the self.

In this context, the maintenance of particular kinds of personality can give politicians expressive latitude that reaches beyond the conventional realms of political language. The following example is the opening paragraph of a UK *Daily Telegraph* column by then London Mayor Boris Johnson – a well-known and eccentric UK politician – lamenting the prospects for socialism, in the context of a debate over the then-leadership of the UK Labour Party:

1 Uh-oh, folks, this is starting to look serious. There really does appear to be a plot to remove Ed
2 Miliband. One paper has reported that there are 20 shadow ministers who are 'on the verge'
3 of asking him to step down. Nameless Labour MPs have said that the rebellion against Ed has
4 reached 'critical mass' – and one has a vision of fuel rods starting to shudder in a nuclear
5 reactor. Toxic steam is spurting from the innards; cracks are showing in the casing. Any minute
6 now the whole thing is going to go ka-boom, they say.
7 Tristram Hunt has turned up the pressure, by suggesting that his party leader is not much good
8 on TV. Clive Soley says Miliband is 'not getting his message across' – which is a way of saying
9 that he is useless. Half the Parliamentary Labour Party seems to be on the phone to the media,
10 whispering about the hopelessness of Miliband, while the other half is burnishing its own
11 leadership credentials.

(Johnson 2014)

This passage works to position Johnson as an explicitly 'anti-political' performer, given to endearingly whimsical outbursts. These aspects of Johnson's political identity are discussed at length by Ruddock (2006), who describes how Johnson has cultivated a public image directed towards a particular construction of the authentic. This is a persona that is nation-specific and class-identified, 'tapping cherished English upper class stereotypes (the naughty public schoolboy, the 'upper class twit')' (Ruddock 2006, p. 265), instanced here by the upper class associated pronoun 'one' (line 4). Every bit as accident-prone as the P G Wodehouse characters he often resembles, Johnson is also beguilingly shambolic, combining 'disarming charm, wit and intellect' (Ruddock 2006, p. 276). In a study of public responses to one of his many 'gaffes', Ruddock (2006, p. 276) points to a widely-reported admiration for Johnson as a 'distinctive figure in an otherwise "grey" political environment'.

Given the extent of his profile and the readership of the Conservative-supporting *Daily Telegraph*, it is reasonable to assume that the reader will be familiar with Johnson's style of speech, and recognise the manner in which the short, declarative sentences that open the extract give way to elaborate metaphor. Johnson also deploys the hedging identified by Montgomery (1999) in 'sincere' media public pronouncements, using 'seems' to playfully exaggerate the extent of his opponent's dissent ('Half the Parliamentary Labour Party seems to be on the phone to the media, whispering about the hopelessness of Miliband, while the other half is burnishing its own leadership credentials' on lines 9 to 11). Crucially, what Chouliaraki (2000, p. 297) describes as the 'intertextual' character of political discourse is manifest here as items from the lexicon of the British comic book ('uh-oh folks' on line 1, 'ka-boom' on line 6), that sit in contrast with phrasings more readily associable with the political field ('on the verge' on line 2, 'critical mass' on line 4); the latter conspicuously outsourced using quotation marks. This opposition between the straightforward language of 'Boris' and the implied prevarication of conventional politicians is then rendered unequivocal, as Johnson reformulates opposing politician Clive Soley's mannered euphemism 'not getting his message across' to Johnson's preferred style of 'a way of saying that he is useless' (lines 8 to 9).

Using Johnson as an example of the populist politician – and Campus (2010) and Niemi (2013) point to many others who are similar – we can see how the use of a popular lexical field works at cultivating certain kinds of mediated political persona. But, according to Brookes, Lewis and Wahl-Jorgensen (2004), there are other tactics of alignment dedicated towards claiming ownership of the link that media provides between the politicians and their electorate, such as in the way that media texts routinely claim to represent the 'public' in the pursuit of a shared interest. Higgins (2008) goes further, arguing that mediated political discourse routinely involves a struggle between media and politicians to be seen to speak on behalf of this 'public'. This is particularly noticeable in 'the accountability interview', where politicians vie with interviewers to align themselves with public concerns and sentiments (Montgomery 2007). Just as politicians seek a public mandate through election to office, in the context of media they are obliged to engage in a parallel and continual struggle for their claim to public representativeness.

The extract is from an interview between the above-mentioned Boris Johnson and BBC journalist Eddie Mair from 23 March 2013 on the news analysis programme the *Andrew Marr Show*. We pick up the interview as it turns to a forthcoming documentary 'exposing' elements of Johnson's personal history. In addition to the conventions outlined prior to the above extract, square brackets indicate overlap between speakers:

1 EM let me ask you about some of the things that came up in the docume[ntary
2 BJ [r right well I I haven't seen it [so
3 EM [but this happened in your life so you know about this (..) [The
4 BJ [clearly
5 EM Times let you go after you made up a quote (..) why did you make up a quote?
6 BJ (...) well ah (.) this this again y'know (.) these are these are (.) b:big terms for what
7   happened w I can tell you the whole thing I mean it was [mumbles] y'know ar are you
8   sure our viewers wouldn't want to hear more (.) about housing in London?
9   [about I can tell you
10 EM [if you don't want to talk about made up quotes let me talk about something
11 BJ it was a long it was a long and lamentable story
12 EM okay

(BBC 24 March 2013)

In terms of phrasing, it is clear that both interviewer and interviewee have temporarily absented themselves from the lexical field associated with politics. Interviewer Marr emphasises the topicality of the personal over political with 'this happened in your life' and offers two variations of the conspicuously informal construction 'made up quote'. While this seems at odds with the role of the interviewing journalist as a publicly appointed expert advocate (Clayman 2002; Higgins 2010), it bears comparison with the plain-speaking 'populist ventriloquism' described in Brunsdon and Morley's (1978) classic analysis of popular news. In response, Johnson produces markers of spontaneous and sincere speech, including punctuating 'discourse markers' 'well, ah' and 'y'know'; although in this instance they may betray a genuine rather than rehearsed hesitancy. Notably, however, Johnson's third turn produces the kind of claim to an alternative configuration of the public interest described by Brookes, Lewis and Wahl-Jorgensen (2004) and Higgins (2008): 'y'know ar are you sure our viewers wouldn't want to hear more (.) about housing in London?' (lines 8 and 9). Even when edging round the norms of political discourse, such claims to speak for the polity are at times necessary in a media setting, particularly when it is in the politician's interest to retreat to a claim to the authority of public representativeness. Indeed, in Johnson's case, the doubly articulated reach of the claim is emphasised still further in his formulation of this political public as 'our viewers'.

Political leaflets: affinity and intertextuality

At the outset of the chapter, it was claimed this media intimacy extended to printed media. Having looked at Boris Johnson's newspaper column, we now turn to how these qualities of sociability and sincerity are manifest in election literature: a form more associated with political institutions and their reflective processes than with the dialogic spontaneity of individual performance. The page below comes from a leaflet distributed by the 'Yes' campaign in the 2014 referendum for Scottish independence (Yes Scotland 2014):

In terms of its political purpose, this text manifests the anti-elite qualities of populism, articulated with a narrative of national belonging (Wodak et al. 2009) and guided by the principles of media sociability. The thrust of the two paragraphs is to set the actions of centralising politicians apart from the interests of the audience. 'Westminster' as a metonym for the UK political establishment (Higgins 2004, p. 642) is set against the inclusive category of 'our nation', later rendered in the nation-specific terms of 'Scotland'. Indeed, the opposition between formal-political and informal lexicons are used humorously, in a rhetorical opposition between 'Devo Max' and 'devo-a-wee-bit-more' ('wee' being Scots dialect for 'small' or slight').

Also, while this is an official referendum communication, informality and conversationalisation are in play throughout. The externalised Westminster parties' keenness to act is expressed as 'falling over themselves', associating elements of ungainly slapstick with the intentions of political opponents. Elaborated phrasings are deployed for emphasis (Pearce 2005), such as 'actually ever happen', a tactic we have already seen in Tony Blair's use of 'quite' in the spoken extracts above. Calling upon what Horton and Wahl (1982) describe as a technique of 'para-social interaction', through which an audience is addressed as though it were present, rhetorical questions are issued, including one ending in the elaborated verb phrase 'how will they ever agree?'. Also from the rhetorical toolbox of mediatised sincerity, repetition is used in up-shifting 'change' to 'real change'.

We have discussed the imperative of 'sociability' above. In this case, the text of the leaflet is purposively dialogic, such that the discourse of inclusivity extends to the assumption of a

Michael Higgins

Promises, promises.

As the referendum date gets ever closer Westminster parties have been falling over themselves to offer more powers for Scotland. The different packages amount to little more than 'devo-a-wee-bit- more'. Westminster is still not prepared to hand the Scottish Parliament any of the real powers which can change our nation for the better. And why are they making these offers now, when these same politicians wouldn't even let 'Devo Max' be an option on the ballot paper? The answer is obvious; they've woken up to the fact that Scotland wants change, real change. On that point, we all agree.

Definitely, maybe.

If the main Westminster parties can't agree amongst themselves, how will they ever agree on the scale of powers for Scotland? What's more, after the General Election of 2015 it will be all change again, with no guarantee that any one of the parties' proposals will actually ever happen. And let's not forget Westminster has made promises to Scotland many times before and failed to deliver. A Yes vote is the only guarantee of not just more powers for Scotland, but complete power for Scotland.

Scotland's future in Scotland's hands.

Figure 25.2 Yes Scotland, *Why independence will be the best thing for generations*
Source: (Yes Scotland 2014)

shared investment in the development of the position. For example, conversational strategies of amplification are in play, such as 'What's more', serving to accumulate points towards an overall argument. As a contribution to a debate around statehood and sovereignty, the leaflet also has a concern in maintaining what Billig (1995) identifies as a shared assumption of national belonging. This is a mood of common purpose that is manifest in lexical terms. After the rhetorical question deploying the political item of 'Devo Max', the first paragraph marshals the national body within an inclusive pronoun on assent, 'On that point, we all agree'; an assumption of a shared critical faculty that continues with the pronominal phrase 'let's not forget'.

While we have identified a correspondence between conversationalisation and media logic, there remains the possibility that both media and politics merely draw upon a common well of sociability and the comforting rhetoric of mutual regard. However, there are other identifiable qualities here that draw more explicitly from media discourse. Prominent on the leaflet are two brief headlines pertaining to each of the paragraphs. Both of these perform the function of 'soft' intros, by alluding to the content of the main bodies of text without necessarily betraying the detail that follows. We have seen elements of intertexuality in Johnson's hints at comic book language, but the intertextuality of these extracts is more explicitly anchored, drawing upon recognisable items from popular music: one, 'Promises,

Promises' from the name of a Bacharach and David musical, and another, 'Definitely, Maybe' from the title of "Britpop" group Oasis's debut album. Thus, the popular credentials of the text is secured in its language and in the repertoire of cultural references.

The political debate and the semiotics of empathy

The final platform that we will look at in order to understand these aspects of the mediatisation of political language is that of the televised debate. Although long-established in the US, the televised election party leaders' debate was introduced to the UK at the 2010 general election (Drake & Higgins 2012). The following extract is one of two debates held between representatives of the two sides of the 2014 referendum on Scottish independence. This second debate, which was broadcast on the BBC, was one in which Alex Salmond of the Scottish National Party (SNP) was thought to have performed more strongly. This extract is from a turn dealing with a debate on currency, in which Salmond was said to have excelled:

1   I know there's other options for Scotland (.) I mean we could have a (.) eh Scottish currency
2   we'd have flexible currency like Sweden or Norway does (..) we could have a fixed rate a
3   Scottish pound attached to the (.) the pound sterling eh that's what Denmark does with the
4   Euro of what I'm seeking a mandate for (.) is to have the pound sterling (.) so we pay our
5   messages we pay our mortgage (.) we get our wages in the pound

(BBC 25 August 2014)

Even from this brief extract, we can see political rhetoric combined with the qualities we now associate with mediatisation. Although it may appear as though Salmond is making his way through a list of refused options in order to emphasise and settle on his preferred choice (Atkinson 1984), the uncertainty of the currency settlement is such that Salmond is obliged to display his understanding of alternative options. There are markers of spontaneity – and sincerity – in the pauses before delivery of the first and second choices (lines 1 and 2), along with a crafted emphasis on items of the political and economic lexicon ('flexible' on line 2, 'fixed rate' on lines 2–3, 'mandate' and 'pound sterling' on line 4), as well as on individual economic action in 'pay' (lines 4 and 5). The monetary union dilemma is also expressed as a concern shared between Salmond and the listening audience, and their common appreciation of an appropriate informal lexicon is marked in the use of the informal Scots term for grocery shopping, 'messages'.

What recommends this extract over the portion of the address that preceded it is that Salmond has stepped out from behind the podium in order to stand closer to the studio audience and cameras (see figure 25.3). In terms outlined in Peters' (2001) discussion of 'bearing witness', Salmond produces a token of personal investment and a willingness to offer the body as 'collateral' for his words. Exposed in this way, the body constitutes a display of willingness to disregard personal imperilment for the benefits of sharing the same space, engaging with and emphasising. This extra-linguistic performance ventures beyond the conventions of professional practice by foregoing the formality and stuffiness of the stage props. In a gesture of alignment with 'the people' (Wodak 2015), Salmond abandons the podium as a symbol of political institutionalism and a restraint on his desired connection with the ordinary electorate. But of course, this abandonment of the conventionality represented by the podium has become a semiotic resource of itself. The alignment of this type of embodied performance with particular linguistic markers of sincerity and belonging

Michael Higgins

Figure 25.3 Alex Salmond steps out from behind the podium

was also a feature of the analysis of Nick Clegg's contribution to the leader debates of the 2010 UK general election (Drake & Higgins 2012; Parry & Richardson 2011).

Granted, this is only one example of the visual aspect of mediated political performance. A fuller multimodal approach to mediated political expression will be sure to reveal other, related, markers of embodied sincerity among politicians, such as deploying a markedly casual appearance or, as Cameron (1996, p. 95) suggests, speaking with an 'authentically' non-elite accent. Yet, such gestures of affinity remain subject to the norms of political proprietary and can remain subject to the essential elements of a political demeanour. The successful navigation of set-piece events, such as interviews and ritualised debates may demand embodied and linguistic markers of sincerity, but only as part of a dynamic in which political credibility remains the dominant concern. On the basis of what we have seen so far, televised debates show these negotiations in practice, producing what may be described as a semiotics of affective empathy, combining language with embodied performance, directed to achieving formal political ends.

Conclusion

There are few qualities in political language that are solely attributable to mediatisation. The activities of both language and politics draw upon a similar cultural lexicon, and are committed to related imperatives of care over expression and comprehensibility, including developments in emotionality outside media and politics (cf. Eccelstone & Hayes 2008). As critics of the mediatisation thesis point out, media logic is designed to appeal, retain attention and persuade, and can internalise the priorities of other cultural forms that are similarly directed. In producing sociability, for example, media aspires to the pleasures of non-mediated conversation, leaving a tangled relation between media politics and the skills and norms of public address. Nevertheless, there are particular priorities in mediatisation that reflect upon and often reconfigure the composition of political language. Mazzoleni (2014, p. 45) points to 'the spectacularisation of political discourse, "personalisation" involving a focus on personal aspects at the expense of policies [...], the simplification of political speeches – the 'sound-bite' effect – and the 'winnowing' of political actors according to their mediagenic presentation'. We can see that, at least to some extent, the personalisation and 'simplification' of political language are entwined, such that the foregrounding of personality, including the 'synthetic personalisation' of conventional political texts, are bound up with what Scannell (1996) describes as the imperative to provide the easy pleasures of sociability; offering a politics designed to please rather than improve and to reassure rather than challenge.

Future thinking on mediatisation and political language should also account for the persuasive purpose that communication serves within the political realm. Recent discussions of the rise of 'mediated populism' have emphasised the obligation of politically-directed language to avoid appearing 'political' (Higgins 2009). That is, as soon as a rhetorical act becomes exposed as a structured political tactic, its persuasive force gives way to the appearance of manipulative cynicism. As journalism moves towards the production of emotional affect (Richards 2007; Wahl-Jorgensen 2013), this has implications for the language and performance associated with the mediatisation of the political. Also, as van Leeuwen shows in this volume, a multimodal approach is necessary to situate language within a broader communication field, including the networks of association and significance in media format and performance. Across these developing contexts, there is much to be gained in examining the extent to which political language strives towards the sociability and informalisation that has characterised the development of media discourse in general.

Acknowledgements

The author owes thanks to Angela Smith, Mari K Niemi, Burcu Demirdöven and Fiona M McKay for their thoughts and input, as well as for the constructive feedback of the collection's referees and editors.

References

Atkinson, M, 1984, *Our master's voices*, Routledge, London.
BBC, 1996, *Six o'clock news*, 15 March 1996.
BBC, 2013, *The Andrew Marr show*, 23 March 2013.
BBC, 2014, *Scotland decides*, 25 August 2014.
Billig, M, 1995, *Banal nationalism*, Sage, London.
Boorstin, D J, 1963, *The image, or what happened to the American dream*, Athenaeum, New York.
Brookes, R, Lewis, J & Wahl-Jorgensen, K, 2004, 'The media representation of public opinion: British television news coverage of the 2001 General Election', *Media, Culture & Society*, vol. 26, no. 1, pp. 63–80.
Brunsdon, C & Morley, D, 1978, *Everyday television: Nationwide*, BFI, London.
Cameron, D, 1996, 'The accents of politics', *Critical Quarterly*, vol. 38, no. 4, pp. 93–96.
Campus, D, 2010, 'Mediatization and personalisation of politics in Italy and France: The cases of Berlusconi and Sarkozy', *International Journal of Press/Politics*, vol. 15, no. 2, pp. 219–235.
Chouliaraki, L, 2000, 'Political discourse in the news: Democratizing responsibility or aestheticizing politics?' *Discourse & Society*, vol. 11, no. 3, pp. 293–314.
Clayman, S E, 2002, '"Tribune of the people": Maintaining the legitimacy of aggressive journalism', *Media, Culture & Society*, vol. 24, no. 2, pp. 197–216.
Coleman, S, ed., 2000, *Televised election debates: International perspectives*, Macmillan, London.

Corner, J, 2003, 'The celebrity politician: political style and popular culture', in *Media and the restyling of politics*, eds. J Corner & D Pels, Sage, London, pp. 67–84.
Corner, J & Pels, D, 2003 'Introduction: the re-styling of politics', in *Media and the restyling of politics*, eds, J Corner & D Pels, Sage, London, pp. 1–18.
Couldry, N, Livingstone, S & Markham, T, 2007, *Media consumption and public engagement*, Palgrave Macmillan, Basingstoke.
Drake, P & Higgins, M, 2012, 'Lights, camera, election: celebrity, performance and the 2010 general election leadership debates', *British Journal of Politics and International Relations*, vol. 14, no. 3, pp. 375–391.
Eccelstone, K & Hayes, D, 2008, *The dangerous rise of therapeutic education*, Routledge, Abingdon.
Esser, F & Strömbäck, J, eds., 2014, *Mediatization of politics*, Palgrave Macmillan, Basingstoke.
Fairclough, N, 1995, *Media discourse*, Arnold, London.
Fairclough, N, 2000, *New Labour, new language*, Routledge, Abingdon.
Fairclough, N & Mauranen, A, 1997, 'The conversationalisation of political discourse: a comparative view', *Belgian Journal of Linguistics*, vol 11, no. 1, pp. 89–119.
Forchtner, B, Krzyżanowski, M & Wodak, R, 2013, 'Mediatization, right-wing populism and political campaigning: The case of the Austrian Freedom Party', in *Media talk and political elections in Europe and America*, eds. A Tolson & M Ekström, Palgrave Macmillan, Basingstoke, pp. 205–228.
Franklin, B, 2004, *Packaging politics*, 2nd ed., Arnold, London.
Gorman, R, 1945, 'Foreword,' in *Molders of opinion*, ed. D Bulman, Bruce Publishing, Milwaukee, WI, pp. v–viii.
Higgins, M, 2004, 'Putting the nation in the news', *Discourse & Society*, vol 15, no. 5, pp. 633–648.
Higgins, M, 2008, *Media and their publics*, Open University Press, Maidenhead.
Higgins, M, 2009, 'Populism and security in political speechmaking: The 2008 US Presidential Campaign', in *Media, religion and conflict*, eds. L Marsden & H Savigny, Ashgate, Farnham, pp. 129–144.
Higgins, M, 2010, 'The public inquisitor as media celebrity', *Cultural Politics*, vol. 6, no. 1, pp. 93–110.
Hjarvard, S, 2013, *The mediatization of culture and society*, Routledge, Abingdon.
Horton, D & Wohl, R R, 1982, 'Mass communication and para-social interaction: Observation on intimacy at a distance', in *Inter/media: interpersonal communication in a media world*, eds. G Gumpert & R Cathcart, Oxford University Press, New York, pp. 188–210.
Jamieson, K H, 1996, *Packaging the presidency*, 3rd ed., Oxford University Press, New York.
Johnson, B, 2014, 'Ditching Ed Miliband will not change the fact that "socialism" has no relevance these days', *The Daily Telegraph*, 9 November, p. 10.
Langer, A I, 2012, *The personalisation of politics in the UK*, Manchester University Press, Manchester.
Martin, J, 2014, *Politics and rhetoric*, Routledge, Abingdon.
Mazzoleni, G, 2014, 'Mediatization and political populism', in *Mediatization of politics*, eds. F Esser & J Strömbäck, Palgrave Macmillan, Basingstoke, pp. 42–56.
Mazzoleni, G & Schulz W, 1999, 'Mediatization of politics? A challenge for democracy', *Political Communication*, vol. 16, no. 3, pp. 247–261.
Montgomery, M, 1999, 'Speaking sincerely: Public reactions to the death of Diana', *Language and Literature*, vol. 8. no. 1, pp. 5–33.
Montgomery, M, 2007, *The discourse of broadcast news*, Routledge, Abingdon.
Niemi, M K, 2013, 'The true Finns: Identity politics and populist leadership on the threshold of the party's electoral triumph', *Javnost – The Public*, vol. 20, no. 3, pp. 77–92.
Parry, K & Richardson, K, 2011, 'Political imagery in the British general election of 2010: the curious case of "Nick Clegg"', *British Journal of Politics and International Relations*, vol. 13, no. 4, pp. 474–489.
Pearce, M, 2005, 'Informalization in UK party election broadcasts, 1966–97', *Language and Literature*, vol. 14, no. 1, pp. 65–90.
Peters, J D, 2001, 'Witnessing', *Media, Culture & Society*, vol. 32, no. 6, pp. 707–723.

Richards, B, 2007, *Emotional governance*, Palgrave Macmillan, Basingstoke.

Ruddock, A, 2006, 'Invisible centers: Boris Johnson, authenticity, cultural citizenship and centrifugal model of media power', *Social Semiotics,* vol. 16, no. 2, pp. 263–282.

Savigny, H, 2008, *The problem of political marketing*, Continuum, London.

Scannell, P, 1996, *Radio, television and modern life*, Blackwell, Oxford.

Schiffrin, D, 1987, *Discourse markers*, Cambridge University Press, Cambridge.

Smith, A & Higgins, M, 2012, 'The convenient ambiguity of tone: Style and the politics of witnessing in Kate Adie's reporting of the Dunblane tragedy', *Journalism,* vol. 13, no. 8, pp. 1081–1095.

Street, J, 2004, 'Celebrity politicians: Popular culture and political representation', *British Journal of Politics and International Relations,* vol. 6, no. 4, pp. 435–452.

Street, J, 2011, *Mass media, politics and democracy*, 2nd ed., Palgrave Macmillan, Basingstoke.

Thompson, J B, 1995, *The media and modernity*, Polity, Cambridge.

Thompson, J B, 2000, *Political scandal*, Polity, Cambridge.

Wahl-Jorgensen, K, 2013, 'The strategic ritual of emotionality: A case study of Pulitzer Prize-winning articles', *Journalism,* vol. 14, no. 1, pp. 129–145.

Wilson, J, 1990, *Politically speaking*, Blackwell, Oxford.

Wodak, R, 2009, *The discourse of politics in action*, Palgrave Macmillan, Basingstoke.

Wodak, R, 2015, *The politics of fear,* Sage, London.

Wodak, R, de Cillia, R, Reisigl, M & Liebhart, K, 2009, *The discursive construction of national identity*, 2nd ed., Edinburgh University Press, Edinburgh.

Yes Scotland, 2014, *Why independence will be the best thing for generations*, Yes Scotland, Glasgow.

26
Performing politics
From the town hall to the inauguration

Jennifer Sclafani

Political discourse and identity performance

Throughout the course of a campaign, political candidates make hundreds of public appearances, with the goal of connecting with voters, explaining their policy proposals and energising the public to engage in the political process. From town hall meetings to the inaugural ceremony, candidates and electees have multitudinous opportunities to engage directly with constituents, to answer voters' questions and concerns, and to formally address the public about their visions, priorities and intended actions, if and when they are elected to office.

This chapter argues that all forms of public political (inter)action, from town hall question-answer interactions to inaugural addresses, constitute *identity performances* whose discursive structure can be fruitfully analysed using tools of interactional sociolinguistics. Much of the existing body of literature within linguistics examining political discourse has come from Critical Discourse Analysis (CDA), an approach that has traditionally focused on how 'opaque as well as transparent structural relationships of dominance, discrimination, power, and control [are] manifested in language' (Wodak 1995, p. 204). CDA has made great strides in uncovering how language is used to uphold and reinforce relations of dominance and subordination, especially by 'elite' groups in institutions (e.g. Chilton 1996; Fairclough 2001; van Dijk 1993; Reisigl & Wodak 2001). More recently, scholars in this field have investigated the role of discursively constructed political subjectivities – or *political selves,* to borrow Duranti's (2006) term – in accomplishing political action (e.g. Carta & Wodak 2015; Charteris-Black 2013; Chilton 2004; Chilton & Schäffner 2002; Wodak 2011). In order for political actions to be accepted (at least in democratic societies) by a majority as 'necessary', 'justified' or 'logical', they must be constructed as originating from political *individuals* that are deemed in some way 'trustworthy', 'relatable' and 'authentic' (Sclafani 2015; in press). So just how do political individuals manage to convince an electorate that they can be trusted in positions of authority? I suggest that we can answer this question by analysing political performances using tools of interactional sociolinguistics.

It has been argued, especially by scholars of American political communication, that the construction of an authentic political self is of utmost importance (e.g. Duranti 2006;

Lempert & Silverstein 2012; Stewart 2012; Teven 2008), since both the US voting public and the mass media largely evaluate political candidates, not on the basis of their professional qualifications, voting records, or official positions on policy issues, but on the basis of self-presentation, and specifically on account of a number of qualities related to the candidate's perceived *personal* identity. As Polsby et al. (2012) remark:

> A candidate is helped by appearing trustworthy, reliable, knowledgeable, mature, empathetic, pious, even-tempered, kind but firm, devoted to family and country, and in every way normal and presentable. To this end, a great deal of campaign activity is devoted to the portrayal of the candidate as a likable person and typical American.
> (Polsby et al. 2012, p. 158)

Given both voters' attention to a candidate's self-presentation and the related effort and money put into managing political figures' public images (see, e.g. Hacker 2004), the linguistic basis of self-presentation merits more detailed attention than it has been accorded in the fields of political communication and rhetoric. I offer the perspective that public political discourse can be viewed as *discursive performances of identity* in which political actors strategically construct themselves as not only knowledgeable and experienced in the positions they currently hold or aim to hold, but that they are trustworthy, relatable and likeable individuals, and hence, worthy leaders.

I do this by first reviewing recent work in socio-cultural linguistics that has addressed political interaction in this way, focusing on work from the past decade on the American political context because of the unique status that personal identity plays in the American political sphere. Next, I review two particularly fruitful concepts central to discourse-analytic approaches to social identity – namely, framing and positioning – and demonstrate how these may be employed in the study of language and politics through case studies of two prominent women in contemporary American politics – US Senator Joni Ernst and former US Secretary of State and (at the time of writing) second-time presidential candidate Hillary Rodham Clinton. Through a brief examination of the way these political figures position themselves and (re)frame interactions in contexts such as town hall meetings, debates, campaign advertisements and speeches, I highlight the fact that political identity is an interactional achievement, which is both strategically crafted as part of a political figure's brand, but is also emergent and malleable in interactional contexts. I conclude by suggesting fruitful avenues for further study in this field.

Approaches to political identity as performance

The concept of social identity as a performance or an interactional achievement is by no means new in socio-cultural linguistics (e.g. Ochs 1992; 1993) or social theory in general (e.g. Goffman 1959; Berger & Luckmann 1966). However, the various discursive strategies through which identity performances play out, as well as the complex layers of social meaning implicated in such performances, have enjoyed a great deal of attention over the past couple of decades. Bucholtz and Hall's (2005) framework for theorising discursive identity construction identifies key principles associated with the performed and performative nature of identity as opposed to a static, macro-level, analyst-determined category or set of demographic variables. Specifically, they highlight the idea that identity is emergent in interaction, and that both fleeting roles and enduring categories are indexed at multiple levels of discursive structure (see also Ochs 1992, 1993; Silverstein 2003). They also emphasise that identities are always constructed in relation to a variety of other potential subject positions within the dialectic of structure and agency.

Sociolinguistic studies of political identity have drawn on these principles, illustrating how political subjectivities and stances are performed in a variety of public contexts. Within the variationist perspective, for example, Podesva et al. (2012) have investigated how phonological variables in US English, such as final /-d/ release and vowel qualities, pattern out in the public speeches of former US Secretary of State Condoleeza Rice, demonstrating how these patterns construct her as a politically conservative, professional African American. Hall-Lew, Coppock & Starr (2010), however, have investigated the phonetic construction of political identity at the group level by demonstrating a correlation between political party affiliation and the various pronunciations of the second vowel in the word 'Iraq' among members of US Congress.

Given the important interactional function of narrative in positioning the self and others and the construction of socio-cultural worlds (e.g. Bruner 1987; Ochs & Capps 2001; Schiffrin 1996, 2006), narrative analysis has also been influential in the study of political identity construction. Duranti (2006) analyses narrative in US congressional debates, examining how candidates tell stories to construct a 'political self', in which they discursively manage two opposing constraints: the need to appear both logical and authentic. In his words, 'candidates must tell stories of their own actions that are solid enough to stand the scrutiny of others in terms of their logic and at the same time must project a type of commitment to voters that can sound authentic' (p. 468). Duranti demonstrates that narrative serves not only in constructing surface-level textual coherence (i.e. cohesion), but in creating 'existential coherence' (p. 472), which involves candidates' presentation of their current actions as natural extensions of the past, and exposing and resolving potential contradictions of character.

Shenhav (2009) also takes a narrative approach to the analysis of political speeches, examining narratives in closing statements of presidential debates. Shenhav argues that qualitative differences in the relative narrativity of closing statements can be correlated with demographic voting patterns as an indicator of 'the power given by the people to the politicians'. This study takes the important step of considering the dialogical *effects* of narrative in political discourse. Hodges (2011) takes a similar approach, examining how one hegemonic narrative of recent US history – that is, the story of the 'War on Terror' – was shaped and reshaped, circulated and resisted in presidential speeches and media discourse during the US war in Iraq, and how the narrative was received and entextualised in talk about post-9/11 politics among college students. Focusing on pragmatic features such as presupposition, entailment and poetic structures, Hodges demonstrates how narrative serves in the process of discursively constructing Al Qaeda and Iraq as linked antagonists, while portraying US military intervention in Afghanistan and Iraq as causally and temporally linked events in the larger War on Terror.

Intertextual discourse analysis has been particularly illuminating in the study of political performance as it highlights connections across disparate speech events, speakers and discursive contexts, and helps us understand how political figures create existential coherence. Austermühl (2014) also uses intertextuality as a framework to analyse presidential discourse and American identity in the inaugural speeches of US presidents. He shows that linguistic features such as personal pronouns, generic conventions and themes, and direct quotation, establish and reaffirm an overarching presidential identity over time and across individual presidents, thus creating, in Ausermühl's words, a historical 'scaffold' for a timeless national identity.

While intertextual analyses have highlighted how political identities are consolidated over time, and between public and private contexts, other approaches have incorporated insights relating to face maintenance and linguistic politeness (Goffman 1967; Brown & Levinson 1987) in order to better understand how political actors manage their self-presentation locally, especially in interactional genres of political discourse, such as political interviews and debates. For example, Beck (1996) and Clayman (2001) have employed tools of conversation analysis to demonstrate that sequential aspects of talk and floor management in these genres have an important bearing on how political figures manage their identity construction. Clayman (2001) examines question- and-answer pairs in political interviews, illuminating interviewees' tactics of question evasion as they 'gain substantial "wiggle room" for pursuing their own agendas even under the most persistent interrogation' (p. 439). Beck (1996), however, examines similar strategies in a vice-presidential debate, finding that different conversational floor-management tactics affect viewers impressions of candidates' relative leadership potential.

Other studies have taken multimodal approaches to the analysis of political performances, considering how non-verbal communication, including gesture and posture, work in concert with linguistic strategies to construct political personae. Lempert (2011) (see also Lempert & Silverstein 2012) provides a nuanced analysis of former President Barack Obama's 'precision-grip' gesture, showing how an information focus-marking gesture can contribute toward indexing the social act of making a 'sharp' or 'effective' point. Lempert argues that such indexical meanings furthermore accrete over time to construct the speaker's personal qualities, thus contributing to the politician's 'brand' as a sharp, effective speaker.

Another multimodal consideration of political performance is offered by Sheldon (2015), who examines the intersection of linguistic and embodied identity acts performed by Hillary Rodham Clinton in a town hall speech during her 2008 presidential campaign, in which she reacts to a heckler's sexist remarks. Sheldon shows that despite the rehearsed and predictable nature of the town hall speech, there are, nonetheless, occasions for impromptu identity management, and that Clinton successfully capitalises on the disruption in order to reframe the unexpected event as an opportunity to call attention to, and disrupt, dominant ideologies that normalise misogyny in the US political sphere. Sheldon's analysis also reveals how the unique participation format of the town hall speech – with audience members supporting her both in the audience and behind her on stage – reinforce the candidate's self-presentation as a cool yet powerful persona. Given Clinton's status as the most-recognised and most-accomplished woman in contemporary US politics, and the continued discussion over the role and perception of women in positions of power in US political life, I will continue this line of inquiry by examining another case in which Hillary Rodham Clinton had to manage her identity by reframing an interaction below (p. 403).

Interactional sociolinguistic frameworks: framing and positioning

There are clear links between the studies summarised thus far in terms of both their approaches in viewing political performances as interactional achievements and the assumptions they make about the relationship between (political) speaking figures and (voting) hearers. Interactional sociolinguistics, an approach to discourse analysis grounded in the work of John Gumperz (e.g. 1982) and Erving Goffman (e.g. 1959, 1974, 1981), highlights these themes through its focus on the situated nature of meaning-making and its view of language as a form of social action that has tangible effects on social identities and relations between speakers, hearers and contexts of talk. The study of language and politics benefits from viewing public political interaction through the lens of interactional sociolinguistics because it grounds language in dialogic interaction, even when the data under investigation may seem relatively monologic on the surface (e.g. as in a scripted presidential address or a campaign advertisement). In other words, political discourse is always interactional in that language is used to persuade a voting public that a political actor's actions and positions are justified. Politicians also use language to respond to feedback they have received from the public through media coverage and polling data. Because interactional sociolinguistics links language structures and their interactional functions to broader conceptual phenomena, such as knowledge schemas and cultural expectations (Tannen & Wallat 1993), this approach also allows us to bridge micro and macro levels of context in the study of language and society. In what follows, I explain and illustrate the utility of two interactional sociolinguistic concepts – framing and positioning – in the study of political discourse as identity performance.

Framing and reframing in political interaction

Framing is a concept that has been widely applied in studies of individual and group identity construction and in the interpersonal negotiation of meaning. The notion of a 'frame', first put forth by Gregory Bateson (1972), was developed by Goffman (1974) in an attempt to explicate the nature of intersubjective engagement in social interaction. Frames are defined as the definition that individuals attribute to a situation – for example, 'this is play' or 'this is work'. As such, frames play a central role in structuring interaction because they provide an interpretive scaffold on which speakers and hearers rely in order to produce and interpret meaning from linguistic, paralinguistic and non-verbal cues. Frames govern pragmatic interpretations of language use in the immediate interactional context, they guide participants' expectations of what is to occur in the following talk and they retrospectively shape understandings of what has occurred in the preceding talk. For example, first-name introductions set the expectation that the following encounter is friendly, informal, or outside an institutional setting, while ending a conversation with the expression 'that's what she said!' reframes a prior utterance (with a presumably innocent illocutionary force) as a sexual innuendo.

Framing is important for understanding political performances because much of what political figures do in their public performances is project, uphold and reinforce a sense of their political self in a certain social world full of problems that can be ameliorated by individuals in their roles as elected leaders. As such, they must draw on a variety of available resources within the particular socio-political field to construct their identities as credible leaders. I have shown elsewhere that US presidential candidates use their identities as mothers, fathers and grandfathers – that is, as effective leaders within their families – as a widely relatable leadership role that frames their projected role in leading the nation (Sclafani 2015). When such 'transportable' identities (Zimmerman 1998) are not available to candidates, or they could jeopardise the identity that they wish to project, candidates may borrow other available identities to construct an alternative type of leader, thus *reframing* the presidential self.

Framing and reframing have been analysed as key political communication strategies, most notably discussed by G Lakoff (2014 [2004]), as well as others analysing metaphors as conceptual framing devices in political and media discourse (e.g. Charteris-Black 2013; Chilton 1996; Santa Ana 2002). However, scholars of political discourse have largely focused on frames in the abstract cognitive sense and have ignored frames as an interactional achievement that are open to negotiation. Sheldon's (2015) analysis of Hillary Rodham Clinton's town hall address, summarised earlier (p. 401), is an exception in this regard, as she describes in great detail how Clinton's verbal and non-verbal reaction to a disruptive audience member *reframes* an unexpected move that could have potentially derailed her performance as an opportunity to openly address broader issues of sexism in the US political sphere.

The speech that Sheldon analyses is by no means an exceptional situation, although considering Clinton's political trajectory and the 'double bind' for women in politics more generally (following R Lakoff 2004 [1975]; see also Jamieson 1995), the discursive balancing act that a figure such as Clinton must regularly perform may have an intensified semiotic potential. Given the prominence of Hillary Clinton in the US political sphere over the past two decades due to both her individual achievements and the intense public scrutiny she has received in her political and familial roles, I now turn to another episode in which Clinton was forced to interactively reframe a conversation and her gender-political identity. The context I examine is a 2008 nationally televised presidential primary debate in which Clinton was questioned by the debate co-moderator about her disputed 'likability'.

Framing case study: Clinton's 'That hurts my feelings'

One of the most talked-about moments of the 2008 Democratic primary election cycle was the 5 January debate between Barack Obama and Hillary Clinton at St Anselm College in Manchester, New Hampshire, aired on ABC, in which co-moderator Scott Spradling asked Clinton the following question:

(1) 2008 Democratic Primary Debate[1]
Spradling: The University of New Hampshire Survey Center has been consistently trying to probe the minds of New Hampshire voters and get a sense of what they think about all of you. I'd be happy to report that the experience vs. change debate seems to be sinking it... My question to you is simply this: What can you say to the voters of New Hampshire on this stage tonight, who see your resume and like it, but are hesitating on the likability issue, where they seem to like Barack Obama more.
Clinton: Well that hurts my feelings. {Clinton closes eyes and grimaces ironically; laughter in audience}
Spradling: I'm sorry, Senator. {Continued laughter, scattered applause.} I'm sorry.
Clinton: But I'll try to go on. {Laughter.} He's *very* likable. I- I agree with that. I don't think I'm that bad.
Obama: You're likable enough, Hillary. No doubt [about it.
Clinton: [Thank you, I appreciate that. {Bobbling head humorously} You know, I think this is one of the most serious decisions that the voters of New Hampshire have ever had to make. And I really believe that the most important question is, who is ready to be president on day one?...you know, in 2000 we, unfortunately, ended up with a president who people said they wanted to have a beer with... So I am offering 35 years of experience making change and the results to show for it... But I think if you want to know what change each of us will bring about, look at what we've done.
(5 January Obama & Clinton debate, New Hampshire, ABC 2008)

In this excerpt, Spradling's question regarding Clinton's likability constitutes an abrupt topic/focus transition from his previous statement about the debate theme of 'experience versus change'. The only cohesive device tying his question regarding Clinton's likability to his previous statement is his reference to her 'resume' (which highlights her more extensive experience in national politics than her opponent), which Spradling posits that New Hampshire voters 'like'. This assertion, which is embedded in a non-restrictive clause, sets up a contrast with his next assertion – that voters 'seem to like Obama more'. This question challenges Clinton's presentation of self – specifically threatening what is referred to in theories of linguistic politeness as her 'positive face' (Brown & Levinson 1987) – by calling into question an aspect of her identity that cannot be refuted by any of her professional credentials that qualify her for the presidency. This question is perhaps the most illustrative example of the double bind for women in politics: Clinton, despite her extensive experience in the male-dominated political arena, and perhaps because of it, is cast as 'unlikable' precisely because, according to dominant ideologies of gender and leadership, femininity and political power mix like oil and water.

Clinton's response to this question is reminiscent of her reaction in the event that Sheldon analyses. Rather than visibly 'losing her cool' in the face of thinly masked sexism, she responds by *reframing* the conversation, enacting a play frame in response to an ostensibly serious question. By answering with 'Well that hurts my feelings', Clinton plays into the subtext of the question, which highlights one side of the double bind – that is, a powerful woman isn't likeable because powerful isn't 'feminine' – by bringing into relief the *other* side of the double bind: to present the self as likably feminine, it is necessary to display powerlessness.

And what would a powerless woman do in the face of such an accusation? She would bow down. And Clinton pretends to do just this: her verbal response – 'Well that hurts my feelings' – conjures up the stereotypical, powerless woman who lacks emotional control (Lutz 1994). Her embodied response, however – the ironic grimace cued by the closed, dismissive eyes – indicates that her feelings are in fact *not* hurt at all, and that she is just playing the script that has been set up by the moderator's question for the amusement of the audience. The laughter and applause in the co-present audience that follow signal to the viewer of the televised event that the ironic keying and frame shift has been understood.

Clinton then continues in the play frame, stating 'but I'll try to go on' (i.e. as if her feelings were so hurt that she might have otherwise quit right then). She then performs a series of moves that could be considered a threat to her own face: she acknowledges the moderator's claim that Obama is 'likable' (a calculated 'very', but not 'more') and makes a self-deprecating remark, 'I don't think I'm that bad' – which sets Obama up to pay her a compliment. Obama indeed takes this serve, responding 'You're likeable enough, Hillary' (also calculated!), for which she thanks him, still displaying her footing within a play frame through the embodied cues of smiling and head bobbling.

The frame shifts abruptly when Clinton declares, 'You know, I think this is one of the most serious decisions that the voters of New Hampshire have ever had to make'. Her explicit reference to this 'serious decision' brings the previous non-serious exchange to a close and marks her following talk as a return to the matrix frame of the debate. She then contrasts the two topics embedded in the moderator's questions – the 'experience vs. change' issue and the 'likable character' issue – by comparing the electorate's previous presidential choice as an 'unfortunate' one based on character, contrasting it with her own identity as a candidate whose experience *illustrates* change.

This example of interactional reframing works to Clinton's benefit, as it did in the town hall meeting analysed by Sheldon, by providing her the opportunity to confront and ridicule implicitly sexist challenges to her character and her compatibility, particularly as a woman, with arguably the most powerful leadership position in the world.

Positioning political identity

Positioning theory, which hails from the field of discursive psychology, is another framework that has been widely applied in discourse-analytic approaches to identity performance. First articulated by Davies and Harré (1990) and developed in Harré and van Langenhove (1999), positioning is presented as a 'mutually determining triad' connecting subject positions with 'relatively determinate speech acts' and broader 'story-lines,' within which, subject positions can be understood as discursively negotiating coherent selves and others.[2] Originally conceived of as dialogically grounded in conversation, positioning theory enables an analysis of how micro-level interactional identities relate to broader ideologies and cultural archetypes (e.g. Bamberg 1997; De Fina & Georgakopoulou 2012).

Positioning has been particularly useful in the study of narrative and interaction. Bamberg's extension (1997; see also Bamberg & Georgakopoulou 2008) elaborates on how positions emerge at three structural levels in the analysis of narratives: (1) within the story-world of the narrative; (2) in the interactional context of narration, and (3) in relation to the individual's own identity as it extends beyond the narrative, in relation to dominant discourses and ideologies, which reflexively lend coherence to the lower-level story-world and interactional contexts. As such, positioning analysis also offers a solution to the dialectic between micro-level and macro-level styles of discourse analysis. As De Fina (2013) argues, 'positioning analysis... offers a middle ground between approaches to identity that keep a very narrow focus on the here and now of interactions (such as Conversation-Analysis-influenced studies) and orientations that focus much more on wide social processes such as the circulation of ideologies and the exercise of control over social and cultural roles' (p. 43).

Positioning theory provides a useful scaffolding for the analysis of political identity since any politician's performance can be seen as an attempt to actively position themselves as a certain type of person in relation to a particular audience, and at the same time, as a response to the way they have been positioned by others, including both individuals (e.g. other candidates) and collectives (e.g. the media). In effect, any political performance creates subject positions (both self and other) through speech acts, and not forgetting the third point in the positioning triad, also constructs a larger 'story-line' or social world against which these positions can be read. Taking into account these three levels, candidates may construct themselves and others: (1) within the stories they tell; and (2) to counteract and resist previous acts of positioning done *to* them. At level (3), political performances reinforce particular story-lines about the nation as a whole, while potentially suppressing or erasing alternative narratives that have surfaced, or may surface, in public discourse.

Positioning case study: Ernst's 'Give me a shot'

In order to illustrate how positioning might be applied to the analysis of political performance, I provide a case study of junior US Senator Joni Ernst, the first woman to represent the state of Iowa in the US Congress and the first female veteran in the US Senate. Less than a month after assuming office in January 2015, Ernst was showcased as a major new voice within the Republican Party when she provided the Republican rebuttal to the 2015 Presidential State of the Union Address. Here, I develop an argument made by McCrimlisk (ND) in her narrative analysis of Ernst's senatorial campaign advertisements by illustrating how positioning theory sheds light on how Ernst strategically employs narrative subjectivities to position herself in relation to both her immediate audience as well as dominant ideologies of gender and leadership.

Jennifer Sclafani

McCrimlisk's study shows how the use of both first and third-person narration in Ernst's campaign advertisements enable her to 'construct an image linked to both traditionally male-associated traits and traditionally female-associated traits without sacrificing her existential coherence' (citing Duranti 2006). McCrimlisk illustrates that the two narrators in Ernst's advertisements – Ernst herself and an unknown male voice – are able to emphasise different aspects of Ernst's personal identity in order to negotiate the double bind that female candidates (and especially those with extensive military experience and leadership credentials) face when trying to project a strong, yet relatable, identity to voters.

Here, I focus on one third-person narrated campaign advertisement entitled 'Give me a shot', which is published on Ernst's campaign website and YouTube channel.[3] The spoken text and a description of the accompanying visual imagery of the 30-second advertisement, which aired throughout Iowa during the 2014 election cycle, is provided in the following transcript.

Line	Speaker	Spoken Text	Imagery
1	Male Narrator	**She's not your typical candidate.**	*{lower body view} Person pulls up to closed white garage door on a motorcycle, wearing jeans and leather bomber jacket.*
2		**Conservative Joni Ernst. Mom. Farm girl.**	*{upper body view, reveals person in 1 as Ernst} Ernst takes off helmet and walks through entrance.*
3		**And a Lieutenant Colonel who carries more than just lipstick in her purse.**	*Ernst enters artillery shop, grabs handgun, and enters target practice room.*
4		**Joni Ernst will take aim at wasteful spending.**	*{close-up of handgun} Ernst loads handgun.*
5		**And once she sets her sights on Obamacare,**	*{from front} Ernst aims handgun*
6		**Joni's gonna unload.**	*{from behind} Ernst aims handgun*
7		**{6 shots fired}**	*Ernst shoots at target {from multiple angles; angle changes with each shot fired}*
8		**Oh, and one more thing: Joni doesn't miss much.**	*{Close-up of target} Target advances toward camera; reveals 15 holes, all in bulls-eye range*
9	Ernst	**Give me a shot. I'm Joni Ernst and I approve this message.**	*{Profile of Ernst, direct gaze into camera}*

(Ernst 2014)

This advertisement, which received heightened media attention (e.g. Sullivan 2014; Wysocki 2014) because of the 'gun-happy' image it presents of Ernst, is a particularly illustrative example of positioning as an analytical tool because, like the examples of Clinton described above, it seeks to navigate the double bind of traditional femininity and political leadership – this time, not through the candidate's interactional reframing but via third-person narrative.

In order to see how this is accomplished, let us first break down the analysis of this advertisement into the three positioning levels, beginning with story-world positions. In this advertisement, Ernst is presented linguistically in an oppositional manner, as 'not your typical candidate', followed by a list of identity categories: 'conservative', 'mom', 'farm girl', and 'a lieutenant colonel who carries more than just lipstick in her purse' (i.e. she also carries a handgun). This text reconfigures aspects of Ernst's personal identity that may seem inconsistent according to dominant ideologies of gender and leadership as a political advantage, rendering Ernst as independent, iconoclastic, and authentic (i.e. as a 'maverick', a salient identity category within the Republican Party, especially following the 2008 presidential campaign of John McCain). As such, this first-level positioning also contributes to third-level positioning by constructing Ernst as a particular *type* of Republican, and one that is consistent with party leaders of the recent past, such as former presidential candidate John McCain. Such positioning of individual candidates along a broader trajectory of the nation's political history, as has been analysed elsewhere (Austermühl 2014; Sclafani 2015), contributes not only to the existential coherence of the political individual, but also the larger political party.

Let us now consider the interactional level, at which the unidentified male narrator provides the description of Ernst to the viewing audience. At this level, Ernst is not only constructed as an authentic character, but as one that has been *authenticated* by a third party (Bucholtz & Hall 2005), and importantly, by a voice that is associated with traditional male-linked ideologies of power. As McCrimlisk has argued, the use of the third-person narrator in this ad allows Ernst to portray a 'tough' image of herself through the voice of another, which contrasts sharply with linguistic strategies employed in her first-person narrated campaign advertisements. This strategy accomplishes political identity work that Ernst could not perform on her own, circumventing the double bind of presenting herself as both feminine and powerful. The third-person narration in this interactional context also allows the advertisement to anticipate and address viewers' potential scepticism by explicitly acknowledging these potential contradictions through oppositional language and syntactic negation ('not your typical candidate,' 'who carries more than just lipstick,' 'doesn't miss much'), a hallmark intertextual strategy of advertising discourse (Fairclough 1995, 2001).

These second-level positioning strategies also contribute to the third level of positioning, in which individual identities are made recognisable as broader archetypes and individual stories are recognised in relation to dominant cultural narratives. Specifically, the intertextual strategy of using negation to describe what Ernst is *not* encourages viewers to consider how Ernst stands out as a unique individual within the history of her political party. Given that women as national leaders within the US Republican Party have been few and far between, the average American voter viewing Ernst's campaign advertisement is likely to draw a comparison between Ernst and former Republican vice-presidential candidate Sarah Palin, which the negation and comparative syntax used in this advertisement seems to address. By introducing the candidate first as 'conservative,' 'mom,' and 'farm girl,' the similarities between Ernst and former vice-presidential candidate Sarah Palin are highlighted. However, when the advertisement continues to say that Ernst 'carries more than just lipstick in her purse,' the distinction between Ernst and Palin is clear. The specific lexical choice of lipstick as a metonym for traditional powerless femininity here may be a direct intertextual reference to one of the most famous 'Palinisms' during the 2008 election season, in which Palin told a joke at a campaign event about lipstick being the one differentiating factor between aggressive 'hockey moms' (including herself) and pit bulls.

In essence, the broader identity work being accomplished in this advertisement involves constructing Ernst as a powerful, conservative, female leader who embodies a Republican 'type' deemed valuable by dominant party ideologies, but distant enough from a recent instantiation of that type who was widely illegitimated in public discourse. This brief analysis of Ernst's campaign advertisement illustrates the utility of the three-tiered positioning framework for examining political discourse as identity performances and demonstrates how interactional sociolinguistics provides a dialogical perspective on what has been considered a relatively monologic genre of public discourse.

Conclusion

In this chapter, I have argued that all forms of political interaction, from interactive town hall meetings to monologic inaugural addresses, can be viewed as identity performances. I have summarised recent studies in sociolinguistics and CDA that have examined various linguistic and embodied features of political performances, and I have proposed that the interactional sociolinguistic frameworks of framing and positioning offer useful insight into how political identities are co-constructed interactively in public discourse. I have illustrated these perspectives with brief analyses of how two prominent women in contemporary American politics have navigated the double bind of presenting themselves as strong leaders while attending to potential conflicts imposed by hegemonic gender ideologies. I demonstrated that while Clinton extemporaneously co-opted the stereotype of the defenceless woman to ironically reframe a serious political debate as a matter of 'hurt feelings' in order to bring to the surface the latent sexism present in her interlocutor's speech, Ernst employed a third-person male narrator in her campaign advertisement to authenticate her maverick identity while it simultaneously distanced her from earlier, less successful female candidates from her party on the national political scene.

While I have chosen to examine the performance of political identities that have been rendered problematic because of conflicting dominant ideologies of gender and leadership, it should be emphasised that frame analysis and positioning theory are much more widely applicable to the study of political identity construction, as all political performances involve a double bind of some sort. Any successful political actor must present himself or herself as trustworthy of holding the leadership position in question, while also coming off as relatable to a wide swath of voters, so presenting an authentically consistent, yet mutable and context-dependent, persona is essential. Political actors must also navigate how their political identities as leaders are both coherent with a broader group identity (i.e. of the party, of the state and of the nation), but are also distinguishable as emanating from an individual subject position. The discursive resolution of contradictions such as these – same yet different, old but new, individual but part of a collective – are the stuff of which political rhetoric is made, and detailed attention to the linguistic devices for performing, justifying and transforming tenable political identities in the face of these oppositions should be a central objective in the study of language and politics.

Notes

1 Ellipses indicate stretches of speech omitted for the sake of brevity. The full official transcript of the debate can be found here: www.presidency.ucsb.edu/ws/index.php?pid=76224.
2 It should be noted that the sense of 'positioning' discussed here is distinct from the concept of 'subject position' in the tradition of Althusser and Foucault in that it focuses on the emergence of identities in conversational interaction rather than the ideological workings of state apparatuses.
3 At the time of writing, the video is available here: www.youtube.com/watch?v=I3mG9fNOZp4.

References

Austermühl, F, 2014, *The great American scaffold: Intertextuality and identity in American presidential discourse*, John Benjamins, Amsterdam.

Bamberg, M, 1997, 'Positioning between structure and performance', *Journal of Narrative and Life History* 7(1–4), pp. 335–342.

Bamberg, M & Georgakopoulou, A, 2008, 'Small stories as a new perspective in narrative and identity analysis', *Text & Talk – An Interdisciplinary Journal of Language, Discourse Communication Studies* 28(3), pp. 377–396.
Bateson, G, 1972, *Steps to an ecology of mind: Collected essays in anthropology, psychiatry, evolution, and epistemology*, University of Chicago Press, Chicago, IL.
Beck, C S, 1996, '"I've got some points I'd like to make here": The achievement of social face through turn management during the 1992 vice presidential debate', *Political Communication* 13(2), pp. 166–180.
Berger, P L & Luckmann, T, 1966, *The social construction of reality: A treatise in the sociology of knowledge*, Anchor Books, New York.
Brown, P & Levinson, S C, 1987, *Politeness: Some universals in language usage*, Cambridge University Press, New York.
Bruner, J, 1987, 'Life as narrative', *Social Research* 54(1), pp. 11–31.
Bucholtz, M & Hall, K, 2005, 'Identity and interaction: A sociocultural linguistic approach', *Discourse Studies* 7(4–5), pp. 585–614.
Carta, C & Wodak, R, 2015, 'Discourse analysis, policy analysis, and the borders of EU identity', Special issue: *Journal of Language and Politics* 14(1), pp. 1–17.
Charteris-Black, J, 2013, *Analysing political speeches: Rhetoric, discourse and metaphor*, Palgrave Macmillan, Basingstoke and New York.
Chilton, P, 1996, *Security metaphors: Cold War discourse from containment to common house*, Peter Lang, New York.
Chilton, P, 2004, *Analysing political discourse: Theory and practice*, Routledge, London.
Chilton, P & Schäffner, C, eds., 2002, *Politics as text and talk: Analytic approaches to political discourse*, John Benjamins, Amsterdam.
Clayman, S E, 2001, 'Answers and evasions', *Language in Society* 30(3), pp. 403–442.
Davies, B & Harré, R, 1990, 'Positioning: The discursive production of selves', *Journal of the Theory of Social Behaviour* 20(1), pp. 43–63.
De Fina, A, 2013, 'Positioning level 3: Connecting local identity displays to macro social processes', *Narrative Inquiry* 23(1), pp. 40–61.
De Fina, A & Georgakopoulou, A, 2012, *Analyzing narrative: Discourse and sociolinguistic perspectives*, Cambridge University Press, Cambridge.
Duranti, A, 2006, 'Narrating the political self in a campaign for US Congress', *Language in Society* 35(4), pp. 467–497.
Fairclough, N, 1995, *Media discourse*, Edward Arnold, London.
Fairclough, N, 2001, *Language and power*, 2nd ed., Longman, London.
Goffman, E, 1959, *The presentation of self in everyday life*, Doubleday, New York.
Goffman, E, 1967, *Interaction ritual: Essays on face-to-face behavior*, Pantheon, New York.
Goffman, E, 1974, *Frame analysis: An essay on the organization of experience*, Harvard University Press, Cambridge, MA.
Goffman, E, 1981, *Forms of talk*, University of Pennsylvania Press, Philadelphia.
Gumperz, J J, 1982, *Discourse strategies*, Cambridge University Press, New York.
Hacker, K L, ed., 2004, *Presidential candidate images*, Rowman & Littlefield, Lanham, MD.
Hall-Lew, L, Coppock, E & Starr, R L, 2010, 'Indexing political persuasion: Variation in the Iraq vowels', *American Speech* 85(1), pp. 91–102.
Harré, R & van Langenhove, L, 1999, *Positioning theory: Moral contexts of intentional action*, Blackwell, Oxford.
Hodges, A, 2011, *The 'War on Terror' narrative: Discourse and intertextuality in the construction and contestation of sociopolitical reality*, Oxford University Press, New York.
Jamieson, K H, 1995, *Beyond the double bind: Women and leadership*, Oxford University Press, Oxford.
Lakoff, G, 2014 [2004], *The ALL NEW Don't Think of an Elephant!: Know Your Values and Frame the Debate*, Chelsea Green Publishing, White River Junction, VT.

Lakoff, R T, 2004 [1975], 'Language and woman's place', in *Language and woman's place: Text and commentaries; revised and expanded edition*, ed. M Bucholtz, Oxford University Press, Oxford.

Lempert, M, 2011, 'Barack Obama, being sharp: Indexical order in the pragmatics of precision-grip gesture', *Gesture 11*(3), pp. 241–270.

Lempert, M & Silverstein, M, 2012, *Creatures of politics: Media, message and the American presidency*, Indiana University Press, Bloomington.

Lutz, C A, 1994, 'Engendered emotion: Gender, power, and the rhetoric of emotional control in American discourse', in *The emotions: Social, cultural and biological dimensions*, eds. R Harré & W Gerrod Parrott, Sage, London, pp. 151–170.

McCrimlisk, J, ND, 'Projecting a consistent image: First and third persona narration in Joni Ernst's 2014 Senate Campaign', Unpublished paper, Georgetown University.

Ochs, E, 1992, Indexing gender, in *Rethinking Context*, eds. A Duranti & C Goodwin, Cambridge University Press, Cambridge, pp. 335–358.

Ochs, E, 1993, 'Constructing social identity: A language socialization perspective', *Research on language and Social Interaction*, *26*(3), pp. 287–306.

Ochs, E & Capps, L, 2001, *Living narrative: Creating lives in everyday storytelling*, Harvard University Press, Cambridge, MA.

Podesva, R J, Hall-Lew, L, Brenier, J, Starr, R L & Lewis, S, 2012, 'Condoleezza Rice and the sociophonetic construction of identity', in *Style-shifting in public: New perspectives on stylistic variation*, eds. J M Hernandez Campoy & J A Cutillas Espinosa, John Benjamins, Amsterdam, pp. 65–80.

Polsby, N W, Wildavsky, A, Schier S E & Hopkins D A, 2012, *Presidential elections: Strategies and structures of American politics*, 13th ed., Rowman & Littlefield, Lanham, MD.

Reisigl, M & Wodak, R, 2001, *Discourse and discrimination: Rhetorics of racism and antisemitism*, Routledge, London.

Santa Ana, O, 2002, *Brown tide rising: Metaphors of Latinos in contemporary American public discourse*, University of Texas Press, Austin, TX.

Schiffrin, D, 1996, 'Narrative as self–portrait: The sociolinguistic construction of identity', *Language in Society 25*(2), pp. 167–203.

Schiffrin, D, 2006, *In other words: Variation in reference and narrative*, Cambridge University Press, Cambridge.

Sclafani, J, 2015, 'Family as a framing resource for political identity construction: Introduction sequences in presidential primary debates', *Language in Society 44*(3), pp. 369–399.

Sclafani, J, in press, 'The presidential self: Discourse and identity in presidential primary debates'.

Sheldon, A, 2015, '"Thank you for heckling me:" Hillary Rodham Clinton's discursive management of her public persona, her political message and the "Iron my shirt!" hecklers in the 2008 presidential election campaign', in *Discourse, politics and women as global leaders*, eds. J Wilson & D Boxer, John Benjamins, Amsterdam, pp. 193–216.

Shenhav, S R, 2009, 'We have a place in a long story: Empowered narratives and the construction of communities: The case of US presidential debates'. *Narrative Inquiry 19*(2), pp. 199–218.

Silverstein, M, 2003, 'Indexical order and the dialectics of sociolinguistic life', *Language & Communication, 23*(3), pp. 193–229.

Stewart, P A, 2012, *Debatable humor: Laughing matters on the 2008 presidential primary campaign*, Lexington Books, Lanham, MD.

Sullivan, S, 2014, 'GOP Senate hopeful Ernst fires gun in ad vowing to 'unload' on Obamacare', *Washington Post*, 14 May 2014, available from: www.washingtonpost.com/blogs/post–politics/wp/2014/05/05/gop–senate–hopeful–ernst–fires–gun–in–ad–vowing–to–unload–on–obamacare/ [accessed 26 March 2016].

Tannen, D & Wallat C, 1993, 'Interactive frames and knowledge schemas in interaction: Examples from a medical examination/interview', in *Framing in discourse*, ed. D Tannen, Oxford University Press, New York, pp. 57–76.

Teven, J, 2008, 'An examination of perceived credibility of the 2008 presidential candidates: Relationships with believability, likeability, and deceptiveness', *Human Communication 11*(4), pp. 391–408
van Dijk, T A, 1993, *Elite discourse and racism*, Sage, Newbury Park, CA.
Wodak, R, 1995, 'Critical linguistics and critical discourse analysis' in *Handbook of pragmatics*, eds. J Verschueren, J-O Östman & J Blommaert, John Benjamins, Amsterdam, pp. 204–210.
Wodak, R, 2011, *The discourse of politics in action: Politics as usual*, 2nd ed., Palgrave Macmillan, Houndmills.
Wysocki, A, 2014, 'Gun–totin' mom's trigger happy campaign commercial', available from: www.tytnetwork.com/2014/05/12/gun–totin–moms–trigger–happy–campaign–commercial/ [accessed 26 March 2016].
Zimmerman, D, 1998, 'Identities, context and interaction', in *Identities in talk*, eds. C Antaki & S Widdicombe, Sage, Thousand Oaks, CA, pp. 87–106.

27
Genres of political communication in Web 2.0

Helmut Gruber

Introduction: the affordances of Web 2.0 social-media platforms for political communication

The internet and its different forms of communication (as many previous technological innovations) has been hailed as providing enhanced opportunities for reshaping political communication by some authors, whereas others have been less optimistic (Larsson 2013). This chapter reviews research on social-media platforms' affordances for the key 'players' of political communication (politicians, citizens) and how these players use social media when they engage in political communication. It will then try to provide a preliminary answer to the question that underlies the two positions sketched here, namely, whether or not social media provide participants of political communication with qualitatively new communicative possibilities. For this reason (and because of the limited space available for this literature overview), studies that use social-media texts from other contexts (such as media discussion boards) in order to investigate 'traditional' topics of critical discourse scholarship such as racist communication (e.g. Dorostkar & Preisinger 2012; Angouri & Wodak 2014), or (social) identity issues (KhosraviNik & Zia 2014; KhosraviNik 2014; Barton & Lee 2013) will not be considered here.

Internet communication tools (ICTs) did not become ubiquitous before the advent of the World Wide Web in the early 90s. The early websites (static personal or commercial websites, or frequently-asked-question lists, FAQs) became more dynamic and interactive in the late 1990s with the inclusion of discussion boards and other tools facilitating user interaction with website owners. Around this time, blogs became the heralds of what was later called Web 2.0 forms of communications as they facilitate frequent updating and easy interaction between bloggers and their audiences (Herring 2013; Miller & Shepherd 2004). Although not uncontroversial, the term 'Web 2.0' is widely used for all internet applications that allow users the easy creation and sharing of various contents (text messages, photos, music, videos, etc.) and enable them to engage in co-operative activities (such as blogging, contributing to wikis and tagging content with individually chosen tags; see Herring 2013).

The new communication technologies' constraining – as well as enabling – factors have been termed their 'affordances' by Hutchby (2001), utilising a concept introduced by cognitive psychologist James J Gibson in the late 1970s. Social-media platforms' affordances cannot be assessed independently from their different groups of users as well as from the hardware devices on which they run; for example, the use of social media for organising protest movements was only made possible by the availability of mobile devices on which activists could use these media on-site. The devices and the software running on them thus represent network agents in the sense of Latour's actor-network theory (see Bennett & Segerberg 2012) that actively change (and enhance) human users' social, semiotic and cognitive capabilities. Viewing social media platforms (used on various devices) in terms of their affordances allows a differentiated assessment of the communicative practices they offer for different user groups and facilitates establishing connections between political scientists' conceptions of collective vs. connective actions (Bennett & Segerberg 2012), specific social media technologies and the genres different user groups realise when using them.

Social-media platforms not only provide affordances for users, but also for the companies that own them and for those who are in control of internet connections: many social-media applications are free for users, but this monetary advantage comes at the price of users' content being constantly monitored by the respective companies in order to provide custom-tailored advertising. Furthermore, various state authorities may also monitor (and in special cases, shut down) internet connections in order to identify users producing content that is not in the respective authorities' interest, or in order to prevent citizens from engaging in connective actions (as incidents in countries such as China, Iran, but also in the UK, have shown, see, e.g. Earl et al. 2013). Social media thus provide simultaneously affordances for business companies and state authorities as well as for different user groups and their communicative needs. This chapter will try to consider all these different aspects when providing an overview on the research literature on genres of political communication in Web 2.0.

The remainder of this chapter is organised as follows: first, the most relevant linguistic concepts used in this chapter will be introduced, and then, different areas of political communication and the use of social-media genres in them will be discussed. The internal division of this section (pp. 414–421, politician-to-citizen communication, citizen-to-citizen communication) roughly follows Bennet & Segerberg's (2012) differentiation between collective and connective action networks. The last section provides an outlook on promising lines for further inquiries.

Relevant genre theoretic concepts

Under a linguistic perspective, genres are abstractions derived from the analysis of texts (i.e. functional communicative units realised mono- or multimodally; Gruber 2008) which are used in a certain type of communicative situation for achieving the same communicative purpose(s). Most current genre theories agree that genres are internally structured, typified forms of purposive social semiotic action used and recognised by members of 'communities of practice' (Lave & Wenger 1991), and emerging as situated rhetorical responses to recurring communicative 'challenges' (for an overview of recent genre theories, see Mäntynen & Shore 2014; Gruber 2013, pp. 31–39). This view entails that genres are conceptualised at the level of context-sensitive social practices, taking into consideration producer and audience positions (and positioning), social purposes, and semiotic modes of their production. Genres are often related to certain discourses ('particular way[s] of constructing a subject matter' Fairclough 1993, p. 128), and are realised through specific registers (situation-adequate semiotic resources for realising a genre; see Gruber 2013,

p. 38). Genre theories differ, however, in the relevance they assign to either their structural ('intrinsic') or their social activity related ('extrinsic') aspects (Kwaśnik & Crowston 2005; Gruber 2013). For analysing genres in the new media, an activity-orientated approach is better suited as it allows a focus on what people are doing with a genre across media and communication platforms. In Web 2.0 communication applications, traditional genres may be (a) simply reproduced on the Web (Askehave & Nielsen 2005; Kwaśnik & Crowston 2005), or they may be (b) adapted (i.e. new media-specific features may be added), or (c) new media-specific genres may emerge (Crowston & Williams 2000).

The concept of recontextualisation (van Leeuwen 2008) provides the appropriate theoretical tool for investigating the effects of 'genre travels' from one (media) context to another. It allows analysis of the effects of taking social action units (e.g. genres) out of their original context (in which they emerged) and putting them into a new context. Using a genre in a new context entails the loss of some original features, whereas others (and their semiotic meanings) are transferred into the new context where new, context-specific meaning aspects may be added. Recontextualisation of social practices thus always involves both semiotic loss and semiotic enrichment.

For the investigation of Web 2.0 genres in general, the above considerations show that investigators would be better not focusing on genres in a single context, but on their travel across various media and communication platforms and the recontexualisation effects of this travel. For scholars of political communication in Web 2.0 in particular, the corollary is that the use of traditional genres of political communication in new media environments deserves the same attention as the emergence of new genres that are facilitated through the affordances of social media for certain user groups.

Domains of political Web 2.0 communication

Most studies of the use of social media in political communication so far have not been conducted within an explicitly linguistic, discourse-analytic or pragmatic framework, but rather, in the fields of political science and communication studies. The activity-orientated genre conception proposed above, however, enables us to discuss the results of many of these studies under a genre perspective.

The following section is divided into two parts. The first part deals with politicians' and political parties' use of social media in their communication with the public; the second part focuses on citizens' use of social media in political activities.

Politician-to-citizen communication: political campaigning revisited

In political science, the use of Web 2.0 communication tools in politician–citizen communication has been studied almost exclusively in the context of Western liberal democracies. Two complementary assumptions have provided the general framework for these investigations (Larsson 2013): the innovation and the normalisation hypothesis. Whereas the innovation hypothesis assumes that the internet (and especially Web 2.0 technologies) will enhance politicians' possibilities for disseminating information and establishing and maintaining contact with their voters, the normalisation hypothesis expects that offline organisational and political structures will also shape political-communication structures on the internet; in other words, that politicians' use of new information and communication technologies will amount to 'more of the same' rather than result in genuinely new and (in whatever sense) 'better' communication with their audience.

Larsson's (2013) literature review shows that far more studies seem to support the normalisation hypothesis, and that innovative uses of both Web 1.0 and 2.0 communication tools by politicians seem to be the exception. The reviewed studies show, however, quite marked geographical differences regarding the use of ICTs. In the US political system, the internet has been used for more than a decade, though for rather traditional communicative goals such as targeting supporters and activists, rather than persuading undecided voters (Vaccari 2008a). The 2008 Obama election campaign that has become internationally famous for its use of internet communication technologies (albeit rather 'traditional' ones such as email field reports for volunteers and journalists, see Chadwick 2013, p. 133) thus marks only the tip of an iceberg of ICT use by US politicians.

In Europe, a north–south divide has been reported insofar as politicians in Northern European countries (including the UK and Germany) tend to use ICTs more often (although not extensively) than politicians in Southern Europe (including France; Larsson 2013). Similar to the US case, the use of traditional web techniques (such as web sites and email) seems to be more frequent than the adoption of Web 2.0 communication technologies. This communication style has been coined 'Web 1.5' use by Jackson and Lilleker (2009). Studies show that audience characteristics (i.e. the 'consumer side' of politician–citizen communication) also support the normalisation hypothesis as mainly (younger) people (in the US and in Europe) who are engaged in offline political activities use the internet for acquiring additional political information (Larsson 2013).

The obvious support of the normalisation hypothesis of Larsson's (2013) review underpins Bennett and Segerberg's (2012) distinction between 'collective' and 'connective' action logics. The former refers to conventional collective actions that are based on overarching social characteristics (e.g. class, gender, race, etc.), and organised by traditional membership-based institutions. The latter are issue-based and rely on similar individual disaffections, rather than on shared collective characteristics (see p. 418). The extensive verification of the normalisation hypothesis thus suggests that traditional political organisations (and actors), following a collective action logic, will display traditional communication behaviour in Web 2.0.

The studies on the overall use of ICTs by politicians leave questions open, such as whether there are differences regarding the communication tools used, the characteristics of politicians who use ICTs, and the communicative goals for which they are used. Concerning the first question, Larsson found in a series of studies, that (at least Swedish and Norwegian) politicians use micro-blogging (i.e. Twitter) more often than Facebook. This result is in line with investigations in other countries showing that Twitter is a communication platform that is mainly used by elites (Ausserhofer & Maireder 2013; Larsson & Moe 2012), where the term 'elites' may refer to rather different groups such as politicians, journalists, celebrities, and so on. Social network analyses show that although ordinary users often contribute most messages to Twitter interactions, politicians (and journalists) tend to be the centres (nodes) of Twitter communication networks (Ausserhofer & Maireder 2013; Larsson 2014). Regarding politicians' use of Twitter messages, Jackson and Lilleker (2011) found that those few (i.e. 7.9 per cent, Jackson & Lilleker 2011, p. 94) UK politicians who use Twitter (in 2007) at all are mostly younger (35–54), female MPs from the three largest parties, and most of their messages are clearly aimed at personal impression management.

Rather different sender characteristics were found in a study that compiled Twitter data from Members of the European parliament (MEPs) in 2013 (Larsson 2013). Although this study also found younger politicians using Twitter more often than older ones, the gender variable was not relevant here. Rather, MEPs who were integrated into denser Twitter networks (i.e. who had more followers, but also followed others) tended to be more active than others. Furthermore, the study did not support previous claims that politicians from established democracies would make more use of Web 2.0 communication facilities than those from younger democracies. Larsson (2013) concludes that (at least with regard to Twitter use) younger, 'innovative' politicians from all European countries who are well integrated in internet communication networks use Twitter as a means for communication with those members of their electorate who share these characteristics (i.e. being young, ardent users of Web 2.0 ICTs) with them. A further study focusing on Norway and Sweden showed that politicians who are not in central, but rather, at mid-level positions in their respective parties, tend to be the most active Twitter users (Larsson & Kalsnes 2014).

Most of the studies reported here (except Jackson & Lilleker 2011) investigated politicians' use of Twitter on the level of network integration and activity, that is, they did not explore the content of the messages and/or the activities they performed and thus leave the question open as to which genres are used in politicians' Twitter use.

Whereas politicians' Twitter use has received some scholarly attention (albeit mainly on the 'macro'- level described above), the use of Facebook by politicians has been rarely studied. In a study of US congressional candidates' use of Facebook during the 2006 and 2008 elections, Williams & Gulati (2013) conducted a content analysis of politicians' Facebook pages. Results show a major increase in politicians' use of Facebook during the investigated period (from about 16% use in 2006 to 72% in 2008). Furthermore, their results reveal that Democrats used this social network more than Republicans, and that challengers and candidates in competitive district races with a more highly educated electorate used Facebook earlier than others did. Early adoption, however, did not correlate with frequency of use (i.e. updating), which means that whereas challengers tend to be early adopters of social media in political campaigning, incumbents (who have more organisational and financial support) use them more often and more professionally.

In a comparative study, Larsson and Kalsness (2014) studied the use of Twitter (see above) and Facebook by Swedish and Norwegian politicians during their routine political activities. Their study also found that politicians in challenger positions used both services more often than incumbents. In an additional investigation, Larsson (2014) compared the Facebook use of Swedish and Norwegian politicians during elections. He found that politicians of marginalised (i.e. either small or politically isolated) parties and less-known politicians tended to use this social-media platform more often than politicians of big parties (probably to overcome a media bias that privileges central political actors). Their postings were also more often liked and shared by users, which Larsson interprets as a kind of audience's mirroring politicians' heavier use of the media platform.

Similar to the Twitter studies discussed above, the few investigations of politicians' use of Facebook provide only limited information on the activities (and hence genres) for which politicians use this social-media platform.

Websites (of both political parties and single politicians), although at first glance typical 'Web 1.0' forms of communication, increasingly include interactive elements (such as discussion boards, chat facilities, links to social media, etc.) and have been studied under a perspective that allows an interpretation of their results in terms of genre use. The applied framework (see Foot & Schneider 2006) provides a broad classification of the communicative activities a website allows: 'information' comprises all traditional communicative activities politicians and parties are expected to provide for their voters; 'involvement' activities refer to website features that allow users to interact with each other or with a party representative (i.e. discussion boards, live-chats, etc.); 'connecting' activities integrate a website into the context of other online actors (i.e. providing outside links to relevant other organisations' and/or individuals' websites); through 'mobilising' activities, a website offers users the opportunities for offline support and activism. These four types of communicative activities entail the use of different genres.

Although it would seem plausible that minor parties may rely more on their web-presence (as online activities are cheaper than offline campaigns), the majority of studies has found that major parties provide more sophisticated websites (Jackson & Lilleker 2009; Schweitzer 2008), which facilitate a greater variety of communicative activities. This is probably a result of their superior financial and organisational resources.

Apart from these global findings, some studies investigated the relation between parties' ideological orientation and website functionalities. Analyses of candidates' websites during the French presidential election campaign (Lilleker & Malagón 2010; Vaccari 2008c) as well as an investigation of Italian parties' websites during parliamentary elections (Vaccari 2008b) showed that right-wing parties tend to provide more information materials on their websites, whereas left-wing parties provide more opportunities for involvement and mobilisation. In a study of Swedish party websites during an election year, Larsson (2011) reports similar results. Although 'informing' activities were employed most often by all parties under scrutiny and peaked during the election period, centre and centre-right parties included involving and mobilising features least often in their websites, whereas left-wing parties (and the tech-savvy Pirate party) made more use of these features. These results seem to indicate that ideological differences result in parties' different communicative styles in terms of discursive activities they engage in with their voters: right-wing parties seem to apply a more 'top-down' communication style, whereas left-wing parties employ more grass-roots communication styles.

In a study of candidates' personal websites in the 2009 elections for the European Parliament, Hermans & Vergeer (2013) focused on the 'informing' activities (and thus on the most traditional party-political communicative activity). They distinguished three topical dimensions ('professional', 'personal preferences', 'home and family'), which allowed differentiated interpretations of the candidates' websites. Results show that the majority of the EP candidates provided information on professional-, home- and family-related topics, but very little information on personal preferences. Candidates from the post-communist countries scored highest on the first two dimensions, whereas candidates from countries with longer democratic traditions received the lowest scores. Although Hermans and Vergeer concede that their measurement of personalisation strategies was basic (2013, pp, 87), their results are, in some respects, parallel with Jackson and Lillekers' (2011) study of British MPs' Twitter use as both studies suggest that politicians tend to use web facilities for personal impression management.

The review of studies on politicians' (and political parties') use of social media and Web 2.0 facilities integrated in web sites shows rather clearly that: (1) these social actors are quite slow in adopting Web 2.0 communication tools; (2) they seem to transfer offline communicative strategies and activities stemming from a 'collective action' logic (Bennet & Segerberg 2012) to their social-media use; and (3) their usage preferences do not match the preferences of the public they intend to represent. Politicians prefer the 'elitist' Twitter service and use Facebook much less often, whereas the usage patterns of their audience are reverse. Traditional politicians and politics thus make use of those communicative affordances of Web 2.0 communication tools that allow them to extend their traditional communicative genre use onto the internet. Furthermore, the results of the studies reported here show that left and right parties seem to use ICTs for different communication strategies and hence use different genres.

Citizen-to-citizen communication: move on, but where to?

Since the early 1980s, ICTs have been considered to provide new possibilities for citizens' political participation and self-organisation, which would eventually lead to a new era of deliberative democracy in a Habermasian sense (see Chouliaraki 2010). Expectations concerning the first aspect have been largely disappointed, as the overview of studies presented on p. 414 has shown. This section will deal with social media's possible contributions to citizens' self-organisation processes in the sense of Bennet and Segerberg's (2012) concept of 'connective action'.

In an overview of early studies that deal with the use of ICTs by new social movements, Garrett (2006), based on McAdam et al. (1996), identifies three relevant factors of social movements that communication technologies can influence: mobilising structures, opportunity structures and framing processes. The first factor refers to possibilities for ICTs to provide fast and widespread access to political information that is relevant for persons who are concerned with a certain political issue. In terms of communicative activities, the 'mobilisation' affordances of ICTs resemble traditional political-communication activities, yet they involve different social actors: in traditional political communication, political parties provide information for their supporters on their web sites (see above, p. 414), whereas ICTs enable activists to provide and spread their own personal views and information concerning movement-relevant issues that may lead to the rapid diffusion of social movements across geographical boundaries.

The second of Garrett's factors, opportunity structures, concerns mainly technological factors of ICT accessibility and availability, and is therefore not directly relevant for a communication-activity perspective. The last factor, framing processes, concerns the opportunities ICTs offer new social movements for propagating their own accounts of relevant issues, without depending on traditional gatekeepers in the public and in the traditional media. Garrett's framework provides a useful meta-perspective from which studies of social-media use by new social movements can be grouped and compared; it will be used to organise the following overview.

Although social-media platforms provide citizens with the opportunity to publicly express their views on various social and political problems without depending on media gatekeepers, the expression of individual political comments often amounts to 'mediated self-representation' (i.e. the public performance of identity), rather than to enduring participatory political engagement (Chouliaraki 2010). In a corpus study of postings to five blogs, Myers (2010) found an abundance of personal stance markers in blog posts as compared to a reference corpus from the British National Corpus. This result, Myers argues, reflects bloggers' attempts to develop an original own position within a discussion, rather than contributing to an argumentation. Comparable results have been reported by van Zoonen et al. (2007) in their investigation of a bulletin board on the website of a popular US TV talk show and in Valera Ordaz's (2012) study of political discussions on Facebook pages of Spanish politicians. Her results show that the majority of participants contributed only one posting, and that most of these postings supported (or even exaggerated) the politicians' view on the issue under discussion. Furthermore, most postings do not realise deliberative argumentative – but rather, commenting – genres, as the following example from her data shows:

[1] I don't know if we live in a country of gullible idiots or crazy people. [2] ETA hasn't said anything different. [3] They've said that they're not going to kill anyone as long as their conditions are met. [4] Nothing more, nothing less. [5] They're not in any way defeated. [6] They have the necessary infrastructure to attack, [7] they have an entire province, [8] they have tax information on all of us, [9] have we gone nuts? [10] Even the PP is celebrating the fact that ETA hasn't said anything. [11] It seems, Rosa, that you are the only politician who has her wits about her along with Mayor Oreja and Esperanza Aguirre. [Retrieved from Rosa Díez's[1] wall and published on October 21 [2012] at 14:41]

(Valera Ordaz 2012, p. 161, translated to English by Valera Ordaz, clause numbers added by HG)

This posting shows some quite characteristic features of the personal comment genre: the author uses a considerable range of evaluative lexis ('gullible idiots', 'crazy people', 'have we gone nuts') and many markers of informal speech (e.g. the high number of contractions (clitics)). Furthermore, the posting is only vaguely argumentative insofar as clauses 2–8 (presenting explicit and implicit negative characterisations of ETA) can be understood as backings for the evaluative statement in clause 1. The rhetorical contrast between clauses 11 and the final clause 12 then serves as a booster for the positive appraisal of three politicians (including the page owner, Rosa Diez) whom the author obviously does not classify as being 'idiots' or 'crazy'.

This example and the aforementioned studies seem to suggest that at least some of the Web 2.0 communication facilities have stimulated personal political expression without concern for an audience and thus merely serve as pressure-relief valves for frustrated citizens.

A similar, partly pessimistic view of the role of citizens' self-produced content for new social movements can be found in Thorson et al.'s (2013) study of YouTube videos on the Occupy movement. The authors investigated the content of YouTube videos on the Occupy movement and traced the video-sharing practices that link YouTube and Twitter (i.e. tweeted links to YouTube videos, etc.) in order to analyse which roles social media play in new protest movements. They analysed all videos with Occupy-related keywords, as well as videos that were linked to Occupy-related tweets during November 2011. Thorson et al.'s results show that although the majority of videos in their corpus was footage of the protests, those videos tweeted (i.e. recommended by a Twitter user to their followers) and often watched were more-or-less professionally produced ('cut and mix'), whereas genuine amateur videos received little attention. From the latter result, the authors concluded that social-media platforms such as YouTube (that are promoted as sites for sharing content) are also used for individual archival purposes. Thorson et al.'s results are interesting in two ways. First, the obvious archival use of YouTube shows that a social-media platform's affordances may (at least for certain users) differ from the primary use it is promoted for. Second, their finding that it was mainly (semi-) professionally edited videos of the Occupy protests that went viral (i.e. were spread over several social-media platforms and were often watched) cautions against premature enthusiasm about the direct access a wider audience may have to ordinary citizens' first-hand eye-witness documents through content-sharing platforms.

All the aforementioned studies show that, in terms of framing processes (see above), social-media platforms seem to facilitate the emergence of new genres of citizens' political expressions (blog postings, video documents), but that these genres (1) may not (yet) be optimally developed for the social purpose they are intended to fulfil, or that these genres (2) may reflect qualitatively new forms of citizens' political expression that are not compatible with the current political system in modern Western democracies.

In the studies reported so far, citizens' web activities accompanied (or commented on) real-life political events, which may be responsible for the disconnectedness between online and offline activities. Political events, however, that take place entirely on the web, may lead to different dynamics because of the mobilising effects ICTs provide. In a study of YouTube videos that reacted to a notorious anti-Islamic video produced and distributed via the internet by a right-wing populist Dutch politician, van Zoonen et al. (2010) identified three genres of citizens' protest expressions: jamming, cut and mix, and vlogging (i.e. video-blogging). While jamming videos exploited YouTube's tagging feature to complicate the search for the original video, and to express disagreement with the politician-producer of the film, cut-and-mix videos applied either satire or rational argumentation in order to counter the original video message. In the vlog genre, speakers (mostly representatives of organisations or frequent vloggers) provided rational argumentations against the original film. The authors conclude that these three video genres construct different forms of producers' virtual citizenship and project different audiences. They further argue that their results would show that social media can serve as platforms for borderless political participation and interaction, and would thus present counter evidence to the pessimistic view adopted in the earlier studies reported above. As van Zoonen et al. do not present a systematic investigation of the numbers of viewers the videos in their corpus attracted, this interpretation may, however, be premature and both positions (the pessimistic and the optimistic) might be defendable.

Evidence for direct influence of citizens' online activities on offline political action seems to be provided by Harlow's (2012) study of a Guatemalan protest movement that was triggered by the murder of a lawyer. Harlow identified several genres ('action frames' in her terminology), which were used in Facebook groups created immediately after the incident. The most frequent genres were calls for action and the conveying of information. These online activities spurred massive offline protests. However, as Harlow reports, three months later, both offline protests and online activities in the Facebook groups had decreased substantially. Therefore, Harlow's study, while providing evidence that online political activities can result in offline political action, also seems to suggest a certain flash-in-the-pan effect of these activities.

Some studies have focused on the use of Web 2.0 communication technologies during political activities. Theocharis (2013) and Earl et al. (2103) studied various aspects of Twitter use during protests. In his social network study, Theocharis found that student groups, during the 2010 university occupations in the UK, deliberately created horizontally linked Twitter account networks without clear centres in order to keep their communication lines intact, even when single nodes were shut down. The protesters thus actively took advantage of affordances of the communication platform in order to pursue their political goals.

In countries such as Spain, Egypt and Greece, social-media platforms played a substantial role in networking new social movements' activities during protests on public squares. The activities resulted in hybrid spaces composed of multimodal representations and communications on different occupied squares (Martin Rojo 2014). The political and social effects of these recontextualisation practices, are, however, far from being obvious and clear. More research of the different local reinterpretations of shared images and videos would be needed to estimate how these signs are taken up by actors in different places (Chun 2014).

Forwarding relevant messages to followers ('retweeting') seems to have become a new, technology-supported communicative practice in citizens' use of social media, as the study of Lotan et al. (2011) shows. The authors intended to identify the major participant roles of micro-blogging information flows in the Arab Spring Revolutions in Tunisia and Egypt, but as a by-product, they found a high number of retweets in their data. Retweeting, thus, is a candidate (emerging) genre in which communicative needs and technological affordances converge.

Tweets sent during the protests against the 2009 G20 meeting in Pittsburgh were content analysed by Earl et al. (2013). Scrutinising the tweets' topics, as well as applying a rough genre classification ('information' vs. 'opinion' vs. 'question' tweets), their results show a clear peak of Twitter activity during the protests and a focus on the broadcasting of (mainly location-related) information. In tweets concerning the police, the information component prevailed during the protests, whereas afterwards, opinion-related tweets peaked. An in-depth analysis of the police-related tweets showed that protesters monitored police activities and equipment closely in order to develop real-time tactics for pre-empting police actions. Earl et al.'s results show that protesters may use services such as Twitter in order to enhance their online-mobilising structures, which may eventually lead to a threat of the authorities' information monopoly during protests and riots. This advantage, however, lasts only as long as the opportunity structures (in Garrett's sense) are intact, that is, as long as ICTs are available and not monitored by the authorities. As events have shown during the uprisings in Egypt (where the authorities shut down services such as Twitter, albeit with limited success), in Iran and in Britain after the 2011 riots (where authorities used Twitter data to identify and prosecute key figures of the protests), or the situation in China (where the internet is constantly monitored by the authorities), the state powers are well aware of the opportunities ICTs provide for protesters and use their own technological capacities for counteracting protesters' counteractions. Theocharis' results, however, show that new protest movements may consciously attempt to circumvent the potential weaknesses of the communication tools they use.

Research on citizens' use of social media and ICTs for their political participation and organisation reviewed above shows mixed results. ICTs facilitate fast dissemination and sharing of information, which offers participants advantages during protests and allows them to share experiences across geographically dispersed social movements. However, as Earl et al. (2013) caution, authorities are well aware of the advantages protesters gain through ICTs and may in turn use features of the new technologies for impeding protests and/or identifying and neutralising key figures or organisations. Furthermore, as Bennet & Segerberg (2012) show, not all internationally shared content 'goes viral'. The political and social conditions for adopting messages, slogans, pictures, etc. in new contexts (i.e. the local terms of recontextualisation) may enhance or hinder the local adoption of political content shared via social media. The reported results also show that the often-hailed availability of first-hand eye-witness accounts of political events facilitated through social media has to be viewed with caution; as Thorson et al.'s (2012) study shows, those videos that attracted a wider audience were more-or-less professionally produced, whereas the genuine eye-witness accounts did not receive much attention. Sharing information (of various kinds and in different semiotic modes), which is often viewed as the key advantage new social movements gained from Web 2.0 technologies, thus turns out to be sensitive to local recontextualisation practices, as well as to (more-or-less) professional production practices. Furthermore, as Harlow's study shows, social movements may be quickly sparked through the use of ICTs, but they may also disappear just as quickly.

Conclusions and outlook

The studies of ICT and Web 2.0 facility use in political communication have demonstrated a clear difference between parties' and politicians' communicative activities and the uses citizens make of these communicative tools. Whereas most political parties seem to use internet communication as a mere extension of their typical offline communication practices (i.e. mainly providing online information for their supporters), politicians use social media for various kinds of self-presentation. Both social actors thus merely seem to transfer traditional genres of political communication from offline to online communication environments.

The review of studies on citizens' use of social media and ICTs for communicating on and during political events reveals mixed results. While studies that focus on citizens' commenting activities on political events (blogging, discussion boards, sharing of video documents) seem to indicate a predominance of mediated self-presentation practices over genuine political-discussion activities, studies that investigate citizens' use of social-media tools during political events show the emergence of genuinely new 'genres' of citizens' political communication (e.g. sharing information on police locations and equipment during demonstrations, developing online tactics for pre-empting police actions). Viewed from a more abstract point of view, these results seem to indicate that citizens' political participation through Web 2.0 communication tools does not enhance new social movements' framing processes, but rather, it improves their mobilising structures (although the sustainability of movements that are exclusively based on ICT mobilisation has not yet been proven). Under a genre perspective, the review has shown that while in politician–citizen communication, the recontextualisation of traditional genres into new communicative forms prevails, in citizen–citizen political communication, genuinely new genres emerge.

The interpretation of the studies' results in terms of genres of political communication has, however, to be taken with caution as most of the studies reviewed here were not conducted within a linguistic, discourse-analytic framework and provide, therefore, only few toeholds for an interpretation under a genre perspective. Most linguistic studies of Web 2.0 communication apply a corpus linguistic approach (Myers 2010; Zappavigna 2011), which does not allow for scrutinising communicative activities (genres) realised in and through social-media communication tools. Furthermore, the role of social-media companies that provide the platforms for – and influence – the software architecture used in communication practices have only rarely been accounted for (see, e.g. Eisenlauer 2014, albeit not on political-communication practices). The scarcity of studies of Web 2.0 political communication under a genre perspective may be due to the methodological-technological difficulties of the acquisition of data sufficient for the needs of discourse-analytical research, but these difficulties may be outweighed by the insights into communicative practices that shape many aspects of our daily lives to an increasing extent.

A further promising field for research under a genre perspective represents the 'hybrid media system' (Chadwick 2013). With this term, Chadwick refers to new media formats (genre networks) that combine genres of traditional electronic media with social-media genres (e.g. live Twitter streams that provide the input for political live TV discussions; Atifi & Marcoccia 2015). Investigating these hybrid genre networks (in which the boundaries between political and media communication become increasingly blurred), however, requires even more sophisticated methodological and technical tools and skills than the study of single social-media genres (see Elmer 2013). Overall, this survey of research has shown that political communication in social media provides discourse scholars and students with rich and promising opportunities for future investigations.

Note

1 Diez was then head of the Spanish leftist party Union, Progress and Democracy (UPyD).

References

Angouri, J & Wodak, R, 2014, '"They became big in the shadow of the crisis" The Greek success story and the rise of the far right', *Discourse & Society*, vol. 25, no. 4, pp. 540–565.
Askehave, I & Nielsen, A E, 2005, 'Digital genres: A challenge to traditional genre theory', *Information Technology & People*, vol. 18, no. 2, pp. 120–141.
Atifi, H & Marcoccia, M, 2015, 'Follow-ups and dialogue in online discussions on French politics. From Internet forums to social TV' in *The dynamics of political discourse. Forms and functions of follow-ups*, eds. A Fetzer, E Weizman & L Berlin, John Benjamins Publishing Company, Amsterdam and Philadelphia, pp. 109–141.
Ausserhofer, J & Maireder, A, 2013, 'National politics on Twitter', *Information, Communication & Society*, vol. 16, no. 3, pp. 291–314.
Barton, D & Lee, C, 2013, *Language online. Investigating digital texts and practices*, Routledge, London.
Bennett, W L & Segerberg, A, 2012, 'The logic of connective action', *Information, Communication & Society*, vol. 15, no. 5, pp. 739–768.
Chadwick, A, 2013, *The hybrid media system*, Oxford, Oxford University Press.
Chouliaraki, L, 2010, 'Self-mediation: New media and citizenship', *Critical Discourse Studies*, vol. 7, no. 4, pp. 227–232.
Chun, C W, 2014, 'Mobilities of a linguistic landscape at Los Angeles City Hall Park', *Journal of Language and Politics*, vol. 14, no. 3, pp. 653–675.
Crowston, K & Williams, M, 2000, 'Reproduced and emergent genres of communication on the World Wide Web', *The Information Society*, vol. 16, no. 3, pp. 201–215.
Dorostkar, N & Preisinger, A 2012, 'CDA 2.0 – Leserkommentarforen aus kritisch-diskursanalytischer Perspektive. Eine explorative Studie am Beispiel der Online-Zeitung derStandard.at', *Wiener Linguistische Gazette*, vol. 76, pp. 1–47.
Earl, J, McKee Hurwitz, E J H, Mejia Mesinas, A, Tolan, M & Arlotti, A 2013, 'This protest will be tweeted', *Information, Communication & Society*, vol. 16, no. 4, pp. 459–478.
Eisenlauer, V, 2014, 'Facebook as a third author – (Semi-)automated participation framework in social network sites', *Journal of Pragmatics*, vol. 72, pp. 73–85.
Elmer, G, 2013, 'Live research: Twittering an election debate', *New Media & Society*, vol. 15, no. 1, pp. 18–30.
Fairclough, N, 1993, *Discourse and social change*, Polity Press, Cambridge.
Foot, K A & Schneider, S, 2006, *Web campaigning*, MIT Press, Cambridge, MA.
Garrett, K R, 2006, 'Protest in an information society: A review of literature on social movements and new ICTs', *Information, Communication & Society*, vol. 9, no. 2, pp. 202–224.
Gruber, H, 2008, 'Analyzing communication in the new media', in *Qualitative discourse analysis in the social sciences*, eds. R Wodak & M Krzyżanowski, Palgrave Macmillan, London, pp. 54–76.
Gruber, H, 2013, 'Genres in political discourse: The case of the parliamentary "inaugural speech" of Austrian chancellors', in *Analyzing genres in political communication: Theory and practice*, eds. P Cap & U Okulska, John Benjamins Publishing Company, Amsterdam and Philadelphia, pp. 29–73.
Harlow, S, 2012, 'Social media and social movements: Facebook and an online Guatemalan justice movement that moved offline', *New Media & Society*, vol. 14, no. 2, pp. 225–243.
Hermans, L & Vergeer, M, 2013, 'Personalization in e-campaigning: A cross-national comparison of personalization strategies used on candidate websites of 17 countries in EP elections 2009', *New Media & Society*, vol. 15, no. 1, pp. 72–92.

Herring, S C, 2013, 'Discourse in Web 2.0: Familiar, reconfigured, and emergent' in *Georgetown University round table on languages and linguistics 2011: Discourse 2.0: Language and new media*, eds. D Tannen & A M Tester, Georgetown University Press, Washington, DC, pp. 1–25.

Hutchby, I, 2001, 'Technologies, texts and affordances', *Sociology*, vol. 35, no. 2, pp. 441–456.

Jackson, N A & Lilleker, D G, 2009, 'Building an architecture of participation? Political parties and Web 2.0 in Britain', *Journal of Information Technology & Politics*, vol. 6, no. 3-4, pp. 232–250.

Jackson, N & Lilleker, D, 2011, 'Microblogging, constituency service and impression management: UK MPs and the use of Twitter', *The Journal of Legislative Studies*, vol. 17, no. 1, pp. 86–105.

KhosraviNik, M, 2014, 'Critical discourse analysis, power and new media: Issues and debates' in *Why discourse matters: Negotiating identity in the mediatized world*, eds. J Kalyango & M W Kopytowska, Peter Lang, Verlag, Frankfurt Main, pp. 287–306.

KhosraviNik, M & Zia, M, 2014, 'Persian nationalism, identity and anti-Arab sentiments in Iranian Facebook discourses: Critical Discourse Analysis and social media communication', *Journal of Language and Politics*, vol. 13, no. 4, pp. 755–780.

Kwaśnik, B H & Crowston, K, 2005, 'Introduction to the special issue', *Information Technology & People*, vol. 18, no. 2, pp. 76–88.

Larsson, A O, 2011, '"Extended infomercials" or "Politics 2.0"? A study of Swedish political party web sites before, during and after the 2010 election', *First Monday*, vol. 16, no. 4, available from: http://firstmonday.org/ojs/index.php/fm/article/view/3456 [accessed 19 November 2014].

Larsson, A O, 2013, '"Rejected bits of program code": Why notions of "Politics 2.0" remain (mostly) unfulfilled', *Journal of Information Technology & Politics*, vol. 10, no. 1, pp. 72–85.

Larsson, A O, 2014, 'Everyday elites, citizens, or extremists? Assessing the use and users of non-election political hashtags', *MedieKultur. Journal of Media and Communication Research*, vol. 30, no. 56, pp. 61–87.

Larsson, A O & Kalsnes, B, 2014, '"Of course we are on Facebook": Use and non-use of social media among Swedish and Norwegian politicians', *European Journal of Communication*, vol. 29, no. 6, pp. 653–667.

Larsson, A O & Moe, H, 2012, 'Studying political microblogging: Twitter users in the 2010 Swedish election campaign', *New Media & Society*, vol. 14, no. 5, pp. 729–747.

Lave, J & Wenger, E, 1991, *Situated learning. Legitimate peripheral participation*, Cambridge University Press, Cambridge.

Lilleker, D G & Malagón, C, 2010, 'Levels of interactivity in the 2007 French presidential candidates' websites', *European Journal of Communication*, vol. 25, no. 1, pp. 25–42.

Lotan, G, Graeff, E, Ananny, M, Gaffney, D, Pearce, I & Boyd, D, 2011, 'The Arab Spring – the revolutions were tweeted: Information flows during the 2011 Tunisian and Egyptian Revolutions', *International Journal of Communication*, vol. 5, np.

Mäntynen, A & Shore, S, 2014, 'What is meant by hybridity? An investigation of hybridity and related terms in genre studies', *Text & Talk*, vol. 34, no. 6, pp. 737–758.

Martin Rojo, L, 2014, 'Taking over the square: The role of linguistic practices in contesting urban spaces', *Journal of Language and Politics*, vol. 14, no. 3, pp. 623–653.

McAdam, D, McCarthy, J D, & Zald, M N, 1996, *Comparative perspectives on social movements: Political opportunities, mobilising structures, and cultural framings*, Cambridge University Press, Cambridge and New York.

Miller, C R & Shepherd, D, 2004, 'Blogging as social action: A genre analysis of the weblog' in *Into the Blogosphere*, eds. L Gurak, S Antonijevic, L A Johnson & C Ratcliff, available from: http://blog.lib.umn.edu/blogosphere/, np [accessed 19 November 2014].

Myers, G, 2010, 'Stance-taking and public discussion in blogs', *Critical Discourse Studies*, vol. 7, no. 4, pp. 263–275.

Schweitzer, E J, 2008, 'Innovation or normalisation in e-campaigning? A longitudinal content and structural analysis of German party websites in the 2002 and 2005 national elections', *European Journal of Communication*, vol. 23, no. 4, pp. 449–470.

Theocharis, Y, 2013, 'The wealth of (occupation) networks? Communication patterns and information distribution in a Twitter protest network', *Journal of Information Technology & Politics*, vol. 10, no. 1, pp. 35–56.

Thorson, K, Driscoll, K, Ekdale, B, Edgerly, S, Thompson, L G, Schrock A, Swartz L, Vraga, E, Wells, C, 2013, 'Youtube, Twitter and the Occupy Movement', *Information, Communication & Society*, vol. 16, no. 3, pp. 421–451.

Vaccari, C, 2008a, 'From the air to the ground: The internet in the 2004 US presidential campaign', *New Media & Society*, vol. 10, no. 4, pp. 647–665.

Vaccari, C, 2008b, 'Research note: Italian parties' websites in the 2006 elections', *European Journal of Communication*, vol. 23, no. 1, pp. 69–77.

Vaccari, C, 2008c, 'Surfing to the Élysée: The internet in the 2007 French elections', *French Politics*, vol. 6, no. 1, pp. 1–22.

Valera Ordaz, L, 2012, 'Deliberation 2.0 or radicalized partisan discourse? An analysis of political discussions conducted on the Facebook pages of Spanish political candidates', *Textual & Visual Media*, vol. 5, pp. 139–168.

van Leeuwen, T, 2008, *Discourse and practice*, Oxford University Press, Oxford.

van Zoonen, L, 2007, 'Audience reactions to Hollywood politics', *Media, Culture & Society*, vol. 29, no. 4, pp. 531–547.

van Zoonen, L, Vis, F & Mihelj, S, 2010, 'Performing citizenship on YouTube: Activism, satire and online debate around the anti-Islam video Fitna', *Critical Discourse Studies*, vol. 7, no. 4, pp. 249–262.

Williams, C B & Gulati, G J, 2013, 'Social networks in political campaigns: Facebook and the congressional elections of 2006 and 2008', *New Media & Society*, vol. 15, no. 1, pp. 52–71.

Zappavigna, M, 2011, 'Ambient affiliation: A linguistic perspective on Twitter', *New Media & Society*, vol. 13, no. 5, pp. 788–806.

28
Music and sound as discourse and ideology
The case of the national anthem

David Machin

Introduction

Like all semiotic resources, sound and music have very specific affordances, which means they can be used in special ways. Scholars have argued that music has a special kind of force as a carrier of collective memory and tradition, working more in 'an emotional and almost physical sense' (Eyerman 1999, p. 119). Unlike texts and pictures, the sounds in music enter and flow through our bodies, calling us to move with their rhythms, and feel the texture of their pitches and sound qualities (Machin & Richardson 2011). A migrant child sitting in a classroom while their classmates sing the daily national anthem may not understand the words, but they will physically experience its power (Abril 2012). In this chapter, I show how we can document and analyse the way this power and the ideas, values and identities that it communicates, are realised. I explain how we can approach sound as discourse using the case study of two national anthems: 'The Star-Spangled Banner' and 'O Canada'. The first part of the chapter introduces what a Multimodal Critical Discourse Analysis (MCDA) approach to sound looks like. It then moves on to apply these ideas to the anthems by looking at the lyrics and then at how these are realised through sound.

Sound, ideology and discourse

MCDA assumes that communicators deploy different kinds of semiotic resources to achieve particular goals, to communicate specific ideas, attitudes and identities, in other words, to disseminate discourses that support their own interest. In this chapter, I show that it is productive to take these principles to approach sound in a social-semiotic sense where we identify the underlying resources available to communicators, presenting these as a kind of inventory of meaning potentials. In the analysis of specific texts, it is then possible to look at how these meaning potentials are used to achieve particular communicative goals and meanings. In practice, this kind of analysis, by identifying the building blocks of sound as communication, allows us to look, not just at what sound communicates, but how it does so. Barthes (1977) argued the need for a critical approach to sound, but urged that a systematic analysis of sound must be able to go beyond the kinds of adjectives we commonly use when we say a sound or piece of music is 'romantic' or 'uplifting'. The aim of MCDA when applied to sound should be to do just this, by describing the details of the features of the music that might communicate such things, and to show how these are used for ideological purposes.

Important in a social-semiotic approach is that semiotic resources will always carry traces of the socio-political contexts in which they were formed (Bezemer & Kress 2010) and will have certain meanings, therefore, built into them (Kress & Selander 2012), which reflect the ideologies and kinds of social relations of this context. To some extent, these meanings are regulated and crucially will then go on to shape social interaction. In this sense, we are interested in the underlying resources available for communication in sound and music, but we depart from a fundamentally social question: what semiotic resources are drawn upon in communication, or discourse, in order to carry out ideological work? Here, we ask this specifically of the national anthem.

But how can all this apply to sound and music? Tagg (1984) has worked on how sounds and music emerge over time as a set of established associations that can communicate specific ideas, attitudes and identities. He was interested in the emergence of sounds and music as communicative acts in hunting-and-gathering-type societies and how they could be used to communicate about the nature of activities, such as initiation rites, marriage ceremonies, harvests and the hunt. Tagg suggests:

> Obviously, the pace required in conjunction with a hunt – intensity of heartbeat, speed of eye, of hands, arms, feet and breathing – will be far greater than that needed for singing a child to sleep […] In the case of the hunt, quick, sudden movements enacted with the precision of split seconds are vital ingredients of the activity, but they would be detrimental when trying to send a child to sleep.
>
> (Tagg 1984, p. 8)

What is clear here is that there are much more precise and predictable aspects of sound as communication than we tend to assume and that these can convey quite clear ideas, attitudes, and sequences of events and identities. So, we cannot use sharp sounds to mean relaxed, nor soft lingering sounds to convey urgency. It is not just that music is 'scary' or 'fun', but that it can communicate specific things about what goes on in a social practice, about how it should be evaluated and what kinds of identities are involved. Here, we begin to see the sense of sound and music being used to code the world.

What Tagg does not address in this case is the ideological nature of this coding. Scholars have pointed to the ideological nature of marriage ceremonies as part of promoting a 'princess' model of femininity and serving to legitimise patriarchal notions of gender relations (Wolf 1991; Otnes & Pleck 2003). The music of the wedding ceremony is part of this process.

So too, anthropologists have drawn attention to the way that hunting as an activity is deeply related to power and politics within a society, often providing little in terms of food supply compared to the agricultural work of women, which also requires skills, planning and collective work (Lee 1969). But the sound and music used to represent the hunt foregrounds and positively evaluates certain kinds of skills, activities and identities.

From a social-semiotic perspective, we can see in the case of both the hunt and the wedding that the communicator draws on a set of available meanings in sound, as regards things like pitch and roughness and as regards different kinds of rhythms, all of which come – to some extent – loaded with meaning potentials, to provide an account of social practices, of what happens, of what attitudes and identities are required. It is this kind of observation that I want to extend here to think about the sounds used to communicate about the nation and nationalism.

There has, in fact, been a lack of scholarly work into the details of music semantics. One notable exception, drawn on extensively in this chapter is Cooke's (1959) attempt to identify the language of music through a study of classical and opera music, looking for the kind of patterns in uses of pitch, melodies, articulation, notation and rhythms that were used for different purposes. So, for example, he established that certain patterns of expanded or limited pitch ranges in melodies clearly related to how emotionally expressive or contained a character was to be depicted. Abrupt and more sudden articulation in how notes were sounded related to confidence, arrogance or certainty, whereas longer lingering notes would be used for emotional dwelling and thoughtfulness.

One rare example of scholarship that related sound meanings to ideology was McClary (1991) who considered gender representations in music. She argued that there is a long tradition of representing men and women in European music using particular kinds of instruments, rhythms and phrasing. For men, we find dotted rhythms, melodies that ascend, notes that are played sharply with staccato. We find louder brass instruments and a wide pitch range in the melodies. In contrast, for women, we find softer, connected and longer articulation of notes, softer instruments such as woodwind and strings and a narrower pitch range in the melodies. The difference between the two, she suggests, is that the male is more precise, outward-looking and assertive. The female is more subjective, inward-looking and gentle.

It is this level of observation about sound qualities, connecting them to ideology, that is the aim in this chapter in the case of the national anthem and the kinds of ideas, values, attitudes and identities they communicate, not only through lyrics, but also through specific semiotic choices in music, rhythm and arrangement.

The national anthem as discourse

In Critical Discourse Studies, it has been shown how nationalism and the idea of a monolithic nationalist identity have been used for ideological purposes (Wodak et al. 2009), as a means to go to war (Graham et al. 2004), to delegitimise migrant populations (Krzyżanowski & Wodak 2008) and to distract from social inequalities based on distribution of wealth and resources (Abousnouga & Machin 2013) – in short, to mobilise populations around deeply ideological projects (O'Doherty & Augoustinos 2008, p. 578). These discourses are communicated through political speeches and news media, but also routinely through banal everyday events and objects, such as weather maps, school books and international sporting events (Billig 1995). Through these processes, the idea of a 'world of nations' become naturalised (Malešević 2011, p. 272). It is clear that discourses of nationalism and national identity are realised and disseminated by different modes and through different kinds of communicative genre. But, given what has been said so far in this chapter about sound and music, what can we learn about their role in this nationalist project? Before analysing examples of anthems, I look first at the history of the national anthem and show its part in the nation-building project.

The origins and deployment of the national anthem

The origin of the national anthem, like nationalism itself, lies in the eighteenth century, although most anthems are much more recently composed, or have gone through many modifications due to local political and power changes. And even where some anthems do date back several hundred years as musical compositions, it is only recently that they have become understood in the present sense of a national anthem, such as the Dutch 'Wilhelmus', composed originally in the sixteenth century, yet not officially recognised as an anthem until 1932. Two of the very first national anthems were the German '*Deutschlandlied*' and France's '*La Marseillaise*', which provided models for many that followed.

The '*Deutschlandlied*' had its origins in the growth of nationalism in the newly unified German state from 1871, where there was a need for national symbols around which the population, from many formerly distinct territories, could be mobilised (Reimer 1993). The first song to be used as such a national symbol was '*Deutschlandlied*' based on a composition by Joseph Haydn, written in Vienna at the end of the eighteenth century. While initially being a song about heart, land and brotherhood, it was later adapted in the First World War to become more aggressive (Hermand 2002). As with many of the earlier national anthems, it only became widely recognised through the nation-building and intensive propaganda of the First World War.

'*La Marseillaise*' was originally called '*Chant de guerre pour l'Armee du Rhin*' (War Song for the Army of the Rhine). It was composed in 1792 by Claude-Joseph Rouget de Lisle as part of the mobilisation against armies from Prussia and Austria that had entered France to stop the Revolution. (It was also called '*Auf, Brüder, auf dem Tag entgegen*' as many of the soldiers were non-French speaking). The lyrics are highly aggressive, referring to fighting on the streets and spilling the blood of the invaders. But this was not used properly as a national song until the end of the nineteenth century and – like other anthems – gained its full recognition through the propaganda of the First World War (Marshall 2015). Its lyrics have been criticised as militaristic and xenophobic (Riding 1992). Marshall (2015) notes the uncomfortable nature of the present-day use of the song with its colonial legacy and as a tool by the far right where the lyrics 'Let's water the fields with impure blood' can allude to contemporary immigrants.

The 'Star-Spangled Banner' (SSB) was originally written as a poem in 1814 called *The Defence of Fort McHenry*, based on a melody by a British composer, which was already popular in the US in sheet-music books (Lichtenwanger 1978). It has therefore always had military associations. By the Civil War, the song had become associated with the North as opposed to the whole of the US (Abril 2012). It was not until the late nineteenth century that the song was taken on as a more official national anthem as it became officially required for all armed forces ceremonies (Weybright 1935), although some commentators complained that the military associations were an unsuitable identity for the country (Weybright 1935). But it was only during the First World War that the SSB took force, when it became a requirement at public events (Tischler 1986).

The rising interest in nationalistic symbolism in nineteenth-century Europe also spread to the colonies as in the case of the Canadian national anthem 'O Canada' (OC), where there was rising French nationalism. One song written for this movement was OC, which was commissioned by the governor of Quebec in 1880. English lyrics were added in 1901 for a visit by British royalty. These were rewritten several times through periods of nation-building. Again, there was little public acknowledgement of the song until the First World War, when it was heavily promoted by the authorities (Cook 2008).

What are now presented as timeless national anthems were part of a deliberate nation-building process by the ruling classes; for the most part, anthems only became more widely known during the intense nationalism of the First World War. As Veblen (2012) points out, anthems were used as an instrument to gloss over and suppress the internal diversity of populations in the interests of what was represented as a monolithic dominant culture, often creating experiences of exclusion for minority groups (Avila 2006; Yudkoff 2012). Here is acknowledgement that music and sound have a crucial role to play in political ideology.

The lyrics of national anthems

I begin with the lyrics of two anthems. I then go on to discuss the manner in which these are realised as melodies and how they are articulated rhythmically. Here, I take the first two verses of each anthem, which are those commonly sung during ceremonies.

The lyrics of the SSB claim to tell a story relating to a battle, where America won its freedom, and OC tells of guarding a land of hope. But in many ways, the two sets of lyrics share features that are typical of many other anthems. To begin with, we find a lexis that positively evaluates the nation, in SSB, words such as 'glory', 'brave' 'gallant' and in OC in 'strong', 'free', 'hope', 'glorious'.

Anthem lyrics often refer to features of dramatic natural landscape where it is commonly thought that the spirit of a nation dwells (Thurlow & Jaworski 2010), such as high mountains, broad rivers and deep oceans, and celebrating a united people willing to defend its borders. In SSB, we find references to the sea (the deep), the shore and the sun shining on the stream. In OC, too, we find the same references to nature and to landscape: oceans, great prairies, lordly rivers, pines and maples.

Table 28.1 US and Canada national anthem lyrics

'Star-Spangled Banner'	'O Canada'
Oh, say, can you see, by the dawn's early light, What so proudly we hail'd at the twilight's last gleaming? Whose broad stripes and bright stars, thro' the perilous fight, O'er the ramparts we watch'd, were so gallantly streaming? And the rockets' red glare, the bombs bursting in air, Gave proof thro' the night that our flag was still there. O say, does that star-spangled banner yet wave O'er the land of the free and the home of the brave? On the shore dimly seen thro' the mists of the deep, Where the foe's haughty host in dread silence reposes, What is that which the breeze, o'er the towering steep, As it fitfully blows, half conceals, half discloses? Now it catches the gleam of the morning's first beam, In full glory reflected, now shines on the stream: 'Tis the star-spangled banner: O, long may it wave O'er the land of the free and the home of the brave!	O Canada! Our home and native land! True patriot love in all thy sons command. With glowing hearts we see thee rise, The True North strong and free! From far and wide, O Canada, We stand on guard for thee. God keep our land, glorious and free! O Canada, we stand on guard for thee; O Canada, we stand on guard for thee. O Canada! Where pines and maples grow, Great prairies spread and Lordly rivers flow! How dear to us thy broad domain, From East to Western sea! The land of hope for all who toil, The true North strong and free! God keep our land, glorious and free. O Canada, we stand on guard for thee! O Canada, we stand on guard for thee!

Also in anthems, the nation tends to become fused with natural cycles, such as the changes of the seasons, sunrise and sunset, or of harvests, and to natural elements, such as the wind (Aboussnouga & Machin 2013). In SSB, we find the 'coming of the dawn', 'the twilight', a 'beam of sunlight' and the 'blowing breeze'. In this way, nations become as eternal as these natural cycles and the features of the natural landscape. In the lyrics of these anthems, we find, therefore, a form of legitimation based on the authorisation (van Leeuwen 2007, p. 92) of the timelessness, inevitability and purity of nation. This lays claim to moral evaluation, because when nation is fused with nature and beginning-less time, it becomes natural and unquestionable.

We can also think about representation of the social actors and transitivity in anthem lyrics. Typically, we find collective pronouns such as 'we' and 'us'. Although in the SSB we also find 'you' being addressed personally as in 'Say can *you* see'. We also find reference to 'foes' in SSB, which are implied in OC, since it is repeated that people must 'stand guard'. In OC, we also find 'sons' of the nation, also typical of anthems where nation is related to a family. Plaques commemorating war often refer to 'the sons of the nation who gave their lives'. Finally, in OC, we have the reference to God.

As regards what the participants do, we find 'proudly we hail'd', 'we watched', in this sense, the collective is bearing witness. In OC, people 'hold true' and 'stand guard' and we find a positive evaluation of the citizens as dedicated workers in 'all who toil'. We also find legitimation in reactions (van Leeuwen 2007) where, in SSB, people are proud seeing the flag and in OC, people have glowing hearts.

In sum, we find the nation as fused with cycles in nature and rural features. All are timeless and somehow pure and spiritual. We find a lexis of 'glory' and 'bravery'. Collective pronouns are used where people are selfless and doubtless as regards the nation, which God will protect.

Analysis of sound

I now turn to the sounds of the anthems, here taking a typical case of their performance at the 2012 Olympic Games. In order to do so, I break down the anthems into a number of components, necessary for the purpose of analysis.

Creating emotion in a melody

Melodies can communicate about mood and emotional engagement through a number of semiotic means. I begin with pitch, which relates to how high or low a sound is: a scream would be a high note, thunder a low note. Pitch itself has lots of meaning potential, but, importantly, it is how pitches shift in melodies that can communicate more complex meanings.

At a basic level, pitch is rich in metaphorical associations. Cooke (1959, p. 102) shows that in the history of classical music and opera, high pitch has been associated with high levels of energy and brightness and low pitch with its opposite – in other words, low levels of energy, being contained, or something substantial, or even grave and dangerous. Both can have negative meanings: higher pitches can mean flighty and superficial, and lower pitches immobile and static. Higher pitch can also extend to mean agitation, and lower pitch can mean low, drooping despair. I summarise these in Table 28.2.

We would not expect a national anthem to use only extreme high pitches, which might suggest something light, flighty, or even hysterical, nor only deep, grave and gloomy pitches. Of course, melodies involve changing pitches, which we come on to now.

David Machin

Table 28.2 Meaning potentials of pitch

Pitch	Positive meaning	Negative meaning
High	Bright/energetic/happy	Lightweight/trivial/flighty
Low	Important/solid	Clumsy/depressed/dangerous

Figure 28.1 'Star-Spangled Banner'

Figure 28.2 'O Canada'

A melody line will usually rise and fall in pitch, which can create meaning at two levels. These are *direction* of pitch movement and *extent* of pitch movement.

Beginning with pitch direction, a movement from a high pitch to a low pitch can communicate a sense of falling energy, of bleakness, or inward contemplation (Cooke 1959). The opposite, a gradual slide from low to high pitch, can give a sense of spirits picking up, or of an outburst of energy. Where there is no pitch movement, there would be a sense of stasis, or of emotional containment. These are summarised in Table 28.3.

We can now begin to consider what may or may not be appropriate for the melody of a national anthem. It would not be appropriate, for example, for a melody to begin at a very

Music and sound as discourse and ideology

Table 28.3 Meaning potentials of direction of pitch movement

Pitch direction	Meaning potential
Ascending melody	Building of mood/outward expression/increase in energy
No pitch movement	Emotional stasis/containment/reservation
Descending melody	Drooping of emotions/inward contemplation/decreased energy

high pitch and then descend to a very low pitch. Should this be used for SSB, it would suggest a shift from hysteria to a bleak falling away of emotional energy.

Many national anthems use stepped increases in pitch to suggest a steady and regulated building of emotion and brightness associated with the national spirit. This will be interspersed with some use of lower pitch to suggest inner reflection on the gravity of the nation. These regulated, rather than flamboyant, sequences are also important for the co-ordination of voice, and therefore sense of social unity, that the anthems are designed to bring about.

We learn more about the kind of emotion communicated by melodies when we also consider the *extent* of pitch movement. Cooke (1959) shows that in music, a large pitch range communicates a sense of letting more energy out, whereas a small pitch range means holding more energy in. Linguists show that larger pitch ranges in speech are heard as more emotionally expressive, whereas more restricted pitch ranges are heard as more contained, reserved or closed. Brazil et al. (1980) note that pitch range in speech is akin to excitement, surprise or anger. These are summarised in Table 28.4.

We can now apply what we have seen in the three tables to the two melodies.

Looking at the pattern of notes for the SSB, we can see a pattern of descending notes and then stepped ascending notes. It starts by going down in pitch for the words 'Oh say'. This is a sense of inward reflection – a shift to something important. The choice of notes here, which I do not want to deal with in detail, communicates a sense of grounding, since they go down through the major or happy note, to the root note of the tune, which creates a feeling of grounding. The melody then ascends in a stepped, regular fashion, as opposed to one that is emotional wavering or flamboyant, to rise steadily over 'say can you see, by'. This marks a considerable level of emotional expression, rising a whole octave. This pattern then repeats.

'O Canada' has similar qualities. We begin with deeper notes for 'O Canada', with a rise for the words 'our home and native'. In fact, these are the very same combination of notes as SSB, including the happy major note for the 'Oh' and the grounding root note of the key for the last note of 'Canada'. The lower pitches for 'Oh' and 'Cana-da' also suggest weight and importance. Had the same phrase been carried out with higher-pitched notes, we could imagine a different meaning. What we find in the rest of the opening line 'Our home and native land' are a sequence of stepped, regulated increases in pitch, resolving again to lower, introspective and, in musical terms, grounding notes.

In sum, the anthems use a considerable pitch range, although not to the extent, for example, of a soul or rock singer who may use two octaves. There is the use of stepped,

Table 28.4 Meaning potentials of pitch range

Pitch range	Meaning potential	Effect
High	Emotionally expansive	Emotionally open/subjective
Low	Emotionally contained	Repressed/contained/objective

regulated and gradually rising melodies, rather than those that might waver about with fluctuations and hesitations. This regulated expression of emotion relates to subjection to the state. This is organised emotional expression. There are higher bright notes as well as lower notes, which suggest importance and inward contemplation. There are lots of happy major notes and certainly no discordant notes.

Certainty and commitment in music

McClary (1991), in her study of classical music, observed that where male characters are represented, we tend to find a more staccato type articulation of note, which bring a sense of liveliness and abruptness. In contrast, where female characters are represented, we tend to find longer legato articulation, which is more emotionally lingering. These observations can be related to those observations made in linguistics where shorter phrases are associated linguistically with sincerity, certainty, weight and therefore authority. In contrast, longer, lingering articulation suggests the opposite (Bell & van Leeuwen 1993). This creates a useful meaning potential for communicating attitudes and identities in musical compositions. Table 28.5 summarises these.

In the history of the national anthem, as in the case of the German anthem, it was important that the music connoted industriousness and the national spirit. Longer lingering notes tend not to communicate industriousness, but rather contemplation, as we might find in a jazz ballad. Longer notes would point to subjective experience, perhaps to suggest something like longing for the homeland. This would suggest something too baleful, self-searching, or individualistic and would be inappropriate for a sense of collective spirit. Dotted notes, however, suggest certainty and commitment to the nation. What we usually find is a dominance of shorter notes with some slightly more lingering notes to point to emotional contemplation.

The opening melody of SSB on 'Oh say can you see' has shorter dotted phrasing through the individual syllables. In the first line, words such as 'see' and 'light' have slightly longer duration. But for the most part, SSB is about dotted phrasing. There is rising and extensive regulated emotional expression, but this is articulated through short, certain phrasing.

'O Canada' opens with ever-so-slightly more lingering notes for the words 'O Cana-da', but then shifts to more dotted notes for 'our home and native land' and the pattern then continues.

In sum, the music of anthems does point to inner contemplation, the ideas for which can be provided in the lyrics. But it also points to certainty. Emotions are clearly present, but always build in a steady, structured fashion suitable for subordination to the state.

Table 28.5 Meaning potentials of note articulation

Articulation of notes	*Meaning potential*
Shorter dotted notes	Abrupt, lively, hurried, certain, objective/clumsy if played in deep-pitched brass or woodwind
Longer lingering notes	Emotionally lingering, subjective

The sound qualities of nationalism

Earlier in the chapter, I suggested that we cannot use sharp sounds to mean relaxed, nor soft lingering sounds to convey urgency. It is this level of observation to which I now turn. What kinds of sound qualities are suitable, or unsuitable, for a national anthem? Here, I draw upon both van Leeuwen (1999) and Machin (2010).

Anthems are recorded with many different kinds of instrumentation, genre and voices, and even in parody. In this case, I have chosen official public performances of SSB and OC from the Olympic Games in London 2012.

- *Tension*: This is related, in some ways, to speech and the difference between having a closed, restricted throat when we are tense, or an open throat when we are relaxed. In other ways, it relates to musical sounds, such as where a piano note is allowed to ring out, or restricted and played in a controlled and muted way.
- *Breathiness*: The meaning potential here relates to contexts where we hear people's breath, usually in moments of confidentiality if they whisper in our ear and share their thoughts with us. This can be in moments of sensuality.
- *Loud/soft*: According to Schaffer (1977), louder sounds can mean weight and importance. Loud sounds can take up physical and social space. Loud sounds can be used to suggest power, status, threat or danger. They can also be overbearing and unsubtle. In contrast, softness can suggest subtlety and measure, and also gentleness or weakness.
- *Distortion/degrees of raspiness*: Raspiness can mean worn or dirty, or suggest aggression, excitement or difficulty. Smoothness can mean natural, simple and easy.
- *Reverb/echo*: Reverb can create a sense of huge space as in a large religious building or a rocky valley. This can suggest something momentous, sacred, magical, or it can suggest isolation and internal mental states (Doyle 2006).
- *Focused versus spread sounds:* This is a sound quality musicians often speak of to distinguish a sound made by an instrument such as a trumpet from that made by a tenor saxophone. It is a little like the tension from lack of tension. It is useful to think about the way that sounds suggest precision and focus, or the lack of these. Often in comedy music, lower-pitched instruments with spread sounds can be used as they sound less precise and more clumsy.
- *Vibrato:* van Leeuwen (1999) relates vibrato to our physical experience of trembling. Its meaning in music will depend on its speed, depth and regularity. Highly regular can suggest something mechanical. Where it increases and decreases can suggest increasing or decreasing levels of emotion, excitement or stress.

Both performances of the anthems share the same sound qualities. We find tension neither in vocals, nor the brass instrument accompaniment. Voices and instruments are allowed to freely resonate. Cymbal clashes ring out openly: unrestrained. This communicates that national belonging is an easy and unproblematic matter, even though, at another level, the melodies are highly regulated. Brass instruments boom out rather than being played with muted tension as we might find in some kinds of blues or jazz. It is common, however, to find some tension in snare-drum roles. These are often used at the start of anthems, along with brass section fanfares in nineteenth-century military style. The tension is then released as the lively and expansive singing begins.

As regards breathiness, the public performances of the two anthems are not whispered or strained, nor are they confidential or sensual (and with microphone technology it would be possible to do so). The anthems are about social and public events, about open sharing of national pride. The public performance of the anthems takes up social space through loudness. Olympic winners are granted social space to their national anthem, which everyone in the arena must hear and experience. The anthems often start with louder drumrolls, cymbal crashes and brass fanfares. Brass sections boom out the accompaniment. However, it can be the case that louder brass sections are accompanied by lighter-sounding instrumentation. At the Olympic performance of OC, lighter, higher-pitched, quieter bells, were also played, thereby accenting beats that brought a feeling of delicacy and brightness – suitable for the magical moment of the victory, which nevertheless moves along with the rhythms and melodies of the overall arrangement.

As regards levels of raspiness/smoothness, public performances of anthems are played on brass instruments, usually with crashing cymbals and snare drumrolls. Brass instruments themselves tend towards a more raspy sound than strings. In McClary's (1991) account of masculine and feminine sounds in opera, she explains that women tend to be associated with softer, smoothly articulated strings and men with dotted brass notes. The brass brings slightly more aggression and power in this sense.

As regards reverb, anthems are often recorded with reverb to bring this sense of scale and sacredness. Performance of anthems in large roofed stadiums can also bring natural reverb and echo.

When it comes to vibrato, we find none on the brass instruments that provide the backing or melodies for the two anthems. In this sense, it appears that anthems are not about quivering emotions, but about the joy of belonging. Where this is emotional, as we have seen, it is regulated and certain, expressed through stepped increases in pitch and through dotted notes.

As regards focused/spread sounds, what we find is more focused instrumentation. We could imagine the effect where anthems use the bottom-range notes of a bassoon or tuba. This would act against the liveliness and movement communicated by other semiotic resources. The nation would become cumbersome, vague or clumsy.

In sum, anthems, use a relaxed sound quality that takes up social space, using focused and dotted instrument sounds and articulation. Emotional expression is regulated and structured and not fluctuating or trembling, and where possible, reverb will be used to add to the timelessness and sacredness communicated by the lyrics.

Moving with the nation: the meaning of rhythm

Here I draw on Cooke's (1959) inventory of rhythm, which draws attention to how music implies some kind of movement and structuring of movement in time, which can be used to activate a set of associations. Tagg (1984) pointed out that music associated with a hunt, for example, will include quick and sudden musical movements, perhaps punctuated with periods of waiting. A lullaby, in contrast, would utilise a gentle and regular rhythm.

- *Even/uneven:* Rhythms can be even (as in much pop music) or uneven (as may be the case in jazz). Uneven rhythms can communicate a sense of difficulty, or if the unevenness is repeated, a sense of being prevented from moving forwards or remaining in one particular place. Unevenness can also suggest creativity as movement changes, reacting and refusing to conform.
- *Fast/slow:* Rhythms can suggest energy, relaxation or sluggishness – hurry versus leisure; rush versus patience.

- *Lightness/heaviness:* Rhythm can be due to instrumentation. For example, if dominated by a deep, loud bass drum, or in contrast, by a flute, it can suggest heaviness versus lightness, clumsiness or mobility, strength or weakness, importance versus unimportance. van Leeuwen (1999) observed that rhythms can be more or less artificial. An example of a more artificial rhythm is the waltz. It suggests lightness as opposed to the forwards-moving binary rhythms used in most pop music.
- *Stasis/motion:* Through constant beat tones (such as a single bass-drum pulse), rhythms can suggest stasis, waiting, hesitation or restriction. Forwards motion can be suggested by alternating tones, such as between a snare and bass drum. There can be degrees of this such as in reggae music, which suggests a feeling of hesitation. Furthermore, some music suggests a side-to-side or rocking movement rather than a forwards motion, which is often used to suggest emotional dwelling.
- *Metronomic time/no metronomic time:* Lack of rhythm can be used to suggest timelessness, sacredness or spirituality (Tagg 1984). We find this in Gregorian chant music, where rhythms are deliberately suppressed, and also in new-age type music.

Both the SSB and OC have even rhythms. It would be problematic for a national anthem to have an uneven rhythm, which stuttered, moved quickly and then slowed again. It would also be problematic for anthems to have rhythms that suggest stasis and hesitation. Nor must they be rushed. Slowness itself can connote importance and thoughtfulness. They must also combine a sense of weight to communicate substantiality with sufficient lightness to allow for mobility.

In the Olympic performance of SSB, cymbals strike at the first beat of each bar, giving a sense of clockwork regularity and repetition. These strikes also bring additional momentousness to each step forwards. The national spirit here is dependable, powerful and emotional.

In fact, SSB uses a waltz-type basic beat structure, giving it a lightness. This brings more of a sense of a gentle side-to-side sway than the full forwards momentum of a march. But it remains even and is fairly slow. There is no sense of urgency.

Likewise, OC is fairly slow in pace and has an even, marked, rhythm. This also suggests not fast, forwards motion, but something unrushed. It also uses cymbal crashes to give emotional bursts to the rhythm. These are sometimes accompanied by taut snare drumrolls, which bring tension. The combination suggests steady and certain forwards motion, where each step is important. In contrast to SSB, OC sounds slightly heavier in motion and, in combination with other sound features, slightly more contemplative.

Conclusion

In this chapter, I have shown how we might critically approach how the sounds of the national anthem also play an important role in nationalism. In the lyrics, there are ideas of glory, freedom and gallantry related to a former era of colonial warfare. There are references to mountains and rivers, and to cycles in nature and the cosmos, pointing to eternity and spiritual connection with natural cycles. These ideas enter our bodies through sound. The music brings regulated rises of emotion and moments of inward contemplation, all done through happy notes and through articulation, which suggests certainty and rhythms that move gently forwards. We must not overlook how these different modes play a crucial role in the legitimation of discourse. Foucault (1972) noted that discourses are never really present in one place, or one instance of communication, but are infused throughout social practice, material culture and in our very embodiment of them through clothing and how we move our bodies. And it is because of this that they appear to be natural, which further acts in making them appear legitimate and more difficult to challenge.

This analysis has shown the potential for including analysis of sounds in other kinds of communication. Political advertisements tend to carry music and sound, as do documentaries and soundtracks for movies, television programmes, news bulletins, Youtube clips and computer games. With its unique set of affordances, in each case, how does music call on us to emotionally and physically relate to the discourses communicated through other semiotic modes?

References

Abousnouga, G, & Machin, D, 2013, *The language of war monuments*, Bloomsbury, London.
Applegate, C & Potter, P, eds., 2002, *Music and German national identity*, University of Chicago Press, Chicago, IL and London.
Avila, O, 2006, 'Star-studded Star Spangled but in Spanish', *Chicago Tribune*, 26 April 26 2006, A1, p. 16.
Barthes, R, 1977, *Image, music, text*, Fontana, London.
Bell, P & van Leeuwen, T, 1993, *The media interview*, University New South Wales Press, Kensington, NSW.
Bezemer, J & Kress, G, 2010, 'Changing text: A social semiotic analysis of textbooks', *Designs for learning*, vol. 3 nos. 1–2, pp. 10–29.
Billig, M, 1995, *Banal nationalism*, London, Sage.
Brazil, D, Coulthard, M & Johns, C, 1980, *Discourse intonation and language teaching*, Longman Higher Education, London.
Cook, N, 1990, *Music, imagination and culture*, Clarendon, Oxford.
Cook, T, 2008, *Shock troops: Canadians fighting the Great War, 1917–1918*, Viking, Toronto.
Cooke, D, 1959, *Language of music*, Clarendon, Oxford.
Doyle, P, 2005, *Echo and reverb: Fabricating space in popular music recording, 1900–1960*, Wesleyan University Press, Middletown, CT.
Eyerman, R, 1999, 'Moving culture', in *Spaces of culture: City, nation, world*, eds. M Featherstone & S Lash, Sage, London, pp. 116–137.
Graham, P, Keenan, T & Dowd, A M, 2004, 'A call to arms at the end of history: A Discourse–Historical Analysis of George W. Bush's declaration of War on Terror', *Discourse & Society*, vol. 15, nos. 2–3, pp. 199–221.
Hermand, J, 2002 'On the history of the "Deutschlandlied"', in *Music and German national identity*, eds. C Applegate & P Potter, University of Chicago Press, Chicago, IL and London, pp. 251–268.
Kress, G & Selander, S, 2012, 'Multimodal design, learning and cultures of recognition', *The internet and higher education*, vol. 15, no. 4, pp. 265–268.
Krzyżanowski, M & Wodak, R, 2008, *The politics of exclusion: Debating migration in Austria*, Transaction, New Brunswick, NJ.
Lee, R, 1969, 'Kung bushmen subsistence: An input–output analysis', in *Environment and Cultural Behaviour*, ed. A Vayda, Natural History Press, Garden City, NY, pp. 47–79.
Lichtenwanger, W, 1977, *The music of the Star-spangled banner from Ludgate Hill to Capitol Hill*, Washington, Library of Congress.
Machin, D, 2010, *Analysing popular music*, Routledge, London.
Machin, D & Richardson, J E, 2012 'Discourses of unity and purpose in the sounds of fascist music: a multimodal approach', *Critical Discourse Studies*, vol. 9, no. 4, pp. 329-345.
Malešević, S, 2011, 'The chimera of national identity', *Nations and Nationalism*, vol. 17, no. 1, pp. 272–290.

Marshall, A, 2015, 'La Marseillaise: Has France's controversial anthem finally hit the right note?', available from: www.theguardian.com/world/2015/nov/17/la-marseillaise-has-controversial-french-anthem-finally-hit-right-note [accessed 26 January 2016].

McClary, S, 1991, *Feminine endings – Music, gender and sexuality*, University of Minnesota Press, Minneapolis, MN.

O'Doherty, K & Augoustinos, M, 2008, 'Protecting the nation: Nationalist rhetoric on asylum seekers and the "Tampa"', *Journal of Community & Applied Social Psychology*, vol. 18, no. 6, pp. 576–592.

Otnes, C, & Pleck, E H, 2003, *Cinderella dreams: The allure of the lavish wedding*, University of California Press, Berkeley, CA.

Reimer, E, 1990, 'Nationalbewusstsein und Musikgeschichtsschreibung in Deutschland 1800–1850', *Die Musikforschung*, vol. 46, pp. 20–24.

Riding, A, 1992, 'Aux Barricades! "La Marseillaise" is besieged', *The New York Times*, 5 March 1992, available from: www.nytimes.com/1992/03/05/world/aux-barricades-la-marseillaise-is-besieged.html [accessed 26 January 2016].

Schafer, R M, 1977, *The tuning of the world*, McClelland and Stewart, Toronto.

Tagg, P, 1984, 'Understanding musical time sense' in *Tvarspel – Festskrift for Jan Ling (50 år)*, Göteborg, SkriftenfranMusikvetenskapligaInstitutionen, available from: www.tagg.org/articles/xpdfs/timesens.pdf [accessed 10 December 2016].

Thurlow, C & Jaworski, A, 2010, *Semiotic Landscapes*, Continuum, London.

Tischler, B, 1986, 'One hundred percent Americanism and music in Boston during World War I', *American Music*, vol. 4, no. 2, pp. 164–176.

van Leeuwen, T, 1999, *Speech, music, sound*, Macmillan, London.

van Leeuwen, T, 2007, 'Legitimation in discourse and communication', *Discourse and Communication*, vol. 1, no. 1, pp. 91–112

van Leeuwen, T, 2009, *Discourse and practice*, Routledge, London.

Veblen, K K, 2012, '"We stand on guard for thee": National identity in Canadian music education', in *Patriotism and nationalism in music education*, eds. D Hebert & A Kertz-Weizel, Ashgate, Farnham pp. 141–156.

Veblen, K K, 2013, 'Patriotism, nationalism, and national identity in music education: "O Canada," how well do we know thee?', *International Journal of Music Education*, vol. 31, no. 1, pp. 78–90.

Weybright, V, 1935, *Spangled banner: The story of Francis Scott Key*, Gyan Books, Delhi, India.

Wodak, R, de Cillia, R, Reisigl, M & Liebhart, K, 2009, *The discursive construction of national identity*, Edinburgh University Press, Edinburgh.

Wolf, N, 1991, *The beauty myth: How images of beauty are used against women*, London, Vintage Books.

Yudkoff, A R, 2012, 'Nationalism and patriotism. The experience of an Indian diaspora in South Africa', in *Patriotism and nationalism in music education*, eds. D G Lebert & A Kertz-Welzel, Ashgate, England, pp. 95–110.

29

The language of party programmes and billboards

The example of the 2014 parliamentary election campaign in Ukraine

Lina Klymenko

Introduction

This chapter is devoted to an analysis of the political language of party programmes and billboards. As genres of political action, party programmes and billboards represent interesting examples of discourse-constituted and discourse-constitutive mechanisms. Adopting the Discourse-Historical Approach (DHA) as the method of analysis, the chapter highlights the linguistic and semiotic characteristics of these genres (Reisigl & Wodak 2009; Richardson & Wodak 2013). To exemplify the topic, the chapter examines programmes and billboards used by three political parties in the 2014 parliamentary election campaign in Ukraine. The analysis of billboards (and to some extent party programmes) as multimodal domains involves the study of both images and words. This is in turn connected to an analysis of colours and types of images, as well as the positioning of images and text objects. Similar to linguistic structures, visual structures represent particular experiences and forms of social interaction (Kress & van Leeuwen 2006).

This study does not offer a systematic analysis of the political discourse in Ukraine. Rather, the chapter aims to unveil the genre-specific characteristics of party programmes and billboards as genres of political action. It focuses on the forms of the election material, thematic choices, and also linguistic devices. Through the use of words and images, the political parties in Ukraine communicate their notions of defence, security, war and national unity to the electorate. The study also illustrates how different political standpoints can be articulated through different representations of the Russian–Ukrainian relations.

The chapter proceeds as follows. The next section focuses on genre-specific characteristics of party programmes and billboards, which is followed by an outline of the DHA as a method of analysis. Then, the socio-historical context of the analysed party programmes and billboards is addressed, followed by a section devoted to the analysis of the party programmes and billboards themselves. Finally, there is a summary of the particularities of the language used by political parties in their election material.

Party programmes and billboards as genres of political action

The specific way of using language tied to a particular social activity is called a genre. It is characterised through the selection of lexical, phraseological and grammatical resources, and compositional structures (Wodak 2008, pp. 14–20; Fairclough 1992; Bakhtin 1990, pp. 944–963; Cap & Okulska 2013). Reisigl and Wodak cite a long list of genres that are both attached to a specific field of action and vary within the spheres of state domain, private sphere and civil society. These fields of action range from law-making procedures, the political executive, political control, media and party-internal development to the formation of working and personal relationships. These activities are respectively expressed through genres such as laws, bills, debates, speeches, press releases, conferences, books, articles, leaflets, party programmes, meetings with politicians, phone calls, or letters (Reisigl & Wodak 2001, p. 38). Linguists have intensively studied various genres of political communication, focusing on the classification of genres and their components within three domains: national and transnational levels (governments, parliaments, political parties, elections and debates), the sphere of governmental and non-governmental institutions (businesses, non-governmental organisations, educational organisations and workplaces), and the media system. Their particular interest has been in genres such as political speeches, political interviews, policy documents, television election broadcasting, political meetings, presidential debates and political blogging (Cap & Okulska 2013, pp. 7–8). Although the number of linguistics-oriented studies dedicated to party programmes and billboards is rather limited, they deserve broader attention as they remain among the more widely used communication genres of political parties.

Previous studies argue that during an election campaign, a party usually formulates an election manifesto (or a programme) to inform citizens about their policy objectives, commitments and promises. A manifesto is usually employed by a political party striving for power, and in election campaigning it is seen as important as the face-to-face appearances of politicians and reports in mass media (Aman 2009, p. 663). Manifestos create a coherent party identity that can be communicated to non-party members, and seem to convey authority as they are usually amended and approved by party members in the party's general assembly. They become focal points during election campaigns and can be referred to after an election, for example, to hold parties accountable to their promises. Party programmes are set within a particular time and space frame (the date of an election in a national territory), and are thus constrained by this framework (Kaal 2012, p. 10). Some studies note that the form of a party manifesto (sometimes also called a platform) depends on the political system of a country. For example, the difference between federal and unitary systems of the United States and the UK leads to specific processes being followed when writing a party programme (Smith & Smith 2000, pp. 459–461).

A number of previous studies have explored party programmes within the framework of discourse studies and semiotic analysis. Using a discourse space model, Kaal identified differences in the conceptual structures of Dutch party programmes (Kaal 2012). Employing Corpus Analysis as a base, Edwards compared various manifestos of the British National Party (BNP) to gauge how language is used by the party to construct a national community and to appeal to a wider electorate (Edwards 2012). Work by Aman looked into how the Barisan Nasional coalition of parties in Malaysia utilised language in order to gain political power. Using a Critical Discourse Analysis (CDA) approach, Aman particularly investigated the textual features and discursive properties of the party manifestos, focusing on discursive practice (production, intertextuality, interdiscursivity and semiotics) and textual analysis

(analysis of grammar, vocabulary and the generic structure of the text) (Aman 2009). A study by Smith and Smith highlighted the rhetorical construction of political realities by political parties in the UK. The authors examined the packaging and layout of the manifestos of the British parties (including graphs, tables and pictures), as well as the policy narratives put forth by the parties in their programmes (Smith & Smith 2000). Breeze also focused on the discursive construction of key issues of the main British parties in an election campaign. Adopting a discourse-analytical approach, the author conducted a detailed linguistic analysis of the manifestos to explore their role in setting a relationship between the parties and the electorate (Breeze 2011).

Billboards and their related posters are another genre of political action, indicative of political party development. A primary means of media communication in the nineteenth century, posters are still an influential mode of political advertising today. This is particularly the case in countries where legislation restricts the use of other media, or where political parties cannot afford to buy expensive television air time. Although television has now become dominant during election campaigns in many countries of the world, posters still help politicians to establish their names and to communicate their political goals to potential voters (Seidman 2007, p. 1). As a genre of communicative action, a billboard or poster is a multimodal text. In a commercial poster, two elements are linked: the image and the word. Slogans on posters have played an important part in poster-driven successes. To be memorable, the slogan on a poster is usually short and simple, and slogans often contain rhyme, alliteration and assonance (Bernstein 1998, pp. 142–143).

Several scholarly studies have offered a semiotic-oriented analysis of posters. A study by Teo uncovered the ideological standpoints of posters produced by Singaporean state structures during their 'Productivity', 'Speak Mandarin', and 'Courtesy' public campaigns (Teo 2004). Work by Oyebode explored the communicative and representational strategies of HIV/AIDS posters found in hospitals in Nigeria (Oyebode 2013). Discourse-orientated studies of posters and billboards have uncovered the ways in which posters work specifically as a means of persuasion for political parties, particularly involving examinations of right-wing discourses in Austria, the UK and Italy. Work by Richardson and Colombo examined right-wing ideological discourse using the example of the Italian political party Lega Nord. Adopting the DHA, the authors explored how the party put forward anti-immigrant and xenophobic arguments by combining linguistic and visual elements in its posters (Richardson & Colombo 2013). Richardson and Wodak also traced the histories of right-wing discourses, exemplified through the positions of the BNP and the Freedom Party of Austria (FPÖ). Particular attention was paid to how their election posters recontextualised the political rhetoric of pre-Second World War colonialism and antisemitism (Richardson & Wodak 2009). Additionally, Forchtner et al. (2013) have focused on the construction of an 'us' versus 'them' dichotomy in the FPÖ posters during one of its election campaigns.

The Discourse-Historical Approach as a method of analysis

One way to analyse the political language of a specific genre is to employ the DHA. As part of the CDA agenda, the DHA denotes a cluster of semiotic practices that are situated in a specific social context or embedded in a specific social action. Discourse is both socially constituted and socially constitutive. It is shaped by social structures, classes, institutions, norms and conventions, but it also contributes to the construction of objects and concepts. It is manifested in a macro-topic and linked to the argumentation strategies of social actors who have different points of view (Reisigl & Wodak 2009, p. 89). The constructive effects of a discourse are realised through identity, as well as through the relational and ideational functions of language. The identity function refers to the way in which language shapes certain identities; the relational aspect addresses how social relations are enacted between the discourse participants, and the ideational function is concerned with the meanings through which the discourse signifies processes and relations (Fairclough 1992, p. 64).

Situated within the broader context of Critical Discourse Studies (CDS), the DHA relies on the main concepts of critique, power and ideology. Adhering to the socio-philosophical orientation of critical theory, the DHA focuses on three aspects: it discovers inconsistencies and contradictions, either in the texts, or in the discourse-internal structures; it unveils the 'manipulative' character of discursive practices; and it seeks to contribute to the improvement of communication. For the DHA, ideology embodies mental presentations, opinions and attitudes that are shared by a particular social group. Ideologies serve as a means of establishing power and retaining unequal relations through a discourse, or even through controlling access to specific public spheres. In this respect, the DHA views language as a medium of power. Power refers to an asymmetric position of social actors who have different social standings and are attached to different social institutions (Reisigl & Wodak 2009, pp. 87–89; Wodak 2013; Forchtner 2011).

Thus, the study of party programmes and billboards through the DHA entails an analysis of the political discourse, and it includes an inquiry into intertextuality and interdiscursivity. Intertextuality means the linkage of texts to other texts through a reference to an event, actor or topic, or a transfer of argumentation from one text to another. Interdiscursivity refers to the connection of a discourse to other discourses, that is, to other sub-topics (Reisigl & Wodak 2009, p. 90). As a three-dimensional approach to discourse analysis, the DHA aims to identify the specific content or topics of a discourse, and the discursive strategies and linguistic means used for the articulation of these topics. The latter aspect is manifested in how the specific actors and processes are named, what characteristics are attributed to them, what arguments are employed regarding them, from what perspective they are used, and to what extent these arguments are intensified or mitigated. This stretches to the identification of rhetorical tropes (metaphors, personifications, metonymies, etc.), and the analysis of grammar (personal pronouns, temporal and modal verbs, etc.) (Reisigl & Wodak 2009, pp. 93–95).

The DHA also encompasses the analysis of four levels of context: the immediate text-internal context; the intertextual and interdiscursive context of the relationship between utterances, texts, genres and discourses; the institutional context in which the texts were produced; and the broader socio-political and historical context of the analysed discourse (Reisigl & Wodak 2009, p. 93). This focus on context is necessary to understand both the texts and the discourse. As an interdisciplinary approach, the DHA seeks to cross the linguistic boundary of discourse analysis and to draw upon the historical, political, sociological and psychological dimensions in which the interpretation of a specific discursive event is embedded (Wodak 2008, pp. 10–14).

The context of the 2014 parliamentary election in Ukraine

The early parliamentary election on 26 October 2014 in Ukraine took place in a highly complex environment. The Euromaidan Revolution in the winter of 2013–2014 led to the emergence of new societal groups, political parties and civil-society organisations. The popular uprising eventually ousted the authoritarian President Viktor Yanukovych, who then fled the country. Russia's annexation of Crimea in March 2014 violated the territorial integrity of Ukraine. The ensuing armed conflict between separatist forces backed by Russia and the Ukrainian army in the Donbas has further destabilised the country. Preceding the 2014 parliamentary election campaign in Ukraine, the conflict in the Donbas resulted in thousands of casualties. According to the UN, more than 3,500 people had been killed in the conflict by September 2014, including the victims of the Malaysian Airlines plane crash (Interfax-Ukraine 2014b). Since April 2014, the Anti-Terror Operation (ATO) by the Ukrainian army in the Donbas has triggered public debates on the nature of the military operation, martial law and conscription into the Ukrainian army. An early presidential election in May 2014 brought the country a new President, Petro Poroshenko, who eventually dissolved the Ukrainian parliament *Verkhovna Rada* (which consisted of deputies elected under the old authoritarian regime), and called for an early parliamentary election.

The election turnout was only 52.42 per cent, and although there was no voting in Crimea and some of the constituencies in the Donbas, the international observers classified the 2014 early parliamentary election in Ukraine as being in line with democratic standards that respected fundamental human freedoms (Interfax-Ukraine 2014a). Following the results of the election, out of 29 political parties who were registered, six parties passed the 5 per cent threshold and moved into the Ukrainian parliament (see Table 29.1). The parliamentary coalition, which was swiftly formed in November of the same year, declared itself as being pro-European, pro-Western, and reform-oriented. However, although all of the leading politicians in the coalition stood for the territorial unity of Ukraine and condemned Russia's annexation of Crimea and its involvement in the Donbas, the coalition partners seemed to disagree on the question of Ukraine's policy towards Russia (Stratievski 2014, p. 2).

Despite the seemingly successful stabilisation of the system of political parties and some restructuring of the party space preceding and following the parliamentary election, many scholars agree that the political parties in Ukraine remained highly undeveloped. As Whitmore points out, some parties that participated in the early parliamentary election did undertake some reconfiguration and electoral alliance-building by including some of the Euromaidan civil-society activists and combatants from the Donbas. However, the key players of the political parties remained the same. Scholarly studies have already underlined various problematic features of the Ukrainian political party system, such as institutional constraints, the influence of financial-industrial groups, extreme personalisation, the weakness of structural and ideological positions, the regionalised basis of electoral support, and the gap between political parties and civil-society organisations. The loyalty of deputies to a party also remains highly fluid. The political parties in Ukraine encompass a rather loose collection of politicians who are grouped under main party brands. Parties often act as the projects of particular individuals, and even the core teams of these parties remain fluid

Table 29.1 Political parties that entered the Ukrainian parliament in the 2014 parliamentary election (Tsentralna Vyborcha Komisiia 2014)

Political parties	Percentage of votes
People's Front	22.14 %
Petro Poroshenko Bloc	21.82 %
Self-Reliance	10.97 %
Opposition Bloc	9.43 %
Radical Party of Oleh Liashko	7.44 %
Fatherland	6.68 %

as party members often switch their affiliation between elections (Whitmore 2014, p. 2). As Whitmore argues in this respect: 'Applying Western definitions of political parties, few, if any, parties of Ukraine can claim to aggregate interests, reflect societal cleavages, offer alternative governments or act as a linkage mechanism between state and society' (Whitmore 2014, p. 3).

Defence discourse in the 2014 parliamentary election campaign

Petro Poroshenko Bloc

In the programme of the Petro Poroshenko Bloc, the defence of the country is one of the five policies that the party proposes to follow (Petro Poroshenko Bloc 2014). This defence policy is subsumed under the heading 'To Live Secure!', and it touches upon the themes of Ukrainian national unity and the Ukrainian armed forces. The party appeals to the voters by suggesting that a united Ukrainian nation is important in the fight against the occupiers. The party's message is transmitted in the programme primarily through nominal sentences without personal pronouns, as in the following examples: 'The most effective defence against the foreign aggressor is the unity of the nation […]' and 'The political and diplomatic fight will become the priority […]'. The use of personal pronouns has been identified by previous studies as one of the main linguistic features in the creation of a connection between the electorate and the party (Breeze 2011, pp. 15–17). From this perspective, the analysed party programme appears relatively impersonal and distanced to the voters. Only occasionally the party uses the personal pronoun 'we' to create a common Ukrainian identity. This can be seen in the conclusion section of the programme where it is argued: 'We can listen and understand each other and unite for the sake of a worthy future for Ukraine and a common victory'.

The party promises to fight politically and diplomatically to return Crimea, and to secure the territorial integrity of Ukraine. However, in its discourse on defence, the party does not explicitly mention the identity of the enemy to be fought. Instead (and in contrast to the other party programmes analysed in this chapter), the programme of the Petro Poroshenko Bloc presents Russia as Ukraine's enemy only implicitly. This is evident through the party's naming of Crimea as a temporally occupied territory. This term is intertextually connected to other Ukrainian legislative documents, which determine Russia as an aggressor in the territory of Ukraine. For example, in April 2014, the Ukrainian parliament adopted a law about the legal regime in the temporally occupied territory. This law classified Crimea as a Ukrainian territory, temporarily occupied under military aggression by the Russian Federation (Verkhovna Rada Ukrainy 2014a).

In its discourse on defence, the programme also refers to the theme of the Ukrainian armed forces. The party calls for an extension of the country's military-industrial complex. In this context, the following examples of intertextuality are worthy of attention. The programme cites two sayings that urge the Ukrainian population to support the Ukrainian army: 'If one wants peace, one should prepare for war' and 'If one does not feed one's own army, one is feeding the foreign one'. Previous studies have already discovered that the use of proverbs in political discourse adds power and authority to the political message, and thus to the politicians. This effect derives from the sentiment that proverbs commonly condense complicated and long messages into one sentence, and also transmit ideas that are commonly regarded as containers of conventional wisdom and communal identification (Orwenjo 2009, pp. 124–125). In the setting of the analysed party programme, the use of proverbs brings credibility to the party's agenda and justifies the president's actions towards strengthening the Ukrainian military.

The theme of national unity is furthermore accentuated on one of the party's billboards (see Figure 29.1). The billboard's slogan 'Час єднатись' (It is time to unite) is set in the imperative mood and calls for unification. However, the slogan's addressees (i.e. the people being urged to unite) remain unclear. The appeal for unification seems to be kept deliberately broad as it suggests that each Ukrainian citizen identifies with this message, regardless of their ethnicity, age, or place of residence. Akin to the strategy of the party programme, the billboard strives to attract as many voters as possible who will come up with their own concepts of national belonging. At the same time, the phrase 'Блок Петра Порошенка' (Petro Poroshenko Bloc) placed below the slogan suggests that everybody should recognise the party as the leading force of national unification.

The positioning of the slogan on the billboard and the coloration of the two phrases support the party's message. According to the image-reading theory of Kress and van Leeuwen, the placement of information on the top and the bottom of a multimodal text form a particular interactive meaning. In a visual composition of this kind, the information placed on the top is presented as 'ideal', and the information on the bottom presented as 'real'. The top part is essential and most salient, whereas the bottom part is more specific and down to earth (Kress & van Leeuwen 2006, pp. 186–187). On the analysed billboard, the party's invitation to unite is positioned at the top. Painted in an intense red colour, the slogan is potentially memorable to the electorate. The slight upwards-inclination of the slogan (in the

Figure 29.1 Billboard of the Petro Poroshenko Bloc (photograph by the author, Poltava, Ukraine, September 2014)

direction of reading) implies a progressive development of the party's promises. The absence of photographs or pictures makes the slogan the most important element on the billboard. The intense red colour represents not only the colour of the party, but also functions as a warning signal and offers a strong appeal. The party's name, which is placed on the bottom, is presented as a real force of national unification. Placed on a white background and painted in black, the party's name potentially attracts viewers' attention.

The Fatherland Party

Of the nine policy fields that the Fatherland Party addresses, one is dedicated to defence (All-Ukrainian Union Fatherland 2014). In the party programme, the corresponding section is entitled 'A decisive victory over the aggressor instead of the illusion of peace', and it is divided into four thematic sections with the characteristic titles: 'For achieving peace, it is necessary to introduce a totally new negotiation process', 'It is urgently necessary to strengthen the defence of Ukraine', 'The organisation of counter-activity against the Russian aggression' and 'The urgent entry of Ukraine into NATO'. Additionally, the programme's introduction is entitled 'Do not surrender! Ukraine will win', and its conclusion has the title 'We will never surrender. Ukraine will definitely win'. These titles explicitly relate to the discourse on defence as being a central point of the party's programme. In contrast to the Petro Poroshenko Bloc, the Fatherland Party explicitly presents Russia as Ukraine's enemy. This reference can already be found in the introduction of the party's programme where it is argued: 'Ukraine's independence is threatened by the military intervention of Russia. The events in the Donbas should not be classified as an ATO, but as a real war and as an occupation of Ukrainian cities by the Russian Army'. The party programme contains vocabulary that is characteristic of the discourse on defence, employing words such as peace, military intervention, aggression, retreat, occupation, victory, front, allies, and so on.

By referring to the theme of peace, the party criticises the peace negotiations initiated by the Ukrainian president with the separatists in the Donbas. It does this by intertextually referring to the (first) Minsk peace agreement and to the law adopted by the Ukrainian parliament in September 2014 following the Minsk Protocol. This law provided special regulations for the local self-governing authorities in some areas of the Luhansk and Donetsk *oblasts* (Verkhovna Rada Ukrainy 2014b). In its promise to establish a reliable peace, the party further calls for co-operation with other countries. It creates a shared identity between Ukraine, the US and the EU member states by utilising the wording 'our allies'. This can be seen in the following passage: 'The plan of victory includes the organisation of a principally new type of co-operation with the Western countries – our allies – against the aggression of the Russian Federation'. A leading role for the party (and particularly its leader Yuliia Tymoshenko) in a proposed new peace-negotiation process is accentuated in the programme through the inclusion of a photograph that portrays Tymoshenko surrounded by her party members.

Another key theme addressed by the party in its programme is the status of the Ukrainian armed forces. As with the previous theme, the party's position on this issue is contrasted with the position of the Ukrainian government. The party proposes to improve the situation by strengthening the country's defence, by getting rid of weak and incompetent generals, and by buying highly effective weapons and equipment. The party's promise is made through the frequent use of the modal modifier 'it is necessary' (*neobkhidno/treba*), as shown in the following examples: 'It is urgently necessary to strengthen our defence […]' and 'It is necessary to defend our native land with dignity, force, and self-sacrifice'. The party's support for the Ukrainian army is additionally illustrated by a photograph depicting Tymoshenko shaking hands with men in military uniforms.

The party further proposes to organise counter-activity against Russia. In this context, it terms the Russian Federation as an aggressor and sponsor of terrorism, and the leadership of the self-proclaimed Luhansk and Donetsk republics as terrorist organisations. The party promises to gain official international recognition of this classification. Moreover, the party includes certain internal Ukrainian political actors in the category of enemies. It promises to investigate the cases of some Ukrainian generals, who in the party's view sell off weapons and military equipment, and send Ukrainian soldiers, officers and volunteers to their deaths. These generals are metaphorically labelled as 'the fifth column' of the Kremlin, a term that usually denotes forces that internally undermine a country by supporting an external enemy.

Moreover, the party calls for Ukraine's North Atlantic Treaty Organization (NATO) accession. This claim is supported in the programme by inclusion of a picture of various national flags, with the Ukrainian national flag placed in the foreground. As an international organisation, NATO is presented in the programme as a group of 28 countries, always ready to defend each other. In the party programme, NATO represents a strong and modern army, weapons, economic development, foreign investment, freedom, democracy, human rights and the rule of law. The adherence of the party to the theme of Ukraine's NATO accession is an interesting example of interdiscursivity as in this case the discourse on defence is linked to Ukraine's NATO membership discourse. As is well known, this issue has been central in political debates in Ukraine and abroad for a long time (Malek 2009).

In contrast to its programme, the party's billboard avoids any reference to Russia, albeit engaging in the discourse on defence (see Figure 29.2). The slogan 'Україна переможе!' (Ukraine will win!) on the left of the billboard is printed in intense red. The additional slogan 'Не здаватись!' (Do not surrender!) is placed above the main message in saturated black. The combination of intense red and black highlights the information and catches viewers' immediate attention. Using the imperative mood and exclamation marks, both phrases urge Ukrainian citizens to continue fighting in order to ensure victory for their country. However, the question of the enemy's identity remains open on this billboard. The vocabulary of the slogans is not strictly military and could be used in any context of struggle, fight, or challenge. The party leader, Tymoshenko, is portrayed on the right-hand side of the billboard and evokes association with Ukraine as a country. Since in Ukrainian, the grammatical gender of the word 'Ukraine' is feminine, Tymoshenko might be seen as a personification of the country, and such a representation of Tymoshenko serves as a projection area of victory for both herself and Ukraine.

As noted by Kress and van Leeuwen, the composition of images in multimodal texts bears significant meaning. An element placed on the left of a billboard is presented as 'given', and an element placed on the right as 'new'. The right side usually contains the key information, something that previously has not been known to the viewer, and to which the viewer should pay more attention. The left side presents something that is understood to be common sense and self-evident (Kress & van Leeuwen 2006, pp. 180–181). In the context of the Fatherland Party's billboard, the slogan on the left projecting Ukraine's victory is presented as self-evident, but the depiction of Tymoshenko on the right implies that she is the person who would lead the country to that victory. The portrait of Tymoshenko as a close-up directly addresses the viewers and creates a closeness with the target audience. At the same time, however, the picture of the party leader does not establish eye contact with the viewers. Rather, it depicts her seriously looking off-frame. According to van Leeuwen,

The language of party programmes

Figure 29.2 Billboard of the Fatherland Party (photograph by the author, Poltava, Ukraine, September 2014)

such depiction of a figure functions as an invitation to viewers to dispassionately scrutinise the depicted figure (van Leeuwen 2008, pp. 140–141).

Radical Party of Oleh Liashko

Of the seven policies that the Radical Party addresses in its programme, one is devoted to defence. The corresponding section of the programme is entitled 'Victory and deseparatisation', and is organised around themes of counter-activities against the perceived enemies of Ukraine (Radical Party of Oleh Liashko 2014). Similar to the Fatherland Party's standpoint, the Radical Party explicitly presents Russia as Ukraine's enemy. This is conceptualised through the party's call to the Ukrainian population to counteract Russia and support the eastern front in Ukraine. The party further suggests creating partisan units and to begin training the civic population to defend big cities. Similar to the Fatherland Party's discourse, the Radical Party also positions itself as an anti-establishment party. It promises potential voters that it will make state authorities work for the front, replace generals with experienced officers, and ensure that social benefits are made available to the injured and their families. The party even ambitiously argues that Ukraine should return to the status of a nuclear power. The leading role of the party in achieving these goals is visible from the use of the personal pronoun 'we', as in the following sentences: 'We will change the government [...]' and 'We will enable the return of Ukraine to the status of a nuclear power [...]'.

In categorising their enemies, the party additionally points to certain political actors in Ukraine. The list includes some deputies in the Ukrainian parliament, Ukrainian state officials in the east of the country, Ukrainian police officers, and oligarchs. In fighting these political actors, the party proposes to carry out a 'deseparatisation' (*deseparatyzatsiia*) process. This neologism seems to refer to counteracting secessionist activities in Ukraine. Other linguistic devices in the programme, through which the party attempts to create a personal connection with its electorate, include the use of metaphors and a specialised vocabulary. For example, the programme calls deputies from the Ukrainian parliament 'shapeshifters' (*perevertni*). This metaphor likely denotes corrupt deputies that commonly change their political party affiliation between elections. Police officers are named in the programme as corrupt '*menty*'. Originating in criminal slang, this term is familiar to the Ukrainian population and is used to convey the citizens' low level of trust in the Ukrainian police. Another interesting example is the use of compound nouns that refer to particular groups of people. In these nouns, a second word is used to describe the qualities of a societal group. For example, the term '*chynovnyky-separatysty*' (officials-separatists) describes state authorities who are allegedly involved in secessionist movements, and the term '*kradii-biznesmeny*' (thieves-businessmen) refers to businesspeople who are allegedly stealing from the state.

The presentation of Russia as Ukraine's enemy is exceedingly clear on one of the party's billboards, where Russia is personified through its President Vladimir Putin (see Figure 29.3). The president's portrait is placed on the left of the billboard, and it immediately

Figure 29.3   Billboard of the Radical Party of Oleh Liashko (photograph by the author, Poltava, Ukraine, September 2014)

attracts viewers' attention. The close-up of Putin directly faces the audience. However, the image is intimidating rather than inviting: the president is portrayed with open mouth and discomforting stare. The party's rhymed slogan 'Путін–Ху#ло! Переможе добро!' on the right of the billboard is an interesting example of intertextuality. The first part of the slogan in intense black mocks President Putin as in Ukrainian, the second word of the phrase can be roughly translated as 'dickhead'. First sung in March 2014 as a fan chant in a Ukrainian football club, this phrase later became widely known in Ukraine and even abroad. In June 2014, after a Ukrainian transport aircraft was shot down by pro-Russian separatists, the then-acting Ukrainian foreign minister Deshchytsia sang this chant in front of a furious crowd outside the Russian embassy in Kyiv as he desperately tried to calm the crowd. The incident triggered intense public debate and also received significant international media coverage (Walker 2014).

The second part of the billboard's slogan 'Переможе добро!' (Good will win!) is printed in saturated red. In combination with the first phrase, this line metaphorically implies that the Russian president is evil and will be defeated by good. The claim is supported by the use of different colours: intense black representing evil and intense red referring to good. An exclamation mark placed after each phrase gives the slogan an authoritative character. Along the lines of Kress and van Leeuwen's theory on the positioning of images (Kress & van Leeuwen 2006, pp. 180–181), the placement of Putin's portrait on the left of the billboard and the slogan on the right bears a significant meaning. It implies that the Russian president is a well-known figure to everyone, but at the same time, the slogan frames him in a new light: he is presented as an evil that can be overcome by good. The fight with Putin's Russia is metaphorically portrayed through three thick red lines covering the president's face. These lines are reminiscent of prison bars, thus implying that the Russian president is guilty, but they also resemble a pitchfork, which is a well-known emblem of the Radical Party of Oleh Liashko and symbolises the party's fight with the political establishment in Ukraine. A similar, but smaller pitchfork – reminiscent of the Ukrainian national coat of arms – is visible in the name of the party in the lower-right corner of the billboard.

Conclusion

This chapter has demonstrated how political parties put language and images to use in order to persuade the electorate during the 2014 parliamentary election campaign in Ukraine. The analysed party programmes are organised around particular policies that the political parties promise to address once elected. Similar to the structural features of party programmes discussed in previous studies (Smith & Smith 2000; Breeze 2011; Aman 2009), the generic structure of the party programmes analysed in this chapter involves various fonts, numeration, bullet points and so on. Previous works have also shown that party programmes can take the form of multimodal texts by combining words and images. Among the analysed party programmes, only the programme of the Fatherland Party contains pictures. This seems to be due to the format of the programme: as it has been created in PDF format, it is presumably designed for distribution beyond the internet pages on which it is found. This is unlike the two other programmes, which are also accessible online, but only as part of the parties' websites. However, the pictures in the programme of the Fatherland Party serve merely as illustrations that accompany the text and do not have a strong value of their own.

The billboards analysed in this chapter function as multimodal texts. The parties operate with simple right–left and top–down geometrical dimensions in the positioning of their images on the billboards. The colour schemes of the slogans are limited to saturated red and black colours that potentially attract viewers' attention. Overall, the billboards of the analysed political parties transmit central themes of their respective political campaigns by condensing messages in laconic slogans that evoke emotions rather than rationality. Indeed, it has been argued elsewhere that visual texts used in election campaigns are usually designed to elicit feelings (Richardson & Wodak 2013, p. 251).

As genres of political action, party programmes and billboards function as a medium to create a connection between the party and the electorate. Previous studies have underlined that through its election campaign material, a party attempts to attract potential voters and provide a sense of commonality between the party and the electorate (Richardson & Colombo 2013; Breeze 2011; Smith & Smith 2000). To this end, both the analysed party programmes and the billboards work using intertextuality and interdiscursivity, employing discursive strategies and a particular choice of vocabulary. In particular, the frequent use of personal pronouns (we/our), time verbs (will) and modal modifiers (should/it is necessary) in the analysed party programmes is similar to observations made in previous studies (Aman 2009, p. 677; Breeze 2011, pp. 15–17). This study also showed that the meaning of images and words in party programmes and billboards remains vague. As previous studies have pointed out, such vagueness is an inherent feature of political communication, particularly when expressed in genres that strive for the construction of common identities (Richardson & Wodak 2013, p. 250).

References

All-Ukrainian Union Fatherland, 2014, 'Program of the party "All-Ukrainian Union Fatherland"', available from: http://batkivshchyna.com.ua/document.html [accessed 3 November, 2014].

Aman, I, 2009, 'Discourse and striving for power: An analysis of Barisan Nasional's 2004 Malaysian general election manifesto', *Discourse & Society*, 20(6), pp. 659–684.

Bakhtin, M, 1990, 'From the problem of speech genres', in *The rhetorical tradition: Readings from classical times to the present*, eds. P Bizzell & B Herzberg, Bedford Books of St. Martin's Press, Boston, pp. 944–963.

Bernstein, D, 1998, *Advertising outdoors: Watch this space!*, Phaidon Press, London.

Breeze, R, 2011, 'Variations on a theme: Party manifesto discourses in the UK 2010 Election', *Cultura, Lenguaje y Representación/Culture, Language and Representation*, 9, pp. 9–30.

Cap, P & Okulska, U, eds., 2013, *Analyzing genres in political communication: Theory and practice*, John Benjamins Publishing Company, Amsterdam.

Edwards, G O, 2012, 'A comparative discourse analysis of the construction of "in-groups" in the 2005 and 2010 manifestos of the British National Party', *Discourse & Society*, 23(3), pp. 245–258.

Fairclough, N, 1992, *Discourse and social change*, Polity, Cambridge.

Forchtner, B, 2011, 'Critique, the Discourse-Historical Approach, and the Frankfurt School', *Critical Discourse Studies*, 8(1), pp. 1–14.

Forchtner, B, Krzyżanowski, M & Wodak, R, 2013, 'Mediatization, right-wing populism and political campaigning: The case of the Austrian Freedom Party', in *Media talk and political elections in Europe and America*, eds. M Ekström & A Tolson, Palgrave Macmillan, Basingstoke, pp. 205–228.

Interfax-Ukraine, 2014a, OSCE Report, available from: http://en.interfax.com.ua/news/general/231241.html [accessed 15 February, 2015].

Interfax-Ukraine, 2014b, UN Report, available from: http://en.interfax.com.ua/news/general/225196.html [accessed 15 February, 2015].

Kaal, B, 2012, 'Worldviews: Spatial ground for political reasoning in Dutch election manifestos', *Critical Approaches to Discourse Analysis Across Disciplines (CADAAD)*, 6(1), pp. 1–22.

Kress, G & van Leeuwen, T, 2006, *Reading images: The grammar of visual design*, Routledge, London.

Malek, M, 2009, 'The "Western vector" of the foreign and security policy of Ukraine', *The Journal of Slavic Military Studies*, 22(4), pp. 515–542.
Orwenjo, D O, 2009, 'Political grandstanding and the use of proverbs in African political discourse', *Discourse & Society*, 20(1), pp. 123–146.
Oyebode, O, 2013, 'Coping with HIV/AIDS: A multimodal discourse analysis of selected HIV/AIDS posters in south-western Nigeria', *Discourse & Society*, 24(6), pp. 810–827.
Petro Poroshenko Bloc, 2014, 'Program of the Petro Poroshenko Bloc', available from: http://solydarnist.org/?page_id=874 [accessed 3 November, 2014].
Radical Party of Oleh Liashko, 2014, 'Program of the Radical Party of Oleh Liashko', available at: http://liashko.ua/program [accessed 3 November, 2014].
Reisigl, M & Wodak, R, 2001, *Discourse and discrimination: Rhetorics of racism and antisemitism*, Routledge, London.
Reisigl, M & Wodak, R, 2009, 'The discourse-historical approach (DHA)', in *Methods for Critical Discourse Analysis*, eds. R Wodak & M Meyer, Sage, London, pp. 87–121.
Richardson, J E & Colombo, M, 2013, 'Continuity and change in anti-immigrant discourse in Italy: An analysis of the visual propaganda of the "Lega Nord"', *Journal of Language and Politics*, 12(2), pp. 180–202.
Richardson, J E & Wodak, R, 2009, 'Recontextualising fascist ideologies of the past: Right-wing discourses on employment and nativism in Austria and the United Kingdom', *Critical Discourse Studies*, 6(4), pp. 251–267.
Richardson, J E & Wodak, R, 2013, 'The impact of visual racism: Visual arguments in political leaflets of Austrian and British far-right parties', in *Critical Discourse Analysis*, ed. R Wodak, Sage, London, pp. 245–274.
Seidman, S A, 2007, *Posters, propaganda, and persuasion in election campaigns around the world and through history*, Peter Lang, New York.
Smith, C & Smith, K B, 2000, 'A rhetorical perspective on the 1997 British party manifestos', *Political Communication*, 17(4), pp. 457–473.
Stratievski, D, 2014, 'Die Koalition steht. Neue Machtverhältnisse im ukrainischen Parlament', *Ukraine-Analysen*, 143, pp. 2–4.
Teo, P, 2004. 'Ideological dissonances in Singapore's national campaign posters: A semiotic deconstruction', *Visual Communication*, 3(2), pp. 189–212.
Tsentralna Vyborcha Komisiia, 2014, 'Pozacherhovi vybory narodnykh deputativ Ukrainy 26 zhovtnia 2014 roku (Early parliamentary election in Ukraine on 26 October, 2014)', available at: www.cvk.gov.ua/vnd_2014/ [accessed 20 November, 2015].
van Leeuwen, T, 2008, *Discourse and practice: New tools for critical analysis*, Oxford University Press, Oxford.
Verkhovna Rada Ukrainy, 2014a, Zakon Ukrainy 1207–VII (Law of Ukraine 1207–VII), available from: http://zakon5.rada.gov.ua/laws/show/1207-18 [accessed 3 February, 2015].
Verkhovna Rada Ukrainy, 2014b. Zakon Ukrainy 1680–VII (Law of Ukraine 1680–VII), available at: http://zakon5.rada.gov.ua/laws/show/1680-18 [accessed 10 February, 2015].
Walker, S, 2014, 'Ukraine minister's abusive remarks about Putin spark diplomatic row', available from: www.theguardian.com/world/2014/jun/15/ukraine-minister-deshchytsia-abusive-putin-russia [accessed 2 February, 2015].
Whitmore, S, 2014, 'Political party development in Ukraine', *Helpdesk Research Report*, University of Birmingham, available from: www.gsdrc.org/docs/open/hdq1146.pdf [accessed 28 March, 2017].
Wodak, R, 2008, 'Introduction: Discourse studies – important concepts and terms', in *Qualitative Discourse Analysis in the social sciences*, eds. R Wodak & M Krzyżanowski, Palgrave Macmillan, Basingstoke, pp. 1–29.
Wodak, R, 2013, 'Critical Discourse Analysis: Challenges and perspectives', in *Critical Discourse Analysis*, ed. R Wodak, Sage, Los Angeles, CA, pp. xix–xliii.

30
Caricature and comics

Randy Duncan

Political cartooning, declares Fatma Müge Göçek, has the potential to generate change by 'freeing the imagination, challenging the intelligence, and resisting state control' (Göçek 1998, p. 1). When text forms of rhetoric address political issues, they often put us on the defensive, but we tend to let our defences down when we read comics. Because we perceive them as 'enjoyable rather than manipulative', they can have a powerful impact on our attitudes (Turner 1977, p. 27).

Most readers of comics take them lightly, but those who are the targets of drawn satire can react violently. The Holy Inquisition considered anyone who produced images that lampooned the church or its doctrine to be a heretic. Oliver Cromwell made it a capital offence to create demeaning images of him. Honoré Daumier's cartoon depicting King Louis-Philippe as a bloated monster cost him six months in prison (Regan, Sinclair & Turner 1988, p. 11).

Today, we tend to think of a political cartoon as a single panel drawing on the editorial page (or web page) of a newspaper, but over the centuries, the power of cartooning has manifested in diverse forms (e.g. a single caricature of an individual, a series of satirical paintings, a multiple-page picture story, a web-based comic strip).

In the following sections, I will define concepts associated with caricature and comics, explain how the comics form creates meaning and engages emotions, and provide a historical overview of the development of caricature and cartooning, including a few examples of how they were employed, sometimes to great effect, in political campaigns and conflicts of the day.

The terms caricature, cartoon and comics will appear frequently in this chapter. Unfortunately, not only has the meaning of these terms varied over time and across cultures, but the usage has been inconsistent even in a particular culture at a particular time. The definitions below provide a general understanding of the forms of communication covered in this essay, but in perusing the history of caricature and comics, we should expect to encounter some variance in how these terms are used by the sources cited.

A **caricature** is a portrait in which the subject is recognisable, but one or more features, usually facial features, are distorted or exaggerated. In England, the term caricature was sometimes used broadly to refer to any humorous or satirical drawing (Bryant & Heneage 1994, p. vii).

The term **cartoon** was originally used to refer to a preliminary sketch for a painting. In the July 15, 1843 issue of the humour magazine *Punch*, a satirical drawing was labelled 'Cartoon, No. 1.' Five more similarly labelled drawings appeared in subsequent issues. This usage helped establish the cartoon as a product in its own right, rather than simply a part of the process of making a piece of art. In contemporary usage, cartoon usually refers to a drawing done in a single panel, such as an editorial or gag cartoon.

Walter Herdeg and David Pascal define **comics** as multiple static, juxtaposed drawn pictures forming a sequence that is printed on paper and, usually, presents a narrative (1972, pp. 9–10). In *Understanding comics: The invisible art*, Scott McCloud builds on Herdeg and Pascal to create what has become the most oft-repeated definition of the art form: 'Juxtaposed pictorial and other images in deliberate sequence, intended to convey information and/or produce an aesthetic response in the viewer' (1993, p. 9). These definitions are meant to apply the term comics to the comic strip, the comic book and the graphic novel, and exclude single-panel cartoons. However, in common usage, single-panel forms of cartooning are often called comics, and perhaps there is some justification for the classification. David Carrier believes understanding a caricature or single-panel cartoon often requires consideration of what happened before, or is likely to happen after, the depicted action (2000, p. 12). Therefore, he argues, some caricatures operate as 'protocomics because understanding them requires imagining a later moment of the action' (Carrier 2000, p. 16).

Drawing comics for any medium is referred to as **cartooning**, and the person who does the drawing, whether it be a comic strip for the *Boston Globe*, an editorial cartoon for the *Washington Post*, a satirical cartoon for *The New Yorker* magazine, or an issue of *Batman*, is referred to as a cartoonist.

Over the centuries, cartoonists have produced a variety of forms of comics. Because artists are seldom concerned with the boundaries articulated by theorists, the simplistic distinctions offered below often get blurred in practice, particularly for cartooning distributed in a digital environment.

The purpose of the **editorial cartoon** is not so much to tell a story as it is to make an argument or communicate a concept. Editorial cartoons rely heavily on visual metaphor and do not always require dialogue. Single-panel editorial cartoons have traditionally been placed in the opinion section of a newspaper, but can increasingly be found online at sites such as *The Nib*.

Comic strips generally present a narrative told in a sequence of panels. Most comic strips use character dialogue or thoughts as one means of advancing the narrative. For most of their existence, comic strips have appeared grouped together on one or two pages, or in their own section of a newspaper. There are now many more comic strips that appear exclusively online than there are strips printed in newspapers.

Comic books are multiple-page comics – the exact form of which often varies by culture (e.g. relatively thin, paper-cover pamphlets in the US, thick manga in Japan, or hard-cover albums in Europe). Comic books typically present genre narrative (e.g. romance, superhero) meant for entertainment, but they have also been used for education and propaganda.

As a marketing strategy, the term **graphic novel** is likely to be applied to any long comic book or trade paperback collection of comic-book issues. However, there are increasing numbers of graphic novels that occupy a distinct cultural space because they are issued by mainstream book publishers and are largely read by people who would never deign to read a comic book.

Arguably, the various formats and means of distributing comics constitute distinct mediums of communication, yet they all make use of the attributes of the comics art form that stimulates readers to perform the operations that construct meaning.

Perhaps the most important attribute of the form is that comics are reductive in creation and additive in reading.

The reduction involves both simplification and exaggeration. During the act of creating a comic, the stories and concepts in the comics creators' minds are necessarily reduced and simplified by the economy of expression of the comics art form. The best single-panel comics usually involve the 'condensation of a complex idea in one striking and memorable image' (Gombrich 1963, p. 130). In comic books and graphic novels, only a fraction of the moments from an imagined narrative are actually shown on the page. Will Eisner claims it is in this act of 'encapsulation that the artist employs the skill of narration' (1985, p. 39).

The use of stereotypes simultaneously exaggerates and simplifies. Stereotypes exaggerate some characteristic of a group, usually to accentuate the difference between the stereotyped group and others. American superhero comics published during the Second World War, provide 'extreme examples of caricature and rhetorical exaggeration' of the physiognomy and morality of the German and Japanese enemy (Murray 2011, p. 182). Simplification comes into play because once stereotypes exist in someone's mind it takes only a few key words or images to activate concepts such as the noble savage or the greedy businessperson. Even when not alluding to a pre-existing stereotype, physical characteristics, personality traits and actions can be exaggerated to quickly communicate information about a person or a situation (Harrison 1981, p. 69). The ancient idea that outward appearance reflects the quality of the soul permeates mainstream superhero comics; the heroes are almost always beautiful and the villains are often grotesque. Stereotypes are a useful, probably inescapable, tool for constructing conceptions of a world 'altogether too big, too fleeting for direct acquaintance' (Lippmann 1965, p. 16)

Cartoonists create comics by reducing the ideas or narratives they have in mind to static pictures and (usually) words within panels. Readers expand the comic into their own imagined narratives or ideas by supplying information or context not explicitly present in the images. Marshall McLuhan (1964) classifies comics as a cool medium because of the high degree of reader participation and Kathleen Turner calls comics 'enthymematic' because they require 'participation in order to be completed' (1977, p. 28). Most of the information readers add to expand the narrative is derived from ideology, intertextuality and inferences.

The nature of each reader's additions is greatly influenced by the reader's world-view. Roland Barthes cautions that with a popular text considered to be entertainment, readers are not fully engaging their critical-thinking skills. Instead, they are likely to be unconsciously in a mythic mode of thinking, applying the values that seem natural to each reader's world-view, in order to construct the meaning of the text (1993, p. 11).

Some of the ways in which readers fill in the gaps are less a matter of ideology and more a reflection of specific cultural information. For instance, the broadsheets sponsored by William III, King of England, sometimes used the thistle – well known at the time as part of the coat of arms of the House of Stuart – rather than a person to represent the king's Stuart rivals. In nineteenth-century Europe, a drawing of a bicorn hat was a widely recognised symbol for Napoleon or the Bonaparte dynasty, but could also be used to imply that someone had dictatorial ambitions (Scully 2014a, p. 31). Images such as the thistle and the bicorn hat are making use of intertextuality, referring to another text. Because intertextual references prompt readers to add information from historical events, popular culture, or well-known literature, the symbolic visual lexicon of comics is usually tied to a certain time and place, and virtually meaningless in other cultures and other eras. However, some visual metaphors, such as the Statue of Liberty or Uncle Sam used to personify the United States, become known across cultures and can endure for generations.

Determining whether an image should be treated as a visual metaphor or taken literally, requires the reader to make an inference about the function the image serves within the comic. Not all images are easily categorised, but, generally, an image in a comic performs one of three functions. Sensory Diegetic Images represent people, creatures, places, objects, or forces within the diegesis (the world of the narrative). Non-Sensory Diegetic Images represent those aspects of the world of the diegesis, such as thoughts, emotions, states of mind, or sensations, that cannot be detected by the senses. Hermeneutic Images are not part of the diegesis and should not be read literally. Hermeneutic Images, as the name implies, require interpretation by the reader (Duncan 2012, pp. 44–45).

In satirical and editorial cartoons, very few of the images are meant to be taken literally, and hermeneutic images often take the form of visual metaphors and intertextuality. Most comic strips, comic books and graphic novels present a narrative, and therefore, the majority of images in these forms are diegetic. However, readers of comics risk missing the point of a narrative if they fail to identify and interpret hermeneutic images.

Brief history of political caricature and cartooning

This overview is admittedly focused on the European and North American traditions of cartooning, but as Richard Scully points out 'It has ultimately been the Western (combining a European and Anglo-American) mode that has shaped the political cartoon as a global form' (2014b, p. 336). Marc Baer claims that in Europe, it was the eighteenth-century satirical caricature prints – influenced by a number of economic, technological, sociological, and aesthetic factors –that evolved into nineteenth-century cartoons (2012, p. 244). Yet, cartooning – using drawings for commentary or story-telling – certainly occurred long before the nineteenth century.

A case can be made that sequences of pictures on cave walls, urns, friezes, tapestries, and so on display some of the formal properties of the comics art form. Closer to the common meaning of comics are the illustrations that appeared in some illuminated manuscripts. There are numerous instances of books that use a sequence of pictures to relate an incident (Herdeg & Pascal 1972, p. 8). The fourteenth-century *Holkham Bible Picture Book* contains a few pages on which there are multiple panels, and character conversations are sometimes depicted in word scrolls (the predecessor of the word balloon). A precursor of caricature can be found in many illuminated manuscripts because it was a common practice to depict the sinful as exaggeratedly ugly.

Telling stories with pictures seems to be as old as civilisation, but it was only after Gutenberg introduced moveable type printing to Europe in the mid fifteenth century that comics in the Western world began to be identifiable as both an art form and a medium of communication. Woodblock and copper-engraving technology allowed for the addition of pictures to the products of the printing press.

The 'long sixteenth century'

Printing technology was used to produce beautiful and expensive works, such as the *Gutenberg Bible*, but the presses also churned out inexpensive and more widely distributed media, such as broadsides and broadsheets. These large single sheets of paper (broadsides were printed on only one side and broadsheets were printed on both sides) were used for a variety of purposes. Many Christians who were illiterate, or could not afford a Bible, learned about their faith from broadsheets illustrated with scenes from 'the life of Jesus, Mary, or one of the saints' (Vansummeren 1998, p. 39). From the fifteenth century to the middle of the nineteenth century, inexpensive broadsheets used images to dramatise a wide variety of events – great storms, notorious murders, or the exploits of Francis Drake. Illustrated broadsheets provided the masses with a mediated reality of people and places they would never see in person.

According to W. A. Coupe (1993) developments in Germany – the theological Reformation led by Martin Luther, and the introduction of the moveable type printing press – spurred the birth of political cartoon satire. The propaganda aspect of the Thirty Years War (1618–1648) led to a resurgence of visual satire, particularly in the Netherlands. Protestants and Catholics were skewering each other, not only with swords, but with acerbic visual satire on broadsheets.

Cartooning in northern Europe would soon become even more caustic as it assimilated a new element – caricature. The practice of exaggerating the features of the subject of a drawn portrait, what became known as *caricatura*, began in Renaissance Italy (McPhee & Orenstein 2001, p. 5). The Italian painters Annibale and Agostino Carracci are generally credited with the development, or at least popularisation, of modern caricature. Caricature, in its original incarnation, was an amusing diversion, a playful teasing of a friend or acquaintance.

Gianlorenzo Bernini (1598–1680) saw caricature as a way of exaggerating elements of appearance and personality to reveal 'a truer portrait of an individual' (Moyle 2004, p. 30). Irving Lavin calls Bernini's caricature of Pope Innocent XI 'as a bedridden, sickly dwarf wearing an oversized papal crown' (Posèq 2006, p. 16), the first true caricature of such an important person, 'a monumental watershed in the history of art' and the beginning of a new kind of social satire (Lavin 1983, p. 365). The once-amusing technique of caricature began to be used to belittle, to criticise.

Caricature became a valuable tool for cartoonists, whether their intent was to amuse or destroy. Moyle claims 'cartooning in its modern sense was an outgrowth of caricature' (2004, p. 37). In the late seventeenth and early eighteenth century, King Louis XIV of France, whose expansionism and aggressively anti-Protestant stance increased tensions throughout Europe, was the target of what might be considered 'the first modern cartoon campaign' (Ames). When Louis XIV banned caricature, many French cartoonists had their work published in the Netherlands (Wright 1875, p. 357). William of Orange of the Netherlands, later King of England, employed a number of print-makers to produce satirical broadsheets ridiculing Louis and bolstering the Protestant movement in England (Schulz & Robbins 1971, p. 10).

The eighteenth century

Satirical illustration had traditionally displayed or implied a narrative and presented exaggerated actions, rather than the exaggerated physical characteristics of caricature. In England, there was a 'melding of caricature and satirical print' (Moyle 2004, p. 38). The painter and print-maker William Hogarth (1697–1764) is sometimes mentioned as participating in this convergence, but Hogarth wanted to make it clear he had no truck with caricature. He produced the print *Characters and caricaturas* (1743) to demonstrate the difference between his character studies and caricatured figures. Hogarth rejected the idea of

Italian *caricatura*, dismissing it as bad drawing, and denied using the technique in his pictorial satires (Hogarth quoted in Paulson 1970, p. 238). Hogarth referred to his own work as comic history painting (Moyle 2004, p. 38) or modern moral subjects. According to Moyle, Hogarth 'developed a new genre of satirical narrative and was effectively the father of topical political cartooning in Britain' (*ibidem*).

William Hogarth's 1721 *Emblematical print on the South Sea scheme*, with its focus on secular politics, is often considered to be a prime example of the transition from satirical print to political cartoon. However, Hogarth wanted to reach a wider audience, not all of whom would know or care about specific policies or political events, but many of whom took joy in seeing the upper classes ridiculed. Thus, in the decades following the *South Sea scheme* print, Hogarth was only mildly political, choosing instead to focus on social satire (Press 1981, p. 34).

In the mid 1700s, artists such as George Townshend (1724–1807) began combining Hogarth's symbolic approach with caricature. Townshend's 1757 drawing, *The Recruiting Serjeant* [sic], with a cast of characters in a specific setting and word balloons used for their dialogue, prefigures the new style of cartooning. In the 1760s, Townshend began creating caricatures that were distributed on cards. They were very popular and widely imitated. Townsend's caricatures began appearing in magazines such as *Town and Country* and *Political Register*. Schulz and Robbins refer to Townshend's drawings as 'the basis of the English political cartoon' (1971, p. 10).

By the end of the eighteenth century, more affordable prints and democratic societies that supported freedom of expression helped usher in a golden age of European cartooning. Political factions in multiple European nations engaged in bitter rhetorical battles, made more personal by the use of satirical prints.

James Gillray (1756–1815) was a more outrageous and offensive cartoonist than most of his contemporaries. The breadth of his cartooning skills – he could effectively use vulgarity and scatological humour, but also create deft and layered satire – made Gillray popular. He might have been the first person to make a living as a political cartoonist. For nearly two decades, his cartoons commented on all the important people and events in England and on the continent (Schulz & Robbins 1971, p. 11).

The drawings of Thomas Rowlandson (1756–1827) gravitated towards social satire rather than caustic political commentary. Even though his caricatures of public figures often made them look foolish or ineffectual, he tended to employ mild, rather than vicious, distortions of features. Rowlandson produced some proto-comics; his print *The loves of the fox and the badger, or the coalition wedding* (1784) had panels and word balloons. However, Rowlandson's greatest impact on the development of comics probably came from his illustrations, which accompanied William Combe's poems for three Dr. Syntax books published between 1812 and 1821. There was Dr. Syntax merchandise (hats, wigs and coats, etc.) (Hotten 1881), and a hotel in Tasmania was named after the character.

The Dr. Syntax stories were not comics; Rowlandson's drawings, only thirty-one coloured plates in the first book, depicted isolated incidents rather than a narrative flow. However, the style of humour, and even the look of the main character, seem to have inspired the work of the father of the comic book: Rodolphe Töpffer.

In the late eighteenth century, 'the English were afflicted with a cartoonomania' (Schulz & Robbins 1971, p. 10). London had scores of print-seller shops catering to the upper-middle class. The century had begun with English artists inspired by Italian caricature, but by the end of the 1700s, the work of Rowlandson and Gillray was displaying a new approach to political satire and was influencing cartoonists on the continent (Schulz & Robbins 1971, p. 10).

The nineteenth century

In the nineteenth century, many cartoonists sought to leave behind their ribald past and their work shifted from vituperation to gentle satire, from vulgarity to 'harmless fun' suitable for children (Low 1942, p. 26; Kunzle 1990, p. 1). This was particularly true in England. For example, during the course of his career, both George Cruikshank (1792–1878) and his work became more genteel and in tune with the conservative sensibilities of the time (Jensen 1997, p. 14). The change in tone during the century was such that, by 1901, Prime Minister Balfour was able to say of the satirical magazine *Punch*, 'I do not believe that the satire of that journal has ever left a wound' (quoted in *Punch* 1914, p. 5).

The barbs of the French satirical cartoonists, most notably Charles Philipon, J J Grandville and Honoré Daumier, were still drawing blood and the ire of those in power. Charles Philipon (c. 1802–1862) co-founded the Paris publishing house Maison Aubert and launched *La Caricature*, a monthly satirical magazine, in 1830. *La Caricature* was aimed at an upper-class audience, but Philipon also edited the less expensive daily broadsheet, *Le Charivari*.

La Caricature soon became notorious for its aggressive attacks on citizen-King Louis-Philippe. Philipon's four drawings transforming Louis-Philippe's head into a pear captured the popular imagination and the pear image was soon appropriated by other artists and became a symbol of opposition to Louis-Philippe's rule (Childs 1997, p. 156). Philipon declared of his magazines' use of caricature: 'We use it in turn to make a mirror for the ridiculous, a whistle for the stupid, a whip for the wicked' (Goldstein 1989, p. 10). The magazines were repeatedly seized by the authorities. Philipon was prosecuted more than a dozen times and spent most of 1832 in prison (Melby 2009; Cuno 1983, p. 351). Moyle claims the 'Modern political newspaper cartooning with its principles of symbolism and personalisation is very much the creation of Philipon' (2004, p. 41).

While the French caricaturists were doing battle with their government, a Swiss professor named Rodolphe Töpffer (1799–1846) was creating gentler, but highly significant, cartoons that helped usher in a new era of narrative cartooning (Baetens & Surdiacourt 2013, p. 349). Töpffer was certainly not the first artist to make use of narrative comics, and while the visual conventions and story-telling techniques that came together in Töpffer's work had been developing for centuries, there is something about the nature of his picture stories – his use of panels, juxtaposition and sequence – that seems to indicate that the gestation period was over and a new art form had been born. It is certainly justifiable to say that Töpffer laid the foundation for what has become known as comic books and graphic novels.

Töpffer's work was fairly widely disseminated throughout Europe and even in the US. Some of the stories, such as the 1845 adaptation of *Histoire de Monsieur Cryptogame* in *L'Illustration*, appeared with his permission. In other instances, the stories were pirated. Three Töpffer albums were plagiarised in England in the 1880s, and one of those was re-used in the North American magazine *Brother Jonathan* as *The adventures of Obadiah Oldbuck* (Kunzle 2007, p. 175).

Inspired by Töpffer's picture stories, Gustave Doré (1832–1883) was attempting graphic narrative by the time he was ten. While still a teenager, he wrote, drew and lithographed *The Labours of Hercules* (1847), the last in a series of picture-story albums published by Maison Aubert. Doré seemed to have a natural affinity for the comics art form and was more aware of the page as a unit of composition than Töpffer had been (Mainardi 2007). Presaging a basic element of comics language, Doré uses lines to indicate force or speed. When the Golden Hind leaps off a cliff with Hercules holding onto its tail, Doré draws their bodies as just a blur of lines to indicate the speed of their fall.

Hercules was very much in the style of Töpffer, but the precocious youngster soon moved beyond imitation. In *(Dis)Pleasures of a pleasure trip* (1851), Doré experiments with page layout, panel shape and narrative technique. Doré was only twenty-two when he undertook a project more ambitious than any cartoonist before him had attempted. At 207 pages, *Dramatic and picturesque history of holy Russia in caricature* (1854) 'is by far the largest comic strip album of the century' and Doré employs 'a dazzling array of graphic devices' (Kunzle 1990, p. 129). Mainardi (2007) believes *History of holy Russia* marks 'the close of the second chapter in the creation of modern comic books.'

In the UK, the picture story developed two rather distinct traditions in what Thierry Smolderen terms 'the serious and the comic illustrated press' (2014, p. 76). The picture stories that appeared in supplements of illustrated newspapers, such as the *Graphic* and the *Illustrated London News*, were subject to tight editorial control and tailored to the perceived tastes of a middle-class readership. The humour magazines allowed a greater range of styles and ribald satire that harkened back to Gillray and Cruikshank (Smolderen 2014, p. 76).

The English humour magazine *Punch*, founded in 1841, had the subtitle *The London Charivari* to indicate a debt to the French predecessor, but perhaps also to piggyback on an established brand name. *Punch* eventually eclipsed in popularity, if not quality, all its rivals in the UK and even the Paris magazines.

Early on, drawings in *Punch* were limited to spot illustrations, gag cartoons, and caricatures of well-known, mostly political, figures. A portent of content to come was the 'Punch Pencilling', a full-page, single-panel cartoon of social commentary that appeared in each issue. These pages functioned much like a modern editorial cartoon and often made use of visual metaphor. In 1843, the *Punch* editors changed our vocabulary by applying the term 'cartoon' to such satirical drawings (*The Economist* 2012).

Punch had an incredible influence on cartooning and visual satire. Rather radical in its early days, *Punch* satire gradually became more moderate in a successful attempt to expand readership by amusing without offending (Scully 2014b, p. 347). At the height of its popularity *Punch* was exported across the globe, and its influence on visual humour was magnified by many imitators that used the Punch brand name. There were many others, such as *Vanity Fair* (1859–1863) and *Fun* (1861–1901), that did not use the name, but attempted to copy the style.

Two notable humour magazines were *Judy* (1867–1910) and *Puck* (1871–1872, 1876–1918). Ally Sloper, the character that Roger Sabin (2003) calls the first comics superstar, debuted in the British magazine *Judy* in 1867. He was the first comics character to have a weekly magazine (*Ally Sloper's Half Holiday*) devoted to him. *Puck*, first as a German-language magazine and then as a better-known English-language version, was the first successful humour magazine in the US. *Puck's* attacks on monopolies, the women's suffrage movement, and particular politicians had real impact on policy and elections. The satirical style of Joseph Keppler, *Puck's* founder and lead cartoonist, influenced generations of cartoonists and the very nature of contemporary editorial cartoons.

While *Punch* imitators might have begun by aping the style of the original, many of them 'came to embody aspects of the emerging national consciousness' (Scully 2013, p. 9), often by embodying the qualities of the nation in a visual symbol.

According to Roger Butterfield (1947), cartoonists tried a wide array of visual symbols, from bucking horse to pine tree, to represent the American colonies and then the new nation. When the British derisively referred to the American colonists as Yankee Doodle or Brother Jonathan, it was meant to stress how uncouth they were, but the Americans soon co-opted these figures, employing them as down-to-earth, common-sense contrasts to the effete snobs of the old world. Yankee Doodle was a creation of song and theatre, but it was in cartoons that Brother Jonathan took form. The 1813 cartoon *A Salutary Cordial* shows Brother Jonathan rather roughly pouring a dose of perry down the throat of John Bull, the national symbol of England. Readers at the time would understand that 'perry' referenced both a paregoric and Commodore Oliver Hazard Perry, the naval hero of the War of 1812. Brother Jonathan and Yankee Doodle eventually morphed into the Uncle Sam figure (Press 1981, pp. 216–221), a mainstay of US cartoons well into the twentieth century.

In the mid nineteenth century, the national consciousness of the US was torn asunder by the Civil War. Photography was still too primitive to truly provide a visual record of the conflict so it fell to the newly emerged illustrated press, an amalgam of journalism and cartooning, to make the brutality of the Civil War vivid for readers far from the front lines. *Frank Leslie's Illustrated Newspaper* and *Harper's Weekly* were the leading publishers of drawn journalism in the US, and they sent scores of artists into the field to sketch battles and camp life. Many of Thomas Nast's (1840–1902) engravings for *Harper's Weekly* were produced in the comfort of his New York City studio, yet he created powerful images that helped raise the morale of soldiers and citizens on the Union side of the conflict. Nast is best known for his relentless cartoon campaign against corrupt New York politician William 'Boss' Tweed, dehumanising him by depicting him as a vulture, or as a man with a money bag for a head.

Nineteenth-century cartoonists, such as Charles Philipon and Thomas Nast, were incorporating some of the visual conventions of the previous centuries, but they were also developing a new style of cartooning that would flourish in new venues, magazines and newspapers, and push aside some of the older forms of cartooning. Satirical prints flourished in the first half of the nineteenth century, with print runs of hundreds of thousands in the 1850s (Göçek 1998, p. 4). Yet, demand declined precipitously, and by the end of the nineteenth century, there was almost no market for the stand-alone satirical print in the tradition of Hogarth and Gillray (Leary 2010, p. 35). In the 1860s, a satirical magazine with many cartoons cost less than one stand-alone print. The humour magazines had pushed aside the satirical prints, but before the end of the nineteenth century, the magazines faced competition from a new form of cartoons that began appearing in newspapers.

The twentieth century

While the newspaper comic strip – as it appeared in the US – owed much to the cartoons that appeared during the final decades of the nineteenth century in weekly humour magazines such as *L'Asino, Puck, Judge,* and *Life* (Harvey 2009, p. 35), not all newspaper comics had the political edge of the cartoons in the humour magazines. Cartooning in newspapers rather quickly assumed two forms – the comic strip and the editorial cartoon – clearly differentiated by their placement in the paper and their formal qualities.

Many of the early newspaper comics were humour strips (Katzenjammer Kids, 1897; Happy Hooligan, 1900) with the 'punchline', often visual in nature, delivered in the final panel. The humour strips were soon joined by comics that presented fanciful adventures (*Little Nemo in Slumberland*, 1905), amusing misadventures (*Hairbreadth Harry*, 1906), or serious adventures (*Tarzan*, 1929). Early political comic strips such as *Lil' Abner* (1934) and *Pogo* (1948) existed primarily to entertain, but they often engaged in political satire. The latter half of the twentieth century saw the appearance of intensely political comics, such as *Doonesbury, Bloom County, Boondocks* and *Tom the Dancing Bug*, that looked like comic strips, but functioned as editorial cartoons.

Walter Hugh McDougal's series of cartoons that ran in the New York *Extra* during 1884 'are probably the very first daily newspaper cartoons on political subjects' (Press 1981, p. 264). *Extra* was short-lived, but later in the year when Joseph Pulitzer hired McDougall to create cartoons for *The World*, 'daily editorial cartooning as a profession was born' (Press 1981, p. 264). When it became clear that McDougall's cartoons were increasing circulation, other newspapers in New York, and then throughout the nation, began to hire their own editorial cartoonists.

By the twentieth century, technological advances made it economically feasible for newspapers to run cartoons commenting on very recent events. Compulsory schooling and increasing democratisation of the political process in the Western world created a newspaper readership with the interest and background knowledge to appreciate editorial cartoons. Newspapers began to lure some of the most talented cartoonists away from the humour magazines and illustrated weeklies. The newspaper political cartoon became the most prestigious form of cartooning when the Pulitzer Prize added a category for editorial cartoons in 1922.

Comic books were far less prestigious. Popular newspaper comic strips were reprinted and sold in booklets that became known as comic books. Malcolm Wheeler-Nicholson, who started the company that would eventually become DC Comics, realised hiring young talent to create original material for his comic books was cheaper than paying the reprint rights for comic strips. Most of this original material was created as multi-page stories, and creators began to make use of the page as a unit of composition. The art form for which Töpffer and Doré had laid the foundations was re-established in a new medium – comic books.

The news-stands were soon flooded with superheroes, funny animals and lovesick teens, but early on, it was evident that the comic book medium could be used for more than entertainment. Malcolm Ater was not the first to produce comic books for a political campaign, but from *The Story of Harry S. Truman* (1948) and *A Man Named Stevenson* (1952) to *The Little Judge, George Wallace for the Big Job* (1962), Ater made a career of using comic books to promote candidates. Comic books have also been used to promote world-views. Ariel Dorfman and Armand Mattelart (1971) argue that Disney comics, especially those featuring Uncle Scrooge, subtly inculcated young readers with a capitalist world-view. However, the US underground comix of the 1960s and 1970s were blatantly anti-establishment. In Europe, comics, magazines and albums were the 'main channels of youth protest in the second half of the 1960s' (Baetens & Surdiacourt 2013, p. 356). The superhero conflict in the Civil War storyline (2006–2007) spanning various Marvel Comics titles was a thinly veiled metaphor for the debate over how much privacy and personal freedom a citizen must give up for national security.

The twenty-first century

Modern cartoonists can construct their comics with an arsenal of techniques developed over the centuries by the likes of Bernini, Townshend, Töpffer, Philipon, Doré and Nast. Seth Tobocman's six-page comic 'The Carlyle Group,' from the anthology *The Bush Junta* (2004), bestialises a subject, condenses a concept into an image and visually blends concepts. Tobocman's controlling visual metaphor is the Carlyle Group as a serpent; sometimes a literal snake and sometimes a snake head coming out of a business suit. An elephant's trunk terminating in a snake head visually links the Grand Old Party and the Carlyle Group. The stripes of a US flag, planted in an Iraqi oil field, morph into a huge snake (see Figure 30.1). The links between the Bush and Bin Laden families suggested in the text are reinforced by

Randy Duncan

Figure 30.1 Visually blending and associating concepts. 'The Carlyle Group' by Seth Tobacman from *The Bush Junta* (2004)

the picture – a snake visually intertwines them and the facial expressions imply a conspiratorial connection (see Figure 30.2).

Yet, even as cartoonists continue to employ age-old techniques, technology is changing the production and distribution of the comics medium and even some aspect of the art form. As the twenty-first century dawned, it was clear that some aspects of the Herdeg and Pascal definition of comics were becoming less applicable. Comics no longer have to be printed. Thousands of cartoonists who could not afford even a small print run can now make their work accessible to the entire world online. Comics no longer have to be drawn. There have been syndicated comic strips that utilise clipart or a few simple, often repetitive, drawings (e.g. *Dinosaur Comics*, *This Modern World*). Having something to say, or a keen sense of humour, has become more important than the ability to draw. The pictures in digital comics are not always static. When elements such as movement of characters, panning of the 'camera,' or music, are used extensively the work is arguably no longer comics but animation. Done deftly, however, as with *Operation Ajax*, a work can remain true to the comics art form while being more palatable to digital natives. Digital comics can also

Figure 30.2 Caricature and cartooning create visual rhetoric. 'The Carlyle Group' by Seth Tobacman from *The Bush Junta* (2004)

provide layers of information not possible, or at least unwieldy, in print comics. For instance, some of the comics published at the web site *The Nib*, or in the digital magazine *Symbolia* include features such as clickable links, embedded videos and additional information that pops up when the cursor is moved over a panel.

Conclusion

From the Protestant Reformation to the Vietnam War to the War on Terror, caricature and comics have been on the front line of ideological conflict. The rhetoric of comics can range from the obvious persuasion of editorial cartoons and government propaganda to subtle and indirect influence, such as comic books that depict anti-capitalism forces as evil.

It is still a dangerous world for cartoonists. In recent years, cartoonists have been jailed in Turkey, India and Tunisia. More recently, cartoonists have been murdered in Paris and Copenhagen. In the wake of the attack on the Charlie Hebdo offices, one commentator noted that comics are powerful because they 'pack so much information, thought and provocation into such a small space' (Phiddian 2015), and another observed that 'political cartoons are a uniquely potent art form because images impact the human mind more quickly than almost any other form of communication' (Heer 2015).

References

Ames, W, 2016, 'Caricature and cartoon,' *Encyclopedia Britannica online*, available from: www.britannica.com/EBchecked/topic/1347521/caricature-and-cartoon> [accessed 5 April 2015].

Baer, M, 2012, *The rise and fall of radical Westminster, 1780–1890*, Palgrave Macmillan, Basingstoke.
Baetens, J & Surdiacourt, S, 2013, 'European graphic narratives: Toward a cultural and mediological history', in *From comics strip to graphic novels: Contributions to the theory and history of graphic narrative*, eds. D Stein & J Thon, De Gruyter, Berlin, pp. 241–253.
Barthes, R, 1993, *Mythologies*, tr. A Lavers, Vintage, London.
Bryant, M & Heneage, S, 1994, *Dictionary of British cartoonists and caricaturists 1730–1980*, Scolar Press, Aldershot.
Carrier, D, 2000, *The aesthetics of comics*, Pennsylvania State University Press, University Park, PA.
Childs, E C, 1997, 'The body impolitic: Censorship and the caricature of Honoré Daumier', in *Suspended license: Censorship and the visual arts*, ed. E C Childs, University of Washington Press, Seattle, WA and London, pp. 148–184.
Coupe, W A, 1993, *German political satires from the Reformation to the Second World War*, 2 Volumes, Kraus International, White Plains, NY.
Cuno, J, 1983, 'Charles Philipon, La Maison Aubert, and the business of caricature in Paris, 1829–41.' *Art Journal*, vol. 43, no. 4, pp. 347–354.
Duncan, R, 2012, 'Image functions: Shape and colour as hermeneutic images in Asterios Polyp', in *Critical approaches to comics: Theories and methods*, eds. M J Smith & R Duncan, Routledge, New York, pp. 43–54.
Economist, 2012, 'Triumph of the nerds: The internet has unleashed a burst of cartooning creativity', 22 December 2012, available from: www.economist.com/news/christmas-specials/21568586-internet-has-unleashed-burst-cartooning-creativity-triumph-nerds [accessed 13 September 13 2015].
Eisner, W, 1985, *Comics and sequential art,* Poor House Press, Tamarac, FL.
Göçek, F M, 1998, 'Political cartoons as a site of representation and resistance in the Middle East', in *Political cartoons in the Middle East*, ed. F M Göçek, Markus Wiener Publishers, Princeton, NJ, pp. 1–11.
Goldstein, R J, 1989, 'The debate over censorship of caricature in nineteenth-century France', *Art Journal*, vol. 48, no. 1 pp. 9–15.
Gombrich, E H, 1963, *Meditations on a hobby horse and other essays on the theory of art*, Phaidon Press, London.
Harrison, R P, 1981, *The cartoon: Communication to the quick*, Sage Publications, Beverly Hills, CA.
Harvey, R C, 2009, 'How comics came to be', in *A comics studies reader*, eds. J Heer & K Worcester, University Press of Mississippi, Jackson, MS. Adapted in part from R C Harvey, 2001 'Comedy at the juncture of word and image', in *The language of comics*, eds. R Varnum & C T Gibbons, University Press of Mississippi, Jackson, MS, pp. 75–96.
Heer, J, 2015, 'The Charlie Hebdo attack underscores the visceral power of political cartoons', *The Globe and Mail*, 7 January 2015, available from: www.theglobeandmail.com/arts/books-and-media/the-charlie-hebdo-attack-underscores-the-visceral-power-of-political-cartoons/article22346511/ [accessed April 4, 2015].
Herdeg, W & Pascal, D, 1972, *The art of the comic strip Die Kunst des Comic Strip L'art de la bande dessinee*, The Graphic Press, Zürich.
Hotten, J C, 1881, 'The life and adventures of the author of *Doctor Syntax*' (introduction to *Doctor Syntax's three tours* by W Combe & Thomas Rowlandson), Chatto and Windus, London.
Jensen, J, 1997, 'The end of the line? The future of British cartooning', in *A sense of permanence: Essays on the art of the cartoon*, ed. R Edwards, The Centre for the Study of Cartoons and Caricature, Canterbury, pp. 11–18.
Kunzle, D, 1973, *The history of the comic strip volume I: The early comic strip*, University of California Press, Berkeley, CA.
Kunzle, D, 1990, *The history of the comic strip volume II: The nineteenth century*, University of California Press, Berkeley, CA.
Kunzle, D, 2007, *Father of the comic strip: Rodolphe Töpffer*, University Press of Mississippi, Jackson, MS.

Lavin, I, 1983, 'Bernini and the art of social satire', *History of European Ideas*, vol. 4 no. 4, pp. 365–420.
Leary, P, 2010, *The Punch brotherhood: Table talk and print culture in Victorian London*, The British Library, London.
Lippmann, W, 1922, *Public opinion*, Allen & Unwin, London [reprinted Macmillan, New York, [1965].
Low, D, 1942, *British cartoonists, caricaturists and comic artists*, Collins, London.
Mainardi, P, 2007, 'The invention of comics', *Nineteenth-century art worldwide* 6.1, available from: www.19thc-artworldwide.org/index.php/spring07/145-the-invention-of-comics [accessed 8 October 2015].
McCloud, S, 1993, *Understanding comics: The invisible art*, Tundra Publishing, Northhampton, MA.
McFee, C C & Orenstein, N M, 2011, *Infinite jest: Caricature and satire from Leonardo to Levine*, The Metropolitan Museum of Art, New York.
McLuhan, M, 1964, *Understanding media: The extensions of man*, McGraw-Hill, New York.
Melby, J L, 2009, 'Charles Philipon's La Caricature', *Graphic Arts*, 4 February, 2009, available from: http://blogs.princeton.edu/graphicarts/2009/02/charles_philipons_la_caricatur.html [accessed 2 October 2015].
Moyle, L R, 2004, *An imagological survey of Britain and the British and Germany and the Germans in German and British cartoons and caricatures, 1945–2000*, unpubl. PhD thesis, Universität Osnabrück, Osnabrück.
Murray, C, 2011, *Champions of the oppressed?: Superhero comics, popular culture, and propaganda in America during World War II*, Hampton Press, Cresskill, NJ.
Paulson, R, 1970, *Hogarth's graphic works*, rev. ed., 2 vols., Yale University Press, New Haven, CT.
Phiddian, R, 2015, 'Cartoonists are defiant in their response to Charlie Hebdo attack', *The Conversation*, 8 January 2015, available from: http://theconversation.com/cartoonists-are-defiant-in-their-response-to-charlie-hebdo-attack-36014 [accessed 4 April 2015].
Posèq, A W G, 2007, 'A note on Bernini's two- and three-dimensional caricatures', *Notes in the History of Art*, vol. 26, no. 2 pp. 16–22.
Press, C, 1981, *The political cartoon*, Associated University Presses, London.
Punch, 1914, 'A special supplement to commemorate Tenniel's career following his death three days short of his 94th birthday', 4 March 1914, p. 5.
Regan, C, Sinclair, S & Turner, M, 1988, *Thin black lines: Political cartoons & development education*, Development Education Centre, Birmingham.
Schulz, J & Robbins, D, 1971, *Caricature and its role in graphic satire*, Museum of Art, Rhode Island School of Design, Providence, RI.
Scully, R, 2013, 'A comic empire: The global expansion of *Punch* as a model publication, 1841–1936', *International Journal of Comic Art*, vol. 15, no. 2 pp. 6–35.
Scully, R, 2014a, 'Towards a global history of the political cartoon: Challenges and opportunities', *International Journal of Comic Art*, vol. 16, no. 1, pp. 29–47.
Scully, R, 2014b, 'Accounting for transformative moments in the history of the political cartoon', *International Journal of Comic Art*, vol. 16, no. 2 pp. 332–364.
Smolderen, T, 2000, *The origins of comics: From William Hogarth to Winsor McCay*, Les Impressions Nouvelles, tr. B Beaty & N Nguyen 2014, University Press of Mississippi, Jackson, MS.
Turner, K J, 1977, 'Comic strips: A rhetorical perspective', *Central States Speech Journal*, vol. 28, no. 1 pp. 24–35.
Vansummeren, P, 1998, 'From "Mannekensbald" to comic strip' in *Forging a new medium: The comic strip in the nineteenth century*, eds. P Lefèvre & C Dierick, VUB University Press, Brussels pp. 37–48.
Wright, T, 1875, *A history of caricature and grotesque in art and literature*, Chatto & Windus, London.

31
Meetings

Jo Angouri and Lorenza Mondada

Introduction

Meetings have attracted significant interest over the years given their frequency and importance for participants and organisations. The term – as it is globally used by social actors as well as by scholars – covers heterogeneous gatherings in which people meet for professional and institutional purposes and work together on a common task and goal. On one side, meetings are a common way in which political activities are organised among large numbers of participants, allowing politicians to talk to large audiences as well as to enable citizens' participation. On the other side, in the professional context, meetings always have a political dimension in that their organisation fosters or reduces issues of asymmetry, power and participation. More generally, meetings are a form of social activity that concerns a number of people engaged in institutions, organisations and professions (Schwartzman 1989). They involve a variable number of participants (from two to hundreds), the presence or absence of organising figures such as moderators, chairpersons, facilitators, and so on, a restricted versus public right to participate, and the use of artefacts (e.g. an agenda). As argued in early research, the form and function of the meeting varies considerably, but the participants always 'commonsensically' recognise it (Cuff & Sharrock 1985) despite the variations.

In this chapter, we refer to a diversity of political, business-orientated and institutional meetings, and we discuss similarities and differences in the genre. In a nutshell, *business/corporate meetings* research has drawn on different contexts from relatively small/medium enterprises to large firms and in some cases multinational companies. *Institutional meetings* research has largely focused on health-care, notably on collective discussions of clinic cases, and academic settings – notably in supervision contexts. *Political meetings* have been studied by mainly focusing on official political speeches and on mediated political talk (on radio and TV), and less on co-presented and more grass-roots participatory gatherings. Here, we draw on meetings from a diversity of settings to illustrate key issues raised by this form of institutional gathering.

We bring together scholarship from three areas, namely, conversation analysis (CA), interactional sociolinguistics (IS) and Critical Discourse Analysis (CDA). CA has studied meetings as social interactions within which institutions are brought into being through specific turn-taking systems, choice of linguistic and embodied resources, and the detailed sequential organisation of actions such as proposing, accepting/rejecting, formulating, rebutting, assessing, and so on. Workplace analysts taking an IS perspective have approached the meeting as a context where the participants negotiate and jointly construct roles and responsibilities, relationships and ways of 'doing'. Analysts have addressed the ways groups make decisions, agree on problems and priorities and bring their practices and processes under scrutiny. Researchers taking a CDA approach have also found in meetings fertile ground for the analysis of power ab/use and the ways the more/less powerful in professional contexts are silenced, and the power distribution is resisted and challenged.

Overall, the study of meetings has been confronted with common challenges, which all methodologies have had to address. Common challenges occur while doing fieldwork and gathering data of different sorts (such as written documents, email exchanges, web pages, situated talk, elicited declarations) from contexts in which there are issues of confidentiality, hierarchy and competition. Getting authorisation to collect documents, to interview people, or to record actual meetings is often difficult, and may be constrained and restricted by confidential contents, but also by delicate hierarchical relationships. Even if the authority or top management delivers the authorisation to conduct the study, this does not always match the consent of all of the involved parties, who might be obliged to accept without fully agreeing. This might impact the choice of the terrains to access and the phenomena to study, as well as the type of feedback – or 'counter-gift', or even 'counter-service' to offer. As a consequence, lots of research has been carried out on institutions such as universities, and less on enterprises; medium/large enterprises have been studied more than smaller ones, white collars more than blue collars, and so on.

Different methodologies have been sensitive to a variety of approaches to meetings. Some insist on the importance of ethnography for a better understanding of how the institution or enterprise works; others use ethnography to produce the most adequate audio-video recordings and collect better data. Some methodologies have favoured various forms of triangulation of data, collecting a diversity of documents, historical information, interview data and recorded data. Other methodologies might prefer to focus on the meeting itself, as it is locally accomplished, and the materials (documents, PowerPoint, notes, etc.) that are actually used during that meeting. These methodological variations depend on different conceptualisations of meetings as historical events produced by a complex web of social, institutional and power relationships, or as social practices through which organisations and institutions come into being, are reproduced and transformed. Some approaches focus on the organisation of single meetings, most often various meetings are considered, either to draw studies of systematic cross-contextual practices, or to conduct a longitudinal study of how problems and relations are established and managed over time.

In this chapter, we choose to focus on one crucial type of data: audio-video recordings of meetings. We also opt for exemplary analyses of small fragments of recorded meetings. These analyses emanate from different analytical sensitivities, aiming to give examples of how data might be approached in different ways. We identified four areas of study that represent crucial issues and challenges for meetings. First, we focus on the specific turn-taking organisation of meetings, mediated by a facilitator or chairperson, who selects the next speakers and distributes opportunities to speak. Second, we point at the multiple identities that are made relevant in meetings, related to the management of talk (such as 'chairperson', 'facilitator', 'presenter', etc.), but also to expertise and knowledge, as well as to other aspects such as national or ethnic categories in multilingual meetings, or gender. Third, we develop issues related not only to the identity of participants, but also to the choice of languages, especially in international contexts, intertwining issues of language competence and participation. Fourth, we describe how topical aspects of the meeting are managed, such as elaborating on solutions, taking decisions, arguing and (dis)agreeing. For each of these areas, we offer a brief state of the art as well as an example, aiming at not only summarising findings, but showing how they can be empirically discussed. These examples aim at showing how different theoretical and methodological traditions address data details and relevances for the issues at hand.

Turn-taking and the management of meetings

The organisation of meetings crucially relies on how the floor is successively given to participants. Turn-taking organisation has been described within CA for ordinary conversation as well as for institutional settings. Whereas in conversation turn-taking is mostly unconstrained and takes a diversity of forms (Sacks, Schegloff & Jefferson 1974), in institutional settings, the system has been described as being more restricted and specialised (Drew & Heritage 1992). Moreover, this specification of the turn-taking system indexes the way in which participants locally and reflexively accomplish the institutionality of the setting, both by adapting to its normative expectations and by contributing to this normativity through their ordered conduct. Particular turn-taking formats shape the opportunities for action and participation.

For institutional situations in which large numbers of participants gather together, such as meetings, specialised formats restrict the number of persons allowed to speak and who can initiate talk, contributing to focusing the activity on a main participant and to defining the audience as constituting a single *party* rather than a number of possible *persons* (Schegloff 1995). There are two particular ways to manage larger groups (Heritage & Clayman 2010): within the *turn-type pre-allocation system* (such as in interviews, courts and formal academic events), the type of person and action performed is restricted (the interviewee is expected to answer questions and does not engage in other types of action); within the *mediated turn-taking system*, a chairperson mediates the distribution of turns, controlling both speakers and topics. Mixed systems exist, in which a mediator can impose restrictions on the type of action or turn allowed for given participants.

Studies of political meetings in CA have focused on mediated political interactions, such as news interviews (Clayman & Heritage 2002) and broadcasted debates (Bovet 2009). Political speeches have been treated as events in which the speaker addresses the audience treated as one *party*. Specific practices by which the speaker invites the audience to respond, as well as the organisation of responses, either in the form of applause (Atkinson 1984) or booing (Clayman 1993), have been examined. Occasions in which the audience participates more actively have been less studied, such as when it participates in public debates in differentiated and not exclusively choral ways (but see Llewellyn 2005; McIlvenny 1996; Mondada 2012).

Studies of turn-taking management in professional meetings (Boden 1994; Ford 2008) have focused on the actions of the chair (Boden 1994; Mondada 2013; Pomerantz & Denvir 2007; Svennevig 2008) and on how turn-taking practices shape opportunities to participate, manage asymmetries and restrict access to the floor. Participation can be facilitated or obstructed, access to the floor can be enabled in a distributed or in a centralised way (Ford 2008). Turn formats and access to the floor define participants' categories, such as 'chairperson', 'speaker', 'expert' or 'guest star' in a locally situated way (Antaki & Widdicombe 1998; Sacks 1972, 1992). As shown by Goodwin and Goodwin (2004), revisiting Goffman's classical paper on participation frameworks (1979), participation is designed in a highly dynamic way and is made possible by the step-by-step opportunities offered by the sequential organisation of talk, which are offered and taken (or not) thanks to various multimodal resources (Goodwin 2007). In meetings, these are deployed *gesturally*, by displaying the status of the imminent speaker (Ford 2008; Mondada 2013), *visually,* by gazing and orientating bodily towards the next speaker, thereby recognising them as such (Ford 2008; Markaki & Mondada 2012).

Turn-taking practices in political meetings with larger groups of participants are a perspicuous setting in which to observe how the practical problems of managing the interactional order are situatedly solved in embodied ways, with important political consequences on issues of transparency, participation, democracy and fairness (Mondada 2013). We give an example in the fragment below, taken from a political meeting in grass-roots democracy, in which citizens contribute to an urban-planning project aimed at transforming a military site into a public park (for further analyses, see Mondada 2011, 2012). According to the golden standards of the field, the participants in all examples quoted in this paper have given their formal agreement to be recorded, analysed and represented in transcripts (including screen shots). The transcript uses pseudonyms in order to anonymise the speakers. We join the meeting as citizens make proposals about structuring features of the park, mediated by a facilitator.

The sequence is initiated by the facilitator selecting the next citizen uttering a proposal: he walks towards her, looking at her (1), in a way that makes publicly visible her emergent status as the next speaker. But also, even before she answers, he repositions himself (2) facing the room, although continuing to gaze at her – in a double orientation of the upper versus the lower part of the body (which Schegloff [1998] calls *body-torque*). When Turenne responds (3), the facilitator looks at her (Figure 1 in Fragment 31.1) and then immediately turns to the room (Figure 2 in Fragment 31.1), self-selecting, although her turn is not complete, and repeating her proposal with an interrogative intonation, 'closed at night?' (4).

With his body-torque, the facilitator exhibits the relevance of two distinct spaces within the room: one, on his right, is where the author of the proposal is located, the other, in front of him, is where the co-participants he addresses are distributed. By repeating Turenne's turn while looking at the co-participants, the facilitator re-addresses it to the entire audience (Mondada 2015); he *collectivises* the proposal that was initially addressed to him.

Next, the facilitator continues to look in front of him, with a circular gaze monitoring the responses of the audience (Figure 3 in Fragment 31.1). Progressively, a disagreement emerges (6–11). Although it is expressed by various people scattered around the room, the facilitator identifies two persons in particular, Rossi and Maurane, sitting at the same table, in front of him. By saying 'OH not agreeing here' (12), the facilitator performs several actions: he completes his monitoring and exhibits its result; he not only states that there is a disagreement, but, by pointing at a particular table (Figure 4 in Fragment 31.1), he localises it within space, 'here' (12). Thereby, he also constitutes the table as a group having an opposite opinion – a *party* in a double sense, interactional (Schegloff 1995) and political. Pointing at other participants at the back of the room (14), the facilitator identifies two antagonistic camps (Figures 4 & 5 in Fragment 31.1), located in two different spots, and organises the space of the controversy. Next, he selects the party defending the proposal (14) – interestingly, *not* the first author – before he comes back to the opponents.

```
1  FAC   *y     avait    *aut'cho:*se?
         was there something else?
         *turns to TUR*points---*walks tow her-->
2        (0.4) *  (0.2)
         --->*stops in front of the room and looks at TUR-->
3  TUR   donc euh: ferm- fermé# la nui:t, [(   )             *
         so ehm: clos- closed at night,  [(   )
4  FAC                                   [fermé# la nuit,* # h
                                         [closed at night, h
                                                          -->*looks R/L-->
   fig                  #fig.1                      #fig.2    #fig.3
```

[figures 1, 2, 3]

```
5  ?     °fermé la nuit°
         °closed at night°
6  ?     n[on
         n[o
7  ?      [non
          [no
8  ?      [non
          [no
9  ?     non
         no
10 ROS   °non on [n'est pas d'accord, [nous°
         °no we [aren't agreeing,     [we°
11 MAU           [non                 [non
                 [no                  [no
12 FAC   A:*H, pas d'accord ic#i,
         O:H, not agreeing here,
         ->*points at ROS and MAU's table in front of him-->
   fig                   #fig.4
13 ?     °pas d'accord°
         °not agreeing°
14 FAC   AH* (.) alors monsieur, pour#quoi? fermé la *nuit?*
         OH  (.) so mister, why closed at night?
   fig                                    #fig.5
         ->*points at CUN in the back of the room-----*,,,,,*
```

[figures 4, 5]

Fragment 31.1 (Corpus_LM_CAB)

This fragment shows how turn-taking organisation in political meetings manages much more than the turn-by-turn distribution of talk between participants; it not only establishes rights and obligations to speak, providing opportunities to participate, but also organises, makes publicly visible and identifies individual versus collective opinions, and therefore manages agreements and disagreements, and also spatialises controversies in intelligible and spectacular ways. In this sense, turn-taking management of political debates achieves political accountability for what is debated, and who debates.

Identity and role

Researchers in workplace discourse, the young but established sub-field of sociolinguistics, have also paid special attention to the meeting event (Holmes & Stubbe 2003) characterised as a 'microcosm of an organisation's communication' (Tannen 1994, p. 277). Meetings are seen as a discourse site within which the participants claim and project roles and identities to the self and others. In a business meeting, participants perform membership in the organisation, and claim and project status and expertise. Context-specific positions, notably the role of the chairperson, have been particularly prominent in this respect (Bargiela-Chiappini & Harris 1997; Holmes & Stubbe 2003; Schwartzman 1989). The role of the chairperson is often one of the criteria used by researchers for distinguishing a meeting from other work-related communicative events. A chairperson is in the powerful position of the meeting controller and this may (or not) be aligned with their overall status in the organisation. Hence, recent work (Angouri & Marra 2011) has focused on the ways that meeting chairpersons construct their role and identity in the community within which they operate.

Within CA, identity issues have been tackled mainly within the framework of Membership Categorisation Analysis developed by Sacks (1972, 1992; see also Hester & Eglin 1997; Jayyusi 1984). The main issue is how a given category – which might belong to different 'collections of categories' (such as profession, expertise, nationality, language, gender...) – is made endogenously relevant in a situated way at a given interactional moment by the participants (rather than decided upon by the analyst). For meetings, this has been elaborated on in different directions: categories bound to speech activities have been studied (such as 'chair': Boden 1994, 99ff; Pomerantz & Denvir 2007; Svennevig 2008), with a specific focus on opportunities to enhance or restrict participation and on the rights and obligations exhibited through practices for allocating turns. However, categories related to the local identities of participants have been analysed in their emergent, fluid and transient character: gender (Ford 2008), multiple expertise (Housley 2003), nationality and cultural background (Markaki & Mondada 2012), institutional roles (Schmitt 2002) as well as language competence (see p. 475).

At the same time, researchers taking a critical perspective have approached the meeting as a site where the power imbalance, inherent in any organisational context (Wodak 2000, 2009), becomes evident (van Dijk 1996), power struggle may be manifested (Krzyżanowski 2008; Wodak 2013) and power is actively used by those in leadership positions in organisations (Wodak et al. 2011). Current work focuses on the importance of consensus in decision making (Angouri & Angelidou 2012) as well as the different discourse styles, notably authoritarian versus egalitarian styles, participants adopt in meetings (Wodak et al. 2011). These styles index different positions in the local context and are negotiated as the event unfolds. Depending on the task at hand, the meeting participants orientate towards different *in-groups* (the organisation, or their own team, for instance), and align (or not) their positions.

By bringing together different sociolinguistic approaches to the study of the meeting genre, new insights emerge. The meeting provides the analyst with a frame for studying how participants, through specific discourse practices, take positions and are *being* positioned by others in relation to specific roles and identities. Current research moves away from static universal and essential categories and understands this process as being dynamic and context-specific. This is in line with the social constructionist paradigm, according to which, 'identity' is socially situated and actively negotiated by participants in relation to the situation, interactional agenda and their goals, among others (Bucholtz & Hall 2005). The meeting participants draw on their institutional roles in constructing their professional identities. The relationship between role and identity is not straightforward, despite being used interchangeably in workplace discourse literature (Sarangi 2010). The operationalisation of the former can shed light on the latter, which is best understood as an abstract notion (Angouri 2015).

Overall, the meeting participants bring to the event their habitus (in Bourdieu's sense; Bourdieu 1984), standing in the organisation, their specific responsibilities and their perception of the nexus of relationships within which their activity takes place. In this context, they perform their roles, drawing on local practices and anchored positions outside the temporary context of the meeting event. The participants negotiate roles specific to their professional expertise (e.g. 'sales expert'), but also in relation to their team (e.g. 'sales department director'). These are not static, but fluid positions, constructed through a set of discourse practices: participants negotiate and balance the here and now of interaction and issues that go beyond it. For instance, the accountability for decisions taken, the implications for their own team and their own agenda play a key role in the positions the meeting participants take.

Fragment 31.2 aims to illustrate some of these issues. The excerpt draws on the case of four senior managers in a small consultancy business (here named LeadingCom UK), who are debating how to best engage their membership, constituting small–medium businesses, in the activities of the organisation. The three interactants collaborate, share the floor and enact a 'we' the organisation and 'them' the membership divide throughout the excerpt. The interactants know each other well and have long discourse histories developed through their collaboration. Dan introduces the metaphor of a family whereby the senior board (the interactants) are the parents and the members are positioned as the children – building an *in-group* constituted by the team of senior executives. The use of metaphors is a common strategy for team-building (Vaara et al. 2003). The particular position here alludes to an evident power imbalance, which is reinforced with the positioning of Tom (the company's director) in the frustrated parent's role who goes as far as to 'bang the kids' heads together' (line 4). Paul takes a softer line on a cost–benefit analysis of what the members 'get' for their membership (an argument introduced earlier in the meeting) and mitigates the strong metaphor introduced by Dan (lines 2–10). This is resisted by Tom who, in line with Dan, expands on the members' responsibility for creating 'belonging'. Although all three interactants are senior, Tom's role as the meeting chairperson and company director can be seen in the foregrounding of 'I' in the positions taken in the interaction (e.g. lines 19–22). The way, however, that the three managers enact their roles is dependent on the norms of the community, the agenda and the meeting participants (see also Angouri 2015). This is a closed-doors meeting, and the fact that the participants share practices is also relevant to the force of the utterances. Through successfully creating common ground, the meeting participants can debate different positions, scrutinise perceived problems (note the explicit position by Tom 'we've got a bigger problem', lines 18/19) and reach solutions. This,

```
1    Dan                         (...) for them (.) and be a parent we and i
2                think tom's ((inaudible)) reaction sometimes is he becomes like a
3                frustrated parent (.) for fucks sake you know (.) bang the kids
4                heads together whatever (.) and i think what we gotta say is look
5                we've all (.) you know the members have got to step up from being
6                (.) well some of the members have got to stop behaving like
7                children (.) they've got to become adults and [LeadingCom] to an
8                extent has got to say right were not going to be the parents here
9                (.) we're not gonna lead this all the time (.) it's down you know
10               to you have just an equal responsibility=
11   Paul                                                   =that's good theory and I
12               agree with you whole heartedly but at a very sensitive time when
13               were trying to actually do a cost benefit analysis on their behalf
14               (.) or show them a way through a cost benefit analysis (.) i
15               wouldn't want to come down too heavy on ((inaudible))[...]
16   Tom                                                            [...] it it may
17               well be (.) but i don't believe the membership has ever seen itself
18               as a membership (.) because ther's been nothing to belong to so i
19               think we:ve we:ve got a bigger problem uh (.) than the one that's
20               being articulated at the moment (.) and i don't believe that there
21               is a feeling of belonging to anything (.) and i think what i hear
22               dan saying is that in order to create that there has to be a
23               responsibility taken by the members
24   Dan                                            yea
25   Tom                                                to build something to belong
26               to (.) because we cant do that (.) or can we?
```

Fragment 31.2 (Corpus_JA)

however, is not a linear process: the architecture of meetings is complex and we discuss this further in the next two sections.

Multilingual meetings

The fact that meetings increasingly take place within a cosmopolitan context generates considerable interest about their multilingual, intercultural and cross-cultural dimensions. International meetings can adopt diverse linguistic solutions: choice of a lingua franca, use of various languages, everybody speaking their language, use of code-switching, punctual use of improvised translations, and so on, which have been variously described in the literature.

Sociolinguistic scholars have studied code-switching and language choice in meetings. These choices, as well as the specific moments at which participants switch from one language to another, are revelatory of both local negotiations and reproduction of relationships and asymmetries (Gumperz 1982, 1987; Gumperz & Cook-Gumperz 1992). This has also prompted research on intercultural meetings (e.g. Bargiela-Chiappini & Harris 1997; Mariott 1997, on business meetings; Unger, Krzyżanowski & Wodak 2014; Wodak et al. 2012 on institutional settings).

Within the now-established field of study of English as a Lingua Franca (ELF) (Seidlhofer 2009), the use of ELF has been described as having very different consequences. In some contexts, it has been seen as a 'neutral code', facilitating the participation of employees of different languages through a 'shared communication code' – as, for example, in the fusion of Swedish and Finnish companies studied by Louhiala-Salminen, Charles and Kankaanranta (2005), in which ELF is adopted to avoid asymmetries between native and non-native speakers. In other contexts, although ELF remains the reference, the switch to other languages has a 'solidarity-building function' and fosters complicity and personal relationships in business (Poncini 2004). In other cases, miscommunication has been highlighted (House 1999; Wei et al. 2001; Ulijn & Xiangling 1995).

From a conversation-analytic perspective, Firth (1996) shows that participants negotiate actively and collaboratively the 'lingua-franca' character of the language they use, namely by perspicuously disattending non-standard features of talk and normalising them actively, orientating to the work being done skilfully rather than to linguistic deficiencies. Pointing at the fact that a linguistic choice is never fully established and might be constantly renegotiated, Mondada (2012) and Markaki et al. (2014) show how lingua-franca meetings can convert into plurilingual gatherings in order to achieve or adjust to changing participants' constellations.

Thus, language choices possibly concern a multitude of issues, from securing mutual understanding to managing identities, participation and asymmetries. As we will see with the next example, multilingual and multicultural meetings enhance the plurality of identities of the participants, who have multiple types of expertise and various institutional roles – and thus can be orientated to by making different categories relevant (see p. 473).

Fragment 31.3 is extracted from a meeting in which French immunologists and medical specialists are discussing the possibility of developing a new vaccine (see Mondada 2012). They host Mary, a well-known biologist from London, with whom they want to initiate collaboration. Although most of the participants are not fluent in English, the meeting is held in English lingua franca because Mary does not speak French. We join the meeting as a member of the local medical team, Mederic, is giving a presentation, in which he mentions a category of patients who could be good candidates for collecting human samples necessary for the experiments planned within the project. At this point, the chairperson, Gilbert, makes an observation about the necessity of obtaining the adequate ethical authorisations. In the unfolding discussion, our analytical attention focuses on the conditions that progressively lead to a change of language in the meeting.

Gilbert self-selects and addresses Mederic (Figure 6 in Fragment 31.3): although his turn is presented as an observation, it can also be understood as a request, projecting a response. But after a pause (3), Mederic only acknowledges this minimally, without offering any solution to the problem. At this point, Gilbert pursues his action: he repeats his point about ethical issues and changes his addressee, now turning to the audience (5), thereby disqualifying Mederic as a possible interlocutor for obtaining an answer. Another participant, Robert, the director of the local research programme, sitting behind Gilbert, also turns back towards the audience. He nominates Blandine (6), who is selected as the next speaker and as a person knowledgeable about how to solve ethical problems.

So, a progressive reorientation of the participants occurs. The relevant interactional space, designed by the disposition of the participants' bodies (Mondada 2011), is no longer orientated towards the front where the official speaker stands, but is reorientated towards the back, with the selection of a member of the audience. These participation shifts and reorientations within the interactional space of the room correspond to the search for a person able to give a response to the problem raised by Gilbert (Figure 7 in Fragment 31.3).

When she responds, Blandine contributes to a further enlargement of the interactional space, by introducing a new person, Anne Rambeau, pointed to as having a solution to the problem. Blandine responds with a body-torque (Schegloff 1998) both maintaining her orientation forwards, to Gilbert and Robert, and adding a new orientation backwards, to Anne.

```
1   GIL    #maybe we need to start thinking the the difficulties,
           >>looks at Med-->
    fig    #fig.6
2          >i mean,< we need to ha:ve (0.3) a comité d'éthique,
                                              an ethical committee,
3          (0.4)
4   MED    >yeah< h
```

```
5   GIL    we *need to: start* building those questions. ↓°i mean:° ah=
           ->*............*turns back toward the audience--->>
    rob                                                        ↓turns to Bla->>
6   ROB    =blandine you contacted °(    )°
7   BLA    so[rry ?
8   ROB      [°ethic committee° or #ethics [(    )°°
    fig                                   #fig.7
```

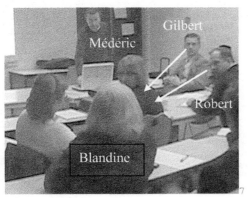

```
9   BLA                                   [yeah %i mean,
                                                %turns back->
10         (2.2)
    bla    --extends her arm backwards-->
11  BLA    anne ram%beau# is [ehm
           -->%points back--> line 20
    fig                      #fig.8
```

Fragment 31.3   continued overleaf

Jo Angouri and Lorenza Mondada

```
12  GIL            [*°°°maybe you can (specify) (    )°°°]*
                    *lower voice, talking to Rob---------*
13  BLA   *but we c- since] >she really prefers to discuss this in french<
    gil   *looks at Bla-->
14        so [eh ann- *we +i mean+ we- you know anne rambeau is* the person
15  GIL      [>oui<
             [>yes<
    gil              ->*looks at Ann---------------------------*at Bla->
    ann                +nods+
16        who is (0.6) *have been for* the collections
    gil               -->*............*stands up and looks at Ann-->
17  GIL   <yeah yeah> #on peut y aller en †en français hein, y a pas:
                      we can go on    in in French right,  there is no:
    mar                                †turns towards Ann-->
    fig               #fig.9
```

```
18  ANN   +oui+ j'préfère ((laughs))
          yes   I prefer
          +nods+
19        ((laughter))
```

Fragment 31.3 (corpus_LM_IDEM)

The latter is introduced by a pointing gesture (emerging line 10), towards her (Figure 8 in Fragment 31.3). Blandine reveals Anne's name (11) while she points at her. But before going on, she mentions Anne's linguistic preferences (13), thus accounting for her silence and pinpointing a linguistic problem hindering the progression of the activity. Gilbert aligns in French ('oui/yes' 15) with this insertion, thereby confirming the possibility of a change

478

of language. Then Blandine reintroduces Anne and describes her tasks and responsibilities (14–16). During her turn, Gilbert progressively focuses on Anne and stands up, turning towards her (Figure 9 in Fragment 31.3), producing a mild acknowledgement. His invitation to continue includes an authorisation to change the language, uttered in French (17). At this point, Anne is established as the next speaker by him as well as by other participants turning towards her, like Mary (Figure 9 in Fragment 31.3). Anne's first response acknowledges the change of language (18), with laughter. Others join in with this laughter, displaying an affiliation concerning the problem of language choice.

In this brief sequence, the language of a meeting that was held in ELF until then is changed into French, while giving the floor to a new participant, silent until then. This is not the only change happening in the fragment: the co-participants' attention, which was orientated towards the presenter at the front of the room, is now reorientated to the last row, where the French speaker is sitting. The radical reorganisation of the interactional space, of the participation framework and of the linguistic resources available operates a reconfiguration of the distribution of talk and knowledge.

Solving problems and reaching decisions

We have already shown that the 'meeting' constitutes a focal interactional site in which the participants build the organisation's knowledge and negotiate perceptions of the joint reality. In this context, the participants scrutinise their norms and processes in negotiating routine and critical issues that shape the organisation's future action/s. Most meetings are multifunctional and although participants often label them according to predominant task/s on an (explicit or tacit) agenda, the boundaries between the activities the meeting participants handle are anything but clear-cut. Workplace discourse studies have gone beyond analysis of the form and structure of the meeting event to unpacking some of its key functions, notably the ways in which participants solve problems and reach decisions (Holmes & Marra 2010).

Problems and their resolution constitute a common agenda for meetings in all professional contexts. What 'counts' as problem is negotiated between the professionals in their own setting (Angouri & Bargiela 2011). Both the organisational 'problem' and the 'decision' are fluid and temporary positions that are recycled and revisited in an organisation's life cycle. This process is 'discursively dispersed and fragmented' (Atkinson 1999), and typically it is difficult to spot the moment when a problem is ratified as such or a decision is made (Boden 1994). Sarangi and Roberts point out that 'decision making is not simply out there waiting to be realised in some common-sense way' (1999, p. 34). Hence the need for understanding the local interactional context within which this process takes place has been highlighted by all workplace approaches. The meeting event provides a key site for organisational learning and for developing the necessary expertise in handling the tasks that form an organisation's set of activities. Interactants negotiate different ways of *doing* depending on their role and professional expertise. This process also involves disagreement (Marra 2012), a term that typically carries negative connotation, although it is a common stage in the problem-solving encounter. The way participants enact disagreement depends on a range of contextual factors, such as: who they are with, the discourse histories of the participants, the agenda, whose responsibility the 'problem' is, and so on. In some communities, heated and direct disagreement is the norm and represents an unmarked way (Angouri 2012) for reaching a commitment to action – a decision.

Conversation-analytic studies have been interested in how mutual intelligibility, intersubjectivity and understanding are both established and repaired in social interaction

(Heritage 1984; Schegloff 1992). In meetings, the common understanding of what is going on might be achieved through different practices – such as *formulations* (Heritage & Watson 1979), which might be used to summarise points that have been discussed and negotiated in the preceding talk and provide an entry into transitions and closings (Barnes 2007), as well as to reorientate a proposal and transform it from an individual suggestion into a collectively agreed matter (Mondada 2015). Such practices build agreement and common concerns (Huisman 2001). However, meetings are also the locus of disagreements and disaffiliative actions. These can be formatted in a bold, aggravated and direct way, but also in a cautious way orientated to the preference for agreement, using delays, mitigations, prefaces and accounts (Ford 2008). Moreover, meetings are characterised by the use of artefacts (notes and formal documents, whiteboards, and so on (see Knoblauch [2008] and Rendle-Short [2006] about PowerPoint presentations; Ochs, Jacoby & Gonzales [1994] and Mondada [2012b] about visualisations). Through these interactional resources and practices, problems, topics and knowledge are collectively established, negotiated, challenged or stabilised.

In the field of workplace discourse, it is common to adopt a Communities of Practice (CofP) framework in order to relate the interaction in a particular context with the norms of a group. Wenger (1998, p. 73) identifies three dimensions of a CofP: namely a) what it is about – its joint enterprise as understood and continually renegotiated by its members; b) how it functions – the mutual engagement that binds members together into a social entity; and c) what capability it has produced – the shared repertoire of communal resources (routines, sensibilities, artefacts, vocabulary, styles, etc.) that members have developed over time. The latter has been discussed by discourse analysts arguing that CofPs develop a specific discourse repertoire that distinguishes one community from others. This co-constructed and constantly renegotiated repertoire is a powerful resource that interactants draw upon in order to construct a collective 'we' identity, while interacting within various communities in their workplace (Angouri 2015).

Conclusion: the politics of meetings

Currently, a massive amount of collective work in organisations is carried out in the form of meetings. From political meetings (Fragment 31.1) to business meetings (Fragment 31.2) and institutional meetings (Fragment 31.3), very different matters – ranging from political opinions and scientific issues through to socio-economic problems – are established, discussed and decided. These meetings can take different forms, managed through specific organisational practices, such as mediated turn-taking systems, which adapt to, and in turn reflexively shape, opportunities to integrate or to exclude participants (p. 470). In these meetings, different persons come together, achieving different tasks, displaying different identities, making relevant issues of expertise, but also nationality and gender (p. 473). These identity displays are further made publicly intelligible through the linguistic choices of the participants, which enhance or minimise differences, competences, asymmetries and forms of participation (p. 475). Turn-taking, identity displays and choice of communicative resources contribute to shape the way in which (dis)agreements are managed, convergences and divergences interpreted and common decisions are taken (p. 479). Despite differences between them, a case can be made for a meeting genre, one that is recognisable to the participants and presents similarities in its organisation despite contextual variation.

The discussion shows that there is indeed a *politics of meetings*. These *political meetings* are one specific form, among others, in which positions, problems, facts and solutions are debated – and in which political rights to talk and be listened to – and where representativeness and participation are shaped. However, the *politics of meetings* pervades the variety of forms and procedures that characterise institutional and entrepreneurial gatherings: in all of these cases, participants are confronted with turn-taking choices that favour different forms of participation; linguistic choices that enhance or limit access to the floor of different categories of participants; and types of actions and sequences that implement the tasks at hand and impose various constraints on the way in which issues are discussed and decided. These issues might be even stronger in contemporary institutions and workplaces, becoming increasingly complex, delocalised, technologically mediated, multilingual and multi-professional – constantly posing new challenges within established routines.

Transcript conventions

Talk is transcribed according to the conventions developed by Gail Jefferson (2004). Multimodal details are transcribed according to the conventions described in Mondada (2001).

References

Angouri, J, 2012, 'Managing disagreement in problem solving meeting talk', *Journal of Pragmatics*, vol. 44, no. 12, pp. 1565–1579.

Angouri, J, 2015, 'Studying identity', in *Research methods in intercultural communication*, ed. Z Hua, Blackwell, Oxford, pp. 37–52.

Angouri, J & Angelidou, E, 2012, 'Managing the director's views: Personal and professional identities in action', in *Professional communication across languages and cultures*, eds. S Mada, R Saftoiu & M Gheorghe, Benjamins, Amsterdam, pp. 61–83.

Angouri, J & Bargiela-Chiappini, F, 2011, '"We are all here today to solve problems right?" Problem solving talk at work', *Discourse and Communication*, vol. 5, no. 3, 209–229.

Angouri, J & Marra, M, 2011, '"Ok one last thing for today then": Constructing corporate identities in meeting talk', in *Constructing identities at work*, eds. J Angouri & M Marra, Palgrave Macmillan, London,
pp. 85–103.

Antaki, C & Widdicombe, S, 1998, *Identities in talk*, Sage, London.

Atkinson, J M, 1984, *Our masters' voices: The language and body language of politics*, Methuen, London.

Atkinson, P, 1999, 'Medical discourse evidentiality and the construction of professional responsibility', in *Talk, work and institutional order*, eds. S Sarangi & C Roberts, de Gruyter, Berlin, pp. 75–109.

Bargiela-Chiappini, F & Harris, S, 1997, *Managing language: The discourse of corporate meetings*, Benjamins, Amsterdam.

Barnes, R, 2007, 'Formulations and the facilitation of common agreement in meetings talk', *Text & Talk*, vol. 27, no. 3, pp. 273–296.

Boden, D, 1994, *The business of talk. Organizations in action*, Polity Press, Cambridge.

Bourdieu, P, 1984, *Distinction. A social critique of judgment of taste*, Harvard University Press, Cambridge, MA.

Bovet, A, 2009, 'Configuring a television debate: Categorisation, questions and answers', in *Media, policy and interaction*, eds. R Fitzgerald & W Housley, Ashgate, Aldershot, pp. 27–48.

Bucholtz, M & Hall, K, 2005, 'Identity and interaction: A sociocultural linguistic approach', *Discourse Studies*, vol. 7, nos. 4–5, pp. 585–614.

Clayman, S, 1993, 'Booing: The anatomy of a disaffiliative response', *American Sociological Review*, vol. 58, no. 1, pp. 110–130.

Clayman, S E & Heritage, J, 2002, *The news interview*, Cambridge University Press, Cambridge.

Cuff, E C & Sharrock, W W, 1985, 'Meetings', in *Handbook of discourse analysis*, vol. 3, ed. T van Dijk, Academic, New York, pp. 149–160.

Drew, P & Heritage, J, 1992, 'Talk at work: Interaction in institutional settings', in *Talk at work*, eds. P Drew & J Heritage, Cambridge University Press, Cambridge, pp. 418–469.

Firth, A, 1996, 'The discursive accomplishment of normality. On "lingua franca" English and Conversation Analysis', *Journal of Pragmatics*, vol. 26, no. 2, pp. 237–259.

Ford, C, 2008, *Women speaking up: Getting and using turns in meetings*, Macmillan, Hampshire.

Goffman, E, 1979, 'Footing', *Semiotica*, vol. 25, no. 1, pp. 1–29.

Goodwin, C, 2007, 'Participation, stance and affect in the organization of activities', *Discourse & Society*, vol. 18, no. 1, pp. 53–73.

Goodwin, C & Goodwin, M H, 2004, 'Participation', in *A companion to linguistic anthropology*, ed. A Duranti, Blackwell, Oxford, pp. 222–244.

Gumperz, J J, 1982, *Discourse strategies*, Cambridge University Press, Cambridge.

Gumperz, J J, 1987, 'Linguistic and social characteristics of minorization/majorisation in verbal interaction', in *Minorization in language*, ed. B Py, University of Neuchatel, Switzerland, pp. 21–37.

Gumperz, J J & Cook-Gumperz, J, 1992, 'Interethnic communication in committee negotiations', in *Talk at work*, eds. P Drew & J Heritage, Cambridge University Press, Cambridge, pp. 145–162.

Heritage, J, 1984, *Garfinkel and ethnomethodology*, Polity Press, New York.

Heritage, J & Clayman, S, 2010, *Talk in action*, Blackwell, Oxford.

Heritage, J & Watson, R, 1979, 'Formulations as conversational objects', in *Everyday language: Studies in ethnomethodology*, ed. G Psathas, Irvington, New York, pp. 123–162.

Hester, S & Eglin, P, 1997, *Culture in action: Studies in Membership Categorisation Analysis*, University Press of America, Washington, DC.

Holmes, J & Marra, M, 2010, 'Leadership and managing conflict in meetings', *Pragmatics*, vol. 14, no. 4, pp. 439–462.

Holmes, J & Stubbe, M, 2003, *Power and politeness in the workplace. A sociolinguistic analysis of talk at work*, Longman, London.

House, J, 1999, 'Misunderstanding in intercultural communication: Interactions in English as a lingua franca and the myth of mutual intelligibility', in *Teaching and learning English as a global language*, ed. C Gnutzmann, Stauffenburg, Tübingen, pp. 73–89.

Housley, W, 2003, *Interaction in multidisciplinary teams*, Ashgate, Aldershot.

Huisman, M, 2001, 'Decision-making in meetings as talk-in-interaction', *International Studies of Management & Organization*, vol. 31, no. 3, pp. 69–90.

Jayyusi, L, 1984, *Categorization and the moral order*, Routledge, London.

Jefferson, G, 2004, 'Glossary of transcript symbols with an introduction', in *Conversation analysis: Studies from the first generation*, ed. G H Lerner, Amsterdam, Benjamins, pp. 13–31.

Knoblauch, H, 2008, 'The performance of knowledge: Pointing and knowledge in Powerpoint presentations', *Cultural Sociology*, vol 2, no. 1, pp. 75–97.

Krzyżanowski, M, 2008, 'Analysing focus groups', in *Qualitative discourse analysis in the social sciences*, eds. R Wodak & M Krzyżanowski, Palgrave Macmillan, Basingstoke, pp. 162–181.

Llewellyn, N, 2005, 'Audience participation in political discourse: A study of public meetings', *Sociology*, vol. 39, no. 4, pp. 697–716.

Louhiala-Salminen, L, Charles, M & Kankaanranta, A, 2005, 'English as a lingua franca in Nordic corporate mergers: Two case companies', *English for Specific Purposes*, vol. 24, no. 4, pp. 401–421.

Markaki, V & Mondada, L, 2012, 'Embodied orientations towards co-participants in multinational meetings', *Discourse Studies*, vol. 14, no. 1, pp. 31–52.

Markaki, V, Merlino, S, Mondada, L, Oloff, F & Traverso, V, 2014, 'Language choice and participation management in international work meetings', in *Multilingual encounters in Europe's institutional spaces*, eds. J Unger, M, Krzyżanowski, R, Wodak, Bloomsbury, London, pp. 43–74.

Marra, M, 2012, 'Disagreeing without being disagreeable: Negotiating workplace communities as an outsider', *Journal of Pragmatics*, vol. 44, no. 12, pp. 1580–1590.

Marriott, H, 1997, 'Australian–Japanese business interaction: Some features of language and cultural contact', in *The languages of business: An international perspective*, eds. F Bargiela-Chiappini & S Harris, Edinburgh University Press, Edinburgh, pp. 49–71.

McIlvenny, P, 1996, 'Heckling in Hyde Park: Verbal audience participation in popular public discourse', *Language in Society*, vol. 25, no. 1, pp. 27–60.

Mondada, L, 2001, 'Conventions for multimodal transcription', available from: https://franz.unibas.ch/fileadmin/franz/user_upload/redaktion/Mondada_conv_multimodality.pdf [accessed 23 January 2016].

Mondada, L, 2011, 'The interactional production of multiple spatialities within a participatory democracy meeting', *Social Semiotics*, vol. 2, no. 3, pp. 283–308.

Mondada, L, 2012a, 'The dynamics of embodied participation and language choice in multilingual meetings', *Language in Society*, vol. 41, no. 2, pp. 1–23.

Mondada, L, 2012b, 'Video analysis and the temporality of inscriptions within social interaction: The case of architects at work', *Qualitative Research*, vol. 12, no. 3, pp. 304–333.

Mondada, L, 2013, 'Embodied and spatial resources for turn-taking in institutional multi-party interactions: The example of participatory democracy debates', *Journal of Pragmatics*, vol. 46, no. 1, pp. 39–68.

Mondada, L, 2015, 'The facilitator's task of formulating citizens' proposals in political meetings', *Gesprächsforschung*, vol. 16, pp. 1–62, available from: www.gespraechsforschung-ozs.de/fileadmin/dateien/heft2015/ga-mondada.pdf [accessed 23 January 2016].

Ochs, E, Jacoby, S & Gonzales, P, 1994, 'Interpretive journeys. How physicists talk and travel through graphic space', *Configurations*, vol. 2, no. 1, pp. 151–171.

Pomerantz, A & Denvir, P, 2007, 'Enacting the institutional role of a chairperson in upper management meetings: The interactional realization of provisional authority', in *Interacting and organizing*, ed. F Cooren, Erlbaum, London, pp. 31–52.

Poncini, G, 2004, *Discursive strategies in multicultural business meetings*, Lang, Bern.

Rendle-Short, J, 2006, *The academic presentation: Situated talk in action*, Ashgate, London.

Sacks, H, 1972, 'An initial investigation of the usability of conversational materials for doing sociology', in *Studies in social interaction*, ed. D Sudnow, Free Press, New York, pp. 31–74.

Sacks, H, 1992, *Lectures on conversation [1964–72]* (2 vols.), Blackwell, Oxford.

Sacks, H, Schegloff, E A & Jefferson, G, 1974, 'A simplest systematics for the organization of turn-taking for conversation', *Language*, vol. 50, no. 4, pp. 696–735.

Sarangi, S, 2010, 'Reconfiguring self/identity/status/role: The case of professional role performance in healthcare encounters', in *Actors, identities and roles in professional and academic settings: Discursive perspectives*, eds. J Archibald & G Garzone, Lang, Bern, pp. 27–54.

Sarangi, S & Roberts, C, 1999, *Talk, work and institutional order: Discourse in medical, mediation and management settings*, de Gruyter, Berlin.

Schegloff, E A, 1992, 'Repair after next turn: The last structurally provided for place for the defence of intersubjectivity in conversation', *American Journal of Sociology*, vol. 95, no. 5, pp. 1295–1345.

Schegloff, E A, 1995, 'Parties and talking together: Two ways in which numbers are significant for talk-in-interaction', in *Situated order: Studies in social organisation and embodied activities*, eds. P T Have & G Psathas, University Press of America, Washington, DC, pp. 31–42.

Schegloff, E A, 1998, 'Body torque', *Social Research*, vol. 65, no. 3, pp. 535–586.

Schmitt, R, 2002, 'Hierarchie in Arbeitsgruppen als stilbildender Aspekt', in *Soziale Welten und kommunikative Stile*, eds. I Keim & W Schütte, Narr, Tübingen, pp. 113–135.

Schwartzman, H, 1989, *The meeting. Gatherings in organizations and communities*, Plenum Press, New York.

Seidlhofer, B, 2009, 'Accomodation and the idiom principle in English as a lingua franca', *Intercultural Pragmatics*, vol. 6, no. 2, pp. 195–215.

Svennevig, J, 2008, 'Exploring leadership conversations', *Management Communication Quarterly*, vol. 21, no. 4, pp. 529–536.

Tannen, D, 1994, *Talking from 9–5: How women's and men's conversational styles affect who gets credit and what gets done*, William Morrow, New York.

Ulijn, J M & Xiangling, L, 1995, 'Is interrupting impolite? Some temporal aspects of turn-taking in Chinese–Western and other intercultural business encounters', *Text*, vol. 15, no. 4, pp. 589–627.

Unger, J W, Krzyżanowski, M & Wodak, R, 2014, *Multilingual encounters in Europe's institutional spaces*, A&C Black, London.

Vaara, E, Tienari, J & Säntti, R, 2003, 'The international match: Metaphors as vehicles of social identity-building in cross-border mergers', *Human Relations*, vol. 56, no. 4, pp. 419–451.

van Dijk, T A, 1996, 'Discourse, power and access', in *Texts and practices: Readings in Critical Discourse Analysis*, eds. C R Caldas-Coulthard & M Coulthard, Routledge, London, pp. 84–104.

Wei, L, Hua, Z & Yue, L, 2001, 'Conversational management and involvement in Chinese–English Business Talk', *Language and Intercultural Communication*, vol. 1, no. 2, pp. 135–150.

Wenger, E, 1998, *Communities of Practice: Learning, meaning, and identity*, Cambridge University Press, Cambridge.

Wodak, R, 2000, 'Recontextualization and the transformation of meaning: A Critical Discourse Analysis of decision making in EU meetings about employment policies', in *Discourse and social life*, eds. S Sarangi & M Coulthard, Longman, New York, pp. 185–206.

Wodak, R, 2009, *The discourse of politics in action: 'Politics as usual'*, Palgrave Macmillan, Basingstoke.

Wodak, R, 2013, 'Comparing meetings in political and business contexts', in *Genres in political discourse*, eds. P Cap & U Okulska, Benjamins, Amsterdam, pp. 187–221.

Wodak, R, Krzyżanowski, M & Forchtner, B, 2012, 'The interplay of language ideologies and contextual cues in multilingual interactions: Language choice and code-switching in EU institutions', *Language in Society*, vol. 41, no. 2, pp. 157–186.

Wodak, R, Kwon, W & Clarke, I, 2011, 'Getting people on board: Discursive leadership for consensus building in team meetings', *Discourse & Society*, vol. 22, no. 5, pp. 592–644.

Part IV

Applications and cases I: language, politics, and contemporary socio-cultural challenges

32
Climate change and the socio-ecological crisis

Anabela Carvalho

A discursive outlook at climate change

Discourse-analytical research on climate change is not only fully justified, but badly needed. Proposing and deciding what this 'wicked issue' is about and what ought to be done about it involves discursive struggles between a range of social actors in science, politics, business, civil society and other domains. Values, world-views and ideologies, as well as multiple forms of power, are deeply interconnected with meaning-making practices on climate change. Discourse-minded academics thus have a responsibility to contribute to identifying, analysing and exposing the ways in which debates are often managed and distorted, and how that connects to issues of power and justice.

Humanity has never been faced with an environmental crisis of the type and scale of climate change. Deeply embedded in structures and practices that are central to current societies, it is tied in multiple ways to other issues, such as loss of biodiversity, deforestation and desertification. The transformations brought about by climate change to bio-physical and socio-economic systems can create a 'before' and 'after' divide in the history of a planet that has never been shared by so many humans. Whereas, according to accepted scientific knowledge, a wide range of impacts that are already being felt will continue to aggravate in terms of frequency and intensity,[1] some projections identify 'tipping points' (Pearce 2007) that would lead to a fast acceleration in the destruction of natural and human systems, and result in a world that would be dramatically different from what we know.

A maximum rise of 2° C in global average temperature has been naturalised in many discourses as the key to averting danger, but is contested by small-island states and other vulnerable groups that are already suffering strong impacts from a rise of about 1° C. Even to stay at around the 2° C limit, it would be necessary to reduce global emissions of greenhouse gases to between 50 and 85 per cent of current levels by 2050, and they would need to continue decreasing rapidly after that. The changes needed in energy generation and energy use, including transportation, industrial processes, heating and cooling of buildings, and so on, are massive. Some have called for a 'great turning', a 'great transition' or a 'great transformation' (e.g. New Economics Foundation 2010). But it has been slow to come. Instead, many forces are invested in preventing any modification of the status quo. Climate change is viewed as a threat to many economic and political interests in the richest countries, such as the US, and to 'development' in others, including China (currently the world's biggest emitter of greenhouse gases; GHG).

From the above, it starts to become clear that climate change constitutes a rich terrain for discourse analysis. There is more, however. Climate change has a set of characteristics, such as many 'invisible causes' (to our senses), various 'distant impacts', and 'delayed or absent gratification for taking action' (Moser 2010), that make it difficult to grasp, or challenging to feel engaged with. Therefore, discursive constructions are of vital importance to define and negotiate meaning. Furthermore, climate change is a multi-faceted matter that can be looked at from a variety of angles. It is a scientific, political, social and economic issue. It is also a key ethical issue, posing questions of equity and fairness between generations, regions of the world, peoples and social classes: the poor have the lowest contributions to the enhanced greenhouse effect, but are among the most vulnerable victims of the impacts of a changed climate.

Multiple voices, arguments and claims compete for attention in various arenas. As one such space, which is constantly influxed by others, the media are decisive as to the social amplification and legitimation of some views and the marginalisation of others. Media(ted) discourses therefore deserve the degree of attention they will receive in this chapter. Climate change requires expert skills and knowledge to be understood: scientists were the ones who first brought it to light and will continue to play a key role. Science has important connections to policy and policy-making, and climate change has been subjected to variegated interpretations in the realm of politics, governmental and otherwise, partly via the media.

The chapter will start by presenting a short summary of the science and politics of climate change and discuss how they unfolded in different arenas. Given the centrality of knowledge claims to the analysis of climate change, processes of social construction of scientific knowledge and the nexus with policy-making will be discussed. This will be followed by an examination of discourses that have dominated the politics of climate change and their socio-political implications. Finally, the chapter will point out some emerging and, as yet, under-researched issues.

Introducing climate change science and politics

As Bodansky (2001, p. 24) has noted, the 'development of the climate change issue initially took place in the scientific arena as understanding of the greenhouse problem improved'. In the late 1980s, it became a political issue and a matter of intergovernmental relevance that saw a process of scientific and political institutionalisation. The Intergovernmental Panel on Climate Change (IPCC) was established in 1988, 'in part as a means of reasserting governmental control over the climate change issue' (Bodansky 2001, p. 28). Bringing together the world's leading atmospheric scientists, by appointment of national governments, it aimed at producing a full assessment of scientific, technical and socio-economic information on climate change and formulating response strategies. Whereas the press in both the US and the UK (as well as other countries) had only dedicated a few occasional pieces to this topic, from 1988, coverage intensified significantly (Carvalho 2005; Mazur 1998), thereby constituting climate change as a topic for public attention.

The IPCC's *First Assessment Report* was published in 1990 and the following key moment in the development of the international regime on climate change was the signature of the United Nations Framework Convention on Climate Change (UNFCCC) at Rio's Earth Summit in 1992. The Convention embodies a broad commitment to the reduction of

GHG emissions by developed countries. The principle of 'common but differentiated responsibilities' (UNFCCC) was translated in the creation of two groups of countries: 'Annex 1 countries', the 'developed' countries, which committed to stabilising their GHG emissions, and 'Non-Annex 1', the 'developing' countries, which were not given specific responsibilities. A Protocol to the UNFCCC was formally accepted at the third Conference of the Parties (COP-3), which took place in Kyoto in 1997. The Kyoto Protocol mandated an average cut of 5.2 per cent in GHG emissions, to be attained in the following 15 years. On the scientific front, the IPCC issued its *Second Assessment Report* in 1995, which spoke of a 'discernible human influence' on climate. The *Third Assessment Report*, published in 2001, revised forecasts of global warming upwards. For the twenty-first century, the IPCC estimated the temperature rise to be between 1.4 and 5.8°C.

Further to a post-Kyoto drop, levels of media coverage of climate change started rising again after the year 2000, pushed by a rather tense COP-6 in The Hague (2000), George W Bush's withdrawal from the Kyoto Protocol (2001) and the release of the *Third Assessment Report* of the IPCC (2001). In 2006 and 2007, three factors led to a peak in media attention: the publication of a report in the UK by Lord Stern on the economics of climate change, the release of Al Gore's book and documentary *An Inconvenient Truth* and the publication of the *Fourth Assessment Report* of the IPCC, which heightened again the level of risk – the top range of projected warming under one scenario was set at 6.4° C. Grundmann and Krishnamurthy (2010) examined media coverage of climate change in France, Germany, the UK and the USA and identified a 138 per cent rise in the number of news pieces in 2007 compared to the previous year.

Levels of media interest in 2007 would only be superseded, in some regions, in 2009 with the so-called Climategate, the illegal hacking and release of email correspondence falsely proclaimed as proof of scientific manipulation of climate data, and the COP-15 in Copenhagen. COP-15 generated enormous momentum as it was expected to produce an agreement to replace the Kyoto Protocol, which was to expire in 2012. Unprecedented levels of civic mobilisation led to large-scale demonstrations in several parts of the world and to a significant participation in Klimaforum09, a civil society climate conference on the side of the COP. However, political negotiations failed to lead to agreement, and only a non-binding 'Accord' was produced by the US, China, India, Brazil and South Africa, which was critically received by many governments, NGOs and other social actors. The Copenhagen Summit thus generated a widespread sense of disappointment and was followed by a sharp drop in the volume of media coverage. At the time of writing, there was hope that COP-21, to happen in Paris at the end of 2015, would lead to a new global agreement, and levels of media and public interest had risen again.

The three parts of the latest IPCC *Assessment Report* (AR5) were launched in 2013 and 2014. AR5 maintained that it is 'extremely likely' that human influence has been the dominant cause of observed warming since 1950. Climate impacts are said to be already occurring in all continents and across the oceans. The level of risk is projected to increase significantly over the coming years regarding death, ill-health, food and water insecurity, loss of ecosystems, extinctions, and so on.

The social construction of scientific knowledge and the science-policy nexus

When compared to other science domains, research and knowledge on climate change has several distinctive characteristics: it draws on a wide variety of disciplines and areas of expertise, from biology to climatology; it involves a variety of spatial and time-scales; the most valuable contributions it can offer to policy-making are estimates of future changes, not descriptions of an existing reality; and it involves a large degree of not only uncertainty, but also, inevitably, of indeterminacy. These traits render climate change into a particularly non-self-evident and non-stable matter where constructions of knowledge claims are especially sensitive, politically and socially.

Given its diffuse and highly complex nature, scientific tools, methods and models have been crucial to bring climate change out into symbolic existence. The procedures and the 'machinery' of collection and interpretation of climate-related data have themselves been the subject of some critical work with commonalities with discourse analysis. Demeritt (2001), for example, has exposed the assumptions involved in some of the early Global Circulation Models and showed that they appraised the value of human lives differently in different parts of the world. Attention to 'mediations' in scientific knowledge, that is, the conceptual and technical devices that are both products and producers of knowledge, is therefore called for, and this kind of 'constructivist critique' (Demeritt 2006) ought to remain as part of the research agenda of social studies of science and technology. Discourse analysts could certainly infuse it with valuable tools.

Climate change is also a prime example of what has been termed 'post-normal science' (Funtowicz & Ravetz 1993), in which facts are uncertain, values are disputed, stakes are high and decisions are urgent. Those traits and other contextual factors may be part of the explanation of why climate change has been prone to intense contestation and to 'diversionary reframing' (Freudenburg & Gramling 1994). A number of social actors have offered different definitions of the issue, associated with different values and priorities (some would say 'interests'), in some cases attempting to make the debate appear to be about something else. Those definitions have received a disproportionate amount of space and attention in media and other public arenas, as exemplified in the following.

One of the most prominent topics of research on climate change communication has been the media 'translation' of uncertainty. Studies on media reconstructions of scientific knowledge have shown a very different picture across the world as regards the presence of climate change scepticism – or, as arguably preferable, denialism – in the media. In the US, Boykoff and Boykoff (2004) examined news reports' depictions of anthropogenic climate change and concluded that most offered a 'balanced' image with mentions of both the anthropogenic nature of climate change and its denial. The journalistic norm of balance, closely tied to 'objectivity', when applied to actors and claims that are distinct in their professional authority and credibility, leads to (and is used to legitimate) bias in media discourse.

McCright and Dunlap (e.g. 2000) and Oreskes and Conway (2010) have shown that there has been intense activity by the fossil-fuel industry, pro-market think-tanks, political conservatives and others in the generation of doubts regarding the occurrence of climate change, its anthropogenic nature and/or the significance of its impacts; in other words, in the construction of what Freudenburg (2000) has termed the 'non-problematicity' of climate change. In a study of numerous US newspapers, Antilla (2005, p. 350) concluded that 'some of the news outlets repeatedly used climate sceptics – with known fossil-fuel industry ties – as primary definers'. Research on Australian media has revealed a similar situation. In the case of news outlets such as *The Australian*, extreme levels of distortion of scientific knowledge have been found, with a frequent alignment with the positions of neo-liberal think-tanks and other sceptical sources (McKewon 2012).

These findings raise questions at the level of what Fairclough (1995) calls 'sociocultural practice', encompassing the 'situational context', 'institutional context', and 'socio-cultural context', as well as at the level of 'discourse practice', that is, the conditions of production of texts by journalists, editors and other media professionals (including news values and norms in operation, forms of pressure, and relation to audiences). Both dimensions are worth continuous consideration and work by discourse-minded researchers and can certainly offer crucial leads to understanding the cultural politics of climate change.

In a Critical Discourse Analysis of the British press, Carvalho (2007) showed that media discourses on scientific knowledge related to climate change are connected to the 'ideological cultures' of news institutions. The selection of research to be reported in news texts, the 'authorized agents of definition' and the interpretations of the meaning of scientific claims for politics and society were all derived from, and sustained, the dominant ideology in each of the newspapers, which involved particular prescriptions for (in)action on climate change.

Instances of climate scepticism/denialism found in the UK press were not as prevalent as in the US or Australia (cf. Painter 2011). Nevertheless, in an analysis of assertions, presuppositions, and factives, among other discursive features of US news, Kuha (2010) pointed out that the degree of certainty in US reports on climate change increased after 2007. More recently, though, Bailey, Giangola and Boykoff compared the language of US and Spanish newspaper reports on climate change and concluded that the former still had a 'higher density of epistemic markers', including references to 'activities that produce inherently uncertain products, such as *predicting, estimating,* and *projecting*; quantitative descriptors of uncertainty, such as *probabilities* and *likelihoods*; common hedging verbs, such as *believe, consider* and *appear*' (2014, p. 202), and 'more ambiguous grammatical constructs of uncertainty' (2014, p. 197). This type of linguistic analysis of texts on climate change has been sparse and could contribute to a better understanding of the implications of word and grammar choices for the construction of the meaning of the issue.

Much research is also needed beyond the press. Focusing on sceptical bloggers, Nerlich (2010) offered one of the first and few discursive studies on new media. She showed how a 'paradoxical mixture of religious metaphors and demands for "better science"' allowed "sceptics" to "undermine the authority of science and call for political inaction" (p. 429). Examples of metaphorical expressions suggesting that 'science is religion' included: 'dogma' about scientific theories, 'zealots' about scientists, and 'doomsday prophecies' about scientific predictions (*ibidem*). Forchtner and Kølvraa examined discourses of the British National Party and the Danish People's Party and found that, in contrast with a position in favour of the conservation of 'nature as national countryside and landscape', they deny or cast doubt on climate change. As the 'transnational undermines the nationalist ideal of sovereignty' (2015, p. 199), populist radical right parties attempt to refute the threat of climate change and refocus the debate on energy self-sufficiency. A Critical Discourse Analysis of books, online discussions and other sources in China pointed to a conspiratorial reading of climate change as part of a Western plot to impede Chinese development, which is strongly grounded in national identity politics (Liu 2015). Although not officially supported, this particular breed of climate scepticism is an important undercurrent in public debate (*ibidem*).

Whereas climate scepticism is present in many spaces, it is not universal. For instance, in Germany (Peters & Heinrichs 2008), Portugal (Carvalho 2011), Sweden (Olausson 2009), France, India, China and Brazil (Painter 2011), sceptical views are given little room in the media. A combination of socio-cultural, political and media-related factors (Painter 2011) is likely to contribute to these inter-country differences.

As we have seen, uncertainty in scientific knowledge has been discursively appropriated and used to refute political, social and economic changes. However, it should not be inferred from this that uncertainty in climate-related knowledge should be hidden or overlooked in climate change communication. Doing so would likely do a bad service to public trust in science. As can be inferred from the following paragraph, while scientific consensus on fundamental aspects of anthropogenic climate change should be made clear, there should also be acknowledgement of aspects of uncertainty and indeterminacy.

Unfounded certainty in media discourses, for instance regarding the future occurrence of given weather events, or the representation of impacts projected by some emissions scenarios as inevitable, has been identified in multiple countries, often combined with some form of sensationalism, such as the use of fatalistic vocabulary or imagery. In Germany, Weingart, Engels and Pansegrau noted a tendency to report climate change in catastrophist terms since the mid-1980s, which they attributed to the media's preference for 'sensationalism, negativity and unequivocal clearness' (2000, p. 275) as well as to scientific and political discourses in the country. Peters and Heinrichs (2008, p. 34) have shown that in more recent times the German media reconstruction of climate change has closely followed the IPCC reports and has therefore toned down certainty. According to Ereaut and Segnit, 'alarmism' was one of the dominant 'linguistic repertoires' in the UK press (the other being optimistic). They view 'linguistic repertoires' as 'systems of language that are routinely used for describing and evaluating actions, events and people', offering structured ways of thinking and talking, and functioning as 'resources that people can draw on' to make sense of an issue (2006, p. 7). In their media analysis, they argue that:

> The alarmist repertoire is typified by an inflated or extreme lexicon. It incorporates an urgent tone ('We have to act. Now. Today!') and cinematic codes, with images and ways of speaking that are familiar from horror and disaster films [...] It employs a quasi-religious register of doom, death, judgement, heaven and hell, using words such as 'catastrophe', 'chaos' and 'havoc'.
>
> (Ereaut & Segnit 2006, p. 13)

Some have spoken of an 'apocalyptic genre' (Smith 2012), or labelled this kind of media representation as 'climate porn' (Lowe 2006). Its appeal to fear has been criticised. More specifically, it has been considered ineffective in mobilising people as it can generate disbelief or apathy ('if the world is doomed there is nothing that can be done about it'). For example, in a study with visual representations of climate change, O'Neill and Nicholson-Cole (2009) concluded that the most dramatic representations made people feel the least empowered to act (whereas images of a low-energy light bulb, a cyclist and a thermostat made them feel most able to act). Perceived agency is key to engagement with climate change. However, there is some evidence suggesting that a negative imaginary is widespread and that response possibilities are not prominent in people's mental representations (Lorenzoni et al. 2006).

Further exploring connections between discursive structures and understandings of climate change, and identifying alternative definitions of the issue itself and, crucially, of citizens' roles is an important task. The functions of rhetorical devices, such as metaphors (cf. Asplund, Hjerpe & Wibeck 2013, on 'greenhouse', 'war' and 'game' metaphors and Nerlich & Koteyko 2009, on 'carbon compounds', such as 'carbon footprint' or 'carbon ration'), in the development of frameworks for communicating and acting 'materially' upon the world will continue to deserve analysts' attention. Maintaining a sense of urgency and gravity and, simultaneously, pointing to possible responses that may engage a variety of social actors is a tricky but crucial challenge in climate change communication.

Although this section has focused mostly on scientific aspects, science, society and politics are never separate. 'Processes of knowledge-making', says Hulme (2010, p. 563), 'are intimately bound up with the assumptions about political and social ordering which lie implicit in the institutions which enable and endorse this knowledge'. Indeed, as the sociology of scientific knowledge has taught us, social contexts and values weigh heavily on the production and the use of knowledge. Likewise, news texts about science both reproduce and challenge world-views, thereby serving important social and political functions, such as legitimating certain political plans for action or inaction.

In the end, climate change science is unlikely to 'save the world'. The kind of science-based consensus that much literature (mostly north American) appears to aspire to is, in all probability, not going to happen, and it would not be automatically translated into concerted action either. As Hulme (2009) notes in *Why we disagree about climate change*, it is much more about values, culture and politics than it is about science.

Techno-managerialism and alternative discourses

In the last few decades, several developments in policy-making processes and the widespread neo-liberal movement have played a part in erasing the space for public debate and citizen involvement. Those trends constitute the backdrop for examining the options available to address climate change and for imagining new ones. Dominant discourses have thus constructed climate change in ways that have tended to depoliticise it. While climate change raises fundamental social, ethical and value-related matters, the techno-managerial discourses (and material practices) that have come to be hegemonic have transformed it into a narrow and exclusionary language of numbers, models and legal jargon. Responses to climate change have been largely privatised through carbon markets, energy-investment decisions, price speculation, and so on, which displace non-expert voices. In Rothe's words (2011, p. 341), there has been a progression towards a 'post-political condition in climate politics where policies are chosen by economic and scientific technocrats rather than by a democratic decision-making process.'

Multiple discursive practices have contributed to the reduction of public debate on climate change. Given their privileged power position, the ways in which formal political bodies frame the issue are key to its wider circulation. Analysing discourses of the WTO, IMF, World Bank and OECD, Methmann (2010) has noted that those international organisations have claimed to embark on climate protection while remaining silent about their role in causing the problem. By discursively appropriating climate change in ways that serve the agenda of continuous economic growth, they leave out any debate on the economic and political structures that are at the basis of the current environmental crisis. For instance, the WTO has argued that the 'increase in income that trade brings about can lead society to demand better environmental quality' and the World Bank has put the emphasis on 'low carbon growth strategies' (*ibidem*). Politics is increasingly missing from discussions about sustainability that involve institutions, markets and technology, and the power relations that shape possible responses to climate change are absent from most debates.

Several studies have shown that governments and intergovernmental organisations have strongly shaped media agendas and discourses. In fact, fluctuations in the volume of media coverage of the last two decades in various countries have revealed an important impact of political initiatives, with most peaks in media attention in, for instance, the UK, Sweden and Japan coinciding with intergovernmental summits (Carvalho 2005; Olausson 2009; Sampei & Aoyagi-Usui 2009). Analysis of references to different social actors in newspaper articles also suggests a clear predominance of governmental sources in several countries (e.g. Yun et al. 2012), at the cost of alternatives, most strikingly from civil society. Ironically, a lot of media space is awarded to political actors (but typically only those in power positions) and to policy issues (measures and proposals put forth by governments), but not in ways that contribute to *the political*, in Mouffe's terms (2005). Discourse analysis of media coverage has pointed to a frequent reproduction and legitimation of governmental discourses promoting techno-managerial approaches and to the marginalisation of more transformative discourses (Carvalho 2005; Carvalho 2011). While we should be weary of homogenising analyses of media discourses and should acknowledge the existence of alternative (re) constructions of climate change, it is fair to say that most of the mainstream media have helped produce consent towards neoliberalism and free-market capitalism (e.g. Edwards & Cromwell 2006).

Aitken (2012, p. 226) maintains that '[t]he dominance of narrow, modernist framings of climate change serves to shut down debate and alternative framings are largely excluded from public and policy discourse'. Echoing Blühdorn's arguments about 'post-ecologism', Aitken (*ibidem*) claims that:

> despite vocal commitments to addressing climate change, society is largely unwilling to make significant sacrifices and lifestyle changes in order to meet this goal [...]. Therefore, more radical framings are not advanced since they are perceived to be adverse to individuals' and society's interests.
>
> (Aitken 2012, p. 226)

These assumptions about 'society' are of course unduly uniform, but there is an indication that they are quite influential over decisions of policy-making bodies and others contributing to a perpetuation of existing models.

The production of (seemingly) consensual views on how to address climate change has also been helped by the discourse of 'sustainable development' and its derivatives, such as ecological modernisation and its present epitome of the 'green economy' (Kenis & Lievens 2014; UNEP 2011). As a promise of conciliation of economic, social and environmental needs and wishes, 'sustainable development' has been as attractive as it is prone to ambiguous uses. However, that very ambiguity and open-endedness has contributed to dissolve discursive conflict, bringing all sorts of social actors on board (Krieg-Planque 2010). More radical forms of environmental discourse and mobilisation, including appeals for transformation of social, economic and political structures, have been pushed aside. As Swyngedouw notes:

> the sustainability argument has evacuated the politics of the possible, the radical contestation of alternative future socio-environmental possibilities and socio-natural arrangements, and has silenced the antagonisms and conflicts that are constitutive of our socio-natural orders by externalizing conflict.
>
> (Swyngedouw 2010, p. 228)

Research suggests that mainstream media have often naturalised and neutralised such 'sustainable development' discourses. For instance, Saunders, Grasso and Price (2012) state that analysis of 'four British newspapers reveals consensus around a light-touch approach to sustainable development. Despite increased frequency of reporting [...] over time, very few articles challenge the status quo or corporate affairs.'

Many of the discourses on climate change that are found in the media have become increasingly technical in the last few years, thereby limiting citizen comprehension, let alone engagement. Koteyko has referred to a 'market-driven sustainability' regarding British media discourses on carbon emissions. She found that the media have often set up:

> equivalences between the application of the marketplace instruments of carbon trading and investment and sustainability practices. Such reporting promotes recontextualisation […] of sustainability within the confines of corporate discourse through the use of carbon compounds and accompanying finance terms.
>
> (Koteyko 2012, p. 33)

Through the analysis of 'framing devices', metaphors and lexical co-occurrences, Koteyko's analysis suggests that the media have aided the appropriation of the discourse of 'sustainable development' by business.

Framing the future in 'sustainable development' terms often seems to be inescapable in democratic societies as most other discourses have been marginalised to a point where it would be hard to win a significant support basis. Still, there are ample variations in understandings of sustainable development, and it is crucial that those differences are spelled out and the implications of each option debated (see Hopwood, Mellor & O'Brien 2005). Hardly any discourses on climate change have contemplated this. Discourses that refer to fundamental transformations in current political-economic systems, such as the discourse on degrowth, are systematically excluded from mainstream media (with the occasional exception of an opinion piece).

Outstanding issues open to research

Climate change is an ever-evolving domain and that is not just true at the atmospheric and bio-physical levels. Understandings of the problem and of the challenges it involves may not progress as fast as necessary, but they undergo transformations. For instance, the 2015 encyclical published by Pope Francis on climate change brought a new voice to the debate and stirred it towards questions that are often ignored in many sectors of society, creating new opportunities for discourse-related research. Also, as societies develop responses to climate change, important new issues arise. For example, there is significant interest in the development of large-scale technological 'fixes', such as the reduction of solar radiation on the planet via aerosols, or the increase of carbon sinking via iron fertilisation of the seas. These and other geo-engineering projects involve major new risks and unknowns that have been mostly kept away from public scrutiny. On a more encouraging note, the movement in favour of divestment in fossil fuels has grown in the last few years, and the specific campaign led by the *Guardian* in 2015, amounts to a new and potentially significant form of climate activism (Bratman et al. 2016). Examining discourses (and silences) on such pathways to our collective future is of vital importance.

As apparent in the previous section, the politics and the 'non-politics' of climate change ought to continue to be subjected to (Critical) Discourse Analysis. Researchers should single out and investigate ongoing struggles over climate justice and political power, and also over nature, lifestyles and money, among other matters to which climate change is connected. A discourse-political analysis will be concerned with the choices and non-choices, as well as the rights and duties, of countries, corporations, social classes and individuals. This should include both powerful actors, such as the European Union

(Krzyżanowski 2013) or large fossil-fuel companies (Ihlen 2009), and under-studied (from a discourse-analytical perspective, at least) groups and social movements, such as the Climate Justice Movement, Climate Action Camps and Transition. The creation of consensuses on depoliticising policies, such as emissions trading (Felli 2015), and the imagined alternative possibilities advanced by those social movements involve discursive processes of key interest.

Attention to the meanings of climate change in public spheres will continue to be warranted. More research is needed on television, the medium that is (still) the chief source of information (and arguments, values and opinions) for many people around the world. The extraordinary development of digital communication calls for more and better studies. Twitter exchanges on climate change have recently been a focal point of several new publications (e.g. Kirilenko & Stepchenkova 2014), but none are discourse-analytical. Undertaking that kind of work on social media would be an important contribution to knowledge.

Research should also diversify in geographical terms. There are wide differences in what we know about media (and other) discourses in the so-called Western world and developing countries (Schäfer & Schlichting 2014). Academics should develop a greater sensitivity to the specificities of different countries in the (global) politics of climate change and ask questions accordingly (Olausson & Berglez 2014).

Both questions and tools shape research findings. Given the large amounts of text on climate change currently available, researchers need to make choices and compromises. Some have explored various questions via computational linguistics (e.g. Grundmann & Krishnamurthy 2010) and others have combined it with Critical Discourse Analysis (Bevitori 2010) for deeper understanding. Some approaches and methods are scarce in climate change research: such is the case of Multimodal Discourse Analysis, which would, for instance, be highly relevant for the analysis of television and new media. Reisigl and Wodak (2015) have recently contributed to filling this gap by applying the multi-theory and multi-method Discourse-Historical Approach (DHA) to online news texts on climate change. More generally, the DHA has a strong potential for productive analysis of any climate-related discourses and their contexts.

Finally, discourse analysts should continue to critically examine relations between texts on climate change (science reports, political speech, materials from corporations, media reports, etc); their producers (multiple social actors, journalists, public relations professionals – see Anderson 2009); and consumers (who are increasingly 'prosumers'), as highlighted by others (Olausson & Berglez 2014). A range of questions may be raised about that circuit involving, among others, textual representations, behaviours, social conditions, cultures and subjectivities. To the extent that discourse does not just have a function of representing the world, but also of constructing social relations and identities, examining subject positions on climate change as 'places of enunciation' (Rothe 2011, p. 334) that are 'contingent and continually negotiated' may contribute to understanding social and political (dis)engagement, a key issue if we are to succeed in constructing a sustainable future in a democratic manner.

Note

1   For more information about, and publications from, the Intergovernmental Panel on Climate Change, go to www.ipcc.ch.

References

Aitken, M, 2012, 'Changing climate, changing democracy: A cautionary tale', *Environmental Politics*, vol. 21, no. 2, pp. 211–229.

Anderson, A, 2009, 'Media, politics and climate change: Towards a new research agenda', *Sociological Compass*, vol. 3, no. 2, pp. 166–182.

Antilla, L, 2005, 'Climate of scepticism: US newspaper coverage of the science of climate change', *Global Environmental Change*, vol. 15, no. 4, pp. 338–352.

Asplund, T, Hjerpe, M & Wibeck, V, 2013, 'Framings and coverage of climate change in Swedish specialized farming magazines', *Climatic Change*, vol. 117, nos. 1/2, pp. 197–209.

Bailey, A, Giangola, L & Boykoff, M T, 2014, 'How grammatical choice shapes media representations of climate (un)certainty', *Environmental Communication*, vol. 8, no. 2, pp. 197–215.

Bevitori, C, 2010, *Representations of climate change: News and opinion discourse in UK and US quality press: A corpus-assisted discourse study*, Bononia University Press, Bologna.

Bodansky, D, 2001, 'The history of the global climate change regime', in *International relations and global climate change*, eds. U Luterbacher & D F Sprinz, MIT Press, Cambridge, MA, pp. 23–40.

Boykoff, M & Boykoff, J, 2004, 'Balance as bias: Global warming and the US prestige press', *Global Environmental Change*, vol. 14, no. 2, pp. 125–136.

Bratman, E, Brunette, K, Shelly, D C & Nicholson, S, 2015, 'Justice is the goal: Divestment as climate change resistance', *Journal of Environmental Studies and Sciences*, vol. 6, no. 4, pp. 677–690.

Carvalho, A, 2005, 'Representing the politics of the greenhouse effect: Discursive strategies in the British media', *Critical Discourse Studies*, vol. 2, no. 1, pp. 1–29.

Carvalho, A, 2007, 'Ideological cultures and media discourses on scientific knowledge. Re-reading news on climate change', *Public Understanding of Science*, vol. 16, no. 2, pp. 223–243.

Carvalho, A, ed., 2011, *As alterações climáticas, os media e os cidadãos*, Grácio editor, Coimbra.

Demeritt, D, 2001, 'The construction of global warming and the politics of science', *Annals of the Association of American Geographers*, vol. 91, no. 2, pp. 307–337.

Demeritt, D, 2006. 'Science studies, climate change and the prospects for constructivist critique', *Economy and Society*, vol. 35, no. 3, pp. 453–479.

Edwards, D & Cromwell, D, 2006, *Guardians of power: The myth of the liberal media*, Pluto Press, London.

Ereaut, G & Segnit, N, 2006, *Warm words: How are we telling the climate story and can we tell it better?* Institute for Public Policy Research, London.

Fairclough, N, 1995, *Media discourse*, Edward Arnold, London.

Felli, R, 2015, 'Environment, not planning: The neoliberal depoliticisation of environmental policy by means of emissions trading', *Environmental Politics*, vol. 24, no. 5, pp. 641–660.

Forchtner, B & Kølvraa, C, 2015 'The nature of nationalism: Populist radical right parties on countryside and climate', *Nature & Culture*, vol. 10, no. 2, pp. 199–224.

Freudenburg, W R, 2000, 'Social constructions and social constrictions: Toward analyzing the social construction of "the naturalized" as well as "the natural"', in *Environment and global modernity*, eds. G Spaargaren, APJ Mol & F H Buttel, Sage, London, pp. 103–19.

Freudenburg, W R & Gramling, R, 1994, *Oil in troubled waters*, State University of New York Press, Albany, NY.

Funtowicz, S & Ravetz, J, 1993, 'Science for the post-normal age', *Futures*, vol. 25, no. 7, pp. 739–755.

Grundmann, R & Krishnamurthy, R, 2010, 'The discourse of climate change: A corpus-based approach', *Critical Approaches to Discourse Analysis across Disciplines*, vol. 4, no. 2, pp. 125–146.

Hopwood, B, Mellor, M & O'Brien, G, 2005, 'Sustainable development: Mapping different approaches', *Sustainable Development*, vol. 13, no. 1, pp. 38–52.

Hulme, M, 2009, *Why we disagree on climate change: Understanding controversy, inaction and opportunity*, Cambridge University Press, Cambridge.

Hulme, M, 2010, 'Problems with making and governing global kinds of knowledge', *Global Environmental Change*, vol. 20, p. 4, pp. 558–564.

Ihlen, Ø, 2009, 'Business and climate change: The climate response of the world's 30 largest corporations', *Environmental Communication: A Journal of Nature and Culture*, vol. 3, no. 2, pp. 244–262.
Kenis, A & Lievens, M, 2014, *The limits of the green economy*, Routledge, London.
Kirilenko, A P & Stepchenkova, S O, 2014, 'Public microblogging on climate change: One year of Twitter worldwide', *Global Environmental Change*, vol. 26, pp. 171–182.
Koteyko, N, 2012, 'Managing carbon emissions: A discursive presentation of "market-driven sustainability" in the British media', *Language & Communication*, vol. 32, no. 1, pp. 24–35.
Krieg-Planque, A, 2010, 'La formule "développement durable": Un opérateur de neutralisation de la conflictualité', *Langage et Société*, vol. 134, no. 4, pp. 5–29.
Krzyżanowski, M, 2013, 'Policy, policy communication and discursive shifts: Analyzing EU policy discourses on climate change', in *Analyzing genres in political communication. Theory and practice*, eds. P Cap & U Okulska, John Benjamins, Amsterdam, pp. 101–133.
Kuha, M, 2010, 'Uncertainty about causes and effects of global warming in U.S. news coverage before and after Bali', *Language & Ecology*, vol. 2, no. 4, pp. 1–18.
Liu, J C-E, 2015, 'Low carbon plot: Climate change skepticism with Chinese characteristics', *Environmental Sociology*, vol. 1, no. 4, pp. 280–292.
Lorenzoni, I, Leiserowitz, A, Doria, M F, Poortinga, W & Pidgeon, N F, 2006, 'Cross-national comparisons of image associations with "global warming" and "climate change" among laypeople in the United States of America and Great Britain', *Journal of Risk Research*, vol. 9, no. 3, pp. 265–281.
Lowe, T D, 2006, *Is this climate porn? How does climate change communication affect our perceptions and behaviour?*, Tyndall Centre Working Paper 98, Norwich.
Mazur, A, 1998, 'Global environmental change in the news', *International Sociology*, vol. 13, no. 4, pp. 457–472.
McCright, A & Dunlap, R, 2000, 'Challenging global warming as a social problem: An analysis of the conservative movement's counter-claims', *Social Problems*, vol. 47, no. 4, pp. 499–522.
McKewon, E, 2012, 'Talking points AMMO: The use of neoliberal think tank fantasy themes to delegitimise scientific knowledge of climate change in Australian newspapers', *Journalism Studies*, vol. 13, no. 2, pp. 277–297.
Methmann, C P, 2010, '"Climate protection" as empty signifier: A discourse theoretical perspective on climate mainstreaming in world politics', *Millennium – Journal of International Studies*, vol. 39, no. 2, pp. 345–372.
Moser, S, 2010, 'Communicating climate change: History, challenges, processes and future directions', *WIREs Climate Change*, vol. 1, pp. 31–53.
Mouffe, C, 2005, *On the political*, Routledge, London.
Nerlich, B, 2010, '"Climategate": Paradoxical metaphors and political paralysis', *Environmental Values*, vol. 19, pp. 419–442.
Nerlich, B & Koteyko, N, 2009, 'Compounds, creativity and complexity in climate change communication: The case of "carbon indulgences"', *Global Environmental Change*, vol. 19, no. 3, pp. 345–353.
New Economics Foundation, 2010, *The great transition*, NEF, London, available from www.neweconomics.org/publications/entry/the-great-transition [accessed 10 June 2014].
Olausson, U, 2009, 'Global warming-global responsibility? Media frames of collective action and scientific certainty', *Public Understanding of Science*, vol. 18, no. 4, pp. 421–436.
Olausson, U & Berglez, P, 2014, 'Media and climate change: Four long-standing research challenges revisited', *Environmental Communication*, vol. 8, no. 2, pp. 249–265.
O'Neill, S & Nicholson-Cole, S, 2009, '"Fear won't do it": Promoting positive engagement with climate change through visual and iconic representations', *Science Communication*, vol. 30, no. 3, pp. 355–379.
Oreskes, N & Conway, E M, 2010, *Merchants of doubt: How a handful of scientists obscured the truth on issues from tobacco smoke to global warming*, Bloomsbury Press, New York.

Painter, J, 2011, *Poles apart: The international reporting of climate scepticism*, Reuters Institute for the Study of Journalism, Oxford.
Pearce, F, 2007, *With speed and violence: Why scientists fear tipping points in climate change*, Beacon Press, Boston.
Peters, H P & Heinrichs H, 2008, 'Legitimizing climate policy: The "risk construct" of global climate change in German mass media', *International Journal of Sustainability Communication*, vol. 3, pp. 14–36.
Reisigl, M & Wodak, R, 2015, 'The discourse-historical approach (DHA)', in *Methods of Critical Discourse Studies*, eds. R Wodak & M Meyer, 3rd ed., Sage, London, pp. 23–61.
Rothe, D, 2011, 'Managing climate risks or risking a managerial climate: State, security and governance in the international climate regime', *International Relations*, vol. 25, no. 3, pp. 330–345.
Sampei, Y & Aoyagi-Usui, M, 2009, 'Mass-media coverage, its influence on public awareness of climate change issues, and implications for Japan's national campaign to reduce greenhouse gas emissions', *Global Environmental Change*, vol. 19, no. 2, pp. 203–212.
Saunders, C, Grasson, M & Price, S, 2012, 'From issue attention cycle to carbon consensus: British newspaper coverage of climate change (1997–2009)', Working paper from the COMPON project.
Schäfer, M & Schlichting, I, 2014, 'Media representations of climate change: A meta-analysis of the research field', *Environmental Communication*, vol. 8, no. 2, pp. 142–160.
Smith, P, 2012, 'Narrating global warming', in *The Oxford handbook of cultural sociology*, eds. J C Alexander, R Jacobs & P Smith, Oxford University Press, Oxford, pp. 745–760.
Swyngedouw, E, 2010, 'Apocalypse forever? Post-political populism and the spectre of climate change', *Theory, Culture & Society*, vol. 27, nos. 2–3, pp. 213–232.
UNEP, 2011, *Towards a green economy: Pathways to sustainable development and poverty reduction*, available from: www.unep.org/greeneconomy/GreenEconomyReport [accessed 29 June 2014].
UNFCCC, 2015, *Feeling the heat: Climate science and the basis of the Convention*, available from: https://unfccc.int/essential_background/the_science/items/6064txt.php [accessed 29 May 2015].
Weingart, P, Engels, A & Pansegrau, P, 2000, 'Risks of communication: Discourses on climate change in science, politics, and the mass media', *Public Understanding of Science*, vol. 9, no. 3, pp. 261–283.
Yun, S J, Ku, D, Park, N B & Han, J, 2012, 'A comparative analysis of South Korean newspaper coverage on climate change: Focusing on conservative, progressive, and economic newspapers', *Development and Society*, vol. 41, no. 2, pp. 201–228.

33
Old and dependent
The construction of a subject position for politics and care

Bernhard Weicht

Introduction

In a thought-provoking essay, Améry (1968) describes ageing as a conglomeration of symbols and associations which, all together, indicate decrement and the end of an era. Ageing in that sense does not describe a continuous process of time passing within a life-course perspective; rather, ageing demarcates the boundaries between the young and active on the one hand, and the old, passive and dependent on the other:

> When we have passed the prime of life, society forbids us a self-image for the future, and culture becomes a burdensome culture which we no longer understand, which rather gives us to understand that, being the scrap iron of the mind, we belong to the waste dumps of the era. In the process of ageing, finally, we have to live with dying, a scandalous imposition, a unique humiliation we have to bear, not with humility, but as the humiliated.
> (Améry 1968, p. 148; tr. Weicht)

In times of demographic changes in the Western world, most importantly ageing societies, the structuring concept of age, as well as the boundaries between young and old, functions as one of the main categories among which social struggles manifest themselves. An increasingly older population leads to pressures related to social security and pension systems, the availability of labour and the provision of care. All of these areas shape the connotations of the process of ageing but are, likewise, strongly informed by the associations with ageing themselves. In this chapter, I present some of the semantic processes through which ageing and old age gain their specific symbolic meaning, which, as a consequence, informs other social practices.

A broad literature on the discursive constructions of old age and the (socio)linguistics of ageing investigating several fields can be found (Coupland 2009; Rozanova 2010). In this chapter, I want to focus on an example that is only obvious on first sight – the field of ageing and care (see also Weicht 2015). While the relationship between care and ageing might seem logical, the specific points of demarcation and construction are often hidden under general assumptions and associations. Furthermore, the field of care makes it possible to trace the specific steps through which a semantic construction of ageing takes place and which, eventually, informs policy-making.

Going beyond its function as a social structure, the idea of ageing represents individual and collective challenges and threats, which are continuously translated into political problems and demands. Like all discourses, the discourse on ageing is experienced as both a social and psychological process. Wetherell & Potter (1992) explain that in order to make sense of the world around us, people draw on different repertoires or resources, which can be described as predefined attitudes and ideologies that build a common moral framework. In the political context, this means that debates and, consequentially, political decisions and legislation need to be framed within existing discursive contexts, drawing on existing semantic resources. A politics of ageing is thus inevitably based within the internal logics of the concept of ageing and old age. The particular use of language limits and delineates political possibilities, on all levels of decision-making processes. Verloo (2005) demonstrates how the framing of political issues can be identified and analysed in several intersecting domains, such as the diagnosis or the prognosis of the problem. Any political formulations or considerations require a language to talk about the issue under question, so discourses function as an 'internalised structuring impetus' (De Cillia et al. 1999). In a simplified way, it could be stated that politics and political interventions need one identifiable subject group, one clearly defined concept and one thoroughly defined problem. The construction of an imagined client group, or an imagined target group, builds the basis for (social) policies, as, for example, Wilińska and Henning (2011) demonstrate, and 'particular "identity categories" function either as legitimating or disciplinary within discourses of entitlement and disentitlement' (Taylor 1998, p. 333). Policies about and for the elderly undoubtedly need the category of the elderly. In turn, however, politics and policies shape the very category of the elderly. The analysis of the semantic practices and the use of language therefore allow a focus on the interrelation between structure and action (see Fairclough 2001) in which language-use functions here first as the tool of construction and categorisation and, second, as an ideal focus for an analysis of the very construction. With van Dijk (1991) it could be stated that through language the macro-level of society is translated into the micro-level of everyday routines and vice versa. The general public, as well as policy-makers, try to implement what is considered 'the proper thing to do' (Williams 2004, p. 17). What is right and wrong, which policies are necessary, justified and desirable, and whether or not politics should intervene or act in the first place, are all questions that are framed using a particular language. Investigating the language used to negotiate ageing and care in society offers then the possibility to understand the very framework in which policy-making takes place.

In analysing the semantic construction of ageing and care, I utilise Reisigl and Wodak's (2001) analytical steps, moving from the identification of referential and predication strategies to a discussion of the related argumentation strategies, drawing on empirical case studies (see Weicht 2015), which investigated the discourses on ageing and care in two European countries, Austria and the UK. In both countries, elderly care is predominantly provided informally, usually by family members, and only supplemented by formal care arrangements. However, due to demographic changes, both countries face enormous challenges to continue this kind of care provision, and social policies are put in place to either support informal carers and enable increasing possibilities for market-organised care (in particular in the UK), or to allow marketised care options in people's households by fostering the employment of migrant care workers (particularly in Austria). The empirical material consists of different genres in different discursive fields, which together should enable sketching the mechanisms of textual chains. In the concrete context, this means that a public outcry (for example, about the unbearable future challenges of organising care for older people) is followed up by some (journalistic) analysis, which in turn is complemented by people's personal narratives and stories and, finally, the negotiations for specific legislation in that field. Importantly, these textual chains do not necessarily reflect a chronological order; rather, I want to point to the similarities in constructions, and how different perspectives and genres apply the same concepts, drawing on the same language. Specifically, I will present some examples from both countries, which stem from the same time period, (2006–2007) reflecting the use of language in the media (here, I draw on an analysis of national newspapers), everyday discussions (I organised focus groups in both countries) and the political debate (I draw on data from parliamentary discussions). The role of the media in this context is, as Aldridge (1994, p. 18) reminds us, 'to set the news agenda in terms of both topics and discursive framework' and the media help to define what is both acceptable and socially thinkable (Aldridge 1994, p. 35; see also Richardson 2007). Focus groups, consisting of 4–10 participants from various backgrounds, ages and relationships to care and ageing, offer data of how individuals talk about care and ageing and so collectively make sense of a particular topic. With the aim of discussing textual continuities and similarities in different genres, focus-group data offer a possibility to investigate how:

> the public sphere influences […] individuals' views on politics and society and how, conversely, the ideas crucial to the 'social' (individual) level penetrate […] into politics, into the media and into other constituents of the public sphere.
> (Krzyżanowski 2008, p. 169)

The pool of empirical data is finally complemented by data on the political rhetoric (Reisigl 2008), which shows how both subjectivities and argumentation strategies are influencing the political discussion and thus shape the frames and possibilities for policy-making.

In the following sections, whose structure is informed by Reisigl and Wodak (2001, p. 45ff), I raise in particular the following questions: How are older people named and referred to, and what traits and characteristics are attributed to them? In this section, I want to specifically analyse the language used to describe the imagined category of the elderly that is used in both public discourses and legislation negotiations. Second, which arguments are presented to justify and/or legitimise a particular treatment of older people, both politically and publicly, and how are these arguments structured linguistically? And finally, which conclusions should be drawn by the public and by politicians, resulting from the structure of the discursive construction of these arguments?

Naming the elderly: Referential strategies

As mentioned earlier the concept of ageing describes much more than a continuous process of time passing over the life-course. Taken-for-granted categories such as child, adult, youth, middle age or old age mark and describe particular stages during life, which entail specific associations (Coupland et al. 1993). Ageing thus demarcates groups and establishes boundaries; the concept is linked to symbols, associations and metaphors. In particular, ageing allows the creation of a dichotomy between the young on one side and an ageing population on the other. Dichotomies are a fundamental and powerful tool to distinguish people and to create in- and out-groups (Weicht 2015). The construction of dichotomies, which is representative of most areas of social life (see Jenks 1998) not only constructs different groups, but associates those with moral rules and normative judgements. As Derrida (1981) shows, taking up de Saussure's (1972) insight that dichotomous categories, such as good and evil, depend on each other, the meanings of these binaries are not neutral, but created within moral and social hierarchies. In the context of ageing and care, this means that being old, being dependent and being passive are all contrasted with the positive ideal of youth, activity and independence. Associations and imaginations of these dichotomous categories (and related categories such as home/institution, private/public etc., see Weicht 2015) are therefore not linked to materialist, objective differences but stem, as Gal (2004, p. 261) shows, from semiotic processes. In that sense, the elderly person represents a specific image which is, to a certain extent, dissociated from the actual chronological age. Elderly people are positioned in opposition to other groups, such as the young, the economically active, carers or family members. Drawing on linguistic categories described by van Leeuwen (1995) and also applied by Reisigl and Wodak (2001) I present in the following some of the main referential strategies by which older people are named, described and thus established as a group.

Aggregation

Aggregation, that is, the presentation of people as numbers or unities, fulfils several functions. First, it allows the reduction of a diverse group to easily graspable figures and concepts. Second, aggregation already suggests the construction of a particular societal problem or challenge. And third, by presenting impressive (in most cases particularly high) numbers the path is already laid for the call for immediate (political) reactions. In the context of ageing, this can be exemplified with the following quote from a popular Austrian tabloid newspaper:

> More than 300,000 Austrians need care – often day and night. And this number is rising quickly!
>
> (*Kronen Zeitung* 15 August 2006)

Van Leeuwen (1995) emphasises that when 'hard facts' and statistics are presented, an imagined group of human beings is replaced by a statistical category. This establishment of challenging 'facts' is furthermore related to metaphors describing and mitigating an objective crisis situation, as for example the Austrian newspaper *Die Presse* (10 August 2006) puts it: '*Social dynamite [...] People are ageing more healthily*'. Terms such as 'demographic time-bomb' or the '*explosion of the number of people in need of care*' (*Kronen Zeitung* 10 May 2007) relate the presented numbers to an inevitable collapse of a societal system and depict (apocalyptic) consequences for the future – a process that, in the context of ageing, can be found in several national circumstances (see Mullen 2002). Statistics and apocalyptic scenarios are in turn extremely influential in shaping people's ideas and opinions about a certain subject matter. Since numbers tend to appear as unchangeable truth, they frame a group (here: the elderly) as already a problem, as Andy's comment in a focus group indicates:

> Andy: there are going to be fewer and fewer young people, who will have to work for more and more older people. How should that work out? In my opinion, at some point, that can't work out any longer. And this point comes closer and closer. [...] and at some moment it's collapsing.

Bernhard Weicht

Collectivisation

In the extracts above, older people are reduced to numbers or statistical categories; they themselves remain, however, without qualifications and identities. Moving from the macro-scale of societal developments and challenges to the micro-level of individual encounters and narratives, this feature becomes more apparent. A process of collectivisation, meaning the establishment of one collective group and category of 'the elderly', which can be characterised in a certain way and associated with particular traits, wishes and opinions, can be found in both descriptions of individual experiences and more generalised accounts. The following focus-group exchange starts with a personal story, but draws immediately on the formation of a particular distinction between the young and the old:

> Pamela: Because of the way that families have changed completely, they don't get an opportunity, to get used to old people [...]. I mean my son came up for his Granny's 100th birthday party, and he had his lunch with her, [...] which I thought was a nice way before the party. He had to get back, and he said afterwards, it was awful, you can shoot me before I get to that stage, because...
> Larry: Because he, I imagine, he hadn't had the experience
> Pamela: He hadn't experienced that
> Larry: That environment
> Pamela: He hadn't experienced that environment. But they had their lunch in a separate area; it wasn't in the main dining room. He was just talking to his granny, and she [...] for an old person she's extraordinary. But he hasn't got
> Will: because he doesn't get into contact with old people, presumably in his job?
> Pamela: He doesn't, no.

Old people are seen as a particular category of people who are fundamentally different to other members of society. Someone needs to 'experience' older people, in order to understand them; to not be scared or appalled by their presence and characteristics. This feature, in which the elderly person is presented as the quintessential other can also be found in Wilińska's (2010) identification of a normative 'age order'. Through collectivisation, clearly drawn positions are established, which not only inform people's day-to-day understandings, but, as resources, build the prerequisites for (social) policy-making.

Problematisation

In relation to the discursive strategy of aggregation, I have already mentioned the possibilities for creating an image of problems and challenges related to an undefined, but clearly demarcated, group. References to natural disasters ('the ageing tsunami') or martial language ('the demographic time-bomb') shape the image of a challenge that dramatically hits (the rest of) society. But also, here, the macro-level is accompanied by a process of problematisation on the micro-level. The established group of the elderly is identified with causing difficulties, problems and challenges both for society in general and their families or carers in particular. In the following three extracts from different focus-group discussions, the category of the older people (in particular older people in need of care) is associated with character traits that have negative impacts on their surroundings:

Hilde: But older people, of course, also turn more and more difficult [...].
Mona: Some really become aggressive.
Hannah: And they can be really nasty and mean.

It is important to emphasise that not only are negative traits and actions described, but that they are associated with the established group of the elderly in general. The statements move beyond a particular personal narrative or experience and stand for the elderly as a category and group. Personal situations and relations are expressed as general truths and vice versa. The language of describing older people in relation to problems caused makes it possible for everyone to join the discussion and draw on their own experiences, as shown in the following extract:

Walter: He's always been like that [...] He's always been like that. [...] he doesn't know himself differently. He doesn't know at all how mean he is.
Barbara: No, no, it is also because of the illness.
Walter: Dementia comes on top of that, on top of that.
Barbara: The illness, it's causing a lot as well. And [...] it changes constantly. I see that as well, especially with people with dementia, one time they're aggressive, and really egomaniac. [...] and also blame the others as well [...] and then they fall into misery.

Below I will also discuss the referential strategy of somatisation, which identifies a group with illnesses and malfunctions of body and mind. What is important here is the link between these illnesses (which also stand for a whole group and not just for individually experienced cases) and the consequences for the speakers' group, representing the young, the active, the family members and the carers. The other (the elderly) thus causes a challenging impact on the self.

Relational identification

These relationships, which are already put in focus by the emphasis on problems for people's surroundings, are also a significant semantic feature on their own. Related to the aforementioned strategy to strip older people of their own agency and to avoid representing them as actors in their own right, a process of relational identification takes place in which the use of personal pronouns, for example, in discussions about 'our' elderly people, becomes a striking facet. Similarly, newspaper articles often feature references to close family relations with terms such as *grannie, nana,* or *grandpa.* Importantly, these nominations do not necessarily refer to concrete and specific family relations, but express more generally the situation of older people within their respective family contexts. Additionally, they become family members to society as a whole, which also already establishes certain connotations of responsibility and obligation. Marion replies during a focus-group discussion to the question of which option of care is preferable:

Marion: Of course, psychologically, I think it is more ideal if it was the family, being there for her [...]. Because, [...] the family knows what the elderly person needs. [...] My mother, my grandmother doesn't need to talk. I know what she wants.

This frequently expressed sentiment that 'the family knows best' establishes an inevitable link between the older person's life, condition and circumstances and his/her family and relatives. Because they are established as family members, others (here: the speakers) know what is best for them. This referential strategy culminates in another association and representation that depicts older people as similar to children. In the following focus-group extract it becomes apparent that family relations are here not referred to as concrete, specific familial bonds; rather, the elderly person is identified with generally well-established family dynamics, in particular, the parent–child relationship:

> Barbara: And on the other hand, somebody has given me this recommendation […] that you can indeed also scold the ill person a bit, and also the person in need of care […] and not having to always do everything for them, and having to give in. Because they forget it, that you have told them off, this they forget again anyways, but somewhere, something remains with them, that it isn't entirely fine, what they're doing […] So you can really once, of course not all the time, but you can really once also have a strict word with them.
> Vanessa: And they, I think, like small children, test the boundaries.
> Barbara: That's it, yes, that's it, yeah. […]
> Walter: Yes, that's it. It is like, that you can really say, they become small children again. […]
> Adam: And children test the boundaries, how far they can go, but the old people do it as well.

Being identified as children is a common feature, which Shakespeare (2000, p. 15) discusses in relation to disabled people, where he finds a dichotomy constructed 'between dependent, vulnerable, innocent, asexual children and competent, powerful, sexual, adult citizens'. Likewise, older people are infantilised, disempowered and, at the same time, by being identified as similar to children, the responsibility for them is linked to other family members.

Physical identification and somatisation

Featherstone and Hepworth (1990) argue that for humans, each other's bodies are usually absent in everyday discourses, but that in relation to certain periods in life which are, not least semantically, marked by decay and decrement (Coupland et al. 1991), the body comes back into focus. In some of the nomination strategies above, older people's illnesses and malfunctions of the body already functioned as a description device by which a particular identity and subjectivity is shaped. The old, vulnerable body becomes the physical expression of decay, passivity and dependency (Oakley 2007; Weicht 2011). This focus on the vulnerable body also abstracts from concrete and specific malfunctions or limitations and rather stands for an association with particular images and stereotypes:

> Hence, the very embodiment of a particular 'dated' body image can itself devalue the old person's social image independently of the perception of the actual physical effects of ageing manifest in such features as sagging flesh, wrinkling, greying hair or restricted movement, and further help to reinforce the negative stereotype.
> (Featherstone & Hepworth 1990, p. 253)

Apart from physical functions, people's mental capacities and performances (such as communicative skills) are an important component of the construction of the group of the elderly. One illness that marks the idea of decrement, both bodily and mentally, is dementia, which not only causes people difficulties in day-to-day encounters, but also challenges notions and experiences of personhood and is thus constructed as a loss of the self (Tanner 2013). Particular bodily malfunctions (such as incontinence) stand for a reference to the body as decay. John, in a focus-group discussion, describes his experience of a care home:

> John: And then slowly, you start getting a picture. I suppose if I go into a care home and if I – if I smell, unfortunately can't but say urine, that immediately puts me off [...] if I go into that place.

The smell of urine stands for the association with bodily malfunctions (in the context of incontinence see also Mitteness & Barker 1995) which, in turn, encompasses a description of old age. Stripped from any agency, stripped from any individuality, the older person is defined by particular features of a malfunctioning body.

Demarcating the group: predication strategies

Discursive strategies are almost always used to establish in- and out-groups and to 'demarcate the boundaries' of those groups (Reisigl & Wodak 2001). In the context of ageing and care, this happens particularly through predication strategies that describe 'the elderly' in a particular way and which connect 'the elderly' to certain characteristics, attributes and circumstances. Starting with the nominations and other referential strategies, it has already become apparent that a dichotomy is created between the young, active, independent speaker on the one side, who defines, on the other side, the old, passive and dependent elderly. Linguistically, older people are referred to by passive sentence constructions, as for example in a report in the Austrian newspaper, *Der Standard* (29 August 2006), '*the elderly people [...] are kept as fit as possible by the committed staff*'.

Other descriptions use formulations which express that things for elderly people have to be arranged by others and link this passivity to the more general notion of decline. The elderly person is sketched and described in a passively vegetating state of sadness, as exemplified by a commentary in *Kronen Zeitung* (30 May 2007):

> I think of the many old people who, often alone, without family, lonely and unhappy, remain without support in their houses. Who don't have anyone who organises help for them. It's not that important whether they have 'dementia' in a medical sense. They don't have the energy to keep their apartment tidy, to do the shopping. Also, trips to the doctor don't happen as nobody is organising those. Let alone a walk or even an excursion. That's all gone.

Van Leeuwen (1995) in this context points out that '[a]s the power of social actors decreases, the amount of emotive reactions attributed to them increases' (van Leeuwen 1995, p. 88). The description of older people as suffering, lonely and unhappy represents a prime example for this attribution. Passivity is thus linked with powerlessness and requires therefore interventions by others (carers, families, the state). Furthermore, van Leeuwen (1995) distinguishes between transactive actions (actions through which others are affected) and non-transactive actions. Older people are explicitly described as not being able to 'affect' or to 'act' but, on the contrary, are dependent on others' actions and interventions. Additionally, the power of social actors, van Leeuwen (1995, p. 87) argues, is also mitigated by attributing cognitive rather than affective actions to them, as the following focus-group exchange exemplifies:

> Lisa: I think it's very difficult to preserve, a person's dignity, and sense of worth, when they, become, less, yeah, a bit helpless. And I think they, I think they need to be aware that they are treated with respect for them, and for their dignity and their pride, uh, in as gentle way as possible. And an understanding way. And I also think it's important, to help them keep their sense of purpose in life. When so much, gradually goes from them. That they need to feel wanted.
> Carol: And a helpful citizen.

The other in this example is responsible for thinking about preserving the older person's dignity and sense of worth. While the old person is feeling helpless (an emotive action) the other needs to act in an understanding way (a cognitive action). As the elderly are mainly presented as a particular, largely homogenous group, differences in degrees of passivity, dependency or vulnerability are furthermore avoided and ignored (see Weicht 2011, 2013). This becomes even more apparent when looking at subject positions of elderly people constructed as active, independent and fit. In the following focus-group exchange, two participants who are part of a voluntary group linked to a church discuss one of their church members:

> Patricia: Our favourite lady at the moment is 98
> Nathan: They are all favourites
> Patricia: Yes, but this one's even more. [laughs]
> Nathan: She said she wants to go to Australia
> Patricia: Next year
> Nathan: For a holiday. At 99
> John: It's amazing
> Patricia: And she came in the other week and she said 'I'm a bit worried', I say 'Why, what's the matter?' She says: 'I'm beginning to feel my age' [all laughing] and I: 'I'd worry about it when you start acting your age', [all laughing] because she doesn't act her age at all.

It is interesting to note that while in the beginning the expression is rather infantilising, the description of the person in question changes substantially to present an active position. While active subject positions are a rarity in the description of the elderly, in particular in the context of care, this nuance allows an even stronger demarcation of the actual group of passive elderly. By picking out and praising those older people who are 'still' active, the general dichotomy between active and passive is reproduced and emphasised. Identities and references relating to successful and/or so-called healthy ageing reproduce the boundary constructed (Gilleard & Higgs 2011; Rozanova 2010). In the literature, this separation is often described as the split between the third and fourth age (Gilleard & Higgs 2011) in which the former refers to the active, independent elderly and the latter to those characterised by passivity, infirmities and shortcomings. In line with the referential strategies described, the dichotomy between passive and active clearly situates the earlier-presented elderly people within the symbolic realm of passivity and dependency. For these older people, so the argument goes, interventions by the active, that is, the speakers and those addressed, are required.

Because we have to take care of them: argumentation strategy

The use of terminology in referential and predication strategies has, as I have pointed out, often already implied particular responsibilities for others, or normative assumptions about particular treatments. In the analysis of the following argumentation strategies, I will demonstrate how the referential strategies are translated into clear demands for both political and societal reactions. Based on the categories established above, the existence of the dependent elderly people presents, first, a problem for 'us', to which we should, second, respond out of gratefulness and reciprocity. How 'we' should treat older people is, third, based on natural preferences that require, fourth, loving family care. These argumentation strategies need to be understood as interrelated *topoi* (describing 'conclusion rules' that connect the argument to a necessary conclusion; see Reisigl & Wodak 2001), which, together, present one coherent argumentation for both the general public and the political decision-makers.

Topos of responsibility

A striking aspect of the discourses on ageing and care is that older people themselves are usually not given their own voice. In the media, they hardly feature in articles or other contributions as individual agents, and their needs, wishes and desires are all defined and shaped by others. In line with the earlier described referential strategies, which do not establish older people as agents in their own right, this present *topos* requires communal responsibility and answers by 'us' for 'them'. *Because we (the speakers) are established in opposition to the passive, dependent elderly, we are in charge of the required answers to societal and individual demands and challenges.* A newspaper headline illustrates the argumentation strategy in which 'we' as the speakers are active and responsible for 'them', the passive, dependent elderly:

> How can we say we are civilised when we treat our elderly no better than prisoners?
> (*Daily Mail* 23 January 2007)

This first argumentation, that 'we' are responsible for caring for 'them' and for arranging society in a way that treats 'them' well, is then furthermore based on particular reasoning that establishes relationships between the different groups, but also demarcates the differences between the active and the passive.

Topos of gratefulness

It has been established that through the language used to describe older people they have been constructed as requiring help, support and care and that we, the active, are responsible for offering this support. The *topos* of gratefulness bases this claim within a construction of reciprocity over time. The terms recurrently used refer, for example, to *elderly people who need care, those who have built up the country and made the country what it is now* (*Kronen Zeitung* 20 July 2007). *Because elderly people have done something for 'us' in the past they ought to be cared for.* This positive reference to older people could, according to Binstock (2005), be described as 'compassionate ageism', in which a particular group's actions are, however, firmly situated in the past.

In a commentary in the *Guardian* newspaper on children exploiting their parents, another argumentation strategy representing this *topos* demonstrates several features already indicated. First, family relationships are a central focus. Second, elderly people are described as passive victims, who are difficult to deal with. Third, and this in turn establishes the argumentation of children's responsibility, they are described as victims of the very people they have brought up and raised:

> But it appears that children are the main culprits. How can they be so callous? Their parents are sitting ducks, of course. They tend to trust their children and can't imagine that they would want to do them any harm. [...] It seems incredible that they should allow greed to override their natural affection for, and duty of care towards, the men and women who brought them into the world and nurtured them through childhood.
>
> (*The Guardian* 23 February 2007)

The *topos* of gratefulness thus works again on both a macro-societal-level as well as the individual-family-level. Personal and societal care and responsibility are established as necessary and logical answers to the actions older people have performed in the past.

Topos of natural preferences

How should this care then be designed, and who is in charge of shaping the particular interventions? Unsurprisingly, and in line with the earlier-presented arguments, these very facts are established by 'us', the young; those who are not in a position to require care at the moment. Importantly, however, these decisions are framed as logical, natural and obvious preferences, which certainly entail the idea that everyone wants to stay at home (see Ceci et al. 2012; Lawson 2007). *And because everyone wants to stay at home, politics ought to enable care at home.* The following extract is taken from an Austrian parliamentary speech about the (then-illegal) employment of migrant care workers in people's households:

> Please imagine: You, me, in a care home – and from there on to the graveyard. Many would say: I don't want that. All of us would probably react like that. At home instead of the care home! That's what the majority of Austrians wish for. 82 percent say I only want to go to a retirement home if nothing else is possible. They only wish for one thing: to stay within their own home for as long as possible. [...] At home instead of a care home! – That should be possible for all those who want it!
>
> (Gertrude Aubauer, ÖVP, 29 November 2006)

Through the establishment of such fixed and unchanging preferences, policies can be presented as logical, obvious and unquestionable answers to the challenges.

Topos of loving care

This final step in establishing an integrated argumentation strategy of how ageing and care should be dealt with, comprises many of the aforementioned semiotic strategies. In particular, it links the establishment of natural preferences to the relational identification and the emphasis on affective needs and desires. While responsibilities are clearly established ('we', the active, need to provide for 'them', the passive elderly), the language used suggests that this support and care should be provided out of love, ideally within families and in people's private homes. *Because we have a natural affection to care for our relatives, this care should take place informally in people's private houses.*

This nostalgically idealised concept of caring is related to a natural disposition to care for 'our' elderly. The language used here often points to affections and dedication, which 'our' generation, however, has lost, due to the current conditions and requirements in society.

This ideal has important political consequences since it pushes responsibilities to care away from a bureaucratic, professionalised context, towards the private family sphere. Gordon Brown, then UK prime minister, used this *topos* in a guest article in a daily newspaper:

> It is far more a matter of love than of duty – caring that expresses itself in the priceless gift of sustained and dedicated support for people close to them.
>
> (*Daily Mail* 21 February 2007)

Political responsibility for older people who require care is thus fulfilled by allowing and fostering families' caring potentials. Ageing and care are, in this context, fundamentally situated within an apolitical realm, as also expressed in another statement made during the Austrian parliamentary debate on migrant care workers:

> This topic is way too sensitive to talk about it polemically. It's a concern for family and social policy which we all – please! – must more than take to our heart, and we should also seriously negotiate about it.
>
> (Ridi Steibl, ÖVP, 29 November 2006)

A dichotomy is created between care, family and affection on one side and the state, professional interventions and political actions on the other. Ageing and care are talked about in such a way that the political sphere is seen (and sees itself) as antipode to the fulfilment of the natural preferences and requirements of older people. In that sense, not only caring, but also ageing in general, is situated outside the political realm and thus stripped of most of its responsibility.

Concluding remarks

In this chapter, I have demonstrated that the language used to talk about ageing and care creates a strong dichotomy of the passive, dependent elderly being in need of care by the active, independent young. The semiotic construction of 'the elderly' then calls for particular care arrangements which then, in turn, reproduce the language used. Ultimately, ageing is constructed as an abstract challenge that hits both individuals and society from the outside. The challenge itself is, however, not a primarily political issue; rather 'we' have to do the one specific right thing for 'them', according to natural, logical preferences. The constant demarcation between the groups allows the establishment of clearly identifiable responsibilities and duties. Politics then only secures the circumstances for the logical answer to the obvious humanity.

Williams (1996) therefore urges the researcher to deconstruct categories in order to understand the meaning for both policy-makers and individuals. The language used to refer to individuals and groups, and to individual and societal challenges and problems, shapes the cognitions and actions of everyone in society and thus also (social) policy (Rudman 2006). By shaping policies according to the existing concepts and categories, these discursive strategies are reproduced and, in that, policies play an important role in the definition and reiteration of social issues (Biggs 2001). Discourses defining the meaning of old age suggest (through argumentation strategies) certain political answers. A politics beyond, or in contrast to, the constructed subject positions and discursive strategies simultaneously requires discursive interventions to open the space for other societal challenges, subject positions and political demands.

References

Aldridge, M, 1994, *Making social work news*, Routledge, London.
Améry, J, 1968, *Über das Altern: Revolte und Resignation*, Ernst Klett Verlag, Stuttgart.
Biggs, S, 2001, 'Toward critical narrativity: Stories of aging in contemporary social policy', *Journal of Aging Studies,* vol. 15, no. 4, pp. 303–316.
Binstock, R, 2005, 'Old-age policies, politics, and ageism', *Generations*, vol. 29, no. 3, pp. 73–78.
Ceci, C, Björnsdóttir, K & Purkis, M, 2012, 'Introduction: Home, care, practice – changing perspectives on care at home for older people', in *Perspectives on care at home for older people,* eds. C Ceci, K Björnsdóttir & M Purkis, Routledge, New York, pp. 1–22.
Coupland, J, 2009, 'Discourse, identity and change in mid-to-late life: Interdisciplinary perspectives on language and ageing', *Ageing & Society*, vol. 29, no. 6, pp. 849–861.
Coupland, N, Coupland, J & Giles, H, 1991, *Language, society & the elderly: Discourse, identity and ageing*, Blackwell, Oxford.
Coupland, N, Nussbaum, J & Grossman, A, 1993, 'Introduction: Discourse, selfhood, and the lifespan', in *Discourse and lifespan identity,* eds. N Coupland & J Nussbaum, Sage, London: pp. x–xxviii.
de Cillia, R, Reisigl, M & Wodak, R, 1999, 'The discursive construction of national identities', *Discourse & Society*, vol. 10, no. 2, pp. 149–173.
de Saussure, F, 1972, *Course in general linguistics*, Open Court Publishing, Peru.
Derrida, J, 1981, *Positions*, University of Chicago Press, Chicago, IL.
Fairclough, N, 2001, 'Critical discourse analysis as a method in social scientific research', in *Critical Discourse Analysis: Theory and Interdisciplinarity,* eds, G Weiss & R Wodak, Palgrave Macmillan, Basingstoke, pp. 121–138.
Featherstone, M & Hepworth, M, 1990, 'Images of aging', in *Aging in society: An introduction to Social Gerontology,* eds. J Bond & P Coleman, Sage, London, pp. 250–275.
Gal, S, 2004, 'A semiotics of the public/private distinction', in *Going public: Feminism and the shifting boundaries of the private sphere,* eds. J W Scott & D Keates, University of Illinois Press, Urbana, IL, pp. 261–277.
Gilleard, C & Higgs, P, 2011, 'Ageing abjection and embodiment in the fourth age', *Journal of Aging Studies*, vol. 25, pp. 135–142.
Jenks, C, ed., 1998, *Core sociological dichotomies*, Sage, London.
Krzyżanowski, M, 2008, 'Analyzing focus group discussions', in *Qualitative Discourse Analysis in the social sciences,* eds. R Wodak & M Krzyżanowski, Palgrave Macmillan, Basingstoke, pp. 162–181.
Lawson, V, 2007, 'Geographies of care and responsibility', *Annals of the Association of American Geographers*, vol. 97, no. 1, pp. 1–11.
Mitteness, L & Barker, J, 1995, 'Stigmatising a "normal" condition: Urinary incontinence in late life', *Medical Anthropology Quarterly*, New Series, vol. 9, no. 2, pp. 188–210.
Mullen, P, 2002, *The imaginary time bomb: Why an ageing population is not a social problem*, Tauris, London.
Oakley, A, 2007, *Fracture: Adventures of a broken body*, The Policy Press, Bristol.
Reisigl, M, 2008, 'Analyzing political rhetoric', in *Qualitative Discourse Analysis in the social sciences,* eds. R Wodak & M Krzyżanowski, Palgrave Macmillan, Basingstoke, pp. 96–120.
Reisigl, M & Wodak, R, 2001, *Discourse and discrimination: Rhetorics of racism and antisemitism*, Routledge, London.
Richardson, J, 2007, *Analysing newspapers: An approach from Critical Discourse Analysis*, Palgrave Macmillan, Basingstoke.
Rozanova, J, 2010, 'Discourse of successful aging in *The Globe & Mail*', *Insights from Critical Gerontology*, vol. 24, no. 4, pp. 213–222.
Rudman, D, 2006, 'Shaping the active, autonomous and responsible modern retiree: An analysis of discursive technologies and their links with neo-liberal political rationality', *Ageing & Society*, vol. 26, no. 2, pp. 181–201.

Shakespeare, T, 2000, *Help*, Venture Press, Birmingham.

Tanner, D, 2013, 'Identity, selfhood and dementia: Messages for social work', *European Journal of Social Work*, vol. 16, no. 2, pp. 155–170.

Taylor, D, 1998, 'Social identity and social policy: Engagements with postmodern theory', *Journal of Social Policy*, vol. 27, no. 3, pp. 329–350.

van Dijk, T A, 1991, *Racism and the press*, Routledge, London.

van Leeuwen, T, 1995, 'Representing social action', *Discourse & Society*, vol. 6, no. 1, pp. 81–106.

Verloo, M, 2005, 'Mainstreaming gender equality in Europe. A Critical Frame Analysis approach', *The Greek Review of Social Research*, vol. 117, pp. 11–34.

Weicht, B, 2011, 'Embracing dependency: Rethinking (in)dependence in the discourse of care', *The Sociological Review*, vol. 58, no. s2, pp. 205–224.

Weicht, B, 2013, 'The making of "the elderly": Constructing the subject of care', *Journal of Aging Studies*, vol. 27, no. 2, pp. 188–197.

Weicht, B, 2015, *The meaning of care: The social construction of care for elderly people*, Palgrave Macmillan, Basingstoke.

Wetherell, M & Potter, J, 1992, *Mapping the language of racism: Discourse and the legitimation of exploitation*, Harvester Wheatsheaf, Hemel Hempstead.

Wilińska, M & Henning, C, 2011, 'Old age identity in social welfare practice', *Qualitative Social Work*, vol. 10, no. 3, pp. 346–363.

Williams, F, 1996, 'Postmodernism, feminism and the question of difference', in *Social theory, social change and social work*, ed. N Parton, Routledge, London, pp. 61–76.

Williams, F, 2004, *Rethinking Families*, ESRC CAVA Research Group, Calouste Gulbenkian Foundation, London.

34
Language and gendered politics
The 'double bind' in action

Tanya Romaniuk and Susan Ehrlich

Introduction

Much has been written about the under-representation of women holding elected office around the world. According to the international organisation of parliaments, the Inter-Parliamentary Union (2015), women constitute just over 20 per cent of members of parliament in upper and lower houses world-wide (22.4% in single or lower houses, and 20.4% in upper houses or senates). Of 179 serving heads of government, 22 are women, only 15 of whom were elected. With women making up nearly half of the world's population of over 7 billion, these statistics speak to an alarming and persistent gendered divide in the domain of institutional politics.[1]

Despite an increasing number of women gaining entry into this domain over recent decades, feminist scholars contend that it remains a distinctively masculine culture (Edwards 2009). At least two factors contribute to the perception of politics as a gendered (i.e. masculine) environment: first, the 'presence or even predominance' of one gender (i.e. men) and, second, 'cultural norms and interpretations of gender that dictate who is best suited' for electoral office (McElhinny 1995, pp. 221). For example, we know that in US politics, the presidency remains a 'bastion of masculinity' (Anderson 2002, p. 105) and that any viable contender for the position of commander in chief is forced to run against the deeply entrenched cultural image of *man as president* (Carroll 2009). This means that even if a woman in a political leadership position, such as the presidency, employs leadership styles that are culturally understood as masculine, she is judged more negatively than a man employing these same styles (Eagly & Carli 2003). Many have written about this 'double-bind' situation faced by women in politics (e.g. Carroll 2003; Jamieson 1995; Ross 2014). That is, adopting so-called masculine patterns of behaviour 'leads women politicians to be seen as strange specimens' (Martin Rojo 2006, p. 744) in relation to the normative expectations of appropriate femininity while, at the same time, women politicians run the risk of appearing 'weak and ineffectual' (Martin Rojo 2006, p. 744) if they behave in accordance with these normative expectations of appropriate femininity (see also Felderer 1997; Gomard & Krogstad 2001).

Recent formulations of the relationship between language and gender, following Butler (1990), have emphasised the *performative* aspect of gender. Under such an account, gender is not a stable, pre-discursive construct residing in individuals; rather it *emerges* in discourse and in other semiotic practices. While the theorising of gender as 'performative' has encouraged language and gender researchers to focus on the agency of social actors in the constitution of a wide and diverse range of gendered identities (Cameron 2005), there has been less emphasis placed on another dimension of Butler's framework – the idea that performances of gender are always subject to regulation and constraint. That is, gendered performances are produced within what Butler (1990, p. 32) calls a 'highly rigid regulatory frame', which 'operates as a condition of cultural intelligibility' (Butler 2004, p. 52). This means that certain enactments of gender are rendered appropriate and intelligible by this 'frame' while others – those that depart from cultural norms – are rendered unintelligible and run the risk of sanctions or penalties. For women politicians, however, there does not seem to be any enactment of gender free of social sanctions: the 'cultural norms and interpretations of gender that dictate who is best suited' for electoral office render any woman's performance of gender in this context as problematic. In what follows, we consider in more detail this 'double bind' encountered by many women politicians: we first briefly review research that has examined women 'doing' politics and how this has been represented, especially in the mainstream media.[2] Then, we turn to a case study of Hillary Clinton and the 'double bind' in action. Finally, we conclude with a consideration of how women politicians fare in more egalitarian political contexts, which we suggest provides further evidence that women's political identities are rendered culturally unintelligible no matter what they do.

Women 'doing' politics and their representations

As noted above, many feminist scholars have argued that politics is a 'masculine culture' in the sense that the characteristics associated with effective political leadership are also those associated with hegemonic masculinity (Tannen 2008, p. 127). Within the discursive realm specifically, it has been claimed that 'masculinist discursive norms have assumed the status of gender-neutral professional norms' (Walsh 2001, p. 1). So, how do women represent themselves as credible political leaders in a context where masculine discursive norms have become naturalised as 'professional norms'? And, how are they represented and evaluated by others?

Some research has documented differential linguistic practices on the part of women and men in political contexts. In the British House of Commons, for example, where debate is characterised by a highly adversarial discursive style, Shaw (2000, 2006) found that, while women and men took 'legal' turns in debates in proportion to their overall representation in the House, male MPs were far more likely than female MPs to produce 'illegal' interventions, such as interrupting, jeering, heckling or filibustering. (And this meant that men dominated the debate floor.) When asked why they did not participate in these kinds of illegal interventions, some female MPs said that they consciously chose not to participate in 'male activities' (Shaw 2006, p. 95).

In contrast, other research has demonstrated that women politicians readily take on linguistic norms symbolically associated with masculinity. This is not surprising, given that, as many language and gender scholars have argued, phenomena such as 'women's language' or 'men's language' are resources available to all speakers in the enactment of various kinds of identities. Perhaps the most notable example of a female politician adopting 'masculinist discursive norms' is Margaret Thatcher. Not only did she receive training in order to lower the pitch of her voice, Wilson and Irwin (2015) have documented her aggressive and adversarial style during Prime Minister's *Question Time*. But, although Thatcher was famously described as 'the best man in the cabinet', Fairclough (1989 as cited by Walsh 2001, p. 72) notes that her rhetorical style was, in fact, a 'hybrid' one because it contained carefully-selected features of white middle-class femininity, along with authoritative features associated with male politicians. According to Fairclough, this particular combination of features allowed Thatcher to assimilate into the dominant culture of the House of Commons without posing any kind of feminist challenge or threat to its masculinist norms. Davies (2015) identifies a similar kind of 'hybrid' discourse in Sarah Palin's (former Republican VP candidate in the US) tweets: Palin 'performs' her traditionally feminine roles as mother and wife, while at the same time deploying an informal, vernacular style associated with working-class masculinity. According to Davies, this hybrid style may resonate well with her political base: extreme conservatives/libertarians/populists who are members of the Republican Party and are mostly older, married, white men.[3]

The linguistic style of Hillary Clinton has also been described as inconsistent with stereotypical norms of femininity; however, in Clinton's case, the negative reaction to it and other features of her political persona have been, arguably, more extreme than reactions to other women in the political spotlight. Indeed, the title of a widely cited article on Clinton's rhetorical style is indicative: 'The Discursive Performance of Femininity: *Hating Hillary*' (emphasis ours). Writing about Clinton's tenure as the First Lady of the United States when she worked to reform the US health-care system with her husband, Bill Clinton, Campbell (1998) argues that Clinton's forceful and highly developed rhetorical skills garnered negative reactions because they did not constitute a discursive enactment of femininity.[4] Interestingly, Campbell also suggests that Clinton's 'gender violations' on the discursive level forced her to adopt more feminine practices in non-linguistic domains (for example, 'softer hairdos, pastel suits and smaller "more feminine" jewelry [sic]' (Campbell 1998, p. 14), leading to what could be construed as a further example of a 'hybrid' style, in Fairclough's terms.[5]

So, while it seems clear that women politicians adopt a variety of leadership styles,[6] including those associated with hegemonic masculinity, Martin Rojo (2006, p. 746) has suggested, in keeping with our argument about the double bind, that 'the style adopted by women politicians in power in government or parliament is sometimes not as important as how these styles are perceived and represented.'[7] Indeed, media discourse has been a fertile site for investigating how female political leaders are perceived and represented. Much research exists, for example, on the sexist, stereotypical or asymmetrical nature of such representations in terms of the amount, type or tone of coverage (see, e.g. Conroy et al. 2015; Lakoff 2003). Other research has demonstrated that female political leaders are subject to negative evaluations regardless of whether they attempt to conform to, or transgress, gender stereotypes (see, e.g. Appleby 2015; Carlin & Winfrey 2009).

Some of this latter research has considered how women politicians are portrayed in media when they attempt to conform to stereotypical notions of 'femininity'. For example, Bengoechea (2011) examined the communicative identity of Spain's first woman Minister of Defence, Carme Chacón, as interpreted by the Spanish press. Bengoechea argued that the strong association between leadership and masculinity in Spain's government and military placed Chacón in a 'perilous and precarious' position (2011, p. 416). When Chacón departed from the conventional chain of command with respect to ordering the withdrawal of troops from Kosovo – adopting a more collaborative approach, long considered a symbolically 'feminine' leadership style – she was criticised extensively in media representations that described her as naïve, weak and incompetent. Her more cooperative ('feminine') style of leadership was reported as indicating a lack of leadership, and, as a consequence, her status as a capable leader was challenged and undermined.[8]

Given the masculinist culture of politics, what about media representations of women who attempt to transgress gender stereotypes? In attempting to demonstrate their suitability for executive office, women who try to utilise more 'masculine' styles of leadership still face the problem of being seen as 'unfeminine' (Murray 2010). For example, in a dual case study of Tarja Halonen, former President of Finland, and Angela Merkel, Chancellor of Germany since 2005, van Zoonen (2006) argues that the popularisation of politics has created an even more unfavourable context for women politicians who eschew the expectations of normative femininity. According to van Zoonen, the hyper-femininity and personalisation associated with 'celebrity politics' render Halonen's and Merkel's 'thoroughly political and professional' styles and their 'rigid' concealment of their personal lives (2006, p. 295) as 'other' in relation to dominant images of femininity, at the same time that Halonen and Merkel 'remain "others" in the political sphere' (2006, p. 298).

An additional issue faced by both Halonen (e.g. Mäkelä, Isotalus & Ruoho 2015) and Merkel (e.g. Lünenborg & Maier 2015), that of managing 'toughness' versus compassion, has been regarded a longstanding problem for other female politicians (Johnson 2015). These and other women heads of state (or candidates) such as Helen Clark of New Zealand (e.g. Trimble & Treiberg 2010), Julia Gillard of Australia (e.g. Hall & Donaghue 2013) and Hillary Rodham Clinton of the United States (e.g. Ritchie 2013) have all been criticised by media for their 'toughness' – a trait that is viewed as admirable in male politicians, yet one that remains incompatible with dominant notions of appropriate 'femininity' (e.g. warmth, empathy and compassion) (Johnson 2015). Indeed, each of these powerful female politicians has been depicted as cold and ruthless, and they have frequently had the authenticity of their respective political identities called into question.[9]

What should be clear from this brief survey of research is that the 'doing' of leadership continues to be associated with masculine communicative practices and styles, and that women's performance and behaviour within such contexts is subject to gendered (typically negative) evaluations. Like Baxter's (2012, p. 103) characterisation of female leaders in workplace contexts, 'the linguistic agency' of women who run for political office is clearly 'constrained by the social category of gender'. In what follows, we summarise research concerning Hillary Rodham Clinton's bid for the Democratic nomination for president of the United States in 2007–2008. This case study illustrates in detail how the rigid regulatory frame may shape and constrain the electoral experiences and outcomes of women political candidates who seek public office.

Clinton and 'the cackle'

During the Democratic primary in autumn 2007, Clinton's laughter became the subject of much media attention following her appearance on all five Sunday morning political news programmes on the same day: ABC's *This Week*, CBS's *Face the Nation*, CNN's *Late Edition*, FOX's *Fox News Sunday* and NBC's *Meet the Press*. After these interviews, several journalists, media commentators and pundits in the mainstream media adopted the term, 'The Clinton Cackle', as a way of characterising Clinton's laughter, and began an extended discussion of 'What's behind the laugh?' In order to understand more fully what may have motivated these responses to Clinton and her laughter, Romaniuk (2009), investigated Clinton's laughter from a conversation analytic perspective as it occurred in the kinds of broadcast news interviews that provoked these media responses in the first place.

The analysis was based on a collection of video recordings and transcripts of 25 live interviews – televised on the 'Big Four' US commercial TV networks (ABC, CBS, FOX, NBC) and the national cable and satellite TV channel, CNN – that Clinton participated in during and following her bid for the Democratic nomination (September 2007–September 2009). In keeping with two fundamental assumptions of conversation analysis (Schegloff 2009), the analysis sought, first, to discover the extent to which Clinton produced laughter in orderly ways and, second, to describe the social actions her laughter seemed to accomplish within these interviews (as opposed to focusing on the exchange of propositional content). While Romaniuk (2013a) identified a range of interactional environments in which Clinton's laughter occurred in these news interviews, the type of laughter that seemed most relevant to the media reporting just described was laughter that responded to, or occurred in the course of, serious interviewer questions.

To illustrate, we present the following example from an interview with Harry Smith on *The Early Show* (transcripts follow CA conventions, see Hepburn & Bolden 2013). At the time of the interview, Clinton had just received an endorsement from the *Des Moines Register*, a newspaper in Des Moines, Iowa. This was a significant moment for her campaign since, Barack Obama was polling increasingly well, and the Iowa Caucuses – the first major electoral event of the nominating process – were less than a month away. Prior to where excerpt (1) begins, Smith suggests that, in spite of the newspaper endorsement, many Americans still hold negative perceptions of Clinton because of her failed attempt at healthcare reform in the 1990s. After Smith unsuccessfully attempts to have Clinton address the issue of these negative perceptions, he follows up with the prefaced question in excerpt (1):

```
(1)     2007Dec17-CBS_TheEarlyShow-2: Rubs
        IR:   Harry Smith; IE: Hillary Rodham Clinton

16      IR:   Here's the thing though. So one of the rubs about
17            your campai:gn:=they say it (.) feels like it's
18            focus-group driven:, that it's too: run too tightly,
19            that [.h [people in Iowa don ]'t get to see=
20      IE:        [uheh[hih h↑ih hehheh]
21      IR:   =e[nough of the [re::al ] you::,=
22      IE:     [.hh           [u(h)h::]    =Well th[at's cert-=
24      IR:                                         [>to run
25            counter to< what you just sai[d.=
26      IE:                                [Well that's certainly
27            not my imp(h)r↑ession. (.)
28      IR:   Right (.)
29      IE:   It's not the first time I've disagreed with the
30            p(h)ress=
31      IR:           =k[hhuh
32      IE:             [and I £p(h)robably don't think it's
33            the last time£ […]
```
                                                    (Clinton interview on *The Early Show* 2007)

Smith's question preface offers three critical perspectives of Clinton's campaign which, in keeping with the journalistic norm of neutrality (Clayman 2012), are attributed to a third party, albeit an anonymous one. That is, Smith says that 'they' say that 'it feels like it is focus-group-driven', 'that it's too run too tightly', and 'that people in Iowa don't get to see enough of the re::al you,' (lines 17–19; 21). But Clinton does not wait until the third of these assertions is produced before responding; instead, she begins to laugh once he completes the second assertion and laughs through the third criticism. Clinton's subsequent verbal response begins with the discourse marker, 'well' (Schiffrin 1987), projecting a non-straightforward response (Schegloff & Lerner 2010), and then Clinton explicitly disagrees with the substance of the question preface. In this case, and others like it, Clinton displays a disaffiliative stance towards the interviewer's talk-in-progress, not just through her laughter, but also visually (e.g. by shaking her head).

This example is illustrative of a practice Clinton engaged in systematically in the broadcast news interviews analysed by Romaniuk – laughing during, or at the completion of, serious interviewer questions. Romaniuk argued that this kind of laughter can be viewed as a public display of disaffiliation in the sense that it expresses disagreement or dissociation from critical or otherwise problematic commentary put forward by an interviewer. For a politician like Clinton, then, laughing in such contexts acts as a form of 'damage control'; that is, the laughter treats the talk as laughable, and, in combination with other embodied stance displays, it functions to mitigate the potential damaging effects of such talk on her, or her campaign (Romaniuk 2013b).

However, was Clinton's laughter an idiosyncratic feature of her interactional style, as media representations such as 'The Clinton Cackle' would have us believe? In order to examine whether and to what extent *other* politicians deployed this practice of laughing in response to serious interviewer questions, Romaniuk collected a second set of video recordings: 50 live interviews televised on the same networks and featuring other politicians from within the same time period.[10] Remarkable similarities emerged between the two collections, both in terms of the overall frequency of laughter's occurrence and the distribution of the types of laughter. The results reported in Table 34.1 indicate that Clinton and other politicians did not differ in their initiation of laughter in the interviews even though, based on the media representations described above, it might have been expected that Clinton would have volunteered laughter much more frequently than other politicians.

In considering the type of laughter that had generated media attention for Clinton (i.e. laughter that occurred in response to interviewers' serious questions), Romaniuk also found that, although Clinton did produce laughter during interviewer questions much more frequently than other politicians (see Table 34.2), again, the difference was not significant.

Table 34.1 Distribution of overall occurrences of laughter, Clinton and 'other politicians'

Distributions compared	Clinton	Other politicians
Overall occurrences of laughter	91% (53/58)	90% (145/161)
Overall volunteered laughter	79% (42/58)	86% (124-161)

Table 34.2 Distribution of overall occurrences in relation to interviewer's (IR's) talk

Overall in relation to IR talk	Clinton	Other politicians
During IR question	78% (28/36)	72% (52/72)
At question completion	22% (8/36)	28% (20/72)

Indeed, excerpt (2) illustrates how a male politician uses laughter in the course of an interviewer's question in a comparable way to Clinton, as exemplified in excerpt (1). The interview features Tim Russert and then-candidate for the Republican nomination, Rudolph Giuliani. In line 1 of excerpt (2), Russert introduces a general criticism of Giuliani and then cites specific examples of Giuliani's questionable associations.

```
(2)     2007Dec09-Meet The Press-Serious accusations
        IR:    Tim Russert; IE: Rudolph Giuliani

01    IR:    People are calling into question yer ju:dgment,=
02           =they a:lso (.) c[ite that yer law: firm, (0.2)
03    IE:                    [hT°(h)im°
04           your law firm, uh did (.) w-work for: Hugo Chavez.
05           (0.2) the head of Venezuela.=
06    IE:    =[(th-)hhehh T(h)im]
07    IR:    =[They-they've now-] they've now quit that,
08           but they [did represent=
09    IE:             [( )
10    IR:    =CIT[GO,
11    IE:        [hi hu [huh °huh°]°huh°   [Hahh]
12    IR:               [which is ru]n by Hu [go C]ha:vez,=
13    IE:    =£T(h)im th(h)at's a st(h)re(h)tch,£ hh
```
                                    (Giuliani Interview, Meet The Press 2007)

Space limitations prevent us from including a more extended excerpt (but see Romaniuk 2013b for a lengthier discussion); however, the key point here is that Giuliani laughs throughout Russert's attempt to justify the association between Giuliani's law firm and Chavez, thus treating it as a laughable rather than a serious matter. Giuliani's subsequent verbal response produced with a smile, 'Tim that's a stretch' (line 13), which is similar to Clinton in excerpt (1), provides the grounds for understanding his affective displays up to that point as disaffiliative.

Excerpts (1) and (2), then, are illustrative of a generic interactional practice that Romaniuk found politicians employing in the course of serious interviewer questioning. As noted above, this practice functions as a public display of disaffiliation, while still technically abiding by the constraints of the news interview format (i.e. waiting until a question is complete to provide a verbal response). Moreover, as an interactional practice that was deployed by *both* male and female politicians in the corpus, Romaniuk concluded that it was *not* an idiosyncratic feature of Clinton's interactional style, nor was it a gendered interactional practice. And, yet, subsequent representations of Clinton's laughter by various news media nevertheless treated it, not only as a unique character trait, but also a gendered one. What follows is a brief discussion of how a particularly negative gendered meaning became associated with Clinton's laughter as representations of it circulated across a range of discursive contexts in the public domain.

In general, media coverage of politics constructs 'catchy' phrases or sound bites to characterise select portions of politicians' talk and other conduct (Talbot, Atkinson & Atkinson 2003). While there was certainly a range of media responses to Clinton's laughter, the characterisation that gained the status of an authoritative representation – 'The Clinton Cackle' – was a decontextualised one. That is, her laughter was extracted from its originating contexts of occurrence (i.e. news interviews) and was recontextualised in media discourse in a way that imbued it with a particularly negative, gendered meaning.[11] But how did this meaning come about?

Since the social construction of meaning is an ongoing process that occurs across multiple contexts, indexicality is a fundamental concept in understanding how linguistic forms come to be associated with social categories such as gender. Whereas early studies of language and gender assumed a one-to-one mapping of linguistic form onto the social category of gender, Ochs' (1992) model of indexical relations demonstrates how the relation between language and gender 'is mediated by and constituted through a web of socially organized pragmatic meanings' (1992, p. 341). The indexicality of gender, according to Ochs (1992), involves (at least) two semiotic processes: with respect to *direct indexicality*, linguistic forms 'most immediately' index particular social roles, activities, stances or acts, whereas in the process of *indirect indexicality*, these same linguistic forms become associated with particular social types and personas believed to embody those roles, to engage in those activities or to take/perform such stances and acts – types and personas that become culturally coded as gendered (Bucholtz 2009, p. 148). It is at the level of indirect indexicality, as Bucholtz (2009, p. 148) points out, where *ideology* comes to play a crucial role 'since it is at this level that [the particular social roles, activities, stances or acts] acquire more enduring semiotic associations'. In media discourse, ideology can manifest itself through the use of lexical choices that convey a range of meanings beyond the strictly referential, denotational ones. So, what is the referential, denotative meaning of 'cackle' and how do speakers who perform the act of 'cackling' take on gendered meanings that move beyond the referential and denotative ones?

Dictionaries such as the *Oxford English Dictionary* suggest that 'cackle' (as a noun) refers to an expressive act (i.e. a particular kind of sound or 'noise' quality), characteristic of hens. This expressive act characteristic of hens can be thought of as what 'cackle' directly indexes. Notably, however, none of the term's denotative meanings or the examples used to illustrate usage suggests 'cackle' is a negatively valenced term – one associated with a negative, gendered persona, that of witches. Despite this absence, Romaniuk (2016) illustrates how such an association is overtly recognisable and recognised both in contemporary usage (as evidenced by insights from corpus linguistics) and in media representations of Clinton's laughter, each of which will be discussed.

Corpus linguistics is particularly valuable in investigating the role that lexical choice plays in constructing ideological representations (Cotterill 2001). To provide evidence for the negative valence of 'cackle' and the implicit and ideological meanings indexed by its use, Romaniuk (2016) examined the term's semantic shape and patterns of collocation in the *Corpus of Contemporary American English*, the largest freely available corpus of American English, containing over 450 million words, including 20 million words each year between 1990–2012 (Davies 2008). Based on this analysis, Romaniuk (2016) found that the term's principal active associations were narrow and restricted, and indirectly indexed the laugh of an undesirable negative persona. More specifically, 'cackle's' collocational profile, and the connotations associated with it, embody what is called a *negative semantic prosody*; that is, the strongest collocates are overwhelmingly negative or unpleasant (Stubbs 1996). Indeed, the restricted set of meanings communicated via its use is strongly associated with an undesirable gendered persona, namely, witches.

As for the mass media representations of Clinton's laughter, Romaniuk (2016) suggested that both the negative semantic prosody of the term 'cackle' and its indirect association with witches were simultaneously evoked when used in media reports. For example, numerous representations alluded to or depicted Clinton as the Wicked Witch of the West (from *The Wizard of Oz*), a fictional character, but also a quintessential emblem of women who occupy powerful positions.[12] This association was often made explicit in television and print news coverage. Excerpt (3), which is commentary by conservative pundit and then-host of his own TV show, Glenn Beck, stands as but one example:

(3) *Glenn Beck*, October 7, 2007
America's starting to pay attention to the real issues that America faces, namely Clinton's laugh. I've never noticed it but critics have. They've called it, and I'm quoting 'less of a laugh and more of a cackle'. **Some have been a little more cruel as to even compare her laugh to the wicked witch of the West,** which is just a little unfair ((laughingly)). Here is the actual wicked witch of the Wizard of Oz. [((Video clip of the Wicked Witch of the West is played))]. **Okay, and here's the wick- uh the junior Senator from New York.** [((Plays video clip of same example of Clinton's laughter that Hannity played an audio clip of))].

(*Glenn Beck* 2007)

Using satire, Beck reproduces a characterisation of Clinton's laugh as a 'cackle' in a way that draws attention to this indirect association with witches while at the same time purporting not to be doing precisely that. That is, he suggests that likening Clinton's laugh to the Wicked Witch of the West is 'a little unfair', but then proceeds to highlight this association anyway (note the strategic use of self-initiated repair in introducing the clip of Clinton: 'here's the wick- uh the junior Senator from New York'). And, in replaying a decontextualised clip of a single instance of Clinton laughing immediately after showing a clip of the Wicked Witch of the West doing so, the indirect association between Clinton and this unflattering negative persona is made explicit. Romaniuk (2016) argued that over time, as this 'cackle' characterisation of Clinton's laughter travelled across discursive contexts and formed links in an intertextual series (see also Romaniuk 2014), the association between 'cackle' and Clinton (and not just the indirect indexical 'witches') became so strong that it too came to be ideologically perceived as direct (cf. Bucholtz 2009; Ochs 1992).

One piece of evidence that captures the strength of the association that developed between Clinton and 'cackle' is afforded by Google technology, which, according to Hill (2005), provides a powerful avenue for exploring dimensions of indexicality, and specifically, how non-linguistic semiotic elements of representations can co-occur with linguistic ones. Nearly ten years have passed since the majority of the 'cackle' coverage appeared, and yet, if the word 'cackle' is entered into Google's search engine, the images that result illustrate not only the indirect indexical association of 'cackle' with witches (via pictures of ugly, fairy-tale-like witches), but also the strong semiotic association of the term with Clinton specifically (indeed, many of the images revealed are of Clinton herself, depicted in unflattering ways).

Thus, what this analysis reveals is that, in spite of Clinton's laughter being a generic interactional practice, employed by both male and female politicians in the context of broadcast news interviews, it was ultimately perceived and evaluated in gendered, and even sexist, ways in the media and public discourse more generally. Here, we see yet another situation in which the social meanings ascribed to women's public performances of politics – performances that may not in fact be gendered in and of themselves – are shaped and constrained by the social category of gender.

Women 'doing' politics in more egalitarian contexts

Although the bulk of this chapter has focused on how women's performances in politics have been (negatively) perceived and represented in traditionally masculine domains, a remaining question concerns the status of women in political institutions that are more egalitarian in nature and where women are better represented. Following Walsh (2001), Shaw (2013) goes some way towards answering this question in her work on devolved parliaments in the United Kingdom. After the Devolved Assemblies Act of 1998, Scotland, Wales and Northern Ireland were given considerable freedom in their creation of new political institutions, and, in contrast to the House of Commons, women have been involved in their development since their inception, and the assemblies themselves have been quite deliberately constructed in accordance with egalitarian principles. Moreover, because of different kinds of voting practices, there is a better representation of women in these institutions than in the House of Commons. For example, Shaw reports that women hold 40 per cent and 35 per cent of the seats in the National Assembly for Wales and the Scottish Parliament, respectively, with the House of Commons lagging behind with 23 per cent of seats held by women members.[13]

One of the questions Shaw investigated in her study of these devolved parliaments was how women members, relative to their male counterparts, participate in debates. In contrast to her findings in the House of Commons, where female and male MPs behaved differently with respect to 'illegal' turns in debates, in the devolved assemblies' debates, Shaw determined that men and women participated equally (relative to their proportional representation) in both types of speaking turns – 'legal' and 'illegal.' According to Shaw (2013, pp. 85–86), the taking of illegal turns 'was not a gendered activity: men and women spoke or shouted out of turn in proportion to their overall numbers'.

The fact that female *and* male members of the devolved parliaments display similarly combative behaviour in political debates is evidence, according to Shaw, that a 'degree of equality' has been reached in these devolved political institutions due to, among other things, the status of women as founding members and their increased numbers relative to the House of Commons. Instead of being made to feel like 'interlopers' (Eckert 2000), Shaw suggests that the women representatives have the status and confidence in these contexts to participate fully (i.e. also in adversarial ways). Yet, like the case study of Clinton's laughter, Shaw's work on devolved parliaments demonstrates that 'the social category of gender [still] *matters*' (Holmes & Meyerhoff 2003, p. 9, emphasis in original) in terms of perception and evaluation. That is, even though debate participation was *not* a gendered activity, the assessment of this participation *was* gendered. Based on interviews with assembly members, Shaw reports that barracking was viewed as 'unladylike behaviour' and was judged more harshly when done by women than by men: when barracking, the women's voices were deemed 'the more strident voices' (2013, p. 88). Thus, while the 'degree of equality' that Shaw speaks of characterises well women's participation in the discourse of devolved parliaments, it does not extend to the way that gendered norms of intelligibility construct women's adversarial participation in negative ways –as 'unladylike' and 'strident'.[14]

Conclusion

We began this chapter by reflecting on Butler's notion of the 'rigid regulatory frame' – the idea that cultural norms specify a range of practices and behaviours that are intelligible as gendered. Identities are produced within this frame; thus, to depart from the range of norms regarded as culturally appropriate is to run the risk of social and physical penalties and sanctions. The problem for women in institutionalised politics, however, is that there are virtually no subject positions that seem to be free of such penalties and sanctions. Whether in masculinist institutions or more egalitarian ones, women politicians are caught between cultural norms of appropriate femininity and deeply entrenched beliefs that link competence in leadership positions with masculinity. Both the Clinton case study and Shaw's work on devolved parliaments show that women's performances as politicians are evaluated according to a dominant, cultural script steeped in masculine hegemony – a script in which powerful women who vie for leadership positions are damned no matter what they do.[15]

While recent work in language, gender and leadership has moved beyond overly general and essentialist claims about gendered speech styles, demonstrating the complex and dynamic ways that women leaders discursively construct their identities, the persistence of 'biological sex' as a 'powerful categorization device' (Wodak 1997, p. 12) belies the complexity of these identities. Indeed, these practices of 'gender polarization' (Bem 1993) may constitute, to borrow Shaw's (2013, p. 91) words, 'the single main barrier to women's entry into, and progress within, politics'. As Julia Gillard, the Australian Prime Minister between 2010–2013 said in a National Address in 2013, 'Smashing through a glass ceiling is a dangerous pursuit. It is hard not to get lacerated on the way through.'

Notes

1 We draw a distinction between formal, institutional politics – i.e., parliamentary, legislative and government politics – and what might be called 'everyday politics', and in this chapter, we focus on the former.
2 Given space limitations, our review is not exhaustive; rather, we focus on research from Western contexts. However, just as this chapter was going to press, we became aware of a new book by Cameron & Shaw (2016) entitled *Gender, power and political speech*, an investigation of women and language in the 2015 UK general election. As a result, we have been unable to include it in this review. For recent work on women, gender and politics in global contexts, see, e.g. the edited collections by Murray (2010); Raicheva-Stover & Ibroscheva (2014); Wilson & Boxer (2015).
3 See Gibson & Heyse (2010) for a similar argument about Sarah Palin's speech at the 2008 Republican convention.
4 See Sheldon (2015) for an analysis of Clinton's discursive versatility in a town hall meeting where Sheldon argues Clinton is able to 'sidestep the trap of the double-bind'.
5 In attempting to explain the hybrid or 'fractured' nature of women politicians' styles, Walsh (2001, p. 201) suggests that women in leadership positions may be much more likely than their male counterparts to encounter 'competing, and often contradictory norms and expectations'.
6 While the research described up to now focuses on women's political performances as gendered, Wodak (2003) draws attention to the 'multiple identities' enacted by women politicians in the context of the European Parliament, highlighting other relevant dimensions of their identities, such as nationality or political affiliation.
7 See Holmes (2014) for a similar argument about workplace contexts.
8 For a similar case of a symbolically 'feminine' style of leadership being negatively evaluated by mainstream media in France, see O'Grady (2011).
9 Similarly, Clark, Clinton, Gillard, Halonen and Merkel have all had their expressed sexuality called into question, facing accusations that they were lesbians.
10 For details on both collections, see Romaniuk (2013a).
11 See Romaniuk (2014) for an elaboration of this process.
12 Both Thatcher and Gillard have also been frequently characterised according to this 'witch' trope (Johnson 2015).
13 Compare this with the current situation in the US: as of 1 February, 2015, the US ranks 72nd out of 190 countries in terms of the number of women in national legislatures, and women constitute approximately 20% of the country's total political representation: 19.4% in the House, and 20% in

the Senate (IPU 2015). These percentages are but one indication that the public sphere of politics (at least in the US) remains a distinctively gendered culture.
14 Shaw also noted that women who were non-combative were 'seen as ineffectual' (p. 91).
15 Almost ten years have passed since Clinton first ran for the Democratic nomination. When we wrote this conclusion, Clinton had officially announced her Presidential bid for 2016. We believe her recent electoral loss to now President Donald J. Trump speaks to the persistence of the deeply entrenched cultural beliefs about women and politics that we have described in this chapter.

References

Anderson, K V, 2002, 'From spouses to candidates: Hillary Rodham Clinton, Elizabeth Dole, and the gendered office of U.S. President', *Rhetoric and Public Affairs*, vol. 5 no. 1, pp. 105–132.
Appleby, R, 2015, 'Julia Gillard: A murderous rage', in *Discourse, politics, and women as global leaders*, eds. J Wilson & B Boxer, John Benjamins, Amsterdam, pp. 149–167.
Baxter, J, 2012, 'Women of the corporation: A sociolinguistic perspective of senior women's leadership language in the UK', *Journal of Sociolinguistics*, vol. 16, no. 1, pp. 81–107.
Bem, S, 1993, *The lenses of gender*, Yale University Press, New Haven, CT.
Bengoechea, M, 2011, 'How effective is "femininity"? Media portrayals of the effectiveness of the first Spanish Woman Defence Minister', *Gender and Language*, vol. 5, no. 2, pp. 405–429.
Bucholtz, M, 2009, 'From stance to style: Gender, interaction, and indexicality in Mexican immigrant youth slang', in *Stance: Sociolinguistic perspectives*, eds. A Jaffe, Oxford University Press, New York, pp. 146–170.
Butler, J, 1990, *Gender trouble: Feminism and the subversion of identity*, Routledge, New York.
Butler, J, 2004, *Undoing gender*, Routledge, New York.
Cameron, D, 2005, 'Language, gender, and sexuality: Current issues and new directions', *Applied Linguistics*, vol. 26, no. 4, pp. 482–502.
Cameron, D & Shaw, S, 2016, *Gender, power and political speech: Women and language in the 2015 UK general election*, Palgrave Macmillan, London.
Campbell, K K, 1998, 'The discursive performance of femininity: Hating Hillary', *Rhetoric & Public Affairs*, vol. 1, no. 1, pp. 1–20.
Carlin, D B & Winfrey, K L, 2009, 'Have you come a long way, baby? Hillary Clinton, Sarah Palin, and sexism in 2008 campaign coverage', *Communication Studies*, vol. 60, no. 4, pp. 326–343.
Carroll, S J, ed., 2003, *Women and American politics: New questions, new directions*, Oxford University Press, New York.
Carroll, S J, 2009, 'Reflections on gender and Hillary Clinton's presidential campaign: The good, the bad, and the misogynic', *Politics and Gender*, vol. 5, no. 1, pp. 1–20.
Clayman, S E, 2012, 'Conversation analysis in the news interview context', in *The handbook of Conversation Analysis*, eds. J Sidnell & T Stivers, Wiley-Blackwell, Malden, MA, pp. 630–656.
Conroy, M, Breckenridge-Jackson, I, Oliver, S, & Heldman, C, 2015, 'From Ferraro to Palin: Sexism in coverage of female vice presidential candidates in old and new media', *Politics, Groups and Identities*, vol. 4, no. 4, pp. 1–21.
Cotterill, J, 2001, 'Domestic discord, rocky relationships: Semantic prosodies in representations of marital violence in the O.J. Simpson trial', *Discourse & Society*, vol. 12, no. 3, pp. 291–312.
Davies, C E, 2015, 'Twitter as political discourse: The case of Sarah Palin' in *Discourse, politics, and women as global leaders*, eds. J Wilson & B Boxer, John Benjamins, Amsterdam, pp. 93–119.
Davies, M, 2008, *The Corpus of Contemporary American English: 450 million words, 1990–present*, available from: http://corpus.byu.edu/coca/ [accessed 8 August 2012].
Eagly, A H & Carli, L L, 2003, 'The female leadership advantage: An evaluation of the evidence', *Leadership Quarterly*, vol. 14, pp. 807–834.
Eckert, P, 2000, 'Gender and linguistic variation' in *Language and gender: A reader*, ed. J Coates, Blackwell, Oxford, pp. 64–75.

Edwards, J L, 2009, *Gender and political communication in America: Rhetoric, representation, and display*, Lexington Books, Lanham, MD.

Felderer, B, 1997, 'Do's and don'ts: Gender representation in a political debate', in *Communicating gender in context*, eds. H Kotthoff & R Wodak, John Benjamins, Amsterdam, pp. 371–400.

Gibson, K L, & Heyse, A, 2010, '"The difference between a hockey mom and a pit bull": Sarah Palin's faux maternal persona and performance of hegemonic masculinity at the 2008 Republican National Convention', *Communication Quarterly*, vol. 58, no. 3, pp. 235–256.

Gomard, K & Krogstad, A, 2001, *Instead of the ideal debate: Doing politics and doing gender in Nordic political campaign discourse*, Aarhus University Press, Åarhus.

Hall, LJ & Donaghue, N, 2013, '"Nice girls don't carry knives": Constructions of ambition in media coverage of Australia's first female Prime Minister', *British Journal of Social Psychology*, vol. 52, no. 4, pp. 631–647.

Hepburn, A & Bolden, G B, 2013, 'The conversation analytic approach to transcription', in *The handbook of conversation analysis*, eds. J Sidnell & T Stivers, Blackwell, West Sussex, pp. 57–76.

Hill, J, 2005, 'Intertextuality as source and evidence for indirect indexical meanings', *Journal of Linguistic Anthropology*, vol. 15, no. 1, pp. 113–124.

Holmes, J & Meyerhoff, M, 2003, 'Different voices, different views: An introduction to current research in language and gender', in *The handbook of language and gender*, eds. J Holmes & M Meyerhoff, Blackwell, Malden, MA, pp. 1–17.

Inter-Parliamentary Union, 2015, available from: http://www.ipu.org/wmn-e/classif.htm [accessed 26 April 2015].

Jamieson, KH 1995, 'Hillary Clinton as Rorschach test', in *Beyond the double bind: Women and leadership*, ed. K H Jamieson, Oxford University Press, New York, pp. 22–52.

Johnson, C, 2015, 'Playing the gender card: The uses and abuses of gender in Australian politics', *Politics & Gender*, vol. 11, no. 2, pp. 291–319.

Lakoff, R, 2003, 'Language, gender, and politics: Putting "women" and "power" in the same sentence', in *The handbook of language and gender*, eds. J Holmes & M Meyerhoff, Blackwell, Malden, MA, pp. 161–178.

Lünenborg, M & Maier, T, 2015, 'Governing in the gendered structure of power: The media discourse on Angela Merkel and her power-driven leadership style', in *Discourse, politics, and women as global leaders*, eds. J Wilson & B Boxer, John Benjamins, Amsterdam, pp. 275–291.

Mäkelä, J, Isotalus, P, & Ruoho, I, 2015, 'The ball is in the women's court: The portrayal of Finnish women as political leaders in newspapers' in *Discourse, politics, and women as global leaders*, eds. J Wilson & B Boxer, John Benjamins, Amsterdam, pp. 293–313.

Martin Rojo, L, 2006, 'Gender and political discourse' in *Encyclopaedia of languages and linguistics*, ed. K Brown, Elsevier, Oxford, pp. 742–749.

McElhinny, B, 1995, 'Challenging hegemonic masculinities: Female and male police officers handling domestic violence', in *Gender articulated: language and the socially constructed self*, K Hall & M Bucholtz, Routledge, New York, pp. 217–243.

Murray, R, 2010, 'Introduction: Gender stereotypes and media coverage of women candidates', in *Cracking the highest glass ceiling: A Global Comparison of women's campaigns for executive office*, ed. R Murray, Praeger, Santa Barbara, CA, pp. 3–28.

Ochs, E, 1992, 'Indexing gender', in *Rethinking context: Language as an interactive phenomenon*, eds. A Duranti & C Goodwin, Cambridge University Press, Cambridge, pp. 335–358.

O'Grady, G, 2011, 'The unfolded imagining of Segolene Royal', *Journal of Pragmatics*, vol. 43, no. 10, pp. 2489–2500.

Raicheva-Stover, M & Ibroscheva, E, 2014, *Women in politics and media: Perspectives from nations in transition*, 3rd ed., Bloomsbury, London.

Ritchie, J, 2013, 'Creating a monster: Online media constructions of Hillary Clinton during the Democratic Primary Campaign, 2007–8', *Feminist Media Studies*, vol. 13, no, 1, pp. 102–119.

Romaniuk, T, 2009, 'The "Clinton cackle": Hillary Rodham Clinton's laughter in news interviews', *Crossroads of Language, Interaction, and Culture*, vol. 7, pp. 17–49.

Romaniuk, T, 2013a, *Cracks in the glass ceiling?: Laughter and politics in broadcast news interviews and the gendered nature of media representations*, unpublished PhD dissertation, York University, Toronto.

Romaniuk, T, 2013b, 'Interviewee laughter and disaffiliation in broadcast news interviews', in *On laughing: Studies of laughter in interaction*, eds. P Glenn & E Holt, Bloomsbury, London, pp. 201–220.

Romaniuk, T, 2014, 'Text trajectories and media discourse: Tracking gendered representations in presidential politics', *Gender and Language,* vol. 8, no. 2, pp. 245–268.

Romaniuk, T, 2016, 'On the relevance of gender in the analysis of discourse: A case study from Hillary Rodham Clinton's presidential bid in 2007–2008', *Discourse & Society*, vol. 27, no. 5, pp. 533–553.

Ross, K, 2014, 'A nice bit of skirt and the talking head: Sex, politics, and news' in *The Routledge companion to media and gender*, eds. C Carter, L Steiner & L McLaughlin, Routledge, New York, pp. 290–299.

Schegloff, E A, 2009, *Sequence organization*, Cambridge University Press, Cambridge.

Schegloff, E A & Lerner, G H, 2009, 'Beginning to respond: Well-prefaced responses to wh-questions', *Research on language and social interaction,* vol. 42, no. 2, pp. 91–115.

Schiffrin, D, 1987, *Discourse markers,* Cambridge University Press, Cambridge.

Shaw, S, 2000, 'Language, gender and floor apportionment in political debates', *Discourse & Society,* vol. 11, no. 3, pp. 401–418.

Shaw, S, 2006, 'Governed by the rules?: The female voice in parliamentary debates', in *Speaking out: The female voice in public contexts,* ed. J Baxter, Palgrave Macmillan, Basingstoke, pp. 81–101.

Shaw, S, 2013, 'Gender and politics in the devolved assemblies', *Soundings: A Journal of Politics and Culture,* vol. 55, no. 1, pp. 81–93.

Sheldon, A, 2015, '"Thank you for heckling me": Hillary Rodham Clinton's discursive management of her public persona, her political message and the "Iron my shirt!" hecklers in the 2008 presidential election campaign', in *Discourse, politics, and women as global leaders*, eds. J Wilson & B Boxer, John Benjamins, Amsterdam, pp. 195–216.

Stubbs, M, 1996, *Text and corpus analysis: Computer-assisted studies of language and culture*, Blackwell, Oxford.

Talbot, M, Atkinson, K, & Atkinson, D, 2003, *Language and power in the modern world,* University of Alabama Press, Tuscaloosa, AL.

Tannen, D, 2008, 'The double bind', in *Thirty ways of looking at Hillary,* ed. S Morrison, Harper Collins, New York, pp. 126–139.

Trimble, L & Treiberg, N, 2010, 'Either way, there's going to be a man in charge', *Cracking the highest glass ceiling: A global comparison of women's campaigns for executive office,* ed. R Murray, Praeger, Santa Barbara, CA, pp. 115–136.

van Zoonen, L, 2006, 'The personal, the political and the popular: A woman's guide to celebrity politics', *European Journal of Cultural Studies,* vol. 9, no. 3, pp. 287–301.

Walsh, C, 2001, *Gender and discourse: Language and power in politics, the church and organizations*, Longman, London.

Wilson, J & Boxer, B, eds., 2015, *Discourse, politics, and women as global leaders,* John Benjamins, Amsterdam.

Wilson, J & Irwin, A, 2015, '"Why can't a woman be more like a man?": Margaret Thatcher and the discourse of leadership', in *Discourse, politics, and women as global leaders,* eds. J Wilson & B Boxer, John Benjamins, Amsterdam, pp. 21–41.

Wodak, R, 1997, 'Introduction: Some important issues in the research of gender and discourse', in *Gender and discourse,* ed. R Wodak, Sage, London, pp. 1–20.

Wodak, R, 2003, 'Multiple identities: The roles of female parliamentarians in the EU Parliament', in *The handbook of language and gender*, eds. J Holmes & M Meyerhoff, Blackwell, Malden, MA, pp. 671–698.

35
Queering multilingualism and politics
Regimes of mobility, citizenship and (in)visibility

Tommaso M. Milani and Erez Levon

Introduction

In June 2014, Harriet Nakigudde, a Ugandan self-identified lesbian in the UK, was denied refugee status on the grounds of sexual orientation, and consequently deported by the British Home Office, because she had been 'single for five years', and hence could not convince immigration officials that she was 'really' lesbian (Morgan 2014). A perhaps less tragic, but nonetheless painful, story is that of Dario Kosarac, who 'recounts his feelings of never totally belonging in Bosnia because his parents were of mixed Serbian-Croatian ethnic backgrounds; and never being totally accepted in the USA because he was from Bosnia and is gay' (*LGBT Asylum News* 2011). By the same token, in a series of interviews with anthropologist David Murray (2014), a Nigerian man called Odu shared his distressing experience of linguistic anomie ensuing from a tension between resisting sexual-identity categories and the necessity of embracing the category 'gay' in order to gain refugee status in Canada. Finally, a South African same-sex couple on their way to Reunion was recently 'harassed, intimidated and humiliated' (DeBarros 2014) by a border official at O R Tambo international airport in Johannesburg after they presented their identity documents together at passport control. According to a news report, the official asked the couple who was the 'man' and who the 'woman' in the relationship, and went on to question 'who put whose penis in whose anus, and how it felt' (DeBarros 2014).

These are telling examples of three main points we want to make in this chapter. First, they illustrate that sexuality plays a key role in the (re)production of specific *regimes of mobility*. Openly identifying as gay or lesbian and being able to 'prove' such sexual identities can be the *sine qua non* for being granted the right to stay in a particular socio-political space, and being invested with some degree of political recognition, such as citizenship. Second, they demonstrate that there is an *affective element* that exceeds well-established understandings of citizenship as a contract of rights and duties between an individual and one or more political entities. A passport is not enough of a warrant for the right to be treated equally irrespective of sexual orientation, nor is a passport a good indicator of the emotional pushes and pulls between different, conflicting feelings of belonging. Third, these examples remind us that semiosis – not only language, but also images and body movements – plays a pivotal function in the regulation of the relationships between sexuality, mobility and citizenship: in some contexts, using the identity categories gay or lesbian as signifiers of one's sense of selfhood may be the only way through which to become *visible*, and consequently be *recognised* by the state. In this sense, knowing which identity labels to use, and when, works as a shibboleth that determines who is allowed to be included in a polity and who instead should be excluded. But, of course, the same visibility and recognition may also be springboards to harassment, humiliation, violence and expulsion (see also Kerfoot and Hyltenstam (in press) for a discussion about the relationships between mobility and visibility).

Against this backdrop, the aim of the chapter is to investigate the intersections of mobility, sexuality and citizenship, and the role played by multilingualism and multi-semioticity in mediating such relationships. In addressing these nexus points, we aim to offer a fresh, *queer* perspective on the growing scholarship on language and citizenship, an important body of work that has nonetheless largely ignored the gendered and sexual facets of the politics of mobility. We also believe that a tight analytical focus on multilingualism and multi-semioticity could constitute a new analytical contribution to the budding field of *queer migration* (e.g. Luibhéid & Cantù 2005), an interdisciplinary enterprise that has, however, paid relatively 'little attention [...] to the border-zones of linguistic and sexual contact, and the attendant struggles for meaning and belonging that are produced through this contact' (Murray 2014, p. 3; see however Cashman 2015 for a notable exception).

We begin with a discussion of the concept of citizenship, and how it has been employed in recent sociolinguistic scholarship. In reviewing the existing literature, we highlight the heuristic potential of the notion of *belonging* as a broad conceptual umbrella that encapsulates the relationships between mobility, sexuality and the domain of the affective. We then move on to offer a concrete example of the ways in which sexuality, multilingualism and mobility intersect in a recent documentary about a group of Palestinian gay men who leave the Occupied Territories. The chapter ends with a discussion of the double bind inherent in a liberal politics of citizenship that dispenses rights and recognition on the basis of (self-) ascription to pre-determined sexual-identity categories.

Language, citizenship and belonging

Debates about language and culture tests for the naturalisation of migrants are perhaps the most fraught discursive terrain in which frictions between mobility and the multilingual diversity that comes with it, as well as forms of surveillance geared to the (re)production of an unachievable monolingual national ideal, have manifested themselves in the first ten years of the twenty-first century (see Horner 2015 for an overview in the European context). Typically involving the terms of citizenship and/or nationality, these discussions revolve around the criteria to be employed by state institutions and their delegated agencies in order to determine which of 'them' (migrants) is most like 'us' and can be officially recognised as part of 'our' polity on 'our' terms.

Part of the problem in analysing these debates lies in the conflation – confusion even – between nationality and citizenship in popular parlance. To be an Italian national, the argument goes, is synonymous with being an Italian citizen, which, in turn, boils down to the wielding of a particular passport. Nationality and citizenship, however, belong to different semantic fields. The former is strongly related to the idea of the nation, an imagined sense of commonality (re)produced through a variety of banal material artefacts (e.g. the national flag) and discursive performances (e.g. the personal pronouns 'we' and 'our' in the daily press) (Billig 1995). The latter, in contrast, carries historical links with forms of political agency in matters pertaining to the Greek *polis* – the city. So, while nationality might be more indicative of a symbolic inclusion in an 'imagined community' (Anderson 1983) – the in-group of the national 'we' – citizenship suggests forms of participation for the common good. Of course, we might wonder whether such political agency is at all possible for those who lack prior symbolic recognition (see also Wodak 2012).

In order to account for the complex connections between symbolic recognition, material structures, and people's practices, political theorist Engin Isin proposes a tripartite model of citizenship as *status, habitus* and *acts.* As *status,* citizenship is a form of membership, usually in the (nation-)state. In this sense, citizenship is a social contract about the rights and duties between an individual, and one or several states. Looking exclusively at citizenship-as-status, however, might unnecessarily limit our analytical range to state-level legislation, obscuring the dynamics through which individuals *acquire* and consequently *enact* citizenship in their daily lives. The understanding of citizenship as a form of embodied practice is informed by: (1) Bourdieu's theorisation of *habitus* as 'systems of durable, transposable dispositions ... which generate and organise practices and representations' (1980, p. 53; see also Unger 2013); and (2) Foucault's (1991) notes on governmentality, that is, 'conduct of conduct' (Gordon 1991, p. 48; see also Milani 2009; Kauppinen 2013). In this sense, citizenship is not so much the sum of the rights individuals are granted and the duties they must comply with; nor is it a position endowed on an individual by the state upon fulfilment of certain requirements (e.g. naturalisation) – rather, it is a *mode of conduct* that is acquired through a multiplicity of 'routines, rituals, customs, norms and habits of the everyday' (Isin 2008, p. 17).

That citizenship is a series of norms and behaviours learned through socialisation does not mean that individuals cannot break with *habitus*, or even act without having official *status*. Echoing Butler's (1997, p. 156) critique of Bourdieu that *habitus* fails to take seriously the possibility of agency, opposition or resistance 'from the margins of power', Isin's notion of *acts of citizenship* seeks to capture those performances of radical dissent that often happen 'when one may be led to least expect it – in the nooks and crannies of everyday life, outside of institutionalised contexts that one ordinarily associates with politics' (Besnier 2009, p. 11). And these are performances that might operate at the boundaries of what is considered legal (see, in particular, Milani's 2015b discussion about a protest against Johannesburg Pride in 2012).

Taken together, status, habitus and acts offer a rich picture. There is however an aspect that has not been developed fully by Isin: the *affective/emotional* dimension with which these three aspects of citizenship are imbued. Fortier, for example, has recently pointed out that 'citizenship constitutes a site of emotional investment not only on the part of applicants and "new" citizens but also on the part of the state' (2013, p. 697). The state differentiates between desirable and undesirable bodies, turning the former into citizens and expelling the latter; it also 'produces itself as desirable' (*ibidem*), through affective processes such as naturalisation ceremonies and their preparations. A cogent example is offered in a carefully nuanced ethnographic account of a migrant's journey to British citizenship (Khan & Blackledge 2015). UK citizenship applicants are expected to acquire a monoglot, authoritative discourse that 'demands unconditional allegiance' (Bakhtin 1981, p. 343) to the nation-state. But, as Khan and Blackledge (2015, p. 402) point out, the applicants' acquisition of the oath of allegiance is not the manifestation of habitus change in that 'they may be moving their lips without uttering the authoritative text'. This, in turn, leads us to wonder '[w]hether the ceremony had created a greater sense of belonging and made becoming British more meaningful' (*ibidem*). Either way, the silent lip movements are important acts of resistance against the affective inculcation promoted by the nation-state. The UK might be producing British citizenship as desirable, but, in Khan and Blackledge's study, it is nothing but a valuable commodity – a *status* – that needs to be achieved by playing the rules of the game, seemingly not involving any deeper emotional attachment (*habitus*).

Granted, emotions are not reducible to affective states with ontological stability, but, as Ahmed emphasises, have the performative capacity to 'do things, [...] align individuals with communities – or bodily space with social space – [and] mediate the relationship between the psychic and the social, and between the individual and the collective' (Ahmed 2004, p. 119). Taking a performative approach to emotions, Milani (2015b) investigated a protest against the annual pride parade in Johannesburg enacted by *One in nine,* an activist group of mainly black women. The analysis demonstrates how the mobilisation of shame enabled the *One in nine* to:

> crack and perturb the very idea of a South African lesbian and gay 'community,' [...] [and] questioned a liberal post-apartheid sexual identity politics that recognizes equality for everyone, but has actually benefited sexually non-normative individuals differently depending on the intersections of race and social class.
>
> (Milani 2015a, p. 330)

No doubt, Isin's distinction between status, habitus and acts is analytically useful. But the notion of citizenship itself, we believe, is too static and lacking in heuristic precision to grasp the complex relationships between ideological structures and processes, (the possibility of) individual and collective agency, and the affective components of both of these dimensions. The concept of *belonging*, instead, may provide a more dynamic and multi-faceted tool (see also Caldas-Coulthard & Iedema 2007). In saying so, we have been inspired by Yuval-Davis' (2011) argument that belonging is relational – it involves a subject and an object – the latter being home, the nation, the LGBT community, or any other concrete or symbolic entity. Moreover, belonging is political; it entails constant negotiation as well as 'the dirty work of boundary maintenance' (Favell 1999, cited in Yuval-Davis 2011, p. 20). Such border policing – which may be physical and/or symbolic – 'involve[s] not only the maintenance and reproduction of the boundaries of the community of belonging by the hegemonic political powers (within and outside the community) but also their contestation, challenge and resistance by other political agents' (Yuval-Davis 2011, p. 20). People's attachments (or detachments) are also affective, multidimensional, multi-scalar, and multi-temporal; not only do these connections involve a degree of emotional investment, but they also relate to different objects, spaces and times that may be in conflict with one another.

It is specifically because of the affective dimension it encodes that belonging is, in our view, particularly apt for a discussion of the relationship of multilingualism, mobility and sexuality. As Cameron and Kulick (2003) remind us, sexuality cannot and should not be reduced to explicit linguistic acts of self, or other identifications such as heterosexual, gay, bisexual, asexual, and so on. It should also include the domain of desire. The distinction between *identity* (what the individual identifies with) and *desire* (what the individual longs for) is not a terminological triviality. Foucault reminds us that the congealment of erotic desires and practices into specific identities (homosexual/heterosexual) is part and parcel of a specific power/knowledge configuration that aims to rule and control modern subjects in capillary ways, through subtle, but no less pernicious, forms of (self-)monitoring. For, as Cuddon explains, '[k]nowledge gives one power to make valid or invalid truth claims about specific "subjects" as well as to control what can be said about them' (2013).

Foucault's reflections are particularly useful for an understanding of the sexual regimentation of mobility that is under investigation in this chapter. Sexual-identity based asylum/refugee legislation and its implementation performatively bring into being a regime of truth that regulates what counts as 'acceptable' versus 'deviant' sexual subjectivities: the only way asylum/refugee applicants can receive political recognition is by openly embracing a non-normative sexual-identity category, 'coming out' and thus making themselves visible and intelligible to the state. Such regulatory processes simplify individuals' lived experiences, whose sexual self-identification (e.g. as heterosexual) may be at odds with their sexual desires and practices (e.g. their erotic involvement with both men and women). They also fail to account for the constraints of making the self seen and heard as a non-normative sexual being, including 'the ongoing difficulties to express oneself as a non-heteronormative subject, and to find the words to do so without fear of repression, rejection, ridicule or misunderstanding; especially since words may not be the only way we tell this story' (Ricard 2014, p. 50). Or, as we will see below, since there might be tensions between the *ideological affordances* offered by different languages in a refugee applicant's linguistic repertoire, as is the case with the different historical baggage carried by Hebrew versus Arabic in relation to non-normative sexualities.

A methodological note: why *The invisible men*? Why a documentary?

The examples that are analysed below are taken from *The invisible men*, a documentary by the Israeli filmmaker, Yariv Mozer, which tells the story of three gay Palestinians – Louie, Abud and Fares – and their lives hiding in Tel Aviv. Winner of several film awards, it received strong opposition from many international critics of the Israeli occupation of the Palestinian Territories, and the attendant homonationalist discourses that paint Israel as a beacon of sexual liberation in the Middle East vis-à-vis a retrograde homophobic Palestinian society.

Admittedly, the choice of a cinematic text is not particularly common in either the work on language and citizenship, or in queer-migration scholarship, both of which have tended to investigate policy documents, interview data and ethnographic field notes. However, following developments in sociolinguistics and Critical Discourse Analysis (e.g. Fairclough 1995; Kelly-Holmes & Milani 2011; Forchtner et al. 2013), we argue that media texts are no less important than any other linguistic/discursive output. They constitute prisms that 'reflect their time and [...] representations of particular contexts of production', and so 'can contribute to the understanding of past and present developments and societal forms of expression' (Pollak 2008, p. 77). Specifically because of their claims to truth, objectivity and credibility, documentaries in particular 'play a significant part in the production and reproduction of societal images and in the formation, affirmation or contestation of world views' (*ibidem*).

Doing citizenship – (re)negotiating belonging

The principal goal of our analysis is to illustrate how citizenship is not a static property or state of being, but rather an interactional accomplishment. Citizenship is something that individuals repeatedly claim and contest as they negotiate between their own sense of attachment and affiliation, and the strictures imposed by dominant social, cultural and institutional forces. We have argued that capturing this more dynamic and processual understanding of citizenship requires reconceptualising it as one type of a broader phenomenon that Yuval-Davis (2011) labels the *politics of belonging*. That said, we nevertheless believe that Isin's (2008) tripartite model of citizenship as comprised of status, habitus and acts, provides a useful heuristic for investigating how citizenship is negotiated in specific interactional contexts. In what follows, we therefore adopt Isin's framework and examine how individuals struggle to define their own status, habitus and acts as a way of ultimately achieving a sense of national belonging.

That we illustrate our arguments with the example of sexuality and belonging in Israel/Palestine is not accidental. For decades, struggles for recognition and for cultural and political legitimacy have been particularly heightened in the region. Without going into a discussion of the various social and historical reasons for this (though see, e.g. Biale 1997; Kimmerling 2001; Shafir & Peled 2002; Pappé 2006, 2012; Levon 2010), the situation today is one where a supposedly 'progressive' and 'Western' Israel is set in symbolic opposition to a more 'traditional' and 'Middle Eastern' (i.e. Muslim) Palestine.[1] Sexuality is often recruited to embody this contrast, pitting the enfranchisement of lesbian and gay citizens of Israel against the discrimination and violence experienced by lesbians and gays in Palestine. As an ideological schema, this dichotomy erases a huge amount of variation in actual lived experience. While it is true that lesbian and gay Israelis enjoy a wide range of legal rights and protections that are denied to those in the Palestinian territories, there nevertheless still exist institutionalised patterns of sexuality-based discrimination in Israel (e.g. Walzer 2000; Levon 2010), particularly outside Tel Aviv and for those individuals who do not conform to a homonormative configuration of lesbian or gay sexuality (Seidman 2002; Duggan 2002).[2] Nevertheless, a belief in Israel as a 'haven' for lesbians and gays has become a powerful trope both in the region and further afield, and to a certain extent has become part of the way in which Israeli society is imagined. Lesbian and gay Palestinians, however, panic this imagining because they sit uneasily in relation to Israel's other dominant (and foundational) discourse, that of Jewish ethno-nationalism (Shafir & Peled 2002). Israel, after all, is, and remains, a Jewish state, and all claims to belonging are contingent on prior acceptance into the Israeli polity – an acceptance that is granted on ethno-national terms. Lesbian and gay Palestinians in Israel thus find themselves in the position of having to discursively negotiate the borders between what it means to be Israeli and what it means to be Palestinian in order to belong as non-heterosexuals.

We find a clear example of this type of negotiation in the practice of Louie, one of the principal protagonists of *The invisible men*. Louie is from Nablus in the West Bank, and has been living as an undocumented migrant in Tel Aviv for over ten years. Towards the beginning of the film, Louie is shown seeking advice about applying for political asylum based on his sexuality. The lawyers who Louie speaks to explain that the request for asylum has to be made to a foreign country (i.e. not Israel) since the Israeli government does not consider asylum applications from Palestinians (for whatever reason). Despite his reticence to be forced to leave what he describes as 'his culture' and 'his land', Louie ultimately completes and submits his application for political asylum abroad. Immediately preceding excerpt (1), Louie receives a letter informing him that his application has been successful for asylum in an un-named country. Louie responds to this news as follows:

Transcriptions follow a simplified version of the conventions described in Jefferson (2004).

(1) Louie: tišma yeš po ba'aja retsinit (3) mamaš ba'aja retsinit (3) kehilu benadam še hu nolad ba'arets (1) ani noladeti ba'arets (.) ani nola- le'umat još li kehilu (.) ata jode'a še benadam nolad ba-bet xolim xatimat medinat israel naxon (.) ani jehere lexa jěš li etsli ba-baj- ba-n ba-tik (.)thailandi još lo zxujot la'avod po la-lexet laxzor xofši etiopim ha-kol (.) ani še noladeti ba-arets (.) azov lo noladeti be-Tel Aviv noladeti be-šxem ein li zxujot lehijot po ba-arets?
listen there's a serious problem here (3) a really serious problem (3) like a person who was born ba-arets *((in Israel)) (1) I was born* ba-arets *((in Israel)) (.) I was bor- I mean I have a like (.) you know when someone is born in the hospital a stamp from the Israeli government right (.) I'll show you I have it at ho- in my- in my bag (.) a Thai has rights to work here to go to come back no problem Ethiopians everything (.) me that was born* ba-arets *((in Israel)) (.) fine I wasn't born in Tel Aviv I was born in* šxem *((Nablus)) I don't have rights to be here* ba-arets *((in Israel))?*

Yariv: (2) kol ha-zman ata mexake la-hizdamnut ha-zot ve hine ata mekabel et ha-hizdamnut ve axšav ata xošev pa'amajim?
(2) all the time you're waiting for this opportunity and here you get the opportunity and now you're having second thoughts?

Louie: ani ma'adif lehijjot po kol ha-zman bet ha-sohar (.) ze'u (.)ba-sof ani: ani jestader po bexlal
I prefer to be here all the time in jail to go there (.) and that's it (.) in the end I'll manage here

(Louie and the filmmaker, Yariv, in *The invisible men*)

Confronted with the concrete possibility of expatriation, Louie claims that *there's a serious problem here*. He goes on to describe how the root of this *problem* is the perceived inequity of forcing someone who was *born in Israel* to seek refuge abroad, while *Ethiopians* and foreign workers from Thailand can remain. It is interesting to note that when claiming his (birth)right to remain in Israel, Louie continually refers to the country with the colloquial term *ha-arets* (Heb. 'the land'). While it is true that this is the most common term used to refer to Israel in informal spoken Hebrew, the use of *ha-arets* by Louie is somewhat marked. For one, it is a term that carries connotations of Jewish nationalism with it, making implicit reference to the Zionist project of 'enracination' in the (Promised) land (e.g. Almog 2000). It is also a term that Louie uses nowhere else. Throughout the rest of the film, Louie either refers to *medinat Israel* (Heb. 'the State of Israel') or specifically to Tel Aviv, or makes more oblique reference to *po* (Heb. 'here') versus *šam* (Heb. 'there'). But what is most striking about Louie's use of *ha-arets* is what he uses it to refer to. Four times in excerpt (1), Louie states that he was born in Israel, though he goes on to admit that he was not born in Tel Aviv but in Šxem (Heb. 'Nablus'), a city in the West Bank.[3] In making this claim, Louie effectively re-designates Nablus as part of Israel proper, allowing him to assert his right to remain in the country by virtue of his *status* as a citizen (exemplified in the extract by the official stamp on Louie's birth certificate). Louie's doing so would be commonplace were it not for the fact that Nablus sits across the border from Israel in the occupied West Bank. Louie's claim to citizenship is thus a dissident act (Isin 2008), one which attempts to destabilise existing political borders so as to enact a new definition of the national polity to which he belongs. Note that our claim that Louie works to assert his status as a citizen via a discursive renegotiation of the Israeli border does not imply that he is successful in this regard. Louie's capacity to redefine the terms of Israeli citizenship (at least from the point of view of the state) is tightly constrained by ideological and institutional forces beyond his control. What interests us in (1), however, is not so much whether Louie's claim to citizenship is recognised. Instead, we focus on how the very act of claiming is part of what constitutes Louie's own sense of belonging.

While we take excerpt (1) to illustrate how language can be used to actively negotiate *citizenship-as-status*, we argue that the interaction in excerpt (2) is an example of contesting and reconfiguring *citizenship-as-habitus*. Immediately prior to the exchange in excerpt (2), Louie is chatting with Abud, another of the main protagonists of the film, about Abud's imminent emigration from Israel after having received asylum abroad. Abud declares that he does not plan to call his parents to tell them he is leaving since they have already made it clear to him that they no longer consider him a member of the family. Louie and Abud have this conversation while walking down the beach-front promenade in southern Tel Aviv. The film then immediately cuts to the two of them walking in the park at the end of the promenade while singing traditional Arabic songs together. As they sit down on the grass, Louie asks Abud if he knows any songs by the popular Egyptian singer from the mid twentieth century, Umm Koulthum. The two of them then begin to sing together (**Arabic** in boldface, Hebrew underlined):

(2) Abud: ((singing)) **illi šufto // xarrif 'anno // qabl ma tšu:fak 'e:najja**
 ((singing)) *what I've seen // tell me about it // before my eyes see you*
 Louie: pšš eize šir jafe ha?
 wow what a beautiful song right?
 Abud: ((singing)) **'omri d'a::ji'**
 ((singing)) *I've been lost all my life*
 Louie: **bti'ref 'abdo kadde:š illi tna'šar sane ho:n? s'a:r li zama:n 'a:jiš ho:n?**
 you know Abdo how long have I been here (.) 12 years? I've lived here for a long time.
 Abud: ((continues singing))
 Louie: ya'ani lo xašavti pa'am exat še ani efgoš eize exad 'aravi ba-roš oto roš ata mevin? lehatxil lašir e- lašir e:: šir be-a'aravit (.)lo xašavti kehilu amarti ze'u ani::: (.)ein li xaverim 'aravim
 and like I never thought even once that I'd meet another Arab with the same mindset do you understand? to start singing (.) e to sing e sing a song in Arabic (.) I didn't think, like, I said, that's it I::: (.) I don't have Arab friends

(Abud and Louie in *The invisible men*)

At the start of excerpt (2), Louie stops singing to comment (in Hebrew) on what a wonderful song it is. Louie's switch to Hebrew here is very much a marked one (Myers-Scotton 1983), given that talk between Louie and Abud, including that immediately preceding excerpt (2), normally takes place entirely in Arabic. What is more, from both a topical and a situation perspective, it is interesting to have a native Arabic speaker switch into Hebrew with another native Arabic speaker when discussing the beauty of an Arabic song. Abud makes no response to the comment, and Louie switches back into Arabic while shifting the topic to a discussion of how long he has been living in Israel. When Abud again fails to reply, Louie

535

switches back to Hebrew and tells Abud that before they met each other, Louie never thought that he would meet another *Arab with the same mindset* and with whom he could *sing a song in Arabic*. Louie concludes by claiming (still in Hebrew) that he had given up on having Arab friends. Though he does not say so explicitly, we are led to understand that all of this changed when Louie met Abud and discovered the possibility of being his 'true self' with another Palestinian.

The content and the form of Louie's comments in excerpt (2) perform a number of semiotic functions. At the most basic level, Louie's assertion that he never thought he would meet another *Arab* with the same *mindset* relies on a presumed incompatibility between homosexuality and Palestinian subjectivity. By accepting this presumed incompatibility as the narrative background to his subsequent comments (Linde 1993; Ochs & Capps 2001), Louie's statements have the effect of reproducing the dominant ideology and of (re) positioning a 'Palestinian habitus' and a 'gay habitus' as mutually exclusive constructs. At the same time, Louie also actively challenges this habitus through the discursive deployment of contrasting chronotopes (Bakhtin 1981). He clearly places his belief in the impossibility of meeting another gay Palestinian in the past in Palestine – a chronotopic node that is implicitly contrasted with the *I-here-now* (Baynham 2003) of his intimacy with Abud performed on an Israeli beach.

Crucially, the very juxtaposition of languages – Arabic and Hebrew – is ideologically relevant for the achievement of concomitant, conflicting negotiations of belonging. On one level, the *I-here-now* intimacy is discursively and visually produced through the proximities of Abud's and Louie's bodies singing Umm Koulthum songs together in Arabic. It is important to note that Umm Koulthum has the status of a near-mythic figure in many Arabic societies, particularly those of the Middle East and North Africa, and her songs are iconic of Arabic culture in the region. So Abud's singing Umm Koulthum's famous love song 'Enta Omri' (You are my life), compounded with Louie's comments, conjure up a moment of Bakhtinian double-voicing: they are the manifestations of these two Palestinian men's declaration of affection for each other; as such, they are also important discursive tactics through which Abud and Louie position same-sex intimacy as legitimately belonging in Arab culture and Palestinian society.

In sum, the interactions in excerpt (2) are simultaneously embodiments of, and acts against, a well-formed habitus (Bourdieu 1986) that views gay subjectivities as irreconcilable with dominant ideas of Palestinian selfhood. The song line 'I've been lost all my life' and the sentence 'I never thought even once I'd meet an Arab with the same mindset' rely on, and hence reproduce, normative conceptualisations of nation and sexuality for their illocutionary force; yet their very vocalisation challenges the validity of such normativity by making same-sex desire and love between two Palestinian men a tangible reality.

What is most interesting, however, is that Louie's semiotic manoeuvring in this regard takes place entirely in Hebrew. This is notable since, as Bakhtin (1981) reminds us, language is never innocuous. Instead, using a particular language serves to position a speaker within a given moral universe and helps to legitimate a speaker's belonging in that socio-semiotic space (Hill 1995). While there might be no attempt on the part of Abud to bring his sense of loss to a closure in Arabic, Louie's use of Hebrew might be symptomatic of an attempted reconciliation of 'gay' and 'Palestinian' with the moral universe of Israeli society. In other words, by using Hebrew to make his arguments, Louie effectively reiterates a belief in the impossibility of gayness in Arabic and instead presents gay subjectivity as an exclusively Israeli (i.e. Western) phenomenon. However, we suggest that Louie's use of Hebrew also serves as an attempt to redefine Israeli habitus itself by locating the behaviour of Umm Koulthum-singing gay Palestinians firmly within its bounds. In this sense, then, Louie's switching to Hebrew not only portrays Israel as the only culture in which his brand of gayness is possible, but also allows him to stake his claim as rightfully belonging in Israeli society.

Conclusions

Isin has urged scholars of citizenship to understand 'how status becomes contested by investigating practices through which claims are articulated and subjectivities are formed' (2008, p. 17). This is precisely what we have sought to do in this chapter, giving a glimpse of certain *acts of citizenship* through which two Palestinian men discursively negotiate struggles for belonging in relation to mobility, space and sexuality. In the first example, we illustrated how Louie contests his (lack of) *status* in Israel via a discursive reconfiguration of *the border*. In the second case, we showed how Abud and Louie make their affection for each other visible, and, in doing so, simultaneously reproduce and contest citizenship *habituses* that view Israel and Palestine as proxies of gay empowerment and repression, respectively.

Such examples are, in our view, powerful empirical testimonies of the dynamic, active and multi-faceted life of the politics of belonging (Yuval-Davis 2011), as produced and negotiated through discursive and multilingual means. The implications of such interactional work, however, should not be overstated, given the far-ranging material and discursive constraints that *regiment* what can be said and done in a particular context. The wall that separates Israel from the Occupied Territories is real, made of cement and barbed wire, and occasionally interrupted by check-points that police Palestinians' movement into Israel. No matter how Abud and Louie redraw the cartographies of desire and belonging in Israel/Palestine, the end of the documentary speaks loud and clear: they are both ultimately forced to leave and seek asylum in a Scandinavian country. Yet their discursive exchanges are fleeting moments of 'cruising utopias' (Munoz 2009), of a queer dream of a different future, perhaps a future that has no future (see Edelman 2004; Halberstam 2012).

Their stories also question an overly hopeful reliance on the rhetoric of *visibility* – we are here; we are gays/lesbians; we want to be recognised as such – as a political strategy for the enfranchisement of non-normative sexualities. For men like Abud and Louie, 'coming out' is not straightforwardly liberating, but instead instantiates a discursive double bind. Coming out is the prerequisite to recognition as non-heterosexual and hence the key to aspiring to Israeli status. However, paradoxically, by coming out, Abud and Louie are forced to become *invisible* as gay in Palestine and as Palestinian in Israel. What is impossible then is the visibility of the intersection of these two axes in either end of the Israel/Palestine dyad.

Notes

1 Sensitive to the highly charged politics of labelling in the region, we use the term 'Israel/Palestine' to designate the entirety of British Mandatory Palestine (i.e. the territory between the Mediterranean Sea and the Jordan River). 'Israel' refers to the internationally recognised borders of the State of Israel, as delineated by the UN Green Line, while 'Palestine' is used to refer to those territories currently under military and administrative occupation by the State of Israel (sometimes also called the Occupied Territories).

2   Same-sex sexual activity is illegal in the Gaza Strip (a remnant of British Mandatory regulations), but legal in the West Bank (having been decriminalized by Jordan in 1951). No anti-discrimination legislation or other legal protections exist for lesbians and gays in Palestine.
3   It is also telling that Louie chooses to use the Hebrew name for the city, which, while current in spoken Israeli Hebrew, is normally dispreferred among Palestinians (as well as people abroad) who instead refer to the city with its Arabic name, Nablus.

References

Ahmed, S, 2004, 'Affective economies', *Social Text*, 22(2), pp. 117–139.
Almog, O, 2000, *The Sabra: The creation of the new Jew*, University of California Press, Berkeley, CA.
Anderson, B, 1983, *Imagined communities: Reflections on the origin and spread of nationalism*, Verso, London.
Bakhtin, M, 1981, *The dialogic imagination: Four essays*, ed. Michael Holquist, University of Texas Press, Austin, TX.
Baynham, M, 2003, 'Narratives in space and time: Beyond "backdrop" accounts of narrative orientations', *Narrative Inquiry*, 13(2), pp. 347–366.
Besnier, N, 2009, *Gossip and the everyday production of politics*, University of Hawai'i Press, Hawai'i, HI.
Biale, D, 1997, *Eros and the Jews: From biblical Israel to contemporary America*, University of California Press, Berkeley, CA.
Billig, M, 1995, *Banal nationalism*, Sage, Thousand Oaks, CA.
Bourdieu, P, 1980, *The logic of practice*, Stanford University Press, Stanford, CA.
Bourdieu, P, 1986, 'The forms of capital', in *Handbook of theory and research for the sociology of education*, ed. J G Richardson, Greenwood, New York, pp. 241–258.
Butler, J, 1997, *Excitable speech: A politics of the performative*, Routledge, New York.
Caldas-Coulthard, C & Iedema, R, eds., 2007, *Identity trouble*, Palgrave Macmillan, Basingstoke.
Cameron, D & Kulick, D, 2003, *Language and sexuality*, Cambridge University Press, Cambridge.
Cashman, H, 2015, 'Intersecting communities, interwoven identities: Questioning boundaries, testing bridges, and forging a queer Latinidad in the U.S. Southwest', *Language and Intercultural Communication*, 15(3), pp. 424–440.
Cuddon, J A, 2013, 'power/knowledge', *Blackwell Reference Online*, available from: www.blackwellreference.com/public/tocnode?id=g9781444333275_chunk_g978144433327517_ss1-183 [accessed 31 March 2017].
DeBarros, L, 2014, 'Joburg gay couple humiliated by airport official', *Mambaonline*, 24 October 2014, available from: www.mambaonline.com/2014/10/24/joburg-gay-couple-humiliated-airport-official/ [accessed 31 March 2017].
Duggan, L, 2002, 'The new homonormativity: The sexual politics of neoliberalism', in *Materializing democracy: Toward a revitalized cultural politics*, eds. R Castronovo & D D Nelson, Duke University Press, Durham, NC, pp. 175–94.
Edelman, L, 2004, *No future: Queer theory and the death drive*, Duke University Press, Durham, NC.
Fairclough, N, 1995, *Media discourse*, Arnold, London.
Forchtner, B, Krzyżanowski, M & Wodak, R, 2013, 'Mediatization, right-wing populism and political campaigning: The case of the Austrian Freedom Party', in *Media talk and political elections in Europe and America*, eds. A Tolson & M Ekström, Palgrave Macmillan, Basingstoke, pp. 205–228.
Fortier, A-M, 2013, 'What's the big deal? Naturalization and the politics of desire', *Citizenship Studies*, 17(6-7), pp. 697–711.
Foucault, M, 1991, 'Governmentality', in *The Foucault effect: studies in governmentality with two lectures by and an interview with Michel Foucault*, eds. G Burchell, C Gordon, & P Miller, University of Chicago Press, Chicago, IL, pp. 87–104.

Gordon, C, 1991, 'Governmental rationality: An introduction' in *The Foucault effect: Studies in governmentality with two lectures by and an interview with Michel Foucault*, eds. G Burchell, C Gordon & P Miller, University of Chicago Press, Chicago, IL. pp. 1–52.

Halberstam, J J, 2012, *Gaga feminism: Sex, gender and the end of the normal*, Beacon Press, Boston, MA.

Hill, J, 1995, 'The voices of Don Gabriel: Responsibility and self in a modern Mexicano narrative', in *The dialogic emergence of culture*, eds. D Tedlock & B Mannheim, University of Illinois Press, Urbana, IL, pp. 97–147.

Horner, K, 2015, 'Discourses on language and citizenship in Europe', *Language and Linguistics Compass*, 9(5), pp. 209–218.

Isin, E F, 2008, 'Theorizing acts of citizenship', in *Acts of citizenship*, eds. E F Isin & G M Nielsen, Zed Books, London, pp. 15–43.

Jefferson, G, 2004, 'Glossary of transcript symbols with an introduction', in *Conversation analysis: Studies from the first generation*, ed. G Lerner, John Benjamins, Amsterdam, pp. 13–31.

Kauppinen, K, 2013, '"Full power despite stress": A discourse analytical examination of the interconnectedness of postfeminism and neoliberalism in the domain of work in an international women's magazine', *Discourse & Communication*, 7(2), pp. 133–151.

Kelly-Holmes, H & Milani, T M, eds., 2011, 'Thematising multilingualism in the media', Special issue of *Journal of Language and Politics*, 10(4), pp. 467–614.

Kerfoot, C & Hyltenstam, K, eds., in press, *Entangled discourses: South–North orders of visibility*, Routledge, London.

Khan, K & Blackledge, A, 2015, '"They look into our lips": Negotiation of the citizenship ceremony as authoritative discourse', *Journal of Language and Politics*, 14(3), pp. 382–405.

Kimmerling, B, 2001, *The invention and decline of Israeliness: State, society and the military*, University of California Press, Berkeley, CA.

Levon, E, 2010, *Language and the politics of sexuality: Lesbians and gays in Israel*. Palgrave Macmillan, Basingstoke.

LGBT Asylum News, 2011, 'Articles', 13 November 2011, available from: http://anti-wycliffite.rssing.com/chan-1375744/all_p84.html [accessed 31 March 2017].

Linde, C, 1993, *Life stories: The creation of coherence*, Oxford University Press, Oxford.

Luibhéid, E & Cantú, L, Jr, eds., 2005, *Queer migrations: Sexuality, U.S. citizenship, and border crossings*, University of Minnesota Press, Minneapolis.

Milani, T M, 2009, 'At the intersection of power and knowlegde: An analysis of a Swedish policy document on language testing for citizenship', *Journal of Language and Politics*, 8(2), pp. 287–304.

Milani, T M, 2015a, 'Language and citizenship: Broadening the agenda', *Journal of Language and Politics*, 14(3), pp. 319–334.

Milani, T M, 2015b, 'Sexual cityzenship: Discourses, spaces and bodies at Joburg Pride 2012', *Journal of Language and Politics*, 14(3), pp. 431–454.

Morgan, J, 2014, 'UK to deport lesbian to Uganda for "being single for five years"', *Gaystarnews*, 9 June 2014, available from: www.gaystarnews.com/article/uk-deport-lesbian-uganda-being-single-five-years090614 [accessed 31 March 2017].

Munoz, J E, 2009, *Cruising utopia: The then and there of queer futurity*, New York University Press, New York.

Murray, D, 2014, 'Queering borders: Language, sexuality and migration', *Journal of Language and Sexuality*, 3(1), pp. 1–5.

Myers-Scotton, C, 1983, 'The negotiation of identities in conversation: A theory of markedness and code choice', *International Journal of the Sociology of Language*, 44, pp. 115–136.

Ochs, E & Capps, L, 2001, *Living narrative: Creating lives in everyday storytelling*, Harvard University Press, Cambridge, MA.

Pappé, I, 2006, *A history of modern Palestine: One land, two peoples*, Cambridge University Press, Cambridge.

Pappé, I, 2012, *The idea of Israel: A history of power and knowledge*, Verso, London.

Pollak, A, 2008, 'Analyzing TV documentaries', in *Qualitative discourse analysis in the social sciences*, eds. R Wodak & M Krzyżanowski, Palgrave Macmillan, Basingstoke, pp. 77–95.

Ricard, N, 2014, 'Testimonies of LGBTIQ refugees as cartographies of political, sexual and emotional borders', *Journal of Language and Sexuality*, 3(1), pp. 28–59.

Seidman, S, 2002, *Beyond the closet: The transformation of gay and lesbian life*, Routledge, New York.

Shafir, G & Peled, Y, 2002, *Being Israeli: The dynamics of multiple citizenship*, Cambridge University Press, Cambridge.

Unger, J W, 2013, *The discursive construction of the Scots language*, John Benjamins, Amsterdam.

Walzer, L, 2000, *Between Sodom and Eden: A gay journey through today's changing Israel*, Columbia University Press, New York.

Wodak, R, 2012, 'Language, power and identity', *Language Teaching*, 45(2), pp. 215–233.

Yuval-Davis, N, 2011, *The politics of belonging: Intersectional contestations*, Sage, London.

36
Language and globalisation

Melissa L. Curtin

Introduction

Taking a critical, transformationalist view of contemporary globalisation, this chapter examines ways in which linguistic practices and ideologies are shaped by – and contribute to – dynamic social conditions in our globalising world. The first section summarises different approaches to understanding globalisation and argues that the *language of globalisation* is central to both the ideological framing and the enactment of globalising processes. The second section considers the *globalisation of language*, focusing on factors that position a language as a 'world language', while also noting the prevalence of 'differential multilingualism'. The third section explores linguistic practices and ideologies situated in specific 'glocalised' contexts. Overall, the chapter highlights that a critical sociolinguistics of globalisation illuminates the need for refined conceptualisations of language, linguistic practices and communicative competencies, and concludes by suggesting ways in which these reconceptualisations might fruitfully inform social-justice-orientated positions of alter-globalisation.

The language (and discourses) of globalisation

What is 'globalisation'?

Generally agreed-upon features of contemporary globalisation include that: (1) it entails a complex set of processes that 'intensify and extensify' the circulation of ideas, goods, information, capital and people; (2) these processes have brought about a 'widening, deepening, and speeding up of global interconnectedness in which the local and global are deeply enmeshed and their boundaries are increasingly blurred'; and (3) consequently, the impacts of globalisation 'can be located on a continuum with the local, national, and regional' (Held et al. 1999, pp. 14–15). Thus, our era of technological globalisation has resulted in an accelerated 'compression of time and space' (Giddens 1990; Harvey 1989), accompanied by a rising 'global imaginary' in which people the world over have a heightened sense of global connectivity (Steger 2013).

As with all labels, however, the term 'globalization' is polysemic and subject to contestation. Common critiques include that it is a fuzzy concept, conflates processes with conditions, and/or is a new buzzword for long-existing economic, political, social and cultural phenomena (e.g. Garrett 2010; Schirato & Webb 2003; Steger 2013). For critical scholars, an over-riding concern is that dominant representations of globalisation elide causality, thus naturalising current processes and conditions as if they were an independent 'techno-economic juggernaut' propelling humankind to inevitable social, political, and economic conditions (Marcuse 2000, p. 23).

While allowing for variation within each grouping, Held et al. (1999) outline three main camps of scholars in the 'great globalization debate': hyperglobalisers, sceptics, and transformationalists. *Hyperglobalisers* emphasise economic globalisation and argue that the 'borderless' neo-liberal global market has ushered in a new epoch with social formations superseding (eventually supplanting) nation-states' economic and political power. However, this new world order is envisioned differently: the optimist camp foresees an emerging global civilisation; the critical camp sees a rising cultural homogenisation with a 'consumerist ideology ... displacing traditional ... ways of life' (Held et al. 1999, p. 4).

Conversely, the *sceptic* camp argues against a historical disjuncture for contemporary economic globalisation. They note that economic liberalisation continues to depend upon national governments' regulatory powers; they also note that there is a continued regionalisation of the economy in three primary blocs: Europe, Asia-Pacific and North America. Overall, then, this camp perceives a continuation of global economic relations, including long-entrenched patterns of inequality and hierarchy.

Transformationalists observe an overall restructuring of global relations wherein the power and function of national governments is continuing yet *shifting* via constant negotiation with public and private entities at local, national, regional and global levels. Also, rather than viewing the economy as the primary force of globalisation, or global processes as mainly West-centric, they note multi-centric networks of interpenetrated, complex global systems: financial, technical, political, cultural, ecological.

Regarding cultural globalisation, hyperglobalisers emphasise pressures towards cultural homogenisation, especially from the spread of American popular culture and Western consumerism. Sceptics, however, see a continued strength of national cultures in contrast to the 'ersatz quality' of thin 'global cultures' (Held et al. 1999, p. 327). Indeed, (ethno) national identification is intensifying in many places as people react to pressures from economic globalisation and rising numbers of immigrants and refugees. Transformationalists hold a third viewpoint, noting an increased 'intermingling of cultures and peoples', which produces a veritable 'global mélange' (Nederveen Pieterse 2015) of 'cultural hybrids and new global cultural networks' (Held et al. 1999, p. 327).

Not surprisingly, popular discourse also carries differing perceptions about globalisation. In a survey of university students in Australia, China, Japan, New Zealand, the UK and the USA, Garrett (2010) found that certain domains were commonly listed – culture, economy, politics/power and communication; however, respondents varied considerably as to whether 'globalisation' carries a positive or negative valence. In Asia, Koh (2005) notes that 'globalisation' has indigenised in various ways. In Korea, *segyehwa* conveys economic liberalisation as well as political, cultural and social open-mindedness. In Japan, *kokusaika* (internationalisation) is cautiously balanced by 'Japanization', to protect national identity while engaging in the global economy. In Thailand, *logapiwatana* signifies spread around the world and change all over the world; however, Thais primarily perceive globalisation as economic. In Singapore, globalisation denotes competitiveness and entrepreneurship, but also creativity and foreign talent. Koh thus concludes that *discourses of globalisation are heteroglossic* (multi-voiced).

Globalisation as a keyword

These different understandings of 'globalisation' remind us that the meaning(s) of any term varies according to how individuals are positioned in particular contexts at particular points in time and in relation to particular ideologies. In fact, 'globalisation' is best understood as a 'keyword' emerging during a period of rapid social change (Williams 1983; Grossberg 2005). As with all keywords, 'globalisation' involves both 'ideas and values'; certain uses are bound together with 'certain ways of seeing culture and society'; and 'the problems of its meaning [are] inextricably bound up with the problems it [is] being used to discuss' (Williams 1983, pp. 12–17). Nevertheless, for 'globalisation' to have purchase as an analytic construct, conceptual usage should be clarified. Rather than taking Williams' historical semantic approach, however, I adopt Steger's (2013) strategy of using different terms when discussing particular facets of globalisation. These terms are *globalisation, globalism* and *globality*, and they are used to differentiate between *processes, ideologies*, and the *resulting conditions* of globalisation.

A working definition of globalisation

Held et al. describe 'globalization' as a set of processes that 'embodies a transformation in the spatial organisation of social relations and transactions – assessed in terms of their extensity, intensity, velocity and impact – generating transcontinental or interregional flows and networks of activity, interaction, and the exercise of power' (1999, p. 16). Thus, globalisation involves flows and networks across space and time as these operate in a dynamic relationship with more spatially delimited processes on local, national and regional levels. Regarding these flows and networks, Appadurai (1990) outlines five primary, intertwined (yet disjunctive) 'scapes' – ethnoscapes, mediascapes, technoscapes, finanscapes and ideoscapes. Importantly, language is central to each dimension.

Finanscapes involve the incredibly rapid movement of global capital. Language is vital to information-based 'New Capitalism', which also relies upon hyper-commodification of language (Heller 2010) and 'discourses of flexibility' (Weiss 2000). Ethnoscapes involve flows of people, including immigrants, guest workers, refugees, tourists and the international elite. These large-scale movements include flows of linguistic repertoires and language ideologies, which both challenge and reinforce longstanding language attitudes and practices. Ideoscapes involve turbulent flows of state and counter-ideologies – including competing discourses of globalism as well as ideologies about language, identity and territory.

Technoscapes, the rapid flows of new and old technologies, both shape and respond to financial flows and are tightly imbricated with mediascapes, the flow of information with increasingly blurred boundaries between news, politics and commodities. Language is clearly central to technoscapes and mediascapes, such as in transnational news (e.g. Al Jazeera, BBC, CNN), the discourse of international organisations (e.g. the United Nations, the European Union, Greenpeace) (Fairclough 2006), and the worldwide flow of popular culture (Otsuji & Pennycook 2010). In fact, to underscore the importance of linguistic/discursive practices in all five dimensions of globalisation, as well as the multi-centric flows of linguistic resources around the world, one may argue for a 'sixth scape': *linguascape*. (Blommaert [2010] similarly argues that language is intrinsic to globalisation.)

Globalism(s)

Globalisms are 'ideologies that endow the concept of globalisation with particular values and meanings' (Steger 2013, p. 104). Steger outlines three main types of globalism with specific political agendas that seek to shape the global imaginary and future conditions of globality: *market globalism, justice globalism* and *religious globalism.*

Religious globalisms are conservative ideologies that envision a single, all-encompassing religious community superseding all state and political structures. While many religions imagine a global unity, religious globalists are understood as extreme fundamentalists. For example, Al Qaeda's discourse of *jihad* and *umma* presents an imagined global community in a struggle against market globalism (Steger 2013). In the United States, Fairclough (2006, 2009) sees an interaction between religious and market globalisms where the 'War on Terror' discourse combines with neo-liberal market discourse, thus 'legitimising' a continued US global hegemony.

Market globalism presents globalisation in reductive neo-liberal economic terms, equating it with trade liberalisation. This discourse is *itself* commodified such as in *Business Week, The Economist, Financial Times* and *The Wall Street Journal* (Steger 2013). Moreover, its iterative dissemination – in media, education, business, and government – forms a hegemonic 'new order of discourse' that idealises a world of consumerism and free markets (Fairclough 2009).[1] This rhetoric of globalisation and competitiveness also absolves governments of responsibility to address structural problems of un/underemployment (Weiss & Wodak 2000). For example, Weiss describes a two-step, transformative argument in globalisation rhetoric. First, confidence in the deregulated financial market guides assessments of all national economic decisions; this is depoliticised by constructing global economic constraints as both necessary and beyond the nation-state's control. Second, these constraints are rendered a *virtue* and all political action is directed towards meeting this economic framework via the 'magic formula' of 'competitiveness and flexibility' (Weiss 2000, p. 48). Globalisation rhetoric especially affects the unemployed who are seen as personally responsible for their plight, and advised to acquire flexible work skills as well as 'flexible minds' through life-long learning (Weiss 2000, p. 35). It also creates a milieu of instability and anxiety for *all* workers, and consequently disciplines the aims of workers and trade unions. Operating as a *doxa* (Bourdieu 1977), then, market globalism largely forecloses considerations of more humane forms of globalisation (Schirato & Webb 2003). However, the hegemony of an ideological discourse is never complete, which brings us to justice globalism.

Justice globalisms is defined in respect to citizens' groups which have long striven for a central role in shaping the economic and political order (Smith 2008). Especially since the late 1990s, however, activists have mobilised to combat neo-liberal practices considered responsible for many of the world's social, political, economic and environmental problems. In the dominant discourse of business, bureaucracies and media, these 'anti-globalization' efforts are repeatedly described as misinformed, disorganised and unrealistic (Schirato & Webb, 2003). However, while some activists focus on local communities and 'de-globalization' (Moghadam 2013), social-justice movements are largely efforts towards *alternative* forms of globalisation based on co-operation and inclusion, *not* economic competition (Smith 2008).

Justice globalism is evidenced in democracy movements, such as in the Arab Spring demonstrations, Taiwan's Sunflower Movement and Hong Kong's Umbrella Movement. It has also been central to Occupy Movements and anti-austerity protests around the world. For example, Martín Rojo (2014) analyses how the *15-M* (or *Indignados*) movement both drew upon and contributed to the discourse of the global justice movement (GJM) by promoting new understandings of politics, citizenship and the economy. Demanding 'Real Democracy Now' and marching under the slogan 'We are not commodities in the hands of bankers and politicians', activists occupied Puerta del Sol, Madrid's central square, along with public spaces in other cities in Spain and Europe. Martín Rojo describes the emergence of 'intertextual chains' (from 2011 to 2013) expressing a solidarity with other protest movements and connecting with the GJM. The display of Arabic and Greek scripts indexed a solidarity with the Arab Spring democracy movements and anti-austerity protests in Greece. A trilingual, hand-made cardboard sign proclaimed 'Truth is with Us' and listed Tunisia, Egypt, Sahara, Palestine, Yemen and Spain – all in Spanish, English and Arabic. English expressions of 'Stop New World Order' and 'People of Europe Rise Up!' called for a new global economic order. The combined message of languages, scripts and symbols signalled a public recognition of diversity and ties across movements, potentially foreshadowing 'another possible world' (2014, p. 648).

'Another World is Possible' is, in fact, the central tenet of The World Social Forum (WSF), which organises an annual forum for tens of thousands of delegates from a broad range of civil organisations around the world. Held as a stark alternative to the elite capitalist World Economic Forum, the convention has been held annually since 2001 – in Brazil, India, Mali, Venezuela, Pakistan, Kenya, Tunisia, Senegal and Canada. It has also spawned many local, national, regional and online social forums. WSF is thus envisioned as:

> an open meeting place for reflective thinking, democratic debate of ideas, formulation of proposals, free exchange of experiences and interlinking for effective action, by groups and movements of civil society that are opposed to neoliberalism and to domination of the world by capital and any form of imperialism, and are committed to building a planetary society directed towards fruitful relationships among Humankind and between it and the Earth.
> (World Social Forum 2016)[2]

However, does the GJM have an *ideological coherence*, with practical alternatives to market globalism? Employing a 'morphological discourse analysis' of materials from 45 organisations associated with the WSF, Steger and Wilson argue that the GJM does have a 'congealing political ideology' with a 'sophisticated alternative vision of global politics' (2012, p. 440). This alternative vision brings us to our third term, 'globality'.

Globality/ies

Whereas *globalisation* concerns complex, interpenetrated (yet disjunctive) social processes and *globalisms* entail ideologies shaping these processes, *globalities* are future social conditions of ever-tightening, global interconnections (Steger 2013). There are many possible globalities (Axford 2013), but two primary, opposing teleologies contrast 'a completely deregulated world economy' versus 'one driven by worldwide solidarity' (Slembrouck 2011, p. 153). That is, do we imagine a social system of globality based primarily on 'individualism, competition, and laissez-faire capitalism' (and exploitation and environmental degradation), or one founded on 'more communal and cooperative norms' (Steger 2013, p. 9)?

In sum, distinguishing between *processes of globalisation, globalisms* and *globalities* helps address shortcomings common to discussions about globalisation. This approach can also unmask ideologies driving neo-liberal global capitalism and encourage consideration of alternative ideologies towards building a more just social world.[3] We now turn to the second main thread of this discussion, the globalisation and hegemonic positioning of certain 'world languages'.

The globalisation of language

World languages (WLs)

According to Ethnologue, there are approximately 7,000 – albeit unevenly distributed – living languages.[4] The 13 most commonly spoken languages – counting both 'native and non-native speakers' (NS and NNS) – are Mandarin, English, Hindi/Urdu, Spanish, Arabic, Malay/Indonesian, Bengali, Portuguese, Russian, Japanese, French, German, and Italian.[5] Yet, a WL is not determined by number of speakers alone. For instance, de Swaan (2001) provides a model in which languages are hierarchised by their 'connectivity', the number of other languages (and speakers) to which a single language is connected via multilingualism. English, with the highest direct connectivity, is the 'hypercentral' WL. There are 11 'supercentral' languages: Arabic, Chinese, French, German, Hindi, Japanese, Malay (Indonesian), Portuguese, Russian, Spanish and Swahili – all but Swahili have over 100-million speakers. These 12 are joined by about 140 other 'central' languages which, together, are spoken by about 95 per cent of humankind. These languages are used in institutions and media, are usually national or official languages, and are highly standardised varieties.

Ammon (2010) ranks the 'global reach' of WLs by their key functions: (1) number of speakers (native and non-native); (2) official status (in countries and international organisations); (3) number of global companies using the language; and, importantly, (4) economic strength of native speakers. While English is the predominant WL, Ammon emphasises the persistent identity function of non-English languages and the *plurality of WLs* used in (mostly) bilateral contexts.

Seidlhofer (2011) agrees that English as an international language (EIL) is an unprecedented phenomenon superseding all WLs in domains of use and global coverage. However, because most English-as-a-lingua-franca (ELF) speakers are 'non-native', she argues that the status of EIL is *not* mainly due to the economic and political power of Anglophone nations, but rather to the global need for a lingua franca. She agrees, however, that users of ELF do not experience a threat to their cultural identities – because ELF is part of a multilingual diversity, not wedded to particular identity/ies (admittedly, however, ELF is linked to the colonial past and to global capitalism). Friedman observes an *increase* in alternative identifications based on immigrant status, regional location and indigenousness, as people search for more stable and rooted identifications; these 'reconfigurations of identification' are forming new hierarchical relations 'reflected in ranked local usages of languages' (2003, p. 744). Thus, despite nationalistic 'language defender' discourses, many scholars foresee little likelihood of shifting from individual/societal multilingualism to Global English only. However, 'all multilingualisms are not considered equal' in our globalising world.

Globalisation and differential multilingualism

In Europe, Gal (2010) observes a shift in the language regime – from 'coercive monolingualism' to 'coercive multilingualism'. This valorisation of multilingualism is due to the need for a 'knowledge society' and to democratic efforts recognising regional languages and conditions of superdiversity. However, Zappettini (2014) sees a heterogeneity in official discourses on multilingualism, with tensions between ongoing reifications of language and static national identities (Europe as a 'sum of its parts') versus languages as new, post-national commodified entities dissociated from identities.

Not surprisingly, different multilingual repertoires are not equally valued – what we might term 'differential multilingualism(s)'. Gal (2010) notes pan-European elite status is usually indexed via proficiency in English, French/German and another language. Wodak, Krzyżanowski and Forchtner (2012) observe that in EU institutions, multilingualism is interactionally situated, with context-dependent factors shaping an individual's 'performing multilingualism'. Sometimes, more prestigious languages (i.e. English, French, German) are used as a strategy of 'hegemonic multilingualism' for setting meeting agendas and managing interactions between participants (who may speak any of the 23 official EU languages). At other times, the goal of efficient communication determines which linguistic resources to use, regardless of a language's relative prestige. Blommaert argues against traditional views of multilingualism altogether (as a co-ordinated use of separate 'languages'), proposing instead the notion of 'truncated multilingualism', with speakers drawing upon 'a complex of *specific* semiotic resources [accents, varieties, registers, genres, modalities], some of which belong to a conventionally defined "language", while others belong to another "language"' (2010, p. 102). Truncated multilingualisms are also not valued equally across contexts (linguistic markets); thus, in the unequal world of contemporary globalisation, some linguistic resources have much greater 'semiotic mobility' than others (2010, p. 3).

Thus, local, regional and global language ecologies are deeply dynamic. The complexity of these ecologies is evidenced in language and globalisation scholars' divergent viewpoints, often summarised using Held et al.'s (1999) typology: hyperglobalists, who focus on global linguistic imperialism and concerns of linguistic homogenisation; sceptics, who observe ongoing processes of linguistic localisation and heterogenisation (language variation and speciation); and transformationalists, who emphasise new, glocalised language mixing (linguistic hybridisation) such that traditional notions of 'bounded language and bounded culture' should be completely refashioned (James 2009; Pennycook 2011).

The hyperglobalists: homogenising WLs?

Despite widespread societal and individual multilingualism, hyperglobalists see the hegemonic spread of English as a homogenising force. The optimistic branch envisions the widespread use of ELF as marching towards the near-utopic development of a Global English 'in which intelligibility and identity happily coexist' (Crystal 2003, p. 22). The more pessimistic branch holds a linguistic imperialism viewpoint, seeing the spread of Global English (especially American English) and Anglophone market globalism as forcing linguistic and cultural homogenisation (Phillipson 1992). Some describe Global English as a 'killer language' responsible for the rapid disappearance of many of the world's languages (Skutnabb-Kangas 2003).

It is true that the world's languages are disappearing at an alarming rate. With one language 'dying' every two weeks on average, linguists estimate that 50 to 90 per cent will no longer be spoken within a hundred years. However, while English did largely supplant indigenous and immigrant languages in *settler* colonies, such as the US and Australia, it is questionable whether the use of English as a WL is exerting direct pressure on indigenous languages elsewhere. Mufwene (2010) asserts that a widespread shift to English, and consequent loss of indigenous languages, is not highly likely to occur in former British *exploitation* colonies, especially in Africa. Rather than experiencing pressures from WLs, ethnic vernaculars are primarily experiencing language-shift pressure from urban vernaculars and regional lingua francas, such as Lingala in the Democratic Republics of Congo, Swahili in East Africa and Town Bemba in Zambia (Mufwene, 2006). In Spanish-speaking Latin America, we see similar processes even in places with much ELF-based tourism, such as in Teotitlán del Valle, Oaxaca, Mexico, where many children are shifting from Zapotec to Spanish.

The sceptics: heterogeneous, localising language processes (language variation and linguistic speciation)

Rather than anticipating the emergence of a homogeneous Global English, this camp focuses on World Englishes (WEs), locally indigenised varieties that are important for national or regional identifications and are 'languages in their own right' and 'testimony to a healthy – Anglophone – glossodiversity' (James 2009, p. 85). These linguists note there has *always* been language spread and language contact, language death and language birth, as well as historical moments in which a dominant lingua franca stretched across vast expanses of territory, such as Latin during the time of the Roman Empire, Arabic throughout the vast Islamic Arabic Empire of the eighth century, and written Chinese (pre-classical, classical and post-classical) during many dynasties in China. And, just as Latin indigenised into new vernaculars (varieties of which were later 'standardised' as national languages), WEs will likely continue to diverge (Crystal 2003). Thus, '[r]ather than driving the world towards monolingualism, the differential evolution of English appears to be substituting a new form of diversity for an older one'; that is, we are likely witnessing language birth as well as death (Mufwene 2010, p. 50). Some scholars tend to celebrate the plurality of WEs. However, these varieties co-exist in unequal, hierarchical relationships (Tupas 2015), in part because 'native Englishes' (where people of European descent are the majority) are legitimised over 'indigenized Englishes' in non-European descent environs (Mufwene 2010).

The transformationalists: a call for new understandings of language, culture and identity

Transformationalist sociolinguists also emphasise the localising processes of language spread. However, with the acceleration of linguistic diversity, multilingualism and (non-standard) language mixing in 'glocalised' linguistic repertoires, these scholars apprehend a *historical disjuncture* in language spread and practices. Rather than presuming homogeneity, stability and boundedness of languages and speakers, transformationalists emphasise an unprecedented degree of linguistic hybridisation, and argue for a paradigm shift in a sociolinguistics of globalisation that takes as a *starting point* the conditions of 'superdiversity' (Blommaert 2010). This brings us to the chapter's remaining thread, examining linguistic practices in specific – globally influenced but locally grounded – contexts.

Linguistic repertoires (and hierarchies) in glocalised contexts

Depending upon interactional contexts, language mixing has been labelled as 'heteroglossia' (Bakhtin 1981), 'translanguaging' (Creese & Blackledge 2010), 'translingual practices' (Canagarajah 2013), 'transidiomaticity' (Jacquemet 2005), 'supervernaculars' (Blommaert

2012), 'language crossing' (Rampton 1995), 'polylingualism' (Jørgensen 2008) and 'metrolingualism' (Otsuji & Pennycook 2010). While some scholars examine linguistic hybridity in educational and other institutional settings, much work focuses on linguistic creativity (particularly by youth) in 'recreational, artistic and/or oppositional contexts' (Blommaert & Rampton 2012, p. 15).

One notable multi-centric flow is that of Global Hip-Hop, which, via 'Hip-Hop indigenization', is paradigmatic of the dialectic of 'cultural globalization' and 'cultural localization' (Alim, Ibrahim, & Pennycook 2009). For example, Auzanneau (2002) describes the linguistic bricolage in the Libreville, Gabon rap scene wherein artists mix French (exonormative and endonormative forms, *verlan* and slang), local languages such as Téké and Fang, and English (standard and African-American vernacular). Hybrid practices vary widely in lexical and code choice as these are made consciously to suit an artist's particular stylisation and situational identification, as well as the poetics and theme of the song. As one example, the lyrics of 'To Kill La Wana', by Siya Po'ossi X, combine (1) Fang, (2) standard urban African-French, (3) non-standard French (slang from France and from local coinage), and (4) a little English, as illustrated in these lines:

> *Voici le quartier pourri, tard le soir, minuit* (standard French; setting the scene)
> *L.B.V. by night* (English; 'LBV' for Libreville; setting the scene)
> *Les bizz en patrouille* ('The bizz on patrol', French slang = 'police' from Fang *biz ma*)
> *Djogué me za bîme wa* ('Clear out or I'll punch you', Fang)
> *J'emprunte un tacla* ('I jump a taxi'; *tacla* = French slang: drops final and resuffixes)
> ('To Kill La Wana' by Siya Po'ossi X 1997)

Combined, these practices signify an identification with a dynamic *culture métissée*, mixing traditional Gabonese and Western elements, while simultaneously differentiating from both traditional society and the dominance of Western societies. The creative use of vernacular languages and 'relexified' French indexes a rooted, urban Gabonese authenticity, simultaneously revalorising these languages in the (g)local hierarchy where standard French is the national language and accepted linguistic norm.

In Nigeria, Inyabri (2016) notes a similar function of linguistic stylisation in Naija Afro Hip-Hop. For example, in the song 'Owusagi', the artist, Wizboy, mixes Igbo (standard and slang), standard Nigerian English, Nigerian Pidgin English and 'core slang' from Nigeria's Eastern state, Anambra. This linguistic bricolage indexes the artist's hyperlocal authenticity, as well as a pan-Nigerian identity that resists 'the linguistic ("English-as-a second-language") hegemony of the establishment' (2016, p. 101). Such glocalised practices mark African Hip-Hop as both *part of* and *distinctive from* other Global Hip-Hop cultures.

Besnier's (2003) study of the linguistic repertoires of Tonga's socio-economically marginalised, transgendered *Leitī* provides another example of 'translocalization'. Despite their rather limited English proficiency, *Leitī* mix English and Tongan to assert their authenticity as (trans)local Tongans, claim a sophisticated cosmopolitan distinctiveness, and index their femininity and transgendered identity. However, mainstream Tongans interpret *Leitīs'* limited English proficiency as *confirmation* that they are 'fake' – as women, speakers of English *and* cosmopolitans – which reinforces *Leitī* marginalisation. For example, during the annual *Leitī* 'Miss Galaxy' beauty pageant, if a contestant speaks in fluent Tongan, she is ridiculed for not using English – the language indexing translocality and femininity. But if she stumbles when searching for a word in English, she is mocked and laughed off the stage for having exposed her 'inauthenticity'.

While creative, hybrid linguistic practices are often exercised by youth cultures and marginalised groups as resistance to hegemonic hierarchies, studies such as Besnier's reveal the limitations of these strategies in bringing about more equitable structural conditions. In addition, especially in globalised business and institution settings where language is viewed as a flexible commodity, Hall (2014) notes that transnational subjects often experience linguistic anxiety; instead of embracing linguistic hybridity, they seek *semiotic stability*, viewing language as rooted in communal identity.

This discussion reveals several key points regarding language and globalisation/glocalisation. One concerns a heated friction between our late modern condition of highly porous boundaries of territory, language and identity versus enduring ideological constructs of their fixity and boundedness. Another point is that linguistic repertoires are ascribed different value (socially, politically, economically) according to the particular, scaled linguistic market(s) in which they are situated. A closely related point is that New Capitalism features an intensified, restructured commodification of language, with language circulating as a 'resource' in a globalised 'linguistic market', with unequal networks and power relations preserving the position of the elites (Heller 2010). These linguistic issues have serious social consequences throughout the world and highlight the need for a more concerted language and globalisation social-justice movement – a point to which we now turn.

Mobilities, human rights, and social inclusion: time for a Language and Globalisation Social Justice Movement (LG-SJM)

According to the World Bank, in 2015, there were over 250 million international migrants worldwide (the vast majority of employment age) and about 20 million refugees.[6] Additionally, there was a record high of 1.184 billion international tourists.[7] Clearly Appadurai's (1990) ethnoscape continues to be a central dimension of globalisation. Thus, many sociolinguists of globalisation emphasise that we are living in a time of unprecedented superdiversity (e.g. Blommaert & Rampton 2012),[8] conditions which raises issues about evaluations of linguistic practices in a broad range of contexts including human rights, transnational migration and employment.

For example, when evaluating asylum seekers' narratives, officials and consultants often use a 'Language analysis for the determination of origin' (LADO) assessment. These frequently entail 'folk linguistic belief and prescriptivism' for determining a person's linguistic 'authenticity' (Eades 2010) and are 'fraught with unexamined assumptions about language, national identity, and communicative competence' (Jacquemet 2009, p. 525). Forensic linguists thus advocate for more sophisticated analyses of asylum seekers' ways of speaking, which take into account porous borders, language variation, and – especially for those with traumatic life histories – the likelihood of more fractured language socialisation and truncated linguistic repertoires. In one case, Blommaert (2009) argues that an asylum seeker was likely misevaluated by the UK Home Office as not 'Rwandan' because of his 'abnormal' linguistic repertoire. The Home Office held the modernist view that all Rwandans should be proficient in the national languages, Kinyarwanda and French. However, 'Joseph' had no formal education, had lived a marginalised existence in several super-diverse areas and had consequently developed a truncated multilingualism. Blommaert cogently argues that, because his truncated multilingualism *supports* his life narrative of enduring ethnic strife, war and genocide, Joseph likely *was* a Rwandan refugee.

Linguists have tried to address government agencies' (mis)use of language analysis to determine country of origin. In June 2004, an international group of linguists drafted a set of guidelines for governments and agencies to consider when conducting LADO assessments. These guidelines were endorsed by professional organisations, including the British Association for Applied Linguistics and the International Association of Forensic Linguists. Unfortunately, neither the UK Home Office nor Sprakab – a Swedish company that provides linguistic analysis services to that office as well as the governments of Canada, Australia and the Netherlands – follow these guidelines (Maniar 2014).

Language proficiency also serves as a gatekeeper for employment for migrants. However, even when migrants have a high level of proficiency in a 'host country's language(s)', there are often penalties for a perceived lack of 'legitimate' communicative competence (Bourdieu 1991). This point is evidenced in many employment contexts which have an 'accent ceiling' effect whereby linguistic discrimination serves as a proxy for other forms of discrimination (Piller & Takahashi 2011). It is also at play when migrant applicants experience a 'linguistic penalty' when striving to convey the equivalence of their foreign work experience during job interviews that follow strict, standardised formats in the name of 'equality' (Roberts 2012).

With the flow of humans, issues of language proficiency and communicative competencies will continue to inhere within a broad range of human-rights' contexts, including asylum hearings, health services, educational opportunities, employment equity and occupational safety, social, economic and political integration, and legal protection. Unfortunately, market globalism largely places the burden of adjustment, linguistic and otherwise, on disadvantaged individuals (e.g. immigrants, service workers in tourism, sex workers) as well as on the global South (e.g. English language education in the Philippines to train overseas Filipino workers, which comprise 10 per cent of the national population; Tupas 2008).

A central question, then, concerns whether or not receiving locales (towns/cities, provinces/states, countries, federations), which for the most part *need* immigrant labour (and taxes) and tourist expenditures, should share the 'communicative burden' of human mobility (Piller & Takahashi 2011). For example, some locales (governments; NGOs) provide free language and/or health education for migrants, such as Australia's federally funded Adult Migrant Education Program (Piller & Takahashi 2011) and Taiwan's distribution of multilingual health literacy materials for new immigrants (Yen & Wu 2014). Another example is that of the 'AMES Australia' non-profit programme,[9] which encourages everyone – the community, business and government, as well as new arrivals – to make necessary adjustments in language training, intercultural pragmatics, employment and social support (Piller & Takahashi 2010). A third example is that of EMPOWER, a non-profit organisation in Thailand organised by and for migrant sex workers (and other activists), whose educational centres offer free classes in language, mental and physical health, law and pre-college education, as well as research programmes on human trafficking.[10]

Although not a panacea for all language and human-rights issues, these programmes can provide inspiration for developing a broader justice-globalism approach towards these challenges. There is no doubt that many critical scholars in discourse studies, linguistic ethnography and sociolinguistics are dedicated to promoting social justice. However, a pressing question is, 'can we do more towards building a language and globalisation social justice movement' (LG-SJM)? This is not to discount the efforts by those working on social-justice issues, such as endeavours documented by the Language on the Move research site 'devoted to multilingualism, language learning and intercultural communication in a transnational world' and focuses on ways in which 'language intersects with consumerism, family life, globalisation, tourism, identity, migration and social justice.'[11] Other efforts include the (still-developing) Society for Linguistic Anthropology's Committee on Language and Social Justice,[12] as well as the Language & Asylum Research Group site (unfortunately no longer updated).[13] Although we face the common challenges of limited time and resources, there is a clear need for critical scholars and other activists to expand the scope and efficacy of their efforts through a more co-ordinated LG-SJM. Ideally, this movement would join the vibrant 'network of networks' and 'movements of movements' of the GJM, working together to promote sustainable, social-justice alternatives for our globalising world.

Concluding comments

Much more could be said about the complexity of language and globalisation in the contexts discussed thus far, as well as about language in many other domains, such as education, the environment, new and traditional media, the military, politics, religion and tourism (e.g. Blommaert 2010; Coupland 2010; Piller 2016). For all contexts, it is perhaps best to think of contemporary globalisation in terms of both continuity and change, with ongoing, multi-scalar tensions between centrifugal and centripetal forces resulting in contestations of authenticity, legitimacy and belonging. Regarding language ideologies, we must continue to argue against enduring Herderian, (ethno)nationalistic ideologies which promote a fixed, triadic relationship between language, people and territory – and argue for a recognition of the communicative validity (as well as brilliant creativity) of different multilingualisms and linguistic hybridisations, and the particular identifications that these afford. Nevertheless, we should acknowledge that some feel a legitimate need for more semiotic stability, for a degree of boundedness of 'language' and of 'identity' in our world of disjunctive flows. These differing needs will continue as dialectical tensions, and should be evaluated according to particular contexts.

Overall, we should consider the importance of the *linguascape* to contemporary globalisation. Discourses of globalisation must be critically examined to unmask ways in which market globalism naturalises a world of increasing socio-economic inequities; alternative discourses of justice globalism should be supported as these strive for a more equitable, interconnected world. As for the globalisation of language, we must recognise that a more just, interconnected world will likely rely upon WLs and multilingualism; nevertheless, efforts can be made to stem the hegemony of particular languages as well as to (re)valorise indigenous language varieties and multilingualisms whose value is restricted to limited linguistic markets. And despite the power of language hierarchies and 'ideologies of boundedness' – or rather, because of these – we should persist in advocating an alternative politics of language that takes into account the many complexities of diverse, and yet locally situated, linguistic practices. Such strategies are called for in this world of contemporary globalisation which is both 'contingent and contradictory'; which both universalises and particularises; which both fragments and integrates; and which engenders co-operation as well as conflict (Held et al. 1999, p. 14).

Notes

1 While Blommaert (2010) lauds Fairclough's (2006) focus on discourse (rather than 'language') in discussing globalisation, he soundly critiques Fairclough's 'theoretically flawed' timeframe of globalization and 'de-historicized' Critical Discourse Analysis of documents concerning education reform in Romania. There are strengths and limitations to both scholars' approaches to language and globalisation. My focus, here, concerns the importance of terminology in understanding processes, discourses, and conditions of 'globalisation,' including that '(market) globalism' naturalises/legitimises neo-liberal economic globalisation as necessary and beneficial.

2 Available from: https://fsm2016.org/en/sinformer/a-propos-du-forum-social-mondial/.
3 There are, of course, other approaches to understanding the complexities of current-day globalisation. Beck, for example, distinguishes between *globalisation* and *cosmopolitanisation*. While often equating 'globalisation' with economic globalisation (promoted by 'globalism' 2006), he has acknowledged political and cultural dimensions (Beck & Grande 2010). His work, however, emphasizes *cosmopolitanisation* (Beck & Grande 2010, p. 417) and distinguishes between two dimensions of cosmopolitanism: (1) 'cosmopolitan imperatives' to address global risks, and (2) a cosmopolitanism of diversity or dynamic intermingling of different modernities. While space precludes addressing cosmopolitan theorisations, this paper generally aligns with Beck and Grande's discussion, such as by discussing the cosmopolitan imperative of language-related justice issues and arguing for a cosmopolitan acceptance of dynamic language practices.
4 Available from: www.ethnologue.com. Counting languages and their speakers is a highly problematic task. Linguists estimate between 5,000 and 7,000 living languages worldwide; Ethnologue estimates 7,102.
5 Arabic, Chinese, and, arguably, Malay/Indonesian may be understood as 'macrolanguages' comprised of closely related varieties without a high degree of mutual intelligibility, yet speakers share a single language identity and a domain such as ethnicity or religion (and script).
6 Available from: https://openknowledge.worldbank.org/bitstream/handle/10986/24012/9781464809132.pdf.
7 Available from: http://cf.cdn.unwto.org/sites/all/files/pdf/annual_report_2015_lr.pdf.
8 Czaika & de Haas dispute that there has been 'a global increase in volume, diversity, and geographical scope of migration'; rather, there is a directional shift with migrants coming from an 'increasingly diverse array of non-European-origin countries concentrating in a shrinking pool of prime destination countries'– the US, Germany, France, Canada, Australia and the Gulf countries (2015, p. 283); thus, the notion of 'superdiversity' may largely be a Eurocentric worldview. This can have serious social justice consequences by marking immigrants and refugees as 'deviating' from an imaginary 'non-diverse' norm (Piller 2016).
9 Available from: www.ames.net.au/about.html.
10 Available from: www.empowerfoundation.org/index_en.html.
11 Available from: www.languageonthemove.com/.
12 Available from: http://linguisticanthropology.org/socialjustice/.
13 Available from: www.essex.ac.uk/larg/Default.aspx.

References

Alim, H S, Ibrahim, A & Pennycook, A, 2009, *Global linguistic flows: Hip-Hop cultures, youth identities, and the politics of language*, Routledge, New York and Oxon.

Ammon, U, 2010, 'World languages: Trends and futures', in *The handbook of language and globalization*, ed. N Coupland, Wiley-Blackwell, Oxford, pp. 101–122.

Appadurai, A, 1990, 'Disjuncture and difference in the global cultural economy', *Theory, Culture & Society*, 7(2), pp. 295–310.

Auzanneau, M, 2002, 'Rap in Libreville, Gabon: An urban sociolinguistic space', in *Black, blanc, beur: Rap music and Hip-Hop culture in the Francophone world*, ed. A-P Durand, The Scarecrow Press, Lanham, MD, pp. 106–123.

Axford, B, 2013, *Theories of globalization*, Polity Press, Cambridge and Malden, MA.

Bakhtin, M M, 1981, *The dialogic imagination*, Texas University Press, Austin, TX.

Beck, U, 2006, *The cosmopolitan vision*, Polity Press, Cambridge and Malden, MA.

Beck, U & Grande, E, 2010, 'Varieties of second modernity: The cosmopolitan turn in social and political theory and research', *The British Journal of Sociology*, 61(3), pp. 409–443.

Besnier, N, 2003, 'Crossing genders, mixing languages: The linguistic construction of transgenderism in Tonga', in *The handbook of gender and language*, eds. J Holmes & M Meyerhoff, Blackwell, Malden, MA, pp. 278–301.

Blommaert, J, 2009, 'Language, asylum, and the national order', *Current Anthropology*, 50(4), pp. 415–441.

Blommaert, J, 2010, *The sociolinguistics of globalization*, Cambridge University Press, Cambridge.
Blommaert, J, 2012, 'Supervernaculars and their dialects', *Dutch Journal of Applied Linguistics*, *1*(1), 1–14.
Blommaert, J & Rampton, B, 2012, 'Language and superdiversity', *MMG Working Paper 12–05*, Max Planck Institute for the Study of Religious and Ethnic Diversity, Göttingen.
Bourdieu, P, 1977, *Outline of a theory of practice*, Cambridge University Press, Cambridge.
Bourdieu, P, 1991, *Language and symbolic power*, Polity Press, Cambridge.
Canagarajah, A S, 2013, *Translingual practices: Global Englishes and cosmopolitan relations*, Routledge, New York.
Coupland, N, 2010, 'Introduction: Sociolinguistics in the global era', in *The handbook of language and globalization*, ed. N Coupland, Wiley-Blackwell, Oxford, pp. 1–27.
Creese, A & Blackledge, A, 2010, 'Translanguaging in the bilingual classroom: A pedagogy for learning and teaching?', *The Modern Language Journal*, *94*(1), pp. 103–115.
Crystal, D, 2003, *English as a global language*, 2nd ed., Cambridge University Press, Cambridge.
Czaika, M & de Hass, H, 2015, 'The globalization of migration: Has the world become more migratory?', *International Migration Review*, *48*(2), pp. 283–323.
de Swaan, A, 2001, *Words of the world: The global language system*, Polity, Cambridge.
Eades, D, 2010, 'Nationality claims: Language analysis and asylum cases', in *The Routledge handbook of forensic linguistics*, eds. M Coulthard & A Johnson, Routledge, Abingdon and New York, pp. 411–422.
Fairclough, N, 2006, *Language and globalization*, Routledge, Abingdon.
Fairclough, N, 2009, 'Language and globalization', *Semiotica*, *173*(1/4), pp. 317–342.
Friedman, J, 2003, 'Globalizing languages: Ideologies and realities of the contemporary global system', *American Anthropologist*, *105*(4), pp. 744–752.
Gal, S, 2010, 'Linguistic regimes and European diversity. Plenary talk of LINEE Conference', *New Challenges for Multilingualism in Europe*, Dubrovnik, 12 April 2010.
Garrett, P, 2010, 'Meanings of "globalization": East and West', in *The handbook of language and globalization*, ed. N Coupland, Wiley-Blackwell, Oxford, pp. 447–474.
Giddens, A, 1990, *The consequences of modernity*, Polity Press, Cambridge.
Grossberg, L, 2005, 'Globalization', in *New keywords: A revised vocabulary of culture and society*, eds. T Bennett, L Grossberg & M Morris, Blackwell, Oxford, pp. 146–150.
Hall, K, 2014, 'Hypersubjectivity: Language, anxiety, and indexical dissonance in globalization', *Journal of Asian Pacific Communication*, *24*(2), pp. 261–273.
Harvey, D, 1989, *The condition of postmodernity: An enquiry into the origins of cultural change*, Blackwell, Oxford.
Held, D, Mcgrew, A G, Goldblatt, D & Perraton, J, 1999, *Global transformations: Politics, economics, culture*, Stanford University Press, Stanford.
Heller, M, 2010, 'Language as resource in the globalized new economy', in *The handbook of language and globalization*, ed. N Coupland, Wiley-Blackwell, Oxford, pp. 349–365.
Inyabri, I T, 2016, Youth and linguistic stylization in Naija Afro Hip-Hop, *Sociolinguistic Studies*, *10*(1–2), pp. 89–108.
Jacquemet, M, 2005, 'Transidiomatic practices: Language and power in the age of globalization', *Language and Communication*, *25*(3), pp. 257–277.
Jacquemet, M, 2009, 'Transcribing refugees: The entextualization of asylum seekers' hearings in a transidiomatic environment', *Text & Talk*, *29*(5), pp. 525–546.
James, A, 2009, 'Theorising English and globalization: Semiodiversity and linguistic structure in Global English, World Englishes and Lingua Franca English', *Apples: Journal of Applied Language Studies*, *3*(1), pp. 79–92.
Jørgensen, J N, 2008, 'Polylingual languaging around and among children and adolescents', *International Journal of Multilingualism*, *5*(3), pp. 161–176.
Koh, A, 2005, '"Heteroglossic" discourses on globalization: A view from the "East"', *Globalizations*, *2*(2), pp. 228–239.

Maniar, A, 2014, 'Language testing of asylum claimants: A flawed approach', *Institute of Race Relations*, available from: www.irr.org.uk/news/language-testing-of-asylum-claimants-a-flawed-approach/ [accessed 15 May 2016].

Marcuse, P, 2000, 'The language of globalization', *Monthly Review*, 52(3), pp. 23–27.

Martín Rojo, L, 2014, 'Taking over the square: The role of linguistic practices in contesting urban spaces', *Journal of Language and Politics*, 13(4), pp. 623–652.

Moghadam, V M, 2013, *Globalization & social movements*, Rowman & Littlefield, Plymouth.

Mufwene, S, 2006, 'Myths of globalization: What African demolinguistics reveals', public lecture, University of Georgia, 15 February 2006.

Mufwene, S S, 2010, 'Globalization, global English, and world English(es): Myths and facts', in *The handbook of language and globalization*, ed. N Coupland, Wiley-Blackwell, Oxford, pp. 31–55.

Nederveen Pieterse, J, 2015, *Globalization and culture: Global mélange*, 3rd ed., Rowman & Littlefield, Lanham, MD.

Otsuji, E & Pennycook, A, 2010, 'Metrolingualism: Fixity, fluidity and language in a flux', *International Journal of Multilingualism*, 5(3), pp. 217–236.

Pennycook, A, 2011, 'Global Englishes', in *The Sage handbook of sociolinguistics*, eds. R Wodak, B Johnstone & P Kerswill, Paul, Sage, London, pp. 513–526.

Phillipson, R, 1992, *Linguistic imperialism*, Oxford University Press, Oxford.

Piller, I, 2016, *Linguistic diversity and social justice*, Oxford University Press, Oxford.

Piller, I & Takahashi, K, 2010, 'At the intersection of gender, language, and transnationalism', in *The handbook of language and globalization*, ed. N Coupland, Wiley-Blackwell, Oxford, pp. 540–554.

Piller, I & Takahashi, K, 2011, 'Language, migration, and human rights', in *The SAGE handbook of sociolinguistics*, eds. R Wodak, B Johnstone & P Kerswill, Sage, London, pp. 583–597.

Rampton, B, 1995, *Crossing: Language and ethnicity among adolescents*, Longman, London.

Roberts, C, 2012, 'Translating global experience into institutional models of competency: Linguistic inequalities in the job interview', *Diversities*, 14(2), pp. 49–71.

Schirato, T & Webb, J, 2003, *Understanding globalization*, Sage, London and Thousand Oaks, CA.

Seidlhofer, B, 2011, *Understanding English as a Lingua Franca*, Oxford University Press, Oxford.

Skutnabb-Kangas, T, 2003, 'Linguistic diversity and biodiversity: The threat from killer languages', in *The politics of English as a world language: New horizons in postcolonial cultural studies*, ed. C Mair, Rodopi, Amsterdam and New York, pp. 31–52.

Slembrouck, S, 2011, 'Globalization theory and migration', in *The Sage handbook of sociolinguistics*, eds. R Wodak, B Johnstone & P Kerswill, Sage, London, pp. 153–164.

Smith, J, 2008, *Social movements for global democracy*, The Johns Hopkins University Press, Baltimore, MD.

Steger, M B, 2013, *Globalization: A very short introduction*, 3rd ed., Oxford University Press, Oxford.

Steger, M B & Wilson, E K, 2012, 'Anti-globalization or alter-globalization? Mapping the political ideology of the global justice movement', *International Studies Quarterly*, 56(3), pp. 439–454.

Tupas, R F, 2008, 'Anatomies of linguistic commodification: The case of English in the Philippines vis-a-vìs other languages in the multilingual marketplace', in *Language as commodity: Global structures, local marketplaces*, eds. PKW Tan & R Rubdy, Continuum Press, London and New York, pp. 89–105.

Tupas, R F, ed., 2015, *Unequal Englishes: The politics of Englishes today*, Palgrave Macmillan, Basingstoke.

Weiss, G, 2000, 'Labor markets, unemployment and the rhetoric of globalization', in *European Union discourses on un/employment*, eds. P Muntigl, G Weiss & R Wodak, John Benjamins, Amsterdam, pp. 27–50.

Weiss, G & Wodak, R, 2000, 'The EU Committee regime and the problem of public space', in *European Union discourses on un/employment*, eds. P Muntigl, G Weiss & R Wodak, John Benjamins, Amsterdam, pp. 185–207.

Williams, R, 1983, *Keywords: A vocabulary of culture and society*, 2nd ed., Oxford University Press, New York.

Wodak, R, Krzyżanowski, M & Forchtner, B, 2012, 'The interplay of language ideologies and contextual cues in multilingual interactions: Language choice and code-switching in European Union institutions', *Language in Society*, *41*(2), pp. 157–186.

Yen, F T & Wu, H, 2014, 台灣新移民的健康網絡 ('Health networks for new immigrants in Taiwan', 護理雜誌 (*The Journal of Nursing*), *61*(4), pp. 35–45.

Zappettini, F, 2014, '"A badge of Europeanness": Shaping identity through the European Union's institutional discourse on multilingualism', *Journal of Language and Politics*, *13*(3), pp. 375–402.

37
A cultural political economy of Corporate Social Responsibility
The language of 'stakeholders' and the politics of new ethicalism

Ngai-Ling Sum

Introduction

This chapter presents a cultural political economy (CPE) approach to the discourses and practices of Corporate Social Responsibility (CSR) in the context of global neo-liberal capitalism. It has four parts. The first briefly explains the main features of the CPE approach. The second examines the changing nature of global capitalism with special reference to the rise of global production-retail chains, such as Wal-Mart. The term 'Wal-Martisation' is introduced to capture the changing social relations between retailers, suppliers and labour along these chains. As these extended into developing countries, there was mounting criticism of their impact on local labour and environmental conditions. This is evident in growing demands for more corporate responsibility reflected in the rise of consumer activism, local protests and non-governmental organisation (NGO) name-and-shame activities. Part three examines corporate responses to such criticisms. It focuses on attempts to reinvent corporate relations with society by promoting a business case for Corporate Social Responsibility. This is reflected in the institutionalisation of codes of conduct and then the 'stakeholder-engagement' discourses and practices. Part four investigates how 'stakeholders' are constructed as objects of governance and illustrates this from two cases. These show how stakeholder-engagement discourses and practices are managerialised and technicalised through the UN Global Compact and World Bank Stakeholder Analysis methodology. The cases indicate how CSR involves a 'new ethicalism' that is continuously resisted by civic activism. The chapter ends with some theoretical and empirical remarks on CPE's contribution to understanding language and politics.

What is cultural political economy?

CPE integrates the 'cultural turn' (a concern with sense- and meaning-making) into the critique of political economy (Jessop & Sum 2006; Sum & Jessop 2013). It explores the articulation of structural features of capitalist economic–political relations (without

557

denying that they also have semiotic properties) with the more contingent discursive features of language use, knowledge production, the problematisation of truth regimes,[1] modes of calculation and the remaking of social relations. More specifically, it explores the interface between these semiotic and material moments as they transform social relations and political processes. The contingent nature of these interactions becomes more visible during crisis conjunctures, when previously sedimented social relations (e.g. capital–labour or capital–nature relations) are challenged and new ones are imagined (e.g. capital–community). One response to such crises is that networks of actors imagine new policies and practices that might resolve these challenges. This can be seen in the case of CSR as a repository of new hopes and social obligations. This case is explored in terms of what neo-Foucauldian scholars, inspired by Foucault's micro-level work on governmentality and power–knowledge relations, call knowledging technologies (Dean 1999; Miller & Rose 2008). In this regard, CPE explores both 'how' knowledge is constructed and how its transformative impact is mediated through discursive networks of actors.

This entry examines the relations between language and politics in the current phase of neo-liberal capitalism, with special reference to CSR, especially since the 1990s. In this context, the CPE agenda is re-specified to include the following questions: (1) when do particular economic imaginaries emerge in changing structural contexts; (2) who participates in the discursive networks that construct/promote new objects of corporate governance and energise feelings for change; (3) what additional ideas and practices are selected and deployed to recontextualise these proposed objects in the interdiscursive space; (4) what governmental knowledging technologies are involved in constituting particular subjectivities and identities related to the furtherance of these schemes; (5) how far, and in what ways, do such schemes impact unevenly on people's everyday experiences; and (6) how are they represented and resisted by differently situated agencies as they engage in the uneven and contested remaking of social relations? Adequate answers require attention to hegemony, discourse, power and structural constraints.

Neo-liberal globalisation of production/retail: towards Wal-Martisation

The idea that corporations have social obligations to serve the public interest dates back to the late nineteenth century. However, in the US, formal writing on social responsibility did not emerge until the twentieth century. Prominent work in the 1950s included Howard R Bowen on *Social responsibilities of the businessman* (1953), which appealed to the social conscience of individual businesspeople rather than to firms. Later work in the 1960s and 1970s (e.g. Joseph W McGuire on *Business and society* in 1963; the Committee for Economic Development on *Social responsibilities of business corporations* in 1971) called for firms to recognise social responsibilities towards their environment that went beyond their legal and economic obligations. This short chapter cannot present the full evolution of this discursive construct (but see Carroll 1999) and will concentrate instead on its development since the 1980s with the rise of neo-liberalism and globalisation of the production and retail trade.

Neo-liberal globalisation of production and retail

In structural terms, the 1980s saw the stretching of global commodity (Gereffi & Korseniewicz 1994) and retail chains in the broader context of the rise and spread of neoliberalism. This was partly facilitated by the free-trade agenda pushed by the World Trade Organization in securing free-trade/export processing zones as well as opening of services, including the retail sector (Sum 2009). These global changes allow transnational corporations (e.g. Wal-Mart, Nike, Apple) to engage in global production and retail by integrating cheap land and workers from the Global South into their networks. In critical political economy, this process of transnationalisation has been related to changes in labour regimes, capital–labour relations, and class formation and struggles. For example, Pun (2005) identified a new work regime in southern China, the labour-dormitory system, which supports global production. Workers are housed in dormitories close to the factories so that they can be mobilised to perform overtime work at any time. A report by the *Catholic Agency for Overseas Development* (2004, pp. 30–34) on electronic-sector workers in China showed that they had to work illegal overtime (making a total of 15–16 hours per day under very poor conditions) to earn the minimum wage. Likewise, in Thailand, sub-contracted workers earned a 'minimum wage' that does not even cover food and household expenses. Such sweat-shop conditions occur not only at specific sites where class, gender, ethnicity and caste intersect to facilitate labour exploitation in specific ways, but elsewhere around the globe to form the nexus of sites that facilitate what Selwyn (2015) calls 'the making of the global labouring class'. Global producers and buyers resort to local sub-contractors at different sites to optimise control over labour so that they can benefit from transnational low-cost production and surplus value extraction on a global scale.

Wal-Martisation as a low-cost accumulation strategy

This chapter will use Wal-Mart's approach to the globalisation of retail chains, described here as Wal-Martisation, to illustrate some of the strategies and stakes in this more general process. As a global discount chain, Wal-Mart thrived on its '*Always Low Prices*' label but replaced this in 2008 with '*Save Money. Live Better*'. Its bargain-based accumulation strategy depends on global–local factors that include: (1) entering into 'glocal' partnerships at specific sites; and (2) using micro-management techniques such as 'category management' and 'scorecards'. First, Wal-Mart entered national markets by forming partnerships with local governments (e.g. the state-owned *Shenzhen International Trusts and Investment Company* in China) as well as with private commercial concerns (e.g. *ASDA* in the UK, *Seiyu* in Japan, *Best Price* in India and *Massmart* in South Africa). These and other ventures enable Wal-Mart both to sell and source in these countries.

Second, underlying these partnership strategies is the use of information technology that integrates retailing and sourcing within the global supply chain. Wal-Mart has developed its own communication-logistical-inventory system that enables it to link the retailer with its suppliers worldwide. Since 1983, Wal-Mart has installed bar-code readers in all its distribution centres and introduced radio-frequency identification in 2005. It has also deployed a software programme since 1991 called *Retail Link* that connects all stores, distribution centres and suppliers. This innovation has made Wal-Mart into the largest private satellite-communication operator in the world. It operates a four-petabyte data warehouse that collects and analyses point-of-sale data (e.g. store number, item number, quantity sold, selling cost, etc.) as well as keeping track of inventory down to item level. These capacities allow Wal-Mart and its suppliers to examine and forecast consumer-demand patterns as well as to co-ordinate product sales and inventory data through the *Retail Link* system. Mainstream economic and management studies argue that this technological prowess enables Wal-Mart to 'share information' with its suppliers and gain cost advantages based on automation, joint demand forecasting, and the 'just-in-time' supply system (e.g. bar-code-triggered replenishment, vendor-managed inventory and faster inventory turnover time) (Holmes 2001; Basker 2007). However, this kind of 'information-sharing' in lean retailing (Bonacich & Wilson 2006, pp. 234–235) can also be employed coercively (Free 2008, pp. 14–16). Given that price-value and cost competitiveness drive supply chains of this kind (Christopher 2005, p. 123), the everyday operations of mega-retailers are based on particular calculating practices that manage costs and margins. More specifically, these practices include 'category management' and 'open-book accounting'.

'Category management', which is a business practice that began in the supermarket business, allows giant retailers to improve sales and profits by managing product categories (e.g. apparel, toys) as separate business units with their own pricing. Wal-Mart's category managers work with suppliers to develop category plans and such routine contacts are facilitated by the *Retail Link*. To monitor profitability and efficiency, suppliers are trained and required to submit scorecards to the *Retail Link*. This entails opening their accounting details (e.g. inventory, pricing, performance and sales) to the retailer (called 'open-book accounting'), with the aim of co-ordinating activities to reduce costs and/or maximise margins.

From a neo-Foucauldian viewpoint, these scorecards operate as a discursive apparatus that provides a form of selective and asymmetrical knowing. It allows Wal-Mart category managers (and their assistants) keyhole views into the suppliers' 'sales', 'markdown', 'margins', 'inventory' and 'return' (see Table 37.1). This produces a new knowledge space that renders suppliers' financial conditions visible in order to identify cause-and-effect relations bearing on the chain's efficiency and profitability (Edenius & Hasselbladh 2002, pp. 249–57; Norreklit 2003, p. 601). Under constant pressure to review product categories, the identification of these cause-and-effect relations provides the everyday bases of calculation, intervention, hard-nosed negotiation and control. Mechanisms of control enable category managers to perform the following routine activities: (1) evaluating the change of each supplier's costs and margins, and requiring it to match its lowest price or even cut it; (2) comparing each supplier's costs and margins with the average; (3) introducing a form of co-ordinated competition between suppliers (e.g. asking a specific supplier to match the lower prices of competing suppliers); (4) asking for alternatives based on a panoramic view of the suppliers' costs and margins; and (5) clawing back funds in the forms of suppliers' contribution towards 'volume incentives, warehouse allowances, and reimbursements for specific programmes such as markdowns, margin protection and advertising' (Wal-Mart 2007, p. 44).

Seen through the micro-accounting practice of scorecards, this 'information-sharing' in the supply chain also sustains a kind of organisational control based on informational 'supervision'. The visibility and benchmarking of suppliers enable Wal-Mart's 'category managers' to demand lower prices, benchmark the average, and demand refunds from suppliers. This way of disciplining suppliers can be seen, in neo-Foucauldian terms, as a virtual panopticon.[2] Computerised corporate 'wardens' conduct organisational surveillance of suppliers who are also enrolled in their own disciplinary gaze. In short, the use of scorecards and similar micro-accounting practices enable Wal-Mart to expropriate margins from suppliers. This seemingly 'managerial-logistical-information fix' is not only techno-economic in nature but also political. In the latter regard, it exhibits asymmetrical power relations that assist the transformation of capital-to-capital social relations, in particular by tilting the balance in favour of the retailers vis-à-vis the suppliers-manufacturers in buyer-driven commodity chains (Gereffi & Korseniewicz 1994; French 2006).

Table 37.1 Knowledge produced through Wal-Mart supplier scorecards

Measurement criteria	Elements of measure
Sales measurements	• Overall % increase • Comparable same-store sales • Average sales/store • Sales at full prices vs. markdown
Markdown measurements	• Markups and markdowns (dollars, units and %) • Prior and current retail price
Margin measurements	• Initial margin • Average retail price • Average cost • Gross profit at item level • Gross profit/item/store • Margin mix
Inventory measurements	• Replenishable store inventory • Non-replenishable store delivery • Warehouse inventory • Lost sales from out-of-stocks • Excess inventory • Past date codes • Total owned inventory
Return measurements	• Customer defective returns • Store claims

(American Logistics Association, Exchange Roundtable 2005)

Aided by this informational 'super-vision', Wal-Mart's procurement staff members are constantly making deals with thousands of suppliers to produce goods tailored to Wal-Mart's own stringent specifications, including pricing, quality assurance, sales, efficiency, delivery and, more recently, sustainability requirements. This firm grip over suppliers-manufacturers and the unrelenting push for cost and price-value competitiveness mean that manufacturers, in turn, must pass on their costs and production insecurity (e.g. termination of orders) to their workers. Workers in Wal-Mart's supplier factories, which the International Labour Rights Fund terms 'Wal-Mart Sweatshops', see their wages cut and safety and welfare measures ignored. This was evident in a report produced by *Students and Scholars Against Corporate Misbehaviour* (SACOM 2007), a Hong Kong-based NGO, that monitored Wal-Mart activities. This report identified extensive labour abuses (e.g. wage and hour violations, unsafe working conditions, deprivation of labour-contract protection) in five toy factories in China that manufactured for Wal-Mart. Similar problems were identified by the Clean Clothes Campaign in its *Cashing In* report (2009). The latter focused on the garment supply chains of the five big retailers (Wal-Mart, Tesco, Carrefour, Aldi and Lidl) and highlighted the poor conditions of their workers in Thailand, India, Bangladesh and Sri Lanka.

This overall process can be summarised as Wal-Martisation. Building on the definition provided by SACOM (2007) and concentrating on the production side, this paper treats Wal-Martisation as a change in the social relations of production where power shifts from suppliers-manufacturers to giant retailers, with the former trickling insecurity and poverty downwards to their flexible workforce in their search for a disciplinary low-cost strategy. This process is mediated by changes in technological-logistical and managerial-calculative practices that enable: (1) giant retailers to more effectively conduct organisational surveillance of suppliers; and (2) suppliers to engage in self-monitoring as well as, to some extent, tactical manoeuvres in the buyer-supplier game.

Reinvention of CSR since the 1980s: 'stakeholder' languages and practices

Wal-Martisation and its cost-reduction practices have prompted (trans-)national and local concern among unions, NGOs and community groups such as AFL-CIO's Eye on WalMart, Wake-Up Walmart, Wal-Mart Watch, Clean Clothes Campaign, and SACOM targeting the activities of the corporation (Sum 2010, p. 60). In general, these groups are challenging its lack of support for improvement of suppliers' safety standards, low wages, worker intimidation, gender-based discrimination, unpaid overtime, replacing full-time workers with part-timers, and firing workers who complain or seek to organise their co-workers (Wang 2013). These forms of labour subjugation are not unique to global retail chains. In fact, civic groups challenging global production and retail have taken aim at brand-name producers such as Nike, Levi-Strauss, the GAP and Reebok since the late 1980s. Such practices have gained more publicity since the 1990s as civic activism has adopted name-and-shame strategies to highlight labour and environment abuses. These movements and their broader 'alter-globalisation' campaigns keep a close eye on corporate activities and try to hold them accountable. Well-known campaign and civic groups in the garment industry include Clean Clothes Campaign (Europe), Maquila Solidarity Network (Canada), United Students Against Sweatshops (the US), Oxfam's Clothes Code Campaign, and the Interfaith Centre on Corporate Responsibility (the US). They participate in the new politics of consumption to challenge sweat-shop abuses. This new politics includes calls for transnational corporations (TNCs) to assume more responsibility for their employees; consumers to look behind the label and think about which products they buy, and for the general public to address issues of global and local inequality.

Corporations, with expensive advice from management consultants and development practitioners, responded to these counter-hegemonic challenges by reinventing the discourses on CSR. Moving on from the 1960s and 1970s constructs, they recast their CSR knowledge to incorporate new themes such as stakeholder management, corporate social performance and business ethics (Carroll 1999, p. 290). Other corporations broadened them further to include corporate citizenship, sustainable development, corporate philanthropy and community engagement, and so on (Itanen 2011, p. 14). The multiplication of such polysemic and overlapping discourses led Pearson (2008) to argue that CSR is a new interdiscursive (dis-)order that has resulted from socio-political struggles (Fairclough 1992, pp. 115–120; Wodak 2001, p. 67). Given its unstable and ambiguous nature, it is also appropriated and reinterpreted by strategic actors in specific conjunctures. The rest of this entry examines one such moment, which Sum and Pun (2005) call the 'code-rush' conjuncture, when corporations – aided and abetted by policy gurus, management consultants and development advisers – selectively deployed the discourses and practices of 'stakeholder theory/management' to reinvent CSR in new directions.

'Stakeholder' languages and practices

The code-rush conjuncture occurred in the late 1980s as these corporations adopted their own company codes (e.g. Wal-Mart's Code of Ethics) and carried out self-regulatory auditing of their suppliers in accordance with the stated standards. Given their in-house nature, some of their auditing practices were criticised for: (1) window-dressing and being self-serving as most audits were conducted by their own internal or associated monitors; (2) announcing their site visits beforehand to suppliers; and (3) coaching workers to give the right answers to assessors (Sum & Pun 2005). In response to these criticisms, management consultants sought to go 'beyond audit' and rebuild corporate reputation and performance by recontextualising particular management fads to fill the regulation gap.

From many such fads, it was 'stakeholder theory' that was selected to reorient CSR in a social direction. This theory of the firm was initially popularised by Freeman (1984) who posited that corporations should address not only their shareholders' interests, but also those of their other stakeholders, such as consumers, workers, NGOs and governments. He defined 'stakeholder' as an organisation that enters into relationships with many groups that influence, or are influenced by, the company. This made managing stakeholder relationships essential to effective enterprise management.

This narrative had various foci, ranging from the normative (e.g. Austrom & Lad 1989) through the managerial (Mitchell, Agle & Wood 1997) to the relational-communicative aspects of stakeholder relations (Clarkson 1995; Harrison & St. John 1996). The original discourse of 'stakeholder management' now co-exists with 'stakeholder-relationship management' and 'stakeholder engagement'. The specific implications for power dynamics depend on which discourse prevails. 'Stakeholder-management' language implies that all stakeholders can be 'managed' by companies (Andriof & Waddock 2002), and makes it hard for external stakeholders to influence corporate practices. 'Stakeholder-relationship management' recognises the inherent mutuality of stakeholder relationships in a network structure that is not necessarily centred on the firm's interests. 'Stakeholder engagement' denotes power sharing, interaction and partnership.

This set of discourses and its associated knowledging practices continued to gain popularity as corporations faced mounting challenges to go 'beyond audit'. But their fluidity has enabled 'stakeholder management' to morph into 'stakeholder relationships' and 'stakeholder engagement' and vice versa. In the 2000s, this rhetoric was given a central place in important works such as the Post, Preston and Sachs book, *Redefining the corporation* (2002a), and a related paper in *California Management Review*, 'Managing the extended enterprise: The new stakeholder view' (2002b). Further, this 'stakeholder' language began to circulate in the consultancy, corporate and policy worlds and acquired certain hegemony in formulating major CSR schemes.

On the corporate level, in the early 2000s, Wal-Mart broadened its stakeholder base from shareholders and customers to include external stakeholders such as suppliers, NGOs, academic leaders and governments. In 2004, Wal-Mart, through Martha Montag Brown and Associates, a global head-hunter, advertised a new position using the stakeholder language. A 'Senior Director on Stakeholder Engagement' would '*pioneer a new model of how Wal-Mart works with outside stakeholders resulting in fundamental changes in how the company does business*' (2004). This model could be described as a communicative–management one in which new techniques such as 'stakeholder analysis/mapping' and communicative strategies such as global responsibility reports,[3] newsletters, web sites, podcasts and blogs have been deployed since 2008.

These changes in Wal-Mart were informed and mediated by the concurrent development of global norm-based CSR schemes/standards such as the United Nations Global Compact, the Global Reporting Initiative and AccountAbility's AA1000 Stakeholder Engagement Standard. These are mainly formulated in terms of multi-stakeholder schemes that combined a principle-based platform for dialogue with emphasis on 'best practice' learning between partners. The UN Global Compact was designed by John Ruggie, the Kirkpatrick Professor of International Affairs in the Harvard Kennedy School of Government, and officially launched in 2000 (Sum & Jessop 2013, p. 320). Drawing from his constructivist theory of international relations, Ruggie sees the Compact as a network that will socialise and stimulate corporations about CSR 'to bring about convergence in corporate practices around universally shared values' (Kell & Ruggie 1999, p. 104). Firms are encouraged to learn and adopt socially responsible principles such as human rights, labour standards, environment and anti-corruption, and thereby improve their governance and performance on these issues wherever they operate. The making of this network-based mechanism also requires discursive practices that can reinvent the relationship between corporations and their NGO/union critics.

The 'stakeholder' languages, which moved round the corporate-consultancy-policy circuits, were selected and reinvented in two ways. First, the language of 'stakeholder engagement' was selected rather than 'stakeholder management' to denote network partnership. Second, the link between CSR and stakeholder engagement was embedded within 'social-risk management' and articulated to the alleged economic rationality of 'competitive necessity'. This new combination can be seen from a 2005 working paper by the Corporate Social Responsibility Initiative of the Harvard Kennedy School of Government:

> Current network-based operating models highlight the growing importance of the extended enterprise by establishing greater connectivity among and between stakeholders across the globe. This connectivity has also created entirely new stakeholders and requires innovative forms of risk management. These changes in the operating model have led to a significant shift in market power – not just to customers and traditional investors but also, and more importantly, toward stakeholders: communities, employees, regulators, politicians, suppliers, NGOs and even the media. As a result of this shift in market power, 'social risk' is a rising area of concern for global corporations.
>
> From a company perspective, social risk, like any other risk, arises when its own behaviour or the action of others in its operating environment creates vulnerabilities. In the case of social risk, stakeholders may identify those vulnerabilities and apply pressure on the corporation for behavioural changes. As the ability to listen to corporate stakeholders' perspectives on social issues becomes a competitive necessity, managing social risks will need to become more fully embedded in corporate strategy.
>
> (Kytle & Ruggie 2005, p. 1)

Thus, CSR programmes are seen as essential to effective 'risk management' and, in turn, 'stakeholder engagement' is functionalised as a counter-measure for these risks, especially those along the supply chains (Kytle & Ruggie 2005, p. 2). This pragmatic meaning-making was ripe for further functionalisation as 'social risks' were translated into economic objects that might serve as means to the ends of product innovation. This is evident in a subsequent 2006 Harvard Kennedy School working paper by Bekefi, Jenkins and Kytle on 'social risks':

> Social risks flag opportunities for companies to innovate around products, business processes, and leadership methods to translate risk into opportunity and position themselves for more sustainable, long-term success. A proactive and strategic approach

to social risk management can therefore lead to new shareholder value creation in addition to existing shareholder value protection.

(Bekefi, Jenkins & Kytle 2006, p. 2)

The reification of 'social risk' and identification of 'stakeholder engagement' as a social risk-management tool create opportunities, not only for the companies, but also for the consultancy-policy world. Stakeholders become objects of governance, and companies introduce newly invented positions such as director of stakeholder engagement (see above) or stakeholder-relations manager. Consultancies such as *APCO Worldwide* offer advice on corporate communicative practices for these managers. For example, one position announced by Shell in 2015 described the task of its 'NGO and Stakeholder Relations Manager' as being to assist the Vice-President of this section to 'deliver stakeholder strategy, policy, standards, guidelines, tools and processes related to Stakeholder Management and dialogue techniques'.[4]

Stakeholders as objects of governance

These stakeholder-engagement guidelines and tools are available on the consultancy-policy market. Consultancies such as SustainAbility design and facilitate engagement for firms such as Wal-Mart, Microsoft, Shell, Starbucks, and so on. Sedex and Twentyfifty provide management-training programmes to country-based networks of firms that have subscribed to the UN Global Compact. Many of these programmes problematise social risks and create stakeholder engagement as a tool to manage their risks and reputation. They construct knowledge products that include methodologies for identifying, prioritising, mapping and engaging stakeholders. From a neo-Foucauldian viewpoint, these products embody the art of identifying and visibilising stakeholders as objects of governance that are pertinent to governmental calculations. These calculations produce a whole new pedagogy of stakeholder engagement that governs and/or disciplines them. New governing tools such as surveys, methodologies, manuals, charts, matrices and scales co-exist with practices that include dialogues, document feedback, advisory panels, focus groups, interviews, information gathering, data analysis/mining, and so on.

These constellations of power configurations are uneven, with some more intrusive than others in the organisation of stakeholder-engagement life. For example, the arrangements recommended in the United Nations Economic and Social Commission for Asia and the Pacific's *United Nations Global Compact Training of Trainers Course Guidance Manual* (2013) can be seen as promoting a lighter touch of stakeholder engagement. In its manual, stakeholders are sorted into two broad types. The first is 'reflective stakeholders'; these comprise individuals/groups who identify themselves as stakeholders and have expressed interest in the firm. The second type is 'strategic'; it consists of those who may be able to influence other stakeholders and the firm's management decisions and are therefore important agents to help achieve the firm's objectives. Some stakeholders may belong to both types. As a process-focused mode of engagement, stakeholder liaison uses tools and practices such as regular dialogues, surveys, document feedback, advisory panels, focus groups, interviews, local networks, and so on (see Figure 37.1), to facilitate participation, learning and communicative action.

This scheme has been criticised on three grounds. First, the Global Compact deploys the languages of management, 'best practice' learning and partnership, rather than accountability and obligation. The former largely supplement and complement market relations in which

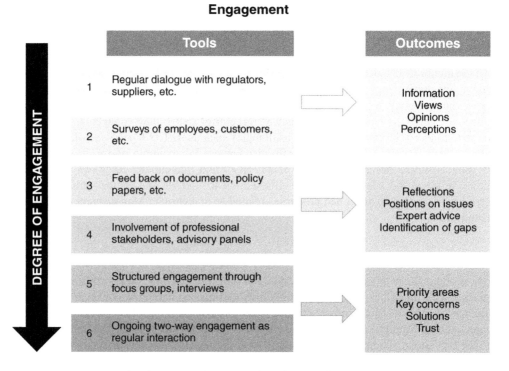

Figure 37.1 An example of UNESCAP's way of identifying and prioritising stakeholders
(Source: Adapted from UNESCAP's *United Nations Global Compact of Trainers Course Guidance Manual* 2013, p. 27)

businesses can choose to be involved in the ways that best suit their strategies. The latter, which emphasises building a social and equitable economy that directly addresses the excesses of capitalism, is avoided. Second, this premier global forum is designed in the light of 'best practice' learning and focuses chiefly on communication rather than legal-material actions such as third-party monitors, legal regulation or sanctions (Knight & Smith 2008, pp. 4, 7–8). Third, they involve largely top-down dialogues that are dominated by business participants and international organisations, with good attendance by market-oriented NGOs. Thus, they are largely learning events to elicit participation of elites to discuss the business case on socially responsible principles (Gregoratti 2012, p. 99). Accordingly, Global Compact has been criticised as an instrument for public-relations 'bluewash' (i.e. draping themselves with the UN flag), which helps to reproduce and legitimate the existing power of corporations (Bruno & Karlina 2000; Banerjee 2008).

This communicative mode can be contrasted with a scaled-up version that focuses on 'stakeholder analysis' as a key part of stakeholder engagement. For example, the World Bank's anti-corruption effort introduced this methodology (its term) in 2002. Stakeholders and stakeholder analysis are seen as follows:

> A stakeholder is any entity with a declared or conceivable interest or stake in a policy concern. The range of stakeholders relevant to consider for analysis varies according to the complexity of reform area targeted and the type of reform proposed and, where the stakeholders are not organized, the incentive to include them. Stakeholders can be

of any form, size and capacity. They can be individuals, organizations, or unorganized groups [...]

Four major attributes are important for Stakeholder Analysis: the stakeholders' position on the reform issue, the level of influence (power) they hold, the level of interest they have in the specific reform, and the group/coalition to which they belong or can reasonably be associated with. These attributes are identified through various data collection methods, including interviews with country experts knowledgeable about stakeholders or with the actual stakeholders directly.

(World Bank 2015)

This World Bank narrative sees stakeholders as objects of policy governance, with diverse political and social attributes that can influence the policy outcomes. They become time-sensitive targets for data collection, profiling and monitoring. Data generating and organising tools, such as *Darzin* software, charts, weightings, matrices and continuums are deployed to construct stakeholder profiles. Based on this data, they are mapped on:

a continuum indicating support for the reform on a scale of 0 to 100 from low (far left) to high (far right). Their varying degrees of support are marked on the line with a value indicating their reform preference. This implement also provides a quick visual of the 'lay of the land', illuminating clusters of groups that support, oppose or are indifferent to reform.

(World Bank 2015)

This form of engagement rule may facilitate participation, but it is also overlaid by 'panoptic-style' systems of disciplinary tools and practices that are designed to: (a) map and contain resistance towards policy reforms; (b) visibilise the micro-political economy of a policy area; (c) build stakeholder coalition and support; and (d) produce value for the firms and policy agencies.

Technique of obfuscation and the politics of new ethicalism

These constellations of discourses and practices based on stakeholderism are promoted with great rhetorical energy in consultancy-corporate-policy circuits. Its pro-capitalist versions cohere and consolidate a new CSR strategy that foregrounds the stakeholder community, while older collective identities (e.g. fractions of capital, workers, unions, NGOs, etc.) recede. Whereas, before the 1990s, globalisation of production and retail denoted changing social relations between retail and manufacturing capital, as well as capital and labour, it now seems only to signify companies and communities of stakeholders who contribute towards economic value production for the firms. This shift in meaning can be seen as a 'technique of obfuscation' (Neilson & Rossiter 2005) that diverts attention from the dark side of exploited suppliers and labour to the bright face of stakeholder communication, engagement and control. This way of obfuscating contradictions can be seen as an ideological instrument of passive revolution where challenges by civic activism are resolved in favour of business interests (and a ruling group).

This passive revolution reveals the emergence of 'new ethicalism' in which strategies such as 'stakeholder engagement' aim to reconnect economic policies with (new) social-community norms that are dominated by the use of techno-managerial tools and practices (e.g. training, interviews, dialogues, data gathering/profiling, charts, matrices, etc.). In this regard, 'new ethicalism' can be seen as an ethicalised-managerial regime that seeks to stabilise/enhance neo-liberalism through 'managerialisation' and 'technification' of CSR with disciplinary and/or governmental effects. These efforts to build neo-liberal CSR produce temporary strategic fixes; however, they cannot prevent opposing discourses and continuous challenges arising from and/or responding to the contradictions rooted in the global production and supply chains. Beside the promotion of 'new ethicalism', we find the attempts of 'progressive' workers and glocal movement-orientated NGOs to resist these changes. For example, they criticised 'stakeholder engagement' as a divide-and-rule strategy that was recommended to TNCs by public-relations gurus 'to isolate the radicals, cultivate the idealists and educate them into becoming realists; then co-opt the realists into agreeing with industry' (John & Thompson 2002, p. 44). CorpWatch (2005, p. 20) resisted these governing techniques because '"radicals" feel not only isolated by NGO/corporate engagement but sold out by it'. It therefore calls for the continual use of confrontational language such as 'social and ecological justice' and 'equality', rather than of compromise narratives such as 'stakeholder engagement' and 'dialogues'. The former informs their solidaristic actions rather than as being absorbed as stakeholders in the micro-political economy of data collection, profiling and monitoring of civic activism.

Concluding remarks

Theoretically, this chapter has argued that a CPE approach can contribute to our understanding of the relationship between language and politics in two ways. First, it explores the articulation of structural features of capitalist economic–political relations (without neglecting their semiotic properties) to the more contingent discursive features of language construction, selective knowledge production, and remaking of social relations. Second, it adds to the agenda of Critical Discourse Studies by highlighting the importance of structural contexts for the emergence of new economic imaginaries. It examines which individuals, groups, or organisations participate in this discursive network, what ideas and practices are selected, what disciplinary and governmental technologies are involved, and how are they resisted in the remaking of social relations.

Empirically, this chapter has used CPE to examine how capitalism is changing in the neo-liberal age. It concentrated on the rise of global retail chains and the consolidation of Wal-Martisation as a low-cost accumulation strategy. With the development of scorecards and data supervision, these global retailers seek to maintain a firm grip over suppliers-manufacturers and pass their costs and production insecurity to their workers. Labour unions and NGOs have challenged their labour and environmental excesses via mixed use of outright criticisms and name-and-shame strategies. In response, corporations, with advice from policy gurus, management consultants and development practitioners, have constructed the language of Corporate Social Responsibility. They started by introducing in-house codes of conduct and have gradually moved towards stakeholderism since the 1990s. The unstable and polysemic nature of this discourse is also subjected to appropriation and interpretation by strategic actors at specific conjuncture. The discourses of 'stakeholder engagement' were repeatedly selected, managerialised and technicalised by TNCs, international organisations, global communication consultancies, and so on. The UN's Global Compact and its reporting initiative have been criticised as instruments for public-relations 'bluewashing'. This resonates with the critique of 'greenwashing' levelled by some NGOs at the close relations between TNCs and pseudo-green groups. Stakeholders gradually become objects of governance and subject to governmental calculations. New governing tools and practices include dialogues, information gathering, methodologies, data analysis, profiles, charts and matrices. This complex constellation of stakeholder discourses, techniques and procedures helps to divert attention from the deep-rooted capital–capital, capital–labour and capital–nature tensions. These quick fixes can be seen as the emergence of new ethicalism that is continuously challenged by workers' and movement-oriented NGOs and community groups based on the language of social/ecological justice and solidarity.

Notes

1 Problematisation is one of Foucault's analytical methods: it questions accepted 'truths' and examines the thinking that comes to constitute our condition (Foucault 1977, pp. 185–186).
2 Panopticon was first proposed by Jeremy Bentham as an architectural form for a circular prison characterized by a central observation tower from which guards could survey all inmates. Foucault (1975) used this idea of an all-seeing, all-controlling space as a metaphor to examine the oppressive use of information and knowledge in modern disciplinary society. This chapter explores the development of a 'virtual panopticon' that rests on Wal-Mart's disciplinary use of database information, such as 'RetailLink', and calculating practices in the scorecards.
3 Wal-Mart adopts the Global Reporting Initiative (GRI) reporting standard in its Global Responsibility Report published in 2014 and 2015. For a critical analysis of the GRI standard, see Joannides and Miller (2011).
4 For details of this post, see: www.rigzone.com/jobs/postings/524749/NGO_and_Stakeholder_ Relations_Manager.asp?utm_source=ind_sp-euaf_uk&utm_medium=aggregator&utm_campaign= indeed_sponsored.

References

Andriof, J & Waddock, S, 2002, 'Unfolding stakeholder engagement', in *Unfolding stakeholder thinking*, eds., J Andriof, S Waddock, B Husted & S Rahman, Greenleaf, Sheffield, pp. 19–42.
Austrom, D & Lad, L, 1989, 'Issues management alliances: New responses, new values and new logics', in *Research in corporate social performance and policy*, 11, ed. J Post, JAI Press, Greenwich, CT, pp. 233–56.
Banerjee, S, 2008, 'Corporate social responsibility: The good, the bad and the ugly', *Critical Sociology*, 34 (1), pp. 51–79.
Basker, E, 2007, 'The causes and consequences of Wal-Mart's growth', *Journal of Economic Perspectives*, 21 (3), pp. 177–98.
Bekefi, T, Jenkins, B & Kytle, B, 2006, 'Social risk as strategic risk, Corporate Social Responsibility initiative', *Harvard Kennedy School of Government Working Paper No. 30*, December, available from: www.daedalusadvising.com/Social_Risk_Strategic_Risk.pdf [accessed 30 March 2017].
Bonacich, E & Wilson, J, 2006, 'Global production and distribution: Wal-Mart's global logistic empire', in *Wal-Mart world: The world's biggest corporation in the global economy*, ed., S D Brunn, Routledge, London, pp. 227–242.
Bruno, K & Karlinerm J, 2000, 'Tangled up in blue: Corporate partnerships at the United Nations', available from: www.corpwatch.org/article.php?id=996 [accessed 30 March 2017].
Carroll, A, 1999, 'Corporate social responsibility: Evolution of a definitional construct', *Business Society*, 38 (3), pp. 268–95.
Catholic Agency for Overseas Development, 2004, *Dire conditions in computer production*, available from: www.hartford-hwp.com/archives/26/203.html [accessed 30 March 2017].
Christopher, M, 2005, *Logistics and supply chain management*, Pearson Education, Harlow.
Clarkson, MBE, 1995, 'A stakeholder framework for analyzing and evaluating corporate social performance', *Academy of Management Review*, 20 (1), pp. 92–117.

Clean Clothes Campaign, 2009, *Cashing in: Giant retailers, purchasing practices and working conditions in the garment industry*, available from: www.cleanclothes.org/resources/publications/cashing-in.pdf/view [accessed 30 March 2017].

CorpWatch, 2005, *What's wrong with corporate social responsibility?*, available from: https://corporatewatch.org/sites/default/files/CSRreport.pdf [accessed 30 March 2017].

Dean, M, 1999, *Governmentality: Power and rule in modern society*, Sage, Thousand Oaks, CA.

Edenius, M & Hasselbladh, H, 2002, 'The balanced scorecard as an intellectual technology', *Organization*, 9 (2), pp. 29–73.

Fairclough, N, 1992, *Discourse and social change*, Polity, Cambridge.

Foucault, M, 1975, *Discipline and punish: The birth of the prison*, Allen Lane, London.

Free, C, 2008, *Walking the talk? Supply chain accounting and trust among UK supermarkets and supplies*, IDEAS, available from: https://ideas.repec.org/a/eee/aosoci/v33y2008i6p629-662.html [accessed 30 March 2017].

Freeman, R, 1984, *Strategic management: A stakeholder approach*, Pitman Books, Marshfield, MA.

French, J, 2006, 'Wal-Mart, retail supremacy and the relevance of political economy', *Labour Studies in Working-Class History of the Americas*, 4 (1), pp. 33–40.

Gereffi, G & Korseniewicz, M, 1994, *Commodity chain and global capitalism*, Greenwood Press, Westport, CT.

Gereffi, G & Ong, R, 2007, 'Wal-Mart in China: Can the world's largest retailer succeed in the world's most populous market?', *Harvard Asia Pacific Review*, 9 (1), pp. 46–9.

Gregoratti, C, 2012, 'The United Nations global compact and development', in *Business regulation and non-state actors*, eds. D Reed, P Utting & A Mukherjee-Reed, Routledge, London, pp. 95–108.

Harrison, J S & St John, C H, 1996, 'Managing and partnering with external stakeholders', *Academy of Management Executive*, 10 (2), pp. 46–59.

Holmes, T, 2001, 'Bar codes lead to frequent deliveries and superstores', *RAND Journal of Economics*, 34 (4), pp. 708–25.

Itanen, M-E, 2011, *CSR discourse in corporate reports – exploring the socially constructed nature of corporate social responsibility*, International Business, MA thesis, School of Economics, Aalto University, Finland, available from: http://epub.lib.aalto.fi/en/ethesis/pdf/12664/hse_ethesis_12664.pdf [accessed 30 March 2017].

Jessop, B & Sum, N-L, 2006, *Beyond the regulation approach: Putting the economy in its place in political economy*, Edward Elgar, Cheltenham, UK.

Joannides, V & Miller, B, 2011, 'Authorship and authority – competing claims within Corporate Social Responsibility report guidance providers', available from: http://docs.business.auckland.ac.nz/doc/bob-miller.pdf [accessed 30 March 2017].

John, S & Thomson, S, eds., 2002, *New activism and the corporate response*, Palgrave Macmillan, Basingstoke.

Kell, G & Ruggie, J G, 1999, 'Global markets and social legitimacy: The case for the global compact', *Transnational Corporations*, 8 (3), pp. 101–20.

Knight, G & Smith. J, 2008, 'The global compact and its critics: Activism, power relations, and Corporate Social Responsibility', in *Discipline and punishment in global politics: Illusions of control*, ed. J Leatherman, Palgrave Macmillan, Basingstoke, pp. 191–214.

Kytle, B & Ruggie, J, 2005, *Corporate Social Responsibility and risk management*, Corporate Social Responsibility Initiative, Harvard Kennedy School of Government Working Paper No. 10, available from: www.ksg.harvard.edu/m-rcbg/CSRI/publications/workingpaper_10_kytle_ruggie.pdf [accessed 30 March 2017].

Martha Montag Brown & Associates, 2004, 'Position description: Wal-Mart senior director stakeholder engagement', available from: www.caseplace.org/usr_doc/Wal-Mart_-_Sr_Dir_Stakeholder_Engagement_Job_Description.pdf [accessed 1 January 2016].

Miller, P & Rose, N, 2008, *Governing the present*, Polity, Cambridge.

Mitchell, R, Agle, B R & Wood, D J, 1997, 'Toward a theory of stakeholder identification and salience: Defining the principle of who and what really counts', *Academy of Management Review*, 22 (4), pp. 853–86.
Neilson, B & Rossiter, N, 2005, 'From precarity to precariousness and back again: Life and unstable network', *The Fibreculture Journal*, iss. 5, available from: http://five.fibreculturejournal.org/fcj-022-from-precarity-to-precariousness-and-back-again-labour-life-and-unstable-networks/ [accessed 30 March 2017].
Norreklit, H, 2003, 'The balanced scorecard: What is the score?', *Accounting, Organizations and Society*, 28 (6), pp. 591–619, available from www.sciencedirect.com/science/article/pii/S0361368202000971 [accessed 30 March 2017].
Post, J, Preston, L & Sachs, S, 2002a, *Redefining the corporation*, Stanford University Press, Stanford, CA.
Post, J, Preston, L & Sachs, S, 2002b, 'Managing the extended enterprise: The new stakeholder view', *California Management Review*, 45 (1), pp. 6–28.
Pun, N, 2005, *Made in China*, Duke University Press, Durham, NC.
SACOM, 2007, *Wal-Mart's sweatshop monitoring fails to catch violations: The story of toys made in China for Wal-Mart*, June, available from: http://sacom.hk/wp-content/uploads/2008/07/walmart-reportsacomjun2007.pdf [accessed 30 March 2017].
Selwyn, B, 2015, 'Commodity chains, creative destruction and global inequality: A class analysis', *Journal of Economic Geography*, 5 (2), pp. 253–74.
Sum, N-L, 2009, 'Wal-Martisation and CSR-ization in developing countries', in *Corporate Social Responsibility and regulatory governance*, eds. P Utting & J C Marques, Palgrave Macmillan, London and UNRISD, Geneva, pp. 50–76.
Sum, N-L & Jessop, B, 2013, *Towards a cultural political economy: Putting culture in its place in political economy*, Edward Elgar, Cheltenham, UK.
Sum, N-L & Pun, N, 2005, 'Globalization and paradoxes of ethical transnational production', *Competition & Change*, 9 (2), pp. 181–200.
United Nations Economic and Social Commission for Asia and the Pacific, 2013, *United Nations Global Compact Training of Trainers Course Guidance Manual*, available from: www.unescap.org/resources/united-nations-global-compact-training-trainers-course-guidance-manual [accessed 30 March 2017].
Wang, E, 2013, 'As Wal-Mart swallows China, workers fight back', *The American prospect*, 23 April, available from: http://prospect.org/article/wal-mart-swallows-chinas-economy-workers-fight-back [accessed 30 March 2017].
Wodak, R, 2001, 'The discourse-historical approach', in *Methods of Critical Discourse Analysis*, eds. R Wodak & M Meyer, Sage, London, pp. 63–95.
World Bank, 2015, 'What is stakeholder analysis?', available from: www1.worldbank.org/publicsector/anticorrupt/PoliticalEconomy/stakeholderanalysis.htm [accessed 30 March 2017].

38
The fictionalisation of politics

Ruth Wodak and Bernhard Forchtner

Introduction

This chapter addresses a genre that has become increasingly successful in recent years: TV soap operas dealing with politics and the actions of politicians, such as *The West Wing*, *Borgen*, *House of Cards*, *In the Thick of it*, *Yes Minister*, and *Im Kanzleramt*. Even more recently, *UKIP: The first 100 Days* presents the viewer with a scenario of the *United Kingdom Independence Party* (UKIP) winning the British national elections 2015 – and the possible consequences of such an event. What all these political television fictions share is their portrayal of what is usually inaccessible for the wider public: the 'backstage' of politics (Wodak 2015, 2011, 2010, 2009; Wodak & Forchtner 2014; Corner, Richardson & Perry 2012; van Zoonen & Wring 2012; Holly 2008; Corner & Pels 2003).

By turning to the far-less strategically planned and polished backstage of contemporary politics (at least in comparison to the thoroughly manufactured frontstage), this genre represents what is assumed, presupposed or even (half)known about the everyday life of politicians, about their private lives, their advisers and spin-doctors, possible scandals or conflicts, as well as the strategies and processes of political problem-solving (cf. Crawley 2006; Parry-Giles & Parry-Giles 2006; Challen 2001). As van Zoonen and Wring (2012, p. 265) rightly suggest, these modern dramas 'function as a source of political imagination and understanding, complementing or even contrasting with the standard sources that journalism offers'.

This is arguably at least one of the reasons why the media have started to recreate the backstage via films, soap operas, and other media, in order to satisfy the widespread demand, as expressed in opinion polls and surveys, to know more about how decisions are taken, how politicians live, and what their everyday lives might consist of, that is, what 'doing politics' might mean and imply. By providing an apparent window into the 'realities behind politics', such programmes construct a proximity that allows viewers to relate more closely to politics and politicians. In other words: emotionalisation, personalisation, aestheticisation, decreased distance and dramatisation all allow for easy identification and comprehensibility by the audience. Citizens and viewers disillusioned by present-day politics, disinformation and the so-called democratic deficit (Hay 2007) are thus offered more-or-less suggestive representations of the *backstage of politics* (Wodak 2011; Goffman 1967). Such representations are, however, not without danger as the displayed worlds frequently construct heroic politicians who seem to be able to: (1) reconcile various, highly demanding requirements of modern life; (2) remain distant from any *realpolitik*; and/or (3) display a political world that is similar to 'sex and crime' scenarios, full of dirty intrigues and even murder.

Against this background, we explore the socio-cultural function/s of such fictional dramas as a form of 'politicotainment' (Holly 2008; Richardson 2006) by asking: how do these TV dramas represent the world of politics, and what do these narratives imply for the field of politics and our understanding of it? We assume that the worlds created in such fictional dramas – a process we label, following Wodak (2011), the *fictionalisation of politics* and *the politicisation of fiction* – provide templates for how politics is both increasingly viewed by, as well as projected to, audiences who, in this genre, encounter a reduction in complexity of real-world problems thanks to seemingly wise, benevolent or simply power-hungry politicians. What we are addressing is thus firmly rooted in the new media ecology of the twenty-first century; in particular, in the shift towards 'media democracy' (Pels 2003; Grande 2000), with its focus on politics in terms of media personalities.

This trend towards mediatisation of modern societies implies a fundamental change in how contemporary societies operate as various areas (politics being only one of them) are increasingly affected by the rising significance of media logic (see Hjarvard 2013). Hjarvard (*ibidem*, p. 17), in fact, points to politics as a sphere that has integrated the media and which, simultaneously, leads to more and more of its operations taking place via the media.

In this chapter, we first provide some theoretical background on the notions of 'backstage and frontstage' before introducing relevant concepts from the Discourse-Historical Approach (DHA) in Critical Discourse Studies (CDS) (Reisigl & Wodak 2015; Wodak 2015, 2011) and narrative theory (Ricoeur 1992, 1984; Propp 1968). Subsequently, we turn to our empirical analysis. First, we point to *The West Wing* as one of the paradigmatic cases of this genre, which is centred on US President Josiah Bartlett as a largely unchallenged positive hero (Rollins & O'Connor 2003). Second, we turn to the acclaimed Danish soap *Borgen*, which depicts a world of coalition governments with a female Prime Minister, Birgitte Nyborg. Due to space limitations, we can only provide indicative examples instead of a thorough critical discourse analysis of the histories, marketisation and construal as brand of *The West Wing* and *Borgen*, and thus focus on the portrayal of two different types of heroes. Bartlett is presented as a *wise man* able to solve the huge problems of a complex world; a man with some (humanising) faults, yet much strength, a hero-type we summarise under the tag of *nurturing patriarch*. Nyborg, in turn, is represented as a tough, emotional, but also overstressed, ambitious and multitasking, caring politician – a leader who is described as 'a lonely and triumphant goddess',[1] and 'a virtuous politician who can't be as decent as she would like'.[2] She is represented as *mother and partner*, with personal problems, which partly emerge due to her prominent role in government. Nyborg is unexperienced, has to learn her role as decision-maker and big player, and she is forced to drop many ideals and illusions about 'doing politics' – we thus label her as a *nurturing multitasker*, both similar and different from Bartlett.

These two tags draw on insights developed by George Lakoff (2004) in the context of his concern for frames and conceptual metaphors in/and of the social world. By introducing the two frames of the 'Nurturing Parent' and the 'Strict Father', Lakoff (2004) presents an ideal–typical contrast between progressive and conservative world-views by depicting and constructing each as a style of parenting, thus conceptualising the President and government authorities of the nation, conceptualised as a family. We believe that both Bartlett and Nyborg relate to the frame of the 'Nurturing Parent' – though subtle differences exist – where it is assumed that the world is basically good, or at least that the good would win, after various struggles. However dangerous and difficult the world may be at present, it can thus only become better. In this kind of family, the highest moral values are empathy and responsibility. Responsibility is critical, since being a good nurturer means being responsible not only for looking after the well-being of others, but also being responsible to ourselves so that we can take care of others. In society, nurturant morality is expressed as social responsibility. This requires co-operation rather than competition, and recognition of interdependence (Lakoff 2004, p. 6).

This frame is juxtaposed with the 'Strict Father', struggling in a competitive world where there are necessarily winners and losers. As children (or people) are viewed as potentially weak and bad, they have to be disciplined. Morality and success are thus linked through discipline. Punishment is required to balance the moral books: if you do wrong, you must suffer a negative consequence. 'Strict Father' morality thus implies a natural traditional and conservative moral order.

In our conclusion, we speculate what such globalised views and beliefs about politics and politicians might imply for people's attitudes and opinions about politics; what are the consequences when our understandings of politics stem largely from this world of 'fictionalised politics'?

Staging and doing politics

Most examples in media studies cast their gaze on the work and life of politicians from outside, rather than within, the world of politics. These are official genres, designed for the public (Wodak 2011). This is what Erving Goffman (1959) referred to as 'frontstage' where actors perform in sanctioned public arenas, stage their work and are perceived by their various audiences. As Goffman noted:

> A correctly staged and performed character leads the audience to impute a self to a performed character, but this imputation – this self – is a product of a scene that comes off, and not the cause of it. The self, then, as a performed character, is not an organic thing that has a specific location, whose fundamental fate is to be born, to mature, and to die; it is a dramatic effect arising diffusely from a scene that is presented, and the characteristic issue, the crucial concern, is whether it will be credited or discredited.
> (Goffman 1959, pp. 252–253)

These activities follow specific norms and rules and are ritualised, as Murray Edelman (1967) claimed in his seminal book *The symbolic use of politics*. However, in contrast to this frontstage, we rarely have access to the backstage, to the '*politics de couloir*', the many conversations and the gossip in the corridors when politicians meet informally (Wodak 2015; Wodak et al. 2012; Krzyżanowski & Oberhuber 2007).

Backstage is where performers are present, but the wider audience is not. Here, the performers can step out of character without fear of disrupting the performance; 'the back region is the place where the impression fostered by the performance is knowingly contradicted as a matter of course' (Goffman 1959, p. 112). It is where facts suppressed in the frontstage and various kinds of informal actions may appear, which are not accessible to outsiders. Putting on a performance becomes a more difficult matter once a member of the audience is backstage. Politicians would not want to be seen by a member of the public practising a speech or being briefed by an adviser. The backstage is completely separate from the frontstage. No members of the audience can or should appear in the back. The actors adopt many strategies to ensure this; thus, access is controlled by gatekeepers (for example, visitors to the European Parliament are issued with special 'backstage entrance passes', which must be worn visibly, like an identification card).

Backstage, we need to stress, is a relative concept; it exists only in relation to a specific audience, at a specific time and in a specific place. In its truest sense, there can almost never be a genuine access 'behind the scenes'. Moreover, the media have created specific cinematic devices linking frontstage and backstage; usually by introducing long corridors that lead from one location to the next (for example from a backstage room to the frontstage press conference). Advisers accompany politicians, running to a specific event and briefing them on the way, which is a specific sub-genre termed '*walk-and-talk*' (Wodak 2011). The walk-and-talk scenes not only link front- and backstage; they establish hierarchies of knowledge and information (who talks about what to whom; who is informed about what and is allowed to pass on information to whom; who briefs whom; who addresses which topics; and so forth). In this way, walk-and-talk scenes establish the social order in the White House team, set the agenda, deliver important knowledge on events and social relations, and create a sense of urgency, of 'doing', of the immediate fast working of politics and political decision-making.[3]

Although the media focus primarily on the kind of 'grand politics' well documented in Edelman (1967), its more recent preoccupation with the cult of celebrity has led to interest in the private lives of politicians (Talbot 2007). Thus, private lives are perceived as newsworthy and scandalised, while news stories try to plot the genesis of important political decisions, searching for intrigues and conspiracies, especially at times of crisis or controversy (Brennan 2015; Klarer 2015; Ming 2015; Eriksson 2013; Tenenboim-Weinblatt 2013; Machin 2006; Richardson & Corner 2012). And as journalists and the media do not have access to the '*politics de couloir*', to the backstage and everyday life of politicians and their advisers, rumours and speculations find fertile ground in contemporary 24/7 news cycles.

Our natural curiosity for this unknown realm perhaps accounts for the popularity of other media forms that use an alternative, fictional route by which to represent and construct the everyday lives of politicians and the intricacies of decision-making: namely, films and soaps such as *Yes Minister*, *The West Wing* or *Im Kanzleramt*. These include culturally available repertoires, such as the Western genre in the case of *The West Wing* (Wright 1977). Although quite different in many ways, both *The West Wing* and *Borgen* have, for example, attracted

Figure 38.1 The West Wing advisers rushing through the corridors of the White House

millions of viewers across the globe and are arguably part of one particular genre. A 'genre' may be characterised, following Fairclough (1995, p. 14), as the conventionalised, more-or-less schematically fixed use of language associated with a particular activity, as 'a socially ratified [that is, socially accepted] way of using language in connection with a particular type of social activity'. Similar to Fairclough's definition, Bakhtin (1986, p. 60) spoke already of genre in terms of '[e]ach separate utterance is individual, of course, but each sphere in which language is used develops its own relatively stable types of these utterances'. What characterises the series we are interested in, what makes such series so attractive? Which interests and needs among mass audiences are they satisfying? As Rollins and O'Connor (2003) elaborate, there is no simple answer to these questions. There are many possible factors motivating audiences to watch these programmes, ranging from simple curiosity to the identification with 'alternative' politics.

For example, viewers might appreciate the portrayal of politicians and their advisers as so-called normal human beings, as 'one of us'. However, Levine (2003, p. 62) rightly states that 'curiously, it [*The West Wing*] turns a blind eye to the stories of staff politics and factionalism inside the White House'. This indicates that, although politicians are depicted as emotional, irrational and ambivalent human beings, they all seem to identify with the 'noble cause' and rarely compete with each other or contradict each other. *The West Wing* thus creates an impression of peace and unity unlikely to mirror actual conditions (Podhoretz 2003). Such fiction might, however, acquire the status of reality, the case of the fictionalisation of politics, and Crawley therefore makes the interesting point that the:

> lure of television is that it promises to bring a new opportunity that is as much about 'intellectual intimacy' as it is about emotional closeness. Intellectually, the public may recognize the players of the familiar presidential performance but what allows them to repeatedly watch the 'soap opera' is, in part, the hope that the next politician will make them feel better.
>
> (Crawley 2006, pp. 128–129)

As in any representation, soaps like *The West Wing* and *Borgen* offer a specific perspective on how 'politics is done' for the US-American or European lay audiences (and because the series have been dubbed in many languages, also almost worldwide). However, while watching these series (and similar productions in other countries), we might ask ourselves whether or not this is the *only* way, or whether it is instead just *one* way of 'doing politics'. Indeed, we might question whether the representation of 'doing politics' in soap operas does in fact resemble the 'real' everyday life of politics at all. In both cases, we need to ask *how* the media represent politics in this particular way.

Narratives and myths

Central in how stories (*narrative* and *story* are used synonymously in the following) such as these are presented are, first, a couple of concepts that capture relations between texts and discourses through which meaning arises. *Intertextuality* refers to the fact that all texts are linked to other texts, both in the past and in the present. Such links can be established in different ways: through continued reference to a topic or the main actors throughout the TV series; through reference to the same events; or by the transfer of central arguments from one text into the next. The latter process is also known as *recontextualisation*. By taking an argument and restating it in a new context, we first observe the process of decontextualisation, and then, when the respective element is implemented in a new context, of recontextualisation. The element then acquires a new meaning because meanings are formed in use (Wittgenstein 1967). *Interdiscursivity*, however, indicates that discourses are linked to each other in various ways. If we define discourse as primarily topic-related, that is a discourse on a political actor, event, object or process, then a discourse on terrorism, for example, may typically refer to the topics or sub-topics of other discourses, such as religion, gender, threat, security or racism.

Second, we point to the narrative form (Bruner 1991; Ricoeur 1984) and some of its particularities in order to make sense of these series and their appeal (cf. also Forchtner 2016; Forchtner & Kølvraa 2015). Narratives enable us to depict changes or developments, in other words, the succession of *events*, involving the selection of events, their fore- and backgrounding, and the choice to arrange them according to the fundamental schema of beginning, middle, and ending. An event, Paul Ricoeur (1984, p. 65) claims, 'only gets its definition from its contribution to the development of the [narrative's] plot'. The force of narrative derives from its linear arrangement of (selected) events in a unified plotline, making the succession, the (implicit) causalities and the conclusions of the story appear natural (Ricoeur 1992, p. 142). What we want to focus on here, is the particular status of the hero in narratives – due to the fact that it is in the figure of the hero that a story becomes 'condensed'.

This character is also one of the categories Vladimir Propp (1968) derived from his seminal analysis of folk tales.[4] His thoughts on 'the hero' point to at least two crucial dimensions. First, heroes are always in search of, or even locked in a struggle for, something. Second, the position given to this character implies that the audience will be invited to associate/identify itself with the hero. Here, we return to Ricoeur (1992, p. 147) whose notion of narrative identity rests on the claim that '*[i]t is the identity of the story that makes the identity of the character*', that is:

> that the traits of the main hero cannot be at odds with the kind of story narrated about him. It is only heuristically [possible,] that one can separate a 'stable' categorical identity, which is associated with the listing of certain personality traits, from the narrative identity developed in the unfolding of the story, in order to analyze how these two are interwoven (Ricoeur, 1991).
>
> (Forchtner & Kølvraa 2015, p. 132)

This construal of the hero relates to classical myths and sagas (Achilles, Siegfried, and many others) which have, in turn, informed meaning-making in contemporary societies. For example, Wright was able to illustrate that the genre of Wild West films fulfils important functions for American society in creating myths about the pioneers colonising and exploring the frontiers. Moreover, the simple Manichean division of 'good' and 'bad' represented by hero and villain forms a basis for the perception and interpretation of historic events where the good win and the bad lose. As we have already noted, individual texts (episodes) are embedded in a web of contexts through which the good and the bad gain their particular meaning. In line with this, Wright maintains that:

> If the form of a myth as narrative is a model for making sense of experience, then the content of particular myths embodies and makes possible this model. [...] The social meanings of myth may become identified with the fundamental organization of understanding by which the mind knows itself and its world. For this reason, it is apparent that if we are fully to understand and explain specific human actions, we must

be able to relate those actions to the social narratives or myths of the society to which the actor belongs. It is at least partly through these myths that he makes sense of his world, and thus the meaning of his actions – both to himself and his society – can only be grasped through a knowledge of the structure and meaning of the myth.

(Wright 1977, p. 184)

When viewing the enormously positive reception of *The West Wing* and the emotional identification with the character of President Bartlett, it makes sense to relate the above to this form of politicotainment. Indeed, Crawley (2006, p. 141) suggests that this fictional President conforms to stereotyped conceptions of a President for the show's US audience, with all his flaws as human being and President: he is intellectual, moral, fatherly and authoritative, and creates a unique meaning system which complies with US traditions and viewers' expectations. Furthermore, Crawley (2006, p. 129) quotes several instances in the US where this fictional world is held up as an exemplary model to the real world of politics. Even organisations such as the teachers' union, the National Education Association, or journalists in the *New York Times* and the *Detroit Free Press* refer to Bartlett's policies as a good model to be followed, or mention characteristics of President Bartlett that the-then presidential candidates Gore and Bush 'would be wise to copy'. The recontextualisation is also apparent outside of the US: the *Guardian* (5 July 2009), in a long report describing then Conservative leader David Cameron's ideas about his possible role as Prime Minister, should the Labour Party lose the 2010 general election (as they did in 2010), frequently referred to *The West Wing*. This illustrates how *The West Wing* serves as both global-knowledge brand and context model for the 'ideal politician' and 'politics as usual' (see also Wodak 2010, p. 56 for an extensive discussion): it is a typical example of presenting specific protagonists (spin-doctors, advisers and strong Presidents) as models for real politicians.

Vignette 1: *The West Wing*, or, the story of a nurturing patriarch

The episode ('Commencement'), which first aired in 2003, takes place on the eve of Bartlett's daughter Zoey's commencement. Bartlett, represented as a rather traditional hero, gains authority through wisdom. He is the nurturing parent, overcoming resistance, as in a romantic story (Frye 1957). There is never any doubt who the good guys are, and who is bad and evil. It is certainly the case that Bartlett is not a strict father – yet, he also does not transcend the very form of a traditional hero. Instead, he represents an authoritative voice, but one which is good and wise.

Moreover, as already mentioned, Bartlett depicts the liberal US-American values found in many films (Wodak 2010). The White House and the West Wing are metonyms for the biggest power hubs in US-American politics – this is where the President takes decisions, receives advice, meets staff, welcomes foreign state visits, and negotiates with oppositional politicians and the press. This is where US-American politics is done. The opposition, in this case, the Republican Party, always attempts to oppose and obstruct via their seats in the Senate and Congress; however, due to the two-party system in the US, there are no possibilities (or any tradition) for coalition governments. Thus, the President in the US is not a representative figure (as in some European countries), but effectively the most powerful politician in the US government. In this way, the socio-political and historical contexts in *The West Wing* and *Borgen* are very different – when watching these soaps, the contexts have to be kept in mind in order to understand the subtle underlying intertextual meanings and insinuations as well as presuppositions.

In the following extracts, Bartlett briefs the staff on his past role in a covert killing after five alleged terrorists go missing. Fearing the controversy this may create, press secretary C. J. Cregg is forced to strike a deal with her former boyfriend and influential journalist, Danny, in order to keep the truth buried. Meanwhile, a new Secret Service agent is assigned to protect the graduate Zoey, who wants to spend three months in Paris with her boyfriend after graduation. Bartlett is represented as a shrewd politician, coping with potential terrorists, but also as a concerned father who wants to persuade his daughter to stay in the US. However, Zoey vanishes. Meanwhile, the wife of the President's personal adviser, Toby, gives birth to twins. Furthermore, throughout the whole episode, we observe the President preparing for commencement and the speech he is due to give there. His – African-American – adviser, Will, helps him prepare the speech at the very last minute. A recurrent theme in *The West Wing,* is that Bartlett excels when giving speeches, even – and sometimes especially – when they are given spontaneously and without notes.

In this scene, Will is instructed to make a start on the speech. Bartlett casually throws out for consideration a number of historical quotes in a gesture that alludes to his broad knowledge. However, Will also reminds the President of his wish to convince Zoey to stay in the US, suggesting that the speech might be counter-productive; while the speech exhorts the nation to embrace change and adventure, Bartlett is concerned to keep his daughter safe at home.

> BARTLETT: I've been thinking I'd like to talk about creativity. Why don't you get started on some thoughts and I'll join you.
> WILL: yes sir.
> BARTLETT: what do you think about using the Eudora Welty quote instead of the Gandhi.
> WILL: Well, I think they both work, but since I wouldn't make any more changes, I'd stay with Gandhi…
> BARTLETT: 'You must be the change'– is that it – 'You must be the change you wish to see in the world,' it sounds too much like Eastern philosophy.
> WILL: Well, it was bound to, Sir.
> BARTLETT: 'Cause Gandhi lived in India.
> WILL: Yeah. Sir, this speech is about creativity and in my judgement it's a home run. Now what it isn't is a speech that will convince Zoey not to go to France tomorrow.
> BARTLETT: Well let's write that one.
> *And we HEAR the double quintet strike up Pomp and Circumstance.*

Nevertheless, Will observes that as it stands the first draft is a 'home run'. This sports metaphor (from baseball) serves to create identification with the American audience, as perhaps does the protective urge to keep his daughter at home. The President's response is short and unequivocal: what is needed is a speech that will keep his daughter safe. When it comes to it, Bartlett's paternal instincts win out, creating yet a further point of identification for the audience. In this brief interaction, the structure and content of the speech are decided; now it only remains to be written. Although the aide, Will, addresses the President with the deferential epithet 'Sir', the interaction nevertheless resembles a brain-storming between peers; hierarchy remains latent, and the President readily accepts advice and criticism.

In this scene, the hero's exceptional ability is foregrounded. With the casual confidence of a skilful orator, the President has not bothered to write up the whole speech, he merely has notes written on napkins stuffed in his pockets. Unfortunately, by putting on his university gown, he cannot retrieve the notes, and thus, he suddenly discovers when desperately searching for – and not finding – his notes that he will have to speak without consulting them.

> AIDE: Mr. President?
> BARTLETT *understands it's time. He zips up his gown, which includes the requisite chevrons for his degrees, honours and disciplines and two cowls. The uniform of academic knighthood.*
> CHANCELLOR: Are you ready, Mr. President?
> BARTLETT: Yeah. Thanks, Will, for the help.
> WILL: (smiles) Use the Eudora Welty, it's better.
> BARTLETT: Thank you.
> *And BARTLETT and the CHANCELLOR, also impressively decked out in academic badges, lead the procession of FACULTY in their gowns and as they come out, the SPECTATORS all stand and APPLAUD.*
> CHANCELLOR: I understand you're not using the Tele Prompter.
> BARTLETT: Yeah, no, I've got it down here folder…and on some napkins in pockets. In this my
> CHANCELLOR: Are you gonna be all right with that?
> BARTLETT: Oh yeah, I'll be fine, you know unless something comes up.
> CHANCELLOR: like what?
> BARTLETT: Well for instance I just realized I don't have access to my pockets anymore, but you know, what are you gonna do?!

The rhetorical question at the end of this brief sequence manifests both the President's witty self-irony (at not being able to find his notes; a safe and humorous moment of human frailty) and his jovial self-assurance that he will just have to manage without his notes, which – as we are meant to infer – will not cause any problems for him. Our hero's exceptional ability is further underlined in the preceding sequence, where the university chancellor is surprised that the President will not make use of the tele-prompter. Earlier in the scene, we again see the human, approachable side of our hero as he takes time to thank his aide, Will, who in turn throws out a last-minute word of advice about which quote to use.

These two sequences illustrate several important characteristics of the President: he has a sense of humour, accepts advice and criticism, and is knowledgeable (even about Eastern philosophy). He also proposes the rather abstract notion of 'creativity' as the general topic for his speech, further adding to this portrayal of a liberal-minded and intellectual hero. He interacts quite informally with his aides and team, is spontaneous and flexible, capable of accommodating new situations quickly, and subtly strategic (he would like to convince his daughter to stay at home, so crafts a speech specifically tailored so as to persuade his daughter). As we have seen, he is also self-confident (he knows that he can manage without notes). Indeed, one might speculate whether this performance (speaking without notes) was staged so that he would have the opportunity to display his oratory prowess. Thus, in sum this hero-type can be described as a nurturing patriarch, an essentially good and wise man who takes equal care of both the nation as well as his family. It is, however, also a subject-type that comes close to a traditional, romantic hero who, in our case due to expertise and knowledge instead of his sword, is poised to steer his people through difficult periods and overcome such obstacles. As such, this patriarch invites unproblematic identification by the audience.

Through this scene, and of course many more throughout this episode, a wise, amiable and paternal hero is constructed who will ultimately protect his daughter and save the country from terrorists. This basic plot structure is repeated in other episodes, suggesting that *The West Wing* genre resembles traditional (that is, simple) plots where heroes save the country from dangerous villains and win in the end. This also means, however, that the series implicitly constructs politics as a series of stories where the good and the bad are easily distinguished and the wise President will finally make the right decisions.

Borgen however, as will become apparent below, differs in some relevant aspects; featuring a less generic plot and offering a less melodramatic separation into good and bad.

Vignette 2: *Borgen*, or, the story of a nurturing multitasker

At the centre of the (so-far) final season, season 3, we encounter two women; first, Nyborg who has returned to politics after her meteoric rise to Prime Minister in season 1 was followed by her exit in order to care for her children in season 2, and, second, Katrine Fønsmark, her spin-doctor. Both are single mothers, but, as middle-upper class, highly educated women, they remain distant from the reality that most single mothers in low-paid, insecure jobs experience. Nevertheless, this context alone provides a different background for the fictionalisation of politics than the stories of male heroes analysed above. Of course, President Bartlett cares for his daughter and mobilises the FBI and the army whenever she is in danger; however, he has a dedicated wife who is in charge of the everyday life routines of the family. The US-American family is characterised by traditional gender roles and does not require the President to deal with the dilemmas faced by single parents.

These differences are embedded in a much wider set of diverging structures: it is certainly no coincidence that it is a Scandinavian political soap that has put a female Prime Minister centre-stage. The political system in which Nyborg operates is also evidently different from that of the US, given that the former is a multi-party system, a factor that contributes much to the drama. However, similar to *The West Wing*, the political scene is closely mapped onto real-world conflicts and dynamics. While *The West Wing* alludes extensively to the conflict between Democrats and Republicans, the difference between former President Clinton and the-then President Bush, those familiar with Danish politics will easily recognise how closely the parties – and in many cases, characters – in *Borgen* map onto the country's political landscape.

In order to elaborate on the difference between the two series, let us consider episode 9 of the third season of *Borgen*. The election campaign is in full swing and Nyborg's party, the New Democrats, have become established and stable; the party looks forward to winning four to six mandates. This would be a success for a new party, but it would not be enough to influence politics and would thus only be another small party in opposition. This is largely due to the fact that one member of the party's inner circle, Nete Buch, had forwarded strategic information to their main rivals, the also centrist Moderates under Jacob Kruse. The latter were thus able to appropriate proposal after proposal by the New Democrats (greenwashing their programme, taking a harder stance against the anti-immigrant Freedom Party, etc.) and have thereby squeezed the political space.

In this situation, Brigitte decides to take a risk by attacking the Moderates, unmasking their hypocrisy and positioning the New Democrats as the true 'party of the centre'. At a public debate with Kruse, she attacks their policies, literally tearing apart their programme. In consequence, the Moderates start a campaign against her, by attacking her personality (*ad hominem*), to which Brigitte reacts by stating concisely that 'We'll stick to politics. Let Kruse wear himself out with personal attacks'. However, Fønsmark, her spin-doctor, is sceptical, a stance which is fuelled by Kasper Juul, the former spin-doctor of Nyborg, and father of Fønsmark's son, who offers Fønsmark proof of what would be a major scandal: the young and married Kruse had caused a car accident under the influence of alcohol (with a mistress at his side). Being aware of the contemporary media logic, Fønsmark is convinced that the story needs to be published:

> FØNSMARK: It's a good one.
> JUUL: Amazing.

While showing her close up and absolutely delighted for several seconds, Fønsmark then turns her head in anticipation of Nyborg's stance, saying '[i]t's not our kind of thing'. Juul, in turn, acts as a manipulator, suggesting to practice the dark arts of leaking materials to the public while protecting his boss from any accusation of involvement. In fact, we see Fønsmark calling a newspaper but, ultimately, hanging up and trying to convince Nyborg to receive authorisation for using the material without discrediting her; something the latter, however, rejects on moral grounds. As Kruse's attacks increase, her colleagues expect Nyborg to react, but she sticks to her commitment not to attack her opponent personally. Instead, she commissions a serious calculation of the credibility of the Moderates' economic policy (making the viewer wonder whether or not Nyborg actually understands the public which – as is presupposed as common knowledge – is receptive to scandals).

One day later, we see Fønsmark in her messy flat, searching for her son's shoe, bumping her head and taking a phone call (she is late). As Juul arrives to look after their son, Gustav, he tells her that he had seen Kruse with two journalists responsible for the witch hunt and is surprised that the New Democrats have not followed his advice to publish the aforementioned materials.

The situation changes in the evening of the very same day (two days before the election) when a tabloid journalist harasses Laura, Nyborg's daughter. When informed about this event, Nyborg (who is meeting her mentor Bent Sejrø, as well as Katrine Fønsmark) loses control – the safety of her children is an absolute priority.

> NYBORG: They have to leave my children alone.
> SEJRØ: You know how it is.
> NYBORG: They can call me a hypocrite. But they have to lay off my children. It is
>   definitely Kruse's doing. [2] Run it.

Bent is surprised as he has not heard of this opportunity but protests:

> SEJRØ: Birgitte, don't do it.
> NYBORG (walking up and down like a tiger in a cage): He's gone too far.
> SEJRØ: It's not politically relevant.
> NYBORG: He went for my children.

While viewers might sympathise with this account of political life, as it triggers identification with Brigitte and a mother's reaction, and also reminds them of their own emotions, it is important to note the presence of Bent Sejrø, who clearly tells the audience (and Nyborg) what the 'right' thing to do would be. Indeed, *Borgen* does not seem to justify Nyborg's response, not even at this point – given that she calls her partner later in the night, telling him, 'I am afraid, I have gone over to the dark side'.

When she goes through the newspapers the next morning, but cannot find the story, she calls Fønsmark. The latter confesses to not submitting the information and is prepared to get fired. However, Nyborg says that 'It was a bit... hasty of me. I'm grateful you didn't'. Ultimately, this tactic proves to be successful as, in the final debate, Nyborg takes Kruse by surprise with her detailed economic critique of the Moderates' programme and thereby, ultimately, secures her triumph in the election in a rational and unemotional way.

When comparing this episode to *The West Wing's* values and gist, what does the audience learn from this vignette? When approaching this question, we suggest the tag of nurturing multitasker for Nyborg: she is undoubtedly 'nurturing' and 'good', thus inviting identification. However, she is also troubling and troubled, never simply represented as a stereotypical female politician, thus as 'tough, cold, and ambitious' or 'motherly, emotional, and caring', but rather as a politician who learns and then knows how to play the game. At the same time, there are clear limits: she is not prepared to play dirty and, when she finally does, it is presented as a failure. Indeed, she ultimately regrets her decision and, luckily, it was not implemented anyway. However, while this episode seems to offer a happy ending, the latter is only enabled by a friend, Katrine, while Nyborg acknowledges her wrong decision and judgement.

This plot – a good person fails but, together with the support of her loyal team, ultimately succeeds in doing the 'right thing' – is not an isolated incident. After all, in another major storyline in season 3, when Nyborg is diagnosed with breast cancer, she tries to fight the illness on her own. After a series of private and professional setbacks, she realizes her 'weakness', tells her children and colleagues about her illness, and succeeds in overcoming the cancer. Thus, she is also more than a stereotypical patriarch, not simply standing above things and managing everything with ease. Rather, she is constantly multitasking, trying to cope with many challenges. Bondebjerg (2015, p. 7) offers a convincing model by proposing four 'spaces' that Nyborg has to confront daily: political, media, private and social – something that 'realistically' must result in unsatisfactory outcomes: multitasking tends to cause failure and, consequently, leads to a rather fragmented hero-type who, while still inviting identification by the audience, nevertheless does so in a less affirmative, more complex way.

Conclusion

Throughout *The West Wing*, heroes are, even in situations related to private and intimate issues, constructed as (charismatic) authorities and assigned mythical qualities (such as being able to solve the 'big problems of the world'). The complexity of politics in a global world is thus simplified; complex, multi-dimensional processes across space and time, and a diversity of social fields are reduced to telegenic personalities, distinct events and simple solutions. The above-mentioned reactions of the audience and press demonstrate that such representations produce and reproduce stereotyped expectations towards, and beliefs about, politics, exploiting cognitive and emotional schemata or shared 'mental models' of the behaviour and life of politicians, which in fact do not relate to the complex reality in political institutions. In effect, such stories construct a banal and romanticised version of politics that often bears very little resemblance to the real world. Nevertheless, part of the appeal of these programmes is that they appear to offer viewers a 'behind the scenes' look at a familiar yet inaccessible social practice. For this reason, they need to offer a recognisable representation of that practice.

Borgen is not fundamentally different in this respect; however, it asks the audience to identify with a 'modern family': first, a career woman who is accused of neglecting her husband and her children, and then learns to set her priorities in a different way. Second, a female politician who learns 'doing politics' the hard way, becomes successful and manages the daily negotiations and setbacks, the strategies and tactics (*realpolitik*) very well. And third, learning to cope with challenges in her private and public life in independent ways, taking decisions for which she is responsible without relying too much on her advisers.

In both, and also in other similar programmes, politics becomes manageable in space and time, divisible into temporal sequences and units. Politics is thus packaged and glamorised through plot devices and dramatic tropes, taking place amid anxiety, panic, danger, imminent disaster, intrigue, illness, comic moments, love affairs, and so on. Problems are solved and each story given a moral. The hero lastly wins and 'good' values triumph. In contrast, empirical research on the everyday life of real politicians illustrates (Wodak 2011) that their life is far from neatly packaged into stories, isolated problems and straightforward plots. Rather, it is a hectic life, filled with a variety of activities ranging from repetitive routines to complex decision-making and the management of urgent affairs. Themes, agendas and topics merge into one another; there seems to be no explicit temporal order as to when and how agendas are finalised and implemented; and many different agendas are pursued at the same time. Disturbances can always – and unpredictably – occur.

The *fictionalisation of politics* (and the *politicisation of fiction*), therefore, has several consequences: creating a world that is still manageable through the traditional routines of politics; through diplomacy, press conferences, speeches and negotiations. This is a world where 'good' values prevail – (where what is 'good' is defined by the series, the presupposed morals, and represented by the fictional characters). This world also, potentially, 'educates' by exploiting the passivising medium of televised politicotainment to socialise the audience into the 'good values' it constructs and, perhaps, to stimulate greater interest in politics in an increasingly apathetic electorate.

As the preceding analyses demonstrate, *The West Wing* creates a myth about the activities and characters of US politics, in contrast to the existing experiences of incomprehensibility that draw on particular schemata with a long tradition in the US, in the genre of Western (cowboy) films. Moreover, *The West Wing* has to be interpreted against the background of enormous dislike and critique of the Bush government after 9/11 and nostalgia – wishing back a liberal Clinton-like President. In contrast, *Borgen* depicts the trajectory of an ambitious and successful woman, struggling with multiple challenges in her family and working lives. Both TV soaps offer a range of options for identification. As *The West Wing* and *Borgen* are also translated and aired worldwide, the various storylines are recontextualised in other countries and cultures. They carry implications for audience beliefs about, and engagement with, the real world of politics. Given the manifest popularity of these programmes, we hope that critical reflection on the impact of the *fictionalisation of politics* will inform future research.

Notes

1 www.imdb.com/title/tt1526318/reviews
2 www.npr.org/2014/02/04/271525839/borgen-is-denmarks-west-wing-but-even-better
3 This is, by the way, also true for the everyday life of politicians in huge organisations such as the European Parliament. In the first author's own observations, briefing and updating of politicians by their advisors takes place in the long corridors, running from one meeting to the next (Wodak 2011).

4 Propp extended the Russian Formalist approach to the study of narrative structure. In the Formalist approach, sentence structures were broken down into analysable elements termed *morphemes*. Drawing on this approach, Propp devised an analogous method for analysing Russian folktales, identifying 31 generic functions performed by archetypal characters (hero, villain, victim, and so forth – see Propp 1968, pp. 25–65 and 84–86).

References

Bakhtin, M M, 1986, 'The problem of speech genres', in *Speech genres and other late essays*, University of Texas Press, Austin, TX, pp. 60–102.
Bondebjerg, I, 2015, 'The mediatization of politics in contemporary Scandinavian film and television', *Palgrave Communications*, vol. 1, available from: www.palgrave-journals.com/articles/palcomms20153 [accessed 12 May 2016].
Brennan, N P, 2015, 'Authority, resistance, and representing national values in the Brazilian miniseries', *Media, Culture & Society*, vol. 37, no. 2, pp. 686–702.
Bruner, J, 1991, 'The narrative construction of reality', *Critical Inquiry*, vol. 18, no. 1, pp. 1–21.
Challen, P, 2001, *Inside the West Wing. An unauthorized look at television's smartest show*, ECW Press, Toronto, ON.
Corner, J & Pels, D, eds., 2003, *Media and the restyling of politics*, Sage, London.
Crawley, M, 2006, *Mr. Sorkin goes to Washington. Shaping the president on television's The West Wing*, McFarland and Company, Jefferson, NC.
Edelman, M, 1967, *The symbolic uses of politics*, University of Illinois Press, Chicago, IL.
Eriksson, B, 2013, 'Pure and public, popular and personal and the inclusiveness of *Borgen* as a public service blockbuster'. *Akademisk Kvarter*, vol. 7, pp. 80–92.
Fairclough, N, 1995, *Critical Discourse Analysis: The critical study of language*, Longman, London.
Forchtner, B, 2016, *Lessons from the past? Memory, narrativity and subjectivity*, Palgrave Macmillan, Basingstoke.
Forchtner, B & Kølvraa, C, 2015, 'Peace and unity: Imagining EUrope in the founding fathers' housemuseums', in *Cultural memories of nonviolent struggle: powerful times*, eds. A Reading & T Katriel, Palgrave Macmillan, Basingstoke, pp. 128–146.
Frye, N, 1957, *Anatomy of criticism: four essays*, Princeton University Press, Princeton, NJ.
Goffman, E, 1959, *The presentation of self in everyday life*, Anchor Books, New York.
Goffman, E, 1981, *Forms of talk*, University of Pennsylvania Press, Philadelphia.
Grande, E, 2000, 'Charisma und Komplexität: Verhandlungsdemokratie, Mediendemokratie und der Funktionswandel politischer Eliten', *Leviathan*, vol. 28, no. 1, pp. 122–141.
Hay, C, 2007, *Why we hate politics*, Polity Press, Cambridge.
Holly, W, 2008, 'Tabloidization of political communication in the public sphere', in *Communication in the public sphere. Handbook of Applied Linguistics*, vol. IV, eds. R Wodak & V Koller, De Gruyter, Berlin, pp. 317–342.
Klarer, M, 2015, 'Putting television "aside": novel narration in House of Cards', *New Review of Television and Film Studies*, vol. 12, no. 2, pp. 203–220.
Krzyżanowski, M & Oberhuber, F, 2007, *(Un)Doing Europe. Discourses and practices of negotiating the EU constitution*, Peter Lang, Brussels.
Lakoff, G, 2004, *Don't think of an elephant!* Chelsea Green, Berkeley.
Levine, M, 2003, '*The West Wing* (NBC) and the West Wing (D.C.): Myth and reality in the television's portrayal of the White House', in *The West Wing*, eds. J E O'Connor & P C Rollins, Syracuse University Press, Syracuse, NY, pp. 42–62.
Machin, D & Niblock, S, 2006, *News production. Theory and practice*. Routledge, London.
Ming, J, 2015, 'Prohibition and production of the past: Representation of the Cultural Revolution in TV dramas', *Media, Culture & Society*, vol. 37, no. 5, pp. 671–685.
Parry-Giles, T & Parry-Giles, S, 2006, *The prime-time presidency: The West Wing and U.S. nationalism*, University of Illinois Press, Chicago, IL.

Pels, D, 2003, 'Aesthetic representation and political style: rebalancing identity and difference in media-democracy' in *Media and the restyling of politics: Consumerism, celebrity and cynicism*, eds. J Corner & D Pels, Sage, London, pp. 41–66.

Podhoretz, J, 2003, 'The liberal imagination' in *The West Wing*, eds. J E O'Connor & P C Rollins, Syracuse University Press, Syracuse, NY, pp. 222–234.

Propp, V, 1968, *Morphology of the folktale*, University of Texas Press, Austin, TX.

Reisigl, M & Wodak, R, 2015, 'The discourse-historical approach (DHA)' in *Methods of Critical Discourse Studies*, eds. R Wodak & M Meyer, Sage, London, pp. 23–61.

Richardson, K, 2006, 'The dark arts of good people: how popular culture negotiates "spin" in NBC's "The West Wing"', *Journal of Sociolinguistics*, vol. 10, no. 1, pp. 52–69.

Richardson, K, Parry, K & Corner, J, 2012, *Political culture and media genre: Beyond the news*, Palgrave Macmillan, London.

Ricoeur, P, 1984, *Time and narrative, vol. 1*, University of Chicago Press, Chicago, IL.

Ricoeur, P, 1991, 'Narrative identity', *Philosophy Today*, vol. 35, no. I, pp. 73–81.

Ricoeur, P 1992, *Oneself as another*, University of Chicago Press, Chicago, IL.

Talbot, M, 2007, *Media discourse: Representation and interaction*, Edinburgh University Press, Edinburgh.

Tenenboim-Weinblatt, K, 2013, 'The path to political substance: Exploring the mediatized discourse surrounding controversial media texts', *Political Communication*, vol. 30, no. 4, pp. 582–601.

Wittgenstein, L, 1967, *Philosophische Untersuchungen*, Suhrkamp, Frankfurt am Main.

Wodak, R, 2009, 'Language and politics' in *English language: Description, variation and context*, eds. J Culpeper, F Katamba, P Kerswill, R Wodak & T McEnery, Palgrave Macmillan, Basingstoke, pp. 576 – 593.

Wodak, R, 2010, 'The glocalization of politics in television: fiction or reality?', *European Journal of Cultural Studies*, vol. 13, no. 1, pp. 1–20.

Wodak, R, 2011, *The discourse of politics in action. Politics as usual*, 2nd revised edition, Palgrave Macmillan, Basingstoke.

Wodak, R, 2015, *The politics of fear. What right-wing populist discourses mean*, Sage, London.

Wodak, R & Forchtner, B, 2014, 'Embattled Vienna 1683/2010: Right-wing populism, collective memory and the fictionalization of politics', *Visual Communication*, vol. 13, no. 2, pp. 231–255.

Wodak, R, Krzyżanowski, M & Forchtner, B, 2012, 'The interplay of language ideologies and contextual cues in multilingual interactions: Language choice and code-switching in European Union organizations', *Language in Society*, vol. 41, no. 2, pp. 1–30.

Wright, W, 1977, *Sixguns and society. A structural study of the Western*, University of California Press, Berkeley.

Zoonen, L & Wring, D, 2012, 'Trends in political television fiction in the UK: Themes, characters, and narratives, 1965–2009', *Media, Culture & Society*, vol. 34, no. 3, pp. 263–279.

39
Religion and the secular

Teemu Taira

Introduction

US Secretary of State, John Kerry, wrote in 2015 that 'if I headed back to college today, I would major in comparative religions rather than political science. That is because religious actors and institutions are playing an influential role in every region of the world' (Kerry 2015). He referred to religion having an influence on politics, diplomacy, violence and peace-building, among others. Indeed, such topics are common among scholars in disciplines and subject areas such as religious studies, International Relations, politics, history and sociology. However, only some of the approaches consider the role of language. This chapter explores how the modern distinction between religion and the secular has become a debated and contested discursive tool in the political organisation of contemporary societies. Although the terms are old, the distinction itself – locating the 'secular' as the 'non-religious' sphere of public politics, as distinct from the private, non-political sphere of 'religion' – has a specific modern history. This discourse is in operation in scholarly works as well as in public debates (media, politics).

For the sake of simplicity, the area of study can be divided into two main approaches, although there are significant differences within each approach. The first one uses religion and the secular as analytical concepts, defining them and exploring the ways in which the two are separated or integrated in theory and practice. It sees them as two different languages with two different rationalities, often ending up offering a normative standpoint that should guide the organisation of society and politics. Section one will examine this approach. The second one does not define the terms, but studies their uses in different contexts and explores what various actors are trying to achieve by separating religion and the secular. The second section introduces this approach and contrasts it with the approach presented in the first. The next section will focus on recent ways in which religion and the secular have been distinguished from each other in public discourse. The concluding section will summarise the argument and suggest ways forward.

Two languages: religion and the secular as analytical concepts

Habermas and the post-secular

The key dividing line in current scholarly debate concerning religion and the secular in different disciplines is between those who see the distinction as analytically meaningful and those who see the distinction as an object of discursive study. For instance, the influential work of Jürgen Habermas is a good example of the former. Habermas (2010, 2011) sees religion and the secular as two different rationalities. Religious language is the language of a particular community, whereas secular language is supposedly universal, common to all. This is typical for the modern discourse that is predicated on the idea that religion should be a private matter, whereas secular language dominates public and political spheres. Habermas' writings on the post-secular address the problem that follows from modern discourse: people who are 'authorized to practice their religion and to lead a pious life in their role as citizens are supposed to participate in a democratic process whose results must be kept free of any religious "contamination"' (Habermas 2011, p. 24). The writings begin with the assumption that religion has (or should have) been separated from the rational conversation of the public sphere, but now the norm has to be re-evaluated: religion should not be excluded from public discussion, although religion remains subordinated to the rules of public discussion, because religious arguments and utterances should be translated into secular, 'generally accessible language' (Habermas 2011, p. 25).

One of the rare examples of translations Habermas provides is that the biblical idea that humans are created in the image of God can be translated as a defence of human freedom and autonomy. The reasons why Habermas seeks to find bridges between two supposedly different languages in politics, and more generally in the public sphere, are at least two-fold. First, that is how the public discussion becomes more inclusive and more democratic, thus providing a more solid foundation for society. Second, Habermas assumes that religions are moral resources. Understood in this manner, religions appear as special cases supplementing what is lacking in secular rational discussion. In this sense, Habermas' way of conceptualising two distinct languages is rather conservative if secular language and morality are not enough to protect people against the potential risks of technology, science and global capitalism. Therefore, there are two ways of interpreting Habermas' vision of the relationship between religion and the secular in his writings on the post-secular: (1) the slightly anti-religious way, which sees religions in need of translation in order to be part of rational (and secular) deliberation; and (2) the moderately pro-religious way, which sees secular deliberation in need of moral support from religions.

Habermas is widely discussed, but many others have addressed religion/secular models by which societies are organised and should be organised. For instance, the distinction between religion and the secular has been operationalised differently in different nation-states. The United States works as a case for pro-religious secularism. This means that secularism is meant to guarantee freedom of religion and equality for all groups and practices in such a way that they can flourish in the private sphere and civil society. France offers another model by applying a strong principle of state neutrality towards religions by not supporting any of them. The UK model is built upon the established church (Church of England). It guarantees a privileged role to one institution, but it is argued that with 'moderate secularism', minority religions are also protected. The model thus functions as a facilitator for religions in public life and operates with institutional compromises (see Berg-Sørensen 2013). British political scientist Tariq Modood (2010) has defended the relative separation of Church and State as opposed to what he calls an 'absolute separation' between them. Relative separation allows for the existence of an established church. The justification is made by suggesting that because the Church of England has contributed so much to British society, it is possible to accept its privileged existence. A further step is to question whether the situation should be changed. Modood has asked whether the situation should be levelled down or levelled up. A more secularist approach is to level down (to diminish the role of religion in politics and the public sphere), whereas a more pro-religious approach is to level up (to extend the role of religion in politics and the public sphere by including minority religions). If there are so many models of secularism and so many meanings of what secularism is, it is a question of persuading others to consent to any proposed meaning. One way to analyse different positions is to study where the arguments come from. At least three positions are at play: (1) some think religion and the secular should be as far apart as possible; (2) some defend moderate secularism, but limit the privileges to dominant religion (e.g. the Church of England); and (3) some (like Modood) approach the issue from a point that tries to see what is best for 'religious minorities', particularly Muslims. What all such positions share is the conviction that religion and the secular are essentially different rationalities and languages.

Maximalist and minimalist models

Another way of looking at the debates between religion and the secular has been developed by US historian of religion, Bruce Lincoln, who pays special attention to language and discourse. He defines religion as 'discourse whose defining characteristic is its desire to speak of things eternal and transcendent with an authority equally transcendent and eternal' (Lincoln 2012, p. 1). He suggests that societies operate with what he calls maximalist and minimalist models, or ideal-types of religion. Maximalist style is based on the conviction that religion ought to permeate all aspects of social existence. Minimalist style restricts religion to 'an important set of (chiefly metaphysical) concerns, protects its privileges against state intrusion, but restricts its activity and influence to this specialized sphere' (Lincoln 2003, p. 5). A typical example of the maximalist type is Sayyid Qutb (1906–1966) who was a leading member of the Egyptian Muslim Brotherhood; an example of the minimalist type is Immanuel Kant (1724–1804) who argued that religion is best suited to metaphysical questions and gave it a significant but marginal role. This model functions in mapping the relationship between religion and the secular.

The heuristic value of the model is that it helps us to understand the widespread discourse in which Islam, for instance, is divided into two forms, moderate and radical/extreme. The binary translates into good and bad forms of Islam and a distinction between those who integrate into dominant liberal societies by showing loyalty (minimalist style) and those who do not (maximalist style) (McCutcheon 2005, p. 77; Wijsen 2013). The first term in the binary is often named as true Islam, whereas the latter term signifies what is not really Islam but politics. In February 2015, President Obama referred to the spokespersons of ISIS and Al Qaeda suggesting that 'they are not religious leaders, they are terrorists' (Obama 2015). The linguistic construction of these binaries and the politics they convey are relevant objects of study in our attempts to explain and understand how religion, language and politics are entangled, and not the detection of whether acts we call extremist, radical or terrorist are truly religious or not.

Overall, Lincoln's reading of the final instructions for the September 11 hijackers, and comparisons between Osama Bin Laden's video-taped address from 7 October 2001 and

George W Bush's address to the nation given on 7 October 2001, clarify how religious discourse functions in politics. Furthermore, he puts an emphasis on the empirical, rather than normative, approach (Lincoln 2012, p. 1; Habermas 2011, p. 26; Modood 2010). What his approach shares with Habermas and other aforementioned scholars is that religion and the secular are used as analytical concepts. The same is the true for so-called political theology – a debate that combines empirical analysis with normative deliberation.

Political theology

It has become commonplace to talk about a so-called 'return of the religious' in political theory. This is also known as political theology, which investigates how theological concepts, ideas and discourses relate to politics. German jurist and political theorist Carl Schmitt argued in his *Political theology* that 'all significant concepts in the modern theory of the state are secularized theological concepts' (Schmitt 1985 [1922], p. 36). His ideas have inspired many interesting disputes about whether contemporary politics can do without theological and religious language. Furthermore, it is relevant to study how the separation of religion and the secular has never been as clear as hoped for in modern political theory, as well as how the leaking of 'religious' language into a supposedly 'secular' sphere has taken place in the past and in the present, either consciously or unconsciously. However, there is a tendency in these examinations to see theological and religious concepts everywhere, and to reduce the notion of 'secular' into almost an impossibility.

  British philosopher Simon Critchley argues in *The faith of the faithless: Experiments in political theology* (2014) that modernity 'can best be viewed as a series of *metamorphoses of sacralisation*' (Critchley 2014, p. 10). This approach rejects the all-too-simple story that sets secular modernity in opposition to pre-modern religion and explores the traces of theological language in politics. Furthermore, it leaves the door open to study how various practices are sacralised independently of whether they are classified as religious or secular. This approach is fruitfully developed in Durkheimian cultural sociology of the sacred, particularly in the works of Robert Bellah, Jeffrey Alexander and, more recently, Gordon Lynch (see Lynch 2014). The more problematic part appears in normative statements and in some readings of various political theorists. Critchley (2014, p. 24) notes that politics is not practicable without religion. It cannot be effective in mobilising people without a religious dimension. Similar arguments can be found in theorists such as Giorgio Agamben, Alain Badiou, Terry Eagleton, John Milbank and Slavoj Žižek (Hyman 2013). Theorists are seeking the middle ground between theism and atheism, but the problem here is that practically everything becomes theological (or religious). A good example is Critchley's reading of John Gray's political philosophy.

  Gray's critique of the modern emancipatory project as surrogate religion is predicated on the idea that 'humans are an animal species much like any other' (Gray 2003, p. 108): there is no progress in society, no perfectibility of humankind, and all we can do is to learn to live with conflict (Gray 2002, 2003). Critchley (2014, pp. 109–117) argues that Gray's dystopian idea that humans are killer apes assumes that humans are flawed and potentially wicked creatures. He sees this as a naturalised version of the idea of original sin. There are at least two problems in this equation. First, the closeness is superficial, as almost any rejection of the idea that humans can become more perfect would count as an example of a version of original sin. Second, such theorising leaves very little space for what is not religious. If even brutal criticism of the surrogate religiosity of modern politics, without any other form of salvation, is just another version of theological and religious discourse, the whole idea of the non-religious 'secular' appears almost useless.

Discourses on religion and the secular as objects of study

If Habermas maintains a clear epistemic break between religious and secular languages, the break has practically vanished in much of political theology by reducing the notion of the secular to a minimum. Yet another way of approaching these issues is to study how the categories of 'religion' and the non-religious 'secular' have developed and are used in practice in relation to other categories. This approach has been condensed to the idea that despite countless studies focusing on the relation between religion and politics, they are not studies 'of the formation and function of categories in rhetorical discursive constructions' (Fitzgerald 2007, p. 25).

The basic idea is to look at how claims to have a religion (or its denials) are strategic discursive tools used by individuals, groups, institutions and governments in organising social practices. These approaches have very little or no use for analytical definitions of 'religion' and the 'secular'. Furthermore, they agree that modern discourse on religion – religion as a distinct private, non-political sphere of life that has to do with personal commitments and experiences of the divine and salvation of the soul – developed in seventeenth- and eighteenth-century Europe and the United States, although earlier discourses are still in operation. These approaches have focused on 'religion', but when the genealogy of religion and contemporary discourses are explored, they also tend to analyse 'secular'.

Nation-states

One of the most significant contexts in understanding the formation of modern discourses on 'religion' is related to the nation-states. Russell T McCutcheon (2003, p. 241) has argued that religion is a discursive tool by which dissent is domesticated. Rather than seeing groups, practices and ideas as political (potential threats to the powers that be), designating them as 'religious' (private experiences that have to do with meaning, but not with collective action) makes public dissent impotent. Dissent can be thought of (in private), but not acted upon in public. If 'religions' become public actors, they are not labelled as religious any more. They are political fanatics, fundamentalist, terrorists or not 'really religious' at all. This modern invention of the 'religious' sphere is, according to this line of thinking, a governmental strategy by which large-scale social identities are controlled, domesticated and marginalised. Thus, in the context of the rise of nation-states, religion has been a category utilised in creating a peripheral space separate from the political sphere. It has domesticated forms of utopian social and collective action that were at odds with the state by labelling them as private matters. 'Religion', then, became the space in which collective goals are individualised and made into a question of personal preference and conviction (Arnal & McCutcheon 2013, pp. 29, 60–61).

In the modern era, 'religion' has been potentially at odds with governance and sovereignty (Stack 2015, p. 7), but at the same time, it has worked for nation-states. McCutcheon (2003, p. 261) goes as far as to speculate that the liberal nation-state may not have been possible without the modern concept of religion. Timothy Fitzgerald (2007, p. 6) has argued similarly that in order to imagine politics – an area of supposedly rational action – it has been historically necessary to invent a discourse on religion that naturalises Euro–American secular rationality.

Although the individualisation and castration of collective sentiments and passions may have been one of the functions of discourse on religion from the point of view of nation-states and governments, the development would not have been so smooth if the groups themselves would not have benefited from that. Modern nation-states pushed 'religious' groups towards homogenisation while privileging one institution (e.g. Protestant, Catholic, Orthodox). In his analysis of John Locke's distinction between private and public, Craig Martin (2010) contends that the distinction did not simply marginalise groups and institutions deemed religious, but secured their right to socialise their children in the dominant ideology that guaranteed the privileged status of Christian institutions and norms while making the imbrication of Church and State largely invisible. Thus, rather than seeing the distinction between private and public, or Church and State, as two fully separate spheres, they should be seen as interlinked in a way that helps us to analyse the circulation of power from one sphere to another. These two aspects of the function of the discourse on 'religion' in modern nation-states – governing by the state and maintenance of the privileged position of dominant 'religious' groups – have been nicely captured by Talal Asad (1993, p. 28), who concludes that the modern discourse on religion is 'at once part of a strategy (for liberal seculars) of the confinement, and (for liberal Christians) of the defence of religion'.

The domestication of potentially disruptive groups is not only enacted by the state, but both majority and minority groups themselves take active part in negotiating whether they are a religion or not, often with the implication that if they are religious they are not political. Groups themselves employ the discourse on religion, thus seeking protection, recognition and privileges, as well as a representative position with people using the same identity tag (Owen & Taira 2015; Taira 2010). Negotiation over the religiosity of Judaism in minority positions is a case in point. Judaism began to be conceived as a religion in eighteenth- and nineteenth-century Prussia. Prior to the modern era, there were Jewish communities with specific rules of conduct – including laws with punishments, rules for excommunication, and so on – but Judaism was not understood as a distinct, 'religious' sphere of life. The discourse on Judaism as a religion developed as an answer to the problem concerning Jewish integration into the German state: the classification of Judaism as a religion was a strategic attempt to assimilate Jews into a modern nation-state by suggesting that Judaism is something different from 'the supreme political authority of the sovereign state and may in fact complement the sovereign state' (Batnitzky 2011, p. 6). Hence, Judaism is rendered into its own domesticated sphere where it is relatively separate from a political (as well as scientific and economic) sphere of life.

One of the key authors arguing for the religiosity of Judaism was Moses Mendelssohn (1729–1786) who wrote during a time when Jews had no civil rights in Prussia. Judaism was accused of being a state within a state that could not be integrated into the Prussian one. It was understood in political terms, but Mendelssohn defined Judaism as a religion as opposed to politics in *Jerusalem: Or on religious power and Judaism* (originally 1783). There is Jewish law, according to Mendelssohn, but it does not have any political power or coercion as states have. As such, there is no problem integrating Jews into the modern nation-state (Batnitzky 2011, pp. 13–28).

Colonialism

Colonialism is another significant context for the emergence and proliferation of the category of religion (Arnal & McCutcheon 2013; Asad 1993; Chidester 1996, 2014; Dubuisson 2003; Fitzgerald 2000, 2007), although it is by no means separate from the development of the modern nation-states. Discourse on religion has been entangled with modern colonialism in at least two related ways: Western colonialism asserted its superiority by extending their categories outside Western societies, and colonised people have been governed by negotiating their religiosity (or lack thereof) in concrete colonial contexts.

Daniel Dubuisson (2003) argues that the development of the modern discourse on religion became the West's central reference point, around which it organised itself. Of course, there was discourse about gods, rituals, and so on before the modern era, as well as many uses of Latin 'religio' and pre-modern uses of English-language 'religion' referring to Christian truth that did not stand in opposition to politics, economics and the state (Fitzgerald 2007; Nongbri 2013), but not the kind of sphere or domain resulting from selecting and isolating certain ideas and practices that formed a unity of some kind. Christianity was conceived as the only proper religion, whereas others were similar to it, but considered inferior. Various binaries, such as monotheistic religions/polytheistic religions, universal religions/ethnic religions, historical religions/cosmic religions, were not neutral classificatory tools, but indicated different stages in the evolutionary history of religions. In each binary, Christianity was on top, the most advantageous religion, thus integrated into colonialist discourse of the supremacy and superiority of the West (Dubuisson 2003). This mapping of the world in terms of 'religions' universalised the category, but at the same time, it projected Western concepts and hierarchies onto others.

To give a more concrete example, the discovery of 'indigenous religion' in Southern Africa in the nineteenth century depended upon colonial conquest and containment. Earlier travellers, missionaries and colonial agents reported the absence of religion among Africans. The lack of religion was part of a larger colonial classification in which the humanity of others was denied. They were practically seen as uncivilised animals. As David Chidester suggests, 'the assertion that people lacked a religion signified, in general terms, an intervention in local frontier conflicts over land, trade, labor, and political autonomy' (1996, p. 14): 'Without religion, like animals, the indigenous people of the Cape had no right to the land' (1996, p. 38). Once an African community was placed under the colonial administration of a magisterial system, it was discovered to have an indigenous religious system, thus demonstrating how negotiations over religiosity were part of local control mechanisms (Chidester 1996, p. xv; 2014, p. x). The knowledge gathered was useful for Britain, which was, to use the words of theologian F D Maurice, from 1847, 'engaged in trading with other countries, or in conquering them, or in keeping possession of them' (quoted in Chidester 1996, p. 131).

Southern Africa is just one case among many. In his study of English-language uses of the word 'religion', Timothy Fitzgerald (2007) argues that discourse on religion, in addition to being about private meanings and experiences marginalising dissent, has been a discourse on civility and barbarity. The European West has considered itself civilised as opposed to others who are barbarians. Civilised people are Enlightened or have Christian religion, whereas others have no religion at all, or they have a false religion. One example of such a discourse is to be found in Charles Darwin's notes. He wrote about the (non-European) 'savages' in Tierra del Fuego who were very different from civilised Europeans. The difference, according to Darwin, was 'greater than between a wild and domesticated animal' (Darwin 2010, p. 15). He suggested that there is no reason to believe that these 'savages of the lowest grade' (Darwin 2010, p. 29) 'perform any sort of religious worship', or have 'religious feelings' (Darwin 2010, pp. 24–25). What makes this a particularly curious example is that we see Darwin – the idol for many contemporary secularists and atheists – speaking highly of religion. However, religion – here, practically synonymous with civility and Christianity – was seen not as the endpoint of history, but, at least for the educated elite, something to be surpassed in the course of history. In this sense, colonialist discourse on religion was entangled with evolutionary stages in which 'religion' played an intermediary and temporary role between pre-modern savages and the future secular society.

What has been offered here is not a short history of religion and the secular, but a short history of modern discourses on 'religion' and the (non-religious) 'secular' and their political functions. The importance of nation-states and colonialism has been emphasised, although the development of the modern discourse on religion and its relation to other categories (secular, political, economic) has been more complex and a more long-ranging process. Furthermore, such discourse has not remained the same throughout the centuries and, what is perhaps more important, it has never been possible to reduce the functions of discourse on religion to one or two aspects. In order to demonstrate the multi-functional and heterogeneous nature of discourse on religion and its continuing connections with politics, the next section focuses on more recent examples.

Discourses on religion and the secular in contemporary public life

Problematic conceptualisations of religion

One of the most relevant recent contributions for the conversation about the topic of this chapter is Timothy Fitzgerald's *Religion and politics in International Relations: The modern myth* (2011). The study analyses the ways in which scholars of International Relations (IR) distinguish religion and the secular, and thus legitimate what he calls the modern myth: the idea that politics is a sphere of (Euro-modern) rational activity, as distinguished from the 'religious' sphere full of irrational and supernatural ideas. His point is that recent interest in studying religion among IR scholars fails because they apply the category of religion without paying attention to its highly contested nature, without deconstructing the myth by examining how the categories are employed, and for what purposes.

Fitzgerald's historical argument is that the idea of 'religion' and 'politics' as two separate spheres emerged in the late seventeenth century, at least in English sources. This discourse with its essentialised concept of religion is prevalent in the recent interest in religion among scholars of politics and IR. Religion was largely ignored in those fields for a long time: of about 1,600 articles published in selected IR journals, only six featured religion as an important influence between 1980 and 1999 (Fitzgerald 2011, p. 29). Vendulka Kubálková (2013) locates the so-called 'turn to religion' in IR to the latter part of the first decade of the twenty-first century, although she notes that one of the foundational conferences took place in 1998. It is one thing to examine why this took place, but another to examine how religion and (secular) politics have been conceptualised, with Fitzgerald concluding that there is a 'tendency to talk about religion as though it is a thing or even an agent with an essentially different nature from politics' (Fitzgerald 2011, p. 107). In practice, this often means that religion is seen as being a cause of the world's problems, or that pure religion is contaminated by politics (see Hurd 2015).

Indeed, public discourse is filled with influential commentators who first generalise in the name of religion and consequently explain actions with reference to people's religiosity. A well-known example is Samuel Huntington's thesis on the clash of civilisations (Huntington 1996 [1993]) in which he takes Islam as one civilisational identity among others. According to Huntington, civilisations are differentiated from each other most importantly by religion, and these differences, though not necessarily violent in themselves, 'have generated the most prolonged and the most violent conflicts' (Huntington 1996, p. 4). One problem with this is that in order to reach the idea of Islamic civilisation as a relatively homogeneous unit, it is necessary to put together more than one-and-a-half billion adherents who cover a third of the inhabited area of the world, approximately a dozen societies and half a dozen main languages (Said 1993, 1994). Another problem is that religion becomes an agent-like being in the world, or that adherents' acts are explained by religious motives. A recent provocative, but illustrative, example was given by Sam Harris, popular US critic of religion who is known as one of the 'New Atheists', who suggested that if he could wave a magic wand and get rid of either rape or religion, he would not hesitate to get rid of religion (Harris 2006). This statement makes sense only if religion is understood as an agential cause of problems and a motivational force of people's behaviour. It goes directly against scholarly advice given by Arnal and McCutcheon (2013, p. 6) who question the usefulness of religion as an explanatory term. In other words, people do not do this or that because they are 'religious'; they act on the basis of a variety of practical reasons that require empirical examination (see also Hurd 2015).

Disputes about what counts as religion and the secular

In addition to exploring the language use of scholars and popular authors, negotiations that concern the religiosity of groups, practices and symbols are fruitful cases for demonstrating how religion, language and politics are intertwined, and how discourse on religion plays a part in the organisation of social and political practices. Two developments are particularly prominent. First, minorities are increasingly making strategic claims to have a religion in order to get recognition and benefits of various kinds. Second, the (usually Christian) majority tries to maintain its position in ever-more diverse societies by relabelling practices and symbols that have been previously considered 'religious' as 'cultural' or part of 'tradition'.

One of the British Druid organisations – the Druid Network – achieved charitable status on the basis of advancement of religion in 2010 after a process that took several years (Owen & Taira 2015). Finnish Wiccans failed to obtain the status of a religious community in the early 2000s after the Supreme Administrative Court decided against them in a tight vote (4–3) (Taira 2010). They did not achieve official recognition, but another Pagan group 'Karhun kansa' (People of the Bear) succeeded, after an initial rejection, in 2013. These successes and failures are partially dependent on language use. For instance, using attributes such as sacred and spiritual, and saying 'worship' and 'ritual', rather than celebration and festival, improves the chances of being regarded as a religion, as was the case with the Druid Network (Owen & Taira 2015, p. 102). In the UK, many consider Jediism – a 'religion' based on the popular film *Star Wars* – as a joke, but hundreds of thousands have announced in a Census that Jediism is their religion. Furthermore, claiming Jediism as a religion has been a successful rhetorical strategy for being heard in public, and even getting public apologies from officials in instances where wearing a hooded top was challenged. As one Jedi stated: 'Muslims can walk around in whatever religious gear they like, so why can't I?' (Taira 2013, p. 485). In Turkey, Alevis – a group traditionally considered part of Islam – have been using the language of 'religion' rather than 'culture' since the late 1980s in order to distinguish themselves from Sunni Muslims, because the laicist order, with its homogenising ambition, does not recognise Alevi identity separately from Sunni Islam (Dressler 2011).

What is common to these examples is that people are appropriating discourse on religion, claiming their identity and/or practice as 'religious', thus aiming to achieve a better public image and distinctive voice in the public sphere, recognition from the state and dominant culture, and more concrete material and legal benefits (financial aid, legal protection, tax reliefs, possibility for being integrated into religious education in schools, and so on).

A related development is that in many cases 'religion' disappears and becomes 'cultural', thus supporting the dominant churches. One recent example is the Lautsi case (Beaman 2015). Finnish-born Italian resident Soile Lautsi made a case of the presence of crucifixes in state-school classrooms. She suggested that they violate the principle of religious freedom. After losing her case in the Veneto Administrative Court in March 2005, she appealed to the Supreme Administrative Court, who upheld the earlier decision. She appealed again, and in November 2009, the European Court of Human Rights decided the case in favour of Lautsi. Finally, in March 2011, the Grand Chamber of the European Court of Human Rights overturned the judgement of the lower chamber, holding that the crucifixes do not violate religious freedom and parents' right to educate their children. What is interesting in the case from the point of view of this chapter, is how the nature of a crucifix was negotiated from ostensibly 'religious' to sufficiently 'secular' by implying that a crucifix is a symbol of Italian culture and suggesting explicitly that Lautsi was attacking both the 'dominant religion of the State and the unity of the Nation' (*Lautsi and Others v. Italy 2011*, at para 19, quoted in Beaman 2015, p. 43). The reasoning of the court was such that, although the cross is 'certainly a religious symbol', 'it evoked principles that could be shared outside Christian faith'. The 'democratic values' were seen to be rooted in the 'message of the cross'; the message could be 'read independently of its religious dimension', thus being 'perfectly compatible with secularism and accessible to non-Christians and non-believers' (*Lautsi v. Italy 2009*, at para. 35, quoted in Beaman 2015, p. 44).

Heated media debates and court cases concerning garments that signal collective belonging are relatively similar, often focusing on veils (Muslims) and turbans (Sikhs), and as a result, temporarily classifying a particular garment as either a religious obligation or sufficiently secular – the choice of an autonomous individual or as an ethnic/cultural symbol. Although veiling has been a contentious issue for some time, with turban campaigns taking place in Britain in the 1970s and 1980s, debates on 'religious' dress have become commonplace in twenty-first century Europe. Changes in media technology have made it possible for these local and national cases to become part of an ever-more global mediatised consciousness in which 'religion' and 'secular' constitute one of the organising binaries.

Despite the recent rise in scholarly interest in secularism, not many studies have focused on discourses on 'secularism'. Studies examining different models of secularity and normative political debates concerning the best possible model have flourished, but usually these do not ask explicitly how the word is used, and for what purposes. One exception is *Media portrayals of religion and the secular sacred* (Knott, Poole & Taira 2013); it analyses, among other things, the ways in which British media employ the term.

Their study of British media found that 'secularism' in the local British context is something negative that threatens people's beliefs, convictions and even British lifestyle, whereas 'secularism' elsewhere, particularly outside Europe and in non-Christian contexts, is a significant political instrument that protects people from religious fanatics. In this discourse, good secularism is supportive of moderate religiosity, especially Christianity, and bad secularism – mainly the British one – is limiting as it, according to a media commentator, does not 'allow space for imagination and fantasy, for the sense of mystery, myth and morality' (Knott, Poole & Taira 2013, p. 115). The media deals with very different systems in their examples of secularism, but the media uses the same word for all varieties and does not provide enough background information for understanding different national histories. Therefore, it can be argued that the discourse functions by legitimating moderate and liberal Christianity at home and Euro-modern values elsewhere. The conclusion about the nature of domestic language use is supported by Steven Kettell (2014) who demonstrates the growth of anti-secular discourse in British public debate. Such discourse is prevalent in MPs' statements in all the biggest parties, although it is more common among Conservatives than Liberal Democrats or the Labour Party. The so-called secularists are increasingly labelled as aggressive, intolerant or militant. Consequently, secularism is increasingly seen as anti-British, and it serves those politicians whose interest it is to promote a greater role for faith-based organisations in British society.

There are plenty of other relevant examples about strategic uses of secularism in contemporary society. For instance, US Republican politician and former presidential candidate, Rick Santorum, suggested in 2014 that 'we should start calling secularism a religion' (Garcia 2014). The obvious political context of this statement was his worry about the exclusion of Christianity from education because it is classified as religion. If secularism were classified similarly, it too could be banned from education. Such examples demonstrate that the disputes about what counts as religion go hand in hand with what counts as secular. Both concepts are used strategically for achieving concrete benefits and recognition, and they deserve attention from scholars interested in language and politics.

Conclusion

There are plenty of studies focusing on religious language and the intertwinement of religion and politics. Studies addressing all three – language use, politics and religion – have been rare. This chapter has mapped various ways in which language, politics and religion are entangled with each other and, more specifically, how discourses on religion and the (non-religious) secular have developed in relation to politics and functioned as strategic governmental tools. The increased interest in religion is clear among scholars who analyse the role and function of religion in contemporary politics and explore different models of secularism. This trend is likely to continue in the future. As long as religion is seen as a salient political force in world politics, scholars will find it relevant to study it empirically. Scholars with normative aspirations will continue to debate which model of secularism works best in a given context, and some will continue to suggest that liberal-democratic politics can do without the language of secularism (Bader 2013). These approaches pay attention to the relationship between religious and secular languages. In addition, this chapter has introduced a slightly different approach to studying discourses on religion and the secular by paying more attention to what is achieved by deploying such categories and distinctions. It is likely to provoke both appreciative and critical responses by those who consider the terms analytically useful. While it is unlikely that any strand or approach introduced in this chapter is becoming so dominant that it would absorb others, more effective conversation between them would at least render visible the blind spots of each approach and further contribute to the need to pay attention to religion and the secular in the study of language and politics.

References

Arnal, W & McCutcheon, R T, 2013, *The sacred is the profane: The political nature of 'religion'*, Oxford University Press, Oxford.

Asad, T, 1993, *Genealogies of religion: Discipline and reasons of power in Christianity and Islam*, The Johns Hopkins University Press, Baltimore, MD.
Bader, V, 2013, 'Priority for liberal democracy or secularism?', in *Contesting secularism: comparative perspectives*, ed. A Berg-Sørensen, Ashgate, Farnham, pp. 43–68.
Batnitzky, L, 2011, *How Judaism became a religion: An introduction to modern Jewish thought*, Princeton University Press, Princeton, NJ.
Beaman, L G, 2015, 'Freedom of and freedom from religion: Atheist involvement in legal cases', in *Atheist identities: Spaces and social contexts*, eds. L G Beaman & S Tomlins, Springer, Cham, pp. 39–52.
Berg-Sørensen, A ed., 2013, *Contesting secularism: Comparative perspectives*, Ashgate, Farnham.
Chidester, D, 1996, *Savage systems: Colonialism and comparative religion in Southern Africa*, University Press of Virginia, Charlottesville, VA.
Chidester, D, 2014, *Empire of religion: Imperialism and comparative religion*, The University of Chicago Press, Chicago, IL.
Critchley, S, 2014, *The faith of the faithless: Experiments in political theology*, Verso, London.
Darwin, C, 2010, *Evolutionary writings*, Oxford University Press, Oxford.
Dressler, M, 2011, 'Making religion through secularist legal discourse: The case of Turkish Alevism' in *Secularism and religion-making*, eds. M Dressler & APS Mandair, Oxford University Press, Oxford, pp. 187–208.
Dubuisson, D, 2003, *The Western construction of religion: Myths, knowledge, and ideology*, The Johns Hopkins University Press, Baltimore, MD.
Fitzgerald, T, 2000, *The ideology of religious studies*, Oxford University Press, Oxford.
Fitzgerald, T, 2007, *Discourse on civility and barbarity: A critical history of religion and related categories*, Oxford University Press, Oxford.
Fitzgerald, T, 2011, *Religion and politics in International Relations: The modern myth*, Continuum, London.
Garcia, A, 2014, 'Rick Santorum: Let's call secularism a religion so it can be banned from classroom', *Raw Story*, 9 September, available from: www.rawstory.com/2014/09/rick-santorum-lets-call-secularism-a-religion-so-it-can-be-banned-from-the-classroom/ [accessed 16 March 2015].
Gray, J, 2002, *Straw dogs: Thoughts on humans and other animals*, Granta Books, London.
Gray, J, 2003, *Al Qaeda and what it means to be modern*, Faber and Faber, London.
Habermas, J, 2010, 'An awareness of what is missing', in *An awareness of what is missing: Faith and reason in a post-secular age*, ed. J Habermas, Polity Press, Cambridge, pp, 15–23.
Habermas, J, 2011, '"The political": The rational meaning of a questionable inheritance of political theology', in *The power of religion in the public sphere*, J Butler, J Habermas, C Taylor & C West, Columbia University Press, New York, pp. 15–33.
Harris, S, 2006, 'The temple of reason. Interview by Bethany Saltman', *The Sun Magazine*, iss. 369, September, available from: http://thesunmagazine.org/issues/369/the_temple_of_reason?page=2 [accessed 3 April 2015].
Huntington, S, 1996, 'The clash of civilizations', in *The clash of civilizations? The debate*. Foreign Affairs, New York, pp. 1–25.
Hurd, E S, 2015, *Beyond religious freedom: The new global politics of religion*, Princeton University Press, Princeton, NJ.
Hyman, G, 2013, *Traversing the middle: Ethics, politics, religion*, Cascade, Eugene, OR.
Kerry, J, 2015, 'Religion and diplomacy: Toward a better understanding of religion and global affairs', *America: The national Catholic review*, 14 September, available from: http://americamagazine.org/issue/religion-and-diplomacy [accessed 6 November 2015].
Kettell, S, 2014, 'The Militant Strain: An analysis of anti-secular discourse in Britain', *Political Studies*, vol. 63, no. 3, pp. 512–528.
Knott, K, Poole, E & Taira, T, 2013, *Media portrayals of religion and the secular sacred: Representation and change*, Ashgate, Farnham.

Kubálková, V, 2013, 'The "turn to religion" in International Relations Theory', *E-International Relations*, 3 December, available from: www.e-ir.info/2013/12/03/the-turn-to-religion-in-international-relations-theory/ [accessed 4 October 2015].

Lincoln, B, 2003, *Holy terrors: Thinking about religion after September 11*, The University of Chicago Press, Chicago, IL.

Lincoln, B, 2012, *Gods and demons, Priests and scholars: Critical explorations in the history of religions*, The University of Chicago Press, Chicago, IL.

Lynch, G, 2014, *The sacred in the modern world: A cultural sociological approach*, Oxford University Press, Oxford.

Martin, C, 2010, *Masking hegemony: A genealogy of liberalism, religion and the private sphere*, Equinox, London.

McCutcheon, R T, 2003, *The discipline of religion: Structure, meaning, rhetoric*, Routledge, London.

McCutcheon, R T, 2005, *Religion and the domestication of dissent: Or, how to live in a less than perfect nation*, Equinox, London.

Modood, T, 2010, 'Moderate secularism: Religion as identity and respect for religion', *Political Quarterly*, vol. 81, no. 1, pp. 4–14.

Nongbri, B, 2013, *Before religion: A history of a modern concept*, Yale University Press, New Haven, CT.

Obama, B, 2015, 'Isis – not Islam – is the enemy', *The Guardian*, 19 February, available from: www.theguardian.com/us-news/video/2015/feb/19/isis-islam-barack-obama-america-video [accessed 7 August 2015].

Owen, S & Taira, T, 2015, 'The category of 'religion' in public classification: Charity registration of the Druid Network in England and Wales', in *Religion as a category of governance and sovereignty*, eds. T Stack, N Goldenberg & T Fitzgerald, Brill, Leiden, pp. 90–114.

Said, E, 1993, 'The phony Islamic threat', *New York Times Magazine*, 21 November.

Said, E, 1994, *Representations of the intellectual*, Vintage, New York.

Schmitt, C, 1985, *Political theology: Four chapters on the concept of sovereignty*, The University of Chicago Press, Chicago, IL.

Stack, T, 2015, 'Introduction', in *Religion as a category of governance and sovereignty*, eds. T Stack, N Goldenberg & T Fitzgerald, Brill, Leiden, pp. 1–20.

Taira, T, 2010, 'Religion as a discursive technique: The politics of classifying Wicca', *Journal of Contemporary Religion*, vol. 25, no. 3, pp. 379–394.

Taira, T, 2013, 'The category of "invented religion": A new opportunity for studying discourses on "religion"', *Culture and Religion*, vol. 14, no. 4, pp. 477–493.

Wijsen, F, 2013, '"There are radical Muslims and normal Muslims": An analysis of the discourse on Islamic extremism', *Religion*, vol. 26, no. 1, pp. 70–88.

Part V

Applications and cases II: language, politics, and (de)mobilisation

40
Discursive depoliticisation and political disengagement

Matthew Flinders and Matt Wood

Depoliticisation has recently emerged as an important concept for critically analysing the effect of contemporary elite discourses on declining levels of public participation in politics (Marsh & Fawcett 2014). Analysts have argued that neo-liberal discourses, in particular those surrounding globalisation, the efficiency of markets over state service provision, and the self-interested nature of public figures, have effectively led to public disengagement (Stoker 2006; Hay 2007). This is because they 'shift the political character of decision making' (Burnham 2001), shaping people's preferences by making otherwise contestable policy agendas appear inevitable, natural or simple matters of 'fate' (Gamble 2000). If the public cannot see why engaging with politics would concretely change anything – how it would enable them to exercise their political agency (Jenkins 2011) – they will understandably disengage from voting for, and joining, political parties, institutions at the heart of liberal democratic governance.[1] Recently, Wood and Flinders (2014) have suggested the concept of 'discursive depoliticisation' to highlight aspects of this process involving the linguistic or rhetorical 'denial' of politics. A number of questions, however, remain unanswered: how and in what particular ways do discourses 'deny' the political character of decision-making; which logics within these particular discourses make politics appear absent; and what is being 'denied' in the act of 'denying' politics? This chapter argues that answering these questions requires integration of the concept of discursive depoliticisation within existing frameworks of discourse analysis, which to date has not happened, despite obvious theoretical links.

The chapter does not, however, offer a review of the universe of different approaches and frameworks of discursive, linguistic or rhetorical analysis and theory (something that the other chapters in this book do in great detail). Rather, it argues that integrating the concept of discursive depoliticisation within one particular framework, namely Glynos and Howarth's (2007) framework of discursive 'logics', provides a useful framework for analysts to *critically explain* how discursive depoliticisation shifts the political character of decision-making by *denying*, in particular ways, its political character. Glynos and Howarth's framework of three logics of explanation underlying dominant forms of discourse – 'political', 'social' and 'fantasmatic' – is useful for our purposes because it enables *critical explanation*, the generation of explanations that systematically 'provide the basis for a possible critique and transformation of existing practices and social meanings' (Howarth 2000, p. 129). We argue that integrating the concept of discursive depoliticisation within this framework enables this type of explanation by offering explanations of how politicians (and other elite actors) deny the possibility of collective human agency in relation to the *past, present* and *future*. Discursive depoliticisation, we argue, denies collective human agency in three ways:

1 The argument that previously dominant political paradigms were inherently 'failed' (denial in relation to the past);
2 The presentation of supposedly scientific social 'rules' that cannot be broken at a particular moment (denial in relation to the present);
3 The generation of a fantasy that change could lead to societal chaos and collapse (denial in relation to the future)

In order to briefly show the utility of this framework of critical analysis – specifically how it nuances or provides *theoretical depth* to the concept of 'denial', while recognising the increasingly contingent and interdependent reality of politics (*empirical fluidity*) – we use the illustrative example of austerity discourse in the United Kingdom under David Cameron's Coalition Government. In sum, the key contribution of this chapter is conceptual innovation: integrating the concept of discursive depoliticisation within a framework of discourse theoretic analysis, thus enabling political analysts to critically explain – through a three-fold approach – how politicians discursively 'deny' the political character of decision-making.

The chapter proceeds in four sections. First, it argues that existing explanations of the 'supply-side' causes of political disengagement convalesce around the concept of depoliticisation. It is, however, argued that the deeply discursive nature of this process is not fully recognised. The second section therefore turns to existing literature that has developed the concept of 'discursive depoliticisation', albeit not directly to analyse political disengagement. It integrates the focus of this concept on the discursive 'denial' of human agency with Glynos and Howarth's (2007) concept of 'logics' developing the critical typology of three 'logics of denial' – denial in relation to the 'past', 'present' and 'future'. The third section then illustrates how this conceptual integration can facilitate useful critical explanation, emphasising *theoretical depth*, but recognising *empirical fluidity*, using the UK Coalition Government's austerity discourse as an example. The chapter then concludes by suggesting how this framework is particularly salient in a social and political world characterised by 'hyper-democracy', namely because it highlights the 'radical contingency' and volatility of contemporary forms of political disaffection.

Discursive depoliticisation and the 'supply side' of political disengagement

The causes of growing political disaffection and disengagement in Western democracies are manifold; therefore, in this chapter, we do not intend to offer a comprehensive review of all the different variables that impact upon it (for a recent systematic analysis see Norris 2011). Rather, we focus specifically on the discursive, rhetorical or linguistic drivers of disengagement, in particular those used by politicians, which the section argues can be encapsulated by the concept of *depoliticisation* (Wood & Flinders 2014). These have been termed the 'supply side' or 'elite' factors driving political disenchantment (Davies 2014; Kisby & Sloam 2011). 'Supply-side' factors are 'changes in the content of the appeals that ...

parties make to potential voters, changes in the character of electoral competition, changes in the substantive "goods" that politics offers to political "consumers", and changes in the capacity of national-level governments to deliver political choice to consumers' (Hay 2007, p. 55). Spelt out in these economistic terms, disengagement from politics is driven not by what the public demands from politicians, but what politicians can – or *say they can* – 'supply' the public with, if they get into office. Hay (2007) specifically identifies four supply-side factors that potentially impact upon disengagement. These are set out in Table 40.1.

What is first notable about these drivers is that they are all consequences of political action, rather than inexorable material structures or contextual factors. Marketisation is a process involving the growth of ideas that equate political parties with businesses, envisaging them as essentially utility-maximising, non-ideological entities competing in the marketplace of electoral competition for the votes of consumer-citizens (Scammell 2014). This is not, however, because they have naturally 'become' businesses, rather, because they *act as if they were businesses*, aiming 'to mould the party cosmetically to appease what are perceived to be the preferences of the target voter' (Hay 2007, p. 56). The voter, treated as a rational consumer, thus becomes disengaged in a self-fulfilling prophecy: 'as the rational voter model predicts, rational consumers will rationally disengage' (Hay 2007, p. 57). Some literature on political marketing has touched upon this issue (see Lilleker 2005a). Lilleker's (2005b) work has shown that political marketing can erode the connection between parties and their base supports. Moreover, through their study of the British New Labour Government, Lilleker and Negrine (2003) show that the nationally orchestrated marketing campaign run by Tony Blair's central party office increasingly led local voters and activists to become disengaged and disillusioned.

The second point – 'policy convergence' – is similarly self-fulfilling. Political parties have *chosen* to emphasise their 'brand' or 'competence' in place of substantive ideological preferences (Johansen 2012): 'parties increasingly compete on the basis of more ephemeral differences in branding and on the images of trust and competence *they seek to construct for themselves*' (Hay 2007, pp. 56–57, italics added). As a result, in a similar case of self-fulfilling prophecy, voters are left to make 'assessments of party leaders' character traits …

Table 40.1 'Supply-side' causes of public disengagement with politics

Phenomenon	Content	Key reference
'Marketisation'	Inter-party electoral competition comes to be seen as analogous to businesses competing in the market	Lilleker 2005
'Policy Convergence'	Political parties compete on ephemeral issues regarding the personal trust and competence of leaders, as they hold essentially similar policies	Manning & Holmes 2014
'Public-choice theoretic assumptions'	Political elites internalise ideas about the inefficiency of the public sector and the incapacity of politics to deliver public goods	Bøggild 2015
'Depoliticisation'	The displacement of responsibility for policy-making or implementation to independent public authorities	Mair 2013

(Source: Adapted from Hay 2007, p. 56)

which arguably the electorate are singularly ill-placed to judge' (Hay 2007, p. 57). The literature on the 'personalisation' of politics in particular supports this argument (Garzia 2011). While scholars such as Mazzoleni (2003) show how politicians may be able to connect with voters on a personal level and enthuse them through personalised narratives, a crucial caveat is that their engagement tends to be more based around the construction of emotional relationships with politicians, and disappointment and disenchantment become more likely (Manning & Holmes 2014).

Third, the growth of 'public choice theoretic assumptions' refers to how 'political elites throughout the advanced liberal democracies … have come to embrace and internalize … public choice theory [which] is predicated on the projection on to politicians … of narrowly self-interested assumptions' (Hay 2007, p. 57). Originating in the work of Anthony Downs and Kenneth Arrow, these theories assume for analytical purposes that actors are self-interested utility-maximising agents. By internalising such assumptions, we risk creating an insidious pathology that assumes all officials seeking public office have such self-interested motives, with debilitating consequences for political trust. It is Hay's (2007) contention that elite politicians and their supervisors have done just this, and by projecting such ideas in their rhetoric and policies, they have encouraged the public to think in just that way – that they are selfish and only in it for themselves. While systematic evidence for this assertion has yet to emerge in existing literature, there has been a growing focus on the expectations the public have of their representatives, and the need to 'manage expectations' about their goals and aims (Flinders 2009). Bøggild (2015), for example, finds through survey experiments that politicians who are seen as self-interested in seeking re-election receive a lot less support for their policies than those who appear not to have ulterior motives. The outcome being that if politicians are not more honest with the public about their goals and aims, they risk alienating them even further.

Lastly, 'depoliticisation' refers (in Hay's description here at least) to the shifting of responsibility for political decisions to non-elected quasi-public bodies, staffed by technocratic 'experts'. 'It is hardly surprising', Hay (2007, p. 58) argues, 'that in a context in which even politicians concede that "politics" is something we need rather less of, public political disaffection and disengagement is rife'. Existing research has tended not to evaluate whether the structure of governance directly impacts upon public engagement with political issues, although several studies provide strong theoretical evidence (e.g. Gamble 2000; Jenkins 2011). For Wood and Flinders (2014), depoliticisation is a multifaceted process that ought to be broken down into several forms in order to assess whether such a process is genuinely at work. However, Peter Mair's (2013) book *Ruling the void* is perhaps the most sustained attempt at demonstrating this thesis. Mair (2013, ch. 3) systematically tracks the growth of expert-led agencies and decentralised governance alongside growing public disenchantment with politics, making a strong case that 'technocratic' governance leads to feelings of exclusion and disillusion with traditional parliamentary politics.

The above 'supply-side' arguments are all based on the problem of self-fulfilling prophecies – politicians have internalised negative theories of themselves, which has then influenced their behaviour but, more importantly, has also influenced the way they *communicate* with the electorate. By convincing themselves that they 'hate' politics, they in turn have convinced the public that they also 'hate' politics and anything deemed 'political', because they have internalised the negative notion of politics assumed by the political authorities. Now, this argument at first sight appears quite a heavily constructivist one. We have all come to believe, through a set of ideas translated to each other in political discourse and reinforced by the behaviour those ideas construct, that politics is a bad thing. If we could only purge ourselves of these assumptions and construct a better image of genuinely altruistic public service, then democratic politics would have a much better future. The objection would be that this is to move towards an unwarranted idealism, which arguably lets politicians off the hook as much as it places them under scrutiny. Ultimately, the blame is pinned on the ideas themselves, politicians have just been foolish for imbibing their toxic substance.

This assessment would, however, do Hay's analysis a disservice, because it goes further than a purely constructivist account, arguing instead that the shifting character of 'politics' *itself*, and innovative ways of exercising power, may be at hand. This is because the identification of *depoliticisation* as a supply-side variable seems to also hang over the other factors. Indeed, much of the remainder of Hay's book is an analysis of depoliticisation – one of his key points of inquiry being 'to assess the extent to which the contemporary condition of formal political disaffection and disengagement ... is connected with contemporary processes of depoliticization' (Hay 2007, p. 89). The following chapters then show how most of the supply-side factors identified above can be subsumed under the umbrella concept of depoliticisation – they all serve, in effect, to drive a process which covers up or, as Peter Burnham (2001) argued, 'places at one remove the political character of decision making'. The marketisation problem, policy convergence, the growth of public-choice theoretic assumptions and what Hay calls depoliticisation – but in other terms might simply be called delegated governance (Flinders 2008) – may all themselves be considered in some way forms of, or drivers of, depoliticisation. This is because they cover up or shroud the political nature of public decision-making and party competition. The argument here is that recognising this entails focusing more intently on *depoliticisation* as a central driving 'supply-side' force of political disengagement, as a key object of inquiry with regards to discerning and interrogating the causes of disengagement, and arguably just as crucially, how disengagement may be challenged. However, in order to do so, we need to recognise the distinctly *discursive nature of these processes.*

Discourse involves the making of speech acts and their reception by an audience of actors who subjectively interpret, internalise and relay the ideas contained in the speech act to other actors (for reviews see Schiffrin 1994; Howarth 2000). When actors – say, politicians – make speeches in which they proclaim policies to be beyond the realms of their control, and therefore not subject to 'politics' of any meaningful sort, then the 'political nature' of those policies does not automatically get shifted away into the ether. Rather, it *attempts such a shift*, which may or may not be accepted by the 'audience'. That in turn may mean that the audience is less likely to recognise in future that the policy in question actually *is* political, and to act upon that acknowledgement by engaging substantively in raising the issue as a political problem in a public forum. Of course, the opposite may be equally as likely – the audience may reject the assertion that the policy in case is non-political, and instead re-engage with the issue, perhaps even more virulently than previously. We shall return to this argument presently. For now though, it is critical to emphasise that, from the perspective of political disengagement, the supply-side argument is one concerned properly with *depoliticisation as a discursive process*. In order to critically assess the supply-side drivers of political disengagement, we require a framework for unearthing and exposing the different aspects of discourses that make them depoliticising, and facilitating an analytical approach that enables criticism of when elites (or indeed, any actors) attempt to use such tools.[2] The following section argues that integrating the concept of discursive depoliticisation within a framework of logics of critical explanation enables us to do precisely this.

Discursive depoliticisation: conceptualising 'denial'

The concept of discursive depoliticisation has been posited by Wood and Flinders (2014) as a distinct form of depoliticisation, separate from what they term 'governmental depoliticisation' (the extent of government control over arm's-length bodies) and 'societal depoliticisation' (policy issues are simply left off the agenda). Discursive depoliticisation 'focuses on the role of language and ideas to depoliticise certain issues and through this define them as little more (than) elements of fate' (Wood & Flinders 2014, p. 165). It is essentially this process that analysts of the 'supply side' of political disengagement are concerned with – to identify and interrogate how particular elite discourses shift the political nature of decisions. Explicit conceptualisations of discursive depoliticisation have been developed by Jenkins (2011) and Wood (2015) (for an empirical application see Bates et al. 2014). Jenkins (2011) develops a conception of 'the political' as relating broadly to contingency and human agency (for theoretical specification of this concept of the political see Gamble 2000), defining depoliticisation as explicit social strategies of recognising or *denying the presence of human agency in social situations*. She hence stipulates a broad definition of depoliticisation: 'A strategy of depoliticisation entails forming necessities, permanence, immobility, closure and fatalism and concealing/negating or removing contingency' (Jenkins 2011, p. 160).

From this broad definition, Wood (2015) defines discursive depoliticisation more specifically as the '*denial by humans of their capacity to alter their collective practices, institutions and social conditions*'. This is distinguished from discursive politicisation, which includes discursive practices that *recognise* human capacities to alter their collective practices, institutions and social conditions. Second, it is distinguished from 'social learning processes', which involve neither recognition, nor denial, but merely *silence* on altering collective practices, institutions and social conditions, instead focusing on tweaking or 'nudging' individual behaviours in order to achieve policy goals. Depoliticisation includes discourses that actively deny or 'push back' against the capacity to collectively change common practices, institutions and social conditions.

To date, this conceptual debate has moved the literature towards more specific definitions. However, the notion of discursive 'denial' has yet to be unpacked conceptually or empirically. What constitutes a 'denial' and how is politics 'denied', linguistically? Despite 'denial' being arguably a critical concern in the study of political language and discourse, it is difficult to find a sustained treatment of the concept of depoliticisation within this literature. Often, we find emphasis on 'sedimentation' (Jessop 2010), or other concepts that essentially describe how 'identities and their nodal points obtain fixity' (Carpentier & De Cleen 2007, p. 266; see also Moon 2013, p. 117), with fixity clearly relating to the denial that alternative ideas or collective action is possible or desirable. The wider literature on language, communication, rhetoric, argumentation and performance addresses denial, but does not link it to depoliticisation. Teun van Dijk (1992) sets out a schema of different forms of denial in the case of racial discrimination:

1. 'Act denial' ('I did not do/say that at all');
2. 'Control denial' ('I did not do/say that on purpose', 'It was an accident');
3. 'Intention denial' ('I did not mean that', 'You got me wrong');
4. 'Goal denial' ('I did not do/say that, in order to…').

(van Dijk 1992, p. 92)

This framework can be applied at individual, institutional and societal scales, either referring to counter-attack against accusations, or pre-emptory denial of responsibility or blame for negative outcomes. At an individual or personal level, Mitchell et al. (2011) examine personal denial strategies for not challenging racist statements in everyday conversations, identifying internal personal justifications of not being able to overcome broad structures of discrimination. At an institutional level, Hansson (2015) applies this analysis to public administration, drawing on Christopher Hood's concept of 'blame games' to show how, among other rhetorical strategies, politicians and civil servants practice forms of 'denial' to shift responsibility for policy problems. He identifies forms of 'total problem denial, partial problem denial, and problem denial accompanied by a counter-attack' in which policy- makers attempt to 'win an argument over culpability in its own terms by offering persuasive excuses and justifications' (Hansson 2015, p. 305). Moreover, at a macro-societal scale, Wodak and de Cillia (2007) show how denial works as a way of displacing collective political/psychological traumas, using the example of post-1945 Austria, in which public discourse constructed the country as a 'newly born child' and the country's complicity with the Third Reich as a 'dark' period not to be discussed.

Our concern in this chapter is to link denial strategies to depoliticisation – or rather, linking strategies of denial similar to those outlined above with the higher-level aim of 'placing at one remove the political nature of decision making' – not merely 'denying' responsibility or blame, but the very *political nature* of those decisions to begin with. Here, we argue that a fruitful engagement can be made with Jason Glynos and David Howarth's (2007) framework for critical explanation through the concept of 'logics'. Glynos and Howarth's 'discourse theoretic approach' (further expanded in Glynos 2001; Howarth 2010), can be applied in critically explaining *how* discursive depoliticisation works, that is, how politicians (in our case) 'deny' discursively the capacity for altering collective practices, institutions and social conditions through different 'logics'. The reason we turn to Howarth and Glynos' approach is because of its critical focus on the deeper meanings (logics) underlying discourse, rather than merely their linguistic construction. We are interested in promoting a framework for *critically explaining* how discursive depoliticisation works, rather than simply determining whether it exists and has causal efficacy or not (for causal evidence see Hay 2007; Stoker, 2006). As Howarth (2000) usefully puts it, 'discourse theory seeks to provide novel interpretations of events and practices by elucidating their meaning', rather than being concerned with 'causal' explanation as such.

Other frameworks of discourse analysis could also be integrated. Notably, the various approaches to Critical Discourse Analysis (CDA) (for a review see Hart & Cap 2014) are similar, being concerned 'to investigate critically social inequality as it is expressed, constituted, legitimized, and so on, by language use (or in discourse)' (Wodak 2004, p. 187). Fairclough's (1992) *Discourse and social change* offers arguably the closest contender, integrating, as it does, micro- and macro-levels of 'how a discursive event stands in relation to hegemonies' (p. 10). However, Glynos and Howarth's approach can be distinguished from CDA approaches due to their 'different methodologies, with detailed linguistic analysis of actual instances of discourse by CDA ... juxtaposed to a more general analysis of the discursive articulation of political identities' (Carpentier & De Cleen 2007, p. 278). For our purposes, the 'discourse theory approach' 'allows one to historicize, scrutinize, and de-naturalize the seemingly fixed interests and identities assigned to subjects' (Paul 2009, p. 243), as expressed in the central concern with *logics* 'understood in a very specific way, as capturing the point, rules and ontological preconditions of a practice or regime of practices' (Glynos & Howarth 2008, p. 165). The 'deeper' meanings underlying discourse are uncovered and critically analysed, as opposed to their strategic, socio-political construction, which is the concern of CDA.

What, then, is this approach and how can it be integrated into the analysis of discursive depoliticisation? Put briefly, due to space constraints, Glynos and Howarth's framework develops an eclectic set of insights from post-structuralist socio-political theory into a typology of three logics of critical explanation: social logics, political logics and fantasmatic logics.[3] As Howarth argues, with a logics framework 'the function' of power 'is to *conceal* the radical contingency of social relations and to *naturalize* relations of domination' (Howarth 2010, p. 310). This is similar to the definition of discursive depoliticisation as discursive *denial*, the shielding, obfuscating or veiling of the capacity of humans to collectively alter their common institutions, practices and social conditions. 'Social logics', they argue, 'enable us to characterize practices in a particular social domain' (p. 133). A particular discourse has a logically stated set of rules and 'laws' that support its dominance at any one particular time, and uncovering social logics enables analysts to highlight the contingent aspects of these 'laws'. Second, 'political logics' 'provide the means to explore how social practices are instituted, contested and defended' (2007 p. 133). When analysing a political logic, the analyst 'disclos(es) and render(s) visible the contingent character of any practice, policy or institution by showing the role of power and exclusion in its formation'. Analysing political logics involves analysing *the past*, analysing a logic that justifies the dominance of a set of ideas by *rationalising* the previous political struggles that it has survived in order to become dominant. Lastly, 'fantasmatic logics' or 'logics of fantasy' aim 'to capture a particularly powerful way in which subjects are rendered complicit in concealing or covering over the radical contingency of social relations' (Glynos & Howarth 2007, p. 134; see Glynos 2008). A logic of fantasy includes 'the different types of "enjoyment" subjects procure in identifying with discourses and believing things they do' (Howarth 2010, p. 326), or in other words, underlying or overt narratives that dramatise the world, in the manner of a film, abstracting what it could, in theory, become. Often, then, analysing logics of fantasy involves analysing how discourse conceives *the future*.

These logics are clearly overlapping and interconnected. Any appeal to a particular rule or law (social logic), will often rely upon historical evidence about how it has proved superior to other ideas (political logic) and (usually implicit) appeal to a fantasy of what might be achieved were the rule to be followed, or what catastrophe might ensue were the rule to be violated (logic of fantasy). Analytically, however, Glynos and Howarth (2007) argue that examining the domination of a particular discourse by interrogating these three logics 'has a role to play in furnishing us with a complete explanatory account'. Accounting systematically for how a discourse dominates within a particular context requires an analysis of how it dominates discourse about how society has come to be (the political logic), how it is currently (social logic) and how it should or could be in the future (logic of fantasy). Table 40.2 therefore applies this framework of logics to the analysis of discursive depoliticisation.

The logics of denial are not exhaustive, but they do provide the most encompassing framework available, drawing from a comprehensive approach to analysing 'logics'. The three 'logics of denial' – teleological assertions, restatements of assumed rules or laws, and evoking disastrous fictions – construct a multidimensional picture of how discursive depoliticisation works. The following section shows how this framework can be used to analyse the critical case study of the depoliticisation of austerity policies during the post-global financial crisis era in UK politics.

Table 40.2 Typology of different logics of discursive depoliticisation

Indicator of discursive depoliticisation	Denial in relation to...	Empirical trope of denial	Example – Coalition Austerity Discourse in the UK	Explanatory logic (Glynos & Howarth 2007)	Focus
Denial	The past	'Things were worse in the old days'	The sick man of Europe in the 1970s	'Political'	Refuting genealogical arguments stating things 'could be otherwise'
	The present	'This rule holds in all circumstances'	Capital-flight thesis	'Social'	Restating logically assumed 'rule' or 'law'
	The future	'If things change, disaster will ensue'	Danger of becoming 'like Greece'	'Fantasy'	Attempting to captivate audience through the politics of fear

Theoretically deep, empirically fluid: Analysing austerity discourse through discursive depoliticisation

Since the 2008 global financial crisis, and in particular since the European Union sovereign debt crisis – which resulted in several governments, including Greece, Ireland and Portugal, seeking assistance from the International Monetary Fund – governments across Europe have sought to impose austerity policies. These include reductions in central-government funding for welfare benefits, education, health-service provision and other public services instead of tax increases. A number of analysts have argued that the imposition of austerity has been 'depoliticising', further entrenching neo-liberalism as an ideological paradigm and stifling political opposition (Kerr et al. 2011; Macartney 2011; Paudyn 2013; Radice 2014; Macartney 2014). Despite the growth of depoliticising discourse, however, empirical evidence shows that political opposition and participation is greater than would be expected. This section argues that the discursive depoliticisation framework is able to deal with this apparent paradox by generating theoretically *deep* nuanced analysis of the logics behind particular acts of depoliticisation, while allowing for the increasingly dynamic, contingent or *fluid* causal relationships between depoliticisation and political disengagement. It illustrates this through a brief analysis of depoliticising discourses employed in the case of the UK, analysing George Osborne and David Cameron's political speeches, and identifies each 'logic of denial' within this selection.

The first is a logic of denial in relation to the past, made up of 'The dank, "declinist" colloquialisms ("cap-in-hand", "sick man of Europe", "winter of discontent", "break-up of Britain") piled up like uncollected rubbish' (Black 2012, p. 175). These references to Britain in the 1970s as an economically backward 'third-world' country before the advent of Thatcherism in the 1980s continue to provide justificatory symbols for how any change of course from neo-liberal economic policies is unthinkable. As George Osborne argued in a 2012 speech to the Conservative Party conference:

> Yes we've cut the budget deficit by a quarter. But it tells you something about just how big it was that the deficit is still higher today than when a British government went begging to the IMF in the 1970s. This Wednesday I'm also going to a meeting of the IMF. Don't worry. Because of the resolve of the British people, I go representing a country that is seen as part of the solution, not part of the problem.
>
> (Osborne 2012)

David Cameron's 2013 speech to the party conference made a similar argument:

> With its brains and research centres, let's make Manchester the world leader in advanced materials. We're building an economy for the North and South, embracing new technologies, producing things and selling them to the world. So make no mistake who's looking forward in British politics ... we'll leave the 1970s-style socialism to others ... we are the party of the future.
>
> (Cameron 2013)

Here, Cameron is appealing to the image of the 'bad old days' of the 1970s, and how reverting to similar policies or practices as then is simply unthinkable. The 1970s was 'the problem' and Cameron's Government, is, apparently, part of 'the solution'. Collective human agency is denied in this instance because of the juxtaposition of the past as purely 'bad' and the present as purely 'good', such that any 'return' is old-fashioned and outdated. Looking 'forward', in Cameron's words, hence means forgetting alternatives and continuing on an unquestionably 'righteous' path.

The second logic of denial is the appeal to the rule that increased taxation and regulation of business leads to capital flight. The logic here assumes, in line with 'business-school' globalisation theory, that increasing rates of taxation leads to capital flight and disinvestment. While such assumptions have received much empirical refutation, they nonetheless retain significant weight discursively. Since 2010, the UK's Coalition Government employed such logics to further justify austerity. A speech by David Cameron to the Confederation of British Industry (CBI) demonstrates this well:

> Corporation tax – coming down to the lowest rate in the G7 and yes, the top rate of tax has been cut too because you cannot on the one hand say 'Britain's open for business' and on the other have the highest top rate of tax in the G20. So this is what being tough means. Doing what's right for our future; taking on all the noisy lobby groups that want to pour money into today and forget about tomorrow. And this approach is working. The deficit cut by 25 per cent. Interest rates at record lows. A million new private sector jobs created in two years. Exports up dramatically. That's what tough government has helped deliver
>
> (Cameron 2012)

Cameron emphasised this point again at length at the 2013 party conference:

> To get decent jobs for people, you've got to recognise some fundamental economic facts. We are in a global race today. No one owes us a living. Last week, our ambition

to compete in the global race was airily dismissed as a race to the bottom ... that it means competing with China on sweatshops and India on low wages. No – those countries are becoming our customers ... and we've got to compete with California on innovation; Germany on high-end manufacturing; Asia on finance and technology. And here's something else you need to recognise about this race. The plain fact is this. All those global companies that employ lots of people – they can set up anywhere in the world. They could go to Silicon Valley. To Berlin. And yes, here in Manchester. And these companies base their decisions on some simple things: like the tax rates in each country. So if those taxes are higher here than elsewhere, they don't come here. And if they don't come here, we don't get those jobs.

(Cameron 2013)

Here, the desirability of Britain to international investors and high taxation rates are presented as directly, and logically, contradictory. The theory is simply assumed as fact, and any alternative to this is skirted over. 'Tough government' is thus, apparently, needed to enforce this 'rule' in order to achieve specified outcomes (creation of jobs, low interest rates, deficit reduction) – tough government meaning, in this case, austere government.

Finally, the logic of denial in relation to the future can be found in comparisons with political conflict elsewhere, and the claim that any diversion away from austerity policies will lead to such political collapse. In the case of Britain, the comparison is often Greece, where large-scale political disruption, widespread unemployment and declining gross domestic product have been prevalent, particularly since the Eurozone crisis began in 2011. George Osborne again provides us with a prime example, this time in a speech responding to Ed Miliband (then British Labour Party Leader), who provoked debate about a 'cost of living crisis', and a potential alternative to austerity:

> More borrowing and more debt remains their economic policy. But they no longer dare talk to the British people about it. Instead, they'd much rather just talk about the cost of living. As if the cost of living was somehow detached from the performance of the economy. Well you ask the citizens of Greece what happens to living standards when the economy fails. You ask someone with a mortgage what happens to their living standards when mortgage rates go up. Just a 1% rise means an extra £1,000 on the average mortgage bill. You ask the citizens of this country what would be an absolute disaster for living standards. They'll tell you. Higher borrowing. Higher welfare costs. Higher taxes. Meaning: higher mortgage rates. And higher unemployment.
>
> (Osborne 2013)

David Cameron made a similar statement days later:

> I see that Labour have stopped talking about the debt crisis and now they talk about the cost of living crisis. As if one wasn't directly related to the other. If you want to know what happens if you don't deal with a debt crisis ... and how it affects the cost of living ... just go and ask the Greeks. So finishing the job means sticking to our course until we've paid off all of Labour's deficit, not just some of it.
>
> (Cameron 2013)

Here, the case of Greece is evoked in a spectral manner as a worst-case scenario, and is then linked to the danger of an 'absolute disaster' for 'citizens of this country', were the government to change course and introduce higher taxes. Because changing course would lead to a Greek-style socio-economic collapse, and at least an extra £1,000 on any mortgage bill, austerity must remain. Collective human agency is enclosed by appealing to a 'fantasy' of economic collapse, thereby evoking fear and insecurity.

The critical analysis of the quotations from Cameron and Osborne provides only a small taster of what a full critical analysis of austerity discourse in Britain – using our discursive depoliticisation framework – would look like. What is important about the brief analysis is that we do not assume any necessary relationship between the logics of denial and their effects. We do not assume that the logics are necessarily convincing or effective in achieving their intended aims (whatever those may be), nor do we assume they are uncontested or even necessarily dominant at any one particular time (the third quote from George Osborne in response to an arguably more powerful alternative speech by Ed Miliband is indicative of this). There is an assumption of *empirical fluidity*. But critical discourse theory, as Howarth explains, 'does not simply attempt to retrieve and reconstruct the meanings of social actors ... nor, on the other hand, does it seek to uncover the true underlying meanings of texts and actions'. Rather, it seeks to 'provide novel interpretations of events and practices ... so that they may acquire a different significance and provide the basis for possible critique and transformation of existing practices and social meanings' (Howarth 2000, p. 129). This *different significance* or *theoretical depth* comes from drawing out these three logics and thus emphasising the multiple ways in which the Coalition Government's austerity discourse attempts to construct particular meanings that seek to close down or delimit people's understandings of the choices that are available in liberal democratic societies. These are worthy of critical analysis in themselves – as worthy as it would be highlighting in a conversation in a pub or a seminar room that an argument or set of assumptions degrades or belittles politics as a worthwhile and important activity of deciding for ourselves how we should be governed.

Conclusion: communication and the politics of hyper-democracy

In this chapter, we have argued for integrating the salient concept of depoliticisation with a well-established 'logics of critical analysis' model developed by Glynos and Howarth (2007) in order to address the 'supply side' of political disengagement. We posited three 'logics of denial' underlying depoliticising discourse – denial in relation to the past, present and future. Critically assessing these, we suggested, is important for the purposes of calling out attempts at shaping negatively the public's attitudes towards politics. Importantly, conceived in this way, depoliticisation may lead to political disengagement, as argued in Hay's *Why we hate politics*, or it may even, perversely, lead to greater disengagement based on a distorted and vicious conception of the public interest. What is critical though, in relation to our framework, is that it offers *theoretical depth* to the critical analysis of 'denial' and its different forms, but makes room for *empirical fluidity*, in a way that a more rigid approach focused purely on causal relationships, or an approach assuming *a priori* that depoliticisation is uncontested, would not.

It is with this thought in mind that we conclude this chapter, not by setting out a future 'research agenda' (we believe that this appears obvious enough from the three-fold framework we have presented), but rather to point to why we believe that our framework – specifically Glynos and Howarth's (2007) 'post-structuralist' insights – can be salient at this moment. Glynos and Howarth's framework is particularly important, not merely because it provides an accessible three-fold distillation of the systematic – but often impenetrable –

post-structuralist approaches to political discourse found in political theory (of which we are not experts ourselves), but rather because it is arguably especially applicable in a time when political structures are becoming more 'liquid' (Bauman 2000) and political authority is increasingly being scrutinised and contested (Hajer 2009). Put simply, we arguably live in an era of what Welch (2013) calls 'hyper-democracy'. In essence, hyper-democracy, as Welch (2013, p. 2) defines it, refers 'neither [to] "more democracy" nor "an excess of democracy"' but 'the *intensification* of democracy'. If (liberal) democracy refers to a system of rule wherein authorities are responsive and accountable to public demand, then 'hyper-democracy' refers to a system whereby the political pressures required to make that system work – or as David Easton (1957) seminally called them, 'inputs' – intensify, putting the system itself under strain.

In this system, politicians try to depoliticise their decisions by portraying them as inevitable or necessary. And yet, as Gamble (2015, p. 42) argues, while structural hierarchies still exist, within those hierarchies, 'governments still face myriad demands for increased spending ... [and] strong external pressures to take control of their public finances'. The implications of this for analysts of political discourse is that the frameworks they use should be open and inclusive of the 'indeterminacy' of contemporary society, and while still 'speaking truth to power', analysts ought to be aware of the increasingly unstable and uncertain conditions within which power operates, and within which they analyse power. This chapter has aimed to provide a framework for critically analysing depoliticising discourse in such a way – critical of its consequences for politics, but recognising its contingent and indeterminate operation.

Notes

1 These aspects of 'formal' politics are clearly not all there is to political participation. 'Alternative' forms of participation in the form of activism in social movements, local participation and 'everyday making' are arguably on the rise (Li & Marsh 2008). For our purposes here, though, the causes of disengagement from 'formal politics' – parties, parliaments and electoral procedures – are taken as a key research question, setting aside questions of how 'participation' can or should be defined.
2 Critically addressing 'powerful elites' is important to any approach for analysing the 'supply side' drivers of political disengagement. It could be argued that such an approach tends to privilege a focus on the specific actions of politicians (their 'agency') at the expense of a focus on broader structures driving disengagement (class-based disengagement, for example). This raises interesting questions about who ought to be 'held accountable' for political disengagement, which we cannot address here. We would agree with Corbett (2015), however, who calls for more research on the internal practices of politicians themselves to assess the extent to which their 'supply side' practices are driven more by structural pressures, or are due to an internalized culture.
3 Note that these logics refer both to the logics used by researchers in their explanation *and* to the logics used by the political actors they are studying in the discourses they adopt. In discourse theoretic analysis, the line between the researcher and the world they are studying is self-consciously blurred or problematised, so as to move beyond overtly positivist approaches to research.

References

Bauman, Z, 2000, *Liquid modernity*, Polity, Cambridge.
Black, L, 2012, 'An enlightening decade? New histories of 1970s' Britain', *International Labor and Working-Class History*, 82, pp. 174–186.

Bøggild, T, 2015, 'How politicians' reelection efforts can reduce public trust, electoral support, and policy approval', *Political* Psychology, *37*(6), pp. 901–919.

Burnham, P, 2001, 'New Labour and the politics of depoliticisation', *The British Journal of Politics and International Relations*, *3*(2), pp. 127–149.

Cameron, D, 2012, 'Speech to CBI', CBI Conference, 19 November, London, available from: www.telegraph.co.uk/finance/economics/9687688/David-Cameron-CBI-speech-in-full.html [accessed 3 December 2014].

Cameron, D, 2013, 'Speech to Conservative Party Conference', 2 October, Manchester, available from: www.telegraph.co.uk/news/politics/david-cameron/10349712/Conservative-Party-Conference-David-Camerons-speech-in-full.html [accessed 3 December 2014].

Carpentier, N, & De Cleen, B, 2007, 'Bringing discourse theory into media studies', *Journal of Language and Politics*, *6*(2), pp. 265–293.

Corbett, J, 2015, 'Diagnosing the problem of anti-politicians', *Political Studies Review*, *14*(4), pp. 534–543.

Easton, D, 1957, 'An approach to the analysis of political systems', *World Politics*, *9*(3), pp. 383–400.

Fairclough, N, 1992, *Discourse and social change*, Polity, Cambridge.

Fawcett, P & Marsh, D, 2014, 'Depoliticisation, governance and political participation', *Policy and Politics*, *42*(2), pp. 171–188.

Flinders, M, 2008, *Delegated governance and the British state: Walking without order*, Oxford University Press, Oxford.

Flinders, M, 2009, 'Bridging the Gap: Revitalising Politics and the Politics of Public Expectations', *Representation*, *45*(3), pp. 337–347.

Gamble, A, 2000, *Politics and fate*, Polity, Cambridge.

Gamble, A, 2015, 'Austerity as statecraft', *Parliamentary Affairs*, *68*(1), pp. 42–57.

Garzia, D, 2011, 'The personalization of politics in Western democracies', *The Leadership Quarterly*, *22*(4), pp. 697–709.

Glynos, J, 2001, 'The grip of ideology', *Journal of Political Ideologies*, *6*(2), pp. 191–214.

Glynos, J & Howarth, D, 2007, *Logics of critical explanation in social and political theory*, Routledge, London.

Glynos, J & Howarth, D, 2008, 'Structure, agency and power in political analysis: Beyond contextualised self-interpretations', *Political Studies Review*, *6*(2), pp. 155–169.

Hajer, M A, 2009, *Authoritative governance: Policy making in the age of mediatization*, Oxford University Press, Oxford.

Hansson, S, 2015, Discursive strategies of blame avoidance in government: A framework for analysis, *Discourse &Society*, *26*(3), pp. 297–322.

Hart, C. & Cap, P, eds., 2014, *Contemporary Critical Discourse Studies*, Bloomsbury Publishing, London.

Hay, C, 2007, *Why we hate politics*, Polity Press, Cambridge.

Howarth, D, 2000, *Discourse: Concepts in the social sciences*, Open University, Buckingham.

Howarth, D, 2010, 'Power, discourse, and policy', *Critical Policy Studies*, *3*(3–4), pp. 309–335.

Jenkins, L, 2011, 'The difference genealogy makes', *Political Studies*, *59*(1), pp. 156–174.

Jessop, B, 2010, 'Cultural political economy and critical policy studies', *Critical Policy Studies*, *3*(3–4), pp. 336–356.

Johansen, H, 2012, *Relational political marketing in party-centred democracies*, Ashgate, Farnham.

Kerr, P, Byrne, C & Foster, E, 2011, 'Theorising Cameronism', *Political Studies Review*, *9*(2), pp. 193–207.

Kisby, B & Sloam, J, 2012, 'Citizenship, democracy and education in the UK', *Parliamentary Affairs*, *65*(1), pp. 68–89.

Li, Y & Marsh, D, 2008, 'New forms of political participation', *British Journal of Political Science*, *38*(02), pp. 247–272.

Lilleker, D G, 2005a, 'Political marketing: The cause of an emerging democratic deficit in Britain?', *Journal of Nonprofit & Public Sector Marketing*, *14*(1–2), pp. 5–26.

Lilleker, D G, 2005b, 'The impact of political marketing on internal party democracy', *Parliamentary Affairs*, 58(3), pp. 570–584.

Lilleker, D G & Negrine, R, 2003, 'Not big brand names but corner shops: Marketing politics to a disengaged electorate', *Journal of Political Marketing*, 2(1), pp. 55–75.

Macartney, H, 2011, 'Crisis for the state or crisis of the state?', *The Political Quarterly*, 82(2), pp. 193–203.

Macartney, H, 2014, 'The paradox of integration? European democracy and the debt crisis', *Cambridge Review of International Affairs*, (ahead-of-print), 27(3), pp. 401–423.

Manning, N & Holmes, M, 2014, 'Political emotions: A role for feelings of affinity in citizens' (dis) engagements with electoral politics?', *Sociology*, 48(4), pp. 698–714.

Mazzoleni, G, 2000, 'A return to civic and political engagement prompted by personalised political leadership?', *Political Communication*, 17(4), pp. 325–328.

Mitchell, M, Every, D & Ranzijn, R, 2011, 'Everyday antiracism in interpersonal contexts', *Journal of Community & Applied Social Psychology*, 21(4), pp. 329–341.

Moon, D S, 2013, '"Tissue on the bones": Towards the development of a post-structuralist institutionalism', *Politics*, 33(2), pp. 112–123.

Osborne, G, 2012, 'Speech to Conservative Party Conference', 8 October, Birmingham, available from: www.newstatesman.com/blogs/politics/2012/10/george-osbornes-speech-conservative-conference-full-text [accessed 3 December 2014].

Osborne, G, 2013, 'Speech to Conservative Party Conference', 30 September, Manchester, available from: www.politics.co.uk/comment-analysis/2013/09/30/george-osborne-s-conference-speech-in-full [accessed 3 December 2014].

Paudyn, B, 2013, 'Credit rating agencies and the sovereign debt crisis', *Review of International Political Economy*, 20(4), pp. 788–818.

Paul, K T, 2009, 'Discourse analysis: An exploration of methodological issues and a call for methodological courage in the field of policy analysis', *Critical Policy Studies*, 3(2), pp. 240–253.

Radice, H, 2014, 'Enforcing austerity in Europe', *Journal of Contemporary European Studies*, 22(3), pp. 318–328.

Scammell, M, 2014, *Consumer democracy: The marketing of politics*, Cambridge University Press, Cambridge.

Schiffrin, D, 1994, *Approaches to discourse*, Blackwell, Oxford.

Stoker, G, 2006, *Why politics matters*, Palgrave Macmillan, Basingstoke.

van Dijk, T A, 1992, 'Discourse and the denial of racism', *Discourse & Society*, 3(1), pp. 87–118.

Welch, S, 2013, *Hyperdemocracy*, Palgrave Macmillan, Basingstoke.

Wodak, R, 2004, 'Critical Discourse Analysis' in *Qualitative Research Practice*, eds. C Seale, G Gobo, G Gubrium & D Silverman, Sage, London, pp. 185–202.

Wodak, R & De Cillia, R, 2007, 'Commemorating the past: The discursive construction of official narratives about the "rebirth of the second Austrian republic"', *Discourse & Communication*, 1(3), pp. 337–363.

Wood, M, 2015, 'Puzzling and powering in policy paradigm shifts', *Critical Policy Studies*, 9(1), pp. 2–21.

Wood, M & Flinders, M, 2014, 'Rethinking depoliticisation', *Policy and Politics*, 42(2), pp. 151–170.

41
Identity politics, populism and the far right

Anton Pelinka

The term 'populism' tends to overshadow the debate concerning democracy and the far right. 'Populism' sometimes seems to be the escape route to prevent any substantial discourse about contemporary anti-democratic trends. This chapter argues that populism is a phenomenon rooted in the very concept of democracy. If democracy is defined by the competition of two or more parties or candidates for votes (Schumpeter 1950), this leads to a populist policy of appeasing the existing interests of the electorate, or of specific electoral segments. The consequence is a usually polemic language of simplified exclusion and inclusion. The question 'Who is a populist?' can only be answered by saying that, in a democracy, every party and every candidate running for election is, in a certain way, a populist. That means it is necessary to look for the differences between different kinds of populism.

To distinguish between populists, specific variables have to be considered – such as 'left' and 'right'. As the chapter's focus is primarily on far-right populism (Wodak, KhosraviNik & Mral 2013), it tries to:

- Provide an overview of the populist far right's defining other, that is, whom does the populist far right exclude from 'us'.
- Underline the differences and similarities between the far right of the past and today's far right.
- Stress that contemporary far-right populism does not confront democracy directly, but claims to defend it against specific enemies.
- Distinguish between far-right tendencies in societies and political systems, especially concerning their recent past outside or inside the 'communist bloc' defined by a one-party system of the Soviet type.

The far right: a conceptual history of far-right parties and movements in the nineteenth, twentieth and early twenty-first centuries

The political meaning of 'left' and 'right' is the product of the sitting order of the French parliament during the revolutionary period. Since then, 'right' has been a term to define the position opposing radical reforms; 'left' became synonymous with deep reforms, be they based on a revolutionary – or an evolutionary – understanding of political strategies. In the Europe of the twenty-first century, the existence of party families – more or less transformed into European parties – followed that tradition. The European Parliament has given the left–right structure developed in national parliaments an all-European meaning (Almeida 2012). Left, respectively, far left indicates a socialist or communist position; right, respectively, far right stands for the different varieties of apolitical understanding based on ethnic or national identity.

Hannah Arendt and her ground-breaking study on totalitarianism underlined another systematic distinction: there are fundamentally shaped anti-democratic tendencies on the right as well as on the left. Arendt has summarised these tendencies, based on the evidence of Nazism and Stalinism (Arendt 1951). The knowledge of similarities between the systems identified with the names Hitler and Stalin has become deeper as a result of further research (see, e.g. Montefiore 2003; Mazower 2008) The similarities between the systems that made the most significant impact on the twentieth century do not imply that the two can be seen as identical: Marxism-Leninism has been a doctrine based on European Enlightenment. Leninism – an interpretation of Marxism – included a cosmopolitan and humanitarian core, despite being used by the century's two most dreadful regimes. Nazism was, in its very essence, the principle antithesis to this core.

It has been the reality of personalised dictatorship without any kind of checks and balances that was the common denominator distinguishing the two totalitarian traditions from any democratic systems based on a universal understanding of basic human rights. Contemporary far-left and far-right political parties are still bound by opposing such democracies – even if they are not in the programmatic tradition of Nazism and Stalinism. This of course means that the moderate, anti-authoritarian forces left of centre (e.g. social democratic or green parties) and the moderate forces right of centre (e.g. Christian democratic or liberal parties) share a common distinction from the extremists of both left and right. The European Union, the product of the centrist forces of moderate parties, has to face the more-or-less principled opposition of the far left and the far right (Pelinka 2015).

Among the political traditions and parties to be considered 'right' in Europe at the beginning of the twenty-first century, significant distinctions have to be made. Beginning with post-1945 development in Europe, significant parties of the politically conservative right parties became forerunners of liberal democracy – such as the Italian, French, and (West-) German Christian democrats (DC, MRP, CDU, respectively). In some cases, the moderate-right parties became a 'hegemonic party' – but always with a clear distinction from the fascist dictators of the past. (Sartori 2005, pp. 204–216) And when the French Fifth Republic started in 1958 as a project distinctly designed by the political right (Charles De Gaulle and his party), Gaullist France stayed within the framework of the French republican tradition and did not fulfil some expectations of turning France into a fascist system.

This 'centrist' or moderate part of the political right was challenged from the very beginning by rightist parties positioned outside the liberal-democratic mainstream of post-1945 Western Europe: post- or neo-fascist parties such as the Italian MSI (Italian Social Movement) or the French Poujadists, who became the forerunners of the Front National. Despite significant elements of revisionism, of pre-democratic and fascist nostalgia, the stability of Europe's liberal democracies started to suck the more traditional right-wing extremists into the competitive party system that defines liberal democracies. In 2000, neo-fascism has ceased to be of any significance in Italy. The right spectrum of Italian politics became dominated by Silvio Berlusconi's Forza Italia, which – regarding its electorate and its foreign and European policies – was more the successor of the Christian democrats than of the neo-fascists. By taking over the role of political dominance for the right of centre, Forza Italia did not have to deal with the competition of the traditional moderates of the old Christian democrats, nor with the old (neo-)fascists, but with the regional, tentatively secessionist populism of the Lega Nord (Ruzza & Balbo 2013).

In France, Poujadism has been replaced by the Front National, which represents probably the most instructive case of the new time of European far-right extremism: the Front National is not nationalistic in the traditional sense, not playing (for example) the anti-German card; it is also not representing the anti-republican resentments that dominated Vichy-France. The Front National is – in a broader sense – republican and egalitarian by excluding those who are not truly French from its understanding of 'us'. The Front National represents the anti-elitist character of the populist far right, criticising traditional elites of destroying France's national identity by opening the French state as well as society to mass immigration (Beauzamy 2013).

At the beginning of the twenty-first century, Europe's far right is different from the far right so typical for most of the twentieth century. The far-right parties have stopped being 'reactionary' in the traditional sense. They do not defend any 'ancient regime' against the forces of democracy. They, rhetorically, have turned around the old discourses. They are against elites – especially against elites representing the '*demos*', the people. The new far right claims to speak on behalf of the people against those who (according to the populist rhetoric) have betrayed the people.

The new far right even defends basic values identified with democracy, and defends civic and human rights. The Dutch Freedom Party (PVV), in the tradition of Pim Fortuyn, claims to articulate the interests of women, principles of free speech and religious freedom – against the perceived danger coming from migrants with an Islamic background (Oudenampsen 2013). This new far right tries to portray itself as the main defender of a civilisation based on enlightenment. It is not the values and principles enshrined in the PVV's (and other far-right parties') programmatic declaration. It is the ethnically exclusive – and in that respect, xenophobic – and at least indirectly, potentially racist character that allows qualifying parties (such as the PVV) as right-wing extremists.

This is in many respects a long way from the anti-democratic far right of the past, such as the Catholic 'Ultra-Montanists' who fought French republicanism in the name of the pope, Russian (and other) aristocrats who were unable to accept the idea of progress as articulated in even the moderate liberal attitudes of Alexis de Tocqueville, all the reactionaries – reactionaries in the original meaning – who saw the modern evil in the revolutions of the eighteenth and nineteenth centuries. This kind of far right may exist today, but it does not have any significant impact.

The European far right of the first decades of the twentieth century – a far right for which the term 'fascism' has been used as an umbrella concept, despite the vagueness of the rather volatile reality – used some techniques of mass democracy to destroy democracy. These included mass parties mobilising significant numbers of people, representatives in parliament to undermine parliament, and – especially – a rather new understanding of 'them': the people was not the enemy, but rather, foreign peoples. Fascism stood for an ethnic and national exclusiveness within newly established democracies, using democratic instruments against democratic principles (Mudde 2007; Müller 2011, pp. 91–124).

'Right' in political terms has always been seen as opposition to any egalitarian agenda. It may have been enlarging the right to vote and bringing what used to be called 'the lower classes' as well as women, into the political arena in an active role, or may it have been defending the privileges of birth and property against any kind of reform labelled liberal or socialist. The right defended the status quo, or even tried – fulfilling the real meaning of the term 'reactionary' – to return to the status quo ante.

This started to change in the twentieth century. The Italian fascists represented a kind of nationalistic egalitarianism and its German cousin was now called the 'National Socialist Party': the party was not just a traditional right-wing bourgeois party promoting extreme reactionary policies. In promoting '*völkischen Sozialismus*' (ethnically exclusive socialism), the party spoke on behalf of a significant part of the German working-class electorate – blue-collar voters who believed they had reason to prefer Hitler's party to social democrats or communists (Falter 1991).

The fascists of the early twentieth century represented a tendency not to see 'class' as the decisive cleavage of the time – as the defenders of the 'ancient regime' and the different socialist factions did. The fascists declared 'nation' and (or) 'race' as the defining conflict of the time. And in some respects, this has not much changed for the far right of the early twenty-first century. The 'defining other' is not the revolutionary at home; it is the foreigner – or whoever is branded as foreign – that is the enemy against whom 'we' have to defend ourselves.

The far right of today does not use the blatant racism as has been the case in the past. 'The others' are not defined by biological fantasies such as the Jewish race, or by superficial misinterpretations of skin colour. 'The others' are defined by characteristics such as 'culture' or 'civilisation' (Wodak 2013). On the surface, the exclusion of 'the others' is usually accompanied by promises of respect for the otherness – as long as they abstain from coming to 'us'.

To justify the construction of a principal difference between 'us' and 'them', specific narratives are used to define a specific nation (Serbia, Hungary, Greece, or others) as the bulwark of Christian or European civilisation against the forces of darkness (Moguls, Muslims, Communists, or others). In this role, 'we' have been not much thanked by our neighbours, 'we' have not been the perpetual victims of the onslaught from the real enemies, and 'we' are not respected in our role as victims. The self-perception of being permanently the victim is a narrative used by nationalistic parties in general, and by right-wing populist parties in particular, and it serves as a significant motivation for historical revisionism (Kopecek 2008).

As the example of the Hungarian Jobbik Party demonstrates, it is especially in the former communist parts of Europe where a kind of old-fashioned, revisionist nationalism (plus a traditional racism directed against 'Jews' and 'Roma') co-exists with the kind of grass-roots democratic claim that contemporary populism represents (Kovács 2013). The 'own' nation is the victim of deeply unjust treaties of the past, the nation has no right to fight against the consequences of those treaties, nor to ask to undo them. At the same time, the search is on for culprits living within the 'own' nation; traditional scapegoats who easily can be defined as agents of foreign interests.

Specific interpretations of historical events (from the battle of Kosovo in the late Middle Ages to the Treaty of Trianon 1920) help to underline a specific identity. By defining 'us' as the permanent victim, it simplifies inclusion as well as exclusion: Over centuries, there seems to be a tradition of enemies to conspire and to act against 'us'.

The research on political parties in Central-Eastern Europe has put much emphasis on the 'nationalist-cosmopolitan' divide, on the gap between the renaissance of nationalist narratives, more or less suppressed by communist rule for decades, and an orientation on transnational values as exemplified by the European Union (Kitschelt, Mansfeldova,

Markowski & Tóka 1999, pp. 223–260) The revival of nationalist tendencies (an unavoidable result of democratic transformation) opens a field for populist tendencies as they already existed in Western Europe. The former communist part of Europe, for decades not integrated in the European integration process, which aimed from its very beginning in the 1950s to overcoming nationalism, is now the region in which a more traditional, revisionist nationalism is allied with populism (Havlík & Pinková 2012, pp. 17–38).

The old (fascist) far right had one common denominator despite all the differences between nations and nationalisms: antisemitism. 'Jews' were constructed as the 'defining others' of those who constructed themselves as true members of a nation or people. Even the communist regimes used this stereotype immediately after 1945 when, in Czechoslovakia, Rudolf Slansky and other victims of the Stalinisation process were called 'cosmopolitans' – a code word for Jews (Applebaum 2013, pp. 281–283). The contemporary far right is still anti-cosmopolitan – even if in some regions (especially in Western Europe) the traditional antisemitism plays a significantly lesser role than in the past, or in some other regions (such as contemporary Central-Eastern Europe).

The old far right can still be seen in the rhetoric of the contemporary far right – in the construction of a seemingly self-evident 'us' and 'them'. In her programmatic declaration, Marine Le Pen – co-president of the ENF-group (Europe of Nations and Freedom) in the European Parliament – declared: 'Day after day, the Europe of Brussels reveals its deadly plan: to deconstruct the nation states in order to create a new globalised order, one that threatens the security, prosperity, identity and survival of the peoples of Europe.'[1]

This is the very essence of contemporary far-right thinking and strategy – a constructed 'other' ('the Europe of Brussels'), a devilish conspiracy ('deadly plan'), and the simplified acceptance of 'nation' and 'people'.

Populism: a theoretical explanation of a specific understanding of democracy

Populism is a vague concept. Populist tendencies, populist thinking, populist traditions have been, and still are, part of the history of democracy. Populism *per se* is not directed against democracy. The term has become a synonym for far-right tendencies that claim they are not anti-democratic, but represent the 'true' understanding of democracy.

Yves Mény and Yves Surel raise the question of whether populism should not be seen as the 'pathology of democracy': an essential democratic phenomenon going out of control (Mény & Surel 2002, pp. 3–7).

In the past, the far right as it existed in the form of fascist parties – especially the National Socialist German Workers' Party (NSDAP) – have been outspoken against the basic principles of democracy. The traditional far right opposed any understanding of universal basic rights as enshrined in the tradition of enlightenment expressed by the declarations of the American and French revolutions. The populist far right argues that contemporary democracy in the liberal ('Western') system has fallen victim to elitist tendencies. The populist far right argues that it is necessary to defend the essence of democracy against elites.

This argument is, of course, not typical for the far right. At the beginning of the twentieth century, Robert Michels used it to describe democratically elected representatives becoming oligarchies without violating the rules of democracy (Michels 1911). And this criticism was considered more 'leftist' than 'rightist'.

The far-right populism is characterised by two 'defining others'. On one side, it mobilises against 'them above' – against ruling parties, against the powerful few in society and the economic sphere. On the other side, it mobilises against 'them below' – against ethnic minorities, against migrants, against any segment in society that can be pictured as 'foreign'. The first front against 'them' is not exclusively owned by far-right traditions. It is also used by leftist tendencies. It is the bridge between the populism of the far right and the populism of the left. It is the second front against 'them' that gives the populist far right its distinct flavour.

Contemporary populism is – differently from anti-democratic, authoritarian or totalitarian movements and parties from the past – not *per se* anti-democratic. The claim populist parties of the twenty-first century have is to represent 'true' democracy as can be seen in the cases of the Sweden Democrats and the 'True Finns' (Freeland 2013; Oja & Mral 2013). Populist parties criticise the existing structures and institutions of liberal political systems as being democratic in name only. Populist parties want to be seen as the 'real' democratic parties.

Concerning right-wing populist parties, this is linked to an outspoken, or at least implicit, ethnic exclusiveness: 'the people' consists of persons from the 'own nation'. Excluded from the 'own' ethnic group are usually minorities who are seen as not 'really belonging' to 'the people' – such as Jews or Roma – and especially migrants who seem not to be fully assimilated into the cultural/religious mainstream, such as Muslims in Europe (Wodak 2015).

Populism speaks on behalf of the majority, even if representing only a minority of the electorate. The consequence of this imagined, perceived role as advocates of the majority is a strong preference for plebiscitarian techniques and an open mistrust directed against the institutions of representative democracies, such as parliaments. Of course, this has an old tradition: Robert Dahl's analysis of the beginning of US-American democracy distinguished between what he called 'Madisonian Democracy' – a system based on representation with a significant degree of mistrust directed against 'the masses' and 'Populist Democracy' – opposing all or most representative institutions (Dahl 1970).

Ernst Fraenkel defined the mainstream understanding of democratic theory: a stable democracy must keep a balance between representative democratic institutions and plebiscitarian instruments, such as referenda. Fraenkel's argument against a pure plebiscitarian understanding of democracy is especially based on historical evidence, on the manipulation of direct (pseudo-) democratic methods by anti-democratic forces such as the German NSDAP (Fraenkel 1964).

It is also part of the dominant understanding of democracy that democracy cannot be reduced to the rule of majority. Any democracy has to be based on a combination of majority rule and minority rights, which have to be guaranteed beyond the decisions and interests of the majority. In their understanding of democracy, right-wing populist parties tend to neglect this aspect of democratic theory: respect for minorities, be they ethnic, religious or political minorities in a pluralistic polity (Müller 2011). This is the consequence of a simplistic understanding of '*demos*', the democratic sovereign. Populism tends to construct 'the people' as a homogenous entity whose 'nature' seems to be undermined by specific (especially external) enemies. Populism – especially right-wing populism – tends to identify 'the people' as a body with one dominating (national) interest. Deviant interests and opinions are considered either the results of 'wrong conscience', or even the expression of a fully illegitimate agenda, orchestrated by an evil conspiracy.

The group 'Europe of Freedom and Direct Democracy' in the European Parliament formulates in its charter: '…the group subscribes to the concept of direct democracy believing it to be the ultimate check on political elites'.[2] This simplified understanding of democracy as an unlimited rule of the majority is representative for the populism of the far right.

Anton Pelinka

Identity politics: the aspect of inclusion and exclusion with particular reference to the ethno-nationalistic (racist) tendencies of the far right

Every political movement is the result of cleavages, of conflict lines, running through any society. Every party that has risen to some success has – and still is – positioning itself on one side of this line. And any position implies a certain understanding of identity. In Europe, the late nineteenth century saw the rise of class parties, based on a specific view of social conflicts as first and foremost class conflicts. Religious parties at the same time defined themselves as opposition to a secular state seen as unfriendly to a specific religion – or as articulating the interests of one religious denomination against another. National parties justified their existence and their policies on the basic interests of one nation or nationality (Duverger 1959). In the late twentieth century, parties entered the political market in prosperous societies based on an ideological perspective – claiming to defend 'nature' against the life-threatening consequences of unlimited economic growth.

In all cases, identity was necessary to mobilise people along the line of conflict. The followers of a party had to distinguish between 'us' and 'them'. However, any specific identity was not an objective given, but the subjective interpretation of a reality that was always open to a different interpretation. Identity has been – and is always – imagined, as Benedict Anderson (2006) has demonstrated with respect to national identities (Anderson 2006).

Identities are constructed; they are rising or declining – they can never be seen as permanent. What it means to be 'Austrian' has changed over the last hundred years – from imperial transnational to ethnic German-national to post-ethnic Austrian republican (Pelinka 1998). To have a 'Yugoslav' identity was a major factor during most of the twentieth century, but it has subsequently disappeared. The conflict between identities of Catholics and Protestants in the Netherlands dominated Dutch politics until the last decades of the twentieth century – it has not disappeared in the twenty-first century, but has lost most of its former political implications. The 'pillarisation' of Dutch politics – the system of segmental autonomy that gave Protestants as well as Catholics significant power to decide their own affairs – started to break down with the merger of the Catholic party and the two Protestant parties (Lijphart 1977, pp. 42–52).

Democracy is challenged by the contradiction between the normative assumption of an existing '*demos*' and the reality of a society that is too complex to be defined by one criterion only – by 'nation', 'culture', or 'religion'. Society can be seen – as David Lloyd George put it in 1917 – as a mass, 'more or less molten and you can stamp upon that molten mass almost anything as long as you do it with firmness and determination.' (quoted in Müller 2011, p. 7) In any society, there is a strong urge to define the self, to be a specific self, to seek an identity. The search for identity implies the exclusion of others – or better – of social segments defined as others.

Populism – any kind of populism – tends to play down the complexities of identities in society. 'Us' is declared as a given – 'us' as a nation or a religious denomination or as a 'race' or as a class. The phenomenon of cross-cutting identities as seen (for example) in Switzerland where cleavages run across each other (e.g. linguistic–ethnic cleavages cutting through religious cleavages) not only reflects the reality of complex societies, but helps to bridge the deep gaps running through a country. Another case of how cross-cutting cleavages help overcome simplistic identities is India where ethnic–linguistic and caste cleavages are creating an identity mix that helps to promote social integration (Lijphart 1977). Populist attitudes reduce such complexities – they favour a clear distinction between one identity and another. By trying to force people to opt for one identity or the other, populism endangers integration across social differences.

Yesterday's far right was based on national identities separated from each other. Polish nationalists perceived Russian or German nationalists as their main enemy. Today's far right is based on a more complex, potentially transnational identity. The French Front National (FN) no longer sees Germany as the arch enemy of France. The Dutch PVV is not afraid of the Netherlands being dominated by a mighty neighbour state. Front National, PVV and other right-wing populist parties claim more and more to defend 'Western civilisation', 'liberal democracy', or basic human (e.g. female) rights, not against other European nations, but against a defining other not associated with a specific nation or state: It may be Islam, or it may be migrants with a specific skin colour or just a perceived specific culture.

Populism of any kind is based on the tentatively naïve and simplistic understanding of an objectively given identity. Right-wing populism as it currently exists, especially in the European party systems, may have broken with the old-fashioned, pre-Second World War nationalism that set one nation against another. But one element – perhaps the decisive element of this nationalism – still does exist: the defence of national sovereignty. The contemporary far right in Europe may be able to form an all-European front against immigrants coming from outside Europe. But this has not – at least not yet – resulted in a common far-right policy within the European Union. Right-wing populist parties gained substantially at the 2014 European Parliament elections.

Soon after the elections of 2014, the far-right parties were able to form a party group within the European Parliament (EP): 'Europe of Nations and Freedom' (ENF/ENL). The founding members were the French FN, the Dutch Freedom Party (PVV), the Austrian Freedom Party (FPÖ), the Italian Lega Nord, and the Flemish (Belgian) Vlaams Belang. Outside this group, another partly similar group exists in the EP – 'Europe for Freedom and Direct Democracy', with membership comprising the United Kingdom Independence Party (UKIP), the Alternative for Germany (AfD) and the Italian Five Star Movement. These parties are – not incidentally – not from the former communist part of Europe. Some of the parties (the Vlaams Belang and the Lega Nord) are more concerned with a separatist agenda, but all are united in their opposition to the EU's ongoing deepening and to the European integration process: national identity (be it Flemish or French) must dominate and must be above European identity.[3]

The sovereignty narrative prevents the far-right populist parties from seeing European integration as a possibility for promoting a far-right agenda. This is still a British message coming from the UKIP, a Swedish message coming from the Sweden Democrats and a Hungarian message coming from Jobbik. And despite some common elements – as can be seen in the somewhat pro-Russian policies these parties promote regarding the crisis (and the war) in Ukraine – the far-right populist parties oppose integration as exemplified by the EU because they see the Union (and rightly so) as an important step away from the nation-state they still want to defend.

The European Union as an attempt to overcome the disasters nationalism has been responsible for in the past challenges by its very existence the assumption of a 'naturally' given identity along national lines. The emerging European identity, which the European integration process is built upon, is anathema to the parties of the populist far right – as it would have been for the traditional nationalist far-right parties of the first half of the twentieth century (Bruter 2005, pp. 23–40).

Contemporary issues

Politics in the twenty-first century is defined by the end of the clearly definable bipolar world of the Cold War. From the viewpoint of the 'West', defined as the two sides of the North Atlantic, the world is particularly influenced by the rising significance of new major players (especially the BRICS states: Brazil, Russia, China, India, South Africa), by the absence of any general explaining pattern, but – clearly – by the decline of the state as the sovereign organisation of human society. The state, as has been known since the Peace of Westphalia 1648, is less and less able to control the consequences of globalisation. The system defined in 1648 as an international order under the control of sovereign states has come to an end (Kissinger 2014, pp. 361–374).

The state – as it has been known – is the main, often repressive authority internally and also the independent actor, deciding over war and peace externally, but the state as an organisational type is in decline. The state's decline is indicated by the phenomenon of wars within and beyond, but without, states. George W Bush's 'War on Terror' was an attempt to bring a war against a phenomenon that was clearly not a state into a traditional terminology. Wars in the Middle East, like the different – and at the same time parallel – wars devastating countries such as Syria and Iraq are wars that state governments seem unable to control.

The state's decline can also be seen in the difficulties that the democratic welfare state has run into. The state's capability to preserve internal social peace by combining economic growth and mass prosperity – as developed especially in European countries such as Sweden and the United Kingdom in the twentieth century – seems to be less and less able to guarantee near full employment as well as paying for everybody's social security.

The reason is economic globalisation. Economic interests have been able to emancipate themselves from governments still bound by territorial limitations. The globalised economy has become stateless, but politics is still state-based. If a corporation thinks it can increase its profit in another region, it will leave the state's territory in which it has prospered for some time in the past. The result is an increasing inequality, especially in the economically better developed, more prosperous parts of the world – in Europe and in North America.

This is the main source of the social unrest that populism (especially right-wing populist parties) articulates. They use their message of national exclusiveness ('us') to mobilise the 'modernisation losers'. In the more prosperous parts of today's world, 'modernisation losers' are particularly the less prosperous social segments; those which can be called working class and lower-middle class. The high degree of unemployment in Europe (greater than the United States is experiencing) reflects national governments' inability to guarantee the welfare state's social network.

Populism defines the result of the declining capacity of national governments *per se*, not as the inability of mainstream political elites, but their unwillingness. In the view of populist rhetoric, the price the lower classes have to pay is the result of elitist class egoism – and not of structural changes in an increasingly globalised economy. Right-wing populism adds to this perspective a significant flavour of ethnic (national) flavour: The structural weaknesses of governments are defined as the product of an alliance of national elites and transnational interests. National elites accept or even promote immigration as an instrument for their rule over the domestic electorate.

This is the case in countries with a comparatively high degree of social security, that is, the countries of Western and Northern Europe. Working-class people in those countries react to decreasing government power not by moving to the left, but to the right.

There is an institutional factor, which as an independent variable, influences the impact that far-right populism has. In the US, in the first two decades of the twenty-first century, the Tea Party demonstrated its mobilising energy by focusing on topics that fit broadly into the concept of far-right populism: a combination of anti-elitist and indirectly xenophobic (anti-immigrant) messages, plus an insistence on defending the core values of liberal democracy, such as women's basic rights (Wodak 2013, p. 28). However, the US Tea Party is not a party in the sense of competing with other parties for votes. The Tea Party is a (neo)conservative lobby within an existing party, the Republican Party, and competes for influence with other interest groups – especially before and during the Republican primaries. As the US electoral system on both state and federal levels is a system of 'first past the post', giving victory to any candidate with the plurality of votes, the US-party system denies third parties a realistic chance of succeeding at the polls. What can be called the US equivalent of European far-right populist parties tries taking over an existing party – and not to compete within an existing party system that has proven quite stable due to the specificities of the US electoral system.

In Central and Eastern Europe, the far-right parties articulate in different form an anti-Western resentment. This resentment may be directed against different 'others', depending on the specific national narratives. And, different to today's West European far right, the post-communist countries are still (or again) the region where traditional anti-Jewish and anti-Roma prejudices can be mobilised for political purposes (Mudde 2005). However, the West and the East European far right have one common enemy – the concept of a United Europe that limits the interpretation of a fully sovereign nation-state as well as any simplified understanding of national 'purity'.

Conclusion

Contemporary far-right populism tends to abstain from openly racist positions. Additionally, today's populist far right has made its peace with the mainstream understanding of democracy – at least on paper. Parties such as the French FN or the Dutch PVV accept the principle of free and fair elections, and even defend basic freedoms such as the freedom of speech – at least rhetorically. It is their exclusionary understanding of democracy that stands for continuity between the extremist right of the past ('fascism') and the populist far right of today.

The definition of 'us' in the far-right policies of today is based on cultural exclusiveness bordering on 'biological' exclusiveness. Using migration as a central topic to construct the image of a rather homogenous society ('us') threatened by a foreign 'them' ignores the complexities of present societies and sees the reality of globalisation with its unavoidable aspect of transnational and transcontinental mobility as a danger that can be fought off by building walls to fight off 'the others'.

The need to define criteria of inclusion and exclusion is part of any democratic order. According to the mainstream understanding of democracy, this has to be done in a way that is consistent with universal human rights and especially without any discrimination based on gender, religion, 'race', ethnicity, mental or physiological disability, generation or sexual orientation. This is best summed up in Robert Dahl's concept of 'citizenship as a categorical right' in its 'modified' version: 'Every adult subject to a government and its laws must be presumed to be qualified as, and has the unqualified right to be, a member of the *demos*' (Dahl 1989, p. 127).

Right-wing populism is not a quality allowing for a clear distinction between populist parties and non-populist parties, between parties incompatible with liberal democracies and parties fully fitting into such systems. As can be seen in cases such as the UK and France, parties of the political mainstream will be tempted to take over some elements of the exclusionary rhetoric and policies of the far right as soon as such an integration of far-right positions is seen to be promising for the electoral outcome.

Notes

1 Available from: www.enfgroup-ep.eu/.
2 Available from: www.europarl.europa.eu/elections-2014/en/political-groups/europe-of-freedom-and-direct-democracy.
3 See www.europarl.europa.eu 2016.

References

Almeida, D, 2012, *The impact of European integration on political parties*, Routledge, New York.
Anderson, B, 2006, *Imagined communities. Reflections on the origin and spread of nationalism*, Verso, London.
Applebaum, A, 2013, *Iron curtain. The crushing of Eastern Europe 1944–1956*, Anchor Books, New York.
Arendt, H, 1951, *The origins of totalitarianism*, Harcourt Brace Jovanovich, New York.
Beauzamy, B, 2013, 'Explaining the rise of the Front National to electoral prominence, multi-faceted or contradictory models?', in *Right-wing populism in Europe: Politics and discourse*, eds. R Wodak, M KhosraviNik & B Mral, Bloomsbury, London, pp. 177–190.
Bruter, M, 2005, *Citizens of Europe? The emergence of a mass European identity*, Palgrave Macmillan, Houndmills.
Dahl, R A, 1970, *A preface to democratic theory. How does popular sovereignty function in America?*, University of Chicago Press, Chicago, IL.
Dahl, R A, 1989, *Democracy and its critics*, Yale University Press, New Haven, CT.
Duverger, M, 1959, *Die politischen Parteien*, C B Mohr, Tübingen.
Falter, J W, 1991, *Hitlers Wähler*, C H Beck, München.
Fraenkel, E, 1964, *Deutschland und die westlichen Demokratien*, Kohlhammer, Stuttgart.
Fryklund, B, 2013, 'Populism – changes over time and space. A comparative and retrospective analysis of populist parties in the Nordic countries', in *Right-wing populism in Europe: Politics and discourse*, eds. R Wodak, M KhosraviNik & B Mral, Bloomsbury, London, pp. 267–276.
Havlík, V & Pinková, A, 2012, *Populist parties in East-Central Europe*, Masaryk University Press, Brno.
Kissinger, H, 2014, *World order. Reflections on the character of nations and the course of history*, Penguin Press, London.
Kitschelt, H, Mansfeldova, Z, Markowski, R & Tóka, G, 1999, *Post-Communist Party systems. Competition, representation, and inter-party cooperation*, Cambridge University Press, Cambridge.
Kopecek, M, 2008, ed., *Past in the making. Historical revisionism in Central Europe after 1989*, CEU University Press, Budapest.
Kovács, A, 2013, 'The post-communist extreme right, the Jobbik Party in Hungary', in *Right-wing populism in Europe: Politics and discourse*, eds. R Wodak, M KhosraviNik & B Mral, Bloomsbury, London, pp. 223–234.
Lijphart, A, 1977, *Democracy in plural societies. A comparative exploration*, Yale University Press, New Haven, CT.
Mazower, M, 2008, *Hitler's empire. How the Nazis ruled Europe*, Penguin Press, New York.
Mény, Y & Surel, Y, 2002, eds., *Democracies and the populist challenge*, Palgrave Macmillan, Houndmills.

Michels, R, 1911, *Zur Soziologie des Parteiwesens in der modernen Demokratie. Untersuchungen über die oligarchischen Tendenzen des Gruppenlebens*, Werner Klinkhardt, Leipzig.

Montefiore, S S, 2003, *Stalin. The court of the Red Tsar*, Vintage Books, New York.

Mudde, C, 2005, *Racist extremism in Central and Eastern Europe*, Routledge, London.

Mudde, C, 2007, *Populist radical right parties in Europe*, Cambridge University Press, Cambridge.

Müller, J-W, 2011, *Contesting democracy. Political ideas in twentieth-century Europe*, Yale University Press, New Haven, CT.

Oja, S & Mral, B, 2013, 'The Sweden Democrats came in from the cold, how the debate about allowing the SD into media arenas shifted between 2002 and 2010', in *Right-wing populism in Europe: Politics and discourse*, eds. R Wodak, M KhosraviNik & B Mral, Bloomsbury, London, pp. 277–292.

Oudenampsen, M, 2013, 'Explaining the swing to the right, The Dutch debate on the rise of right-wing populism', in *Right-wing populism in Europe: Politics and discourse*, eds. R Wodak, M KhosraviNik & B Mral, Bloomsbury, London, pp. 191–208.

Pelinka, A, 1998, *Austria. Out of the shadows of the past*, Praeger, Boulder, CO.

Pelinka, A, 2015, *Die unheilige Allianz. Die rechten und die linken Extremisten gegen Europa*, Böhlau, Vienna.

Ruzza, C & Balbo, L, 2013, 'Italian populism and the trajectories of two leaders, Silvio Berlusconi and Umberto Bossi', in *Right-wing populism in Europe. Politics and discourse*, eds. R Wodak, M KhosraviNik, B Mral, Bloomsbury, London, pp. 163–176.

Sartori, G, 2005, *Parties and party systems. A framework of analysis*, 2nd ed., ECPR Press, Colchester.

Schumpeter, J A, 1950, *Capitalism, socialism and democracy*, Harper and Row, New York.

Wodak, R, 2013, '"Anything Goes" – The Haiderization of Europe', in *Right-wing populism in Europe: Politics and discourse*, eds. R Wodak, M KhosraviNik & B Mral, Bloomsbury, London, pp. 23–28.

Wodak, R, 2015, *The politics of fear. What right-wing populist discourses mean*, Sage, London.

Wodak, R, KhosraviNik, M & Mral, B, 2013, eds., *Right-wing populism in Europe. Politics and discourse*, Bloomsbury, London.

42
Race, racism, discourse

Dávid Kaposi and John E. Richardson

Introduction

This chapter will examine race and racism, and the relations between social ideas (e.g. the existence of races; the association of qualities/characteristics with particular racial/ethnic/religious groups), social stratification based on these ideas, and discourse. After introductory and contextualising sections, where we introduce the historic and conceptual bases of the subject, the empirical and analytic sections of the chapter will be structured in such a way that we gradually examine levels and details that the reader may not have initially considered. We start with the most obviously prejudicial texts, produced and circulated by European extreme-right political parties. Next, we will examine a case that appears to have a racial dimension without race being explicitly articulated: a televised interview with the actor Samuel L Jackson, in which the interviewer mistook him for Laurence Fishburne. Finally, we will consider British conservative broadsheet newspapers' reporting of a conflagration of the Israel/Palestine conflict ('Operation Cast Lead'), and the ways they related this act of reporting to acts of antisemitism. The chapter will thus progressively move to less conspicuous and more dilemmatic waters, and in so doing demonstrate the value of close analysis when examining discourse on this topic.

Race and racism

Conventional, lay understandings of racism – as revealed, for example, in dictionary definitions – continue to consider racism to be a system of beliefs, or a (false) mode of thinking. Such interpretations underlie classroom discussions with our students too, wherein racism tends (initially at least) to be approached as simplified and misrepresentative ideas about others (typically 'others with differently coloured skin'); a racist, consequently, is one who agrees with and vocalises such beliefs. Systems of white privilege are especially absent from such conventional understandings of racism, given the ways they inevitably highlight the ways that white liberals and even white anti-racists benefit from racism. This conventional tendency, 'to define racism as a mental phenomenon, has continually led to an under-theorisation of the relationship between the mental classification involved and the practices in which they are inserted' (Hage 1998, p. 29). Donald and Rattansi (1992) have made a similar point, arguing that racism ought to be approached from a position that assumes it is 'rooted in broader economic structures and material interests' (p. 3). From such a position:

> Meanings and beliefs do not become irrelevant, but the coherence and falsity of racist ideas [are] now ascribed to the function they serve in legitimating social practices that reinforce an unequal distribution of power between groups differentiated in racial and/or ethnic terms.
>
> (Donald & Rattansi 1992)

Explicit in this critique of racism is not just an acknowledgement of the differentiation and stratification of 'racialised' individuals and groups, but also the very practical functions of racism in maintaining inequitable systems of social power and behavioural manifestations of racism. The forms that racism takes are not fixed – to the degree that it may be more appropriate to talk of *racisms*.

However, Anthias (1995, p. 288) argues that it is important to acknowledge that all racisms are 'underpinned by a notion of a natural relation between an essence attributed to a human population, whether biological or cultural, and social outcomes that do, will or should flow from this'. A key dimension of this 'essence attribution' is *differentiation*: the processes through which social groups are made 'other'. Differentiation simultaneously constructs and applies the (biological or cultural) qualities considered important enough to distinguish social groups. It should go without saying that such criteria are – somatically, genetically and culturally – *arbitrary*. (Thus, shoe size is *not* a criterion, but nose size *can* be; equally, whether someone wears a scarf is *not* a criterion, but whether someone wears a *head* scarf *can* be; and so on.) However, such criteria are socially, politically and historically highly relevant since they present the specific – but, equally, the highly adaptable and mutable – features that define social groups and, consequently, are used to constitute an in-group 'us' through rejecting the out-group 'them'.

Accordingly, racism is 'a discourse and a practice whereby ethnic groups are inferiorised' (Anthias 1995, p. 294); such groups can be differentiated in and through their perceived 'racial' (that is somatic), religious or cultural characteristics (invoking, *inter alia*, language, clothing, values and practices); and the practices of inferiorisation and discrimination may be more or less severe (see Allport 1954 for further discussion). To illustrate this point, during the High Middle Ages, while skin colour was an important criterion for Venetians in differentiating and inferiorising Byzantine troops, it had less significance elsewhere in Europe (Bethencourt 2013, p. 53): 'The illuminated manuscripts commissioned by the Castilian king Alfonso the Wise (1221–84) [...] represented visible differences between Christians and Muslims based more on clothing than physical appearances' (*ibidem*). That said, although skin colour was considered unimportant (to some, in some contexts), familiar patterns and relations of racist structuration were already crystallising. Thus, by this period, black Africans were being associated with extensive negative characteristics, particularly with various barbarous and animalistic qualities. For example, in his *Muqaddimah*, Ibn Khaldûn argued that black people 'are submissive to slavery, because [they] have little that is essentially human and possess attributes that are quite similar to those of dumb animals' (cited in Bethencourt 2013, p. 53).

A further logic of racism – in addition to differentiation and inferiorisation – is that of *transmission*, across time and between members of the vilified human population. It is not sufficient that a human population is marked out, deemed inferior and discriminated against;

the inferior (and, concomitant *superior*) qualities imputed to reside in populations are additionally presumed and argued to be transferred across time – they exist as a birthright, passed from one generation to the next. In biological racisms, this transmission occurs genetically; in cultural/neo-racisms this occurs through socialisation or enculturation. From the vantage point of Anthias' inclusive definition of racism, 'Undesirable groups need not be conceptualised in explicit racial terms, but as Others more generally. [...] This population is endowed with fixed, unchanging and negative characteristics, and subjected to relations of inferiorisation and exclusion' (1995, p. 294).

The strength of this particular account of racism is that it is not restricted to 'biological' racism – in other words, it challenges the belief that racism only relates to prejudice and discrimination suffered by populations who share specific genotypic or phenotypic characteristics, transmitted as biological hereditary. (And, *in extremis*, that 'to be racist' is to discriminate on the basis of skin colour.) The assumption that racism is based on physical or 'biological' characteristics has often been a sticking point in past discussion of prejudice and discrimination suffered by populations marked as religiously different.[1] Yet, as early as the end of the Middle Ages (in the thirteenth to fifteenth centuries), ethnicity and religion – and not simply genes, skin colour, and so on – *had* been built into racial theories. In Europe, both Jews and Muslims were subject to ongoing discrimination, based on 'the idea of *ethnic descent*; it was expected that they would continue to show the "qualities of character" of their ancestors, and would inevitably revert to their former faith. Permanent war on various fronts between Christians and Muslims also created a prejudice based on religious allegiance that deepened the idea of ethnic descent' (emphasis added, Bethencourt 2013, p. 60). The Spanish Inquisition institutionalised such racist practice, against both Jews and Muslims. Such insights are especially important to take into account in relation to contemporary discourse, wherein 'an absolute fixing of the difference between cultures' (Meyer 2001, p. 33) has, essentially, ensured that 'culture acquires an immutable character, and hence becomes a homologue for race' (Malik 1996, p. 150).

This can be illustrated by considering the re-emergence of the extreme right as a political force in Western Europe since the 1990s and particularly after 2001. The European extreme right includes many parties, such as the British National Party, the Republikaner in Germany, the Lega Nord in Italy, the Sweden Democrats, the French Front National, the Belgian Vlaams Blok, the Austrian Freedom Party (FPÖ), Jobbik Magyarországért Mozgalom (Movement for a Better Hungary) and the Danish People's party. These parties share a fundamental core of ethno-nationalist xenophobia (based on 'ethno-pluralist' doctrine) and anti-political-establishment populism (Rydgren 2007). At all levels of discourse, their 'new' racism is not always expressed in overtly (biologically) racist terms, or in the terms of neo-fascist discourse. This form of racism, which Taguieff (1988) calls '*racisme différencialiste*' and Wieviorka (1995) calls '*racisme culturelle*', stresses the incompatible difference between ethnic or religious groups that are described in cultural terms without specifically mentioning race or overtly racial criteria.

Crucially, however, this does not mean that racialised minorities are not the targets of this 'new' racism, merely that the grounds of their alleged incompatibility with 'us' are expressed using 'cultural' and religious, rather than biological, criteria. Indeed, the historic examples described briefly above reveal that there is little 'new' about 'new racism': cultural, religious, ethnic and 'racial' characteristics have been used interchangeably to differentiate and exclude for centuries. For this reason, we maintain that (biological) racism, antisemitism, anti-Muslimism and other forms of ethnicised discrimination (e.g. against Roma/Sinti) are variations of the same racist logic:

differentiation, inferiorisation and presumed transmission of negative characteristics across time and between members of the vilified population.

Race, racism and discourse

This chapter assumes that racism, like all aspects of social life, is in part discursive: it is simultaneously a product of, and a factor contributing to, the continuation of hierarchical and unjust social relations. Put another way, racism simultaneously constructs social relations between individuals and groups in society – predominantly hierarchies of the sort already mentioned – and, at the same time, is constructed by these social relations. This is not to suggest that racisms are wholly constructed phenomena – that racist practices are assembled and reassembled 'as social actors interact with each other and exchange interpretative meanings' (Manning 2001, p. 21) – or that racism can be collapsed into, and conceptualised wholly in relation to discourse. Rather, it is to suggest that racism, like all social phenomena, should be approached in relation to questions of structure and agency typical of critical social analysis. Such a position focuses upon, and aims at illuminating, the subtle interplay between the economic, the political, the social and the symbolic (see Golding & Murdock 2000), and so reveals that racism and racialisation are 'criss-crossed by ethnic, national, gender, class and other social constructions and divisions' (Wodak & Reisigl 2015, p. 578). The cultural studies and critical race analysis of theorists such as Robert Miles, Stuart Hall, Étienne Balibar and Colette Guillaumin 'conceptually integrate[s] the structural and discursive aspects of racism', theorising:

> how stereotypes, racist images and metaphors – the totality of racism as an ideology in the strongest sense – are socially reproduced and institutionalized as part of the superstructure of a social formation [...] how this superstructure is retroactive related to exclusionary practices and understand how racism, understood not as a tool but a social relation, produces racialized identities.
>
> (Opratko & Müller-Uri 2014, p. 7)

The grammatical processes described in Anthias' account of racism above – 'conceptualised', 'characterised', 'endowed' – point to the significant role that discourse plays in racialisation, in terms of both the *enactment* and the *reproduction* of racism. As van Dijk et al (1997, p. 165) have argued, 'racist talk and text themselves are discriminatory practices, which at the same time influence the acquisition and confirmation of racist prejudices and ideologies'. Similarly, Wodak and Reisigl (2015, p. 576) point out:

> Racism, as both social practice and ideology, manifests itself discursively. On the one hand, racist attitudes and beliefs are produced and promoted by means of discourse, and discriminatory practices are prepared, promulgated, and legitimated through discourse. On the other hand, discourse serves to criticize and argue against racist opinions and practices, that is, to pursue anti-racist strategies.
>
> (Wodak & Reisigl 2015, pp. 576)

Van Dijk (2004, pp. 352–353) identifies three main topical clusters in racist discourse: the differences of 'others', and so their dissimilarity to 'us'; the ways that the behaviour of 'others' breaches 'our' norms and values; and topics constructing 'them' in terms of threat. There is a rich tradition of studies describing the structure and function of xenophobic discourse (van Dijk 1984; van Dijk et al. 1997; Quasthoff 1987; Billig 1991; Essed 1991; Wetherell & Potter 1992; Reisigl & Wodak 2001), its diffusion through the mass media (Jäger & Link 1993; Jiwani & Richardson 2011; Richardson 2004, 2009; van Dijk 1991; Wodak & Forchtner 2014; Wodak & Matouscheck 1993), and its semantic organisation in political discourse (Richardson & Colombo 2013, 2014; van Dijk 1997; van der Valk 2002, 2003). The accomplishment and negotiation of prejudiced/unprejudiced identities has been documented in several studies (cf. Edwards 2003; Rapley 2001), as have the processes through which those designated as 'others' are represented in discourse (Augoustinous, Tuffin & Rapley 1999; Tileagă 2006; Verkuyten 1998, 2001; Wetherell & Potter 1992; Wodak & Matouscheck 1993).

Extensive research in the critical discourse-analytic tradition has focused on the crucial role exerted by the elites in the production, the diffusion and legitimation of both overt and covert forms of xenophobia and racist discourse over time (Wodak & Van Dijk 2000). This chapter now turns towards the discourse of such elites, examining: first, two leaflets produced by European extreme-right political parties; second, an interview broadcast on the US television network CNN; and third, the opinions of conservative broadsheet newspapers on Israeli 'Operation Cast Lead' (the war in Gaza, 2008–2009), as represented in their editorials.

Case study 1: extremist political discourse

The core exoteric message of the extreme right amounts to a base opposition to immigration and, frequently, settled minority ethnic communities.[2] Here, we present a leaflet (also produced as a poster), which had an impact on both an anti-Muslim referendum in Switzerland and on propaganda produced by other European extreme-right parties (see also Wodak 2015).[3] In the past two decades, the Swiss People's Party has established itself as one of the most powerful far-right parties in Western Europe. The Swiss People's Party advertising is distinctive in the way that it uses graphic illustrations rather than more widespread and traditional photos. Their posters/leaflets generally contain very few words; the core of the message is communicated visually, typically accompanied by a brief slogan.

On these images, silhouettes of minarets are pictured, superimposed over the national flags of Switzerland and Britain.[4] As with other nationalist political discourse (extremist and otherwise), the flags clearly act as metonyms for their respective nations (see Billig 1995); the meaning potential of the minarets, however, is a little more complex. Viewed in conjunction with the veiled woman, they function, first, to represent Islam in a metonymic replacement of a building by the faith of the people *using* the building. However, they also act to represent a more specific process – a process through which, in the view of these parties, their respective national spaces are gradually being taken over by Muslims. Combined with the linguistic element of the leaflets (either the imperative 'Stopp', or the 'Facts' in the British National Party leaflet), it is clear that these respective parties view the presence of Islam in the(ir) national space as objectionable. Oskar Freysinger, the SVP member of parliament, has confirmed as much – that their campaign is directed not at Muslim buildings of worship in themselves, but against minarets as a 'symbol of a political and aggressive Islam' (quoted in Betz 2013, p. 73). Political discourse, in both the news media and public policy, has constructed Islam and Muslims as a threat (Poole 2002; Richardson 2004). The leaflets therefore recall the widespread questioning – by both politicians and mainstream news media – of whether Muslims can, or *should*, be integrated into European society.

The placement of these fantasy minarets over the flags suggests they are either piercing *through* the flags or have been imposed, or built *on top* of them. The suggested violence of this process is heightened by the ways the minarets evoke spear-tips, or perhaps the cones of missiles.[5] Given the wide variety of minaret designs, they did not have to be this 'sharp ended', suggesting that this choice and its meaning potential – *weaponry* – is deliberate. Indeed, minarets, in the view of the SVP's Freysinger, have an 'imperialist connotation' (Betz 2013, p. 73). This meaning is picked up explicitly in the linguistic material included on the BNP leaflet, where an overtly militaristic lexicon of war (bayonets, helmets, barracks and army) is invoked as part of a discourse of conquest – 'Islamification' being the putative goal of Turkey and, *pars pro toto*, of Muslims in general. (Otherwise this process would have been named 'Turkification', rather than the more general 'Islamification'.) The rhetoric of conquest and colonisation, and the negative prosody of the terms employed to substantiate the standpoint and, thereby, the threat that 'they' pose to 'us', work to substantiate and 'naturalise' the stance of these parties as defensive rather than aggressive and driven by base antipathy towards (all) Muslims.

However, the leaflets do not simply suggest that 'Islamification' is a threat that will affect 'us' all in the same way. The presence of the second key pictorial element of these leaflets works to implicitly suggest a more specific battleground: the bodies of women. 'The veiled/concealed Muslim woman' has become part of a visual iconography of anti-immigrant discourse in general, and anti-Muslim discourse in particular, that has been developed by European parties of the right (Durham 2015). The leaflets position women – and the bodies of women specifically – as sites where this conflict between Islam and 'us' is played out. The BNP has pushed this argument to the forefront of its propaganda campaigns, to the extent that it argues, more or less explicitly, that 'we need to defend *our women*, otherwise they will end up looking *like this*' (Jiwani & Richardson 2011; Richardson 2011; Richardson & Wodak 2009b). That is, women's bodies are invoked, in a *pars pro toto* synecdoche, as the site for this putative process of colonisation (or Islamification) and reconquest. This battle for control over ('our') women and ('our') women's bodies utilises and subverts a liberal discourse of gender equality, apportions women's rights as the purview of nationalist men and objectifies the very women that it claims to honour. 'Nationalist' (that is, extreme-right-wing) men are positioned as protectors of 'our' women – the passivised, embodied nation space – and ethnic managers with the power and responsibility to reject Islam.

Case study 2: implicit racism

As Case study 1 demonstrated, 'thinly veiled' racism remains part and parcel of European and Western politics. Indeed, at the time of writing this chapter, Donald Trump, then the frontrunner for the Republican nomination for the president of the United States, was considering a full-scale ban on Muslim people entering the country (*Guardian* 2015a), and the Danish parliament adopted a law approving the seizure of asylum seekers' assets worth more than $1,453 (*Guardian* 2016). Meanwhile, young black men in 2015 were five times more likely to be killed by US police officers than white men of the same age; despite making up 2% of the entire population, African American males between the ages of 15 and 34 comprised more than 15% of all deaths (*Guardian* 2015b).

Having said that, the fact that even political parties that publish or propagate blatantly racist rhetoric are unlikely to describe themselves or their messages *as* racist, demonstrates that racism has also become taboo in modern Western discourse. One outcome of this, of course, was demonstrated in the previous section, as we examined how racist intentions and aims now have to be expressed through linguistic and visual codes. In what follows, Case study 2 now engages with a second outcome: implicit or inadvertent racism.

In a live interview on 10 February 2014, US actor, Samuel L. Jackson (SLJ), should have been interviewed by CNN host, entertainment reporter Sam Rubin (SR), about his recent movie *RoboCop*. The interview turned out to be about something else:[6]

```
1    SR    .hhH uhh .hh I, >I tell y'u what< you::  workin for Ma:rvel, the super bowl commercial
2          did you get a lot o' reaction to tha' super bowl commer↑↑cial?
3          (1.9)
4    SLJ   What su↓per bowl commer↓cial.
5          (3.0)
6    SR    ↓↓O:h, you know wha: t I didn- nu- bu- my mistake I,=
7          =[       >you know wha-<   (.) deh.]
8    SLJ   [> ↑↑↑D'you know what<   (.) See:,]  (.) yo:u? (.) yo:u're as crazy <as the people on
9          Twitter.=
10   SR    =↑Righ-=
11   SLJ   =I'm not Laurence Fishburne.
12         (0.9)
13   SR    ↓That's my fault (.) I know that (.) that w's my fault I:, my mistake. (.) >You know
14         what,<=
```

(Jackson & Rubin CNN 2014)

As we see, the interview starts with what is consensually established by both participants as Rubin confusing Jackson with fellow actor, Laurence Fishburne. *Something* therefore has happened.

Yet what, exactly, is this 'something'? What has happened? Has Rubin confused two human beings, two actors or two black actors? Rubin immediately offers an apology and does this in terms of having made a 'mistake'. This remains his position throughout the interview, repeatedly apologising, yet repeatedly apologising for making a 'mistake' (l. 40) and being 'dumb' (l. 33). As such, he implicitly categorises the event of confusion as a matter of accident and, at worst, a matter of unprofessional conduct – no offence, so to speak.

On one level, this is in line with Jackson's reference to Rubin being 'as crazy as the people on Twitter' (ll. 9–10). This formulation conveys no additional understanding and therefore does not identify the source of his outrage. His next interruption, however, clearly does:

```
13   SR    ↓That's my fault (.) I know that (.) that w's my fault I:, my mistake. (.) >You know
14         what,<=
15   SLJ   =We don't all: look ali:ke.
16   SR    (  ) you're e[xactly    right.
17   SLJ                [We may be all:=
18         =black and fa:mous (.) but we a:ll don't look ALI:KE=
19   SR    =I'm I'm I'm guil[t:y.
20   SLJ                    [Uh:::
21   SR    [I'm]
```

22	SLJ	[You]'re bus↓ted.
23	SR	I'm guilty.
24		(1.0)
25	SR	Ri:ght,
26	SLJ	Ye-
27		(0.7)
28	SR	°That's right.°
29		(0.5)

(ibidem)

Clearly, then, what happened, in Jackson's understanding, is more than a mere accidental confusion around the identity of two celebrities; he is not hurt as a famous actor and is not (just) angry on his own behalf. As he makes relevant the race he has in common with Laurence Fishburne, he also makes it clear that the case is not simply that two actors have just been confused, but that *two black actors have just been confused*. Indeed, by emphatically repeating the scalar quantifier 'a:ll' twice, he immediately expands the perceived mistake as a perceived insult to the whole black community. This way, his anger too gets transformed from what could possibly be perceived as an egoistic rant to righteous outrage over past and present mistreatment of black people.

Significantly, however, this important – if implicit – change in Jackson's rhetoric is left unattended to by Rubin. He repeatedly continues to own up to his 'mistake' – without specifying *what* he considers his 'mistake'/'fault' to be and *what* exactly he is 'guilty' *of*. As such, though explicitly agreeing with Jackson that he (i.e. Rubin) did something wrong, Rubin may be seen as trying to implicitly accomplish two acts: first, disagreeing with Jackson by reflectively characterising his own action as an accidental mistake and, therefore, the non-specific confusion of *any two faces*; and second, turning the tables by reflectively presenting the enraged Jackson as the bully.

What we see during the interview is the constant repetition of precisely this dynamic of discourse: there is explicit agreement between Jackson and Rubin that something happened, but there is implicit disagreement as to what exactly happened.

40	SR	=My mistake, ↓my: mistake. I apologise. Really my big mistake.
41		↑Let's talk abo[u t u-]
42	SLJ	[↓There must be] a ve:ry short li:ne for your ↓job=
43		=[<↓outside] ↓there.>
44	SR	[I:' l l s a y]
45		Now there's somethin- uh ha:h .HH it probably would not be hard to get another person
46		to sit right here.
47		Let's ta:lk about RoboCop,=
48	SLJ	↑↑ ↑= Oh:: He::ll: no::.

(Ibidem)

Jackson keeps implying that what happened connotes or even enacts a hurtful racial stereotype while Rubin keeps implicitly denying it, both by referring to a non-specific 'mistake' and by pushing the interview to the new and supposedly more important topic of Jackson's film, *RoboCop*. Rubin's clear message here is that *RoboCop* is more important than a 'mistake' he made or him being just 'dumb'. Similarly, even a 'big mistake' is no warrant for Jackson's aggressively interrupting Rubin countless times, let alone abusing him as happens in lines 43–44. A possible act of *racism*, however, *is*. But Jackson does not offer an explicit alternative to Rubin's non-specific 'mistake', and as such starts turning from a victim of a 'mistake' to a perpetrator of more-or-less unwarranted aggression.

Arguably, there is one exception to this dynamic during the interview. In a sarcastic move to prove his point, Jackson starts to list the TV commercials in which black actors other than him feature, repeatedly adding that 'I am not that guy. (...) I am not that guy either.' Towards the end of this sequence, something interesting happens:

```
86   SLJ  [There's a heavier=
87        =weight black guy that's like putting ca:sh down in the seats in a, in a baseball
88        ↓stadium but he's ↑a:lso the black guy that turns off (.) ↓the ((silence for 0.3s, as if
90        recording was stopped)) house, the water and the li:ghts .hh when his kid tells him
91        the ho:use is cool.
92   SR   Righ(h)-=
93   SLJ  =↑I'm not that guy either.
94        (0.5)
95   SR   .HHa? (0.6) Do we wanna do a list of all the people that you're not?=
96   SLJ  =And I've actually never done a MacDonald's o:r a Kentucky Fri:ed Chicken=
97        =[commercial.
98   SR    [Uh(h)
99        Fa:ir enough.
100  SLJ  I know that's su:'prising.
101  SR   ↓↓Right. (1.2) Fair enough, fair enough.
102       (0.8)
103  SR   Uh: (0.4) to the ori[ g i nal  u h : : :
104  SLJ                      [And I'm the o:nly=
105       =black gu:::y (0.6) in RoboCop that's not a cri:minal.
```

(*Ibidem*)

For once, Rubin's rhetorical strategy changes in line 95. From an apologetic yet non-specific and non-committal 'that's right', 'my mistake', 'you are right', he changes to a more active way of re-categorising the 'mistake' he made, as he teasingly asks Jackson the question: 'Do we wanna do a list of all the people that you're not?' In other words, he ignores Jackson's act of enlisting exclusively *black people for a minute or so*. Interestingly, it is precisely at this point that Jackson too becomes more overt about the exact source of his anger. Namely, his rant concludes at the point where he asserts who he actually is: 'And I'm the o:nly black gu:::y (0.6) in RoboCop that's not a cri:minal.' (ll. 104–105) By this, he broadens the context of his utterances beyond the studio. His problem becomes not just the incident that has just happened in the studio, but an America which still readily countenances representing/consuming black people mostly *as criminals*. This, incidentally, is where the detour finishes before the participants start to discuss the actual topic the interview was assigned to cover.

From the perspective of this chapter, the tragedy of this encounter is not simply that it is still possible to be racist on mainstream television. Rather, the tragedy is that while everything in this interview happened in front of our eyes, it still somehow *happened in darkness*. That is, while a hurtful racist stereotype, with the connotation that the skin colour of black people matters more than their individuality, was *objectively* enacted, and while both participants immediately recognised this transgression of morality, they could not incorporate this objective state of affairs in their discourse. Racism was there – but still somehow not there. Not there for Jackson to explicitly spell out, and not there for Rubin to explicitly own up to or deny. As such, rather than the fact of racism that occurred, it was the discourse around it that created a *taboo*. A topic, that is, which is there to be seen, but not there to be touched, to be discussed, to be engaged with, and ultimately to be genuinely changed.

Case study 3: racism as threat

So far, we have encountered a case where racism was clearly intended *as such*, and one where, arguably, it was less about acting out a conscious intention and more about (racialised) misrecognition. This combination of the power of racism and its occasionally unintentional nature has led to some distinct developments in the contemporary discourse of racism, which can be categorised as 'racism as dilemmatic'. In what follows, an example of this will be presented, drawing on some extracts from British conservative broadsheets' editorial engagement with the first Gaza War between Israel and Hamas (cf., Kaposi 2014, 2016).

Before doing so, however, some preliminary remarks are in place regarding the coming case study. The previous cases dealt with issues of racism; the present one concerns antisemitism. While antisemitism may be considered simply to be a specific instance of racism, arguments abound that it is, in fact, *sui generis*, as the unique nature of its ultimate manifestation, the Holocaust, attests (cf., Wodak 2015, pp. 97–124; Bauer 2002, pp. 1–68). In addition, as the coming examples will bear out, the existence of an officially Jewish state (the State of Israel) leads to further ambiguities. While criticism is a legitimate and necessary element of politics, it is easy to see how such acts with regard to the State of Israel may possibly stem from antisemitic intentions, or even lead to antisemitic effects (cf. Kaposi 2014, pp. 15–19).

It is with these dilemmas in mind that we ask readers to read the following paragraph:

> The first reaction of most commentators was that the air attacks on Gaza were unnecessarily savage. The deaths of nearly 300 Palestinians, including civilians, seems disproportionate to the small number of Israelis killed by rocket attacks. Hamas was not expecting retribution on this scale, but we can be sure that it will extract the maximum possible propaganda advantage from the slaughter. Israel's enemies in the liberal West are already pinning the blame squarely on 'Zionists'. So are most Muslims.
> (*Daily Telegraph*, 29 December 2008)

Interestingly, the *Daily Telegraph*'s first paragraph on the war starts not with the presentation of the conservative newspaper's stance on the morality of the war, but with the exposition of an alternative political-moral position to what will be revealed as the newspaper's own. Why is this alternative position relevant? Why is it important to cite those 'commentators' who see the war as 'disproportionate' and 'unnecessarily savage'?

As their opinions are discounted as mere 'first reactions', it appears that it is not so much their intellectual worth that makes them important. Rather, they seem relevant because these gut-reactions might be taken as embodiments of political-moral *dispositions*. Who are these people ('most commentators')? Why are they jumping to condemn Israel's conduct as 'savage' and 'disproportionate'? The paragraph concludes by naming them as 'Israel's enemies in the liberal West' as well as 'most Muslims'. More importantly, though, we also learn that these groups' ultimate account is to put the blame 'squarely on "Zionists"'. It is not for nothing that the *Telegraph* uses 'scare' quotes to refer to Zionists. First, given that arguing for the Jewish people's collective right to a homeland/state certainly does not equal arguing for the Jewish state's army sustaining an offensive on Gaza, Zionists may or may not have supported the war. Second, the war was launched by the Israeli Defense Forces (IDF), instructed by an Israeli government carrying the democratic mandate of the Israeli people. Political-moral responsibility may belong to them. The designation *Zionist*, however, implicates many millions of people living outside Israel, certainly with no direct political responsibility for the events.

What is more, quite apart from the question of whether Zionism would warrant an accusation of this sort, it is not an *idea* but a group of people that is designated. And if so, we might infer that at the core of putting the 'blame squarely on "Zionists"' is a motive to blacken not an idea at all, but an *ethnic-religious community*. And by the same token, what the *Telegraph*'s 'scare' quotes around the word 'Zionist' appear to alert us to is that by blaming 'Zionists', they actually mean to blame *the Jewish community*. The shadow of the imagined 'other', in the presence of which the *Daily Telegraph*'s account of the war starts, is, therefore, the shadow of antisemitism.

Interestingly enough, the role of the 'other' equally emerged in the argumentation of the other conservative British broadsheet, *The Times*. To examine this, let us look at a remarkable paragraph where the newspaper appears to formulate firm criticism of *Israeli* action.

> White phosphorus is illegal under international law when used in built-up areas, but a legitimate weapon of war when used to provide cover for troops in open country. There is scant evidence of the IDF using it deliberately against civilians, but northern Gaza, where the fighting is concentrated, is one of the most densely populated places in the world. Civilian casualties were inevitable, and the deep burns that white phosphorus can cause are virtually untreatable. The longer that the IDF equivocate about its use, the more ammunition they hand to those who would accuse them of war crimes.
>
> (*The Times*, 16 January 2009)

This is the concluding paragraph of *The Times*' editorial criticism of Israel's use of white phosphorous.[7] It is also an odd paragraph. It features two premises and a conclusion that seem to be in a gross mismatch. The newspaper argues that white phosphorous is illegal when used in built-up areas, and that Israel appears to be using it in 'one of the most densely populated areas in the world', but instead of concluding that IDF's conduct of war needs to be independently investigated, it merely calls for less equivocation on its part.

Puzzling as that is, what is of importance for the purposes of this chapter is that where we would expect a call for independent investigation into Israel's apparently illegal use of a weapon (and hence, by definition, a possible war crime), we encounter yet another figure of *the other*. Namely, not only does *The Times* refrain from substantial criticism of Israeli conduct, but it raises the spectre of Israeli equivocation providing 'ammunition (...) to those who would accuse them of war crimes.'

Thus, just as in the case of the *Telegraph*, the presence of an 'other', an alternative political-moral position, is therefore relevant to *The Times*' political-moral perspective.[8] What is more, and again in line with the *Telegraph*, that 'other' appears to be a rather suspect character; where we might have expected the activity of an independent and impartial investigation of a factual nature, we find the act of 'accusation'. *Those* people are not interested in finding out facts about Israel, but in accusing it. And, as a corollary, they are not interested in the description of the world, but attempt some act for which the information they get is 'ammunition'. That is, metaphorically, they attempt a military activity against Israel.

Who exactly are these people? And why do they do what they are doing? It is difficult to obtain more information from the passage. For a more precise description, we might have to turn to an earlier editorial from *The Times*. The following passage concludes the conservative newspaper's first critical exposition of Israel's use of white phosphorous:

> (...) Israel has a powerful ally in the United States.
>
> Its critics are wont to condemn this alliance as a Jewish axis blind to heart-rending realities in Gaza and to the sacrifices necessary for peace.
>
> No one can be unmoved by the suffering witnessed by the Norwegian surgeon who texted friends to tell them 'we're wading in death, blood [and] amputees'. But the way to end it is not to abandon Israel. It is to defeat Hamas. As Washington contemplates an opening to Iran, its reluctance to condemn Israel is not ideological but rational. The alternative would be to open talks with Tehran while its proxy in Gaza still threatened much of Israel with Iranian-built rockets.
>
> (*The Times*, 10 January 2009)

The explicit referent of the 'other' here is Israel's 'critics'. This is a category that, despite strong words about Israel's use of phosphorous, *The Times* clearly does not belong to. What we learn about these critics is that their preferred way of ending the suffering in Gaza would be to 'abandon Israel', and that they condemn the US–Israel alliance as a cold-hearted 'Jewish axis'. The first attribute could perhaps in itself, and in a different context, come under the umbrella of anti-Zionism; the second though, is a clear instance of antisemitism as it invokes the anti-Jewish *trope* of a worldwide and malicious Jewish conspiracy responsible for the suffering of the world. In this remarkable paragraph concluding *The Times*' position on Israeli use of white phosphorous, then, Israel's 'critics' turn out to be plain and simple anti-Semites. No wonder, perhaps, that the conservative newspaper would go out its way not to be counted among them.

To summarise, when putting forward editorial arguments on the Israeli–Palestinian conflict, both British conservative broadsheets found it relevant to refer to an alternative political-moral perspective to their own – and that alternative appeared to be a complete non-alternative since, in both cases, it turned out to be antisemitic. This meant that the newspapers could not, and *did not have to*, engage with the argumentative position of the 'other' that was critical towards the conduct of Israel.

Indeed, as pointed out earlier, it may be the case that the *prima facie* political nature of the Israeli–Palestinian conflict can be useful to serve as cover for the airing of antisemitic (or anti-Muslim) perspectives otherwise undesirable in public discourse (cf., Harrison 2006; Rosenfeld 2006). At the same time, the facts that, first, when British conservative broadsheets introduced a perspective critical of Israel's conduct it inevitably proved to be antisemitic; and, second, that *The Times* itself explicitly dubbed 'Israel's critics' as antisemitic, might make us feel uneasy when antisemitism (or anti-Muslimism) is rhetorically invoked in political debates. Namely, as argued by a number of authors (Bunzl 2007; Butler 2004), through calculation or genuine fear, it clearly closes down political-moral imaginaries by branding them as antisemitic/anti-Muslim. As such, not only does it hinder the solution of a political conflict like that between Israel–Palestine, but will contribute to the taboo where racism does not disappear, only becomes impossible to be touched, discussed, engaged with and transformed.

Conclusion

In three case studies, this chapter has examined what we think are three prominent ways in which racism features in contemporary Western public discourse. The point that we tried to make was that while in the West *the idea of racism* (as opposed to its practice) has by and large become taboo, racist discourse nonetheless operates on three levels.

With our first case study, we demonstrated how racism can still be invoked in an essentially explicit form in extreme-right discourse. Of course, since racism is variously proscribed in contemporary politics, racist discourse might have to be coded to a greater or lesser extent, and/or package its hateful message in appealing contemporary forms (see Wodak & Forchtner 2014, for analysis of comics produced by the FPÖ, for example). But nevertheless, such discourses constitute a 'thinly veiled' and by-and-large *explicit* version of political racism.

Second, the *idea* of racism having become taboo has led to developments where racism is not only coded and implicit, but arguably unintentional. This means that racists do not simply seek to deceive the mainstream public and communicate to audiences with coded messages, but rather that racism manages to *deceive the very self that emits it*. We offered Case study 2 as an example of this, showing not only how racism can be implicitly invoked in public discourse, but also how it becomes virtually impossible to discuss: it can be seen by everyone but cannot be touched.

Our third example further developed this line of thinking. In Case study 3, the issue at stake was the threat of racism and the awareness of the ways it is perceived to contaminate political discourse. The conservative broadsheets analysed were extraordinarily wary of not becoming (or being perceived as, or accused of being) racist – to the extent that it stopped them from fully developing critical lines of political thinking. As such, they demonstrated another way that racism, banished as taboo, comes back to haunt modern Western societies: from a system of ideas and practices legitimating the stratification of society, it becomes a *fear of thinking and criticism* that, once again, petrifies the political status quo and immunises it from change.

Notes

1. It behoves us to point out that Islamophobia does, indeed, 'pose a challenge to traditional understandings of race and racism' (Opratko & Müller-Uri 2014, p. 1), and one that is being answered differently in different countries. In Germany, for example, the 2011 'Deutsche Islam Konferenz', a state agency initiated by the Federal Ministry of the Interior, rejected the term 'Islamophobia' in favour of the neologism '*Muslimfeindlichkeit*' (hostility towards Muslims) (Opratko & Müller-Uri 2014, p. 3).
2. Though see Richardson (2011, 2013, 2015) and Richardson & Wodak (2009a, 2009b) for analysis of fascist esoteric arguments.
3. For an extended analysis of these and other leaflets, see Richardson & Colombo (2014).
4. Given copyright restrictions, we cannot include images of these leaflets in this chapter. We therefore point the reader to the following links: http://imgur.com/2UL5xV5; http://imgur.com/gsuY7c9.
5. See the silhouettes of missiles in this article, for example: www.scienceclarified.com/Ro-Sp/Rockets-and-Missiles.html.
6. The video of the interview is available from: www.hollywoodreporter.com/live-feed/ktla-anchor-apologizes-mistaking-samuel-679048. It is worth watching it before reading our analysis of the case. Transcripts follow the conventions for CA transcription (see Jefferson 2004).
7. White phosphorous is a self-igniting, and therefore highly incendiary chemical substance, which the Israeli Army claim to use as an obscurant. However, due to the fact that it used it within densely

populated urban areas and that white phosphorous can by definition be used with little precision, it arguably led to many avoidable civilian casualties (Human Rights Watch 2009; also see Kaposi 2014, 2016).

8   Incidentally, the paragraph is preceded by the following thoughts: 'Israelis grieve as all humans do for the children cut down in Gaza's maelstrom, and their leaders know full well the damage that this conflict is doing to the country's reputation, *especially where images of Palestinian suffering are broadcast more as propaganda than news*'. (*The Times* 16 January 2009 – emphasis ours.) Again, we witness the emergence of suspicious figures who are defined not by any positive motive (i.e. by their genuine interest in Palestinian suffering), but by their clear and inexplicable animosity towards the State of Israel.

References

Allport, G W, 1954, *The nature of prejudice*, Addison-Wesley, Cambridge, MA.

Augoustinous, M, Tuffin & K, Rapley, M, 1999, 'Genocide or failure to gel? Racism, history and nationalism in Australian talk', *Discourse & Society*, 10(3), pp. 351–378.

Bauer, Y, 2002, *Rethinking the Holocaust*, Yale Nota Bene Book, New York.

Bethencourt, F, 2013, *Racisms: From the Crusades to the twentieth century*, Princeton University Press, Princeton, NJ.

Betz, H.-G, 2013, 'Mosques, minarets, burqas and other essential threats: The populist right's campaign against Islam in Western Europe', in *Right-Wing Populism in Europe*, eds. R Wodak, M KhosraviNik & B Mral, Bloomsbury, London, pp. 71–88.

Billig, M, 1991, *Ideology and opinions: Studies in rhetorical psychology*, Sage, London.

Billig, M, 1995, *Banal nationalism*, Sage, London.

Bunzl, M, 2007, *Anti-Semitism and Islamophobia: Hatreds old and new in Europe*, Prickly Paradigm Press, Chicago, IL.

Butler, J, 2004, 'The charge of anti-Semitism: Jews, Israel and the risks of public critique', in *Precarious life: The powers of mourning and violence*, J Butler, Verso, London, pp. 101–127.

Donald, J & Rattansi, A, 1992, 'Introduction', in *'Race', culture and difference*, eds. J Donald & A Rattansi, Sage, London, pp. 1–9.

Durham, M, 2015, 'Securing the future for our race: Women in the culture of the modern-day BNP', in *Cultures of post-war British fascism*, eds. N Copsey & J E Richardson, Routledge, Oxon, pp. 68–85.

Edwards, D, 2003, 'Analyzing racial discourse: The discursive psychology of mind–world relationships', in *Analyzing race talk: Multidisciplinary approaches to the interview*, eds. H van den Berg, M Wetherell & H Houtkoop-Steenstra, Cambridge University Press, Cambridge, pp. 31–48.

Essed, PJM, 1991, *Understanding everyday racism: An interdisciplinary approach*, Sage, Newbury Park, CA.

Golding, P & Murdock, G, 2000, 'Culture, communications and political economy', in *Mass media and society*, eds. J Curran & M Gurevitch, Arnold, London, pp. 70–92.

Guardian, 2015a, 'Donald Trump: Ban all Muslims from entering US', available from: www.theguardian.com/us-news/2015/dec/07/donald-trump-ban-all-muslims-entering-us-san-bernardino-shooting [accessed 8 February 2016].

Guardian, 2015b, 'Young black men killed by US police at highest rate in year of 1,134 deaths, available from: http://www.theguardian.com/us-news/2015/dec/31/the-counted-police-killings-2015-young-black-men, [accessed 8 February 2016].

Guardian, 2016, 'Danish parliament approves plans to seize assets from refugees', available from: www.theguardian.com/world/2016/jan/26/danish-parliament-approves-plan-to-seize-assets-from-refugees [accessed 8 February 2016].

Hage, G, 1998, *White nation: Fantasies of white supremacy in a multicultural society*, Pluto Press, Annandale, NSW.

Harrison, B, 2006, *The resurgence of anti-Semitism: Jews, Israel, and liberal opinion*, Rowman & Littlefield, New York.

Human Rights Watch, 2009, *Rain of fire: Israel's unlawful use of white phosphorous in Gaza*, Human Rights Watch, New York.
Jäger, S & Link, J, 1993, *Die vierte Gewalt. Rassismus and die Medien*, Duisburg Institute for Language and Social Research, Duisburg.
Jefferson G, 2004, 'Glossary of transcript symbols with an Introduction,' in ed. G H Lerner, *Conversation analysis: Studies from the first generation*, Philadelphia, John Benjamins, pp. 13–23.
Jiwani, Y & Richardson, J E, 2011, 'Discourse, ethnicity and racism', in *Discourse Studies*, 2nd ed., ed. T A van Dijk, Sage, London, pp. 241–262.
Kaposi, D, 2014, *Violence and understanding in Gaza: The British broadsheets' coverage of the war*, Palgrave Macmillan, London.
Kaposi, D, 2016, 'On the possibility of critiquing Israel: *The Times*' engagement with Israel's deployment of white phosphorous during the first Gaza war', *Media, War & Conflict*, 9(2), pp. 272–289.
Malik, K, 1996, *The meaning of race: Race, history and culture in Western society*, Macmillan, Houndsmill.
Manning, P, 2001, *News sources: A critical introduction*, Routledge, London.
Meyer, T, 2001, *Identity mania: Fundamentalism and the politicisation of cultural differences*, Zed Books, London.
Opratko, B & Müller-Uri, F, 2014, 'L'islamophobie et les théories critiques du racism', in *Période*, 7 March 2014.
Poole, E, 2002, *Reporting Islam: Media representations of British Muslims*, I.B.Tauris, London.
Quasthoff, U, 1987, 'Linguistic prejudice/stereotypes', in *Sociolinguistics. An international handbook of the science of language and society*, eds. U Ammon, N Dittmar & K J Mattheier, de Gruyter, Berlin, pp. 785–799.
Rapley, M, 2001, 'How to do X without doing Y?: Accomplishing discrimination without "being racist" – "doing equity"', in *Understanding prejudice, racism and social conflict*, eds. M Augoustinous & K J Reynolds, Sage, London, pp. 231–250.
Reisigl, M & Wodak, R, 2001, *Discourse and discrimination: Rhetorics of racism and antisemitism*, Routledge, London.
Richardson, J E, 2004, *(Mis)Representing Islam: The racism and rhetoric of British broadsheet newspapers*, John Benjamins, Amsterdam.
Richardson, J E, 2009, 'Get shot of the lot of 'em': Election reporting of Muslims in British newspapers', *Patterns of Prejudice*, 43(3–4), pp. 355–377.
Richardson, J E, 2011, 'Race and racial difference: The surface and depth of BNP ideology, in *British National Party: Contemporary perspectives*, eds. N Copsey & G Macklin, Routledge, London, pp. 38–61.
Richardson, J E, 2013, 'Racial populism in British fascist discourse: The case of COMBAT and the British National Party (1960–67)', in *Analysing fascist discourse: European fascism in talk and text*, eds. R Wodak & J E Richardson, Routledge, London, pp. 181–202.
Richardson, J E, 2015, '"Cultural-Marxism" and the British National Party: A Universal neo-fascist discourse?', in *Cultures of post-war British fascism*, eds. N Copsey & J E Richardson, Routledge, London, pp. 202–226.
Richardson, J E & Colombo, M, 2013, 'Continuity and change in populist anti-immigrant discourse in Italy: An analysis of Lega leaflets', *Journal of Language and Politics*, 12(2), pp. 180–202.
Richardson, J E & Colombo, M, 2014, 'Race and immigration in far- and extreme-right European discourse', *Contemporary studies in Critical Discourse Analysis*, eds. C Hart & P Cap, Continuum, London, pp. 521–542.
Richardson, J E & Wodak, R, 2009a, 'Recontextualising fascist ideologies of the past: Rightwing discourses on employment and nativism in Austria and the United Kingdom', *Critical Discourse Studies*, 6(4), pp. 251–267.

Richardson, J E & Wodak, R, 2009b, 'The impact of visual racism: Visual arguments in political leaflets of Austrian and British far-right parties', *Controversia: An International Journal of Debate and Democratic Renewal*, 6(2), pp. 45–77.

Rosenfeld, A, 2006, *'Progressive' Jewish thought and the new anti-Semitism*, American Jewish Committee, available from: www.ajc.org/atf/cf/%7B42D75369-D582-4380-8395-D25925B85EAF%7D/PROGRESSIVE_JEWISH_THOUGHT.PDF [accessed 7 April 2017].

Rydgren, J, 2007, 'The sociology of the radical right', *Annual Review of Sociology*, 33, pp. 241–262.

Taguieff, P.-A, 1988, *La force du préjugé. Essai sur le racisme et ses doubles*, La Découverte Paris.

Tileagă, C, 2006, 'Representing the "other": A discursive analysis of prejudice and moral exclusion in talk about Romanies', *Journal of Community & Applied Social Psychology*, 16(1), pp. 19–41.

van der Valk, I, 2002, *Difference, deviance, threat?: Mainstream and right-extremist political discourse on ethnic issues in the Netherlands and France (1990–1997)*, Aksant Academic Publishers, Amsterdam.

van der Valk, I, 2003, 'Right-wing parliamentary discourse on immigration in France', *Discourse & Society*, 14, pp. 309–348.

van Dijk, T A, 1984, *Prejudice in discourse*, Benjamins, Amsterdam.

van Dijk, T A, 1991, *Racism and the press*, Routledge, London.

van Dijk, T A, 1997, 'Political discourse and racism', in *The language and politics of exclusion: Others in discourse*, S H Riggins, ed., Sage, Thousand Oaks, CA, pp. 31–64.

van Dijk, T A, 2004, 'Racist discourse', in *Routledge encyclopedia of race and ethnic studies*, ed. E Cashmore, Routledge, London, pp. 351–355.

van Dijk, T A, Ting-Toomey, S, Smitherman, G & Troutman, D, 1997, 'Discourse, ethnicity, culture and racism', in *Discourse Studies: A multidisciplinary introduction*, vol 2., ed. T A van Dijk, Sage, London, pp. 144–180.

Verkuyten, M, 1998, 'Self-categorisation and the explanation of ethnic discrimination', *Journal of Community & Applied Social Psychology*, 8(6), pp. 395–407.

Verkuyten, M, 2001, 'Abnormalization of ethnic minorities in conversation', *British Journal of Social Psychology*, 40(2), pp. 257–278.

Wetherell, M & Potter, J, 1992, *Mapping the language of racism*, Columbia University Press, New York.

Wieviorka, M, 1995, *The arena of racism*, Sage, London.

Wodak, R, 2015, *The politics of fear: What right-wing populist discourses mean*, London, Sage.

Wodak, R & Forchtner, B, 2014, 'Embattled Vienna 1683/2010: Right-wing populism, collective memory and the fictionalisation of politics', *Visual Communication*, 13(2), pp. 231–255.

Wodak, R & Matouscheck, B, 1993, '"We are dealing with people whose origins one can clearly tell just by looking": Critical Discourse Analysis and the study of neo-racism in contemporary Austria', *Discourse & Society*, 4(2), pp. 225–248.

Wodak, R & Reisigl, M, 2015, 'Discourse and racism', in *The handbook of Discourse Analysis*, 2nd ed., vol. II, eds. D Tannen, H E Hamilton & D Schiffrin, Wiley, Oxford, pp. 576–596.

Wodak, R & van Dijk, T A, eds., 2000, *Racism at the top: Parliamentary discourses on ethnic issues in six European states*, Drava, Klagenfurt.

43
The materiality and *semiosis* of inequality and class struggle and warfare
The case of home-evictions in Spain

David Block

Introduction

> A woman died Friday in the outlying Malagan neighborhood of *Los Corazones* after leaping from the balcony of her flat situated on the fourth floor. Earlier this week, she allegedly received an eviction notice for non-payment of her mortgage.
> (*La Vanguardia* 2012)[1]

Suicides due to inability to pay mortgages, as described here, are fortunately not an everyday occurrence in Spain, although they have been more common in recent years than was previously the case. And when they do occur, they bring to the fore general issues around growing inequality in Spanish society beyond the family tragedy that they represent. As in many parts of the world, inequality in Spain has risen markedly since the beginning of the economic recession of 2007–2008, and one aspect of this state of affairs is the crude reality of many individuals and families who cannot pay their mortgages or rents and are therefore evicted from their homes. And as we see in this newspaper excerpt, in extreme cases, the victims of eviction are pushed to a sense of despair that makes life too hard to bear and ultimately not worth living.

This chapter is about inequality and class struggle and warfare, which both engender and are engendered by events such as home-evictions. It begins with an attempt to make clear what is meant by inequality and class struggle, drawing on a range of work: from Plato's (2007 [380]) and Rousseau's (2004 [1754]) early reflections on the topic to more current scholarship (e.g. Atkinson 2015; Dorling 2011, 2014a; Duménil & Lévy 2011, 2014; Harvey 2014; Piketty 2014). There is then a discussion of how inequality and class struggle and warfare are made in context, both materially and via *semiosis*, or multimodal meaning making (Fairclough 2010). The chapter then moves on to the concrete example of home-evictions and examines how inequality and class struggle and warfare come together around them.

Inequality and class struggle and warfare

References to inequality can be found as far back as the fourth century BC, when Plato discussed both the inevitability and danger of inequality. In book IV of *The Republic*, he wrote that a state 'always contains at least two states, the rich and the poor, at enmity with each other' (Plato 2007, p. 124), and in Book V of *The Laws*, he wrote that '[i]n a state which is desirous of being saved from the greatest of all plagues ... there should exist among the citizens neither extreme poverty nor, again, excessive wealth, for both are productive of great evil' (Plato 2014 [360]). The early philosophy of Plato is alive and well in Jean Jacques Rousseau's (2004) oft-cited essay *Discourse on the origin of inequality*, first published some twenty centuries after Plato in 1754. Rousseau's starting point is the existence of 'two species of inequality': *physical* inequality, which is about *natural* differences between individuals in terms of body, mind and health; and *moral* or *political* inequality, which is based on convention, is established, accepted and authorised by society, and leads to differences in wealth and power in society. Controversially, Rousseau developed the idea that existing stratification in society is not just about the natural abilities and propensities of individuals; rather, there are social conditions, human-made certainly, which create, strengthen and maintain existing political, economic and social orders. Significantly, Rousseau positions the ownership of property as what Marx (1990, p. 873) would later call the 'original sin' of political economy, and as the wellspring of inequality:

> The first man who after enclosing a piece of ground, took it into his head to say, "This is mine", and found people simple enough to believe him, was the true founder of civil society. How many crimes, how many wars, how many murders, how many misfortunes and horrors, would that man have saved the human species, who pulling up the stakes or filling up the ditch should have cried to his fellows: Be sure not to listen to this impostor; you are lost, if you forget that that the fruits of the earth belong equally to us all, and the earth itself to nobody!
>
> (Rousseau 2004, p. 27)

More recently, Göran Therborn (2006) further develops the notion of inequality as a moral concern, arguing that it is inevitably about qualifying differences between individuals and collectives as good/right and bad/wrong. For Therborn, inequality itself is based on difference, but it is not just a matter of dissimilarity between and among individuals. First, it is about difference that limits the life possibilities of the disadvantaged: either directly, by concentrating resources among the privileged; or indirectly, via social, psychological mechanisms of humiliating signals of superiority and inferiority. Second, as a difference, inequality is too large and harsh for it to be accepted by a substantial proportion of society, even those who might benefit from it. Third and finally, inequality goes against notions of fairness in society, giving underserved, unfair advantages to people on the basis of power, rather than work and sacrifice. Of course, such notions of fairness have not always been in operation, as we see in recent surveys of inequality (Milanovic 2011; Piketty 2014).

Therborn also outlines three general types of inequality. First, there is *vital inequality*, which is about basic life-and-death chances, and individuals and collectives' relative exposure to life-threatening natural phenomena, such as disease, famine, flooding and drought; self-inflicted human conditions, such as violence, alcoholism, and obesity; and larger human-made disasters, such as war, pollution and the inability to reach and use vital natural resources. Second, there is *existential inequality*, which is about systems of oppression that deny individuals and collectives what are understood today to be basic human rights. Social structures such as patriarchy, slavery, caste systems, racism, religious persecution, homophobia and other forms of social ostracism, or attacks on ways of being, fall into this category. Third, there is *resource inequality*, which refers to the variable access that individuals and collectives have to material and symbolic resources, from property to money to culture; contacts and social networks; and recognised legitimacy and respect (see Bourdieu's capital metaphors).

As many authors such as Duménil and Lévy (2011, 2014) and Piketty (2014) have noted, from roughly the late 1940s to the mid 1970s, the economies of the wealthy countries of Western Europe, North America and elsewhere operated according to a dominant Keynesian social-democratic consensus (*de facto* or conscious), and during this period, inequality was reduced. However, since the mid 1970s, there has been a considerable increase in Therborn's *resource inequality*, especially material inequality, as this Keynesian consensus was first of all discredited and then effectively dismantled to a great extent. This turnaround came about as neo-liberal economic policies and practices rose to prominence, albeit in different ways across different geographical locations (Mirowski 2013; Peck 2010). These policies and practices have generated social and political changes that have brought with them greater differences between the rich and the poor, and the weakening and diminishing of the traditional middle class, not only in economic and material terms (around the ownership of assets, the relative stability of employment and the amount of income), but also in terms of the status and legitimacy that accompany it. In addition, and to make matters worse, this inequality has increased even more rapidly in the years since the current economic crisis first began to emerge in 2007–2008 (Piketty 2014). In the midst of this situation, it is worthwhile noting how – among the populations of those countries most affected by the crisis, such as the southern-most states of the EU – there is a growing realisation that the persistence and growth of *resource inequality* lead inevitably to a rise in another of Therborn's categories. In this sense, there is a concomitant increase in *vital inequality*, the collateral negative effects that come with society-wide impoverishment, such as ill-health (both physical and psychological) and a decrease in the quality of social services and publicly available resources (Dorling 2011, 2014a).

Of course, in order to study inequality and social stratification and/or do something about it, it is necessary to elaborate some sort of descriptive framework, which informs both researchers and lay people about what it is that they are challenging and trying to overturn. Grusky and Ku (2008) have elaborated a typology of eight key 'assets' around which groups and individuals may be considered stratified, and hence advantaged and disadvantaged. Assets here are understood as the resources that individuals struggle over in societies, or the social realities according to which they can be classified and ultimately stratified. Grusky and Ku's assets, which may be seen as transcending Therborn's *vital*, *existential* and *resource* inequalities, are outlined in Table 43.1.

Grusky and Ku's list might be expanded somewhat to include overt reference to the continuing deficits in recognition of, and respect for, difference in contemporary societies, that is, enduring discrimination based on race, ethnicity, gender, nationality, sexual orientation, age, religion and disability. In addition, a more material domain – housing and shelter – deserves a separate mention, even if this aspect is perhaps implied in Grusky and Ku's 'economic' category. Indeed, whether we frame housing in terms of its use value (a roof over our head), or its exchange value, as an asset generating greater wealth, there is little doubt that it marks divisions in society ((see Bourdieu 2005, for an examination of the housing market in 1990s France and Dorling 2014b, for a more recent discussion of the UK).

Table 43.1 Typology of assets related to inequality

Asset	Gloss
Economic	Relative wealth, income, ownership of consumer goods
Power	Relative political power, workplace authority, household authority
Cultural	Relative knowledge, digital culture, 'good' manners
Social	Membership in social clubs, workplace associations, informal networks
Honorific	Relative respect received based on merit, social status, age
Civil	Relative rights to work, to vote, to legal processes
Human	Relative education and training: on-the-job, general schooling, vocational
Physical	Relative fitness, illness, disease

(Based on Grusky & Ku 2008)

My starting point for exploring how stratification and inequality are *made* in the ongoing flux-and-flow social events, activity and communication is the premise that we are living in times of class *struggle* as class *warfare*, where class is understood in terms of a *constellation of dimensions* model (Block 2014, 2015, 2016). This model draws on the foundational political economic work of Marx (1990); the later, more sociocultural models of class elaborated by Durkheim (1984) and above all, Weber (1968); and the more recent work of Bourdieu (1984), Wright (2005) and Savage et al. (2013). It frames class in terms of a long list of factors, including property owned, material possessions (e.g. electronic goods, clothing, books, art, etc.), income, occupation, education, social networking, consumption patterns, symbolic behaviour, pastimes, mobility, neighbourhood and type of dwelling inhabited. These dimensions of class cluster together and index points of contrast between and among individuals in class-based societies where class struggle and class conflict are a part of daily life, albeit in ways that are often subtle, and equally often, go unnoticed.

Eric Olin Wright defines class struggle as:

> Conflicts between the practices of individuals and collectivities in pursuit of opposing class interests. These conflicts range from the strategies of individual workers within the labour process to reduce their level of toil, to conflicts between highly organized collectivities of workers and capitalists over the distribution of rights and powers within production.
>
> (Wright 2005, pp. 20–21)

Class warfare is a more vivid term that I will use here to capture how the neo-liberal policies adopted over the past four decades have constituted not only a point of conflict and struggle, but an actual attack on the well-being and even survival of the popular class in countries around the world across the dimensions outlined above. Nowhere has such an attack been more evident than in the transfer of capital assets from the less wealthy in society to the wealthiest since the beginning of the economic crisis in 2007. To capture this trend, David Harvey (2010, 2014) updates Marx's notion of 'primitive accumulation', discussing what he calls 'accumulation by dispossession'. Primitive accumulation was Marx's term for the 'historical process of divorcing the producer from the means of production' (Marx 1990, p. 875), which began with waves of land expropriations going back as far as the late fifteenth century in England. These expropriations, which ranged from the feudal lords being dispossessed of land by the emerging industrial capitalist class to the reformation-era spoliation of land held by the Catholic Church, had the common effect of divesting the peasant class of access to a livelihood as they were driven towards their historical destiny as the industrial proletariat.

Moving to more recent times, Harvey sees a new form of accumulation at work – accumulation by dispossession – in the range of activities and practices carried out by governments and financial institutions, which have the function of transferring wealth from the less well-off to the wealthy. First, there is the privatisation of state-owned and operated industries and services, which began in earnest some four decades ago, and more recently, there is the sale of state-owned assets – which, in theory, belong to 'the people' – to private investors eager to pick up architectural jewels and prime property at knock-down prices. Second, there are activities in the financial sector such as Ponzi schemes (Frankel 2012), in which unassuming investors, often of modest incomes, are cheated out of their savings. Finally, and most relevant to this chapter, there are the massive defaults on mortgages and subsequent home-evictions that have come with the current economic crisis. In this case, the executors are banks, aided and abetted by governments serving the interests of capital over citizens at large, an alignment of interests denounced long ago by Marx (1973; 1990; see also Marx & Engels 1998).

Given the discussion above, in which we have moved from inequality to class struggle and warfare fairly rapidly, there is the key issue of how to operationalise these constructs in empirical research, or perhaps it would be better to say, how to document how these phenomena are constituted in, and indeed how they emerge from, the social world of events, activity and communication. I turn to this issue in the next section.

Exploring the material and the discursive construction of inequality and class struggle and warfare: Critical Discourse Analysis

In order to explore the issues just identified, I draw on the work of Norman Fairclough over recent decades (Fairclough 2006, 2010; see also Wodak & Meyer 2012). Central to Fairclough's approach is the study of *semiosis*, or the making of meaning via the use of semiotic resources (speech, written script, visuals, body movement, gaze, etc.) as a way of understanding how power relationships are symbolically established and reproduced in society. Fairclough defines discourse as:

> a complex set of relations including relations of communication between people who talk, write and in other ways communicate with each other, but also, for example, describe relations between concrete communicative events (conversations, newspaper articles, etc.) and more abstract and enduring complex discourses and genres.
> (Fairclough 2010, p. 3)

Crucially, he sees 'relations between discourse and other such complex "objects" ... in the physical world, persons, power relations and institutions, which are interconnected elements in social activity ...' (Fairclough 2010, p. 3). It is also worth noting that discourses, as defined above, are always 'positioned' ways of presenting social practices, and the world and life in general, which means that they are not casual, but always *come from somewhere*. In addition, discourses about social events and phenomena do not normally exist in isolation; indeed, the norm, as Weedon (1997) notes, is for there to be multiple discourses around a same social reality, and for these to be contested and in conflict with each other. Thus, at the time of writing, the Spanish central government is engaged in a continuous campaign to convince a progressively demoralised and sceptical public that the economy is going well. However, their efforts are constantly contested by academics, journalists and lay people who simply do not trust the official version of events, and based on study, experience, or both, have developed their own counter-discourses.

A final point about discourses is that they often exist as integral historical artefacts, which means that they are potential resources for communication in the present. In different ways, both Bakhtin (1981) and Kristeva (1986) capture this general notion in their respective work on 'heteroglossia' and 'intertextuality'. For his part, Fairclough makes the point that it is often possible to find that the producer of a text brings forward to the present elements found in communication in the past. This can mean, for example, a mixing of genres (e.g. personalising a formal speech with anecdotes), or the adoption of a variety of recognisable social voices in the telling of story (often the choice of voices tells us great deal about the person producing them), or the use of simplified versions of material and discursive realities from the past (as we shall see below, all too often, references to Hitler and the Nazis are used as a quick and easy way to discredit an interlocutor or political opponent).

Exploring the material and the discursive construction of inequality, and class struggle and warfare

In this discussion of inequality and class warfare, there are two key participating collectives. First, there is the *Partido Popular* (PP), the Spanish conservative party, which governed Spain with an absolute majority from 2011 to 2015. From early 2012, the PP began to apply extreme austerity measures according to the dictates of the 'troika', composed of the European Central Bank, the European Commission and the International Monetary Fund. The measures taken by PP, which included across-the-board (*and* ongoing) pay cuts for civil servants, as well as cutbacks in funding for essential services (e.g. universal health care, education) had begun to produce a slight amelioration of the profound economic crisis in Spain in macro-economic terms by the end of 2014, although the PP tended to exaggerate such developments while the 'troika' continued to show a degree of scepticism. However, even if the Spanish government could claim that at the macro-level the economy was emerging from the recession by late 2014, the majority of the Spanish people were not feeling the effects and this, coupled with massive corruption scandals (the majority of which involved prominent past and present members of the PP) had served to submerge the population in despair. One key development from 2011 onwards was the increase in home-evictions, a phenomenon that led directly to the formation and rise to media prominence of the second key participating collective in this discussion, the *Plataforma de Afectados por la Hipoteca* (Platform for those Affected by Mortgages; PAH).

The PAH is a grass-roots organisation that campaigns on behalf of individuals and families who, because of unemployment or other events, find that they are unable to make mortgage or rent payments and therefore are either threatened with eviction from their homes or are actually evicted. Evictions normally occur with no provision whatsoever of alternative accommodation, and as we observed in the newspaper excerpt with which this chapter began, they can be extremely traumatic experiences for those who are evicted. On PAH's web site, the following explanation of the campaign it organised appears under the heading, 'Origin and justification':

Text 1: PAH: Origin and justification

This campaign was born in September 2011 in the street ... The motives behind the campaign are simple: they steal our homes and condemn us to continue paying for them. We are left in the street without any housing alternative. Banks, including those which were rescued, continue to display an antisocial attitude, evicting families and accumulating a huge stock of empty houses disregarding the social function of housing. The government protects such actions: it neither stops them nor offers solutions such as social rent, putting a halt to evictions or waiver of payment. PAH's social project consists of a campaign of occupations and the recovery of the right to housing in response to a generalized state of housing emergency generated artificially and intentionally by banks and the government. To address this situation, we propose the recovery of empty housing held by banks for the homeless and our main demand is a social rent for families, in accordance with their income. The social project connects seamlessly with the trajectory of the PAH: the defense of the population when their rights are amputated, disobedience to recover these rights and in this way drive solutions.

(PAH 2014)

Importantly, this text traces clear lines of demarcation between the empowered capitalist class (backed by the government) and the relatively disempowered popular classes – the former 'they' against the interest of 'we' – and thus outlines a kind of class warfare (practised but denied by the government, and identified and felt by the popular classes). And it makes clear the inequality existing in contemporary Spanish society in the form of: (1) *resource* inequality (unequal access to wealth, property and housing); and (2) *existential* inequality (unequal access to political power and civil rights based on unequal access to the appropriate cultural and social assets).

It is worth noting at this stage that the Spanish mortgage law, which was passed in 1946 and remained unaltered through 30 years of the Franco regime and almost 40 years of democratic rule, was extremely biased in favour of the interests of banks. It left homebuyers and renters with few rights if they could not make mortgage payments or pay their rent. The most abusive – and as a result, controversial – section of this law was the impossibility of waiving the remainder of a mortgage, even after home-eviction for default and the permanent cession of the home to the lending bank. In essence, mortgage defaulters not only lost their homes, along with all of the money they had paid up to the time of default, but they were also still legally bound to paying off the remainder of their mortgage at such a point in time when it was deemed they were able to do so. A new law was passed in May 2013, with the sole support of the majority PP in parliament, which alleviated some of the more egregious and crueller aspects of the earlier law (preventing the eviction of families living in absolute destitution), but the obligation to pay off mortgages, even after home cession to a bank, remained. And as regards the prevention of evictions, the law seemed to have had little effect, as official statistics produced by the Spanish National Statistics Institute (Instituto Nacional de Estadística) for 2014 showed that there were 34,680 evictions, up 7.4% from the previous year.

In the midst of this drama, members of the PAH developed three types of activity. First, they held assemblies, during which information was shared about past or impending evictions, and victims were provided with legal, practical and emotional support. Second, they set up and maintained an active web site on which new and updated information was constantly posted on a range of topics, from Spanish law to strategies for dealing with eviction. Third, there was direct action, which included a physical presence at evictions, with the aim of stopping them, and participation in mass demonstrations. More controversially, in 2013, some members of the PAH began to engage in a form of direct action, called *escraches*, which were more focused demonstrations in which groups of activists protested outside the homes and/or workplaces of politicians. The objects of these *escraches* were individuals deemed to have decision-making capacity with regard to the legislation of banks and practices such as home-evictions (mainly PP members in the parliament). It is precisely these more 'in-your-face' demonstrations which led to a public discursive conflict with the PP in 2013.

Home-evictions and *escraches* are, without a doubt, material events involving the physical presence of actors (evictors, evictees, *escrache* protestors and the objects of *escraches*) and physical spaces (homes and streets). But what actually occurs in a home-eviction and an *escrache* when these events are framed as acts of semiosis that exemplify and structure inequality and class warfare? Lorenzo (2013) provides a vivid portrayal (via written text and a photograph) of a home-eviction in which we first note that there are two main actors: protestors and the police or military. There is a physical confrontation as police officers physically remove protestors from the entrance of a building in which evictees live, while the protestors do everything in their power to prevent this from happening. The use of violence by the police, provoked or not, is not uncommon in evictions, consisting of anything from the pulling of hair and pushing, to the use of batons to strike protestors. The corporality and positioning of the police officers during a home-eviction stands in contrast to those of the protestors: while the former are only focused on the removal of evictees, the protestors are engaged in a range of activities, which include attempts to talk to police officers, and outright physical resistance, such as hanging on to rails and other fixed objects to prevent physical removal from the scene. Protestors are likely to use phone technologies to contact associates or the press and above all to take photographs of unfolding events. There is, thus, a contrasted *semiosis* of the two groups in conflict. What this contrast means to those observing a home-eviction will no doubt depend on their views on a range of issues, from the morality of home-evictions to the role of the police in society (as guardians of security and order, or as the oppressive arm of the state ideological apparatuses and the interests of capital).

Applying the parameters of inequality outlined above to the home-eviction as event, we see that it is an instance of Therborn's *vital inequality* and an instance of unequal allocation of physical assets in Grusky and Ku's model. Evictees in effect have their physical integrity compromised in that they are at risk of not having access to basic shelter. The eviction also raises issues around Therborn's *existential inequality*, and Grusky and Lu's *civic inequality* as it may be seen as an act of denial and withdrawal of the evictees' basic human rights (the right to housing). Of course, the root of the problem is the evictees' lack of economic and political assets in contrast with the substantial economic and political assets possessed by banks as the ultimate instigators of eviction for mortgage default. And further to this, there is the state as guarantor of the banks' interests. However, the PAH enters the conflict, providing cultural and social assets to the victims of eviction to counteract the cultural and social assets held by the banks and the state. In effect, members of the PAH are well informed about the legality and procedure of home-evictions, and they are well organised, with well-established networks. Importantly, in this battle of assets, it is sometimes the PAH that wins, as they are often able to stop an eviction and/or to rehouse a family.

Meanwhile, the *escrache* shows us a different *semiosis* from the home-eviction, even if the same two parties – members of the PAH and police officers – are involved. However, the two groups' behaviour differs here, as we move from evictees as the focal point of the activity to politicians. In *escraches*, the objects of the activity are seldom seen, except when rushing from their home or office to an official car to avoid contact with protestors and the press. By far the most interesting contrast between an eviction and an *escrache* is the behaviour of the police officers: while they are active in home-evictions, executing eviction orders, in an *escrache*, they are relatively static as they stand, wait and contain. Indeed, for most *escraches*, the police only intervene when the target appears, ostensibly to prevent any possible physical contact between the latter and the protestors. Meanwhile, the PAH has always maintained that it neither engages in physical attacks on targets nor uses abusive and insulting language towards them, and there has never been any reliable evidence to suggest the contrary, despite uncorroborated claims by some members of the PP. At most, there have been instances in which PAH demonstrators have shouted phrases such as '*sin verguenza*' (shameless) at their targets. Threats against life and harsh language do not seem to be part of the normal repertoire of those participating in *escraches*, and the PAH has publicly expressed low tolerance for such extremism. More typically, protestors hold placards with slogans, such as '*no criminalización*' (no criminalisation), in reference to the way that from 2012 onwards, parts of the media and the PP began a campaign to frame many forms of public protest as illegal.[2]

As a political party with strong survival instincts, the PP could not be expected to stand idly by while the PAH's discourses around the unfairness of home-evictions, the unethical and uncaring actions of banks, and the inactivity and insensitivity of the government gained traction in the press and among the wider public. However, PP politicians were finding it difficult to defend their position in public, given that in the run-up to the passing of the 2013 mortgage law, it had become clear that they would be offering only minor palliatives to the rising number of people affected by mortgage default and inability to pay rent. Above all, they made clear that they would not be changing the most controversial aspect of the 1946 law, whereby mortgage defaulters not only lose their home, but are still liable to pay off the remainder of the mortgage.

The arrival of *escraches* changed matters substantially for the PP. For many people in Spain, moving protests outside people's homes, and therefore close to the border between the public and the private, was a questionable tactic. Perhaps seeing this, the PP embarked on a frontal attack on the PAH and attempted to shift public opinion, such that its members were no longer seen as saints, rather as something akin to political thugs. On 13 April 2013, as the number of *escraches* was increasing in the run-up to the parliamentary vote on the new mortgage law, Maria Dolores de Cospedal, the General Secretary of the PP, made the following statement during a meeting of PP party members (see p. 657 for transcription conventions):

> … we have in our memory/fortunately it is well documented/how in the 30s certain people were pointed out/for belonging to certain political/ethnic/cultural/or religious groups/and they said/<u>there they are/and you have to go and attack them</u> (1) but what is this attempt to violate the vote? (1) this is pure Nazism (1.5) I know they are going to criticize me for this (1.5) [smiling] but this is pure Nazism …
>
> (Rachide 2013)

Cospedal's words received a good deal of media attention, not least because of their incendiary content. However, they were not improvised or idiosyncratic; rather, they were integral to an organised campaign by the PP to get a particular message across about *escraches* and, of course, about the PAH. Just one day later, Esperanza Aguirre, Head of the PP in the Autonomous Community of Madrid, wrote about members of the PAH in similar terms in a blog on her web site, referring to their 'impudence', 'cockiness' and 'impunity' while likening *escraches* to 'the worst totalitarian tactics of the last century' (with a reference to the Hitler Youth) and 'the bullying tactics of ... ETA in the Basque Country' (Aguirre 2013).

The Cospedal and Aguirre texts both contain an element of interdiscursivity as they involve 'the insertion of history into a text and of this text into history' (Kristeva 1986, p. 39). They also employ what Ruth Wodak et al. (1999, p. 85) have called the '*topos* of history as teacher', and more specifically what Bernhard Forchtner (2014) has called the 'rhetorics of judging', a discursive strategy that 'links the data (a past wrongdoing committed by an out-group) and the conclusion (that similar actions proposed today by *others* should be avoided)' (Forchtner 2014, p. 26). In short, '[s]ince history teaches that specific actions have specific consequences, one should perform or omit a specific action in a specific situation (allegedly) comparable with the historical example referred to' (Forchtner 2014, p. 26). Using wording such as 'certain people were pointed out/for belonging to certain political/ethnic/cultural/or religious groups', and lexical items ranging from the bald 'Nazism' to 'totalitarian tactics', the two PP members draw on a discourse that frames the horrors of the Nazi era in Germany: PP party members, who are the object of *escraches*, are the persecuted Jews of our time, while PAH members (home evictees and those who help them) are Hitler's henchmen. Apart from its outright crassness and insensitivity to the descendants of Holocaust victims, this intertextual twist is rather shaky for two reasons.

First, there is Spain's well-documented contact with the Nazi regime both before and during the Second World War. From 1936 to 1939, Spain was occupied with the Spanish Civil War, during which Nazi Germany provided Franco's insurrectionary fascist forces with valuable material and logistical support, among other things, bombing Spanish cities and transporting forces (Beevor 2006). After Franco's victory in 1939, Spain was then officially 'neutral' during the Second World War, as Franco sought and achieved formal recognition of his regime by the allied powers after the war. Such historical events (and I apologise to readers for the elliptical nature of this foray into Spanish history) mean that references to the Nazis and Hitler in the Spanish public sphere often ring hollow, and they never have the kind of visceral value and impact among Spaniards that they would have with British or French audiences, to cite just two examples. Second, the PP itself has clear and unequivocal historical links to the Franco regime, as its earlier incarnation, the *Alianza Popular* (Popular Alliance), was founded in 1978 by a former Franco-era minister, Manuel Fraga. In addition, some of the policies and practices of the PP today – its close relationship with ultra-conservative elements in the Catholic Church, its latent authoritarianism (see endnote 2), its overt support for and celebration of 'national symbols' such as bull-fighting, and so on – are consistent with *nacionalcatolicismo* (national Catholicism), which was the ideological base of the Franco regime, dependent on the support of both Catholic fundamentalism and fascism. In sum, the PP arguably has far more links to the persecutors of Jews in 1930s Germany than the persecuted Jews themselves, and the PAH-as-Nazis intertextual turn therefore comes across as a cynical rhetorical ploy.

Nevertheless, members of the party, led by Cospedal and Aguirre, showed no sense of what Forchtner (2014, p. 28) calls the 'self-critical narrative of *our* past failing', and they went on to use the Nazi-based '*topos* of history as teacher' (Ruth Wodak et al. 1999, p. 85) for a period of time in 2013. Ultimately, this was an attempt of Orwellian proportions to do what governments defending capital (in this case, the interests of banks) have always done:

turning reality on its head and then trying to convince the general public that it is true. In other words, the PP's claim of victim status is a classic example of Marx and Engels' (1998, p. 42) metaphor of ideology as a 'camera obscura' as '[actors] and their relations appear upside down'. But did this strategy work in the sense of allowing the PP to win the battle of ideas with the PAH (to win, in short, a symbolic victory over the PAH)?

This is a difficult question to address and answer because it is hard to find direct evidence in one direction or the other. Thus, while monthly reports provided by the official Spanish statistical office, the Sociological Research Centre (the *Centro de Investigaciones Sociológicas;* CIS),[3] show that home-evictions are hardly ever cited as being among the top problems facing Spaniards on a day-to-day basis, this could hardly be expected in a country facing persistently high unemployment and a continuing parade of corruption scandals. Still, if we consider that the responsibility for economic problems, such as unemployment, are generally attributed to the government in power (the PP), and the fact that the PP is by far the political party most associated with corruption, then it seems that in both the short and long term, the effect of the attack on the PAH for *escraches* could only ever move the right-wing media and unconditional supporters of the PP cause. It seems then, that the obvious absurdity of the two-part equation – PAH = Nazis and PP members = persecuted Jews – has militated against the prospect of any kind of symbolic victory of the PP over the PAH with regard to *escraches*. Meanwhile, the material victories of the state and capital over evictees in the ongoing class war, exacerbated by the economic crisis, continue. To say the least, the materiality and *semiosis* of inequality and class struggle and warfare is complex and multi-levelled in its characteristics, a veritable moving object over time and space.

Conclusion

Inequality and class struggle and warfare are on the rise around the world, and in particular in countries such as Spain, where the recession has hit particularly hard. As noted above, inequality is multidimensional, existing, as it does, around and through unequal basic life-and-death chances (*vital inequality)*, unequal human, civil and material rights (*existential inequality*) and unequal access to material and symbolic resources (*resource inequality*). And these dimensions mediate specific instances of class struggle and warfare, as defined and exemplified in this chapter, where I have provided a brief and admittedly limited analysis of how inequality and class struggle and warfare are constructed via processes of semiosis, focusing on the specific case of home-evictions in Spain.

From Rousseau to Marx, the ownership (or not) of property has been seen as a foundation of inequality in societies, and more recently, it is home ownership (or not), which has had a similar function (Piketty 2014; Dorling 2014b). Grusky and Ku (2008) note how the different assets that mediate and index inequality are interrelated and tend to co-occur, or 'crystallise'. For example, as we have seen in this chapter, control over housing by banks and the wealthy in society is interrelated with (and crystallises around) not only the latter's extensive economic assets, but also with their political power, their social networking, their legal know-how and the human resources that they have at their disposal. The class warfare emergent in the clash between the PP and the PAH, in general over home-evictions and more specifically over *escraches* as a means of protest, shows how different access to crystallised assets comes to map inequality. Where the PAH has been able to match the PP – in terms of grass-roots political power, social networking, legal know-how and human resources – they have on occasion been victorious, and have therefore won a class battle, as opposed to a war, by overthrowing housing equality, albeit momentarily. Such small-scale victories are encouraging and no doubt have made a big difference to the individuals and families involved. In addition, the Spanish municipal elections of May 2015 brought to power left-wing coalitions led by parties with a manifesto promise to stop home-evictions in most of the country's largest cities, including Barcelona, where Ada Colau, one of the founding members of the PAH, was sworn in as mayor in June 2015. This development provides some hope and relief to those living in precarious conditions. However, as I somewhat pessimistically noted above, the ongoing historical process of the interests of capital over the interests of the majority, in more recent times framed as the 1 per cent over the 99 per cent, carries on inexorably, and it will surely take more than a mayor to overturn matters to a significant degree.[4]

Appendix: Transcription conventions

Slash (/) shows the end of a chunk of talk, normally paced.
Pauses are timed to the nearest second, and the number of seconds is put in brackets: (.5).
Question mark (?) indicates question intonation.
Square brackets ([) are used for comments.
Underlining indicates the adoption of a second-party voice as a rhetorical device.

Notes

1 All cited texts that originally appeared in Spanish have been translated into English by the author. The reader can find the original texts in the cited sources.
2 This campaign culminated in the passing of a new public order law in March 2015, the *Ley Orgánica de Seguridad Ciudadana* (Organic Law of Public Security), known to many as the *Ley Mordaza* (the gag law), with the sole support of the PP. This law severely limits the right to freedom of speech in Spain, affecting not only activities such as *escraches*, but also more traditional forms of protest.
3 Available from: www.cis.es/cis/opencms/ES/index.html.
4 Whether real and profound change will come with a new Spanish parliament, after the PP lost a third of its seats and came up short of a majority in the national elections of December 2015 and June 2016, remains to be seen at the time of writing.

References

Aguirre, E, 2013, 'El acoso a los políticos del Partido Popular' ('The harassment of members of the Partido Popular'), available from: http://esperanza.ppmadrid.es/el-acoso-a-politicos-del-partido-popular/ [accessed 1 December 2014].
Atkinson, T, 2015, *Inequality*, Harvard University Press, Cambridge, MA.
Bakhtin, M, 1981, *The dialogic imagination: Four essays*, University of Texas Press, Austin, TX.
Beevor, A, 2006, *The battle for Spain: The Spanish Civil War 1936–1939*, Phoenix, London.
Block, D, 2014, *Social class in applied linguistics*, Routledge, London.
Block, D, 2015, 'Identity and social class: Issues arising in applied linguistics research', *Annual Review of Applied Linguistics*, vol. 35, pp. 1–19.
Block, D, 2016, 'Social class in language and identity research', in *The Routledge handbook of language and identity*, ed. S Preece, Routledge, London, pp. 241–254.
Bourdieu, P, 1984, *Distinction*, Routledge, London.
Bourdieu, P, 2005, *The social structures of the economy*, Cambridge University Press, Cambridge.
Dorling, D, 2011, *Injustice: Why social inequality persists*, The Policy Press, Bristol.
Dorling, D, 2014a, *Inequality and the 1%*, Verso, London.

Dorling, D, 2014b, *All that is solid: How the great housing disaster defines our times, and what we can do about it*, Allen Lane, London.
Duménil, G & Lévy, D, 2011, *The crisis of neoliberalism*, Harvard University Press, Cambridge, MA.
Duménil, G & Lévy, D, 2014, *La gran bifurcation*, Le Découverte, Paris.
Durkheim, E, 1984 [1893] *The division of labor in society*, The Free Press, New York.
Fairclough, N, 2006, *Language and globalization*, Routledge, London.
Fairclough, N, 2010, *Critical discourse analysis: The critical study of language*, 2nd ed., Longman, Harlow.
Forchtner, B, 2014, '*Historia magistra vitae*: The *topos* of history as a teacher in public struggles over self and other representation', in *Contemporary critical discourse studies*, eds. C Hart & P Cap, Bloomsbury, London, pp. 19–43.
Frankel, T, 2012, *The Ponzi scheme puzzle: A history and analysis of con artists and victims*, Oxford University Press, New York.
Grusky, D & Ku, M, 2008, 'Gloom, doom, and inequality', in *Social stratification: Class, race, and gender in sociological perspective*, ed. D Grusky, Westview Press, Boulder, CO, pp. 2–28.
Harvey, D, 2010, *The enigma of capital*, Profile Books, London.
Harvey, D, 2014, *Seventeen contradictions and the end of capitalism*, Profile Books, London.
Kristeva, J, 1986, 'Word, dialogue and novel', in *The Kristeva reader*, ed. T Moi, Blackwell, Oxford, pp. 34–61.
Lorenzo, A, 2013, 'Escrache: Cuando falla la democracia', available from: http://hordago.org/escrache-cuando-falla-la-democracia/ [accessed 10 April 2013].
Marx, K, 1973 [1858], *Grundrisse*, Penguin, Harmondsworth.
Marx, K, 1990 [1867], *Capital: A critique of political economy*, vol. 1, Penguin, Harmondsworth.
Marx, K & Engels, F, 1998 [1846], *The German ideology*, Lawrence & Wisart, London.
Milanovic, B, 2011, *The haves and the have-nots: A brief and idiosyncratic history of global inequality*, Basic Books, New York.
Mirowski, P, 2013, *Never let a serious crisis go to waste*, Verso, London.
PAH, 2014, 'Origin and justification', available from: http://afectadosporlahipoteca.com/ [accessed 10 January 2015].
Peck, J, 2010, *Constructions of neoliberal reason*, Oxford University Press, Oxford.
Piketty, T, 2014, *Capital in the twenty-first century*, Harvard University Press, Cambridge, MA.
Plato, 2007 [380 BC], *The republic, book IV*, Penguin, Harmondsworth.
Plato, 2014 [360 BC], *Laws, book V*, available from: http://classics.mit.edu/Plato/laws.5.v.html [accessed 15 June 2015].
Rachide, I, 2013, 'Cospedal tilda de "nazismo puro" los escraches de los ciudadanos contra políticos', Cadena SER, available from: http://cadenaser.com/ser/2013/04/13/espana/1365810617_850215.html [accessed 13 April 2013].
Savage, M, Devine, F, Cunningham, N, Taylor, M, Li, Y, Hjellbrekke, J, Le Roux, B, Friedman, S & Miles, A, 2013, 'A new model of social class? Findings from the BBC's Great Class Survey Experiment', *Sociology*, vol. 47, no. 2, pp. 219–250.
Therborn, G, 2006, 'Meaning, mechanisms, patterns, and forces: An introduction', in *Inequalities of the world: New theoretical framework, multiple empirical approaches*, ed. G Therborn, Verso, London, pp. 1–58.
Vanguardia, 2012, 'Una mujer se suicida en Málaga tras recibir la orden de desahucio', *La Vanguardia*, 14 December 2012, available from: www.lavanguardia.com/sucesos/20121214/54356355075/mujer-suicida-malaga-recibir-orden-desahucio.html [accessed 15 October 2014].
Weber, M, 1968 [1922], *Economy and society*, vols. 1 & 2, University of California Press, Berkeley, CA.
Weedon, C, 1997 *Feminist practice and poststructuralist theory*, 2nd ed., Blackwell, Oxford.
Wright, E O, 2005, 'Foundations of a neo-Marxist class analysis', in *Approaches to class analysis*, ed. E O Wright, Cambridge University Press, Cambridge, pp. 4–30.

Wodak, R & Meyer, M, eds., 2012, *Methods for critical discourse analysis*, Sage, London.
Wodak, R, de Cillia, R, Reisigl, M & Liebhart, K, 1999, *The discursive construction of national identities*, Edinburgh University Press, Edinburgh.

44
Language under totalitarian regimes
The example of political discourse in Nazi Germany

Andreas Musolff

Introduction: what is special about language use under totalitarian regimes?

Language as a system does not change with political regimes, but the way it is used does, and the changes under totalitarian rule are arguably the most drastic. In his satirical utopia, *1984,* George Orwell characterised these changes as *Newspeak*, a jargon designed to 'meet the ideological needs' of the ruling dictatorship of the fictitious state of 'Oceania'. Its purpose is to establish 'doublethink', the 'power of holding two contradictory beliefs in one's mind simultaneously, and accepting both of them' (Orwell 1984), which finds its most (in)famous expression in the deliberately paradoxical slogans of the 'Ministry of Truth' (i.e. the Ministry of Propaganda): 'WAR IS PEACE, FREEDOM IS SLAVERY, IGNORANCE IS STRENGTH' (Orwell 1984). Orwell based *Newspeak* on the experiences of contemporary propagandistic language during the National Socialist and Stalinist dictatorships, in particular, obfuscation of references to historical events, denial and euphemistic cover-up of state crimes, vilification of dissent, and formulaic and hyperbolic discourse. In the following sections, we will argue that these functional features do indeed form a coherent type of political language use that is of specific socio-political significance and thus needs to be on the agenda of any critically interested and engaged theory of political communication.

Any classification of language use as 'totalitarian' depends on the extra-linguistic category of 'totalitarianism'. This concept was first developed in early and mid-twentieth-century political theory to capture the emergent new forms of dictatorship, that is, involving a state leadership controlling all aspects of society on the basis of a coherent ideology, rather than any 'partial political control' that leaves some social and private niches free from state interference (Arendt 1951; Bracher 1981; Lams et al. 2014; Shorten 2012; Žižek 2001). The notion of such a special new form of dictatorship has been vigorously contested, not least due to its use as a political stigma in the Cold War era (Gleason 1995). Typical examples of totalitarian states are Nazi Germany and its chief ally, the Fascist Dictatorship of Mussolini in Italy, the USSR under Lenin and Stalin, communist China under Mao Zedong, as well as state-like structures originating from the military establishment of terrorist movements as rulers over a territory, such as the so-called 'Islamic State' in Iraq and Syria in 2014 (Barrett 2014). Even this core group of totalitarian states is characterised by considerable variation in terms of power structures. If less typical cases are taken into consideration, 'totalitarianism' as a political category becomes harder to define.

If even political-systems theories find it difficult to agree on a definition of totalitarianism, how can discourse analysis make it into an operative concept? Perhaps, however, this is not the right question to ask as it assumes a primacy of political theory over political discourse. From a critical, Discourse-Historical Approach perspective (within the wider field of Critical Discourse Studies, whose objective is to uncover and analyse the establishment and justification of power hierarchies through discourse, see Fairclough 2014; Wodak 2001, 2013), we can reformulate it so that totalitarian political systems are defined as those that use totalitarian discourses. The latter's purpose is evidently to propagate and legitimise a 'total' control of society through a maximally strict demarcation of '"insiders" vs. enemy-"outsiders"' (Faye 2003; Wodak & Kirsch 1995), so that the latter can be stigmatised, isolated and possibly destroyed. We can then ask the empirical question: which communicative means are being, or have been, used to achieve these purposes? As National Socialist Germany (1933–1945) provides probably the best-documented and most-researched historical case of a (self-consciously) totalitarian state, its discourse will be at the centre of the following sections, with cross-references to similarities to other historical and contemporary discourses.

Analyses of Nazi discourse

The study of National Socialist discourse has been a central feature of linguistic criticism and research and cultural studies for three-quarters of a century. It is powered not least by the ethical and intellectual embarrassment about the fact that its canonical foundation text, that is, Hitler's *Mein Kampf*, published in 1925–26, was in the public domain for several years before the Nazis came to power, so that contemporaries 'could have known' to some extent what was coming. Evidently, the German public sphere showed insufficient resistance to prevent the rise of Nazi propaganda to 'hegemonic' status (Laclau & Mouffe 1985); a few warning voices of journalistic and cultural critics, such as those of Karl Kraus in Austria and Kurt Tucholsky in Germany (Tucholsky 1960 [1930]; Kraus 1933) and abroad were not heard (for overviews of contemporary Anglo-American critiques see Michael & Doerr 2002; Deissler 2003). After the Nazis had gained power in Germany, and later in annexed Austria after 1938 and in the conquered countries after 1939, open criticism of their discourse was impossible in Germany. Instead, the Nazi 'Minister for Public Enlightenment [!] and Propaganda', Joseph Goebbels, and his academic sympathisers advertised their own jargon as expressing a 'liberating' new national world-view (Pechau 1935; Six 1936). They viewed the German language as a 'mirror' of the German people's 'soul', which would be enhanced by the addition of lexical material related to Nazism and the reinterpretation of 'old' words that were allegedly 'infected' by Jewish Marxist ideology. While the scientific value of these publications was minimal (Hachmeister 1998; Simon 2012), such writings are evidence of the Nazis' claim to create a new language that would match the national/racial 'instincts' of the German people. In German academic linguistics, this stance led to a boom in studies of supposed *volk*-ish roots of modern German vocabulary and grammar in archaic Germanic world-views and to academics' co-operation with the SS *Institut Ahnenerbe* ('Forefathers' legacy') (Ahlzweig 1989; Ehlich 1989; Hutton 1999; Kater 2006; Knobloch

2005; Maas 1987; Römer 1989; Simon 1989). Up until the end of the Second World War, Nazi propaganda remained assertive and self-affirming (Evans 2008).

Soon after the war, however, two seminal publications on Nazi discourse came out in East and West Germany, which were based on 'critical insider' observations. One was authored by the Jewish Holocaust survivor and Professor of Romance Philology at Dresden University, Victor Klemperer; it was entitled *LTI* (short for the Latin, *Lingua Tertii Imperii*, (*Language of the Third Reich*), Klemperer 1975). The other publication was a series of articles by the anti-Nazi political scientists and journalists Gerhard Storz, Dolf Sternberger and Wilhelm E Süskind, which was later re-edited as the *Dictionary of inhumanity* (Sternberger, Storz & Süskind 1989). The main objectives of these two – and many following – analyses were: (1) documentation and critique of the Nazis' hate and heroism propaganda; and (2) stigmatisation of lexemes and formulas that expressed Nazi ideology, as a warning to future generations about the deceptive power of manipulative language.

For several decades afterwards, detailed studies on Nazi-language use concentrated on the oratorical performances of Hitler and Goebbels (Beck 2001; Fetscher 1998; Hachmeister & Kloft 2005; Kegel 2006; Kopperschmidt 2003) and on the compilation of detailed dictionaries that documented Nazi-specific lexemes and phrases and their historical origins, as well as on their post-war thematisation as 'Nazi-typical' vocabulary (Brackmann & Birkenhauer 2001; Schmitz-Berning 1998; Wulf 1963). Valuable though such analyses were, they failed to explain Nazi-language use as an integral part of a totalitarian socio-political system. In order to understand this aspect, the contribution of social and political historians in the area of media and propaganda research on Nazi Germany proved essential. One of their major insights from this research was the recognition of the Nazi leadership's unprecedented control over the media through daily supervision of print media, radio and the film industry (Evans 2005, 2008; Tegel 2007; Welch 2007; for comparison with Soviet media, see Taylor 1998; Weiss 2005). This control was by no means monolithic because there was still competition and confusion about competencies within the National Socialist ruling elite (Abel 1990), but such Nazi-internal competition meant only that the public had to put up with a surfeit of propaganda, never with a shortage, and the public was 'educated' to always note and 'learn' the latest discourse-rules (*Sprachregelungen*). Officially approved phrases were constantly refined, reproduced and disseminated, while 'deviant' uses were sanctioned and could only be uttered in private and/or in clandestine contexts. However, even such contexts were monitored by the Nazis' State Police *Gestapo* and the SS's secret 'security service', the SD (*Sicherheitsdienst*), which throughout the whole period of Nazi rule produced reports on privately and clandestinely voiced popular opinion from across the *Reich* (Boberach 1971, 1984; Kulka & Jäckel 2004).

The constant barrage of propaganda events and rituals (e.g. party congresses, national and militaristic memorial events and celebrations), the heavily censored and biased news and development of a 'homely' aesthetics of supposedly indigenous cultural forms, as well as their organisational underpinning (e.g. in the Hitler Youth, Nazified trade unions, the school and university system, and professional institutions) have to be taken into account when assessing the conditions for communication in Nazi Germany. While these aspects have been thoroughly researched from social, cultural and political history perspectives (Bachrach & Luckert 2009; Diesener & Gries 1996; Flessak 1977; Frei & Schmitz 1989; Friedländer 1982), their integration with linguistic and discourse studies, especially with the Discourse-Historical Approach (DHA) are still, to some extent, a desideratum. The DHA aims to 'transcend the purely linguistic dimension' by combining and comparing it with 'the historical, political, sociological and/or psychological dimension' in order to 'triangulate' its research findings in an interdisciplinary account (Reisigl & Wodak 2001; Wodak 2001). Such triangulation is necessary in order to assess which communicative and social weight certain speech acts by specific speakers in particular situations have in shaping discourse overall.

Hitler's *Mein Kampf,* for instance, published several years before his dictatorship had come to power, functioned as a key text throughout the rule of the 'Third Reich', that is, as a blueprint for countless follow-up discourses produced under the Nazi regime. These discourses cannot be properly interpreted without taking into consideration their derivative relationship with Hitler's 'master' version and their uptake in a 'streamlined' public, where open ideological dispute was impossible. These socio-political conditions distinguish totalitarian discourses from other uses of discriminatory and belligerent rhetoric and require a DHA-triangulation of linguistic, socio-psychological and historical factors. In the following section, I attempt such a triangulation of the impact of Hitler's speech at the 1935 Party Congress.

Before we can embark on that case study, however, we need to study one further analytical approach to totalitarian language in addition to the philological-lexicographic and discourse-historical approaches, that is, cognitive (semantic) analysis. Within the wider field of cognitive studies that encompass Cognitive Grammar, psychology and neuro-linguistic approaches, cognitive semantics and especially Conceptual Metaphor Theory (CMT) have reformulated traditional research questions with a view to explaining the *conceptual* conditions of producing and understanding linguistic meaning (Croft & Cruse 2004). Instead of viewing metaphors and other figurative language use as 'special' poetic or rhetorical ornaments, CMT stresses their fundamental function for cognitive 'mappings' and 'blendings' across conceptual domains that underlie all language use (Lakoff & Johnson 1980, 1999; Fauconnier & Turner 2002). Conceptual mappings enable humans to connect diverse domains of experience and knowledge and 'frame' them mentally and communicatively as new concepts. A number of cognitive studies have, for instance, focused on Hitler's use of metaphor in *Mein Kampf* as a case of racist figurative framing (e.g. Chilton 2005; Hawkins 2001; Musolff 2007, 2008, 2010; Rash 2006; for further observations, see Charteris-Black 2005; Goatly 2007). The mapping of biological and religious source inputs (i.e. PARASITE-DISEASE-POISON and DEVIL-PERSONIFIED EVIL) onto the socio-cultural/religious target category of JEWISHNESS resulted in a special type of frame/scenario that depicted the supposed racially constituted 'people's body' (*Volkskörper*) as threatened by a deadly infection caused by the devil-like Jewish 'parasite'-race, which had to be annihilated.

This mapping, which was elaborated in *Mein Kampf,* was reiterated publicly on innumerable occasions after the Nazi takeover in 1933. It appeared in every prominent Nazi speech and was omnipresent by way of public posters, public stalls and propaganda films, such as *The Eternal Jew*. It was explicitly linked to Hitler's repeated 'justifications' for the extermination of European Jewry as a result of their allegedly having unleashed both World Wars against Germany (Herf 2006), and it was even included in manuals of the SS and police units that carried out the mass murders in Eastern Europe (Browning 2004). While the genocide was perpetrated, this PARASITE-ANNIHILATION scenario featured in speeches by Hitler, Goebbels and other Nazi leaders as a 'prophecy' that was 'coming true', that is, that was being implemented literally to ensure that all Jews would physically disappear from the territories under German control. The conceptual framing achieved by this deep discursive entrenchment was much more than a merely occasional use of discriminatory terminology: it served as an invitation to the whole populace to assist or at least collude in the ongoing genocide.

Such an analysis of Nazi genocide propaganda as part of a self-fulfilling metaphor scenario goes beyond its traditional treatment that concentrated on their rhetorical function as a means of stigmatisation (Drommel & Wolf 1978; Volmert 1989). The use of metaphors to denigrate adversaries is indeed a staple of discriminatory discourse and is by no means restricted to totalitarian systems (Sontag 1978; van Dijk 1991). It is, however, only in the latter that it gains policy-shaping force by being turned into a self-confirming scenario that triggers genocidal actions, such as the Nazi Holocaust. *Gestapo* reports on popular opinion and German prisoners of war's secretly recorded conversations show that the PARASITE-ANNIHILATION scenario was in fact well known and understood as announcing the Jewish genocide among the wider German public (Kulka & Jäckel 2004; Musolff 2010; Neitzel & Wälzer 2011). The Nazi-framing of JEWS-AS-PARASITES went far beyond the 'othering' of opponents that is normal in adversarial political discourse. The 'other' of the totalitarian discourse was, as one of the theoreticians of the 'total state', the Nazi jurist Carl Schmitt (1932, 1940), formulated, not just an enemy opposed to the collective national 'self'; rather, it is conceived of as an existential 'foe' whose continued existence implies a fundamental threat to the self, which therefore has the 'sovereign' right to eliminate that 'other'.

Similar uses of the PARASITE-ANNIHILATION scenario as a means to denounce large groups of people as 'anti-social' enemies and justify their elimination can also be found in Soviet Russian discourses in the Leninist and Stalinist eras (Figes 1996; Fitzpatrick 2006) and in Maoist slogans in Communist China (Lu 1999; Lynteris 2013). These 'leftist' versions of PARASITE-ANNIHILATION discourse can be traced back through nineteenth-century Marxism to the 'Jacobin' terrorist strand of French Revolutionary discourse, where it was first used to stigmatise monarchy and aristocracy as corrupted and corrupting parts of the 'people's body' in analogy to bio-parasites (de Baecque 1997; Musolff 2014). Obviously, the precise historical circumstances of such uses of the PARASITE-ANNIHILATION scenario differ from those of the racist versions, but they all have as their common denominator the absolute other-vilification as a frame for genocidal policies. They combine a radical denunciation of whole classes or 'races' as deadly enemies of the supposed elite people with the pseudo-scientific certainty of 'explaining' their impending destruction as objectively necessary and ethically justified.

Case study: how to deliver a perfect speech in a totalitarian state

The annual National Socialist Party Rally in Nuremberg of 1935 was billed as the 'Congress of Freedom', in celebration of the Nazis supposedly having freed Germany from the Versailles Treaty obligations. Today, however, it is chiefly remembered as the occasion when the race laws 'for the Protection of German Blood and Honour' and a newly defined citizenship were proclaimed, which lay at the core of judicial terror against Jews in Germany. The 'Nuremberg laws' excluded Jewish people in principle from German citizenship and from marriage or sexual relations with 'Aryan' (= non-Jewish) Germans (Kershaw 1999, 2008; Longerich 2006). In his main Congress speech, Hitler justified these laws as designed to 'make it possible for the German people to have a tolerable relationship with the Jewish people'; at the same time, he denounced Jews as the 'enemy within' (*innere Feinde*) and threatened that if legal and bureaucratic means did not suffice, the 'living' German nation itself would 'solve' the problem, as quoted in the Nazi newspaper *Völkischer Beobachter* (16 September 1935).

This speech has been thoroughly analysed by historians and political scientists as a milestone in the prosecution of Jewish people in Nazi Germany, and so has its reception in the German public (Gellately 2001; Kulka 1984; Longerich 2006). We have, thus, a detailed picture of the socio-historical context on which to base a discourse-historical assessment of Hitler's announcement; in addition, there is a unique 'reading help' for it by no other than his propaganda chief, Goebbels. On the last day of the Congress, in a special meeting for party propaganda leaders from across the Reich, Goebbels commended Hitler's speech as an exemplary feat of clever propaganda:

> If I make clear in my propaganda that the Jews have absolutely nothing to lose – well, then we mustn't be surprised that they fight back. [...] No, you have to always leave it open-ended, just as the *Führer* did in his masterly speech yesterday: 'We hope that the laws concerning the Jews have opened the chance for a tolerable relationship between the German and the Jewish peoples and ...' [laughter]. That's what I call *skill*! That *works*! [...] if you leave a little chance to them open, then the Jews will say, 'Hey, if we start atrocity propaganda from outside, it'll get worse, so let's keep quiet, *and maybe we can stay on after all*' [laughter, applause]. Above all: the Jews are not going to run away.
>
> (Goebbels 1971)

As their reactions show, the audience was in no doubt about the laws being intended as a basis for the destruction of Jewish life in Germany. Goebbels could use their shared insider knowledge to give them a master-class, as it were, in misleading the wider German and international public, including Jewish people. Colluding or sympathising groups in the Nazi party and the wider populace were thus given to know that antisemitic practices would be condoned as long as they could be 'legitimised' within the terms of the new laws. The non-committed German and international public were discouraged from showing any solidarity or sympathy with the victims, and at the same time reassured that all measures taken would be legal. The Jewish victims were kept in the dark about the future repression and given illusionary hopes until it would be too late for them to take counter-measures. As *Gestapo* reports, diaries and resistance groups' documents show, Hitler and Goebbels' strategy worked: the party's most zealous anti-Jewish activists felt vindicated; the wider German and international public perceived the Führer's proclamation as restoring calm and proving foreign 'atrocity propaganda' about state terror against the Jews wrong; Jewish groups inside and outside Germany were isolated and individuals fooled into postponing immigration and toning down protests (Behnken 1980; Kershaw 2008; Klemperer 1995; Kulka & Jäckel 2004). The only true 'discourse-insiders', that is, ardent party members, were 'promised' the chance for future repression and power-gain beyond the momentary measures, without having to fear criticism or sanction.

This quasi-conspiratorial practice of signalling genocidal intentions to insiders through vague and metaphorical statements was not restricted to prominent public pronouncements, but extended right to the centre of the totalitarian regime and its internal, backstage discourses. The protocol of the so-called 'Wannsee-conference' of January 1942 on logistical details of the Holocaust, which included its top administrators, who among themselves, spoke openly and drastically about the mass-murder methods to be implemented, was, as the minute-taker and policy-implementer, Adolf Eichmann, himself testified in his trial in Jerusalem, deliberately redacted in such a way that any 'over-plain talk and jargon expressions' were replaced by abstract 'office language' (Cesarani 2004; see also Roseman 2002).

Andreas Musolff

Such 'gatekeeping' (Shoemaker & Vos 2009) over access to insider interpretation of official discourse is to some extent a general characteristic of political discourse, but it assumes an extreme form in totalitarian discourse. In less tightly monitored political systems, meanings of official statements remain still negotiable. In totalitarian systems, however, the vast majority of the receivers of political statements are left guessing, with only small circles of insiders having definite knowledge about the concrete implications of policy statements formulated by the power-holders. As long as the latter maintain this privileged access, they maintain an unassailable power over the discourse community, with the added advantage of presiding over a competition among their second- and third-ranking followers for access to authoritative interpretations and membership in central parts of the ruling elite. Observers and critics on the outside are reduced largely to guesswork, as experienced not only by many international commentators on Nazi Germany, but also of the Soviet Union ('Kremlinology'), on Maoist China, or of state-building terrorist groups such as Al Qaeda and 'Islamic State' (Barrett 2014; Matusitz 2013; Schwarz-Friesel & Kromminga 2014).

Absolute control over the public sphere is also a precondition for the seemingly paradoxical tendency in totalitarian discourse to advertise its oppressive practices and treat them at the same time as state secrets or taboos, the very mention of which can trigger repression and genocide. This feature is different from, but complements, the already-discussed 'vagueness': instead of under-determining informative content, it over-determines it through explicitly denying *and* at the same time triumphantly asserting it, leading to a cognitively dissonant mental representation for non-insiders. After the so-called *Kristallnacht* (Crystal Night) state pogrom on 9 November 1938, for instance, which cost several hundred lives and led to the brutal arrest of about 30,000 Jewish people, the *Völkischer Beobachter* (11 November 1938) claimed that 'not a single hair had been touched on a Jewish head'. Anyone who contradicted such obviously misleading information in public was likely to be arrested, given a 'sharp' warning in *Gestapo* custody and put under observation (Kershaw 2008). During the war, reference to the ongoing genocide and/or war crimes, or doubting final victory for Germany would be classed as crimes to 'undermine the war effort', punishable by death. Such bans on any counter-discourse conferred on official propaganda a ritualistic status, so that topics not covered by it became 'taboo' in the sense that even the fact of them being banned fell under a ban.

In order to maintain its taboos, Nazi propaganda operated not just a combination of threats, lies, denials and vague hints, but also used a camouflage terminology, especially for referring to the institutions or practices of oppression. Labels such as *Schutzstaffel* (SS) (protection corps), or *Schutzhaft* (protective custody) for arrest by *Gestapo* or SS, often including transfer to and torture and/or murder in a *Konzentrationslager* (KZ) (concentration camp) suggested a 'protective' character for Nazi repression institutions. Other terms belonged to the field of administrative vocabulary, for example, *Umsiedlung/Transport* (deportation and transport) for transfer to extermination camps in Eastern Europe, *Sonderbehandlung* (special treatment) for torture/murder by *Gestapo*/SS, or *Einsatzgruppen* (task forces) for the murder units (Forster 2009; Klemperer 1975; Wulf 1963). Semantically, such terminology can be classified as 'euphemistic' insofar as neutral- or even positive-sounding labels cover up referents that would normally be given a negative evaluation. Pragmatically, however, the cover-terms, like most euphemisms (Burridge 1998), quickly lost their power to conceal secret facts because the latter were in fact 'open secrets' (Kaplan 1998; Taussig 1999), which everyone was meant to know about and be terrified by. The true referents of SS, KZ, and so on as parts of a system of brutal oppression and state terror were well known to the public, and parts of it actively collaborated with them, for example, by way of mass denunciations (Bankier 1992; Gellately 1990, 2001; Kershaw 1983; Longerich 2006), or stood by passively when witnessing the public humiliation, brutalisation and dehumanisation of the regime's 'enemy'-victims. The post-1945 conceit that adult members of German-speaking communities were fooled by Nazi propaganda's euphemisms is as disingenuous as the excuses of having misunderstood Hitler's PARASITE-ANNIHILATION prophecies and boasts as mere metaphor. In Nazi Germany, as well as in Stalinist Russia and Maoist China, the existence of a secret police that had the task of arresting, torturing and killing enemies of the state was made widely known through the mass media and supported by mass experience, but officially denied and violently suppressed by the 'security agencies' when mentioned in public.

Descriptions of totalitarian discourse as 'euphemistic', 'manipulative' or as 'othering' their victims are in fact understatements because they gloss over their qualitative difference to the biased and polemical character of *all* political language use. Polemical disputes in open societies that allow for public debate without imposing violent sanctions can be antagonising and highly divisive and manipulating (and hence also socially problematic), but they are still based on the assumption that counter-discourses are possible in principle. By contrast, the deceitful discourse of a totalitarian dictatorship takes place against the background of latent state-terrorism, that is, the threat and enactment of denunciation and brutal punishment of any counter-discourse. This special communicative context does not change the conventional meanings of words or utterances, but it distorts their socio-pragmatic value and significance so as to turn them into matters of life and death.

The afterlife of totalitarian discourse and lessons for its critical analysis

The breakdown of a totalitarian regime does not lead automatically to the disappearance of its discourse from the public sphere. Even if the regime's institutions of propaganda and repression are dismantled, as happened in West Germany after 1945, or in the more gradual process of de-Stalinisation in the Soviet Union and Eastern Europe, societies retain for some time totalitarian attitudes, not least due to many of their members being implicated in the former repression systems. These attitudes encouraged, for instance, parts of the Nazi elites and historical 'revisionists' to deny or belittle Nazi atrocities (Engel & Wodak 2013; Lipstadt 1994; Shermer & Grobman 2000; Wodak 2011; for similar tendencies in post-Stalinist Russia and in Eastern Europe: Applebaum 2003; Getty & Naumov 1999; Jones 2013; Kozlov 2013; Kreß 2013; for post-Maoist China: MacFarquhar & Schoenhals 2008). Relying on the public's short memory, these former elites continue to use metaphors and argumentation *topoi* to stigmatise specific victim groups, while at the same time pretending that they are neutral, for example, German and Austrian post-war right-wing politicians reviving antisemitic stereotypes, denouncing opponents as 'rats and flies' or immigrants as 'parasites' (Keller-Bauer 1983; Musolff 2014; Posch et al. 2013; Wodak et al. 1990).

A different, though no less problematic, form of instrumentalisation of Nazi discourse has been its use as a label to denounce political opponents by blaming them for manipulating language 'like the Nazis'. This *topos*, as used in Western countries, fitted the equation of Nazism and Communism as variants of 'totalitarianism', which was particularly fashionable during the Cold War (Dieckmann 2007; Eitz & Stötzel 2007; Forchtner 2013; Niven 2002, 2006; von Polenz 2005). Such ascriptions have little or no basis in scientific discourse-historical research. By contrast, analysing present-day discourses by way of highlighting parallels with empirically based studies of historical-totalitarian language use can help deconstruct the pseudo-rational underpinnings and taboos of recent totalitarian movements, for example, fledgling terror-states such as the 'Islamic State' and Al Qaeda, but also uncover emergent proto-totalitarian discourse tendencies in countries whose publics consider themselves democratic and therefore immune to them, for example, trends to establish globalised neo-liberalism as the only rational form of social order, or the erosion of minority rights through scapegoating. Whether it is immigrants, socially deprived, sexually 'deviant' or 'disabled' groups, any community that allows itself to stigmatise people as 'parasites' on its social self's 'body' is in danger of reinforcing and reifying its boundary-maintaining mechanisms (Douglas 1966) into totalitarian power structures and practices of exclusion.

References

Abel, K-D, 1990, *Presselenkung im NS-Staat: Eine Studie zur Geschichte der Publizistik in der nationalsozialistischen Zeit*, Colloquium Berlin, Berlin.

Ahlzweig, K, 1989, 'Die deutsche Nation und ihre Muttersprache', in *Sprache im Faschismus*, ed. K Ehlich, Suhrkamp, Frankfurt, pp. 35–57.

Applebaum, A, 2003, *Gulag: A history*, Doubleday, New York.

Arendt, H, 1951, *The origins of totalitarianism*, Harcourt Brace, New York.

Bachrach, S & Luckert, S, 2009, *State of deception: The power of Nazi propaganda*, W W Norton, New York.

Bankier, D, 1992, *The Germans and the Final Solution: Public opinion under Nazism*, Blackwell, Oxford.

Barrett, R, 2014, *The Islamic State*, The Soufan Group, New York.

Beck, H-R, 2001, *Politische Rede als Interaktionsgefüge: Der Fall Hitler*, Niemeyer, Tübingen.

Behnken, K, ed., 1980, *Deutschland-Berichte der Sozialdemokratischen Partei Deutschlands (Sopade) 1934–1940*, 7 vols., Petra Nettelbeck/Zweitausendeins, Frankfurt.

Boberach, H, ed., 1971, *Berichte des SD und der Gestapo über Kirchen und Kirchenvolk in Deutschland 1934–1944*, Matthias Grunewald Verlag, Mainz.

Boberach, H, ed., 1984, *Meldungen aus dem Reich, 1938–1945: Die geheimen Lageberichte des Sicherheitsdienstes der SS*, 17 vols., Pawlak, Herrsching.

Bracher, K D, 1981, 'The disputed concept of totalitarianism', in *Totalitarianism reconsidered*, ed. E A Menze, Kennikat Press, Port Washington, NY, pp. 11–33.

Brackmann, K-H & Birkenhauer, R, 2001, *NS-Deutsch. 'Selbstverständliche Begriffe und Schlagwörter aus der Zeit des Nationalsozialismus*, Straelener Manuskripte Verlag, Straelen.

Browning, C, 2004, *The origins of the Final Solution: The evolution of Nazi Jewish policy, September 1939 – March 1942*, with contributions by J Matthäus, Heinemann, London.

Burridge, K, 1998, 'Euphemism with attitude: Politically charged language change', in *Historical linguistics*, eds. M Schmid, J Austin & D Stein, Benjamins, Amsterdam, pp. 57–76.

Cesarani, D, 2004, *Eichmann. His life and crimes*, Heinemann, London.

Charteris-Black, J, 2005, *Politicians and rhetoric. The persuasive power of metaphor*, Palgrave Macmillan, Basingstoke.

Chilton, P, 2005, 'Manipulation, memes and metaphors: The case of *Mein Kampf*', in *Manipulation and ideologies in the twentieth century*, eds. L de Saussure & P Schulz, Benjamins, Amsterdam, pp. 5–45.

Croft, W & Cruse, D A, 2004, *Cognitive linguistics*, Cambridge University Press, Cambridge.

de Baecque, A, 1997, *The body politic. Corporeal metaphor in revolutionary France 1770–1800*, Stanford University Press, Stanford, CA.

Deissler, D, 2003, 'The Nazis may almost be said to have "invented" a new German language'. Der anglo-amerikanische Diskurs über nationalsozialistischen Sprachgebrauch im Zweiten Weltkrieg und in der Besatzungszeit', *Germanistische Linguistik*, vol. 169–170, pp. 319–337.

Dieckmann, W, 2007, '"Belastete Wörter" als Gegenstand und Resultat sprachkritischer Reflexion', *Aptum. Zeitschrift für Sprachkritik und Sprachkultur*, vol. 3, no. 1, pp. 62–80.

Diesener, G & Gries, R, eds., 1996, *Propaganda in Deutschland. Zur Geschichte der politischen Massenbeeinflussung im 20. Jahrhundert*, Wissenschaftliche Buchgesellschaft, Darmstadt.

Douglas, M, 1966, *Purity and danger: An analysis of the concepts of pollution and taboo*, Routledge, London.

Drommel, R H & Wolff, G, 1978, 'Metaphern in der politischen Rede', *Der Deutschunterricht*, vol. 30, pp. 71–86.

Ehlich, K, 1989, 'Über den Faschismus sprechen – Analyse und Diskurs', in *Sprache im Faschismus*, ed. K Ehlich, Suhrkamp, Frankfurt, pp. 7–34.

Eitz, T & Stötzel, G, 2007, *Wörterbuch der "Vergangenheitsbewältigung": Die NS-Vergangenheit im öffentlichen Sprachgebrauch*, Olms, Hildesheim.

Engel, J & Wodak, R 2013, '"Calculated ambivalence" and Holocaust denial in Austria', in *Analysing fascist discourse. European fascism in talk and text*, eds. R Wodak and J E Richardson, Routledge, London, pp. 73–96.

Evans, R J, 2005, *The Third Reich in power, 1933–1939*, Allen Lane, London.

Evans, R J, 2008, *The Third Reich at war, 1939–1945*, Allen Lane, London.

Fairclough, N, 2014, *Language and power*, Longman, London.

Fauconnier, G & Turner, M, 2002, *The way we think: Conceptual blending and the mind's hidden complexities*, Basic Books, New York.

Faye, J-P, 2003, *Introduction aux langages totalitaires*, Hermann, Paris.

Fetscher, I, 1998, *Josef Goebbels im Berliner Sportpalast 1943: "Wollt Ihr den totalen Krieg?"*, Europäische Verlagsanstalt, Hamburg.

Figes, O, 1996, *A people's tragedy. The Russian Revolution 1891–1924*, Pimlico, London.

Fitzpatrick, S, 2006, 'Social parasites: How tramps, idle youth, and busy entrepreneurs impeded the Soviet march to communism', *Cahiers du Monde Russe*, vol. 47, nos. 1–2, pp. 377–408.

Flessak, K-I, 1977, *Schule und Diktatur. Lehrpläne und Schulbücher des Nationalsozialismus. Eine notwendige Erinnerung*, Ehrenwirth, Munich.

Forchtner, B, 2013, 'Legitimizing the Iraq War through the genre of political speeches. Rhetorics of judge-penitence in the narrative reconstruction of Denmark's cooperation with Nazism', in *Analyzing genres in political communication*, eds. P Cap & U Okulska, Benjamins, Amsterdam, pp. 240–265.

Forster, I, 2009, *Euphemistische Sprache im Nationalsozialismus. Schichten, Funktionen, Intensität*, Hempen Verlag, Bremen.

Frei, N & Schmitz, J, 1989, *Journalismus im Dritten Reich*, C H Beck, Munich.

Friedländer, S, 1982, *Kitsch und Tod. Der Widerschein des Nazismus*, tr. M Grendlacher, dtv, Munich.

Gellately, R, 1990, *The Gestapo and German society: Enforcing racial policy 1933–1945*, Oxford University Press, Oxford.

Gellately, R, 2001, *Backing Hitler: Consent and coercion in Nazi Germany*, Oxford University Press, Oxford.

Getty, J A & Naumov, O V, 1999, *The road to terror: Stalin and the self-destruction of the Bolsheviks, 1932–1939*, Yale University Press, New Haven, CT.

Gleason, A, 1995, *Totalitarianism: The inner history of the Cold War*, Oxford University Press, Oxford.

Goatly, A, 2007, *Washing the brain. Metaphor and hidden ideology*, Benjamins, Amsterdam.

Goebbels, J, 1971, *Reden*, ed. H Heiber, 2 vols., Heyne, Munich.

Hachmeister, L, 1998, *Der Gegnerforscher. Die Karriere des SS-Führers Franz Alfred Six*, C H Beck, Munich.

Hachmeister, L & Kloft, M, eds., 2005, *Das Goebbels-Experiment. Propaganda und Politik*, Deutsche Verlags-Anstalt, Munich.

Hawkins, B, 2001, 'Ideology, metaphor and iconographic reference', in *Language and Ideology, vol. II*, in *Descriptive cognitive approaches*, eds. R Dirven, R Frank & C Ilie, John Benjamins, Amsterdam, pp. 27–50.

Herf, J, 2006, *The Jewish enemy: Nazi propaganda during World War II and the Holocaust*, Belknap Press, Cambridge, MA.

Hutton, C M, 1999, *Linguistics and the Third Reich: Mother-tongue fascism, race and the science of language*, Routledge, London.

Jones, P, 2013, *Myth, memory, trauma: Rethinking the Stalinist past in the Soviet Union, 1953–70*, Yale University Press, New Haven, CT.

Kaplan, M A, 1998, *Between dignity and despair: Jewish life in Nazi Germany*, Oxford University Press, Oxford.

Kater, M H, 2006, *Das Ahnenerbe der SS 1935–1945: Ein Beitrag zur Kulturpolitik des Dritten Reiches*, Oldenbourg, Munich.

Kegel, J, 2006, *"Wollt ihr den totalen Krieg?" Eine semiotische und linguistische Gesamtanalyse der Rede Goebbels' im Berliner Sportpalast am 18. Februar 1943*, Niemeyer, Tübingen.

Keller-Bauer, F, 1983, 'Metaphorische Präzedenzen', *Sprache und Literatur in Wissenschaft und Unterricht*, vol. 51, pp. 46–60.

Kershaw, I, 1983, *Popular opinion and political dissent in the Third Reich: Bavaria 1933–1945*, Oxford University Press, Oxford.

Kershaw, I, 1999, *Hitler, 1889–1936: Hubris*, Allen Lane, London.

Kershaw, I, 2008, *Hitler, the Germans, and the Final Solution*, Yale University Press, New Haven, CT.

Klemperer, V, 1975 [1947], *LTI. Notizbuch eines Philologen*, P Reclam Jr., Leipzig.

Klemperer, V, 1995, *Ich will Zeugnis ablegen bis zum letzten: Tagebücher 1933–1945*, 2 vols., Aufbau-Verlag, Berlin.

Knobloch, C, 2005, *Volkhafte Sprachforschung. Studien zum Umbau der Sprachwissenschaft in Deutschland zwischen 1918 und 1945*, Niemeyer, Tübingen.

Kopperschmidt, J, ed., 2003, *Hitler der Redner*, Fink, Munich.

Kozlov, D, 2013, *The readers of Novyi Mir. Coming to terms with the Stalinist past*, Harvard University Press, Cambridge, MA.

Kraus, K, 1933, 'Man frage nicht', *Die Fackel*, no. 888, p. 4.

Kreß, B, ed., 2013, *Totalitarian political discourse? Tolerance and intolerance in Eastern and East Central European Countries – Diachronic and Synchronic Aspects*, in collaboration with K Senkbeil, P Lang, Frankfurt.

Kulka, O D, 1984, 'Die Nürnberger Rassengesetze und die deutsche Bevölkerung im Lichte geheimer NS-Lage- und Stimmungsberichte', *Vierteljahreshefte für Zeitgeschichte*, vol. 32, pp. 582–624.

Kulka, O D & Jäckel, E, eds, 2004, *Die Juden in den geheimen NS-Stimmungsberichten 1933–1945*, Droste, Düsseldorf.

Laclau, E & Mouffe, C, 1985, *Hegemony and socialist strategy: Towards a radical democratic politics*, Verso, London.

Lakoff, G & Johnson, M, 1999, *Philosophy in the flesh: The embodied mind and its challenge to Western thought*, Basic Books, New York.

Lakoff, G & Johnson, M, 2003 [1980], *Metaphors we live by*, University of Chicago Press, Chicago, IL.

Lams, L, Crauwels, G & Șerban, H A, 2014, *Totalitarian and authoritarian discourses. A global and timeless phenomenon?*, P Lang, Frankfurt/M.

Lipstadt, D, 1994, *Denying the Holocaust: The growing assault on truth and memory*, Penguin, London.

Longerich, P, 2006, *"Davon haben wir nichts gewusst!" Die Deutschen und die Judenverfolgung*, Siedler, Munich.

Lu, X, 1999, 'An ideological/cultural analysis of political slogans in communist China', *Discourse & Society*, vol. 10, no. 4, pp. 487–508.

Lynteris, C, 2013, *The spirit of selflessness in Maoist China: Socialist medicine and the new man*, Palgrave Macmillan, Basingstoke.

Maas, U, 1987, *'Als der Geist der Gemeinschaft eines Sprache fand' – Sprache im Nationalsozialismus*, Westdeutscher Verlag, Opladen.

MacFarquhar, R & Schoenhals, M, 2008, *Mao's last revolution*, Belknap Press, Cambridge, MA.
Matusitz, J, 2013, *Terrorism and communication: A critical introduction*, Sage, London.
Michael, R & Doerr, K, 2002, *Nazi-Deutsch/Nazi German: An English lexicon of the Third Reich*, Greenwood Press, Westport, CT.
Musolff, A, 2007, 'Which role do metaphors play in racial prejudice? – The function of antisemitic imagery in Hitler's *Mein Kampf*', *Patterns of Prejudice*, vol. 41, no. 1, pp. 21–44.
Musolff, A, 2008, 'What can Critical Metaphor Analysis add to the understanding of racist ideology? Recent studies of Hitler's antisemitic metaphors', *Critical Approaches to Discourse Analysis Across Disciplines (CADAAD)*, vol. 2, no. 2, pp. 1–10.
Musolff, A, 2010, *Metaphor, nation and the Holocaust. The concept of the body politic*, Routledge, London.
Musolff, A, 2014, 'Metaphorical *parasites* and "parasitic" metaphors: Semantic exchanges between political and scientific vocabularies', *Journal of Language and Politics*, vol. 13, no. 2, pp. 218–233.
Neitzel, S & Wälzer, H, 2011, *Soldaten. Protokolle vom Kämpfen, Töten und Sterben*, S. Fischer, Frankfurt.
Niven, W, 2002, *Facing the Nazi past: United Germany and the legacy of the Third Reich*, Routledge, London.
Niven, W, ed., 2006, *Germans as victims: Remembering the past in contemporary Germany*, Palgrave Macmillan, Basingstoke.
Orwell, G, 1984, *1984*, with a critical introduction and annotations by B Crick, Clarendon Press, Oxford.
Pechau, M, 1935, *Nationalsozialismus und deutsche Sprache*, Hans Adler, Greifswald.
Posch, C, Stopfner, M & Kienpointner, M, 2013, 'German postwar discourse of the extreme and populist right', in *Analysing fascist discourse. European fascism in talk and text*, eds. R Wodak & J E Richardson, Routledge, London, pp. 97–121.
Rash, F, 2006, *The language of violence. Adolf Hitler's Mein Kampf*, P Lang, Frankfurt.
Reisigl, M & Wodak, R, 2001, *Discourse and discrimination. Rhetorics of racism and antisemitism*, Routledge, London.
Römer, R, 1989, *Sprachwissenschaft und Rassenideologie in Deutschland*, Fink, Munich.
Roseman, M, 2002, *The villa, the lake, the meeting. Wannsee and the Final Solution*, Allen Lane, London.
Schmitt, C, 1932, *Der Begriff des Politischen*, Duncker & Humblot, Berlin.
Schmitt, C, 1940, 'Totaler Feind, totaler Krieg, totaler Staat,' in *Positionen und Begriffe im Kampf mit Weimar-Genf-Versailles, 1923–1939*, Hanseatische Verlagsanstalt, Hamburg, pp. 268–273.
Schmitz-Berning, C, 1998, *Vokabular des Nationalsozialismus*, de Gruyter, Berlin.
Schwarz-Friesel, M & Kromminga, J-H, eds., 2014, *Metaphern der Gewalt. Konzeptualisierungen von Terrorismus in den Medien vor und nach 9/11*, Francke, Tübingen.
Shermer, M & Grobman, A, 2000, *Denying history: Who says the Holocaust never happened and why do they say it?* University of California Press, Berkeley, CA.
Shoemaker, P J & Vos, T P, 2009, *Gatekeeping theory*, Routledge, London.
Shorten, R, 2012, *Modernism and totalitarianism: Rethinking the intellectual sources of Nazism and Stalinism, 1945 to the present*, Palgrave Macmillan, Basingstoke.
Simon, G, 1989, 'Sprachpflege im "Dritten Reich"', in *Sprache im Faschismus*, ed K Ehlich, Suhrkamp, Frankfurt, pp. 35–57.
Simon, G, 2012, *NS-Sprache aus der Innensicht. Der Linguist Manfred Pechau und die Rolle seines SS-Sonderkommandos bei dem Massenmord in den Sümpfen Weisrusslands*, available from: http://homepage.uni-tuebingen.de/gerd.simon/pechau.pdf [accessed 10 November 2015].
Six, F A, 1936, *Die politische Propaganda der NSDAP im Kampf um die Macht*, Winter, Heidelberg.
Sontag, S, 1978, *Illness as metaphor*, Vintage Books, New York.
Sternberger, D, Storz, G & Süskind, W E, 1989 [1945], *Aus dem Wörterbuch des Unmenschen*, Ullstein, Berlin.

Taussig, M, 1999, *Defacement. Public secrecy and the labor of the negative*, Stanford University Press, Stanford, CA.
Taylor, R, 1998, *Film propaganda. Soviet Russia and Nazi Germany*, I.B.Tauris, London.
Tegel, S, 2007, *Nazis and the cinema*, Continuum, London.
Tucholsky, K, 1960 [1930], 'Das Dritte Reich', in *Gesammelte Werke in 10 Bänden,* eds., M Gerold-Tucholsky & F J, Raddatz, Rowohlt, Reinbek, vol. 8, pp. 127–128.
van Dijk, T, 1991, *Racism and the press,* Routledge, London.
Volmert, J, 1989, 'Politische Rhetorik des Nationalsozialismus' in *Sprache im Faschismus,* ed. K Ehlich, Suhrkamp, Frankfurt, pp. 137–161.
von Polenz, P, 2005, 'Streit über Sprachkritik in den 1960er Jahren', *Aptum*, vol. 2, pp. 97–111.
Weiss, D, 2005, 'Stalinist vs. fascist propaganda. How much do they have in common?', in *Manipulation and ideologies in the twentieth century,* eds., L de Saussure and P Schulz, Benjamins, Amsterdam, pp. 250–274.
Welch, D, 2007, *Propaganda and the German cinema 1933–1945*, I.B.Tauris, London.
Wodak, R, 2001, 'The discourse-historical approach', in *Methods of Critical Discourse Analysis. Introducing qualitative methods,* eds. R Wodak & M Meyer, Sage, London, pp. 63–94.
Wodak, R, 2011, 'Suppression of the Nazi past, coded languages, and discourses of silence: Applying the Discourse-Historical Approach to post-war antisemitism in Austria', in *Political Languages in the Age of Extremes,* ed. W Steinmetz, Oxford University Press, Oxford, pp. 351–379.
Wodak, R, ed., 2013, *Critical Discourse Analysis*, 4 vols., Sage, London.
Wodak, R & Kirsch, F P, 1995, *Totalitäre Sprache = Langue de bois = Language of dictatorship,* Passagen Verlag, Vienna.
Wodak, R, Nowak, P, Pelikan, J, Gruber, H, de Cillia, R & Mitten, R, 1990, *'Wir sind alle unschuldige Täter'. Diskurshistorische Studien zum Nachkriegsantisemitismus,* Suhrkamp, Frankfurt.
Wulf, J, 1963, *Aus dem Lexikon der Mörder. "Sonderbehandlung" und verwandte Wörter in nationalsozialistischen Dokumenten,* Mohn, Gütersloh.
Žižek, S, 2001, *Did somebody say totalitarianism?* Verso, London.

45
Discursive underpinnings of war and terrorism

Adam Hodges

Introduction

War and terrorism are two forms of political violence that are salient to current debates and future challenges faced both by scholars and the wider public. Whether agreeing with von Clausewitz (1976 [1832]) that war is simply the continuation of politics, or preferring Foucault's (2003, p. 15) suggestion that politics has become 'the continuation of war by other means', it is clear that the collective exercise of, and struggle for, power – one element of politics (Chilton 2004, p. 3) – is all too often associated with violence. Moreover, discourse is central to enabling that violence and formulating responses to it. War as a form of organised group behaviour 'relies upon the organizational capacity of discourse to mobilize forces, direct resources, and legitimize actions' (Hodges 2013a, p. 3). Terrorism as a conceptual category relies upon the discursive practices that define and label the actors and actions involved. How one characterises forms of violence – for example, as 'terrorism' or 'insurgency' or 'guerilla warfare' or 'crimes' – and the actors involved in that violence – for example, as 'terrorists' or 'freedom fighters' or 'criminals' or 'activists' – shapes understandings and constrains responses. Therefore, a better understanding of the discursive processes that undergird political violence can inform projects that seek to rescue politics from violence (Arendt 1970) and engage in a more productive politics based on that other element of the craft: co-operation (Chilton 2004, p. 3).

The analysis provided in this chapter starts with the widely recognised premise among discourse scholars that language does not simply mirror a pre-existing world, but rather, actively constructs that world. Discourse shapes meanings and constrains understandings. With this in mind, I aim to make several points about discourse, war and terrorism in the five main sections that follow. First, discourse constructs the normative ethical principles that legitimise certain forms of violence as acceptable or unacceptable. These ways of thinking in turn influence definitions of terrorism that circulate within and between academic communities and the wider public. Second, from an academic perspective, terrorism can be viewed as a form of political communication that uses violence to communicate a message, even though popular conceptualisations may diverge from this understanding out of political expediency. Third, given the definitional issues surrounding terrorism, it is important to underscore that terrorism is itself a social construct that relies upon the discursive processes that give it meaning. As Jackson (2008, p. 28) notes, 'In an important sense, terrorism does not exist outside of the definitions and practices that seek to enclose it.' Conceptualising forms of violence as terrorism draws upon familiar domains of experience (such as ideas about crime, war and ideological movements) to construct understandings and shape/ constrain responses. Fourth, justifications for political violence, including the 'call to arms' that rallies a nation to war, utilise political narratives that construct understandings of the world. Narrative excels at organising perceptions and drawing causal connections to shape experience; and narrative represents a potent tool in the political domain to shape images of socio-political reality. Finally, central to such narratives is the 'us' versus 'them' binary that undergirds all forms of political violence. 'This division of humanity into groups draws from the need to organize and categorize the world around us, but during times of war this process becomes exaggerated to produce invidious distinctions with deadly consequences' (Hodges 2013a, p. 6). Semiotic processes are central to forming this in-group versus out-group opposition. I develop these points further in the sections that follow.

Legitimacy and political violence

As a form of 'organized, purposeful group action, directed against another group…involving the actual or potential application of lethal force' (Ferguson 1984, p. 5; 1990, p. 26), the modern view of war prototypically conceptualises it as armed conflict between the military forces of nation-states (interstate war) or between factions within a state (intrastate, or civil war). The centrality of the nation-state within this modern conception of war arises from the political ordering of the world after the Peace of Westphalia in 1648, which recognised the sovereignty of territorial states. Although the Westphalian system did not eliminate war, it attempted to regulate it as a contest between sovereign states and abolish the type of ideologically driven wars of annihilation experienced during the Holy Roman Empire (Kochi 2007, p. 271). Along with the Westphalian order came recognition of the state's monopoly on the legitimate use of violence (Weber 2004 [1919]).

Legitimacy in the realm of warfare depends greatly upon a discursive process that positions some forms of political violence as 'legitimate' versus other forms as 'illegitimate.' Moreover, as van Leeuwen (2007) discusses, legitimisation always occurs within a framework of accepted norms. The legitimisation of the violence associated with modern warfare rests upon the normative philosophical framework of Just War Theory (Moseley 2009; Orend 2005), an ethical doctrine that reaches back to Aristotle, Cicero and Augustine, with contributions by thirteenth-century theologian and philosopher Thomas Aquinas (Aquinas 1985 [1274]). As the moral justification for war continues to be discussed and debated by contemporary philosophers (Walzer 2000, 2008 *inter alia*), Just War Theory provides a robust scaffold upon which states construct the right to enter into war (*jus ad bellum*), the actions taken during war (*jus in bello*), and the agreements entered into after war (*jus post bellum*). The tenets of Just War Theory are not merely important for understanding the way modern wars are legitimised, but also for understanding the way other forms of political violence, such as terrorism, are conceptualised. Although violent actions are typically legitimised or delegitimised vis-à-vis this normative framework, the outcome of such discursive processes does not necessarily guarantee that a close fit exists between the actions and normative categories in actual fact. In other words, categorising and justifying political violence is very much a political act open to varying degrees of contestation.

The seeds for understanding terrorism as a form of political violence can be seen in Schmitt's (2004 [1963]) *Theory of the partisan* in which he outlines what he saw as a new type of warfare emerging in the twentieth century. For Schmitt, the partisan refers to an irregular fighter that rises up to defend the homeland from outside attack. The national resistance movements against Nazi Germany during the Second World War provide models for the partisan, with the most effective being the Yugoslav Partisans led by Josip Broz Tito. Although conceptually distinct from regular uniformed troops, and hence lying outside the Westphalian conception of 'legal' forms of warfare, partisans are nevertheless afforded legitimacy by Schmitt insofar as they exhibit a defensive and *telluric* (i.e. tied to a specific territory) character. The partisan fights a 'real enemy' (e.g. foreign invader) that threatens the territory in which the partisan resides; once that territory is liberated, the fighting ceases. This 'fundamental restriction of enmity' (Schmitt 2004, p. 66) to a limited territorial conflict conforms to the Westphalian order, and the defensive posture aligns with Just War Theory, even if the forms of irregular warfare adopted by the partisan do not.

Schmitt contrasts the legitimate 'true partisan' with what he describes as the revolutionary fighter – a partisan whose political goals extend beyond the aims of territorial liberation. For the revolutionary 'terrorist,' violence is employed for a political cause that reaches beyond spatially limited resistance movements. Unlike the restriction of enmity exhibited by the true partisan, for the revolutionary fighter – modelled after Lenin – the political struggle is taken up against an absolute (even if vague) enemy. Whereas both the true partisan and revolutionary partisan blur the line between civilians and military as they employ irregular and hence illegal tactics, only the true partisan holds legitimacy per the modern conception of warfare. As Schmitt's discussion implies, it is not so much the tactics or forms of violence employed, but rather who employs those tactics and towards what ends, which determines the legitimacy of the violence. Political violence tied to the state – including irregular forces linked to the state – is often legitimised while political violence practised by non-state actors is delegitimised.

While in theory the revolutionary zeal of the terrorist may be cleanly viewed as conceptually distinct from the 'true partisan,' in practice, the legitimacy of political violence exercised by any actor relies upon a discursive process whereby 'who is considered a civilian, how innocence can be measured, what the real intentions of often clandestine actors might be and what counts as a political aim, are all highly contested and subject to competing claims' (Jackson 2008, p. 28). As Wodak (2006) shows in her study of the discourse in Austria over the *Wehrmacht's* role in war crimes during the Second World War, political violence perpetrated by traditional state militaries during times of war is subject to extensive legitimisation strategies to exculpate those involved in actions that violate the norms of modern warfare. Likewise, in a study of Israeli secondary school history textbooks, Peled-Elhanan (2010) shows how excesses carried out by the Israeli Defense Forces during the 1948 war are legitimised as within the acceptable bounds of war. In contrast to legitimisation strategies employed to justify the state's monopoly on the use of force, political organisations that represent threats to established political orders are often subject to delegitimisation through their labelling as 'terrorist organisations'. This can be seen in the cases of the Palestinian Liberation Organisation in its struggle for the liberation of Palestine, or the African National Congress during South Africa's apartheid era, both of which have histories of being discursively dismissed as terrorist organisations.

Crucially, acts of political violence do not contain their own meaning. We must give them meaning by constructing their significance out of frameworks of prior experience, and interpreting the meanings of the contested concepts that are used to categorise certain actions as 'illegitimate', as targeting 'innocents', and so forth. In this way, there is nothing inherent in violent acts labelled 'terrorism' that automatically makes them so (Jackson 2008, p. 28; Schmid & Jongman 1988, p. 101). As Jackson (2008, p. 28) argues, 'The reality is that terrorism is a social fact rather than a brute fact. Although acts of violence are experienced as brute facts, the wider cultural-political meaning of those acts as "terrorism"… is decided through symbolic labelling, social agreement and a range of inter-subjective practices'.

The ontologically unstable and politically malleable status of terrorism as a conceptual category can be seen in the many instances where governments refer to resistance fighters engaged in civil warfare as 'terrorists', even if they attack traditional military targets. The ubiquitous and unqualified use of the term 'terrorists' by US officials to refer to any fighter engaged in insurgent warfare during the prolonged conflict in Iraq after the 2003 invasion is a case in point. Many of the fighters could just as easily have been characterised as 'partisans' in Schmitt's (2004) terms, engaged in a defensive resistance against the invaders and post-invasion government.

Just as ubiquitous are instances where governments refer to street protestors or oppositional political movements as 'terrorists', as they seek to banish the groups from the political process and deny legitimacy to their cause. This can be seen in the political struggles in Egypt after the Arab Spring uprising. As power changed hands over the years that followed, from Hosni Mubarak to Mohamed Morsi to Abdel Fattah el-Sisi, the only consistency in the use of the term 'terrorists' was the way each government in turn used it as a label against its own domestic political rivals. Through its use to label various actors, from student pro-democracy protestors to ex-President Morsi, who was tried and sentenced to death (later overturned) for conspiring to commit 'terrorist acts', the fungibility of terrorism as a political concept becomes evident.

As Jackson (2008, p. 28) emphasises, 'as a phenomenon, terrorism is constituted by and through the discursive practices which make it a concrete reality for politicians, law enforcement officials, the media, the public, academics and so on'. The next two sections examine some of the practices through which official definitions of terrorism are formulated and, in turn, by which public understandings and government policies are shaped.

Terrorism as a form of political communication

As a form of political communication that could be potentially employed by any actor involved in political struggle, terrorism involves 'the deliberate targeting of innocents in an effort to convey a message to another party' (Richardson 2000, p. 29). The use of violent acts to convince or persuade audiences stretches back to the invention of modern terrorism in the nineteenth century when, as Schmid (2004, p. 205) points out, it 'was known as "propaganda by the deed"' (see also, Schmid & de Graaf 1982). In combining the coercive effects of violence with the persuasive effects of propaganda, terrorism employs violence in an effort to coerce and persuade a wider audience into some type of action. The ultimate addressees of terrorist acts – the 'overhearers' in Goffman's (1976, 1981) terms – are therefore not the directly targeted victims, but a wider audience that simultaneously targets multiple addressees with multiple messages. The addressees may include 'others from the group of the victim, the public at large, or, more narrowly, members of the constituency of the terrorist' (Schmid 2004, p. 207). Given the communicative dimension of the violence, the targets and the manner in which they are attacked carry symbolic meaning. Moreover, the responses to the acts – particularly the resulting media coverage – work to generate publicity for the terrorists' cause and amplify the message.

This perspective on terrorism, widely held among scholars, places a focus on the 'characteristics of the act itself' (Jackson 2008, p. 26). Namely, terrorism involves an indirect strategy whereby one entity (the direct victim) is deliberately targeted in an effort to pressure another entity (the wider public or government bodies). In this way, terrorism is defined as a form of violent coercion intended to propagate fear and intimidation beyond the immediate scene of the violence to achieve political aims. The political motives behind the acts distinguish terrorism from other forms of violence (e.g. violence used to commit a crime for monetary gain such as during an armed bank robbery). In addition, the fact 'that terrorism instrumentalizes its victims' separates it from the use of violence during war that seeks to directly degrade an opponent's ability to fight (Jackson 2008, p. 29; see also, Schmid 2004, p. 203). According to this perspective, terrorism could be adopted as a strategy by any type of organisation. Just as it can be used by non-state actors, it could equally be used by states as a strategy against enemies during war (or peacetime) or to quash domestic dissent.

Yet, given the contested nature of what forms of violence constitute legitimate uses of force, labelling acts as terrorism often hinges on how that question of legitimacy is resolved; one way to resolve the question is through the use of actor-based definitions that focus on who carries out the violence. The labelling of certain acts as terrorism therefore comes down to who is afforded political legitimacy. Although such an approach tends to be favoured by politicians and security officials, as Jackson (2008, p. 25) points out, 'it is not uncommon to see researchers adopt an actor-based definition in the literature'. As a result, the interests of Western states can be ratified by the authoritative pronouncements of academics. Note, in particular, the US Department of State's definition, which appears in Title 22 of the United States Code, Section 2656f(d): 'The term "terrorism" means premeditated, politically motivated violence perpetrated against noncombatant targets by subnational groups or clandestine agents, usually intended to influence an audience' (US Department of State 2001; see also Federal Bureau of Investigation, ND; National Institute of Justice 2007). Here, acts of terrorism are confined to 'subnational groups,' which works to exclude states from consideration as users of terrorism, and thereby preserve the state's monopoly on the legitimate use of violence (Weber 2004 [1919]).

This definitional move is quite intentional. The Deputy Director of the White House Task Force on Terrorism in 1985, Edward Peck, noted of the working group's attempts to define terrorism, '...they asked us to come up with a definition of terrorism that could be used throughout the government. We produced about six, and each and every case, they were rejected, because careful reading would indicate that our own country had been involved in some of those activities' (Peck 2006). From an academic perspective, actor-based definitions prove problematic in that they exclude repressive forms of political violence carried out by governments against their own populations as well as violent actions carried out by state militaries against civilian targets in other nations. As Jackson (2008, p. 27) argues, 'scholars should be highly suspicious of any and all attempts by states to define terrorism in ways that conveniently absolve what they or their agents do from being considered terrorism'. Public conceptions of terrorism ultimately rest upon the outcomes of political debates that call into question the assumptions that undergird officially ratified definitions.

Conceptualisations of terrorism

Beyond explicit definitions, the central frameworks that have commonly been invoked in public discourse to make sense of terrorist acts are the war frame, the crime frame, or a combination of the two. As Lakoff (2001) writes, 'The crime frame entails law, courts, lawyers, trials, sentencing, appeals, and so on'. Alternatively, the war frame talks of 'enemies', 'battles', 'casualties', and whole nations (rather than just individuals or particular groups) being under attack (Hodges 2011, p. 27). Importantly, the way in which acts of terrorism are conceptualised holds implications for how governments respond. Whereas a violent crime is dealt with through the criminal justice system, an act of war is dealt with on the battlefield. As then-President George W Bush positioned the US response to the events of 9/11 within the framework of war, the resulting 'war on terror' discourse effectively erased the criminal justice perspective from consideration in favour of a highly militarised response that led to very real wars in Afghanistan and Iraq. The approach, of course, was not without its critics; public discourse sometimes featured explicit debate over how best to make sense of, and respond to, terrorism, as can be seen in the following excerpt from President Bush's 2004 State of the Union Address (quoted in Hodges 2011, p. 28; the italicised words represent elements that invoke the crime and war frames).

> I know that some people question if America is really in a war at all. *They view terrorism more as a crime*, a problem to be solved mainly with *law enforcement* and *indictments*. After the World Trade Center was first attacked in 1993, some of *the guilty* were *indicted*, and *tried*, and *convicted*, and *sent to prison*. But the matter was not settled. The terrorists were still training and plotting in other nations, and drawing up more ambitious plans. After the chaos and carnage of September the 11th, *it is not enough to serve our enemies with legal papers*. The terrorists and their supporters *declared war* on the United States, and *war* is what they got.
> (George W Bush's 2004 State of the Union Address, quoted in Hodges 2011, p. 28)

From the perspective of terrorists themselves, the conceptualisation of terrorism as war (rather than as crime) merges well with the political motivations behind the acts. As Schmid (2004, pp. 202–203) notes, 'terrorists, rather than seeing themselves as criminals, generally prefer to view themselves as "warriors"'. After all, to be viewed as a 'criminal' is to be universally condemned as a lawbreaker acting out of selfish motives, but to be viewed as a 'warrior' is to be seen as a hero, much like Schmitt's (2004) 'partisan', carrying out brave actions for a shared cause. Likewise, given the widely accepted pejorative connotations of 'terrorism' and 'terrorists' in contemporary discourse, those engaged in political violence often eschew those labels in favour of the warrior model. As with 'criminal', to be branded a 'terrorist' is to be stripped of the political legitimacy afforded real soldiers and warriors. Within the framework of war, terrorism implies involvement in the excesses of war – that is, the types of actions routinely condemned by the tenets of *jus in bello* and codified in The Hague Regulations and Geneva Conventions. Therefore, to be a terrorist is to be denied recognition as a heroic warrior and to be stripped of political legitimacy. In this way, even though governments such as the US government may militarise their response to terrorism and deal with it primarily outside the criminal justice model, the discourse emphasises that the enemy consists of 'terrorists' rather than 'soldiers'.

Yet an imperfect fit exists between terrorism and war; therefore, in President Bush's 'war on terror' narrative, he emphasises that this is 'a new kind of war' (Hodges 2011, p. 47), one that is fought against an enemy that represents an ideological movement: 'Our war against terror is not a war against one terrorist leader, or one terrorist group. Terrorism is a movement, an ideology that respects no boundary of nationality, or decency' (Hodges 2011, p. 37). In this way, terrorism is conceptualised not only through the war frame, but it is defined as an ideology or movement. That is, terrorism comes to be seen as the ends rather than the means. The strategy morphs into a creed. This discursive move obscures the perspective discussed earlier that defines terrorism as a strategy with underlying political motivations. It works to erase those motivations along with the socio-historical origins of the acts in favour of viewing them as pure 'evil'. In turn, this sets up the binary opposition in the war narrative between 'good' and 'evil', which helps justify a war against a dehumanised enemy.

Although viewing terrorism as an ideology works well from the perspective of politicians seeking to rally a nation to war, it fails to fully grasp the complexities of terrorism as a form of political violence. As Tilly (2004, pp. 11–12) notes, 'Properly understood, terror is a strategy, not a creed. Terrorists range across a wide spectrum of organizations, circumstances, and beliefs. Terrorism is not a single causally coherent phenomenon. No social scientist can speak responsibly as though it were'. However, as Jackson (2008, p. 25) points out, 'a surprising number of researchers and pundits', in addition to 'political leaders and security officials', have accepted the conceptualisation of terrorism as a totalising ideology. This merely reinforces the view that to deal with terrorism demands war as the only viable strategy, foreclosing other understandings and approaches to the problem. Moreover, it positions the 'war on terror' as a type of war that, as Devji (2005, p. 156) describes, 'leaves behind all enemies of a traditional kind to contend with something more metaphysical than empirical'. The global scope of such a war against an abstract enemy (i.e. 'terror' or 'terrorism') is quite similar to the way Schmitt's revolutionary partisan moves beyond a defensive, telluric position to wage war against an absolute enemy that must not only be defeated, but annihilated (Chandler 2009). In many ways, the 'war on terror' does represent a 'new kind of war', as Bush exhorts, a war that disrupts traditional conceptions of war, as evidenced from various actions, policies and legal strategies associated with the US response to 9/11, from the use of so-called 'extraordinary rendition' (i.e. government-sponsored abduction) to the designation of prisoners as 'enemy combatants' to the adoption of torture under the euphemistic label 'enhanced interrogation methods'.

Ultimately, to recognise terrorism as a discursive construction – as with the justifications of war discussed in the next section – is to recognise that our understandings of the world are very much dependent upon the way language operates in the service of interested positions to construct socio-political reality. The next section elaborates on the way language serves to bring about the reality of war.

Narrative constructions of war

Central to political discourse as it relates to war is the need to legitimise the use of force and mobilise group support for any campaign of violence. To build a following, leaders must outline a history and construct an image of events and actors in the world that brings the group to the 'inevitability' of conflict. Narrative is a prime means towards those ends. After all, 'we organize our experience and our memory of human happenings mainly in the form of narrative – stories, excuses, myths, reasons for doing and not doing, and so on' (Bruner 1991, p. 4). With this in mind, van Leeuwen (2007) includes *mythopoesis* as one of four major legitimisation strategies.

The power of narrative in constructing group understandings of the world comes from the common view of 'narratives as icons of events' (Bauman 1986, p. 6). That is, narratives are seen as simply mirroring events as external referents. As Bauman (1986, p. 6) points out, this view that events are 'somehow antecedent or logically prior to the narratives that recount them' holds even for fictional narratives. This view is helped along by the language ideology of referentialism (Silverstein 1979), which maintains that the role of language is simply to convey information. As a result, events are positioned as pre-existing information to 'report'. Narrative becomes the tool to do the reporting, ostensibly representing the external world in a transparent manner. Yet, as discourse scholars widely recognise, narrative does not merely reflect a pre-existing world, but discursively constructs that world – whether the fictional world of literature or the real world of everyday interaction. In this sense, as Bauman (1986, p. 6) explains, 'events are not the external raw materials out of which narratives are constructed, but rather the reverse: Events are abstractions from narrative. It is the structures of signification in narrative that give coherence to events in our understanding.' In other words, through the use of narrative, we give meaning to the people, places and events that surround us by naming protagonists, defining who we are in relation to them, attributing motivations to others, and providing explanations of the world in which we live. Importantly, this narrative process provides an important means for constructing social reality in line with one or another group's view of the world.

In the 'call to arms' rhetoric that operates to manufacture public consent for war in democracies, the 'justification [for war] is embodied in a dramatic narrative from which, in turn, an argument is extracted' (Campbell & Jamieson 2008, p. 224). Forming the dramatic starting point for the narrative is what Labov and Waletzky (1967) term a 'precipitating event'. This event represents a 'breach' from the canonical expectations of everyday life (Bruner 1991). In the 'call to arms' narratives rehearsed by US presidents, this breach corresponds to what is invariably described as 'an act of raw aggression' that is 'deliberate' and 'unprovoked', coming from an enemy 'without warning' (Hodges 2013b, p. 53). The precipitating event forms the *casus belli* for the impending conflict, setting up a military response as necessary and inevitable, even if it is said to be regrettable. Furthermore, it positions the 'enemy' as the aggressor who started the conflict, and thereby positions the narrator's side as simply acting in self-defence. Any shared culpability for bringing about the conflict is dealt with through the ideological process of *erasure* whereby '[f]acts that are inconsistent with the ideological scheme either go unnoticed or get explained away' (Irvine & Gal 2000, p. 38). That is, regardless of whether the narrator's role in the conflict is defensive or offensive in actual fact, the narration works to position it strictly as defensive (Hodges 2013b, p. 56). The construction of the 'call to arms' narrative in this manner works to justify subsequent military actions in line with the tenets of *jus ad bellum* (Hodges 2013b, pp. 51–53).

As seen here, narratives 'depict a temporal transition from one state of affairs to another' (Ochs 1997, p. 189). Although this transition entails recounting a series of past events as the basis for the narrative, narratives can also be future orientated. For example, Dunmire examines the narrative of the future in US national security documents, which serves 'to legitimize US global supremacy as a military power' (Dunmire 2013, p. 8). The exigency for the future-orientated narrative is the need to convince a US public expectant of a lasting post-Cold War peace of 'an unprecedented range of threats and actors' (Dunmire 2013, p. 28; quoting USCNS/21st Century, 1999, p. 46) to justify increased military expenditures and postures.

Notably, 'the kinds of things people do in narratives seem to repeat themselves over and over again' across different narratives (Toolan 1988, p. 4). In other words, as Toolan describes, there is a certain degree of 'prefabrication'. Another way of discussing this is in terms of genre. As 'orienting frameworks' (Hanks 1987, p. 670) or 'conventional guidelines or schemas' (Bauman 2004, p. 5), genres aid 'the hermeneutic task of making sense of human happenings' (Bruner 1991, p. 5). On top of a pre-fabricated generic framework, the 'particulars' of a given narrative are 'filled in' so that the '"suggestiveness" of a story lies, then, in the emblematic nature of its particulars, its relevance to a more inclusive narrative type' (Bruner 1991, p. 7). This provides for what Chandler (2007, p. 67) terms 'generic realism', where the narrative adheres closely to our expectations (based on generic precedents) for the types of characters we encounter and the actions they undertake. In other words, the more tightly a particular narrative adheres to a widely recognised generic precedent, the easier it is to be taken in by 'narrative seduction' (Bruner 1991, p. 7), or to 'fall into a "suspension of disbelief" so that alternative scenarios or interpretations fail to be considered or given adequate play' (Hodges 2013b, p. 51).

In constructing understandings of terrorism, narratives have commonly revolved around the 'familiar human plights' (Bruner 1991, p. 12) of war and crime. The narrative of the 'war on terror' promoted by the Bush administration after the events of 9/11, as discussed earlier, exemplifies the use of the war genre for constructing a war narrative, and thereby building consensus for a response to terrorism in line with that genre's expectations (Hodges 2011). By adhering to the 'generic presidential war narrative' (Hodges 2013b) discussed earlier, President Bush set up a convincing narrative that worked to foreclose all but a single interpretation for the events of 9/11 and the US's subsequent response to Al Qaeda's atrocities. The 'call to arms' narrative succeeded in garnering public support for, not just a war in Afghanistan, but also a second (and arguably unrelated) war in Iraq.

The power and import of the 'war on terror' narrative employed by the Bush administration can be seen in the way it has been taken up and 'colonized' (Chouliaraki & Fairclough 1999) in settings removed from the US response to 9/11. For example, Erjavec (2009) and Erjavec and Volcic (2007) illustrate the way Serbian intellectuals and media appropriated the 'war on terror' discourse to recharacterise the conflict in the former Yugoslavia. As one of Erjavec and Volcic's (2007, p. 196) interviewees describes it, 'We were fighting the Osama terrorists by ourselves already then'. This illustrates how the 'war on terror' narrative, once established and widely circulated around the world, can be appropriated and recontextualised to legitimise divergent political goals.

As van Leeuwen (2007) discusses, there are various ways that narrative can be employed in the process of legitimisation, such as through the telling of moral tales, or cautionary tales. Forchtner (2013) illustrates one type of cautionary tale in his analysis of then-Prime Minister of Denmark Anders Fogh Rasmussen's speech to justify the Iraq war. In his speech, Rasmussen pointed to Denmark's past wrongdoing during the Second World War to make the case for justifying its role in the 2003 invasion of Iraq. The self-critical stance allowed Rasmussen to claim to have learned the lessons of history and to stake out the moral high ground as he made his case for war.

Clearly, as Foucault (1971) argues, discourse is the power to be seized. In particular, the power of political narratives to construct particular visions of socio-political reality holds real-world consequences in terms of manufacturing consent for war. In this vein, Dunmire (2013) raises an important point relevant to all the examples of political narrative discussed in this section – namely, the issue of 'narrative rights'. As Ochs (1997, p. 203) argues of narrative more generally, the ability to 'represent and reflect upon events…may be asymmetrically allocated, granting reflective rights to some more than others'. Within the political arena, leaders and official government commissions are imbued with 'the *delegated power* of the spokesperson' (Bourdieu 1991, p. 107). Critically, that power affords such speakers and writers, as Gal (1991, p. 197) says of power more generally, 'more than an authoritative voice in decision making', but also 'the ability to define social reality, to impose visions of the world'.

Discourse of us versus them

Central to any narrative are the characters that populate the plotline. Since to wage war requires an 'enemy' and a united front to fight against that enemy, political war narratives revolve around the delineation of a clearly defined out-group (qua 'enemy') in contradistinction to a united alliance that sets aside internal differences (even if only temporarily) to form a distinct in-group. The constitution of the in-group and out-group relies upon 'constructive strategies' in discourse (van Leeuwen & Wodak 1999, p. 92). As socio-cultural linguists emphasise, the identity of groups in times of war (as with identity more generally) 'is the product rather than the source of linguistic and other semiotic practices' (Bucholtz & Hall 2005, p. 585). This means that rather than viewing identity as an internal psychological state, or fully formed social position that exists prior to interaction, identity emerges from social and cultural interaction. Within the narrative construction of socio-political reality, the identities that populate that reality are very much a product of semiotic processes that construct the binary of 'us' versus 'them'.

In their discussion of identity construction, Bucholtz and Hall (2004, *inter alia*) put forth several *tactics of intersubjectivity* language users adopt to position the self, and others in relation to that self. These tactics revolve around the relations of similarity/difference, genuineness/artifice and authority/delegitimacy (Bucholtz & Hall 2005, p. 598). For example, in the 'war on terror' narrative discussed earlier, President Bush employs the tactic of *adequation* to position Saddam Hussein's Iraq and the terrorist group Al Qaeda as two faces of the same overarching 'enemy' in the 'war on terror' (Hodges 2011, p. 64ff). 'The term *adequation* emphasizes the fact that in order for groups or individuals to be positioned as alike, they need not – and in any case cannot – be identical, but must merely be understood as sufficiently similar for current interactional purposes' (Bucholtz & Hall 2005, p. 599). The adequation of Iraq and Al Qaeda is accomplished by placing them in the same conceptual category of 'terrorists', equating the otherwise disparate actors in world affairs by imposing upon them a moral and political equivalence (Hodges 2011, p. 71ff). In part, this is accomplished through the incorporation of the lexeme 'terror' into alliterative phrases that draw together the two throughout President Bush's speeches (e.g. 'terror cells and terror states', 'terrorists and tyrants') and the general characterisation of Saddam Hussein's Iraq in terms of terror (e.g. 'practices terror', 'its drive toward an arsenal of terror') in reference to his alleged possession of weapons of mass destruction, or WMDs. The historically contingent nature of the 'enemy' in times of war is well represented in this example through the effective creation of sufficient sameness between a nation-state governed by a repressive dictatorial regime, but also a non-state terrorist organisation that had openly professed hostility to Saddam's regime and others like it in the Middle East (Hodges 2011, p. 67).

Van Dijk's (1998, p. 267) concept of the 'ideological square' provides further insight into the ideological underpinnings of the construction of identities in times of war. As narrators set up the binary distinction between 'us' and 'them', they fit either side of the divide into different parts of the square through the common process of positive self-presentation and negative other-presentation. On one side of the divide, speakers express/emphasise positive aspects and suppress/de-emphasise negative aspects about 'us'. On the other side of the binary, speakers express/emphasise negative aspects and suppress/de-emphasise positive aspects about 'them'. Through *erasure* (Irvine & Gal 2000, p. 38) negative traits about 'us' and positive traits about 'them' are often concealed through their simple absence in the discourse. In turn, the largest investment of discursive work occurs in the form of expressing and emphasising positive characteristics about 'us' and negative characteristics of 'them'.

Through this process, the resulting out-group becomes the polar opposite of the in-group. This can be seen in the generic presidential war narrative discussed earlier where the attributes assigned to the out-group – namely, practice aggression and deception, break international agreements, lack legal and moral authority, lack unity – are diametrically opposed to those assigned to the in-group – namely, defend against aggression, follow the rule of law, possess legal and moral authority, possess unity (Hodges 2013b, p. 61). The construction of this dichotomy works to increase the social, political and moral distance between the in-group and the out-group. In particular, the moral distancing is accomplished through the 'out-casting' of the enemy (Lazar & Lazar 2004). In this out-casting, the values of the out-group are positioned as wholly other than the values of the in-group. Where in-groups stand for peace and freedom, out-groups become the 'enemies of freedom' and 'enemies of peace' (Lazar & Lazar 2004, p. 227). Notably, the vilification of the other – which works to strip the enemy of its humanity (a prerequisite for carrying out organised group violence against another group) – contains decidedly religious underpinnings in President Bush's post-9/11 discourse (Chernus 2006; Silberstein 2002). Such moral evaluation represents one of the four common legitimisation strategies used in discourse (van Leeuwen, 2007; van Leeuwen & Wodak 1999). Lazar and Lazar (2004, p. 236) use the term '(e)vilification' to underscore this type of vilification 'based upon the spiritual/religious dichotomy between "good" and "evil"'. They note that '(e)vilification effectively banishes the other from the moral order that is fundamentally good and godly, and invokes a moral duty to destroy that evil'. In general, the process of out-casting in war discourse creates invidious distinctions and denies the other its humanity, paving the way for war. This is what separates the everyday discursive construction of identities from the process as it is applied in legitimising organised group violence.

Conclusion

As this chapter has illustrated, the forms of political violence encapsulated within the concepts of war and terrorism are very much dependent upon language and social interaction to enable them, to give them meaning, and to shape and constrain understandings and responses. Discourse supplies the socially negotiated frameworks that serve to legitimise certain forms of group violence and delegitimise others. Discourse mobilises polities for war and formulates responses to terrorism. Discourse categorises the world and divides humanity into groups, which can lead to exaggerated distinctions that dehumanise in the service of justifying violent actions against the other. This chapter has aimed to provide greater clarity into the discursive processes that underlie the forms of political violence associated with war and terrorism. In taking a discourse-centred approach, the analysis has sought to disrupt the taken-for-granted assumptions upon which war and terrorism are built and legitimised. What may be taken to be a mere reflection of a pre-existing socio-political reality in political discourse is in fact the product of discursive processes fraught with struggle. To misrecognise those discursive processes as a mirror of 'the way things simply are' is to misread the importance of language in constructing war and terrorism as political concepts, and, by implication, to miss the opportunity to critically consider alternatives to the use of violence as a means to solve political disputes.

References

Aquinas, T, 1985 [1274], *Summa Theologica*, Hayes Barton Press, Raleigh, NC.

Arendt, H, 1970, *On violence*, Harcourt, Brace, Jovanovich, New York.
Bauman, R, 1986, *Story, performance, and event: Contextual studies of oral narrative*. Cambridge University Press, Cambridge.
Bauman, R, 2004, *A world of others' words: Cross-cultural perspectives on intertextuality*, Blackwell, Malden, MA.
Bourdieu, P, 1991, *Language and symbolic power*, Harvard University Press, Cambridge, MA.
Bruner, J, 1991, 'The narrative construction of reality', *Critical Inquiry* 18(1), pp. 1–21.
Bucholtz, M & Hall, K, 2004, 'Language and identity', in *A Companion to Linguistic Anthropology*, ed. A Duranti, Blackwell, Hoboken, NJ, pp. 369–394.
Bucholtz, M, Hall, K, 2005, 'Identity and interaction: A sociocultural linguistic approach', *Discourse Studies* 7(4/5), pp. 585–614.
Campbell, K K, Jamieson, K H, 2008, *Presidents creating the presidency: Deeds done in words*, University of Chicago Press, Chicago, IL.
Cap, P, 2013, *Proximization: The pragmatics of symbolic distance crossing*, John Benjamins Publishing, Amsterdam.
Chandler, D, 2007, *Semiotics: The basics*, 2nd ed. Routledge, London.
Chandler, D, 2009, War without end(s): Grounding the discourse of 'Global War', *Security Dialogue* 40(3), pp. 243–262.
Chernus, I, 2006, *Monsters to destroy: The neoconservative war on terror and sin*, Paradigm Publishers, Boulder, CO.
Chilton, P A, 2004, *Analysing political discourse: Theory and practice*, Routledge, London.
Chouliaraki, L & Fairclough, N, 1999, *Discourse in late modernity: Rethinking Critical Discourse Analysis*, Edinburgh University Press, Edinburgh.
Devji, F, 2005, *Landscapes of the Jihad: Militancy, morality, modernity*, Cornell University Press, Ithaca, NY.
Dunmire, P L, 2013, '"New world coming": Narratives of the future in U.S. post-Cold War national security discourse', in *Discourses of war and peace*, ed. A Hodges, Oxford University Press, Oxford and New York, pp. 23–46.
Erjavec, K, 2009, 'The "Bosnian war on terrorism"', *Journal of Language and Politics*, 8(1), pp. 5–27.
Erjavec, K & Volcic, Z, 2007, '"War on terrorism" as a discursive battleground: Serbian recontextualization of G.W. Bush's discourse', *Discourse and Society*, 18(2), pp. 123–137.
Federal Bureau of Investigation, ND, 'Definitions of Terrorism in the U.S. Code' available from: www.fbi.gov/about-us/investigate/terrorism/terrorism-definition [accessed 20 May 2014].
Ferguson, R B, 1984, *Warfare, culture, and environment*, Academic Press, Cambridge, MA.
Ferguson, R B, 1990, 'Explaining war', in *The Anthropology of War, School of American Research Advanced Seminars*, ed. J Haas, Cambridge University Press, Cambridge, pp. 26–55.
Forchtner, B, 2013, 'Legitimizing the Iraq War through the genre of political speeches: Rhetorics of judge-penitence in the narrative reconstruction of Denmark's cooperation with Nazism', in *Analyzing genres in political communication: Theory and practice*, eds. P Cap, & U Okulska, John Benjamins Publishing, Amsterdam, pp. 239–266.
Foucault, M, 1971, *L'Ordre Du Discours*, Gallimard, Paris.
Foucault, M, 2003, *'Society must be defended': Lectures at the Collège de France, 1975–1976*, Picador, New York.
Gal, S, 1991, 'Between speech and silence: The problematics of research on language and gender', in *Gender at the crossroads of knowledge: Feminist anthropology in the post-modern era*, ed. M di Leonardo, University of California Press, Berkeley, CA, pp. 175–203.
Goffman, E, 1976, 'Replies and responses', *Language and Society* 5(3), pp. 257–313.
Goffman, E, 1981, *Forms of talk*. University of Pennsylvania Press, Philadelphia, PA.
Hanks, W F, 1987, 'Discourse genres in a theory of practice', *American Ethnologist* 14(4), pp. 668–692.
Hodges, A, 2011, *The 'war on terror' narrative: Discourse and intertextuality in the construction and contestation of sociopolitical reality*, Oxford University Press, Oxford and New York.

Hodges, A, 2013a, 'War, discourse and peace', in *Discourses of war and peace*, ed. A Hodges, Oxford University Press, New York, pp. 3–19.

Hodges, A, 2013b, 'The generic U.S. presidential war narrative: Justifying military force and imagining the nation', in *Discourses of war and peace*, ed. A Hodges, Oxford University Press, Oxford and New York, pp. 47–68.

Irvine, J T & Gal, S, 2000, 'Language ideology and linguistic differentiation', *Regimes of language: Ideologies, polities and identities, School of American Research Advanced Seminar Series*, ed. P V Kroskrity, School of American Research Press, Santa Fe, NM, pp. 35–83.

Jackson, R, 2008, 'An argument for terrorism', *Perspectives on Terrorism* 2(2), pp. 25–32.

Kochi, T, 2007, 'The partisan: Carl Schmitt and terrorism', *Law and Critique* 17(3), pp. 267–295, available from: doi:10.1007/s10978-006-9002-2.

Labov, W, Waletzky, J, 1967, 'Narrative analysis: Oral versions of personal experience', in *Essays on the verbal and visual arts*, ed. J Helm, University of Washington Press, Seattle, WA, pp. 12–24.

Lakoff, G, 2001, *Metaphors of Terror. Days Essays Writ. Aftermath Sept. 11 2001*, University of Chicago Press, Chicago, IL.

Lazar, A & Lazar, M M, 2004, 'The discourse of the new world order: "out-casting" the double face of threat', *Discourse and Society* 15(2/3), pp. 223–242.

Moseley, A, 2009, 'Just war theory', *Internet Encyclopedia of Philosophy*, pp. 1–13.

National Institute of Justice, 2007, 'Terrorism', available from: www.nij.gov/topics/crime/terrorism/Pages/welcome.aspx [accessed 20 May 2014].

Ochs, E, 1997, 'Narrative', in *Discourse as structure and process*, ed. T A van Dijk, Sage, Thousand Oaks, CA, pp. 185–207.

Orend, B, 2005, 'War', in *The Stanford encyclopedia of philosophy*, ed. E N Zalta, The Metaphysics Research Lab, Stanford, CA.

Peck, E, 2006, 'Democracy now, Friday, July 28', available from: www.democracynow.org/2006/7/28/national_exclusive_hezbollah_leader_hassan_nasrallah [accessed 20 May 2014].

Peled-Elhanan, N, 2010, 'Legitimation of massacres in Israeli school history books', *Discourse and Society* 21(4), pp. 377–404.

Richardson, L, 2000, 'Terrorists as transnational actors', in *The future of terrorism*, eds. J Horgan & M Taylor, Routledge, New York, pp. 209–219.

Schmid, A P, 2004, 'Frameworks for conceptualizing terrorism', *Terrorism and Political Violence* 16(2), pp. 197–221.

Schmid, A P & de Graaf, J, 1982, *Violence as communication: Insurgent terrorism and the Western news media*, Sage, Thousand Oaks, CA.

Schmid, A P & Jongman, A J, 1988, *Political terrorism: A new guide to actors, authors, concepts, data bases, theories, and literature*, Transaction Publishers, Piscataway, NJ.

Schmitt, C, 2004 [1963], 'The theory of the partisan', *CR: The New Centennial Review* 4, p. 67.

Silberstein, S, 2002, *War of words: Language, politics, and 9/11*, Routledge, New York.

Silverstein, M, 1979, 'Language structure and linguistic ideology', in *The elements: A parasession on linguistic units and levels*, eds. P R Clyne, W F Hanks & C L Hofbauer, Chicago Linguistic Society, Chicago, IL, pp. 193–247.

Tilly, C, 2004, 'Terror, terrorism, terrorists', *Sociological Theory* 22(1), pp. 5–13.

Toolan, M J, 1988, *Narrative: A critical linguistic introduction*, Routledge, London.

USCNS/21st Century, T.U.S.C. on N.S.C, 1999, *New world coming: American security in the 21st century: Supporting research and analysis*, US Government Printing Office, Washington, DC.

US Department of State, 2001, 'Patterns of Global Terrorism', available from: www.state.gov/j/ct/rls/crt/2000/2419.htm [accessed 20 May 2014].

van Dijk, T A, 1998, *Ideology: A multidisciplinary approach*, Sage, London.

van Leeuwen, T, 2007, 'Legitimation in discourse and communication', *Discourse and Communication* 1(1), pp. 91–112.

van Leeuwen, T & Wodak, R, 1999, 'Legitimizing immigration control: A discourse-historical analysis', *Discourse Studies* 1(1), pp. 83–118.

von Clausewitz, C, 1976, *On war*, Princeton University Press, Princeton, NJ.
Walzer, M, 2000, *Just and unjust wars: A moral argument with historical illustrations*, Basic Books, New York.
Walzer, M, 2008, *Arguing about war*, Yale University Press, New Haven, CT.
Weber, M, 2004, *The vocation lectures*, Hackett Publishing, Indianapolis, IN.
Wodak, R, 2006, 'History in the making/The making of history: The "German Wehrmacht" in collective and individual memories in Austria', *J. Lang. Polit.*, 5, pp. 125–154.

Index

15-M (*Indignados*) movement 544–5
1984 (Orwell) 2, 660

AA1000 Stakeholder Engagement Standard 563
Abbas, Mahmud 269, 271, 294
Abercrombie, Ida 162, 163
academia, scholastic fallacy 113–14
Academic Discourse (Bourdieu) 112, 116
accountability 48, 53, 143, 287, 309–10, 345, 380, 390, 473–4, 565
accumulation 559–62; by dispossession 649, 650; mortgage defaults 650; Ponzi schemes 650; primitive 649; privatisation of state-owned assets 650
actio (delivery) 248, 249
action schemas 190
action, social theory of 109
active/passive dichotomy of ageing 508; *see also* aging
actor-network theory 413
Adorno, Theodore W. 2, 12, 142, 232
Adult Migrant Education Program 551
adversarialism, norm of 286
adversarialness 287, 350
advertising: conformity 226; contraception 224–5; influence on discourse 219; legitimation and 219; moral evaluations 227; role model authority 224; tradition, stressing 225; use of signifiers 224
affect 7, 84, 91, 92, 97, 105, 107, 120, 198, 219, 238, 384, 395, 551–2

ageing: active/passive dichotomy 508; aggregation 503; argumentation strategy 508–11; boundaries between young and old 500, 502; collectivisation 504; demarcation of groups 507–8, 511; dementia 506–7; description of 500; dichotomies 502–3; discourse on 501; gratefulness, *topos* of 509–10; loving care, *topos* of 510–11; natural preferences, *topos* of 510; physical identification and somatisation 506–7; political responsibility for 511; politics of 501; problematisation 504–5; relational identification 505–6; respect and dignity 508; responsibility, *topos* of 509 agency 241
aggregation 503
aggressive questioning 287
agreement (*Einverständnis*) 49, 50, 54; *see* Habermas
Aguirre, Esperanza 655
Aitken, Mhairi 494
Alceste software 174
aleatory materialism 40; *see also* Althusser
Alevis 595
algorithms 170–1; Saussurean and Lacanian 85
alienation 83; *see also* Lacan
Alliance of Free Democrats (AFD) 294
alliteration 255
Althusser, Louis 37–40; base-superstructure 38; differences from Gramsci 38; on Gramsci 39; ideological state apparatus (ISA) 38, 39, 40; ideology 37–8; repressive state apparatus (RSA) 38, 39, 40; state, the 38–40

Index

Americanism 35
Améry, Jean 500
AMES Australia non-profit programme 551
analogy 269, 270; moral evaluations 227–8
analytics of power, Foucault 75–7
anaphora 255–6
ANC (African National Congress) 675
anchorage plane 191–2
Ancient Greece 1; Ancient Greeks 17; rhetoric in 1, 18–20; *see also* rhetoric
Ancient Rome 20–2
Andrews, Molly 236, 238, 240
antagonism 104–5, 144, 271; *see also* Laclau
AntConc linguistic tool 175
Anthropology of the Contemporary 78
anti-austerity protests 544–5
anti-globalisation 544
anti-Muslim discourse 634–5
antisemitism 269, 270, 622, 639; *see also* fascism; Nazism; racism
APCO Worldwide 565
appeal to pity, fallacy 254
applause 284–5
appropriation, concept of 362–3; Philadelphia school district 363–4
Aquinas, Thomas 24
Arabic language 535–7
Arab Spring 421, 544, 545
archaeology, Foucauldian perspective 71
Archaeology of Knowledge, The (Foucault) 69, 72–3, 122
Archer, Margaret 118–19
Arendt, Hannah 619; political power 3–4
argumentatio (argumentation) 371; *see also* argumentation and argumentation analysis
argumentation 17, 19, 25; of commemorative speeches 371; definition 268; government officeholders 332; informal logic 249–50; logical structure analysis of 251–2
argumentation analysis 32, 262–3; Benjamin Netanyahu speech 269–72; Critical Discourse Analysis (CDA) and 264, 265, 266–8; discourse analysis (DA) and 264–8; formal 267; functional 267; macro structural 267; meaning of 263–4; non-normative approaches 268; patterns of reasoning 265; *see also* political discourse
argumentation schemas 332
argumentative strategies 251
arguments: emotive language 252; fallacious 253–4; inventio (invention) 20, 25, 248; schemas 254; semantics of 252–3; structures of 252; two sides of 18

argumentum ad misericordiam (appeal to pity) 254
Aristotle 17, 19–20, 26, 247; arguments 248; man as political animal 1–2; rhetoric 248
arms race 204, 210
articulacy 110
articulation: concept of 140; Laclau 97–8, 99
artistic writing 156, 162
arts of distribution, Foucault 71–2
Asad, Talal 592
Asia, globalisation and 542
Assessment Report (AR5) (IPCC) 489
asylum/refugee legislation 532
asylum seekers: Kosovers 238–9; narratives 238, 550
Atlanta Constitution, The 157, 161, 164
Atlanta Journal, The 155, 156, 161
audiences 264; parliamentary 315
Augustine of Hippo 23
austerity, metaphor 208
austerity policies: across Europe 611; in Greece 613; in Spain 651; in the United Kingdom 611–14
Australian parliament 319; *see also* parliament(s)
Austria 253; commemorative speeches 373
Austrian parliament 318; *see also* parliament(s)
authentic personalities 389–91, 407
authenticity 388–9, 517, 549, 552
authorised interruptions 318
authority legitimation 221; authority of conformity 226; authority of tradition 225; commendation legitimation 221, 223–5; impersonal authority 222–3; legitimation by custom 221, 225–6; moral evaluation legitimation 226–8; personal authority 221–2
autonomy: civic 53; collective 45; individual 45; personal 48; private 53

backstage of politics 6, 10, 145, 294, 297, 309, 321, 331, 337, 360, 369, 374, 385, 573, 574–5, 572, 665
Bacon, Francis 25
Barthes, Roland 87–92, 229, 456
Bartlett, Josiah (TV character) 573, 574, 578; speeches 579–80; *see also* fictionalisation
Bartoli, Matthew 34
base space 191
base-superstructure: Althusser 38; Gramsci 33, 35; Marx 31–2
Bastille, storming of (14 July) 372
Beauvoir, Simone de 71
Beck, Glenn 522

688

Begriffsgeschichte 122, 132, 146; *see also* conceptual history
belletristic movement 26
belonging 391–3; Arabic and Hebrew languages 536; Israeli polity 533; language and citizenship 529–32; politics of 533
Benjamin, Walter 292–3
Berger, John 227
Berger, Peter & Luckmann, Thomas 2, 219–20
Berlusconi, Silvio 239
Bernini, Gianlorenzo 458
billboards: discourse-historical approach to studying 443; of the Fatherland Party 448–9; as genres of political action 441–2; as multimodal texts 451–2; of the Petro Poroshenko Bloc 446–7; of the Radical Party of Oleh Liashko 2014 449–50; *see also* Ukrainian parliamentary election campaign (2014)
biological racisms 632
biopolitics 76
biopower 76
Blair, Hugh 26
Blair, Tony 212, 213, 386–8; speed element 213–14
blame avoidance 333–4, 337, 346
blame games, concept of 609
Blank, Andreas 125
Bloch, Marc 122
blocked learning 143, 144
block of plural pronouns 347; *see also* press conference
blogs 412, 415, 418, 563, 655
blood libel 269, 270; *see also* antisemitism
Bödeker, Hans-Erich 130
Boethius 23–4
Boltanski, Luc 118
booing 285–6
Borgen (TV series) 573, 574, 575–6, 581–3, 584; comparison with *West Wing, The* 581, 583
Boston Transcript 155
Bourdieu, Pierre 109–10; action, social theory of 109; capital 112, 112–13; class racism 117; discourse analysis 109; emotions, disregard for 119; fatalism 118–19; fields 111–12; fields of struggle 116–17; games 111; habituation 115; habitus 110–11, 115, 118, 119; hegemony 114; interactionist approaches 111; markets 111–12, 116; misrecognition 115–16; political discourse 117–18; scholastic fallacy 113–14, 118; signifier and signified 92; social theory 144–6; soft forms of domination 109, 115; strategy, notion of 145; sub-markets 112; symbolic power 114–15, 116; symbolic profit 112; symbolic violence 4; *see also* dominant classes
brain, left side/right side 118
Brandt, Willy 376
breathiness in sound/music 435, 435–6
Britain *see* United Kingdom
British National Party (BNP) 441
broadsheets 458
Brother Jonathan 462
Brown, Gordon 511
bulletin boards 418
Bunin, Ivan 156, 160
Burkhardt, Armin 3
Bush administration 106
Bush, George W. 221, 222, 238, 255, 363; crime and war frames 678; press conferences 348–9; questioning of 286–7; tactic of adequatation 682; War on Terror *see* War on Terror
business/corporate meetings 468
Butler, Judith 78
bystanders 316

cackle 521–2
CA (Conversation Analysis) 276–7; actions 277–8; analytic claims 279–81; applause 284–5; booing 285–6; collections 281; direct interactional encounters 276–7; exemplary studies 282–8; identity construction 401; interaction, study of 277; journalistic and infotainment interviews 286–7; language practices 276; meetings 468–9; methodology 277–82; news conferences 287–8; participatory democracy meetings 282; political speeches 284–6; practices 278, 281; quantitative extensions 282; question-and-answer sessions 348; radio phone-in shows 283–4; sequences of action 277; tasks and norms 277; turn-taking systems 277
Caldicott, Helen 219
call and response song structure 225
call to arms 680
Cambridge School 129, 132
Cameron, David 203, 204, 211; on competition 612–13; competition 212; on the debt crisis 613; global race metaphor 210, 212; looking forward speech 612; Magna Carta 225; speed references 212; on taxation 612, 630
Cameroonian Parliament 321; *see also* parliament(s)
campaigning, political 414–18
campaign interviews 286

Campbell, George 26
candidate metaphors 207, 208
candidates, political: likeability 403–4; personal identity of 399; personal impression management, websites 417; personal websites 417; political self 398–9, 400; question evasion in interviews 401; self-presentation 101, 399
Canguilhem, Georges 68
capital, Bourdieusian metaphor 112, 112–13
capital flight 612–13
capital, global 543
capitalism 10, 32, 35, 103, 128, 203, 210–16, 267, 293, 494, 543–7, 557–8, 588; CPE (cultural political economy) approach 566–8; international 211
carbon sinking 495
care 501–2; active/passive dichotomy 508; aggregation 503; argumentation strategy 508–11; dichotomies 503; loving care, *topos* of 510–11; natural preferences, *topos* of 510; political responsibility for 511; relational identification 505–6; responsibility 509; *see also* ageing
caricatura 458, 459
caricature(s) 455, 457; definition 454; origins of 458; as tool for cartoonists 458; *see also* political caricature(s)
Carlyle Group 463
Carracci, Annibale; Carracci, Agostino 458
Carter, Jimmy 301
cartooning: definition 455; eighteenth century 458–9; history 457; in newspapers 462–3; nineteenth century 460–2; in northern Europe 458; sixteenth century 457–8; twentieth century 462–3; twenty-first century 463–5; *see also* political cartooning
cartoonists 455, 456; caricature as tool for 458
cartoon(s): definition 455; editorial 455; single-panel 455
Casasanto, Daniel 197
category management 560
CDA (Critical Discourse Analysis) 97, 109, 132, 137, 171, 173, 179–80, 237, 273, 408, 426, 441–2, 609–10; comparison with argumentation analysis 264, 265, 266–8; integration of documentation 267; meetings 468, 469; political actions 398; political discourse and 398; political language and 383; vocation of 266
CDS (Critical Discourse Studies) 7, 167, 247, 443; approaches within 135, 136; *Begriffsgeschichte* and 146; Bourdieu's social theory 144–6; Critical Theory, influence of 141–4; DHA (discourse-historical approach) 145; disciplinary boundaries 137; Marx(ism), influence of 137–9; nationalism 428; post-structuralist approaches, influence of 139–41; views on 135–6; *see also* CL-CDS (Cognitive Linguistics CDS)
celebrity talk-show interviews 287
Central European parliaments 320; *see also* parliament(s)
Chacón, Carme 516–17
chain of equivalences 102, 103; *see also* Laclau
chairpersons, meetings 473; *see also* meeting
Chidester, David 593
Chilton, Paul 136, 326
China 421; illegal overtime 559; labour abuses 561
chi-square tests 177
Christianity 593–7
Cicero 20–1
citizenry 45; models of 46
citizens: use of social media and ICTs 421, 422
citizenship 10, 43, 309, 420, 545, 562; acts of 530, 531; affective/emotional dimension 530; democracy and 46–7, 54; as habitus 530, 531, 535; as an interactional accomplishment 532–3; language and belonging 529–32; nationality and 529–30; rights and duties 528–9; as status 530, 531, 535
citizen-to-citizen communication 418–21
civic activism 562
civic autonomy 53
civic inequality 653
civic life 17, 18, 25, 27
civilisations 594–5
civil rights 46
civil servants 328; impartiality 337; use of language 337
class: dimensions of 649; framing of 649; *see also* class struggle; social class
class antagonism 4
class parties/conflicts 624
class racism 117
class struggle and warfare 31, 40, 649, 656–7; Bourdieu 119; definition 649; home evictions 646, 651, 653, 656, 657; in Spain 652; violence in home evictions 653; *see also* inequality
classical music 428, 434
classical myths and sagas 577
CL-CDS (Cognitive Linguistic Critical Discourse Studies): analysis of conceptualisation in discourse 188; Critical

Metaphor Analysis 188; differences with socio-cognitive approaches 187–8; Discourse Space Theory 189; image schema analysis 189–90, 191–2, 193; mental processes 187; multimodal approaches 194–8; point-of-view specifications 191–2, 193, 195–6, 197–8; political protests 195–7; reciprocal constructions 191, 193; regular transitive constructions 191, 193
Clean Clothes Campaign 561, 562
Clegg, Nick 394
Clifford, James 291
Climate Action Camps 496
climate change 10, 143, 321; construction of scientific knowledge 489–93; controls, richer countries opposition to 488; crucial role of science and scientists 488; denial 490–1; Discourse-Historical Approach (DHA) 496; discursive outlook 487–8; impact on small-island states 487; issues open to research 495–6; media attention 489; Multimodal Discourse Analysis 496; scepticism 491; science and politics of 488–9; technical nature of reportage 495; techno-managerialism and alternative discourses 493–5
Climate Justice Movement 496
Clinton, Hillary 401, 403–4, 408; Clinton Cackle 517–22; Democratic nomination 517–22; feminine practices in non-linguistic domains 516; linguistic style 516; as Wicked Witch of the West 522
Clinton, Bill 278; framing case study 403–4
Clothes Code Campaign (Oxfam) 562
CMT (Conceptual Metaphor Theory) 188, 663
code books 171
code-rush conjuncture 562–3
coding categories 155, 156
coercion 326, 327, 335
Cognitive Grammar 189, 191
Cognitive Linguistic Critical Discourse Studies (CL-CDS) *see* CL-CDS
Cognitive Linguistics 198
Colau, Ada 657
collective action logics 415
collective autonomy 45
collective identity 92
collective political subject 369
collective self-determination 45
collective solidarity 45
collective sovereignty 48–9
collective will-formation 52
collectivisation 504

collocates 175–6
colloquial language 385, 389, 534
colonialism 442, 592–4
colonial territories 291
comic books 455, 463
comics 454; art form 456, 464; common meaning 457; definition 455; digital 464–5; images 457; newspaper 462–3; single-panel 456; stereotypes, use of 456; technology and 464
comic strips 455, 461, 464; newspaper 463
commemoration(s) 368; as a multimodal semiotic process and event 374–7; *see also* political commemoration
commemoration(s), official 237
commemorative speeches 370–4; apologies in 373–4; argumentation (*argumentatio*) 371; deliberative purposes of 372; epideictic purposes of 372; failing 373, 374; final part (*peroratio*) 371; introduction (*exordium*) 371; narration (*narratio*) 371; purpose of 372; for something (*probatio*) 371; against something (*refutatio*) 371
commendation legitimation 221, 223–5; *see also* legitimation
commodity, government communication as 329
common memory 369, 378
communication: context and 129; Habermas, Jürgen 49, 50, 54; non-verbal 379, 401; public 329, 330; verbal 379; *see also* government communication
communicative action and discourse ethics, model of 4; *see* Habermas
communicative power 46
communicative rationality, democracy and 49–50, 54; agreement (*Einverständnis*) 49, 50, 54; communication (*Verständigung*) 49, 50, 54; intelligibility (*Verständlichkeit*) 49, 50, 54; reason (*Verstand*) 49, 50, 54; understanding (*Verstehen*) 49, 50, 54; *see also* Habermas
communicative reason 113
communism 102–3, 143; censorship in parliament 320
Communities of Practice (CofP) framework 413, 480
community, essence of 105
compassionate ageism 509; *see also* aging
competition: David Cameron on 212; normalisation of 211
competition metaphors 206
competitiveness 544
Competitive Race metaphors 203, 208–15; contextual information 209–10; David

Cameron on international performance 204; Ed Miliband on competing nations 203–4; global race 204, 209, 210, 212–14; league tables 204; metaphor keywords 209; race 209; rat race 210, 211–12
computational linguists 170–1
computer-aided textual analysis 169
concepts: basic 131; counterconcepts 126; democratisation 130; distributional 126; insertion into ideologies 130; politicisation of 130; supraconcepts temporalisation of 130; totalising 126; words and 131
conceptual history 122–3; action and context 129–30; basic concepts and politics 131; distinction between semantics and pragmatics 129–30; language 123–4; linguistics and 132; onomasiological approach 124, 125; pragmatics 129–30; reference 126–9; referentiality 129; representation 123, 124–6; social history and 127; *see also* *Begriffsgeschichte*
conceptualisation 188; levels of mental representation 194
conceptual mappings 663
conceptual metaphors 188, 202, 205, 256, 573; areas of contested ideological outlook 205; country is container 189; immigration is flood 188–9; inferences of 204; international financial crisis 256; motivations of 205; state as container 188
Conceptual Metaphor Theory (CMT) *see* CMT (Conceptual Metaphor Theory)
concise narratives 240; *see* narrative
concordancing 175–6; *see* corpus analysis
condensation 131, 456
condescension 110, 115, 116
conflict theory 329
conformity legitimation 226; *see also* legitimation
connective action logics 415, 418
consciousness 31, 40; false 329; mediatised 596; national 461, 462
consistency analysis 177; *see* corpus analysis
constitutional law, democracy and 52–3, 55
content analysis: artistic writing 156, 162; coy approach 162; dealing with texts 154–6; development of 154; manifest interest 162; purpose of 153; reading between the lines 162, 163; techniques of 154
context, meaning of 129
contraception, advertising of 224–5
contrast, rhetorical device 285
Convention on the Future of Europe (2002) 310–11

conversationalisation 138, 385–6
Conversation Analysis (CA) *see* CA (Conversation Analysis)
co-occurrence analysis 175; *see* corpus analysis
Copenhagen Summit 489
corpora 170–1; *see also* corpus analysis
corporations: social obligations of 558; *see also* CSR (Corporate Social Responsibility)
corpus analysis: analytical strategy 179–80; approaches to 170–2; benefits of 170; concordancing in corpus linguistics 175–6; contrasting in corpus linguistics 177; contrasting in lexicometrics 174–5; corpus-based approaches 169, 173; corpus-driven approaches 169, 173; crisis discourse, study in 179–83; definition of corpus 170; demand for 169; dilemmas of conducting corpus research 172–3; focus and procedures of 173–9; implications of the corpus-analytical view 177–9; linguistic categories 172; methods 181–3; periodised intra-corpus comparison 181–3; philosophy of science 173; popularity of techniques 169; scientific approaches 173; size of text collections 172; supervised approaches 169; unsupervised approaches 169; using in political discourse studies 183–4
corpus linguistics 174; concordancing in 175–6; contrasting in 177; lexical choice 521
Coseriu, Eugenio 125
Cosmopolitan magazine 223, 224
cosmopolitan 622
cosmopolitanisation 553n3
Cospedal, Maria Dolores de 654
Council of Europe 310
CPE (cultural political economy) approach 568; features of 557–8
Crimea 443–4, 445
crime frame of terrorism 678
crisis, concept of 126
crisis conjunctures 558
crisis discourse, study in 179–80
crisis journalists 182
crisis labels 182
crisis narratives 180; *see also* narrative
Critchley, Simon 590
Critical Discourse Studies (CDS) *see* CDS (Critical Discourse Studies)
critical explanation 603–4, 608–9
Critical Metaphor Analysis 188, 189, 206
critical ontology 69; *see also* Foucault
Critical Social Analysis 267
Critical Theory 69, 136, 141–4, 443

critique 31, 32, 40, 48, 69, 71, 77, 109, 110, 113, 120, 171, 176, 219, 264–7, 270, 273, 284, 293, 302, 347, 376, 379, 443, 490, 530, 557, 583, 590, 604, 614, 631, 661, 662; meaning of 136; prospective (retrospective) 136; socio-diagnostic 136; text-imminant 136
Croce, Benedetto 34
Cromwell, Oliver 454
crucifixes 596; *see* religion
Cruikshank, George 460
Crystal Night (*Kristallnacht*) state pogrom 666; *see* antisemitism; Nazism
CSR (Corporate Social Responsibility): code-rush conjuncture 562–3; corporations' broadening of 562; development of norm-based schemes/standards 563–4; neoliberal 568; reinvention since the 1980s 562–7; risk management and 564; social risks 564–5; stakeholder languages and practices 562–5; stakeholder theory 563; Wal-Mart 563; Wal-Martisation and 562; *see also* stakeholders
cultural capital 112–13; *see also* Bourdieu
cultural globalisation 542
cultural political economy (CPE) *see* CPE (cultural political economy) approach
customer satisfaction 329
custom, legitimation by 221, 225–6; *see also* legitimation

DACA (Deferred Action for Childhood Arrivals) 242, 243
Dahl, Robert 623, 627
Daily Telegraph 639–40
Danish politics *see Borgen* (TV series); Nyborg, Birgitte (TV character)
Darwin, Charles 594
Dasein (being-there) 53; *see also* Habermas
data, Foucault's use of 71
Daumier, Honoré 454
Davutoğlu, Ahmet 138
Day of Liberation (8 May 1945) 372
debates in parliament *see* parliamentary debates
decision-making in meetings 479–80; *see* meetings
declamation 21
De doctrina Christiana (Augustine of Hippo) 23
defensive learning 143–4
de-legitimation 220
delegitimisation 327
deliberation 5; definition 262; democracy and 43–4, 50, 53; rhetorical argumentation 262, 263

deliberative democracy 43, 49, 50, 142
deliberative genre 371
deliberative speech 248
dementia 506–7
democracy 266, 276, 282, 288, 301–3, 328, 345, 350, 359, 373, 448, 471, 573, 615, 627; agonistic model of 4; citizenship and 46–7, 54; communicative rationality and 49–50, 54; constitutional law and 52–3, 55; deficit 330; deliberation and 43–4, 53; genuine 55; government communication and 330–1; grass roots 55; hyper-democracy 604, 615; majority rule and minority rights 623; movements 544–5; populism and 618, 622–3; reciprocity and 44–5, 53; regulation and 50–1, 54; self-determination and 45–6, 54; social interaction 50; sovereignty and 48–9, 54; state and 47, 54; will-formation and 51–2, 54–5; Zapatistas' usage 141
democratic oligarchy 20
democratic politics 294; description in theatrical terms 294
democratisation 130
demographic 53, 378, 399–400, 500; demographic time-bomb 503–4
demonstrative speech 248
denial: discursive 608–11; government officeholders 332; institutional level 609; personal 609
de Niro, Robert 224
denotation 126
De Oratore (Cicero) 21
depoliticisation 603–4, 605, 606; definition 608; *see also* discursive depoliticisation
Derrida, Jacques 85
desire 93, 94n3, 531–2
determinate market 35
Deutschlandlied (national anthem) 429
deviant cases 281; *see also* CA
Devolved Assemblies Act (1988) 523
DHA (Discourse Historical Approach) 136, 141, 143, 144, 250–1, 442–3; application to climate change 496; argumentation and 267–8; aspects of 443; in CDS (Critical Discourse Studies) 145; explanatory power of 145; ideology and 443; language as medium of power 443; normative 268; political commemoration 377–8; study of party programs and billboards 443
dialectics 24, 137, 250
dichotomies 502–3; *see also* aging
Die deutsche Ideologie (Marx and Engels) 31
differential multilingualism 546–7

digital comics 464–5; *see* comics
digitisation 169
dignity of the elderly 508
Dionysius of Halicarnassus 22
diplomacy press conferences 346, 347; *see* press conferences
disaffiliation 519, 520
disagreement in meetings 479; *see* meetings
disciplinary power 76; *see* Foucault
discourse analysis (DA) 109, 160–2; approach to critical reading 267; argumentation analysis and 264–8; object of 264; *see also* CDA; CDS; CL-CDS; DHA
discourse genre, parliamentary 312–14; *see also* parliament(s)
Discourse Historical Approach (DHA) *see* DHA (Discourse Historical Approach)
discourse(s): analytical strategies 179; analytics of 72–5; concept of 136; content of 120; definition of 650; discriminatory 253; dominant 120; as Foucauldian concept 70; integral historical artefacts 651; multiple 650–1; order of 139; political 117–18; representation 373; social practices, presenting 650; strands 140; strategy/ies 255, 312; technologisation of 139; worlds 189
Discourse Space Theory 189; *see also* CL-CDS
discourse theory, Laclau 96–8; discursive and non-discursive practices 98–9; dislocation, concept of 90, 100–1; elements 98; field of discursivity 99; fullness of society 100–1; meaning 99; meaningful totality 98; moments 98; nationalism 99; political subjectivity 100; political, the 100; reformulation of 140; sedimentation 99–100; social, the 100; subject positions 98
discrimination 631
discursive depoliticisation 603–4; austerity discourse in the UK 611–14; conceptualising denial 608–11; definition 608; discourse theoretic approach 609–10; Glynos and Howarth's framework 609–10, 614–15; supply side of political disengagement 604–7; *see also* logics of denial
discursive order/structure 98–9
discursive politicisation 608
discursive reciprocity 44
discursive strategies 145, 255, 312
discussion boards 412
disengagement, political 604–7
dislocation, Laclau concept 90, 100–1, 104
dispositions 145–6; Bourdieu 110
dispositive(s) 140; as Foucauldian concept 70–1

disposito (disposition) 248, 249
Distinction (Bourdieu) 109
dogmatic learning 143
doing politics 292, 331, 572, 573, 576; women and their representations 515–17; women in egalitarian contexts 523
Dole, Bob 280
dominant classes: cultural capital 112–13; linguistic capacities of 111; styles of speaking and writing 112; symbolic power 114–15; symbolic violence 115; time and leisure of 113
dominated class: compliance 116, 170; condescension 116; constitution of 92; deference 116; envisaging radical alternatives 114; fatalism 118–19; habitus 117, 118; language 115; reproducing own position 118; resistance of 117, 119; symbolic violence 115
Donbas 444, 447
Doré, Gustave 460–1
double bind 403, 404, 406, 407, 408; leadership styles, variety of 516; *see also* women in politics
doublethink 660
doxa 114, 264
Dreamers movement 242–3
Dr. Syntax books 459
Druid Network 595
Dry September (Faulkner) 160, 161, 163
Dubuisson, Daniel 593
Duisburg School of CDS 140
Dumézil, Georges 68
Dunblane 386–8
Dutch Freedom Party (PVV) 620, 625

Eastern European parliaments 320
eavesdroppers 316, 317
economic globalisation 542, 626
economism 180, 205
economy, regionalisation of 542
ecopower 77
editorial cartoonists 463
editorial cartoons 455
educational capital 113
Egypt 421; terrorism and 676
Eichmann, Adolf 665
Eighteenth Brumaire of Louis Bonaparte, The (Marx) 33
electoral discourse 263
elites, political: far-right opposition to 622, 626
elocutio (formulation) 25, 248, 249
eloquence 20, 23, 25
Elton, G.R. 165

emancipatory cognitive interest 48
emotions: disregard for 119; knowledge of 19; in melodies 431–4
emotive language 252
empathy, semiotics of 393–4
empirical research 207–8
EMPOWER 551
empty signifiers 90–1, 103–4, 105
Engels, Friedrich 30–3
English as a Lingua Franca (ELF) 475–6, 546, 547
English as an international language (EIL) 546, 547
enlightenment 69
EP (European Parliament) 310, 321, 359
epideictic genre 312, 371
epideictic mode of political discourse 263
epideictic speech 248
epistemology 235
equivalence 102, 103
Erasmus, Desiderius 24
Erdoğan, Recep Tayyip 373
Ernst, Joni 405–7
escraches (direct action) 653–4, 655, 656
ethnic groups: discrimination against 631; inferiorised 631
ethnography 291, 292; limitations 302; political institutions 292; political processes 292; politics of storytelling 292–3; staging processes 294; untimliness 302; *see also* Hungarian parliament building; Hungary
ethnoscapes 543
ethos 19, 262, 272
ethos construction 269
EU (European Union): multi-level organisation 359; multilingual structure 358–9; policy genres 358–60; relation to member states' policies 359; sovereign debt crisis 611
euphemisms 255, 327, 666–7
Euromaidan Revolution 443
European Commission (EC) 310, 359
European Council 359
European Parliament (EP) *see* EP (European Parliament)
European parliaments 320
European Union (EU) *see* EU (European Union)
European Union Language and Multilingualism Policy (EULMP) 146
Europe for Freedom and Direct Democracy 625
Europe of Nations and Freedom (ENF/ENL) 625
Euro-sclerosis metaphor 214–15
event-space 191

eventualisation 70
even/uneven rhythms 436
existential inequality 647–8, 652, 653, 656
existentialism 67, 68
exordium (introduction) 20, 371
experiential rationalisations 230
experimentation, Foucauldian notion 67
expert authority legitimation 223–4
external sovereignty 48
extreme right 632, 634; *see also* far right; fascism; populism; populist
extreme-right political parties 630, 634; extreme-right parties 634
EZLN (*Ejército Zapatista de Liberación*) 141

Facebook: genres 420; Guatemalan protest movement 420; Swedish and Norwegian politicians 416; use by politicians 416
facilitators, meetings 471
factor analyses 175
facts, linguistic construction of 162–3
Fairclough, Norman 137–8, 139–40, 576; definition of discourse 650; semiosis 650
fallacies 143, 252, 266; *argumentum ad* 254; definition 253; formal and informal 254; straw-man 333
fallacious arguments 253–4
false consciousness 329
family *see* ageing; care
fantasmatic logics 610
far right 618; anti-democratic tendencies 619; anti-Muslim discourse 634–5; antisemitism 269, 270, 622; conceptual history of parties and movements 618–22; contrast with left-wing politics 619; distinction between parties 619; exclusion of 'the others' 621; in France 619, 620; in Italy 619–20; mobilising against 'them above' 622–3; mobilising against 'them below' 623; neo-fascism 619–20; in the Netherlands 620; opposition to political elites 622, 626; Swiss People's Party 634; twenty-first century in Europe 620; us and them narrative 621, 622; in Western Europe 632; *see also* extreme right; fascism; Nazism; racism; right-wing politics/parties
fascism 372–3, 620; in Italy 621; twenty-first century in Europe 621; *see also* Nazism; neo-fascism
fast/slow rhythms 436
fatalism 118–19
Fatherland Party 447–9, 451
Faulkner, William 160
Febvre, Lucien 122

femininity, modern 142
fictionalisation of politics 572–3; backstage 574–5; frontstage 574; functions of 584; good and bad, division of 577; heroes, status of 577; interdiscursivity 577; intertextuality 576; narratives 577; recontextualisation 576–7; stories and myths 576–8; *see also Borgen* (TV series); *West Wing, The* (TV series)
field of discursivity 99
fields, Bourdieu 111–12, 116
fields of action 441
fields of struggle 116–17
figures of speech (FSP) 254–6
filibustering 320
finanscapes 543
Finnish Wiccans 595
First Assessment Report (IPCC) 488
first past the post system 627
first-person plural nouns 319
first-person plural pronouns 319
Firthian assumption 174
Fishburne, Laurence 636, 637
fitness 207
Fitzgerald, Timothy 591, 594
flash mob events 242
flexible work skills 544
floating signifiers 102, 103
focused versus spread sounds 435, 436
Fogel, R. 165
folk tales 577
Fønsmark, Katrine (TV character) 581
football metaphors 206
footing shifts 280, 286, 349
Fordism 33, 35
forensic genres 312
forensic speech 248
formal logic 249
formation concepts 73
formation of enunciative modalities 73
formation of objects, Foucault 73
formation of strategies 73
formulations 480
Forza Italia 619–20
fossil-fuel industry 490
Foucault, Michel 2, 67–8; academic background 67; analytic and diagnostic concepts 68; analytics of discourse(s) 72–5; analytics of power 75–7; archaeology 71; arts of distribution 71–2; biopolitics 76; biopower 76; CDS (Critical Discourse Studies) 139–41; concern and intent 68–9; discourse 70, 681; dispositive 70–1; enlightenment 69; erotic desires and practices 531–2; eventualisation 70; experimentation 67; games of truth concept 74; genealogy 71; governmentality 76–7; history of the present 69; influences on 68; knowledge 74; methodology of experimenting 69–72; modern subjects 68–9; order of discourse 139; order of things, the 72; Pierre Rivière case 75; power 74, 218; problematisation 70; relations of strategy 76; rules of formation 73
Fourth Assessment Report (IPCC) 489
Fraenkel, Ernst 623
frame analysis 163–5, 408
frames 402; structuring interaction 402
framing 114, 206, 236, 374, 418, 422, 490, 494–5, 541, 663–4; case study, Hillary Clinton 403–4; government officeholders 332; identity construction 402; as key political communication strategies 402; notion of 402; political performances 402; *see also* reframing
framing processes, social movements 418, 422
France: articulacy and command of language valued 110; far-right parties 619, 620; satirical cartoonists 460–1; secularism 588
Franco, General 655
Frankfurt School 2, 330
Frank Leslie's Illustrated Newspaper 462
free association 45
freedom of action 76
freedom of information laws 328
Freedom Party of Austria (FPÖ) 442
French Revolution 222
Freud, Sigmund 84
Freysinger, Oskar 634, 635
Front National (FN) 620, 625
frontstage of politics 145, 294–7, 309, 321, 574
fullness of society 100–1

G20 meeting (2009) 421; police-related tweets 421
Gabon 549
Gadamer, Hans Georg 123, 127
games, Bourdieusian metaphor 111
games of truth, Foucauldian concept 74
gay citizens: in Israel 533; in Palestine 533; rhetoric of visibility 529, 535
Gaza War 269, 639–41
Gemeinschaft 50, 51
gender: highly rigid regulatory frame 515; indexicality of 521; performative aspects of 514–15; regulation and constraints 515
gendered politics: masculine culture of politics 514; politics as a gendered environment 514; *see also* Clinton, Hillary; women in politics

gender roles in parliament 320–1
genealogy, Foucauldian perspective 71
General Inquirer, The 171
generic realism 681
genocide 269, 270, 271, 663–4
genres 139; characterisation of 576; commemorative speeches 371; definition 355, 441; deliberative 371; epideictic 312, 371; EU (European Union) 358–60; Facebook 420; forensic 312; heterogeneity of 312; interactive 373; judicial 371; parliamentary discourse 312–14; policy, analysis of 357–60; political communication 441; press conferences 345; social media 419–20; theories 413–14; war 680, 681; Wild West films 577; *see also* commemorative speeches
Gentle breath (Bunin) 156
genuflection 376
genuine democracy 55
Georgias 18
Gephi 158, 159
Gerő, András 294
German parliament 320
German Unity Day (3 October) 372
Germany: climate change reportage 492; National Socialism 142; National Socialist Party 621, 622; 'new right' 140; political cartooning 458
Gesellschaft 50, 51
Getty Image Bank 228
Gillard, Julia 524
Gillray, James 459
GIS modelling 158
Giuliani, Rudolph 520
global capital 543
Global English 547, 548
global financial crisis (2008) 611
Global Hip-Hop 549
globalisation 101, 211; concept of 541–3; economic 542, 626; hyperglobalisers 542, 547; as a keyword 543; Language and Globalisation Social Justice Movement (LG-SJM) 550–2; language of 541–6; linguistic repertoires in glocalised contexts 548–50; neoliberal production 558–62; positive/negative valance 542; rhetoric 544; sceptics 542, 547, 548; state and 626; transformationalists 542, 547–8, 548; working definition 543
globalisation of language: differential multilingualism 546–7; world languages (WLs) 546
globalism(s) 544–5

globality/ies 545–6
global justice movement (GJM) 545
global planning 143
global race, metaphor 204, 209, 210, 212–14
global relations 542
Global Reporting Initiative 563
global warming 489
Glynos, Jason and Howarth, David 609–10, 614–15
Goebbels, Joseph 661, 665
Goetsch, Paul 239
Goffman, Erving 294, 574
gold standard 88–9
Google Earth Pro 158, 160
Google ngrams 164
Gorgias (Plato) 19
governance: decentralised 606; delegated 607
governmental depoliticisation 608
governmentality 76–7
government communication: activities 327–8; as a commodity 329; communication and communicators 326–8; compromised impartiality of non-elected administrators 337; conceptualising 328–31; conflictual aspects of 336–7; employees 328; examples of 331–6; as a factor in doing or undoing democracy 330–1; freedom of information laws 328; functions of language in 326–7; 'go home or face arrest' campaign 334–5; instrumental-language use 335; intra-governmental strikes 336–7; managerial discourse 330; managing actions 335–6; as manipulation 329–30; mediated scandals and blame avoidance 337; as a policy instrument 328–9; strategic use of language 326; using language to exert power 334; using language to hold on to power 331–2; Whitehall waste story 332–4; *see also* officeholders, government
grammar 23, 157–8, 443
Gramsci, Antonio 33–7, 329; Americanism and Fordism 33, 35; economic essentialism 96; hegemony 34, 36–7, 39, 137–8; historical bloc 35–6; intellectuals, studies of 36–7; misleading interpretations of 33; philological method 34; redefinition of base 35; stratification of language use 34; vernacular materialism 34–5
graphemes 174
graphic novels 455
grass roots democracy 55
gratefulness, *topos* of 509–10
Gray, John 590–1

Index

Greece 93; anti-austerity movements 545; impact of austerity policies 613
Greek parliament 320
green economy 494
green papers 359
groups, demarcation of 507–8
Guardian, The 226
Guatemalan protest movement 420
Guilhaumou, Jacques 132
Gusztos, Péter 294–5, 296–7

Habermas, Jürgen 4, 43; citizenship and democracy 46–7, 54; communicative rationality and democracy 49–50, 54; communicative reason 113; constitutional law and democracy 52–3, 55; Critical Theory 142–3; deliberation and democracy 43–4, 53; everyday practices 218; parliament 311; political deliberation 311; reciprocity and democracy 44–5, 53; regulation and democracy 50–1, 54; religion and the secular 588; self-determination and democracy 45–6; sovereignty and democracy 48–9, 54; the state and democracy 47, 54; will-formation and democracy 51–2, 54–5
habituation 115
habitus 110–11, 115, 118, 119, 145, 474; citizenship as 530, 531, 535; gay subjectivities and Palestinian selfhood 536; *see also* Bourdieu
Hall, Stuart 78
Halonen, Tarja 517
Hamas 269
handshake, symbolism of 376
Hansard 209
Hansard Debates 318
Harding, Warren 343
Harper's Weekly 462
Harris, Sam 595
Hartvic, Bishop 300
Harvard Kennedy School of Government 564
Harvey, David 649–50
hate speech 295
headline-punchlines 285
head-scarves, Islamic 142
health 207
Hebrew language 535–7
Hegel, Georg Wilhelm Friedrich 30, 31, 35, 83, 137
hegemonic masculinity 515
hegemonic multilingualism 547

hegemony 4, 329; apparatuses 36; Bourdieu 114; Gramscian notion of 34, 36–7, 39; Laclau 96; practices 36
hegemony, Laclau 96; chain of equivalences 102; empty signifiers 90–1, 103–4, 105; logic of difference 101, 102; logic of equivalence 101–2, 103; political spaces 101
Held, David and Leftwich, Andrew 4–5
heraldic music 222–3
hermeneutic images 457
hermeneutics 123
Hermogenic corpus 22
hero, status of 577, 579–81
Hip-Hop: Global 549; Naija Afro 549
Hirschauer, Stefan 302
historians 122–4; long-term perspectives 131; *see also* Koselleck, Reinhart
historical bloc, concept of 35–6
historical change 22, 122, 125–30, 368, 377
historical materialism 31, 35
history of the present 69
Hitler, Adolf: justification of Nuremberg laws 664–5; *Mein Kampf* 661, 663; *see also* Nazi discourse; Nazism
Hobbes, Thomas 25
Hogarth, William 458–9
Holkham Bible Picture Book 457
Holocaust 203, 270, 639, 664, 665; *see also* antisemitism
Holy Crown of Hungary 299
Holy Inquisition 454
home evictions 646, 651, 653, 656, 657; physical confrontation 653; violence 653
Home Office (UK) 334–5
horizons of expectations 128; *see also* Koselleck, Reinhart
Horkheimer, Max 141–2
Horthy, Miklós 294, 300
House of Commons (UK) 309; dominant masculine culture 516; interventions in debate 515; representation of women 523
human agency, denial of 604
human mobility 551
human reality 83; division between reality and the real 83
humorous narratives 240
humour 319, 320; visual 461
humour strips 462
Hungarian Parliament building 293–7; Constitution 298; construction of 293; Cupola Hall 300; debates 298; hate speech 295; laws 298; majorities 298; National Assembly 294, 298; *Official Journal of the House Of*

698

Representatives 299; politics of storytelling 301–2; royal jewels 299–300; as site of Hungarian politics 293–4; Standing Orders 298; stenographers 298–9; Third Republic 294, 299, 301
Hungarian Socialist Party (HSP) 294
Hungarian Socialist Workers' Party 294
Hungary: Constitutional Court 301; Department of File Registry 298; Holy Crown 299, 300, 301, 302; invasion by German forces 300–1; legislative bills 297–8; National Museum 299, 301; political decision-making in 294; political extremism 295
hunting 427
Huntington, Samuel 594–5
Hussein, Saddam 682
Hutchby, Ian 283–4
Hyperbase software 174
hyperglobalisers 542, 547; homogenising world languages 547–8
hyperlinks 242
hyper-democracy 615

ICTs (Internet communication tools) 412; 2008 Obama election campaign 415; framing processes 418, 422; geographical differences in use of 415; mobilising structures 418, 422; North-South European divide 415; opportunity structures 418, 422; politicians' use of 415; protesters 421; sharing information 421
identity: complexity of 624–5; construction 402, 682; construction, conversation analysis 401; cross-cutting identities 624–5; discursive performances of 399; personal 399, 406; political identity as performance 399–400; political self 398–9; social 399; Social Constructionist paradigm 474; *see also* framing; positioning
identity formation 370
identity performance 398–9
identity politics 624–5
ideological learning 144
ideological metaphors 202–3, 205; researching 207–8
ideological square, concept of 682
ideological state apparatus (ISA) 38, 39, 40
Ideologiekritik 32; *see also* Marx
ideology/ideologies 32, 203; Althusser on 37–8; discourse-historical approach (DHA) and 443; indirect indexicality 521; insertion of concepts into 130
ideoscapes 543
Illich, Ivan 224

image repair 272
image schema analysis 189–90; point of view 191–2, 193, 195–6, 197–8
images, in comics 457
imaginary, Lacan 37, 82, 83, 84, 86–7
imitation, theory of 22
immersed experiencers 194–5
immigration 188–9, 253; 'go home or face arrest' campaign 334–5; topic in parliamentary debates 317
impartiality 337
impartiality of civil servants 328
impersonal authority legitimation 222–3; *see* legitimation
implicit racism 635–9
impoliteness in parliament 319
inadvertent racism 635–9
incipient legitimation, 219–20; *see* legitimation
Independence Day 372
independence, Scotland 391–3
indexicality 521, 522; direct 521; indirect 521
India, cross-cutting cleavages 624–5
indigenous groups 291
indirect indexicality 521
indirection, technique of 272
individual autonomy 45
individualism 82, 214, 215
individual self-determination 45
individual sovereignty 48
inequality 656–7; civic 653; existential 647–8, 652, 653, 656; impact of global financial crisis (2008) 648; as a moral concern 647; moral/political 647; physical 647; Plato 647; property 647; resource 648, 652, 656; Rousseau 647; in Spain 646; typology of assets 648–9; vital 647, 648, 653, 656; *see also* class struggle and warfare
inferiorisation 631
informal logic 249–50
infotainment 286–7
in-groups 142, 203, 319, 331, 332; dichotomies 502, 683; discursive strategies 507; governments 336; meetings 473, 474; national 377; solidarity 378; us versus them discourse 682, 683; war and terrorism 674, 682; 'We' 142, 530
innovation hypothesis 414
Instagram 220
institutional discourse 74
institutional meetings 468
Institutio oratoria (Quintilian) 21–2
instrumental rationalisation legitimation 230; *see* legitimation

Index

intellectuals: Gramsci's study of 36–7; organic 36–7; traditional 37
intelligibility (*Verständlichkeit*) 43, 49, 50, 54
intensifying devices 332
interactional sociolinguistics (IS) 401–2, 468, 469; *see also* framing; positioning
interactionist approaches 111
interactionist fallacy 113
interaction, study of 277
interactive genre 373
interdisciplinarity 137
interdiscourse 265–6
interdiscursivity 443, 577
Interfaith Centre on Corporate Responsibility 562
internal sovereignty 48
international capitalism 211
International Labour Rights Fund 561
international meetings 475
International Relations (IR) 594
Internet 412
Internet communication tools (ICTs) *see* ICTs (Internet communication tools)
Inter-Parliamentary Union 514
interpellations 38, 312
interruptions 318–19
intersubjectivity: communicative 49, 52; critical 46, 48; everyday 46; experiences of 44
intertextual chains 545
intertextual discourse analysis 400
intertextuality 238, 392–3, 400, 443, 445, 451, 576
interventions, political debate 515
interviews: celebrity talk-shows 287; journalistic and infotainment 286–7
intra-corpus comparison 181–3
intra-governmental stripes 336–7
introduction (*exordium*) of commemorative speeches 371
introductory speeches 347
inventio (invention) 20, 25, 248
inventory measurements 561
Invisible Men, The 532, 533; Abud 535, 536; Arabic and Hebrew languages 535–7; claim to citizenship 534–5; Louie 533–7; political asylum 533–4
IPCC (Intergovernmental Panel on Climate Change) 488
irony 319–20
Isin, Engin 530
Isocrates 18–19
Israel: belonging 533; gay and lesbian citizens 533; Gaza War 639–41; progressive, symbolic opposition to traditional Palestine 533; *see also Invisible Men, The*
Israeli Defense Forces (IDF) 640
issue-specific corpora 171
Italian parliament 320–1
Italy: caricature, origins of 458; fascism 621; neo-fascism 619–20

Jackson, Samuel L. 636–8
Jacquemet, M. 238
Jäger, Siegfried 139
Japan, globalisation and 542
Jediism 595
Jenninger, Phillip 373
Jewish people *see* antisemitism; Israel; Nazi discourse
Jobbik Party 621
Johnson, Boris 389–91
Johnstone, Barbara 268
Jones, Owen 157, 161, 163
jouissance 83, 84, 106; language and 89–91
journalism: aggressive questioning 287, 349–50; news journalism 350–2; process of moments/phases 351; roll of 350
journalist-controlled press conferences 349
journalistic and infotainment interviews 286–7
journalists: aggressiveness of questioning 349–50; attributes of 287; crisis 182; interrogations by 349–50; post-interviews 350; press conferences 342, 343–5, 346; question-and-answer sessions 348–9; self-perception 350; *see also* press conferences
Judaism 592
judgements 161, 280, 319, 596
judicial genre 371
justice 105
justice globalisms 544–5, 552
Just War Theory 674

Kant, Immanuel 68, 69, 589
Kantorowicz, Ernst 300
Karhun kansa 595
Kerry, John 587
keyword analysis 177
Kienpointner, Manfred 247, 248, 255
Kitchener, Lord 222
Klaus, Václav 143
Klemperer, Victor 2, 662
Klimaforum09 489
knowledge: power and 74; reconstruction of 140
knowledge-constitutive interests 48
knowledge technologies 558
Kohl, Helmut 376

700

Korea, globalisation and 542
Kosarac, Dario 528
Koselleck, Reinhart 122–3; action and context 129–30; basic concepts and politics 131; crisis, concept of 126; distinction between structure and event 127; language 123–4; language as a tension between representation and world 127; metonymisation 125; polysemy 125; reference 126–9; representation 124–6; revolution, concept of 126, 128; semantic fields 124–5; state, concept of 128
Kosovers 238–9
Kracauer, Siegfried 142
Kraus, Karl 661
Kress, Gunther 136
Kroebner, Richard 122
Kubálková, Vendulka 594
Küçükali, Can 138, 139
KWIC (key words in context) 126
Kyoto Protocol (1997) 489

Labov, William 157, 161; narrative of personal experience 234
Lacan, Jacques 37; algorithms 85; division between reality and the real 83; Freud and 84; humans becoming subjects in language 83; imaginary, the 34, 82, 83, 84, 86–7; *jouissance* 83, 84, 89–91, 106; language and *jouissance* 89–91; linguistics 82; myth 87–8; *objet petit a* 90, 91; psychoanalysis 82, 106; real, the 83, 84, 86–7, 89–90; retroactivity 83, 93; Return to Freud 87–9; Saussure and 84, 85; semiotics 84–6; signifier 83, 84, 91; signifier and signified 85–7; split subject 82–3; symbolic, the 83–4, 91; Thing, the 106; transference 87, 88, 91; trees 86
La Caricature magazine 460
Laclau, Ernesto 4, 90; antagonism 104–5; articulation 97–8, 99; better society, pure idea of a 103, 104; discourse theory *see* discourse theory, Laclau; dislocation 90, 100–1, 104; empty signifier, category of 90–1, 103–4, 105; hegemony *see* hegemony, Laclau; Lacanian psychoanalysis 106; nodal point 99; populism, theory of 92, 93
LADO (language analysis for the determination of origin) assessment 550, 551
Lakoff, George 141, 188, 205, 332, 573–4, 676
La Marseillaise (national anthem) 429
land expropriations 649–50
language: articulation of interests 31; citizenship and belonging 529–32; conceptual history 123–4; controlling 2; historians and 122; legitimation and 218–19; mixing 548–9; as object of struggle 116; as practical consciousness 31, 40; representation 123, 124–6; tension between representation and world 127; *see also* linguistics
Language & Asylum Research Group 551–2
Language and Globalisation Social Justice Movement (LG-SJM) 550–2
language and politics: interdisciplinary endeavour 5–6
language-constitutive interests 48
language discrimination 551
language of globalisation 541–6
language ideology/ies 361, 543, 552; *see* ideology
language policy arbiters 363
language proficiency 550–1
languages, command of 110
Lascoumes, Pierre 77
Lasswell, Harold D 2, 153; coy approach 162; Freudian psychiatry 153–4; judgements 161; newspaper articles 154–5; propaganda symbols 153; psychoanalytic interviews 153–4; symbols 154, 164–5; university career 153, 154; vision 164; words as data 158–60; *see also* content analysis; Nazism
laughter 517–22
Lautsi, Soile 596
law 51; constitutional, democracy and 52–3; legitimacy of 218; *see also* policy-making
Lazarsfeld, Paul 2
learning: blocked 143, 144; defensive 143–4; dogmatic 143; ideological 144; regressive 144
left-wing parties 417
left-wing politics 618, 619; contrast with right-wing politics 619
legal system, plain meaning rule 362
legal texts 356–7
Lega Nord 442
legislation process as a complex collective work on texts 297–8
legitimacy: narrative 681; political violence and 674–6
legitimate language 116
legitimate law 53
legitimation: government officeholders 332; language and 218–19; law 218; multimodal approaches 219; persuasive role of 219–20; practices and 218–19; social practices 218, 290; visual and musical realisation 220; *see also* authority legitimation; moral evaluation legitimation; rationalisation legitimation

legitimisation 327
Leites, Nathan 2; *see* Lasswell
Leitī 549
Lemkin, Raphael 270
Leninism 619
Le Pen, Marine 622
lesbian citizens: in Israel 533; in Palestine 533; rhetoric of visibility 529, 537
Lévi-Strauss, Claude 37, 68
lexeme 174
lexical-semantic techniques 3
lexicometrics 171–2, 174; contrasting in 174–5; software 174–5
Lexico software 174
liberal democracy 619
Liberation Day, Italy (25 April) 372
lifestyle identities 224
lightness/heaviness in rhythms 437
likeability 403–4
Lincoln, Bruce 589–90
lingua-franca: meetings 476; need for 546
linguascape 543, 552
linguistica spaziale (spatial linguistics) 34
linguistic capital 113
linguistic discourse analysis 268
linguistic habitus 112
linguistic modality 189
linguistic repertoires 548–50
linguistic representations 327
linguistic rhetorical analysis 250
linguistics: capacities 111; conceptual history and 132; *see also* language
linguistic triangle 123–4
Lisbon Treaty 146
Lloyd George, David 624
logic 23; fallacies 252
logic of difference 101, 102
logic of equivalence 101–2, 103
logics framework 609–10
logics of denial 609–14; Britain in the 1970s 611–12; capital flight 612–13; comparisons with political conflict elsewhere 613–14
logics of fantasy 610
log-likelihood (LL) 175, 177
logos (rational appeal) 19, 262, 264, 271
loud/soft sounds 435, 436
Louis XIV 458
loving care, *topos* of 510–11
lynchings 155, 160; evaluation in newspaper articles 161; Georgia 157, 160–1; hanging body on display 163–4; Jones, Owen 157, 161, 163; Stamps, Peter 160–1, 161–2, 163–4

Macgilchrist, Felicitas 141
Machiavelli, Niccolò 40, 329
Madisonian Democracy 623
Magna Carta 225
Maingueneau, Dominique 267
Mair, Eddie 390–1
majority groups 592
majority rule 623
Major, John 386–8
management of meetings 470–3; mediated turn-taking system 470; turn-type pre-allocation system 470
man as political animal 1–2
manifestos 441; British political parties 442
manipulation 18, 33, 54, 136, 143, 233, 266, 277, 328, 489, 623; government communication as 329–30
Manning, Souto 239
manual labour 31
Maquila Solidarity Network 562
margin measurements 561
markdown measurements 561
markers of personal deixis 390
market globalisms 544, 551
marketisation 605
markets, Bourdieusian metaphor 111–12, 116
Martianus Capella 23
Martin, Craig 592
Marxism: CDS (Critical Discourse Studies) 137–9; conflict theory 329; economic essentialism 96
Marxism-Leninism 619
Marx, Karl 30–3; CDA (Critical Discourse Analysis) 137; ideologies 32; language as practical consciousness 31, 40; political economy 31–2; primitive accumulation 649
masculine culture of politics 514
masculine gender norms 320
mass communication 2
mass media 2, 40, 349, 383, 399, 441, 521, 631, 667
mass mediation 169
master-narratives 236–7, 239
materialism: aleatory 40; historical 31, 35
materiality 33, 41, 83, 127, 656
Maude, Francis 333
McCrimlisk, J., ND. 405–7
McCutcheon, Russell T 591
MCDA (Multimodal Critical Discourse Analysis) 426; application to climate change 496; application to sound 427
McDougal, Walter Hugh 463

702

McNair, Brian 5, 6
meaning-making 220
meaning(s) 99; discourses and 99; fragmentation of 219; legitimation and 219; understanding of 97
media: climate change and 490–1, 495; sustainable development 494, 495
media democracy 573
media logic 384, 385
mediascapes 543
mediated populism 395
mediated self-representation 418
mediated turn-taking system 470
mediated visibility 384
mediatisation: authentic personalities and the language of the popular 389–91; media sociability and the conversationalisation of political discourse 385–6; mediated political sincerity 386–8; mediated visibility and political personality 384; political debate and the semiotics of empathy 393–4; political leaflets 391–3; politics and 5, 6, 345, 384–5; *see also* political language
meetings 468–70; audience participation 470; business/corporate 468; categories 473; chairperson role of 473; Conversational Analysis (CA) approach 468–9; Critical Discourse Analysis (CDA) approach 468, 469; definition 468; disagreements 479, 480; institutional 468; interactional sociolinguistics (IS) approach 468, 469; international 475; lingua-franca meetings 473–5; mediated turn-taking system 470; methodological approaches to 469; multilingual 475–9; political 468, 471–2; politics of 480–1; solving problems and reaching decisions 479–80; studying, common challenges 469; turn-taking and management of 470–3; turn-type pre-allocation system 470
Mein Kampf (Hitler) 661, 663
melodies 431–4; pitch 431–3
Membership Categorisation Analysis 473
Members of Parliament (MPs) *see* MPs (Members of Parliament)
Members of the European Parliament (MEPs) *see* MEPs (Members of the European Parliament)
memoria (memory) 248, 249
Mendelssohn, Moses 592
mental labour 31
mental representations 194, 195
mental simulation 194

MEPs (members of the European Parliament) 310, 321; Twitter, use of 415–16
mercato determinato (determinate market) 35
mere rhetoric 247
Merkel, Angela 517
message/discourse-centred approaches to political communication 5
metadiscourse 317–18
meta-narratives 239
metaphorisation 125, 126
metaphor keywords 208, 209
metaphors 141, 188, 189; austerity 208; candidate 207, 208; characterising and influencing thought 204; classification 208; comparisons of 205; competition 206; Euro-sclerosis 214–15; football 206; nation-as-a-family 141; in political genres 202; political issues 208; reconstructing 256; reiteration of 202; relay 214; speed-related 212; sports 205; struggle 205; teambuilding 474; use by Nazis 663–4; visual 208; war 205; *see also* CMT (Conceptual Metaphor Theory); Competitive Race metaphors; conceptual metaphors; ideological metaphors; purposeful metaphors
metonymisation 125
metonymy 255
metronomic time/no metronomic time 437
Mexican parliament 318–19
Michels, Robert 622
micro-blogging 415
microphysics of power 76
Middle Ages, rhetoric in 22–4
middle-range theories 179, 180
migrants 550; language proficiency 551
migration, 240
Miliband, Ed 203
milieu, social and economic 45
Miller, Max 143
minimum wage 559
ministerial statements 312
minority groups 592
minority rights 623
Minsk Protocol 447
misrecognition 115–16
misrepresentation 327
Miteinandersein (being-with-one-another) 53; *see* Habermas
mitigating devices 332
mitigation/intensification 251
Mitterrand, François 376
mobilising structures, social movements 418, 422

Index

mobility, human 551
modernisation losers 626
modernity 130, 590
modern subjects 68–9
Modood, Tariq 588–9
modus inveniendi 23
modus proferendi 23
Montesano Montessori, Nicolina 140–1
moral evaluation legitimation 226–8; abstraction 228–9; analogy 227–8; evaluation 227; *see* legitimation
moral inequality 647
morality 51
moral values 228, 272
More, Thomas 89
morphology 255
mortgage defaults 650
motifs 157
Mouffe, Chantal 4, 96; *see also* discourse theory, Laclau; hegemony, Laclau
movable type printing 457
Mozer, Yariv 532
MPs (Members of Parliament) 309; as addressees and audience members 315; in a co-performance 317; as direct participants 316; discourse of 311; parliamentary questions 313–14; parliamentary speeches 312–13; political line of 317; in the public eye 315; responsibilities of 312
multicultural politics 47
multidisciplinarity 137
multilingualism 146, 529, 546; differential 546–7
multilingual meetings 475–9
Multimodal Critical Discourse Analysis (MCDA) *see* MCDA (Multimodal Critical Discourse Analysis)
multimodality 194–8; advertising and 219; legitimation and 219; meaning-making 220; studies 195
multi-party dialogues 315–16
multi-semioticity 529
Murph, Karen 236
music: certainty and commitment in 434; classical 428, 434; as communicative act in hunting 427; conformity 226; emotive power of 222; gender representations in 428; heraldic function of 222–3; language of 428; legitimation and 220; lyrics of national anthems 430–1; melodies 431–4; moral values 228–9; opera 428; rhythm 436–7; tradition 225; wedding ceremonies 427; *see also* national anthem, the; sound

musical signifiers 222
Mutual Information (MI) score 175, 176
mutual understanding 43
myth 87–8; *see also* fictionalisation

Naija Afro Hip-Hop 549
Nakigudde, Harriet 528
naming 117, 332
narrative analysis 156–8, 233–4; dealing with texts 157–8; political identity construction 400; widened scope of 241–2
narrative (*narratio*) of commemorative speeches 371
narrative rights 681
narrative(s): asylum seekers 238; coming-out 242; concise 240; definitions of 234–5; difference from stories 234; in the discourse of politicians 239–40; everyday discourse practices and genres 233; fictionalised TV series of politics 577; grand 236–9; humorous 240; master 233, 236–7, 239; as methodology or epistemology 235; of personal experience 234; as political sense making 240–4; politics and 235–6; positioning and 405; theory 73, 144; trends 233; truth commissions 238; video 242–3
narrotology 234
Nast, Thomas 462
national anthem, the: as discourse 428; lyrics of 430–1; melodies 432–4; nationalism and 429–30; origins and deployment 428–30; pitch 431–3; shorter notes 434; sound qualities of 435–6
National Assembly (Wales) 523; debating turns 523
national identities 237; Austrian 253
National Institute of Music 222
nationalism 99, 101, 149, 374, 428, 533, 621, 625; colonies 429; French 429; German state 429; sound qualities of 435–6
nationality, citizenship and 529–30
national-popular 35, 40
National Socialism *see* Nazism
National Socialist Party 621, 622
national sovereignty 48; defence of 625
nations: arms race 204; competing 203–4; identities of 237
nation-states 591–2; war and 674; Westphalian system 674
NATO (North Atlantic Treaty Organization) 448
naturalisation 227
naturalism 88
natural language 264

Natural Language Processing (NPL) *see* NPL (Natural Language Processing)
natural preferences, *topos* of 510
Nazi discourse: camouflage terminology 666–7; censorship 662; claim to new language 661–2; CMT (Conceptual Metaphor Theory) approach 663; conceptual mapping 663–4; counter-discourse 666, 667; *Dictionary of inhumanity* (Sternberger et al.) 662; discourse-historical approach (DHA) 662–3; discourse-rules (*Sprachregelungen*) 662; euphemisms 666–7; genocidal intentions, signalling of 665; Gestapo documentation 665; insider information 665–6; Jews-as-parasites 664; *LTI* (*Lingua Tertii Imperii*) (Klemperer) 662; media, control of 662; *Mein Kampf* (Hitler) 661, 663; Nuremberg laws 664–5; parasite-annihilation scenario 663, 664, 667; propaganda 662, 666; public sphere, control of 666; speeches, case study 664–7; taboos 666
Nazism 2, 142, 210, 222, 372–3, 373, 619, 621; genocide 663–4; *see also* Hitler, Adolf
negative interrogatives 278
negative politeness in parliament 319
negative semantic prosody 521
neo-fascism 619–20
neoliberal globalisation of production 558–62
neoliberal model 46–7
neoliberal values 228
neolinguistics 34
Netanyahu, Benjamin 269–72
Netherlands: Catholics/Protestants political identity 624; far-right politics 620
neuroscience 118
neutralism, norm of 286
New Atheists 595
New Capitalism 543, 550
new ethicalism 567–8
New Labour 212
new media 242
New Rhetoric 264, 266
news conferences 287–8
news interviews 276–8, 286, 343, 470, 517–21
newspaper comics 462–3
newspaper comic strips 463
newspaper political cartoons 463
Newspeak 660
news production 350–2
Nietzsche, Friedrich 68, 71
Nigeria 549
Nixon, Richard 287
No Child Left Behind Act (NCLB) 363–4

nodal points 99
nomination 251; *see* discursive strategies; DHA
non-sensory diegetic images 457
non-verbal communication 379, 401
normalisation hypothesis 414, 415
normativity 51
norms: adversarialism 286; neutralism 286; policies and laws 357
Norway, politicians' use of Twitter and Facebook 416
Norwegian Constitution Day (17 May) 372
NPL (Natural Language Processing) 170, 171, 174; tools 172
Nuremberg laws 664–5
Nyborg, Birgitte (TV character) 573–4, 581–3; *see* fictionalisation

Obama, Barack 106, 401, 589; debate with Hillary Clinton 403–4
objectivity 49, 162, 286, 490, 532
objet petit a, Lacan 90, 91, 92
O Canada (OC) 429, 430–1; dotted notes 434; pitch (melody) 433; rhythm 437
Occupy Movement 419, 544
October Revolution (7 November 1917) 372
officeholders, government 327, 330; argumentation schemes 332; denial 332; exerting power 334; framing 332; intensifying and mitigating devices 332; language of 331; legitimation 332; managing actions 335–6; naming and attributing 332; perspective-taking 332; social actor and action representation 332; warrants 332
official commemorations 237
off-the-record press conferences 343
Olbrechts-Tyteca, Lucie 249
Olofsson, Maud 347–8
One in Nine group 531
one-sided schemas 190
open-book accounting 560
opportunity structures, social movements 418, 422
oppositional discourse 117, 220
oral ministerial statements 312
oral parliamentary questions 313
orators 18, 19; functions of 21; ideal role and education of 21; skills of 22; *see also* rhetoric
oratory 19
Ordaz, Valera 419
order of discourse, Foucault 139, 544
order of the things, Bourdieu 114
order of things, Foucault 72
organic intellectuals, Gramsci 36–7

Orwell, George 2, 660
Osborne, George 612, 613
out-groups 193, 203, 332; constructive strategies 682; dichotomies 502, 683; discursive strategies 507; Europe as 334; officeholders 337; political war narratives 682; racism 631; segregation and discrimination 378; us versus them discourse 682, 683
overhearers 316
overtime, illegal 559
overt impoliteness in parliament 319
Owens, Jared 225
Oxford English Dictionary (OED) 209

paganism 595
Pahor, Borut 361
PAH (Platform for those Affected by Mortgages) 656–7; assemblies 652; direct action 653; home-evictions 653–4; non-violence 654; website 652–3
Palestine 639–41; gay and lesbian citizens 533, 536; traditional, symbolic opposition to Israel 533; *see also Invisible Men, The*
Palin, Sarah 407, 516
Palme, Olof 344
panning 195
Panopticon 71
paradiastole 156, 163
paradigmatic (logical-hierarchical) 174
parallelisms 255
parallel language 285
parasite-annihilation scenario 663, 664, 667
para-social interaction 391
parent-child relationship 506
parliamentary debates 310; addressees and audiences 315; adversariality 311; agonistic features 311; audience-oriented 311; barracking 523; co-operativeness 311; deliberation in parliament 311; discourse genre and its subgenres 312–14; discourse of MPs 311; gender roles 320–1; in the House of Commons 515, 523; humour and irony 319–20; key research topics on 317–21; ministerial statements 312; participant roles 315–17; partisan/planted questions 314; politeness and impoliteness 319; Prime Minister's Questions (PMQs) 313–14; Question Time (QT) 313–14, 318, 319; in the Scottish Parliament 523; speaking turns 523; style of 313; theatre scenarios 311; unparliamentary language 319; in the Welsh National Assembly 523

parliamentary democracy: stability of 297–9; texts 297–9
parliamentary institutions 309–11; committees 309, 310; debate parliaments 309; oversight of the executive 310; plenary chambers 309; questioning of ministers 310; Westminster-system 309, 312; working parliaments 309
parliamentary metadiscourse 317–18
parliamentary parenthicals 318
parliamentary questions 313–14
parliamentary speeches 312–13
parliament(s): addressees 315; censorship in 320; covert impoliteness in 319; deliberation in 311; European, variation in 321; evolution of 320; German 311; interruptions 318–19; reinvention and reactivation of 320; Swiss 311; US Congress 311; Westminster-type 309, 312
parsing, lexical and syntactic 174
participation 18, 44, 53, 277, 312, 330, 401, 603, 611, 615n, 653
participation frameworks 241–2
participatory democracy meetings 282
partisan questions 314
partisans 675
party programmes: compound nouns 450; of the Fatherland Party 447–9, 451; as genres of political action 441–2; metaphors and specialised vocabulary 450; personal pronouns 445; of the Petro Poroshenko Bloc 445–7; proverbs 445–6; of the Radical Party of Oleh Liashko 449–51; studied choosing discourse-historical approach 443; *see also* Ukrainian parliamentary election campaign (2014)
pathos 19, 262, 271
patterns of reasoning 265
pauses in speech 388
Pêcheux, Michel 2
Peck, Edward 677
Perelman, Chaïm 249
performance: identity 398–9; political identity as 399–401
performance of politics 385
periodisation 180
peroratio 371
personal authority, legitimation 221–2
personal autonomy 48
personal dictatorships 619
personal experience, narrative of 234
personal identity 399, 406
personalisation 386
personalisation of politics 606

personalised politics 337
personal pronouns 386, 445, 505
perspectivation, strategies of 251; *see* DHA
persuasion 17, 248; *see also* rhetoric
persuasive role of legitimation 219–20
Petro Poroshenko Bloc 445–7
Philipon, Charles 460
philology 34
philosophy 19
philosophy of science 173
philosophy of the subject 67–8
phonology 255
phoros 269–70
physical identification 506–7
physical inequality 647
picture stories 461
Pieterse, Nederveen 220
pitch (melody) 431–3
plain meaning rule 362
planted questions 314
Plataforma de Afectados por la Hipoteca see PAH (Platform for those Affected by Mortgages)
platforms (party manifestos) 441
Plato 19, 647
plebiscitarian techniques and instruments 623
plenary chambers 310
plenary halls 294
PLO (Palestinian Liberation Organisation) 675
plots 164, 389, 491, 575–7, 581–3, 682; distinction from stories 156–7
point-of-view specifications 191–2, 193, 195–6, 197–8
polemical dimension of political discourse 263
policies *see* policy making
policy appropriation *see* appropriation, concept of
policy convergence 605–6
policy document 326–7, 331, 338, 352, 358, 360, 441
policy implementation 362; bottom-up view 362; top-down view 362
policy instruments, government 328–9
policy making 238, 355–6; analysing policy genres in institutional context 357–60; language of policies and laws 356–7; norms 357; policy genres in the EU 358–60; policy texts 358, 359, 360–2; public 334; research questions 358
policy meanings 362–4
policy texts 358, 359, 364–5; analysing the genesis of 360–2
Polish parliament 320

polis (public affairs) 263
politeness in parliament 319
political action(s) 398; party programmes and billboards as genres of 441–2, 452
political animal, man as 1–2
political apparatus 45
political asylum 533–4
political candidates *see* candidates, political
political caricature(s): sixteenth century 457–8; eighteenth century 458–9; nineteenth century 460–2; twentieth century 462–3; twenty-first century 463–5
political cartooning 454
political cartoon satire 458
political commemoration: argumentation patterns 377–8; commemorative speeches 370–4; common memory 369, 378; discourse-historical focus on 377–8; fundamental characteristics of 369–70; good and bad practice 379; historical politolinguistics 378, 379; individual knowledge of the past 370; integrative function 370; polity 370; secularisation 369; semiotics of 374–7; shared memory 369, 370, 379; socially disintegrative function 370; tripartite question 370; tropes 378
political communication 3; genres of 441; message/discourse-centred approaches to 5; reception-centred approaches to 5; source-centred approaches to 5, 6
political communities 299
political culture 292
political debates 393–4
political deliberation 269
political discourse 2–3; Bourdieu 117–18; epideictic mode 263; framing 402–3; identity performance and 398–9; limits and goals 263; link to argumentation 262, 268; polemical dimension 263; *see also* argumentation analysis
Political Discourse Analysis 267
political disenchantment 330
political disengagement 604–7
political economy 31–2
political events 237
political hegemony 107; *see also* Laclau, Ernesto
political identity 399–401; positioning 405
political inequality 647
political institutions 292; press conferences 345; *see also* ethnography
political issues 3
political language: authentic personalities 389–91; Critical Discourse Analysis (CDA)

707

and 383; personalisation and simplification of 395; *see also* mediatisation
political leaflets 391–3
political logics 610
politically controlled press conferences 349
political meetings 468, 471–2
political organisations, communication within 2–3
political parties: internet communication, use of 422; websites 416–17
political performance: interactional sociolinguistics 401–2; political discourse and identity performance 398–9; political identity as performance 399–401; *see also* framing; positioning
political personality 384
political power 3–4, 46
political processes 292
political protests 195–7
political rhetoric 312
political rhetorical acts 248
political rights 46
political self, the 398–9, 400
political sincerity, mediated 386–8
political speeches 239, 242, 284–6; closing statements 400; as events 470; press conferences 347
political spin 5
political subjectivity, Laclau 100
political, the 4, 236
political theology 590–1
political violence: justifications for 674; legitimacy and 674–6; meaning 675–6; 'us' versus 'them' binary 674; *see also* terrorism; war
political Web 2.0 communication: citizen-to-citizen communication 418–21; Facebook 416; genre theoretic concepts 413–14; Internet 412; during political activities 420; politician-to-citizen communication 414–18; social media platforms 412–13; Twitter 415–16, 420; websites of political parties and politicians 416–17
politicians: claim to public representativeness 390; discourses of 118, 239–40; Facebook, use of 416; honesty and self-interest 606; mediated persona 383; micro-blogging 415; narratives and 236, 239–40; personalising stories 240; populist 390; press conferences 345; private lives 575; question-and-answer sessions 349; social media and Web 2.0 review 417–18; strategies and techniques to attract public attention 6; style of 3; televisual mode of public speaking 387; Twitter, use of 415; use of ICTs 415; websites, use of 416–17; *see also* candidates, political; depoliticisation; fictionalisation
politicisation of fiction 573
politicotainment 573
politics: basic concepts and 130; conflict and co-operation 5; contradictory senses of 326; definition of 4–5; distinction with the political 4; ethnographic studies 292; masculine culture of 514; narratives and 235–6; ordering of social relations 4; personalised 337; thinking about 236; tied to economic relations 4; understanding 3–5; of words 291–3; *see also* fictionalisation of politics; gendered politics; mediatisation
Politics (Aristotle) 1–2
politics beyond words 291, 293, 301
politics of ageing 501
politics of belonging 533
politics of storytelling 292–3, 301–2
politics of words 291–3
Politolinguistics 250
Polsby et al. 399
polysemy 125
Ponzi schemes 650
pop quiz questions 286
popular, the 389–91
populism 618; complexity of identities and 624–5; contemporary 623; defence of national sovereignty 625; European Parliament elections (2014) 625; in former communist Europe 622; identity politics 624–5; perceived role of representing the majority 623; Tea Party 627; theoretical explanation of 622–3; theory of 92, 93; *see also* far right; extreme right
populist politicians 390
populist radical right-wing parties 101, 105
populist ventriloquism 391
Poroshenko, Petro 444
Portuguese parliament 319
positional family 221
positioning 241; case study, Joni Ernst 405–7; first-level 407; narrative and interaction, study of 405; political identity 405; political performance 405; second-level 407; theory 405; third-level 407
positioning power 77
positive face 404
positive impoliteness in parliament 319
positive politeness in parliament 319
post-communist world 47

postdisciplinarity 137
posters 442
post-interviews 350
post-normal science 490
post-structuralist approaches 139–41
Poujadism 620
power: analytics of, Foucault 75–7; communicative 46; disciplinary 76; governmentality 76–7; and knowledge, Foucault 74; language as medium of 443; legitimate 4; microphysics of 76; political 3–4, 46; positioning 77; sovereign 76
power relations 75; historical transformations of 76
PP (Partido Popular) 651, 656; attack on the PAH 654–5, 656; campaign about escraches 654–5, 656; corruption scandals 651, 656; links to Franco regime 655; mortgage law 654; reference to Hitler and Nazism 655
practical reasoning 262, 267
practices: legitimation of 218–19; meanings 219
Pragma-dialectics 250, 253, 254, 266, 267
pragmatics 129–30
pragmatic text-linguistic techniques 3
predication 251; see discourse strategies; DHA
press conferences 287–8, 342–3; boundaries between politicians and journalists 345; communicative strategies 344; diplomacy 346; frontstage activities 352; as genre and sub-genre 345–7; historical development 343–5; joint 344; journalist-controlled 349; managing scandals 346–7; news production and 350–2; politically controlled 349; political speeches 347; post-interviews 350; question-and-answer session 348–9; regular and confidential 344; in Sweden 344, 347, 351, 352; televised 344; in the United States 343–4; US presidential 343–4, 349–50, 351
press officers 344
pride parade (Johannesburg) 531
Prime Minister's Questions (PMQs) 313–14, 318
primitive accumulation 649
Prince, The (Machiavelli) 329
private autonomy 53
privatisation 650
PR managers, managing scandals 346–7
probatio 371
problematisation 70, 504–5
problem-solving in meetings 479–80
Prodicus 18
production: neoliberal globalisation of 558–62; social relations of 561–2; *see also* Bourdieu; relations of production

professionalism 224
profile orientation 196
Pro-Life activists 254
pronouns: block of 347; first-person plural 319; personal 386, 445, 505
propaganda symbols 153
property, inequality and 647, 656
propitious moment (*kairos*) 18
prospective (retrospective) critique 136; *see* DHA
Protagoras 18
Protective Edge (military operation) 269, 272
proverbs 445–6
proximation 189
PR (public relations) 345
pseudo-masculinity/pseudo-femininity 142
psychoanalysis 82; *see also* Lacan, Jacques
public attention, attracting 6
public-choice theoretic assumptions 605, 606
public communication 329, 330
public discourse 237
public representativeness 390
public speaking 26
public sphere 142, 330
Puck 461
Punch 455, 460, 461; Punch Pencilling 461
purposeful metaphors 202
Putin, Vladimir 450–1
puzzle-solutions 285
PVV (Dutch Freedom Party) 620, 625

quadrivium, the 23
quantification 158, 166n5, 282, 287–8
quantitative narrative analysis (QNA) 156–8
Queen's English 116
queer migration 529
question-and-answer sessions 348–9
questioning: answering strategies in parliament 319; EP (European Parliament) 321; parliamentary practices of 318; partisan/planted questions 314; pop quiz 286–7; Prime Minister's Questions (PMQs) 314, 318; progressive 287; question-and-answer session 348–9
Question Time (QT) 313–14, 318, 319, 321
Quintilian 21–2
quoting 74, 318, 351
Quran, The 222
Qutb, Sayyid 589

Rabinow, Paul 78
race: arms 204, 210; entries in the OED 209; global 204, 209, 210, 212–14; space 210

racial stereotypes 220
racial stereotyping 637–8
racism: biological 632; black Africans 631; differentiation 631; essence attribution 631; during the High Middle Ages 631; implicit, case study 635–9, 642; inferiorisation 631; Israeli-Palestinian conflict, case study 639–41, 642; lay understandings of 630–1; race and discourse 633–4; Spanish Inquisition 632; Swiss People's Party, case study 634–5, 642; as threat 639–41; transmission 631–2; *see also* antisemitism; far right
Radical Party of Oleh Liashko 449–51
radio phone-in shows 283–4
Ramus, Petrus 24–5
Rancière, Jacques 118
Rank Xerox 221–2
Rasmussen, Anders Fogh 681
raspiness in sound/music 435, 436
rational appeal (*logos*) 19
rational dispute 266
rationalisation legitimation 229; instrumental 230; theoretical 230–1; *see* legitimation
rat race, metaphor 210, 211–12
Reagan, Ronald 280, 376
reality *see* human reality
real, the (Lacan) 37, 83, 84, 86–7, 89–90
reasoning, patterns of 265
reasoning, practical 262, 267
reason (*Verstand*) 49, 50, 54
reception-centred approaches to political communication 5
reciprocal constructions 191, 193
reciprocity, democracy and 44–5, 53
recontextualisation 33, 135, 144–6, 414, 576–7, 681
redescription 156, 160
reductionism 118; sociological 118, 119
reference 126–9
referentialism 680
referentiality 129
reflective stakeholders 565
reframing: Hillary Clinton, case study 404; as key political communication strategies 402; presidential self, the 402
refugees 550
refutatio 371
regimes of mobility 528
registers of analysis 37
regressive learning 144
regular transitive constructions 191, 193
regulation, democracy and 50–1, 54
Reichardt, Rolf 126

relational identification 505–6
relations of production 38, 39; reproduction of 39; social 33, 35
relations of strategy 76
relay metaphor 214
religion: as an analytical concept 588–91; becoming culture 596; civilised people and 594; colonialism and 592–4; in France 588; Habermas on 588; majority groups 595; maximalist and minimalist models 589–90; minority groups 595; nation-states 591–2; political theology and 590–1; problematic conceptualisations of 594–5; relative separation from the state 589; in the United Kingdom 588–9; in the United States 588; *see also* secularism
religious dress 596
religious globalisms 544
religious language 588
remembrance days 372
Renaissance, rhetoric 24
representation 123, 124–6, 327, 334
repressive state apparatus (RSA) 38, 39, 40
resistance 117, 119
resistance fighters 676
Resolution for a National Language Policy Programme for 2014–2018 (RLP-14) 361
resource inequality 648, 652, 656
respect for the elderly 508
responsibility/ies 312, 469, 474, 489, 508, 558, 574; *topos* of 509
Retail Link system 559–60
retail, neo-liberal globalisation of 558–62
retroactivity 83, 93
return measurements 561
Return to Freud, Lacan 87–9
retweeting 421; *see* Web 2.0
reverb/echo in sound/music 435, 436
revolutionary partisans 675, 679
revolution, concept of 126, 128
rhetoric 26–7, 206; in Ancient Greece 1, 18–20; in Ancient Rome 20–2; Aquinas, Thomas 24; Aristotle 19–20, 247, 248; art of 247; Augustine of Hippo 23; Bacon, Francis 25; belletristic movement 26; Blair, Hugh 26; Boethius 23–4; Campbell, George 26; Capella, Martianus 23; Cicero 20–1; Desiderius Erasmus 24; development of 17–18; Eastern schools of 22; in the eighteenth century 25–6; of globalisation 544; Hobbes, Thomas 25; Isocrates 18; in the Middle Ages 22–4; modernity 26–8; negative connotations of 17; Plato 19; politics and 247;

Quintilian 21–2; Ramus, Petrus 24–5; Rollin, Charles 26; Roman Empire 22; in the seventeenth century 25; in the sixteenth century 24–5; Sophists 18; Western schools of 22; Whately, Richard 26
rhetorical analysis 247–8; analysing rhetorical devices 251; contemporary 249–50; discursive approaches to 250–1; fallacious arguments 253–4; figures of speech (FSP) 254–6; linguistic 250; logical structure analysis of argumentation 251–2; metaphors, reconstructing 256; semantics of arguments 252–3; theoretical perspectives 247; traditional approaches 248–9
rhetorical strategies 347
Rhetoric (Aristotle) 19–20
Rhetoric in Detail (Johnstone) 268
rhythm 436–7
Rice, Condoleeza 400
right-wing politics/parties: in Germany 140; posters 442; print media 140; traditional policies 620–1; websites 417; *see* populism
risk management 564
Rivière, Pierre 75
Rockefeller Foundation 154
Rojo-Martin, Luisa 544–5
role model authority legitimation 224–5
roles, in meetings 473–5
Rollin, Charles 26
Roman Empire: Eastern schools of rhetoric 22; rhetoric and 22; Western schools of rhetoric 22
Romanian parliament 320
Rome 20
Roosevelt, Franklin D. 343
Roosevelt, Theodore 343
Rousseau, Jean-Jacques 647
Rowlandson, Thomas 459
Rubin, Sam 636–9
Ruggie, John 564
rules of formation, Foucault: formation of concepts 73; formation of enunciative modalities 73; formation of objects 73; formation of strategies 73
ruling class 30, 31
Russian Army 141

Sachs, Jeffrey 228, 229, 230
Sacks, Harvey 281
Saïd, Edward 78
sales measurements 561
Salinas, Carlos 141
Salmond, Alex 393–4

salutation (*salutatio*) 371
Sartre, Jean-Paul 67, 68
satire: political cartoon 458; *see also Punch*
satirical illustration 458
Saussure, Ferdinand de 68, 84, 85; algorithms 85; signifier and signified 85–6; trees 86
scandals 337, 346–7
sceptics 542, 547, 548
schematisation 190
Schmitt, Carl 590, 678; partisans 675
scholastic fallacy 113–14; in the social sciences 118
Schröder, Gerhard 296
Schubert, Christoph 239–40, 242
Schulz, Heiner 128
Science and Technology Studies (STS) 292
science, climate change and 489–93
scientific rationalisations 230
scorecards 560, 568
Scotland: debating turns in Parliament 523; independence 391–3; representation of women in Parliament 523
Second Assessment Report (IPCC) 489
secularism: as an analytical concept 588–91; as anti-British 597; colonialism and 592–4; discourses on 596; good and bad 596; Habermas on 588; maximalist and minimalist models 589–90; nation-states 591–2; political theology and 590–1; strategic uses of 596–7; in the United Kingdom 588–9, 596; in the United States 588; *see also* religion
secular language 588
sedimentation 99–100
self-determination, democracy and 45–6, 54
self-direction 45
self-representation: of governments 331–2; mediated 418; of political candidates 399, 401
semantic nets 126
semantics: of arguments 252–3; change 125, 128; distinction from pragmatics 129–30; fields 124–5; metaphorisation 125, 126; metonymisation 125; reference 126–9; relations 126
semiosis 650
semiotic economy 33
semiotics 84–6; of empathy 393–4; *see also* commemoration
semiotics of political commemoration 374–7; elements of 374
semiotic stability 550
semiotic techniques 3
sensory diegetic images 457
sentence and text-semantic procedures 3

sexism 403, 408
sexist jokes 320
sexuality 531; acceptable/deviant 532; symbolic opposites of Israel and Palestine 533
shame 531, 557, 562
shapeshifters (*perevertni*) 450
shared memory 369, 370, 379
Shepherdson, C. 88
side participants 316
signifier, the: in Bourdieu 92; empty, Laclau 90–1, 103–4, 105; floating signifiers 102; in Lacan 83, 84, 85–7, 91; in Saussure 85–6; and signified 85–7, 92
simulation 194, 198
sincerity, political 386–8
Singapore, globalisation and 542–3
singers, role models 225
Skinner, Quentin 122, 129
slogans 239, 442
Slovenia 361–2
small stories 240
Smith, Adam 137
Smith, Harry 518–19
sociability 385, 394
social capital 112
social change 130
social class 37, 110, 229, 448, 495, 531; *see also* class struggle
social cognition 208
Social Constructionist paradigm 474
social constructivism 123
social development 31
social discrimination 46
social history 127
social identity 399
social interaction 50
social-justice movements 544
social learning processes 608
social logics 610
social media 242; affordances 413; custom-tailored advertising 413; genres 419–20; social movements' activities 420; state monitoring of users 413; *see also* political Web 2.0 communication
social movements: citizens' self-produced content 419; framing processes 418, 422; mobilising structures 418, 422; networking through social media 420; opportunity structures 418, 422
social practices 218, 219
social relations 4; Gramsci on 34; Marx and Engels on 32, 33; of production 33, 35
social rights 46

social-risk management 564
social risks 564–5
social security 626
social stratification 648
social theory 144–6
social world, conserving/transforming 117–18
societal depoliticisation 608
societal differentiation, systems of 76
socio-cognitive approach, van Dijk 187–8
socio-diagnostic critique 136
sociological reductionism 118, 119
soft forms of power/domination 109, 115
solar radiation, reduction of 495
somatisation 506–7
songs 225
Sontag, Susan 205
Sophists 18
Against the Sophists (Isocrates) 18
souls (*psychagogia*) 18
sound: application of MCDA 427; as communicative act in hunting 427; ideology and discourse 426–8; melodies 431–4; *see also* music; national anthem, the
soundbites 255
source-centred approaches to political communication 5, 6
source domains 188
Southern Africa 593
sovereign power 76
sovereignty: collective 48–9; democracy and 48–9, 54; external 48; individual 48; internal 48; national 48
space race 210
Spain: austerity measures 651; Civil War 655; class warfare 652; contact with Nazi regime 655; existential inequality 652, 653; home-evictions 646, 651, 653; inequality 646, 652; mortgage law 652; resource inequality 652; suicides 646; *see also* PAH (Platform for those Affected by Mortgages); PP (Partido Popular)
Spanish Inquisition 632
spatial linguistics 34
speaking, part of 18; *see also* rhetoric
species-constitutive interests 48
specificity tests 175
speech: *inventio* 20; parts of 20–1; in politics 1–2; style of 20; *see also* political speeches
speech acts 607
speech genres, rhetorical theory of 248
speed-related metaphors 212
sports metaphors 205

Spradling, Scott 403–4
stakeholder analysis 566–7
stakeholder engagement 563, 564, 565, 568
stakeholder-management 563, 564
stakeholder-relationship management 563
stakeholders: definition 563; identifying and prioritising 566; languages and practices of CSR 562–5; as objects of governance 565–7; selection and reinvention of languages 564
Stalinism 222, 619
Stamps, Peter 160–1, 161–2, 163–4
stance-taking 241
Star-Spangled Banner (SSB) 429, 430–1; pitch (melody) 433; rhythm 437; shorter dotted phrasing 434
stasis/motion in rhythms 437
state, the: Althusser 38–40; concept of in Koselleck 128; decline of 626; democracy and 47, 54; globalisation and 626; ideological state apparatus (ISA) 38, 39, 40; Marx and 31; nation-states 591–2, 674; relative separation from religion 589; repressive state apparatus (RSA) 38, 39, 40
statistical analysis 174
statistics 172
status, citizenship as 530, 531, 535
St Augustine 23
Steindl, Imre 293–4
stenographers 298–9
stereotypes 332; in comics 456; racist 220; visual 220
Sternberger et al. 2, 662
stigmatisation 662, 664
stories: components 234; difference from narratives 234; distinction from plots 156–7; Dreamers movement 243; emplotted 144; prototypical 234–5; small 240; *see also* truth commissions
storytelling 238, 241; by asylum seekers 238; politics of 292–3, 301–2
story-world positions 405, 406–7
strategic manoeuvring, concept 254
strategic purposive intentions 385
strategic stakeholders 565
strategy, Bourdieu's notion of 145
stratification 648, 649; of language use 34
straw-man fallacy 333
street protesters 676
stretching of words 388
strict father morality 574; *see also* metaphor; Lakoff
strong discourses, Bourdieu 118
structuralism 68

structuralist semantics 125
structures and events 127
struggle metaphors 205
St Stephen (Hungarian king) 299–300, 301
student groups 420
style(s) 25; Foucault 139; Gramscian notion of 36; of speech 20
subject: Lacanian notion 83; philosophy of 67–8
subjective vacation, process of 38
subjectivity 82
sub-markets, Bourdieusian metaphor 112
suicide 646
Sunflower Movement 544
superdiversity 547–50; definition of 553n
superstructure *see* base-superstructure
suppliers 560; scorecards 560–1
supply side of political disengagement 604–7
SustainAbility 565
sustainable development 494; media reportage 494, 495
sweatshops 559
Sweden: parliament 319, 320, 321; politicians' use of Facebook and Twitter 416; press conferences 344, 347, 351, 352
Swiss People's Party (SVP) 634–5
Sydney Morning Herald 226
symbolic, Lacanian notion 83–4, 91
symbolic order 37
symbolic power 114–15, 116; *see* Bourdieu
symbolic profit, Bourdieusian metaphor 112
symbolic violence 4, 115; class racism 117; horizontal deflections of 117
symbols 154, 164–5
syntagmatic (sequential) terms 174
syntax 255
Syriza 93
systematic interpretation 362
Szálasi, Ferenc 300
Szűrös, Mátyás 294

tact 387
target domains 188
taxation 612
teambuilding 474
Tea Party 627
technique of obfuscation 567–8
technocratic governance 606
technologies of discipline 77
technologies of dominance 77
technologies of the self 77
technologisation of discourse 139
technology 464; climate change and 495

713

techno-managerialism 493–5
technoscapes 543
televised debates 393–4
temporalisation of concepts 130
tension in sound/music 435
terrorism: academic perspective 673; conceptualisations of 677–9; criminalisation of 678; definition 677; delegitimisation of 675; discourse of us versus them 682–3; discursive practices 673; Egypt 676; as a form of political communication 676–7; as an ideology or movement 678–9; legitimacy and 675; oppositional political movements 676; partisans 675; resistance fighters 676; social construct 674; street protesters 676; war and 678
text-imminant critique 136; see DHA
text mining 169, 172
texts, stabilising role in parliamentary democracy 297–9
Thailand: EMPOWER 551; globalisation and 542; minimum wage 559
Thanksgiving 372
Thatcher, Margaret 212, 213, 515–16
theoretical rationalisation legitimation 230–1
Therborn, Göran 647
Third Assessment Report (IPCC) 489
Third Republic of Hungary 294, 299, 301
three-part lists 285
Times, The 332–3, 640, 641
Title III ('Language Instruction for Limited English Proficient and Immigrant Students') 363–4
TNCs (transnational corporations) 562, 568
Tobocman, Seth 463–4
Todorov, Tzvetan 157
Tomashevsky, Boris 156–7
Tonga 549
tools for corpus analysis 172
top-down view of policy implementation 362
Töpffer, Rodolphe 460
topics 252–3
topoi/topos 138–9, 143, 145, 171, 237, 248–9, 251, 253, 265, 267, 270, 273, 332–3, 377–8, 509–11, 655, 667; see argumentation
topos of responsibility 378, 509
totalitarianism 619; concept of 660–1
totalitarian regimes: afterlife of totalitarian discourse 667–8; Crystal Night (*Kristallnacht*) state pogrom 666; discourses of 661; doublethink 660; examples of 660–1; insider information of official discourse 665–6; language use 660–1; Nazi discourse *see* Nazi discourse; Nazi genocide 663–4; *Newspeak* 660
tough government 612, 613
Toulmin schema 249; *see* argumentation
tourists 550
town hall meetings/speeches 398, 399, 408; Clinton, Hillary 401, 403–4
Townshend, George 459
trade liberalisation 544
traditional intellectuals 37
tradition legitimation 225
transdisciplinarity 137
transference 87, 88, 91
transformationalists 542, 547, 548
trans-generational political community 370
Transition group 496
translocalisation 549
transmission in racism 631–2
transnationalisation 559
TRC (Truth and Reconciliation Commission) 238
Treaty of Lisbon (2007) 310
trees, Saussurean and Lacanian 86
Trier, Jost 124
trivium, the 23
tropes 378, 443; *see* rhetoric
true partisans 675
truncated multilingualism 547
truth 23; games of, Foucauldian concept 74
truth commissions 238; *see also* TRC (Truth and Reconciliation Commission)
T score 175, 176
Tucholsky, Kurt 661
turbans 596
turn-taking systems 277, 470–3, 480; facilitators 471; gestural cues 471; participation 470–1; political meetings 471–2; visual cues 471
turn-type pre-allocation system 470
tweets, 2009 G20 meeting 421
Tweet, William 'Boss' 462
Twitter: elites 415; MEPs 415–16; message content 460; Occupy protests 419; retweeting 421; student groups 420; UK politicians 415; *see* Web 2.0
two-party dialogues 315–16
two-sided schemas 190
Tymoshenko, Yulia 448–9

UK parliament 318, 319, 321; *see also* Westminster-system parliaments
Ukrainian parliamentary election campaign (2014): Anti-Terror Operation (ATO) 444; context 443–5; defence discourse 445–52;

election turnout and results 444; explicit reference to Russia 447, 448, 449, 450–1; Fatherland Party 447–9, 451; implicit reference to Russia 445; Petro Poroshenko Bloc 445–7; political parties entering parliament 444; Radical Party of Oleh Liashko 449–51; undeveloped nature of political parties 444–5; uprising 444
Umbrella Movement 544
Umm Koulthum 536, 537
unauthorised interruptions 318
Uncle Sam 462
underemployment 544
Underhill, James 203–4
understanding (*Verstehen*) 49, 50, 54; *see* Habermas
unemployment 544
UNESCAP 566
United Kingdom (UK): austerity policies 611–14; House of Commons debate 515; middle-class social anxiety 110–11; picture stories 461; political cartooning 459; Queen's English 116; religion 588–9; satirical cartoonists 460; secularism 588–9, 596, 597; 'sick man of Europe' 611–12; working class disdain for articulacy 110; working class notion of masculinity 117
United Nations Framework Convention on Climate Change (UNFCCC) 488–9
United Nations Global Compact 563, 564, 565, 568; criticisms of 565–6
United Nations High Commission on Refugees 238
United States of America (USA): Civil War 462; denial of climate change 490; first past the post system 627; political cartooning 461–2; religion 588; secularism 588; Tea Party 627
United Students Against Sweatshops 562
unparliamentary language 319
uprisings 421
Utopians 89, 90
utterance 86, 126, 130, 145, 179, 194–5, 221, 251, 255–6, 267, 270–1, 318, 332, 347–51, 402, 443, 474, 576, 588, 667

validity: claims 143; context-specific forms of 44; rationally justified claims to 51; symbolically mediated modes of 45
van Dijk, Teun A. 187, 208
veiling 596
verbal communication 379
verbal process causes 222, 223
vernacular materialism 34–5

Verständigung (communication) 49, 50, 54; *see* Habermas
vibrato 435, 436
video narratives 242–3
violence: discourse and 673; *see also* political violence; terrorism; war
visibility, rhetoric of 529, 537
visual analogy 228
visual art, legitimation and 220 220
visual humour 461
visual metaphors 208
visual modality 189
visual personal authority legitimation 222
visual stereotypes 220
vital inequality 647, 648, 653, 656
von Weizäcker, Richard 373
voters 605
Vranitzky, Franz 373
Vygotsky, Lev S. 156, 162

Waldheim, Kurt 145
Wales, representation of women in politics 523
walk and talk sub-genre 575
Wal-Martisation 558–62; category management 560; communication-logistical-inventory system 559; labour abuses in Chinese factories 561; as a low-cost accumulation strategy 559–62; neoliberal globalisation of production and retail 558–9; open-book accounting 560; procurement staff 561; Retail Link software 559–60; stakeholders 563; supplier scorecards 560–1; workers in suppliers' factories 561
Wal-Mart Sweatshops 561
Walton, Douglas 253
war: call to arms 680; definition of 673; discourse and 673; discourse of us versus them 682–3; genre 680, 681; Just War Theory 674; legitimacy 674–6; modern view 674; narrative constructions of 679–81; precipitating events 680; terrorism and 678
War Communications Research Unit 154
war frame of terrorism 678
war metaphors 205
War on Terror 106, 226, 626, 679, 682; criminal Justice and 678; narrative 238, 400, 678, 681
Warsaw Genuflection 376; *see* Willi Brandt
Warsaw, Treaty of 376
watchdog role 286, 345, 348, 349, 351
Web 1.5 415
Web 2.0: definition 412; genres 414; innovation hypothesis 414; normalisation hypothesis 414, 415; *see also* political Web 2.0 communication

web crawlers 172
Weber, Max 330
websites: candidates' personal websites 417; centre and centre-right parties 417; left-wing parties 417; personal impression management 417; political parties and politicians 416–17; right-wing parties 417
wedding ceremonies 427
WEIRD (Western, Educated, Industrialised, Rich and Democratic) 163
welfare state 101, 626
West Germany 373
Westminster-system parliaments 309, 312
Westphalian system 674
West Wing, The (TV series) 573, 574, 575–6, 578–81, 584; comparison with *Borgen* (TV series) 581, 583; fictionalisation of politics 576
Whately, Richard 26
Wheeler-Nicholson, Malcolm 463
white papers 359
Wicked Witch of the West 522
Wild West films 577
will-formation, democracy and 51–2, 54–5
William III 456
William of Orange 458
Williams, Raymond 131
Wilson, Woodrow 343
witnessing 283, 284
women in politics: adopting linguistic norms 515–16; adopting masculine styles of leadership 517; barracking by 523; Chacón, Carme 516–17; double bind *see* double bind; in egalitarian contexts 523; Halonen, Tarja 517; interventions in political debate 515; leadership styles, variety of 516; media portrayal of 516; Merkel, Angela 517; Palin, Sarah 516; perceptions of leadership styles 516; representations 515–17; Thatcher, Margaret 515–16; toughness versus compassion, managing 517; under-representation of elected office positions 514; *see also* Clinton, Hillary
word-cloud software 158

Wordle 158, 159
word lists 177
words: concepts and 131; corpus analysis and 173–4; as data 158–60; pauses and stretching of 388; politics of 291–3; primary and secondary senses of 204
Wordsmith linguistic tool 173, 175, 176
word statistics 174
working classes: flexible work skills 544; illegal overtime 559; instability and anxiety for 544; labour abuses 561, 562; language to formulate demands 33; minimum wage 559; in Wal-Mart's suppliers factories 561; *see* social class
working parliaments 309
workplace discourse 473, 479, 480
World Bank 566–7
World Economic Forum 545
World Englishes (WEs) 548
world languages (WLs) 546; disappearance of 547; homogenising 547–8
world of nations 428
World revolutionary propaganda (Lasswell) 154, 162
World Social Forum (WSF) 545
world-views 203; comic books 463
World Wide Web 412
Wright, Eric Olin 649
Writing Culture workshop 291
written ministerial statements 312
written parliamentary questions 313
WTO (World Trade Organization) 493, 559

xenophobia 632, 634; *see also* racism

Yankee Doodle 461–2
Yanukovych, Viktor 443
YouTube 419

Zapatistas 141
Zarefsky, Daniel 249
Zionism 639–40
Žižek, Slavoj 105